THE IMPORTANCE OF TESTING YOURSELF ON WHAT YOU'VE STUDIED

In our years of teaching, we have found that certain study strategies can greatly improve learning, and so we'd like to offer you, our reader, the following suggestions. Do not try to read this textbook the way you might read a novel, taking in large chunks at a sitting. If you are like most students, your favourite strategy is to read the textbook and your notes, and then simply read them again, but this is not really the best way to learn.

If you could do just one thing that would improve your learning and improve your grades it is this: Test yourself on what you've studied early, often, and repeatedly. Ask yourself questions, answer them, and then go back and restudy what you didn't know. Test yourself again and again until you learn the material. Even when you have learned it, you need to keep testing yourself regularly over the semester so that what you've learned stays learned. At the end of Chapter 1, we provide you with some other proven techniques to help you learn.

To get the most from your studying, we recommend that you read only a part of each chapter at a time. Instead of simply reading silently, nodding along saying "hmmmmm" to yourself, try to restate what you have read in your own words at the end of each section. At specific points in each chapter, you will find a feature called **Recite & Review**, a way to discover what you know or still don't understand. You will be invited to recite out loud (to yourself, a friend, or even a patient pet) what you know about key topics and terms, and to reread what you didn't get the first time around. Do this, and you'll quickly see how it boosts your learning and your grades.

We strongly advise you to make use of *MyPsychLab*, an online resource that provides many more opportunities to test yourself, with immediate feedback to show you exactly how you are doing in your course—what you understand well and where you need more work, so you can study more efficiently. Based on how you do on a pretest, you are provided with your own customized study plan with simulations and activities to help you master the material you are reading. Go to **http://www.mypsychlab.com.**

We have never gotten over our own initial excitement about psychology, and we have done everything we can think of to make the field as lively and absorbing for you as it is for us. However, what you bring to your studies is as important as what we have written. This text will remain only a collection of pages unless you choose to read actively, using the many active-learning and critical-thinking features we have provided.

Psychology can make a real difference in your own life, and we hope you will enjoy studying about it in this book. Welcome to psychology!

Carole Wade
Carol Tavris
Maryanne Garry
Deborah Saucier
Lorin Elias

Allenby!

PSYCHOLOGY

FIFTH CANADIAN EDITION

PSYCHOLOGY

CAROLE WADE

Dominican University of California

CAROL TAVRIS

MARYANNE GARRY

Victoria University of Wellington

DEBORAH SAUCIER

University of Ontario Institute of Technology

LORIN ELIAS

University of Saskatchewan

Toronto

Acquisitions Editor: *Matthew Christian*
Program Manager: *Madhu Ranadive*
Marketing Manager: *Claire Varley*
Developmental Editor: *John Lewis*
Supervising Developmental Editor: *Suzanne Schaan*
Project Manager: *Marissa Lok*
Full Service Vendor Project Manager: *Manvir Singh Chaudhary, Aptara®, Inc.*
Copy Editor: *Susan Bindernagel*
Proofreader: *Ruth Chernia*
Compositor: *Aptara®, Inc.*
Permissions Project Manager: *Kathryn O'Handley*
Photo Researcher: *Dimple Bhorwal, Aptara®, Inc.*
Permissions Researcher: *Phyllis J. Padula*
Cover and Interior Designer: *Anthony Leung*
Cover Image: *Les and Dave Jacobs/Cultura/Corbis*

Credits and acknowledgments for material borrowed from other sources and reproduced, with permission, in this textbook appear on the appropriate page within the text and on page C-1.

Library and Archives Canada Cataloguing in Publication

Wade, Carole, author
   Psychology / Carole Wade (Dominican University of California), Carol Tavris, Maryanne Garry (Victoria University of Wellington), Deborah Saucier (University of Ontario Institute of Technology), Lorin Elias (University of Saskatchewan). —Fifth Canadian edition.

Revision of: Psychology / Carole Wade . . . [et al.]. —4th Canadian ed.
   —Toronto: Pearson, ©2013.
Includes bibliographical references and index.
ISBN 978-0-205-96035-4 (bound)

   1. Psychology—Textbooks.   I. Tavris, Carol, author   II. Garry, Maryanne, author
III. Saucier, Deborah, 1966-, author   IV. Elias, Lorin, 1972-, author   V. Title.

BF121.W28 2014   150   C2014-906169-2

ISBN 978-0-205-96035-4

To Howard, whose support has made it all possible.
Carole Wade

For Ronan, in loving memory.
Carol Tavris

To Devon, Beth, and all the apples.
Maryanne Garry

To Chai and Mia.
Deb Saucier

To Lana, Mileva, and Noam.
Lorin Elias

Brief Contents

Contents

5   Body Rhythms and Mental States   138

6   Sensation and Perception   174

7   Learning and Conditioning   218

Authors' Acknowledgments

Many people contributed to this project, which has evolved through four editions now. Our thanks go out to the following individuals: Jennifer Burkitt, Greg Christie, Farhad Dastur, Chai Duncan, John Elias, Lana Elias, Mileva Elias, Noam Elias, Trista Friederich, Isabelle Gauthier, Peter Hall, Ben Heppner, Duane Janzen, Bryan Kolb, Regan Patrick, Ky Pruesse, Mia Saucier, Rob Sutherland, Matt Tata, Rosalie Byrnes, Krista Hester, Hugo Lehmann, Michael Owen, Tim McTiernan, and Andrew Iwaniuk.

Like any other cooperative effort, writing a book requires a support team. We are indebted to the following reviewers for their many insightful and substantive suggestions during the development of this fifth Canadian edition of *Psychology*:

Dianne Crisp, *Kwantlen Polytechnic University*
Carolyn Ensley, *Wilfrid Laurier University*
Kathy Foxall, *Wilfrid Laurier University*
Stuart J. McKelvie, *Bishop's University*
Susana Phillips, *Kwantlen Polytechnic University*

Heather Schellinck, *Dalhousie University (ret.)*
Nicholas F. Skinner, *King's University College (Western)*
Erin Strahan, *Wilfrid Laurier University, Brantford Campus*
Michael Woloszyn, *Thompson Rivers University*

Additionally, we would also like to thank the many talented people at Pearson Canada and their associates, including Matthew Christian (Acquisitions Editor), John Lewis (Senior Developmental Editor), Madhu Ranadive (Program Manager), Manvir Singh (Aptara Project Manager), and Susan Bindernagel (copy editor).

We have always loved learning about psychological discoveries and introducing them to students. We hope you will enjoy reading and using this book as much as we have enjoyed writing it.

Deborah Saucier
Lorin Elias

About the Authors

CAROLE WADE earned her PhD in cognitive psychology at Stanford University. At the University of New Mexico she taught courses in psycholinguistics and developed the first course there on the psychology of gender. She was professor of psychology for ten years at San Diego Mesa College, then taught at College of Marin and Dominican University of California. In addition to this text, she and Carol Tavris have written *Invitation to Psychology; Psychology in Perspective;* and *The Longest War: Sex Differences in Perspective.* Dr. Wade has long sought to make psychology accessible to students and the general public, focusing on the promotion of critical-thinking skills. She chaired the APA Board of Educational Affairs's Task Force on Diversity Issues at the Precollege and Undergraduate Levels of Education in Psychology, presented a G. Stanley Hall lecture at the APA convention, and served on the steering committee for the National Institute on the Teaching of Psychology. She is a Fellow of two divisions of the American Psychological Association and a Fellow of the Association for Psychological Science.

CAROL TAVRIS earned her PhD in social psychology at the University of Michigan. In addition to her other books with Carole Wade, she is coauthor, with Elliot Aronson, of *Mistakes Were Made (But Not by Me)*, and author of *The Mismeasure of Woman* and *Anger: The Misunderstood Emotion.* She has written on psychological topics for a wide variety of magazines, journals, edited books, and newspapers; some of her essays have been collected in *Psychobabble and Biobunk: Using Psychological Science to Think Critically about Popular Psychology.* Dr. Tavris lectures widely on topics involving science vs. pseudoscience in psychology and many other subjects of contemporary interest. She has taught in the psychology department at UCLA and at the Human Relations Center of the New School for Social Research in New York. She is a Fellow of three divisions of the American Psychological Association, a charter Fellow of the Association for Psychological Science, and a member of the editorial board of the APS journal *Psychological Science in the Public Interest.*

MARYANNE GARRY earned her PhD at the University of Connecticut and did postdoctoral training at the University of Washington before moving to Victoria University of Wellington in 1996. She is best known for her research on the causes and consequences of false memories, including "imagination inflation" and its dangers as a therapeutic technique, the effects of inert substances such as fake alcohol on susceptibility to misleading information, and the power of photographs to rewrite our childhood stories and bias our decisions. In her efforts to apply psychological science to the law, she has worked with the New Zealand Law Commission and police, served as a Director of the Innocence Project New Zealand, and acted as an expert witness in criminal and civil trials worldwide on the (un)reliability of human memory. She is a Fellow of the Association for Psychological Science and served as President of the Society for Applied Research in Memory and Cognition. Dr. Garry has received her university's Merit Awards for Excellence in Research and for Excellence in Teaching.

DEBORAH SAUCIER earned her PhD in psychology at the University of Western Ontario. She earned her BSc and MSc degrees in psychology from the University of Victoria. Currently, she is the Provost and Vice-President Academic at the University of Ontario Institute of Technology. Dr. Saucier researches how individual differences in spatial cognition are related to steroid hormones in human and non-human animals. She receives research funding from the Natural Sciences and Engineering Research Council, and her research has been published in *Nature*, *Behavioural Neuroscience*, *Journal of Neuroscience*, *Brain and Cognition*, *Laterality*, and *Cognitive Brain Research*. When Dr. Saucier is not busy discussing issues like bedtime with her daughter, Mia, she tries to get on top of her gardening and quilting, although she is often out playing with Mia and her soft-coated wheaten terrier (Khali) and black cat (Mr. Barry White).

LORIN ELIAS earned his PhD in behavioural neuroscience at the University of Waterloo. He was then appointed as an assistant professor in the Department of Psychology at the University of Saskatchewan, the same institution where he completed his BA (Honours) degree in psychology. He now serves the Department of Psychology at the University of Saskatchewan as a full professor and the Department Head. Dr. Elias is an active and award-winning teacher and researcher. He has won seven teaching excellence awards and teaches a variety of courses in introductory psychology, cognitive neuroscience, and evolutionary psychology at both the undergraduate and graduate levels while maintaining an active research program. His federally funded research program has mainly focused on the functional differences between the left and right hemispheres of the brain. However, he has also investigated a number of unusual perceptual phenomena, including a condition called synesthesia. Dr. Elias's research has been published in a number of academic journals, including *Neuropsychologia*, *Cortex*, *Brain and Cognition*, *Laterality*, *Neurosurgery*, *Cognitive Brain Research*, and *Behavioural Neuroscience*. When Dr. Elias is not busy writing, teaching, doing research, or performing other professional duties, he is active in the audiophile community and he writes reviews of high-end audio equipment.

Lorin Elias and Deborah Saucier also co-authored *Neuropsychology: Clinical and Experimental Foundations*, for Pearson Allyn & Bacon, published in 2006.

PSYCHOLOGY

1 What Is Psychology?

Ask questions. . . be willing to wonder

How does "pop psych" on the internet and TV differ from the psychology in this book?

———

If you want to think critically, must you always be critical?

———

If you call yourself a psychotherapist, will you be breaking the law?

———

What's the difference between a psychologist, a clinical psychologist, and a psychiatrist?

Would you like to unlock the secret of happiness? Manage your stress? Fall in love? Get over love? Improve your study habits? Stop procrastinating? Get rich? Lose weight? Stop worrying?

If you are like most people, you probably answered "You bet!" to at least some of these questions. If so, the internet is full of advice for you. Some advice comes from experts who know what they're talking about; some comes from bloggers who know as much about psychology as they do about astrophysics; some comes from psychotherapists who will send you a diagnosis and treatment program based solely on what you write in an email. And hundreds of internet companies offer "natural" herbal remedies for anxiety, nervousness, sexual problems, and depression, or prescription drugs at impossibly low prices. A better life may seem to be just a click away.

Perhaps you would prefer a book? There's *Why Your Life Sucks: And What You Can Do About It*; *Idea Mapping: How to Access Your Hidden Brain Power, Learn Faster, Remember More, and Achieve Success in Business*; and *How to Make Anyone Fall in Love with You* (and then you will undoubtedly want the sequel, *How to Make Someone Love You Forever! In 90 Minutes or Less*). If you like things laid out in easy-to-follow lists, you can buy *Ten Secrets for Success and Inner Peace*, and if 10 is too many, you can try *Getting Unstuck: 8 Simple Steps to Solving Any Problem*.

How in the world are you supposed to separate out useful information in this sea of opinions, marketing ploys, and downright rubbish? Fortunately for you, you are taking an introductory psychology course, and by the time you finish it you will have some good answers.

Before you head for the bookstore, however, we want to tell you that the psychology you are about to study—*real* psychology—bears little relation to the popular psychology ("pop psych") seen on television or found in these and thousands of similar books on the web. It is more complex, more informative, and, we think, far more helpful because it is based on scientific research and **empirical** evidence—evidence gathered by careful observation, experimentation, and measurement.

The psychology you will be studying also addresses a far broader range of issues than does popular psychology. When people think of psychology, they usually think of mental and emotional disorders, personal problems, and psychotherapy. But psychologists take as their subject the entire spectrum of brave and cowardly, intelligent and foolish, beautiful and brutish things that people do. They want to know how ordinary human beings—and other animals, too—learn, remember, solve problems,

empirical Relying on or derived from observation, experimentation, or measurement.

Psychologists use scientific methods to study many puzzles of human behaviour. Why do people lose their inhibitions when they dress up in funny outfits? Why do people strive to become champion athletes in spite of physical disabilities? And what would motivate terrorists to kill themselves and thousands of innocent people?

Top Left: Eugenio Marongiu/Fotolia. Bottom Left: John Fryer/Alamy. Right: Stacy Walsh Rosenstock/Alamy.

perceive, feel, and get along (or fail to get along) with others. They are therefore as likely to study commonplace experiences—rearing children, gossiping, remembering a shopping list, daydreaming, making love, and making a living—as exceptional ones.

Psychology can be defined generally as *the discipline concerned with behaviour and mental processes and how they are affected by an organism's physical state, mental state, and external environment*. This definition, however, is a little like defining a car as a vehicle for transporting people from one place to another, without explaining how a car differs from a train or a bus, how a Ford differs from a Ferrari, or how a catalytic converter works. To get a clear picture of what psychology is, you are going to need to know more about its methods, its findings, and its ways of interpreting information. We will begin by looking more closely at what psychology is *not*.

Learning Objectives

1. Compare "psychobabble" and serious psychology.

2. Articulate what's wrong with psychologists' nonscientific competitors, such as astrologers and psychics.

psychology The discipline concerned with behaviour and mental processes and how they are affected by an organism's physical state, mental state, and external environment; the term is often represented by Ψ, the Greek letter psi (usually pronounced "sigh").

psychobabble Pseudoscience and quackery covered by a veneer of psychological and scientific-sounding language.

Psychology, Pseudoscience, and Popular Opinion

In recent decades, the public's appetite for psychological information has created a huge market for "**psychobabble**": pseudoscience and quackery covered by a veneer of psychological and scientific-sounding language. Pseudoscience promises easy fixes to life's problems and challenges, such as resolving your unhappiness as an adult by "reliving" the supposed trauma of your birth, or becoming more creative on the job by "reprogramming" your brain. Some forms of psychobabble play on the modern consumer's love of technology. All sorts of electrical gizmos have been marketed with the promise that they will get both halves of your brain working at their peak: the Graham Potentializer, the Tranquilite, the Floatarium, the Transcutaneous Electro-Neural Stimulator, the Brain SuperCharger, and the Whole Brain Wave Form Synchro-Energizer. (We are not making these up.) And today you can find all sorts of psychobabble on the internet, where promoters promise that a higher IQ, a perfect love life, or a better personality is just a click away.

Because so many pop-psych ideas have filtered into public consciousness, the media, education, and even the law, we all need to distinguish between psychobabble and serious psychology, and between unsupported *popular opinion* and findings based on *research evidence*. Are unhappy memories "repressed" and then accurately recalled years later, as if they had been tape-recorded? Do most women suffer from emotional symptoms of premenstrual syndrome (PMS)? Do policies of abstinence from alcohol reduce rates of alcoholism? Do abused children inevitably become abusive parents, caught in a "cycle of abuse"? If you play Beethoven's symphonies to your infant, will your baby become smarter? Many people would answer "yes" to these questions, but empirical evidence has shown that these and many other widely held ideas about human behaviour are, in fact, wrong.

One purpose of an introductory course like the one you are taking is to correct misconceptions—by teaching you how psychologists study them and showing you how their research might confirm or dispel ideas that many of us take for granted. Two researchers, Annette Kujawski Taylor and Patricia Kowalski (2004), wondered how many students come into their first psych course with a bunch of mistaken ideas in their heads and whether a semester of learning helps dislodge those ideas.

To answer these questions, they gave 90 introductory students a "Psychological Information" questionnaire on the first day of class. The test consisted of 36 true-or-false items—for example, "Under hypnosis you can perform feats that are otherwise impossible," "Too much sugar causes hyperactivity in children," "At any point in time, we use only 10% of our brains," and "Listening to Mozart will enhance your thinking and creativity." The students also rated their confidence in each of their responses on a scale of one (not at all confident) to 10 (very confident). All the items were on topics that the course was scheduled to cover, and all of them were false. As a group, the students failed the test miserably: Their accuracy was only 38.5%, which is actually worse than chance, and they had more confidence in their wrong answers than their correct ones! Moreover, students with high grade-point averages did no better than those with low ones. (See Figure 1.1.) So much for common sense.

During the last week of class, the same students took another test, one that included all of the earlier items plus 12 new true items that were randomly mixed in but not scored. This time, we're happy to say, the students' overall accuracy was much better: 66.3%. The researchers attributed this change in part to the fact that instruction had explicitly focused on the scientific evidence refuting such beliefs. (As you will see, we take the same approach in this book.) Yet even at the end of the course, more than a third of the students' responses were wrong, meaning that there was still plenty of room left for improvement. The researchers then dug deeper into the evidence, analyzing the students' confidence ratings. They found that by the end of the semester, the students had gained confidence in their correct beliefs and lost confidence in those beliefs that were still incorrect, suggesting that they were beginning to be unsure about their misconceptions, were in the process of questioning them, and perhaps were on the way to giving them up. If so, they were learning one of the most important lessons in science: Uncertainty about untested assumptions and beliefs can be a good thing.

The marriage of old-fashioned pseudo-science and modern technology has produced gizmos like the "Synchro-Energizer," which supposedly alters consciousness, boosts intelligence, and enhances sexual functioning, all by simply bombarding you with lights and sounds of different frequencies and intensities.

Peter Menzel

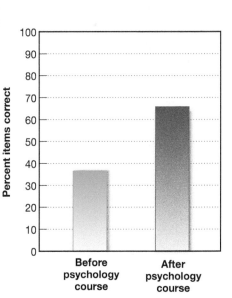

FIGURE 1.1 Psychology: It's Not Just "Common Sense"
On the first day of class, students in an introductory psychology course actually did worse than chance on a true–false psychological information questionnaire. But by the end of the semester, after they had learned to examine the scientific evidence for their beliefs, their performance had greatly improved.

Nonscientific approaches to psychological problems, such as astrology and psychic readings, promise easy answers and quick solutions. But can they deliver?

Jeff Greenberg/Alamy

Throughout this book and your introductory course, you, too, will repeatedly find that popular opinion and "common sense" are not always reliable guides to human behaviour. The kind of research you will be learning about won't always provide the answers you might have wished for, and sometimes it will be unable to provide final answers. Our goal, however, is to show you why the scientific investigation of even our most cherished beliefs can lead to answers that are far more sensible than "common sense."

Common sense, information in the media, and personal experience are not the only sources of misunderstandings about human behaviour. Psychology has many nonscientific competitors: palm reading, graphology, fortune-telling, numerology, and the most popular, astrology. Like psychologists, promoters of these competing systems try to explain people's problems and predict their behaviour. If you are having romantic problems, an astrologer may advise you to choose an Aries instead of an Aquarius as your next love, and a "past-lives channeller" may say it's because you were jilted in a former life. Belief in these unscientific approaches is widespread, even in scientifically advanced countries; between one-third and one-half of Americans and Canadians believe in astrology, and 17% of Americans have sought out a fortune teller or psychic for advice (De Robertis & Delaney, 2000; National Science Board, 2000).

Yet whenever the claims of psychics and astrologers are put to the test, those claims turn out to be so vague as to be meaningless ("Spirituality will increase next year")—or just plain wrong (Park, 2000; Radford, 2005; Shermer, 1997). In 2008, one well-known Canadian psychic, who calls herself the "psychic to the stars," predicted that Sean Penn would be wounded in the Middle East and John Edwards would win the U.S. presidency after Hillary Clinton dropped out of the race. Obviously, she was wrong on all counts. Moreover, contrary to what you might think from watching TV shows like *Medium*, no psychic has ever found a missing child, identified a serial killer, or helped police solve any other crime solely by using "psychic powers." The "help" given by psychics merely adds to the heartbreak the victim's family feels. In 2004, when 11-year-old Carlie Brucia was abducted, her family's hopes were raised by a psychic's report that Carlie was alive. In fact, the child had been raped and murdered.

So why does belief in psychobabble persist? For one thing, it gives people a sense of control and predictability in a confusing world; indeed, our brains are probably wired to look for patterns in events, even when no patterns exist (Hood, 2009). Psychobabble also confirms our existing beliefs and prejudices, whereas scientific psychology often challenges them. You do not have to be a psychologist to know that people do not always take kindly to having their beliefs challenged. You rarely hear someone cheerfully say, "Oh, thank you for explaining to me why my irrational beliefs are mistaken!" The person is more likely to say, "Oh, buzz off, and take your stupid ideas with you."

Psychological findings do not have to be surprising or counterintuitive, however, to be important. Like scientists in other fields, psychological researchers strive not only to discover new phenomena and correct mistaken ideas but also to deepen our understanding of an already familiar world—by identifying the varieties of love, the origins of violence, or the reasons that a great song can lift our hearts.

Learning Objectives

3 Articulate what it means to think critically.

4 Explain why not all opinions are created equal.

5 List eight guidelines for evaluating psychological claims.

Thinking Critically and Creatively about Psychology

In this book, you will gain practice in distinguishing scientific psychology from pseudoscience by thinking critically. **Critical thinking** is the ability and willingness to assess claims and make objective judgments on the basis of well-supported reasons and evidence, rather than emotion or anecdote. Critical thinkers are able to look for flaws in arguments and to resist claims that have no support. They realize that criticizing an argument is not the same as criticizing the person making it, and they are willing to engage in vigorous debate about the validity of an idea. Critical thinking, however, is not merely negative thinking. It includes the ability to be creative and constructive—the ability to come up with alternative explanations for events, think of implications of research findings, and apply new knowledge to social and personal problems. Critical thinking is indispensable in ordinary life. Without it, people cannot formulate a rational argument or see through misleading ads that play on their emotions. They may have trouble assessing a political proposal or candidate, deciding whether or when to have children, or making medical decisions. 👁

Most people know that you have to exercise the body to keep it in shape, but they may not realize that clear thinking also requires effort and practice. All around us we can see examples of flabby thinking. Sometimes people justify their mental laziness by proudly telling you they are open-minded. It's good to be open-minded, many scientists have observed, but not so open that your brains fall out! Open-mindedness does not mean that all opinions are created equal and that everybody's beliefs are as good as anyone else's (Hare, 2009).

On matters of personal preference, all opinions are created equal: If you prefer the look of a Ford Taurus to the look of a Honda Accord, no one can argue with you. But if you say, "The Ford is a better car than a Honda," you have uttered more than mere opinion. Now you have to support your belief with evidence of the car's reliability, track record, and safety (Ruggiero, 2004). And if you say, "Fords are the best in the world and Hondas do not exist; they are a conspiracy of the Japanese government," you forfeit the right to have your opinion taken seriously. Your opinion, if it ignores reality, is *not* equal to any other.

Critical thinking is not only indispensable in ordinary life; it is also fundamental to all science, including psychological science. By exercising critical thinking, you will be able to distinguish serious psychology from the psychobabble that clutters the internet, the media, and bookstores. (In the study of introductory students' misconceptions described earlier, students who did well on a critical-thinking test showed the greatest improvement over the semester.) Critical thinking requires logical skills, but other kinds of skills and dispositions are also important (Anderson, 2005; Halpern, 2002; Levy, 2010; Paul, 1984; Ruggiero, 2004; Stanovich, 2010). Here are eight essential critical-thinking guidelines that we will be emphasizing throughout this book. 👁

Ask Questions; Be Willing to Wonder. What is the one kind of question that most exasperates parents of young children? "Why is the sky blue, Mommy?" "Why doesn't the plane fall?" "Why don't pigs have wings?" Unfortunately, as children grow up, they tend to stop asking "why" questions. (Why do you think this is?)

critical thinking The ability and willingness to assess claims and make objective judgments on the basis of well-supported reasons and evidence rather than emotion or anecdote.

👁—⌐Watch the Video
The Big Picture: Asking the Tough Questions in **MyPsychLab**

👁—⌐Watch the Video
Thinking Like a Psychologist: Thinking Critically in **MyPsychLab**

We often hear that all viewpoints should be taught to students in the name of "fairness" and "open-mindedness," but not all viewpoints, theories, and opinions are equally valid or supported by the evidence.

Universal Uclick

"The trigger mechanism for creative thinking is the disposition to be curious, to wonder, to inquire," observed Vincent Ruggiero (1988). "Asking 'What's wrong here?' and/or 'Why is this the way it is, and how did it come to be that way?' leads to the identification of problems and challenges." We hope that you will not approach psychology as received wisdom but will ask many questions about the theories and findings presented in this book. Be on the lookout, too, for questions about human behaviour that have not yet been asked, or have been asked but not answered—the way a psychological scientist would. In 2005, the editors of *Science*, one of the world's foremost science journals, celebrated the publication's 125th anniversary by identifying 125 scientific puzzles that scientists hope to solve at least partially over the next few decades, and among them were several psychological ones (Kennedy & Norman, 2005). What is the biological basis of consciousness? How are memories stored and retrieved? Why do we sleep and dream? Why are there critical periods for language learning? What causes schizophrenia? What is the biological basis of addiction? Psychological scientists are not discouraged by the fact that questions like these have not yet been answered; they see them as an exciting challenge.

Define Your Terms. Once you have raised a general question, the next step is to frame it in clear and concrete terms. "What makes people happy?" is a fine question for midnight reveries, but it will not lead to answers until you have defined what

THINKING CRITICALLY AND CREATIVELY ABOUT PSYCHOLOGICAL ISSUES

These eight critical-thinking guidelines will help you evaluate psychological findings, claims in the media, and problems that you encounter in your own life.

ASK QUESTIONS; BE WILLING TO WONDER
When faced with a life-threatening disease like cancer, why do some people (like Terry Fox) risk their lives to help their fellow human beings, while others focus all their attention on their own well-being? Social psychologists explore these and many other questions, as we will see in Chapter 8.

The Canadian Press Images

Victoria Times-Colonist/ The Canadian Press Images

DEFINE YOUR TERMS
People refer to intelligence all the time, but what is it exactly? Does the artistic genius of Emily Carr count as intelligence? Is intelligence captured by an IQ score, or does it also include wisdom and practical "smarts"? We will consider some answers in Chapter 9.

you mean by "happy." Do you mean being in a state of euphoria most of the time? Do you mean feeling pleasantly contented with life? Do you mean being free of serious problems or pain?

Vague or poorly defined terms in a question can lead to misleading or incomplete answers. For example, have you ever wondered how common it is for schoolchildren to be bullied? The answer depends on how you define "bullying." If you mean "ever mistreated in any way by another child," then nearly every child has been bullied. If you mean "subjected to repeated verbal harassment and taunting," the numbers are lower. And if you mean "physically attacked and threatened," the numbers are lower still. The definition makes all the difference (Best, 2001).

Examine the Evidence. Have you ever heard someone in the heat of an argument exclaim, "I just know it's true, no matter what you say" or "That's my opinion; nothing's going to change it"? Have you ever made such statements yourself? Accepting a conclusion without evidence, or expecting others to do so, is a sure sign of lazy thinking. A critical thinker asks, "What evidence supports or refutes this argument and its opposition? How reliable is the evidence?"

Or have you ever received some dire warning or funny "true" story emailed by a friend, and then forwarded it on to your entire address book, only to learn later that it was a hoax or an urban legend? A critical thinker would ask, "Is this story something I'd better check out on Snopes.com before I tell 90 000 of my closest friends?"

EXAMINE THE EVIDENCE
When demonstrating "levitation" and other supposedly magical phenomena, illusionists exploit people's tendency to trust the evidence of their own eyes even when such evidence is misleading, as discussed in Chapter 6.

Landov

ANALYZE ASSUMPTIONS AND BIASES
People often assume that drug effects are purely biological, and many Canadians and Americans also share a cultural bias that all psychoactive drugs are inevitably harmful. The Rastafarian church, however, regards marijuana as a "wisdom weed." Will these young Jamaican members react to the drug in the same way as someone who buys it on the street and smokes it alone or at a party? We will find out in Chapters 5 and 15.

Daniel Laine/Corbis

Sometimes, of course, checking the reliability of the evidence for a claim is not practical. In those cases, critical thinkers consider whether the evidence came from a reliable source (Lipps, 2004). Reliable authorities exercise critical thinking themselves.

They have education or experience in the field in which they claim expertise. They don't pressure people to agree with them. They are trusted by other experts in the field. They share their evidence openly. In psychology, they draw on research conducted according to certain rules and procedures, which you will be learning about in the next chapter.

Analyze Assumptions and Biases. *Assumptions* are beliefs that are taken for granted. Critical thinkers try to identify and evaluate the unspoken assumptions on which claims and arguments may rest—in the books they read, the political speeches they hear, and the advertisements that bombard them every day. The assumption might be "All Toronto Maple Leafs fans are idiots" or "You need the product we are selling" or "People have free will, and are entirely responsible for any crimes they commit" (or, conversely, "People's behaviour is a result of their biology or upbringing, so they aren't responsible for anything they do"). Everyone, of course, makes assumptions about how the world works; we could not function otherwise. But if we do not make explicit our own assumptions and those of other people, our ability to judge an argument's merits can be impaired.

When an assumption or belief keeps us from considering the evidence fairly, or causes us to ignore the evidence completely, it becomes a *bias*. Often a bias remains

DON'T OVERSIMPLIFY
When you're feeling angry, is it better to "let it out" (as this man is certainly doing here!) or "keep it bottled up"? Either answer oversimplifies. Depending on the circumstances, sometimes it is helpful to express your feelings, but sometimes venting your anger makes everything worse, as we discuss in Chapter 11.

Vladimir Mucibabic/Shutterstock

Queerstock, Inc./Alamy

AVOID EMOTIONAL REASONING
Intense feelings about controversial issues such as gay marriage can keep us from considering other viewpoints. The resolution of differences requires that we move beyond emotional reasoning and instead weigh point and counterpoint, as discussed in Chapter 9.

hidden until someone challenges our belief and we get defensive and angry. For instance, most of us, psychologists included, believe that parents are the most important influence in shaping a child's personality. Could anything be more obvious? Isn't that what parenting books, therapists, and magazine articles have been telling us for years? In her book *The Nurture Assumption*, Judith Rich Harris (2009) dared to question that assumption. Genes and peers, she argued, are more important influences on a child's personality and behaviour than how the parents raise the child. Because this idea challenged a widespread bias, it immediately provoked a storm of disbelief, outrage, and scorn. Some critics focused on Harris's lack of credentials instead of her facts or her logic (although she had authored a successful developmental psychology text, she does not have a PhD), and many attacked the book without even bothering to read it. That is the nature of a bias: It creates intellectual blinders. (In Chapter 14 we will look more closely at Harris's argument—in as unbiased a manner as possible.)

Avoid Emotional Reasoning. Emotion has a place in critical thinking. Passionate commitment to a view motivates people to think boldly, to defend unpopular ideas, and to seek evidence for creative new theories. But when "gut feelings" replace clear thinking, the results can be dangerous. "Persecutions and wars and lynchings," observed Edward de Bono (1985), "are all a result of gut feeling."

All of us are apt to feel threatened and get defensive whenever our most cherished beliefs are challenged (Tavris & Aronson, 2007). We value these beliefs highly, in part

Stanislav Fridkin/Shutterstock

TOLERATE UNCERTAINTY
Many parents, because they naturally want their children to turn out well, have trouble accepting uncertainty about how to raise them. For example, should they let their baby sleep with them, or will that make the baby too dependent and clingy? In Chapter 14, we will look at why there is often no single right answer to what parents "should" do.

Geraint Lewis/Alamy

CONSIDER OTHER INTERPRETATIONS
Hypnosis has traditionally been considered a "trance state" in which people involuntarily do things they ordinarily couldn't or wouldn't do. But might there be another interpretation of the surprising things that hypnotized people often do? We'll look at competing explanations in Chapter 5.

because they offer explanations for phenomena that might otherwise seem puzzling or frightening—for example, the existence of death and suffering—and because they simplify a complicated world (Preston & Epley, 2005). Because our feelings feel so *right*, so natural, we may not realize that people who hold an opposing viewpoint feel just as strongly as we do. But they usually do, which means that emotional conviction alone cannot settle arguments. You probably hold strong feelings about many topics of psychological interest, such as drug use, the causes of crime, racism, the origins of intelligence, gender differences, and homosexuality. As you read this book, you may find yourself quarrelling with findings that you dislike. Disagreement is fine; it means that you are reading actively and are engaged with the material. All we ask is that you think about why you are disagreeing: Is it because the evidence is unpersuasive or because the results make you feel anxious or annoyed?

Don't Oversimplify. A critical thinker looks beyond the obvious, resists easy generalizations, and rejects either–or thinking. For instance, is it better to feel you have control over everything that happens to you, or to accept with tranquility whatever life serves up? Either position oversimplifies. As we will see in Chapter 11, a sense of control has many important benefits, but sometimes it is best to "go with the flow."

One common form of oversimplification is *argument by anecdote*—generalizing to everyone from a personal experience or a few examples: One crime committed by a paroled ex-convict means that parole should be abolished; one friend who hates her school means that everybody who goes there hates it. Anecdotes are often the source of stereotyping as well: One dishonest welfare mother means they are all dishonest; one encounter with an unconventional Vancouverite means they are all flaky. Critical thinkers want more evidence than one or two stories before drawing such sweeping conclusions.

Consider Other Interpretations. A critical thinker creatively generates as many reasonable explanations of the topic at hand as possible before settling on the most likely one. Suppose a newsmagazine reports that chronically depressed people are more likely than other people to develop cancer. Before concluding that depression causes cancer, you would need to consider some other possibilities. Perhaps depressed people are more likely to smoke and drink excessively, and it is those unhealthy habits that increase their cancer risk. Or perhaps, in studies of depression and cancer, early, undetected cancers were responsible for patients' feelings of depression. Alternative explanations such as these must be ruled out by further investigation before we can conclude that depression is a direct cause of cancer. (It's not, by the way.)

Once several explanations of a phenomenon have been generated, a critical thinker chooses the one that accounts for the most evidence while making the fewest unverified assumptions—a principle known as **Occam's Razor**, after the fourteenth-century philosopher who first formulated it. Thus, if a fortune teller reads your palm and predicts that soon you will fall in love on a blind date, travel to Zanzibar, and have twins, then one of two things must be true (Steiner, 1989):

- The fortune teller can actually sort out the infinite number of interactions among people, animals, events, objects, and circumstances that could affect your life, and can know the outcome for sure. Moreover, this fortune teller is able to alter all the known laws of physics and defy the hundreds of studies showing that no one, under proper procedures for validating psychic predictions, has been able to predict the future for any given individual.

OR

- The fortune teller is faking it.

A critical thinker would prefer the second alternative because it requires fewer assumptions and has the most supporting evidence.

Occam's Razor The principle of choosing the solution that accounts for the most evidence while making the fewest unverified assumptions.

Psychology's Present: Behaviour, Body, Mind, and Culture

If you had a noisy, rude, surly neighbour, and you asked a group of psychologists to explain why this person was so miserable, they might give you different answers. Depending on their theoretical perspective, they might cite your neighbour's biological makeup, his belligerent attitude toward the world, the way he was brought up, an environment that encourages his nasty temper, or the influence of his unconscious motives. Modern psychologists tend to examine human behaviour through several lenses.

The Major Psychological Perspectives

The five lenses that predominate in psychology today are the *biological, learning, cognitive, sociocultural,* and *psychodynamic* perspectives. These approaches reflect different questions about human behaviour, different assumptions about how the mind works, and, most important, different ways of explaining why people do what they do.

1 **The *biological perspective* focuses on how bodily events affect behaviour, feelings, and thoughts.** Researchers such as McGill University's Donald O. Hebb argue that all behavioural and mental phenomena arise as the result of physical activity within the brain (Hebb, 1949). Electrical impulses shoot along the intricate pathways of the nervous system. Hormones course through the bloodstream, telling internal organs to slow down or speed up. Chemical substances flow across the tiny gaps that separate one microscopic brain cell from another. Biological psychologists study how these physical events interact with events in the external environment to produce perceptions, memories, and behaviour.

Researchers in this perspective study how biology affects learning and performance, perceptions of reality, the experience of emotion, and vulnerability to emotional disorder. They study how the mind and body interact in illness and health. They investigate the contributions of genes and other biological factors in the development of abilities and personality traits. And a popular specialty, **evolutionary psychology**, follows in the tradition of functionalism by focusing on how genetically influenced behaviour that was functional or adaptive during our evolutionary past may be reflected in many of our present behaviours, mental processes, and traits (see Chapter 3). The message of the biological approach is that we cannot really know ourselves if we do not know our bodies.

2 **The *learning perspective* is concerned with how the environment and experience affect a person's (or a nonhuman animal's) actions.** Within this perspective, *behaviourists* focus on the environmental rewards and punishers that maintain or discourage specific behaviours. Behaviourists do not invoke the mind or mental states to explain behaviour. They prefer to stick to what they can observe and measure directly: acts and events taking place in the environment. For example, do you have trouble sticking to a schedule? A behaviourist would analyze the environmental distractions that could help account for this common problem. **Behaviourism** was the dominant school of scientific psychology in North America for nearly half a century, through to the 1960s.

Social-cognitive learning theorists, on the other hand, combine elements of behaviourism with research on thoughts, values, expectations, and intentions. They believe that people learn not only by adapting their behaviour to the environment, but also by imitating others and by thinking about the events happening around them.

Donald O. Hebb (1904–1985) argued that all behaviour is the result of physical changes within the nervous system.

Montreal Gazette/The Canadian Press Images

Watch the **Video**
The Basics: Diverse Perspectives
in **MyPsychLab**

biological perspective A psychological approach that emphasizes bodily events and changes associated with actions, feelings, and thoughts.

evolutionary psychology A field of psychology emphasizing evolutionary mechanisms that may help explain human commonalities in cognition, development, emotion, social practices, and other areas of behaviour.

learning perspective A psychological approach that emphasizes how the environment and experience affect a person's or animal's actions; it includes behaviourism and social-cognitive learning theories.

behaviourism An approach to psychology that emphasizes the study of observable behaviour and the role of the environment and priori experience as determinants of behaviour.

As we will see in other chapters, the learning perspective has many practical applications. Historically, the behaviourists' insistence on precision and objectivity has done much to advance psychology as a science, and learning research in general has given psychology some of its most reliable findings.

3 The *cognitive perspective* **emphasizes what goes on in people's heads**—how people reason, remember, understand language, solve problems, explain experiences, acquire moral standards, and form beliefs. (The word *cognitive* comes from the Latin for "to know.") A "cognitive revolution" in psychology during the 1970s brought this perspective to the forefront. One of its most important contributions has been to show how people's thoughts and explanations affect their actions, feelings, and choices. Using clever methods to infer mental processes from observable behaviour, cognitive researchers have been able to study phenomena that were once only the stuff of speculation, such as emotions, motivations, and insight. They are designing computer programs that model how humans perform complex tasks, discovering what goes on in the mind of an infant, and identifying types of intelligence not measured by conventional IQ tests. The cognitive approach is one of the strongest forces in psychology, and it has inspired an explosion of research on the intricate workings of the mind.

4 The *sociocultural perspective* **focuses on social and cultural forces outside the individual, forces that shape every aspect of behaviour, from how we kiss to what and where we eat.** Most of us underestimate the impact of other people, the social context, and cultural rules on nearly everything we do. We are like fish that are unaware they live in water, so obvious is water in their lives. Sociocultural psychologists study the water—the social and cultural environment that people "swim" in every day.

Within this perspective, *social psychologists* focus on social rules and roles, how groups affect attitudes and behaviour, why people obey authority, and how each of us is affected by other people—spouses, lovers, friends, bosses, parents, and strangers. *Cultural psychologists* examine how cultural rules and values—both explicit and unspoken—affect people's development, behaviour, and feelings. They might study how culture influences people's willingness to help a stranger in distress, or how it influences what people do when they are angry. Because human beings are social animals who are profoundly affected by their different cultural worlds, the sociocultural perspective has made psychology a more representative and rigorous discipline.

5 The *psychodynamic perspective* **deals with unconscious dynamics within the individual, such as inner forces, conflicts, or instinctual energy.** Its origins are in Freud's theory of psychoanalysis, but many other psychodynamic theories now exist. Psychodynamic psychologists try to dig below the surface of a person's behaviour to get to its unconscious roots; they think of themselves as archeologists of the mind.

Psychodynamic psychology is the thumb on the hand of psychology—connected to the other fingers, but also set apart from them because it differs radically from the other approaches in its language, methods, and standards of acceptable evidence. Although some psychological scientists are doing empirical studies of psychodynamic concepts, many others believe that psychodynamic approaches belong in philosophy or literature rather than in academic psychology. You are unlikely to find

cognitive perspective A psychological approach that emphasizes mental processes in perception, memory, language, problem solving, and other areas of behaviour.

sociocultural perspective A psychological approach that emphasizes social and cultural influences on behaviour.

psychodynamic perspective A psychological approach that emphasizes unconscious dynamics within the individual, such as inner forces, conflicts, or the movement of instinctual energy.

psychoanalysis mentioned much in mainstream journals of psychological science (Robins, Gosling, & Craik, 1999). Outside empirical psychology, however, many psychotherapists, novelists, and lay people are attracted to the psychodynamic emphasis on such grand psychological issues as relations between the sexes, the power of sexuality, and the universal fear of death. Later in this book, we will candidly discuss the many controversies surrounding psychodynamic ideas.

Review 1.2 summarizes these five perspectives and shows you how they might be applied to a concrete issue: the problem of violence. See if you can apply these perspectives to another issue of your choosing.

Other Influential Movements in Psychology

Throughout psychology's history, various movements and intellectual trends have emerged that do not fit neatly into any of the major perspectives. In the 1960s, proponents of **humanist psychology** rejected the two dominant psychological approaches of the time: psychoanalysis and behaviourism. Humanists regarded psychoanalysis, with its emphasis on dangerous sexual and aggressive impulses, as too pessimistic a

humanist psychology A psychological approach that emphasizes personal growth and the achievement of human potential rather than the scientific understanding and assessment of behaviour.

REVIEW 1.2   Five Major Psychological Perspectives

	Perspective	Major Topics of Study	Sample Finding on Violence
	Biological	The nervous system, hormones, brain chemistry, heredity, evolutionary influences	Brain damage caused by birth complications or child abuse might incline some people toward violence.
	Learning	Environment and experience	
	Behavioural	Environmental determinants of observable behaviour	Violence increases when it pays off.
	Social-Cognitive	Environmental influences, observation and imitation, beliefs and values	Violent role models can influence some children to behave aggressively.
	Cognitive	Thinking, memory, language, problem solving, perceptions	Violent people are often quick to perceive provocation and insult.
	Sociocultural	Social and cultural contexts	
	Social Psychology	Social rules and roles, groups, relationships	People are often more aggressive in a crowd than they would be on their own.
	Cultural Psychology	Cultural norms, values, expectations	Cultures based on herding rather than agriculture tend to train boys to be aggressive.
	Psychodynamic	Unconscious thoughts, desires, conflicts	A man who murders prostitutes may have unconscious conflicts about his mother and about sexuality.

feminist psychology A psychological approach that analyzes the influence of social inequities on gender relations and on the behaviour of the two sexes.

view of human nature, one that overlooked human resilience and the capacity for joy. And humanists regarded behaviourism, with its emphasis on observable acts, as too mechanistic and "mindless" a view of human nature, one that ignored what really matters to most people—their uniquely human hopes and aspirations. In the humanists' view, human behaviour is not completely determined by either unconscious conflicts or the environment. People are capable of free will and therefore have the ability to make more of themselves than either psychoanalysts or behaviourists would predict. The goal of humanist psychology was, and still is, to help people express themselves creatively and achieve their full potential.

Although humanism is no longer a dominant movement in psychology, it has had considerable influence both inside and outside the field. Many psychologists across all perspectives embrace some humanist ideas, although most regard humanism as a philosophy of life rather than a systematic approach to psychology. Further, many topics raised by the humanists, such as creativity, joy, humour, and courage, are now being studied by scientific psychologists from many fields. For example, a contemporary research specialty known as *positive psychology* focuses on the qualities that enable people to be happy, optimistic, and resilient in times of stress (Gable & Haidt, 2005; Seligman & Csikszentmihaly, 2000). And humanism has had a direct influence on psychotherapy and the human potential and self-help movements.

Another important movement, which emerged in the early 1970s, was **feminist psychology**. As women began to enter psychology in greater numbers, they documented evidence of a pervasive bias in the research methods used and in the very questions that researchers had been asking (Bem, 1993; Crawford & Marecek, 1989; Eagly et al., 2012; Hare-Mustin & Marecek, 1990; Shields & Dicicco, 2011). They noted that many studies used only men as participants—and usually only young, white, middle-class men, at that—and they showed why it was often inappropriate to generalize to

✓•—**Study** and **Review**
in **MyPsychLab**

Recite & Review

Recite: Out loud, say as much as you can about these concepts: *biological perspective, evolutionary psychology, learning perspective, behaviourism, cognitive perspective, sociocultural perspective, psychodynamic perspective, humanist psychology, feminist psychology.*

Review: Next, go back and reread this section.

Now take this *Quick Quiz:*

Anxiety is a common problem. To test your understanding of the five major perspectives in psychology, match each possible explanation of anxiety with a perspective listed beside the explanations.

1. Anxious people often think about the future in distorted ways.
2. Anxiety is due to forbidden, unconscious desires.
3. Anxiety symptoms often bring hidden rewards, such as being excused from exams.
4. Excessive anxiety can be caused by a chemical imbalance.
5. A national emphasis on competition and success promotes anxiety about failure.

a. learning
b. psychodynamic
c. sociocultural
d. biological
e. cognitive

Answers:

1.e 2.b 3.a 4.d 5.c

everyone else from such a narrow research base. They spurred the growth of research on topics that had long been ignored in psychology, including menstruation, motherhood, the dynamics of power and sexuality in relationships, definitions of masculinity and femininity, gender roles, and sexist attitudes. They critically examined the male bias in psychotherapy, starting with Freud's own case studies (Hare-Mustin, 1991). And they analyzed the social consequences of psychological findings, showing how research has often been used to justify the lower status of women and other disadvantaged groups.

Feminist psychology greatly advanced efforts to make psychology the study of all human beings, and other groups have made similar contributions. In 1976, black psychologist Robert Guthrie, in *Even the Rat Was White*, wrote a searing and influential indictment of racism in psychological research. Since the 1970s, African-American, Latino, and Asian psychologists, gay and lesbian psychologists, and psychologists with disabilities have hugely expanded the theoretical and empirical vistas of psychology, as we will see throughout this book.

Learning Objectives

12 Explain why you can't assume that all therapists are psychologists, or that all psychologists are therapists.

13 List the three major areas of psychologists' professional activities.

14 Describe the difference between a clinical psychologist and a psychiatrist.

What Psychologists Do

Now you know the main viewpoints that guide psychologists in their work. But what do psychologists actually do with their time between breakfast and dinner?

To most people, the word *psychologist* conjures up an image of a therapist listening intently while a client, perhaps stretched out on a couch, pours forth his or her troubles. Many psychologists do in fact fit this image (though chairs are more common than couches these days). Many others, however, do not. The professional activities of psychologists generally fall into three broad categories: (1) teaching and doing research in colleges and universities; (2) providing health or mental-health services, often referred to as **psychological practice**; and (3) conducting research or applying its findings in nonacademic settings such as business, sports, government, law, and the military (see Review 1.3 on p. 24). Some psychologists move flexibly across these areas. A researcher might also provide counselling services in a mental-health setting, such as a clinic or a hospital; a university professor might teach, do research, and serve as a consultant in legal cases. 👁

👁—⎡Watch the **Video**
So Much to Choose From: Phil Zimbardo
in **MyPsychLab**

Psychological Research

Most psychologists who do research have doctoral degrees (PhDs, or EdDs, doctorates in education). Some, seeking knowledge for its own sake, work in **basic psychology**, doing "pure" research. Others, concerned with the practical uses of knowledge, work in **applied psychology**. The two approaches are complementary: Applied psychology has direct relevance to human problems, but without basic psychology there would be little knowledge to apply. A psychologist doing basic research might ask, "How does peer pressure influence people's attitudes and behaviour?" An applied psychologist might ask, "How can knowledge about peer pressure be used to reduce binge drinking in college and university?"

psychological practice Providing health or mental-health services.

basic psychology The study of psychological issues in order to seek knowledge for its own sake rather than for its practical application.

applied psychology The study of psychological issues that have direct practical significance; also, the application of psychological findings.

REVIEW 1.3 What Is a Psychologist?

Not all psychologists do clinical work. Many do research, teach, work in business, or consult. The professional activities of psychologists with doctorates fall into three general categories.

Academic/Research Psychologists	Clinical Psychologists	Psychologists in Industry, Law, or Other Settings
Specialize in areas of pure or applied research, such as	**Do psychotherapy and sometimes research; may work in any of these settings**	**Do research or serve as consultants to institutions on, for example**
Human development	Private practice	Sports
Psychometrics (testing)	Mental-health clinics	Consumer issues
Health	General hospitals	Advertising
Education	Mental hospitals	Organizational problems
Industrial/organizational psychology	Research laboratories	Environmental issues
Physiological psychology	Colleges and universities	Public policy
Sensation and perception		Opinion polls
Design and use of technology		Military training
		Animal behaviour
		Legal issues

Research psychology is the aspect of psychology least recognized or understood by the public. Ludy Benjamin (2003), bemoaning the fact that psychology has never had a United States postage stamp commemorating the discipline or its founders (unlike dozens of other fields, including poultry farming and truck driving), notes that the public "has minimal understanding of psychology as a science and even less appreciation for what psychological scientists do" or how psychological research contributes to human welfare.

We hope that by the time you finish this book, you will have a greater appreciation for what research psychologists do and how their work contributes to human welfare. Here are just a few of the major nonclinical specialties in psychology:

- *Experimental psychologists* conduct laboratory studies of learning, motivation, emotion, sensation and perception, physiology, and cognition. Do not be misled by the term *experimental*, though; other psychologists also do experiments.

- *Educational psychologists* study psychological principles that explain learning and search for ways to improve educational systems. Their interests range from the application of findings on memory and thinking to the use of rewards to encourage achievement.

- *Developmental psychologists* study how people change and grow over time—physically, mentally, and socially. In the past, their focus was mainly on childhood but many now study adolescence, young adulthood, the middle years, or old age.

- *Industrial/organizational psychologists* study behaviour in the workplace. They are concerned with group decision making, employee morale, work motivation, productivity, job stress, personnel selection, marketing strategies, equipment design, and many other issues.

- *Psychometric psychologists* design and evaluate tests of mental abilities, aptitudes, interests, and personality. Nearly all of us have had firsthand experience with one or more of these tests in school or at work.

and noise affect mental health. They do rehabilitation training for people who are physically or mentally disabled. They assist the police in emergencies involving hostages or disturbed persons. They educate judges and juries about eyewitness testimony. They conduct public-opinion surveys. They run suicide-prevention hotlines. They advise zoos on the care and training of animals. They help coaches improve the athletic performance of their teams. And on and on. Is it any wonder that people are a little fuzzy about what a psychologist is?

BIOLOGY, CULTURE, and *Psychology*
Beyond the Borders

The differences we have described among psychological perspectives and specialties have produced many passionate arguments. Not all psychologists, however, feel they must swear allegiance to one approach or another. Indeed, there is a growing trend in psychology to cross the borders that have traditionally divided one specialty from another. This trend has been fuelled by two developments. One is a revolution in our understanding of biology's influence on behaviour. Neuropsychologists are now studying the workings of the brain and its influence on emotions and behaviour. Cognitive psychologists are looking at the neurological aspects of thinking, decision making, and problem solving. Social psychologists have taken an interest in the brain and have even developed a new specialty called "social neuroscience." Clinical scientists are examining the separate and combined effects of medication and psychotherapy in the treatment of psychological disorders. Behavioural geneticists are documenting the contributions of genetics to everything from the origins of personality to the origins of mental illness. Indeed, researchers who study almost any important phenomenon—aggression, anger, love, sexuality, child development, aging, prejudice, war—often now do so by combining psychological findings and biological ones. We will be covering much of the new biological research throughout this book, and, in most chapters, the heading "Biology and . . ." will alert you to discussions of some exciting, cutting-edge findings that have resulted from these efforts.

The second major development is that psychologists are increasingly looking outward to culture as well as inward to biology. They are documenting the many ways in which culture and ethnicity shape and influence much of what we do. Developmental psychologists are looking at culture's impact on mental, social, and linguistic development. Cognitive psychologists are studying cultural influences on achievement, problem solving, and test performance. Social psychologists are examining how a culture's norms and history affect rates of aggression and cooperation. Clinical researchers are exploring how the cultural backgrounds of therapists and clients affect the bond between them and the ultimate success of psychotherapy. Psychologists studying sensation are discovering how culture affects which tastes and smells delight or disgust us. Accordingly, throughout this book you will find a heading called "Culture and . . . ," which will alert you to some of the most exciting results from research incorporating culture.

The modern field of psychology is like a giant mosaic made up of many fragments, yielding a rich, multicoloured psychological portrait. Psychologists may argue about which part of the portrait is most important, but they also have much in common. All psychological scientists, whatever their specialty, believe in the importance of gathering empirical evidence instead of relying on hunches. And one thing will always unite psychologists: a fascination with the unending mysteries of human behaviour and the human mind. If you too have wondered what makes people tick; if you love a mystery and want to know not only who did it but also why they did it; if you are willing to reconsider what you think you think . . . then you are in the right course. We invite you now to step into the world of psychology, the discipline that dares to explore the most complex topic on earth: *you.*

Are you ready to have some light shed on the mysteries of human behaviour? Then keep reading!

Chanpipat/Shutterstock

Taking Psychology with You

THINKING CRITICALLY IN EVERYDAY LIFE

Psychology Can Help You Get Better Grades

How can you use psychology to improve your grades? Do you remember at the beginning of the chapter where we discussed what psychology is and how it is concerned with behaviour and mental processes? Well, part of psychology studies memory strategies that can help you understand course material, absorb it thoroughly as you study, and successfully retrieve it when you need it. Ideally, these strategies will help you with taking tests and with applying this material during everyday life. So what are you waiting for? Go make psychology work for you!

Read, Recite, Review

Reading is not enough. The types of encoding we discuss in more detail in Chapter 10 (memory), such as *elaborate encoding* and *deep processing*, are useful because they force you to be an active rather than a passive learner. Many students believe that the best way to study for an exam is to read and reread a textbook passage until they think that they've "got it." This passive strategy feels intuitively right, but it is actually much less effective than actively rehearsing and recalling the material. In the *read-recite-review strategy*, you read the passage, close the book, hide your notes, write down (or say out loud) everything you can recall, and then review what you've read to see if you understood and remember the information. In a series of experiments, researchers compared this strategy with simply rereading and taking notes. Participants took free recall tests on the material, answered multiple-choice questions, and took short-answer tests right after studying

and again a week later. The active read-recite-review strategy was the hands-down winner (McDaniel, Howard, & Einstein, 2009).

Retrieval Practice

Most students define "learning" as the ability to retrieve the correct answer to a question from memory. But then what? Once retrieved, say, for an exam, does that answer stay put or vanish quickly like steam on a bathroom mirror? Cognitive psychologists have found that *retrieval practice* is necessary if a memory is going to undergo consolidation and therefore remain available for a long time—even after your course is over. In a series of experiments in which students learned words in foreign languages, once a student had learned a word it was (a) repeatedly studied but dropped from further testing, (b) repeatedly tested but dropped from further studying, or (c) dropped from studying and testing. To the surprise of the students themselves, who were completely unable to predict how they would do on the tests, studying after learning had no effect on their subsequent ability to recall the foreign words. But repeated testing (i.e., practice in repeatedly retrieving the words from memory) had a large, significant benefit (Karpicke & Roediger, 2008). So when your professors (and your textbook authors) want to keep quizzing you, why, it's only for your own good.

Mnemonics

In addition to using elaborative rehearsal, deep processing, strategies such as read-recite-review, and retrieval practice, people who want to give their powers of memory a boost sometimes use mnemonics [neh-MON-iks], formal strategies and tricks for encoding, storing, and retaining information. (Mnemosyne, pronounced neh-MOZ-eh-nee, was the ancient Greek goddess of memory. Can you remember her?) Some mnemonics take the form of easily memorized rhymes (e.g., "Thirty days hath September/April, June, and November . . ."). Others use formulas (e.g., "Please never, never, never question our mother's singing and baking" for the names of the provinces from east to west). Still others use visual images or word associations. The best mnemonics force you to encode material actively and thoroughly. They may also reduce the amount of information by chunking it, which is why, in ads, many companies use words for their phone numbers instead of unmemorable numbers ("1-888-GOT-JUNK").

Apply Your Learning

Add meaning to the material you are learning by applying it to your own experiences. The more meaningful the material, the more likely it is to link up with information already in long-term memory. Meaningfulness also reduces the number of chunks of information you have to learn. Common ways of adding meaning include making up a story about the material, thinking of examples, and forming visual images. If you are trying to remember a difficult concept in a chapter, you might make the concept meaningful by thinking of an example from your own life.

Avoid Cramming

We recommend that you take your time when studying. Leisurely learning, spread out over several sessions, usually produces better results than harried cramming (although reviewing material just before a test can be helpful). In terms of hours spent, "distributed" (spaced) learning sessions are more efficient than "massed" ones. In other words, three separate one-hour study sessions may result in more retention than one session of three hours. Remember, only moderate amounts of stress can help memory; thus, keeping study time distributed can reduce stress associated with studying to a moderate level.

Also take time off from studying. If possible, minimize interference by using study breaks for rest or recreation. Sleep is the ultimate way to reduce interference. In a classic study, students who slept for eight hours after learning lists of nonsense syllables retained them better than students who went about their usual business (Jenkins & Dallenbach, 1924). Sleep is not always possible, of course, but periodic mental relaxation usually is.

Whatever strategies you use, you will find that active learning produces more comprehension and better retention than does passive reading or listening. The mind does not gobble up information automatically; you must make the material digestible. Even then, you should not expect to remember everything you read or hear. Nor should you want to. Piling up facts without distinguishing the important from the trivial is just confusing.

Popular books and podcasts that promise a "perfect," "photographic" memory, or "instant recall" of everything you learn, fly in the face of what psychologists know about how the mind operates. Our advice: Forget them. The fastest route to a good memory is to follow the principles suggested by the findings in this section.

Summary

MyPsychLab can help you get a better grade. Test your knowledge and grasp difficult concepts through
- Custom study plans: See where you are strong and where you are wrong.
- Multimedia, including videos and interactive simulations
- Dynamic Study Modules: flashcards for self-study that ensure you achieve mastery of course concepts

Psychology, Pseudoscience, and Popular Opinion

- *Psychology* is the discipline concerned with behaviour and mental processes and how they are affected by an organism's external and internal environment. Psychology's methods and reliance on *empirical evidence* distinguish it from pseudoscience and "psychobabble." An introductory psychology course can correct many misconceptions about human behaviour.

- Psychologists have many pseudoscientific competitors, such as astrologers and psychics. But when put to the test, the claims and predictions of these competitors turn out to be meaningless or just plain wrong. Psychobabble is appealing because it confirms our beliefs and prejudices; in contrast, psychology often challenges them, although it also seeks to extend our understanding of familiar facts.

Thinking Critically and Creatively about Psychology

- One benefit of studying psychology is the development of *critical-thinking* skills and attitudes. Critical thinking helps people evaluate competing findings on psychological issues that are personally and socially important.

- The critical thinker asks questions, defines terms clearly, examines the evidence, analyzes assumptions and biases, avoids emotional reasoning, avoids oversimplification, considers alternative interpretations, and tolerates uncertainty. Critical thinking is an evolving process rather than a once-and-for-all accomplishment.

Psychology's Past: From the Armchair to the Laboratory

- Psychology's forerunners made some valid observations and had useful insights, but without rigorous empirical methods they also made serious errors in the description and explanation of behaviour, as in the case of *phrenology*.

- The official founder of scientific psychology was Wilhelm Wundt, who formally established the first psychological laboratory in 1879, in Leipzig, Germany. His work led to *structuralism*, the first of many approaches to the field. Structuralism emphasized the analysis of immediate experience into basic elements. It was soon abandoned, in part because of its reliance on *introspection*.

- Another early approach, *functionalism*, was inspired in part by the evolutionary theories of Charles Darwin; it emphasized the purpose of behaviour. One of its leading proponents was William James. Functionalism, too, did not last long as a distinct school of psychology, but it greatly affected the course of psychological science.

- Psychology as a method of psychotherapy has roots in Sigmund Freud's theory of *psychoanalysis*, which emphasizes unconscious causes of mental and emotional problems.

Psychology's Present: Behaviour, Body, Mind, and Culture

- Several points of view predominate today in psychology. The *biological perspective* emphasizes bodily events associated with actions, thoughts, and feelings, and also genetic contributions to behaviour. Within this perspective, a popular new specialty, *evolutionary psychology*, is following in the footsteps of functionalism. The *learning perspective* emphasizes how the environment and a person's history affect behaviour; within this perspective, *behaviourists* reject mentalistic explanations, and *social-cognitive learning theorists* combine elements of behaviourism with the study of thoughts, values, and intentions. The *cognitive perspective* emphasizes mental processes in perception, problem solving, belief formation, and other human activities. The *sociocultural perspective* explores how social contexts and cultural rules affect an individual's beliefs and behaviour. And the *psychodynamic perspective*, which

originated with Freud's theory of psychoanalysis, emphasizes unconscious motives, conflicts, and desires; it differs greatly from the other approaches in its methods and standards of evidence.

- Not all approaches to psychology fit neatly into one of the five major perspectives. For example, two important movements, *humanist psychology* and *feminist psychology*, have influenced the questions researchers ask, the methods they use, and their awareness of biases in the field. A contemporary research specialty called *positive psychology* follows in the tradition of humanism by focusing on the positive aspects of human behaviour.

What Psychologists Do

- Psychologists do research and teach in colleges and universities, provide mental-health services (*psychological practice*), and conduct research and apply findings in a wide variety of nonacademic settings. *Applied psychology* is concerned with the practical uses of psychological knowledge. *Basic psychology* is concerned with knowledge for its own sake. Among the many psychological specialties are experimental, educational, developmental, industrial and organizational, psychometric, counselling, school, and clinical psychology.

- *Psychotherapist* is an unregulated term for anyone who does therapy, including persons who have no credentials or training at all. Licensed therapists differ according to their training and approach. *Clinical psychologists* have a PhD, an EdD, or a PsyD; *psychiatrists* have an MD; *psychoanalysts* are trained in psychoanalytic institutes; and licensed clinical social workers, counsellors with various specialties, and marriage, family, and child counsellors may have a variety of postgraduate degrees. Many psychologists are concerned about an increase in poorly trained psychotherapists who lack credentials or a firm understanding of research methods and findings.

Biology, Culture, and Psychology: Beyond the Borders

- Many, if not most, psychologists draw on more than one school of psychology. Indeed, there is a growing trend in psychology to cross the borders that have traditionally divided one specialty from another, a trend encouraged by increased interest in biological and cultural influences on behaviour.

- Although psychologists differ in their perspectives and goals, psychological scientists, whatever their specialty, generally agree on which methods of study are acceptable, and all psychologists are united by their fascination with the mysteries of behaviour.

Key Terms

Use this list to check your understanding of terms and people in this chapter. If you have trouble with a term, you can find it on the page listed.

empirical **3**

psychology **4**

psychobabble **4**

critical thinking **7**

Occam's Razor **12**

phrenology **15**

structuralism **16**

functionalism **17**

psychoanalysis **18**

biological perspective **19**

evolutionary psychology **19**

learning perspective **19**

behaviourism **19**

cognitive perspective **20**

sociocultural perspective **20**

psychodynamic perspective **20**

humanist psychology **21**

feminist psychology **22**

psychological practice **23**

basic psychology **23**

applied psychology **23**

psychotherapist **25**

psychoanalyst **25**

psychiatrist **26**

How Psychologists Do Research

Ask questions. . . be willing to wonder

If you want to be a psychologist so that you can help people, why in the world do you need to study statistics and research methods?

━━━━

If you hear that TV watching is linked to hyperactivity, can you say which causes which?

━━━━

How could you find out whether driving while talking on a cellphone is dangerous?

━━━━

Why do psychologists study animals— the nonhuman kind?

Here are four words that make many people nervous: *research, statistics, methods,* and *math.* "What do we have to learn this stuff for?" our students have often lamented. "I'm never going to need it anyway. Let's just cut straight to the findings." In this chapter, we hope to persuade you that of all the stuff you are going to learn in psychology, the information in this chapter may be the most important for protecting yourself from making wrong choices, adopting mistaken beliefs, or coming to inappropriate conclusions. Consider these claims:

- Various studies report that playing fast-paced video games such as *The Last of Us* and *Bioshock Infinite* improves players' cognitive abilities, such as visual attention and speed of response. Moreover, these games have a "transfer effect," improving visual skills in other areas of life. Does this mean that you now have a legitimate reason to spend more time playing video games?

- A paper in a major psychology journal claims that the results of nine experiments, involving 1000 university students, found "statistically significant" evidence of extrasensory perception (ESP). The students had to choose which of two curtains on a computer screen had an erotic picture behind it, and they allegedly demonstrated ESP by doing this at a rate that was slightly above chance (Bem, 2011). Was this good evidence of ESP?

- Your nine-year-old son is autistic. He lives in his own private world, cut off from normal social interaction. He does not speak, and he rarely looks you in the eye. He has never been able to function in a public school classroom. You hear about a technique called "facilitated communication" (FC), in which children with autism are placed in front of a keyboard while an adult "facilitator" gently places a hand over the child's hand or forearm. The method's proponents claim that children who have never used words before are able to type out complete sentences, answer questions, and divulge their thoughts. Some children, through their facilitators, have supposedly mastered advanced subjects or have written poetry of astonishing beauty. Should you sign up your child for FC?

THINKING CRITICALLY

Examine the evidence.

A study reported that playing video games may help children's cognitive abilities. Some students happily concluded that video games were beneficial. But how else could these findings be interpreted? Later in this chapter, you will learn the answers.

By the time you finish this chapter, you will know how to think critically about these questions and the many others you encounter. Research methods are the tools of the psychological scientist's trade, and understanding them is crucial for everyone who reads or hears about a new program or an "exciting finding" that is said to be based on psychological research. Trying to practise critical thinking or apply psychological findings to your own life without having these tools is like trying to dig a foundation for your house with teaspoons. You could do it, but it would take a *long* time and the result wouldn't be very sturdy. Knowing the difference between claims based on good research and those based on sloppy research or anecdotes can help you make wiser psychological and medical decisions, prevent you from spending money on worthless programs, and sometimes even save lives.

Learning Objectives

1. List and define the five key characteristics of scientific psychological research.

2. Recognize the biases psychologists encounter in the conduct and publication of their research.

3. Understand the system of checks and balances involved in publishing high quality research.

What Makes Psychological Research Scientific?

When we say that psychologists are scientists, we do not mean they work with complicated instruments and machines (although some do). The scientific enterprise has more to do with attitudes and procedures than with apparatus (Stanovich, 2010). Here are a few key characteristics of the ideal scientist:

1 **Precision.** Scientists sometimes launch an investigation simply because of a hunch they have about some behaviour. Often, however, they start out with a general **theory**, an organized system of assumptions and principles that purports to explain certain phenomena and how they are related. Many people misunderstand what scientists mean by a theory. A scientific theory is not just someone's personal opinion, as in "It's only a theory." Many scientific theories are tentative, pending more research, but others, such as the theory of evolution, are accepted by nearly all scientists.

From a hunch or theory, a psychological scientist derives a **hypothesis**, a statement that attempts to describe or explain a given behaviour. Initially, this statement may be quite general, as in, say, "Misery loves company." But before any research can be done, the hypothesis must be made more precise. "Misery loves company" might be rephrased as "People who are anxious about a threatening situation tend to seek out others facing the same threat."

Watch the Video *The Big Picture: How to Answer Psychological Questions* in **MyPsychLab**

theory An organized system of assumptions and principles that purports to explain a specified set of phenomena and their interrelationships.

hypothesis A statement that attempts to predict or to account for a set of phenomena; scientific hypotheses specify relationships among events or variables and are empirically tested.

A hypothesis, in turn, leads to predictions about what will happen in a particular situation. In a prediction, terms such as *anxiety* or *threatening situation* are given **operational definitions**, which specify how the phenomena in question are to be observed and measured. "Anxiety" might be defined operationally as a score on an anxiety questionnaire, and "threatening situation" as the threat of an electric shock. The prediction might be "If you raise people's anxiety scores by telling them they are going to receive electric shocks, and then give them the choice of waiting alone or with others who are in the same situation, they will be more likely to choose to wait with others than they would be if they were not anxious." The prediction can then be tested using systematic methods.

2 **Skepticism.** Scientists do not accept ideas on faith or authority; their motto is "Show me!" Some of the greatest scientific advances have been made by those who dared to doubt what everyone else assumed to be true: that the sun revolves around the earth, that illness can be cured by applying leeches to the skin, that madness is a sign of demonic possession. In the world of science, skepticism means treating conclusions, both new and old, with caution.

Thus, in the case of facilitated communication, psychological scientists did not simply say, "Wow, what an interesting way to help autistic kids." Rather than accept testimonials about the method's effectiveness, they have done experiments involving hundreds of autistic children and their facilitators (Romanczyk et al., 2003). Their techniques have been simple: They have the child identify a picture but show the facilitator a different picture or no picture at all, or they keep the facilitator from hearing the questions being put to the child. Under these conditions, the child types only what the facilitator sees or hears, not what the child sees or hears. This research shows that what happens in facilitated communication is exactly what happens when a medium guides a person's hand over a Ouija board to help the person receive "messages" from a "spirit": The person doing the "facilitating" unconsciously nudges the other person's hand in the desired direction, remaining unaware of having influenced the responses produced (Wegner, Fuller, & Sparrow, 2003). In other words, facilitated communication is really facilitator communication. This finding is vitally important, because if parents waste their time and money on a treatment that doesn't work, they may never get genuine help for their children, and they will suffer when their false hopes are finally shattered by reality.

"Skepticism" is not simply about debunking some claim, but showing *why* the claim is invalid—so that better methods can replace it. Skepticism and caution, however, must be balanced by openness to new ideas and evidence. Otherwise, a scientist may wind up as shortsighted as the famous physicist Lord Kelvin, who reputedly declared with great confidence at the end of the nineteenth century that radio had no future, X-rays were a hoax, and "heavier-than-air flying machines" were impossible.

3 **Reliance on empirical evidence.** Unlike plays and poems, scientific theories and hypotheses are not judged by how pleasing or entertaining they are, or by whether they fit our prejudices and preferences. An idea may initially generate excitement because it is plausible or imaginative, but it must eventually be backed by empirical evidence. A collection of anecdotes or an appeal to authority will not do, nor will the intuitive appeal of the idea or its popularity. As Nobel Prize–winning scientist Peter Medawar (1979) once wrote, "The intensity of the conviction that a hypothesis is true has no bearing on whether it is true or not." In 2011, Richard Muller, a prominent physicist who had doubted that global warming was occurring, made headlines when he reported, after a two-year investigation, that temperatures really are rising, and the following year, that human beings are a large part of the reason. Muller had been funded in large measure by two conservative oil billionaires who did not welcome his results. But Muller let the evidence trump politics, as a scientist should.

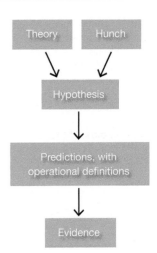

operational definition A precise definition of a term in a hypothesis, which specifies the operations for observing and measuring the process or phenomenon being defined.

principle of falsifiability The principle that a scientific theory must make predictions that are specific enough to expose the theory to the possibility of disconfirmation; that is, the theory must predict not only what will happen but also what will not happen.

confirmation bias The tendency to look for or pay attention only to information that confirms one's own belief.

4 **Willingness to make "risky predictions."** A related principle is that a scientist must state an idea in such a way that it can be *refuted*, or disproved by counterevidence. This important rule, known as the **principle of falsifiability**, does not mean that the idea *will* be disproved, only that it could be if contrary evidence were to be discovered. In other words, a scientist must risk disconfirmation by predicting not only what will happen but also what will *not* happen. In the "misery loves company" study, the hypothesis would be supported if most anxious people sought each other out, but would be disconfirmed if most anxious people went off alone to sulk and worry, or if anxiety had no effect on their behaviour (see Figure 2.1). A willingness to risk disconfirmation forces the scientist to take negative evidence seriously and to abandon mistaken hypotheses.

The principle of falsifiability is often violated in everyday life, because all of us are vulnerable to the **confirmation bias**: the tendency to look for and accept evidence that supports our pet theories and assumptions and to ignore or reject evidence that contradicts our beliefs. If a police officer is convinced of a suspect's guilt, he or she may interpret anything the suspect says, even the person's maintenance of innocence, as confirming evidence that the suspect is guilty ("Of course he says he's innocent; he's a liar"). But what if the suspect *is* innocent? The principle of falsifiability compels scientists—and the rest of us—to resist the confirmation bias and to consider counterevidence.

5 **Openness.** Science depends on the free flow of ideas and full disclosure of the procedures used in a study. Secrecy is a big "no-no"; scientists must be willing to tell others where they got their ideas, how they tested them, and what the results were. They must do this clearly and in detail so that other scientists can repeat, or *replicate*, their studies and verify—or challenge—the findings. Replication is an essential part of the scientific process because sometimes what seems to be a fabulous phenomenon turns out to be only a fluke.

If you think about it, you will see that these principles of good science correspond to the critical thinking guidelines described in Chapter 1. Formulating a prediction

FIGURE 2.1 The Principle of Falsifiability

The scientific method requires researchers to expose their ideas to the possibility of counterevidence, as in row (a). In contrast, people claiming psychic powers, such as dowsers (who say they can find underground water with a "dowsing rod" that bends when water is present), typically interpret all possible outcomes as support for their assertions, as in row (b). Their claims are therefore untestable.

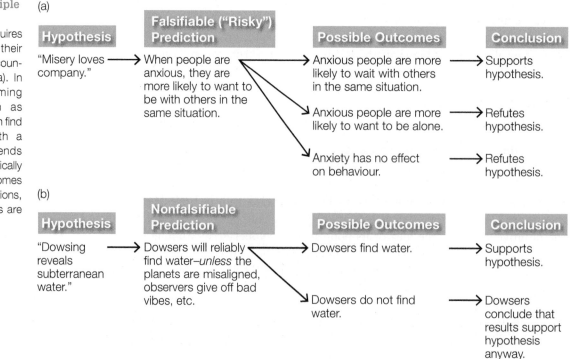

with operational definitions corresponds to "define your terms." Openness to new ideas encourages scientists to "ask questions" and "consider other interpretations." Reliance on empirical evidence helps scientists avoid the temptation to oversimplify. The principle of falsifiability forces scientists to "analyze assumptions and biases" in a fair-minded fashion. And until their results have been replicated and verified, scientists must "tolerate uncertainty."

Do psychologists and other scientists unfailingly live up to these lofty standards? Not always. Being only human, they may put too much trust in their personal experiences, be biased by a conflict of interest when they are funded by private industry, or permit ambition to interfere with openness. Like everyone else, they may find it hard to admit that the evidence does not support their hypothesis; it is far easier to be skeptical about someone else's ideas than about your own (Tavris & Aronson, 2007).

Commitment to one's theories is not in itself a bad thing. Passion is the fuel of progress. It motivates researchers to think boldly and do the exhaustive testing that is often required to support an idea. But passion can also cloud perceptions, causing scientists to misinterpret their own data to confirm what they want to see. Other scientists, motivated by the desire for fame, discovery, or fortune, have even resorted to plagiarism, faking their data, and other deceptive methods. That is why science is a communal activity. Scientists are expected to submit their results to professional journals, which send the findings to experts in the field for evaluation before deciding whether to publish them. This process, called *peer review*, is an effort to ensure that the work lives up to accepted scientific standards. Peer review and scientific publication are supposed to precede announcements to the public through press releases, internet postings, or popular books. The research community acts as a jury, scrutinizing and sifting the evidence, judging its integrity, approving some viewpoints, and relegating others to the scientific scrap heap.

The peer review process is not perfect, but it does give science a built-in system of checks and balances. Individuals are not necessarily objective, honest, or rational, but science forces them to subject their findings to scrutiny and to justify their claims.

Recite & Review

Recite: Out loud, say as much as you can about these concepts: *theory, hypothesis, operational definition, principle of falsifiability,* and *confirmation bias.*

Review: Next, go back and reread this section.

Now take this *Quick Quiz:*

Can you identify which rule of science was violated in each of the following cases?

1. For nine months after being diagnosed with a treatable form of pancreatic cancer, Steve Jobs refused to have surgery and instead tried to heal himself with alternate therapies including herbal treatments and restrictive diet regimens.

2. Sigmund Freud theorized that all men unconsciously experience "castration anxiety." When his fellow analysts questioned this notion and asked for his evidence, he was amused. He wrote: "One hears of analysts who boast that, though they have worked for dozens of years, they have never found a sign of the existence of the castration complex. We must bow our heads in recognition of . . . [this] piece of virtuosity in the art of overlooking and mistaking."

Answers:

1. Jobs did not examine the evidence from scientific studies of the value of these therapies for those with pancreatic cancer. He also may have been vulnerable to the confirmation bias, as he may have looked for and believed reports that supported his desire to avoid surgery. **2.** Freud violated the principle of falsifiability. If analysts saw castration anxiety in their patients, Freud was right; but if they failed to see it, they were "overlooking" and "mistaking" it, and Freud was still right. Thus, no possible counterevidence could refute the theory.

Learning Objectives

4 Understand the process and limitations involved in gathering a study sample. Use the material on WEIRDos to describe how these limitations can affect the generalizability of results.

5 Define case studies, naturalistic and laboratory observation techniques. Compare their strengths and weaknesses.

6 Using projective and objective tests as an example, identify and define the criteria that measure a test's quality, including standardization, reliability, and validity.

7 Understand the pros and cons to using surveys to collect information. List two possible sources of bias.

Descriptive Studies: Establishing the Facts

Psychologists gather evidence to support their hypotheses by using different methods, depending on the kinds of questions they want to answer. These methods are not mutually exclusive, however. Just as a police detective may rely on DNA samples, fingerprints, and interviews of suspects to figure out "whodunnit," psychological sleuths often draw on different techniques at different stages of an investigation.

One of the first challenges facing any researcher, no matter what method is used, is to select the participants (sometimes called "subjects") for the study. Ideally, the researcher would prefer to get a **representative sample**, a group of participants that accurately represents the larger population that the researcher is interested in. Suppose you wanted to learn about drug use among first-year university students in Canada. Questioning or observing every first-year student in the country would obviously not be practical; instead, you would need to recruit a sample. You could use special selection procedures to ensure that this sample contained the same proportion of women, men, immigrants, indigenous peoples, francophones, and so on as in the general population of first-year university students. Even then, a sample drawn just from your own school or town might not produce results applicable to the entire country or even your home province.

A sample's size is less critical than its representativeness. A small but representative sample may yield important results, whereas a large study that fails to use proper sampling methods may yield questionable results. But in practice, those who study human behaviour must often settle for a sample of people who happen to be available—a "convenience" sample—and more often than not, this means undergraduate students. One group of researchers noted that most of these students are WEIRDos—from Western, educated, industrialized, rich, and democratic cultures—and thus hardly representative of humans as a whole. "WEIRD subjects are some of the most psychologically unusual people on the planet," said one of the investigators (Henrich, Heine, & Norenzayan, 2010).

Typically, undergraduates are younger than the general population. They are also more likely to be female and to have better cognitive skills than those who do not go to university. Does that matter? It depends. Many psychological processes, such as basic perceptual or memory processes, are likely to be the same in students as in anyone else; after all, students are not a separate species, no matter what they (or their professors) may sometimes think! When considering other topics, however, we may need to be cautious about drawing conclusions until the research can be replicated with nonstudents. Scientists are turning to technology to help them do this. Amazon runs a site called Mechanical Turk, where people across the world do online tasks that computers cannot do, typically for small rewards that they usually convert into Amazon vouchers. Many of the 500 000 registered Turk workers also participate in research, allowing scientists to quickly and cheaply recruit a diverse sample of thousands of people (Buhrmester, Kwang, &

representative sample A group of individuals, selected from a population for study, that matches the population on important characteristics such as age and sex.

Gosling, 2011). One research team was able to analyze the patterns of moods in people's tweets worldwide (Golder & Macy, 2011) and using search terms from Google, scientists have predicted flu (and other disease) outbreaks (e.g. Ginsberg et al., 2008).

We turn now to the specific methods used most commonly in psychological research. As you read about these methods, you may want to list their advantages and disadvantages in order to remember them better. Then check your list against the one in Review 2.1. We will begin with **descriptive methods**, which allow researchers to describe and predict behaviour but not necessarily to choose one explanation over competing ones.

Case Studies

A **case study** (or *case history*) is a detailed description of a particular individual based on careful observation or formal psychological testing. It may include information about a person's childhood, dreams, fantasies, experiences, and relationships—anything that will provide insight into the person's behaviour. Case studies are most commonly used by clinicians, but sometimes academic researchers use them as well, especially when they are just beginning to study a topic or when practical or ethical considerations prevent them from gathering information in other ways.

Suppose you want to know whether the first few years of life are critical for acquiring a first language. Can children who have missed out on hearing speech (or, in the case of deaf children, seeing signs) during their early years catch up later on? Obviously, psychologists cannot answer this question by isolating children and seeing what happens. So, instead, they have studied unusual cases of language deprivation.

One such case involved a 13-year-old girl who had been cruelly locked up in a small room since the age of 1½, strapped for hours to a potty chair. Her mother, a battered wife, barely cared for her, and no one in the family spoke a word to her. If she made the slightest sound, her severely disturbed father beat her. When she was finally rescued, "Genie," as researchers called her, did not know how to chew or stand erect and was not toilet trained. She spat on anything that was handy, including other people, and her only sounds were high-pitched whimpers. Eventually, she was able to learn some rules of social conduct, and she began to understand short sentences and to use words to convey her needs, describe her moods, and even lie. But even after many years, Genie's grammar and pronunciation remained abnormal. She never learned to use pronouns correctly, ask questions, produce proper negative sentences, or use the little word endings that communicate tense, number, and possession (Curtiss, 1977, 1982; Rymer, 1993). This sad case, along with similar ones, suggests that a critical period exists for language development, with the likelihood of fully mastering a first language declining steadily after early childhood and falling off drastically at puberty (Pinker, 1994).

Case studies illustrate psychological principles in a way that abstract generalizations and cold statistics never can, and they produce a more detailed picture of an individual than other methods do. In biological research, cases of patients with brain damage have yielded important clues to how the brain is organized (see Chapter 4). But in most instances, case studies have serious drawbacks. Information is often missing or hard to interpret; no one knows what Genie's language development was like before she was locked up or whether she was born with mental deficits. The observer who writes up the case may have certain biases that influence which facts are noticed or overlooked. The person who is the focus of the study may have selective or inaccurate memories, making any conclusions unreliable (Loftus & Guyer, 2002). Most important, because that person may be unrepresentative of the group the researcher is interested in, this method has only limited usefulness for deriving general principles of behaviour. For all these reasons, case studies are usually used only as sources, rather than tests, of hypotheses.

descriptive methods Methods that yield descriptions of behaviour but not necessarily causal explanations.

case study A detailed description of a particular individual being studied or treated.

This picture, drawn by Genie, a young girl who endured years of isolation and mistreatment, shows one of her favourite pastimes: listening to researcher Susan Curtiss playing the piano. Genie's drawings were used along with other case material to study her mental and social development.

Susan Curtiss/Elsevier Science (USA)

THINKING CRITICALLY

Don't oversimplify.

Case studies are often enormously compelling, which is why talk shows love them. But often they are merely anecdotes. What are the dangers in using case studies to draw general conclusions about human nature?

Many psychotherapists publish individual case studies of their clients in treatment. These can be informative, but they are not equivalent to scientific research and can sometimes be incorrect or misleading. Consider the sensational story of "Sybil," whose account of her 16 personalities became a famous book and TV movie, eventually launching an epidemic of multiple personality disorder (see Chapter 15). Detective work by investigative journalists and other skeptics later revealed that Sybil was not a multiple personality after all; her diagnosis was created in collusion with her psychiatrist, Cornelia Wilbur, who hoped to profit professionally and financially from the story (Nathan, 2011). Wilbur omitted many facts from her case study of Sybil, such as the vitamin B_{12} deficiency that produced Sybil's emotional and physical problems. Wilbur did not disclose that she was administering massive amounts of heavy drugs to her patient, who became addicted to them. And she never informed her colleagues or the public that Sybil had written to her admitting that she did not have multiple personalities.

Be wary, then, of the compelling case histories reported in the media by individuals or by therapists. Often, these stories are only "arguing by anecdote," and they are not a basis for drawing firm conclusions about anything.

Observational Studies

In **observational studies**, the researcher observes, measures, and records behaviour, taking care to avoid intruding on the people (or animals) being observed. Unlike case studies, observational studies usually involve many participants. Often, an observational study is the first step in a program of research; it is helpful to have a good description of behaviour before you try to explain it.

The primary purpose of *naturalistic observation* is to find out how people or animals act in their normal social environments. Psychologists use naturalistic observation wherever people happen to be—at home, on playgrounds or streets, in schoolrooms, or in offices. In one study, a social psychologist and his students ventured into a common human habitat: bars. They wanted to know whether people in bars drink more when they are in groups than when they are alone. They visited all 32 pubs in a mid-sized city, ordered beers, and recorded on napkins and pieces of newspaper how much the other patrons imbibed. They found that drinkers in groups consumed more than individuals who were alone. Those in groups did not drink any faster; they just lingered in the bar longer (Sommer, 1977).

observational study A study in which the researcher carefully and systematically observes and records behaviour without interfering with the behaviour; it may involve either naturalistic or laboratory observation.

The students who did this study did not rely on their impressions or memories of how much people drank. In observational studies, researchers count, rate, or measure behaviour systematically, to guard against noticing only what they expect or want to see, and they keep careful records so that others can check their observations. Observers must also take pains to avoid being obvious about what they are doing so that those who are being observed will behave naturally. If the students who studied drinking

GET INVOLVED! A Study of Personal Space

Try a little naturalistic observation of your own. Go to a public place where people voluntarily seat themselves near others, such as a movie theatre or a cafeteria with large tables. If you choose a setting where many people enter at once, you might recruit some friends to help you; you can divide the area into sections and give each observer one section to observe. As individuals and groups sit down, note how many seats they leave between themselves and the next person. On average, how far do people tend to sit from strangers? Once you have your results, see how many possible explanations you can come up with.

Psychologists using laboratory observation have gathered valuable information about brain and muscle activity during sleep. Psychologists using naturalistic observation have studied how people in crowded places modify their gaze and body position to preserve a sense of privacy.

Left: Richard Damoret/The New York Times. Right: Michael Lusmore/Alamy.

habits had marched into those bars with camcorders and announced their intentions to the customers, the results might have been quite different.

Sometimes psychologists prefer to make observations in a laboratory setting. In *laboratory observation*, researchers have more control of the situation. They can use sophisticated equipment, determine the number of people who will be observed, maintain a clear line of vision, and so forth. Say you wanted to know how infants of different ages respond when left with a stranger. You might have parents and their infants come to your laboratory, observe them playing together for a while through a one-way window, then have a stranger enter the room and, a few minutes later, have the parent leave. You could record signs of distress in the children, interactions with the stranger, and other behaviour. If you did this, you would find that very young infants carry on cheerfully with whatever they are doing when the parent leaves. However, by the age of about eight months, many children will burst into tears or show other signs of what child psychologists call "separation anxiety."

One shortcoming of laboratory observation is that the presence of researchers and special equipment may cause people to behave differently than they would in their usual surroundings. Further, whether they are in natural or laboratory settings, observational studies, like other descriptive methods, are more useful for describing behaviour than for explaining it. The barroom results we described do not necessarily mean that being in a group makes people drink a lot. People may join a group because they are already interested in drinking and find it more comfortable to hang around the bar if they are with others. Similarly, if we observe infants protesting whenever a parent leaves the room, is it because they have become attached to their parents and want them nearby, or have they simply learned from experience that crying brings an adult with a smile and a cuddle? Observational studies alone cannot answer such questions.

Tests

Psychological tests, sometimes called *assessment instruments*, are procedures for measuring and evaluating personality traits, emotions, aptitudes, interests, abilities, and values. Typically, tests require people to answer a series of written or oral questions. The answers may then be totalled to yield a single numerical score, or a set of scores. *Objective tests*, also called *inventories*, measure beliefs, feelings, or behaviours of which an individual is aware; *projective tests* are designed to tap unconscious feelings or motives (see Chapter 15).

psychological tests Procedures used to measure and evaluate personality traits, emotional states, aptitudes, interests, abilities, and values.

standardize In test construction, to develop uniform procedures for giving and scoring a test.

norms In test construction, established standards of performance.

reliability In test construction, the consistency of scores derived from a test, from one time and place to another.

validity The ability of a test to measure what it was designed to measure.

At one time or another, you no doubt have taken a personality test, an achievement test, or a vocational-aptitude test. Hundreds of psychological tests are used in industry, education, the military, and the helping professions, and many tests are also used in research. Some tests are given to individuals, others to large groups. These measures help clarify differences among people, as well as differences in the reactions of the same person on different occasions or at different stages of life. Tests may be used to promote self-understanding, to evaluate psychological treatments and programs, or, in scientific research, to draw generalizations about human behaviour. Well-constructed psychological tests are a great improvement over simple self-evaluation, because many people have a distorted view of their own abilities and traits.

One measure of a good test is whether it is **standardized**—whether uniform procedures exist for giving and scoring the test. It would hardly be fair to give some people detailed instructions and plenty of time and others only vague instructions and limited time. Those who administer the test must know exactly how to explain the tasks involved, how much time to allow, and what materials to use. Scoring is usually done by referring to **norms**, or established standards of performance. The usual procedure for developing norms is to give the test to a large group of people who resemble the population for whom the test is intended. Norms determine which scores can be considered high, low, or average.

Test construction presents many challenges. For one thing, the test must be **reliable**; it must produce the same results from one time and place to the next or from one scorer to another. A vocational interest test is not reliable if it says that Greg would make a wonderful engineer but a poor journalist, but then gives different results when Greg retakes the test a week later. Psychologists can measure *test–retest reliability* by giving the test twice to the same group of people and comparing the two sets of scores statistically. If the test is reliable, individuals' scores will be similar from one session to another. This method has a drawback, however: People tend to do better the second time they take a test, after they have become familiar with it. A solution is to compute *alternate-forms reliability* by giving different versions of the same test to the same group on two separate occasions. The items on the two forms are similar in format but are not identical in content. Performance cannot improve because of familiarity with the items, although people may still do somewhat better the second time around because they have learned the procedures expected of them.

To be useful, a test must also be **valid**; that is, it must measure what it sets out to measure. A creativity test is not valid if what it actually measures is verbal sophistication. If the items broadly represent the trait in question, the test is said to have *content validity*. If you were testing, say, employees' job satisfaction, and your test tapped a broad array of relevant beliefs and behaviours (e.g., "Do you feel you have reached a dead end at work?" "Are you bored with your assignments?"), it would have content validity. If the test asked only how workers felt about their salary level, it would lack content validity and would be of little use; after all, highly paid people are not always satisfied with their jobs, and people who earn low wages are not always dissatisfied.

Most tests are also judged on *criterion validity*, the ability to predict independent measures, or criteria, of the trait in question. The criterion for a scholastic aptitude test might be grades; the criterion for a test of shyness might be behaviour in social situations. To find out whether your job satisfaction test had criterion validity, you might return a year later to see whether it correctly predicted absenteeism, resignations, or requests for job transfers.

Reliability
How consistent are the test's results?

Test-Retest Reliability

Are scores similar from one session to another?

Alternate-Forms Reliability

Are scores similar on different versions of the test?

Teachers, parents, and employers do not always stop to question a test's validity, especially when the results are summarized in a single, precise-sounding number, such as an IQ score of 115 or a job applicant's ranking of 5. Among psychologists and educators, however, controversy exists about the validity and usefulness of even some widely used tests, including tests like the Test of English as a Foreign Language (TOEFL) or standardized IQ tests. In Canada and 80 other countries, if you are a non-native English speaker, admission to university can depend primarily on your score on the TOEFL. However the relation between TOEFL scores and academic performance for undergraduates is not great (Simner, 1998). This is why the Canadian Psychological Association (CPA) suggested that TOEFL scores should not be used as an admission tool for universities but rather as a test of English proficiency. As we will see in upcoming chapters, not everyone has access to the opportunities that lead to strong test scores and strong real-world performance. And as we will see in Chapter 9, motivation, study skills, self-discipline, practical "smarts," and other traits not measured by IQ or other mental tests are major influences on success in school and on the job.

Criticisms and reevaluations of psychological tests keep psychological assessment honest and scientifically rigorous. In contrast, the pop-psych tests found in magazines, newspapers, and on the internet usually have not been evaluated for either validity or reliability. These questionnaires have inviting headlines, such as "Which Breed of Dog Do You Most Resemble?" or "The Seven Types of Love," but they are merely lists of questions that someone thought sounded good.

Content Validity
Do items broadly represent the trait in question?

Criterion Validity
Do the test results predict other measures of the trait?

surveys Questionnaires and interviews that ask people directly about their experiences, attitudes, or opinions.

volunteer bias A shortcoming of findings derived from a sample of volunteers instead of a representative sample; the volunteers may differ from those who did not volunteer.

Surveys

Everywhere you go, someone wants your opinion. Political polls want to know what you think of some politician. Eat at a restaurant, get your car serviced, or stay at a hotel, and you'll get a satisfaction survey five minutes later. Whereas psychological tests usually generate information about people indirectly, **surveys** are questionnaires and interviews that gather information by asking people *directly* about their experiences, attitudes, or opinions. How reliable are all these surveys?

Surveys produce bushels of data, but they are not easy to do well. Sampling problems are often an issue; when a talk-radio host or TV personality invites people to send comments about a political matter, the results are not likely to generalize to the population as a whole, even if thousands of people respond. Why? As a group, people who listen to talk-radio may be quite different than those who are fans of Jian Ghomeshi. Popular polls and surveys also frequently suffer from a **volunteer bias**: People who are willing to volunteer their opinions may differ from those who remain silent. When you read about a survey (or any other kind of study), always ask who participated. A nonrepresentative sample does not necessarily mean that a survey is worthless or uninteresting, but it does mean that the results may not hold true for other groups.

Yet another problem with surveys, and with self-reports in general, is that people sometimes lie, especially when the survey is about a touchy or embarrassing topic. ("What? Me do that disgusting/illegal/dishonest thing? Never!") Studies comparing self-reports of illicit drug use with the results of urinalysis from the same individuals find that between 30% and 70% of those who test positive for cocaine or opiates deny having used drugs recently (Tourangeau & Yan, 2007). The likelihood of lying is reduced when respondents are guaranteed anonymity and allowed to respond in private. Researchers can also check for lying by asking the same question several times with

THINKING CRITICALLY

Analyze assumptions.

A magazine has just published a survey of its female readers, called "Would you cheat?." It reports that "87% of all married women report that they would cheat in the right circumstance." Is the assumption that the sample represents all married Canadian women justified? Is it relevant that the study was funded by an online dating service? What would be a more accurate title for the survey?

different wording to see whether the answers are consistent. But not all surveys use these techniques, and even when respondents are trying to be truthful, they may misinterpret the survey questions, hold inaccurate perceptions of their own behaviour, or misremember the past.

When you hear about the results of a survey or opinion poll, you also need to consider which questions were (and were not) asked and how the questions were phrased. These aspects of a survey's design may reflect assumptions about the topic or encourage certain responses—as political pollsters well know. Many years ago, the famed sex researcher Alfred Kinsey, in his pioneering surveys of sexual behaviour, made it his practice always to ask, "*How many times have you* (masturbated, had non-marital sex, etc.)?" rather than "*Have you ever* (masturbated, had nonmarital sex, etc.)?" (Kinsey, Pomeroy, & Martin, 1948; Kinsey et al., 1953). The first way of phrasing the question tended to elicit more truthful responses than the second because it removed the respondent's self-consciousness about having done any of these things. The second way of phrasing the question would have permitted embarrassed respondents to reply with a simple but dishonest "No."

Technology can help researchers overcome some of the problems inherent in doing surveys. Because many people feel more anonymous when they 'talk' to a computer than when they fill out a paper-and-pencil questionnaire, computerized questionnaires can reduce lying (Turner et al., 1998). Participants are usually volunteers and are not

REVIEW 2.1   Research Methods in Psychology: Their Advantages and Disadvantages

Method	Advantages	Disadvantages
Case study	Good source of hypotheses. Provides in-depth information on individuals. Unusual cases can shed light on situations or problems that are unethical or impractical to study in other ways.	Vital information may be missing, making the case hard to interpret. The person's memories may be selective or inaccurate. The individual may not be representative or typical.
Naturalistic observation	Allows description of behaviour as it occurs in the natural environment. Often useful in first stages of a research program.	Allows researcher little or no control of the situation. Observations may be biased. Does not allow firm conclusions about cause and effect.
Laboratory observation	Allows more control than naturalistic observation. Allows use of sophisticated equipment.	Allows researcher only limited control of the situation. Observations may be biased. Does not allow firm conclusions about cause and effect. Behaviour may differ from behaviour in the natural environment.
Test	Yields information on personality traits, emotional states, aptitudes, and abilities.	Difficult to construct tests that are reliable and valid.
Survey	Provides a large amount of information on large numbers of people.	If sample is nonrepresentative or biased, it may be impossible to generalize from the results. Responses may be inaccurate or untrue.
Correlational Study	Shows whether two or more variables are related. Allows general predictions.	Usually does not permit identification of cause and effect.
Experiment	Allows researcher to control the situation. Permits researcher to identify cause and effect and to distinguish placebo effects from treatment effects.	Situation is artificial, and results may not generalize well to the real world. Sometimes difficult to avoid experimenter effects.

randomly selected, but because web-based samples are often huge, consisting of hundreds of thousands of respondents, they are more diverse than traditional samples in terms of gender, socioeconomic status, geographic region, and age. In these respects, they tend to be more representative of the general population than traditional samples are (Gosling et al., 2004). Even when people from a particular group make up only a small proportion of the respondents, in absolute numbers, they may be numerous enough to provide useful information about that group. Whereas a typical sample of 1000 representative Canadians might include only a handful of Buddhists, a huge internet sample might draw hundreds.

Internet surveys also carry certain risks, however. It is hard for researchers to know whether participants understand the instructions and the questions and are taking them seriously. Also, many tests and surveys on the web have never been validated, which is why drawing conclusions from them about your personality or mental adjustment could be dangerous to your mental health! Always check the credentials of those designing the test or survey and be sure it is not just something someone made up at his or her computer in the middle of the night.

Recite & Review

Recite: Say aloud to yourself or a study partner everything you can recall about the use of *representative sample, descriptive methods, case study, observational study, psychological tests, standardize, norms, reliablity, validity, surveys,* and *volunteer bias.* Include as much detail as possible about each of these methods, including their strengths and weaknesses.

Review: Next, go back and reread this section.

Now take this *Quick Quiz:*

A. Which descriptive method would be most appropriate for studying each of the following topics? (By the way, psychologists have investigated all of them.)

1.	Ways in which the games of boys differ from those of girls	**a.**	case study
2.	Changes in attitudes toward nuclear power after a major nuclear accident	**b.**	naturalistic observation
3.	The math skills of children in Canada versus Germany	**c.**	survey
4.	Physiological changes that occur when people watch violent movies	**d.**	laboratory observation
5.	The development of a male infant who was reared as a female after his penis was accidentally burned off during a routine surgery	**e.**	test

B. Professor Flummox gives her new test of aptitude for studying psychology to her psychology students at the start of the year. At the end of the year, she finds that those who did well on the test averaged only a C in the course. The test lacks _____.

C. Over a period of 55 years, a British woman snorted large amounts of cocaine, which she obtained legally under British regulations for the treatment of addicts. Yet she appeared to show no negative effects (Brown & Middlefell, 1989). What does this case tell us about the dangers or safety of cocaine?

Answers:

A. 1. b 2. d 3. e 4. c 5. a **B.** Validity (more specifically, criterion validity) **C.** Not much. Snorting cocaine may be relatively harmless for some people, such as this woman, but extremely harmful for others. Also, the cocaine she received may have been less potent than cocaine purchased on the street. Critical thinking requires that we resist generalizing from a single case.

correlational study A descriptive study that looks for a consistent relationship between two phenomena.

correlation A measure of how strongly two variables are related to one another.

variables Characteristics of behaviour or experience that can be measured or described by a numeric scale.

positive correlation An association between increases in one variable and increases in another—or between decreases in one and decreases in another.

negative correlation An association between increases in one variable and decreases in another.

coefficient of correlation A measure of correlation that ranges in value from −1.00 to +1.00.

Variable X   Variable Y

Positive Correlation: The higher X is, the higher Y is.

Variable X   Variable Y

Negative Correlation: The higher X is, the lower Y is.

Learning Objectives

8 Define positive and negative correlations. Give a real world example of each.

9 Interpret the following correlations: −.80; 0; and +.10. List the correlations in order from the strongest association to the weakest.

10 Understand the caution required when interpreting correlational findings and attempting to draw conclusions about causation.

Correlational Studies: Looking for Relations

In descriptive research, psychologists often want to know whether two or more phenomena are related and, if so, how strongly. Are students' grade point averages related to the number of hours they spend watching television, playing video games, or texting? To find out, a psychologist conducts a **correlational study**.

Measuring Correlations

The word **correlation** is often used as a synonym for "relation." Technically, however, a correlation is a numerical measure of the *strength* of the relation between two things. The "things" may be events, scores, or anything else that can be recorded and tallied. In psychological studies, such things are called **variables** because they can vary in quantifiable ways. Height, weight, age, income, IQ scores, number of smiles in a given time period—anything that can be measured, rated, or scored can serve as a variable.

A **positive correlation** means that high values of one variable are associated with high values of the other and that low values of one variable are associated with low values of the other. Height and weight are positively correlated; so are IQ scores and school grades. Rarely is a correlation perfect, however. Some tall people weigh less than some short ones; some people with average IQs are academic superstars and some with high IQs get poor grades. Figure 2.2a shows a positive correlation between scores on a psychology exam and the average number of boiled kumquats eaten per month by students. (Obviously, we made this up.) Each dot represents a student; you can find each student's score by drawing a horizontal line from the person's dot to the vertical axis. You can find the number of kumquats a student ate by drawing a vertical line from the student's dot to the horizontal axis. In general, the more kumquats, the higher the score.

A **negative correlation** means that high values of one variable are associated with *low* values of the other. Figure 2.2b shows a hypothetical negative correlation between scores on a psychology exam and number of *grilled* kumquats eaten per month. In general, the more kumquats eaten, the lower the test score. Here's another more realistic example: In general, the older adults are, the fewer kilometres they can run. How about hours spent watching TV and grade point averages? You guessed it; they're negatively correlated: Spending lots of hours in front of the television is associated with lower grades (Potter, 1987; Ridley-Johnson, Cooper, & Chance, 1983). See whether you can think of other variables that are negatively correlated. Remember that a negative correlation tells you that the *more* of one thing, the *less* of another. If no relation exists between two variables, we say that they are *uncorrelated* (see Figure 2.2c). Shoe size and IQ scores are uncorrelated.

The statistic used to express a correlation is called the **coefficient of correlation**. This number conveys both the size of the correlation and its direction. A perfect positive correlation has a coefficient of +1.00, and a perfect negative correlation has a coefficient of −1.00. Suppose you weighed 10 people and listed them from lightest to heaviest, then measured their heights and listed them from shortest to tallest. If the names on the two lists were in exactly the same order, the correlation between weight and height would be

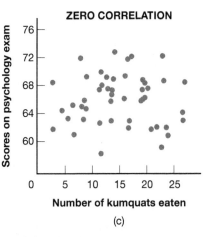

FIGURE 2.2 Correlations
Graph (a) shows a positive correlation between scores on a psychology test and number of boiled kumquats eaten per month: The higher the score, the higher the number of kumquats. Graph (b) shows a negative correlation between test scores and number of grilled kumquats eaten: The higher the scores, the lower the number of kumquats. Graph (c) shows the reality—a zero correlation between kumquat-eating and test scores.

+1.00. If the correlation between two variables is +.80, it means that they are strongly related. If the correlation is −.80, the relation is just as strong, but it is negative. When there is no association between two variables, the coefficient is zero or close to zero.

Cautions about Correlations

Correlational findings are common in psychology and often make the news. But beware: Many supposed "correlations" reported in the media or on the internet are based on rumour and anecdote, and turn out to be small or meaningless. Some are merely *illusory correlations*, apparent associations between two things that are not really related. Illusory correlations can create dangerous beliefs and cause great social harm. Claims of an association between autism and vaccination for childhood diseases were based largely on one paper that linked autism with a preservative, thimerosal, in vaccines. However, no convincing evidence exists that thimerosal is involved in autism. After this preservative was removed from most vaccines, the incidence of autism did not decline, as it would have if thimerosal were to blame. Study after study has failed to find any connection whatsoever (Mnookin, 2011; Offit, 2008). In one major study of all children born in Denmark between 1991 and 1998 (over a half million children), the incidence of autism in vaccinated children was actually a bit *lower* than in unvaccinated children (Madsen et al., 2002) and in early 2010, *The Lancet*, the journal that had published the original report on the correlation, retracted the report, citing numerous problems with the research. Thus, the apparent link between vaccination and autism is almost certainly a coincidence, an illusory correlation, arising from the fact that symptoms of childhood autism are often first recognized at about the same time that children are vaccinated. Thimerisol is used only in multi-dose vaccines in Canada (Public Health Agency of Canada, 2012).

You can see why an understanding of correlations matters. Unfortunately, despite the retraction and the studies that failed to find a connection, some parents continue to avoid vaccinating their children. For many preventable diseases, such as measles and whooping cough, fewer than 65% of Canadian children are fully immunized (Public Health Agency of Canada, 2006). At the same time, because children are not vaccinated, the rates of these preventable diseases are rising and many of these diseases can have serious or fatal consequences (Health Canada, 2009).

Even when correlations are meaningful, they can still be hard to interpret, because *a correlation does not establish causation*. It is often easy to assume that if variable A predicts variable B, A must be causing B—that is, making B happen—but that is not necessarily so. A positive correlation has been found between the number of hours that one-, two-, and three-year-old children watch television and their risk of hyperactivity (impulsivity, attention problems, difficulty concentrating) by age 7 (Christakis et al., 2004). Does this mean that watching TV *causes* hyperactivity? Maybe so, but it is also possible that children with a disposition to become hyperactive are more attracted to television than those disposed to

THINKING CRITICALLY

Consider other interpretations.

The number of hours toddlers spend watching TV is correlated with their risk of being hyperactive later in life. Does that mean TV watching causes hyperactivity problems? Are there other possible explanations for this finding?

Tom Prettyman/PhotoEdit Inc.

Loisjoy Thurstun/Alamy

be calm. Or perhaps the harried parents of distractible children are more likely than other parents to rely on TV as a babysitter. It's also possible that neither variable causes the other directly: Perhaps parents who allow their young kids to watch a lot of TV have attention problems themselves and therefore create a home environment that fosters hyperactivity and inattentiveness. Likewise, the negative correlation between TV watching and grades mentioned earlier might exist because heavy TV watchers have less time to study, because they have some personality trait that causes an attraction to TV *and* an aversion to studying, because they use TV as an escape when their grades are low, . . . you get the idea.

The moral of this story: When two variables are associated, one variable may or may not be causing the other.

Recite & Review

Recite: Out loud, tell us everything you can remember about these concepts. Go on . . . we're listening: *corrrelational study, correlation, variables, positive* versus *negative correlation,* and *coefficient of correlation.*

Review: Next, go back and reread this section.

Now take this *Quick Quiz:*

A. Identify each of the following as a positive or negative correlation.

1. The higher a male monkey's level of the hormone testosterone, the more aggressive he is likely to be.
2. The older people are, the less frequently they tend to have sexual intercourse.
3. The hotter the weather, the higher the crime rate.

B. Now see whether you can generate two or three possible explanations for each of the preceding findings.

Answers:

A. 1. positive **2.** negative **3.** positive **B. 1.** The hormone may cause aggressiveness; acting aggressively may stimulate hormone production; or some third factor, such as age or dominance, may influence aggressiveness and hormone production independently. **2.** Older people may have less interest in sex than younger people; have less time, less energy or more physical ailments; or simply lack partners. **3.** Hot temperatures may make people edgy and cause them to commit crimes; potential victims may be more plentiful in warm weather because more people go outside; criminals may find it more comfortable to be out committing their crimes in warm weather than in cold. (Our explanations for these correlations are not the only ones possible.)

Learning Objectives

11 Define dependent and independent variables.

12 Describe the importance of experimental and control conditions, random assignment, and use of placebos when seeking true effects.

13 Define and be able to recognize single-blind and double-blind studies and their importance in preventing experimenter effects.

Experiments: Hunting for Causes

Researchers gain plenty of illuminating information from descriptive studies, but when they want to track down the causes of behaviour, they rely heavily on the experimental method. An **experiment** allows a researcher to control and manipulate the situation being studied. Instead of being a passive recorder of behaviour, the researcher actively does something that he or she believes will affect people's behaviour and then observes what happens. These procedures allow the experimenter to draw conclusions about cause and effect—about what causes what.

Experimental Variables

Imagine that you are a psychologist whose research interest is multitasking. Almost everyone multitasks these days, and you would like to know whether that's a good thing or a bad thing. Specifically, you would like to know whether or not using a handheld cellphone while driving is dangerous, an important question because most people have done so. Talking on a cellphone while driving is associated with an increase in accidents, but maybe that's just for people who are risk takers or lousy drivers to begin with. To pin down cause and effect, you decide to conduct an experiment.

In a laboratory, you ask participants to "drive" using a computerized driving simulator equipped with an automatic transmission, steering wheel, gas pedal, and brake pedal. The object, you tell them, is to maximize the distance covered while driving on a busy highway, taking care to avoid collisions with other cars. Some of the participants talk on a cellphone for 15 minutes to a research assistant in the next room about a topic that interests them; others just drive. You are going to compare how many collisions the two groups have. The basic design of this experiment is illustrated in Figure 2.3, which you may want to refer to as you read the next few pages.

The aspect of an experimental situation manipulated or varied by the researcher is known as the **independent variable**. The reaction of the participants—the behaviour that the researcher tries to predict—is the **dependent variable**. Every experiment has at least one independent and one dependent variable. In our example, the independent variable is cellphone use (use versus nonuse). The dependent variable is the number of collisions.

Ideally, everything in the experimental situation except the independent variable is held constant, that is, kept the same for all participants. You would not have some people use a stick shift and others drive an automatic, unless shift type were an independent variable. Similarly, you would not have people in one group go through the experiment alone and others perform in front of an audience. Holding everything but the independent variable constant ensures that whatever happens is due to the researcher's manipulation and nothing else. It allows you to rule out other interpretations.

experiment A controlled test of a hypothesis in which the researcher manipulates one variable to discover its effect on another.

independent variable A variable that an experimenter manipulates.

dependent variable A variable that an experimenter predicts will be affected by manipulations of the independent variable.

FIGURE 2.3 Do Cellphone Use and Driving Mix?
The text describes this experimental design to test the hypothesis that talking on a cellphone while driving impairs driving skills and leads to accidents.

Understandably, students often have trouble keeping independent and dependent variables straight. You might think of it this way: The dependent variable—the outcome of the study—*depends* on the independent variable. When psychologists set up an experiment, they think, "If I do X, the people in my study will do Y." The "X" represents the independent variable; the "Y" represents the dependent variable, as illustrated:

Most variables may be either independent or dependent, depending on what the experimenter wishes to find out. If you want to know whether eating chocolate makes people nervous, then the amount of chocolate eaten is the independent variable. If you

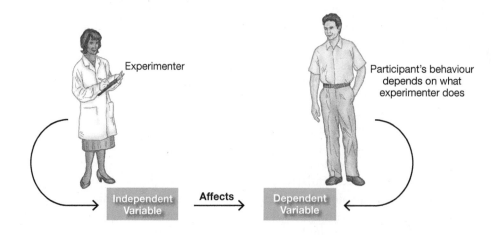

want to know whether feeling nervous makes people eat chocolate, then the amount of chocolate eaten is the dependent variable.

Experimental and Control Conditions

Experiments usually require both an experimental condition and a comparison, or **control condition**. In the control condition, participants are treated exactly as they are in the experimental condition, except that they are not exposed to the same treatment or manipulation of the independent variable. Without a control condition, you cannot be sure that the behaviour you are interested in would not have occurred anyway, even without your manipulation. In some studies, the same people can be used in both the control and the experimental conditions; they are said to serve as their own controls. In other studies, participants are assigned to either an *experimental group* or a *control group*.

In our cellphone study, we could have drivers serve as their own controls by having them drive once while using a cellphone and once without a phone. But for this illustration, we will use two different groups. Participants who talk on the phone while driving make up the experimental group, and those who just drive along silently make up the control group. We want these two groups to be roughly the same in terms of average driving skill. It would not do to start out with a bunch of new drivers in the experimental group and a bunch of experienced drivers in the control group. We also probably want the two groups to be similar in age, education, driving history, and other characteristics so that none of these variables will affect our results. One way to accomplish this is to use **random assignment** of people to one group or another, often by randomly assigning them numbers and putting those with even numbers in one group and those with odd numbers in another. If we have enough participants in our study, individual characteristics that could possibly affect the results are likely to be roughly balanced in the two groups, so we can safely ignore them.

Sometimes researchers use several different experimental or control groups. In our cellphone study, we might want to examine the effects of short versus long phone conversations, or conversations on different topics—say, work, personal matters, and *very* personal matters. In that case, we would have more than one experimental group to compare with the control group. In our hypothetical example, though, we'll just have one experimental group, and everyone in it will drive for 15 minutes while talking on the cellphone.

This description does not cover all the procedures that psychological researchers use. In some studies, people in the control group get a **placebo**, a fake treatment or sugar pill that looks, tastes, or smells like the real treatment or medication, but is phony. If the placebo produces the same result as the real thing, the reason must be the participants' expectations rather than the treatment itself. Placebos are critical in testing new drugs because of the optimism that a potential "miracle cure" often brings with it. Medical placebos usually take the form of pills or injections that contain no active ingredients.

Control groups, by the way, are also crucial in many nonexperimental studies. For example, some psychotherapists have published books arguing that girls develop problems with self-esteem and confidence as soon as they hit adolescence. But unless the writers have also tested or surveyed a comparable group of teenage boys, there is no way of knowing whether low self-esteem is a problem unique to girls or is just as typical for boys (see Chapter 13).

control condition In an experiment, a comparison condition in which participants are not exposed to the same treatment as in the experimental condition.

random assignment A procedure for assigning people to experimental and control groups in which each individual has the same probability as any other of being assigned to a given group.

placebo An inactive substance or fake treatment used as a control in an experiment or given by a medical practitioner to a patient.

THINKING CRITICALLY

Consider other interpretations.

You have developed a new form of therapy that you believe cures anxiety. Sixty-three percent of the people who go through your program improve. What else, besides your therapy, could account for this result? Why shouldn't you rush out to open an anxiety clinic?

single-blind study An experiment in which participants do not know whether they are in an experimental or a control group, but the researchers do.

experimenter effects Unintended changes in study participants' behaviour due to cues that the experimenter inadvertently conveys.

double-blind study An experiment in which neither the people being studied nor the individuals running the study know who is in the control group and who is in the experimental group until after the results are tallied.

Experimenter Effects

Because their expectations can influence the results of a study, participants should not know whether they are in an experimental or a control group. When this is so (as it usually is), the experiment is said to be a **single-blind study**. But participants are not the only ones who bring expectations to the laboratory; so do researchers. And researchers' expectations, biases, and hopes for a particular result may cause them to inadvertently influence the participants' responses through facial expressions, posture, tone of voice, or some other cue.

Many years ago, Robert Rosenthal (1966) demonstrated how powerful such **experimenter effects** can be. He had students teach rats to run a maze. Half of the students were told that their rats had been bred to be "maze bright," and half were told that their rats had been bred to be "maze dull." In reality, there were no genetic differences between the two groups of rats, yet the supposedly brainy rats actually did learn the maze more quickly, apparently because of the way the students were handling and treating them. If an experimenter's expectations can affect a rodent's behaviour, reasoned Rosenthal, surely they can affect a human being's behaviour, and he went on to demonstrate this point in many other studies (Rosenthal, 1994). Even an experimenter's friendly smile or cold demeanour can affect people's responses.

One solution to the problem of experimenter effects is to do a **double-blind study**. In such a study, the person running the experiment, the one having actual contact with the participants, also does not know who is in which group until the data have been tallied. Double-blind procedures are essential in drug research. Different doses of a drug (and whether it is the active drug or a placebo) are coded in some way, and the person administering the drug is kept in the dark about the code's meaning until after the experiment. To run our cellphone study in a double-blind fashion, we could use a simulator that automatically records collisions and have the experimenter give instructions through an intercom so that he or she will not know which group a participant is in until after the results are tallied.

Think back now to the opening story on the alleged benefits of video games. Most of the studies that reported such benefits may suffer from basic mistakes in experimental design. The experimental and control groups were not comparable: Often, the performance of expert gamers was compared with those with no gaming experience. The studies were not blind: Players knew they were chosen to participate precisely because they were expert gamers, an awareness that could have influenced their performance and motivation to do well. And the researchers knew which participants were in the experimental and control groups, knowledge that might have affected the participants' performance (Boot, Blakely, & Simons, 2011).

Because experiments allow conclusions about cause and effect, and because they permit researchers to distinguish real effects from placebo effects, they have long been the method of choice in psychology. However, like all methods, the experiment has its limitations. Just as in other kinds of studies, the participants are typically students and may or may not represent the larger population. Moreover, in an experiment, the

GET INVOLVED! The Power of a Smile

Prove to yourself how easy it is for experimenters to affect the behaviour of a study's participants by giving off nonverbal cues. As you walk around campus, quickly glance at individuals approaching you and either smile or maintain a neutral expression; then observe the other person's expression. Try to keep the duration of your glance the same whether you smile or not. You might record the results as you collect them instead of relying on your memory. Chances are that people you smile at will smile back, whereas those you approach with a neutral expression will do the same. What does this tell you about the importance of doing double-blind studies?

In *Alice in Wonderland*, the Cheshire cat understood the power of a smile. Whenever the cat vanished, it left its smile behind.

Shutterstock

researcher designs and sets up what is often a rather artificial situation, and the participants try to do as they are told. In their desire to cooperate or to present themselves in a positive light, they may act in ways that they ordinarily would not (Kihlstrom, 1995). For this reason, many psychologists have called for more **field research**, the careful study of behaviour in natural contexts such as schools and the workplace (Cialdini, 2009). For instance, have you ever wondered whether women are more "talkative" than men, as the stereotype suggests? A field study would be the best way to answer this question, and indeed such a study has been done. The participants wore an unobtrusive recording device as they went about their normal lives, and the researchers found no gender differences at all (Mehl et al., 2007).

Every research method has both its strengths and its weaknesses. Did you make a list of each method's advantages and disadvantages, as we suggested earlier? If so, compare it now with the one in Review 2.1.

field research Descriptive or experimental research conducted in a natural setting outside the laboratory.

CULTURE and *Research*

Doing good research is demanding enough, but the challenges are multiplied when psychologists venture into societies other than their own to learn which attitudes, behaviours, and traits are universal and which are specific to particular groups. Here are three major concerns that arise in cross-cultural research:

1 **Methods and sampling.** Right off the bat, researchers must worry about how one language translates into another. Speakers of English know that "Mary had a little lamb" means she owned one, not that she gave birth to it, ate it, or had an affair with it. But that's not clear from the words alone! Further, sometimes the term for a concept or emotional experience that is central in one culture (say, the Chinese concept of "filial piety," honouring your ancestors) may have no exact linguistic equivalent in another. In doing cross-cultural research, scientists must also be sure that their samples are similar in all important ways except for ethnicity or nationality. Otherwise, what seems like a cultural difference may really be a difference in education, crowding, or some other noncultural factor.

2 **Stereotyping.** When researchers describe average differences across societies, they may be tempted to oversimplify their findings, which can lead to stereotyping. Of course, cultural rules may make Nigerians different than Australians and Cambodians different from Italians. Yet within every society, individuals vary according to their temperaments, beliefs, and learning histories. The challenge is to understand average cultural differences without implying that everyone in Culture A is as different from everyone in Culture B as chocolate is from cheese (see Chapter 14).

3 **Reification.** To *reify* means to regard an intangible process, such as a feeling, as if it were a literal object. For example, when people say, "I have a lot of anger buried in me," they are speaking of anger as if it were a thing that sits inside them like a kidney, when in fact it is a cluster of mental and physical reactions that come and go. In cultural psychology, reification—treating "culture" as a thing instead of a collection of beliefs and traditions—can lead to circular reasoning, as in "Country A attacks its neighbours because it has a warlike culture, and we know it is a warlike culture because it attacks its neighbours." This is like telling a man with a leg injury that he can't walk because he's lame (Lonner & Malpass, 1994). Cultural psychologists must therefore identify not only the average differences in traits and behaviours across cultures but also the underlying mechanisms that account for them. They ask *why* Country A is "warlike," and why it changed from being peaceful (Matsumoto & Yoo, 2006).

Doing good cross-cultural research can be tricky, requiring the right methods and the ability to interpret them critically. But the results are essential for a deeper, more accurate understanding of human behaviour in all its rich variety.

· ·

Recite & Review

Recite: Tell someone (even if that someone is yourself) all that you remember about these concepts: *experiment*, *independent* and *dependent variables*, *control condition*, *random assignment*, *placebo*, *single-blind study*, *experimenter effects*, *double-blind study*, and *field research*.

Review: Next, go back and reread this section.

Now take this *Quick Quiz:*

A. Name the independent and dependent variables in studies designed to answer the following questions:

1. Whether sleeping after learning a poem improves memory for the poem
2. Whether the presence of other people affects a person's willingness to help someone in distress
3. Whether listening to heavy metal music makes people aggressive

B. Identify three special challenges in doing cross-cultural research.

C. On a TV show, Dr. Blitznik announces a fabulous new program she calls **C**hocolate **I**mmersion **T**herapy (CIT). "People who spend one day a week doing nothing but eating chocolate are soon cured of eating disorders, depression, and poor study habits," claims Dr. Blitznik. What should you find out about CIT before signing up?

Answers:

A. 1. Opportunity to sleep after learning is the independent variable; memory for the poem is the dependent variable. **2.** The presence of other people is the independent variable; willingness to help others is the dependent variable. **3.** Exposure to heavy metal is the independent variable; aggressive behaviour is the dependent variable. **B.** Problems in methodology (e.g., translation problems) and sampling; stereotyping; reification of culture when explaining results. **C.** Some questions to ask: Is there research showing that people who went through CIT did better than those in a control group who did not have the therapy or who had a different therapy—say, **B**roccoli **I**mmersion **T**herapy? If so, how many people were studied? How were they selected, and how were they assigned to the therapy and no-therapy groups? Did the person running the experiment know who was getting CIT and who did the "cures" last? Has the research been peer-reviewed? Has it been replicated?

Learning Objectives

14 Understand the role of descriptive statistics. Recognize what information is conveyed by arithmetic means and standard deviations.

15 Understand the role of inferential statistics. Interpret the meaning of a statistically significant result.

16 Define cross-sectional and longitudinal study designs; compare and contrast their strengths and weaknesses to the previously learned research methods.

Evaluating the Findings

If you are a psychologist who has just done an observational study, a survey, or an experiment, your work has just begun. Once you have some results in hand, you must do three things with them: (1) describe them, (2) assess how reliable and meaningful they are, and (3) figure out how to explain them.

Most people assume that "on average" means "typically"—but sometimes it doesn't! Averages can be misleading if you don't know the extent to which events deviated from the statistical mean and how they were distributed.

Creators Syndicate Inc.

Descriptive Statistics: Finding out What's So

Let's say that 30 people in the cellphone experiment talked on the phone, and 30 did not. We have recorded the number of collisions for each person on the driving simulator. Now we have 60 points of data. What can we do with them?

The first step is to summarize the data. The world does not want to hear how many collisions each person had. It wants to know what happened in the cellphone group as a whole compared to the control group. To provide this information, we need numbers that sum up our data. Such numbers, known as **descriptive statistics**, are often depicted in graphs and charts.

A good way to summarize the data is to compute group averages. The most commonly used type of average is the **arithmetic mean**, which is calculated by adding up all the individual scores and dividing the result by the number of scores. We can compute a mean for the cellphone group by adding up the 30 collision scores and dividing the sum by 30. Then we can do the same for the control group. Now our 60 numbers have been boiled down to 2. For the sake of our example, let's assume that the cellphone group had an average of 10 collisions, whereas the control group's average was only 7.

We must be careful, however, about how we interpret these averages. It is possible that no one in our cellphone group actually had 10 collisions. Perhaps half the people in the group were careless and had 15 collisions, whereas the others were more cautious and had only 5. Perhaps almost all the participants in the group had 9, 10, or 11 collisions. Perhaps the number of accidents ranged from 0 to 15. The mean does not tell us about such variability in the participants' responses. For that, we need other descriptive statistics. The **standard deviation** tells us how clustered or spread out the individual scores are around the mean; the more spread out they are, the less "typical" the mean is. (See Figure 2.4.) Unfortunately, when research is reported in the news, you usually hear only about the mean.

descriptive statistics Statistical procedures that organize and summarize research data.

arithmetic mean An average that is calculated by adding up a set of quantities and dividing the sum by the total number of quantities in the set.

standard deviation A commonly used measure of variability that indicates the average difference between scores in a distribution and their mean.

Inferential Statistics: Asking "So What?"

At this point in our study, we have one group with an average of 10 collisions and another with an average of 7. Should we break out the champagne? Hold a press conference? Call our mothers?

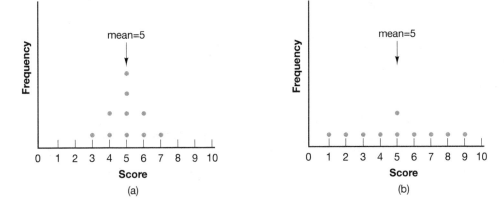

FIGURE 2.4 Same Mean, Different Meaning
In both distributions of scores, the mean is 5, but in (a), the scores are clustered around the mean, whereas in (b), they are widely dispersed, so the standard deviations for the distributions will be quite different. In which distribution is the mean more "typical" of all scores?

inferential statistics Statistical procedures that allow researchers to draw inferences about how statistically meaningful a study's results are.

significance tests Statistical tests that show how likely it is that a study's results occurred merely by chance.

confidence interval A statistical measure that provides, with a specified probability, a range of values within which a population mean is likely to lie.

Better hold off. Perhaps if one group had an average of 15 collisions and the other an average of 1, we may get excited. But rarely does a psychological study hit you between the eyes with a sensationally clear result. In most cases, there is some possibility that the difference between the two groups was due simply to chance. Despite all our precautions, perhaps the people in the cellphone group just happened to be a little more accident-prone, and their extra 3 collisions had nothing to do with talking on the phone.

To find out how meaningful the data are, psychologists use **inferential statistics**. These statistics do not merely describe or summarize the data; they permit a researcher to draw *inferences* (conclusions based on evidence) about how meaningful the findings are. Like descriptive statistics, inferential statistics involve the application of mathematical formulas to the data.

Historically, the most commonly used inferential statistics have been **significance tests**, which tell researchers how likely it was that their result occurred by chance. (We have given you the general meaning; statisticians use a more technical one.) Suppose that in the real world, people who talk on cellphones have no more collisions than people who do not. How likely, then, would you be to obtain the difference you found (or an even larger one) between the experimental group and the control group by chance? It is not possible to rule out chance entirely, but if the likelihood that the result occurred by chance is quite low, we can use significance tests to find out if result is *statistically significant*. This means that there is a high probability that the difference is real.

Psychologists consider a result to be significant if it would be expected to occur by chance only rarely, and "rarely" usually means 5 or fewer times in 100 repetitions of the study. We would then say that the result is significant at the .05 level, or $p < .05$, where p stands for probability and .05 is referred to as the p *value*. If, however, the significance test shows that the p value is greater than .05, many researchers would have little confidence in the study's result, although they might still want to do further research to confirm their judgment.

Statistically significant results allow psychologists to make general predictions about human behaviour: "Talking on a phone while driving increases people's risk of accidents." These predictions are usually stated as probabilities (On average, we can expect 60% of all students to do X, Y, or Z). However, they do not tell us with any certainty what a *particular* person will do in a particular situation. Probabilistic results are typical in all of the sciences, not just psychology. Medical research can tell us that the odds are high that someone who smokes will get lung cancer; but because many variables interact to produce any particular case of cancer, research cannot tell us for sure whether Aunt Bessie, who smokes two packs a day, will come down with the disease.

Today, a growing number of psychologists and other researchers also report their results by using a statistical formula that creates a **confidence interval**. The mean from a particular sample will almost never be exactly the same value as the true mean in the population; instead, it will probably be a little higher or a little lower. A confidence interval draws a range a little higher and lower than the sample mean to help depict where the true mean probably lies, especially in graphs (Fidler & Loftus, 2009; Masson & Loftus, 2003;). As Figure 2.5 shows, if you repeated your study over and over, you would produce a different sample mean and confidence interval each time. But notice something interesting: Although none of the means in each study (the green circles) is exactly the same as the population mean (the straight vertical line), most of the confidence intervals (CIs) contain the true mean. In fact, if you repeated your study over and over, 95% of the CIs would contain the true mean, although you would occasionally produce a rogue CI (the grey bars) (Cumming, 2012). Do you see the problem with drawing strong conclusions on the basis of any one study?

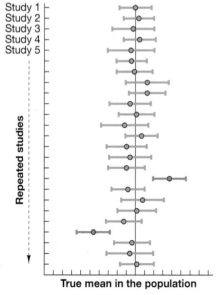

FIGURE 2.5 Confidence Intervals across Repeated Studies

By the way, many studies similar to our hypothetical one have confirmed the dangers of talking on a cellphone while driving. In one study, cellphone users, whether their phones were handheld or handsfree, were as impaired in their driving ability as intoxicated drivers were (Ishigami & Klein, 2009; Strayer, Drews, & Crouch, 2006). Because of such research, some provinces have made it illegal to drive while holding a cellphone to your ear, although handsfree conversations remain a-okay. However, a metaanalysis of 45 studies found that there was no difference between handsfree conversations and those that were handheld (Horrey & Wickens, 2006). So if you drive and talk, be careful! We will revisit this topic and examine the issue of multitasking in Chapter 9.

Interpreting the Findings

The last step in any study is to figure out what the findings mean. Trying to understand behaviour from uninterpreted findings is like trying to become fluent in Swedish by reading a Swedish–English dictionary. Just as you need the grammar rules of Swedish to tell you how the words fit together, psychologists need hypotheses and theories to explain how the facts that emerge from research fit together.

Choosing the Best Explanation. Sometimes it is hard to choose between competing explanations of a finding. Does cellphone use disrupt driving by impairing coordination, by increasing a driver's vulnerability to distraction, by interfering with the processing of information, or by some combination of these or other factors? Several explanations may fit the results equally well, which means that more research will be needed to determine the best one.

In a real study of cellphone use while driving, a participant "drives" in a high-tech driving simulator.

Jim Moulin/David Strayer

Sometimes the best interpretation of a finding does not emerge until a hypothesis has been tested in different ways. Although the methods we have described tend to be appropriate for different questions (see Review 2.2 on page 60), sometimes one method can be used to confirm, disconfirm, or extend the results obtained with another. If the findings of studies using various methods converge, there is greater reason to be confident about them. If they conflict, researchers must modify their hypotheses or do more research.

Here is an example. When psychologists compare the mental-test scores of young people and old people, they usually find that younger people outscore older ones. This type of research, in which different groups are compared at the same time, is called **cross-sectional**:

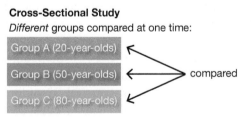

Cross-Sectional Study

Different groups compared at one time:

Group A (20-year-olds)
Group B (50-year-olds)   compared
Group C (80-year-olds)

But **longitudinal studies** can also be used to investigate mental abilities across the lifespan. In a longitudinal study, the same people are followed over a period of time and are reassessed at regular intervals:

Longitudinal Study

Same group compared at different times:

Group A at age 20 → Group A at age 50 → Group A at age 80

cross-sectional study A study in which people (or animals) of different ages are compared at a given time.

longitudinal study A study in which people (or animals) are followed and periodically reassessed over a period of time.

REVIEW 2.2 **Psychological Research Methods Contrasted**

Psychologists may use different methods to answer different questions about a topic. This table shows some ways in which the methods described in this chapter can be used to study different questions about aggression. Sometimes, however, two or more methods can be used to investigate the same question, and findings based on one method may extend, support, or disconfirm findings based on another.

Method	Purpose	Example
Case study	To understand the development of aggressive behaviour in a particular individual; to formulate research hypotheses about the origins of aggressiveness	Developmental history of a serial killer
Naturalistic observation	To describe the nature of aggressive acts in early childhood	Observation of hitting, kicking, etc., during free-play periods in a preschool
Laboratory observation	To find out whether aggressiveness in pairs of same-sex and different-sex children differs in frequency or intensity	Observation through a one-way window of same-sex and different-sex pairs of preschoolers; pairs must negotiate who gets to play with an attractive toy that has been promised to each child
Test	To compare the personality traits of aggressive and nonaggressive people	Administration of personality tests to violent and nonviolent prisoners
Survey	To find out how common domestic violence is in the general population	Questionnaire asking anonymous respondents (in a sample representative of the population) about the occurrence of slapping, hitting, etc., in their homes
Correlational study	To examine the relation between aggressiveness and television viewing	Administration to university students of a paper-and-pencil test of aggressiveness and a questionnaire on number of hours spent watching TV weekly; computation of correlation coefficient
Experiment	To find out whether high air temperatures elicit aggressive behaviour	Arrangement for individuals to "shock" a "learner" (actually a confederate of the experimenter) while seated in a room heated to either 20°C or 30°C

In contrast to cross-sectional studies, longitudinal studies find that as people age, they sometimes perform as well as they ever did on certain mental tests. A *general* decline in ability may not occur until people reach their 70s or 80s (see Chapter 13). Why do results from the two types of studies conflict? Probably because cross-sectional studies measure generational differences; younger generations tend to outperform older ones in part because they are better educated or are more familiar with the tests used. Without longitudinal studies, we might falsely conclude that all types of mental ability inevitably decline with advancing age.

Judging the Result's Importance. Sometimes psychologists agree on the reliability and meaning of a finding but not on its ultimate relevance for theory or practice. Part of the problem is statistical. Traditional tests of significance continue to be used in the overwhelming majority of psychological studies, which is why we have described them here, but these tests have important drawbacks (Cumming, 2012; Cumming et al., 2007; Erceg-Hurn & Mirosevich, 2008). A result may be statistically significant yet be small and of little consequence in everyday life because the independent variable does not explain most of the variation in people's behaviour. Moreover, p values don't guarantee that other researchers (or even the same researchers) will be able to obtain a similar effect if they run their study again; in fact, p values can vary considerably from one replication to another

(Cumming, 2012). That is why so many "findings" that make the news don't pan out in later studies. Remember the ESP study that we mentioned at the start of this chapter? Because the results were just barely statistically significant, the paper was published in an academic journal, which appalled many psychological scientists (Alcock, 2011). As one statistician noted, the article did not show that ESP exists; rather, it showed why a reliance on p values produces too many results that are just flukes (in Miller, 2011).

To gain better protection against spurious, unsubstantial results, many psychology journals now encourage or require the use of alternate methods and statistics. One is to use statistical procedures that reveal the **effect size**. Think of effect sizes as similar to measuring how much something weighs: Regardless of what you're weighing, 100 kilograms is weightier than 10 kilograms. Effect sizes, then, help us to understand how important—how weighty—an effect is. One such measure tells us how much of the variation in the data the independent variable accounts for. If it explains 5% of the variation, it is not not as powerful as one that explains 40%, even if both are statistically significant.

A popular set of statistical techniques called **meta-analysis** combines and analyzes data from a number of related studies instead of assessing each study's results separately. A single result based on a small sample may be just a coincidence. Meta-analysis can be used to reveal how much of the variation in scores across all studies in the analysis can be explained by a particular variable. Meta-analysis can be particularly helpful when studies conflict with each other. For instance, one meta-analysis of nearly 50 years of research found that gender does account for a good deal of the variance in performance on certain spatial-visual tasks, such as the ability to mentally rotate objects, with males doing better on average (Voyer, Voyer, & Bryden, 1995). In contrast, other meta-analyses have shown that gender accounts for very little of the variance in performance on tests of verbal and math ability, usually only 1 to 5% (Hyde, 2005, 2007). Thus, gender effects may depend on the nature of the task that is studied.

Because rarely does one study prove anything, in psychology or any other field, you should be suspicious of headlines that announce a sudden major scientific breakthrough based on a single study. Breakthroughs do occur, but they are rare.

Another approach, growing in popularity among scientists in medicine and other fields as well as psychology, is based on **Bayesian statistics**, named for the eighteenth-century English minister who developed it (Dienes, 2011; McGrayne, 2011). Bayesian statistics involve a formula that takes prior knowledge into consideration when evaluating any finding. In the case of ESP, "prior knowledge" of physics and biology suggests no known or possible mechanism for this phenomenon. And in fact, when a team of mathematical psychologists reassessed the ESP paper using Bayes' formula, they concluded that the data actually support the hypothesis that ESP does *not* exist (Wagenmakers et al., 2011).

One writer nicely summarized the Bayesian approach as the "yeah, right" effect. If a study finds that eating blueberry muffins reduces the risk of heart disease by 90% or that a treatment cures drug addiction in a week, a Bayesian's reaction would be to evaluate that finding against what can be observed in the real world, and the result would have to pass the "yeah, right" test of plausibility (Carey, 2011). A team of researchers compared p values, effect sizes, and Bayes factors as measures of statistical evidence, using 855 published findings (Wetzels et al., 2011). They found that although p values and Bayes factors almost always agreed about which hypotheses were better supported by the data, the measures often disagreed about the strength of this support. In many cases, the Bayes analysis showed that the result was only anecdotal.

effect size An objective, standardized way of describing the strength of the independent variable's influence on the dependent variable.

meta-analysis A set of techniques for combining data from a number of related studies to determine the explanatory strength of a particular independent variable.

Bayesian statistics Statistics that involve a formula for calculating the likelihood of a hypothesis being true and meaningful, taking into account relevant prior knowledge.

The Bayesian approach is still controversial, and arguments continue about how precisely to quantify "prior knowledge," which can vary from strong empirical evidence to more subjective estimates. But its importance is growing among the statistical methods of science.

Recite & Review

Recite: Major scientific breakthrough: Reciting what you've read helps! So go ahead and recite everything you know about these concepts: *descriptive statsitics, arithmetic mean, standard deviation, inferential statistics, significance tests, confidence interval, cross-sectional study, longitudinal study, effect size, meta-analysis,* and *Bayesian statistics.*

Review: Next, go back and reread this section.

Now take this *Quick Quiz:*

A. Check your understanding of the descriptive–inferential distinction by placing a check in the appropriate column for each phrase:

	Descriptive statistics	Inferential statistics
1. Summarize the data	_____	_____
2. Give likelihood that a result occurred by chance	_____	_____
3. Include the mean	_____	_____
4. Give measure of statistical significance	_____	_____
5. Tell you whether to call your mother about your results	_____	_____
6. Examine a confidence interval around the sample mean	_____	_____

B. If a researcher studies the same group over many years, the study is said to be _____.

C. Suppose a researcher wants to know about the effects on memory of energy drinks. Unfortunately, in the 45 studies that have examined this question, the results vary. What statistical method might be used to determine whether the relation between energy drinks and memory is strong or weak?

D. On the internet, you read about a "Fantastic Scientific Breakthrough in Treating Shyness." Why should you be cautious about this announcement?

Answers:

A. 1. descriptive 2. inferential 3. descriptive 4. inferential 5. inferential 6. inferential B. longitudinal C. meta-analysis D. Scientific progress usually proceeds gradually, not all at once. And besides, anyone can post a claim on the internet, so you will want to ask, "What's the original source of this claim? What is the 'science' behind that alleged breakthrough? How was shyness defined, and what was the method of treating it? How was success defined and measured?"

Learning Objectives

17 List the eight major principles of the TCPS2 and CPA codes for conducting ethical research. Discuss why informed consent and deception are serious concerns for psychological research.

18 Discuss the role of animal subjects in psychological research and paraphrase the means by which ethical methods are enforced.

Keeping the Enterprise Ethical

Because rigorous research methods are the very heart of science, psychologists spend considerable time discussing and debating their procedures for collecting and evaluating data. And they are also concerned about the ethical principles governing research and practice. In all institutions that receive federal funding, a review committee must approve all studies and ensure they conform to federal regulations (The Tri-Council Policy Statement, TCPS2). In addition, the Canadian Psychological Association (CPA) has a code of ethics that all members must follow. In general, both the CPA and TCPS2 advocate that research follows these eight major principles (Canadian Institutes of Health Research, Natural Sciences and Engineering Research Council of Canada, and Social Sciences and Humanities Research Council of Canada, 2010): (1) respect for human dignity; (2) respect for free and informed consent; (3) respect for vulnerable persons, such as children; (4) respect for privacy and confidentiality; (5) respect for justice and inclusiveness; (6) balancing harms and benefits; (7) minimizing harm; and (8) maximizing benefit. In practice, these principles mean that, before participating in an experiment, individuals must know what to expect during the session and must voluntarily choose to take part (that is, they must give "informed consent"). ⊙

⊙—⌐Watch the Video
Special Topics: Ethics and Psychological Research in **MyPsychLab**

The Ethics of Studying Human Beings

The TCPS2 and CPA codes call on psychological scientists to respect the dignity and welfare of the people they study. Participants must enter a study voluntarily and must know enough about it to make an intelligent decision about taking part, a doctrine known as **informed consent**. Researchers must also protect participants from physical and mental harm, and if any risk exists, they must warn participants in advance and give them an opportunity to withdraw at any time.

The policy of informed consent sometimes clashes with an experimenter's need to disguise the true purpose of the study. In such cases, if the purpose were revealed in advance, the results would be ruined because the participants would not behave naturally. In social psychology especially, a study's design sometimes calls for an elaborate deception. For example, a confederate of the researcher might pretend to be having a seizure. The researcher can then find out whether bystanders—the uninformed participants—will respond to a person needing help. If the participants knew that the confederate was only acting, obviously they would not bother to intervene or call for assistance.

Sometimes people have been misled about procedures that are intentionally designed to make them uncomfortable so that researchers can learn what people do when they feel this way. In studies of embarrassment and anger, people have been made to look clumsy in front of others, have been called insulting names, or have been told they were incompetent. In studies of dishonesty, participants have been entrapped into cheating and have then been confronted with evidence of their guilt. Today, Canada's ethical guidelines require researchers to show that any deceptive procedures are justified by a study's potential value, to consider alternative procedures, and to thoroughly debrief participants about the true purpose and methods of the study afterward. When people are debriefed and told why deception was necessary, they are rarely resentful and say that they are willing to take part in further studies (Bröder, 1998). But the issues raised by deception will always be with us, and both the Tri-Council and the CPA frequently reevaluate their ethical codes to deal with deception.

Participants also have the right to expect that their responses will be confidential unless they explicitly consent to public disclosure. This requirement can present

informed consent The doctrine that anyone who participates in human research must do so voluntarily and must know enough about the study to make an intelligent decision about whether to take part.

researchers with a dilemma because psychologists often investigate sensitive issues, such as illegal drug use. Because of the need for confidentiality, responses must be anonymous. Confidentiality is also an issue in psychological practice. In Canada, unlike in the United States, communications between the psychologist and the client are not privileged. A court can compel a psychologist to reveal the content of discussions with a client. Further, Canadian law requires that certain types of information must be reported (for example, child abuse), regardless of any potential harm that may come to the client. Many of these conflicts can be avoided by ensuring that a potential participant or client understands the limits of confidentiality before he or she begins to disclose potentially sensitive information.

The Ethics of Studying Animals

Ethical issues also arise in animal research. Animals have always been used in psychological studies and they still play a crucial role. Although sometimes they are not harmed (as in research on mating in hamsters, which is definitely fun for the hamsters), sometimes they are (as when rats are euthanized so that their brains can be examined for any effects of early exposure to toxins). Psychologists study animals for many reasons:

- *To conduct basic research on a particular species.* For example, researchers have learned a great deal about the unusually lusty and cooperative lives of bonobo apes.
- *To discover practical applications.* For example, behavioural studies have shown farmers how to reduce crop destruction by birds and deer without resorting to their traditional method—shooting the animals.
- *To clarify theoretical questions.* For example, we might not attribute the longer lifespans of women solely to lifestyle factors and health practices if we discover that a male–female difference exists in other mammals as well.
- *To study issues that cannot be studied experimentally with human beings because of practical or ethical considerations.* For example, research on monkeys has

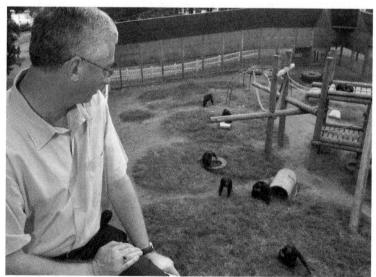

Psychologists sometimes use animals to study learning, memory, emotion, and social behaviour. On the left, John Boitano and Kathryn Scavo observe a swimming rat as it learns the location of platforms in a pool of dark water. On the right, Frans de Waal observes a group of chimpanzees socializing in an outdoor play area.

Left: James Marshall/The Image Works. Right: Yerkes Regional Primate Research Center.

demonstrated the effects of maternal deprivation on emotional development, and the effects of later experience in overcoming early deprivation.

- *To improve human and animal welfare.* For example, animal studies have helped researchers develop ways to reduce chronic pain and rehabilitate human and animal patients with neurological disorders—to name only a few benefits.

In recent decades, some psychological and medical scientists have been trying to find ways to do their research without using animals at all or by reducing the numbers of animals or changing the species of animal studied. When animals are essential to research, the Canadian Council on Animal Care (CCAC), CPA and the Tri-Council all regulate the humane treatment of animals. These codes are comprehensive and cover everything from the housing and care of research animals to encouraging researchers to develop alternative procedures that take advantage of new technology or research innovations. Moreover, thanks to a growing understanding of animals' instinctive, social, and cognitive needs—especially in the widely studied lab rat—many psychological scientists have changed the way they treat animals, which improves their research as well as the animals' well-being (Patterson-Kane, Harper, & Hunt, 2001). The difficult task for scientists is to balance the benefits of animal research with an acknowledgement of past abuses and a compassionate attitude toward species other than our own.

You are now ready to explore more deeply what psychologists have learned about human psychology. The methods of psychological science, as we will see repeatedly in the remainder of the book, have overturned some deeply entrenched assumptions about the way people think, feel, act, and adapt to events in their lives, and have yielded information that greatly improves the well-being of humans and animals. These methods illuminate our human errors and biases and enable us to seek knowledge with an open mind. Biologist Thomas Huxley put it well. The essence of science, he said, is "to sit down before the fact as a little child, be prepared to give up every preconceived notion. Follow humbly wherever and to whatever abyss nature leads, or you shall learn nothing."

Recite & Review

Recite: Major scientific breakthrough: Reciting what you've read helps! So go ahead and recite everything you know about this concept: *informed consent.*

Review: Next, go back and reread this section.

Now take this *Quick Quiz:*

1. Janice wants to conduct a research study about how individuals are affected by social media. To do this, she wants to present individuals with a fake post from one of their friends on Facebook. This procedure involves _____ and as such her study would be subject to enhanced ethical review. The focus of the review would be to ensure _____, _____, and _____.

2. List two reasons that research with non-human animals may be justified.

Answers:

1. deception; that the study had potential value; that there were no alternative ways to conduct the study; that the participants were fully debriefed afterward 2. Research with non-human animals may be justified to study issues that cannot be studied ethically with humans, to improve human and animal welfare, to clarify theoretical answers, to discover practical applications, and to understand particular species.

Taking Psychology with You

Lying with Statistics

We have seen that statistical procedures are indispensable tools for assessing research. But in the real world, statistics can be manipulated, misrepresented, and even made up by people hoping to promote a particular political or social agenda. That is why an essential part of critical and scientific thinking is learning not only how to use statistics correctly but also how to identify their misuse.

A primary reason for the misuse of statistics is "innumeracy" (mathematical illiteracy). For instance, it has been argued that each year, between 62 500 and 80 000 Canadians have used a gun for self-defence (e.g., Mauser & Buckner, 1997). Why haven't we heard these astounding numbers on the news? Well, because the numbers come from a study (Mauser, 1995) in which 1505 Canadians were surveyed and 2.1% (31 people) responded that in the last five years they had used a gun to protect themselves against a person or an animal. This percentage was then multiplied by the population of Canada to obtain the larger figure (note the difference between 31 and 80 000 Canadians), which assumes that the sample was representative and that everyone in Canada has equal access to firearms!

We don't want you to distrust all statistics. Statistics don't lie; people do—or, more likely, they misinterpret what the numbers mean. When statistics are used correctly, they neither confuse nor mislead. On the contrary, they can expose unwarranted conclusions, promote clarity and precision, and protect us from our biases and blind spots. You need to be careful, though. Here are a few things you can do when you hear that "2 million people do this" or "one out of four people are that":

Ask how the number was computed

Suppose someone on your campus gives a talk about a hot social issue and cites some big number to show how serious and widespread the problem is. You should ask how the number was calculated. Was it based on government data, such as the census? Did it come from just one small study or from a meta-analysis of many studies? Or is it pure conjecture?

> 66 Statistics don't lie; people do—or, more likely, they misrepresent or misinterpret what the numbers mean. When statistics are used correctly, they can expose unwarranted conclusions and protect us from our biases and blind spots. 99

Ask about base rates and absolute numbers

If we tell you that the *relative risk* of getting ulcers is increased by 300% in university students who eat a bagel every morning (relax, it isn't!), that sounds pretty scary, but it does not tell you much. You would need to know how many students get ulcers in the first place, and then how many bagel-eating students get ulcers. If the "300% increased risk" is a jump from 100 students in every thousand to 300 in every thousand, then you might reasonably be concerned. If the number shifts from one in every thousand to three in every thousand, that is still a 300% increase, but the risk is very small and could even be a random fluke. Many health findings are presented in alarming terms, as an increased relative risk of this or that when the actual, absolute numbers are quite trivial (Bluming & Tavris, 2009; Gigerenzer et al., 2008).

Ask how terms were defined

If we hear that "one out of every four women" will be raped at some point in her life, we need to ask: How was rape defined? If women are asked if they have ever experienced any act of unwanted sex, the percentages are higher than if they are asked specifically whether they have been forced or coerced into intercourse against their will. (See Chapter 12 for further discussion of this issue.)

Always, always look for the control group

If an experiment does not have a control group, then, as they say in New York, "fuhgeddaboudit." The kinds of "findings" often reported without a control group tend to be those promoting specific products or programs. As you will learn in Chapter 8, people are motivated to justify any program or treatment in which they have invested time, money, or effort. Further, thanks to the placebo effect, people's expectations of success are often what helps them, not the treatment itself. This is why testimonials don't provide a full or accurate picture of a medication's or treatment's benefits or harms. It's like the bartender who says to the customer, "Why are you waving your arms around like that?" And the customer says, "It keeps the gerbils away." "But there aren't any gerbils here," the bartender says. "See?" says the customer, "It works!" All the arm waving in the world won't substitute for a good study.

Be cautious about correlations

We said this before, but we'll say it again: With correlational findings, you usually cannot be sure what's causing what. A study reported that teenagers who listened to music five or more hours a day were eight times more likely to be depressed than those who didn't listen that often (Primack et al., 2011). Does listening to music make you depressed? A more likely explanation is that being depressed causes teenagers to tune out and listen to music, as they don't have the mental energy to do much else. "At this point, it is not clear whether depressed people begin to listen to more music to escape, or whether listening to large amounts of music can lead to depression, or both," said the lead researcher.

The statistics that most people like best are usually the ones that support their own opinions and prejudices. Unfortunately, bad statistics, repeated again and again, can infiltrate popular culture, spread like a virus on the internet, and become difficult to eradicate. The information in this chapter will get you started on telling the difference between numbers that are helpful and those that mislead or deceive. In future chapters, we will give you other information to help you think critically and scientifically about popular claims and findings that make the news.

Summary

MyPsychLab can help you get a better grade. Test your knowledge and grasp difficult concepts through
- Custom study plans: See where you are strong and where you are wrong
- Multimedia, including videos and interactive simulations
- Dynamic Study Modules: flashcards for self-study that ensure you achieve mastery of course concepts

What Makes Psychological Research Scientific?

- Research methods provide a way for psychologists to separate well-supported conclusions from unfounded belief. An understanding of these methods can also help people think critically about psychological issues and become astute consumers of psychological findings and programs.

- The ideal scientist states hypotheses and predictions precisely, is skeptical of claims that rest solely on faith or authority, relies on empirical evidence, resists the *confirmation bias* and complies with the *principle of falsifiability*, and is open about methods and results so that findings can be *replicated*. The public nature of science and the process of *peer review* give science a built-in system of checks and balances.

Descriptive Studies: Establishing the Facts

- In any study, the researcher would ideally like to use a *representative sample*, one that is similar in composition to the larger population that the researcher wishes to describe. But in practice, researchers must often use "convenience" samples, which typically means university undergraduates. In the study of many topics, the consequences are minimal, but in other cases, conclusions about "people in general" must be interpreted with caution.

- *Descriptive methods* allow psychologists to describe and predict behaviour but not necessarily to choose one explanation over others. Such methods include case studies, observational studies, psychological tests, and surveys, as well as correlational methods.

- *Case studies* are detailed descriptions of individuals. They are often used by clinicians and can also be valuable in exploring new research topics and addressing questions that would otherwise be difficult to study. But because the person under study may not be representative of people in general, case studies are typically sources rather than tests of hypotheses.

- In *observational studies*, researchers systematically observe and record behaviour without interfering in any way with the behaviour. *Naturalistic observation* is used to find out how animals and people behave in their natural environments. *Laboratory observation* allows more control and the use of special equipment; behaviour in the laboratory, however, may differ in certain ways from behaviour in natural contexts.

- *Psychological tests* are used to measure and evaluate personality traits, emotional states, aptitudes, interests, abilities, and values. A good test is one that has been *standardized*, is scored using established *norms*, and is both *reliable* and *valid*. Critics have questioned the reliability and validity of even some widely used tests.

- *Surveys* are questionnaires or interviews that ask people directly about their experiences, attitudes, and opinions.

Unrepresentative samples and *volunteer bias* can influence the generalizability of survey results. Findings can also be affected by the fact that respondents sometimes lie, misremember, or misinterpret the questions. Technology and use of the internet can help psychologists minimize some of these problems, but they also introduce some new methodological challenges. People should be cautious about tests they take on the internet because not all of them meet scientific standards.

Correlational Studies: Looking for Relations

- In descriptive research, studies that look for relations between phenomena are known as *correlational*. A *correlation* is a measure of the strength of a positive or negative relation between two variables and is expressed by the *coefficient of correlation*. Many correlations reported in the media or on the internet are based on rumour and anecdote and are not supported by data. Even when a correlation is real, it does not necessarily demonstrate a causal relation between the variables.

Experiments: Hunting for Causes

- Experiments allow researchers to control the situation being studied, manipulate an *independent variable*, and assess the effects of the manipulation on a *dependent variable*. Experimental studies usually require a comparison or control condition and often involve random assignment of participants to *experimental and control groups*. In some studies, those in the control group receive a *placebo*, or fake treatment. *Single-blind* and *double-blind procedures* can be used to prevent the expectations of the participants or the experimenter from affecting the results.

- Because experiments allow conclusions about cause and effect, they have long been the method of choice in psychology. However, like laboratory observations, experiments create a special situation that may call forth behaviour not typical in other environments. Many psychologists, therefore, have called for more *field research*.

Evaluating the Findings

- Psychologists use *descriptive statistics*, such as the *arithmetic mean* and the *standard deviation*, to summarize data. They use *inferential statistics* to find out how impressive the data are. *Significance tests* tell the researchers how likely it is that the results of a study occurred merely by chance. The results are said to be *statistically significant* if this likelihood is very

low. Statistically significant results allow psychologists to make predictions about human behaviour, but, as in all sciences, probabilistic results do not tell us with any certainty what a particular person will do in a given situation.

- Choosing among competing interpretations of a finding can be difficult, and care must be taken to avoid going beyond the facts. Sometimes the best interpretation does not emerge until a hypothesis has been tested in more than one way, as by using both *cross-sectional* and *longitudinal* methods.

- Statistical significance does not always imply real-world importance because the amount of variation in the data accounted for by the independent variable—the *effect size*—may be small. Therefore, many psychologists are now turning to other measures. *Confidence intervals* help researchers evaluate where the real population mean is likely to be if they could repeat their study over and over. *Meta-analysis* is a procedure for combining data from many related studies to determine the overall strength of an independent variable. *Bayesian statistics* take prior knowledge into account in assessing the likelihood that a finding is true and meaningful.

Keeping the Enterprise Ethical

- The Tri-Council Policy Statement and the CPA's ethical code requires researchers to obtain the *informed consent* of anyone who is participating in a study or experiment, protect them from harm, and warn them in advance of any risks. Many studies require deceptive procedures. Concern about the morality of such procedures has led to guidelines to protect participants.

- Psychologists study animals in order to gain knowledge about particular species, discover practical applications of psychological principles, study issues that cannot be studied with human beings for practical or ethical reasons, clarify theoretical questions, and improve human and animal welfare. Debate over the use of animals in research has led to more comprehensive regulations governing their treatment and care.

Taking Psychology with You

- Statistics help scientists understand the complexities of behaviour, but statistics can also be misrepresented and misused. Critical thinkers should ask how numbers were calculated, look at percentages that provide *absolute* risk rather than *relative* risk, ask how terms were defined, make sure there was a control group, and be cautious about inferring a cause from a correlation.

Key Terms

theory 36

hypothesis 36

operational definition 37

principle of falsifiability 38

confirmation bias 38

representative sample 40

descriptive methods 41

case study 41

observational study 42

psychological tests 43

standardize 44

norms 44

reliability 44

validity 44

surveys 45

volunteer bias 45

correlational study 48

correlation 48

variables 48

positive correlation 48

negative correlation 48

coefficient of correlation 48

experiment 51

independent variable 51

dependent variable 51

control condition 53

random assignment 53

placebo 53

single-blind study 54

experimenter effects 54

double-blind study 54

field research 55

descriptive statistics 57

arithmetic mean 57

standard deviation 57

inferential statistics 58

significance tests 58

confidence interval 58

cross-sectional study 59

longitudinal study 59

effect size 61

meta-analysis 61

Bayesian statistics 61

informed consent 63

Genes, Evolution, and Environment

Think of all the ways in which human beings are alike. Everywhere, no matter what their backgrounds or where they live, people love, work, argue, dance, sing, complain, and gossip. They rear families, celebrate marriages, and mourn losses. They reminisce about the past and plan for the future. They help their friends and fight their enemies. They smile with amusement, frown with displeasure, and glare in anger. Where do all these commonalities come from?

Think of all the ways in which human beings differ. Some are extroverts, always ready to make new friends or speak up in a crowd; others are shy and introverted, preferring the safe and familiar. Some are ambitious and enterprising; others are placid, content with the way things are. Some take to academics like a cat to catnip; others struggle in school but have plenty of street smarts and practical know-how. Some are overwhelmed by even petty problems; others remain calm and resilient in the face of severe difficulties. Where do all these differences come from?

For many years, psychologists addressing these questions tended to fall into two camps. On one side were the nativists, who emphasized genes and inborn characteristics, or nature; on the other side were the empiricists, who focused on learning and experience, or nurture. Edward L. Thorndike (1903) staked out the first position when he claimed that "in the actual race of life . . . the chief determining factor is heredity." But in words that became famous, his contemporary, behaviourist John B. Watson (1925), insisted that experience could write virtually any message on the tabula rasa, the blank slate, of human nature: "Give me a dozen healthy infants, well-formed, and my own specified world to bring them up in and I'll guarantee to take any one at random and train him to become any type of specialist I might select—doctor, lawyer, artist, merchant-chief and yes, even beggar-man and thief, regardless of his talents, penchants, tendencies, abilities, vocations, and race of his ancestors."

In this chapter, we examine the contributions of both nature and nurture in shaping our human commonalities and our individual differences. We will focus largely on findings from two related areas: evolutionary psychology and behavioural genetics. Researchers in **evolutionary psychology** emphasize the evolutionary mechanisms that might help explain commonalities in language learning, attention, perception, memory, sexual behaviour, emotion, reasoning, and many other aspects of human psychology. Researchers in **behavioural genetics** attempt to tease apart the relative contributions of heredity and environment to explain individual differences in personality, mental ability, and other characteristics.

evolutionary psychology A field of psychology emphasizing evolutionary mechanisms that may help explain human commonalities in cognition, development, emotion, social practices, and other areas of behaviour.

behavioural genetics An interdisciplinary field of study concerned with the genetic bases of individual differences in behaviour and personality.

The long and short of it: Human beings are both similar and different.

Georgerudy/Fotolia

The long and short of it: Human beings are both similar and different. Keep in mind, however, that virtually no one argues in terms of nature *versus* nurture anymore. Scientists today understand that heredity and environment constantly interact to produce our psychological traits and even most of our physical ones. This interaction works in two directions. First, genes affect the kinds of experiences we have: A teenager with a genetic aptitude for schoolwork may be more likely than other kids to join a spelling-bee team and get books and science kits as birthday presents. These experiences reward and encourage the development of academic skills. Conversely, although most people don't realize it, experience also affects our genes: Stress, diet, emotional events, and hormonal changes can all influence which genes are active or inactive at any given time over a person's lifetime (Fraga et al., 2005; Mischel, 2009). The study of this type of stable change in gene expression (that does not involve changes in the underlying DNA structure) is called *epigenetics*. Try, then, as you read this chapter, to resist the temptation to think of nature and nurture in either–or terms.

Learning Objectives

1 Describe what the chemical code in our genes encodes for.

2 Contrast what a complete map of the human genes reveals—and does not reveal.

3 Compare how gene expression can change over the lifespan. Identify the promise and limitations of epigenetics.

Unlocking the Secrets of Genes

Simulate the **Experiment**
DNA Replication in **MyPsychLab**

genes The functional units of heredity; they are composed of DNA and specify the structure of proteins.

chromosomes Within every cell, rod-shaped structures that carry the genes.

deoxyribonucleic acid (DNA) The chromosomal molecule that transfers genetic characteristics by way of coded instructions for the structure of proteins.

genome The full set of genes in each cell of an organism (with the exception of sperm and egg cells).

Let's begin by looking at what genes are and how they operate. **Genes**, the basic units of heredity, are located on **chromosomes**, rod-shaped structures found in the centre (nucleus) of every cell of the body. Each sperm cell and each egg cell (ovum) contains 23 chromosomes, so when a sperm and egg unite at conception, the fertilized egg and all the body cells that eventually develop from it (except for sperm cells and ova) contain 46 chromosomes, arranged in 23 pairs.

Chromosomes consist of threadlike strands of **deoxyribonucleic acid (DNA)** molecules, and genes consist of small segments of this DNA. Each human chromosome contains thousands of genes, each with a fixed location. Collectively, all the genes together—the best estimates put the number at around 25 000—are referred to as the human **genome**. Most of these genes are found in other animals as well, but others are uniquely human, setting us apart from chimpanzees, wasps, and mice. Many genes contribute directly to a particular trait, but others work indirectly by switching other genes on or off throughout a person's life. Everyone inherits many genes in the same form as everyone else; other genes vary, contributing to our individuality.

Cell nucleus

Cell

Chromosomes containing genes

DNA

Within each gene, four basic chemical elements of DNA—the bases adenine, thymine, cytosine, and guanine, identified by the letters A, T, C, and G—are arranged in a particular order: for example, ACGTCTCTATA. . . . This sequence may contain thousands or even tens of thousands of "letters," which together constitute a code for the synthesis of one of the many proteins that affect virtually every aspect of the body, from its structure to the chemicals that keep it running. But this is a simplification. Many genes can make more than one protein, depending on when and where different "coding" segments of DNA on the gene are activated. Thus our measly 25 000 or so genes—barely more than a common worm has—are able to produce hundreds of thousands of different proteins (Pennisi, 2005).

Identifying even a single gene is a daunting task; biologist Joseph Levine and geneticist David Suzuki (1993) once compared it to searching for someone when all you know is that the person lives somewhere on earth. However, new technologies now allow scientists to survey hundreds of thousands of "letters" at once instead of looking for one gene at a time. Using powerful computer programs, scientists can compare the genes of people who share a particular disease or trait with those of people who do not have it. A catalogue has been developed that describes millions of patterns of human genetic variation so that researchers can study the consequences of those variations. One method, which has been used to search for the genes associated with many physical and mental conditions, involves doing *linkage studies*. These studies take advantage of the tendency of genes lying close together on a chromosome to be inherited together across generations. The researchers start out by looking for a **genetic marker**, a DNA segment that varies considerably among individuals and whose location on the chromosome is already known. They then look for patterns of inheritance of these markers in large families in which a condition—say, depression or impulsive violence—is common. If a marker tends to exist only in family members who have the condition, then it can be used as a genetic landmark: The gene involved in the condition is apt to be located nearby on the chromosome, so the researchers have some idea where to search for it. The linkage method was used, for example, to locate the gene responsible for Huntington's disease, a fatal neurological disorder that affects motor control, intellectual functioning, and memory (Huntington's Disease Collaborative Research Group, 1993). Although in this instance only one gene was involved, the search took a decade of painstaking work.

In 2000, after years of heated competition, an international collaboration of researchers called the Human Genome Project and a private company, Celera Genomics, both announced that they had completed a rough draft of a map of the entire human genome, and since then the map has been greatly refined. Using high-tech methods, researchers have identified the sequence of nearly all 3 billion units of DNA (those As, Cs, Ts, and Gs) and have been able to determine the boundaries between genes and how the genes are arranged on the chromosomes (see Figure 3.1). This project has been costly and time-consuming, but it reflects the view among many scientists that the twenty-first century will be the century of the gene.

Even when researchers locate a gene, however, they do not automatically know its role in physical or psychological functioning. Usually, locating a gene is just the first tiny step in understanding what it does and how it works. Also, be wary of media reports implying that some gene is the *only* one involved in a complex psychological ability or trait, such as autism or shyness. It seems that nearly every year brings another report about some gene that supposedly explains a human trait. A few years back, newspapers even announced the discovery of a "worry gene." Don't worry about it! Most human traits, even such seemingly straightforward ones as height and eye colour, are influenced by more than one gene pair. Psychological traits are especially likely to depend on multiple genes, with each one accounting for just a small part of the variance among people. Conversely, any single gene is apt to influence many different behaviours. So at this point, all announcements of a "gene for this" or a "gene for that" should be viewed with extreme caution.

genetic marker A segment of DNA that varies among individuals, has a known location on a chromosome, and can function as a genetic landmark for a gene involved in a physical or mental condition.

Chromosome 10

FIGURE 3.1 Mapping Human Genes
Genes are located on chromosomes, some of which are shown on the left, magnified almost 55 000 times. On the right, a small portion of the map for chromosome 10 shows 52 genes identified by the Human Genome Project, including some that have been linked to prostate cancer, leukemia, and obesity.

Recite & Review

Recite: We've been through some technical material, so say out loud everything you can remember about *evolutionary psychology*, *behavioural genetics*, *genes*, *chromosomes*, *DNA*, *the genome*, *bases*, *genetic markers*, linkage studies, and epigenetics.

Review: Next, go back and reread this section.

Now take this *Quick Quiz:*

The Human Genome Project has not discovered any quiz-taking genes.

1. What does it mean to say that the gene–environment interaction works in both directions?
2. The basic unit of heredity is called a (a) gene, (b) chromosome, (c) genome, (d) DNA molecule.
3. What does the code within a gene encode for?
4. *True or false*: Most human genetic traits depend on a single gene.

Answers:

1. Genes affect the environments we experience, and environmental factors affect the activity of genes over a person's lifetime. 2. a 3. the synthesis of a particular protein 4. False

"Heard the one about the three humans who went into a bar?" Evolutionary psychologists are interested in the origins of many human behaviours, such as smiling and laughter, which are universal among primates and are part of our shared evolutionary heritage.

James Balog/Getty Images

Learning Objectives

4 Describe the meaning of evolution.

5 Document one reason that some traits become more common during evolution and others become less common.

6 Explain why some evolutionary psychologists assume the existence of innate "mental modules" in the human mind.

7 List some innate human characteristics.

The Genetics of Similarity

What accounts for the similarities among all human beings everywhere in the world, such as the universal capacity for language or loyalty to a family or clan? Evolutionary psychologists believe the answer lies partly in genetic dispositions that developed during the evolutionary history of our species. As British geneticist Steve Jones (1994) writes, "Each gene is a message from our forebears and together they contain the whole story of human evolution."

Evolution and Natural Selection

To read the messages from the past that are locked in our genes, we must first understand the nature of evolution itself. **Evolution** is basically a change in gene frequencies within a population, a change that typically takes place over many generations. As particular genes become more common or less common in the population, so do the characteristics they influence. These developments account for changes within a species, and when the changes are large enough they can result in the formation of new species.

Why do gene frequencies in a population change? Why don't they remain static from one generation to another? One reason is that during the division of the cells that produce sperm and eggs, if an error occurs in the copying of the original DNA sequence, genes can spontaneously change, or undergo **mutation**. In addition, during the formation of a sperm or an egg, small segments of genetic material cross over (exchange places) from one member of a chromosome pair to another, before the final cell division. As genes spontaneously mutate and recombine during the production of sperm and eggs, new genetic variations—and therefore potential new traits—keep arising.

But that is only part of the story. According to the principle of **natural selection**, first formulated in general terms by the British naturalist Charles Darwin in *On the Origin of Species* (1859/1964), the fate of these genetic variations depends on the environment. Darwin did not actually know about genes, as their discovery had not yet been widely publicized, but he realized that a species' characteristics must somehow be transmitted biologically from one generation to the next.

The fundamental idea behind natural selection is this: If, in a particular environment, individuals with a genetically influenced trait tend to be more successful than other individuals in finding food, surviving the elements, and fending off enemies—and therefore better at staying alive long enough to produce offspring—their genes will become more and more common in the population. Their genes will have been "selected" by reproductive success, and over many generations these genes may even spread throughout the species. In contrast, individuals whose traits are not as adaptive in the struggle for survival will not be as "reproductively fit": They will tend to die before reproducing, and therefore their genes, and the traits influenced by those genes, will become less and less common and eventually may even disappear.

Scientists debate how gradually or abruptly evolutionary changes occur and whether competition for survival is always the primary mechanism of change, but they agree on the basic importance of evolution. Over the past century and a half, Darwin's ideas have been resoundingly supported by findings in anthropology, botany, and molecular genetics (Coyne, 2009). Scientists have watched evolutionary developments occurring before their very eyes in organisms that change rapidly, such as microbes, insects, and various plants. Researchers have even identified specific genes that account for evolutionary changes that have occurred in animals in the wild, such as the transformation of mice and lizards from light coloured to dark coloured (or vice versa) as the animals have migrated into different environments (Hoekstra et al., 2006; Rosenblum, 2005). They have also observed rapid evolutionary changes due to human activity. For example, the horns of bighorn rams have been getting smaller because of trophy hunting, which removes animals with larger horns from the breeding population (Coltman et al., 2003).

However, this "survival of the fittest" account of evolution cannot explain all the physical and behavioural traits that reflect a gene's success (that is, increase or decrease within a population). For example, why does a peacock (but not the female of the same species, the peahen) have such an incredibly large and colourful tail? Certainly not to

Darwin's image can be found on countless T-shirts, bumper stickers, and mugs. His theory of evolution forms the basis of modern biology and has had a growing influence in psychology.

Newscom

Simulate the **Experiment** *Mechanisms of Evolution* in **MyPsychLab**

evolution A change in gene frequencies within a population over many generations; a mechanism by which genetically influenced characteristics of a population may change.

mutation Changes in genes, sometimes due to an error in the copying of the original DNA sequence during the division of the cells that produce sperm and eggs.

natural selection The evolutionary process in which individuals with genetically influenced traits that are adaptive in a particular environment tend to survive and to reproduce in greater numbers than do other individuals; as a result, their traits become more common in the population.

Natural selection allows animals to survive by adapting to the environment. In the deserts of Arizona, most rock pocket mice are sandy-coloured and are well camouflaged against the beige rocks they scamper over (a). Their colouring therefore protects them against owls and other predators. But in areas where ancient lava flows have left large deposits of black rock, the same species has evolved to be dark-coated and thus equally well disguised (b). You can see how vulnerable these mice are when their coats do *not* blend with the colour of the rocks (c and d). Researchers have identified the gene involved in the evolution of dark coloration in these mice (Nachman, Hoekstra, & D'Agostino, 2003).

Professor Michael Nachman

avoid being spotted by predators! Darwin himself was puzzled by some of the physical traits he observed in nature and eventually became dissatisfied with natural selection as the only cause (or agent) of evolution. In Darwin's second book on evolution, *The Descent of Man* (1874), he proposed another type of selection: *sexual selection*. In natural selection, nature determines which genes survive and reproduce, and which genes disappear from the planet. In sexual selection, the members of either the other sex or the same sex, with which one is competing, determine a gene's fate. Two types of sexual selection exist:

- **Intersexual selection.** In this type, a member of one sex chooses a mate from the other sex on the basis of certain characteristics. For males, the choice appears to be most influenced by physical factors such as attractiveness and youth. For females, the choice is similarly influenced by physical factors, such as height and muscularity, but the resources that the male has access to also come into play. We will explore the tactics of intersexual selection later in this chapter.

- **Intrasexual selection.** In this type, members of the same sex compete for a partner of the other sex. Males might compete with each other by becoming more muscular or acquiring and displaying resources (such as wealth), whereas females might compete by enhancing their appearance and youthful look through such techniques as hair colouring or using makeup.

A renewed interest in sexual selection over the past 20 years has led to numerous "culturally driven" behaviours being reexamined from an evolutionary framework. In his book *The Mating Mind: How Sexual Choice Shaped the Evolution of Human Nature*, Geoffrey Miller hypothesizes that a number of behaviours, such as artistic innovation, music, and humour, are the result of sexually selected psychological traits dating back to the Pleistocene epoch (Miller, 2000). In order to excel in these areas, one requires considerable intelligence and creativity. These are also traits that are indicative of high genetic quality when viewed in the context of mate selection. In fact, the trait "artistic intelligence" ranked third out of nine (behind kindness and being socially exciting) in a comprehensive survey of preferred partner traits for both males and females (Buss & Barnes, 1986). Thus, an exceptional musician, imaginative painter, or witty comedian may attain higher reproductive success than a physically comparable counterpart owing to enhanced creative intelligence.

Traits and Preferences. Evolutionary biologists often start with an observation about some characteristic and then try to account for it in evolutionary terms. For example, why do male peacocks have such fabulous and flamboyant feathers while females look so drab and dull? Those long plumes certainly did not help the males avoid predators! The evolutionary answer is that during the history of the species, males who put on a flashy display (evidence that they had "good genes" and could afford to carry around the extra plumage) were better able to attract females. In contrast, a female peacock did not have to put on such a display to attract competing males. Instead, all she had to do was hang around and pick the best potential mate: the guy with the best genes and fanciest feathers. She didn't even have to dress up!

Evolutionary psychologists work in the same way as biologists, but some take a slightly different tack: They start by asking what sorts of challenges human beings might have faced in their prehistoric past—say, having to decide which foods were safe to eat, or needing to size up a stranger's intentions quickly. Then they draw inferences about the behavioural tendencies that might have been selected because they helped our forebears solve these survival problems and enhanced their reproductive fitness. (They make no assumption about whether the behaviour is adaptive or intelligent in the *present* environment.) Finally, they do research to see if those tendencies actually exist throughout the world.

For example, our ancestors' need to avoid eating poisonous or rancid food might have led eventually to an innate dislike for bitter tastes and rotten smells; those individuals who happened to be born with such dislikes would have stood a better chance of surviving long enough to reproduce. Similarly, it made good survival sense for our ancestors to develop an innate capacity for language and an ability to recognize faces and emotional expressions. But they would not have had much need for an innate ability to read or drive, inasmuch as books and cars had not yet been invented (Pinker, 1994).

Mental Modules. For many evolutionary psychologists, a guiding assumption is that the human mind is not a general-purpose computer waiting to be programmed. Instead, they say, it developed as a collection of specialized and independent **mental modules** to handle specific survival problems, such as the need to locate food or find a mate (Buss, 1995, 1999; Cosmides, Tooby, & Barkow, 1992; Marcus, 2004; Mealey, 1996; Pinker, 2002). A particular module may involve several dispersed but interconnected areas of the brain, just as a computer file can be fragmented on a hard drive (Pinker, 1997). Critics worry that the idea of mental modules is no improvement over instinct theory, the once-popular notion in psychology that virtually every human activity and capacity, from cleanliness to cruelty, is innate. Frans de Waal (2002), an evolutionary theorist who believes that someday all psychology departments will have a picture of Darwin hanging on the wall, has accused some of his colleagues who argue for mental modules of mistakenly assuming that if a trait exists and has a genetic component, then it must be adaptive and must correspond to a module. This assumption, he points out, is incorrect: Male pattern baldness and pimples, for example, are not particularly adaptive! Many evolved and inherited traits are merely by-products of other traits (for example, your bellybutton is a by-product of being a placental mammal), and some can even be costly; the problems that many people have with aching backs are no doubt an

mental modules A collection of specialized and independent sections of the brain, developed to handle specific survival problems, such as the need to locate food or find a mate.

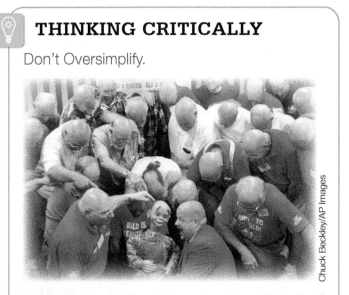

THINKING CRITICALLY

Don't Oversimplify.

Chuck Beckley/AP Images

Many people oversimplify evolutionary theory by concluding that if a trait exists, it must have aided survival by serving some beneficial purpose. Not so! Baldness, for example, may be beautiful, but it is not necessarily adaptive.

unfortunate consequence of our evolved ability to walk on two feet. To understand our evolutionary legacy, de Waal argues, we must consider not just individual traits in isolation but also the whole package of traits that characterizes the species. This is as true for psychological traits as for physical ones.

Those who subscribe to the modules approach respond that evidence from psychology and other disciplines can distinguish behaviour that has a biological origin from behaviour that does not. As Steven Pinker (1994) explains, if a mental module for some behaviour exists, then neuroscientists should eventually discover the brain circuits or subsystems associated with it. Further, he adds, "When children solve problems for which they have mental modules, they should look like geniuses, knowing things they have not been taught; when they solve problems that their minds are not equipped for, it should be a long hard slog."

The debate over modules will undoubtedly continue. But whether or not modules are the best way to describe traits that appear to be inherited, you should be careful to avoid the common error of assuming that if some behaviour or trait exists, it must be adaptive.

Innate Human Characteristics

Because of the way our species evolved, many abilities, tendencies, and characteristics are either present at birth in all human beings or develop rapidly as a child matures. These traits include not just the obvious ones, such as the ability to stand on two legs or to grasp objects with the forefinger and thumb, but also less obvious ones. Here are just a few examples:

1 **Infant reflexes.** Babies are born with a number of reflexes—simple, automatic responses to specific stimuli. For example, all infants will suck something put to their lips; by aiding nursing, this reflex enhances their chances of survival.

2 **An interest in novelty.** Novelty is intriguing to human beings and many other species. If a rat has had its dinner, it will prefer to explore an unfamiliar wing of a maze rather than the familiar wing where food is. Human babies reveal a surprising interest in looking at and listening to unfamiliar things—which, of course, includes most of the world. A baby will even stop nursing momentarily upon seeing someone new.

3 **A desire to explore and manipulate objects.** All birds and mammals have this innate inclination. Primates, especially, like to "monkey" with things, taking them apart and scrutinizing the pieces, apparently for the sheer pleasure of it (Harlow, Harlow, & Meyer, 1950). Human babies shake rattles, bang pots, and grasp whatever is put into their tiny hands. For human beings, the natural impulse to handle interesting objects can be overwhelming, which may be one reason why the command "Don't touch" is so often ignored by children, museum-goers, and shoppers.

4 **An impulse to play and fool around.** Think of kittens, puppies, lion cubs, panda cubs, and young primates who will play with and pounce on each other all day until hunger or naptime calls. Play and exploration may be biologically adaptive because they help members of a species find food and other necessities of life and learn to cope with their environments. Indeed, the young of many species enjoy *practice play*, behaviour that will be used for serious purposes when they are adults (Vandenberg, 1985). A kitten, for example, will stalk and attack a ball of yarn. In human beings, play teaches children how to get along with others and gives them a chance to practise their motor and linguistic skills (Pellegrini & Galda, 1993).

All primates, including human beings, are innately disposed to explore the environment, manipulate objects, play, and "monkey around."

Left: Petro Feket/Fotolia. Right: Christian Prandl/ Alamy.

5 **Basic cognitive skills.** Many evolutionary psychologists believe that people are born with abilities that make it easy to learn to interpret the expressions and gestures of others, identify faces, figure out what others are thinking or feeling, distinguish plants from animals, distinguish living from nonliving things, and acquire language (Geary & Huffman, 2002). Young infants have even been credited with a rudimentary understanding of number (Izard et al., 2009). Of course, tiny infants cannot count. By the age of only one week, however, they will spend more time looking at a new set of three items after getting used to a set of two items, or vice versa, which means that they can recognize the difference. By seven months, most infants prefer to look at videotapes in which the number of adults mouthing a word (two or three adults) matches the number of voices saying the word in synchrony with the images (Jordan & Brannon, 2006). By 18 months, infants know that four is more than three, which is more than two, which is more than one— suggesting that the brain is designed to understand "more than" and "less than" relations for small numbers. Evolutionary psychologists believe that these and other fundamental cognitive skills evolved because they were useful to our ancestors and aided their survival.

Although most archaeological evidence suggests that humans have spent the vast majority of their time on earth as hunter–gatherers on the African savannah (Orians & Heerwagen, 1992), the natural and sexual selection pressures that existed in this environment were quite different from the pressures we face today. For example, on the savannah, vitamins would have been hard to come by. One of the best sources would have been fruits, which were some of the sweetest foods available. Therefore, individuals preferring (and seeking) sweet foods would have been more likely to survive and reproduce. Since our ancestors were the ones who preferred sweets, so do we. However, we now often satisfy that preference with candy, not fruit. A behaviour that *was* adaptive is now maladaptive. Roger Bingham was probably thinking of such ancestral carry-overs when he wrote, "We live in the space age with a brain from the stone age."

In other chapters, we will consider the adaptive and evolutionary aspects of sensory and perceptual abilities (Chapter 6), learning (Chapter 7), ethnocentrism (Chapter 8), cognitive biases (Chapter 9), memory (Chapter 10), emotions and emotional expressions (Chapter 11), stress reactions (Chapter 11), the tendency to gain weight when food is plentiful (Chapter 12), and attachment (Chapter 13). For now, let us look more closely at an are of particular interest to evolutionary psychologists: the nature of mating practices around the world.

Learning Objectives

8 Contrast how evolutionary psychologists explain male–female differences in courtship and mating.

9 List some problems with evolutionary theories of courtship and mating preferences.

10 Identify the basic issue that divides evolutionary psychologists and their critics.

Our Human Heritage: Courtship and Mating

Most psychologists agree that the evolutionary history of our species has made certain kinds of learning either difficult or easy. Most acknowledge that simple behaviours, such as smiling or preferring sweet tastes, resemble instincts, behaviours that are relatively uninfluenced by learning and that occur in all members of the species. And most agree that human beings inherit some of their cognitive, perceptual, emotional, and linguistic capacities. But social scientists disagree heartily about whether biology and evolution can help account for complex social customs, such as warfare, cooperation, and altruism (the willingness to help others). Nowhere is this disagreement more apparent than in debates over the origins of male–female differences in sexual behaviour, so we are going to focus here on that endlessly fascinating topic.

Evolution and Sexual Strategies

In 1975, one of the world's leading experts on ants, Edward O. Wilson, published a book that had a big impact. It was titled *Sociobiology: The New Synthesis,* the "synthesis" being the application of biological principles to the social and sexual customs of both nonhuman animals and human beings. **Sociobiology** became a popular topic for researchers and the public, generating great controversy.

sociobiology An interdisciplinary field that emphasizes evolutionary explanations of social behaviour in animals, including human beings.

Sociobiologists contend that evolution has bred into each of us a tendency to act in ways that maximize our chances of passing on our genes, and to help our close biological relatives, with whom we share many genes, do the same. In this view, just as nature has selected physical characteristics that have proven adaptive, so it has selected psychological traits and social customs that aid individuals in propagating their genes. Customs that enhance the odds of such transmission survive in the form of kinship bonds, dominance arrangements, taboos against female adultery, and many other aspects of social life.

In addition, sociobiologists believe that because the males and females of most species have faced different kinds of survival and mating problems, the sexes have evolved to differ profoundly in aggressiveness, dominance, and sexual strategies (Symons, 1979; Trivers, 1972). In many species, they argue, it is adaptive for males to compete with other males for access to young and fertile females, and to try to win and then inseminate as many females as possible. The more females a male mates with, the more genes he can pass along. (The human record in this regard was achieved by a man who fathered 899 children [Daly & Wilson, 1983]. What else he did with his time is unknown.) But according to sociobiologists, females need to shop for the best genetic deal, as it were, because they can conceive and bear only a limited number of offspring. Having such a large biological investment in each pregnancy, females cannot afford to make mistakes. Besides, mating with a lot of different males would produce no more offspring than staying with just one. So females try to attach themselves to dominant males who have resources and status and are likely to have "superior" genes. The result of these two opposite sexual strategies, in this view, is that males generally want sex more often than females do; males are often fickle and promiscuous, whereas females are usually devoted and faithful; males are drawn to sexual novelty and even rape, whereas females want stability and security; males are relatively undiscriminating in their choice of sexual partners, whereas females are cautious and choosy; and males are competitive and concerned about dominance, whereas females are less so. ◉

◉—Watch the Video *Thinking Like a Psychologist: Evolutionary Psychology* in **MyPsychLab**

Evolutionary psychologists generally agree with these conclusions, but whereas sociobiologists often study nonhuman species and argue by analogy, many evolutionary psychologists consider such analogies simplistic and misleading. For example, because male scorpion flies force themselves on females, some sociobiologists have drawn an analogy between this behaviour and human rape and have concluded that human rape must have the same evolutionary origins and reproductive purposes (Thornhill & Palmer, 2000). But this analogy does not bear scrutiny. Human rape has many motives, including, among others, revenge, sadism, and conformity to peer pressure (see Chapter 12). It is often committed by high-status men who could easily find consenting sexual partners. All too frequently its victims are children or the elderly, who do not reproduce. And sadistic rapists often injure or kill their victims, hardly a way to perpetuate one's genes. In general, therefore, evolutionary psychologists rely less on comparisons with other species than sociobiologists do, focusing instead on commonalities in human mating and dating practices around the world. As a result of this difference, evolutionary psychologists also rely on different assumptions than sociobiologists do. Although both groups assume that human bodies and behaviours have been subject to evolutionary selection pressures, Darwin's account of speciation (the origin of new species) is irrelevant to evolutionary psychologists. Instead, the evolutionary psychologists simply assume that—as mentioned previously in this chapter—humans have spent the vast majority of their time on earth living as hunter–gatherers, probably on the African savannah.

Nevertheless, both groups emphasize the evolutionary origins of many human sex differences that appear to be universal, or at least very common. In one massive project, 50 scientists studied 10 000 people in 37 cultures located on six continents and five islands (Buss, 1994;

THINKING CRITICALLY

Consider Other Interpretations.

Evolutionary theories have been criticized on conceptual and methodological grounds. Do genes hold culture on a tight leash; a long, flexible one; or none at all?

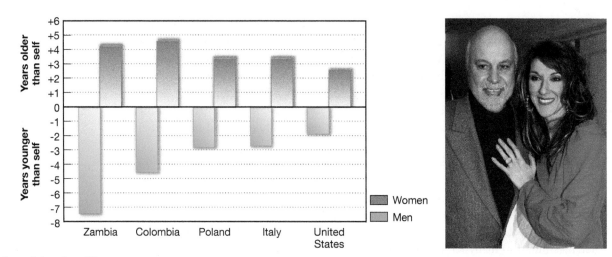

FIGURE 3.2 Preferred Age in a Mate In most societies, men say they prefer to marry women younger than themselves, whereas women prefer men who are older (Buss, 1995). Evolutionary psychologists attribute these preferences to male concern with a partner's fertility and female concern with a partner's material resources and status. Although people may make comments about age differences when the man is much older than the woman, as in the case of Canadian singer Celine Dion and her much older husband, René Angélil, people are far more apt to make disapproving comments when the woman is much older.

Schmitt, 2003). Around the world, they found, men are more violent and more socially dominant than women are. Men are more interested in the youth and beauty of their sexual partners, presumably because youth is associated with fertility (see Figure 3.2). According to their responses on questionnaires, men are more sexually jealous and possessive, presumably because if a man's mate had sex with other men, he could never be 100% sure that her children were genetically his as well. They are quicker than women to have sex with partners they don't know well and more inclined toward polygamy and promiscuity, presumably so that their sperm will be distributed as widely as possible. Women, in contrast, tend to emphasize the financial resources or prospects of a potential mate, his status, and his willingness to commit to a relationship. On questionnaires, they say they would be more upset by a partner's emotional infidelity than by his sexual infidelity, presumably because abandonment by the partner might leave them without the support and resources needed to raise their offspring. Many studies have reported similar results (e.g., Bailey et al., 1994; Buss, 1996, 2000; Buss & Schmitt, 2011; Buunk et al., 1996; Daly & Wilson, 1983; Mealey, 2000; Sprecher, Sullivan, & Hatfield, 1994).

The Genetic Leash

Evolutionary views of sex differences have become enormously popular. Many academics and lay people are persuaded that there are indeed evolutionary advantages for males in sowing their seed far and wide and evolutionary advantages for females in finding a man with a good paycheque.

But critics, including some evolutionary theorists, have challenged this conclusion on conceptual and methodological grounds:

1 **Stereotypes versus actual behaviour.** Many critics argue that current evolutionary explanations of infidelity and monogamy are based on simplistic *stereotypes* of gender differences. The actual behaviour of humans and other animals often fails to conform to images of sexually promiscuous males and coy, choosy females (Barash & Lipton, 2001; Birkhead, 2001; Fausto-Sterling, 1997; Hrdy, 1994; Roughgarden, 2004). In many species of birds, fish, and mammals, including human beings, females are sexually ardent and often have many male partners. The female's sexual behaviour does not seem to depend only on the goal of being fertilized by the male: Females have sex when they are not ovulating and even when they are already pregnant. And in many species, from penguins to primates, males do not just mate and run. They stick around, feeding the infants, carrying them, and protecting them from predators (Hrdy, 1988; Snowdon, 1997).

Human sexual behaviour, especially, is amazingly varied and changeable across time and place. Cultures range from those in which women have many children to those in which they have very few, from those in which men are intimately involved in

A basic assumption of evolutionary approaches to sexuality is that females across species have a greater involvement in child rearing than males do. But there are many exceptions. Female emperor penguins, for example, take off every winter, leaving behind males like this one to care for the young.

child rearing to those in which they take no part at all, from those in which women may have many lovers to those in which women may be killed for having sex outside of marriage (Hatfield & Rapson, 1996/2005). In many places, the chastity of a potential mate is much more important to men than to women; but in other places, it is important to both sexes—or to neither one (see Figure 3.3). In some places, just as evolutionary theory predicts, a relatively few men—those with the greatest wealth and power—have a far greater number of offspring than other men do; but in many societies, including some polygamous ones, powerful men do not have more children than men who are poor or who are low in status (Brown, Laland, & Mulder, 2009). Sexual attitudes and practices also vary tremendously within a culture, as is immediately apparent to anyone surveying the panorama of sexual attitudes and behaviours within the United States and Canada (Laumann et al., 2004; Levine, 2002).

Much of the data cited by evolutionary psychologists have come from questionnaires and interviews. In this research, when people (often undergraduates) are asked to rank the qualities they most value in a potential mate, sex differences appear, just as evolutionary theory would predict (Kenrick et al., 2001). But when we examine the evidence more closely, we find problems. For example, despite their differences, *both* sexes usually rank kindness, intelligence, and understanding over physical qualities or financial status.

2 **Convenience versus representative samples.** In Chapter 2 we saw that "convenience samples" of undergraduates sometimes produce research results that do not apply to nonstudents. This may well be the case in much of the evolutionary research on attitudes toward sex and marriage. In a recent national study, researchers at the U.S. Centers for Disease Control and Prevention (CDC) interviewed more than 12 000 men and women aged 15 to 44 about sex, living together, marriage, divorce, and parenting (Martinez et al., 2006). The agency had conducted similar surveys since 1973 but only with women. This time, the researchers *asked a question* that in retrospect seems obvious: What about men? Thus they were able to draw conclusions about male and female attitudes based on a sample that was far more representative of the general population than those used by most researchers. What they found throws a different light on evolutionary notions of sex differences.

For example, as we've seen, in the evolutionary view, women on the whole value commitment to a relationship more than men do and are more dedicated to parenting. Yet 66% of the men, compared to only 51% of the women, agreed or strongly agreed with the statement "It is better to get married than go through life being single." Further, most women *and* men agreed that "It is more important for a man to spend a lot of time with his family than be successful at his career." Among fathers in their first marriage, 90% were living with their kids and spent considerable time feeding and bathing them, helping them with homework, and taking them to activities. And 94% of both sexes agreed that "The rewards of being a parent are worth it despite the cost and work it takes."

As always, we need to avoid oversimplification. Some results did go in the stereotypical direction. More men than women (60% versus 51%) agreed that it was

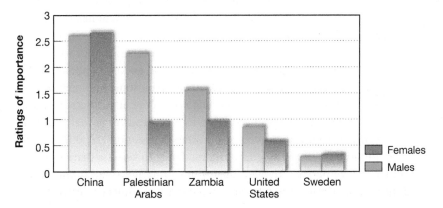

FIGURE 3.3 Attitudes toward Chastity
In many places, men care more about a partner's chastity than women do, as evolutionary psychologists would predict. But culture has a powerful impact on these attitudes, as this graph shows. Notice that in China, both sexes prefer a partner who has not yet had intercourse, whereas in Sweden, chastity is a nonissue. (From Buss, 1995.)

acceptable for unmarried 18-year-olds to have sexual relations "if they have strong affection for each other." Women were also more likely to be married by age 30 than men were. And decades of research have found that men are likely to have more pre-marital sexual partners than women are. But taken as a whole, the CDC findings suggest that men are just as interested in serious family relationships as women are.

3 **What people say versus what they do.** There is yet another problem in surveys inspired by evolutionary theories. Some critics have questioned an assumption underlying those surveys: that people's responses are a good guide to their actual choices and actions. When you ask people which would upset them more, their mate's having sex with someone else or their mate's falling in love with someone else, women are usually likelier than men to say that emotional infidelity would be worse (although there are big variations across cultures). But when one researcher asked people about their *actual* experiences with infidelity, men and women did not differ at all in the degree to which they had focused on the emotional or sexual aspects of their partners' behaviour (C. Harris, 2003). In fact, men, supposedly the more sexually jealous sex, were significantly more likely than women to have tolerated their partners' sexual unfaithfulness, whereas women were more likely to have ended their relationships over it. If you are thinking critically, you may be wondering whether these questionnaire results are any more reliable than those on dating preferences. Good question! The answer is yes. From studies that had people keep diaries of how they spend their time each day, we know that men's behaviour has changed along with their attitudes. Women still do more housework and child care than men do, but since the 1960s, the time men spend on housework has more than doubled, and since the 1980s the time they spend on primary child care has nearly tripled (Bianchi, Robinson, & Milkie, 2006; Wang & Bianchi, 2009).

4 **The Fred Flintstone problem.** Finally, some scientists have questioned evolutionary psychologists' emphasis on the Pleistocene age, which extended from about 2 million to about 11 000 years ago. Recent analysis of the human genome in Africans, East Asians, and Europeans suggests that during the past 10 000 to 15 000 years, natural selection has continued to influence genes associated with taste, smell, digestion, bone structure, skin colour, fertility, and even brain function (Voigt et al., 2006). Some of these changes might have begun when humans abandoned hunting and gathering in favour of agriculture, a switch that made certain genetic dispositions more adaptive and others less so. David Buller (2005), a philosopher who was captivated by evolutionary psychology until he took a closer look, concludes that "There is no reason to think that contemporary humans are, like Fred and Wilma Flintstone, just Pleistocene hunter–gatherers struggling to survive and reproduce in evolutionarily novel suburban habitats."

How large an influence does our Stone Age past have on our current courtship and mating customs?

Corbis

Even if the Pleistocene period did strongly influence human mating preferences, those preferences may differ from the ones usually emphasized by evolutionary theory. Our prehistoric ancestors, unlike the undergraduates in many mate-preference studies, did not have 5000 fellow students to choose from. They lived in small bands, and if they were lucky they might get to choose between Urp and Ork, and that's about it; they could not hold out for some gorgeous babe or handsome millionaire down the road. Because there was a small range of potential partners to choose from, there would have been no need for the kinds of sexual strategies described by evolutionary theorists (Hazan & Diamond, 2000). Instead, evolution might have instilled in us a tendency to select a mate based on similarity (the person's genes, background, and age roughly match our own) and proximity (the person is around a lot). Indeed, similarity and proximity are among the strongest predictors today of the mates people actually choose, whatever they may say on questionnaires (see Chapter 12). Debate over these matters can become quite heated because of worries that evolutionary arguments will be used to justify social and political inequalities and even violent behaviour. In the past, evolutionary ideas have been used to promote **social Darwinism**, the notion that the wealthy and successful are more reproductively fit than other people. Such arguments have also led some people to conclude that men, with less investment in child rearing and more interest in status and dominance, are destined to control business and politics. More than 30 years ago, Edward Wilson (1975) certainly thought so. "Even with identical education and equal access to all professions [for both sexes]," he writes, "men are likely to continue to play a disproportionate role in political life, business, and science."

social Darwinism The notion that the wealthy and successful are more reproductively fit than other people.

Recite & Review

Recite: Yabba dabba doo! Say out loud everything you can remember about *sociobiology*, *social Darwinism*, the evolutionary view of sex differences in human mating and courtship behaviour, and the four key criticisms of that view.

Review: Next, reread this section, paying extra attention to what you didn't remember.

Now take this *Quick Quiz:*

Males and females alike have evolved to be able to answer these questions.

1. Which of the following would an evolutionary psychologist expect to be more typical of males than of females? (a) promiscuity, (b) choosiness about sexual partners, (c) concern with dominance, (d) interest in young partners, (e) emphasis on physical attractiveness of partners

2. What major issue divides evolutionary theorists and their critics in debates over courtship and mating?

3. A friend of yours, who has read some sociobiology, tells you that men will always be more sexually promiscuous than women because during evolution, the best reproductive strategy for a male primate has been to try to impregnate many females. What kind of evidence would you need in order to evaluate this claim?

Answers:

1. all but b 2. the relative influence of biology and culture 3. You would not want to look just for confirming evidence (recall the principle of falsifiability from Chapter 2). You would want to look also for evidence of female promiscuity and male monogamy among humans and other species and changes in human sexual customs in response to changing social conditions.

Learning Objectives

11 State what it means to say that a trait is "heritable."

12 List three important facts about heritability.

13 Describe how researchers estimate a trait's heritability.

The Genetics of Difference

We have been focusing on the origins of human similarities. We turn now to the second great issue in debates about nature and nurture: the origins of the differences among us. We begin with a critical discussion of what it means to say that a trait is "heritable." Then, to illustrate how behavioural geneticists study differences among people that might be influenced by genes, we will examine in detail a single, complex issue: the genetic and environmental contributions to intelligence. In other sections of this book, you will be reading about behavioural–genetic findings on many other topics, including biological rhythms (Chapter 5), taste perception (Chapter 6), weight and body shape (Chapter 12), sexual orientation (Chapter 12), personality and temperament (Chapter 14), addiction (Chapter 15), and mental disorders (Chapter 15).

The Meaning of Heritability

Suppose you want to measure flute-playing ability in a large group of music students, so you have some independent raters assign each student a score from 1 to 20. When you plot the scores, you find that some people are what you might call melodically disadvantaged and should forget about a musical career, others are flute geniuses, and the rest fall somewhere in between. What causes the variation in this group of students? Why are some so musically talented and others so inept? Are these differences primarily genetic, or are they the result of experience and motivation?

To answer such questions, behavioural geneticists compute a statistic called **heritability**, which gives an estimate of the proportion of the total variance in a trait that is attributable to genetic variation within a group. Because the heritability of a trait is expressed as a proportion (such as 0.60, or 60/100), the maximum value it can have is 1.00 (equivalent to "100% of the variance"). Height is highly heritable; that is, within a group of equally well-nourished individuals, most of the variation among them will be accounted for by their genetic differences. In contrast, table manners have low heritability because most variation among individuals is accounted for by differences in upbringing. Our guess is that flute-playing ability—and musical ability in general—falls somewhere in the middle. Differences in the ability to correctly perceive musical pitch and melody appear to be highly heritable; some people, it seems, really are born with a "tin ear" (Drayna et al., 2001). Nonetheless, musical training can enhance normal musical ability, and lack of musical training can keep a person with normal ability from tuning in to the nuances of music. ◉

Many people hold completely mistaken ideas about heritability. But as genetic findings pour in, the public will need to understand this concept more than ever. You cannot understand the nature–nurture issue without understanding the following important facts about heritability:

1 **An estimate of heritability applies only to a particular group living in a particular environment.** Heritability may be high in one group and low in another. Suppose that all the children in community A are affluent, eat plenty of high-quality food, have kind and attentive parents, and go to the same top-notch schools. Because their environments are similar, any intellectual differences among them will have to be due largely to their genetic differences. In other words, mental ability in this group will be highly heritable. In contrast, suppose the children in community B are rich, poor, and in between. Some of them have healthy diets; others live on fatty foods and cupcakes. Some attend good schools; others go to inadequate ones. Some have doting parents, and some have unloving and neglectful ones. These children's intellectual differences could be due to their environmental differences and, if that is so, the heritability of intelligence for this group will be low. Indeed, in a study that followed 48 000 American children from birth to age seven, intelligence did depend greatly on socioeconomic status. In impoverished families, 60% of the variance in IQ was accounted for by environmental factors shared by family members, and the contribution of genes was close to zero. In affluent families, the result was nearly exactly the reverse: Heritability was extremely high, and shared environment contributed hardly at all (Turkheimer et al., 2003).

THINKING CRITICALLY

Define Your Terms.

What does it mean to say that some trait is highly heritable? If you want to improve your flute playing and someone tells you that musical ability is heritable, should you stop practising?

◉⎯Watch the Video *The Basics: Genetic Mechanisms and Behavioural Genetics* in **MyPsychLab**

heritability A statistical estimate of the proportion of the total variance in some trait that is attributable to genetic differences among individuals within a group.

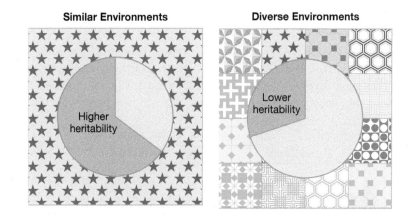

Similar Environments / Diverse Environments

Higher heritability / Lower heritability

2 **Heritability estimates do not apply to individuals, only to variations within a group.** You inherited half your genes from your mother and half from your father, but your *combination* of genes has never been seen before and will never be seen again (unless you have an identical twin). You also have a unique history of family relationships, intellectual training, and life experiences. It is impossible to know just how your genes and your personal history have interacted to produce the person you are today. For example, if you are a great flute player, no one can say whether your ability is mainly a result of inherited musical talent, living all your life in a family of devoted flute players, a private obsession that you acquired at age six when you saw the opera *The Magic Flute*—or a combination of all three. For one person, genes may make a tremendous difference in some aptitude or disposition; for another, the environment may be far more important. Scientists can study only the extent to which differences among people in general are explained by their genetic differences.

3 **Even highly heritable traits can be modified by the environment.** Although height is highly heritable, malnourished children may not grow to be as tall as they would with sufficient food, and children who eat an extremely nutritious diet may grow to be taller than anyone thought they could. Hair colour is genetically determined, but a trip to a hair stylist can transform you from a brunette to a blonde, or vice versa. The same principle applies to psychological traits, although biological determinists sometimes fail to realize this. They argue, for example, that because IQ is highly heritable, IQ and school achievement cannot be boosted much (Herrnstein & Murray, 1994; Murray, 2008). But even if the first part of the statement is true, the second part does not necessarily follow, as we will see.

For instance, most of us have five fingers on each hand, something that is specified in our genetic recipe. If we went out and looked for people who didn't have five fingers per hand—say, those who had four fingers—we would probably conclude that genes had nothing to do with the number of fingers people have. We would find that most people with fewer than five fingers on each hand have lost digits as the result of accidents. This does not mean that their genes did not influence the number of fingers they were born with—just that the environment modified this heritable trait (Ridley, 2000).

Computing Heritability

Scientists have no way to estimate the heritability of a trait or behaviour directly, so they must *infer* it by studying people whose degree of genetic similarity is known. You might think that the simplest approach would be to compare biological relatives within families; everyone knows about families that are famous for some talent or trait. But family traits do not tell us much because close relatives usually share environments as well as genes. If Carlo's parents and siblings all love lasagna, that does not mean a taste for lasagna is heritable! The same applies if everyone in Carlo's family has a high IQ, is mentally ill, or is moody.

A better approach is to study adopted children (e.g., Loehlin, Horn, & Willerman, 1996; Plomin & DeFries, 1985). Such children share half their genes with each birth parent, but they grow up in a different environment, apart from their birth parents. On the other hand, they share an environment with their adoptive parents and siblings but not their genes:

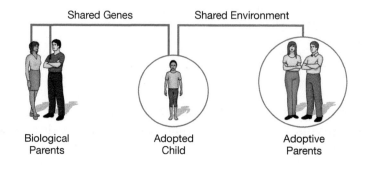

Researchers can compare correlations between the traits of adopted children and those of their biological and adoptive relatives and can use the results to compute an estimate of heritability.

Another approach is to compare identical twins with fraternal twins. **Identical (monozygotic) twins** develop when a fertilized egg (zygote) divides into two parts that then develop as two separate embryos. Because the twins come from the same fertilized egg, they share all their genes. Some surprising recent work, however, suggests that duplicated or missing blocks of DNA (sets of those As, Cs, Gs, and Ts that we discussed earlier) can exist in one identical twin but not the other (Bruder et al., 2008). Also, prenatal accidents or illnesses can modify the genetic expression in only one twin (Plomin, 2011). (Identical twins may be slightly different at birth, however, because of differences in the blood supply to the two fetuses or other chance factors.) In contrast, **fraternal (dizygotic) twins** develop when a woman's ovaries release two eggs instead of one and each egg is fertilized by a different sperm. Fraternal twins are womb mates, but they are no more alike genetically than any other two siblings (they share, on average, only half their genes), and they may be of different sexes:

identical (monozygotic) twins Twins that develop when a fertilized egg divides into two parts that develop into separate embryos.

fraternal (dizygotic) twins Twins that develop from two separate eggs fertilized by different sperm; they are no more alike genetically than are any other pair of siblings.

Behavioural geneticists can estimate the heritability of a trait by comparing groups of same-sex fraternal twins with groups of identical twins. The assumption is that if identical twins are more alike than fraternal twins, then the increased similarity must be due to genetic influences. Perhaps, however, identical twins are treated differently than fraternal twins. To avoid this problem, investigators have studied identical twins who were separated early in life and reared apart. (Until recently, adoption policies and attitudes toward births out of wedlock permitted such separations to occur.) In theory, separated identical twins share all their genes but not their environments. Any similarities between them should be primarily genetic and should permit a direct estimate of heritability.

Recite & Review

Recite: Say out loud everything you can recall about *heritability*, and ways of inferring or computing it, *identical (monozygotic) twins*, and *fraternal (dizygotic) twins*.

Review: Treat this review identically to all others, and reread this section to see what you might have overlooked.

Now take this *Quick Quiz:*

1. Diane hears that basket-weaving ability is highly heritable. She assumes that her own low performance must therefore be due mostly to genes. What is wrong with her reasoning?

2. Bertram hears that basket-weaving ability is highly heritable. He concludes that schools should not bother trying to improve the skills of children who lack this talent. What is wrong with his reasoning?

3. Basket-weaving skills seem to run in Andy's family. Why shouldn't Andy conclude that his own talent is genetic?

4. Why do behavioural geneticists find it useful to study twins?

Answers:

1. Heritability applies only to differences among individuals within a group, not to particular individuals. 2. A trait may be highly heritable and still be susceptible to modification. 3. Family members share not just genes but also environments. 4. Identical twins growing up together share an environment, and so do fraternal twins. So if identical twins are more alike than fraternal twins, then the increased similarity is assumed to be genetic. Identical twins reared apart share only their genes, not their environment, so similarities between them should be primarily genetic also.

Learning Objectives

14 Describe the extent to which intelligence may be heritable.

15 Identify a common error in the argument that one group is genetically smarter than another.

16 List how the environment nurtures or thwarts mental ability.

Our Human Diversity: The Case of Intelligence

Behavioural-genetics research has transformed our understanding of many aspects of behaviour that were once explained solely in psychological terms. Some findings, such as the discovery that certain mental illnesses have a genetic component, have been accepted readily. Other findings, however, have inflamed political passions and upset people. No topic has aroused more controversy than the origins of human intelligence.

intelligence quotient (IQ) A measure of intelligence originally computed by dividing a person's mental age by his or her chronological age and multiplying by 100; it is now derived from norms provided for standardized intelligence tests.

Genes and Individual Differences

In heritability studies, the usual measure of intellectual functioning is an **intelligence quotient (IQ)** score. Scores on an IQ test reflect how a child has performed compared with other children of the same age, or how an adult has performed compared with other adults. The average score for each age group is arbitrarily set at 100. The distribution of scores in the population approximates a normal (bell-shaped) curve, where scores near the average (mean) are the most common and very high or very low scores are rare. Two-thirds of all test-takers score between 85 and 115.

Most psychologists believe that IQ tests measure a general quality that affects most aspects of mental ability, but the tests also have many critics. Some argue that intelligence comes in many varieties, more than are captured by a single score. Others argue that IQ tests are culturally biased, tapping mostly those abilities that depend on experiences in a middle-class environment and favouring white people over people of other ethnicities. We discuss the measurement of intelligence and debates surrounding this concept more fully in Chapter 9. For now, keep in mind that most heritability estimates apply only to those mental skills that affect IQ test scores and that these estimates are likely to be more valid for some groups than for others. You cannot use a heritability estimate from one group of people and apply it to another, different group of people.

Despite these important qualifications, it is clear that the kind of intelligence that produces high IQ scores is highly heritable, at least in the middle-class samples usually studied. For children and adolescents, heritability estimates average around 0.40 or 0.50; that is, about half of the variance in IQ scores is explainable by genetic differences (Chipuer, Rovine, & Plomin, 1990; Devlin, Daniels, & Roeder, 1997; Plomin, 1989). For adults, the estimates until late middle age are even higher—in the 0.60 to 0.80 range (Bouchard, 1995; McClearn et al., 1997; McGue et al., 1993). That is, the genetic contribution becomes relatively larger and the environmental one relatively smaller with age. Some psychologists, however, note that most people who adopt children are screened to make sure they have a secure income, are psychologically stable, and so forth. As a result, critics argue, there is not much "variation" in adopted children's environments, which spuriously inflates the variation due to heredity (Nisbett, 2009). In studies of twins, the scores of identical twins are always much more highly correlated than those of fraternal twins, a difference that reflects the influence of genes. In fact, the scores of identical twins reared *apart* are more highly correlated than those of fraternal twins reared *together*, as you can see in Figure 3.4. In adoption studies, the scores of adopted children are more highly correlated with those of their birth parents than with those of their biologically unrelated adoptive parents; the higher the birth

FIGURE 3.4 Correlations in Siblings' IQ Scores
The IQ scores of identical twins are highly correlated, even when they are reared apart. The figures represented in this graph are based on average correlations across many studies (Bouchard & McGue, 1981).

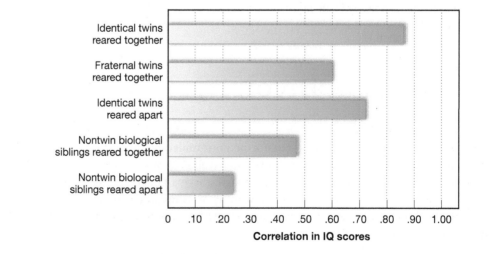

Correlation in IQ scores

parents' scores, the higher the child's score is likely to be. As adopted children grow into adolescence, the correlation between their IQ scores and those of their biologically unrelated family members diminishes, and in adulthood the correlation falls to *zero* (Bouchard, 1997b; Scarr, 1993; Scarr & Weinberg, 1994). (This does not mean that adoption has no positive effects; adopted children score higher on IQ tests than do birth siblings who were not adopted, probably because adoptees grow up in more enriched environments [van Ijzendoorn et al., 2005].)

The Question of Group Differences

If genes influence individual differences in intelligence, do they also help account for differences between groups, as many people assume? Unfortunately, the history of this issue has been marred by ethnic, class, and gender prejudice. As Stephen Jay Gould (1996) notes, genetic research has often been bent to support the belief that some groups are destined by "the harsh dictates of nature" to be subordinate to others. Because this issue has enormous political and social importance, we are going to examine it closely.

Most of the focus has been on black–white differences in IQ, because black children score, on average, some 10 to 12 points lower than do white children. (We are talking about averages; the distributions of scores for black children and white children overlap considerably.) A few psychologists have proposed a genetic explanation of this difference (Jensen, 1969, 1981; Rushton, 1988). As you can imagine, this topic is not merely academic. Racists have used theories of genetic differences between groups to justify their own hatreds, and politicians have used them to argue for cuts in programs that would benefit blacks, other minorities, and poor children. Some researchers themselves have concluded that there is little point in spending money on programs that try to raise the IQs of low-scoring children, of whatever race (Murray, 2008; Rushton & Jensen, 2005; Herrnstein & Murray, 1994).

Genetic explanations, however, have a fatal flaw: They use heritability estimates based mainly on samples of white people to estimate the role of heredity in *group* differences, a procedure that is not valid. This problem sounds pretty technical, but it is really not too difficult to understand, so stay with us.

Consider, first, not people, but tomatoes. (Figure 3.5 will help you visualize the following "thought experiment.") Suppose you have a bag of tomato seeds that vary genetically; all things being equal, some will produce tomatoes that are puny and tasteless, and some will produce tomatoes that are plump and delicious. Now you take a bunch of these seeds in your left hand and another bunch from the same bag in your right hand. Though one seed differs genetically from another, there is no *average* difference between the seeds in your left hand and those in your right. You plant the left hand's seeds in pot A, with some enriched soil that you have doctored with nitrogen and other nutrients, and you plant the right hand's seeds in pot B, with soil from which you have extracted nutrients. You sing to pot A and put it in the sun; you ignore pot B and leave it in a dark corner.

When the tomato plants grow, they will vary *within* each pot in terms of height, the number of tomatoes produced, and the size of the tomatoes, purely because of genetic differences. But there will also be an average difference between the plants in pot A and those in pot B: The plants in pot A will be healthier and bear more tomatoes. This difference *between* pots is owing entirely to the different soils and the care that has been given to them—even though the heritability of the *within*-pot differences is 100% (Lewontin, 1970). The same is true for real plants, by the way; if you take identical, cloned plants and grow them at different elevations, they will develop differently (Lewontin, 2001).

> ### 💡 THINKING CRITICALLY
>
> Analyze Assumptions and Biases.
>
> Most behavioural-genetics studies show the heritability of intelligence to be high. A popular book argues that heredity must play a similarly large role in average IQ differences between ethnic groups. What's wrong with the assumption behind that reasoning?

FIGURE 3.5 The Tomato Plant Experiment
In the hypothetical experiment described in the text, even if the differences among plants within each pot were due entirely to genetics, the average differences between pots could be environmental. The same general principle applies to individual and group differences among human beings.

The principle is the same for people as it is for tomatoes. Although intellectual differences *within* groups are at least partly genetic in origin, that does not mean differences *between* groups are genetic. Blacks and whites do not grow up, on the average, in the same "pots" (environments). Because of a long legacy of racial discrimination and de facto segregation, black children, as well as other minority children, often receive far fewer nutrients—literally, in terms of food, and figuratively, in terms of education, encouragement by society, and intellectual opportunities (Nisbett, 2009). Ethnic groups also differ in countless cultural ways that affect their performance on IQ tests. And negative stereotypes about ethnic groups may cause members of these groups to doubt their own abilities, become anxious and self-conscious, and perform more poorly than they otherwise would on tests (see Chapter 9).

Doing good research on the origins of group differences in IQ is extremely difficult in the United States, where racism affects the lives of even affluent, successful black people. However, the few studies that have overcome past methodological problems fail to reveal any genetic differences between blacks and whites in whatever it is that IQ tests measure. One study found that children fathered by black and white American soldiers in Germany after the Second World War and reared in similar German communities by similar families did not differ significantly in IQ (Eyferth, 1961). Another showed that, contrary to what a genetic theory would predict, degree of African ancestry (which can be roughly estimated from skin colour, blood analysis, and genealogy) is not related to measured intelligence (Scarr et al., 1977). And white and black infants do equally well on a test that measures their preference for novel stimuli, a predictor of later IQ scores (Fagan, 1992).

Even among groups popularly thought to be high achievers, purely genetic explanations are unsatisfactory. For instance, although descendants of the Ashkenazi Jews of Europe tend to have higher IQ scores than their non-Jewish white counterparts, their accomplishments exceed what would be expected on the basis of their IQ scores alone (Nisbett et al., 2012). An intelligent reading of the research on intelligence, therefore, does not direct us to conclude that differences among cultural, ethnic, or national groups are permanent, genetically determined, or a sign of any group's innate superiority. On the contrary, the research suggests that we should make sure that all children grow up in the best possible soil, with room for the smartest and the slowest to find a place in the sun.

The Environment and Intelligence

By now you may be wondering what kinds of experiences hinder intellectual development and what kinds of environmental "nutrients" promote it. Here are some of the influences associated with reduced mental ability:

- *Poor prenatal care.* If a pregnant woman is malnourished, contracts infections, takes certain drugs, smokes, is exposed to secondhand smoke, or drinks alcohol regularly, her child is at risk of having learning disabilities and a lower IQ.

- *Malnutrition.* The average IQ gap between severely malnourished and well-nourished children can be as high as 20 points (Stoch & Smythe, 1963; Winick, Meyer, & Harris, 1975).

- *Exposure to toxins.* Lead, especially, can damage the nervous system, even at fairly low levels, producing attention problems, lower IQ scores, and poorer school achievement (Hornung, Lanphear, & Dietrich, 2009; Lanphear et al., 2005; Needleman et al., 1996). Many children in the United States are exposed to dangerous levels of lead from dust, contaminated soil, lead paint, and old lead pipes, and the concentration of lead in black children's blood is 50% higher than in white children's (Lanphear et al., 2002). Air pollution, which people cannot control directly, also appears to be a serious risk factor. A recent longitudinal study of nonsmoking inner-city women found a link between delayed cognitive development in the women's children and the level of pollutants from fossil fuels that the mothers were exposed to during pregnancy. The culprit appears to be a chemical spewed from vehicles and power plants. Even after controlling for other factors, such as lead exposure, the researchers found that by age three, the children of highly exposed mothers were more than twice as likely as other children to be developmentally delayed (Perera et al., 2006). As well, children exposed in utero to high levels of pesticides (still legal for spraying on farm fields) later have an IQ that is 7 points lower than children with the least exposure (Raloff, 2011).

Severe poverty, exposure to toxic materials, run-down neighbourhoods, and stressful family circumstances can all have a negative impact on children's cognitive development and IQ.

Siphiwe Sibeko/Reuters

- *Stressful family circumstances.* Factors that predict reduced intellectual competence include, among others, having a father who does not live with the family, a mother with a history of mental illness, parents with limited work skills, and a history of stressful events, such as domestic violence, early in life (Sameroff et al., 1987). On average, each risk factor reduces a child's IQ score by 4 points. Children with seven risk factors score more than *30 points lower* than those with no risk factors. And when children live in severely disadvantaged neighbourhoods, their verbal IQs decline over time, even after they have moved to better areas; the drop is comparable to that seen when a child misses a year of school (Sampson, Sharkey, & Raudenbush, 2008).

In contrast, a healthy and stimulating environment can raise mental performance (Guralnick, 1997; Nelson, Westhues, & MacLeod, 2003; Ramey & Ramey, 1998). Attending quality preschool increases the reading and math skills of children from racial and ethnic minorities, especially if they are not getting much cognitive stimulation elsewhere (Tucker-Drob, 2012). In one longitudinal study called the Abecedarian Project, inner-city children who received lots of mental enrichment at home and in child care or school, starting at infancy, had much better school achievement than did children in a control group (Campbell & Ramey, 1995). In another important study, of abandoned children living in Romanian orphanages, researchers randomly assigned some children to remain in the orphanages and others to move to good foster homes. By age four, the fostered children scored dramatically higher on IQ tests than did those left behind. Children who moved before age two showed the largest gains, almost 15 points on average. A comparison group of children reared in their biological homes did even better, with average test scores 10 to 20 points higher than those of the foster children (Nelson et al., 2007). (Since this study was done, Romania has stopped institutionalizing abandoned children younger than two unless they are seriously disabled.)

Although no single activity is going to turn anyone into a genius, certain experiences do appear to contribute to overall intelligence. In general, children's mental abilities improve when their parents talk to them about many topics and describe things accurately and fully, encourage them to think things through, read to them, and expect them to do well. A child's abilities also improve when the child's peers value and strive for intellectual achievement (Harris, 2009). Some kinds of enrichment classes may also help. When Canadian researchers randomly assigned grade 1 students to weekly piano, singing, or drama lessons during the school year, or to a

The children of migrant workers (left) often spend long hours doing backbreaking field work and may miss out on the educational opportunities and intellectual advantages available to middle-class children (right).

Left: Eric Draper/AP Images. Right: Science Source.

control group that received no extracurricular lessons, those children who learned to play the piano or sing showed an average IQ increase of 7 points by the end of the school year—compared to 4.3 points in the other groups. This difference was not large, but it was statistically significant (Schellenberg, 2004). The music lessons might have helped the children pay attention, use their memories, and hone their fine-motor skills, thus contributing to the development of brain areas involved in intelligence.

Perhaps the best evidence for the importance of environmental influences on intelligence is the fact that IQ scores in developed countries have been climbing steadily for at least three generations (Flynn, 1987, 1999) (see Figure 3.6). A similar increase has been documented in Kenya, a developing country: Rural children aged six to eight scored about 11 points higher in 1998 than their peers did in 1984—the fastest rise in a group's average IQ scores ever reported (Daley et al., 2003). Genes cannot possibly have changed enough to account for these findings. Most psychologists attribute the increases to improvements in education, the growth in jobs requiring abstract thought, and better nutrition and health (Neisser, 1998).

We see, then, that although heredity may provide the range of a child's intellectual potential—a Homer Simpson can never become an Einstein—many other factors affect where in that range the child will fall.

FIGURE 3.6 Climbing IQ Scores
Raw scores on IQ tests have been rising in developed countries for many decades at a rate much too steep to be accounted for by genetic changes. Because test norms are periodically readjusted to set the average score at 100, most people are unaware of the increase. On this graph, average scores are calibrated according to 1989 norms. As you can see, performance was much lower in 1918 than in 1989. (Adapted from Horgan, 1995.)

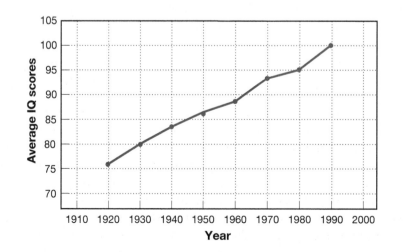

Recite & Review

Recite: Say out loud everything you can recall about *IQ*, the heritability of IQ, group differences in IQ, and environmental influences on IQ and mental abilities.

Review: There was some complicated information in this section, so reread it carefully.

Now take this *Quick Quiz:*

Are you thinking intelligently about intelligence?

1. On average, behavioural-genetics studies estimate the heritability of intelligence to be (a) about 0.90, (b) about 0.20, (c) low at all ages, (d) higher for adults than for children.

2. *True or false:* If a trait such as intelligence is highly heritable within a group, then differences between groups must also be due mainly to heredity.

3. The available evidence (does/does not) show that ethnic differences in average IQ scores are due to genetic differences.

4. Name four environmental factors associated with reduced mental ability.

Answers:

1. d 2. false 3. does not 4. poor prenatal care, malnutrition, exposure to toxins, and stressful family circumstances

Beyond Nature versus Nurture

This chapter opened with two questions: What makes us alike as human beings, and why do we differ? Today, a prevalent but greatly oversimplified answer is: It's all genetic. Genes, it's claimed, make men sexually adventurous and women sexually choosy. You either have a gene for smartness, musical ability, math genius, or friendliness, or you don't. In this climate, many people who believe in the importance of learning, opportunities, and experience feel that they must take an equally oversimplified position: Genes, they say, don't matter at all. As new findings in genetics emerge, scientists are finding that this interaction is even more complex than anyone imagined just a few years ago (Barry, 2007). This is not a text book on genetics, but we think you should know about a few developments in the field that promise to radically alter our understanding of nature and nurture in the coming years.

> ### THINKING CRITICALLY
>
> Tolerate Uncertainty.
>
> Many people would like to specify precisely how much genes and the environment independently contribute to human qualities. But is this goal achievable? Is a human being like a jigsaw puzzle made up of separate components, or more like a cake with blended ingredients that interact to produce its unique taste?

To begin with, scientists are revisiting the whole notion of what a gene is. It turns out that some individual genes may be fragmented and intertwined with other genes, making the search for genes associated with any particular trait or condition even more difficult. Scientists are also rethinking their ideas about noncoding DNA, the DNA that is found outside of genes and that until recently was disparagingly referred to as "junk DNA." Mutations in this DNA could possibly be associated with common diseases. Messages from noncoding DNA, along with random chemical events in cells, may also affect the "expression" (activity) of certain genes.

As we have seen, however, heredity and environment always interact to produce the unique mixture of qualities that make up a human being. At the start of this chapter, we mentioned that genes switch on or off depending on the experiences a person has and on the activity of other genes. Gene expression also varies because of random biochemical processes within bodily cells, which geneticists call "noise." As a result of these extraordinary developments, a specialty called **epigenetics** has emerged to study changes in gene expression due to mechanisms other than structural changes in the DNA itself. In part because of epigenetic influences, identical twins and even cloned,

epigenetics The study of changes in gene expression due to mechanisms other than structural changes in DNA.

Genes are not destiny. In fact, because of "noise" and other influences on gene expression, even identical twins and cloned animals are not exactly alike. The first cat ever cloned (left) was named CC, for "carbon copy," but she's not really a carbon copy of her genetically identical mother. The two have different coat patterns and different personalities.

Left: AP Images. Right: Pat Sullivn/AP Images.

genetically identical animals living in exactly the same environment can differ considerably in appearance and behaviour (Raser & O'Shea, 2005). Yes, you read that right: Even clones can differ (as fans of *Battlestar Galactica* already know). The study of epigenetics is demonstrating that the timing and pattern of genetic activity are critical not only before birth but throughout life (Feinberg, 2008). This means that the genome is not a static blueprint for development but more like a constantly changing network of interlinked influences, including environmental ones. Even more astonishing, work with animals finds that at least some epigenetic changes can be transmitted to the next generation (Champagne, 2009).

Thus we can no more speak of genes, or of the environment, "causing" personality or intelligence in a straightforward way than we can speak of butter, sugar, or flour individually causing the taste of a cake (Lewontin, Rose, & Kamin, 1984). Many people do speak that way, however, out of a desire to make things clearer than they actually are, and sometimes to justify prejudices about ethnicity, gender, or class.

An unstated assumption in many debates about nature and nurture is that the world would be a better place if certain kinds of genes prevailed. This assumption overlooks the fact that nature loves genetic diversity, not similarity. The ability of any species to survive depends on such diversity. If every penguin, porpoise, or person had exactly the same genetic strengths and weaknesses, these species could not survive changes in the environment; a new virus or a change in climate would wipe out the entire group. With diversity, at least some penguins, porpoises, or people have a chance of making it.

Psychological diversity is adaptive, too. Each of us has something valuable to contribute, whether it is artistic talent, academic ability, creativity, social skill, athletic prowess, a sense of humour, mechanical aptitude, practical wisdom, a social conscience, or the energy to get things done. In our complicated, fast-moving world, all these qualities are needed. The challenge, for any society, is to promote the potential of each of its members.

Taking Psychology with You

THINKING CRITICALLY IN EVERYDAY LIFE

Should You Have Genetic Testing?

Imagine that you have been feeling depressed and you go to a clinical psychologist for help.

The psychologist interviews you, gives you a battery of psychological tests, lets you talk about your problems—and then has your blood drawn to check your DNA, to find out if you have a genetic predisposition for depression.

The psychologist has your blood drawn? Right now, this scenario is purely hypothetical, but perhaps not for long. Two leading experts in behavioural genetics, Robert Plomin and John Crabbe (2000), have predicted that in the not-so-distant future, therapists will routinely have their clients' DNA tested to gather information for use in diagnosis and treatment. This

is already possible, they note, for Alzheimer's disease: Having a DNA marker for a gene that codes for a particular protein heightens an individual's risk of developing the disease. Would you want to be tested for a gene that increases the risk of developing Alzheimer's? How would you feel about being tested for a gene that increases the risk of an early death? Would you want to know so that you could plan accordingly, or would you rather let the chips fall where they may? Pregnant women and their partners are often tested to determine whether they are carrying genes that are likely to condemn their children to a fatal or painful disease. When the test results are positive, many choose to abort the pregnancies. But what if you could be tested for a gene that increases your future child's risk of developing a mental or emotional disorder, such as schizophrenia or autism? Would you want to have that sort of test, and what would you do with the results? What if the test were for a more common condition, such as a reading disability or obesity? And what if the condition were homosexuality, which is not a disorder at all but which some people fear; or being very short, which in some quarters is a social disadvantage but is hardly a disability? If prenatal genetic testing revealed that your child had a somewhat increased chance of being gay or short, what would you do with that information? Would you consider aborting the fetus?

In coming years, as noninvasive methods of genetic testing such as blood tests are introduced and become widespread, all of us are going to have to think long and hard about such questions. You can use information from this chapter to evaluate the pros and cons of such testing for yourself or a family member. Here are some things to keep in mind:

Genes are not destiny. It is true that some diseases, such as Huntington's, are caused by a single gene. However, as we have seen, most traits are influenced by many genes, by environmental factors, and by biochemical and other events within cells. That is why knowing that you have markers for one or two genes that may contribute to a trait or disorder does not necessarily tell you much in practical terms.

Knowing about a genetic disposition can create a premature diagnosis or a self-fulfilling prophecy. If parents and school officials know that a child is at risk of developing a learning disorder, they may treat the child as cognitively impaired even though the child has not shown any signs of a problem. If a person is aware of having a genetic predisposition toward depression, he or she may not develop the skills to cope with setbacks, deciding incorrectly that "there's nothing I can do."

Genes do not absolve you of responsibility. Some judges are allowing or even compelling defendants in criminal cases to be genetically tested for mental conditions or behavioural tendencies in order to help determine the extent of their responsibility for the crime or likelihood of repeating it (Hoffmann & Rothenberg, 2005). But "my genes made me do it" is not necessarily a good excuse for bad behaviour. Not only does the environment play a large role in behaviour, but also the flexible human brain allows us to do an end run around many of our genetic tendencies by modifying them, ignoring them, or controlling them. As David Barash (2001), an evolutionary psychologist, put it, a strong case can be made that "we are never so human as when we behave contrary to our natural inclinations, those most in tune with our biological impulses."

Genetic information could be used to discriminate against individuals. Critics of genetic testing worry that insurance companies will refuse coverage to adults and children who are currently healthy but whose DNA reveals them to have some genetic predisposition for developing a physical or psychological disorder later in life. Employers who pay insurance premiums for their workers might be reluctant to hire such individuals. So far, such cases of genetic discrimination have been rare. But some bioethicists and scholars are concerned that current laws may not adequately protect people's right to keep genetic information private.

Knowing your genetic risk does not necessarily tell you what to do about it. If your child has a physical disorder called phenylketonuria (PKU), which prevents the body from assimilating protein and causes mental retardation, the solution is obvious: Limit the intake of protein. But in the case of behavioural, cognitive, or emotional problems, the answer is usually not so straightforward. Often we simply don't yet know how to treat problems that have a genetic component, or many possible approaches exist and we don't know which one is best.

Genetic testing can be liberating or stigmatizing. Knowing that a condition or trait is "not your fault" may help you live with it or accept the limitations it imposes. For example, knowing that your child's autism is genetic and not caused by bad parenting will keep you from feeling unnecessary guilt. On the other hand, genetic testing can activate prejudices against anyone with less-than-ideal looks or abilities.

In the past, such prejudices led to the discredited social movement called *eugenics*, which aimed to "improve" the species through forced sterilization of low-IQ people. As a result, from the beginning of the twentieth century until the mid-1960s, thousands of mentally ill and developmentally delayed North Americans were sterilized against their will (Bruinius, 2006).

Defenders of genetic testing answer that the goal of prenatal screening is not to improve the human species; it is to relieve the suffering of parents and children, and therefore prospective parents should not feel guilty for taking advantage of this technology (Cowan, 2008). But to some social critics, prenatal testing for run-of-the-mill human qualities reflects a view of children as products to be perfected instead of as individuals to be appreciated for who they are (Sandel, 2007).

If abortion would be an option for you, how serious and how likely would an inherited condition have to be before you would consider aborting a fetus? Would a 10% likelihood be enough, or 50%, or would you require near certainty? Would you want to know, while you are still young, that you carry genes associated with some disorder that usually doesn't strike until middle or old age? How might this information change your life?

Summary

MyPsychLab can help you get a better grade. Test your knowledge and grasp difficult concepts through
- Custom study plans: See where you are strong and where you are wrong
- Multimedia, including videos and interactive simulations
- Dynamic Study Modules: flashcards for self-study that ensure you achieve mastery of course concepts

Unlocking the Secrets of Genes

- In general, *evolutionary psychologists* study our commonalities and *behavioural geneticists* study our differences. Historically, *nativists* have emphasized "nature" and *empiricists* "nurture," but scientists today understand that heredity and environment interact to produce our psychological traits and even most of our physical ones. This interaction works in both directions: Genes affect the environments we choose, and the environment affects the activity of genes over our lifetimes.

- *Genes*, the basic units of heredity, are located on *chromosomes*, which consist of strands of *DNA*. Within each gene, a sequence of four elements of DNA constitutes a chemical code that helps determine the synthesis of a particular protein. In turn, proteins affect virtually all the structural and biochemical characteristics of the organism.

- Most human traits depend on more than one gene pair, which makes tracking down the genetic contributions to a trait extremely difficult. One method for doing so involves the use of *linkage studies*, which look for patterns of inheritance of the *genetic markers* whose locations on the genes are already known.

- Researchers have completed a map of the entire human *genome*. However, this map does not automatically tell us what a particular gene does or how it does so, or how multiple genes interact and influence behaviour.

The Genetics of Similarity

- Evolutionary psychologists argue that many fundamental human similarities can be traced to the processes of *evolution*, especially *natural selection*. They draw inferences about the behavioural tendencies that might have been selected because they helped our forebears solve survival problems and enhanced reproductive fitness; they then conduct research to see if such tendencies actually exist throughout the world.

- Many evolutionary psychologists believe that the mind is not a general-purpose computer, but instead evolved as a collection of specialized *mental modules* to handle specific survival problems. Among the candidates for such modules are inborn reflexes, an attraction to novelty, a motive to explore and manipulate objects, an impulse to play, and the capacity for certain basic cognitive skills, including a rudimentary understanding of number. However, because some behaviour or trait exists does not necessarily mean that it is adaptive or the product of natural selection.

Our Human Heritage: Courtship and Mating

- *Sociobiologists* and evolutionary psychologists argue that males and females have evolved different sexual and courtship strategies in response to survival problems faced in the distant past. In this view, it has been adaptive for males to be promiscuous, to be attracted to young partners, and to want sexual novelty, and for females to be monogamous, to be choosy about partners, and to prefer security to novelty.

- Critics argue that evolutionary explanations of infidelity and monogamy are based on simplistic stereotypes of gender differences; that they rely too heavily on answers to questionnaires, which often do not reflect real-life choices; that convenience samples used in questionnaire studies are not necessarily representative of people in general; and that the evolutionary emphasis on the Pleistocene Age may not be warranted. Moreover, our ancestors probably did not have a wide range of partners to choose from; what may have evolved is mate selection based on similarity and proximity. The central issue dividing evolutionary theorists and their critics is the length of the "genetic leash."

The Genetics of Difference

- Behavioural geneticists often study differences among individuals by using data from studies of adopted children and of *identical* and *fraternal* twins. These data yield an estimate of the *heritability* of traits and abilities—the extent to which differences in a trait or ability within a group of individuals is accounted for by genetic differences.

- Heritability estimates do not apply to specific individuals or to differences between groups. They apply only to differences within a particular group living in a particular environment; for example, heritability is higher for children in affluent families than in impoverished ones. Moreover, even highly heritable traits can often be modified by the environment.

Our Human Diversity: The Case of Intelligence

- Heritability estimates for intelligence (as measured by IQ tests) average about 0.40 to 0.50 for children and adolescents and 0.60 to 0.80 for adults. Identical twins are more similar in IQ test performance than fraternal twins, and adopted children's scores correlate more highly with those of their biological parents than with those of their nonbiological relatives. These results do not mean that genes determine intelligence; the remaining variance in IQ scores must owe largely to environmental influences.

- Several studies have reported markers for genes that may influence IQ performance. But each of these genes, if confirmed, is likely to contribute just a tiny piece to the puzzle of genetic variation in intelligence.

- It is a mistake to draw conclusions about *group* differences from heritability estimates based on differences *within* a group. The available evidence fails to support genetic explanations of black–white differences in performance on IQ tests.

- Environmental factors such as poor prenatal care, malnutrition, exposure to toxins, and stressful family circumstances are associated with lower performance on intelligence tests. Conversely, a healthy and stimulating environment, and certain kinds of enrichment activities, can improve performance. IQ scores have been rising in many countries for several generations, most likely because of improved diet and education and the increase in jobs requiring abstract thought.

Beyond Nature versus Nurture

- Neither nature nor nurture can entirely explain people's similarities or differences. New discoveries about the role of noncoding DNA, and findings in the field of epigenetics, show that the interaction between genes and environment is far more complex than anyone once imagined. Genetic and environmental influences blend and become indistinguishable in the development of any individual.

Taking Psychology with You

- When deciding whether to have genetic testing, critical thinkers will consider the personal and social consequences, such as whether test results can reveal a risk that has practical relevance, could be misused by their employer or insurance company, might stigmatize them if others knew about it, would help them accept and live with a problem, or could create a self-fulfilling prophecy.

Key Terms

evolutionary psychology **71**
behavioural genetics **71**
genes **72**
chromosomes **72**
DNA (deoxyribonucleic acid) **72**

genome **72**
genetic marker **73**
evolution **75**
mutation **75**
natural selection **75**
mental modules **77**

sociobiology **80**
social Darwinism **85**
heritability **86**
identical (monozygotic) twins **88**

fraternal (dizygotic) twins **88**
intelligence quotient (IQ) **90**
epigenetics **95**

4

The Brain and Nervous System

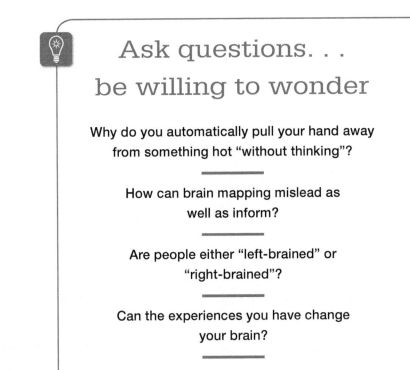

Ask questions. . .
be willing to wonder

Why do you automatically pull your hand away from something hot "without thinking"?

————

How can brain mapping mislead as well as inform?

————

Are people either "left-brained" or "right-brained"?

————

Can the experiences you have change your brain?

————

Are there "his" and "hers" brains?

After suffering damage to the right side of the brain, a Swiss stroke patient developed a puzzling symptom: he became obsessed with fine dining, a phenomenon later dubbed "gourmand syndrome." After recovering, he quit his job as a political journalist and became a food columnist (Regard & Landis, 1997).

Since suffering brain damage when a freight train hit her car, Julie has been unable to recall people and events from either the distant past or a few minutes ago. She cannot remember her daughter, who died in the accident. She knows she has a husband, but he must be reintroduced to her whenever she sees him. She keeps meticulous notes about her day, but she feels she is faking her way through life (Mason, 2008).

These cases, and thousands like them, teach us that the 1500-gram organ inside our skull provides the bedrock for everything we do and think. When injury or disease affects the brain's functioning, life is inevitably altered physically, emotionally, or mentally. Sometimes the changes are subtle and even benign, as in the case of "gourmand syndrome." All too often, they are not.

Nearly every week, discoveries about the brain make headlines, as new research is announced and old puzzles begin to be solved. For example:

- In 2008, two macaque monkeys were taught to control a robotic arm with just their thoughts, by using a computer that was connected to tiny electrodes attached to the brain cells that signal arm and hand movements (Velliste et al., 2008). In 2012, this research was extended to involve a woman who has been paralyzed for 15 years, who used signals from her brain to control a robotic arm to drink a coffee. This research raises hope that men and women who are paralyzed will someday be able to increase their independence in meaningful ways.

- A brain-monitoring technique determines which internet movie clips a person is watching (Nishimoto et al., 2011). Researchers programmed a computer to examine 5000 hours of YouTube trailers, training it to associate brain activity during viewing of the trailers with specific visual images. Later, the computer was able to predict which new trailers people were seeing—a sort of "mind reading."

Neuroscientists in psychology and other disciplines study the brain and the rest of the

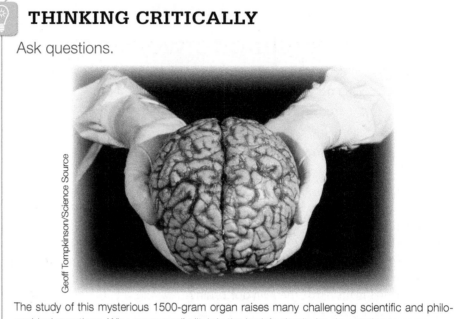

THINKING CRITICALLY

Ask questions.

Geoff Tompkinson/Science Source

The study of this mysterious 1500-gram organ raises many challenging scientific and philosophical questions. Why can a small glitch in the brain's circuits be devastating to some people, whereas others can function with major damage? How do experiences in life alter our brains?

nervous system to gain a better understanding of human behaviour and the brain's potential:

- Cognitive neuroscientists explore the biological foundations of consciousness, perception, memory, and language.
- Social neuroscientists focus on processes such as attachment and attitudes.
- Affective neuroscientists study the nervous system's involvement in emotion, motivation, and stress.
- Behavioural neuroscientists study the biology of such basic processes as learning, conditioning, eating, and sex.

You can see that this list covers basically everything that human beings feel and do. In this chapter, we will examine the structure of the brain and the rest of the nervous system as background for our later discussions of these and other topics.

At this very moment, your own brain, assisted by other parts of your nervous system, is busily taking in these words. Whether you are excited, curious, or bored, your brain is registering an emotional reaction. As you continue reading, your brain will store away much of the information in this chapter. (Reciting and reviewing will help, of course.) Later on, your brain may enable you to smell a flower, climb the stairs, greet a friend, solve a problem, or chuckle at a joke. But the brain's most startling accomplishment is its knowledge that it is doing all these things. This self-awareness makes brain research different from the study of anything else in the universe. Neuroscientists must use the cells, biochemistry, and circuitry of their own brains to understand the cells, biochemistry, and circuitry of brains in general. ◉

The brain is like the main room in a house filled with many alcoves and passageways—the "house" being the nervous system as a whole. Before we can understand the windows, walls, and furniture of this house, we need to become acquainted with the overall floor plan.

◉─ **Watch** the **Video**
*The Big Picture: My Brain Made Me
Do It* in **MyPsychLab**

Brain

Spinal cord

Nerves

The Nervous System: A Basic Blueprint

The function of a nervous system is to gather and process information, produce responses to stimuli, and coordinate the workings of different cells. Even an earthworm has the beginnings of such a system. In very simple organisms that do little more than move, eat, and eliminate wastes, the "system" may be only one or two nerve cells. In human beings, who do such complex things as dance, cook, and take psychology courses, the nervous system contains billions of cells. Scientists divide this intricate network into two main parts: the *central nervous system* and the *peripheral (outlying) nervous system* (see Figure 4.1).

The Central Nervous System

The **central nervous system (CNS)** receives, processes, interprets, and stores incoming sensory information—information about tastes, sounds, smells, colour, pressure on the skin, the state of internal organs, and so forth. It also sends out messages destined for muscles, glands, and internal organs. The CNS is usually conceptualized as having two components: the brain, which we will consider in detail later, and the **spinal cord**, which is actually an extension of the brain. The spinal cord runs from the base of the brain down the centre of the back, protected by a column of bones (the spinal column), and it acts as a bridge between the brain and the parts of the body below the neck.

The spinal cord produces some behaviours on its own without any help from the brain. These *spinal reflexes* are automatic, requiring no conscious effort. If you accidentally touch a hot iron, you will immediately pull your hand away, even before your brain has registered what has happened. Nerve impulses bring a message to the spinal cord (hot!), and the spinal cord immediately sends out a command via other nerves, telling muscles in your arm to contract and to pull your hand away from the iron. (Reflexes above the neck, such as sneezing and blinking, involve the lower part of the brain rather than the spinal cord.)

The neural circuits underlying many spinal reflexes are linked to neural pathways that run up and down the spinal cord, to and from the brain. Because of these connections, reflexes can sometimes be influenced by thoughts and emotions. An example is erection in men, a spinal reflex that can be inhibited by anxiety or distracting thoughts and initiated by erotic thoughts. Some reflexes can be brought under conscious control. If you concentrate, you may be able to keep your knee from jerking when it is tapped, as it normally would. Similarly, most men can learn to voluntarily delay ejaculation, another spinal reflex.

The Peripheral Nervous System

The **peripheral nervous system (PNS)** handles the central nervous system's input and output. It contains all portions of the nervous system outside the brain and spinal cord, right down to the nerves in the tips of the fingers and toes. If your brain could

FIGURE 4.1 The Central and Peripheral Nervous Systems
The central nervous system includes the brain and the spinal cord. The peripheral nervous system consists of 43 pairs of nerves that transmit information to and from the central nervous system. Twelve pairs of cranial nerves in the head enter the brain directly; 31 pairs of spinal nerves enter the spinal cord at the spaces between the vertebrae.

central nervous system (CNS)
The portion of the nervous system consisting of the brain and spinal cord.

spinal cord A collection of neurons and supportive tissue running from the base of the brain down the centre of the back, protected by a column of bones (the spinal column).

peripheral nervous system (PNS)
All portions of the nervous system outside the brain and spinal cord; it includes sensory and motor nerves.

somatic nervous system
The subdivision of the peripheral nervous system that connects to sensory receptors and to skeletal muscles; sometimes called the *skeletal nervous system*.

autonomic nervous system
The subdivision of the peripheral nervous system that regulates the internal organs and glands.

sympathetic nervous system
The subdivision of the autonomic nervous system that mobilizes bodily resources and increases the output of energy during emotion and stress.

parasympathetic nervous system
The subdivision of the autonomic nervous system that operates during relaxed states and that conserves energy.

not collect information about the world by means of a peripheral nervous system, it would be like a smartphone without internet access (not so smart!). In the peripheral nervous system, *sensory nerves* carry messages from special receptors in the skin, muscles, and other internal and external sense organs to the spinal cord, which sends them along to the brain. These nerves put us in touch with both the outside world and the activities of our own bodies. *Motor nerves* carry orders from the central nervous system to muscles, glands, and internal organs. They enable us to move, and they cause glands to contract and to secrete substances, including chemical messengers called *hormones*.

Scientists further divide the peripheral nervous system into two parts: the *somatic* (bodily) nervous system and the *autonomic* (self-governing) nervous system.

- The **somatic nervous system**, sometimes called the *skeletal nervous system*, consists of nerves that are connected to sensory receptors—cells that enable you to sense the world—and also to the skeletal muscles that permit voluntary action.
- The **autonomic nervous system** regulates the functioning of blood vessels, glands, and internal (visceral) organs such as the bladder, stomach, and heart.

When you feel a bug on your arm, turn off a light, or write your name, your somatic system is active. But when you see someone you have a crush on and your heart pounds, your hands get sweaty, and your cheeks feel hot, you can blame your autonomic nervous system.

The autonomic nervous system is itself divided into two parts: the **sympathetic nervous system** and the **parasympathetic nervous system**. These two parts work together, but in opposing ways, to adjust the body to changing circumstances (see Figure 4.2).

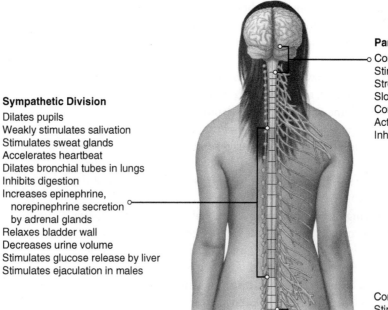

Parasympathetic Division
Constricts pupils
Stimulates tear glands
Strongly stimulates salivation
Slows heartbeat
Constricts bronchial tubes in lungs
Activates digestion
Inhibits glucose release by liver

Sympathetic Division
Dilates pupils
Weakly stimulates salivation
Stimulates sweat glands
Accelerates heartbeat
Dilates bronchial tubes in lungs
Inhibits digestion
Increases epinephrine,
  norepinephrine secretion
  by adrenal glands
Relaxes bladder wall
Decreases urine volume
Stimulates glucose release by liver
Stimulates ejaculation in males

Contracts bladder wall
Stimulates genital erection (both
  sexes) and vaginal lubrication
  (females)

FIGURE 4.2 The Autonomic Nervous System
In general, the sympathetic division of the autonomic nervous system prepares the body to expend energy, and the parasympathetic division restores and conserves energy. Sympathetic nerve fibres exit from areas of the spinal cord shown in orange in this illustration; parasympathetic fibres exit from the base of the brain and from spinal-cord areas shown in blue.

- The sympathetic system acts like the accelerator of a car, mobilizing the body for action and an output of energy. It makes you blush, sweat, and breathe more deeply, and it pushes up your heart rate and blood pressure. As we discuss in Chapter 11, when you are in a situation that requires you to fight, flee, or cope, the sympathetic nervous system whirls into action.

- The parasympathetic system is more like a brake: It does not stop the body, of course, but it does slow things down and keep them running smoothly. It enables the body to conserve and store energy.

If you have to jump out of the way of a speeding motorcyclist, sympathetic nerves increase your heart rate. Afterward, parasympathetic nerves slow it down again and keep its rhythm regular.

Recite & Review

Recite: Put your nervous system into high gear by saying out loud everything you can remember about the *central, peripheral, somatic, autonomic, sympathetic,* and *parasympathetic nervous systems,* and the *spinal cord.*

Review: Next, go back and read this section again, and pay extra attention to what you didn't remember.

Now take this *Quick Quiz:*

Mentally fill in the missing parts of the nervous system "house." Be sure, once more, that you can describe what each part of the system does.

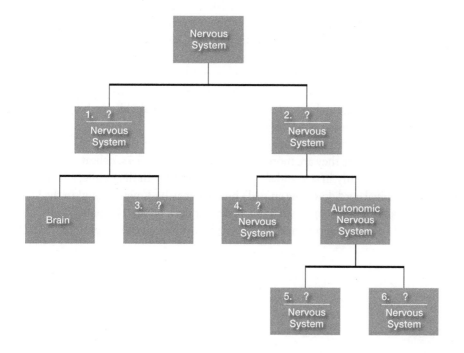

Answers:

1. central: processes, interprets, and stores information and issues orders to muscles, glands, and organs **2.** peripheral: transmits information to and from the CNS **3.** spinal cord: serves as a bridge between the brain and the peripheral nervous system; produces reflexes **4.** somatic: controls the skeletal muscles **5.** sympathetic: mobilizes the body for action and an energy output **6.** parasympathetic: conserves energy and maintains the body in a quiet state

neuron A cell that conducts electrochemical signals; the basic unit of the nervous system; also called a *nerve cell*.

glia [GLY-uh or GLEE-uh] Cells that support, nurture, and insulate neurons, remove debris when neurons die, enhance the formation and maintenance of neural connections, and modify neuronal functioning.

Learning Objectives

(3) Compare the functions of neurons and glial cells in the nervous system.

(4) Describe the three main parts of a neuron, and explain their functions.

(5) Explain why researchers are excited about the discovery of stem cells in the brain.

(6) Describe what happens when levels of neurotransmitters are too low or too high.

(7) Identify which brain chemicals mimic the effects of morphine by dulling pain and promoting pleasure.

(8) List which hormones are of special interest to neuroscientists and other researchers, and explain why.

Communication in the Nervous System

The blueprint we just described provides only a general idea of the nervous system's structure. Now let's turn to the details.

Like the rest of your body, your brain is made of cells—two types of cells, in fact. **Neurons**, or *nerve cells*, are the brain's communication specialists, transmitting information to, from, and within the central nervous system. Neurons are supported by **glia**, or *glial cells* (from the Greek for "glue"), which make up about 90% of the brain's cells.

Glial cells are much more than just "glue," however. They provide the neurons with nutrients, insulate them, help them grow, protect the brain from toxic agents, and remove cellular debris when neurons die. They also communicate chemically with each other and with neurons; without them, neurons could not function effectively. One kind of glial cell appears to give neurons the go-ahead to form connections and to start "talking" to each other (He & Sun, 2007; Ullian, Christopherson, & Barres, 2004). Another kind seems to act like the brain's electrician, identifying and trying to repair problems with the nerves' electrical systems (Graeber & Streit, 2010). And over time, glia help determine which neural connections get stronger or weaker, suggesting that they play a vital role in learning and memory (Bains & Oliet, 2007; Fields, 2004). Neuroscientists are now focusing on more holistic therapies to repair the nervous system; these therapies include the transplantation of glial cells to help repair and regenerate neurons (Almad & Maragakis, 2012).

It's the neurons, though, that are considered the building blocks of the nervous system, though in structure they are more like snowflakes than blocks, delicate and differing from one another greatly in size and shape (see Figure 4.3). In the giraffe, a neuron that runs from the spinal cord down the animal's hind leg may be 3 metres long! In the human brain, neurons are microscopic. An adult brain contains about 171 billion cells, about evenly divided between neurons and glia (Herculano-Houzel, 2009; Lent et al., 2012).

👁—|**Watch** the **Video**
The Basics: How the Brain Works, Part 1 in **MyPsychLab**

Neurons in the outer layers of the brain.

Science Source

FIGURE 4.3 Different Kinds of Neurons

Neurons vary in size and shape, depending on their location and function. More than 200 types of neurons have been identified in mammals.

Spinal cord (motor neuron)   Thalamus   Cerebellum   Cortex

The Structure of the Neuron

As you can see in Figure 4.4, a neuron has three main parts: *dendrites*, a *cell body*, and an *axon*.

- The **dendrites** look like the branches of a tree; indeed, the word *dendrite* means "little tree" in Greek. Dendrites act like antennas, receiving messages from as many as 10 000 other nerve cells and transmitting these messages toward the cell body. They also do some preliminary processing of those messages.
- The **cell body** is shaped roughly like a sphere or a pyramid; it includes the cell's nucleus, which contains genetic information (DNA) and controls the cell's growth and reproduction. The rest of the cell body contains the biochemical machinery for keeping the neuron alive and producing neurochemicals (which you will read about shortly).
- The **axon** (from the Greek for "axle") transmits messages away from the cell body to other neurons or to muscle or gland cells. Axons commonly divide at the end into branches called *axon terminals*. In adult human beings, axons vary from only a few microns to more than a metre in length.

Dendrites and axons give each neuron a double role.

Many axons, especially the larger ones, are insulated by a surrounding layer of fatty material called the **myelin sheath**, which in the central nervous system is made up of glial cells. Constrictions in this covering, called *nodes*, divide it into segments, making it look a little like a string of link sausages (see Figure 4.4 again). One purpose of the myelin sheath is to prevent signals in adjacent cells from interfering with each other. Another purpose, as we will see shortly, is to speed up the conduction of neural impulses. In individuals with multiple sclerosis, loss of myelin results in erratic nerve signaling, leading to loss of sensation, weakness or paralysis, lack of coordination, or vision problems.

In the peripheral nervous system, the fibres of individual neurons (axons and sometimes dendrites) are collected together in bundles called **nerves**, rather like the lines in a telephone cable. The human body has 43 pairs of peripheral nerves; one nerve from each pair is on the left side of the body and the other is on the right. Most of these nerves enter or leave the spinal cord, but 12 pairs in the head, the *cranial nerves*, connect directly to the brain. In Chapter 6, we will discuss the cranial nerves involved in smell, hearing, and vision.

dendrites A neuron's branches that receive information from other neurons and transmit it toward the cell body.

cell body The part of the neuron that keeps it alive and determines whether or not it will fire.

axon A neuron's extending fibre that conducts impulses away from the cell body and transmits them to other neurons.

myelin sheath A fatty insulation that may surround the axon of a neuron.

nerve A bundle of nerve fibres (axons and sometimes dendrites) in the peripheral nervous system.

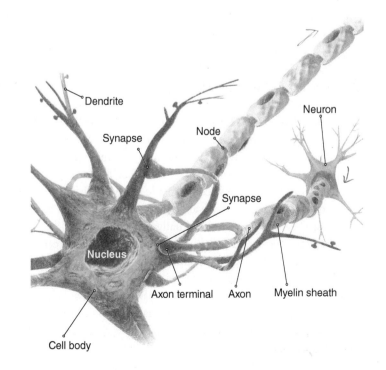

FIGURE 4.4 The Structure of a Neuron
Incoming neural impulses are received by the dendrites of a neuron and are transmitted to the cell body. Outgoing signals pass along the axon to terminal branches.

In an area of the brain associated with learning and memory, immature stem cells give rise to new neurons, and physical and mental stimulation promotes the production and survival of these neurons. These mice, who have toys to play with, tunnels to explore, wheels to run on, and other mice to share their cage with, will grow more cells than mice living alone in standard cages.

Marc Lieberman

👁—⟩Watch the Video
Special Topics: The Plastic Brain
in **MyPsychLab**

neurogenesis The production of new neurons from immature stem cells.

stem cells Immature cells that renew themselves and have the potential to develop into mature cells; given encouraging environments, stem cells from early embryos can develop into any cell type.

Neurogenesis: The Birth of Neurons

For most of the twentieth century, scientists assumed that if neurons in the central nervous system were injured or damaged, they could never grow back (regenerate). But then animal studies showed that severed axons in the spinal cord *can* regrow if you treat them with certain nervous system chemicals (Schnell & Schwab, 1990). Researchers are hopeful that regenerated axons will eventually enable people with spinal-cord injuries to use their limbs again.

In the past two decades, scientists have also had to rethink another entrenched assumption: that mammals produce no new CNS cells after infancy. In the early 1990s, Canadian neuroscientists immersed immature cells from mouse brains in a growth-promoting protein and showed that these cells could give birth to new neurons in a process called **neurogenesis**. Even more astonishing, the new neurons continued to divide and multiply (Reynolds & Weiss, 1992). Since then, scientists have discovered that the human brain and other body organs also contain such cells, which are now known as **stem cells**. Many of these cells, including those in brain areas involved in learning and memory, seem to divide, mature, and remain functional throughout adulthood (Marrone, Ramirez-Amaya & Barnes, 2011). Animal studies have found that physical exercise, effortful mental activity, and an enriched environment promote the production and survival of new cells, whereas aging and stress can inhibit their production and commonly used drugs like nicotine can kill them (Berger, Gage, & Vijayaraghavan, 1998; Kempermann, 2006; Schoenfeld & Gould, 2013; Shors, 2009). 👁

Stem-cell research is one of the hottest areas in biology and neuroscience, because embryonic stem (ES) cells are *pluripotent*, a word that literally means "having many powers." Amazingly, ES cells can generate many types of specialist cells, from neurons to kidney cells. Therefore, stem cells may be useful for treating damaged tissues. ES cells come from aborted fetuses and from embryos that are a few days old, which consist of just a few cells. (Fertility clinics store many such embryos because several "test tube" fertilizations are created for every patient who hopes to become pregnant; eventually, the extra embryos are destroyed.) In Canada, embryonic stem cells (ES) can be obtained only from sources approved by the Assisted Human Reproduction Agency of Canada, a regulatory body for stem-cell research. To reduce the number of embryos used, academic researchers are strongly encouraged to share ES cells and to participate in a national registry (Knowles, 2010).

An alternative to the use of ES cells is to reprogram adult cells from certain organs to become stem cells (Takahashi et al., 2007; Yu et al., 2007). In one study, when stem cells derived from human nasal cells were transplanted into mice that had lesions in a part of the brain involved with memory, the mice performed better on learning and memory tasks (Nivet et al., 2011). Like ES cells, "induced pluripotent stem (iPS) cells" derived from adult tissues seem capable of giving rise to many types of cells. However, these cells are harder to keep alive than embryonic stem cells are, and it is still unclear whether they will prove to be equally versatile.

Patient-advocacy groups hope that transplanted stem cells will eventually help people recover from diseases of the brain (such as Alzheimer's) and from damage to the spinal cord and other parts of the body. Scientists have already had some success in animals. In one study, stem cells recovered from baby teeth have helped rats recover from stroke (Sugiyama et al., 2013). Microscopic analysis showed that many of the cells had helped axons regenerate at the site of the spinal injury by blocking substances that were inhibiting their growth. Exciting research by Rob Sutherland and colleagues has demonstrated

(Legrenzi & Umiltà, 2011; Tallis, 2011; Wade, 2006). Because brain-scan images seem so "real" and scientific, many people fail to realize that these images can convey oversimplified and sometimes misleading impressions (see Figure 4.8). Simply by colouring various regions, researchers can make small contrasts look dramatic, and larger ones seem insignificant (Dumit, 2004). Combining individual brain scans into one average scan—a common practice—can mask significant variability among people's brains.

Further, simply including an image of brain activity can be enough to make a study's conclusions seem more "scientifically reasoned" even when they are not. To illustrate this point, scientists asked people to read some scientific-sounding nonsense. One passage explained that because watching television and doing math problems both caused activation in the temporal lobe, watching television would improve math skills! (This conclusion is, of course, rubbish.) Some people read a version of the passage with no image, and others read the passage featuring either a bar graph of the results or an image of the brain, such as from an fMRI. People who read the version of the passage with the brain images thought it had much better scientific reasoning than did those who read the version with no images, or even the version with the graph (McCabe & Castel, 2008).

Research using fMRI sometimes suffers from poor statistical procedures that produce highly inflated correlations between brain activity and measures of personality and emotion (Vul et al., 2009). Yet the press usually reports these findings uncritically, giving the impression that psychological scientists know more about the relation between the brain and psychological processes than they really do. One clever group of scientists made this point very well by doing an fMRI on a dead Atlantic salmon while asking it to view emotional images and determine what emotions the person in each photo was feeling (Bennett et al., 2010). We know what you're thinking: The salmon is dead, so why would the fMRI detect *any* brain activity? But the scan revealed that the salmon was "thinking" about the pictures and the people in them. That's because fMRI produces a mix of signal and noise, like trying to track a conversation in a crowded bar. Scientists have to use sophisticated techniques to "quiet" the noise and reveal the true signal. Sometimes they can make errors. In this case, the result is funny because we know the salmon is dead. But in real life, too, we may not know if the result is real . . . or another dead salmon.

The real problem is not fMRI as a technology, but bad theories, poorly defined dependent measures, and inappropriate interpretations of results, all of which have produced many dubious findings. The enthusiasm for technology has generated the widespread belief that specific "brain centres" or "critical circuits" explain why you prefer Coke to Pepsi, why you identify as a liberal or conservative, or what your brain is doing when you are in love. These beliefs are certainly appealing because they explain complicated behaviour in simple terms (Beck, 2010). But the attempts to reduce complex behaviour to single locations in the brain will almost certainly fail, just as phrenology failed (Gonsalves & Cohen, 2010; Tallis, 2011; Uttal, 2001). So if you know that one part of the brain is activated when you are thinking about your beloved pet pig, what exactly do you know about love—or your brain? Is the same part activated when you are thinking about a luscious pork chop or another one of your pets (presumably non-edible)?

Whether neuroscientists manipulate different brain areas to determine how behaviour is affected, or manipulate behaviour and then record the effects in the brain, their studies are just one step in understanding brain processes and must be interpreted with the same caution as other studies. Nonetheless, when used appropriately, they do provide an illuminating look at the brain at work and play, and we will therefore be reporting many findings from brain-scan research throughout this text. For scientists, the brain can no longer hide behind the thick fortress of the skull.

FIGURE 4.8 Colouring the Brain
By altering the colours used in brain images, such as in this PET scan, researchers can create the appearance of dramatic brain differences. These scans are actually images of the same brain.

Brian Murphy

THINKING CRITICALLY

Don't oversimplify.

Brain scans provide us with fabulous windows on the brain. But if a scan shows that a brain area is active when you're doodling, does that mean the area is a "doodling centre"?

Recite & Review

Recite: You know the drill: Tell someone or something everything you can recall about the *lesion method, transcranial magnetic stimulation (TMS), transcranial direct current stimulation (tDCS), EEGs, event-related potential (ERP), PET scans, MRI, fMRI,* and . . . the dead salmon.

Review: Next, go back and read this section again.

Now take this *Quick Quiz:*

1. What are the two general approaches to mapping the brain?

2. Why is transcranial magnetic stimulation essentially a virtual lesion method?

3. What does fMRI tell us that structural MRI does not?

4. A researcher scans the brains of gum-chewing volunteers, finds out which part of their brains is most active, and concludes that he or she has discovered the brain's "gum-chewing centre." What's wrong with this conclusion?

Answers:

1. Intervening in the brain and then observing the consequences for behaviour; intervening in behaviour and then observing the effects in the brain 2. TMS disables a part of the brain, though only temporarily and without damaging or removing brain tissue. 3. An fMRI allows us to associate brain activity with specific thoughts or behaviours lasting at least several seconds, instead of just picturing the brain at a moment in time. 4. Many actions and sensations are involved in chewing gum, such as the chewing motion, enjoyment of the flavours, and salivation. A brain scan may tell us where things are happening, but not why or how they are happening. The same areas might also become active when you chew a piece of asparagus. Finally, even if there were a gum-chewing centre (there isn't!), yours might not be in the same place as someone else's. Brains vary a lot, a fact that may be lost when a researcher averages the results of all the brain scans in his or her study.

Learning Objectives

12. Outline the major parts of the brain and describe some of their major functions.

13. Evaluate whether or not it is a good thing that the outer covering of the human brain is so wrinkled.

14. Explain how a bizarre nineteenth-century accident illuminated the role of the frontal lobes.

✳ Explore the **Concept**
Virtual Brain in **MyPsychLab**

localization of function Specialization of particular brain areas for particular functions.

A Tour through the Brain

Most modern brain theories assume that different brain parts perform different (though greatly overlapping) tasks. This concept, known as **localization of function**, goes back at least to Franz Joseph Gall (1758–1828), the Austrian anatomist who thought that personality traits were reflected in the development of specific areas of the brain (see Chapter 1). Gall's theory of phrenology was completely wrongheaded, but his general notion of specialization in the brain had merit.

To learn about what the major brain structures do, let's take an imaginary stroll through the brain. Pretend that you have shrunk to a microscopic size and that you are standing at the lower part of the brain, just above the spine. Figure 4.9 shows the major structures we will encounter along our tour; you may want to refer to it as we proceed. Keep in mind that any activity—feeling an emotion, having a thought, and performing a task—involves many different structures working together. Our description, therefore, is a simplification. ✳

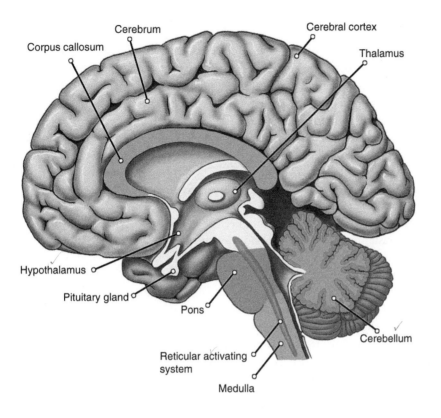

Cerebrum

Corpus callosum

Cerebral cortex

Thalamus

Hypothalamus

Pituitary gland

Pons

Reticular activating system

Medulla

Cerebellum

FIGURE 4.9 Major Structures of the Human Brain
This cross section depicts the brain as if it were split in half. This view is of the inside surface of the right half, and it shows the structures described in the text. For the most part, the same structures appear in the left half too.

The Brain Stem

We begin at the base of the skull with the **brain stem**, which began to evolve some 500 million years ago in segmented worms. The brain stem looks like a stalk rising out of the spinal cord. Pathways to and from upper areas of the brain pass through its two main structures: the medulla and the pons. The **pons** is involved in (among other things) sleeping, waking, and dreaming. The **medulla** is responsible for bodily functions that do not have to be consciously willed, such as breathing and heart rate. Hanging has long been used as a method of execution because when it breaks the neck, nerve pathways from the medulla are severed, stopping respiration.

Extending upward from the core of the brain stem is the **reticular activating system (RAS)**. This dense network of neurons, which extends above the brain stem into the centre of the brain and has connections with areas that are higher up, screens incoming information and arouses the higher centres when something happens that demands their attention. Without the RAS, we could not be alert nor perhaps even conscious.

The Cerebellum

Standing atop the brain stem and looking toward the back part of the brain, we see a structure about the size of a small fist. It is the **cerebellum**, or "lesser brain," which contributes to a sense of balance and coordinates the muscles so that movement is smooth and precise. If your cerebellum were damaged, you would probably become clumsy and uncoordinated. In addition, this structure is involved in remembering certain simple skills and acquired reflexes (Daum & Schugens, 1996; Krupa, Thompson, & Thompson, 1993). But the cerebellum, which was once considered just a motor centre, is not as "lesser" as its name implies; it plays a part in complex cognitive tasks ranging from analyzing sensory information, solving problems and understanding words, to judgments of right and wrong (Demirtas-Tatlidede & Schmahmann, 2013; Fiez, 1996; Gao et al., 1996; Muller, Courchesne, & Allen, 1998; Timmann et al., 2010).

Cerebellum

Pons

Reticular activating system

Medulla

brain stem The part of the brain at the top of the spinal cord, consisting of the medulla and the pons.

pons A structure in the brain stem involved in, among other things, sleeping, waking, and dreaming.

medulla [muh-DUL-uh] A structure in the brain stem responsible for certain automatic functions, such as breathing and heart rate.

reticular activating system (RAS) A dense network of neurons found in the core of the brain stem; it arouses the cortex and screens incoming information.

cerebellum A brain structure that regulates movement and balance, is involved in remembering simple skills and acquired reflexes, and plays a role in cognitive and emotional learning.

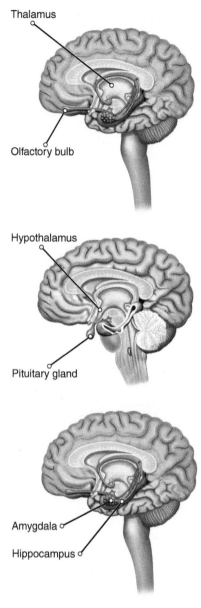

thalamus A brain structure that relays sensory messages to the cerebral cortex.

hypothalamus A brain structure involved in emotions and drives vital to survival; it regulates the autonomic nervous system.

pituitary gland A small endocrine gland at the base of the brain that releases many hormones and regulates other endocrine glands.

amygdala [uh-MIG-dul-uh] A brain structure involved in the arousal and regulation of emotion and the initial emotional response to sensory information.

hippocampus A brain structure involved in the storage of new information in memory.

The Thalamus

Deep in the brain's interior, roughly at its centre, we can see the **thalamus**, the sensory relay station of the brain. As sensory messages come into the brain, the thalamus directs them to higher areas in charge of vision, sound, or touch. The only sense that completely bypasses the thalamus is the sense of smell, which has its own private switching station, the *olfactory bulb*. The olfactory bulb lies near areas involved in emotion, which may be why particular odours, such as the smell of fresh laundry or a steaming bowl of chicken soup, often rekindle vivid memories.

The Hypothalamus and the Pituitary Gland

Beneath the thalamus sits a structure called the **hypothalamus** (*hypo* means "under"). It is constantly monitoring the body's current state and issuing instructions to help the body maintain a steady state called *homeostasis*. It is involved in basic survival drives associated with the "four Fs"—feeding, fighting, fleeing, and . . . sex. It regulates body temperature by triggering sweating or shivering, and it controls the complex operations of the autonomic nervous system. It also contains the biological clock that controls the body's daily rhythms (see Chapter 5).

Hanging down from the hypothalamus, connected to it by a short stalk, is a cherry-sized endocrine gland called the **pituitary gland**, mentioned earlier in our discussion of hormones. The pituitary is often called the body's "master gland" because the hormones it secretes affect many other endocrine glands. The master, however, is really only a supervisor. The true boss is the hypothalamus, which sends chemicals to the pituitary that tell it when to "talk" to the other endocrine glands. The pituitary, in turn, sends hormonal messages out to these glands.

The hypothalamus and several other loosely interconnected structures have often been considered part of the *limbic system;* the term is from the Latin for "border," and these structures were thought to form a border between the "higher" and "lower" parts of the brain. Structures in this region are heavily involved in emotions that we share with other animals, such as rage and fear, so the region is also sometimes called "the emotional brain." But researchers now know that these structures also have other functions, and that parts of the brain outside of the old limbic system are involved in emotion. As a result, the term *limbic system* has been going out of fashion.

The Amygdala

The **amygdala** (from the ancient Greek word for "almond") is responsible for evaluating sensory information, quickly determining its emotional importance, and contributing to the initial decision to approach or withdraw from a person or situation (see Chapter 11). Some people describe the amygdala as the brain's "fear centre," but it is more than that. Your amygdala assesses stimuli for their fit with your current psychological state and even your core personality traits, responding to positive, negative, or even just plain interesting stimuli accordingly. It does so by working with higher brain areas to regulate your response. If you're extroverted, your amygdala responds more actively to photographs of happy people than it does if you are shy, and when you're hungry, your amygdala responds to food (Cunningham & Brosch, 2012). The amygdala also plays a role in mediating anxiety and depression and in forming and retrieving emotional memories.

The Hippocampus

The shape of the **hippocampus** must have reminded someone of a sea horse, for in Latin that is what its name means. The structure compares sensory information with what the brain has learned about the world. When expectations are met, it tells the reticular activating system to "cool it." There's no need for neural alarm bells to go off every time a car goes by, a bird chirps, or you feel your saliva trickling down the back of your throat.

The hippocampus has also been called the "gateway to memory." It enables us to form spatial memories so that we can accurately navigate through our environment. And, along with adjacent brain areas, it enables us to form new memories about facts and events—the kind of information you need to identify a flower, tell a story, or recall a vacation trip. The information is then stored in various parts of the cerebral cortex, which we will be discussing shortly. When you recall meeting someone yesterday, various aspects of the memory—the person's greeting, tone of voice, appearance, and location—are probably stored in different locations in the cortex. But without the hippocampus, the information would never get to these destinations. As we will see in Chapter 10, this structure is also involved in the retrieval of information during recall. We know about the central role the hippocampus plays in memory in part from research on patients with hippocampal damage who exhibit severe memory problems. We will meet some of these patients in Chapter 10.

The Cerebrum

At this point in our tour, the largest part of the brain still looms above us. It is the cauliflower-like **cerebrum**, where the higher forms of thinking take place. The human brain's circuitry is far more complex than that of any computer in existence, and much of its most complicated wiring is packed into this structure. Compared to many other creatures, we humans may be ungainly, feeble, and thin-skinned, but our well-developed cerebrum enables us to overcome these limitations and creatively control our environment (and, some would say, to mess it up).

The cerebrum is divided into two separate halves, or **cerebral hemispheres**, connected by a large band of fibres called the **corpus callosum**. In general, the right hemisphere is in charge of the left side of the body, and the left hemisphere is in charge of the right side of the body. As we will see shortly, the two hemispheres also have somewhat different tasks and talents, a phenomenon known as **lateralization**.

The Cerebral Cortex. Working our way right up through the top of the brain, we find that the cerebrum is covered by several thin layers of densely packed cells known collectively as the **cerebral cortex**. Cell bodies in the cortex, as in many other parts of the brain, produce a greyish tissue, hence the term *grey matter*. In other parts of the brain (and in the rest of the nervous system), long, myelin-covered axons prevail, providing the brain's *white matter*. Although the cortex is only about 3 millimetres thick, it contains almost three-fourths of all the cells in the human brain. Because of the cortex's many deep wrinkles and crevasses, it can contain those billions of neurons in a compact space. Without them, our brains and heads would be too large to be born! In other mammals, the cortex is less crumpled; in rats, it is quite smooth.

Lobes of the Cortex. In each cerebral hemisphere, deep fissures divide the cortex into four distinct regions, or lobes (see Figure 4.10):

- The **occipital lobes** (from the Latin for "in back of the head") are at the lower back part of the brain. Among other things, they contain the *visual cortex*, where visual signals are processed. Damage to the visual cortex can cause impaired visual recognition or blindness.

cerebrum [suh-REE-brum] The largest brain structure, consisting of the upper part of the brain; divided into two hemispheres, it is in charge of most sensory, motor, and cognitive processes. From the Latin for "brain."

cerebral hemispheres The two halves of the cerebrum.

corpus callosum The bundle of nerve fibres connecting the two cerebral hemispheres.

lateralization Specialization of the two cerebral hemispheres for particular operations.

cerebral cortex A collection of several thin layers of cells covering the cerebrum; it is largely responsible for higher mental functions. *Cortex* is Latin for "bark" or "rind."

occipital [ahk-SIP-uh-tuhl] lobes Lobes at the lower back part of the brain's cerebral cortex; they contain areas that receive visual information.

FIGURE 4.10 Lobes of the Cerebrum
Deep fissures divide the cortex of each cerebral hemisphere into four regions.

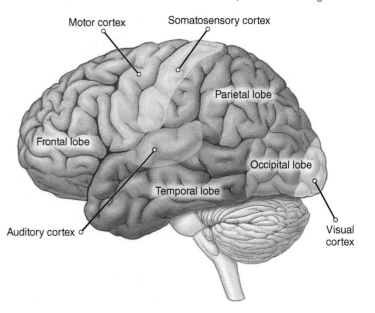

Motor cortex Somatosensory cortex
Parietal lobe
Frontal lobe
Occipital lobe
Temporal lobe
Auditory cortex Visual cortex

parietal [puh-RYE-uh-tuhl]
lobes Lobes at the top of the brain's
cerebral cortex; they contain areas that
receive information on pressure, pain,
touch, and temperature as well as
handle attention and awareness of
spatial relations.

temporal lobes Lobes at the sides of
the brain's cerebral cortex; they contain
areas involved in hearing, memory,
perception, emotion, and (in the left lobe,
typically) language comprehension.

frontal lobes Lobes at the front of the
brain's cerebral cortex; they contain
areas involved in short-term memory,
higher-order thinking, initiative, social
judgment, and (in the left lobe, typically)
speech production.

- The **parietal lobes** (from the Latin for "pertaining to walls") are at the top of the brain. They contain the *somatosensory cortex*, which receives information about pressure, pain, touch, and temperature from all over the body. The areas of the somatosensory cortex that receive signals from the hands and the face are disproportionately large because these body parts are particularly sensitive. Parts of the parietal lobes are also involved in attention and awareness of spatial relations.

- The **temporal lobes** (from the Latin for "pertaining to the temples") are at the sides of the brain, just above the ears and behind the temples. They are involved in memory, perception, and emotion, and they contain the *auditory cortex*, which processes sounds. An area of the left temporal lobe known as *Wernicke's area* is involved in language comprehension.

- The **frontal lobes**, as their name indicates, are located toward the front of the brain, just under the skull in the area of the forehead. They contain the *motor cortex*, which issues orders to the 600 muscles of the body that produce voluntary movement. In the left frontal lobe, a region known as *Broca's area* handles speech production. During short-term memory tasks, areas in the frontal lobes are especially active. The frontal lobes are also involved in emotion and in the ability to make plans, think creatively, and take initiative.

Because of their different functions, the lobes of the cerebral cortex tend to respond differently when stimulated. If a surgeon touches the somatosensory cortex in the parietal lobes, a patient might feel a tingling in the skin or a sense of being gently touched. If the visual cortex in the occipital lobes were electrically stimulated, he or she might report a flash of light or swirls of colour. And, eerily, many areas of the cortex, when stimulated, would produce no obvious response or sensation. These "silent" areas are sometimes called the *association cortex* because they are involved in higher mental processes. (Note that your brain does not feel pain itself, so these surgical stimulations would not hurt at all!)

The Prefrontal Cortex. The most forward part of the frontal lobes is the *prefrontal cortex*. This area barely exists in mice and rats and takes up only 3.5% of the cerebral cortex in cats and about 7% in dogs, but it accounts for approximately one-third of the entire cortex in human beings. It is the most recently evolved part of our brains, and is associated with such complex abilities as reasoning, decision making, and planning.

Neuroscientists have long known that the frontal lobes, and the prefrontal cortex in particular, must also have something to do with personality. The first clue appeared in 1848, when a bizarre accident drove an 2.5 centimetre thick and 1 metre long iron rod clear through the head of a young railroad worker named Phineas Gage. As you can see in the photos, the rod entered beneath the left eye and exited through the top of the head, destroying much of the prefrontal cortex (H. Damasio et al., 1994). Miraculously, Gage survived this trauma and, by most accounts, he retained the ability to speak, think, and remember. But his friends complained that he was "no longer Gage." He had changed from a mild-mannered, friendly, efficient worker into a foul-mouthed, ill-tempered, undependable lout who could not hold a steady job or stick to a plan. His employers had to let him go, and he was reduced to exhibiting himself as a circus attraction.

There is some controversy about the details of this sad incident, but many other cases of brain injury, whether from stroke or trauma, support the conclusion that most scientists draw from the Gage case: that parts of the frontal lobes are involved in social judgment, rational decision making, and the ability to set goals and to make and carry out plans. Like Gage, people with damage in these areas sometimes mismanage their finances, lose their jobs, and abandon their friends. The mental deficits that characterize damage to these areas are accompanied by a flattening out of emotion and feeling, which suggests that normal emotions are necessary for everyday reasoning and the ability to learn from mistakes (H. Damasio et al., 1994; A. Damasio, 2003).

👁—**Watch** the **Video**
Special Topics: Risky Behaviour and Brain Development in **MyPsychLab**

On the far left is a recent digital reconstruction of Phineas Gage's skull, showing the trajectory of the iron rod that penetrated his brain. The photos in the centre and on the right show reconstructions of the interior of the skull from the front and from above. The colours indicate the different fibre pathways that were probably affected, including white-matter pathways between the frontal cortex and other brain parts (Van Horn et al., 2012). After the accident, Gage's behaviour and personality were dramatically altered, and scientists today understand why: The rod passed through an area of the prefrontal cortex associated with emotional processing and rational decision making.

Public Library of Science

The frontal lobes also govern the ability to do a series of tasks in the proper sequence and to stop doing them at the proper time. The pioneering Soviet psychologist Alexander Luria (1980) studied many cases in which damage to the frontal lobes disrupted these abilities. One man kept trying to light a match after it was already lit. Another planed a piece of wood in the hospital carpentry shop until it was gone and then went on to plane the workbench!

Review 4.1 summarizes the major parts of the brain that we have discussed and their primary functions.

REVIEW 4.1 Functions Associated with the Major Brain Structures

The functions listed here are just some of those that have been linked with these structures:

Structure	Functions
Brain stem	
Pons	Sleeping, waking, dreaming
Medulla	Automatic functions such as breathing, heart rate
Reticular activating system (RAS) (extends into centre of the brain)	Screening of incoming information, arousal of higher centres, consciousness
Cerebellum	Balance, muscular coordination, memory for simple skills and learned reflexes, involvement in cognitive and emotional learning
Thalamus	Relay of impulses from higher centres to the spinal cord and of incoming sensory information (except for olfactory sensations) to other brain centres
Hypothalamus	Behaviours necessary for survival, such as hunger, thirst, emotion, reproduction; regulation of body temperature; control of autonomic nervous system
Pituitary gland	Under direction of the hypothalamus, secretion of hormones that affect other glands
Amygdala	Initial evaluation of sensory information to determine its importance; mediation of anxiety and depression; formation and retrieval of emotional memories
Hippocampus	Comparison of new sensory information with existing knowledge in order to regulate the RAS; formation of new memories about facts and events, as well as other aspects of memory
Cerebrum (including cerebral cortex)	Higher forms of thinking
Occipital lobes	Visual processing
Parietal lobes	Processing of pressure, pain, touch, temperature
Temporal lobes	Memory, perception, emotion, hearing, language comprehension
Frontal lobes	Movement, short-term memory, planning, setting goals, creative thinking, initiative, social judgment, rational decision making, speech production

Recite & Review

Recite: Without referring back to Review 4.1 and, using your own brain, say out loud everything you can about these terms: *localization of function*, the *brain stem, pons, medulla, reticular activating system (RAS), cerebellum, thalamus, hypothalamus, pituitary gland, amygdala, hippocampus, cerebrum, cerebral hemispheres, corpus callosum, lateralization, cerebral cortex, occipital lobes, parietal lobes, temporal lobes,* and *frontal lobes.*

Review: Next, go back and read this section again. What did you miss?

Now take this *Quick Quiz:*

A. Match each description on the left with a term on the right:

1. Filters out irrelevant information	**a.** reticular activating system
2. Known as the "gateway to memory"	**b.** cerebrum
3. Controls the autonomic nervous system; involved in drives associated with survival	**c.** hippocampus
	d. cerebral cortex
4. Consists of two hemispheres	**e.** frontal lobes
5. Wrinkled outer covering of the brain	**f.** hypothalamus
6. Site of the motor cortex; associated with planning and taking initiative	

B. Why might the same threat or danger produce a different response in the amygdala in two different people?

Answers:

A. 1. a 2. c 3. f 4. b 5. d 6. e **B.** Because of differences in their personality traits or current psychological state.

Learning Objectives

15 Discuss what would happen if the two cerebral hemispheres could not communicate with each other.

16 Explain why "left-brainedness" and "right-brainedness" are exaggerations.

The Two Hemispheres of the Brain

We have seen that the cerebrum is divided into two hemispheres that control opposite sides of the body. Although similar in structure, these hemispheres have somewhat separate talents, or areas of specialization. Hemispheric specialization is especially apparent in patients who have suffered brain damage, usually as a result of a stroke. Those with left hemisphere damage may lose the ability to speak or understand language, whereas those with right hemisphere damage rarely do. A French neurologist named Paul Broca (the same Broca as *Broca's area*) first made this observation in 1861, and many behavioural and cognitive difficulties associated with left or right hemisphere damage have been documented since then. Patients with left hemisphere damage may have difficulties with reading, identifying objects, making symbolic gestures or pantomimes, and describing events in the correct order. Patients with right hemisphere damage may have difficulty identifying faces, interpreting emotional expressions in a face or voice, or understanding music or art. They may get lost easily, even in their own homes. ✳

✳ **Explore the Concept**

Virtual Brain: Lateralization and Language in **MyPsychLab**

The problem occurs when laypeople wrongly infer that a brain difference is the reason for a behavioural difference—one that doesn't exist! (Fine, 2010).

3 **Some male–female differences in the brain can be the result rather than the cause of behavioural differences.** As we have seen, experiences and cultural influences are constantly sculpting the circuitry of the brain, affecting the way brains are organized and how they function. Women and men, of course, often have different experiences in childhood and throughout their lives. Thus, when researchers find a sex difference in brain structure or function, they cannot automatically assume that the difference is innate or unchangeable.

One reason that scientists differ in their interpretation of the research is that some are focusing on the differences between the sexes and others are focusing on the similarities. Both sides may be right. Yet both would agree that we all should avoid oversimplifying, jumping to conclusions, and thinking in either–or terms (*either* men and women have "different" brains *or* we are all exactly alike). Critical-thinking skills are something both sexes can learn.

We think you'll agree that findings about the brain are pretty fascinating, and we will be discussing many others in the rest of this text. However, these findings should not deflect attention from all the other influences that make us who we are, for better or worse: our relationships, our experiences, our standing in society, our culture. Keep in mind that analyzing a human being in terms of physiology alone is like analyzing the Eiffel Tower solely in terms of the materials that were used to build it. Even if we could monitor every cell and circuit of the brain, we would still need to understand the circumstances, thoughts, and cultural rules that affect whether we are gripped by hatred, consumed by grief, lifted by love, or transported by joy.

Recite & Review

Recite: Has your flexible brain adapted to what you've just read? Recite out loud everything you can recall about *plasticity* and the effects of experience and maturation on the brain, cultural influences on the brain, and sex-related brain differences.

Review: Next, read this section again.

Now take this *Quick Quiz:*

Men and women alike have brains that can answer these questions:

1. During childhood, (a) some synapses are strengthened; (b) some synapses weaken and are pruned away; (c) both a and b; (d) neither a nor b.

2. Name two types of cognitive tasks that may show different patterns of brain activity depending on a person's culture.

3. A new study reports that in a sample of 11 brains, 4 of the 6 women's brains but only 2 of the 5 men's brains had multiple chocolate receptors. (*Note:* We made this up; there's no such thing as a chocolate receptor, sorry.) The researchers conclude that their findings explain why so many women are addicted to chocolate. What concerns should a critical thinker have about this study?

Answers:

1. c **2.** mathematical and visual–spatial **3.** The sample size was very small; have the results been replicated? Were the sex differences more impressive than the similarities? Might eating chocolate affect chocolate receptors rather than the other way around? Most important, was the number of receptors related to the amount of chocolate eaten by the brains' owners in real life?

Taking Psychology with You

Cosmetic Neurology: Tinkering with the Brain

Should healthy people be permitted, even encouraged, to take "brain boosters" or "neuroenhancers," drugs that will sharpen concentration and memory? What about a pill that could erase a traumatic memory? If having cosmetic surgery can change parts of your body that you don't like, what's wrong with allowing "cosmetic neurology" to tinker with parts of your brain that you don't like?

For centuries, people have been seeking ways to stimulate their brains to work more efficiently, with caffeine being an especially popular drug of choice. But people who dislike coffee don't talk about the unfair advantage that coffee drinkers have. Likewise, no one objects to the finding that omega-3s, found in some kinds of fish, may help protect university students against the sudden increases in blood pressure that mental stress causes (Ginty & Conklin, 2012). But when it comes to prescription medications that increase alertness or appear to enhance memory and other cognitive functions, it's another kettle of fish oil, so to speak. What questions should critical thinkers ask and what kind of evidence would they need to make wise decisions about using these medications? A new interdisciplinary specialty, *neuroethics*, has been formed to address the many legal, ethical, and scientific questions raised by brain research, including those raised by the development of neuroenhancing drugs (Farah, 2012; Gazzaniga, 2005).

Much of the buzz has focused on Provigil (modafinil), a drug approved for treating narcolepsy and other sleep disorders, and Ritalin and Adderall, approved for attention deficit disorders. Many students, pilots, business people, and jetlagged travellers are taking one or another of these drugs, either obtaining them illegally from friends or the internet, or getting their own prescriptions. Naturally, most of these users claim the drugs help them, and one review of the literature concluded that Provigil does improve memory for studied material (Smith & Farah, 2011). Recent research suggests that some of the effects that Provigil has on cognition relate to how much individuals enjoyed doing the memory tasks, especially when they were difficult (Mueller et al., 2013). Thus, the effect of these medications is less than what people expect (Repantis et al., 2010) and may relate to other aspects of the testing experience!

But these drugs have downsides. Adderall, like all amphetamines, is addictive, and can cause nervousness, headaches, sleeplessness, allergic rashes, and loss of appetite, and, as the label says, it has "a high potential for abuse." Provigil, too, is habit-forming. Another memory-enhancing drug being studied targets a type of glutamate receptor in the brain. The drug apparently improves short-term memory, but at the price of impairing long-term memory (Talbot, 2009).

Even when a drug is benign for most of its users, there may be surprising and unexpected consequences. For example, cognitive neuroscientists have found that the better people focus and concentrate on a task—the reason for taking stimulants in the first place—the less *creative* they often are. Creativity, after all, comes from being able to let our minds roam freely. One neurologist therefore worries that the routine use of mind-enhancing drugs among students could create "a generation of very focused accountants" (quoted in Talbot, 2009).

Some bioethicists and neuroscientists think that cognitive enhancement is perfectly fine, because it is human nature for people to adapt their environments (Müller & Schumann, 2011). After all, we use eyeglasses to improve vision and hearing aids to improve hearing; why not use pills to improve our memories and other mental skills? One team of scientists has argued that improving brain function with pills is no more objectionable than eating right or getting a good night's sleep. They wrote, "In a world in which human workspans and lifespans are increasing, cognitive enhancement tools . . . will be increasingly useful for improved quality of life and extended work productivity, as well as to stave off normal and pathological age-related cognitive declines" (Greely et al., 2008).

Other scientists and social critics, however, consider cosmetic neurology to be a form of cheating that will give those who can afford the drugs an unfair advantage and increase socioeconomic inequalities. They think the issue is no different from the (prohibited) use of performance-enhancing steroids in athletics. Yes, they say, people wear glasses and hearing aids, but glasses and hearing aids do not have side effects or interact negatively with other treatments. Many neuroethicists also worry that ambitious parents will start giving these medications to their children to try to boost the child's academic performance, despite possible hazards for the child's developing brain.

And what if cognitive enhancement involved not pills but electrical stimulation of your brain? In 2012, neuroscientists at the University of Oxford reported that transcranial direct current stimulation (tDCS) might soon be used with healthy people to improve their math skills, memory, problem solving, and other mental abilities. One said, "I can see a time when people plug a simple device into an iPad so that their brain is stimulated when they are doing their homework, learning French or taking up the piano." And, he added, tDCS would be a great educational aid for children.

Should you get in line to buy your own tDCS machine? Best to wait. As a critical thinker, you would want to ask how much research on tDCS has been done. (Answer: Most is preliminary laboratory work that has been done only on a small scale.) Has research determined whether there are better or worse ways of using tDCS for different mental abilities? (Not yet.) Has the method been tested on children, whose brains are still developing? (Not yet.) Is it known whether boosting ability in one area might affect abilities in other areas? (Not yet.) Has research determined whether the use of tDCS in the lab can improve people's abilities in everyday life? (Not yet.).

Summary

- Neuroscientists and other researchers study the brain because it is the bedrock of consciousness, perception, memory, and emotion.

The Nervous System: A Basic Blueprint

- The function of the nervous system is to gather and process information, produce responses to stimuli, and coordinate the workings of different cells. Scientists divide it into the *central nervous system* (CNS) and the *peripheral nervous system* (PNS). The CNS, which includes the brain and *spinal cord*, receives, processes, interprets, and stores information and sends out messages destined for muscles, glands, and organs. The PNS transmits information to and from the CNS by way of *sensory* and *motor nerves*.

- The peripheral nervous system consists of the *somatic nervous system*, which permits sensation and voluntary actions, and the *autonomic nervous system*, which regulates blood vessels, glands, and internal (visceral) organs. The autonomic system usually functions without conscious control. The autonomic nervous system is further divided into the *sympathetic nervous system*, which mobilizes the body for action, and the *parasympathetic nervous system*, which conserves energy.

Communication in the Nervous System

- *Neurons* are the basic units of the nervous system. They are held in place by *glial cells*, which also nourish, insulate, protect, and repair them. Each neuron consists of *dendrites*, a *cell body*, and an *axon*. In the peripheral nervous system, axons (and sometimes dendrites) are collected together in bundles called *nerves*. Many axons are insulated by a *myelin sheath* that speeds up the conduction of neural impulses and prevents signals in adjacent cells from interfering with one another.

- In the laboratory, neurons have been induced to regenerate. Embryonic *stem cells* are pluripotent, meaning that they can generate many different kinds of cells in the body. These stem cells in various organs, including in brain areas associated with learning and memory, continue to divide and mature throughout adulthood, giving rise to new neurons. A stimulating environment seems to enhance this process of *neurogenesis*.

- Communication between two neurons occurs at the *synapse*. When a wave of electrical voltage (*action potential*) reaches the end of a transmitting axon, *neurotransmitter* molecules are released into the *synaptic cleft*. When these molecules bind to *receptor sites* on the receiving neuron, that neuron becomes either more or less likely to fire. The message that reaches a final destination depends on how frequently particular neurons are firing, how many are firing, what types are firing, their degree of synchrony, and where they are located.

- *Neurotransmitters* play a critical role in mood, memory, and psychological well-being. *Serotonin*, *dopamine*, *acetylcholine*, and *norepinephrine* systems travel different paths through the brain; *GABA* and *glutamate* are distributed through the entire brain. Abnormal levels of neurotransmitters have been implicated in several disorders, such as Alzheimer's disease and Parkinson's disease.

- *Hormones*, produced mainly by the *endocrine glands*, affect and are affected by the nervous system. Neuroscientists are especially interested in *melatonin*, which promotes sleep and helps regulate bodily rhythms; *oxytocin* and *vasopressin*, which play a role in attachment and trust; *adrenal hormones* such as *epinephrine* and *norepinephrine*, which are involved in emotions and stress; and the *sex hormones*, which are involved in the physical changes of puberty, the menstrual cycle (*estrogens* and *progesterone*), sexual arousal (*testosterone*), and some nonreproductive functions, including mental functioning.

- *Neuromodulators* are like the brain's volume control, varying the strength of neural functions. One neuromodulator, a *serotonin transporter*, helps to recycle serotonin back to the neurons that released it. *Endorphins* reduce pain and promote pleasure, and shoot up when an animal or person is afraid or is under stress. Endorphins have also been linked to the pleasures of human attachment.

Mapping the Brain

- Researchers study the brain by observing patients with brain damage; by using the *lesion method* with animals; and by using such techniques as *electroencephalograms (EEGs)*, *event-related potentials (ERP)*, *transcranial magnetic stimulation (TMS)*, *transcranial direct current stimulation (tDCS)*, *PET scans (positron-emission tomography)*, *magnetic resonance imaging (MRI)*, and *functional MRI (fMRI)*.

- These tools reveal which parts of the brain are active during different tasks, but they do not reveal discrete "centres" for particular functions. Because brain-scan images seem so "real" and scientific, many people fail to realize that these images can convey oversimplified and sometimes misleading impressions.

A Tour through the Brain

- All modern brain theories assume *localization of function*, although a particular area may have several functions and many areas are likely to be involved in any particular activity.

- In the lower part of the brain, in the *brain stem*, the *medulla* controls automatic functions such as heartbeat and breathing, and the *pons* is involved in sleeping, waking, and dreaming. The *reticular activating system* (RAS) screens incoming information and is responsible for alertness. The *cerebellum* contributes to balance and muscle coordination, and plays a role in cognitive and emotional learning.

- The *thalamus* directs sensory messages to appropriate higher centres. The *hypothalamus* is involved in emotion and in drives associated with survival. It also controls the operations of the autonomic nervous system, and sends out chemicals that tell the *pituitary gland* when to "talk" to other endocrine glands.

- The *amygdala* is responsible for evaluating sensory information and quickly determining its importance, and thus your initial decision to approach or withdraw from a person or situation, depending on your personality and your psychological state. It is also involved in forming and retrieving emotional memories. The *hippocampus* moderates the reticular activating system. It has also been called the "gateway to memory" because it plays a critical role in the formation of long-term memories for facts and events and other aspects of memory.

- Much of the brain's circuitry is packed into the *cerebrum*, which is divided into two *hemispheres* and is covered by thin layers of cells known collectively as the *cerebral cortex*. The *occipital*, *parietal*, *temporal*, and *frontal lobes* of the cortex have specialized (but partially overlapping) functions. The *association cortex* appears to be responsible for higher mental processes. The *frontal lobes*, particularly areas in the *prefrontal cortex*, are involved in social judgment, making and carrying out plans, and decision making.

The Two Hemispheres of the Brain

- Studies of patients who have had *split-brain surgery* (a severing of the *corpus callosum*) show that the two cerebral hemispheres have somewhat different talents. In most people, language is processed mainly in the left hemisphere, which generally is specialized for logical, symbolic, and sequential tasks. The right hemisphere is associated with spatial–visual tasks, facial recognition, and the creation and appreciation of art and music. In most mental activities, however, the two hemispheres cooperate as partners, with each making a valuable contribution.

The Flexible Brain

- Many synapses have not yet formed at birth. During development, axons and dendrites continue to grow as a result of both physical maturation and experience with the world, and throughout life, new learning results in new synaptic connections in the brain. During childhood, synaptic connections that are useful for helping the child respond to the environment survive and are strengthened whereas those that are not useful wither away, leaving behind a more efficient neural network. But the brain's circuits are not fixed and immutable but are continually changing in response to information, challenges, and changes in the environment, a phenomenon known as *plasticity*. In some people who have been blind from an early age, brain regions usually devoted to vision are activated by sound—a dramatic example of plasticity.

- As discussed in "Culture and the Brain," *cultural neuroscientists* are finding that culture can affect the way the brain perceives, calculates, and experiences the world.

Stefania Follini (left) spent four months in a New Mexico cave (above), nine metres underground, as part of an Italian study on biological rhythms. Her only companions were a computer and two friendly mice. In the absence of clocks, natural light, or changes in temperature, she tended to stay awake for 20 to 25 hours and then sleep for 10. Because her days were longer than usual, when she emerged she thought she had been in the cave for only two months.

Thomas Ives

In most societies, external time cues abound, and people's circadian rhythms become entrained to them, following a strict 24-hour schedule. To identify endogenous rhythms, therefore, scientists must isolate volunteers from sunlight, clocks, environmental sounds, and all other cues to time. Some hardy souls have spent weeks or even months alone in caves and salt mines, linked to the outside world only by a one-way phone line and a cable transmitting physiological measurements to the surface. Nowadays, however, volunteers usually live in specially designed rooms equipped with stereo systems, comfortable furniture, and temperature controls.

When participants in these studies have been allowed to sleep, eat, and work whenever they wished, a few have lived a "day" that is much shorter or longer than 24 hours. If allowed to take daytime naps, however, most participants soon settle into a day that averages about 24.3 hours (Moore, 1997). And when people are put on an artificial 28-hour day, in an environment free of all time cues, their body temperature and certain hormone levels follow a cycle that is very close to 24 hours—24.18 hours, to be precise (Czeisler et al., 1999). These rhythms are remarkably similar in length from one person to the next. For many people, alertness, like temperature, peaks in the late afternoon and falls to a low point in the very early morning (Lavie, 2001). ((•

Listen to the **Chapter Audio** *Brain Time* in **MyPsychLab**

The Body's Clock. Circadian rhythms are controlled by a biological clock, or overall coordinator, located in a tiny teardrop-shaped cluster of cells in the hypothalamus called the **suprachiasmatic nucleus (SCN)**. Neural pathways from special receptors in the back of the eye transmit information to the SCN and allow it to respond to changes in light and dark. The SCN then sends out messages that cause the brain and body to adapt to these changes. Other clocks also exist, scattered around the body, and some may operate independently of the SCN, but for most circadian rhythms the SCN is regarded as the master pacemaker.

The SCN regulates fluctuating levels of hormones and neurotransmitters, and they in turn provide feedback that affects the SCN's functioning. For example, during the dark hours, one hormone regulated by the SCN, **melatonin**, is secreted by the

suprachiasmatic [soo-pruh-kye-az-MAT-ick] nucleus (SCN) An area of the brain containing a biological clock that governs circadian rhythms.

melatonin A hormone, secreted by the pineal gland, that is involved in the regulation of daily biological (circadian) rhythms.

pineal gland, deep within the brain. When you go to sleep in a darkened room, your melatonin level rises; when you wake up in the morning to a lightened room, it falls. Melatonin, in turn, appears to help keep the biological clock in phase with the light–dark cycle (Haimov & Lavie, 1996; Lewy et al., 1992).

Melatonin therapy has been used to treat insomnia and synchronize the disturbed sleep–wake cycles of blind people who lack light perception and whose melatonin production does not cycle normally (Sack & Lewy, 1997). But efforts to treat the insomnia of sighted people by giving them melatonin have had mixed results. Many people take over-the-counter melatonin supplements to help them sleep or to reduce jet lag, but it's unlikely that these supplements are very helpful. There are no federal standards to assure their quality, and no one has yet identified which dosages are effective (if any) or studied their long-term safety.

When the Clock Is out of Sync. Under normal conditions, the rhythms governed by the SCN are synchronized, just as watches can be synchronized. Their peaks may occur at different times, but they occur in phase with one another; if you know when one rhythm peaks, you can predict fairly well when another will. But when your normal routine changes, your circadian rhythms may be thrown out of phase with one another. Such **internal desynchronization** often occurs when people take airplane flights across several time zones. Sleep and wake patterns usually adjust quickly, but temperature and hormone cycles can take several days to return to normal. The resulting jet lag affects energy level, mental skills, and motor coordination.

Travel can be exhausting, and jet lag makes it worse.

Jeff Greenberg/PhotoEdit Inc.

Internal desynchronization also occurs when a worker must adjust to a new shift. Efficiency drops, the person feels tired and irritable, accidents become more likely, and sleep disturbances and digestive disorders may occur. For police officers, emergency room personnel, airline pilots, truck drivers, and operators of nuclear power plants, the consequences can be a matter of life and death. Even relatively small desynchronizations can have deadly effects. University of British Columbia researcher Stanley Coren (1996) studied the records of all accidental deaths in the United States over a three-year period. He found that the spring shift to daylight saving time (and the minimal sleep loss associated with it) produced a short-term increase in the likelihood of accidental death, but that the fall shift back to standard time had little effect.

One reason that scientists have not yet found a simple cure for desynchronization is that circadian rhythms are not perfectly regular in daily life. They can be affected by illness, stress, fatigue, excitement, exercise, drugs, mealtimes, and ordinary daily experiences. In research with mice, these rhythms were even influenced by diet. Mice usually sleep during the day, but putting them on a high-fat diet altered the activity of genes involved in appetite and metabolism, and the mice began waking up and eating during the day (Kohsaka et al., 2007).

internal desynchronization A state in which biological rhythms are not in phase (synchronized) with one another.

chronotype A person's pattern of sleep and wakefulness throughout a typical day.

Further, circadian rhythms differ greatly from individual to individual because of genetic differences (Hur, Bouchard, & Lykken, 1998). For example, a variation in a single gene seems to be the reason that some people are early birds (or "larks"), bouncing out of bed at the crack of dawn, while others are night owls who do their best work late at night and can't be pried out of bed until noon (Archer et al., 2003). Scientists call your identity as a lark or owl your **"chronotype."** Genetic influences may contribute to chronotypes, although early attempts to find "chronotype genes" have proven difficult to replicate (Chang et al., 2011; Osland et al., 2011). Moreover, your chronotype may change as you age: Adolescents are more likely than children and older adults to be owlish (Biss & Hasher, 2012), which may be why many teenagers have trouble adjusting to school schedules. (Schools are not designed to accommodate night owls.) You may be able to learn about your own personal pulses through careful self-observation, and you may want to try putting that information to use when planning your daily schedule.

Moods and Long-Term Rhythms

Long-term cycles have been observed in everything from the threshold for tooth pain to conception rates. Folklore holds that our moods follow similar rhythms, particularly in response to seasonal changes and, in women, to menstrual changes. But do they?

Does the Season Affect Moods?   Clinicians report that some people become depressed during particular seasons, typically winter, when periods of daylight are short—a pattern that has come to be known as **seasonal affective disorder (SAD)** (N. E. Rosenthal, 2009). During the winter months, SAD patients report feelings of sadness, lethargy, drowsiness, and a craving for carbohydrates. To counteract the presumed effects of sunless days, some physicians and therapists treat SAD patients with

> **seasonal affective disorder (SAD)**
> A controversial disorder in which a person experiences depression during the winter and an improvement of mood in the spring.

GET INVOLVED! Measuring Your Alertness Cycles

For at least three days, except when you are sleeping, keep an hourly record of your mental alertness level, using this five-point scale: 1 = extremely drowsy or mentally lethargic, 2 = somewhat drowsy or mentally lethargic, 3 = moderately alert, 4 = alert and efficient, 5 = extremely alert and efficient. Does your alertness level appear to follow a circadian rhythm, reaching a high point and a low point once every 24 hours? Or does it follow a shorter rhythm, rising and falling several times during the day? Are your cycles the same on weekends as during the week? Most important, how well does your schedule mesh with your natural fluctuations in alertness?

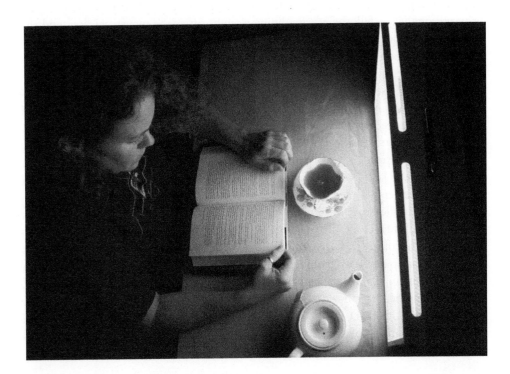

This woman is receiving light therapy for seasonal affective disorder (SAD). This type of treatment has become popular and appears to be effective. But fewer people actually have SAD than is commonly thought, and the causes remain uncertain.

Heather Rousseau/Newcom

phototherapy, having them sit in front of bright fluorescent lights at specific times of the day, usually early in the morning. In some cases, they have also begun prescribing antidepressants and other drugs.

Evaluating the actual prevalence of SAD is difficult, however. Information comes mainly from clinical case reports rather than controlled studies, and as we saw in Chapter 2, case studies have serious drawbacks. As for the effectiveness of light treatments, research on this question too has been flawed. A review of 173 light-treatment studies published between 1975 and 2003 found that only 20 had used an acceptable design and suitable controls (Golden et al., 2005). However, a meta-analysis of the data from those 20 studies did show that SAD patients' symptoms were reduced when they were exposed to either a brief period (such as 30 minutes) of bright light after waking or to light that slowly became brighter, simulating the dawn. Light therapy even helped people with mild to moderate nonseasonal depression (Pail et al., 2011) (see also Wirz-Justice et al., 2005).

Many researchers believe that the circadian rhythms of SAD patients are out of sync—that, in essence, they have a chronic form of jet lag (Lewy et al., 2006). Some researchers have concluded that SAD patients must have some abnormality in the way they produce or respond to melatonin. For example, in one study, SAD patients produced melatonin for about half an hour longer at night in the winter than in the summer, whereas control subjects showed no such seasonal pattern (Wehr et al., 2001). However, why would light therapy also help some people with *non*seasonal cases of depression? True cases of SAD may in fact have a biological basis, but the evidence to date remains inconclusive. When people get the winter blues, the reason could also be that they hate cold weather, are physically inactive, do not get outside much, or feel lonely during the winter holidays.

Does the Menstrual Cycle Affect Moods? Controversy has persisted about another long-term rhythm, the female menstrual cycle, which occurs, on average, every 28 days. During the first half of this cycle, an increase in the hormone estrogen causes the lining of the uterus to thicken in preparation for a possible pregnancy. At mid-cycle, the ovaries release a mature egg, or ovum. Afterward, the ovarian sac that contained the egg begins to produce progesterone, which helps prepare the uterine lining to receive the egg. Then, if conception does not occur, estrogen and progesterone levels fall, the uterine lining sloughs off as the menstrual flow, and the cycle begins again. The interesting question for psychologists is whether these physical changes are correlated with emotional or intellectual changes, as folklore and tradition would have us believe.

Many people seem to think so. In the 1970s, a vague cluster of physical and emotional symptoms—including fatigue, headache, irritability, and depression—associated with the days preceding menstruation came to be thought of as an illness and was given a label: *"premenstrual syndrome" ("PMS")* (Parlee, 1994). Since then, most laypeople, doctors, and psychiatrists have assumed, uncritically, that many women "suffer" from PMS or from its supposedly more extreme and debilitating version, "premenstrual dysphoric disorder" ("PMDD").

What does the evidence actually show? Many women do have *physical* symptoms associated with menstruation, including cramps, breast tenderness, and water retention, although women vary tremendously in this regard. And of course these physical symptoms can make some women grumpy or unhappy, just as pain can make men grumpy or unhappy. But *emotional* symptoms associated with menstruation—notably, irritability and depression—are pretty rare, which is why we put "PMS" in quotation marks. Just as with SAD, more people claim to have symptoms than actually do. In reality, fewer than 5% of all women have such symptoms predictably over their cycles (Brooks-Gunn, 1986; Reid, 1991; Walker, 1994).

Recite & Review

Recite: It's time to say out loud everything you can remember about *biological rhythms, entrainment, endogenous cues, circadian rhythms, suprachiasmatic nucleus (SCN), melatonin, internal desynchronization, chronotype,* and *seasonal affective disorder.*

Review: Next, go back and read this section again.

Now take this *Quick Quiz:*

1. The functioning of the biological clock governing circadian rhythms is affected by the hormone _____.

2. Jet lag occurs because of _____.

3. For most women, the days before menstruation are reliably associated with (a) depression, (b) irritability, (c) elation, (d) creativity, (e) none of these, (f) a and b.

Answers:

1. melatonin 2. internal desynchronization 3. e

Learning Objectives

5 Summarize the five stages of sleep.

6 Describe what happens when we go too long without enough sleep.

7 List the mental benefits of sleep.

The Rhythms of Sleep

Perhaps the most perplexing of all our biological rhythms is the one governing sleep and wakefulness. Sleep, after all, puts us at risk: Muscles that are usually ready to respond to danger relax, and one's senses grow dull. So why is sleep such a profound necessity?

The Stages of Sleep

Let's start with some of the changes that occur in the brain during sleep. Until the early 1950s, little was known about these changes. Then a breakthrough occurred in the laboratory of physiologist Nathaniel Kleitman. He had given one of his graduate students, Eugene Aserinsky, the tedious task of finding out whether the slow, rolling eye movements that characterize the onset of sleep continue throughout the night. To both men's surprise, eye movements did occur but they were rapid, not slow (Aserinsky & Kleitman, 1955). Using electroencephalography (EEG) to measure the brain's electrical activity (see Chapter 4), these researchers, along with another of Kleitman's students, William Dement, were able to correlate the rapid eye movements with changes in sleepers' brain-wave patterns (Dement, 1992). Adult volunteers were soon spending their nights sleeping in laboratories while scientists measured changes in their brain activity, muscle tension, breathing, and other physiological responses.

As a result of this research, today we know that during sleep, periods of **rapid eye movement (REM) sleep** alternate with periods of fewer eye movements, or *non-REM (NREM) sleep,* in a cycle that recurs every 90 minutes or so. The REM periods last from a few minutes to as long as an hour, averaging about 20 minutes in length. Whenever they begin, the pattern of electrical activity from the sleeper's brain changes to resemble that of alert wakefulness. Non-REM periods are themselves divided into distinct stages, each associated with a particular brain-wave pattern (see Figure 5.1).

rapid eye movement (REM) sleep Sleep periods characterized by eye movement, loss of muscle tone, and dreaming.

FIGURE 5.1 Brain-Wave Patterns during Wakefulness and Sleep
Most types of brain waves are present throughout sleep, but different ones predominate at different stages.

When you first climb into bed, close your eyes, and relax, your brain emits bursts of *alpha waves*. On an EEG recording, alpha waves have a regular, slow rhythm and a high amplitude (height). Gradually, these waves slow down even further, and you pass through four stages, each deeper than the previous one:

Stage 1. Your brain waves become small and irregular, and you feel yourself drifting on the edge of consciousness, in a state of light sleep. If awakened, you may recall fantasies or a few visual images.

Stage 2. Your brain emits occasional short bursts of rapid, high-peaking waves called *sleep spindles*. Minor noises probably won't disturb you.

Stage 3. In addition to the waves that are characteristic of stage 2, your brain occasionally emits *delta waves*, very slow waves with very high peaks. Your breathing and pulse have slowed down, your muscles are relaxed, and you are hard to rouse.

Stage 4. Delta waves have now largely taken over, and you are in deep sleep. It will probably take vigorous shaking or a loud noise to awaken you. Oddly, though, if you walk in your sleep, this is when you are likely to do so. No one yet knows what causes sleepwalking, which occurs more often in children than adults, but it seems to involve unusual patterns of delta-wave brain activity Bassetti et al., 2000).

This sequence of stages takes about 30 to 45 minutes. Then you move back up the ladder from stage 4 to 3 to 2 to 1. At that point, about 70 to 90 minutes after the onset of sleep, something peculiar happens. Stage 1 does not turn into drowsy wakefulness, as one might expect. Instead, your brain begins to emit long bursts of very rapid, somewhat irregular waves. Your heart rate increases, your blood pressure rises, and your breathing speeds up and becomes more irregular. Small twitches in your face and fingers may occur. In men, the penis becomes somewhat erect as vascular tissue relaxes

Because cats sleep up to 80% of the time, it is easy to catch them in the various stages of slumber. A cat in non-REM sleep (left) remains upright, but during the REM phase (right), its muscles go limp and it flops onto its side.

Left: Alamy. Right: Vera Kailova/Shutterstock.

and blood fills the genital area faster than it exits. In women, the clitoris enlarges and vaginal lubrication increases. At the same time, most skeletal muscles go limp, preventing your aroused brain from producing physical movement. You have entered the realm of REM. ✳

Because the brain is extremely active while the body is entirely inactive, REM sleep has also been called "paradoxical sleep." It is during these periods that vivid dreams are most likely to occur. People report dreams when they are awakened from non-REM sleep, too, but non-REM dreams tend to be shorter, less vivid, and more realistic than REM dreams, except in the hour or so before a person wakes up in the morning.

Occasionally, as the sleeper wakes up, a curious phenomenon occurs. The person emerges from REM sleep before the muscle paralysis characteristic of that stage has entirely disappeared, and becomes aware of an inability to move. About 30% of the general population has experienced at least one such episode, and about 5% have had a "waking dream" in this state. Their eyes are open, but what they "see" are dreamlike hallucinations, most often shadowy figures. They may even "see" a ghost or space alien sitting on their beds or hovering in a hallway. Some people interpret this experience literally and come to believe they have been visited by aliens or are being haunted by ghosts (Clancy, 2005; McNally, 2003).

REM and non-REM sleep continue to alternate throughout the night. As the hours pass, stages 3 and 4 tend to shorten or even disappear and REM periods tend to lengthen and occur closer together (see Figure 5.2). This pattern explains why you are likely to be dreaming when the alarm clock goes off in the morning. But the cycles are far from regular. An individual may bounce directly from stage 4 back to stage 2 or go from REM to stage 2 and then back to REM. Also, the time between REM and non-REM is highly variable, differing from person to person and also within any given individual.

The reasons for REM sleep are still controversial. If you wake people up every time they lapse into REM sleep, nothing dramatic will happen. When finally allowed to sleep normally, however, they will spend a longer time than usual in the REM phase, and it will be hard to rouse them. Electrical brain activity associated with REM may burst through into non-REM sleep and even into wakefulness, as if the person is making up for something he or she had been deprived of.

Some researchers have proposed that this "something" is connected with dreaming, but that idea has problems. For one thing, in rare cases, brain-damaged patients have lost the capacity to dream, yet they continue to show the normal sleep stages, including REM (Bischof & Bassetti, 2004). Moreover,

✳ **Explore** the **Concept**
Virtual Brain: Sleep and Waking
in **MyPsychLab**

THINKING CRITICALLY

Consider other interpretations.

In a state between sleeping and waking, some people have thought they've seen a ghost or a visitor from space in their bedroom—a pretty scary experience. What other explanation is possible?

FIGURE 5.2 A Typical Night's Sleep for a Young Adult
In this graph, the thin horizontal red bars represent time spent in REM sleep. REM periods tend to lengthen as the night wears on, but stages 3 and 4, which dominate during non-REM sleep early in the night, may disappear as morning approaches (from Kelly, 1981).

Whatever your age, sometimes the urge to sleep is irresistible, especially because in fast-paced modern societies, many people—even young children—do not get as much sleep as they need.

Left: Lee Thompson/123RF. Right: Earl Roberge/ Science Source.

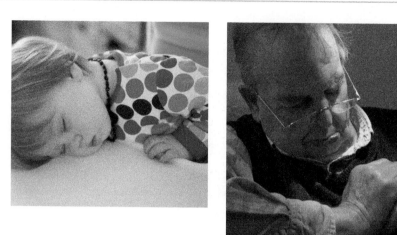

although all mammals experience REM sleep—the only known exceptions are the bottlenose dolphin and the porpoise—it seems unlikely that rats and anteaters have the cognitive abilities required to construct dreams. According to one well-known dream researcher, "no one, but no one, has been able to come up with a convincing explanation for REM sleep" (G. William Domhoff, personal communication).

Why We Sleep

Generally speaking, sleep appears to provide a time-out period, so that the body can eliminate waste products from muscles, repair cells, conserve or replenish energy stores, strengthen the immune system, or recover abilities lost during the day. When we do not get enough sleep, our bodies operate abnormally. For example, levels of hormones necessary for normal muscle development and proper immune system functioning decline (Leproult, Van Reeth, et al., 1997).

Although most people can still get along reasonably well after a day or two of sleeplessness, sleep deprivation that lasts for four days or longer is quite uncomfortable, and soon becomes unbearable. In animals, forced sleeplessness leads to infections and eventually death, and the same seems to be true for people. In one tragic case, a 51-year-old man abruptly began to lose sleep. After sinking deeper and deeper into an exhausted stupor, he developed a lung infection and died. An autopsy showed that he had lost almost all of the large neurons in two areas of the thalamus that have been linked to sleep and hormonal circadian rhythms (Lugaresi et al., 1986). ◉

◉⎯⎡**Watch** the **Video**
The Basics: Rhythms of Consciousness in **MyPsychLab**

The Mental Consequences of Sleeplessness. Sleep is also necessary for normal *mental* functioning. Chronic sleep deprivation increases levels of the stress hormone cortisol, which may damage or impair brain cells that are necessary for learning and memory (Leproult, Copinschi, et al., 1997). Also, new brain cells may either fail to develop or may mature abnormally (Guzman-Marin et al., 2005). Perhaps in part because of such damage, after the loss of even a single night's sleep, mental flexibility, attention, and creativity all suffer. After several days of staying awake, people may even begin to have hallucinations and delusions (Dement, 1978).

Of course, sleep deprivation rarely reaches that point, but people frequently suffer milder versions. According to Statistics Canada, 3.3 million Canadians (about one out of seven people over the age of 15) are plagued by chronic insomnia—difficulty falling or staying asleep (Statistics Canada, 2005). Insomnia can result from worry and anxiety, psychological problems, physical problems such as arthritis, and irregular or overly demanding work and study schedules. The result can be grogginess the next day. In a Canadian study of insomnia, Laval University's Charles Morin followed almost 400 insomniacs undergoing treatment for the condition. More than half the group

The Riddle of Hypnosis

For many years, stage hypnotists, "past-lives channellers," and some psychotherapists have been reporting that they can "age regress" hypnotized people to earlier years or even earlier centuries. Some therapists claim that hypnosis helps their patients accurately retrieve long-buried memories, and a few even claim that hypnosis has helped their patients recall alleged abductions by extraterrestrials. What are we to make of all this?

Hypnosis is a procedure in which a practitioner suggests changes in the sensations, perceptions, thoughts, feelings, or behaviour of the participant (Kirsch & Lynn, 1995). The participant, in turn, tries to alter his or her cognitive processes in accordance with the hypnotist's suggestions (Nash & Nadon, 1997). Hypnotic suggestions typically involve performance of an action ("Your arm will slowly rise"), an inability to perform an act ("You will be unable to bend your arm"), or an experience of distorted perception or memory ("You will feel no pain," "You will forget being hypnotized until I give you a signal"). People usually report that their response to a suggestion feels involuntary, as if it happened without their willing it.

To induce hypnosis, the hypnotist typically suggests that the person being hypnotized feels relaxed, is getting sleepy, and feels the eyelids getting heavier and heavier. In a singsong or monotonous voice, the hypnotist assures the participant that he or she is sinking "deeper and deeper." Sometimes the hypnotist has the person concentrate on a colour or a small object, or on certain bodily sensations. People who have been hypnotized report that the focus of attention turns outward, toward the hypnotist's voice. They sometimes compare the experience to being totally absorbed in a good book, play, or favourite piece of music. Almost always the hypnotized person remains fully aware of what is happening and remembers the experience later, unless explicitly instructed to forget it—and even then, the memory can be restored by a prearranged signal.

Because hypnosis has been used for everything from parlour tricks and stage shows to medical and psychological treatments, it is important to understand just what this procedure can and cannot achieve. We will begin with a general look at the major findings on hypnosis; then we will consider two leading explanations of hypnotic effects.

hypnosis A procedure in which the practitioner suggests changes in the sensations, perceptions, thoughts, feelings, or behaviour of the participant.

The Nature of Hypnosis

Since the late 1960s, thousands of articles on hypnosis have appeared. Based on controlled laboratory and clinical research studies, most researchers agree on the following points (Kirsch & Lynn, 1995; Nash, 2001; Nash & Nadon, 1997):

Watch the **Video**
Thinking Like a Psychologist: The Uses and Limitations of Hypnosis
in **MyPsychLab**

1 **Hypnotic responsiveness depends more on the efforts and qualities of the person being hypnotized than on the skill of the hypnotist.** Some people are more responsive to hypnosis than others, but why they are is unknown. Surprisingly, hypnotic susceptibility is unrelated to general personality traits such as gullibility, trust, submissiveness, or conformity (Nash & Nadon, 1997). And it is only weakly related to the ability to become easily absorbed in activities and the world of imagination (Council, Kirsch, & Grant, 1996; Green & Lynn, 2010; Nash & Nadon, 1997).

2 **Hypnotized people cannot be forced to do things against their will.** Like drunkenness, hypnosis can be used to justify letting go of inhibitions ("I know this looks silly but, after all, I'm hypnotized"). Hypnotized individuals may even comply with a suggestion to do something that looks embarrassing or dangerous. But the individual is choosing to turn responsibility over to the hypnotist and to cooperate with the hypnotist's suggestions (Lynn, Rhue, & Weekes, 1990). There is no evidence that hypnotized people will do anything that actually violates their morals or that constitutes a real danger to themselves or others (Laurence & Perry, 1988).

during times of crisis. Findings on the dreams of divorced people support this view.

- The *cognitive approach to dreams* holds that they are simply a modification of the cognitive activity that goes on when we are awake. The difference is that during sleep we are cut off from sensory input from the world and our bodily movements, so our thoughts tend to be more diffuse and unfocused. This explanation is supported by research on the content of dreams and changes in children's dreams as they mature cognitively.

- The *activation–synthesis theory* of dreaming holds that dreams occur when the cortex tries to make sense of, or interpret, spontaneous neural firing initiated in the pons. The resulting synthesis of these signals with existing knowledge and memories results in a dream. In this view, dreams do not disguise unconscious wishes, but they can reveal a person's perceptions, conflicts, and concerns.

- All the current theories of dreams have some support, and all have weaknesses. Most psychologists today accept the notion that dreams are more than incoherent ramblings of the mind, but many psychologists quarrel with psychoanalytic interpretations. Some psychologists doubt that people can solve problems during sleep. The activation–synthesis theory does not seem to explain coherent, storylike dreams or non-REM dreams. The cognitive approach is now a leading contender, but some of its specific claims remain to be tested.

The Riddle of Hypnosis

- *Hypnosis* is a procedure in which the practitioner suggests changes in a participant's sensations, perceptions, thoughts, feelings, or behaviour, and the participant tries to comply. Although hypnosis has been used successfully for many medical and psychological purposes, it does not produce special abilities. Hypnosis can sometimes improve memory for facts about real events, but it also results in confusion between facts and vividly imagined possibilities. Therefore, "hypnotically refreshed" accounts are often full of errors and pseudo memories.

- A leading explanation of hypnosis and its effects is that hypnosis involves *dissociation*, a split in consciousness. In one version of this approach, the split is between a part of consciousness that is hypnotized and a *hidden observer* that watches but does not participate. In another version, the split is between an executive-control system in the brain and other brain systems responsible for thinking and acting. Dissociation theories are consistent with modern models of the brain.

- Another leading approach, the *sociocognitive explanation*, regards hypnosis as a product of normal social and cognitive processes. In this view, hypnosis is a form of role-playing in which the hypnotized person uses active cognitive strategies, including imagination, to comply with the hypnotist's suggestions. The role is so engrossing that the person interprets it as real. Sociocognitive processes can account for the apparent age and past-life "regressions" of people under hypnosis and their reports of alien abductions: These individuals are simply playing a role based on fantasy, imagination, and suggestion.

- As we saw in Biology and *Hypnosis*, brain-scan studies are increasing our understanding of what happens in the brain during hypnosis. But it is too soon to draw any conclusions from this research about what hypnosis really is and how it works.

Consciousness-Altering Drugs

- In all cultures, people have found ways to produce altered states of consciousness. For example, *psychoactive drugs* alter cognition and emotion by acting on neurotransmitters in the brain. Most psychoactive drugs are classified as *stimulants*, *depressants*, *opiates*, or *psychedelics*, depending on their central nervous system effects and their impact on behaviour and mood. However, some common drugs, such as marijuana, fall outside these categories.

- When used frequently and in large amounts, some psychoactive drugs can damage neurons in the brain and impair learning and memory. Their use may lead to *tolerance*, in which increasing dosages are needed for the same effect, and *withdrawal* symptoms if a person tries to quit. But certain drugs, such as alcohol and marijuana, also have some health benefits when used in moderation. And the effects of Ecstasy are controversial; much of the research has been flawed, and permanent negative effects so far are unproven.

- Reactions to a psychoactive drug are influenced not only by its chemical properties but also by the user's individual condition, prior experience with the drug, environmental setting, and *mental set*—the person's expectations and motives for taking the drug. Expectations can be even more powerful than the drug itself, as shown by the "think–drink" effect. Expectations and beliefs about drugs are affected by a person's culture.

Taking Psychology with You

- People often find it difficult to distinguish drug use from drug abuse, to differentiate between heavy use and light or moderate use, and to separate issues of a drug's legality or illegality from the drug's potential dangers and benefits.

Key Terms

biological rhythm **140**

entrainment **140**

endogenous **140**

circadian rhythm **140**

suprachiasmatic nucleus (SCN) **141**

melatonin **141**

internal desynchronization **142**

chronotype **142**

seasonal affective disorder (SAD) **143**

rapid eye movement (REM) sleep **145**

sleep apnea **149**

narcolepsy **149**

REM behaviour disorder **149**

consolidation **150**

lucid dream **152**

activation–synthesis theory **154**

hypnosis **157**

dissociation **158**

psychoactive drug **163**

stimulants **164**

depressants **164**

opiates **164**

psychedelic drugs **164**

anabolic steroids **165**

tolerance **167**

withdrawal **167**

6 Sensation and Perception

Ask questions. . . be willing to wonder

Why do some people see religious images in a tortilla or a grilled cheese sandwich?

―――――

Why does having a cold make it harder to taste the flavour of food?

―――――

Why does pain sometimes persist long after the reason for it is gone?

―――――

Can subliminal messages affect what you buy and believe?

A university student reports spotting three triangular "UFOs" hovering over the highway during rush hour. An image of Jesus on a garage door draws huge crowds of people who regard the likeness with reverence. A photograph published shortly after September 11, 2001, appears to show a sinister face in smoke billowing from the doomed World Trade Center, which some people interpret as Osama bin Laden's.

We have all heard reports like these. Some of us scoff at them; others take them seriously. Are UFOs, visions of faces in everyday objects, and other strange sightings reported only by people who are silly or gullible, or do smart, savvy people see them too? If such experiences are illusions, then why are they so frequent and so detailed, and why are those who have them so confident that what they saw was real?

In this chapter, we will try to answer these questions by exploring how our senses take in information from the environment and how our brain uses this information to construct a model of the world. We will focus on two closely connected sets of processes that enable us to know what is happening both inside our bodies and in the world beyond our own skins. The first, **sensation**, is the detection of physical energy emitted or reflected by physical objects. The cells that do the detecting are located in the *sense organs*—the eyes, ears, tongue, nose, skin, and internal body tissues. Sensory processes produce an immediate awareness of sound, colour, form, and other building blocks of consciousness. Without sensation, we would lose touch—literally—with reality. But to make sense of the world impinging on our senses, we also need **perception**, a set of mental operations that organizes sensory impulses into meaningful patterns. Our sense of vision produces a two-dimensional image on the back of the eye, but we perceive the world in three dimensions. Our sense of hearing brings us the sound of a C, an E, and a G played simultaneously on the piano, but we perceive a C-major chord. Sometimes, a single sensory image produces two alternating perceptions.

Sensation and perception are the foundation of learning, thinking, and acting, and findings on these processes can often be put to practical use—for example, in the design of hearing aids and industrial robots and in the training of flight controllers, astronauts, and others who must make crucial decisions based on what they sense and perceive. An understanding of sensation and perception can also help all of us think more critically about our own experiences, because although these processes are usually accurate, sometimes they are not.

sensation The detection of physical energy emitted or reflected by physical objects; it occurs when energy in the external environment or the body stimulates receptors in the sense organs.

perception The process by which the brain organizes and interprets sensory information.

175

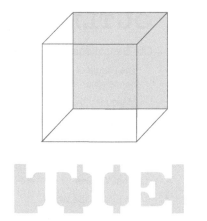

If you stare at the cube, the surface on the outside and front will suddenly be on the inside and back or vice versa, because your brain can interpret the sensory image in two different ways. The other blue-and-white drawing can also be perceived in two ways. Do you see them?

◉—Watch the **Video** *The Big Picture: Taking in the World around Us* in **MyPsychLab**

sense receptors Specialized cells that convert physical energy in the environment or the body to electrical energy that can be transmitted as nerve impulses to the brain.

Learning Objectives

1. Explain why we experience separate sensations even though they all rely on similar neural signals.

2. Describe what kind of code in the nervous system helps explain why a pinprick and a kiss feel different.

3. Detail how psychologists measure the sensitivity of our senses.

4. Describe the bias that influences whether or not you think you hear the phone ringing when you are in the shower.

5. Predict what happens when people are deprived of all external sensory stimulation.

6. Illustrate why we sometimes fail to see an object that we're looking straight at.

Our Sensational Senses

At some point you probably learned that there are five senses, corresponding to five sense organs: vision (eyes), hearing (ears), taste (tongue), touch (skin), and smell (nose). Actually, there are more than five senses, though scientists disagree about the exact number. The skin, which is the organ of touch or pressure, also senses heat, cold, and pain, not to mention itching and tickling. The ear, which is the organ of hearing, also contains receptors that account for a sense of balance. The skeletal muscles contain receptors responsible for a sense of bodily movement.

All of our senses evolved to help us survive. Even pain, which causes so much human misery, is an indispensable part of our evolutionary heritage, for it alerts us to illness and injury. People who are born with a rare condition that prevents them from feeling the usual hurts and aches of life are susceptible to burns, bruises, and broken bones, and they often die at an early age because they can't take advantage of pain's warning signals. ◉

Sensory experiences contribute immeasurably to our quality of life, even when they are not directly helping us stay alive. They entertain us, amuse us, soothe us, inspire us. If we really pay attention to our senses, said poet William Wordsworth, we can "see into the life of things" and hear "the still, sad music of humanity."

The Riddle of Separate Sensations

Sensation begins with the **sense receptors,** cells located in the sense organs. The receptors for smell, pressure, pain, and temperature are extensions (dendrites) of sensory neurons (see Chapter 4). The receptors for vision, hearing, and taste are specialized cells separated from sensory neurons by synapses.

When the sense receptors detect an appropriate stimulus—light, mechanical pressure, or chemical molecules—they convert the energy of the stimulus into electrical impulses that travel along nerves to the brain. Sense receptors are like military scouts who scan the terrain for signs of activity. These scouts cannot make many decisions on their own. They must transmit what they learn to field officers—sensory neurons in the peripheral nervous system. The field officers in turn must report to generals at a command centre—the cells of the brain. The generals are responsible for analyzing the reports, combining information brought in by different scouts, and deciding what it all means.

The "field officers" in the sensory system—the sensory nerves—all use exactly the same form of communication, a neural impulse. It is as if they must all send their messages on a bongo drum and can only go "boom." How, then, are we able to experience so many different kinds of sensations? The answer is that the nervous system encodes the messages. One kind of code, which is *anatomical*, was first

GET INVOLVED! Now You See It, Now You Don't

Sensation depends on change and contrast in the environment. Hold your hand over one eye and stare at the dot in the middle of the circle on the right. You should have no trouble maintaining an image of the circle. However, if you do the same with the circle on the left, the image will fade. The gradual change from light to dark does not provide enough contrast to keep your visual receptors firing at a steady rate. The circle reappears only if you close and reopen your eye or shift your gaze to the X.

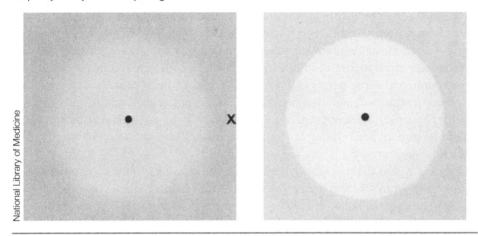

for example, most of the time you have no need to feel your watch sitting on your wrist. Sometimes, however, adaptation can be hazardous, as when you no longer smell a gas leak that you noticed when you first entered the kitchen.

We never completely adapt to extremely intense stimuli—a terrible toothache, the odour of ammonia, the heat of the desert sun. And we rarely adapt completely to visual stimuli, whether they are weak or intense. Eye movements, voluntary and involuntary, cause the location of an object's image on the back of the eye to keep changing, so visual receptors don't have a chance to "fatigue." But in the laboratory, researchers can stabilize the image of a simple pattern, such as a line, at a particular point on the back of a person's eye. They use an ingenious device consisting of a tiny projector mounted on a contact lens. Although the eyeball moves, the image of the object stays focused on the same receptors. In minutes, the image begins to disappear.

What would happen if our senses adapted to *most* incoming stimuli? Would we sense nothing, or would the brain substitute its own images for the sensory experiences no longer available by way of the sense organs? In early studies of **sensory deprivation** conducted at McGill University, researchers studied this question by isolating male volunteers from all patterned sight and sound. A translucent visor restricted vision, a U-shaped pillow and noise from an air conditioner and fan restricted hearing, and cotton gloves and cardboard cuffs restricted touch. The volunteers took brief breaks to eat and use the bathroom, but otherwise they lay in bed, doing nothing. The results were dramatic. Within a few hours, many of the men felt edgy. Some were so disoriented that they quit the

sensory deprivation The absence of normal levels of sensory stimulation.

THINKING CRITICALLY

Don't oversimplify.

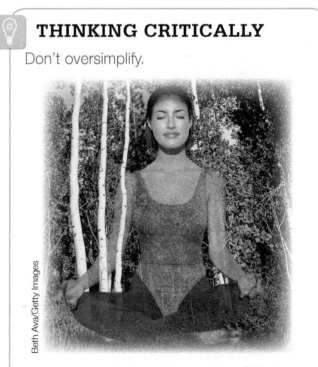

Is sensory deprivation pleasant or unpleasant? The answer isn't "either–or"; it depends on the circumstances and how you interpret your situation. Being isolated against your will can be terrifying, but many people have found meditating alone, away from all sights and sounds, to be calming and pleasant.

In his films, famed director Alfred Hitchcock always appeared briefly in one of the scenes, but few noticed him even when they were aware he would appear—an instance of inattentional blindness.

A.F. ARCHIVE/Alamy

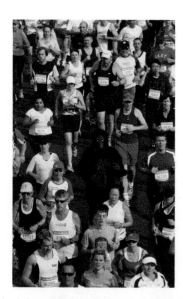

Hard though it is to believe, even a person in a gorilla suit may go unnoticed if people's attention is elsewhere.

Lisa Maree Williams/Getty Images

⊙▶ Simulate the Experiment
Selective Attention in **MyPsychLab**

selective attention The focusing of attention on selected aspects of the environment and the blocking out of others.

inattentional blindness Failure to consciously perceive something you are looking at because you are not attending to it.

study the first day. Those who stayed longer became confused, restless, and grouchy. Many reported bizarre visions, such as a squadron of squirrels or a procession of marching eyeglasses. It was as though they were having the kinds of "waking dreams" described in Chapter 5. Few were willing to remain in the study for more than two or three days (Heron, 1957).

According to research conducted at the University of British Columbia, the notion that sensory deprivation is unpleasant or even dangerous turned out to be an oversimplification (Suedfeld, 1975). In many of the studies, the experimental procedures themselves probably aroused anxiety: Participants were told about "panic buttons" and were asked to sign "release from legal liability" forms. Later research, using better methods, showed that hallucinations are less dramatic and less disorienting than at first thought. In fact, many people enjoy limited periods of deprivation, and some perceptual and intellectual abilities actually improve. Your response to sensory deprivation depends on your expectations and interpretations of what is happening. Reduced sensation can be scary if you are locked in a room for an indefinite period, but relaxing if you have retreated to that room voluntarily for a little time out—at, say, a luxury spa or a monastery.

Still, it is clear that the human brain requires a minimum amount of sensory stimulation in order to function normally. This need may help explain why people who live alone often keep the radio or television set running continuously and why prolonged solitary confinement is used as a form of punishment or even torture.

Sensing without Perceiving

If too little stimulation can be bad for you, so can too much, because it can lead to fatigue and mental confusion. If you have ever felt exhausted, nervous, and headachy after a day crammed with activities, you know firsthand about sensory overload. When people find themselves in a state of overload, they often cope by blocking out unimportant sights and sounds and focusing only on those they find interesting or useful. Psychologists have called this the "cocktail party phenomenon" because, at a noisy cocktail party, a person typically focuses on just one conversation, ignoring other voices, the clink of ice cubes, music, and bursts of laughter across the room.

Even when overload is not a problem, our capacity for **selective attention**—the ability to focus on some parts of the environment and block out others—protects us from being overwhelmed by countless sensory signals that are constantly impinging on our sense receptors. Competing sensory messages all enter the nervous system, however, and they get some processing, enabling the person to pick up anything important, such as her own name spoken by someone several metres away.

That's the good news. The bad news is that selective attention, by its very nature, causes us to miss much that is going on around us; as a result, our conscious awareness of the environment is much less complete than most people think. We may even fail to consciously register objects that we're looking straight at, a phenomenon known as **inattentional blindness**. We look, but we do not see (Mack, 2003). When people are shown a video of a ball-passing game and are asked to count the number of passes, they will often miss something as seemingly obvious as a man in a gorilla suit walking slowly through the ball court and thumping his chest (Simons & Chabris, 1999)! ⊙▶

Selective attention, then, is a mixed blessing. It protects us from overload and allows us to focus on what's important, but it also deprives us of sensory information that we may need. That could be disastrous if you are so focused on listening to a voice on your cellphone while you are driving that you fail to see a pedestrian crossing the street in front of you.

Recite & Review

Recite: Say out loud everything you can remember about *sensation, perception, sense receptors,* the *doctrine of specific nerve energies, synesthesia,* the *absolute threshold,* the *difference threshold, signal-detection theory, sensory adaption, sensory deprivation, selective attention,* and *inattentional blindness.*

Review: Time to go back and read this section again, concentrating on what you couldn't remember.

✓•―**Study** and **Review**
in **MyPsychLab**

Quick Quiz:

If you are not overloaded, try answering these questions.

1. Even on the clearest night, some stars cannot be seen by the naked eye because they are below the viewer's _____ threshold.
2. If you jump into a cold lake but moments later the water no longer seems so cold, sensory _____ has occurred.
3. If you are immobilized in a hospital bed, with no roommate and no TV or radio, and you feel edgy and disoriented, you may be suffering the effects of _____.
4. During a break from your job as a waiter, you are so engrossed in a book that you fail to notice the clattering of dishes or orders being called out to the cook. This is an example of _____.
5. In real-life detection tasks, is it better to be a "naysayer" or a "yea-sayer"?

Answers:

1. absolute 2. adaptation 3. sensory deprivation 4. selective attention 5. Neither; it depends on the consequences of a "miss" or a "false alarm" and the probability of an event occurring. You might want to be a yea-sayer if you are expecting a call about a job interview, and you don't think you hear the phone ringing, and you are on your way to a job interview. You might want to be a naysayer if you are just out the door, you think you hear the phone ringing, and you are expecting a call about a job interview and don't want to be late.

Learning Objectives

7. List how the physical characteristics of light waves correspond to the psychological dimensions of vision.
8. Identify the basics of how the eye works, and why the eye is not a camera.
9. Describe how we see colours, and why we can describe a colour as bluish green but not as reddish green.
10. Tell how we know how far away things are.
11. Articulate why we see objects as stable even though sensory stimulation from the object is constantly changing.
12. Explain why perceptual illusions are valuable to psychologists.

Vision

Vision is the most frequently studied of all the senses, and with good reason. More information about the external world comes to us through our eyes than through any other sense organ. (Perhaps that is why people say "I see what you mean" instead of "I hear what you mean.") Because we evolved to be most active in the daytime, we are equipped to take advantage of the sun's illumination. Animals that are active at night tend to rely more heavily on hearing.

What We See

The stimulus for vision is light; even cats, raccoons, and other creatures famous for their ability to get around in the dark need some light to see. Visible light comes from the sun and other stars and from light bulbs, and it is also reflected off objects. Light

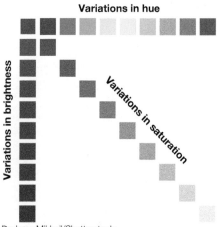

Dudarev Mikhail/Shutterstock

hue The dimension of visual experience specified by colour names and related to the wavelength of light.

brightness Lightness or luminance; the dimension of visual experience related to the amount of light emitted from or reflected by an object.

saturation Vividness or purity of colour; the dimension of visual experience related to the complexity of light waves.

retina Neural tissue lining the back of the eyeball's interior, which contains the receptors for vision.

rods Visual receptors that respond to dim light.

cones Visual receptors involved in colour vision.

travels in the form of waves, and the *physical* characteristics of these waves affect three *psychological* dimensions of our visual world: hue, brightness, and saturation.

1 **Hue,** the dimension of visual experience specified by colour names, is related to the *wavelength* of light—that is, to the distance between the crests of a light wave. Shorter waves tend to be seen as violet and blue, longer ones as orange and red. (We say "tend to" because other factors also affect colour perception, as we will see later.) The sun produces white light, a mixture of all the visible wavelengths. Sometimes, drops of moisture in the air act as a prism: They separate the sun's white light into the colours of the visible spectrum, and we are treated to a rainbow.

2 **Brightness** is the dimension of visual experience related to the amount, or *intensity*, of the light an object emits or reflects. Intensity corresponds to the amplitude (maximum height) of the wave. Generally speaking, the more light an object reflects, the brighter it appears. However, brightness is also affected by wavelength: Yellows appear brighter than reds and blues when physical intensities are actually equal.

3 **Saturation** (colourfulness) is the dimension of visual experience related to the *complexity* of light—that is, to the wideness or narrowness of the range of wavelengths. When light contains only a single wavelength, it is said to be "pure," and the resulting colour is said to be completely saturated. At the other extreme is white light, which lacks any colour and is completely unsaturated. In nature, pure light is extremely rare. Usually, we sense a mixture of wavelengths, and we see colours that are duller and paler than completely saturated ones.

An Eye on the World

Light enters the visual system through the eye, a wonderfully complex and delicate structure. As you read this section, examine Figure 6.2. Notice that the front part of the eye is covered by the transparent *cornea*. The cornea protects the eye and bends incoming light rays toward a lens located behind it. A camera lens focuses incoming light by moving closer to or farther from the shutter opening. However, the lens of the eye works by subtly changing its shape, becoming more or less curved to focus light from objects that are close or far away. The amount of light that gets into the eye is controlled by muscles in the *iris*, the part of the eye that gives it colour. The iris surrounds the round opening, or *pupil*, of the eye. When you enter a dim room, the pupil widens, or dilates, to let more light in. When you emerge into bright sunlight, the pupil gets smaller, contracting to allow in less light. You can see these changes by watching your eyes in a mirror as you change the lighting. ✳

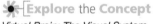 Explore the Concept
Virtual Brain: The Visual System in **MyPsychLab**

FIGURE 6.2 Major Structures of the Eye
Light passes through the pupil and lens and is focused on the retina at the back of the eye. The point of sharpest vision is at the fovea.

The visual receptors are located in the back of the eye, or **retina**. (The retina also contains special cells that communicate information about light and dark to the brain area that regulates biological rhythms, as discussed in Chapter 5.) In a developing embryo, the retina forms from tissue that projects out from the brain, not from tissue destined to form other parts of the eye; thus, the retina is actually an extension of the brain. As Figure 6.3 shows, when the lens of the eye focuses light on the retina, the result is an upside-down image (which can actually be seen with an instrument used by eye specialists). Light from the top of the visual field stimulates light-sensitive receptor cells in the bottom part of the retina, and vice versa. The brain interprets this upside-down pattern of stimulation as something that is right side up.

About 120 to 125 million receptors in the retina are long and narrow and are called **rods**. Another 7 or 8 million receptors are cone-shaped and are called, appropriately enough, **cones**. The centre of the retina, or *fovea*, where vision is sharpest, contains only cones, clustered densely together. From the centre to the periphery, the ratio of rods to cones increases, and the outer edges contain virtually no cones.

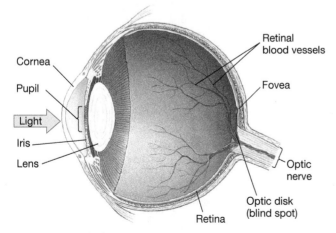

Cornea
Pupil
Light
Iris
Lens
Retinal blood vessels
Fovea
Optic nerve
Optic disk (blind spot)
Retina

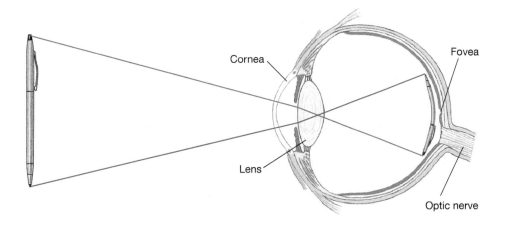

FIGURE 6.3 The Retinal Image
When we look at an object, the light pattern on the retina is upside down. René Descartes (1596–1650) was probably the first person to demonstrate this fact. He cut a piece from the back of an ox's eye and replaced the piece with paper. When he held the eye up to the light, he saw an upside-down image of the room on the paper!

Rods are more sensitive to light than cones are. They enable us to see in dim light and at night. (Cats see well in dim light in part because they have a high proportion of rods.) Because rods occupy the outer edges of the retina, they also handle peripheral (side) vision. But rods cannot distinguish different wavelengths of light so they are not sensitive to colour, which is why it is often hard to distinguish colours clearly in dim light. The cones, on the other hand, are differentially sensitive to specific wavelengths of light and allow us to see colours. However, the cones need much more light than rods do to respond, so they don't help us much when we are trying to find a seat in a darkened movie theatre (see Review 6.1).

We have all noticed that it takes some time for our eyes to adjust fully to dim illumination. This process of **dark adaptation** involves chemical changes in the rods and cones. The cones adapt quickly, within 10 minutes or so, but they never become very sensitive to the dim illumination. The rods adapt more slowly, taking 20 minutes or longer, but are ultimately much more sensitive. After the first phase of adaptation, you can see better but not well; after the second phase, your vision is as good as it will ever get.

Rods and cones are connected by synapses to *bipolar neurons*, which in turn communicate with neurons called **ganglion cells** (see Figure 6.4). The axons of the ganglion cells converge to form the *optic nerve*, which carries information out through the back of the eye and on to the brain. Where the optic nerve leaves the eye, at the *optic disk*, there are no rods or cones. The absence of receptors produces a blind spot in the field of vision. Normally, we are unaware of the blind spot because (1) the image projected on the spot is hitting a different, "non-blind" spot in the other eye; (2) our eyes move so fast that we can pick up the complete image; and (3) the brain fills in the gap. You can find your blind spot by doing the Get Involved exercise on the next page.

dark adaptation A process by which visual receptors become maximally sensitive to dim light.

ganglion cells Neurons in the retina of the eye that gather information from receptor cells (by way of intermediate bipolar cells); their axons make up the optic nerve.

Why the Visual System Is Not a Camera

Although the eye is often compared to a camera, the visual system, unlike a camera, does not passively record the external world. Neurons in the visual system actively build up a picture of the world by detecting its meaningful features.

REVIEW 6.1   Differences between Rods and Cones

	Rods	Cones
How many?	120–125 million	7–8 million
Where most concentrated?	Periphery of retina	Centre (fovea) of retina
How sensitive?	High sensitivity	Low sensitivity
Sensitive to colour?	No	Yes

Light

Light

Light

Ganglion cells

Bipolar neurons

Direction of neural impulse

Rod
Cone

Photoreceptor cells

Optic disk

Optic nerve (to brain)

Direction of neural impulse

Retina

Eyeball

Optic nerve

FIGURE 6.4 The Structures of the Retina

For clarity, all cells in this drawing are greatly exaggerated in size. In order to reach the receptors for vision (the rods and cones), light must pass through the ganglion and bipolar cells as well as the blood vessels that nourish them (not shown). Normally, we do not see the shadow cast by this network of cells and blood vessels because the shadow always falls on the same place on the retina, and such stabilized images are not sensed. But when an eye doctor shines a moving light into your eye, the treelike shadow of the blood vessels falls on different regions of the retina and you may see it—a rather eerie experience.

feature detector cells Cells in the visual cortex that are sensitive to specific features of the environment.

Cases of brain damage support the idea that particular systems of brain cells are highly specialized. One man's injury left him unable to identify ordinary objects, which he said often looked like "blobs." However, he had no trouble with faces, even when they were incomplete or upside down. When shown this painting, he could easily see the face, but he could not see the vegetables from which it was composed (Moscovitch, Winocur, & Behrmann, 1997).

Erich Lessing/Art Resource

Ganglion cells and neurons in the thalamus of the brain respond to simple features in the environment, such as spots of light and dark. But in mammals, special **feature detector cells** in the visual cortex respond to more complex features. This fact was first demonstrated by David Hubel and Torsten Wiesel (1962, 1968) who painstakingly recorded impulses from individual cells in the brains of cats and monkeys. In 1981, they received a Nobel Prize for their work. Hubel and Wiesel found that different neurons were sensitive to different patterns projected on a screen in front of the animal's eyes. Most cells responded maximally to moving or stationary lines that were oriented in a particular direction and located in a particular part of the visual field. One type of cell might fire most rapidly in response to a horizontal line in the lower right part of the visual field, another to a diagonal line at a specific angle in the upper left part of the visual field. In the real world, such features make up the boundaries and edges of objects.

GET INVOLVED! Find Your Blind Spot

A blind spot exists where the optic nerve leaves the back of your eye. Find the blind spot in your left eye by closing your right eye and looking at the magician. Then slowly move the book toward and away from yourself. The rabbit should disappear when the book is 23 to 30 centimetres from your eye.

Since this pioneering work was done, scientists have found that other cells in the visual system have more complex specialties, such as bull's eyes and spirals. Some cells in the right temporal lobe even appear to respond maximally to *face*s (Kanwisher, 2000; Ó Scalaidhe, Wilson, & Goldman-Rakic, 1997; Young & Yamane, 1992). Some scientists have concluded that evolution has equipped us with an innate *face module* in the brain. The existence of such a module could help explain why infants show a preference for looking at faces instead of images that scramble the features of a face, and why a person with brain damage may continue to recognize faces even after losing the ability to recognize other objects. In a case described by Morris Moscovitch at the University of Toronto, a patient could recognize a face made up entirely of vegetables, like the one in the painting, but he could not recognize the component vegetables (Moscovitch, Winocur, & Behrmann, 1997). ◉

A facility for deciphering faces makes evolutionary sense because it would have ensured our ancestors' ability to quickly distinguish friend from foe or, in the case of infants, mothers from strangers. However, the existence of face modules remains controversial among neuroscientists. Some think that infants' apparent preference for faces is really a preference for curved lines, or eye contact, or patterns that have more elements in the upper part (e.g., two eyes) than in the lower part (e.g., just a mouth) (Turati, 2004). Moreover, some of the brain cells that supposedly make up the face module respond to other things, too, depending on a person's experiences and interests. In one fascinating study, cells in the presumed face module fired when car buffs examined pictures of classic cars but not when they looked at pictures of exotic birds, whereas the exact opposite was true for birdwatchers (Gauthier et al., 2000). Cars, of course, do not have faces! In another study by the same researchers, cells in the "face module" fired after people were trained to distinguish among cute—but faceless—imaginary creatures called greebles (Gauthier et al., 1999) (see Figure 6.5).

Even if face modules and other specialized modules do exist, the brain cannot possibly contain a special area for every conceivable object. In general, the brain's job is to take fragmentary information about edges, angles, shapes, motion, brightness, texture, and patterns and figure out that a chair is a chair and that it is next to the dining room table. The perception of any given object probably depends on the activation of many cells in far-flung parts of the brain and on the overall pattern and rhythm of their activity (Bower, 1998).

How We See Colours

For 300 years, scientists have been trying to figure out why we see the world in living colour. We now know that different processes explain different stages of colour vision.

The Trichromatic Theory. The **trichromatic theory** (also known as the *Young-Helmholtz theory*) applies to the first level of processing, which occurs in the retina of the eye. The retina contains three basic types of cones. One type responds maximally to blue (or more precisely, to a range of wavelengths near the short end of the spectrum, which give rise to the experience of blue), another to green, and a third to red. The thousands of colours we see result from the combined activity of these three types of cones.

Total colour blindness is usually due to a genetic variation that causes cones of the retina to be absent or nonfunctional. The visual world then consists of black, white, and shades of grey. Many species of animals are totally colour blind, but the condition is extremely rare in human beings. Most "colour blind" people are actually *colour deficient*. Usually, the person

trichromatic theory A theory of colour perception that proposes three mechanisms in the visual system, each sensitive to a certain range of wavelengths; their interaction is assumed to produce all the different experiences of hue.

◉—|Watch the **Video**
Special Topics: Recognizing Faces in **MyPsychLab**

FIGURE 6.5 Greebles
Researchers trained people to recognize hypothetical "greebles" and to identify the creatures' "family" and "sex" according to subtle differences in their features. During the task, "face modules" in the participants' brains were active—yet greebles have no faces. The researchers concluded that face modules may not be responding to faces per se. Instead, they claimed that these brain areas might be specialized for distinguishing between visually similar objects within a given category. Faces happen to be visually similar (most faces contain similar features in similar places), and therefore the neural architecture for distinguishing between complex, visually similar objects might also be used for distinguishing between faces (Gauthier et al., 1999).

Greebles created by Isabel Gauthier (Vanderbilt University), Scott Yu and Michael J. Tarr

opponent-process theory A theory of colour perception that assumes that the visual system treats pairs of colours as opposing or antagonistic.

is unable to distinguish red and green; the world is painted in shades of blue, yellow, brown, and grey. In rarer instances, a person may be blind to blue and yellow and may see only reds, greens, and greys. Colour deficiency is found in about 8% of white men, 5% of Asian men, and 3% of indigenous men and black men (Sekuler & Blake, 1994). Because of the way the condition is inherited, it is rare in women.

The Opponent-Process Theory. The **opponent-process theory** applies to the second stage of colour processing, which occurs in ganglion cells in the retina and in neurons in the thalamus and visual cortex of the brain. These cells, known as *opponent-process cells*, either respond to short wavelengths but are inhibited from firing by long wavelengths, or vice versa (DeValois & DeValois, 1975). Some opponent-process cells respond in opposite fashion to red and green; that is, they fire in response to one and turn off in response to the other. Others respond in opposite fashion to blue and yellow. (A third system responds in opposite fashion to white and black and thus yields information about brightness.) The net result is a colour code that is passed along to the higher visual centres. Because this code treats red and green, and also blue and yellow, as antagonistic, we can describe a colour as bluish green or yellowish green but not as reddish green or yellowish blue. The existence of opponent-process cells in the visual system was first predicted by Ewald Hering (contradicting claims by Helmholtz), although Hering did not specify that these cells would be in the brain instead of the eye.

Opponent-process cells that are *inhibited* by a particular colour produce a burst of firing when the colour is removed, just as they would if the opposing colour were present. Similarly, cells that *fire* in response to a colour stop firing when the colour is removed, just as they would if the opposing colour were present. These facts explain why we are susceptible to seeing a *negative afterimage* when we stare at a particular hue—why we see, for instance, red after staring at green (see the Get Involved exercise below). A sort of neural rebound effect occurs: The cells that switch on or off to signal the presence of "green" send the opposite signal ("red") when the green is removed—and vice versa.

GET INVOLVED! A Change of Heart

Opponent-process cells that switch on or off in response to green send an opposite message—"red"—when the green is removed, producing a negative afterimage. Stare at the black dot in the middle of this heart for at least 20 seconds. Then shift your gaze to a white piece of paper or a white wall. Do you get a "change of heart"? You may see an image of a red heart with a blue border.

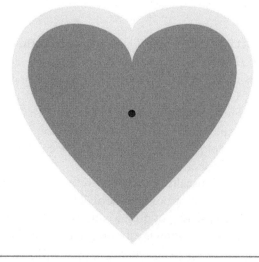

Constructing the Visual World

We do not see a retinal image; that image is merely grist for the mill of the mind, which actively interprets the image and constructs the world from the often fragmentary data of the senses. In the brain, sensory signals that give rise to vision, hearing, taste, smell, and touch are combined from moment to moment to produce a unified model of the world. This is the process of *perception*.

Form Perception. To make sense of the world, we must know where one thing ends and another begins. In vision, we must separate the teacher from the lectern; in hearing, we must separate the piano solo from the orchestral accompaniment; in taste, we must separate the marshmallow from the hot chocolate. This process of dividing up the world occurs so rapidly and effortlessly that we take it completely for granted—until we must make out objects in a heavy fog or words in the rapid-fire conversation of someone speaking a foreign language. The *Gestalt psychologists* (Max Wertheimer, Wolfgang Köhler, & Kurt Koffka) started a movement that began in Germany and was influential in the 1920s and 1930s; they were among the first to study how people organize the world visually into meaningful units and patterns. Gestalt is German for "form" or "configuration." The Gestalt psychologists' motto was "The whole is more than the sum of its parts." They observed that when we perceive something, properties emerge from the configuration as a whole that are not found in any particular component. When you watch a movie, for example, the motion you see is nowhere in the film, which consists of separate static frames projected at 24 frames per second.

One thing the Gestalt psychologists noted was that people always organize the visual field into *figure* and *ground*. The figure stands out from the rest of the environment (see Figure 6.6). Some things stand out as figure by virtue of their intensity or size; it is hard to ignore the blinding flash of a camera or a tidal wave approaching your piece of beach. The lower part of a scene tends to be seen as figure, the upper part as background (Vecera, Vogel, & Woodman, 2002). Unique objects also stand out, such as a banana in a bowl of oranges. Moving objects in an otherwise still environment, such as a shooting star, will usually be seen as figure. Indeed, it is hard to ignore a sudden change of any kind in the environment because our brains are geared to respond to change and contrast. However, selective attention—the ability to concentrate on some stimuli and to filter out others—gives us some control over what we perceive as figure and ground, and sometimes it blinds us to things we would otherwise interpret as figure, as we saw earlier.

Other **Gestalt principles** describe strategies used by the visual system to group sensory building blocks into perceptual units (Köhler, 1929; Wertheimer, 1923/1958). The Gestalt psychologists believed that these strategies are present from birth or develop automatically early in infancy as a result of maturation. Modern research, however, suggests that at least some of them depend on experience (Quinn & Bhatt, 2005). Here are a few well-known Gestalt principles:

1 **Proximity.** Things that are near each other tend to be grouped together. Thus you perceive the dots on the left on page 190 as three groups of dots, not as

Gestalt principles Principles that describe the brain's organization of sensory information into meaningful units and patterns.

FIGURE 6.6 Figure and Ground
Which do you notice first in this drawing by M. C. Escher—the fish, geese, or salamanders? It will depend on whether you see the blue, red, or gold sections as figure or ground.

M.C. Escher Company/Cordon Art, b.v.

12 separate, unrelated ones. Similarly, you perceive the pattern on the right as vertical columns of dots, not as horizontal rows:

2 **Closure.** The brain tends to fill in gaps in order to perceive complete forms. This is fortunate because we often need to decipher less-than-perfect images. The following figures are easily perceived as a triangle, a face, and the letter E, even though none of the figures is complete:

3 **Similarity.** Things that are alike in some way (for example, in colour, shape, or size) tend to be perceived as belonging together. In the figure on the left, you see the circles as forming an X. In the one on the right, you see horizontal bars rather than vertical columns because the horizontally aligned stars share the same colour:

4 **Continuity.** Lines and patterns tend to be perceived as continuing in time or space. You perceive the figure on the left as a single line partially covered by an oval, rather than as two separate lines touching an oval. In the figure on the right, you see two lines, one curved and one straight, instead of two curved and two straight lines, touching at one focal point:

Since the Gestalt principles were discovered, researchers have identified other cues that help us identify which parts of what we see form objects or scenes. But consumer products are sometimes designed with little thought for these cues, which is why it can be a major challenge to find the pause button on your DVD player's remote control or to change from AM to FM on your car radio (Bjork, 2000; Norman, 1988). Good design requires, among other things, that crucial distinctions be visually obvious. For instance, knobs and switches with different functions should differ in colour, texture, or shape, and they should stand out as figure. How would you use this information to redesign some of the products you use?

Depth and Distance Perception. Ordinarily we need to know not only *what* something is, but also *where* it is. Touch gives us this information directly, but vision does not, so we must infer an object's location by estimating its distance or depth.

To perform this remarkable feat, we rely in part on **binocular cues**—cues that require the use of two eyes. One such cue is **convergence**, the turning of the eyes

binocular cues Visual cues to depth or distance requiring two eyes.

convergence The turning inward of the eyes, which occurs when they focus on a nearby object.

inward, which occurs when they focus on a nearby object. The closer the object, the greater the convergence, as you know if you have ever tried to "cross" your eyes by looking at your own nose. As the angle of convergence changes, the corresponding muscular changes provide information to the brain about distance.

The two eyes also receive slightly different retinal images of the same object. You can prove this by holding a finger about 30 centimetres in front of your face and looking at it with only one eye at a time. Its position will appear to shift when you change eyes. Now hold up two fingers, one closer to your nose than the other. Notice that the amount of space between the two fingers appears to change when you switch eyes. The slight difference in lateral (sideways) separation between two objects as seen by the left eye and the right eye is called **retinal disparity**. Because retinal disparity increases as the distance between two objects increases, the brain can use it to infer depth and calculate distance.

Binocular cues help us estimate distances up to about 15 metres. For objects farther away, we use only **monocular cues**, cues that do not depend on using both eyes. One such cue is *interposition*: When an object is interposed between the viewer and a second object, partly blocking the view of the second object, the first object is perceived as being closer. Another monocular cue is *linear perspective:* When two lines known to be parallel appear to be coming together or converging, they imply the existence of depth. For example, if you are standing between railway tracks, they appear to converge in the distance. These and other monocular cues are illustrated on pages 192 and 193.

The perception of distance is also influenced by some factors that have nothing to do with vision, such as your emotional state, a goal you are trying to reach, and the effort necessary to reach that goal (Proffitt, 2006). Suppose you are out walking and, tired and cranky, you see an appealing coffee shop up ahead. You are likely to think it is farther away if you are wearing a heavy backpack than if you are wearing a light one, because of the increased energy it would take you to get there. Likewise, if you are asked to throw a ball into a basket, you will probably estimate the distance of that basket as farther away when the ball is heavy than when it is light. If an object is just out of reach, you may think it is nearer when you can touch it with a baton than when you can't touch it, because touching it makes it seem closer to your "personal space." And if you are looking down from a balcony, you will probably overestimate the distance to the ground if you are afraid of heights, but not if heights don't worry you.

Visual Constancies: When Seeing Is Believing. Your perceptual world would be a confusing place without still another important perceptual skill. Lighting conditions, viewing angles, and the distances of stationary objects are all continually changing as we move about, yet we rarely confuse these changes with changes in the objects themselves. This ability to perceive objects as stable or unchanging even though the sensory patterns they produce are constantly shifting is called **perceptual constancy**. The best-studied constancies are visual, and they include the following:

1 **Shape constancy.** We see objects as having a constant shape even though the shape of the retinal image produced by an object changes when our point of view changes. If you hold a Frisbee directly in front of your face, its image on the retina will be round. When you set the Frisbee on a table and back away from it, its image becomes elliptical, yet you continue to identify the Frisbee as round.

2 **Location constancy.** We perceive stationary objects as remaining in the same place even though the retinal image moves about as we move our eyes, heads, and bodies. As you drive along the highway, telephone poles and trees fly by—on your retina. But you know that these objects do not move on their own, and you also know that your body is moving, so you perceive the poles and trees as staying put.

retinal disparity The slight difference in lateral separation between two objects as seen by the left eye and the right eye.

monocular cues Visual cues to depth or distance that can be used by one eye alone.

perceptual constancy The accurate perception of objects as stable or unchanged despite changes in the sensory patterns they produce.

3 **Size constancy.** We see an object as having a constant size even when its retinal image becomes smaller or larger. A friend approaching on the street does not seem to be growing; a car pulling away from the curb does not seem to be shrinking. Size constancy depends in part on familiarity with objects; you know people and cars do not change size from moment to moment. It also depends on the apparent distance of an object. An object that is close produces a larger retinal image than the same object farther away, and the brain takes this into account. For example, when you move your hand toward your face, your brain registers the fact that the hand is getting closer, and you correctly perceive its unchanging size despite the growing size of its retinal image. There is, then, an intimate relationship between perceived size and perceived distance.

4 **Brightness constancy.** We see objects as having a relatively constant brightness even though the amount of light they reflect changes as the overall level of illumination changes. Snow remains white even on a cloudy day. We are not fooled because the brain registers the total illumination in the scene, and we automatically take this information into account.

5 **Colour constancy.** We see an object as maintaining its hue despite the fact that the wavelength of light reaching our eyes from the object may change as the illumination changes. For example, outdoor light is "bluer" than indoor light, and

MONOCULAR CUES TO DEPTH

Most cues to depth do not depend on having two eyes. Some monocular (one-eyed) cues are shown here.

INTERPOSITION

An object that partly blocks or obscures another one must be in front of the other one and is therefore seen as closer.

Shutterstock

Chrisharvey/Fotolia

LIGHT AND SHADOW

Both of these attributes give objects the appearance of three dimensions.

Fotolia

MOTION PARALLAX

When an observer is moving, objects appear to move at different speeds and in different directions. The closer an object, the faster it seems to move; and close objects appear to move backward, whereas distant ones seem to move forward.

objects outdoors therefore reflect more "blue" light than those indoors. Conversely, indoor light from incandescent lamps is rich in long wavelengths and is therefore "yellower." Yet objects usually look the same colour in both places: An apple looks red whether you look at it in your kitchen or outside on the patio. Part of the explanation involves sensory adaptation, which we discussed earlier. Outdoors, we quickly adapt to short-wavelength (bluish) light, and indoors, we adapt to long-wavelength light. As a result, our visual responses are similar in the two situations. Also, when computing the colour of a particular object, the brain takes into account *all* the wavelengths in the visual field immediately around the object. If an apple is bathed in bluish light, so, usually, is everything around it. The increase in blue light reflected by the apple is cancelled in the visual cortex by the increase in blue light reflected by the apple's surroundings, and so the apple continues to look red. Colour constancy is further aided by our knowledge of the world. We know that many types of apples are red and bananas are usually yellow, and the brain uses that knowledge to recalibrate the colours of those objects when the lighting changes (Mitterer & de Ruiter, 2008).

Visual Illusions: When Seeing Is Misleading. Perceptual constancies allow us to make sense of the world. Occasionally, however, we can be fooled, and the result is a *perceptual illusion*. For psychologists, illusions are valuable because they are systematic errors that provide us with hints about the perceptual strategies of the mind.

RELATIVE SIZE
The smaller an object's image on the retina, the farther away the object appears.

Glow Images

TEXTURE GRADIENTS
Distant parts of a uniform surface appear denser; that is, its elements seem spaced more closely together.

Fotolia

LINEAR PERSPECTIVE
Parallel lines will appear to converge in the distance; the greater the apparent convergence, the greater the perceived distance. Artists often exaggerate this cue to convey an impression of depth.

Dudarev Mikhail/Shutterstock

Alamy

RELATIVE CLARITY
Because of particles in the air—from dust, fog, or smog—distant objects tend to look hazier, duller, or less detailed.

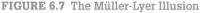

(a)　　　　　　　　(b)

FIGURE 6.7 The Müller-Lyer Illusion
The two lines in part (a) are exactly the same length. We are probably fooled into perceiving them as different because the brain interprets the one with the outward-facing branches as farther away, as if it were the far corner of a room, and the one with the inward-facing branches as closer, as if it were the near edge of a building (b).

◉➤ **Simulate** the **Experiment**
Ambiguous Figures in **MyPsychLab**

FIGURE 6.8 Psychology: It's Not Just "Common Sense"
The way you perceive a colour depends on the colours around it. In this work by Joseph Albers, the adjacent *X*s are actually the same colour, but against different backgrounds they look different.

Josef Albers, "Plate VI-3 from 'Interaction of Color'." © Josef Albers Foundation/Yale University Press. © 2000 The Josef and Anni Albers Foundation/ Artists Rights Society (ARS), New York.

Although illusions can occur in any sensory modality, visual illusions have been the best studied. Visual illusions sometimes occur when the strategies that normally lead to accurate perception are overextended to situations where they don't apply. Compare the lengths of the two vertical lines in Figure 6.7. If you are like most people, you perceive the line on the right as slightly longer than the one on the left. Yet they are exactly the same length. (Go ahead, measure them; everyone does.) This is the Müller-Lyer illusion, named after the German sociologist who first described it in 1889. ◉➤

One explanation for the Müller-Lyer illusion is that the branches on the lines serve as perspective cues that normally suggest depth (Gregory, 1963). The line on the left is like the near edge of a building; the one on the right is like the far corner of a room (see part [b] of the figure). Although the two lines produce retinal images of the same size, the one with the outward-facing branches suggests greater distance. We are fooled into perceiving it as longer because we automatically apply a rule about the relationship between size and distance that is normally useful: When two objects produce the same-sized retinal image and one is farther away, the farther one is larger. The problem, in this case, is that there is no actual difference in the distance of the two lines, so the rule is inappropriate.

Just as there are size, shape, location, brightness, and colour constancies, so there are size, shape, location, brightness, and colour inconstancies, resulting in illusions. For example, the perceived colour of an object depends on the wavelengths reflected by its immediate surroundings, a fact well known to artists and interior designers. Thus, you never see a good, strong red unless other objects in the surroundings reflect the blue and green part of the spectrum. When two objects that are the same colour have different surroundings, you may mistakenly perceive them as different (see Figure 6.8).

Some illusions are simply a matter of physics. Thus, a chopstick in a half-filled glass of water looks bent because water and air refract light differently. Other illusions occur due to misleading messages from the sense organs, as in sensory adaptation. Still others, like the Müller-Lyer illusion, seem to occur because the brain misinterprets sensory information. Figure 6.9 shows some other startling illusions.

In everyday life, most illusions are harmless and entertaining. Occasionally, however, an illusion interferes with the performance of some task or skill. For example, in baseball, two types of pitches that drive batters batty are the rising fastball, in which the ball seems to jump a few centimetres when it reaches home plate, and the breaking curveball, in which the ball seems to loop toward the batter and then fall at the last moment; both of these pitches are physical impossibilities. According to one

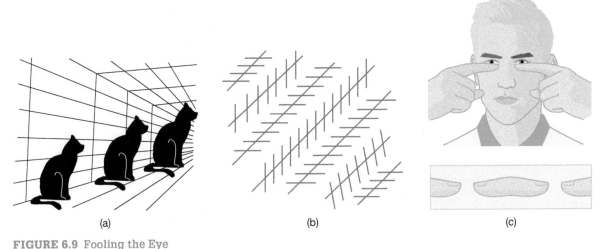

(a)   (b)   (c)

FIGURE 6.9 Fooling the Eye
Although perception is usually accurate, we can be fooled. In part (a) the cats as drawn are all the same size; in part (b) the diagonal lines are all parallel. To see the illusion depicted in part (c), hold your index fingers 13 to 26 centimetres in front of your eyes as shown, then focus straight ahead. Do you see a floating "fingertip frankfurter"? Can you move your fingers to make it shrink or expand?

explanation, such illusions occur when batters wrongly estimate a ball's speed and momentarily shift their gaze to where they think it will cross home plate (Bahill & Karnavas, 1993). ◉

Some illusions can also contribute to industrial and automobile accidents. For example, because large objects often appear to move more slowly than small ones, drivers sometimes underestimate the speed of onrushing trains at railroad crossings and think they can beat the train, with tragic results.

Perhaps the ultimate perceptual illusion occurred when Swedish researchers tricked people into feeling that they were swapping bodies with another person or even a mannequin (Petkova & Ehrsson, 2008). The participants wore virtual-reality goggles connected to a camera on the other person's (or mannequin's) head. This allowed them to see the world from the other body's point of view as an experimenter simultaneously stroked both bodies with a rod. Most people soon had the weird sensation that the other body was actually their own; they even cringed when the other body was poked or threatened. The researchers speculate that some day the body-swapping illusion could be helpful in marital counselling, allowing each partner to literally see things from the other's point of view, or in therapy with people who have distorted body images.

◉—Watch the Video
What's in It for Me? Perceptual Magic in Art in **MyPsychLab**

Talk about an illusion! The person on the left is wearing virtual-reality goggles and the mannequin on the right is outfitted with a camera that feeds images to the goggles. As a result, the person quickly comes to feel as though he has swapped bodies with the mannequin.

Niklas Larsson/AP Images

Recite & Review

Recite: This instruction is no illusion: Recite everything you can remember about *hue*, *brightness*, *saturation*, *retina*, parts of the eye, *rods* and *cones*, *dark adapation*, *ganglion cells*, *feature detector cells*, *trichromatic* and *opponent-process theories of colour vision*, *Gestalt principles*, *binocular* and *monocular cues* to depth and distance, *convergence*, *retinal disparity*, *perceptual constancy*, visual constancies, and visual illusions.

Review: That's a lot of information to learn, so go back and read this section again.

Quick Quiz:

This quiz is no illusion.

1. How can two Gestalt principles help explain why you can make out the Big Dipper on a starry night?

2. *True or false:* Binocular cues help us locate objects that are very far away.

3. Hold one hand about 30 centimetres from your face and the other one about 15 centimetres away. (a) Which hand will cast the smaller retinal image? (b) Why don't you perceive that hand as smaller?

4. From an evolutionary point of view, people are most likely to have a mental module for recognition of (a) flowers, (b) bugs, (c) faces, (d) chocolate, (e) cars.

Answers:

1. Proximity of certain stars encourages you to see them as clustered together to form a pattern; closure allows you to "fill in the gaps" and see the contours of a "dipper." 2. false 3. (a) The hand that is 30 centimetres away will cast a smaller retinal image. (b) Your brain takes the differences in distance into account in estimating size; also, you know how large your hands are. The result is size constancy. 4. c

Learning Objectives

13 List the basics of how we hear.

14 Articulate why a note played on a flute sounds different from the same note played on an oboe.

15 Describe how we locate the source of a sound.

Hearing

Like vision, the sense of hearing, or *audition*, provides a vital link with the world around us. Because social relationships rely so heavily on hearing, when people lose their hearing they sometimes come to feel socially isolated. That is why many hearing-impaired people feel strongly about teaching deaf children American Sign Language (ASL) or other gestural systems, which allow them to communicate and forge close relationships with other signers.

What We Hear

The stimulus for sound is a wave of pressure created when an object vibrates (or, sometimes, when compressed air is released, as in a pipe organ). The vibration (or release of air) causes molecules in a transmitting substance to move together and apart. This movement produces variations in pressure that radiate in all directions. The transmitting substance is usually air, but sound waves can also travel through water and solids, as you know if you have ever put your ear to the wall to hear voices in the next room.

As with vision, *physical* characteristics of the stimulus—in this case, a sound wave—are related in a predictable way to *psychological* aspects of our auditory experience.

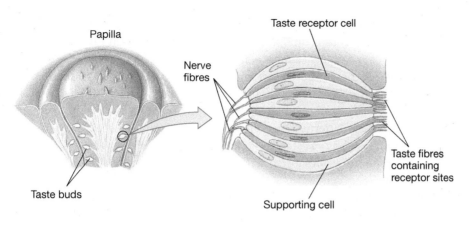

Papilla

Taste receptor cell

Nerve fibres

Taste buds

Supporting cell

Taste fibres containing receptor sites

FIGURE 6.12 Taste Receptors
The illustration on the left shows taste buds lining the sides of a papilla on the tongue's surface. The illustration on the right shows an enlarged view of a single taste bud.

Latin for "pimple"), and they come in several forms. In all but one of these forms, the sides of each papilla are lined with **taste buds**, which up close look a little like segmented oranges (see Figure 6.12). Because of genetic differences, human tongues can have as few as 500 or as many as 10 000 taste buds (Miller & Reedy, 1990). ◉

The taste buds are commonly referred to, mistakenly, as the receptors for taste. The actual receptor cells are *inside* the buds, 15 to 50 to a bud. These cells send tiny fibres out through an opening in the bud; the receptor sites are on these fibres. The receptor cells are replaced by new cells about every 10 days. However, after age 40 or so, the total number of taste buds (and therefore receptors) declines.

Traditionally, researchers have considered four tastes to be basic: *salty*, *sour*, *bitter*, and *sweet*, each produced by a different type of chemical. Today most researchers also include a fifth taste, *umami* (from the Japanese for "delicious"), which is the taste of monosodium glutamate (MSG) and is found in many protein-rich foods, including meat, shellfish, and seaweed. The basic tastes are part of our evolutionary heritage: Bitterness and sourness help us identify foods that are rancid or poisonous; sweetness helps us identify foods that are healthful or rich in calories; salt is necessary for all body functions; and umami may help us identify protein-rich foods.

The basic tastes can be perceived at any spot on the tongue that has receptors, and differences among the areas are small. Interestingly, the centre of the tongue contains no taste buds, and so it cannot produce any sort of taste sensation. But, as in the case of the eye's blind spot, you will not usually notice the lack of sensation because the brain fills in the gap. When you bite into an egg or a piece of bread or an orange, its unique flavour is composed of some combination of the four or five basic tastes, but the physiological details are still hazy. It has even been difficult to identify the receptors for the basic tastes, although recently researchers have proposed candidates for the receptors that process bitter, sweet, and umami (Chaudhari, Landin, & Roper, 2000; Damak et al., 2003; Huang et al., 1999; Max et al., 2001; Montmayeur et al., 2001; Zhang et al., 2003). Researchers are now hot on the trail of the specific receptors that process each of the basic tastes (Chandrashekar et al., 2006).

taste buds Nests of taste receptor cells.

◉─ Watch the **Video**
The Basics: In Full Appreciation of the Cookie in **MyPsychLab**

GET INVOLVED! The Smell of Taste

Demonstrate for yourself that smell enhances the sense of taste. While holding your nose, take a bite of a slice of apple, and then do the same with a slice of raw potato. You may find that you can't taste much difference. If you think you do taste a difference, perhaps your expectations are influencing your response. Try the same thing, but close your eyes this time and have someone else feed you the slices. Can you still tell them apart? It's also fun to do this little test with flavoured jelly beans. They are still apt to taste sweet, but you may be unable to identify the separate flavours.

Everyone knows that people live in different "taste worlds" (Bartoshuk, 1998). Some people love broccoli and others hate it. Some people can eat chili peppers that are burning hot and others cannot tolerate the mildest jalapeño. One reason for these differences is genetic. In the United States, about 25% of people are *supertasters* who find saccharin, caffeine, broccoli, and many other substances unpleasantly bitter. (Women, especially Asian women, are overrepresented in this group.) "Tasters," in contrast, detect less bitterness, and "nontasters" detect none at all. Supertasters also perceive sweet tastes as sweeter and salty tastes as saltier than other people do, and they feel more "burn" from substances such as ginger, pepper, and hot chilies (Bartoshuk et al., 1998; Lucchina et al., 1998). Supertasters have more taste buds than other people, and certain papillae on their tongues are smaller, are more densely packed, and look different from those of nontasters (Reedy et al., 1993).

Other taste preferences are a matter of culture and learning. Many North Americans who enjoy raw oysters, raw smoked salmon, and raw herring are nevertheless put off by other forms of raw seafood that are popular in Japan, such as sea urchin and octopus. And within a given culture, some people will greedily gobble up a dish that makes others turn green. Some of these learned taste preferences seem to begin in the womb or during breastfeeding. Flavours as diverse as vanilla, carrot, garlic, anise, hot spice, and mint can be transmitted to the fetus or newborn through amniotic fluid or breast milk, with long-lasting consequences (Beauchamp & Mennella, 2011; Mennella et al., 2011). Babies fed salty foods prefer salty foods when they become preschoolers (Stein, Cowart, & Beauchamp, 2012).

The attractiveness of a food can be affected by its colour, temperature, and texture. As Goldilocks found out, a bowl of cold porridge is not nearly as delicious as one that is properly heated. And any peanut butter fan will tell you that chunky and smooth peanut butters just don't taste the same. Even more important for taste is a food's odour. Much of what we call "flavour" is really the smell of gases released by the foods we put in our mouths. Indeed, subtle flavours such as chocolate and vanilla would have little taste if we could not smell them (see Figure 6.13). Smell's influence on flavour explains why you have trouble tasting your food when you have a stuffy nose. Most people who have chronic trouble detecting tastes have a problem with smell, not taste.

FIGURE 6.13 Taste Test
The turquoise bars show the percentages of people that could identify a substance dropped on the tongue when they were able to smell it. The gold bars show the percentage that could identify the substance when they were prevented from smelling it. (From Mozell et al., 1969.)

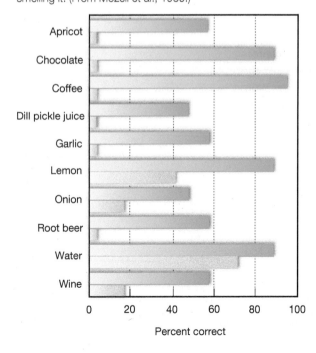

Smell: The Sense of Scents

The great author and educator Helen Keller, who became blind and deaf as a toddler, once called smell "the fallen angel of the senses." Yet our sense of smell, or *olfaction*, although seemingly crude when compared to a bloodhound's, is actually quite good; the human nose can detect aromas that the most sophisticated machines fail to detect. And this sense is also far more useful than most people realize.

The receptors for smell are specialized neurons embedded in a tiny patch of mucous membrane in the upper part of the nasal passage, just beneath the eyes (see Figure 6.14). Millions of receptors in each nasal cavity respond to chemical molecules in the air. When you inhale, you pull these molecules into the nasal cavity, but they can also enter from the mouth, wafting up the throat like smoke up a chimney. These molecules trigger responses in the receptors that combine to yield the yeasty smell of freshly baked bread or the spicy smell of a eucalyptus tree. Signals from the receptors are carried to the brain's olfactory bulb by the *olfactory nerve*, which is made up of the receptors' axons. From the olfactory bulb, they travel to a higher region of the brain.

Figuring out the neural code for smell has been a real challenge. Of the 10 000 or so smells we detect (rotten, burned, musky, fruity,

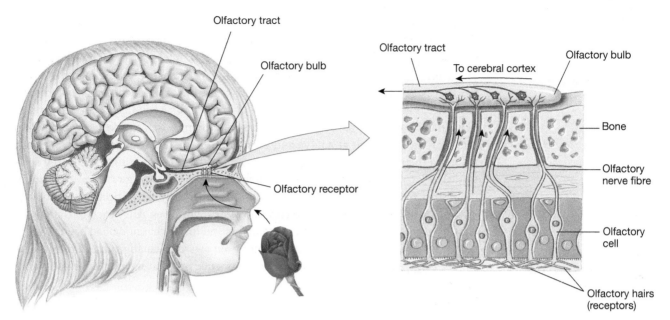

FIGURE 6.14 Receptors for Smell
Airborne chemical molecules (vapours) enter the nose and circulate through the nasal cavity, where the smell receptors are located. The receptors' axons make up the olfactory nerve, which carries signals to the brain. When you sniff, you draw more vapours into the nose and speed their circulation. Vapours can also reach the nasal cavity through the mouth by way of a passageway from the throat.

spicy, flowery, resinous, putrid . . .), none seems to be more basic than any other. Moreover, as many as 1000 kinds of receptors exist, each kind responding to a part of an odour molecule's structure (Axel, 1995; Buck & Axel, 1991). In 2004, Richard Axel and Linda Buck won a Nobel Prize for this discovery. Distinct odours activate unique combinations of receptors, and signals from different types of receptors are combined in individual neurons in the brain. Some neurons seem to respond only to particular mixtures of odours rather than the individual odours in a mixture, which may explain why a mixture of clove and rose may be perceived as carnation rather than as two separate smells (Zou & Buck, 2006).

Although smell is less vital for human survival than for the survival of other animals, it is still important. We sniff out danger by smelling smoke, food spoilage, and gas leaks, so a deficit in the sense of smell is nothing to turn up your nose at. Such a loss can result from infection, disease, injury to the olfactory nerve, or smoking. A person who has smoked two packs a day for 10 years must abstain from cigarettes for 10 more years before the sense of smell returns to normal (Frye, Schwartz, & Doty, 1990).

Odours, of course, have psychological effects on us, which is why we buy perfumes and sniff flowers. Perhaps because olfactory centres in the brain are linked to areas that process memories and emotions, specific smells often evoke vivid, emotionally coloured memories (Herz & Cupchik, 1995; Vroon, 1997). The smell of hot chocolate may trigger fond memories of cozy winter mornings from your childhood; the smell of rubbing alcohol may remind you of an unpleasant trip to the hospital. Odours can also influence people's everyday behaviour, which is why shopping malls and hotels often install aroma diffusers in hopes of putting you in a good mood.

Many dubious, unsupported claims have been made for the powers of particular aromas, but now some serious

Smell has not only evolutionary but also cultural significance. These pilgrims in Japan are purifying themselves with holy incense for good luck and health.

Christophe Boisvieux/Corbis

research is being done. For example, Dutch researchers have found that the citrus scent of an all-purpose cleaner, unobtrusively left in a hidden bucket, can activate the mental concept *cleaning* and can even affect people's "cleaning behaviour" (Holland, Hendriks, & Aarts, 2005). In one of their studies, participants wrote down five activities they were planning to do during the rest of the day. Those who had been exposed to the scent listed a cleaning activity more often than those who had not been exposed to it. In another study, participants did a task and then moved to another room, where they were invited to sit at a table and eat a crumbly biscuit as a hidden video camera recorded their hand movements. People who had been exposed to the cleaning scent while working on the initial task were much more likely to wipe away crumbs from the table than those who had not been exposed! Apparently, activation of the concept *cleaning* made them more likely to clean up after themselves. After each of these studies, the researchers questioned the participants and found that none had been aware of the scent's influence. In fact, most were not even aware of having smelled the scent at all. Clearly, scent can have a nonconscious influence on what we think and do.

Senses of the Skin

The skin's usefulness is more than just skin deep. Besides protecting our innards, our nearly two square metres of skin help us identify objects and establish intimacy with others. By providing a boundary between ourselves and everything else, the skin also gives us a sense of ourselves as distinct from the environment.

The basic skin senses include *touch* (or pressure), *warmth*, *cold*, and *pain*. Within these four types are variations such as itch, tickle, and painful burning. Although certain spots on the skin are especially sensitive to the four basic skin sensations, for many years scientists had difficulty finding distinct receptors for these sensations, except in the case of pressure. But then Swedish researchers found a new kind of nerve fibre that seems responsible for some types of itching (Schmelz et al., 1997). Another team has found that the same fibres that detect pain from a punch in the nose or a burn also seem to detect the kind of pathological itch that is unrelated to histamines and that can't be relieved by antihistamine medications (Johanek et al., 2008). Moreover, scientists recently identified a possible cold receptor (McKemy, Neuhausser, & Julius, 2002; Peier et al., 2002).

Perhaps specialized fibres will also be discovered for other skin sensations. In the meantime, many aspects of touch continue to baffle science—for example, why gently touching adjacent pressure spots in rapid succession produces tickle, why scratching quells (or sometimes worsens!) an itch, and why the simultaneous stimulation of warm and cold spots produces not a lukewarm sensation but the sensation of heat. Decoding the messages of the skin senses will eventually tell us how we are able to distinguish sandpaper from velvet and glue from grease.

The Mystery of Pain

Pain, which is not only a skin sense but also an internal sense, has come under special scrutiny. Pain differs from other senses in an important way: When the stimulus producing it is removed, the sensation may continue—sometimes for years. Chronic pain disrupts lives, puts stress on the body, and causes depression and despair.

The Gate-Control Theory of Pain.
For many years, a leading explanation of pain has been the **gate-control theory of pain**, which was first proposed by Canadian psychologist Ronald Melzack and British physiologist Patrick Wall (1965). According to this theory, pain impulses must get past a "gate" in the spinal cord. The gate is not an actual structure, but rather a pattern of neural activity that either blocks pain messages coming from the skin, muscles, and internal organs or lets those signals

gate-control theory of pain The theory that the experience of pain depends in part on whether pain impulses get past a neurological "gate" in the spinal cord and thus reach the brain.

through. Normally, the gate is kept shut, either by impulses coming into the spinal cord from large fibres that respond to pressure and other kinds of stimulation, or by signals coming down from the brain itself. But when body tissue is injured, the large fibres are damaged and smaller fibres open the gate, allowing pain messages to reach the brain unchecked.

Because the gate-control theory emphasizes the role of the brain in controlling the gate, it correctly predicts that thoughts and feelings can influence our reactions to pain. When we dwell on our pain, focusing on it and talking about it constantly instead of acting in spite of it, we often intensify our experience of it (Sullivan, Tripp, & Santor, 1998). Conversely, when we are distracted from our pain, we may not feel it as we usually would—which is why we hear, from time to time, of athletes who are able to finish a performance despite sprained ankles or even broken bones. The gate-control theory also correctly predicts that mild pressure, or other kinds of stimulation, can interfere with severe or protracted pain by closing the spinal gate. When we vigorously rub a banged elbow or apply ice packs, heat, or stimulating ointments to injuries, we are applying this principle.

Updating the Gate-Control Theory.

The gate-control theory has been highly useful, but it does not fully explain the many instances of severe, chronic pain that occur without any sign of injury or disease whatsoever.

In the strange phenomenon of **phantom pain**, for instance, a person continues to feel pain that seemingly comes from an amputated limb or from an organ that has been surgically removed. An amputee may feel the same aching, burning, or sharp pain from sores, calf cramps, throbbing toes, or even ingrown toenails that he or she endured before the surgery. Even when the spinal cord has been completely severed, amputees often continue to report phantom pain from areas below the break. There are no nerve impulses for the spinal-cord gate to block or let through. So why is there pain?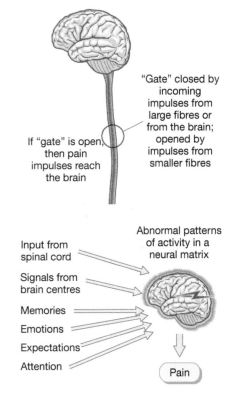

These puzzles led Ronald Melzack (1992, 1993) to revise the gate-control theory. The brain, he says, not only responds to incoming signals from sensory nerves but is also capable of generating pain (and other sensations) entirely on its own. An extensive *matrix* (network) of neurons in the brain gives us a sense of our own bodies and body parts. When this matrix produces abnormal patterns of activity, the result is pain. Such abnormal patterns can occur not only because of input from peripheral nerves, but also as a result of memories, emotions, expectations, or signals from various brain centres. In the case of phantom pain, the abnormal patterns may arise because of a lack of sensory stimulation or because of the person's efforts to move a nonexistent limb. Evidence that brain areas associated with a missing limb continue to function in its absence is consistent with this view (Davis et al., 1998).

At present, however, no general theory completely explains *phantom pain*, or for that matter normal pain, which has turned out to be extremely complicated, both physiologically and psychologically. Different types of pain (from, say, a thorn, a bruise, or a hot iron) involve different chemical changes and different changes in nerve-cell activity at the site of injury or disease, as well as in the spinal cord and brain. These changes may suppress the pain or may amplify it by making neurons hyperexcitable. Further, recent evidence suggests that chronic, pathological pain involves *glia*, the cells that support nerve cells (see Chapter 4). Challenges to the immune system during viral and bacterial infections, and substances released by neurons along the pain pathway after an injury, activate glial cells in the spinal cord. The glia then release inflammatory substances that may worsen the pain and keep it going (Watkins & Maier, 2003). These chemicals can spread to spinal cord areas far from the site where they were released, which may help explain why injured people sometimes report pain in body areas that were not hurt.

A nurse examines Ashlyn Blocker's feet for injuries. Because of a rare condition, Ashlyn cannot feel pain from scrapes and scratches. Despite the suffering that pain causes, it is useful because it alerts us to injury.

Stephen Morton/AP Images

"Gate" closed by incoming impulses from large fibres or from the brain; opened by impulses from smaller fibres

If "gate" is open, then pain impulses reach the brain

Abnormal patterns of activity in a neural matrix

Input from spinal cord
Signals from brain centres
Memories
Emotions
Expectations
Attention

Pain

👁—**Watch** the **Video**
In the Real World: Managing Pain
in **MyPsychLab**

phantom pain The experience of pain in a missing limb or other body part.

After his right leg was destroyed in an explosion while he was in Iraq, Army Sgt. Nicholas Paupore experienced excruciating phantom limb pain—as though the missing leg were constantly being shocked or stabbed. Even morphine didn't help. Then, as part of a clinical trial, he underwent a simple daily treatment. A mirror was placed at a strategic angle to reflect his intact leg, tricking his brain into registering two healthy legs that he could move freely. The pain almost immediately subsided. A year after therapy, he had only occasional, milder pain, and needed no medication. In some patients, mirror therapy has eliminated phantom pain entirely.

US Army Military History Institute

A leading explanation of phantom pain is that the brain has reorganized itself: The area in the sensory cortex that formerly corresponded to the missing body part has been "invaded" by neurons from another area, often one corresponding to the face. Higher brain centres then interpret messages from those neurons as coming from the nonexistent body part (Cruz et al., 2005; Ramachandran & Blakeslee, 1998). Even though the missing limb can no longer send signals through touch and internal sensations, memories of these signals remain in the nervous system, including memories of pain, paralysis, and cramping that occurred prior to amputation. The result is an inaccurate "body map" in the brain and pain signals that cannot be shut off.

Vilayanur Ramachandran, the neurologist who first proposed this theory, has developed an extraordinarily simple but effective treatment for phantom-limb pain. Ramachandran wondered whether he could devise an illusion to trick the brain of an amputee with phantom arm pain into perceiving the missing limb as moving and pain-free. He placed a simple mirror upright and perpendicular to the sufferer's body, such that the amputee's intact arm was reflected in the mirror. From the amputee's perspective, the result was an illusion of two functioning arms. The amputee was then instructed to move both arms in synchrony while looking into the mirror. With this technique, which has now been used with many people, the brain is fooled into thinking its owner has two healthy arms or legs, resynchronizes the signals—and phantom pain vanishes (Ramachandran & Altschuler, 2009). Neurologists have been testing this method with Iraq veterans, and are finding it to be more successful than control therapies in which patients just mentally visualize having two intact limbs (Anderson-Barnes et al., 2009; Chan et al., 2007).

The Environment Within

We usually think of our senses as pipelines to the "outside" world, but two senses keep us informed about the movements of our own bodies. **Kinesthesis** tells us where our body parts are located and lets us know when they move. This information is provided by pain and pressure receptors located in the muscles, joints, and tendons (tissues that connect muscles to bones). Without kinesthesis, you could not touch your finger to your nose with your eyes shut. In fact, you would have trouble with any voluntary movement. Think of how hard walking is when your leg has "fallen asleep" or how clumsy you are at chewing when a dentist has numbed your jaw with Novocaine.

Equilibrium, or the sense of balance, gives us information about our bodies as a whole. Along with vision and touch, it lets us know whether we are standing upright or on our heads and tells us when we are falling or rotating. Equilibrium relies primarily on three **semicircular canals** in the inner ear (refer to Figure 6.11 on page 198). These thin tubes are filled with fluid that moves and presses on hairlike receptors whenever the head rotates. The receptors initiate messages that travel through a part of the auditory nerve that is not involved in hearing.

Normally, kinesthesis and equilibrium work together to give us a sense of our own physical reality—something we take utterly for granted but should not. Oliver Sacks (1985) told the heartbreaking story of Christina, a young British woman who suffered irreversible damage to her kinesthetic nerve fibres because of a mysterious inflammation. At first, Christina was as floppy as a rag doll; she could not sit up, walk, or stand.

kinesthesis [KIN-es-THEE-sís] The sense of body position and movement of body parts; also called *kinesthesia*.

equilibrium The sense of balance.

semicircular canals Sense organs in the inner ear that contribute to equilibrium by responding to rotation of the head.

Then, slowly, she learned to do these things, relying on visual cues and sheer willpower. But her movements remained unnatural; she had to grasp a fork with painful force or she would drop it. More important, despite her remaining sensitivity to light touch on the skin, she said she could no longer experience herself as physically embodied: "It's like something's been scooped right out of me," she told Sacks, "right at the centre."

With equilibrium, we come, as it were, to the end of our senses. Every second, millions of sensory signals reach the brain, which combines and integrates them to produce a model of reality from moment to moment. How does it know how to do this? Are our perceptual abilities inborn, or must we learn them? We turn next to this issue.

These performers from Quebec's famed Cirque du Soleil have turned their kinesthetic talents into artistry.

✓•—**Study** and **Review**
in **MyPsychLab**

Recite & Review

Recite: Don't lose your own sense of equilibrium as you recall everything you can about *papillae*, *taste buds*, *gate-control theory of pain*, *phantom pain*, *kinesthesis*, *equilibrium*, and *semicircular canals*.

Review: Next, read this section again.

Quick Quiz:

Can you make sense of the following sensory problems?

A. What explanation of each problem is most likely?
 1. April always has trouble tasting foods, especially those with subtle flavours.
 2. May, a rock musician, does not hear as well as she used to.
 3. June has chronic shoulder pain, though the injury that initially caused it seems to have healed. (Hint: Think about the gate-control theory and its revisions.)

B. After seeing a new pain-relief ointment advertised on TV, you try it and find that it seems to work. What other explanation is possible for the decrease in your pain?

Answers:

A. 1. April may have an impaired sense of smell, possibly due to disease, illness, or cigarette smoking. **2.** Hearing impairment has many causes, but in May's case we might suspect that prolonged exposure to loud music has damaged the hair cells of her cochlea. **3.** Nerve fibres that normally close the pain "gate" might have been damaged, or a matrix of cells in the brain might be producing abnormal activity. **B.** The relief you feel may be due at least in part to a placebo effect, which has decreased activity in the pain matrix of your brain or has led to increased production of endorphins.

Learning Objectives

21 Differentiate whether babies see the world in the way adults do.

22 Predict what happens when people who are born blind or deaf have their sight or hearing restored.

23 Explain how psychological and cultural factors affect perception.

Perceptual Powers: Origins and Influences

What happens when babies first open their eyes? Do they see the same sights, hear the same sounds, smell the same smells, and taste the same tastes that an adult does? Are their strategies for organizing the world wired into their brains from the beginning?

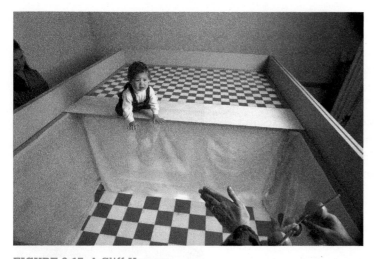

FIGURE 6.15 A Cliff-Hanger
Infants as young as six months usually hesitate to crawl past the apparent edge of a visual cliff, which suggests that they are able to perceive depth.

Joseph Campos

👁—⌐Watch the **Video**
Perception in **MyPsychLab**

FIGURE 6.16 Vision and Early Experience
Cats were reared in darkness for five months after birth, but for several hours each day were put in a special cylinder that permitted them to see only vertical or horizontal lines, and nothing else. Later on, cats who were exposed only to vertical lines had trouble perceiving horizontal ones, and those exposed only to horizontal lines had trouble perceiving vertical ones (Blakemore & Cooper, 1970).

Or is an infant's world, as William James once suggested, only a "blooming, buzzing confusion," waiting to be organized by experience and learning? The truth lies somewhere between these two extremes.

Inborn Abilities

In human beings, most basic sensory abilities, and many perceptual skills, are inborn or develop very early. Infants can distinguish salty from sweet and can discriminate among odours. They can distinguish a human voice from other sounds. They will startle to a loud noise and turn their heads toward its source, showing that they perceive sound as localized in space. Many visual skills are also present at birth or they develop shortly afterward. Human infants can discriminate sizes and colours very early, possibly even right away. They can distinguish contrasts, shadows, and complex patterns after only a few weeks. And depth perception develops very early, during the first few months. 👁

Testing an infant's perception of depth requires considerable ingenuity. One clever procedure that was used for decades was to place infants on a device called a *visual cliff* (Gibson & Walk, 1960). The "cliff" is a pane of glass covering a shallow surface and a deep one (see Figure 6.15). Both surfaces are covered by a checkerboard pattern. The infant is placed on a board in the middle, and the child's mother tries to lure the baby across either the shallow side or the deep side. Babies only six months of age will crawl across the shallow side but will refuse to crawl out over the "cliff." Their hesitation shows that they have depth perception.

Of course, by six months of age, a baby has had quite a bit of experience with the world. But infants younger than six months can also be tested on the visual cliff, even though they cannot yet crawl. At only two months of age, babies show a drop in heart rate when placed on the deep side of the cliff, but no change when they are placed on the shallow side. A slowed heart rate is usually a sign of increased attention. Thus, although these infants may not be frightened the way an older infant would be, it seems they can perceive the difference between the shallow and deep sides of the cliff (Banks & Salapatek, 1984).

Critical Periods

Although many perceptual abilities are inborn, experience also plays a vital role. If an infant misses out on certain experiences during a crucial window of time—a *critical period*—perception will be impaired. Innate abilities will not survive because cells in the nervous system deteriorate, change, or fail to form appropriate neural pathways.

One way to study critical periods is to see what happens when the usual perceptual experiences of early life fail to take place. To do this, researchers usually study animals whose sensory and perceptual systems are similar to our own. For example, like human infants, kittens are born with the visual ability to detect horizontal and vertical lines and other spatial orientations as well; at birth, kittens' brains are equipped with the same kinds of feature detector cells that adult cats have. But if they are deprived of normal visual experience, these cells deteriorate or change and perception suffers (Crair, Gillespie, & Stryker, 1998; Hirsch & Spinelli, 1970).

In one famous study, kittens were exposed to either vertical or horizontal black and white stripes. Special collars kept them from seeing anything else, even their own bodies (see Figure 6.16). After several months, the kittens exposed only to vertical stripes seemed blind to all horizontal contours; they bumped into horizontal obstacles, and they ran to play with a bar that an experimenter held vertically but not to a bar held horizontally. In contrast, those exposed only to horizontal stripes bumped into vertical obstacles and ran to play with horizontal bars but not vertical ones (Blakemore & Cooper, 1970).

Critical periods for sensory development also exist in human beings. When adults who have been blind from infancy have their vision restored, they may see, but often they do not see. Areas in the brain normally devoted to vision may have taken on different functions when these individuals were blind. As a result, their depth perception may be poor, causing them to trip constantly. They cannot always make sense of what they see; to identify objects, they may have to touch or smell them. They may have trouble recognizing faces and emotional expressions. They may even lack size constancy, and may need to remind themselves that people walking away from them are not shrinking (Fine et al., 2003)! But if an infant's congenital blindness is corrected early, during a critical period occurring during the first nine months or so, the prognosis is much better (though visual discriminations may never become entirely normal). In one study of infants who underwent corrective surgery when they were between one week and nine months of age, improvement began after as little as one hour of visual experience (Maurer et al., 1999).

Similar findings apply to hearing. When adults who were born deaf, or who lost their hearing before learning to speak, receive cochlear implants (devices that stimulate the auditory nerve and allow auditory signals to travel to the brain), they tend to find sounds confusing. They are unable to learn to speak normally, and often they ask to have the implants removed. But cochlear implants are more successful in children and in adults who became deaf late in life (Rauschecker, 1999). Young children presumably have not yet passed through the critical period for processing sounds, and adults have already had years of auditory experience.

In sum, our perceptual powers are both inborn and dependent on experience. Because neurological connections in infants' brains and sensory systems are not completely formed, their senses are far less acute than an adult's. It takes time and experience before their sensory abilities fully develop. But an infant's world is clearly not the blooming, buzzing confusion that William James took it to be.

Psychological and Cultural Influences

The fact that some perceptual processes appear to be innate does not mean that all people perceive the world in the same way. A camera doesn't care what it "sees." A digital recorder doesn't ponder what it "hears." A robot arm on a factory assembly line holds no opinion about what it "touches." But because we human beings care about what we see, hear, taste, smell, and feel, psychological factors can influence what we perceive and how we perceive it. Here are a few of these factors:

1 **Needs.** When we need something, have an interest in it, or want it, we are especially likely to perceive it. For example, hungry individuals are faster than others at seeing words related to hunger when the words are flashed briefly on a screen (Radel & Clement-Guillotin 2012; Wispé & Drambarean, 1953).

2 **Beliefs.** What we hold to be true about the world can affect our interpretation of ambiguous sensory signals. For example, if you believe that extraterrestrials occasionally visit Earth, and you see a round object in the sky (where there are few points of reference to help you judge distance), you

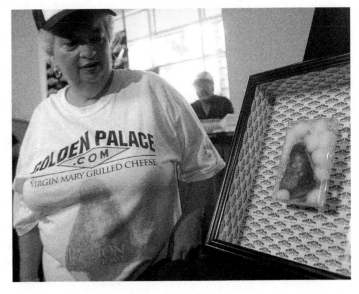

People often see what they want to see. Diana Duyser, a cook at a Florida casino, took a bite out of a grilled cheese sandwich and believed she saw the image of the Virgin Mary in what remained of it. She preserved the sandwich in plastic for 10 years and then decided to sell it. An online casino bought it on eBay for $28,000, even with a bite of it missing!

J. Pat Carter/AP Images

perceptual set A habitual way of perceiving, based on expectations.

may see a spaceship. (Impartial investigations of UFO sightings show that they are really weather balloons, rocket launchings, swamp gas, military aircraft, or ordinary celestial bodies, such as planets and meteors.) Images that remind people of a crucified Jesus have been reported on walls, dishes, and plates of spaghetti, causing great excitement among those who believe that divine messages can be found on everyday objects—until other explanations emerge. Do you remember that image of Jesus on the garage door, in our opening story? It turned out to be caused by two streetlights that merged the shadows of a bush and a "For Sale" sign in the yard.

3 **Emotions.** Emotions can also influence our interpretation of sensory information. A small child afraid of the dark may see a ghost instead of a robe hanging on the door, or a monster instead of a beloved doll. Pain, in particular, is affected by emotion. Soldiers who are seriously wounded often deny being in much pain, even though they are alert and are not in shock. Their relief at being alive may offset the anxiety and fear that contribute so much to pain (although distraction and the body's own pain-fighting mechanisms may also be involved). Conversely, negative emotions such as anger, fear, sadness, or depression can prolong and intensify a person's pain (Fernandez & Turk, 1992; Fields, 1991). Interestingly, when people perceive their pain as resulting from another person's malicious intent (e.g., they think the other person intentionally stepped on their toe), they feel the hurt more than they would if they thought it was simply due to a clumsy accident (Gray & Wegner, 2008).

4 **Expectations.** Previous experiences often affect how we perceive the world (Lachman, 1996). The tendency to perceive what you expect is called a **perceptual set**. Perceptaul sets can come in handy; they help us fill in words in sentences, for example, when we haven't really heard every one. But perceptual sets can also cause misperceptions. In Center Harbor, Maine, local legend has it that veteran newscaster Walter Cronkite was sailing into port one day when he heard a small crowd on shore shouting "Hello, Walter . . . hello, Walter." Pleased, he waved and took a bow. Only when he ran aground did he realize what they had really been shouting: "Shallow water . . . shallow water." (By the way, this paragraph has a misspelled word. Did you notice it? If not, it was probably because you expected all the words in this book to be spelled correctly.)

. . . .

CULTURE and *Perception*
Of Carpenters and Context

Our needs, beliefs, emotions, and expectations are all affected, in turn, by the culture we live in. Different cultures give people practice with different environments. In a classic study done in the 1960s, researchers found that members of some African tribes were much less likely to be fooled by the Müller-Lyer illusion and other geometric illusions than were Westerners. In the West, the researchers observed, people live in a "carpentered" world, full of rectangular structures. Westerners are also used to interpreting two-dimensional photographs and perspective drawings as representations of a three-dimensional world. Therefore, they interpret the kinds of angles used in the Müller-Lyer illusion as right angles extended in space, a habit that increases susceptibility to the illusion. The rural Africans in the study, living in a less carpentered environment and in round huts, seemed more likely to take the lines in the figures literally, as two-dimensional, which could explain why they were less susceptible to the illusion (Segall, Campbell, & Herskovits, 1966; Segall et al., 1999).

Culture also affects perception by shaping our stereotypes, directing our attention, and telling us what to notice or ignore. Westerners, for example, tend to focus mostly on the figure when viewing a scene and much less on the ground. East Asians, in contrast, tend to pay attention to the overall context and the relationship between figure and ground. When Japanese people and Americans were shown underwater scenes containing brightly coloured fish that were larger and moving faster than other objects in the scene, they reported the same numbers of details about the fish, but the Japanese reported more details about everything else in the background (Masuda & Nisbett, 2001). One of the researchers, Richard Nisbett, commented, "If it ain't moving, it doesn't exist for an American" (quoted in Shea, 2001).

Why should the Japanese pay more attention to context than Americans? One possibility is that a greater concern with the social world directs the attention of the Japanese to contexts of all types. Another possibility is that in Japanese environments, specific objects really do stand out less than in comparable American environments, so living in Japan tends to direct a person's attention to the whole visual field. Indeed, when researchers randomly sampled pictures of hotels, elementary schools, and post offices from small, medium, and large cities in Japan and the United States, they found that the Japanese scenes were more ambiguous and contained more elements than comparable American scenes—just the kind of scenes that encourage attention to context (Miyamoto, Nisbett, & Masuda, 2006).

As you can see . . . well, what you see partly depends on the culture you live in! When travellers visit another culture and are surprised to find that its members "see things differently," they may be literally correct.

THINKING CRITICALLY

Consider other interpretations.

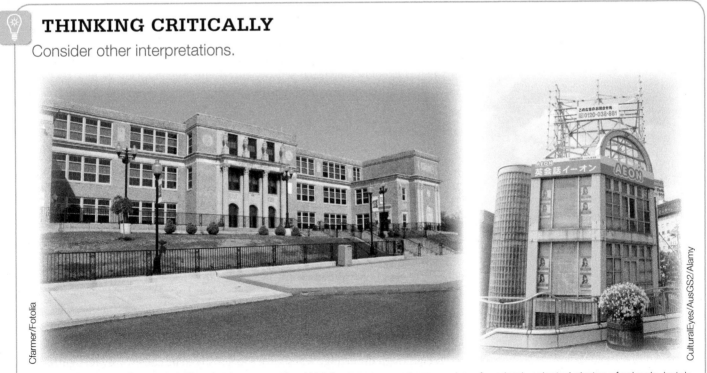

These photos of a U.S. school (left) and a Japanese school (right) were among a large number of randomly selected photos of schools, hotels, and post offices taken in the two countries. Japanese scenes tend to be more ambiguous and complex than American scenes, which may help explain why the Japanese attend more closely to context than Americans do (Miyamoto, Nisbett, & Masuda, 2006).

Recite & Review

Recite: Draw on all your senses to report everything you can remember about *perceptual set*, psychological influences on perception, and cultural influences on perception.

Review: Next, go back and reread this section.

Quick Quiz:

Direct your perceptual attention now to this quiz.

1. On the visual cliff, most six-month-old babies (a) go right across because they cannot detect depth, (b) cross even though they are afraid, (c) will not cross because they can detect depth, (d) cry or get bored.

2. Newborns and infants (a) have few perceptual abilities, (b) need visual experiences during a critical period for vision to develop normally, (c) see as well as adults.

3. "Have a nice . . ." says Dewey, but then he gets distracted and doesn't finish the thought. Yet Clarence is sure he heard Dewey wish him a nice *day*. Why?

Answers:

1. c 2. b 3. perceptual set due to expectations

Learning Objectives

24 Recognize that perception is often unconscious.

25 Predict whether "subliminal perception" tapes will help you lose weight or reduce your stress.

Puzzles of Perception

We come, finally, to two intriguing questions about perception that have captured the public's imagination for years. First, can we ever perceive what is happening in the world when it is below our usual sensory threshold? Second, can we pick up signals from the world or from other people without using our usual sensory channels at all?

Subliminal Perception: How Persuasive?

As we saw earlier in our discussion of selective attention, even when people are oblivious to speech sounds, they are processing and recognizing those sounds at some level. But such sounds and sights are above people's absolute thresholds. Is it also possible to perceive and respond to messages that are below the absolute threshold—too quiet to be consciously heard or too brief or dim to be consciously seen? Perhaps you have seen ads for products that will supposedly help you learn another language or raise your self-esteem (or, our favourite, learn to love housework) by taking advantage of such "subliminal perception." What are the facts?

Perceiving without Awareness. First, a simple visual stimulus can indeed affect your behaviour even when you are unaware that you saw it. For example, people sometimes correctly "sense" a change in a scene (say, in the colour or location of an object) even though the change was shown too quickly to be consciously recognized and identified (Rensink, 2004). And people subliminally exposed to a face will tend to prefer that face over one they did not "see" in this way (Bornstein, Leone, & Galley, 1987).

In many studies, researchers have used a method called **priming**, in which a person is exposed to information (subliminally or explicitly) and is later tested to see whether the information affects performance on another task (see Chapter 10).

priming A method used to measure unconscious cognitive processes, in which a person is exposed to information and is later tested to see whether the information affects behaviour or performance on another task or in another situation.

Researchers have found that when words flashed subliminally are related to some personality trait, such as honesty, people are more likely later to judge someone they read about as having that trait. They have been "primed" to evaluate the person that way (Bargh, 1999).

Several investigators at the University of Waterloo have demonstrated interesting effects while presenting stimuli without participants' being aware of it. Jim Cheesman and Phil Merikle have found that presentations of colour words shown without participant awareness still influence the subsequent naming speed of a colour patch (Cheesman & Merikle, 1986). Also at Waterloo, Erin Strahan and her advisers demonstrated that thirsty people who have been primed by thirst-related words are likely to drink more of a sweet beverage than thirsty people who are not primed, and they also find ads for a thirst-quenching drink more persuasive (Strahan, Spencer, & Zanna, 2002). Findings such as these show that people often know more than they think they know. In fact, nonconscious processing appears to occur not only in perception but also in memory, thinking, and decision making, as we will see in Chapters 9 and 10. However, even in the laboratory, where researchers have considerable control, subliminal perception can be hard to demonstrate and replicate. The strongest evidence comes from studies using simple stimuli (faces or single words such as *bread*) rather than complex stimuli such as sentences ("Eat whole-wheat bread, not white bread").

Perception versus Persuasion. If subliminal priming can affect judgments and preferences, can it be used to manipulate people's attitudes and behaviour? Subliminal persuasion techniques were a hot topic back in the 1950s, when an advertising executive claimed to have increased popcorn and Coke sales at a theatre by secretly flashing the words EAT POPCORN and DRINK COKE on the movie screen. The claim turned out to be a hoax, devised to save the man's struggling advertising company. Ever since, scientists have been skeptical, and most attempts to demonstrate subliminal persuasion have been disappointing.

However, this has not deterred people who market subliminal tapes that promise to help you lose weight, stop smoking, relieve stress, read faster, boost your motivation, lower your cholesterol, stop biting your nails, overcome jet lag, or stop taking drugs, all without any effort on your part. If only those claims were true! But in study after study, placebo tapes—tapes that do not contain the messages that participants think they do—are just as "effective" as subliminal tapes (Eich & Hyman, 1992; Merikle & Skanes, 1992; Moore, 1992, 1995). In one typical experiment, people listened to tapes labelled "memory" or "self-esteem," but some heard tapes that were incorrectly labelled. About half showed improvement in the area specified by the label whether it was correct or not; the improvement was due to expectations alone (Greenwald et al., 1991).

Three Canadian psychologists from the University of Waterloo have suggested that previous efforts at subliminal persuasion left out an important ingredient: the person's motivation. Instead of trying to influence people directly by using a subliminal message such as "Drink Coke," these researchers used subliminal messages—the words *thirst* and *dry*—to make participants feel thirsty and prime them to drink. Later, when given a chance to drink, the primed participants did in fact drink more than control participants did, but only if they had been moderately thirsty to begin with (Strahan, Spencer, & Zanna, 2002).

Does this mean that advertisers can seduce us into buying soft drinks or voting for political candidates by slipping subliminal slogans and images into television and magazine ads? The priming research has renewed the debate. However, given the many studies that have found no evidence of subliminal persuasion and the subtlety of the effects that do occur (you have to be somewhat thirsty already to be primed to want to drink), we think there's little cause for worry about subliminal manipulation. If

> ## THINKING CRITICALLY
>
> Examine the evidence.
>
> For just $29.95, a "subliminal tape" promises to tune up your sluggish motivation. It is true that many perceptual processes occur outside awareness, but does that mean that these tapes can change your behaviour or improve your life?

advertisers want you to buy something, they will probably do better to spend their money on above-threshold messages. And if you want to improve yourself or your life, you'll have to do it the old-fashioned way: by working at it consciously.

As we have seen throughout this chapter, we do not register the world "out there" passively; we mentally construct it. All of us, even those of us who are not usually gullible, have needs and beliefs that can fool us into seeing things we *want* to see. All of us occasionally read meanings into sensory experiences that are not inherent in the experience itself; who has not seen nonexistent water on a hot highway, or felt a nonexistent insect on the skin after merely thinking about bugs?

The great Greek philosopher Plato once said that "knowledge is nothing but perception," but he was wrong. Simple perception is *not* always the best path to knowledge. Because our sense organs evolved for particular purposes, our sensory windows on the world are partly shuttered. But we can use reason, ingenuity, and scientific inquiry to pry those shutters open. Ordinary perception tells us that the sun circles the Earth, but the great astronomer Copernicus was able to figure out nearly five centuries ago that the opposite is true. Ordinary perception will never let us see ultraviolet and infrared rays directly, but we know they are there, and we can measure them. If research can enable us to overturn the everyday evidence of our senses, who knows what surprises science has in store for us?

✓●─ **Study** and **Review**
in **MyPsychLab**

Recite & Review

Recite: Tell someone everything you can remember about perception without awareness, especially *priming* and subliminal persuasion.

Review: Next, read this section again, focusing on what you couldn't remember.

Quick Quiz:

Please remain conscious to answer this question.

A study appears to find evidence of "sleep learning"—the ability to perceive and retain material played on an audio recording while a person sleeps. What would you want to know about this research before deciding to record this chapter and play it by your bedside all night instead of studying it in the usual way?

Answers:

Was there a control group that listened to, say, a musical selection or white noise? How complicated was the material that was allegedly learned: a few key words, whole sentences, a whole lecture by Professor Arbuckle? Were the results large enough to have any practical applications? How did the researchers determine that the participants really were asleep? (When brain-wave measures are used to verify that volunteers are actually sleeping, no "sleep learning" takes place.)

Taking Psychology with You

Extrasensory Perception: Reality or Illusion?

Eyes, ears, mouth, nose, skin—we rely on these organs for our experience of the external world. Some people, however, claim they can send and receive messages about the world without relying on the usual sensory channels, by using extrasensory perception (ESP). Reported ESP experiences involve things like telepathy, the direct communication of messages from one mind to another without the usual sensory signals, and precognition, the perception of an event that has not yet happened. Most ESP claims challenge everything we currently know to be true about the way the world and the universe operate. A lot of people are ready to accept these claims. Should they?

Evidence or Coincidence? Much of the supposed evidence for extrasensory perception comes from anecdotal accounts. But people are not always reliable reporters of their own experiences. They often embellish and exaggerate, or they recall only part of what happened. They also tend to forget incidents that don't fit their beliefs, such as "premonitions" of events that fail to occur. Many ESP experiences could merely be unusual coincidences that are memorable because they are dramatic. What passes for telepathy or precognition could also be based on what a person knows or deduces through ordinary means. If Joanne's father has had two heart attacks, her premonition that her father will die shortly (followed, in fact, by her father's death) may not be so impressive.

The scientific way to establish a phenomenon is to produce it under controlled conditions. Extrasensory perception has been studied extensively by researchers in the field of *parapsychology*. But ESP studies have often been poorly designed, with inadequate precautions against fraud and improper statistical analysis. After an exhaustive review, the National Research Council concluded that there was "no scientific justification . . . for the existence of parapsychological phenomena" (Druckman & Swets, 1988). Other investigators have presented rational explanations for the apparent perception of various "psychic" phenomena. For example, at Laurentian University, Michael Persinger and his colleagues presented evidence that these perceptions are related to signs of temporal lobe epilepsy in otherwise neurologically normal individuals (Persinger & Makarec, 1987). People who report having "psychic" experiences also tend to show some signs of epilepsy!

The history of research on psychic phenomena has been one of initial enthusiasm because of apparently positive results (Bem & Honorton, 1994; Dalton et al., 1996), followed by disappointment when results cannot be replicated (Milton & Wiseman, 1999, 2001). The thousands of studies done since the 1940s have failed to make a convincing case for ESP. One researcher who tried for 30 years to establish the reality of psychic phenomena finally gave up in defeat. "I found no psychic phenomena," she wrote, "only wishful thinking, self-deception, experimental error, and even an occasional fraud. I became a sceptic" (Blackmore, 2001).

The issue has not gone away, however. Many people really, really want to believe that ESP exists. James Randi, a famous magician who is dedicated to educating the public about psychic deception, has for years offered a million dollars to anyone who can demonstrate ESP or other paranormal powers under close observation. Many have taken up the challenge; no one has succeeded. We think Randi's money is safe.

Lessons from a Magician. Despite the lack of evidence for ESP, many people say they believe in it. Perhaps you yourself have had an experience that seemed to involve ESP, or perhaps you have seen a convincing demonstration by someone else. Surely you can trust the evidence of your own eyes. Or can you? We will answer this question with a true story, one that contains an important lesson about why it's a good idea to think critically regarding ESP.

During the 1970s, Andrew Weil (who is now known for his efforts to promote alternative medicine) set out to investigate the claims of a self-proclaimed psychic named Uri Geller (Weil, 1974a, b). Weil, who believed in telepathy, felt that ESP might be explained by principles of modern physics, and he was receptive to Geller's claims. When he met Geller at a private gathering, he was not disappointed. Geller correctly identified a cross and a Star of David sealed inside separate envelopes. He made a stopped watch start running and made a ring sag into an oval shape, apparently without touching them. He also made keys change shape. Weil came away a convert. What he had seen with his own eyes seemed impossible to deny . . . until he went to visit the Amazing Randi.

To Weil's astonishment, Randi was able to duplicate much of what Geller had done. He, too, could bend keys and guess the contents of sealed envelopes. But Randi's feats were tricks, and he was willing to show Weil exactly how they were done. Weil suddenly experienced "a sense of how strongly the mind can impose its own interpretations on perceptions; how it can see what it expects to see, but not see the unexpected."

Weil was disillusioned—literally. Even when he knew what to look for in a trick, he could not catch the Amazing Randi doing it. Weil learned that our sense impressions of reality are not the same as reality. Our eyes, our ears, and especially our brains can play tricks on us.

Summary

- *Sensation* is the detection and direct experience of physical energy as a result of environmental or internal events.

Perception is the process by which sensory impulses are organized and interpreted.

Our Sensational Senses

- Sensation begins with the *sense receptors*, which convert the energy of a stimulus into electrical impulses that travel along nerves to the brain. Separate sensations can be accounted for by *anatomical codes* (as set forth by the *doctrine of specific nerve energies*) and *functional codes* in the nervous system. In *sensory substitution*, sensory crossover from one modality to another occurs and, in *synesthesia*, sensation in one modality evokes a sensation in another modality, but these experiences are rare.

- Psychologists specializing in *psychophysics* have studied sensory sensitivity by measuring *absolute* and *difference thresholds*. *Signal-detection theory*, however, holds that responses in a detection task consist of both a sensory process and a decision process and will vary with the person's motivation, alertness, and expectations.

- Our senses are designed to respond to change and contrast in the environment. When stimulation is unchanging, *sensory adaptation* occurs. Too little stimulation can cause *sensory deprivation*, and too much stimulation can cause *sensory overload*. *Selective attention* prevents overload and allows us to focus on what is important, but it also deprives us of sensory information we may need, as in *inattentional blindness*.

Vision

- Vision is affected by the wavelength, frequency, and complexity of light, which produce the psychological dimensions of visual experience—*hue*, *brightness*, and *saturation*. The visual receptors, *rods* and *cones*, are located in the *retina* of the eye. They send signals (via other cells) to the *ganglion cells* and ultimately to the *optic nerve*, which carries visual information to the brain. Rods are responsible for vision in dim light; cones are responsible for colour vision. *Dark adaptation* occurs in two stages.

- Specific aspects of the visual world, such as lines at various orientations, are detected by *feature-detector cells* in the visual areas of the brain. Some of these cells respond maximally to complex patterns. A heated debate is now going on about the existence of specialized "face modules" in the brain. In general, however, the brain takes in fragmentary information about lines, angles, shapes, motion, brightness, texture, and other features of what we see and comes up with a unified view of the world.

- The *trichromatic* and *opponent-process* theories of colour vision apply to different stages of processing. In the first stage, three types of cones in the retina respond selectively to different wavelengths of light. In the second, *opponent-process cells* in the retina and the thalamus respond in opposite fashion to short and long wavelengths of light.

- Perception involves the active construction of a model of the world from moment to moment. The *Gestalt principles* (for example, *figure and ground*, *proximity*, *closure*, *similarity*, and *continuity*) describe visual strategies used by the brain to perceive forms.

- We localize objects in visual space by using both *binocular* and *monocular* cues to depth. Binocular cues include *convergence* and *retinal disparity*. Monocular cues include, among others, *interposition* and *linear perspective*. *Perceptual constancies* allow us to perceive objects as stable despite changes in the sensory patterns they produce. *Perceptual illusions* occur when sensory cues are misleading or when we misinterpret cues.

Hearing

- Hearing (*audition*) is affected by the intensity, frequency, and complexity of pressure waves in the air or other transmitting substance, corresponding to the experience of *loudness*, *pitch*, and *timbre* of the sound. The receptors for hearing are *hair cells (cilia)* embedded in the *basilar membrane*, in the interior of the *cochlea* (in the *organ of Corti*). These receptors pass signals along the *auditory nerve*. The sounds we hear are determined by patterns of hair-cell movement, which produce different neural codes. When we localize sounds, we use as cues subtle differences in how pressure waves reach each of our ears.

Other Senses

- Taste (*gustation*) is a chemical sense. Elevations on the tongue, called *papillae*, contain many *taste buds*, which in turn contain the taste receptors. The basic tastes include salty, sour, bitter, sweet, and umami. Responses to a particular taste depend in part on genetic differences among individuals; for example, some people are "supertasters." Taste preferences are also affected by culture and learning, and by the texture, temperature, and smell of food.

- Smell (*olfaction*) is also a chemical sense. No basic odours have been identified, and up to 1000 different receptor types exist. But researchers have discovered that distinct odours activate unique combinations of receptor types, and they have started to identify those combinations. Odours also have psychological effects and can affect behaviour even when people are unaware of their influence. Cultural and individual differences also affect people's responses to particular odours.

- The skin senses include touch (pressure), warmth, cold, pain, and variations such as itch and tickle. Except in the case of pressure, it has been difficult to identify specialized receptors for these senses, but researchers have reported a receptor for one kind of itching and a possible receptor for cold.

- Pain is both a skin sense and an internal sense. According to the *gate-control theory*, the experience of pain depends on whether neural impulses get past a "gate" in the spinal cord and reach the brain. According to a revised version of this theory, a matrix of neurons in the brain can generate pain even in the absence of signals from sensory neurons, which may help explain the puzzling phenomenon of *phantom pain*. No one theory, however, completely explains perception of pain, which involves the release of many chemicals all along the pain pathways, and also the involvement of *glial cells*.

- *Kinesthesis* tells us where our body parts are located, and *equilibrium* tells us the orientation of the body as a whole. Together, these two senses provide us with a feeling of physical embodiment.

Perceptual Powers: Origins and Influences

- Many fundamental perceptual skills are inborn or are acquired shortly after birth. By using the *visual cliff*, for example, psychologists have learned that babies have depth perception by the age of six months and possibly even earlier. However, without certain experiences during *critical periods* early in life, cells in the nervous system deteriorate, change, or fail to form appropriate neural pathways, and perception is impaired. This is why efforts to correct congenital blindness or deafness are most successful when they take place early in life.

- Psychological influences on perception include needs, beliefs, emotions, and expectations (which produce *perceptual sets*). These influences are determined by culture, which gives people practice with certain kinds of experiences and affects what they attend to.

Puzzles of Perception

- In the laboratory, studies using *priming* show that simple visual subliminal messages can influence certain behaviours, judgments, and motivational states, such as thirst. However, no evidence indicates that "subliminal-perception" tapes or other commercial subliminal techniques can alter complex behaviours.

Taking Psychology with You

- Years of research have failed to produce convincing evidence for extrasensory perception (ESP). What so-called psychics do is no different from what all good magicians do: capitalize on people's beliefs and expectations.

Key Terms

sensation 175	selective attention 182	trichromatic theory 187	organ of Corti 198
perception 175	inattentional blindness 182	opponent-process theory 188	cochlea 198
sense receptors 176	hue 184		papillae 200
doctrine of specific nerve energies 177	brightness 184	Gestalt principles 189	taste buds 201
synesthesia 177	saturation 184	binocular cues 190	gate-control theory of pain 204
absolute threshold 178	retina 184	convergence 190	phantom pain 205
difference threshold 179	rods 184	retinal disparity 191	kinesthesis 206
signal-detection theory 180	cones 184	monocular cues 191	equilibrium 206
sensory adaptation 180	dark adaptation 185	perceptual constancy 191	semicircular canals 206
sensory deprivation 181	ganglion cells 185	loudness 197	perceptual set 210
	feature detector cells 186	pitch 197	priming 212
		timbre 197	

7

Learning and Conditioning

Ask questions. . . be willing to wonder

Why are so many people scared to death of snakes and spiders?

Why do efforts to crack down on wrongdoers often fail?

Is there anything wrong with paying kids to get good grades?

Why does playing violent video games make some people aggressive and others not?

learning A relatively permanent change in behaviour (or behavioural potential) due to experience.

behaviourism An approach to psychology that emphasizes the study of observable behaviour and the role of the environment and prior experience as determinants of behaviour.

conditioning A basic kind of learning that involves associations among environmental stimuli and an organism's behaviour.

It's January 1, a brand-new year. The sins and lapses of the old year are behind you; the slate is clean and you're ready for a fresh start. Optimistically, you sit down to record your New Year's resolutions: to eat better, study harder, control your temper, get in shape, manage your spending, . . . (you can fill in the rest). How likely are you to achieve these goals? Within weeks, days, or even hours, many people find themselves reverting to their old habits ("Well, maybe just one *small* cookie"). They may decide that trying to mend their ways is pointless because they lack the willpower, brains, or courage to do it. In this chapter, however, we will see that, in fact, willpower, brains, and courage often have little to do with the ability to change your ways.

People do not want to fix just their own behaviour, of course; they are forever trying to improve or fix other people's behaviour as well. We imprison criminals, punish children, shout at spouses, give the finger to a driver who cuts us off, and impose zero-tolerance policies for the slightest infraction of a rule. On the positive side, we give children gold stars for good work, give parents bumper stickers that praise their children's successes, give bonuses to employees, and give out trophies for top performance. Do any of these efforts get the results we hope for? Well, yes and no. Once you understand the laws of **learning**, you will realize that behaviour, whether it's your own or other people's, *can* change for the better—and you will also understand why often it does not.

Research on learning has been heavily influenced by **behaviourism**, the school of psychology that accounts for behaviour in terms of observable acts and events. Unlike the cognitive approach (see Chapter 9), a behavioural perspective emphasizes the influence of prior experience on current behaviour, without reference to mental entities such as "mind" or "will." Behaviourists focus on **conditioning**, which involves associations between environmental stimuli and behaviour. Two types of conditioning, *classical conditioning* and *operant conditioning*, can explain a great deal of behaviour both in animals and in people. But other approaches, including *social-cognitive learning theories*, hold that omitting mental processes from explanations of human learning is like omitting passion from descriptions of sex: You may explain the form, but you miss its essence. To social-cognitive theorists,

219

👁—Watch the **Video**
The Big Picture: What Does It Mean to Learn? in **MyPsychLab**

learning includes not only changes in behaviour but also changes in thoughts, expectations, and knowledge, which in turn influence behaviour in a reciprocal, or two-way, process. 👁

Learning Objectives

1 List four important features of classical conditioning.

2 Summarize what is actually learned in classical conditioning.

Classical Conditioning

At the turn of the twentieth century, the great Russian physiologist Ivan Pavlov (1849–1936) was studying salivation in dogs as part of his Nobel prize-winning research on digestion. One of his procedures was to make a surgical opening in a dog's cheek and insert a tube that conducted saliva away from the animal's salivary gland so that the saliva could be measured. To stimulate the reflexive flow of saliva, Pavlov placed meat powder or other food in the dog's mouth (see Figure 7.1).

Pavlov was a truly dedicated scientific observer. Many years later, as he lay dying, he even dictated his sensations for posterity! He instilled in his students and assistants the same passion for detail. During his salivation studies, one of the assistants noticed something that most people would have overlooked or dismissed as trivial. After a dog had been brought to the laboratory a few times, it would start to salivate before the food was placed in its mouth. The sight or smell of the food, the dish in which the food was kept, and even the sight of the person who delivered the food were enough to start the dog's mouth watering. These new salivary responses clearly were not inborn, so they must have been acquired through experience.

👁—Watch the **Video**
Classic Footage of Pavlov
in **MyPsychLab**

At first, Pavlov treated the dog's drooling as just an annoying secretion. But he quickly realized that his assistant had stumbled onto an important phenomenon, one that Pavlov came to believe was the basis of most learning in human beings and other animals (Pavlov, 1927). He called that phenomenon a "conditional" reflex because it depended on environmental conditions. Later, an error in the translation of his writings transformed "conditional" into "conditioned," the word most commonly used today.

Pavlov soon dropped what he had been doing and turned to the study of conditioned reflexes, to which he devoted the last three decades of his life. Why were his dogs salivating to stimuli other than food? 👁

FIGURE 7.1 Pavlov's Method
The photo shows Ivan Pavlov (with the white beard), flanked by his students and a canine subject. The drawing depicts an apparatus similar to the one he used; saliva from a dog's cheek flowed down a tube and was measured by the movement of a needle on a revolving drum.

The Granger Collection

New Reflexes from Old

Pavlov initially speculated about what his dogs might be thinking and feeling when they drooled before getting their food. Was the doggy equivalent of "Oh boy, dinner!" going through their minds? He soon decided, however, that such speculation was pointless. Instead, he focused on analyzing the environment in which the conditioned reflex arose.

The original salivary reflex, according to Pavlov, consisted of an **unconditioned stimulus (US)**, food in the dog's mouth, and an **unconditioned response (UR)**, salivation. By an unconditioned stimulus, Pavlov meant a thing or event that elicits a response automatically or reflexively. By an unconditioned response, he meant the response that is automatically produced:

In Pavlov's lab, when some neutral stimulus such as the dish—a stimulus that did not typically cause the dog to salivate—was regularly paired with food, the dog learned to associate the dish and the food. As a result, the dish alone acquired the power to make the dog salivate:

More generally, as a neutral stimulus and US become associated, the neutral stimulus becomes a **conditioned stimulus (CS)**. The CS then has the capacity to elicit a learned or **conditioned response (CR)** that is usually similar or related to the original, unlearned one. In Pavlov's laboratory, the sight of the food dish, which had not previously elicited salivation, became a CS for salivation:

The procedure by which a previously neutral stimulus becomes a conditioned stimulus eventually became known as **classical conditioning** and is sometimes also called *Pavlovian* or *respondent* conditioning. Pavlov and his students went on to show that all sorts of things can become conditioned stimuli for salivation if they are paired

unconditioned stimulus (US) The classical-conditioning term for a stimulus that already elicits a certain response without additional learning.

unconditioned response (UR) The classical-conditioning term for a response elicited by an unconditioned stimulus.

conditioned stimulus (CS) The classical-conditioning term for an initially neutral stimulus that comes to elicit a conditioned response after being associated with an unconditioned stimulus.

conditioned response (CR) The classical-conditioning term for a response that is elicited by a conditioned stimulus; it occurs after the conditioned stimulus is associated with an unconditioned stimulus.

classical conditioning The process by which a previously neutral stimulus becomes associated with a stimulus that already elicits a response and, in turn, acquires the capacity to elicit a similar or related response. Also called Pavlovian or respondent conditioning.

extinction The weakening and eventual disappearance of a learned response; in classical conditioning, it occurs when the conditioned stimulus is no longer paired with the unconditioned stimulus.

spontaneous recovery The reappearance of a learned response after its apparent extinction.

higher-order conditioning In classical conditioning, a procedure in which a neutral stimulus becomes a conditioned stimulus through association with an already established conditioned stimulus.

⊙─Watch the **Video**
The Basics 1: Classical Conditioning: An Involuntary Response in **MyPsychLab**

with food: the ticking of a metronome, the musical tone of a bell, the vibrating sound of a buzzer, a touch on the leg, even a pinprick or an electric shock.

Principles of Classical Conditioning

Classical conditioning occurs in all species, from one-celled amoebas to *Homo sapiens*. Many responses besides salivation have been classically conditioned, including heartbeat, blood pressure, alertness, hunger, and sexual arousal. In the laboratory, the optimal interval between the presentation of the neutral stimulus and the presentation of the US is often quite short, sometimes less than a second. Let us look more closely at some of classical conditioning's other important features: extinction, higher-order conditioning, and stimulus generalization and discrimination. ⊙

Extinction. Conditioned responses can persist for months or years. However, if a conditioned stimulus is repeatedly presented without the unconditioned stimulus, the conditioned response will weaken and may eventually disappear, a process known as **extinction** (see Figure 7.2). Suppose that you train your dog Khali to salivate to the sound of a bell, but then you ring the bell every five minutes and do *not* follow it with food. Khali will salivate less and less to the bell and will soon stop salivating altogether; salivation will have been extinguished. Extinction, however, is not the same as unlearning. If you come back the next day and ring the bell, Khali may salivate again for a few trials, although the response will probably be weaker. The reappearance of the response, called **spontaneous recovery**, explains why completely eliminating a conditioned response often requires more than one extinction session.

Higher-Order Conditioning. Sometimes a neutral stimulus can become a conditioned stimulus by being paired with an already established CS, a procedure known as **higher-order conditioning**. Say Khali has learned to salivate to the sight of his food dish. Now you flash a bright light before presenting the dish. With repeated pairings of the light and the dish, Khali may learn to salivate to the light. The procedure for higher-order conditioning is illustrated in Figure 7.3.

FIGURE 7.2 Acquisition and Extinction of a Salivary Response
A neutral stimulus that is consistently followed by an unconditioned stimulus for salivation will become a conditioned stimulus for salivation (left side of graph). But when this conditioned stimulus is then repeatedly presented without the unconditioned stimulus, the conditioned salivary response will weaken and eventually disappear; it has been extinguished.

FIGURE 7.3 Higher-Order Conditioning
In this illustration of higher-order conditioning, the food dish is a previously conditioned stimulus for salivation (left). When the light, a neutral stimulus, is paired with the dish (centre), the light also becomes a conditioned stimulus for salivation (right).

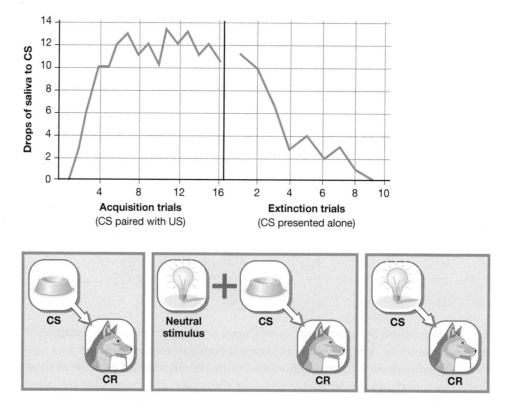

Higher-order conditioning may explain why some words trigger emotional responses in us—why they can inflame us to anger or evoke warm, sentimental feelings. When words are paired with objects or other words that already elicit some emotional response, they too may come to elicit that response (Staats & Staats, 1957). A child may learn a positive response to the word *birthday* because of its association with gifts and attention. Conversely, the child may learn a negative response to ethnic or national labels if the labels are paired with words that the child has already learned are disagreeable, such as *dumb* or *dirty*. Higher-order conditioning, in other words, may contribute to the formation of prejudices.

Stimulus Generalization and Discrimination. After a stimulus becomes a conditioned stimulus for some response, other similar stimuli may produce a similar reaction, a phenomenon known as **stimulus generalization**. If you condition your patient pooch Khali to salivate to middle C on the piano, Khali may also salivate to D, which is one tone above C, even though you did not pair D with food. Stimulus generalization is described nicely by an old proverb: "He who hath been bitten by a snake fears a rope."

The mirror image of stimulus generalization is **stimulus discrimination**, in which *different* responses are made to stimuli that resemble the conditioned stimulus in some way. Suppose that you have conditioned Khali to salivate to middle C on the piano by repeatedly pairing the sound with food. Now you play middle C on a guitar, *without* following it by food (but you continue to follow C on the piano by food). Eventually, Khali will learn to salivate to a C on the piano and not to salivate to the same note on the guitar; that is, he will discriminate between the two sounds. If you keep at this long enough, you could train Khali to be a pretty discriminating drooler!

stimulus generalization After conditioning, the tendency to respond to a stimulus that resembles one involved in the original conditioning; in classical conditioning, it occurs when a stimulus that resembles the CS elicits the CR.

stimulus discrimination The tendency to respond differently to two or more similar stimuli; in classical conditioning, it occurs when a stimulus similar to the CS fails to evoke the CR.

What Is Actually Learned in Classical Conditioning?

For classical conditioning to be most effective, the stimulus to be conditioned should *precede* the unconditioned stimulus rather than follow it or occur simultaneously with it. This makes sense, because in classical conditioning the conditioned stimulus becomes a *signal* for the unconditioned stimulus. Classical conditioning is in fact an evolutionary adaptation, one that enables the organism to anticipate and prepare for a biologically important event that is about to happen. In Pavlov's studies, for instance, a bell, buzzer, or other stimulus was a signal that meat was coming, and the dog's salivation was preparation for digesting food. Today, therefore, many psychologists contend that what an animal or person actually learns in classical conditioning is not merely an association between two paired stimuli that occur close together in time, but rather *information* conveyed by one stimulus about another: "If a tone sounds, food is likely to follow."

This view is supported by the research of Robert Rescorla (1988), who showed, in a series of imaginative studies, that the mere pairing of an unconditioned stimulus and a neutral stimulus is not enough to produce learning. To become a conditioned stimulus, the neutral stimulus must reliably signal, or *predict*, the unconditioned stimulus. If food occurs just as often *without* a preceding tone as with it, the tone is unlikely to become a conditioned stimulus for salivation, because the tone does not provide any information about the probability of getting food. Think of it this way: If every phone call you got brought bad news that made your heart race, your heart might soon start pounding every time the phone rang—a conditioned response. Ordinarily, though, upsetting calls occur randomly among a far greater number of routine ones. The ringtone may sometimes be paired with a racing heart, but it doesn't always signal disaster, so no conditioned heart-rate response occurs.

Rescorla concluded that "Pavlovian conditioning is not a stupid process by which the organism willy-nilly forms associations between any two stimuli that happen to co-occur. Rather, the organism is better seen as an information seeker using logical and perceptual

GET INVOLVED! Conditioning an Eye-Blink Response

Try out your behavioural skills by conditioning an eye-blink response in a willing friend, using classical-conditioning procedures. You will need a drinking straw and something to make a ringing sound; a spoon tapped on a water glass works well. Tell your friend that you are going to use the straw to blow air in his or her eye, but do not say why. Immediately before each puff of air, make the ringing sound. Repeat this procedure ten times. Then make the ringing sound but don't puff. Your friend will probably blink anyway, and may continue to do so for one or two more repetitions of the sound before the response extinguishes. Can you identify the US, the UR, the CS, and the CR in this exercise?

✳ Explore the Concept
What Learning Techniques Do You Use?
in MyPsychLab

relations among events, along with its own preconceptions, to form a sophisticated representation of its world." Not all learning theorists agree; an orthodox behaviourist would say that it is silly to talk about the preconceptions of a rat. The important point, however, is that concepts such as "information seeking," "preconceptions," and "representations of the world" open the door to a more cognitive view of classical conditioning. ✳

Recite & Review

Recite: When you hear the tone, say as much as you remember about these concepts (ding!): *learning, behaviourism, conditioning, unconditioned stimulus, conditioned stimulus, unconditioned response, conditioned response, classical conditioning, extinction, spontaneous recovery, higher-order conditioning, stimulus generalization,* and *stimulus discrimination.*

Review: Next, go back and read this section again.

Now take this *Quick Quiz:*

A. Name the unconditioned stimulus, unconditioned response, conditioned stimulus, and conditioned response in these two situations:
 1. Five-year-old Emily is watching a storm from her window. A huge bolt of lightning is followed by a tremendous thunderclap, and Emily jumps at the noise. This happens several more times. There is a brief lull and then another lightning bolt. Emily jumps in response to the bolt.
 2. Gregory's mouth waters whenever he eats anything with lemon in it. One day, while reading an ad that shows a big glass of lemonade, Gregory finds that his mouth has started to water.

B. In the view of many learning theorists, pairing a neutral and unconditioned stimulus is not enough to produce classical conditioning; the neutral stimulus must _____ the unconditioned stimulus.

Answers:

A. 1. US = the thunderclap; UR = jumping elicited by the noise; CS = the sight of the lightning; CR = jumping elicited by the lightning 2. US = the taste of lemon; UR = salivation elicited by the taste of lemon; CS = the picture of a glass of lemonade; CR = salivation elicited by the picture B. signal or predict

Learning Objectives

3 Describe why advertisers often include pleasant information or music in ads for their products.

4 Illustrate how classical conditioning might be used to explain common fears.

5 Give examples of how you might be conditioned to like certain tastes and odours and dislike others.

6 Break down the factors underlying how placebos make you feel better.

Classical Conditioning in Real Life

If a dog can learn to salivate to the ringing of a bell, so can you. In fact, you probably have learned to salivate to the sound of a lunch bell, the phrase *hot fudge sundae*, and "mouth-watering" pictures on Instagram. But classical conditioning affects us every day in many other ways.

One of the first psychologists to recognize the real-life implications of Pavlovian theory was John B. Watson, who founded behaviourism in North America and enthusiastically promoted Pavlov's ideas. Watson believed that the whole rich array of human emotion and behaviour could be accounted for by conditioning principles. Watson even went so far as to claim that we learn to love another person when that person is paired with stroking and cuddling. Most psychologists, and nonpsychologists too, think Watson was wrong about love, which is a lot more complicated than he thought (see Chapter 12). But he was right about the power of classical conditioning to affect our emotions, preferences, and tastes.

John B. Watson (1878–1958).

Getty Images Inc.

Learning to Like

Classical conditioning plays a big role in our emotional responses to objects, people, symbols, events, and places. It can explain why sentimental feelings sweep over us when we see a school mascot, a national flag, or the logo of the Olympic games. These objects have been associated in the past with positive feelings:

Many advertising techniques take advantage of classical conditioning's role in emotional responses. In one study, students at the University of British Columbia looked at slides of either a beige pen or a blue pen while listening to either a theme song from a recent popular movie or a selection of traditional music from India. (The experimenter made the assumption that the theme music would be more appealing to the students in the study.) Later the students were allowed to choose one of the pens. Almost three-fourths of those who heard the theme music chose a pen that was the same colour as the one they had seen in the slides. An equal number of those who heard the Indian music chose a pen that *differed* in colour from the one they had seen (Gorn, 1982).

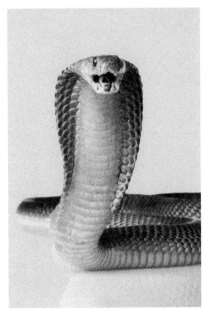

Why do most people fear snakes, and why do some even develop a snake phobia?

Martin Harvey/Getty Images

Learning to Fear

Positive emotions are not the only ones that can be classically conditioned; so can dislikes and fears. A person can learn to fear just about anything if it is paired with something that elicits pain, surprise, or embarrassment. Human beings, however, are biologically primed or "prepared" to acquire some kinds of fears more readily than others. It is far easier to establish a conditioned fear of spiders, snakes, and heights than of butterflies, flowers, and toasters. The former can be dangerous to your health, so in the process of evolution, human beings may have acquired a tendency to learn quickly to be wary of them and to retain this fear (LoBue & DeLoache, 2008; Öhman & Mineka, 2001; but see Tierney & Connolly, 2013 who note some problems with the methods in some of the studies). Evolution may also have instilled in humans a readiness to learn to fear unfamiliar members of groups other than their own, a tendency that may contribute to the emotional underpinnings of prejudice (Navarrete et al., 2009; Olsson et al., 2005).

When fear of an object or situation becomes irrational and interferes with normal activities, it qualifies as a *phobia* (see Chapter 15). To demonstrate how a phobia might be learned, John Watson and Rosalie Rayner (1920/2000) deliberately established a rat phobia in an 11-month-old boy named Albert. Their goal was to demonstrate how an inborn reaction of fear could transfer to a wide range of stimuli; today, we call this stimulus generalization. They also wanted to demonstrate that adult emotional responses, such as specific fears, could originate in early childhood. The research procedures used by Watson and Rayner had some flaws, and for ethical reasons, no psychologist today would attempt to do such a thing to a child. Nevertheless, the study's main conclusion, that fears can be conditioned, is still well accepted. ◉

◉─┤Watch the Video
Special Topics: Learning to Overcome Phobias in **MyPsychLab**

"Little Albert" was a placid child who rarely cried. (Watson and Rayner deliberately chose such a child because they thought their demonstration would do him relatively little harm.) When Watson and Rayner gave Albert a live, furry rat to play with, he showed no fear; in fact, he was delighted. The same was true when they showed him a variety of other objects, including a rabbit and some cotton wool. However, like most children, Albert was innately afraid of loud noises. When the researchers made a loud noise behind his head by striking a steel bar with a hammer, he would jump and fall sideways onto the mattress where he was sitting. The noise made by the hammer was an unconditioned stimulus for the unconditioned response of fear. ◉

◉─┤Watch the Video
Classic Footage of Little Albert in **MyPsychLab**

Having established that Albert liked rats, Watson and Rayner set about teaching him to fear them. Again they offered him a rat, but this time, as he reached for it, one of the researchers struck the steel bar. Startled, Albert fell onto the mattress. A week later, they repeated this procedure several times. Albert began to whimper and tremble. Finally, they held out the rat to him without making the noise. Albert fell over, cried, and crawled away so quickly that he almost reached the edge of the table he was sitting on before an adult caught him; the rat had become a conditioned stimulus for fear:

Tests done a few days later showed that Albert's fear had generalized to other hairy or furry objects, including a white rabbit, cotton wool, a Santa Claus mask, and even John Watson's hair.

Unfortunately, Watson and Rayner lost access to Little Albert, so we do not know how long the child's fears lasted. Further, because the study ended early, Watson and Rayner had no opportunity to reverse the conditioning. However, Watson and Mary Cover Jones did reverse another child's conditioned fear—one that was, as Watson put it, "home grown" rather than psychologist-induced (Jones, 1924). A three-year-old named Peter was deathly afraid of rabbits. To reverse Peter's fear, Watson and Jones used a method called **counterconditioning**, in which a conditioned stimulus is paired with some other stimulus that elicits a response incompatible with the unwanted response. Counterconditioning probably does not eliminate prior learning, but instead leads to new learning that supplants or overrides old learning. In this case, the rabbit (the CS) was paired with a snack of milk and crackers, and the snack produced pleasant feelings that were incompatible with the conditioned response of fear. At first, Watson and Jones kept the rabbit some distance from Peter, so that his fear would remain at a low level. Otherwise, Peter might have learned to fear milk and crackers! Then gradually, over several days, they brought the rabbit closer and closer. Eventually, Peter learned to like rabbits:

> **counterconditioning** In classical conditioning, the process of pairing a conditioned stimulus with a stimulus that elicits a response that is incompatible with an unwanted conditioned response.

Peter was even able to sit with the rabbit in his lap, playing with it with one hand while he ate with the other. A variation of this procedure, called *systematic desensitization*, was later devised for treating phobias in adults (see Chapter 16).

Back when John Watson was using counterconditioning to help young Peter overcome his fear of rabbits, he focused on the observable associations between unconditioned and conditioned stimuli and responses. Techniques for understanding the biological basis of classical conditioning were limited. But today, technology and a better understanding of the brain are letting scientists explore methods for helping people overcome debilitating conditioned fears in ways that Watson could scarcely have imagined.

The amygdala plays a central role in the conditioning of fear, in part because of a receptor for the neurotransmitter glutamate (Bermudo-Soriano et al., 2012). Giving rats a drug that blocks this receptor prevents extinction of a conditioned fear, whereas giving a drug that enhances the receptor's activity speeds up extinction (Walker et al., 2002). Inspired by these results, scientists set out to discover whether the same receptor-enhancing drug, which is safe in humans, could help people with a phobic fear of heights (Davis et al., 2005). Using a double-blind procedure, they gave the drug to 15 people with that phobia and a placebo to 15 others. All participants then underwent two therapy sessions in which they donned virtual-reality goggles and "rode" a glass elevator to progressively higher floors in a virtual hotel—an incredibly scary thing to do if you're terrified of heights. They could also "walk" out on a bridge and look down on a fountain in the hotel lobby. During each session, and again at one-week and three-month follow-up sessions, the participants rated their discomfort at each "floor." Combining the therapy with the drug reduced symptoms far more than combining it with the placebo. Further, in their everyday lives, people who got the drug were less likely than the controls to avoid heights.

Finally, DNA analysis has been used to investigate how genetic differences might explain why some people are more likely than others to become anxious and fearful. In a study done in Sweden, researchers conditioned university students to startle in response to pictures of faces. Only those students who had a particular gene associated with reactivity in the amygdala acquired the conditioned startle response. Moreover, those students who carried a gene associated with impaired cognitive control in the prefrontal cortex showed resistance to extinction of the response (Lonsdorf et al., 2009).

Whether we say "yuck" or "yum" to a food may depend on a past experience involving classical conditioning. This Inuit family is eating mattak, the raw fatty skin of a beluga whale, which is considered a delicacy by this culture. You may not respond as positively to this treat.

Fred Lum/Globe and Mail DIGITAL IMAGE/The Canadian Press Images

Such research helps us to understand the biological mechanisms that underlie our fears, and the principles of behaviourism that may help us control and even overcome them.

Accounting for Taste

Classical conditioning can also explain learned reactions to many foods and odours. In the laboratory, researchers have taught animals to dislike foods or odours by pairing them with drugs that cause nausea or other unpleasant symptoms. One team trained slugs to associate the smell of carrots, which slugs normally like, with a bitter-tasting chemical they detest. Soon the slugs were avoiding the smell of carrots. The researchers then demonstrated higher-order conditioning by pairing the smell of carrots with the smell of potato. Sure enough, the slugs began to avoid the smell of potato as well (Sahley, Rudy, & Gelperin, 1981).

Many people have learned to dislike a food after eating it and then falling ill, even when the two events were unrelated. The food, previously a neutral stimulus, becomes a conditioned stimulus for nausea or other symptoms produced by the illness. Psychologist Martin Seligman once told how he himself was conditioned to hate béarnaise sauce. One night, shortly after he and his wife ate a delicious filet mignon with béarnaise sauce, he came down with the flu. Naturally, he felt wretched. His misery had nothing to do with the béarnaise sauce, of course, yet the next time he tried it, he found to his annoyance that he disliked the taste (Seligman & Hager, 1972).

Notice that unlike conditioning in the laboratory, Seligman's aversion to the sauce occurred after only one pairing of the sauce with illness and with a considerable delay between the conditioned and unconditioned stimuli. Moreover, Seligman's wife did not become a conditioned stimulus for nausea, and neither did his dinner plate or the waiter, even though they also had been paired with illness. Why? In earlier work with rats, John Garcia and Robert Koelling (1966) had provided the answer: the existence of a greater biological readiness to associate sickness with taste than with sights or sounds (the "Garcia effect"). Like the tendency to acquire certain fears, this biological tendency probably evolved because it enhanced survival: Eating bad food is more likely to be followed by illness and death than are particular sights or sounds.

Psychologists have taken advantage of this phenomenon to develop humane ways of discouraging predators from preying on livestock, using conditioned taste aversions instead of traps and poisons. In one classic approach, researchers laced sheep meat with a nausea-inducing chemical; coyotes and wolves fell for the bait, and as a result they developed a conditioned aversion to sheep (Dingfelder, 2010; Gustavson et al., 1974). Similar techniques have been used to control other predators—for example, to deter raccoons from killing chickens, and ravens and crows from eating crane eggs (Garcia & Gustavson, 1997).

Reacting to Medical Treatments

Because of classical conditioning, medical treatments can create unexpected misery or relief from symptoms for reasons that are entirely unrelated to the treatment itself. For example, unpleasant reactions to a treatment can generalize to a wide range of other stimuli. This is a particular problem for cancer patients. The nausea and vomiting resulting from chemotherapy often generalize to the place where the therapy takes place, the waiting room, the sound of a nurse's voice, or the smell of rubbing alcohol. The drug treatment is an unconditioned stimulus for nausea and vomiting, and, through association, the other previously neutral stimuli become conditioned stimuli for these responses. Even *mental images* of the sights and smells of the clinic can become conditioned stimuli for nausea (Dadds et al., 1997; Redd et al., 1993).

Some cancer patients also acquire a classically conditioned anxiety response to anything associated with their chemotherapy (Jacobsen et al., 1995). However, patients may have *reduced* pain and anxiety when they receive *placebos*, pills and injections that have no active ingredients or treatments that have no direct physical effect on the problem. Placebos can be amazingly powerful, especially when they take the form of an injection, a large pill, or a pill with a brand name (Benedetti & Levi-Montalcini, 2001). In fact, placebos can act on the same neural pathways in the brain that real medicines do (Price, Finniss, & Benedetti, 2008; see also Chapter 6).

Why do placebos work? Cognitive psychologists emphasize the role of expectations, at least in humans; expectations of getting better may reduce anxiety, and that reduction may have a positive effect on the immune system. Such expectations may also cause us to act in ways that produce the outcome we hope for (Michael, Garry, & Kirsch, 2012). But behaviourists emphasize conditioning: The doctor's white coat, the doctor's office, and pills or injections all become conditioned stimuli for relief from symptoms because these stimuli have been associated in the past with *real* drugs (Ader, 2000). The real drugs are the unconditioned stimuli, and the relief they bring is the unconditioned response. Placebos acquire the ability to elicit similar reactions, thereby becoming conditioned stimuli.

The expectancy explanation of placebo effects and the classical-conditioning explanation are not mutually exclusive (Kirsch, 2004; Stewart-Williams & Podd, 2004). As we saw earlier, many researchers now accept the view that classical conditioning itself involves the expectation that the conditioned stimulus will be followed by the unconditioned stimulus. Thus, at least some classically conditioned placebo effects may involve the patient's expectations. In fact, the patient's previous conditioning history may be what created those expectations to begin with.

Recite & Review

Recite: Say aloud everything you know about the classical conditioning of positive emotions, phobias, and tastes, *counterconditioning*, and reactions to medical treatments.

Review: Next, read this section again, and notice anything that you didn't catch the first time.

Now take this *Quick Quiz:*

See whether you can supply the correct term to describe the outcome in each of these situations:

1. After Jeff learns to fear spiders, he also responds with fear to ants, beetles, and other crawling bugs.

2. Little Eryn is afraid of the bath, so her father puts just a little water in the tub and gives Eryn a lollipop to suck on while she is being washed. Soon, Eryn loses her fear of the bath.

3. A factory worker's mouth waters whenever a noontime bell signals the beginning of his lunch break. One day, the bell goes haywire and rings every half hour. By the end of the day, the worker has stopped salivating to the bell.

Answers:

1. stimulus generalization 2. counterconditioning 3. extinction

7 Describe how the consequences of your actions affect your future behaviour.

8 List the primary difference between negative reinforcement and punishment.

Operant Conditioning

At the end of the nineteenth century, in the first known scientific study of anger, G. Stanley Hall (1899) asked people to describe angry episodes they had experienced or observed. One person told of a three-year-old girl who broke out in seemingly uncontrollable sobs when she was kept home from a ride. In the middle of her outburst, the child suddenly stopped and asked her nanny in a perfectly calm voice if her father was in. Told no, and realizing that he was not around to put a stop to her tantrum, she immediately resumed her sobbing.

Children, of course, cry for many valid reasons—pain, discomfort, fear, illness, fatigue—and these cries deserve sympathy and attention. The child in Hall's study, however, was crying because she had learned from prior experience that an outburst of sobbing would pay off by bringing her attention and possibly the ride she wanted. Her tantrum illustrates one of the most basic laws of learning: *Behaviour becomes more likely or less likely depending on its consequences.*

This principle is at the heart of **operant conditioning** (also called *instrumental conditioning*), the second type of conditioning studied by behaviourists. In classical conditioning, it does not matter whether an animal's or person's behaviour has consequences. In Pavlov's procedure, the dog learned an association between two events that were not under its control (e.g., a tone and the delivery of food) and the animal got food whether or not it salivated. But in operant conditioning, the organism's response (such as the little girl's sobbing) *operates*—produces effects on—the environment. These effects, in turn, influence whether the response will occur again.

Thus, whereas the central feature of classical conditioning is an association between stimuli (the neutral stimulus and the unconditioned stimulus), in operant conditioning the central feature is an association between a stimulus (consequence) and a response. Classical conditioning and operant conditioning also tend to differ in the types of responses they involve. In classical conditioning, the response is typically reflexive, an automatic reaction to something happening in the environment, such as the sight of food or the sound of a bell. Generally, responses in operant conditioning are complex and are not reflexive—for instance, riding a bicycle, writing a letter, climbing a mountain, . . . or throwing a tantrum.

The Birth of Radical Behaviourism

Operant conditioning has been studied since the start of the twentieth century, although it was not called that until later. Edward Thorndike (1898), then a young doctoral student, set the stage by observing cats as they tried to escape from a complex "puzzle box" to reach a scrap of fish located just outside the box. At first, the cat would scratch, bite, or swat at parts of the box in an unorganized way. Then, after a few minutes, it would chance on the successful response (loosening a bolt, pulling a string, or hitting a button) and rush out to get the reward. Placed in the box again, the cat now took a little less time to escape, and after several trials, the animal immediately made the correct response. According to Thorndike, this response had been "stamped in" by the satisfying result of getting the food. In contrast, annoying or unsatisfying results "stamped out" behaviour. Behaviour, said Thorndike, is controlled by its consequences.

This general principle was elaborated and extended to more complex forms of behaviour by B. F. (Burrhus Frederic) Skinner (1904–1990). Skinner called his approach

operant conditioning The process by which a response becomes more likely to occur or less so, depending on its consequences.

"radical behaviourism" to distinguish it from the behaviourism of John Watson, who emphasized classical conditioning. Skinner argued that to understand behaviour, we should focus on the external causes of an action and the action's consequences. He avoided terms that Thorndike used, such as "satisfying" and "annoying," which reflect assumptions about what an organism feels and wants. To explain behaviour, he said, we should look outside the animal or person, not inside.

The Consequences of Behaviour

In Skinner's analysis, which has inspired an immense body of research, a response ("operant") can be influenced by two types of consequences: ◉

1 **Reinforcement strengthens the response or makes it more likely to recur.** When your dog begs for food at the table, and you give her the lamb chop off your plate, that **reinforcement** means her begging is likely to increase:

Reinforcers are roughly equivalent to rewards, and many psychologists use *reward* and *reinforcer* as approximate synonyms. However, strict behaviourists avoid the word *reward* because it implies that something has been earned that results in happiness or satisfaction. To a behaviourist, a stimulus is a reinforcer if it strengthens the preceding behaviour, whether or not the organism experiences pleasure or a positive emotion. Conversely, no matter how pleasurable a reward is, it is not a reinforcer if it does not increase the likelihood of a response. It's great to get a cheque, but if you get paid regardless of the effort you put into your work, the money will not reinforce "hard-work behaviour."

2 **Punishment weakens the response or makes it less likely to recur.** Any aversive (unpleasant) stimulus or event may be a *punisher*. If your dog begs for a lamb chop off your plate, and you lightly swat her nose and shout "No," that **punishment** means her begging is likely to decrease—as long as you don't feel guilty and then give her the lamb chop anyway:

Parents, employers, and governments resort to reinforcers and punishers all the time—to get kids to behave well, employees to work hard, and taxpayers to pay up—but they do not always use them effectively. For one thing, they often wait too long to deliver the reinforcer or punisher. In general, the sooner a consequence follows a response, the greater its effect; you are likely to respond more reliably when you do not have to wait ages for a grade, your cheque, or a compliment. When other responses occur during a delay, it may be difficult to make the connection between the desired or undesired response and the consequence.

Primary and Secondary Reinforcers and Punishers.

Food, water, light stroking of the skin, and a comfortable air temperature are naturally reinforcing because they satisfy biological needs. They are therefore known as **primary reinforcers**. Similarly, pain and extreme heat or cold are inherently punishing and are therefore known as **primary punishers**. Primary reinforcers and punishers can be powerful, but they have some drawbacks, both in real life and in research. For one thing, a primary reinforcer may be ineffective if an animal or person is not in a deprived state; a glass of water is not much of a reward if you just drank three glasses. Also, for obvious ethical reasons, scientists cannot go around using primary punishers (say, by hitting their research participants) or taking away primary reinforcers (say, by starving their volunteers).

Fortunately, behaviour can be controlled just as effectively by **secondary reinforcers** and **secondary punishers**, which are learned. Money, praise, applause, good grades, awards, and gold stars are common secondary reinforcers. Criticism, demerits, scolding, fines, and bad grades are common secondary punishers. Most behaviourists believe that secondary reinforcers and punishers acquire their ability to influence behaviour by being paired with primary reinforcers and punishers. (If that reminds you of classical

---

Watch the **Video**
The Basics 2: Operant Conditioning: Learning from Consequences in **MyPsychLab**

reinforcement The process by which a stimulus or event strengthens or increases the probability of the response that it follows.

punishment The process by which a stimulus or event weakens or reduces the probability of the response that it follows.

primary reinforcer A stimulus that is inherently reinforcing, typically satisfying a physiological need; an example is food.

primary punisher A stimulus that is inherently punishing; an example is electric shock.

secondary reinforcer A stimulus that has acquired reinforcing properties through association with other reinforcers.

secondary punisher A stimulus that has acquired punishing properties through association with other punishers.

positive reinforcement A reinforcement procedure in which a response is followed by the presentation of, or increase in intensity of, a reinforcing stimulus; as a result, the response becomes stronger or more likely to occur.

negative reinforcement A reinforcement procedure in which a response is followed by the removal, delay, or decrease in intensity of an unpleasant stimulus; as a result, the response becomes stronger or more likely to occur.

conditioning, reinforce your excellent thinking with a pat on the head! Indeed, secondary reinforcers and punishers are often called *conditioned* reinforcers and punishers.) As a secondary reinforcer, money has considerable power over most people's behaviour because it can be exchanged for primary reinforcers such as food and shelter. It is also associated with other secondary reinforcers, such as praise and respect.

Positive and Negative Reinforcers and Punishers. In our example of the begging dog, something pleasant (getting the lamb chop) followed the dog's begging response, so the response increased. Similarly, if you get a good grade after studying, your efforts to study are likely to continue or increase. This kind of process, in which a pleasant consequence makes a response more likely, is known as **positive reinforcement**. But another type of reinforcement, **negative reinforcement**, involves the *removal* of something *unpleasant*. Negative reinforcement occurs when you *escape* from something aversive or *avoid* it by preventing it from ever occurring. If someone nags you to study but stops nagging when you comply, your studying is likely to increase because you will then avoid the nagging:

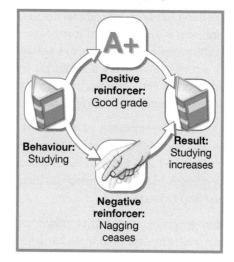

Likewise, negative reinforcement occurs when taking a pill eliminates your pain or when you take a certain route across campus to avoid a rude person.

The positive–negative distinction can also be applied to punishment: Something unpleasant may occur following some behaviour (positive punishment), or something *pleasant* may be *removed* (negative punishment). If your friends tease you for studying (positive punishment) or if studying makes you lose time with your friends (negative punishment), you may stop studying:

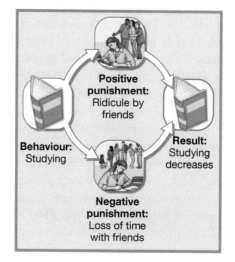

The distinction between positive and negative reinforcement and punishment has been a source of confusion for generations of students. You will master these terms more quickly if you understand that "positive" and "negative" have nothing to do with "good" or "bad." They refer to whether something is given or taken away. In the case of reinforcement, think of a positive reinforcer as something that is added or obtained (imagine a plus sign) and a negative reinforcer as avoidance of, or escape from, something unpleasant (imagine a minus sign). *In either case, a response becomes more likely.* Do you recall what happened when Little Albert learned to fear rats through a process of classical conditioning? After he acquired this fear, crawling away was negatively reinforced by escape from the now-fearsome rodent. The negative reinforcement that results from escaping or avoiding something unpleasant explains why so many fears are long-lasting. When you avoid a feared object or situation, you also cut off all opportunities to extinguish your fear.

Understandably, people often confuse negative reinforcement with positive punishment, because both involve an unpleasant stimulus. With punishment, you are subjected to the unpleasant stimulus; with negative reinforcement, you escape from it or avoid it. To keep these terms straight, remember that punishment, whether positive or negative, *decreases* the likelihood of a response; and reinforcement, whether positive or negative, *increases* it. In real life, punishment and negative reinforcement often go hand in hand. If you use a chain collar to teach your dog to heel, a brief tug on the collar punishes the act of walking; release of the collar negatively reinforces the act of standing by your side.

You can positively reinforce your studying of this material by taking a short break. As you master the material, a decrease in your anxiety will negatively reinforce studying. But we hope you won't punish your efforts by telling yourself "I'll never get it" or "It's too hard"!

Recite & Review

Recite: Say out loud everything you know about these concepts: *operant conditioning*, *reinforcement*, *punishment*, *primary reinforcers and punishers*, *secondary reinforcers* and *punishers*, and *positive* versus *negative reinforcement*.

Review: Next, go back and read this section again.

Now take this *Quick Quiz:*

What kind of consequence will follow if you can't answer these questions?

1. Brittany nags her father for a cookie; he keeps refusing. Finally, unable to stand the nagging any longer, he hands over the cookie. For him, silence from Brittany is a _____. For Brittany, the cookie is a _____.

2. Robert, who is not disabled, has paid a large fine for parking in a handicapped space, and no longer does it. The loss of money is a _____.

3. Identify which of the following are commonly used as secondary reinforcers: coins spilling from a slot machine, a winner's blue ribbon, a piece of candy, an A on an exam, frequent-flyer miles.

4. During late-afternoon "happy hours," bars and restaurants sell drinks at a reduced price and snacks are often free. What undesirable behaviour may be rewarded by this practice?

Answers:

1. negative reinforcer; positive reinforcer 2. punisher—or more precisely, a negative punisher (because something desirable was taken away) 3. All but the candy are secondary reinforcers. 4. One possible answer: The reduced prices, free snacks, and cheerful atmosphere all reinforce heavy alcohol consumption just before rush hour, thus possibly contributing to binge drinking and drunk driving.

extinction The weakening and eventual disappearance of a learned response; in operant conditioning, it occurs when a response is no longer followed by a reinforcer.

Learning Objectives

9 Summarize the key principles of operant conditioning.

10 Formulate a plan to shape your dog to balance a cookie on her nose.

11 Articulate some of the biological limits to what can be learned with operant conditioning.

Principles of Operant Conditioning

Thousands of operant-conditioning studies have been done, many using animals. A favourite experimental tool is the *Skinner box*, a chamber equipped with a device that delivers a reinforcer, usually food, when an animal makes a desired response, or a punisher, such as a brief shock, when the animal makes an undesired response (see Figure 7.4). In modern versions, a computer records responses and charts the rate of responding and cumulative responses across time.

Early in his career, Skinner (1938) used the Skinner box for a classic demonstration of operant conditioning. A rat that had previously learned to eat from the pellet-releasing device was placed in the box. The rat proceeded to scurry about the box, sniffing here and there, and randomly touching parts of the floor and walls. Quite by accident, it happened to press a lever mounted on one wall, and immediately a pellet of tasty rat food fell into the food dish. The rat continued its movements and again happened to press the bar, causing another pellet to fall into the dish. With additional repetitions of bar pressing followed by food, the rat began to behave less randomly and to press the bar more consistently. Eventually, Skinner had the rat pressing the bar as fast as it could. 👁

Watch the Video
Classic Footage of B.F. Skinner and the Skinner Box in **MyPsychLab**

Extinction. In operant conditioning, as in classical conditioning, **extinction** is a procedure that causes a previously learned response to stop. In operant conditioning, however, extinction takes place when the reinforcer that maintained the response is withheld or is no longer available. At first, there may be a spurt of responding, but then the responses gradually taper off and eventually cease. Suppose you put a coin in a vending machine and get nothing back. You may throw in another coin, or perhaps even two, but then you will probably stop trying. The next day, you may put in yet another coin, an example of *spontaneous recovery*. Eventually, however, you will give up on that machine. Your response will have been extinguished.

FIGURE 7.4 The Skinner Box
When a rat in a Skinner box presses a bar, a food pellet or drop of water is automatically released. The photo shows Skinner training one of his subjects.

Nina Leen/Getty Images

Light

Bar
Water

Food tray

Stimulus Generalization and Discrimination. In operant conditioning, as in classical, **stimulus generalization** may occur. That is, responses may generalize to stimuli that were not present during the original learning situation but resemble the original stimuli in some way. For example, a pigeon that has been trained to peck at a picture of a circle may also peck at a slightly oval figure. But if you wanted to train the bird to discriminate between the two shapes, you would present both the circle and the oval, giving reinforcers whenever the bird pecked at the circle and withholding reinforcers when it pecked at the oval. Eventually, **stimulus discrimination** would occur. Pigeons, in fact, have learned to make some extraordinary discriminations. They have learned to discriminate between two paintings by different artists, such as Vincent van Gogh and Marc Chagall (Watanabe, 2001). And then, when presented with a new pair of paintings by those same two artists, they have been able to tell the difference between them! Pigeons have even learned to discriminate beautiful paintings from ugly ones, a discrimination similar to what human beings would make (Watanabe, 2010). On a related note, similar results have been observed when asking mathematicians to make judgments on the beauty of mathematical equations (Zeki et al., 2014).

Sometimes an animal or person learns to respond to a stimulus only when some other stimulus, called a **discriminative stimulus**, is present. The discriminative stimulus signals whether a response, if made, will pay off. In a Skinner box containing a pigeon, a light may serve as a discriminative stimulus for pecking at a circle. When the light is on, pecking brings a reward; when it is off, pecking is futile. Human behaviour is controlled by many discriminative stimuli, both verbal ("Store hours are 9 to 5") and nonverbal (traffic lights, doorbells, the ring of your cell phone, other people's facial expressions). Learning to respond correctly when such stimuli are present allows us to get through the day efficiently and to get along with others.

Learning on Schedule. When a response is first acquired, learning is usually most rapid if the response is reinforced each time it occurs; this procedure is called **continuous reinforcement**. However, once a response has become reliable, it will be more resistant to extinction if it is rewarded on an **intermittent (partial) schedule of reinforcement**, which involves reinforcing only some responses, not all of them. Skinner (1956) happened on this fact when he ran short of food pellets for his rats and was forced to deliver reinforcers less often. (Not all scientific discoveries are planned.) On intermittent schedules, a reinforcer is delivered only after a certain number of responses occur or after a certain amount of time has passed since a response was last reinforced; these patterns affect the rate, form, and timing of behaviour. (The details are beyond the scope of this book.)

Intermittent reinforcement helps explain why people often get attached to "lucky" hats, charms, and rituals. A batter pulls his earlobe, gets a home run, and from then on always pulls his earlobe before each pitch. A student takes an exam with a purple pen and gets an A, and from then on will not take an exam without a purple pen. Such rituals persist because sometimes they are followed, purely coincidentally, by a reinforcer—a home run, a good grade—and so they become resistant to extinction.

Skinner (1948) once demonstrated this phenomenon by creating eight "superstitious" pigeons in his laboratory. He rigged the pigeons' cages so that food was delivered every 15 seconds, even if the birds didn't lift a feather. Pigeons are often in motion, so when the food came, each animal was likely to be doing something. That something was then reinforced by delivery of the food. The behaviour, of course, was reinforced entirely by chance, but it still became more likely to occur and thus to be reinforced again. Within a short time, six of the pigeons were practicing some sort of consistent ritual: turning in counterclockwise circles, bobbing their heads up and down, or

stimulus generalization In operant conditioning, the tendency for a response that has been reinforced (or punished) in the presence of one stimulus to occur (or be suppressed) in the presence of other similar stimuli.

stimulus discrimination In operant conditioning, the tendency of a response to occur in the presence of one stimulus but not in the presence of other similar stimuli that differ from it on some dimension.

discriminative stimulus A stimulus that signals when a particular response is likely to be followed by a certain type of consequence.

continuous reinforcement A reinforcement schedule in which a particular response is always reinforced.

intermittent (partial) schedule of reinforcement A reinforcement schedule in which a particular response is sometimes but not always reinforced.

> ## THINKING CRITICALLY
> Consider other interpretations.
> People cling to superstitious rituals because they think they work. Could this "effectiveness" be an illusion, explainable in terms of operant principles?

shaping An operant-conditioning procedure in which successive approximations of a desired response are reinforced.

swinging their heads to and fro. None of these activities had the least effect on the delivery of the reinforcer; the birds were behaving "superstitiously," as if they thought their movements were responsible for bringing the food.

Now her is one of the most useful things to know about operant conditioning: If you want a response to persist after it has been learned, you should reinforce it *intermittently*, not continuously. If you are giving Harry, your hamster, a treat every time he pushes a ball with his nose, and then you suddenly stop the reinforcement, Harry will soon stop pushing that ball. Because the change in reinforcement is large, from continuous to none at all, Harry will easily discern the change. But if you have been reinforcing Harry's behaviour only every so often, the change will not be so dramatic, and your hungry hamster will keep responding for quite a while. Pigeons, rats, and people on intermittent schedules of reinforcement have responded in the laboratory thousands of times without reinforcement before throwing in the towel, especially when the timing of the reinforcer varies. Animals will sometimes work so hard for an unpredictable, infrequent bit of food that the energy they expend is greater than that gained from the reward; theoretically, they could actually work themselves to death.

It follows that if you want to get rid of a response, whether it's your own or someone else's, you should be careful *not* to reinforce it intermittently. If you are going to extinguish undesirable behaviour by ignoring it—a child's tantrums, a friend's midnight phone calls, a parent's unwanted advice—you must be absolutely consistent in withholding reinforcement (your attention). Otherwise, the other person will learn that if he or she keeps up the screaming, calling, or advice giving long enough, it will eventually be rewarded. From a behavioural point of view, one of the most common errors people make is to reward intermittently the very responses that they would like to eliminate.

Shaping. For a response to be reinforced, it must first occur. But suppose you want to train cows to milk themselves, a child to use a knife and fork properly, or a friend to play terrific tennis. Such behaviours, and most others in everyday life, have almost no probability of appearing spontaneously. You could grow old and grey waiting for them to occur so that you could reinforce them. The operant solution is a procedure called **shaping**.

In shaping, you start by reinforcing a tendency in the right direction, and then you gradually require responses that are more and more similar to the final desired

Behavioural techniques such as shaping have many useful applications. Monkeys have been trained to assist their paralyzed owners by opening doors, helping with feeding, and turning the pages of books. Miniature horses have been trained to help blind people navigate everywhere, even on rocky, uneven terrain. Note the horse's cool little protective sneakers!

Left: Rita Nannini/Science Source. Right: Michael York/AP Images.

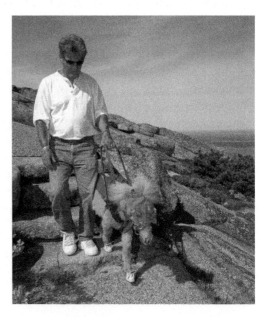

response. The responses that you reinforce on the way to the final one are called **successive approximations**. Take the problem of teaching cows to milk themselves. How can cows possibly do that when they have no hands? Ah, but cows *can* be trained to use a milking robot. In several countries, psychologists have done just that (Stiles, Murray, & Kentish-Barnes, 2011). First, they gave the cow crushed barley (the cow equivalent of a chocolate treat) for simply standing on a platform connected to the robot. Once that response was established, they gave her barley for turning her body toward the spot where the robot attaches the milking cups. After that, they rewarded her for being in the exact spot the robot requires for attaching the cups, and so on until the cow finally learned to milk herself. The key is that as each approximation is achieved, the next one becomes more likely, making it available for reinforcement. Cows allowed to milk themselves do so three or four times a day instead of the traditional twice a day, and show fewer signs of stress than other cows. Farmers show less stress too, because they no longer have to get up at 5 a.m. for the early-morning milking!

Using shaping and other techniques, Skinner was able to train pigeons to play table tennis with their beaks and to "bowl" in a miniature alley, complete with a wooden ball and tiny bowling pins. (Skinner had a great sense of humour.) Animal trainers routinely use shaping to teach animals their parts in movies and TV shows, and to act as the "eyes" of the blind and as the "limbs" of people with spinal cord injuries. These talented animals companions learn to turn on light switches, open refrigerator doors, and reach for boxes on shelves.

Biological Limits on Learning. All principles of operant conditioning, like those of classical conditioning, are limited by an animal's genetic dispositions and physical characteristics. If you try to teach a fish to dance the samba, you're going to get pretty frustrated (and wear out the fish). Operant-conditioning procedures always work best when they capitalize on inborn tendencies.

Years ago, two psychologists who became animal trainers, Keller and Marian Breland (1961), learned what happens when you ignore biological constraints on learning. They found that their animals were having trouble learning tasks that should have been easy. One animal, a pig, was supposed to drop large wooden coins in a box. Instead, the animal would drop the coin, push at it with its snout, throw it in the air, and push at it some more. This odd behaviour actually delayed delivery of the reinforcer (food, which is *very* reinforcing to a pig), so it was hard to explain in terms of operant principles. The Brelands finally realized that the pig's rooting instinct—using its snout to uncover and dig up edible roots—was keeping it from learning the task. They called such a reversion to instinctive behaviour **instinctive drift**.

GET INVOLVED! Shape Up!

Would you like to improve your study habits? Start exercising? Learn to play a musical instrument? Here are a few guidelines for shaping your own behaviour: (1) Set goals that are achievable and specific, as in "jog ten minutes and increase the time by five minutes each day" instead of "get in shape." (2) Track your progress on a graph or in a diary; evidence of progress serves as a secondary reinforcer. (3) Avoid punishing yourself with self-defeating thoughts such as "I'll never be a good student" or "I'm a food addict." (4) Reinforce small improvements (successive approximations) instead of expecting perfection. By the way, a reinforcer does not have to be a thing; it can be something you like to do, like watching a movie.

Above all, be patient. Like Rome, new habits are not built in a day. You can find information on shaping behaviour—yours or anyone else's—in books such as *Don't Shoot the Dog!: The New Art of Teaching and Training,* by Karen Pryor (1999), and *Behaviour Modification: What It Is and How to Do It,* by Garry Martin and Joseph Pear (2011).

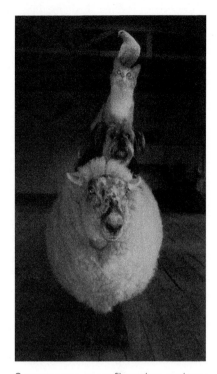

Suppose you are a filmmaker, and you want this pigeon, cat, dog, and sheep to pose in a stack for your movie. A behaviourist will use shaping to get the animals to agree.

Caroline Gridlestone/Hero Animals

successive approximations In the operant-conditioning procedure of shaping, behaviours that are ordered in terms of increasing similarity or closeness to the desired response.

instinctive drift During operant learning, the tendency for an organism to revert to instinctive behaviour.

In human beings, too, operant learning is affected by genetics, biology, and the evolutionary history of our species. As we saw in Chapter 3, human children are biologically disposed to learn language, and they may be disposed to learn some arithmetic operations as well. Further, temperaments and other inborn dispositions may affect how a person responds to reinforcers and punishments. It will be easier to shape belly-dancing behaviour if a person is temperamentally disposed to be outgoing and extroverted than if the person is by nature shy.

Skinner: The Man and the Myth

Because of his groundbreaking work on operant conditioning, B. F. Skinner is one of the best-known psychologists. He is also one of the most misunderstood. Many people (even some psychologists) think that Skinner denied the existence of human consciousness and the value of studying it. In reality, Skinner (1972, 1990) maintained that private internal events—what we call perceptions, emotions, and thoughts—are as real as any others, and we can study them by examining our own sensory responses, the verbal reports of others, and the conditions under which such events occur. But he insisted that thoughts and feelings cannot *explain* behaviour. These components of consciousness, he said, are themselves simply behaviours that occur because of reinforcement and punishment.

Skinner aroused strong passions in both his supporters and his detractors. Perhaps the issue that most provoked and angered people was his insistence that free will is an illusion. In contrast to humanist and some religious doctrines that human beings have the power to shape their own destinies, his philosophy promoted the *determinist view* that our actions are determined by our environments and our genetic heritage. ◉

Because Skinner thought the environment should be manipulated to alter behaviour, some critics have portrayed him as cold-blooded. One famous controversy regarding Skinner occurred when he invented an enclosed "living space," the Air Crib, for his younger daughter Deborah when she was an infant. This "baby box," as it came to be known, had temperature and humidity controls to eliminate the usual discomforts that babies suffer: heat, cold, wetness, and confinement by blankets and clothing. Skinner believed that to reduce a baby's cries of discomfort and make infant care easier for the parents, you should fix the environment. But people imagined, incorrectly, that the Skinners were leaving their child in the baby box all the time without cuddling and holding her, and rumours circulated for years (and still do from time to time) that she had sued her father, gone insane, or killed herself. Actually, both of Skinner's daughters were cuddled and doted on, loved their parents deeply, and turned out to be successful, perfectly well-adjusted adults.

Skinner, who was a kind and mild-mannered man, felt that it would be unethical *not* to try to improve human behaviour by applying behavioural principles. And he practised what he preached, proposing many ways to improve society and reduce human suffering. At the height of public criticism of Skinner's supposedly cold and inhumane approach to understanding behaviour, the American Humanist Association recognized his efforts on behalf of humanity by honouring him with its Humanist of the Year Award.

◉—Watch the **Video**
Classic Footage of Skinner
in **MyPsychLab**

B. F. Skinner invented the Air Crib to provide a more comfortable, less restrictive infant bed than the traditional crib with its bars and blankets. Here the Skinners play with their 13-month-old daughter, Deborah.

AP Images

Recite & Review

Recite: Out loud, say as much as you can about *extinction, stimulus generalization, stimulus discrimination* in operant conditioning, *discriminative stimulus, continuous and intermittent reinforcement, shaping, successive approximations,* and *instinctive drift.*

Review: Next, go back and read this section again to check what you recited.

Now take this *Quick Quiz:*

In each of the following situations, choose the best alternative and give your reason for choosing it.

1. You want your two-year-old to ask for water with a word instead of babble. Should you give him water when he says "wa-wa" or wait until his pronunciation improves?

2. Your roommate keeps interrupting your studying even though you have asked her to stop. Should you ignore her completely or occasionally respond for the sake of good manners?

3. Your father, who rarely calls you, has finally left a voice-mail message. Should you reply quickly, or wait a while so he will know how it feels to be ignored?

Answers:

1. You should reinforce "wa-wa," an approximation of water, because complex behaviours need to be shaped. 2. From a behavioural view, you should ignore her completely because intermittent reinforcement (attention) could cause her interruptions to persist. 3. If you want to encourage communication, you should reply quickly because immediate reinforcement is more effective than delayed reinforcement.

Learning Objectives

12 Recommend when you would choose to use punishment over reinforcement to change behaviour.

13 List three ways in which reinforcement can result in undesired behaviour

Operant Conditioning in Real Life

Operant principles can clear up many mysteries about why people behave as they do. They can also explain why people have trouble changing when they want to, in spite of all the motivational seminars they attend or resolutions they make. If life remains full of the same old reinforcers, punishers, and discriminative stimuli (a grumpy boss, an unresponsive roommate, a refrigerator stocked with junk food), any new responses that have been acquired may fail to generalize.

To help people change unwanted, dangerous, or self-defeating habits, behaviourists have carried operant principles out of the laboratory and into the wider world of the classroom, athletic field, prison, mental hospital, nursing home, rehabilitation ward, child care centre, factory, and office. The use of operant techniques in such real-world settings is called **behaviour modification** (also known as *applied behaviour analysis*).

Behaviour modification has had some enormous successes (Kazdin, 2001; Martin & Pear, 2011). Behaviourists have taught parents how to toilet train their children in only a few sessions. They have trained disturbed and intellectually impaired adults to communicate, dress themselves, mingle socially with others, and earn a living. They have taught brain-damaged patients to control inappropriate behaviour, focus their attention, and improve their language abilities. They have helped autistic children improve their social and language skills. And they have helped ordinary folk get rid of unwanted habits, such as smoking and nail biting, or acquire desired ones, such as practising the piano, exercising more, or studying. In one such example, the Société de l'assurance automobile du Québec (SAAQ) tried to increase seat-belt use

behaviour modification The application of operant-conditioning techniques to teach new responses or to reduce or eliminate maladaptive or problematic behaviour; also called *applied behaviour analysis*.

throughout the province with the use of radio, TV, and print commercials. However, the police also used behavioural techniques. The police reinforced good behaviour by handing out scratch-and-win tickets to individuals who were wearing seat belts. (Those who were not wearing seat belts received tickets of the other kind.) The rate of seat-belt use in the province dramatically increased, from 40% to 67% to over 93%—the highest rate in Canada (Transport Canada, 1998)! Similar programs have been adopted all over Canada and are now used to reinforce the wearing of bicycle helmets and the use of child safety seats. However, when others try to apply the principles of conditioning to commonplace problems without thoroughly understanding those principles, their efforts sometimes miss the mark, as we are about to see.

The Pros and Cons of Punishment

In a novel called *Walden Two* (1948/1976), Skinner imagined a utopia in which reinforcers were used so wisely that undesirable behaviour was rare. Unfortunately, we do not live in a utopia; bad habits and antisocial acts abound.

Punishment might seem to be an obvious solution. Although most western countries have banned the physical punishment of schoolchildren at school, the laws in Canada permit the use of force for correction (for example, spanking) by teachers and parents as long as it is reasonable (notably, there is great debate over what is reasonable!

Many Canadians, teachers and parents alike, would be shocked if a teacher physically disciplined a pupil). Some suggest that spanking or slapping is reasonable punishment, while others suggest that this is child abuse. Even the research about spanking is contentious! For instance, some researchers suggest that spanking may lead to physical abuse (for example, Gershoff, 2002), whereas others have taken the position that the research on spanking is, at best, inconclusive (for example, Baumrind, Larzelere, & Cowan, 2002). And, of course, in their relationships, people punish one another frequently by yelling, scolding, and sulking. Does all this punishment work?

When Punishment Works. Sometimes punishment is unquestionably effective. For example, punishment can deter some young criminals from repeating

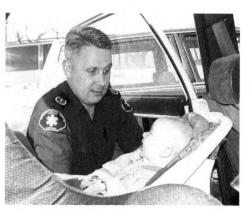

You don't have to be a psychologist to take advantage of behavioural principles. The performer on the left is being rewarded by the attention, applause, and most likely the donations of his admiring crowd. On the right, a police officer in Calgary reinforces law-abiding behaviour by checking a baby seat at an event featuring free food.

Left: Eric Nathan/Getty Images. Right: City of Calgary.

their offences. A study of the criminal records of all Danish men born between 1944 and 1947 (nearly 29 000 men) examined repeat arrests (recidivism) through age 26 (Brennan & Mednick, 1994). After any given arrest, punishment reduced rates of subsequent arrests for both minor and serious crimes, though recidivism still remained fairly high. Contrary to expectation, however, the *severity* of punishment made no difference; fines and probation were about as effective as jail time. What mattered most was the *consistency* of the punishment. This is understandable in behavioural terms: When lawbreakers sometimes get away with their crimes, their behaviour is intermittently reinforced and therefore becomes resistant to extinction.

When Punishment Fails. What about punishment that occurs every day in families, schools, and workplaces? Laboratory and field studies find that it, too, often fails, for several reasons:

1 **People often administer punishment inappropriately or mindlessly.** They swing in a blind rage or shout things they don't mean, use harsh methods with toddlers, apply punishment so broadly that it covers all sorts of irrelevant behaviours, or misunderstand the proper application of punishment.

2 **The recipient of harsh or frequent punishment often responds with anxiety, fear, or rage.** Through a process of classical conditioning, these emotional side effects may then generalize to the entire situation in which the punishment occurs—the place, the person delivering the punishment, and the circumstances. These negative emotional reactions can create more problems than the punishment solves. A teenager who has been severely punished may strike back or run away. A spouse who is constantly insulted, belittled, and criticized will feel bitter and resentful and is likely to retaliate with small acts of hostility. And extreme punishment—physical abuse—is a risk factor, especially in children, for the development of depression, low self-esteem, violent behaviour, and many other problems (Gershoff, 2002; Widom, DuMont, & Czaja, 2007).

THINKING CRITICALLY

Ask questions.

Dennis MacDonald/PhotoEdit Inc.

As we all know, people often do things that they're not supposed to. Have you ever wondered why so many people ignore warnings and threats of punishment?

3 **The effectiveness of punishment is often temporary, depending heavily on the presence of the punishing person or circumstances.** All of us can probably remember some transgressions of childhood that we never dared commit when our parents were around but that we promptly resumed as soon as they were gone and reinforcers were once again available. All we learned was not to get caught. Indeed, when comparing photo radar with speed traps that are manned by police officers, photo radar does not appear to reduce the frequency of crashes. As crashes are most commonly a result of speeding, it may be that the absence of an immediate punishment and the presence of an officer combine to reduce the effectiveness of photo radar on reducing speeding (Tay, 2009).

4 **Most misbehaviour is hard to punish immediately.** Punishment, like reward, works best if it quickly follows a response. But outside the laboratory, rapid punishment is often hard to achieve, and during the delay, the behaviour may be reinforced many times. If you punish your dog when you get home for getting into the doggie biscuits and eating them all up, the punishment will not do any good because you are too late. Your pet's misbehaviour has already been reinforced by all those delicious treats.

5 **Punishment conveys little information.** It may tell the recipient what *not* to do, but it does not communicate what the person (or animal) *should* do. Spanking a toddler for messing in her pants will not teach her to use the potty chair, and scolding a student for learning slowly will not teach him to learn more quickly.

6 **An action intended to punish may instead be reinforcing because it brings attention.** Indeed, in some cases, angry attention may be just what the offender is after. If a mother yells at a child who is throwing a tantrum, the very act of yelling may give him what he wants: a reaction from her. In the schoolroom, teachers who scold children in front of other students, thus putting them in the limelight, may unwittingly reward the very misbehaviour they are trying to eliminate.

Because of these drawbacks, most psychologists believe that punishment, especially when it's severe, is a poor way to eliminate unwanted behaviour. Consider spanking. A Canadian review of two decades of research found that although spanking may put a halt to a child's annoying or dangerous behaviour in the short term, it backfires in the long term, because children who are physically punished tend to become more aggressive and antisocial over time (Durrant & Ensom, 2012). Spanking is also associated with later mental health problems and slower cognitive development. No study has ever established a link between physical discipline and any positive outcome. Parents are starting to get the message. Fifty years ago, in many parts of the world, most parents thought that hitting their children was a good approach to correcting bad behaviour, but today roughly half hold that belief (Roberts, 2000; Straus, 2005). To date, 32 countries, including nations as different as Denmark, Israel, Tunisia, Costa Rica, and New Zealand, have outright bans on hitting children.

In special cases, as when mentally disabled children are in immediate danger of seriously injuring themselves or a school bully is about to beat up a classmate, temporary physical restraint may be necessary. But even in these cases, alternatives are often available. School programs have successfully reduced school violence by teaching kids problem-solving skills, emotional control, and conflict resolution, and by rewarding good behaviour (Hahn et al., 2008; Wilson & Lipsey, 2007). And in some cases, the best way to discourage a behaviour—a child's nagging for a cookie before dinner, a roommate's interruptions when you're studying—is to extinguish it by ignoring it. Of course, ignoring a behaviour requires patience and is not always feasible. If your dog barks all day and night, telling your neighbours that it's best to ignore the racket will not be a winning strategy for long, even if you explain that you learned all about the drawbacks of punishment in your psychology class.

Finally, when punishment must be applied, these guidelines should be kept in mind: (1) It should not involve physical abuse; instead, parents can use time-outs and loss of privileges (negative punishers); (2) it should be consistent; (3) it should be accompanied by information about the kind of behaviour that would be appropriate; and (4) it should be followed, whenever possible, by the reinforcement of desirable behaviour. 👁

👁─Watch the **Video**
Thinking Like a Psychologist: Physical Punishment—You Decide!
in **MyPsychLab**

The Problems with Reward

So far, we have been praising the virtues of praise and other reinforcers. But like punishers, rewards do not always work as expected. Let's look at two complications that arise when people try to use them.

Misuse of Rewards. For many years, teachers everywhere have been handing out lavish praise, happy-face stickers, and high grades, even if students don't deserve them, in hopes that students' performance will improve as they learn to "feel good about themselves." Scientifically speaking, however, this approach is misguided. Study after study finds that high self-esteem does not improve academic performance (Baumeister et al., 2003). Instead, academic achievement requires effort and persistence (Duckworth et al., 2011). It is nurtured not by undeserved rewards but by a teacher's honest appreciation of the content of a student's work, and specific constructive feedback on how to correct mistakes or fix weaknesses (Damon, 1995). These strong findings from psychological science have finally begun to influence some teachers, who are now shifting away from doling out unwarranted "self-esteem boosters" and focusing on helping students appreciate the benefits of effort and persistence.

One obvious result of the misuse of rewards in schools has been grade inflation at all levels of education (Jewell. McPherson, & Tieslau, 2013). Today, at many colleges and universities, Cs (which are supposed to mean average or satisfactory) are nearly extinct; in U.S. universities, 43% of grades are now As (Rojstaczer & Healy, 2012). Compare this to a study of seven universities in Ontario, which found a 5% increase in the number of As in a 20-year period (of which only 21% of all students received an A; Anglin & Meng, 2000). One study found that a third of college students expected Bs just for showing up to class, and 40% felt they were entitled to a B merely for doing the required reading (Greenberger et al., 2008).

We have talked to students who feel that hard work should even be enough for an A. If you yourself have benefited from grade inflation, you may feel good about it—but remember that critical thinking requires us to separate feelings from facts! The problem is that rewards, including grades, serve as effective reinforcers only when they are tied to the behaviour one is trying to increase, not when they are dispensed indiscriminately. Getting a good grade for "showing-up-in-class behaviour" reinforces going to class, but not necessarily learning much once you are there. Would you want to be treated by a doctor, represented by a lawyer, or have your taxes done by an accountant who got through school just by showing up for class? Or who did all the required reading, but without understanding it?

> ## THINKING CRITICALLY
> Don't oversimplify.
>
> Because reinforcers increase desirable behaviour, some teachers give out high grades whether or not students deserve them. Does this practice improve the students' performance or self-esteem? What do these rewards actually reinforce?

Why Rewards Can Backfire. Most of our examples of operant conditioning have involved **extrinsic reinforcers**, which come from an outside source and are not inherently related to the activity being reinforced. Money, praise, gold stars, applause, hugs, and thumbs-up signs are all extrinsic reinforcers. But people

extrinsic reinforcers Reinforcers that are not inherently related to the activity being reinforced.

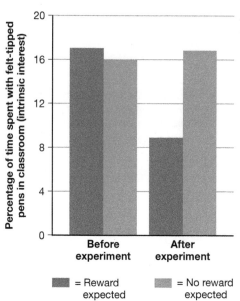

FIGURE 7.5 Turning Play into Work Extrinsic rewards can sometimes reduce the intrinsic pleasure of an activity. When preschoolers were promised a prize for drawing with felt-tipped pens, the behaviour temporarily increased. But after they got their prizes, they spent less time with the pens than they had before the study began (Lepper, Greene, & Nisbett, 1973).

(and probably some other animals as well) also work for **intrinsic reinforcers**, such as enjoyment of the task and the satisfaction of accomplishment. In real-world settings, extrinsic reinforcement sometimes becomes too much of a good thing: If you focus on it exclusively, it can kill the pleasure of doing something for its own sake.

Consider what happened in a classic study of how praise affects children's intrinsic motivation (Lepper, Greene, & Nisbett, 1973). Nursery school children were given the chance to draw with felt-tipped pens during free play and observers recorded how long each child spontaneously played with the pens. The children clearly enjoyed this activity. Then the researchers told some of the children that if they would draw with felt-tipped pens they would get a prize, a "Good Player Award" complete with gold seal and red ribbon. After drawing for six minutes, each child got the award as promised. Other children did not expect an award and were not given one. A week later, during free play, those children who had expected and received an award spent much less time with the pens than they had before the start of the experiment. In contrast, children in a control group who had neither expected nor received an award continued to show as much interest in playing with the pens as they had initially, as you can see in Figure 7.5. Similar results have occurred in other studies when children have been offered a reward for doing something they already enjoy.

Why should extrinsic rewards undermine the pleasure of doing something for its own sake? The psychologists who did the pen study suggested that when we are paid for an activity, we interpret it as work instead of something we do because of our own interests, skills, and efforts. It is as if we say to ourselves, "Since I'm being paid, it must be something I wouldn't do if I didn't have to." Then, when the reward is withdrawn, we refuse to "work" any longer. Another possibility is that we tend to regard extrinsic rewards as controlling, so they make us feel pressured and reduce our sense of autonomy and choice ("I guess I have to do what I'm told to do—but *only* what I'm told to do") (Deci, Koestner, & Ryan, 1999). A third, more behavioural explanation is that extrinsic reinforcement sometimes raises the rate of responding above some optimal, enjoyable level, at which point the activity really does become work.

Findings on extrinsic versus intrinsic reinforcements have wide-ranging implications. Economists have shown that financial rewards can undermine ethical and moral norms like honesty, hard work, and fairness toward others, and can decrease people's willingness to contribute to the common good (e.g., by paying taxes and giving to charity). In other words, an emphasis solely on money encourages selfishness (Bowles, 2008).

We must be careful, however, not to oversimplify this issue. The effects of extrinsic rewards depend on many factors, including a person's initial motivation, the context in which rewards are achieved, and in the case of praise, the sincerity of the praiser (Henderlong & Lepper, 2002). Sometimes extrinsic rewards can help boost achievement. When some American high schools started offering large cash rewards to students who got high scores on Advanced Placement tests for college, achievement skyrocketed at inner city schools. Suddenly, disadvantaged minority students were taking statistics classes on Saturdays and passing the placement tests in larger numbers. But these effects might be limited to a unique combination of already motivated teachers and students. In a study of more than 27 000 students in Dallas, New York City, and Chicago, students were paid to read books, to complete assignments, or for getting good grades. The financial incentives had no effect. Although the students were excited about the money, they did not have the basic study skills to build on in order to achieve the goals (Fryer, 2011).

As for the relationship between intrinsic and extrinsic reinforcement, in general, if you get praise, money, a high grade, or a trophy for doing a task *well*, for achieving a

intrinsic reinforcers Reinforcers that are inherently related to the activity being reinforced.

certain level of performance, or for improving your performance rather than for just doing the task, your intrinsic motivation is not likely to decline; in fact, it may increase (Cameron, Banko, & Pierce, 2001; Pierce et al., 2003). The rewards are apt to make you feel competent rather than controlled. And if you have always been crazy about reading or about playing the banjo, you will keep reading or playing even when you do not happen to be getting a grade or applause for doing so. In such cases, you will probably attribute your continued involvement in the activity to your own intrinsic interests and motivation rather than to the reward.

So, what is the take-home message about extrinsic rewards? First, they are often useful or necessary. Few people would trudge off to work every morning if they never got paid, and in the classroom, teachers may need to offer incentives to some students. But extrinsic rewards should be used carefully and should not be overdone, so that intrinsic pleasure in an activity can blossom. Educators, employers, and policy makers can avoid the trap of either–or thinking by recognizing that most people do their best when they get tangible rewards for real achievement *and* when they have interesting, challenging, and varied kinds of work to do.

Recite & Review

Recite: If you say as much as you can about these concepts loudly enough, maybe it will help drown out the nonstop barking from your neighbour's dog: *behaviour modification*, when punishment works and when it fails, and the effects of *extrinsic* and *intrinsic reinforcers*.

Review: Next, go back and read this section again.

Now take this *Quick Quiz:*

A. According to behavioural principles, what is happening here?
   1. An adolescent whose parents have hit him for minor transgressions since he was small runs away from home.
   2. A young woman whose parents paid her to clean her room while she was growing up is a slob when she moves to her own apartment.
   3. Two parents scold their young daughter every time they catch her sucking her thumb. The thumb sucking continues anyway.

B. Certain school systems are rewarding students for perfect attendance by giving them money, shopping sprees, laptops, and video games. What are the pros and cons of such practices?

C. Some harried parents habitually resort to physical punishment without being aware of its many negative consequences for themselves and their children. What alternatives do these parents have?

Answers:

A. 1. The physical punishment was painful, and through a process of classical conditioning, the situation in which it occurred also became unpleasant. Because escape from an unpleasant stimulus is negatively reinforcing, the boy ran away. **2.** Extrinsic reinforcers are no longer available, and room-cleaning behaviour has been extinguished. Also, extrinsic rewards may have displaced the intrinsic satisfaction of having a tidy room. **3.** Punishment has failed, possibly because it rewards thumb sucking with attention or because thumb sucking still brings the child pleasure whenever the parents are not around. **B.** The rewards may improve attendance (they have in some schools), and students who attend more regularly may become more interested in their studies and do better in school. But extrinsic rewards can also decrease intrinsic motivation, and when they are withdrawn (e.g., when the student goes to another school or leaves for university), attendance may plummet ("If there's no reward, why should I attend?"). Further, students may come to expect bigger and bigger rewards, upping the ante. In some schools, especially those that have de-emphasized penalties for poor attendance, the rewards have backfired and attendance has actually fallen. (Bonus question: Can you now apply these points to parents who pay their children for everything from brushing their teeth to behaving themselves in a restaurant?) **C.** Parents can use time-outs and loss of privileges (negative punishers), which are best accompanied by information about the kind of behaviour that would be appropriate. Negative punishers should be followed, whenever possible, by the reinforcement of desirable behaviour.

GET INVOLVED! What's Reinforcing Your Behaviour?

For each activity that you do, indicate whether the reinforcers controlling your behaviour are primarily extrinsic or intrinsic.

Activity	Reinforcers mostly extrinsic	Reinforcers mostly intrinsic	Reinforcers about equally extrinsic and intrinsic
Studying	_____	_____	_____
Housework	_____	_____	_____
Worship	_____	_____	_____
Grooming	_____	_____	_____
Job	_____	_____	_____
Dating	_____	_____	_____
Attending class	_____	_____	_____
Reading unrelated to school	_____	_____	_____
Sports	_____	_____	_____
Cooking	_____	_____	_____

Learning Objectives

14 Describe the features of the classic experiment (Tolman, 1938) that illustrated latent learning.

15 Differentiate observational learning from latent learning.

16 Summarize how learning occurs without obvious reinforcement.

Learning and the Mind

For half a century, most North American learning theories held that learning could be explained by specifying the behavioural "ABCs": *antecedents* (events preceding behaviour), *behaviours*, and *consequences*. Behaviourists liked to compare the mind to an engineer's hypothetical "black box," a device whose workings must be inferred because they cannot be observed directly. To them, the box contained irrelevant wiring; it was enough to know that pushing a button on the box would produce a predictable response. But even as early as the 1930s, a few behaviourists could not resist peeking into that black box.

Latent Learning

Behaviourist Edward Tolman (1938) committed virtual heresy at the time by noting that his rats, when pausing at turning points in a maze, seemed to be *deciding* which way to go. Moreover, the animals sometimes seemed to be learning even without any reinforcement. What, he wondered, was going on in their little rat brains that might account for this puzzle?

In a classic experiment, Tolman and C. H. Honzik (1930) placed three groups of rats in mazes and observed their behaviour daily for more than two weeks. The rats in Group 1 always found food at the end of the maze and quickly learned to find it without going down blind alleys. The rats in Group 2 never found food and, as you would expect, they followed no particular route. Group 3 was the interesting group. These rats found no food for 10 days and seemed to wander aimlessly, but on the 11th day they received food, and then they quickly learned to run to the end of the maze. By the following day, they were doing as well as Group 1, which had been rewarded from the beginning (see Figure 7.6).

Group 3 had demonstrated **latent learning**, learning that is not immediately expressed in performance. A great deal of human learning also remains latent until

latent learning A form of learning that is not immediately expressed in an overt response; it occurs without obvious reinforcement.

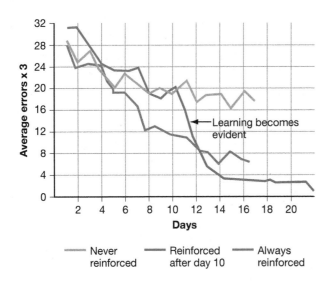

FIGURE 7.6 Latent Learning
In a classic experiment, rats that always found food in a maze made fewer and fewer errors in reaching the food (blue curve). In contrast, rats that received no food showed little improvement (gold curve). But rats that got no food for 10 days and then found food on the 11th day showed rapid improvement from then on (red curve). This result suggests that learning involves cognitive changes that can occur in the absence of reinforcement and that may not be acted on until a reinforcer becomes available (Tolman & Honzik, 1930).

circumstances allow or require it to be expressed. A driver gets out of a traffic jam and finds her way to Fourth and Kumquat Streets using a route she has never used before (without GPS!). A little boy observes a parent setting the table or tightening a screw but does not act on this learning for years; then he finds he knows how to do these things.

Latent learning raises questions about what, exactly, is learned during operant learning. In the Tolman and Honzik study, the rats that did not get any food until the 11th day seemed to have acquired a mental representation of the maze. They had been learning the whole time; they simply had no reason to act on that learning until they began to find food. Similarly, the driver taking a new route can do so because she already knows how the city is laid out. What seems to be acquired in latent learning, therefore, is not a specific response, but *knowledge* about responses and their consequences. We learn how the world is organized, which paths lead to which places, and which actions can produce which payoffs. This knowledge permits us to be creative and flexible in reaching our goals. ⊙➤

Simulate the **Experiment**
Learning in **MyPsychLab**

Social-Cognitive Learning Theories

During the 1960s and 1970s, many learning theorists concluded that human behaviour could not be understood without taking into account the human capacity for higher-level cognitive processes. They agreed with behaviourists that human beings, along with the rat and the rabbit, are subject to the laws of operant and classical conditioning. But they added that human beings, unlike the rat or the rabbit, are full of attitudes, beliefs, and expectations that affect the way they acquire information, make decisions, reason, and solve problems. Today, this view has become very influential.

We will use the term **social-cognitive theory** for all theories that combine behavioural principles with cognitive ones to explain behaviour (Bandura, 1986; Mischel, 1973; Mischel & Shoda, 1995). These theories share an emphasis on the importance of beliefs, perceptions, and observations of other peoples' behaviour in determining what we learn, what we do at any given moment, and the personality traits we develop (see Chapter 14). To a social-cognitive theorist, differences in beliefs and perceptions help explain why two people who live through the same event may come away with entirely different lessons from it (Bandura, 2001). All siblings know this. One sibling may regard being grounded by their father as evidence of his all-around meanness, whereas another may see the same behaviour as evidence of his care and concern for his children. For these siblings, being grounded is likely to affect their behaviour differently.

social-cognitive theories Theories that emphasize how behaviour is learned and maintained through observation and imitation of others, positive consequences, and cognitive processes such as plans, expectations, and beliefs.

observational learning A process in which an individual learns new responses by observing the behaviour of another (a model) rather than through direct experience; sometimes called *vicarious conditioning*.

Learning by Observing. Late one night, a friend living in a rural area was awakened by a loud clattering noise. A raccoon had knocked over a "raccoon-proof" garbage can and seemed to be demonstrating to an assembly of other raccoons how to open it: If you jump up and down on the can's side, the lid will pop off. According to our friend, the observing raccoons learned from this episode how to open stubborn garbage cans, and the observing humans learned how smart raccoons can be. In short, they all benefited from **observational learning**, learning by watching what others do and what happens to them for doing it.

The behaviour learned by the raccoons through observation was an operant one, but observational learning also plays an important role in the acquisition of automatic, reflexive responses, such as fears and phobias (Mineka & Zinbarg, 2006; Olsson & Phelps, 2004). Thus, in addition to learning to be frightened of rats directly through classical conditioning, as Little Albert did, you might also learn to fear rats by observing the emotional expressions of other people when they see or touch one. The perception of someone else's reaction serves as an unconditioned stimulus for your own fear, and the learning that results may be as strong as it would be if you had had a direct encounter with the rat yourself. Children often learn to fear things in this way, perhaps by observing a parent's fearful reaction whenever a dog approaches. Adults can acquire fears even by watching suspenseful movies. After seeing the classic horror film *Psycho*, in which a character is knifed to death in a shower, some people became nervous about taking a shower. Similarly, after seeing *Jaws*, with its horrific scenes of shark attacks and its gripping music, some people became afraid to swim in the ocean.

Behaviourists refer to observational learning as *vicarious conditioning*, and believe it can be explained in stimulus–response terms. But social-cognitive theorists believe that observational learning in human beings cannot be fully understood without taking into account the thought processes of the learner (Meltzoff & Gopnik, 1993). They emphasize the knowledge that results when a person sees a *model*—another person—behaving in certain ways and experiencing the consequences (Bandura, 1977).

None of us would last long without observational learning. Learning would be both inefficient and dangerous. We would have to learn to avoid oncoming cars by walking into traffic and suffering the consequences, or learn to swim by jumping into a deep pool and flailing around. Parents and teachers would be busy 24 hours a day shaping children's behaviour. Bosses would have to stand over their employees' desks, rewarding every little link in the complex behavioural chains we call typing, report writing, and accounting. But observational learning has its dark side as well: People often imitate antisocial or unethical actions (they observe a friend cheating and decide they can get away with it too) or self-defeating and harmful ones (they watch a film star smoking and take up the habit in an effort to look just as cool).

Many years ago, Albert Bandura and his colleagues showed just how important observational learning is for children who are learning the rules of social behaviour (Bandura, Ross, & Ross, 1963). Nursery school children watched a short film of two men, Rocky and Johnny, playing with toys. (Apparently the children did not think this behaviour was the least bit odd.) In the film, Johnny refuses to share his toys, and Rocky responds by clobbering him. Rocky's aggressive actions are rewarded because he winds up with all the toys. Poor Johnny sits dejectedly in the corner, while Rocky marches off with a sack full of loot and a hobbyhorse under his arm.

After viewing the film, each child was left alone for 20 minutes in a playroom full of toys, including some of

Observation is how line dancers learn their steps.

Alamy

the items shown in the film. Watching through a one-way mirror, the experimenters found that the children were much more aggressive in their play than a control group that had not seen the film. Some children imitated Rocky almost exactly. At the end of the session, one little girl even asked for a sack! ◉

Of course, people imitate positive activities that they observe, too. In the *Hunger Games*, the heroine Katniss Everdeen is a superb archer, whose skill with the bow and arrow helps her survive. Denise Parker, CEO of USA Archery, reports that there has been a boom in archery among young women and girls that is being seen beyond the States, in countries including Canada, France, and the UK. Other films and shows involving archery, such as *Brave* and *Game of Thrones*, no doubt help this increase in interest as well.

Findings on latent learning, observational learning, and the role of cognition in learning can help us evaluate arguments in the passionate debate about the effects of media violence. Children and teenagers in Canada and many other countries see countless acts of violence on television, in films, and in video games. Does all this mayhem of blood and guts affect them? Do you think it has affected you? In "Taking Psychology with You," we offer evidence that bears on these questions, and suggest ways of resolving them without oversimplifying the issues. ◉

Although the behavioural and social-cognitive approaches to learning differ in emphasis, they share a fundamental optimism about the possibilities of change for individuals and societies. In the learning view, we do not have to sit around hoping that people will magically have a change of heart and stop harming themselves or others. Instead, we can focus on changing the reinforcers, role models, and media images that affect people's attitudes and actions.

Skinner himself never wavered in his determination to apply learning principles to fashion better, healthier environments for everyone. In 1990, just a week before his death, ailing and frail, he addressed an overflow crowd at the annual meeting of the American Psychological Association, making the case one last time for the approach he was convinced could create a better society. When you see the world as the learning theorist views it, Skinner was saying, you see the folly of human behaviour, but you also see the possibility of improving it.

◉—⌐Watch the Video *Classic Footage of Bandura's Bobo Doll Experiment* in **MyPsychLab**

◉—⌐Watch the Video *In the Real World: Learning Aggression* in **MyPsychLab**

In studies by Albert Bandura and his colleagues, children watched films of an adult kicking, punching, and hammering on a big rubber doll (top). Later, the children imitated the adult's behaviour, some of them almost exactly.

Top left: Albert Bandura. Top right, bottom left and right: Bandura Albert.

Recite & Review

Recite: Maybe someone will overhear you saying everything you know about these concepts, realize how smart you are, and adopt the same useful study habit: *latent learning*, *social-cognitive theories*, and *observational learning*.

Review: Next, go back and read this section again.

Now take this *Quick Quiz:*

1. A friend asks you to meet her at a new restaurant across town. You have never been to this specific address, but you find your way there anyway because you have experienced _____ learning.

2. To a social-cognitive theorist, the fact that we can learn without being reinforced for any obvious responses shows that we do not learn specific responses but rather _____.

3. After watching her teenage sister put on lipstick, a little girl takes a lipstick and applies it to her own lips. She has acquired this behaviour through a process of _____.

Answers:

1. latent 2. knowledge about responses and their consequences 3. observational learning

Taking Psychology with You

THINKING CRITICALLY IN EVERYDAY LIFE

Does Media Violence Make You Violent?

Countries such as Australia, New Zealand, and England have concluded that violent video games can be dangerous enough to children to justify restrictions or even a complete ban; others, including Canada, rate video games but do not necessarily restrict the sales of these games to minors (although many companies will not sell them to minors). Which conclusion is right? Does violence depicted in films, on TV, and in video games lead to real violence?

Psychologists are strongly divided in their answers to this question. One group of investigators concluded, "Research on violent television and films, video games, and music reveals unequivocal evidence that media violence increases the likelihood of aggressive and violent behaviour," both in the short term and long term (Anderson et al., 2003). Their meta-analyses find that the greater the exposure to violence in movies and on television, the stronger the likelihood of a person's behaving aggressively, and this correlation holds for both sexes and across cultures, from Japan to England (Anderson et al., 2010). Video games that directly reward violence, as by awarding points or moving the player to the next level after a "kill," increase feelings of hostility, aggressive thinking, and aggressive behaviour (Carnagey &

> 66 Should we ban *Hamlet*? Bloody graphic comics? Violent action films? 99

Anderson, 2005). Moreover, when grade school children cut back on time spent watching TV or playing violent video games, the children's aggressiveness declines (Robinson et al., 2001). However, most of these studies also use games that differ in difficulty and pace of action and use different measures of aggressiveness (Adachi & Willoughby, 2011)—so when you are interpreting these results, use your critical thinking as any one of these factors may be the reason that behaviour is affected.

Violent media may also desensitize people to the pain or distress of others. In a field study, people who had just seen a violent movie took longer to come to the aid of a woman struggling to pick up her crutches than did people who had seen a nonviolent movie or people still waiting to see one of the two movies (Bushman & Anderson, 2009).

However, an opposing group of psychologists believes that the effects of video games have been exaggerated and sensationalized (Ferguson & Kilburn, 2010). The correlation between playing violent video games and behaving aggressively, they maintain, is too small to worry about (Ferguson, 2007; Sherry, 2001). Other factors that are correlated with violent criminality are far more powerful; they include genetic influences (.75), perceptions of criminal opportunity (.58), owning a gun (.35), poverty (.25), and childhood physical abuse (.22). In their calculations, watching violent video games has the lowest correlation, only

.04 (Ferguson, 2009; Ferguson & Kilburn, 2010). Besides, they observe, rates of teenage violence declined significantly throughout the 1990s, a period in which the number of violent video games was increasing astronomically.

In the social-cognitive view, both conclusions about the relationship of media violence to violent behaviour have merit. Repeated acts of aggression in the media do model behaviour and responses to conflict that a few people may imitate, just as media ads influence what many people buy and what many people think the ideal male or female body should look like. However, children watch many different programs and movies and have many models to observe besides those they see in the media, including parents and peers. For every teenager who is obsessed with playing a video game that involves grim fantasies of blowing up the world, hundreds more think the game is just plain fun and then go off to do their homework.

Moreover, perceptions and interpretations of events, personality dispositions such as aggressiveness and sociability, and the social context in which the violence is viewed can all affect how a person responds (Feshbach & Tangney, 2008). One person may learn from seeing people being blown away in a film that violence is cool and masculine; another may decide that the violent images are ugly and stupid; a third may conclude that they don't mean anything at all, that they are just part of the story.

What should be done, if anything, about media violence? Even if only a small percentage of viewers learn to be aggressive from observing all that violence, the social consequences can be serious, because the total audiences for TV, movies, and video games are immense. But censorship, which some people think is the answer, brings its own set of problems, quite apart from constitutional issues of free speech. Should we ban *Hamlet?* Bloody graphic comics? Films that truthfully depict the realities of war, murder, and torture?

Consider, too, that it's not just video games and other visual media that can increase aggression. In two studies, students read a violent passage from the Bible, with two sentences inserted in which God sanctions the violence. Later, in what they thought was a different study, they played a competitive reaction-time game with a partner. In the game, they were more willing to blast their competitor with a loud noise than were students who had been told the violent passage was from an ancient scroll or students who had read a passage that did not mention God (Bushman et al., 2007). Participants who believed in God were most affected by the passage in which God condones the violence, but many nonbelievers were affected too. Although the general message of the scriptures is one of peace and reconciliation, the Bible is also full of violence, some of it sanctioned by God. Yet few people would be willing to ban the Bible or censor its violent parts.

As you can see, determining a fair and equitable policy regarding media violence will not be easy. It will demand good evidence—and good thinking.

Summary

- Research on *learning* has been heavily influenced by *behaviourism*, which accounts for behaviour in terms of observable events without reference to mental entities such as "mind" or "will." Behaviourists have focused on two types of *conditioning*: classical and operant.

Classical Conditioning

- *Classical conditioning* was first studied by Russian physiologist Ivan Pavlov. In this type of learning, when a neutral stimulus is paired with an *unconditioned stimulus* (US) that already elicits a certain *unconditioned response* (UR), the neutral stimulus becomes associated with the US. The neutral stimulus then becomes a *conditioned stimulus* (CS), and has the capacity to elicit a *conditioned response* (CR) that is similar or related to the UR. Nearly any kind of involuntary response can become a CR.

- In *extinction*, the conditioned stimulus is repeatedly presented without the unconditioned stimulus, and the conditioned response eventually disappears, although later it may reappear (*spontaneous recovery*). In *higher-order conditioning*, a neutral stimulus becomes a conditioned stimulus by being paired with an already-established conditioned stimulus. In *stimulus generalization*, after a stimulus becomes a conditioned stimulus for some response, other similar stimuli may produce the same or similar reaction. In *stimulus discrimination*, different responses are made to stimuli that resemble the conditioned stimulus in some way.

- Many theorists believe that what an animal or person learns in classical conditioning is not just an association between the unconditioned and conditioned stimuli, but also information conveyed by one stimulus about another. Indeed, classical conditioning appears to be an evolutionary adaptation that allows an organism to prepare for a biologically important event. Considerable evidence exists to show that a neutral stimulus does not become a CS unless it reliably signals or predicts the US.

Classical Conditioning in Real Life

- Classical conditioning helps account for positive emotional responses to particular objects and events, fears and phobias, reactions to particular foods and odours, and reactions to medical treatments and placebos. John Watson showed how fears may be learned and then may be unlearned through a process of *counterconditioning*. Work on classical conditioning is now integrating findings on fear, learning, and biology. Using a drug to enhance the activity of a certain receptor in the amygdala speeds up the extinction of a phobia (fear of heights) during virtual-reality treatments. Because of evolutionary adaptations, human beings (and many other species) are biologically primed to acquire some classically conditioned responses easily, such as conditioned taste aversions and certain fears.

Operant Conditioning

- In *operant conditioning*, behaviour becomes more likely or less likely to occur depending on its consequences. Responses in operant conditioning are generally not reflexive and are more complex than in classical conditioning. Research in this area is closely associated with B. F. Skinner, who called his approach "radical behaviourism."

- In the Skinnerian analysis, *reinforcement* strengthens or increases the probability of a response, and *punishment* weakens or decreases the probability of a response. Immediate consequences usually have a greater effect on a response than do delayed consequences.

- *Reinforcers* are called *primary* when they are naturally reinforcing because they satisfy a biological need. They are called *secondary* when they have acquired their ability to strengthen a response through association with other reinforcers. A similar distinction is made for *punishers*.

- Reinforcement and punishment may be either positive or negative, depending on whether the consequence involves a stimulus that is presented or one that is removed or avoided. In *positive reinforcement*, something pleasant follows a response; in *negative reinforcement*, something unpleasant is removed. In *positive punishment*, something unpleasant follows the response; in *negative punishment*, something pleasant is removed.

- *Extinction, stimulus generalization,* and *stimulus discrimination* occur in operant conditioning as well as in classical conditioning. A *discriminative stimulus* signals that a response is likely to be followed by a certain type of consequence.

- *Continuous reinforcement* leads to the most rapid learning. However, *intermittent (partial) reinforcement* makes a response resistant to extinction (and, therefore, helps account for the persistence of superstitious rituals). One of the most common errors people make is to reward intermittently the responses they would like to eliminate.

- *Shaping* is used to train behaviours with a low probability of occurring spontaneously. Reinforcers are given for *successive approximations* to the desired response until the desired response is achieved.

- Biology places limits on what an animal or person can learn through operant conditioning, or how easily it is learned. Animals sometimes have trouble learning a task because of *instinctive drift*.

Operant Conditioning in Real Life

- *Behaviour modification*, the application of operant-conditioning principles, has been used successfully in many settings, but when used inappropriately, reinforcement and punishment both have their pitfalls.

- Punishment, when used properly, can discourage undesirable behaviour, including criminal behaviour. But it is frequently misused and can have unintended consequences. It is often administered inappropriately because of the emotion of the moment; it may produce rage and fear; its effects are often only temporary; it is hard to administer immediately; it conveys little information about the kind of behaviour that is desired; and it may provide attention that is rewarding. Extinction of undesirable behaviour, combined with reinforcement of desired behaviour, is generally preferable to the use of punishment.

- Reinforcers can also be misused. Rewards that are given out indiscriminately, as in efforts to raise children's self-esteem, do not reinforce desirable behaviour. And an exclusive reliance on *extrinsic reinforcement* can sometimes undermine the power of *intrinsic reinforcement*. But money and praise do not usually interfere with intrinsic pleasure when a person is rewarded for succeeding or making progress rather than for merely participating in an activity, or when a person is already highly interested in the activity.

Learning and the Mind

- Even during behaviourism's heyday, some researchers were probing the "black box" of the mind. In the 1930s, Edward Tolman studied *latent learning*, in which no obvious reinforcer is present during learning and a response is not expressed until later on, when reinforcement does become available. What appears to be acquired in latent learning is not a specific response but rather knowledge about responses and their consequences.

- The 1960s and 1970s saw the increased influence of *social-cognitive theories* of learning, which focus on *observational learning* and the role played by beliefs, interpretations of events, and other cognitions in determining behaviour. Social-cognitive theorists argue that in observational learning, as in latent learning, what is acquired is knowledge rather than a specific response. Because people differ in their perceptions and beliefs, they may learn different lessons from the same event or situation. Perceptions, personality traits, and social context can all influence how people respond.

Taking Psychology with You

- Because people differ in their perceptions and beliefs, some people become more aggressive after exposure to violent images in the media, but most people do not. Social-learning research shows that personality traits and the social context influence how people respond to what they see and the lessons they take from any experience.

Key Terms

learning **219**
behaviourism **219**
conditioning **219**
unconditioned stimulus (US) **221**
unconditioned response (UR) **221**
conditioned stimulus (CS) **221**
conditioned response (CR) **221**
classical conditioning **221**
extinction (in classical conditioning) **222**

spontaneous recovery **222**
higher-order conditioning **222**
stimulus generalization (in classical conditioning) **223**
stimulus discrimination (in classical conditioning) **223**
counterconditioning **227**
operant conditioning **230**
reinforcement/ reinforcers **231**
punishment/punishers **231**
primary reinforcers **231**
primary punishers **231**

secondary reinforcers **231**
secondary punishers **231**
positive reinforcement **232**
negative reinforcement **232**
extinction (in operant conditioning) **234**
stimulus generalization (in operant conditioning) **235**
stimulus discrimination (in operant conditioning) **235**
discriminative stimulus **235**
continuous reinforcement **235**

intermittent (partial) schedule of reinforcement **235**
shaping **236**
successive approximations **237**
instinctive drift **237**
behaviour modification (applied behaviour analysis) **239**
extrinsic reinforcers **243**
intrinsic reinforcers **244**
latent learning **246**
social-cognitive theories **247**
observational learning **248**

8 Behaviour in Social and Cultural Context

Obedience, Milgram concluded, was more a function of the situation than of the personalities of the participants. "The key to [their] behaviour," Milgram (1974) summarized, "lies not in pent-up anger or aggression but in the nature of their relationship to authority. They have given themselves to the authority; they see themselves as instruments for the execution of his wishes; once so defined, they are unable to break free."

The Milgram study has had numerous critics. Some consider it unethical because people were kept in the dark about what was really happening until the session was over (of course, telling them in advance would have invalidated the study) and because many suffered emotional pain (Milgram countered that they would not have felt pain if they had simply disobeyed instructions). A "softer" version of the experiment was conducted wherein "teachers" who had not heard of the original Milgram study had to administer shocks only up to 150 volts, when they first heard the learner protest. That amount of shock had been a critical choice point in Milgram's study, and in the replication, nearly 80 percent of those who went past 150 ended up going all the way to the end (Packer, 2008). Overall obedience rates were only slightly lower than Milgram's, and once again, gender, education, age, and ethnicity had no effect on the likelihood of obeying (Burger, 2009). In another, rather eerie cyber-version replication of Milgram's study, participants had to shock a virtual woman on a computer screen. Even though they knew she wasn't real, their heart rates increased and they reported feeling bad about delivering the "shocks." Yet they kept doing it (Slater et al., 2006).

Some psychologists have questioned Milgram's conclusion that personality traits are virtually irrelevant to whether or not people obey an authority. Certain traits, they note, especially hostility, narcissism, and rigidity, do increase obedience and a willingness to inflict pain on others (Blass, 2000; Twenge, 2009). Others have objected to the parallel Milgram drew between the behaviour of the study's participants and the brutality of the Nazis and others who have committed acts of barbarism in the name of duty (Darley, 1995). The people in Milgram's study typically obeyed only when the experimenter was hovering right there, and many of them felt enormous discomfort and conflict. In contrast, most Nazis acted without direct supervision by authorities, without external pressure, and without feelings of anguish.

Milgram's compelling study has had a tremendous influence on public awareness of the dangers of uncritical obedience. As John Darley (1995) observed, "Milgram shows us the beginning of a path by means of which ordinary people, in the grip of social forces, become the origins of atrocities in the real world."

In 2007, guards at the Grand Valley Institution for Women in Kitchener Ontario videotaped Ashley Smith asphyxiating herself while she was under a suicide watch. The guards did not intervene nor did anyone enter her cell for 45 minutes, at which point she was dead. When the guards were asked why they didn't intervene, they responded that they were under orders not to respond to self-strangling attempts by Ms. Smith. Were those guards "just following orders"? Social psychologists think the explanation of their behaviour lies in the roles they were assigned; the implicit permission, if not direct orders, given by their leaders; and the group norms of their peers.

AP Images

The Prison Study

Another famous demonstration of the power of roles is known as the Stanford prison study. Its designers, Philip Zimbardo and Craig Haney, wanted to know what would happen if ordinary university students were randomly assigned to the roles of prisoners and guards (Haney, Banks, & Zimbardo, 1973). And so they set up a serious-looking "prison" in the basement of a Stanford building, complete with individual cells, different uniforms for prisoners and guards, and nightsticks for the guards. The students agreed to live there for two weeks. 👁

Within a short time, most of the prisoners became distressed and helpless. They developed emotional symptoms and physical ailments. Some became apathetic; others became rebellious. One panicked and broke down. The guards, however, began to enjoy their new power. Some tried to be nice, helping the prisoners and doing little favours for them. Some were "tough but fair," holding strictly to "the

👁 **Watch** the **Video**
Nature vs. Nurture and the Stanford Prison Experiment: Phil Zimbardo in **MyPsychLab**

Prisoners and guards quickly learn their respective roles, which often have more influence on their behaviour than their personalities do.

Corbis

rules." But about a third became punitive and harsh, even when the prisoners were not resisting in any way. One guard became unusually sadistic, smacking his nightstick into his palm as he vowed to "get" the prisoners and instructing two of them to simulate sexual acts (they refused). The researchers, who had not expected such a speedy and alarming transformation of ordinary students, ended this study after only six days.

Generations of students and the general public have seen emotionally charged clips from videos of the study made at the time. To the researchers, the results demonstrated how roles affect behaviour: The guards' aggression, they said, was entirely a result of wearing a guard's uniform and having the power conferred by a guard's authority (Haney & Zimbardo, 1998). Some social psychologists, however, have argued that the prison study is really another example of obedience to authority and of how willingly some people obey instructions, in this case from Zimbardo himself (Haslam & Reicher, 2003). Consider the briefing that Zimbardo provided to the guards at the beginning of the study:

> You can create in the prisoners feelings of boredom, a sense of fear to some degree, you can create a notion of arbitrariness that their life is totally controlled by us, by the system, you, me, and they'll have no privacy. . . . We're going to take away their individuality in various ways. In general what all this leads to is a sense of powerlessness. That is, in this situation we'll have all the power and they'll have none. (*The Stanford Prison Study* video, quoted in Haslam & Reicher, 2003)

These are pretty powerful suggestions to the guards about how they would be permitted to behave, and they convey Zimbardo's personal encouragement ("*we'll* have all the power"), so perhaps it is not surprising that some took Zimbardo at his word and behaved quite brutally. The one sadistic guard later said he was just trying to play the role of the "worst S.O.B. guard" he'd seen in the movies. Even the investigators themselves noted at the time that the data were "subject to possible errors due to selective sampling. The video and audio recordings tended to be focussed upon the more interesting, dramatic events which occurred" (Haney, Banks, Zimbardo, 1973).

Despite these flaws, the Stanford prison study remains a useful cautionary tale. In real prisons, guards do have tremendous power, and they too may be given instructions that encourage them to treat prisoners harshly or that enable them to ignore self-destructive behaviour. Thus the prison study provides a good example of how the social situation affects behaviour, causing some people to behave in ways that seem out of character.

Why People Obey

Of course, obedience to authority or to the norms of a situation is not always harmful or bad. A certain amount of routine compliance with rules is necessary in any group, and obedience to authority has many benefits for individuals and society. A nation could not operate if all its citizens ignored traffic signals, cheated on their taxes, dumped garbage wherever they chose, or assaulted each other. An organization could not function if its members came to work only when they felt like it. But obedience also has a darker aspect. Throughout history, the plea "I was only following orders" has been offered to excuse actions carried out on behalf of orders that were foolish, destructive, or illegal. The writer C. P. Snow once observed that "More hideous crimes have been committed in the name of obedience than in the name of rebellion."

Most people follow orders because of the obvious consequences of disobedience: They can be suspended from school, fired from their jobs, or arrested. But they may also obey an authority because they hope to gain advantages or promotions or to gain knowledge or experience. They obey because they are dependent or respect the authority's legitimacy (van der Toorn, Tyler, & Jost, 2011). And, most of all, they obey because they do not want to rock the boat, appear to doubt the experts, or be rude, fearing that they will be disliked or rejected for doing so (Collins & Brief, 1995). But what about all those people in Milgram's study who felt they were doing wrong and wanted to rebel, but who could not untangle themselves from the "cobweb of social constraints"? How do people become morally disengaged from the consequences of their actions?

One answer is **entrapment**, a process in which individuals escalate their commitment to a course of action in order to justify their investment in it (Brockner & Rubin, 1985). The first stages of entrapment may pose no difficult choices, but one step leads to another and before you realize it you've become committed to a course of action that poses real problems. 👁

In Milgram's study, once participants had given a 15-volt shock, they had committed themselves to the experiment. The next level was "only" 30 volts. Because each increment was small, before they knew it most people were administering what they believed were dangerously strong shocks. At that point, it was difficult to justify a sudden decision to quit, especially after reaching 150 volts, the point at which the "learner" made his first verbal protests. Those who administered the highest levels of shock justified their actions by adopting the attitude of "It's his problem; I'm just following orders," handing over responsibility to the authority and absolving themselves of accountability for their own actions (Kelman & Hamilton, 1989; Modigliani & Rochat, 1995). In contrast, individuals who refused to give high levels of shock justified *their* decision by taking responsibility for their actions. "One of the things I think is very cowardly," said a 32-year-old engineer, "is to try to shove the responsibility onto someone else. See, if I now turned around and said, 'It's your fault . . . it's not mine,' I would call that cowardly" (Milgram, 1974).

A chilling study of entrapment was conducted with 25 men who had served in the Greek military police during the authoritarian regime that ended in 1974 (Haritos-Fatouros, 1988). A psychologist interviewed the men, identifying the steps used in training them to use torture in questioning prisoners. First, the men were ordered to stand guard outside the interrogation and torture cells. Then they stood guard inside the detention rooms, where they observed the torture of prisoners. Then they "helped" beat up prisoners. Once they had obediently followed these orders and became actively involved, the torturers found their actions easier to carry out. Similar procedures have been used around the world to train military and police interrogators to use torture on political opponents and criminal suspects, although torture is expressly forbidden under international law (Conroy, 2000; Huggins, Haritos-Fatouros, & Zimbardo, 2003; Mayer, 2009).

From their standpoint, torturers justify their actions because they see themselves as "good guys" who are just "doing their jobs," especially in wartime. And perhaps they are—but such a justification overlooks entrapment. This prisoner might be a murderer or a terrorist, but what if this other one is completely innocent? Before long, the torturer has shifted his reasoning from "If this person is guilty, he deserves to be tortured" to "If I am torturing this person, he must be guilty—and besides, if I am doing it, it isn't torture." And so the abuse escalates (Tavris & Aronson, 2007).

This is a difficult concept for people who divide the world into "good guys" versus "bad guys" and cannot imagine that good guys might do brutal things; if the good guys are doing it, by definition, it's all right to do. Yet in everyday life, as in the Milgram study, people often set out on a path that is morally ambiguous, only to find that they have travelled a long way toward violating their own principles. From Greece's torturers to the African nuns to the guards who watched Ashley Smith choke herself to

entrapment A gradual process in which individuals escalate their commitment to a course of action to justify their investment of time, money, or effort.

👁 **Watch** the **Video**
The Power of the Situation: Phil Zimbardo in **MyPsychLab**

death, from Milgram's well-meaning volunteers to all of us in our everyday lives, from cheating on exams to cheating in business, people face the difficult task of drawing a line beyond which they will not go. For many, the demands of the role and the social pressures of the situation defeat the inner voice of conscience.

Recite & Review

Recite: Step into your role of student and say aloud what you know about *norms*, *roles*, *culture*, the Milgram experiment, the Stanford prison study, and *entrapment*.

Review: Next, read this section again.

Now take this *Quick Quiz:*

1. About what proportion of the people in Milgram's obedience study administered the highest level of shock? (a) two-thirds, (b) one-half, (c) one-third, (d) one-tenth

2. Which of the following actions by the "learner" reduced the likelihood of being shocked by the "teacher" in Milgram's study? (a) protesting noisily, (b) screaming in pain, (c) complaining of having a heart ailment, (d) nothing he did made a difference

3. A friend of yours, who is moving, asks you to bring over a few boxes. Because you are there anyway, he asks you to fill them with books. Before you know it, you have packed up his kitchen, living room, and bedroom. What social-psychological process is at work here?

Answers:

1. a 2. d 3. entrapment

Learning Objectives

3. Classify two general ways that people explain their own or other people's behaviour.

4. List and define two self-serving biases in how people think about themselves and the world.

5. Explain why most people will believe lies and nonsensical statements if they are repeated often enough.

6. Assess whether certain fundamental political and religious attitudes have a genetic component.

Social Influences on Beliefs and Behaviour

Social psychologists are interested not only in what people do in social situations, but also in what is going on in their heads while they are doing it. Those who study **social cognition** examine how people's perceptions of themselves and others affect their relationships and also how the social environment influences their perceptions, beliefs, and values. Current approaches draw on evolutionary theory, neuroimaging studies, surveys, and experiments to identify universal themes in how human beings perceive and feel about one another. In this section, we will consider two important topics in social cognition: attributions and attitudes. 👁

Attributions

A detective's job is to find out *who* did the dirty deed, but most of us also want to know *why* people do bad things. Was it because of a terrible childhood, a mental illness, possession by a demon, or what? According to **attribution theory**, the

---

👁 **Watch** the **Video**
Social Influence: Robert Cialdini
in **MyPsychLab**

social cognition An area in social psychology concerned with social influences on thought, memory, perception, and beliefs.

attribution theory The theory that people are motivated to explain their own and other people's behaviour by attributing causes of that behaviour to a situation or a disposition.

explanations we make of our behaviour and the behaviour of others generally fall into two categories. When we make a *situational attribution*, we are identifying the cause of an action as something in the situation or environment: "Joe stole the money because his family is starving." When we make a *dispositional attribution*, we are identifying the cause of an action as something in the person: "Joe stole the money because he is a born thief."

When people are trying to explain someone else's behaviour, they tend to overestimate personality traits and underestimate the influence of the situation (Forgas, 1998; Nisbett & Ross, 1980). In terms of attribution theory, they tend to ignore situational attributions in favour of dispositional ones. This tendency has been called the **fundamental attribution error** (Jones, 1990):

> **Attributions**
>
> "Why is Aurelia so mean and crabby lately?"
>
> **Situational**   **Dispositional**
>
> "She's under pressure."   "She's self-involved and clueless."
>
> (May lead to)
>
> **Fundamental Attribution Error**
>
> Ignoring influence of situation on behavior and emphasizing personality traits alone.

fundamental attribution error The tendency, in explaining other people's behaviour, to overestimate personality factors and underestimate the influence of the situation.

Were the hundreds of people who obeyed Milgram's experimenters sadistic by nature? Were the student guards in the prison study cruel and the prisoners cowardly by temperament? Were the individuals who pocketed the money from a mailbox on a dirty street "born thieves"? Those who think so are committing the fundamental attribution error. The impulse to explain other people's behaviour in terms of their personalities is so strong that we do it even when we know that the other person was *required* to behave in a certain way (Yzerbyt et al., 2001).

The fundamental attribution error is especially prevalent in western nations, where middle-class people tend to believe that individuals are responsible for their own actions and dislike the idea that the situation has much influence over them. Therefore, they prefer to explain behaviour in terms of people's traits (Na & Kitayama, 2011). They think that *they* would have refused the experimenter's cruel orders and *they* would have treated fellow-students-temporarily-called-prisoners fairly. In

Children learn the value of self-serving attributions at an early age.

Universal Uclick

contrast, in countries such as India, where everyone is embedded in caste and family networks, and in Japan, China, Korea, and Hong Kong, where people are more group oriented than in the west, people are more likely to be aware of situational constraints on behaviour, including their own behaviour (Balcetis, Dunning, & Miller, 2008; Choi et al., 2003). Thus, if someone is behaving oddly, makes a mistake, or commits an ethical lapse, a person from India or China, unlike a westerner, is more likely to make a situational attribution of the person's behaviour ("He's under pressure") than a dispositional one ("He's incompetent").

A primary reason for the fundamental attribution error is that people rely on different sources of information to judge their own behaviour than that of others. We know what we ourselves are thinking and feeling, but we can't always know the same of others. Thus, we assess our own actions by introspecting about our feelings and intentions, but when we observe the actions of others, we have only their behaviour to guide our interpretations (Pronin, 2008; Pronin, Gilovich, & Ross, 2004). This basic asymmetry in social perception is further widened by *self-serving biases*, habits of thinking that make us feel good about ourselves, even (perhaps especially) when we shouldn't. We discuss other cognitive biases in Chapter 9, but here are two types of self-serving biases that are especially relevant to the attributions that people often make:

1 **The bias to choose the most flattering and forgiving attributions of our own lapses.** When it comes to explaining their own behaviour, people tend to choose attributions that are favourable to them, taking credit for their good actions (a dispositional attribution) but letting the situation account for their failures, embarrassing mistakes, or harmful actions (Mezulis et al., 2004). For instance, most North Americans, when angry, will say, "I am furious for good reason; this situation is intolerable." They are less likely to say, "I am furious because I am an ill-tempered grinch." On the other hand, if they do something admirable, such as donating to charity, they are likely to attribute their motives to a personal disposition ("I'm so generous") instead of the situation ("That guy on the phone pressured me into it").

Research performed at the University of British Columbia suggests that culture may affect whether or not we adopt another type of bias: the *group-serving bias*. This term describes our tendency to view the groups to which we belong, or the individuals in these groups, favourably (Heine & Lehman, 1997; Falk, Heine, & Takemura, 2014). In one study, European-Canadian, Asian-Canadian, and Japanese students were asked to evaluate their university and a member of their family. The researchers observed that the Japanese students consistently evaluated their family member and their university less positively than did the Canadians (regardless of their ethnicity). Thus, the Japanese participants (members of a more collectivist society) did not engage in group-serving biases, at either individual or group levels, whereas the Canadian participants (members of a more individualist society) exhibited group-serving biases at all levels of groups to which they belonged. Thus, some group-serving biases result from the degree to which one's culture is collectivist or individualist.

2 **The bias to believe that the world is fair.** According to the **just-world hypothesis**, attributions are also affected by the need to believe that justice usually prevails, that good people are rewarded and bad guys punished (Lerner, 1980). When this belief is thrown into doubt—especially when bad things happen to "good people" who are just like us—we are motivated to restore it (Aguiar et al., 2008; Hafer & Bègue, 2005). Unfortunately, one common way of restoring the belief in a just world is to call upon a dispositional attribution called *blaming the victim:* Maybe that person wasn't so good after all; he or she must have done *something* to deserve what happened or to provoke it. Blaming the victim is virtually universal

just-world hypothesis The notion that many people need to believe that the world is fair and that justice is served, that bad people are punished and good people are rewarded.

when people are ordered to harm others or find themselves entrapped into harming others (Bandura, 1999). In the Milgram study, some "teachers" made comments such as "[The learner] was so stupid and stubborn he deserved to get shocked" (Milgram, 1974). In an innovative series of experiments, Carolyn Hafer of Brock University has found that people who strongly believe that the world is just are more likely to blame the victim than are those who have weaker beliefs in a just world (Hafer, 2000a, 2000b). When their belief in a just world is threatened, such individuals then seek to maintain their belief by finding some reason why the victims deserved what they got (Hafer & Bègue, 2005).

Of course, sometimes dispositional (personality) attributions *do* explain a person's behaviour. The point to remember is that the attributions you make can have huge consequences. For example, happy couples usually attribute their partners' occasional thoughtless lapses to something in the situation ("Poor guy is under a lot of stress") and their partners' loving actions to a stable, internal disposition ("He has the sweetest nature"). But unhappy couples do just the reverse. They attribute lapses to their partners' personalities ("He is totally selfish") and good behaviour to the situation ("Yeah, he gave me a present, but only because his mother told him to") (Karney & Bradbury, 2000). You can see why the attributions you make about your partner, your parents, and your friends will affect how you get along with them—and how long you will put up with their failings.

Recite & Review

Recite: Attribute your willingness to learn to an internal disposition, and state aloud what you know about *social cognition*, *attribution theory*, the *fundamental attribution error*, two central self-serving biases, and the *just-world hypothesis*.

Review: Next, reread this section.

Now take this *Quick Quiz:*

1. What kind of attribution is being made in each case, situational or dispositional? (a) A man says, "My wife has sure become a grouchy person." (b) The same man says, "I'm grouchy because I had a bad day at the office." (c) A woman reads about high unemployment in poor communities and says, "Well, if those people weren't so lazy, they would find work."

2. What principles of attribution theory are suggested by the items in the preceding question?

Answers:

1. a. dispositional b. situational c. dispositional 2. Item (a) illustrates the fundamental attribution error; (b), the bias to choose a flattering or forgiving explanation of our own lapses; and (c), blaming the victim, possibly because of the just-world hypothesis.

Attitudes

People hold attitudes about all sorts of things—politics, food, children, movies, sports heroes, you name it. An *attitude* is a belief about people, groups, ideas, or activities. Some attitudes are *explicit:* We are aware of them, they shape our conscious decisions and actions, and they can be measured on self-report questionnaires. Others are *implicit:* We are unaware of them, they may influence our behaviour in ways we do not recognize, and they are measured in indirect ways (Stanley, Phelps, & Banaji, 2008).

Some of your attitudes change when you have new experiences, and on occasion they change because you rationally decide you were wrong about something. But attitudes also change because of the psychological need for consistency and the mind's

cognitive dissonance A state of tension that occurs when a person simultaneously holds two cognitions that are psychologically inconsistent or when a person's belief is incongruent with his or her behaviour.

familiarity effect The tendency of people to feel more positively toward a person, item, product, or other stimulus the more familiar they are with it.

👁 **Watch** the **Video**
The Basics: Under the Influence of Others in **MyPsychLab**

FIGURE 8.2 The Slippery Slope of Self-Justification
Imagine two people with the same neutral attitude toward cheating. Given an opportunity, one cheats and the other doesn't. Because of the need to reduce cognitive dissonance, each will then justify the action taken so that her or his opinion about cheating is consonant with her or his behaviour. Over time, they both will have moved a long way from their original attitude.

normal biases in processing information. In Chapter 9, we discuss **cognitive dissonance**, the uncomfortable feeling that occurs when two attitudes, or an attitude and a behaviour, are in conflict (are dissonant). To resolve this dissonance, most people will change one of their attitudes. If a politician or celebrity you admire does something stupid, immoral, or illegal, you can restore consistency either by lowering your opinion of the person or by deciding that the person's behaviour wasn't so stupid or immoral after all. Usually—and unfortunately for critical thinking—people restore cognitive consistency by dismissing evidence that might otherwise throw their fundamental beliefs into question (Aronson, 2008). 👁

Here's an example closer to home: cheating. Let's say two students have the same general attitude toward it: It's not an ideal way to get ahead, but it's not the greatest crime, either. Now they take an important exam and freeze on a crucial question. They have a choice: Read their neighbour's answers (to get a better grade) or refrain from doing so (to maintain feelings of integrity). Impulsively, one cheats; the other doesn't. What happens now? The answer is illustrated in Figure 8.2. To reduce dissonance, *each one will justify their action to make it consonant with their beliefs.* The one who refrained will begin to think that cheating is serious after all, that it harms everyone, and that cheaters should be punished—Hey! Expel them! But the one who cheated will need to resolve the dissonance between "I am a fine, honest human being" and "I just cheated." He or she could say, "I guess I'm not an honest person after all," but it is more likely that the person will instead decide that cheating isn't very serious—Hey! Everyone does it!

Understanding how cognitive dissonance works to keep our beliefs and behaviour in harmony is important, because the way we reduce dissonance can have major, unexpected consequences. The student who cheated "just this once" will find it easier to cheat again on an assignment, and then again by turning in a term paper written by someone else, sliding down the slippery slope of entrapment. By the time the cheater has slid to the bottom, it will be extremely difficult to go back up, because that would mean admitting "I was wrong; I did a bad thing." That is how a small act of dishonesty, corruption, or error—from cheating to staying in a bad relationship—can set a person on a course of action that becomes increasingly self-defeating, cruel, or foolhardy . . . and difficult to reverse (Tavris & Aronson, 2007).

Unfortunately for critical thinking, people often restore cognitive consistency by dismissing evidence that might otherwise throw their fundamental beliefs into question (Aronson, 2012). In fact, they often become even *more* committed to a discredited belief. In one study, when people were thrown into doubt about the rightness of a belief or their position on some issue that was very important to them—such as being a vegetarian or carnivore, a Mac or PC user—they reduced dissonance by advocating their original position even more strongly. As the researchers summarized, "When in doubt, shout!" (Gal & Rucker, 2010). This mechanism explains why people in religious cults that have invested heavily in failed doomsday predictions rarely say, "What a relief that I was wrong." Instead, many become even more committed proselytizers.

Shifting Opinions and Bedrock Beliefs. All around you, every day, advertisers, politicians, and friends are trying to influence your attitudes. One weapon they use is the drip, drip, drip of a repeated idea. Repeated exposure even to a nonsense syllable such as *zug* is enough to make a person feel more positive toward it (Zajonc, 1968). The **familiarity effect**, the tendency to hold positive attitudes toward familiar people or things, has been demonstrated across cultures, across species, and across states of awareness, from alert to preoccupied. It works even for stimuli you aren't aware of seeing (Monahan, Murphy, & Zajonc, 2000). A related phenomenon is the **validity effect**, the tendency to believe that something is true simply because it has been repeated many times. Repeat something often enough, even the basest lie, and eventually the public will believe it. Hitler's propaganda minister, Joseph Goebbels, called this technique the "Big Lie."

In a series of experiments, Hal Arkes and his associates demonstrated how the validity effect operates (Arkes, 1993; Arkes, Boehm, & Xu, 1991). In a typical study, people read a list of statements, such as "Mercury has a higher boiling point than copper" or "Over 400 Hollywood films were produced in 1948." They had to rate each statement for its validity, on a scale of 1 (definitely false) to 7 (definitely true). A week or two later, they again rated the validity of some of these statements and also rated others that they had not seen previously. The result: Mere repetition increased the perception that the familiar statements were true. The same effect also occurred for other kinds of statements, including unverifiable opinions (e.g., "At least 75% of all politicians are basically dishonest"), opinions that subjects initially felt were true, and even opinions they initially felt were false. "Note that no attempt has been made to persuade," said Arkes (1993). "No supporting arguments are offered. We just have subjects rate the statements. Mere repetition seems to increase rated validity. This is scary."

On most everyday topics, such as movies and sports, people's attitudes range from casual to committed. If your best friend is neutral about baseball whereas you are an insanely devoted fan, your friendship will probably survive. But when the subject is one involving beliefs that give meaning and purpose to a person's life—most notably, politics and religion—it's another ball game, so to speak. Wars have been fought, and are being fought as you read this, over people's most passionate convictions. Perhaps the attitude that causes the most controversy and bitterness around the world is the one toward religious diversity: accepting or intolerant. Some people of all religions accept a world of differing religious views and practices; they believe that church and state should be separate. But for many fundamentalists in any religion, religion and politics are inseparable; they believe that one religion should prevail (Jost et al., 2003). You can see, then, why these irreconcilable attitudes cause continuing conflict, and sometimes are used to justify terrorism and war. Why are people so different in these views?

validity effect The tendency of people to believe that a statement is true or valid simply because it has been repeated many times.

BIOLOGY and *Beliefs*

Where do your attitudes on these issues come from? Many attitudes result from learning and experience, of course. But research from behavioural genetics has found that some core attitudes stem from personality traits that are heritable. That is, the variation among people in these attitudes is due in part to their genetic differences (Paunonen, 2003; see Chapters 3 and 14). Two such traits are "openness to experience" and "conscientiousness." We would expect people who are open to new experiences to hold positive attitudes toward novelty and change in general—say, in religion, art, music, and social and political events in the larger culture. We would expect people who prefer the familiar and conventional, and who are conscientious about order and obligations, to be drawn to conservative politics, religious denominations, and philosophies. And that is what research finds. In a study of Protestant Christians, fundamentalist Christians scored much lower than liberal Christians on the dimension of openness to experience (Streyffeler & McNally, 1998). Conversely, conservatives score higher than liberals on conscientiousness (Jost, 2006). These differences in conservatism are also associated with changes in the brain—notably in areas of the brain that are associated with threat processing, fear, and inhibition (Jost & Amodio, 2012).

However, religious *affiliation* is not heritable. Most people choose a religious group because of their parents, ethnicity, culture, and social class, and many people

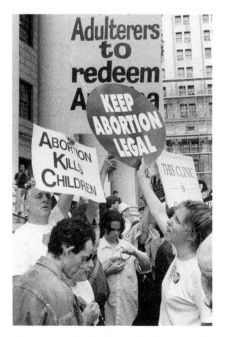

When people hold attitudes that are central to their religious and political philosophies, they often fail to realize that the other side feels just as strongly.

Malcolm Clarke/AP Images

switch their religious affiliation at least once in their lives. Increasingly, people report having no religious affiliation or belief. But, as studies of twins reared apart have found, *religiosity*—a person's depth of religious feeling and adherence to a religion's rules—does have a genetic component. When religiosity combines with conservatism and authoritarianism (an unquestioning trust in authority), the result is a deeply ingrained acceptance of tradition and dislike of those who question it (Olson et al., 2001; Saucier, 2000).

Likewise, political affiliation is not heritable; it is largely related to your upbringing and to the friends you make in early adulthood, the key years for deciding which party you want to join. Nor do the casual political opinions held by many swing voters or people who are politically disengaged have a genetic component. But political conservatism has high heritability: 0.65 in men and 0.45 in women (Bouchard, 2004). Various political positions on emotionally hot topics that are associated with conservative or liberal views are also partly heritable. A team of researchers analyzed two large samples of more than 8000 sets of twins and asked about their personality traits, religious beliefs, and political attitudes (Alford, Funk, & Hibbing, 2005). The researchers compared the opinions of fraternal twins (who share, on average, 50% of their genes) with those of identical twins (who share virtually all of their genes). They calculated how often the identical twins agreed on each issue, subtracted the rate at which fraternal twins agreed, and ended up with a rough measure of heritability. As you can see in Figure 8.3, the attitudes showing the highest heritability were those toward school prayer and property taxes; attitudes showing the lowest influence of genes included those toward nuclear power, divorce, modern art, and abortion.

As a result of such evidence, some psychological scientists maintain that ideological belief systems may have evolved in human societies to be organized along a left–right dimension, consisting of two core sets of attitudes: (1) whether a person advocates social change or supports the system as it is, and (2) whether a person thinks inequality is a result of human policies and can be overcome, or is inevitable and should be accepted as part of the natural order (Graham, Haidt, & Nosek, 2009). Liberals tend to prefer the

FIGURE 8.3 The Genetics of Belief
A study of thousands of identical and fraternal twins identified the approximate genetic contribution to the variation in attitudes about diverse topics. Heritability was greatest for school prayer and property tax, and lowest for divorce, modern art, and abortion. But notice that in almost all cases, a person's unique life experiences (the "nonshared environment") were far more influential than genes, especially on attitudes toward topics as unrelated as the draft, censorship, and segregation (Alford, Funk, & Hibbing, 2005).

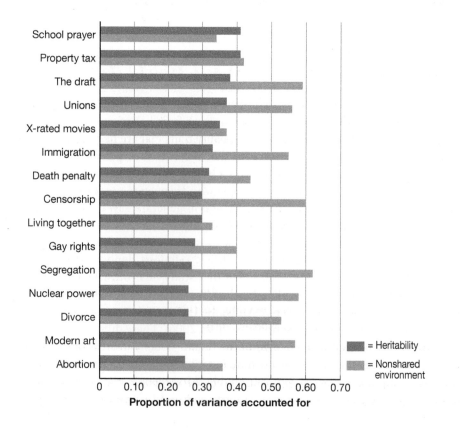

Proportion of variance accounted for

= Heritability

= Nonshared environment

values of progress, rebelliousness, chaos, flexibility, feminism, and equality, whereas conservatives tend to prefer tradition, conformity, order, stability, traditional values, and hierarchy. Those two dimensions underlie a host of specific attitudes. For instance, liberal undergraduates were more likely than conservative students to have favourable attitudes toward atheists, poetry, Asian food, jazz, street people, tattoos, foreign films, erotica, big cities, recreational drugs, and foreign travel—all examples of "openness to experience" rather than preference for the familiar (Jost, Nosek, & Gosling, 2008).

You can see why liberals and conservatives argue so emotionally over issues such as gun control, social protest, and gay marriage. They are not just arguing about the specific issue, but also about each side's underlying assumptions and values that emerge from their personality traits. Evolutionary psychologists point out that both sets of attitudes would have had adaptive benefits over the centuries: Conservatism would have promoted stability, tradition, and order, whereas liberalism would have promoted flexibility and change (Graham, Haidt, & Nosek, 2009).

These findings are provocative, but it is important not to oversimplify them—say by assuming that everyone's political opinions are hardwired and unaffected by events. In fact, the factor that accounts for even more of the variation in political attitudes than heritability is individual life experiences, or what behavioural geneticists call the *nonshared environment* (Alford, Funk, & Hibbing, 2005; see Chapter 14). What do you think might be the personality dispositions that underlie your own ideological commitments? What might be the experiences you have had, because of your family, gender, ethnicity, social class, or unique history, that have shaped your own political views?

Persuasion or "Brainwashing"?

Let's now see how the social-psychological factors discussed thus far might help explain the disturbing phenomenon of cult suicides. Between 1994 and 1997, more than 70 members of the Order of the Solar Temple either committed mass suicide or engaged in murder–suicide, including more than 30 men, women, and children in Quebec. Cult leaders Luc Jouret and Joseph di Mambro persuaded their followers that if they committed suicide, they would be reborn on the star Sirius and avoid the imminent destruction of Earth. Neither of these leaders ever said to new recruits, "If you follow me, you will eventually give up your marriages, homes, children, and your lives"; but by the end, that is just what all of them did. Were these people mentally ill? Had they been "brainwashed"?

"Brainwashing" implies that a person has had a sudden change of mind without being aware of what is happening; it sounds mysterious and strange. On the contrary, the methods of persuasion are neither mysterious nor unusual (Bloom, 2005; Moghaddam, 2005). Some may be more emotionally vulnerable than others to methods of coercive persuasion, but most people who become involved are not easily distinguishable from the general population. Studies of religious, political, and psychological sects and of terrorist cells have identified some of the key processes of coercive persuasion (Bloom, 2005; Moghaddam, 2005; Ofshe & Watters, 1994; Singer, 2003; Zimbardo & Leippe, 1991):

- *The person is subjected to entrapment.* At first, the new recruit to the cause agrees only to do small things, but gradually the demands increase to spend more time, spend more money, make more sacrifices. Ultimately, people take extreme measures because, over time, they have become entrapped in closed groups led by strong or charismatic leaders (Moghaddam, 2005).
- *The person's problems, personal and political, are explained by one simple attribution,* repeatedly emphasized: "It's all the fault of those bad people; we have to eliminate them."
- *The person is offered a new identity and is promised salvation.* There are as many simplistic explanations as there are groups that offer them. Afraid or unhappy?

Sports teams engage in ritualistic behaviour that utilize coercive persuasion. How many hockey players (or fans for that matter) do you think would be willing to shave off a playoff beard during a winning streak?

Action Plus Sports Images/Alamy

Being part of "the group" will fix this. Members may be taught to simplify their problems by blaming a single enemy.

- ***The person's access to disconfirming (dissonant) information is severely controlled.*** As soon as a person is a committed believer, the group or leader limits the person's choices, denigrates critical thinking, and suppresses private doubts. Recruits may be physically isolated from the outside world and thus from antidotes to the leader's ideas. They are separated from their families and indoctrinated and eventually become emotionally bonded to the group and the leader (Atran, 2010).

Not all instances of coercive persuasion are perceived as negative in our culture. Many of the rituals associated with organized sports use tactics of coercive persuasion. The lifestyle required of top athletes in our country often involves hazing and team cohabitation, frequently resulting in little time to socialize with non-team members. Many athletes will take coercive persuasion to the next level and will deliberately harm themselves by taking performance-enhancing drugs and competing while injured because they do not want to be perceived as weak. Further, team-serving biases (that are remarkably similar to group-serving biases) are consistently observed in a variety of sports, especially after teams win (Martin & Carron, 2012).

A key step in increasing resistance to coercive persuasion, therefore, is to dispel people's illusion of invulnerability to these tactics. Another is to teach people how to articulate and defend their own positions and think critically (Sherman & Kim, 2005). These skills prepare people to resist propaganda and make them less vulnerable to manipulation by others (Tormala & Petty, 2002).

Recite & Review

Recite: Speak aloud what you know about *cognitive dissonance*, the *familiarity* and *validity effects*, genetic contributions to certain attitudes, and persuasion techniques used to recruit people into terrorist groups and various sects.

Review: Next, reread this section.

Don't make us brainwash you into taking this *Quick Quiz:*

1. A political party spends $3 million to make sure that its name is seen and heard frequently and to repeat unverified charges that the opposing party is not fit to govern. What psychological processes are at play here?

2. Which of the following has a significant heritable component? (a) religious affiliation, (b) political affiliation, (c) attitudes that favour stability and order versus those favouring equality and change, (d) attitudes toward modern art, (e) political conservatism

3. A friend urges you to join a "life-renewal" group called "The Feeling Life." Your friend has been spending increasing amounts of time with her fellow Feelies, and has already contributed more than $2000 to their cause. You have some doubts about them. What questions would you want to have answered before joining up?

Answers:

1. The familiarity effect and the validity effect 2. c, e 3. A few things to consider: Is there an autocratic leader who suppresses dissent and criticism, while rationalizing this practice as a benefit for members? ("Doubt and disbelief are signs that your feeling side is being repressed.") Have long-standing members given up their friends, families, interests, and ambitions for this group? Does the leader offer simple but unrealistic promises to repair your life and all your troubles? Are members required to make sacrifices by donating large amounts of time and money?

Learning Objectives

7 Analyze the key features that lead to conformity in groups.

8 Predict the features of a group that promotes groupthink.

9 Explain how crowds can create "bystander apathy" and unpredictable violence—or acts of altruism.

10 List the conditions that increase the likelihood that some people will dissent from the majority opinion, take risks to help others, or blow the whistle on wrongdoers.

Individuals in Groups

The need to belong may be the most powerful of all human motivations (Baumeister et al., 2007). This makes good evolutionary sense because, like apes, bees, and elephants, human beings could never have survived without being included and accepted by their tribe. The need for social connection also explains why sending a prisoner to solitary confinement is internationally considered a form of torture: Its psychological consequences are even more devastating than physical abuse (Gawande, 2009). In fact, the *social* pain of being rejected, humiliated, or excluded activates parts of the brain that are highly diagnostic of *physical* pain (Chen et al., 2008; DeWall & Bushman, 2011; Williams, 2009). People who had recently been rejected by their partners were asked to look at photos of the person and think about the experience, while fMRIs recorded their brain activity. Two areas in the brain (the somatosensory cortex and posterior insula) that became active were the same as when people experience actual physical pain (Kross et al., 2011). Rejection hurts—literally.

Accordingly, the most powerful weapon that groups have to ensure their members' cooperation, and to weed out unproductive or disruptive members, is rejection or permanent banishment (Williams & Nida, 2011). Social rejection impedes the ability to empathize, think critically, and solve problems. It can lead to mental disorders, eating disorders, and attempted suicide. No wonder that when people are rejected by a group they care about, some try to mend the rift, change their behaviour, and get back in the group's good graces, whereas others respond with rage and violence (Baumeister et al., 2007). Conversely, social *acceptance*, a sense of belonging, can have many positive effects. Minority students who feel that they belong in school have better grades, health, and well-being (Walton & Cohen, 2011).

Of course, we belong to many different groups, which vary in their importance to us. But the point to underscore is that as soon as we join a bunch of other people, we act differently than we would on our own. This change occurs regardless of whether the group has convened to solve problems and make decisions, has gathered to have a party, consists of anonymous bystanders or members of an internet chat room, or is a crowd of spectators or celebrants.

Conformity

The first thing that people in groups do is conform, taking action or adopting attitudes as a result of real or imagined group pressure. Suppose that you are required to appear at a psychology laboratory for an experiment on perception. You join seven other students seated in a room. You are shown a 25 cm line and asked which of three other lines is identical to it. The correct answer, line A, is obvious, so you are amused when the first person in the group chooses line B. "Bad eyesight," you say to yourself. "He's off by 5 cm!" The second person also chooses line B. "What a dope," you think. But by the time the fifth person has chosen line B, you are beginning to doubt yourself. The

GET INVOLVED! Can You Disconnect?

To see for yourself how "social" you are, try this simple experiment: Turn off your cellphone or tablet. *Off!* You may use your laptop to take notes in class, but no fair using social media while you do. Now, how long can you go without checking Facebook, IMs, tweets, email, or the web? Keep track of your feelings on a (written!) notepad as time passes. Are you feeling anxious? Nervous? How long can you remain "cut off" before you start to feel isolated from your friends and family?

Test line   A   B   C

sixth and seventh students also choose line B, and now you are worried about *your* eyesight. The experimenter looks at you. "Your turn," he says. Do you follow the evidence of your own eyes or the collective judgment of the group?

This was the design for a series of famous studies of conformity conducted by Solomon Asch (1952, 1965). The seven "nearsighted" students were actually Asch's confederates. Asch wanted to know what people would do when a group unanimously contradicted an obvious fact. He found that when people made the line comparisons on their own, they were almost always accurate. But in the group, only 20% of the students remained completely independent on every trial, and often they apologized for not agreeing with the others. One-third conformed to the group's incorrect decision more than half the time, and the rest conformed at least some of the time. Whether they conformed or not, the students often felt uncertain of their decision. As one participant later said, "I felt disturbed, puzzled, separated, like an outcast from the rest." Asch's experiment has been replicated many times and in many countries over the years (Bond & Smith, 1996).

There are two basic motives for conformity, and, remarkably, both motives appear in many other species, from rats to primates, suggesting that conformity has a powerful adaptive function (Claidière & Whiten, 2012). One is the *need for social acceptance*, which is the reason that people can end up doing all kinds of stupid things (or smart things!) simply because their friends are doing them. By understanding the power of this motive, social psychologists have designed interventions to rally people's peer groups to help them stop smoking and binge drinking, stay in school and improve their performance, and make many other beneficial changes they would not do on their own (Wilson, 2011).

Sometimes people like to conform to feel part of the group . . . and sometimes they like to assert their individuality.

Left: Alex Webb/Magnum Photos. Right: Dave Thomson/AP Images.

The second reason for conformity is the *need for information* before deciding on the "right" thing to do (Cialdini, 2009). People often intuitively understand that sometimes the group knows more than they do, and this reliance on group judgment begins in very early childhood. When 3- and 4- year-old children were given a choice between relying on information provided by a three-adult majority or a single adult about the name of an unfamiliar object, they sided with the majority (Corriveau, Fusaro, & Harris, 2009). It works the same way with adults: The belief that "everyone else" is doing something must mean it is the wisest choice or course of action. Again, social psychologists have used this knowledge to induce people to make improvements. When hotels put notices in guest bathrooms saying that "the majority of guests in this room reuse their towels" (in contrast to simply requesting the guest to do the same because it's good for the environment), the number who participate in the reuse program rises markedly (Goldstein, Cialdini, & Griskevicius, 2008). In some parts of England, sensors that monitor a car's speed either reward law-abiding drivers with a smiley face or punish speeders with a frowning face. The end result: fewer fatalities and fewer accidents, and all with a simple cue for conformity.

Like obedience, therefore, conformity has positive aspects. Society runs more smoothly when people feel that they belong and share the same norms. But also like obedience, conformity can have negative consequences, notably its power to suppress critical thinking and creativity. In a group, many people will deny their private beliefs, agree with silly notions, and even repudiate their own values.

Groupthink

Close, friendly groups usually work well together. But they face the problem of getting the best ideas and efforts from their members while avoiding an extreme form of conformity called **groupthink**, the tendency to think alike and suppress dissent. According to Irving Janis (1982, 1989), groupthink occurs when a group's need for total agreement overwhelms its need to make the wisest decision. The symptoms of groupthink include the following:

- *An illusion of invulnerability.* The group believes it can do no wrong and is 100% correct in its decisions.
- *Self-censorship.* Dissenters decide to keep quiet rather than make trouble, offend their friends, or risk being ridiculed.
- *Pressure on dissenters to conform.* The leader teases or humiliates dissenters or otherwise pressures them to go along.
- *An illusion of unanimity.* By discouraging dissent and failing to consider alternative courses of action, leaders and group members create an illusion of consensus; they may even explicitly order suspected dissenters to keep quiet.

Throughout history, groupthink has led to disastrous decisions in military and civilian life. In 1986, NASA officials insulated themselves from the dissenting objections of engineers who warned them that the space shuttle *Challenger* was unsafe; NASA launched it anyway, and it exploded shortly after takeoff. Tragically, NASA did not learn immediately from this disaster. When an expert panel warned in 2002 that the space shuttles still had many safety problems, NASA removed five of the panel's nine members and two of its consultants. Early in 2003, the *Columbia* exploded upon re-entry, killing its entire crew. Although most of us have not had to make these kinds of decisions, we have all likely been in situations where we have gone along with a group, stifling our own private reservations.

Fortunately, groupthink can be minimized if the leader rewards the expression of doubt and dissent, protects and encourages minority views, asks group members

groupthink The tendency for all members of a group to think alike for the sake of harmony and to suppress disagreement.

to generate as many alternative solutions to a problem as they can think of, and has everyone try to think of the risks and disadvantages of the preferred decision. Resistance to groupthink can also be fostered by creating a group identity that encourages members to think of themselves as open-minded problem solvers rather than invulnerable know-it-alls (Turner, Pratkanis, & Samuels, 2003). Leaders who encourage group members to identify strongly with the collective enterprise are also more likely to hear dissenting opinions, because members will be less willing to support a decision they regard as harmful to the group's goal (Packer, 2009).

Not all leaders want to run their groups this way, of course. For many people in positions of power, from prime ministers to movie moguls, the temptation is great to surround themselves with others who agree with what they want to do, and to demote or fire those who disagree on the grounds that they are being "disloyal." Perhaps a key quality of great leaders is that they are able to rise above this temptation.

The Wisdom and Madness of Crowds

On the TV show *Who Wants to be a Millionaire?*, contestants are given the chance to ask the audience how it would answer a question. This gimmick comes straight from a phenomenon known as the "wisdom of crowds": the fact that a crowd's judgment is often more accurate than that of its individual members—a reason for conformity, as we noted earlier (Surowiecki, 2004; Vul & Pashler, 2008). Just as neurons interconnect in networks that create thoughts and actions beyond the scope of any individual neuron, a crowd creates a social network whose "behaviour" is more than individual members may intend or even be aware of (Goldstone, Roberts, & Gureckis, 2008). But crowds can create havoc, too. They can spread gossip, rumours, misinformation, and panic as fast as the flu. They can turn from joyful and peaceful to violent and destructive in a flash.

Diffusion of Responsibility.   Suppose you were in trouble on a city street or in another public place—say, being mugged or having a sudden appendicitis attack. Do you think you would be more likely to get help if (1) one other person were passing by, (2) several other people were in the area, or (3) dozens of people were in the area? Most people would choose the third answer, but that is not how human beings operate. On the contrary, the more people around you, the *less* likely that one of them will come to your aid. Why?

The answer has to do with a group process called the **diffusion of responsibility**, in which responsibility for an outcome is diffused, or spread, among many people, reducing each individual's personal sense of accountability. One result is *bystander apathy*: In crowds, when someone is in trouble, individuals often fail to take action or call for help because they assume that someone else will do so (Darley & Latané, 1968; Fischer et al., 2011). When the crowd consists of online observers, it's even easier to pass the buck. Abraham Biggs Jr., age 19, had been posting to an online discussion board for two years. One day he announced his intention to commit suicide with an overdose of drugs, adding a link to a live video feed from his bedroom. None of the watchers called the police for more than 10 hours, and Biggs died.

A meta-analysis of the many studies done since the first identification of bystander apathy revealed some cause for optimism, though: In truly dangerous, *unambiguous* emergencies—a child is drowning, or people are being shot at by a deranged gunman in a school, movie theatre, or street—people are more likely to rush to help, and in fact are often spurred to do so by the presence of others. One

diffusion of responsibility In groups, the tendency of members to avoid taking action because they assume that others will.

reason is that the person who intervenes counts on getting physical and psychological support from other observers. In addition, dangerous emergencies are most effectively handled by cooperation among observers (Fischer et al., 2011).

Deindividuation. The most extreme instances of the diffusion of responsibility occur in large, anonymous mobs or crowds. The crowds may consist of cheerful sports spectators or angry rioters. Either way, people often lose awareness of their individuality and seem to hand themselves over to the mood and actions of the crowd, a state called **deindividuation** (Festinger, Pepitone, & Newcomb, 1952). You are more likely to feel deindividuated in a large city, where no one recognizes you, than in a small town, where it is hard to hide. (You are also more likely to feel deindividuated in large classes, where you might—mistakenly!—think you are invisible to the teacher, than in small ones.) Sometimes organizations actively promote the deindividuation of their members to enhance conformity and allegiance to the group. This is an important function of uniforms or masks, which eliminate each member's distinctive identity.

People in crowds, feeling anonymous, may do destructive things they would never do on their own. These soccer hooligans are kicking a fan of the opposing team during a night of violence.

Topham/The Image Works

Deindividuation has long been considered a prime reason for mob violence. According to this explanation, because deindividuated people in crowds "forget themselves" and do not feel accountable for their actions, they are more likely to violate social norms and laws than they would be on their own—breaking store windows, looting, getting into fights, or rioting at a sports event. But deindividuation does not always make people more combative. Sometimes it makes them more friendly; think of all the chatty, anonymous people on buses and planes who reveal things to their seatmates they would never tell anyone they knew.

What really seems to be happening when people are in large crowds or anonymous situations is not that they inevitably become mindless or aggressive. Rather, they become *disinhibited*, just as if they were intoxicated on alcohol. That disinhibition, in turn, makes them more likely to conform to the norms of the *specific situation*, which may be either antisocial or prosocial (Hirsh, Galinsky, & Zhong, 2011; Postmes & Spears, 1998). University students who go wild during reading week may be violating the local norms because they are conforming to the "Let's party!" norms of their fellow students. Crowd norms can also foster helpfulness, as they often do in the aftermath of disasters, such as the recent flood in Calgary, when strangers came out to help victims and rescuers, leaving food, clothes, and tributes. Sometimes both norms operate at the same time: In the aftermath of a hockey loss to Boston in the Stanley Cup in Vancouver in 2011, many Canucks fans rioted, burning cars, smashing windows, and looting; but other fans did what they could, sometimes at risk to themselves, to protect cars and other property and maintain the law.

And so, should the deindividuation excuse, like the "I was only following orders" excuse, exonerate a person of responsibility for looting, rape, or even murder? What do you think?

Altruism and Dissent

We have seen how roles, norms, and pressures to obey authority and conform to one's group can cause people to behave in ways they might not otherwise. Yet, throughout history, men and women have disobeyed orders they believed to be wrong and have gone against prevailing cultural beliefs; their actions have sometimes changed the course of history. For instance, until 1929, the government of Canada defined a

deindividuation In groups or crowds, the loss of awareness of one's own individuality.

When we think of heroes, we tend to think of men like the courageous firefighters who work so hard to rescue others after a disaster strikes. But heroism comes in many forms. When Medicins san Frontiers works with Ebola patients, they can pay a steep price—death. Recently, Edward Snowden has leaked thousands of classified documents revealing some of the scope that the Canadian government, among others, conducts surveillance on its own citizens. However, given the leaks, debate rages on as to whether Edward Snowden is a crusader for privacy or someone who has made the world less safe.

Left: Ton Koene/Horizons WWP/Alamy. Right: Glenn Greenwald/Laura Poitras/EPA/Newscom.

person entitled to vote in this country as "A male person, including an Indian, excluding a Mongolian or Chinese. . . . No woman, idiot, lunatic or criminal shall vote." Pioneers such as Nellie McClung, Mary Irene Parlby, Emily Murphy, Henrietta Louise Edwards, and Louise McKinney fought for the right of Canadian women to become persons, a legal status that would grant them the right to vote, hold political office, and take a more active role in society. Similarly, indigenous peoples' leaders, such as Shawn Atleo, are working to ensure self-determination, which would result in autonomous communities within Canada, rather than dependence on Aboriginal Affairs and Northern Development Canada. In trying to ensure sovereignty and treaty rights for indigenous peoples, Idle No More protesters have occupied lands and protested throughout the country.

Sadly, the costs of dissent, courage, and honesty are often high; remember that most groups do not welcome deviance, nonconformity, and disagreement. Most whistle-blowers, far from being rewarded for their bravery, are punished for it. Studies of whistle-blowers find that half to two-thirds lose their jobs and have to leave their professions entirely. Many lose their homes and families (Alford, 2001).

Nonconformity, protest, and *altruism*, the willingness to take selfless or dangerous action on behalf of others, are in part a matter of personal convictions and conscience. However, just as there are situational reasons for obedience and conformity, there are external influences on a person's decision to state an unpopular opinion, choose conscience over conformity, or help a stranger in trouble. Here are some of the situational factors involved in deciding to behave courageously: 👁

Watch the Video
The Basics: Under the Influence of Others
in **MyPsychLab**

1   **You perceive the need for intervention or help.** It may seem obvious, but before you can take independent action, you must realize that such action is necessary. Sometimes people willfully blind themselves to wrongdoing to justify their own inaction ("I'm just minding my business"; "I had no idea what was happening at that residential school"). But blindness to the need for action also occurs when a situation imposes too many demands on people's attention, as it often does for residents of densely populated cities.

2   **Cultural norms encourage you to take action.** Would you tell a passerby that he or she had dropped a pen? Offer to help a person with an injured leg who had dropped an armful of magazines? An international field study investigated strangers' helpfulness to one another with those three nonemergency acts of kindness, in 23 North American cities and 22 cities in other countries. Cultural norms were more

important than population density in predicting levels of helpfulness: Pedestrians in busy Copenhagen and Vienna were kinder to strangers than were passersby in busy New York City or Kuala Lumpur, Malaysia (Levine, 2003; Levine, Norenzayan, & Philbrick, 2001).

3 You have an ally. In Asch's conformity experiment, the presence of one other person who gave the correct answer was enough to overcome agreement with the majority. In Milgram's experiment, the presence of someone who disobeyed the experimenter's instruction to shock the learner sharply increased the number of people who also disobeyed. One dissenting member of a group may be viewed as a troublemaker, but two or three are a coalition. An ally reassures a person of the rightness of the protest, and their combined efforts may eventually persuade the majority (Wood et al., 1994).

4 You become entrapped. Once having taken the initial step of getting involved, most people will increase their commitment. In one study, nearly 9000 U.S. federal employees were asked whether they had observed wrongdoing at work, whether they had told anyone about it, and what happened if they had told. Nearly half of the sample had observed some serious cases of wrongdoing, such as stealing federal funds, accepting bribes, or creating a situation that was dangerous to public safety. Of that half, 72% had done nothing at all, but the other 28% reported the problem to their immediate supervisors. Once they had taken that step, a majority of the whistle-blowers eventually took the matter to higher authorities (Graham, 1986).

As you can see, certain social and cultural factors make altruism, disobedience, and dissent more likely to occur, just as other external factors suppress them.

Recite & Review

Recite: Say aloud what you know about the motives for conformity, *groupthink*, the *diffusion of responsibility*, bystander apathy, *deindividuation*, and the conditions that foster altruism and dissent.

Review: Take responsibility for your learning by rereading this section.

Now take this *Quick Quiz:*

A. Which phenomenon is illustrated in each of the following situations?
1. The prime minister's closest advisers are afraid to disagree with his views on energy policy.
2. You are at a costume party wearing a silly gorilla suit. When you see a chance to play a practical joke on the host, you take it.
3. Walking down a busy street, you see that fire has broken out in a store window. "Someone must already have called the fire department," you say.

B. Imagine you are chief executive officer of a new electric-car company. You want your employees to feel free to offer their suggestions and criticisms to improve productivity and satisfaction. You also want them to inform managers if they find any evidence that the cars are unsafe, even if that means delaying production. What concepts from this chapter could you use in setting company policy?

Answers:

A. 1. groupthink **2.** deindividuation **3.** bystander apathy brought on by diffusion of responsibility **B.** Some possibilities: You could encourage, or even require, dissenting views; avoid deindividuation by rewarding innovative suggestions and implementing the best ones; stimulate employees' commitment to the task (building a car that will help solve the world's pollution problem); and establish a written policy to protect whistle-blowers. What else can you think of?

social identity The part of a person's self-concept that is based on his or her identification with a nation, religious or political group, occupation, or other social affiliation.

ethnic identity A person's identification with a racial or ethnic group.

acculturation The process by which members of minority groups come to identify with and feel part of the mainstream culture.

Learning Objectives

11 Discuss acculturation and its relation to ethic identity.

12 Describe the Eagles and the Rattlers experiment. List the features that lead to conflict. Contrast these with the features that lead to cooperation.

13 Compare how stereotypes benefit us with how they distort reality.

Us versus Them: Group Identity

Each of us develops a personal identity that is based on our particular traits and unique life history. But we also develop **social identities** based on the groups we belong to, including our national, religious, political, and occupational groups (Brewer & Gardner, 1996; Tajfel & Turner, 1986).

Ethnic Identity

In multicultural societies such as Canada, different social identities sometimes collide. In particular, people often face the dilemma of balancing an **ethnic identity**, a close identification with a religious or ethnic group, and **acculturation**, identification with the dominant culture (Phinney, 1996). The hallmarks of having an ethnic identity are that you identify with the group, feel proud to be a member, feel emotionally attached to the group, and behave in ways that conform to the group's rules, values, and norms. Many individuals pick and choose among the values, food, traditions, and customs of the mainstream culture, while also keeping aspects of their heritage that are important to their self-identity.

In these multiethnic times, many people do not want to be pigeonholed into one ethnic category. In 2011, more than 42% of Canadians reported on the National Household Survey having multiple ethnic origins (Statistics Canada, 2013). Compare this to the almost 19% of Canadians who answered this way on the 1996 census (the first time that this category was available), and we can see that our views of ethnicity are changing. Thus, for many Canadians, ethnicity does not reflect where they were born—especially when we consider that most of the people who reported multiple ethnicities were born in Canada. It is also interesting to note that more than 10 000 000 respondents listed their ethnicity as Canadian, an ethnicity that many Canadians find challenging to define (Statistics Canada, 2008)! Some observers think that young people are becoming less likely to define themselves by their ethnic identity than by their youth identity—a hipster, a Whedonite, a 'Little Monster,' and so forth. Do you agree? In your world, are traditional ethnic identities breaking down, or are they as strong as ever? 👁

Of course, most remain identified with their ethnicity of origin, while picking and choosing among the values, foods, and customs of the mainstream culture. However, acculturation is not always easy, in any nation. Many immigrants arrive in their host country with every intention of becoming part of the mainstream culture. If they encounter discrimination or other setbacks, however, they may realize that acculturation is harder than they anticipated and that their original ethnic identity offers greater

👁—⌐**Watch** the **Video**
Bilingual Family in **MyPsychLab**

GET INVOLVED! How Acculturated Are You?

Do you have an ethnic identity? If you are a member of an ethnic minority within your country, city, or school, how acculturated do you feel? Do you feel at ease in more than one culture, or only in your own? Does your comfort level depend on the situation you're in? Now ask five friends, relatives, or acquaintances, ideally from different ethnic groups, how they would answer these questions. If you feel that you do not have an ethnic heritage other than a national identity, why is that? Would your parents and grandparents feel the same as you do?

scarce jobs, white attitudes changed again. Whites now thought the Chinese were "criminal," "crafty," "conniving," and "stupid." (The newspapers did not report the attitudes of the Chinese.)

The oldest prejudice in the world may be sexism, and it, too, serves to legitimize existing sex roles and inequities in power. According to research with 15 000 men and women in 19 nations, *hostile sexism*, which reflects active dislike of women, is different from *benevolent sexism*, which puts women on a pedestal. The latter type of sexism is affectionate but patronizing, conveying the attitude that women are so wonderful, good, kind, and moral that they should stay at home, away from the rough-and-tumble (and power and income) of public life (Glick et al., 2000; Glick, 2006). Because benevolent sexism lacks a tone of hostility to women, it doesn't seem like a prejudice to many people, and many women find it alluring to think they are better than men (Christopher & Wojda, 2008). But both forms of sexism—whether someone thinks women are too good for equality or not good enough—legitimize discrimination against women (Brandt, 2011).

THINKING CRITICALLY

Avoid emotional reasoning.

In times of war, most people fall victim to emotional reasoning about the enemy. They start thinking of "them" as aggressors who are less than human, often as brutes, rats, or pigs. All nations do this. In 2003, students at a Muslim school in Montreal arrived to find that their school had been vandalized, with the words "Death to Arabs" spray-painted on the outside.

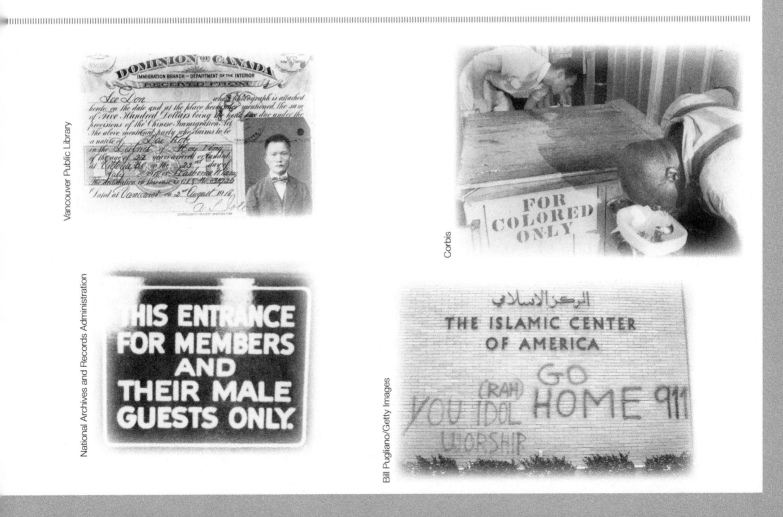

GET INVOLVED! Probing Your Prejudices

Are you prejudiced? No? Is there any group of people you tend to dislike because of their gender, ethnicity, sexual orientation, nationality, religion, physical appearance, or political views? Write down your deepest thoughts and feelings about this group. Take as long as you want, and do not censor yourself or say what you think you ought to say. Now reread what you have written. Which of the sources of prejudice discussed in the text might be contributing to your views? Do you feel that your attitudes toward the group are legitimate, or are you uncomfortable about having them?

Perhaps you are thinking: "What about men? There are plenty of prejudices against men, too—that they are sexual predators, emotionally heartless, domineering, and arrogant." In fact, according to a 16-nation study of attitudes toward men, many people do believe that men are aggressive and predatory, and overall just not as warm and wonderful as women (Glick et al., 2004). This attitude seems hostile to men, the researchers found, but it also reflects and supports gender inequality by characterizing men as being designed for leadership and dominance.

4 **Cultural and national causes.** Finally, prejudice bonds people to their own ethnic or national group and its ways; by disliking "them," we feel closer to our own group. That feeling, in turn, justifies whatever we do to "them" to preserve our customs and national policies. In fact, although many people assume that prejudice causes war, the reverse is far more often the case: War causes prejudice. When two nations declare war, when one country decides to invade another, or when a weak leader displaces the country's economic problems onto a minority scapegoat, the citizenry's prejudice against that enemy or scapegoat will be inflamed. Of course, sometimes anger at an enemy is justified, but war usually turns legitimate anger into blind prejudice: Those people are not only the enemy; they are less than human and deserve to be exterminated (Keen, 1986; Staub, 1999). That is why enemies are so often described as vermin, rats, mad dogs, heathens, baby killers, or monsters—anything but human beings like us.

Review 8.1 summarizes the causes of prejudice.

Defining and Measuring Prejudice

The good news is that on surveys in Canada, prejudice of all kinds has been dropping sharply. The numbers of people who admit to believing that blacks are inferior to

REVIEW 8.1 Sources of Prejudice

Psychological	Social	Economic	Cultural/National
Low self-esteem	Groupthink	Majority's desire to preserve its status	Ethnocentrism
Anxiety	Conformity	Competition for jobs, power, resources	Desire for group identity
Insecurity	Parental messages		The justification of war
Powerlessness			

Examples of resulting prejudice:

"Those people are not as moral and decent as we are."	"My parents taught me that those people are just no good."	"Those people are not smart enough to do this work."	"We have to protect our religion/country/government from those monsters."

whites, women inferior to men, and gays inferior to straights have plummeted in the last 20 years (Dovidio, 2001; Plant & Devine, 1998; Weaver, 2008).

Yet, as Gordon Allport (1954/1979) observed so long ago "Defeated intellectually, prejudice lingers emotionally." Attitudes may change and discriminatory behaviour may be outlawed, but deep-seated negative feelings and bigotry may persist in subtle ways (Dovidio & Gaertner, 2008). As we just saw, prejudices may lie dormant during good times, only to be easily aroused during bad times.

That is why prejudice is like a weasel—hard to grasp and hold on to. Moreover, not all prejudiced people are prejudiced in the same way or to the same extent. Suppose that Raymond wishes to be tolerant and open-minded, but he grew up in a small homogeneous community and feels uncomfortable with members of other cultural and religious groups. Should we put Raymond in the same category as Rupert, an outspoken bigot who detests all ethnic groups other than his own? Do good intentions count? What if Raymond knows nothing about Muslims and mindlessly blurts out a remark that reveals his ignorance? Is that prejudice or thoughtlessness? And what about people who say they are not prejudiced but then make remarks that suggest otherwise? When Mel Gibson was arrested for drunk driving, he spewed forth sexist and anti-Semitic insults to the arresting officer ("Jews are responsible for all the wars in the world!"), yet later denied being prejudiced. Should the public have accepted his claim that he isn't "really" anti-Semitic?

Some social psychologists, while welcoming the evidence that *explicit*, conscious prejudices have declined, have used various measures to see whether *implicit*, unconscious negative feelings between groups have also diminished. They maintain that implicit attitudes, being automatic and unintentional, reflect lingering negative feelings that keep prejudice alive below the surface. They have developed several ways of measuring these feelings (Olson, 2009):

1 **Measures of social distance.** *Social distance* is a possible behavioural expression of prejudice, a reluctance to get "too close" to another group. Does a straight man stand farther away from a gay man than from another heterosexual? Does a nondisabled woman move away from a woman in a wheelchair? How close will you let "those people" into your social life—work with them, live near them, marry them? A review of decades of representative surveys of North Americans found that while overt prejudice among all of these groups has dropped, most people within each ethnic group are still strongly opposed to virtually all the other ethnic groups living in their neighbourhoods or marrying into their families (Weaver, 2008). But does this fact reflect prejudice or merely a comfort with and preference for one's own ethnicity?

THINKING CRITICALLY

Define your terms.

What does it mean to be "prejudiced"? Is prejudice blatant hostility, or does it also include vague discomfort with another group, a patronizing attitude of superiority, or unconscious feelings of dislike? Does ignorance about an unfamiliar culture count as prejudice?

THINKING CRITICALLY

Don't oversimplify.

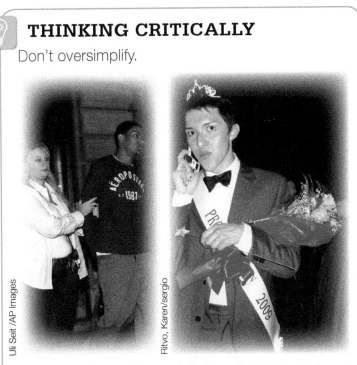

Uli Seit /AP Images

Ritvo, Karen/sergio

In New York, police arrested a man (left), along with six others, on charges of committing a horrific gang attack on three gay men. In Los Angeles, a high school chose an openly gay Hispanic senior, Sergio Garcia, to be its first male prom queen (right). "There were girls who wanted [the title] as much as I did," he said, "but they were so supportive when I won." These stories from the news, revealing the ugly face of prejudice in one place and its virtual eradication in another, show that the question "Is prejudice declining?" oversimplifies. Among which age groups? Which ethnicities? Under what circumstances?

2 **Measures of what people do when they are stressed or angry.** Many people are willing to control their negative feelings under normal conditions, but as soon as they are angry, drunk, or frustrated, their unexpressed prejudice often reveals itself (Aronson, 2012). In one of the first experiments to demonstrate this phenomenon, white students were asked to administer a shock to black or white confederates of the experimenter in what the students believed was a study of biofeedback. In the experimental condition, participants overheard the biofeedback "victim" (who actually received no shock) saying derogatory things about them. In the control condition, participants overheard no such nasty remarks. Then all the participants had another opportunity to shock the victims; their degree of aggression was defined as the amount of shock they administered. At first, white students actually showed *less* aggression toward blacks than toward whites. But as soon as the white students were angered by overhearing derogatory remarks about themselves, they showed *more* aggression toward blacks than toward whites (Rogers & Prentice-Dunn, 1981). The same pattern appeared in studies of how English-speaking Canadians behave toward French-speaking Canadians (Meindl & Lerner, 1985), straights toward gays, non-Jewish students toward Jews (Fein & Spencer, 1997), and men toward women (Maass et al., 2003).

3 **Measures of brain activity.** Social neuroscientists have been using fMRI to determine which parts of the brain are involved in forming stereotypes, holding prejudiced beliefs, and feeling disgust, anger, or anxiety about an ethnic or stigmatized group, such as addicts or the homeless (Cacioppo et al., 2003; Harris & Fiske, 2006; Stanley, Phelps, & Banaji, 2008). In one study, when blacks and whites saw pictures of each other, activity in the amygdala (the brain structure associated with fear, anxiety, and other negative emotions) was elevated. But it was not elevated when people saw pictures of members of their own group (Hart et al., 2000). However, the fact that parts of the brain are activated under some conditions does not mean a person is "prejudiced." In a similar experiment, when participants were registering the faces as individuals or as part of a simple visual test rather than as members of the category "blacks," there was no increased activation in the amygdala. The brain may be designed to register differences, it appears, but any negative associations with those differences depend on context and learning (Wheeler & Fiske, 2005).

4 **Measures of implicit attitudes.** A final, controversial method of assessing prejudice is the *Implicit Association Test (IAT)*, which measures the speed of people's positive and negative associations to a target group (Greenwald, McGhee, & Schwartz, 1998; Greenwald et al., 2009). Its proponents have argued that if white students take longer to respond to black faces associated with positive words (e.g., *triumph, honest*) than to black faces associated with negative words (e.g., *devil, failure*), it must mean that white students have an unconscious prejudice toward blacks. Millions of people have taken the test online, and it has also been given to students, business managers, and many other groups to identify their alleged prejudices toward blacks, Asians, women, old people, and other categories (Nosek, Greenwald, & Banaji, 2007).

We say "alleged" prejudices because other social psychologists believe that whatever the test measures, it is not a stable prejudice (De Houwer et al., 2009). Two experimenters got an IAT effect by matching target faces with nonsense words and neutral words that had no evaluative connotations at all. They concluded that the IAT does not measure emotional evaluations of the target but rather the *salience* of the word associated with it—how much it stands out. (Negative words attract more attention in general.) When they corrected for these factors, the presumed unconscious prejudice faded away (Rothermund & Wentura, 2004). Moreover, as we saw earlier, people find

Typical stimuli used in the IAT.

William A. Cunningham

BLACK FACES **WHITE FACES**

GOOD WORDS
love joy triumph
terrific peace
champion honest

BAD WORDS
maggot poison
hatred agony devil
failure detest filth

familiar names, products, and even nonsense syllables to be more pleasant than unfamiliar ones. Some investigators argue that the IAT may simply be measuring, say, white subjects' unfamiliarity with other ethnicities and the greater salience of their own ethnicities to them, rather than a true prejudice (Kinoshita & Peek-O'Leary, 2005).

As you can see, defining and measuring prejudice are not easy tasks, and it's important not to oversimplify. To understand prejudice, we must distinguish explicit attitudes from unconscious ones, active hostility from simple discomfort, what people say from what they feel, and what people feel from how they actually behave.

Reducing Conflict and Prejudice

The findings that emerge from the study of prejudice show us that efforts to reduce prejudice by appealing to moral or intellectual arguments are not enough. They must also touch people's deeper insecurities, fears, or negative associations with a group. Of course, given the many sources and functions of prejudice, no one method will work in all circumstances or for all prejudices. But just as social psychologists investigate the situations that increase prejudice and animosity between groups, they have also examined the situations that might reduce them. Here are four of them (Allport, 1954/1979; Dovidio & Gaertner, 2010; Pettigrew & Tropp, 2006):

1 **Both sides must have equal legal status, economic opportunities, and power.** This requirement is the spur behind efforts to change laws that permit discrimination. Women would never have gotten the right to vote, attend university, or do "men's work" (law, medicine, bartending . . .) without persistent challenges to the laws that permitted gender discrimination. But changing the law is not enough if two groups remain in competition for jobs or if one group retains power and dominance over the other.

You have probably heard that women who work full time generally earn less in wages than their male counterparts (Desmarais & Curtis, 2001). Research conducted by Serge Desmarais, a social psychologist at the University of Guelph, suggests that men and women often differ not only in the actual pay they receive, but also in their beliefs about the amount of pay they should receive for their work. Desmarais found that when students are allowed to pay themselves for tasks they complete as part of psychology experiments, women participants actually pay themselves less than the men do (Desmarais & Curtis, 1997).

2 **Authorities and community institutions must provide moral, legal, and economic support for both sides.** Society must establish norms of equality and support them in the actions of its officials—teachers, employers, the judicial system, government officials, and the police. Where segregation is official government policy or an unofficial but established practice, conflict and prejudice will continue and seem normal and justified.

3 **Both sides must have many opportunities to work and socialize together, formally and informally.** According to the *contact hypothesis*, prejudice declines when people have the chance to get used to another group's rules, food, customs, and attitudes, thereby discovering their shared interests and shared humanity and learning that "those people" aren't, in fact, "all alike." The contact hypothesis has been supported by many studies in the laboratory and in the real world: young people's attitudes toward the elderly; healthy people's attitudes toward the mentally ill; nondisabled children's attitudes toward the disabled; and straight people's prejudices toward gay men and lesbians (Herek & Capitanio, 1996; Pettigrew & Tropp, 2006; Wilner, Walkley, & Cook, 1955). Remarkably, contact actually works best for the most intolerant and mentally rigid people, perhaps by reducing feelings of threat and anxiety and increasing feelings of empathy and trust (Hodson, 2011).

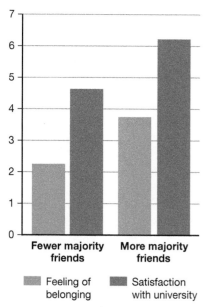

FIGURE 8.5 The Impact of Cross-Ethnic Friendships on Minority Students' Well-Being
Cross-ethnic friendships benefit both parties. In a longitudinal study of minority students at a predominantly white university, many minority students at first felt left out of school life and thus dissatisfied with their educational experience. But the more white friends they made, the higher their sense of belonging (gold bar) and satisfaction with the university (blue bar). This finding was particularly significant for minority students who initially had been the most sensitive to rejection and who had felt the most anxious and insecure about being in a largely white school (Mendoza-Denton & Page-Gould, 2008).

Multiethnic university campuses are a living laboratory for testing the contact hypothesis. White students who have roommates, friends, and romantic relationships across ethnic lines tend to become less prejudiced and find commonalities (Van Laar, Levin, and Sidanius, 2008). Cross-group friendships benefit minorities and reduce their prejudices, too. Minority students who join ethnic student organizations tend to develop, over time, not only an even stronger ethnic identity, but also an increased sense of ethnic victimization. Over time, minority students often come to feel they have less in common with other ethnic groups (Sidanius et al., 2004). But a longitudinal study of minority students at a predominantly white university found that friendships with whites increased their feelings of belonging and reduced their feelings of dissatisfaction with the school. This was especially true for students who had been feeling insecure and sensitive about being rejected as members of a minority (Mendoza-Denton & Page-Gould, 2008). (See Figure 8.5.)

4 **Both sides must cooperate, working together for a common goal.**
Although contact reduces prejudice, it is also true that prejudice reduces contact. And when groups don't like each other, forced contact just makes each side resentful and even more prejudiced, as a longitudinal field survey of students in Germany, Belgium, and England found (Binder et al., 2009). At many multiethnic high schools, ethnic groups form cliques and gangs, fighting one another and defending their own ways.

To reduce the intergroup tension and competition that exist in many schools, Elliot Aronson and his colleagues developed the "jigsaw" method of building cooperation. Students from different ethnic groups work together on a task that is broken up like a jigsaw puzzle; each person needs to cooperate with the others to put the assignment together. Students in such classes, from elementary school through university, tend to do better, like their classmates better, and become less stereotyped and prejudiced in their thinking than students in traditional classrooms (E. Aronson, 2000; J. Aronson, 2010; Slavin & Cooper, 1999). Cooperation and interdependence often reduce us–them thinking and prejudice by creating an encompassing social identity—the Eagles and Rattlers solution.

Each of these four approaches to creating greater harmony between groups is important, but none is sufficient on its own. Perhaps one reason that group conflicts and prejudice are so persistent is that all four conditions for reducing them are rarely met at the same time.

Tensions between groups often subside when people work together on a common goal. When classrooms are structured so that students of different ethnic groups must cooperate to do well on a lesson (left), prejudice decreases. On the right, volunteers from Habitat for Humanity build a new home for low-income people.

Left: Tom Watson/Merrill Education. Right: A. Ramey/PhotoEdit Inc.

Recite & Review

Recite: Try to overcome your prejudice against quizzes by reciting what you know about four major causes of *prejudice*, hostile *and* benevolent sexism, explicit *versus* implicit prejudices, four ways of measuring implicit prejudice, and four conditions necessary for reducing prejudice and conflict.

Review: You have just read a long but important section; you really should reread it.

Now take this *Quick Quiz:*

Surveys find that large percentages of individuals from visible minority groups often hold prejudices about other minorities. What are some reasons that people who have themselves been victims of stereotyping and prejudice would hold the same attitudes toward others?

Answers:

Their own ethnocentrism; low self-esteem, anxiety, or feelings of threat; conformity with relatives and friends who share their prejudices; parental lessons; and economic competition for jobs and resources.

Learning Objectives

17 Describe two examples of how cultural differences can influence explanations of behaviour.

The Question of Human Nature

Throughout this chapter, we have seen that human nature contains the potential for unspeakable acts of cruelty and inspiring acts of goodness. Most people believe that some cultures and individuals are inherently evil and therefore not fully human; if we could just get rid of them, everything would be fine. But from the standpoint of social and cultural psychology, all human beings, like all cultures, contain the potential for both good and evil.

That is why virtually no nation has bloodless hands. The Nazis systematically exterminated millions of Jews, Gypsies, homosexuals, disabled people, and anyone not of the "pure" Aryan "race." But they were not unique. Canadians slaughtered indigenous peoples, Turks slaughtered Armenians, the Khmer Rouge slaughtered millions of fellow Cambodians, the Spanish conquistadors slaughtered indigenous peoples in Mexico and South America, Idi Amin waged a reign of terror against his own people in Uganda, the Japanese slaughtered Koreans and Chinese, despotic political regimes in Argentina and Chile killed thousands of dissidents and rebels, Bosnian Serbs massacred Bosnian Muslims in the name of "ethnic cleansing" . . . to say nothing of ongoing conflicts throughout the world.

It's easy to conclude that outbreaks of violence like these are a result of inner aggressive drives, the sheer villainy of the perpetrators, or age-old tribal hatreds. But in the social-psychological view, they result from the all-too-normal processes we have discussed in this chapter, including mindless obedience to authority, conformity, groupthink, deindividuation, stereotyping, ethnocentrism, and prejudice. These processes are especially likely to be activated when a government feels weakened and vulnerable. By generating an outside enemy, rulers create us–them thinking to impose order and cohesion among their citizens and to create a scapegoat for the country's economic problems (Smith, 1998). The good news is that when circumstances within a nation change, societies can also change from being warlike to being peaceful. Sweden

THINKING CRITICALLY

Don't oversimplify.

Many people like to divide individuals and nations into those that are good and those that are evil. What is the problem with thinking this way?

These paintings done during wartime poignantly illustrate one child's effort to portray the horror of war and another's dream of peace. Can we learn to design a world in which conflicts and group differences, though inevitable, need not lead to violence?

UNICEF

was once one of the most warlike nations on earth, but today it is among the most pacifistic and egalitarian. Less than two decades after Rwanda's Hutu committed genocide against the Tutsi, the country today is one of the safest and most well-functioning African nations (Gourevitch, 2009).

The philosopher Hannah Arendt (1963), who covered the trial of Adolf Eichmann, used the phrase "the banality of evil" to describe how it was possible for Eichmann and other ordinary people in Nazi Germany to commit the monstrous acts they did. (*Banal* means "commonplace" or "unoriginal.") The compelling evidence for the banality of evil is difficult for many people to accept. Clearly, some people do stand out as being unusually heroic or unusually sadistic. But as we have seen, good people can do terribly disturbing things when their roles encourage or require them to do so, when the situation takes over and they do not stop to think critically.

The research discussed in this chapter suggests that ethnocentrism and prejudice are part of our human heritage, awaiting the conditions that will awaken them. But it can also help us formulate ways of living in a diverse world. By identifying the conditions that create the banality of evil, perhaps we can create other conditions that foster the "banality of virtue"—everyday acts of kindness, selflessness, and generosity.

Taking Psychology with You

THINKING CRITICALLY IN EVERYDAY LIFE

Dealing with Cultural Differences

A French salesman worked for a company that was bought by Canadians. When the new Canadian manager ordered him to step up his sales within the next three months, the employee quit in a huff, taking his customers with him. Why? In France, it takes years to develop customers; in family-owned businesses, relationships with customers may span generations. The Canadian manager wanted instant results, as we often do, but the French salesman knew this was impossible and quit. The Canadian view was "He wasn't up to the job; he's lazy and disloyal, so he stole my customers." The French view was "There is no point in explaining anything to a person who is so stupid as to think you can acquire loyal customers in three months" (Hall & Hall, 1987).

Both men were committing the fundamental attribution error: assuming that the other person's behaviour was due to personality rather than the situation, in this case a situation governed by cultural rules. Many corporations now realize that such rules are not trivial and that success in a global economy depends on understanding them. But you don't have to go to another country to encounter cultural differences; they are likely to exist in your own hometown.

If you find yourself getting angry over something a person from another culture is doing or not doing, use the skills of critical thinking to find out whether your expectations and perceptions of that person's behaviour are appropriate. Take the time to examine your assumptions and biases, consider other explanations of the person's actions, and avoid emotional reasoning. For example, people who shake hands as a gesture of friendship and courtesy are likely to feel insulted if a person from a non–hand shaking culture refuses to do the same, unless they have asked themselves the question, "Does everyone have the custom of shaking hands that my culture does?"

> People who shake hands out of courtesy feel insulted if a person from another culture refuses to reciprocate—unless they ask themselves, "Does everyone have the custom of shaking hands that my culture does? 99

Similarly, people from Middle Eastern and Latin American cultures are used to bargaining for what they buy; Canadians and northern Europeans are used to having a fixed price. People who do not know how to bargain, therefore, are likely to find bargaining an exercise in frustration because they will not know whether they got taken or got a great deal. In contrast, people from bargaining cultures will feel just as exasperated if a seller offers a flat price. "Where's the fun in this?" they'll say. "The whole human transaction of shopping is gone!"

Learning another culture's rule or custom is hard enough, but it is much more difficult to comprehend cultural differences that are deeply embedded in its language. In Iran, the social principle of *taarof* describes the practice of deliberate insincerity, such as giving false praise and making promises you have no intention of keeping. Iranians know that they are supposed to tell you what you want to hear to avoid conflict or to offer hope for a compromise. To Iranians, these practices are a part of good manners; they are not offended by them. But Canadians and members of other English-speaking cultures are used to "straight talking," to saying directly and succinctly what they want. Therefore, they find *taarof* hard to learn, let alone to practise. As an Iranian social scientist told *The New York Times* (August 6, 2006), "Speech has a different function than it does in the West"—in the west, "yes" generally means yes; in Iran, "yes" can mean yes, but it often means maybe or no. "This creates a rich, poetic linguistic culture," he said. "It creates a multidimensional culture where people are adept at picking up on nuances. On the other hand, it makes for bad political discourse. In political discourse people don't know what to trust."

You can see why critical thinking can help people avoid the tendency to stereotype and to see cultural differences in communication solely in hostile, negative ways. "Why are the Iranians lying to me?" a Canadian might ask. The answer is that they are not "lying" in Iranian terms; they are speaking in a way that is completely natural for them, according to their cultural rules for communication.

To learn the unspoken rules of a culture, you must look, listen, and observe. What is the pace of life like? Do people regard brash individuality and loud speech as admirable or embarrassing? When customers enter a shop, do they greet and chat with the shopkeeper or ignore the person as they browse? Are people expected to be direct in their speech or evasive? Sociocultural research enhances critical thinking by teaching us to appreciate the many cultural rules that govern people's behaviour, values, attitudes, and ways of doing business. Before you write off someone from a culture different from your own as being rude, foolish, stubborn, or devious, consider other interpretations of that person's behaviour—just as you would want that person to consider other, more forgiving, interpretations of yours.

Summary

MyPsychLab can help you get a better grade. Test your knowledge and grasp difficult concepts through
- Custom study plans: See where you are strong and where you are wrong
- Multimedia, including videos and interactive simulations
- Dynamic Study Modules: flashcards for self-study that ensure you achieve mastery of course concepts

- *Social psychologists* study how social roles, attitudes, relationships, and groups influence individuals; *cultural psychologists* study the influence of culture on human behaviour. Many cultural rules, such as those governing correct *conversational distance*, are unspoken but nonetheless powerful.

Roles and Rules

- The environment influences people in countless subtle ways; observing that others have broken rules or laws increases the likelihood that a passerby will do the same. Two classic studies illustrate the power of *norms* and *roles* to affect individual actions. In Milgram's obedience study, most people in the role of "teacher" inflicted what they thought was extreme shock on another person because of the authority of the experimenter. In the Stanford prison study, university students tended to behave in accordance with the role of "prisoner" or "guard" that they had been assigned.

- Obedience to authority contributes to the smooth running of society, but obedience can also lead to actions that are deadly, foolish, or illegal. People obey orders because they can be punished if they do not, out of respect for authority, and to gain advantages. Even when they would rather not obey, they may do so because they have been *entrapped*, justifying each step and decision they make, and handing over responsibility for any harmful actions they commit to the authority.

Social Influences on Beliefs and Behaviour

- *Social cognition* is the study of how people's perceptions affect their relationships and how the social environment affects their beliefs and perceptions. According to *attribution theory*, people are motivated to search for causes to which they can attribute their own and other people's behaviour. Their attributions may be *situational* or *dispositional*. The *fundamental attribution error* occurs when people overestimate personality traits as a cause of behaviour and underestimate the influence of the situation. A primary reason for the fundamental attribution error is that people rely on introspection to judge their own behaviour but only have observation to judge the behaviour of others. Attributions are further influenced by two *self-serving biases*: the bias to choose the most flattering and forgiving explanations of our own behaviour and the bias that the world is fair (the *just-world hypothesis*).

- People hold many *attitudes* about people, things, and ideas. Attitudes may be *explicit* (conscious) or *implicit* (unconscious). Attitudes may change through experience, conscious decision, or as an effort to reduce *cognitive dissonance*. The process of dissonance reduction can cause entrapment along a "slippery slope" from mild errors or mistakes to more serious ones. One powerful way to influence attitudes is by taking advantage of the *familiarity effect* and the *validity effect*: Simply exposing people repeatedly to a name or product makes them like it more, and repeating a statement over and over again makes it seem more believable.

- As discussed in "Biology and *Beliefs*," many attitudes are acquired through learning and social influence, but some are associated with personality traits that have a genetic component and are deeply ingrained. Religious and political affiliations are not heritable, but religiosity and certain political attitudes do have relatively high heritability. Ideological belief systems may have evolved to be organized along a left–right dimension, consisting of two central sets of attitudes: whether a person advocates or opposes social change; and whether a person thinks inequality is a result of human policies and can be overcome or is inevitable and should be accepted as part of the natural order. Attitudes are also profoundly affected by the *nonshared environment*, an individual's unique life experiences.

Individuals in Groups

- The need to belong is so powerful that the pain of social rejection and exclusion is greater and more memorable than physical pain, which is why groups use the weapon of ostracism or rejection to enforce conformity.

- In groups, individuals often behave differently than they would on their own. Conformity permits the smooth running of society and allows people to feel in harmony with others like them. But as the Asch experiment showed, most people will conform to the judgments of others even when the others are plain wrong.

- Close-knit groups are vulnerable to *groupthink*, the tendency of group members to think alike, censor themselves, actively suppress disagreement, and feel that their decisions are invulnerable. Groupthink often produces faulty decisions because group members fail to seek disconfirming evidence for their ideas. However, groups can be structured to counteract groupthink.

- Sometimes a group's collective judgment is better than that of its individual members—the "wisdom of crowds." But crowds can also spread panic, rumour, and misinformation. *Diffusion of responsibility* in a group can lead to inaction on the part of individuals, as in *bystander apathy*. In truly dangerous, *unambiguous* emergencies, however, people are more likely to help, and in fact are often spurred to do so by the presence of others. The diffusion of responsibility is likely to occur under conditions that promote *deindividuation*, the loss of awareness of one's individuality. Deindividuation increases when people feel anonymous, as in a large group or crowd or when they are wearing masks or uniforms. In some situations, crowd norms lead deindividuated people to behave aggressively, but in others, crowd norms foster helpfulness.

- The willingness to speak up for an unpopular opinion, blow the whistle on illegal practices, or help a stranger in trouble and perform other acts of *altruism* is partly a matter of personal belief and conscience. But several situational factors are also important: The person perceives that help is needed; cultural norms support taking action; the person has an ally; and the person becomes entrapped in a commitment to help or dissent.

Us versus Them: Group Identity

- People develop *social identities* based on their ethnicity, including nationality, religion, occupation, and other social memberships. In culturally diverse societies, many people face the problem of balancing their *ethnic identity* with *acculturation* into the larger society.

- *Ethnocentrism*, the belief that one's own ethnic group or religion is superior to all others, promotes "us–them" thinking. One effective strategy for reducing us–them thinking and hostility between groups is *interdependence*, having both sides work together to reach a common goal.

- *Stereotypes* help people rapidly process new information, organize experience, and predict how others will behave. But they distort reality by exaggerating differences between groups, underestimating the differences within groups, and producing selective perception.

Group Conflict and Prejudice

- A *prejudice* is an unreasonable negative feeling toward a category of people. Psychologically, prejudice wards off feelings of anxiety and doubt and bolsters self-esteem when a person feels threatened (by providing a scapegoat) and, according to *terror management theory*, protects against the fear of death. Prejudice also has social causes: People acquire prejudices mindlessly, through conformity and parental lessons. Prejudice also serves to justify a majority group's economic interests and dominance. Finally, prejudice serves the cultural and national purpose of bonding people to their social groups and nations, and in extreme cases justifying war. *Hostile sexism* is different from *benevolent sexism*, although both legitimize gender discrimination. During times of economic insecurity and competition for jobs, prejudice rises.

- Psychologists disagree on whether racism and other prejudices are declining or have merely taken new forms. Some are trying to measure prejudice indirectly, by measuring *social distance*; seeing whether people are more likely to behave aggressively toward a target when they are stressed or angry; observing changes in the brain; or assessing unconscious positive or negative associations with a group, as with the *Implicit Association Test* (IAT). However, the IAT has many critics who claim it is not capturing true prejudice.

- Efforts to reduce prejudice need to target both the explicit and implicit attitudes that people have. Four conditions help to reduce two groups' mutual prejudices and conflicts: Both sides must have equal legal status, economic standing, and power; both sides must have the legal, moral, and economic support of authorities and cultural institutions; both sides must have opportunities to work and socialize together informally and formally (the *contact hypothesis*); and both sides must work together for a common goal.

The Question of Human Nature

- Although many people believe that only bad or evil people do bad deeds, the principles of social and cultural psychology show that under certain conditions, good people can be induced to do bad things too. Everyone is influenced to one degree or another by the social processes of obedience, entrapment, conformity, persuasion, bystander apathy, groupthink, deindividuation, ethnocentrism, stereotyping, and prejudice.

Taking Psychology with You

- Sociocultural research enhances critical thinking by identifying the cultural rules that govern people's behaviour, values, communication, and ways of doing business. Understanding these rules can help people examine their assumptions about people in other cultures, and avoid the tendency to jump to conclusions and reason emotionally about group differences.

Key Terms

norms (social) **256**
role **256**
culture **257**
entrapment **261**
social cognition **262**
attribution theory **262**

fundamental attribution error **263**
just-world hypothesis **264**
cognitive dissonance **266**
familiarity effect **266**
validity effect **267**

groupthink **273**
diffusion of responsibility **274**
deindividuation **275**
social identity **278**
ethnic identity **278**

acculturation **278**
ethnocentrism **279**
stereotype **281**
prejudice **282**

Thinking and Intelligence

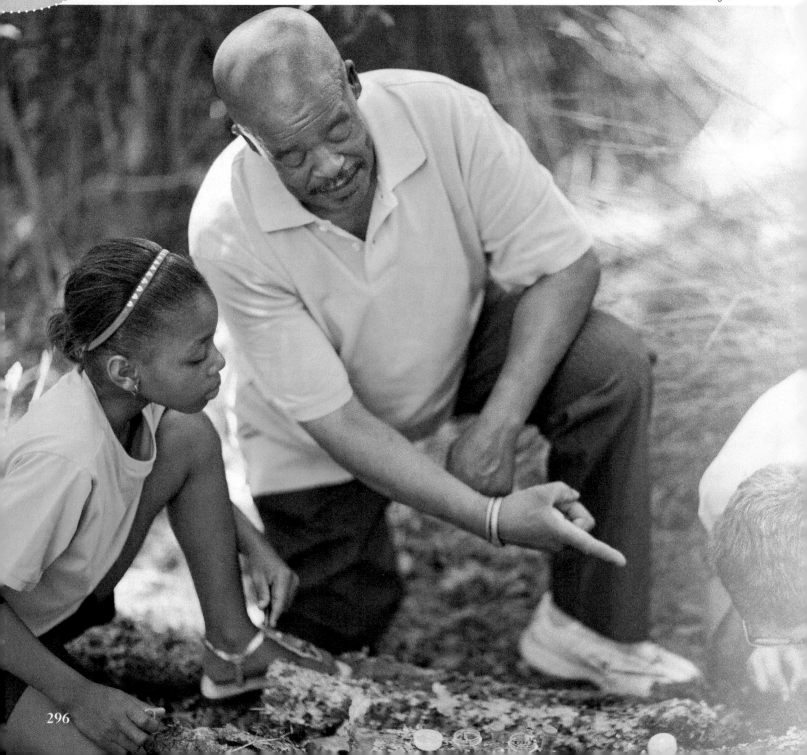

Glow Images

Ask questions. . . be willing to wonder

Is all of our thinking conscious?

Why is it often so hard for people to reason rationally?

Does a high IQ guarantee success in school and in life?

Can animals think—and if so, what do they think about?

Each day, in the course of ordinary living, we all make decisions, draw up plans, draw inferences, construct explanations, and organize and reorganize the contents of our mental world. Descartes' famous declaration "I think, therefore I am" could just as well be reversed: "I am, therefore I think." Our powers of thought and intelligence have inspired humans to immodestly call ourselves *Homo sapiens*, Latin for wise or rational man.

But just how "sapiens" are we, really? As children, we all learn how clocks arbitrarily divide time into hours, minutes, and seconds. Yet each spring, when daylight saving time begins, some people fret about tampering with "normal time." One woman complained to her local newspaper that the "extra hour of sunlight" was burning up her front lawn! In Nottingham, England, the mayor decided to distribute flyers to visitors telling them that Robin Hood and his pals never actually lived in nearby Sherwood Forest, inasmuch as they were not real persons; tourism plummeted. In Sochi, a video purportedly showing a wolf roaming the residences of the Olympic Village went viral. Before being revealed as a prank pulled by Jimmy Kimmel and Kate Hansen, many of those in the media reported on it with many people weighing in on whether or not it was a real wolf or a dog (it was a wolf), without questioning whether or not it was likely that a wolf would be wandering about the Olympic village . . . We could go on.

Of course, our cognitive abilities are also pretty impressive. Think for a moment about what thinking does for you. It frees you from the confines of the immediate present: You can think about a trip taken three years ago, a party next Saturday, or the First World War. It carries you beyond the boundaries of reality: You can imagine unicorns and utopias, Martians and magic. You can make plans far into the future and judge the probability of events, both good and bad. Because you think, you do not need to grope your way blindly through your problems but can apply knowledge and reasoning to solve them intelligently and creatively.

Yes, the human mind, which has managed to come up with poetry and penicillin, is a miraculous thing. But the human mind has also managed to come up with traffic jams, spam, and war. To better understand why the same species that figured out how to get to the moon is also capable of breathtaking bumbling here on Earth, we will examine in this chapter how people reason, solve problems, and grow in intelligence, as well as some sources of their mental shortcomings. These topics are the focus of *cognitive psychology*, the study of cognition (mental processes).

Learning Objectives

1. Describe how concepts and prototypes are the building blocks of thought.

2. Give an example in your life of subconscious thinking and describe one way that this differs from nonconscious thinking.

3. Articulate the key way in which an algorithm differs from a heuristic. From real life, give one example of each.

Thought: Using What We Know

Many cognitive scientists liken the human mind to an information processor, analogous to a computer but far more complex. Information processing approaches capture the fact that the brain actively processes information by altering it, organizing it, and using it to make decisions. Just as computers internally manipulate representations of 0s and 1s to "think," so we *mentally* manipulate internal representations of objects, activities, and situations. 👁

The Elements of Cognition

One type of mental representation is the **concept**, a mental category that groups objects, relations, activities, abstractions, or qualities having common properties. The instances of a concept are seen as roughly similar: *golden retriever, cocker spaniel*, and *border collie* are instances of the concept *dog*; and *anger, joy*, and *sadness* are instances of the concept *emotion*. Concepts simplify and summarize information about the world so that it is manageable and so that we can make decisions quickly and efficiently. You may never have seen a *Basenji* or eaten *escargots*, but if you know that the first is an instance of *dog* and the second an instance of *food*, you will know, roughly, how to respond (unless you do not like to eat snails, which is what escargots are).

Basic concepts have a moderate number of instances and are easier to acquire than those having either few or many instances (Rosch, 1973). What is the object pictured in the margin? You will probably call it an apple. The concept *apple* is more basic than *fruit*, which includes many more instances and is more abstract. It is also more basic than *McIntosh*, which is quite specific. Children seem to learn basic-level concepts earlier than others, and adults use them more often than others, because basic concepts convey an optimal amount of information in most situations.

The qualities associated with a concept do not necessarily all apply to every instance: Some apples are not red; some dogs do not bark (Basenjis!); some birds do not fly. But all the instances of a concept do share a family resemblance. When we need to decide whether something belongs to a concept, we are likely to compare it to a **prototype**, a representative instance of the concept (Rosch, 1973). Which dog is doggier, a golden retriever or a Chihuahua? Which fruit is more fruitlike, an apple or a pineapple? Which activity is more representative of sports, football or weight lifting? Most people within a culture can easily tell you which instances of a concept are most representative, or *prototypical*.

The words used to express concepts may influence or shape how we think about them. Many decades ago, Benjamin Lee Whorf, an insurance inspector by profession and a linguist and anthropologist by inclination, proposed that language moulds cognition and perception. According to Whorf (1956), because English has only one word for snow and Inuktitut has many (for snow on the ground, snow in which one sinks, falling snow, . . .), the Inuit notice differences in snow that English speakers do not. He also argued that grammar—the way words are formed and arranged to convey tense and other concepts—affects how we think about the world.

👁—⎡**Watch** the **Video**
The Basics: The Mind is What the Brain Does in **MyPsychLab**

What is this?

Vaclav Volrab/Shutterstock

concept A mental category that groups objects, relations, activities, abstractions, or qualities having common properties.

basic concepts Concepts that have a moderate number of instances and that are easier to acquire than those having few or many instances.

prototype An especially representative example of a concept.

Some instances of a concept are more representative or prototypical than others. A "bachelor" is an unmarried man. For example, Justin Bieber is an unmarried man and thus a bachelor but what about the Pope?

Left: Allstar Picture Library/Alamy. Right: Marco iacobucci/Alamy.

Whorf's theory was popular for a while and then fell from favour. After all, English speakers can see varieties of snow and they have plenty of adjectives to describe them. But Whorf's ideas have once again gained attention. Vocabulary and grammar may affect how we perceive the location of objects, think about time, attend to shapes and colours, and remember events (Boroditsky, 2003; Gentner & Goldin-Meadow, 2003). A language spoken by a group in Papua, New Guinea, refers to blue and green with one word, but to distinct shades of green with two separate words. On perceptual discrimination tasks, New Guineans who speak this language handle green contrasts better than blue–green ones, whereas the reverse holds true for English speakers (Roberson, Davies, & Davidoff, 2000). Similar results on the way language affects colour perception have been obtained in studies comparing English with certain African languages (Özgen, 2004).

Here's another example: In many languages, speakers must specify whether an object is linguistically masculine or feminine (in French and Spanish), where *la clé*, the key, is feminine but *le pont*, the bridge, is masculine. It seems that labelling a concept as masculine or feminine affects the attributes that native speakers ascribe to it. Thus, a German speaker will describe a key (masculine in German) as hard, heavy, jagged, serrated, and useful, whereas a Spanish or French speaker is more likely to describe a key (a feminine noun) as golden, intricate, little, lovely, and shiny. German speakers will describe a bridge (feminine in German) as beautiful, elegant, fragile, peaceful, and slender, whereas French or Spanish speakers are more likely to describe a bridge (a masculine noun) as big, dangerous, strong, sturdy, and towering (Boroditsky, Schmidt, & Phillips, 2003). ◉

Concepts are the building blocks of thought, but they would be of limited use if we merely stacked them up mentally. We must also represent their relations to one another. One way we accomplish this may be by storing and using **propositions**, units of meaning that are made up of concepts and that express a unitary idea. A proposition can express nearly any sort of knowledge ("Emily raises Border collies") or belief ("Border collies are smart"). Propositions, in turn, are linked together in complicated networks of knowledge, associations, beliefs, and expectations. These networks, which psychologists call **cognitive schemas**, serve as mental models of aspects of the world. Gender schemas represent a person's beliefs and expectations about what it means to be male or female (see Chapter 13). People also have schemas about cultures, occupations, animals, geographical locations, and many other features of the social and natural environment.

Mental images—especially visual images—are also important in thinking and in constructing cognitive schemas. Although no one can directly see another person's visual images, psychologists are able to study them indirectly. One method is to measure how long it takes people to rotate an image in their imaginations, scan from one

How do you divide up these hues? People who speak a language that has only one word for blue and green, but separate words for shades of green, handle green contrasts better than the blue–green distinction. English speakers do the opposite.

Eky Chan/Fotolia

◉—|**Watch** the **Video**
Thinking Like a Psychologist: Speaking One's Mind in **MyPsychLab**

proposition A unit of meaning that is made up of concepts and expresses a single idea.

cognitive schema An integrated mental network of knowledge, beliefs, and expectations concerning a particular topic or aspect of the world.

mental image A mental representation that mirrors or resembles the thing it represents; mental images occur in many and perhaps all sensory modalities.

subconscious processes Mental processes occurring outside of conscious awareness but accessible to consciousness when necessary.

⊙▶⎤Simulate the Experiment
Mental Rotation in **MyPsychLab**

point to another in an image, or read off some detail from an image. The results suggest that visual images are much like images on a computer screen: We can manipulate them, they occur in a mental space of a fixed size, and small ones contain less detail than larger ones (Kosslyn, 1980; Shepard & Metzler, 1971). Most people also report auditory images (such as a song, slogan, or poem you can hear in your "mind's ear"), and many report images in other sensory modalities as well—touch, taste, smell, or pain. Some even report kinaesthetic images, imagined feelings in the muscles and joints. ⊙▶

Here, then, is a visual summary of the elements of cognition:

How Conscious Is Thought?

When we think about thinking, we usually have in mind those mental activities that are carried out in a deliberate way with a conscious goal in mind, such as solving a problem, drawing up plans, or making calculated decisions. However, not all mental processing is conscious.

Subconscious Thinking. Some cognitive processes lie outside of awareness but can be brought into consciousness with a little effort when necessary. These **subconscious processes** allow us to handle more information and to perform more complex tasks than if we depended entirely on conscious deliberate thought. Many automatic routines are performed "without thinking," though they might once have required careful, conscious attention: texting, driving a car, reading.

Because of the capacity for automatic processing, people can eat lunch while reading a book or drive a car while listening to music; in such cases, one of the tasks has become automatic. However, this does not mean you should go ahead and text your friends while driving. Not only is texting while driving illegal in Canada, but *multitasking* rarely works well. In fact, multitasking increases the time required to complete both tasks, increases stress and errors, and impairs memory (Lien, Ruthruff, & Johnston, 2006). This is *especially* true for people who consider themselves to be good at multitasking, who were routinely impaired in task performance by multitasking (Ophir, Nass, & Wagner, 2009). Of relevance to this course, in a study titled 'no A 4 U" more than 1800 university students were surveyed about their multitasking (e.g. using Facebook, texting, IMing) while studying (Junco & Cotton, 2012). Researchers found those who had the poorest grades engaged in the most multitasking. Thus, in real life, multitasking while studying for this course may negatively impact your GPA.

Even overhearing one side of someone else's cell phone conversation siphons your attention away from a task you are doing, possibly because of the effort required to make sense of just one half of a conversation. In one experiment, when people listened to a "halfalogue" while they were doing a visual task, they made more than six times as many errors on the task than when they listened to an ordinary two-person conversation (Emberson et al., 2010). And as we saw in Chapter 2, cell phone use greatly impairs a person's ability to drive, whether the phone is hands-free or not; a driver's attention is diverted far more by a phone conversation

Some well-learned skills do not require much conscious thought and can be performed while doing other things, but multitasking can also get you into serious trouble. It's definitely not a good idea to talk on your cell phone, eat, and try to drive all at the same time.

Spencer Grant/PhotoEdit Inc.

than by listening to music (Strayer & Drews, 2007). And having an emotionally charged conversation with a passenger may negatively affect driving even more than other distractions (Lansdown & Stephens, 2013). However, drivers have been caught on camera checking their stocks, applying makeup, flossing their teeth, and putting in contact lenses—all while hurtling down the highway at high speeds (Klauer et al., 2006). When an engineer of a commuter train texted while driving, he didn't see the oncoming freight train, resulting in an accident that killed 25 people, including the engineer himself. 👁

Nonconscious Thinking. Other kinds of thought processes, **nonconscious processes**, remain outside of awareness, even when you try to bring them back. As we will see shortly, people often find the solution to a problem when it suddenly pops into mind after they have given up trying to figure it out. And sometimes people learn a new skill without being able to explain how they perform it. For instance, they may discover the best strategy for winning at a card game without ever being able to consciously identify what they are doing (Bechara et al., 1997). With such **implicit learning**, you learn a rule or an adaptive behaviour, either with or without a conscious intention to do so; but you don't know how you learned it, and you can't state, either to yourself or to others, exactly what it is you have learned (Frensch & Rünger, 2003; Lieberman, 2000). Many of our abilities, from the grammar of our first language to riding a bike, are the result of implicit learning. But implicit learning is not always helpful, because it can also generate biases and prejudices. We can learn an association between "stupidity" and "those people" without ever being aware of how we learned it or who taught it to us.

Even when our thinking is conscious, often we are not thinking very *hard*. We may act, speak, and make decisions out of habit, without stopping to analyze what we are doing or why we are doing it. *Mindlessness*—mental inflexibility, inertia, and obliviousness to the present context—keeps people from recognizing when a change in a situation requires a change in behaviour. In a classic study of mindlessness, a researcher approached people as they were about to use a photocopier and made one of three requests: "Excuse me, may I use the Xerox machine?" "Excuse me, may I use the Xerox machine, because I have to make copies?" or "Excuse me, may I use the Xerox machine, because I'm in a rush?" Normally, people will let someone go before them only if the person has a legitimate reason, as in the third request. In this study, however, people also complied when the reason sounded like an authentic explanation but was actually meaningless ("because I have to make copies"). They heard the form of the request but they did not hear its content, and they mindlessly stepped aside (Langer, Blank, & Chanowitz, 1978).

Problem Solving and Decision Making

Conscious and nonconscious processes are both involved in solving such everyday problems as finding a missing word in a crossword puzzle, assembling a cabinet, or doubling a cookie recipe. In well-defined problems, the nature of the problem is clear ("I need more cookies for the party tomorrow"). Often, all you need to do to solve the problem is apply the right **algorithm**, a set of procedures guaranteed to produce a correct (or a best) solution even if you do not understand why it works. To increase a cookie recipe, you can simply multiply the number of cookies you want per person by the number of people you need to feed. If the original recipe produced 10 cookies and you need 40, you can then multiply each ingredient by four. The recipe itself is also an algorithm (add flour, stir lightly, add raisins . . .), though you probably won't know the chemical changes involved when you combine the ingredients and heat the batter in an oven.

nonconscious processes Mental processes occurring outside of and not available to conscious awareness.

implicit learning Learning that occurs when you acquire knowledge about something without being aware of how you did so and without being able to state exactly what it is you have learned.

algorithm A problem-solving strategy guaranteed to produce a solution even if the user does not know how it works.

👁—|Watch the Video
What's In It For Me?: The Myth of Multitasking in **MyPsychLab**

Advertisers sometimes count on mindlessness in consumers.

Jennifer K. Berman

heuristic A rule of thumb that suggests a course of action or guides problem solving but does not guarantee an optimal solution.

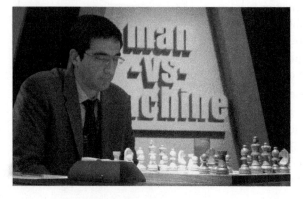

Watch the Video
What's In It For Me?: Making Choices in **MyPsychLab**

Whether you are a chess grand master, pondering your next move in a match against a computer, or just an ordinary person solving ordinary problems, you need to use heuristics, rules of thumb that help you decide on a strategy.

ADAM JAN/AFP/Newscom

Other problems are fuzzier. There is no specific goal ("What should I have for dinner tomorrow?") and no clearly correct solution, so no algorithm applies. In such cases, you may resort to a **heuristic**, a rule of thumb that suggests a course of action without guaranteeing an optimal solution ("Maybe I'll browse through some recipes online, or go to the market and see what catches my eye"). Many heuristics, like those used when playing chess, help you limit your options to a manageable number of promising ones, reducing the cognitive effort it takes to arrive at a decision (Galotti, 2007). Heuristics are useful to a student trying to choose a major, an investor trying to predict the stock market, a doctor trying to determine the best treatment for a patient, and a factory owner trying to boost production. All of them are faced with incomplete information with which to reach a solution, and may therefore resort to rules of thumb that have proven effective in the past.

As useful as algorithms and heuristics are, sometimes the conscious effort to try to solve a problem seems to get you nowhere. Then, with insight, you suddenly see how to solve an equation or finish a puzzle without quite knowing how you found the solution. Insight probably involves different stages of mental processing (Bowers et al., 1990). First, clues in the problem automatically activate certain memories or knowledge. You begin to see a pattern or structure to the problem, although you cannot yet say what it is; possible solutions percolate in your mind. Although you are not aware of it, considerable mental work is guiding you toward a hypothesis, reflected in your brain as patterns of activity that differ from those associated with ordinary, methodical problem solving (Kounios & Beeman, 2009). Eventually, a solution springs into mind, seemingly from nowhere ("Aha, now I see!").

People also say they sometimes rely on intuition—hunches and gut feelings—rather than conscious thinking when they make judgments or solve problems. Why do we trust such feelings? One possibility is that changes in our bodies signal that we are close to success. Long before people can consciously identify the best strategy for winning a card game, their bodies already seem to "know" it: Changes in their sweat and heart rate occur as soon as they make a wrong move (Bechara et al., 1997). What's more, people who are better at paying attention to their heart rates tend to be better at figuring out the best strategy (Dunn et al., 2010).

Should you therefore go with your gut or take your pulse when answering questions or solving problems on your next test? Not necessarily. Daniel Kahneman's book *Thinking, Fast and Slow* (2011) explains why. "Fast" thinking applies to our rapid, intuitive, emotional, almost automatic decisions; "slow" thinking requires intellectual effort. Naturally, most people rely on fast thinking because it saves time and effort, but it is often wrong. Here is one of his examples: Suppose that a bat and ball together cost $1.10 and that the bat costs one dollar more than the ball. How much does the ball cost? Most people answer with fast thinking and say 10 cents. But the correct answer is five cents. Think (slowly) about it.

Jerome Kagan (1989) once likened consciousness to firefighters who are quietly playing cards at the station house until an alarm goes off, calling them into action. The rest of the time, we rely on automatic processes and unconscious impressions. Usually that's a good thing; walking around in a state of fully conscious awareness would be impossible, and undesirable as well; we would never get anything done if we had to examine "thoughtfully" every little thing we do, say, decide, or overhear. But multitasking, mindlessness, and operating on automatic pilot can also lead to errors and mishaps, ranging from the trivial (misplacing your keys) to the serious (walking into traffic because you're texting). Therefore, most of us would probably benefit if our mental firefighters paid a little more attention to their jobs. How can we improve our capacity to reason rationally and think critically? We turn to that question next.

Recite & Review

Recite: Mindfully, say out loud what you know about *concepts, basic concepts, prototypes, propositions, cognitive schemas, mental images, subconscious and nonconscious processes,* multitasking, *implicit learning, algorithms,* and *heuristics.*

Review: Next, consciously as well as conscientiously, reread this section.

Now take this *Quick Quiz:*

1. Which concept is most basic: *furniture, chair,* or *high chair?*

2. Which example of the concept *chair* is prototypical: *high chair, rocking chair,* or *dining room chair?*

3. What two findings in the previous section support Whorf's theory that language affects perception and cognition?

4. Peter's mental representation of *Thanksgiving* includes associations (e.g., to turkeys), attitudes ("It's a time to be with relatives"), and expectations ("I'm going to gain weight from all that food"). They are all part of his _____ for the holiday.

5. Mina discovers that she has called her boyfriend's number instead of her mother's, as she intended. Her error can be attributed to _____.

6. When you solve a long-division problem, which are you using, an algorithm or a heuristic?

Answers:

1. chair 2. A plain, straight-backed dining room chair will be prototypical for most people. 3. Colour terms can affect how people respond to colours on visual discrimination tasks, and the linguistic gender of a word can affect people's descriptions of the concept it represents. 4. cognitive schema 5. mindlessness 6. an algorithm

Learning Objectives

4   List and define the seven stages of dialectical reasoning. Assess whether individuals may demonstrate more

than one stage of dialectical thinking when engaging in reasoning about complex issues.

Reasoning Rationally

Reasoning is purposeful mental activity that involves operating on information to reach a conclusion. Unlike impulsive ("fast") or nonconscious responding, reasoning requires us to draw specific inferences from observations, facts, or assumptions. In *formal reasoning problems*—the kind you might find, say, on an intelligence test or an entrance exam for medical or law school—the information needed for drawing a conclusion or reaching a solution is specified clearly, and there is a single right (or best) answer. In *informal reasoning problems*, there is often no clearly correct solution. Many approaches, viewpoints, or possible solutions may compete, and you may have to decide which one is most "reasonable."

To do this wisely, a person must be able to use **dialectical reasoning**, the process of comparing and evaluating opposing points of view to resolve differences. Philosopher Richard Paul (1984) once described dialectical reasoning as movement "up and back between contradictory lines of reasoning, using each to critically cross-examine the other." Dialectical reasoning is what juries are supposed to do to arrive at a verdict: consider arguments for and against the defendant's guilt, point and counterpoint. It is also what voters are supposed to do when thinking about whether the government should raise or lower taxes, or about the best way to improve public education.

reasoning The drawing of conclusions or inferences from observations, facts, or assumptions.

dialectical reasoning A process in which opposing facts or ideas are weighed and compared, with a view to determining the best solution or resolving differences.

GET INVOLVED! Practice Your Dialectical Reasoning

Choose a controversial topic, such as Quebec sovereignty or enhanced treaty rights for indigenous peoples. First, list all the arguments you can to support your own position. Then list all the arguments you can on the other side of the issue. You do not have to agree with these arguments; just list them. Do you feel a mental block or emotional discomfort while doing this? Can you imagine how opponents of your position would answer your arguments? Having strong opinions is fine; you should have an informed opinion on matters of public interest. But does that opinion get in the way of even imagining a contrary point of view or of altering your view if the evidence warrants a change?

One reason that Auguste Rodin's *The Thinker* became world famous and has been much imitated is that it captures so perfectly the experience of thinking reflectively.

Shutterstock

Many adults clearly have trouble thinking dialectically; they take one position, and that's that. When do people develop the ability to think critically—to question assumptions, evaluate and integrate evidence, consider alternative interpretations, and reach conclusions that can be defended as most reasonable?

To find out, Patricia King and Karen Kitchener (1994, 2002, 2004) provided a large, diverse sample of adolescents and adults with statements describing opposing viewpoints on various topics. Each person then had to answer several questions, such as "What do you think about these statements?" "On what do you base your position?" and "Why do you suppose disagreement exists about this issue?" From the responses of thousands of participants, King and Kitchener identified seven cognitive stages on the road to what they call *reflective judgment* and we have called critical thinking. At each stage, people make different assumptions about how things are known and use different ways of justifying their beliefs.

In general, people in the two *prereflective thinking* stages tend to assume that a correct answer always exists and that it can be obtained directly through the senses ("I know what I've seen") or from authorities ("They said so on the news"; "That's what I was brought up to believe"). If authorities do not yet have the truth, prereflective thinkers tend to reach conclusions on the basis of what "feels right" at the moment. They do not distinguish between knowledge and belief or between belief and evidence, and they see no reason to justify a belief. One respondent at this stage, when asked about evolution, said, "Well, some people believe that we evolved from apes and that's the way they want to believe. But I would never believe that way and nobody could talk me out of the way I believe because I believe the way that it's told in the Bible."

During three *quasi-reflective stages*, people recognize that some things cannot be known with absolute certainty, and they realize that judgments should be supported by reasons, yet they pay attention only to evidence that fits what they already believe. They seem to think that because knowledge is uncertain, any judgment about the evidence is purely subjective. Quasi-reflective thinkers will defend a position by saying, "We all have a right to our own opinion," as if all opinions are created equal. One undergraduate at this stage, when asked whether one opinion on the safety of food additives was right and others were wrong, answered: "No. I think it just depends on how you feel personally because people make their decisions based upon how they feel and what research they've seen. So what one person thinks is right, another person might think is wrong. . . . If I feel that chemicals cause cancer and you feel that food is unsafe without it, your opinion might be right to you and my opinion is right to me."

In the last two stages, a person becomes capable of *reflective judgment*. They understand that although some things can never be known with certainty, some judgments are more valid than others because of their coherence, their fit with the available evidence, their usefulness, and so on. *They* are willing to consider evidence from a variety of sources and to reason dialectically. This interview with a graduate student illustrates reflective thinking:

Interviewer: Can you ever say you know for sure that your point of view on chemical additives is correct?

Student: No, I don't think so. . . . [But] I think that we can usually be reasonably certain, given the information we have now, and considering our methodologies. . . . It might be that the research wasn't conducted rigorously enough. In other words, we might have flaws in our data or sample, things like that.

Interviewer: How then would you identify the "better opinion"?

Student: One that takes as many factors as possible into consideration. I mean one that uses the higher percentage of the data that we have, and perhaps that uses the methodology that has been most reliable.

Interviewer: And how do you come to a conclusion about what the evidence suggests?

Student: I think you have to take a look at the different opinions and studies that are offered by different groups. Maybe some studies offered by the chemical industry, some studies by the government, some private studies. . . . You have to try to interpret people's motives and that makes it a more complex soup to try to strain out.

Sometimes a person's reasoning varies across two or three stages, depending on the kind of problem or issue they are thinking about. They might be able to use reflective judgment for some issues yet be prereflective on others that hold deep emotional meaning for them (Haidt, 2012; King & Kitchener, 2004). Most people, however, show no evidence of reflective judgment until their middle or late twenties, if ever. A longitudinal study found that many students graduate without learning to distinguish fact from opinion, evaluate conflicting reports objectively, or resist emotional statements and political posturing (Arum & Roksa, 2011). Still, there's reason for hope. When students get ample support for thinking reflectively, have opportunities to practise it in their courses, and apply themselves seriously to their studies, their thinking tends to become more complex, sophisticated, and well grounded (Kitchener et al., 1993). As one writer noted, the gradual development of thinking skills among these students represents an abandonment of "ignorant certainty" in favour of "intelligent confusion" (Kroll, 1992). It may not seem so, but this is a big step forward! You can see why, in this book, we emphasize thinking about psychological findings, and not just memorizing them.

Recite & Review

Recite: State out loud what you know about *reasoning* and *dialectical reasoning*.

Review: Next, reread this section.

Now be reasonable and take this *Quick Quiz:*

1. Yvonne is arguing with Henrietta about whether real estate is a better investment than stocks. "You can't convince me," says Yvonne. "I just know I'm right." Yvonne needs training in _____ reasoning.

2. Seymour thinks the media have a liberal political bias, and Sophie thinks they are too conservative. "Well," says Seymour, "I have my truth and you have yours. It's purely subjective." Which of King and Kitchener's stages of thinking describes Seymour's statement?

Answers:

1. dialectical 2. quasi-reflective

affect heuristic The tendency to consult one's emotions instead of estimating probabilities objectively.

Learning Objectives

5 Give examples of four major biases in reasoning that impair the ability to think rationally and critically.

6 Analyze why people worry more about rare but vivid disasters than about commonly occurring dangers.

7 Explain why people will choose a medical treatment that has a 70% chance of success rather than one with a 30% chance of failure.

8 Describe the research that demonstrates that people often value fairness above rational self-interest. Interpret this result in light of the work in behavioural economics.

9 List three conditions that are likely to produce cognitive dissonance.

THINKING CRITICALLY

Analyze assumptions and biases.

Most people assume they make decisions and judgments logically and rationally. But are human beings biased to be biased?

👁—**Watch the Video**
In the Real World: Changing Your Mind
in **MyPsychLab**

Because of the affect and availability heuristics, many of us overestimate the chances of suffering a shark attack. Shark attacks are extremely rare, but they are terrifying and easy to visualize.

Mark Conlin /Alamy

Barriers to Reasoning Rationally

Although most people have the capacity to think logically, reason dialectically, and make judgments reflectively, it is abundantly clear that they do not always do so. One obstacle is the need to be right; if your self-esteem depends on winning arguments, you will find it hard to listen with an open mind to competing views. Other obstacles include limited information and a lack of time to reflect carefully. But human thought processes are also tripped up by many predictable, systematic biases and errors. Psychologists have studied dozens of these cognitive pitfalls (Kahneman, 2003, 2011). Here we describe just a few. 👁

Exaggerating the Improbable (and Minimizing the Probable)

One common bias is the inclination to exaggerate the probability of rare events. This bias helps to explain why so many people enter lotteries and buy disaster insurance, and why some irrational fears persist. As we discuss in Chapter 7, evolution has equipped us to fear certain natural dangers, such as snakes. However, in modern life, many of these dangers are no longer much of a threat; the risk of a rattler sinking its fangs into you in Victoria or Waterloo is pretty low! Yet the fear lingers on, so we overestimate the danger. Evolution has also given us brains that are terrific at responding to an immediate threat or to acts that provoke moral outrage even though they pose no threat to the survival of the species (for instance, inequity). Unfortunately, our brains were not designed to become alarmed by serious *future* threats that do not seem to pose much danger right now, such as global warming (Gilbert, 2006b).

When judging probabilities, people are strongly influenced by the **affect heuristic**, the tendency to consult their emotions (affect) to judge the "goodness" or "badness" of a situation instead of judging probabilities objectively (Slovic & Peters, 2006; Slovic et al., 2002). Emotions can often help us make decisions by narrowing our options or by allowing us to act quickly in an uncertain or dangerous situation. But emotions can also mislead us by preventing us from accurately assessing risk. One unusual field study looked at how people in France responded to the "mad cow" crisis that occurred several years ago. (Mad cow disease affects the brain and can be contracted by eating meat from contaminated cows.) Whenever many newspaper articles reported the dangers of "mad cow disease," beef consumption fell during the following month. But when news articles, reporting the same dangers, used the technical names of the disease—Creutzfeldt-Jakob disease and bovine spongiform encephalopathy (BSE)—beef consumption stayed the same (Sinaceur, Heath, & Cole, 2005). The more alarming labels caused people to reason emotionally and to overestimate the danger. (During the entire period of the supposed crisis, only six people in France were diagnosed with the disease.) Canada has also had cases of BSE, and as was the case in France, there was a similar negative relation between beef consumption and reports about "mad cow disease" in the media (Peng, McCann-Hiltz, & Goddard, 2004). 👁

Our judgments about risks are also influenced by the **availability heuristic**, the tendency to judge the probability of an event by how easy it is to think of instances of it (Tversky & Kahneman, 1973). The availability heuristic often works hand in hand with the affect heuristic. Catastrophes and shocking accidents evoke an especially strong emotional reaction in us, and thus stand out in our minds, becoming more available mentally than other kinds of negative events. (An image of a "mad cow"— that sweet, placid creature running amok!—is highly "available.") This is why people overestimate the frequency of deaths from tornadoes and underestimate the frequency of deaths from asthma, which occur dozens of times more often but do not make headlines. It is why news accounts of avalanches make people fearful, even though skiing without a helmet is more dangerous.

Avoiding Loss

In general, people try to avoid or minimize risks and losses when they make decisions. That strategy is rational enough, but people's perceptions of risk are subject to the **framing effect**, the tendency for choices to differ depending on how the choice is presented. When a choice is framed in terms of the risk of losing something, people will respond more cautiously than when the very *same* choice is framed in terms of gain. They will choose a ticket that has a 1% chance of winning a raffle over one that has a 99% chance of losing. Or they will rate a condom as effective when they are told it has a 95% success rate in protecting against the AIDS virus, but not when they are told it has a 5% failure rate—which of course is exactly the same thing (Linville, Fischer, & Fischhoff, 1992).

Suppose you had to choose between two health programs to combat a disease expected to kill 600 people. Which would you prefer: a program that will definitely save 200 people, or one with a one-third probability of saving all 600 people and a two-thirds probability of saving none? (Problem 1 in Figure 9.1 illustrates this choice.) When asked this question, most people, including physicians, say they would prefer the first program. In other words, they reject the riskier though potentially more rewarding solution in favour of a sure gain. However, people will take a risk if they see it as a way to *avoid loss*. Suppose now that you have to choose between a program in which 400 people will definitely die and a program in which there is a one-third probability of nobody dying and a two-thirds probability that all 600 will die. If you think about it, you will see that the alternatives are exactly the same as in the first problem; they are merely worded differently (see Problem 2 in Figure 9.1). Yet this time, most people choose the second solution. They reject risk when they think of the outcome in terms of lives saved, but they accept risk when they think of the outcome in terms of lives lost (Kahneman, 2002; Kahneman, 2011; Tversky & Kahneman, 1981).

Few of us will have to face a decision involving hundreds of lives, but we may have to choose between different medical treatments for ourselves or a relative. Our decision may be

availability heuristic The tendency to judge the probability of a type of event by how easy it is to think of examples or instances.

framing effect The tendency for people's choices to be affected by how a choice is presented, or framed, such as whether it is worded in terms of potential losses or gains.

👁 **Watch** the **Video**
The Big Picture: I Am, Therefore I Think
in **MyPsychLab**

FIGURE 9.1 A Matter of Wording
The decisions we make can depend on how the alternatives are framed. When asked to choose between the two programs in Problem 1, which are described in terms of lives saved, most people choose the first program. When asked to choose between the programs in Problem 2, which are described in terms of lives lost, most people choose the second program. Yet the alternatives in the two problems are actually identical.

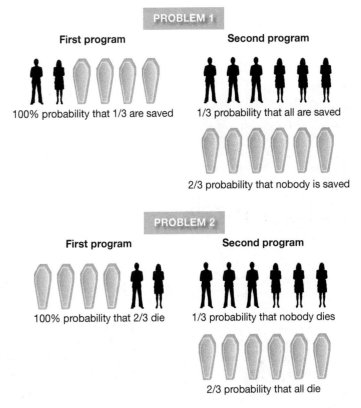

PROBLEM 1

First program

100% probability that 1/3 are saved

Second program

1/3 probability that all are saved

2/3 probability that nobody is saved

PROBLEM 2

First program

100% probability that 2/3 die

Second program

1/3 probability that nobody dies

2/3 probability that all die

affected by whether the doctor frames the choice in terms of chances of surviving or chances of dying.

The Fairness Bias

Interestingly, in certain circumstances, we do not try to avoid loss altogether, because we are subject to a *fairness bias*. Imagine that you are playing a two-person game called the *Ultimatum Game*, in which your partner gets $20 and must decide how much to share with you. You can choose to accept your partner's offer, in which case you both get to keep your respective portions, or you can reject the offer, in which case neither of you gets a penny. How low an offer would you accept?

If you think about it, you'll see that it makes sense to accept any amount at all, no matter how small, because then at least you will get *something*. But that is not how people respond when playing the Ultimatum Game. If the offer is too low, they are likely to reject it. In industrial societies, offers of 50% are typical and offers below 20–30% are commonly rejected, even when the absolute sums are large. In other societies, the amounts offered and accepted may be higher or lower, but there is always some amount that people consider unfair and refuse to accept (Henrich et al., 2001). People may be competitive and love to win, but they are also powerfully motivated to cooperate and to see fairness prevail.

This finding has intrigued scientists from many disciplines, including psychology, philosophy, economics, anthropology, evolutionary biology, and neuroscience. Using the Ultimatum Game and other laboratory games, they are exploring how a sense of fairness often takes precedence over rational self-interest when people make economic choices. Their work, which belongs to a field called *behavioural economics*, verifies and extends the pioneering work of Nobel Prize–winner Herbert Simon (1955), who first showed that economic decisions are not always rational. Psychologist Daniel Kahneman also won a Nobel Prize for his work on the irrational processes of decision making, but because there is (as yet) no Nobel Prize in psychology, he won it in economics. This was a delicious irony, because many economists still have a difficult time accepting the evidence of human irrationality.

In this drawing, made from a video, the monkey on the right watches as the one on the left exchanges a token for a reward. Later, the observing monkey may refuse a lesser reward.

Dr. Sarah Brosnan

BIOLOGY and
Economic Choice

Why does a desire for fair play sometimes outweigh the desire for economic gain? Evolutionary theorists suggest that cooperative tendencies and a desire for fairness and reciprocity evolved because they were beneficial to our forebears (Fehr & Fischbacher, 2003; Trivers, 2004). Different cultures develop their own rules to promote cooperation and punish cheaters, but a concern with fairness appears to be universal, part of our evolutionary prehistory. The idea that the Golden Rule has a basis in biology has gained support from studies of nonhuman primates and human babies.

In one study, capuchin monkeys received a token that they could then exchange for a slice of cucumber. The monkeys regarded this exchange as a pretty good deal—until they saw a neighbouring monkey exchanging tokens for an even better reward, a grape. At that point, they began to refuse to exchange their tokens, even though they were then left with no reward at all (Brosnan & de Waal, 2003). Sometimes they even threw the cucumber slice on the ground in apparent disgust!

Human babies also have a sense of fairness. In ingenious studies with 19- and 21-month-old infants, researchers took advantage of the fact that infants will look longer at something when it violates their expectations. When the experimenter failed to distribute rewards equally to two adult women who were doing a chore, the infants' expectation of fair play was violated. But it was not violated when the experimenter simply opened a box to reveal the items rather than distributing them, or when the rewards were distributed by an inanimate object (Sloane, Baillargeon, & Premack, 2012). Although the experimenters noted that young children might be learning about fair play from early interactions with adults, the early age at which infants seem to know at least some rules of fairness suggests a biological predisposition to acquire such rules.

Some behavioural economists have studied fairness by using fMRI to examine brain activity when people play variations of the Ultimatum Game (Camerer, 2003; Sanfey et al., 2003). Typically, while a person is deciding whether to accept a low or unfair offer, two brain areas are active: a part of the prefrontal cortex linked to rational problem solving and an area called the anterior insula, which is associated with pain, disgust, and other unpleasant feelings. According to economist Colin Camerer (quoted in D'Antonio, 2004), "Basically the brain toggles between 'Yes, money is good' and 'Ugh, this guy is treating me like crap.'" People with greater activation of the prefrontal cortex are likely to accept low offers; they do the economically smart thing and let the insult slide. In contrast, those with greater activation of the anterior insula are likely to refuse. In fact, Camerer estimates that researchers can predict the outcome 70% of the time simply by looking at participants' brain scans. In an interesting twist, when people are given drugs that reduce anxiety, not only did the acceptance rate of unfair offers increase, but they were also associated with less brain activity in the amygdala, a part of the brain that is often active when people respond emotionally (Gospic et al., 2011).

Now, if only the apparently innate desire for fairness didn't lead human beings to inflict suffering so often on those whom they perceive as being unfair, and if only their ability to cooperate didn't lead so often to cooperation in waging war.

The Hindsight Bias

There is a reason for the saying that hindsight is 20/20. When people learn the outcome of an event or the answer to a question, they are often sure that they "knew it all along." Armed with the wisdom of hindsight, they see the outcome that actually occurred as inevitable, and they overestimate their ability to have predicted what happened beforehand (Fischhoff, 1975; Hawkins & Hastie, 1990). This **hindsight bias** shows up all the time from evaluations of relationships ("I always knew they would break up") to medical judgments ("I could have told you that mole was cancerous"), and beyond.

The hindsight bias can be adaptive. When we try to make sense of the past, we focus on explaining just one outcome, the one that actually occurred, because explaining outcomes that did not occur can be a waste of time. Then, in light of current knowledge, we reconstruct and misremember our previous judgment (Hoffrage, Hertwig, & Gigerenzer, 2000). But as Scott Hawkins and Reid Hastie (1990) wrote, "Hindsight biases represent the dark side of successful learning and judgment." They are the dark side because when we are sure that we knew something all along, we are also less willing to find out what we need to know in order to make accurate predictions in the future. In medical conferences, when doctors are told what the postmortem findings were for a patient who died, they tend to think the case was easier to diagnose than it actually was ("I would have known it was a brain tumour"), and so they learn less from the case than they should (Dawson et al., 1988).

hindsight bias The tendency to overestimate one's ability to have predicted an event once the outcome is known; the "I knew it all along" phenomenon.

confirmation bias The tendency to look for or pay attention only to information that confirms one's own belief.

Perhaps you feel that we are not telling you anything new because you have always known about the hindsight bias. But then, you may just have a hindsight bias about the hindsight bias.

The Confirmation Bias

When people want to make the most accurate judgment possible, they usually try to consider all of the relevant information. But as we saw in Chapter 2, when they are thinking about an issue they already feel strongly about, they often succumb to the **confirmation bias**, paying attention only to evidence that confirms their belief and finding fault with evidence or arguments that point in a different direction (Edwards & Smith, 1996; Kunda, 1990; Nickerson, 1998). You rarely hear someone say, "Oh, thank you for explaining to me why my lifelong philosophy of childrearing (or politics or investing) is wrong. I'm so grateful for the facts!" The person is more likely to say, "Oh, get lost, and take your nonsense with you."

Once you start looking for it, you will see the confirmation bias everywhere. Politicians brag about economic reports that confirm their party's position and dismiss counterevidence as biased or unimportant. Police officers who are convinced of a suspect's guilt take anything the suspect says or does as evidence that confirms it, including the suspect's claims of innocence (Davis, 2010). The confirmation bias also affects jury members. Instead of considering and weighing possible verdicts against the evidence, they quickly construct a story about what happened and then consider only the trial evidence that supports their version of events. These same people are the most confident in their decisions and most likely to vote for an extreme verdict (Kuhn, Weinstock, & Flaton, 1994). We bet you can see the confirmation bias in your own reactions to what you are learning in psychology. In thinking critically, most of us apply a double standard; we think most critically about results we dislike. That is why the scientific method can be so difficult. It forces us to consider evidence that *disconfirms* our beliefs.

GET INVOLVED! Confirming the Confirmation Bias

Suppose someone deals out four cards, each with a letter on one side and a number on the other. You can see only one side of each card:

Your task is to find out whether the following rule is true: "If a card has a vowel on one side, then it has an even number on the other side." Which two cards do you need to turn over to find out?

The vast majority of people say they would turn over the E and the 6, but they are wrong. You do need to turn over the E (a vowel), because if the number on the other side is even, it confirms the rule, and if it is odd, the rule is false. However, the card with the 6 tells you nothing. The rule does *not* say that a card with an even number must always have a vowel on the other side. Therefore, it doesn't matter whether the 6 has a vowel or a consonant on the other side. The card you do need to turn over is the 7, because if it has a vowel on the other side, that fact disconfirms the rule.

People do poorly on this problem because they are biased to look for confirming evidence and to ignore the possibility of disconfirming evidence. Don't feel too bad if you missed it. Most judges, lawyers, and people with PhDs do, too.

GET INVOLVED! Connect the Dots

Copy this figure, and try to connect the dots by using no more than four straight lines without lifting your pencil or pen. A line must pass through each point. Can you do it?

Most people have difficulty with this problem because they have a mental set to interpret the arrangement of dots as a square. They then assume that they can't extend a line beyond the apparent boundaries of the square. Now that you know this, you might try again if you haven't yet solved the puzzle. Some solutions are given at the end of this chapter.

Mental Sets

Another barrier to rational thinking is the development of a **mental set**, a tendency to try to solve new problems by using the same heuristics, strategies, and rules that worked in the past on similar problems. Mental sets make human learning and problem solving efficient; because of them, we do not have to keep reinventing the wheel. But mental sets are not helpful when a problem calls for fresh insights and methods. They cause us to cling rigidly to the same old assumptions and approaches, blinding us to better or more rapid solutions.

One general mental set is the tendency to find patterns in events. This tendency is adaptive because it helps us understand and exert some control over what happens in our lives. But it also leads us to see meaningful patterns even when they do not exist. For example, many people with arthritis think that their symptoms follow a pattern dictated by the weather. They suffer more, they say, when the barometric pressure changes or when the weather is damp or humid. Yet when 18 arthritis patients were followed for 15 months, no association whatsoever emerged between weather conditions and the patients' self-reported pain levels, their ability to function in daily life, or a doctor's evaluation of their joint tenderness (Redelmeier & Tversky, 1996). Of course, because of the confirmation bias, the patients refused to believe the results.

The Need for Cognitive Consistency

Mental sets and the confirmation bias cause us to avoid evidence that contradicts our beliefs. But what happens when disconfirming evidence finally smacks us in the face, and we cannot ignore or discount it any longer? As the twentieth century rolled to an end, predictions of the end of the world escalated. Similar doomsday predictions have been made throughout history and continue today; after all, you are reading this despite the alleged Mayan prophecy that the world would end in December, 2012. When these predictions fail, why do we never hear believers say, "Boy, what a fool I was"?

According to the theory of **cognitive dissonance**, people will resolve such conflicts in predictable, though not always obvious, ways (Festinger, 1957; see Chapter 8). *Dissonance*, the opposite of consistency (*consonance*), is a state of tension that occurs when you hold either two cognitions (beliefs, thoughts, attitudes) that are psychologically inconsistent with one another, or a belief that is incongruent with your behaviour. This tension is psychologically uncomfortable, so you will be motivated to reduce it.

mental set A tendency to solve problems using procedures that worked before on similar problems.

cognitive dissonance A state of tension that occurs when a person holds two cognitions that are psychologically inconsistent or when a person's belief is incongruent with his or her behaviour.

THINKING CRITICALLY

Ask questions.

Time and again, doomsday predictions fail. Why don't people who wrongly predict a devastating earthquake or the end of the world feel embarrassed when their forecasts flop?

You may do this by rejecting or modifying one of those inconsistent beliefs, changing your behaviour, denying the evidence, or rationalizing:

COGNITIVE DISSONANCE

Years ago, in a famous field study, Leon Festinger and two associates explored people's reactions to failed prophecies by infiltrating a group of people who thought the world would end on December 21 (Festinger, Riecken, & Schachter, 1956). The group's leader, whom the researchers called Marian Keech, promised that the faithful would be picked up by a flying saucer and whisked to safety at midnight on December 20th. Many of her followers quit their jobs and spent all their savings, waiting for the end to come. What would they do or say, Festinger and his colleagues wondered, to reduce the dissonance between "The world is still muddling along on the 21st" and "I predicted the end of the world and sold off all my worldly possessions"?

Festinger predicted that believers who had made no public commitment to the prophecy, who awaited the end of the world by themselves at home, would simply lose their faith. However, those who had acted on their conviction by selling their property and waiting with Keech for the spaceship would be in a state of dissonance. They would have to *increase* their religious belief to avoid the intolerable realization that they had behaved foolishly and others knew it. That is just what happened. At 4:45 a.m., long past the appointed hour of the saucer's arrival, the leader had a new vision. The world had been spared, she said, because of the impressive faith of her little band.

Cognitive dissonance theory predicts that in more ordinary situations, people will resist or rationalize information that conflicts with their existing ideas, just as the people in the arthritis study did. For example, cigarette smokers are often in a state of dissonance, because smoking is dissonant with the fact that smoking causes illness. Smokers may try to reduce the dissonance by trying to quit, by rejecting evidence that smoking is bad, by persuading themselves that they will quit later on, by emphasizing the benefits of smoking ("A cigarette helps me relax"), or by deciding that they don't want a long life, anyhow ("It will be shorter but sweeter").

You are particularly likely to reduce dissonance under three conditions (Aronson, 2012):

1 **When you need to justify a choice or decision that you made freely.** All car dealers know about buyer's remorse: The second that people buy a car, they worry that they made the wrong decision or spent too much, a phenomenon called **postdecision dissonance**. You may try to resolve this dissonance by deciding that the car you chose (or the toaster or house or spouse) is really, truly the best in the world. *Before* people make a decision, they can be open-minded, seeking information on the pros and cons of the choice at hand. *After* they make that choice, however, the confirmation bias will kick in, so that they will now notice all the good things about their decision and overlook or ignore evidence that they might have been wrong.

2 **When you need to justify behaviour that conflicts with your view of yourself.** If you consider yourself to be honest, cheating will put you in a state of dissonance. To avoid feeling like a hypocrite, you will try to reduce the dissonance by justifying your behaviour ("Everyone else does it"; "It's just this once"; "I had to do it to get into med school and learn to save lives"). Or if you see yourself as a kind

postdecision dissonance In the theory of cognitive dissonance, tension that occurs when you believe you may have made a bad decision.

FIGURE 9.2 The Justification of Effort
The more effort you put into reaching a goal, the more highly you are likely to value it. As you can see in the graph on the left, after people listened to a boring group discussion, those who went through a severe initiation to join the group rated it most highly (Aronson & Mills, 1959). In the photo, soldiers undergo special and difficult training to join an elite unit. They will probably become extremely devoted members.

Newscom

person and you harm someone, you may reduce your dissonance by blaming the person you have victimized or by finding other self-justifying excuses.

3 **When you need to justify the effort put into a decision or choice.** The harder you work to reach a goal, or the more you suffer for it, the more you will try to convince yourself that you value the goal, even if the goal turns out to be not so great after all (Aronson & Mills, 1959). This explains why hazing, whether in social clubs, on athletic teams, or in the military, turns new recruits into loyal members (see Figure 9.2). You might think that people would hate the group that caused them pain and embarrassment, but the cognition "I went through a lot of awful stuff to join this group" is dissonant with the cognition "only to find I hate the group." Therefore, people must decide either that the hazing was not so bad or that they really like the group. This mental reevaluation is called the **justification of effort**, and it is one of the most popular methods of reducing dissonance.

Some people are secure enough to own up to their mistakes instead of justifying them, and individuals and cultures vary in the kinds of experiences that cause them to feel dissonance. However, the need for cognitive consistency in those beliefs that are most central to our sense of self and our values is universal (Tavris & Aronson, 2007).

Overcoming Our Cognitive Biases

Sometimes our mental biases are a good thing. The ability to reduce cognitive dissonance helps us preserve our self-confidence and avoid sleepless nights second-guessing ourselves, and having a sense of fairness keeps us from behaving like self-centred louts. From this point of view, such biases are not so irrational after all. But our mental biases can also get us into trouble. The confirmation bias, the justification of effort, and a need to reduce postdecision dissonance permit people to stay stuck with decisions that eventually prove to be self-defeating, harmful, or incorrect. Physicians may continue using outdated methods, crown prosecutors may overlook evidence that a criminal suspect might be innocent, and managers may refuse to consider better business practices.

To make matters worse, most people have a "bias blind spot." They acknowledge that *other* people have biases that distort reality, but they think that they themselves are free of bias and see the world as it really is (Pronin, Gilovich, & Ross, 2004; Ross, 2010). This blind spot is itself a bias, and it is a dangerous one because it can prevent individuals, nations, ethnic groups, and religious groups from resolving conflicts with others. Each side thinks that its own proposals for ending a conflict, or its own analyses of a situation are reasonable and fair but the other side's are "biased."

Fortunately, the situation is not entirely hopeless. For one thing, people are not equally irrational in all situations. When they are doing things in which they have

justification of effort The tendency of individuals to increase their liking for something that they have worked hard or suffered to attain; a common form of dissonance reduction.

some expertise or are making decisions that have serious personal consequences, their cognitive biases often diminish (Smith & Kida, 1991). Further, once we understand a bias, we may, with some effort, be able to reduce or eliminate it, especially if we make an active, mindful effort to do so and take time to think carefully (Kida, 2006).

Some people, of course, seem to think more rationally than others a great deal of the time; we call them "intelligent." Just what is intelligence, and how can we measure and improve it? We take up these questions next.

Recite & Review

Recite: Make a rational decision now to say aloud what you know about the *affect heuristic*, the *availability heuristic*, the *framing effect*, the *fairness bias*, the *hindsight bias*, the *confirmation bias*, *mental set*, *cognitive dissonance*, *postdecision dissonance*, and the *justification of effort*.

Review: In hindsight, you might feel you know this material already, but read it again to be sure.

Now take this *Quick Quiz:*

1. In 2001, an unknown person sent anthrax through the mail, causing the deaths of five people. Many people became afraid to open their mail, although the risk for any given individual was extremely small. What heuristics help to explain this reaction?

2. *True or false:* Research on the Ultimatum Game shows that people usually act out of rational self-interest.

3. Stu meets a young woman at the student cafeteria. They hit it off and eventually get married. Says Stu, "I knew when I woke up that morning that something special was about to happen." What cognitive bias is affecting his thinking, charmingly romantic though it is?

4. In a classic experiment on cognitive dissonance, students did some boring, repetitive tasks and then had to tell another student, who was waiting to participate in the study, that the work was interesting and fun (Festinger & Carlsmith, 1959). Half the students were offered $20 for telling this lie and the others only $1. Based on what you have learned about cognitive dissonance reduction, which students do you think decided later that the tasks had been fun after all? Why?

Answers:

1. the affect and availability heuristics 2. false 3. the hindsight bias 4. The students who got only $1 were more likely to say that the task had been fun. They were in a state of dissonance because "The task was as dull as dishwater" is dissonant with "I said I enjoyed it—and for a mere dollar, at that." Those who got $20 could rationalize that the large sum (which really was large in the 1950s) justified the lie.

Learning Objectives

10 Discuss the the original purpose of intelligence testing and how it changed when IQ tests came to North America.

11 Evaluate the efforts to design intelligence tests that are free of cultural influence.

Measuring Intelligence: The Psychometric Approach

intelligence An inferred characteristic of an individual, usually defined as the ability to profit from experience, acquire knowledge, think abstractly, act purposefully, or adapt to changes in the environment.

Intelligent people disagree on just what intelligence is. Some equate it with the ability to reason abstractly, others with the ability to learn and profit from experience in daily life. Some emphasize the ability to think rationally, others the ability to act purposefully. These qualities are all probably part of what most people mean by **intelligence**, but theorists weigh them differently.

The traditional approach to intelligence, the **psychometric** approach, focuses on how well people perform on standardized aptitude tests, which are designed to measure the ability to acquire skills and knowledge. A typical intelligence test asks you to do several things: Provide a specific bit of information, notice similarities between objects, solve arithmetic problems, define words, fill in the missing parts of incomplete pictures, arrange pictures in a logical order, arrange blocks to resemble a design, assemble puzzles, use a coding scheme, or judge what behaviour would be appropriate in a particular situation. A statistical method called **factor analysis** helps to identify which basic abilities underlie performance on the various items. This procedure identifies clusters of correlated items that seem to be measuring some common ability, or factor.

More than a century of research has focused on a general ability, or *g* **factor**, that is purported to underlie various abilities and talents measured by intelligence tests (Gottfredson, 2002; Jensen, 1998; Lubinski, 2004; Spearman, 1927; Wechsler, 1955). The *g* factor is divided into **crystallized intelligence**, knowledge and skills that allow you to do arithmetic, define words, and make political decisions; and **fluid intelligence** or the capacity to reason and use information to solve new problems (Horn & Cattell, 1966). Although tests of *g* do a good job of predicting academic achievement, occupational success, and eminence in many fields (Kuncel, Hezlett, & Ones, 2004; Schmidt & Hunter, 2004; Simonton & Song, 2009), some scientists dispute the existence of a global quality called "intelligence," observing that a person can be smart in some areas and not in others (Gould, 1994; Guilford, 1988). Indeed, recent research by Adrian Owen at Western University suggests that there are many independent components to intelligence that rely on different areas of the brain (Hampshire et al., 2012). These different types of intelligence map onto known functions of distinct areas of the brain that appear to be independent. 👁

The Invention of IQ Tests

The first widely used intelligence test was devised in 1904, when the French Ministry of Education asked psychologist Alfred Binet (1857–1911) to find a way to identify children who were slow learners so that they could be given remedial work. The ministry was reluctant to let teachers identify such children because the teachers might have prejudices about poor children, or might assume that shy or disruptive children were mentally impaired. The government wanted a more objective approach. 👁

Binet's Brainstorm. Wrestling with the problem, Binet had a great insight: In the classroom, the responses of "dull" children resembled those of ordinary children of younger ages. Bright children, on the other hand, responded like children of older ages. The thing to measure, then, was a child's **mental age (MA)**, or level of intellectual development relative to that of other children. Then instruction could be tailored to the child's capabilities.

The test devised by Binet and his colleague, Théodore Simon, measured memory, vocabulary, and perceptual discrimination. Items ranged from those that most young children could do easily to those that only older children could handle, as determined by the testing of large numbers of children. A scoring system developed later by others used a formula in which a child's mental age was divided by the child's chronological age to yield an **intelligence quotient**, or **IQ** (a quotient is the result of division). With this formula, all average children, regardless of their age, would have an IQ of 100 because their mental age and their actual age would be the same. But a child of 8 who performed like the average 10-year-old would have a mental age of 10 and an IQ of 125 (10 divided by 8, times 100). 👁

Unfortunately, this method of computing IQ had serious flaws. At one age, scores might cluster tightly around the average, whereas at another age they might be more

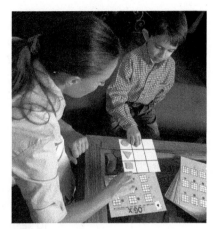

A child taking an intelligence test.

Laurent/AgeFotostock

👁—Watch the **Video**
The Basics: Theories of Intelligence in **MyPsychLab**

👁—Watch the **Video**
Are Intelligence Tests Valid: Robert Guthrie in **MyPsychLab**

👁—Watch the **Video**
Special Topics: Intelligence Testing, Then and Now in **MyPsychLab**

psychometrics The measurement of mental abilities, traits, and processes.

factor analysis A statistical method for analyzing the intercorrelations among various measures or test scores; clusters of measures or scores that are highly correlated are assumed to measure the same underlying trait, ability, or aptitude (factor).

g **factor** A general intellectual ability assumed by many theorists to underlie specific mental abilities and talents.

crystallized intelligence Cognitive skills and specific knowledge acquired over a lifetime; it is heavily dependent on education and tends to remain stable over time.

fluid intelligence The capacity to reason and use information to solve problems; it is relatively independent of education.

mental age (MA) A measure of mental development expressed in terms of the average mental ability at a given age.

intelligence quotient (IQ) A measure of intelligence originally computed by dividing a person's mental age by his or her chronological age and multiplying by 100; it is now derived from norms provided for standardized intelligence tests.

FIGURE 9.3 Expected Distribution of IQ Scores

In a large population, IQ scores tend to be distributed on a normal (bell-shaped) curve. On most tests, about 68% of all people will score between 85 and 115; about 95% will score between 70 and 130; and about 99.7% will score between 55 and 145. In any actual sample, however, the distribution will depart somewhat from the theoretical ideal.

▶ Watch the Video *Classic Footage of Language Assessment Portions of Stanford-Binet Intelligence Scale* in **MyPsychLab**

dispersed. As a result, the score necessary to be in the top 10% or 20% or 30% of your age group varied, depending on your age. Also, the IQ formula did not make sense for adults; a 50-year-old who scores like a 30-year-old does not have low intelligence! ([50/30] × 100 = 60.) Today, therefore, intelligence tests are scored differently. The average is usually set arbitrarily at 100; tests are constructed so that about two-thirds of all people score between 85 and 115; and individual scores are computed from tables based on established norms. These scores are still informally referred to as IQs, and they still reflect how a person compares with other people, either children of a particular age or adults in general. At all ages, the distribution of scores approximates a normal (bell-shaped) curve, with scores near the average more common than high or low scores (see Figure 9.3).

The IQ Test Comes to North America. Stanford psychologist Lewis Terman revised Binet's test and established norms for North American children. His version, the *Stanford–Binet Intelligence Scale*, was first published in 1916, and has been updated several times since. The test asks a person to perform a variety of tasks—to fill in missing words in sentences, answer questions requiring general knowledge, predict how a folded paper will look when unfolded, measure a quantity of water using two containers of different sizes, and distinguish between concepts that are similar but not exactly the same (such as, say, *vigour* and *energy*). The older the test taker is, the more the test requires in the way of verbal comprehension and fluency, spatial ability, and reasoning. ◉

Two decades later, David Wechsler designed another test expressly for adults, which became the *Wechsler Adult Intelligence Scale (WAIS)*; it was followed by the *Wechsler Intelligence Scale for Children* (WISC). Although the Wechsler tests produced a general IQ score, they also provided specific scores for different abilities: verbal comprehension, perceptual reasoning, processing speed, and working memory (the ability to hold information in mind so that it can be used for a task). Items measure a range of abilities, including vocabulary, arithmetic abilities, the ability to recognize similarities (e.g., "How are books and movies alike?"), general knowledge and comprehension (e.g., "Who was Sir John A. MacDonald?" "Why do people who want a divorce have to go to court?"), and nonverbal skills, such as the ability to re-create a block design within a specified time limit or to identify a part missing from a picture. (See Figure 9.4 for some sample items.)

FIGURE 9.4 Performance Tasks on the Wechsler Tests

Nonverbal items such as these are particularly useful for measuring the abilities of those who have poor hearing, are not fluent in the tester's language, have limited education, or resist doing classroom-type problems. A large gap between a person's verbal score and performance on nonverbal tasks such as these sometimes indicates a specific learning problem. (Object assembly, digit symbol, and picture completion are adapted from Cronbach, 1990.)

Picture arrangement
(Arrange the panels to make a meaningful story)

Object assembly
(Put together a jigsaw puzzle)

Digit symbol
(Using the key at the top, fill in the appropriate symbol beneath each number)

Picture completion
(Supply the missing feature)

Binet had emphasized that his test merely *sampled* intelligence and did not measure everything covered by that term. A test score, he said, could be useful, along with other information, for predicting school performance, but it should not be confused with intelligence itself. The tests were designed to be given individually, so that the test giver could tell when a child was ill or nervous, had poor vision, or was unmotivated. The purpose was to identify children with learning problems, not to rank all children. But when intelligence testing was brought from France to the North America, its original purpose got lost. IQ tests were not widely used to bring slow learners up to the average, but to categorize people in school and in the armed services according to their presumed "natural ability." The testers overlooked the fact that in North America, with its many ethnic groups, people did not all share the same background and experience (Gould, 1996).

CULTURE and *Intelligence Testing*

Intelligence tests developed between World War and the 1960s for use in schools favoured city children over rural ones, middle-class children over poor ones, and white children over nonwhite children. One item asked whether the Emperor Concerto was written by Beethoven, Mozart, Bach, Brahms, or Mahler. (The answer is Beethoven.) Critics complained that the tests did not measure the kinds of knowledge and skills that indicate intelligent behaviour in a minority neighbourhood or in the Far North. They feared that because teachers thought IQ scores revealed the limits of a child's potential, low-scoring children would not get the educational attention or encouragement they needed. ◉

Sometimes, despite your best intentions, you may have only limited success trying to reduce cultural bias. For instance, to illustrate this problem, Darou (1992) uses the following intelligence-test item: "Saw is to whine as snake is to _____". Because the item deals with tools and animals, it seems fairly culturally neutral. However, when Darou tested the item, he rapidly found out that indigenous peoples of the Far North had limited experience with snakes and that they had more experience with chain saws or hand saws, neither of which make the mechanical "whining" sound of table saws. As such, Darou quickly learned that despite his best intentions, this test item was biased.

Test-makers tried to incorporate knowledge and skills common to many different cultures. But these efforts were disappointing. One reason was that cultures differ in the problem-solving strategies they emphasize (Serpell, 1994). In the west, white, middle-class children typically learn to classify things by category—to say that an apple and a peach are similar because they are both fruits, and that a saw and a rake are similar because they are both tools. But children who are not trained in middle-class ways of sorting things may classify objects according to their sensory qualities or functions; they may say that an apple and a peach are similar because they taste good. Although a charming and innovative answer, it is one that test-givers have interpreted as less intelligent (Miller-Jones, 1989).

It is not the case that middle-class urban children always excel on intelligence tests. For instance, using a pictorial test of intelligence, researchers at McGill University found that Inuit children from northern Quebec consistently scored higher than predicted by the U.S. norms (Wright, Taylor, & Ruggiero, 1996). The intelligence test they used in this study required participants to pick a patterned piece to fit

◉—Watch the Video
Cultural Biases: Robert Guthrie
in **MyPsychLab**

💡 **THINKING CRITICALLY**

Consider other interpretations.

When tests find IQ differences between groups of children from different cultures, many people assume that the children who score lower are inherently less intelligent. What other explanations are possible?

stereotype threat A burden of doubt a person feels about his or her performance, due to negative stereotypes about his or her group's abilities.

into a hole cut from a larger pattern. It appears that individuals with intensive hunting and navigating experience tend to excel on tests that measure spatial or pattern discrimination and/or pattern reproduction, like the one used in the study by McGill researchers (Morton, Allen, & Williams, 1994).

Testing experts also discovered that cultural values and experiences affect many things besides responses to specific test items. These include a person's general attitude toward exams, comfort in the settings required for testing, motivation, rapport with the test-giver, competitiveness, comfort in solving problems independently rather than with others, and familiarity with the conventions for taking tests (Anastasi & Urbina, 1997; López, 1995; Sternberg, 2004). Further, Sternberg suggests that the kinds of activities that are considered intelligent in one culture may be incomprehensible to another (Sternberg, 2014).

Moreover, people's performance on IQ and other mental-ability tests may depend on their own expectations about how they will do, and those expectations are affected by cultural stereotypes. Stereotypes that portray women or members of certain ethnic, age, or socioeconomic groups as unintelligent can actually depress the performance of people in those groups. You might think that a woman would say, "So, sexists think women are dumb at math? I'll show them!" or that an indigenous person would say, "So racists believe that I'm not as smart as whites? Just give me that exam." But often that is not what happens.

On the contrary, such individuals commonly feel a burden of doubt about their abilities, creating an insecurity known as **stereotype threat** (Steele, 1992, 1997). The threat occurs when people believe that if they do not do well, they will confirm the stereotypes about their group. Negative thoughts intrude and disrupt their concentration ("I hate this test," "I'm no good at math") (Cadinu et al., 2005). The resulting anxiety may then worsen their performance or kill their motivation to even try to do well. 👁

👁—Watch the Video
In the Real World: Intelligence Tests and Stereotypes in **MyPsychLab**

STEREOTYPE THREAT

More than 300 studies have shown that stereotype threat can affect the test performance of many minorities, low-income people, women, and elderly people, all of whom perform better when they are not feeling self-conscious about themselves as members of negatively stereotyped groups (e.g., J. Aronson, 2010; Brown & Josephs, 1999; Inzlicht & Ben-Zeev, 2000; Levy, 1996; Quinn & Spencer, 2001; Steele & Aronson, 1995; Thomas & Dubois, 2011). Anything that increases the salience of group stereotypes can increase stereotype threat and affect performance, including taking the test in a setting where you are the only member from your group, or being asked to state your ethnicity before taking the test. The media and even some scholars have sometimes misinterpreted these results to mean that stereotype threat is the *only* reason for group differences in test performance, which it is not (Sackett, Hardison, & Cullen, 2004). It can be, however, an important contributing factor. Regardless, Sternberg reminds us that most of these differences rely on social categories rather than other definitions of ethnicity, such as biological factors related to where your ancestors came from (Sternberg, 2014).

What can be done to reduce stereotype threat? One possibility is simply to tell people about it (Good, Aronson, & Harder, 2008; Johns, Schmader, & Martens, 2005). But these solutions are unlikely to eliminate all group differences in test scores, and

Whether or not you feel "stereotype threat" depends on what category you are identifying with at the time. Asian women do worse on math tests when they see themselves as "women" (stereotype = poor at math) rather than as "Asians" (stereotype = good at math) (Shih, Pittinsky, & Ambady, 1999).

Bob Daemmrich/PhotoEdit Inc.

points to a dilemma at the heart of intelligence and mental-ability testing. Intelligence and other mental-ability tests put some groups of people at a disadvantage, yet they also measure skills and knowledge useful in the classroom. How can psychologists and educators recognize and accept cultural differences and, at the same time, promote the mastery of the skills, knowledge, and attitudes that can help people succeed in school and in the larger society?

Recite & Review

Recite: Check your Quiz Quotient (QQ) by saying aloud everything you can about *intelligence, psychometrics, factor analysis, g factor, crystallized and fluid intelligence, mental age, intelligence quotient*, IQ tests, and *stereotype threat*.

Review: Next, reread this section and make sure you really understand it.

Now take this *Quick Quiz:*

1. What was Binet's great insight?

2. *True or false:* IQ tests designed to avoid cultural bias frequently fail to eliminate such biases.

3. Hilda, who is 68, is about to take an IQ test, but she is worried because she knows that older people are often assumed to have diminished mental abilities. Hilda is being affected by _____.

Answers:

1. Mental age does not necessarily correspond to chronological age. 2. true 3. stereotype threat

Learning Objectives

12 List the three components of the triarchic theory of intelligence. Provide an example of each one.

13 Based on your reading in this section, defend the statement "Genius is 1% inspiration and 99% perspiration."

Dissecting Intelligence: The Cognitive Approach

Critics of standard intelligence tests point out that such tests tell us little about *how* a person goes about answering questions and solving problems. Nor do the tests explain why people with low scores often behave intelligently in real life, making smart consumer decisions, winning at the racetrack, and making wise choices in their relationships instead of repeating the same dumb patterns. Therefore, many scientists believe that the psychometric approach yields an incomplete picture of intelligence. Their aim is to identify the cognitive processes and strategies that people use when they are thinking and behaving intelligently. ◉

Watch the **Video**
The Big Picture: What Is Intelligence?
in **MyPsychLab**

Elements of Intelligence

One cognitive ingredient of intelligence is *working memory*, a complex capacity that enables you to manipulate information retrieved from long-term memory and interpret it appropriately for a given task. It permits you to juggle your attention while you

metacognition The knowledge or awareness of one's own cognitive processes, and the ability to monitor and control those processes.

triarchic [try-ARE-kick] theory of intelligence A theory of intelligence that emphasizes analytic, creative, and practical abilities.

are working on a problem, shifting your attention from one piece of information to another while ignoring distracting or irrelevant information. (We discuss working memory further in the next chapter.) People who do well on tests of working memory tend to be good at many complex real-life tasks requiring the control of attention, including reading comprehension, writing, and reasoning (Engle, 2002). In contrast, people with less working-memory capacity often have trouble keeping their minds on the job at hand and do not get better on a task, even with practice (Kane et al., 2007). Instead of trying to help people do better on individual tasks, therefore, might it be possible to improve their working memories, and thereby improve a crucial component of intelligence? Some scientists have reported success with working-memory training programs (Klingberg, 2010). Unfortunately, more rigorous recent research suggests that although, with practice, people do get better at specific working-memory tests, those gains do not translate to better performance on other tests of working memory or intelligence (Redick et al., 2012).

Another cognitive ingredient of intelligence is **metacognition**, the knowledge or awareness of your own cognitive processes and the ability to monitor and control those processes. Students who are weak in metacognition fail to notice when a passage in a textbook is difficult, and they do not always realize that they haven't understood what they've been reading. As a result, they spend too little time on difficult material and too much time on material they already know. They are overconfident about their comprehension and memory, and are surprised when they do poorly on exams (Dunlosky & Lipko, 2007). In contrast, students who are strong in metacognition check their comprehension by restating what they have read, testing themselves, backtracking when necessary, and questioning what they are reading. When time is limited, they tackle fairly easy material (where the payoff will be great), and then move on to more difficult material; as a result, they learn better (Metcalfe, 2009).

It works in the other direction, too: The kind of intelligence that enhances academic performance can also help you develop metacognitive skills. Students with poor academic skills typically fail to realize how little they know; they think they're doing fine (Dunning, 2005). The very weaknesses that keep them from doing well on tests or in their courses also keep them from realizing their weaknesses. In one study, students in a psychology course estimated how well they had just done on an exam relative to other students. As you can see in Figure 9.5, those who had performed in the bottom quartile greatly overestimated their own performance (Dunning et al., 2003). In contrast, people with strong academic skills tend to be more realistic. Often, they even underestimate slightly how their performance compares with the performance of others.

FIGURE 9.5 Ignorance Is Bliss
In school and in other settings, people who perform poorly often have poor metacognitive skills and therefore fail to recognize their own lack of competence. As you can see, the lower that students scored on an exam, the greater the gap between how they thought they had done and how they actually had done (Dunning et al., 2003).

Perceived Test Performance   Actual Test Performance

The Triarchic Theory. Having a good working memory and strong metacognitive skills, however, does not explain why some smart people keep making the same dumb choices in their relationships, or why people who don't seem especially bright are wildly successful in their jobs. That is why some psychological scientists reject the idea of a *g* factor as an adequate description of intelligence, and prefer to speak of different kinds of intelligence.

Robert Sternberg (1988, 2004, 2012), developed the **triarchic theory of intelligence** (*triarchic* means "three-part") that defines intelligence as "the skills and knowledge needed for success in life, according to one's own definition of success, within one's sociocultural context." A guitar player, builder, scientist, and farmer can all be called successful if they make the most of their strengths, correct their weaknesses, and adapt to, select, and shape their environments to improve their lives. According to Sternberg, successfully intelligent people another shell, which it will open in the same way. Incidents such as these and scores of others have convinced some biologists, psychologists, and ethologists that we are not the only animals with cognitive abilities—that "dumb beasts" are not so dumb after all. But how smart are they?

Animal Intelligence

In the 1920s, Wolfgang Köhler (1925) put chimpanzees in situations in which some tempting bananas were just out of reach and watched to see what the apes would do. Most did nothing, but a few turned out to be quite clever. If the bananas were outside the cage, the chimp might pull them in with a stick. If they were hanging overhead, and there were boxes in the cage, the chimp might pile up the boxes and climb on top of them to reach the fruit. Often the solution came after the chimp had been sitting quietly for a while. It appeared as though the animal had been thinking about the problem and was struck by a sudden insight.

Learning theorists felt that this seemingly impressive behaviour could be accounted for perfectly well by the standard principles of operant learning, without resorting to mental explanations (see Chapter 7). Because of their influence, for years any scientist who claimed that animals could think was likely to be ignored or laughed at. Today, however, the study of animal intelligence is booming, especially in the interdisciplinary field of **cognitive ethology**. (Ethology is the study of animal behaviour, especially in natural environments.) Cognitive ethologists argue that some animals can anticipate future events, make plans, and coordinate their activities with those of their comrades (Griffin, 2001).

When we think about animal cognition, we must be careful, because even complex behaviour that appears to be purposeful can be genetically prewired and automatic (Wynne, 2004). The assassin bug of South America catches termites by gluing nest material on its back as camouflage, but it is hard to imagine how the bug's tiny dab of brain tissue could enable it to plan this strategy consciously. Yet explanations of animal behaviour that leave out any sort of consciousness at all and that attribute animals' actions entirely to instinct do not seem to account for some of the amazing things that animals can do. Like the otter that uses a stone to crack mussel shells, many animals use objects in the natural environment as rudimentary tools, and in some nonhuman primates, the behaviour is learned.

cognitive ethology The study of cognitive processes in nonhuman animals.

In an early study of animal intelligence, Sultan, a talented chimpanzee studied by Wolfgang Köhler, was able to figure out how to reach a cluster of bananas by stacking some boxes and climbing on top of them.

SuperStock

Dodger, a 2-year-old dolphin in Shark Bay, Australia, carries a sea sponge on her sensitive beak as protection against stinging creatures and sharp coral. Dolphin "sponge moms" apparently teach the behaviour to their daughters.

Janet Mann/AP Images

Chimpanzee mothers occasionally show their young how to use stones to open hard nuts (Boesch, 1991). Orangutans in one particular Sumatran swamp have learned to use sticks as tools held in their mouths to pry insects from holes in tree trunks and to get seeds out of cracks in a bulblike fruit, whereas nearby groups of orangutans use only brute force to get to the delicacies (van Schaik, 2006). Even some nonprimates may have the capacity to learn to use tools, although the evidence remains controversial among ethologists. Female bottlenose dolphins off the coast of Australia attach sea sponges to their beaks while hunting for food, which protects them from sharp coral and stinging stonefish, and they seem to have acquired this unusual skill from their mothers (Krützen et al., 2005). Is this yet another case of mothers telling their daughters what to wear?

In the laboratory, nonhuman primates have accomplished even more surprising things. For example, dozens of studies have found that chimpanzees have a rudimentary sense of number. In one study, chimpanzees compared two pairs of food wells containing chocolate chips. One pair might contain, say, 5 chips and 3 chips, the other 4 chips and 3 chips. Allowed to choose which pair they wanted, the chimps almost always chose the one with the higher combined total, showing some sort of summing ability (Rumbaugh, Savage-Rumbaugh, & Pate, 1988). Chimpanzees can even remember over a period of 20 minutes which of two containers holds more bananas (e.g., 5 versus 8, or 6 versus 10), after watching the bananas being placed one at a time into the containers. In fact, they do as well as young children on this task (Beran & Beran, 2004).

One of the most controversial questions about animal cognition is whether any animals besides human beings have a **theory of mind**, a system of beliefs about the way one's own mind and the minds of others work, and an understanding of how thoughts and feelings affect behaviour. A theory of mind enables you to draw conclusions about the intentions, feelings, and beliefs of others; empathize with others ("What would I experience if I were in the other person's position?"); deceive others; recognize when someone else is lying; recognize yourself in a mirror; and know when others can or cannot see you. In human beings, a theory of mind starts to develop in the second year and is clearly present by about age 3 or 4 (see Chapter 13).

Some researchers believe that the great apes (chimpanzees, gorillas, and orangutans), dolphins, and elephants have certain abilities that reflect a theory of mind (de Waal, 2001; Plotnik, de Waal, & Reiss, 2006; Suddendorf & Whiten, 2001). In addition, chimpanzees console other chimps who are in distress, use deceptive tactics when competing for food, and point to draw attention to objects, suggesting that they are able to grasp what is going on in another chimp's mind. In the wild, when one male African chimp makes an exaggerated scratching movement on part of its body during social grooming—say, on the forehead—a comrade will then groom the indicated spot, even if he was already grooming some other spot (Pika & Mitani, 2006). Chimps and even monkeys may also be capable of some metacognition, the ability to understand and monitor their own cognitive processes. When they are tested on a new task, they will sometimes avoid difficult trials in which they are likely to be wrong. And they will press an icon on a touch screen to request "hints" provided by their human observers when they are unsure of the correct response, even when seeking a hint means getting a lesser reward for a correct answer (Kornell, 2009). These findings suggest that the animals know what they know and don't know.

Recently, reports have suggested that these abilities are not just limited to apes and monkeys. For instance, placing dogs in fMRIs has resulted in research that demonstrates a remarkable similarity between dog and human brains in the ability to process the emotional tone in speech (Andics et al., 2014) and use a touch screen to answer questions about basic concepts, like 'Which one of these pictures is a landscape?' (Range et al., 2008). When dogs are presented with unexpected answers to math questions they

theory of mind A system of beliefs about the way one's own mind and the minds of others work, and of how individuals are affected by their beliefs and feelings.

behave like the babies in the fairness experiment discussed previously. That is, when dogs were presented with a math problem that has the wrong answer (1+1=3), they spent more time looking at wrong answer than a problem with the right answer (West & Young, 2002). And with respect to the theory of mind, some researchers have demonstrated that dogs can follow gaze and other forms of communication as well as or better than apes (Hare et al., 2002). This dog cognition research has led some people to conclude that "dogs are people too!" We suggest that these studies remind us that there are many unresolved issues in animal cognition and that oversimplifications abound.

Animals and Language

A primary ingredient of human cognition is *language*, the ability to combine elements that are themselves meaningless into an infinite number of utterances that convey meaning (see Chapter 13). Do animals have anything comparable? Many people have wished they could ask their pet what it's like to be a dog, or a cat, or a horse. If only animals could speak!

To qualify as a language, a communication system must use combinations of sounds, gestures, or symbols that are *meaningful*, not random. It must permit *displacement*, communication about objects and events that are not present here and now but rather are displaced in time or space. And it must have a grammar (syntax) that permits *productivity*, the ability to produce and comprehend an infinite number of new utterances. By these criteria, no nonhuman species has its own language. Animals do communicate, of course, using gestures, body postures, facial expressions, vocalizations, and odours. Some of these signals have highly specific meanings: Vervet monkeys seem to have separate calls to warn about leopards versus eagles versus snakes (Cheney & Seyfarth, 1985). But vervets cannot combine these sounds to produce entirely novel utterances, as in "Look out, Harry, that eagle-eyed leopard is a real snake-in-the-grass."

Perhaps, however, some animals could acquire language if they got a little help from their human friends. Because the vocal tract of an ape does not permit speech, most investigators have used innovative approaches that rely on gestures or visual symbols. In one project, chimpanzees learned to use geometric plastic shapes arranged on a magnetic board (Premack & Premack, 1983). In another, they learned to punch symbols on a keyboard monitored by a computer (Rumbaugh, 1977). In yet another, they learned hundreds of signs in American Sign Language (ASL) (Fouts & Rigby, 1977; Gardner & Gardner, 1969). ◉

Animals in these studies learned to follow instructions, answer questions, and make requests. They even seemed to use their newfound skills to apologize for being disobedient, scold their trainers, and talk to themselves. Koko, a lowland gorilla, reportedly used signs to say that she felt happy or sad, to refer to past and future events, to mourn for her dead pet kitten, and to lie when she did something naughty (Patterson & Linden, 1981). Most important, the animals combined individual signs or symbols into longer utterances that they had never seen before.

Unfortunately, in their desire to talk to the animals and their affection for their primate friends, some early researchers overinterpreted the animals' utterances, reading all sorts of meanings and intentions into a single sign or symbol, ignoring scrambled word order ("banana eat me") and unwittingly giving nonverbal cues that might enable the apes to respond correctly. But over the past few decades, as researchers have improved their techniques, they have discovered that with careful training, chimps can indeed acquire some aspects of language, including the ability to use symbols to refer to objects. Some animals have also used signs spontaneously to converse with each other, suggesting that they are not merely imitating or trying to get a reward (Van Cantfort & Rimpau, 1982). Bonobos (a type of ape) are especially adept at language.

◉ **Watch** the **Video**
Classic Footage of Chimpanzees and Sign Language in **MyPsychLab**

Kanzi, a bonobo who answers questions and makes requests by punching symbols on a specially designed computer keyboard, also understands short English sentences. Kanzi is shown here with researcher Sue Savage-Rumbaugh.

Georgia State University/Department of Psychology

Alex was a remarkably clever bird. His abilities have raised intriguing questions about the intelligence of animals and their capacity for specific aspects of language.

Michael Goldman/Getty Images

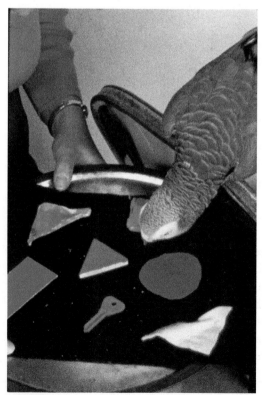

One bonobo named Kanzi has learned to understand English words, short sentences, and keyboard symbols without formal training (Savage-Rumbaugh & Lewin, 1994; Savage-Rumbaugh, Shanker, & Taylor, 1998). Kanzi responds correctly to commands such as "Put the key in the refrigerator" and "Go get the ball that is outdoors," even when he has never heard the words combined in that particular way before. He picked up language as children do—by observing others using it and through normal social interaction. He has also learned, with training, to manipulate keyboard symbols to request favourite foods or activities (games, TV, visits to friends) and to announce his intentions.

Research on animal language and comprehension of symbols is altering our understanding of animal cognition, and not only of primates. Dolphins have learned to respond correctly to requests made in an artificial language consisting of either computer-generated whistles or hand and arm gestures (Herman, Kuczaj, & Holder, 1993; Herman & Morrel-Samuels, 1996). Taking the meaning of symbols and their order (syntax) into account, they were able to understand the difference between "To left Frisbee, right surfboard take" and "To right surfboard, left Frisbee take."

Some psychologists are calling Border collies "the new chimps," ever since a Border collie named Rico and another named Betsy have acquired vocabularies of more than 200 words (Kaminski, Call, & Fisher, 2004; Morell, 2008). Since then, another Border collie, Chaser, has stunned the public and psychologists alike by showing that she knows more than 1100 words! When Chaser is asked to retrieve an object from another room, she can do it with astonishing accuracy. Even more impressive, when a new toy she had never seen (a Darwin doll) was placed among a dozen of her familiar toys and she was asked to fetch it, she did. She paused and walked among the toys, seemingly making an inference: Because none of the familiar toys matched the request, the new Darwin toy must be the one that was wanted.

Most amazingly, we now know that birds are not as bird-brained as once assumed. Irene Pepperberg (2000, 2002, 2008) has been working since the late 1970s with African grey parrots. Her favourite, named Alex, could count, classify, and compare objects by vocalizing English words. When he was shown up to six items and was asked how many there were, he responded with spoken (squawked?) English phrases, such as "two cork(s)" or "four key(s)." He even responded correctly to questions about items specified on two or three dimensions, as in "How many blue key(s)?" or "What matter [material] is orange and three-cornered?" Alex also made requests ("Want pasta") and answered simple questions about objects ("What colour [is this]?" "Which is bigger?"). When presented with a blue cork and a blue key and asked "What's the same?" he would correctly respond "colour." He actually scored slightly better with new objects than with familiar ones, suggesting that he was not merely "parroting" a set of stock phrases. He could sum two small sets of objects, such as nuts or jelly beans, for amounts up to six (Pepperberg, 2006).

Alex was also able to say remarkably appropriate things in informal interactions. He would tell Pepperberg, "I love you," "I'm sorry," and, when she was feeling stressed out, "Calm down." One day, Alex asked Pepperberg's accountant, "Wanna nut?" "No," said the accountant. "Want some water?" "No," she said. "A banana?" "No." After making several other suggestions,

Alex finally said, "What *do* you want?" (quoted in Talbot, 2008). To the sorrow of thousands of his admirers all over the world, Alex died suddenly in 2007. Pepperberg is continuing her work with other African greys.

Thinking about the Thinking of Animals

These results on animal language and cognition are impressive, but scientists are still divided over just what the animals in these studies are doing. Do they have true language? Are they thinking, in human terms? How intelligent are they? Are Kanzi, Chaser, and Alex unusual, or are they typical of their species? In their efforts to correct the centuries-old *under*estimation of animal cognition, are modern researchers now reading too much into their data and *over*estimating animals' abilities?

On one side are those who worry about *anthropomorphism*, the tendency to falsely attribute human qualities to nonhuman beings (Balter, 2012; Wynne, 2004). They like to tell the story of Clever Hans, a "wonder horse" at the turn of the last century who was said to possess mathematical and other abilities (Spitz, 1997). Clever Hans would answer math problems by stamping his hoof the appropriate number of times. But a little careful experimentation by psychologist Oskar Pfungst (1911/1965) revealed that when Clever Hans was prevented from seeing his questioners, his powers left him. It seems that questioners were staring at the horse's feet and leaning forward expectantly after stating the problem, then lifting their eyes and relaxing as soon as he completed the right number of taps. Clever Hans was indeed clever, but not at math or other human skills. He was merely responding to nonverbal signals that people were inadvertently providing. (Perhaps he had a high EQ.)

On the other side are those who warn against *anthropodenial*, the tendency to think, mistakenly, that human beings have nothing in common with other animals, that are, after all, our evolutionary cousins (de Waal, 2001; Fouts, 1997). The need to see our own species as unique, they say, may keep us from recognizing that other species, too, have cognitive abilities, even if not as sophisticated as our own. Those who take this position point out that most modern researchers have gone to great lengths to avoid the Clever Hans problem.

The outcome of this debate is bound to affect the way we view ourselves and our place among other species. Perhaps we can find a way to study and think about animal abilities and emotions without assuming sentimentally that they are just like our own. There is no disputing, however, that scientific discoveries about the cognitive abilities of our animal relatives are teaching us to have greater respect for animal minds.

We human beings are used to thinking of ourselves as the smartest species around because of our astounding ability to adapt to change, find novel solutions to problems, invent endless new gizmos, and use language to create everything from puns to poetry. Yet, as this chapter has shown, we are not always as wise in our thinking as we might think. We can, however, boast of one crowning accomplishment: We are the only species that tries to understand its own misunderstandings and improve itself (Gazzaniga, 2008). We want to know what we don't know; we are motivated to overcome our mental shortcomings. This uniquely human capacity for self-examination is probably the best reason to remain optimistic about our cognitive abilities.

💡 **THINKING CRITICALLY**

Consider other interpretations.

The Granger Collection

This old photo shows Clever Hans in action. His story has taught scientists to beware of anthropomorphism when they interpret findings on animal cognition.

Recite: Recite aloud to the smartest animal you can find what you know about *cognitive ethology*, animal intelligence, evidence that some animals have a *theory of mind* and a degree of metacognition, and animals' capacity for language.

Review: Next, reread this section.

Now take this *Quick Quiz:*

1. Which of the following abilities have primates demonstrated, either in the natural environment or the laboratory? (a) the use of objects as simple tools; (b) the summing of quantities; (c) the use of symbols to make requests; (d) an understanding of short English sentences

2. A honeybee performs a little dance that communicates to other bees the direction and distance of food. Because the bee can "talk" about something that is located elsewhere, its communication system shows _____. But because the bee can create only utterances that are genetically wired into its repertoire, its communication system lacks _____.

3. Barnaby thinks his pet snake Curly is harbouring angry thoughts about him because Curly has been standoffish and won't curl around his neck anymore. What error is Barnaby making?

Answers:

1. all of them 2. displacement, productivity 3. anthropomorphism

Taking Psychology with You

THINKING CRITICALLY IN EVERYDAY LIFE

Becoming More Creative

Throughout this book, we emphasize the importance of asking questions, thinking of nonobvious explanations, and examining assumptions and biases. These critical-thinking guidelines involve creativity as much as they do reasoning.

Take a few moments to test your own creativity by answering these items based on the Remote Associates Test, a test of mental flexibility. Your task is to come up with a fourth word that is associated with each item in a set of three words (Mednick, 1962). For example, an appropriate answer for the set *news–clip–wall* is *paper*. Got the idea? Now try these (the answers are given at the end of this chapter):

1. piggy—green—lash
2. surprise—political—favour
3. mark—shelf—telephone
4. stick—maker—tennis
5. cream—cottage—cloth

Creative thinking requires you to associate elements of a problem in new ways by finding unexpected connections among them, as on the Remote Associates Test. People who are uncreative rely on *convergent thinking*, following a particular set of steps that they think will converge on one correct solution. Then, once they have solved a problem, they tend to develop a mental set and approach future problems the same way. Creative people, in contrast, exercise *divergent thinking*; instead of stubbornly sticking to one tried-and-true path, they explore side alleys and generate several possible solutions. They come up with new hypotheses, imagine other interpretations, and look for connections that are not immediately obvious. For artists and novelists, of course, creativity is a job requirement, but it also takes creativity to invent a tool, put together a recipe from leftovers, find ways to distribute unsold food to the needy, or decorate your room. Creative people tend to have three characteristics (Helson, Roberts, & Agronick, 1995; McCrae, 1987; Schank, 1988):

> ❝Creativity is not just 'in you'; it depends also on the situations you're in. It flourishes when schools and employers encourage intrinsic motivation instead of just handing out gold stars.❞

Nonconformity

Creative individuals are not overly concerned about what others think of them. They are willing to risk ridicule by proposing ideas that may initially appear foolish or off the mark. Geneticist Barbara McClintock's research was ignored or belittled by many for nearly 30 years. But she was sure she could show how genes move around and produce sudden changes in heredity. In 1983, when McClintock won the Nobel Prize, the judges called her work the second-greatest genetic discovery of our time, after the discovery of the structure of DNA.

Curiosity

Creative people are open to new experiences; they notice when reality contradicts expectations, and they are curious about the reason. Wilhelm Roentgen, a German physicist, was studying cathode rays when he noticed a strange glow on one of his screens. Other people had seen the glow, but they ignored it because it didn't jibe with their understanding of cathode rays. Roentgen studied the glow, found it to be a new kind of radiation, and thus discovered X-rays.

Persistence

After that imaginary lightbulb goes on over your head, you still have to work hard to make the illumination last. Or, as Thomas Edison, who invented the real lightbulb, reportedly put it, "Genius is one percent inspiration and ninety-nine percent perspiration." No invention or work of art springs forth full-blown from a person's head. False starts and painful revisions occur along the way.

If you are thinking critically (and creatively!), you may wonder whether these qualities are enough. Do you recall the "Termites" who were the most successful? They were smart, but they also got plenty of encouragement for their efforts. Likewise, some individuals may be more creative than others, but *circumstances* can foster or inhibit creative accomplishment. Creativity flourishes when schools and employers encourage intrinsic motivation (a sense of accomplishment, intellectual curiosity, the sheer love of an activity) and not just extrinsic rewards such as gold stars and money (see Chapter 7 and Chapter 12). It thrives when you work with others who have different ideas, perspectives, and occupational training, because they tend to jolt you out of your familiar way of seeing problems. But individual creativity often requires solitude—having "lazy" time to daydream productively—and the freedom to perform a task or solve a problem independently. "Brainstorming" sessions tend to produce more storm than brain (Amabile, 1983; Amabile & Khaire, 2008). Finally, organizations encourage creativity when they let people take risks, give them plenty of time to think about problems, and welcome innovation.

In sum, if you hope to become more creative, you can do two things. One is to cultivate your own talents and qualities of curiosity, intrinsic motivation, and self-discipline. The other is to seek out the kinds of situations that will permit you to express your abilities and experiment with new ideas. ✳

✳ **Explore** the **Concept** *What Is Creativity?* in **MyPsychLab**

Summary

MyPsychLab can help you get a better grade. Test your knowledge and grasp difficult concepts through
- Custom study plans: See where you are strong and where you are wrong
- Multimedia, including videos and interactive simulations
- Dynamic Study Modules: flashcards for self-study that ensure you achieve mastery of course concepts

Thought: Using What We Know

- Thinking is the mental manipulation of information. Our mental representations simplify and summarize information from the environment.

- A *concept* is a mental category that groups objects, relations, activities, abstractions, or qualities that share certain properties. *Basic concepts* have a moderate number of instances and are easier to acquire than concepts with few or many instances. *Prototypical* instances of a concept are more representative than others. The language we use to express concepts may influence how we perceive and think about the world.

- *Propositions* are made up of concepts and express a unitary idea. They may be linked together to form *cognitive schemas*, which serve as mental models of aspects of the world. *Mental images* also play a role in thinking.

- Not all mental processing is conscious. *Subconscious processes* lie outside of awareness but can be brought into consciousness when necessary. They allow us to perform two or more actions at once when one action is highly automatic. But *multitasking*—toggling between tasks that are not automatic—is usually inefficient, introduces errors, and can even be dangerous, as when done while driving. *Nonconscious processes* remain outside of awareness but nonetheless affect behaviour; they are involved in *implicit learning*, when we learn something but don't know how we learned it and aren't able to state exactly what we've learned. Even conscious processing may be carried out in a *mindless* fashion if we overlook changes in context that call for a change in behaviour.

- Conscious and nonconscious processes are both involved in problem solving and making decisions. When problems are well defined, they can often be solved by applying an *algorithm;* when problems are fuzzier, however, people often must apply rules of thumb called *heuristics*. Some problems lend themselves to nonconscious processes such as *intuition* and *insight*. "Fast" thinking applies to rapid, intuitive, emotional, almost automatic decisions; "slow" thinking requires intellectual effort, which is why most people rely on the former—and make mistakes.

Reasoning Rationally

- *Reasoning* is purposeful mental activity that involves drawing inferences and conclusions from observations, facts, or assumptions. *Formal reasoning problems* provide the information necessary to reach a conclusion or solution and permit a single correct or best answer; *informal reasoning problems* often have no clearly correct solution and thus require *dialectical thinking* about opposing points of view.

- Studies of *reflective judgment* show that many people have trouble thinking dialectically. *Prereflective* thinkers do not distinguish between knowledge and belief or between belief and evidence. *Quasi-reflective* thinkers believe that because knowledge is sometimes uncertain, any judgment about the evidence is purely subjective. Those who think *reflectively* understand that although some things cannot be known with certainty, some judgments are more valid than others, depending on their coherence, fit with the evidence, and so on. Supported opportunities to engage in reflective thinking moves people gradually closer to reflective judgment.

Barriers to Reasoning Rationally

- The ability to reason clearly and rationally is affected by many cognitive biases. People tend to exaggerate the likelihood of improbable events in part because of the *affect* and *availability heuristics*. They are swayed in their choices by the desire to *avoid loss* and by the *framing effect*—how the choice is presented. They forgo economic gain because of a *fairness bias*, which, as discussed in "Biology and Economic Choice," appears to have evolutionary roots and is being studied in primates and human toddlers, and by using brain scans. They often overestimate their ability to have made accurate predictions (the *hindsight bias*) and attend mostly to evidence that confirms what they want to believe (the *confirmation bias*). Another barrier to reasoning is that people tend to form *mental sets*, seeing patterns where none exist.

- The theory of *cognitive dissonance* holds that people are motivated to reduce the tension that exists when two cognitions, or a cognition and a behaviour, conflict. They can reduce dissonance by rejecting or changing a belief, changing their behaviour, or rationalizing. Dissonance is most uncomfortable, and motivates efforts to reduce it, under three conditions: after a decision has been made (*postdecision dissonance*); when people's actions violate their concept of themselves as honest and kind; and when they have put hard work into an activity (the *justification of effort*).

Measuring Intelligence: The Psychometric Approach

- *Intelligence* is hard to define. The *psychometric approach* focuses on how well people perform on standardized aptitude tests. Most psychometric psychologists believe that a general ability, a *g factor*, underlies this performance. However others argue that a person can do well in some kinds of reasoning or problem solving but not others and that these differences reflect the known functions of the brain.

- The *intelligence quotient*, or *IQ*, represents how well a person has done on an intelligence test compared to other people. Alfred Binet designed the first widely used intelligence test to identify children who could benefit from remedial work. But in North America, people assumed that intelligence tests revealed natural ability and used the tests to categorize people in school and in the armed services.

- IQ tests have been criticized for being biased in favour of white, middle-class people. However, as discussed in "Culture and Intelligence Testing," efforts to construct tests that are free of cultural influence have been disappointing. Culture affects nearly everything to do with taking a test, from attitudes to problem-solving strategies. Negative stereotypes about a person's ethnicity, gender, or age may cause the person to feel *stereotype threat*, which can lead to anxiety that interferes with test performance.

Dissecting Intelligence: The Cognitive Approach

- *Cognitive approaches* to intelligence emphasize several kinds of intelligence and the strategies people use to solve problems. An important cognitive ingredient of intelligence is *working memory*, which allows you to juggle your attention when thinking or working on a problem and to ignore distractions. Another is *metacognition*, the understanding and monitoring of your own cognitive processes.

- Sternberg's *triarchic theory* proposes three aspects of intelligence: *componential/analytic*, *experiential/creative*, and *contextual/practical*. Contextual intelligence allows you to acquire *tacit knowledge*, practical strategies that are important for success but are not explicitly taught. *Emotional intelligence* is also important—the ability to identify your own and other people's emotions accurately, express emotions clearly, and regulate emotions in yourself and others.

- Intellectual achievement also depends on motivation, hard work, and self-discipline. Cross-cultural work shows that beliefs about the origins of mental abilities, parental standards, and attitudes toward education play a big role in creating differences in academic performance.

Animal Minds

- Some researchers, especially those in *cognitive ethology*, argue that nonhuman animals have greater cognitive abilities than has previously been thought. Some animals can use objects as simple tools. Chimpanzees and birds have shown evidence of a simple understanding of number. Some researchers believe that the great apes, dolphins, and elephants have aspects of a *theory of mind*, an understanding of how their own minds and the minds of others work. In some apes and monkeys, these aspects may include some metacognition.

- In projects using visual symbol systems or American Sign Language (ASL), primates have acquired linguistic skills. Some animals (even nonprimates such as dolphins and African grey parrots) seem able to use simple grammatical ordering rules to convey or comprehend meaning. However, scientists are divided about how to interpret the findings on animal cognition, with some worrying about *anthropomorphism* and others about *anthropodenial*.

Taking Psychology with You

- Creativity is part of critical thinking. Creative people rely on *divergent* rather than *convergent* thinking when solving problems. They tend to be nonconformist, curious, and persistent, but certain circumstances also foster creative accomplishment.

Key Terms

concept **298**
basic concepts **298**
prototype **298**
proposition **299**
cognitive schema **299**
mental image **299**
subconscious processes **300**
nonconscious processes **301**
implicit learning **301**
algorithm **301**

heuristic **302**
reasoning **303**
dialectical reasoning **303**
affect heuristic **306**
availability heuristic **307**
framing effect **307**
hindsight bias **309**
confirmation bias **310**
mental set **311**
cognitive dissonance **311**

postdecision
    dissonance **312**
justification of effort **313**
intelligence **314**
psychometrics **315**
factor analysis **315**
g factor **315**
crystallized intelligence **315**
fluid intelligence **315**
mental age (MA) **315**

intelligence quotient
    (IQ) **315**
stereotype threat **318**
metacognition **320**
triarchic theory of
    intelligence **320**
tacit knowledge **321**
emotional intelligence **321**
cognitive ethology **325**
theory of mind **326**

Some solutions to the nine-dot problem in the Get Involved exercise on page 311 (from Adams, 2001):

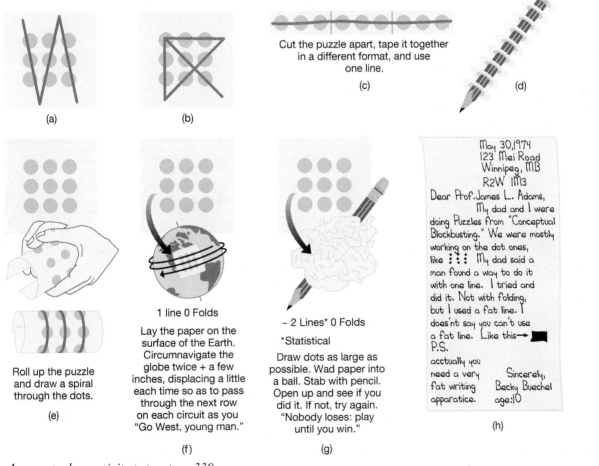

(a)

(b)

Cut the puzzle apart, tape it together in a different format, and use one line.

(c)

(d)

1 line 0 Folds

Roll up the puzzle and draw a spiral through the dots.

(e)

Lay the paper on the surface of the Earth. Circumnavigate the globe twice + a few inches, displacing a little each time so as to pass through the next row on each circuit as you "Go West, young man."

(f)

~ 2 Lines* 0 Folds

*Statistical

Draw dots as large as possible. Wad paper into a ball. Stab with pencil. Open up and see if you did it. If not, try again. "Nobody loses: play until you win."

(g)

May 30, 1974
123 Mei Road
Winnipeg, MB
R2W 1M3
Dear Prof. James L. Adams,
    My dad and I were doing Puzzles from "Conceptual Blockbusting." We were mostly working on the dot ones, like ⋮⋮⋮ My dad said a man found a way to do it with one line. I tried and did it. Not with folding, but I used a fat line. I does'nt say you can't use a fat line. Like this→ ▰
P.S.
acctually you need a very fat writing apparatice.
    Sincerely,
    Becky Buechel
    age: 10

(h)

Answers to the creativity test on page 330:
back, party, book, match, cheese

10 Memory

Ask questions. . . be willing to wonder

Is everything that ever happened to us stored in the brain?

———

What strategies can help us remember better?

———

Why can't we remember events from our first two years?

———

Do people repress traumatic memories?

In 1982, Thomas Sophonow was arrested for the murder of Barbara Stoppel, a waitress in a doughnut shop in Winnipeg. In 1983 and 1985 he was convicted of murder, largely due to the eyewitness testimony of four individuals who identified him as the killer. However, the courts overturned his conviction in 1986 due to problems with the trial. With a fourth trial looming, in 1986 the Supreme Court of Canada ordered him acquitted. What happened? Given that four eyewitnesses came forward, did a guilty man get away with murder because of some legal technicality? Often, individuals (like Thomas Sophonow) are sent to prison based on the strength of eyewitness testimony. But is an eyewitness's account always reliable? In the absence of corroborating evidence, should a witness's confidence in her memory be sufficient for establishing guilt? A lot is at stake when answering these questions: justice for the victims and avoiding false convictions.

The Sophonow case did not end in 1986. At the conclusion of this chapter we will tell you what ultimately happened.

This chapter will raise some fascinating but troubling questions about memory: When should we trust our own memories and when should we be cautious about doing so? We all forget things that *did* happen; do we also "remember" things that *never* happened? Are memory malfunctions the exception to the rule or are they commonplace? And if memory is not always reliable, how can any of us hope to know the story of our own lives? How can we hope to understand the past?

335

THINKING CRITICALLY

Ask questions.

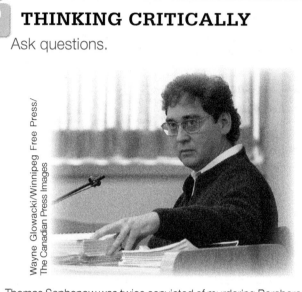

Thomas Sophonow was twice convicted of murdering Barabara Stoppel, based largely on eyewitness testimony. In thinking about cases in which an eyewitness provides the only evidence against a suspect, a critical thinker would ask: How accurate is eyewitness testimony, even when the witness is the victim? How trustworthy are our memories, even of traumatic events? Psychologists have learned some startling answers, as this chapter will show.

Learning Objectives

1. Criticize the commonly held view that memory works like a camera. Describe a more accurate view of how memory does work.

2. Describe the features of a flashbulb memory.

3. List three features of an event that can lead to confabulation.

Reconstructing the Past

Memory refers to the capacity to retain and retrieve information, and also to the structures that account for this capacity. Human beings are capable of astonishing feats of memory. Most of us can easily remember the words to *O Canada*, how to use a bank machine, the most embarrassing experience we ever had, and zillions of other details. Memory confers competence; without it, we would be as helpless as newborns, unable to carry out even the most trivial of our daily tasks. Memory also endows us with a sense of personal identity; each of us is the sum of our recollections, which is why we feel so threatened when others challenge our memories. Individuals and cultures alike rely on a remembered history for a sense of coherence and meaning; memory gives us our past and guides our future.

Can you imagine what life would be like if you could never form any new memories? That does happen for older people who are suffering with dementia; sometimes this happens to younger people who have brain injuries or diseases. Henry Molaison's case is the most intensely studied in the annals of medicine (Corkin, 1984; Corkin et al., 1997; Hilts, 1995; Milner, 1970; Ogden & Corkin, 1991). In 1953, when Henry, known in the scientific literature as H. M., was 27, surgeons made a last-ditch effort to cure his severe and life-threatening epilepsy by removing his hippocampus, most of his amygdala, and a portion of his temporal lobes. The operation did achieve its goal: Henry's seizures were milder and were controlled by medication. However, McGill's

Brenda Milner observed that his memory had been affected profoundly. Although he appeared to recall most events that had occurred before the operation, he could no longer remember new experiences for much longer than 15 minutes. Facts, songs, stories, and faces all vanished like water down the drain. He would read the same magazine over and over without realizing it. He could not recall the day of the week, the year, or even his last meal. ◉

Henry loved to do crossword puzzles and play bingo, skills he had learned long before the operation. Curiously, he knew he had memory problems. He would occasionally recall an unusually emotional event, such as the assassination of someone named Kennedy, and he sometimes remembered that both of his parents were dead. But according to Suzanne Corkin, who studied H. M. extensively, these "islands of remembering" were the exceptions in a vast sea of forgetfulness. This good-natured man never knew the scientists who studied him for decades. He always thought he was much younger than he really was, and he was unable to recognize a photograph of his own face; he was stuck in a time warp from the past. Henry died in 2008 at age 82, and one neuroscientist remarked that H. M. gave science the ultimate gift: his memory (Ogden, 2012). He taught neuroscientists a great deal about the biology of memory; before his surgery, scientists did not realize the important role played by the hippocampus. We will meet H. M. again at several points in this chapter.

The Manufacture of Memory

People's descriptions of memory have always been influenced by the technology of their time: from wax tablets to print libraries to smartphones that automatically capture every moment of their lives (Simons & Chabris, 2011). Popular and appealing though this belief about memory is, it is utterly wrong. Not everything that happens to us or impinges on our senses is tucked away for later use. Memory is selective. If it were not, our minds would be cluttered with mental junk: the temperature at noon on Thursday, the price of milk two years ago, a phone number needed only once. Moreover, recalling a memory is not at all like replaying a recording of an event. It is more like watching a few unconnected frames and then figuring out what the rest of the scene must have been like.

One of the first scientists to make this point was the British psychologist Sir Frederic Bartlett (1932). Bartlett asked people to read lengthy, unfamiliar stories from other cultures and then tell the stories back to him. As the volunteers tried to recall the stories, they made interesting errors: They often eliminated or changed details that did not make sense to them, and they added other details from their own culture—details that made the story make more sense. Memory, Bartlett concluded, must therefore be largely a *reconstructive* process. We may reproduce some kinds of simple information by rote, said Bartlett, but when we remember complex information, we typically alter it in ways that help us make sense of the material, based on what we already know or think we know. Since Bartlett's time, numerous studies have supported the original observation, showing that it applies to all kinds of memories.

In reconstructing their memories, people often draw on many sources. Suppose that someone asks you to describe one of your early birthday parties. You may have some direct recollection of the event, but you may also incorporate information from family stories, photographs, or home videos, and even from accounts of other people's birthdays and re-enactments of birthdays on television. You take all these bits and pieces and build one integrated account. Later, you may not be able to distinguish your actual memory from information you got elsewhere—a

◉—⌐Watch the Video
Special Topics: When Memory Fails
in MyPsychLab

If this happy child remembers this birthday party later in life, her constructions may include information picked up from family photographs, videos, and stories. And she may be unable to distinguish their actual memories from information they got elsewhere.

Zak Waters/Alamy

source misattribution The inability to distinguish an actual memory of an event from information you learned about the event elsewhere.

confabulation Confusion of an event that happened to someone else with one that happened to you, or a belief that you remember something when it never actually happened.

phenomenon known as **source misattribution**, or sometimes *source confusion* (Johnson, Hashtroudi, & Lindsay, 1993; Mitchell & Johnson, 2009).

A dramatic instance of reconstruction once occurred with H. M. (Ogden & Corkin, 1991). After eating a chocolate Valentine's Day heart, H. M. stuck the shiny red wrapping in his shirt pocket. Two hours later, while searching for his handkerchief, he pulled out the paper and looked at it in puzzlement. When a researcher asked why he had the paper in his pocket, he replied, "Well, it could have been wrapped around a big chocolate heart. It must be Valentine's Day!" But a short time later, when she asked him to take out the paper again and say why he had it in his pocket, he replied, "Well, it might have been wrapped around a big chocolate rabbit. It must be Easter!" Sadly, H. M. *had* to reconstruct the past; his damaged brain could not recall it in any other way. But those of us with normal memory abilities also reconstruct, far more often than we realize.

Of course, some shocking or tragic events—such as earthquakes or accidents—do hold a special place in memory, especially when we have experienced them personally (Talarico, 2009; Tinti et al., 2009). Years ago, these vivid recollections of emotional and important events were labelled *flashbulb memories*, to capture the surprise, illumination, and seemingly photographic detail that characterize them (Brown & Kulik, 1977). As such, it should be no surprise that flashbulb memories can occur for positive events, such as starting university or joining a highly coveted club (Kraha & Boals, 2014; Talarico, 2009) and that they can last for years. In a Danish study, older people who had lived through the Nazi occupation of their country in World War II retained accurate memories, for decades, of the day that the radio announced liberation (Berntsen & Thomsen, 2005).

However, flashbulb memories are not usually complete or accurate. People typically remember the *gist* of a startling, emotional event they experienced or witnessed, but when researchers question them about their memories over time, errors creep into the details, and after a few years, some people even forget the gist (Neisser & Harsch, 1992; Talarico & Rubin, 2003). Just one day after the 2001 attacks on the World Trade Centre and the Pentagon, researchers asked university students when they had first heard the news of the attacks, who had told them the news, and what they had been doing at the time. They also asked the students to report details about a mundane event from the days immediately before the attacks, to allow a comparison of ordinary memories with flashbulb ones. The students were retested at various intervals up to eight months later. Over time, the vividness of the flashbulb memories and the students' confidence in these memories remained higher than for the everyday memories. Their confidence, however, was misplaced. The details the students reported became less and less consistent (and equally inconsistent) for *both* types of memories (Talarico & Rubin, 2003; 2007).

Even with flashbulb memories, then, facts tend to get mixed with fiction. Remembering is an active process, one that involves not only dredging up stored information but also putting two and two together to reconstruct the past. Sometimes, unfortunately, we put two and two together and get five.

The Conditions of Confabulation

Because memory is reconstructive, it is subject to **confabulation**—confusing an event that happened to someone else with one that happened to you, or coming to believe that you remember something that never really happened. Such confabulations are especially likely under certain circumstances (Garry et al., 1996; Hyman & Pentland, 1996; Mitchell & Johnson, 2009):

NEVER FORGETS   SOMETIMES FORGETS   ALWAYS FORGETS

Sidney Harris

1 **You have thought, heard, or told others about the imagined event many times.** Suppose that at family gatherings you keep hearing about the time that Uncle Gord got so excited during a soccer game that he began pounding the couch with his fist so hard that the wall collapsed. The story is so colourful that you can practically see it unfold in your mind. The more you think about this event, the more likely you are to believe that you actually were there and that it happened as you "remember" it, even if you were sound asleep in another house. This process has been called *imagination inflation*, because your own active imagination inflates your belief that the event really occurred as you assume it did (Garry & Polaschek, 2000). Even merely explaining how a hypothetical childhood experience *could* have happened inflates people's confidence that it really did occur. Explaining an event makes it seem more familiar and thus real (Sharman, Manning, & Garry, 2005).

2 **The image of the event contains lots of details that make it feel real.** Ordinarily, we can distinguish imagined events from real ones by the amount of detail we recall; memories of real events tend to contain more details. But the longer you think about an imagined event, the more likely you are to embroider those images with details—what Gord was wearing, the collapsing couch, the sound of the TV—and these added details will persuade you that you really do remember the event and aren't just confusing other people's reports with your own experience (Johnson et al., 2011).

3 **The event is easy to imagine.** If imagining an event takes little effort (as does visualizing a man pounding the couch with his fist), then we are especially likely to think that a memory is real rather than false. In contrast, when we must make an effort to form an image of an experience, a place we have never seen, or an activity that is utterly foreign to us, we use our cognitive effort as a cue that we are merely imagining the event or have heard about it from others.

As a result of confabulation, you may end up with a memory that feels emotionally, vividly real to you and yet is false (Mitchell & Johnson, 2009). This means that your feelings about an event, no matter how strong they are, do not guarantee that the event really took place. In fact, it is important to know that false memories can be as stable over time as true ones (Roediger & McDermott, 1995). There's just no getting around it: Memory is reconstructive.

In the 1980s, Whitley Strieber published *Communion*, in which he claimed to have had encounters with nonhuman beings, possibly aliens from outer space. An art director designed this striking image for the cover. Ever since, many people have assumed that this is what an extraterrestrial must look like, and some have imported the image into their own confabulated memories of alien abduction.

Moviestore collection Ltd/Alamy

Recite & Review

Recite: Reconstruct what you just read and say what you can remember about why memory is reconstructive, and about *source misattribution*, flashbulb memories, and *confabulation*.

Review: Next, go back and read this section again.

Now take this *Quick Quiz:*

1. Memory is like (a) a wax tablet, (b) a giant file cabinet, (c) a video camera, (d) none of these.

2. *True or false:* Because they are so vivid, flashbulb memories remain perfectly accurate over time.

3. Which of the following confabulated "memories" might a person be most inclined to accept as having really happened to them, and why? (a) getting lost in a shopping centre at the age of five, (b) taking a class in astrophysics, (c) visiting a monastery in Tibet as a child, (d) being bullied by another kid in the fourth grade

Answers:

1. d 2. false 3. a and d, because they are common events that are easy to imagine and that contain a lot of vivid details. It would be harder to induce someone to believe that he or she had studied astrophysics or visited Tibet because these are rare events that take an effort to imagine.

Memory and the Power of Suggestion

The reconstructive nature of memory helps the mind work efficiently. Instead of cramming our brains with infinite details, we can store the essentials of an experience and then use our knowledge of the world to figure out the specifics when we need them. But precisely because memory is so often reconstructive, it is also vulnerable to suggestion—to ideas implanted in our minds after the event, which then become associated with it. This fact raises thorny problems in legal cases that involve eyewitness testimony or people's memories of what happened, when, and to whom.

The Eyewitness on Trial

Without the accounts of eyewitnesses, many guilty people would go free. Lineups and photo arrays don't necessarily help, because witnesses may simply identify the person who looks most like the perpetrator of the crime (Wells & Olson, 2003). Further, even the instructions given at the lineup can result in false identification— presumably because the instruction increases the motivation of the witness to help find the guilty person (Quinlivan et al., 2012; Leach et al. 2009). As a result, some convictions based on eyewitness testimony turn out to be tragic mistakes.

Eyewitnesses are especially likely to make mistaken identifications when the suspect's ethnicity differs from their own. Because of unfamiliarity with other ethnic groups, the eyewitness may focus solely on the ethnicity of the person they see committing a crime ("He's Asian"; "She's white") and ignore the distinctive features that would later make identification more accurate (Levin, 2000; Meissner & Brigham, 2001).

In a program of research spanning nearly four decades, Elizabeth Loftus and her colleagues have shown that memories are also influenced by the way in which questions are put to the eyewitness and by suggestive comments made during an interrogation or interview. In one classic study, the researchers showed how even subtle changes in the wording of questions can lead a witness to give different answers. Participants first watched short films depicting car collisions. Afterward, the researchers asked some of them, "About how fast were the cars going when they hit each other?" Other viewers were asked the same question, but with the verb changed to *smashed, collided, bumped,* or *contacted.* Estimates of how fast the cars were going varied, depending on which word

THINKING CRITICALLY

Analyze assumptions and biases.

Corbis

On TV crime shows, witnesses often identify a criminal from a lineup or a group of photos. But these methods can mislead real witnesses, who may wrongly identify a person simply because he or she resembles the actual culprit more closely than the other people standing there or in the photos do. Based on psychological findings, many law enforcement agencies are now using better methods, such as having witnesses look at photos of suspects one at a time without being able to go back to an earlier one.

was used. *Smashed* produced the highest average speed estimates (40.8 mph, 65.3 km/h), followed by *collided* (39.3 mph, 62.9 km/h), *bumped* (38.1 mph, 61.0 km/h), *hit* (34.0 mph, 54.4 km/h), and *contacted* (31.8 mph, 50.9) (Loftus & Palmer, 1974). ◉

Misleading information from other sources also can profoundly alter what witnesses report. Consider what happened when students were shown the face of a young man who had straight hair, then heard a description of the face supposedly written by another witness—a description that wrongly said the man had light, curly hair (see Figure 10.1). When the students reconstructed the face using a kit of facial features, a third of their reconstructions contained the misleading detail, whereas only 5% contained it when curly hair was not mentioned (Loftus & Greene, 1980). In real life, misleading information about a perpetrator's appearance can reduce an eyewitness's ability to identify the real perpetrator later in a lineup (Zajac & Henderson, 2009).

Does the number of eyewitnesses affect a person's susceptibility to misleading information? In a study of this question, people first watched a video of a simulated crime and later read three eyewitness reports about the crime, each report containing the same misleading claim—such as about the location of objects, the thief's actions, or the name on the side of the suspect van. One group was told that a single person wrote all three reports, whereas another group was told that each report was written by a different person. It made no difference; a single witness's report proved to be as influential as the reports of three different witnesses. Such is the power of a single witness's voice (Foster et al., 2012).

Leading questions, suggestive comments, and misleading information affect people's memories not only for events they have witnessed but also for their own experiences. Researchers have successfully used these techniques to induce people to believe they are recalling complicated events from early in life that never actually happened, such as getting lost in a shopping mall, being hospitalized for a high fever, being harassed by a bully, getting in trouble for playing a prank on a first-grade teacher, or spilling punch all over the mother of the bride at a wedding (Hyman & Pentland, 1996; Lindsay et al., 2004; Loftus & Pickrell, 1995; Mazzoni et al., 1999). When people were shown a phony Disneyland ad featuring Bugs Bunny, about 16% later recalled having met a Bugs character at Disneyland (Braun, Ellis, & Loftus, 2002). In later studies, the percentages were even higher. Some people even claimed to remember shaking hands with the character, hugging him, or seeing him in a parade. But these memories were impossible, because Bugs Bunny is a Warner Brothers creation and would definitely be rabbit non grata at Disneyland! ◉

◉—[Watch the Video
Memory: Elizabeth Loftus
in **MyPsychLab**

◉—[Watch the Video
Thinking Like a Psychologist: Police Line-Up in **MyPsychLab**

FIGURE 10.1 The Influence of Misleading Information
In a study described in the text, students saw the face of a young man with straight hair and then had to reconstruct it from memory. On the left is one student's reconstruction in the absence of misleading information about the man's hair. On the right is another person's reconstruction of the same face after exposure to misleading information that mentioned curly hair (Loftus & Greene, 1980).

Dr. Elizabeth Loftus

Children's Testimony

The power of suggestion can affect anyone, but its impact on children who are being questioned about possible sexual or physical abuse is especially worrisome. How can adults determine whether a young child has been sexually molested without influencing what the child says? The answer is crucial. Throughout the 1980s and 1990s, accusations of child abuse in daycare centres skyrocketed. One widely publicized case of child abuse associated with an unlicensed daycare centre occurred in Martensville, Saskatchewan, in 1992. The RCMP arrested nine people, including the owners of the service as well as several police officers, and charged them with more than 100 counts of sexual and physical abuse. In no case had parents actually seen such mistreatment and none of the children had complained to their parents, although one parent had noticed a diaper rash on her child—prompting the investigation. During the investigation, the children at the centre were repeatedly questioned by a police officer about the abuse. The officer used suggestive techniques to obtain testimony of abuse. Rumours of child mutilation, satanic cults, and other ritualistic abuse spread rapidly through the community. Were these people really guilty or had the children been persuaded to make up fanciful stories?

> ### THINKING CRITICALLY
>
> Don't oversimplify.
>
> Some people claim that children's memories of sexual abuse are always accurate; others claim that children cannot distinguish fantasy from reality. How can we avoid either–or thinking on this emotional issue? Is the question "Are children's memories accurate?" even the right one to ask?

Thanks largely to research by psychological scientists, the hysteria eventually subsided and people were able to assess more clearly what had gone wrong in how the children had been interviewed. Today we know that most children do accurately recall events. Like adults, children can also be influenced by an interviewer's leading questions, suggestions, or pressure to report certain information (Ceci & Bruck, 1995). Moreover, in the courtroom, the style of questions put to children under cross-examination often leads them to be highly inaccurate (O'Neill & Zajac, 2012). The question to ask, therefore, is not "Can children's memories be trusted?" but "Under what conditions are children apt to be suggestible, and to report that something happened to them when in fact it did not?"

The answer, from many experimental studies, is that a child is more likely to give a false report when an interviewer strongly believes that the child has been molested and then uses suggestive techniques to get the child to reveal molestation (Bruck, 2003). Interviewers who are biased in this way seek only confirming evidence and ignore discrepant evidence and other explanations for a child's behaviour. They reject a child's denial of having been molested and assume the child is "in denial." They use techniques that encourage imagination inflation ("Let's pretend it happened!") and that blur reality and fantasy in the child's mind. They pressure or encourage the child to describe terrible events, badger the child with repeated questions, tell the child that "everyone else" said the events happened, or use bribes and threats (Poole & Lamb, 1998).

A team of researchers analyzed the actual transcripts of interrogations of children in the first highly publicized sexual abuse case (a case in California which ended in a hung jury). Then they applied the same suggestive techniques in an experiment with preschool children (Garven et al., 1998). A young man visited children at their preschool, read them a story, and handed out treats. The man did nothing aggressive, inappropriate, or surprising. A week later, an experimenter questioned the children individually about the man's visit. She asked children in one group leading questions ("Did he bump the teacher? Did he throw a crayon at a kid who was talking?" "Did he tell you a secret and tell you not to tell?"). She asked a second group the same questions but also applied influence techniques used by interrogators in the McMartin and other daycare cases: telling the children what "other kids" had supposedly said, expressing disappointment if answers were negative, and praising the children for making allegations.

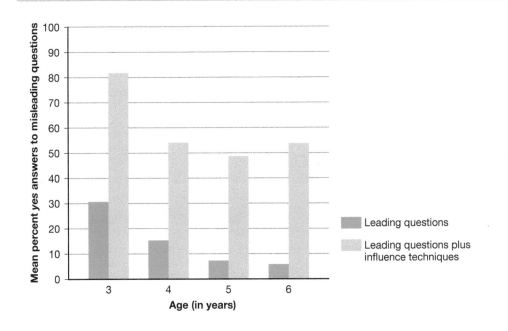

FIGURE 10.2 Social Pressure and Children's False Allegations
When researchers asked three-year-olds leading questions about events that had not occurred—such as whether a previous visitor to their classroom had committed aggressive acts—nearly 30% said that yes, he had. This percentage declined among older children. But when the researchers used influence techniques taken from actual child-abuse investigations, most of the children agreed with the false allegation, regardless of their age (Garven et al., 1998).

In the first group, children said "Yes, it happened" to about 17% of the false allegations about the man's visit. And in the second group, they said "yes" to the false allegations suggested to them a whopping 58% of the time. As you can see in Figure 10.2, the three-year-olds in this group, on average, said "yes" to over 80% of the false allegations, and the four- to six-year-olds said "yes" to over half of the allegations. Note that the interviews in this study lasted only 5 to 10 minutes, whereas in actual investigations, interviewers often question children repeatedly over many weeks or months.

Many people believe that children cannot be induced to make up experiences that are truly traumatic, but psychologists have shown that this assumption, too, is wrong. When schoolchildren were asked for their recollections of an actual sniper incident at their school, many of those who had been absent from school that day reported memories of hearing shots, seeing someone lying on the ground, and other details they could not possibly have experienced directly. Apparently, they had been influenced by the accounts of the children who had been there (Pynoos & Nader, 1989). Indeed, rumour and hearsay play a big role in promoting false beliefs and memories in children, just as they do in adults (Principe et al., 2006).

As a result of such findings, psychologists have been able to develop ways of interviewing children that reduce the chances of false reporting. If the interviewer says, "Tell me the reason you came to talk to me today," and nothing more, most actual victims will disclose what happened to them (Bruck, 2003). The interviewer must not assume that the child was molested, must avoid leading or suggestive questions, and must understand that children do not speak the way adults do. Young children often drift from topic to topic, and their words may not be the words adults would use (Poole & Lamb, 1998). One little girl being interviewed thought her "private parts" were her elbows!

In sum, children, like adults, can be accurate in what they report and, also like adults, they can distort, forget, fantasize, and be misled. As research shows, their memory processes are only human.

Children's testimony is often crucial in child sexual abuse cases. Under what conditions do children make reliable or unreliable witnesses?

Buddy Norris/Newscom

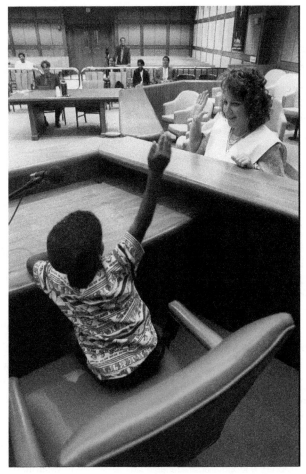

Learning Objectives

6 Analyze why multiple-choice test items are generally easier than short-answer or essay questions.

7 Define implicit memory. Describe 2 methods that psychologists use to study implicit memory.

In Pursuit of Memory

Now that we have seen how memory *doesn't* work—namely, like an infallible recording of everything that happens to you—we turn to studies of how it *does* work.

Measuring Memory

Conscious, intentional recollection of an event or an item of information is called **explicit memory**. It is usually measured using one of two methods. The first method tests for **recall**, the ability to retrieve and reproduce information encountered earlier. Essay and fill-in-the-blank exams require recall. The second method tests for **recognition**, the ability to identify information you have previously observed, read, or heard about. The information is given to you, and all you have to do is say whether it is old or new, or perhaps correct or incorrect, or pick it out of a set of alternatives. The task, in other words, is to compare the information you are given with the information stored in your memory. True–false and multiple-choice tests call for recognition. 👁

Recognition tests can be tricky, especially when false items closely resemble correct ones. Under most circumstances, however, recognition is easier than recall. Recognition for visual images is particularly impressive. If you show people 2500 slides of faces and places, and later you ask them to identify which ones they saw out of a larger set, they will be able to identify more than 90% of the original slides accurately (Haber, 1970).

👁—⎡Watch the **Video**
Classic Footage of Assessment of Memory with the Stanford-Binet Intelligence Scale in **MyPsychLab**

explicit memory Conscious, intentional recollection of an event or of an item of information.

recall The ability to retrieve and reproduce from memory previously encountered material.

recognition The ability to identify previously encountered material.

GET INVOLVED! Recalling Rudolph's Friends

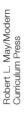

You can try this test of recall if you are familiar with the poem that begins "'Twas the Night Before Christmas" or the song "Rudolph the Red-Nosed Reindeer." Rudolph had eight reindeer friends; name as many of them as you can. After you have done your best, turn to the Get Involved exercise on page 346 for a recognition test on the same information.

The superiority of recognition over recall was once demonstrated in a study of people's memories of their high school classmates (Bahrick, Bahrick, & Wittlinger, 1975). The participants, aged 17 to 74, first wrote down the names of as many classmates as they could remember. Recall was poor; even when prompted with yearbook pictures, the youngest people failed to name almost a third of their classmates, and the oldest failed to name most of them. Recognition, however, was far better. When asked to look at a series of cards, each of which contained a set of five photographs, and to say which picture in each set showed a former classmate, recent graduates were right 90% of the time—and so were people who had graduated 35 years earlier. The ability to recognize names was nearly as impressive.

Sometimes, information encountered in the past affects our thoughts and actions even though we do not consciously or intentionally remember it, a phenomenon known as **implicit memory** (Schacter, Chiu, & Ochsner, 1993). To get at this subtle sort of memory, researchers must rely on indirect methods instead of the direct ones used to measure explicit memory. One common method, **priming**, asks you to read or listen to some information and then tests you later to see whether the information affects your performance on another type of task.

Suppose that you had to read a list of words, some of which began with the letters *def* (such as *define*, *defend*, or *deform*). Later, you were asked to complete word fragments (such as *def-*) with the first word that came to mind. Even if you could not recognize or recall the original words very well, you would be more likely to complete the word fragments with words from the list than if you had not seen the list (Richardson-Klavehn & Bjork, 1988; Roediger, 1990). The words on the list have "primed" (made more available) your responses on the word-completion task. Priming isn't limited to words; priming people with unusual sentence constructions causes them to adopt those constructions a week later (Kaschak et al., 2011). Fragments of pictures can also act as primes. In one study, people briefly saw fragments of drawings depicting objects and animals. Then, *17 years later*, they were mailed the same fragments and also fragments of new drawings, with a request to name what the fragments depicted. Even when people couldn't remember having been in the original experiment, they identified the primed objects much better than the new objects (Mitchell, 2006). These studies show that people know more than they think they know—and that they can know it for a very long time.

implicit memory Unconscious retention in memory, as evidenced by the effect of a previous experience or previously encountered information on current thoughts or actions.

priming A method used to measure unconscious cognitive processes, in which a person is exposed to information and is later tested to see whether the information affects behaviour or performance on another task or in another situation.

PRIMING

"Defend" → Influences → "Def–" → "Defend"

Exposure to information | Responses to *different* task

GET INVOLVED! Recognizing Rudolph's Friends

If you took the recall test in the Get Involved exercise on page 345, now try a recognition test. From the following list, see whether you can identify the correct names of Rudolph the Red-Nosed Reindeer's eight reindeer friends. The answers are at the end of this chapter—but no fair peeking!

Blitzen	Dander	Dancer	Masher
Cupid	Dasher	Prancer	Comet
Kumquat	Donder	Flasher	Pixie
Bouncer	Blintzes	Trixie	Vixen

Which was easier, recall or recognition? Can you speculate on the reason?

---

relearning method A method for measuring retention that compares the time required to relearn material with the time used in the initial learning of the material.

Another way to measure implicit memory, the **relearning method**, or *savings method*, was devised by Hermann Ebbinghaus (1885/1913) in the nineteenth century. The relearning method requires you to relearn information or a task that you learned earlier. If you master it more quickly the second time around, you must be remembering something from the first experience.

Models of Memory

Although people usually refer to memory as a single faculty, as in "I must be losing my memory" or "He has a memory like an elephant's," the term *memory* actually covers a complex collection of abilities and processes. If a video camera is not an accurate metaphor for capturing these diverse components of memory, what metaphor would be better?

Many cognitive psychologists liken the mind to an information processor, along the lines of a computer, though more complex. They have constructed *information-processing models* of cognitive processes, liberally borrowing computer-programming terms such as *input*, *output*, *accessing*, and *information retrieval*. When you type something on your computer's keyboard, a software program encodes the information into an electronic language, stores it on a hard drive, and retrieves it when you need to use it. Similarly, in information-processing models of memory, we *encode* information (convert it to a form that the brain can process and use), *store* the information (retain it over time), and *retrieve* the information (recover it for use). In storage, the information may be represented as concepts, propositions, images, or *cognitive schemas*, mental networks of knowledge, beliefs, and expectations concerning particular topics or aspects of the world. (If you can't retrieve these terms, see Chapter 9.)

In most information-processing models, storage takes place in three interacting memory systems. A *sensory register* retains incoming sensory information for a second or two, until it can be processed further. *Short-term memory (STM)* holds a limited amount of information for a brief period of time, perhaps up to 30 seconds or so, unless a conscious effort is made to keep it there longer. *Long-term memory (LTM)* accounts for longer storage, from a few minutes to decades (Atkinson & Shiffrin, 1968, 1971). Information can pass from the sensory register to short-term memory and in either direction between short-term and long-term memory, as illustrated in Figure 10.3. ✳

✳ Explore the **Concept**
Stages of Memory: The Atkinson-Shiffrin Model in **MyPsychLab**

This model, which is known informally as the "three-box model," has dominated research on memory since the late 1960s. The problem is that the human brain does not operate like your average computer. Most computers process instructions and data sequentially, one item after another, and so the three-box model has emphasized sequential operations. In contrast, the brain performs many operations simultaneously,

FIGURE 10.3 Three Memory Systems

In the three-box model of memory, information that does not transfer out of the sensory register or short-term memory is assumed to be gone forever. Once in long-term memory, information can be retrieved for use in analyzing incoming sensory information or performing mental operations in short-term memory.

in parallel. It recognizes patterns all at once rather than as a sequence of information bits, and it perceives new information, produces speech, and searches memory all at the same time. It can do these things because millions of neurons are active at once, and each neuron communicates with thousands of others, which in turn communicate with millions more.

Because of these differences between human beings and machines, some cognitive scientists prefer a **parallel distributed processing (PDP)** or *connectionist* model. Instead of representing information as flowing from one system to another, a PDP model represents the contents of memory as connections among a huge number of interacting processing units, distributed in a vast network and all operating in parallel—just like the neurons of the brain (McClelland, 1994, 2011; Rumelhart, McClelland, & the PDP Research Group, 1986). As information enters the system, the ability of these units to excite or inhibit each other is constantly adjusted to reflect new knowledge.

In this chapter, we emphasize the three-box model, but keep in mind that the computer metaphor that inspired it will become as outdated as the metaphor of memory as a camera.

parallel distributed processing (PDP) model A model of memory in which knowledge is represented as connections among thousands of interacting processing units, distributed in a vast network, and all operating in parallel. Also called a *connectionist model*.

Recite & Review

Recite: To find out how well you've encoded and stored the preceding material, retrieve it by saying out loud everything you can about *recall*, *recognition*, *explicit* versus *implicit memory*, *priming*, the *relearning method*, *parallel distributed processing (PDP)*, and models of memory.

Review: Next, go back and read this section again.

Now take this *Quick Quiz:*

1. Alberta solved a crossword puzzle a few days ago. She no longer recalls the words in the puzzle, but while playing a game of Scrabble, she unconsciously tends to form words that were in the puzzle, showing that she has _____ memories of some of the words.

2. The three basic memory processes are _____, storage, and _____.

3. Do the preceding two questions ask for recall, recognition, or relearning? (And what about *this* question?)

4. One objection to traditional information-processing theories of memory is that, unlike most computers, the brain performs many independent operations _____.

Answers:

1. implicit 2. encoding, retrieval 3. The first two questions both measure recall; the third question measures recognition. 4. simultaneously, or in parallel

If the visual sensory register did not clear quickly, multiple images might interfere with the accurate perception and encoding of memory.

Bruce Brander/Science Source

sensory register A memory system that momentarily preserves extremely accurate images of sensory information.

short-term memory (STM) In the three-box model of memory, a limited-capacity memory system involved in the retention of information for brief periods; it is also used to hold information retrieved from long-term memory for temporary use.

Learning Objectives

8 Define the three components that make up the three-box model of memory.

9 Contrast short-term memory with working memory.

10 Define the following terms: *procedural memory*, *declarative memory*, and *semantic memory*.

11 Diagram the serial position effect.

The Three-Box Model of Memory

The information model of three separate memory systems—sensory, short-term, and long-term—remains a leading approach because it offers a convenient way to organize the major findings on memory, does a good job of accounting for these findings, and is consistent with the biological facts about memory. Let us now peer into each of the "boxes."

The Sensory Register: Fleeting Impressions

In the three-box model, all incoming sensory information must make a brief stop in the **sensory register**, the entryway of memory. The sensory register includes a number of separate memory subsystems, as many as there are senses. Visual images remain in a visual subsystem for a maximum of a half second. Auditory images remain in an auditory subsystem for a slightly longer time, by most estimates up to two seconds or so.

The sensory register acts as a holding bin, retaining information in a highly accurate form until we can select items for attention from the stream of stimuli bombarding our senses. It gives us time to decide whether information is extraneous or important; not everything detected by our senses warrants our attention. And the identification of a stimulus on the basis of information already contained in long-term memory occurs during the transfer of information from the sensory register to short-term memory.

Information that does not quickly go on to short-term memory vanishes forever, like a message written in disappearing ink. That is why people who see an array of 12 letters for just a fraction of a second can only report four or five of them; by the time they answer, their sensory memories are already fading (Sperling, 1960). The fleeting nature of incoming sensations is actually beneficial; it prevents multiple sensory images—"double exposures"—that might interfere with the accurate perception and encoding of information.

Short-Term Memory: Memory's Notepad

Individuals with brain injury, such as H.M., demonstrate the importance of transferring new information from **short-term memory** into long-term memory. H. M. was able to store information on a short-term basis; he could hold a conversation and his behaviour appeared normal when you first met him. Yet, for the most part, he could not retain explicit information about new facts and events for longer than a few minutes. His terrible memory deficits involved a problem in transferring explicit memories from short-term storage into long-term storage. With a great deal of repetition and drill, patients like H. M. can learn some new visual information, retain it in long-term memory, and recall it normally (McKee & Squire, 1992). But usually information does not get into long-term memory in the first place.

The Leaky Bucket. People such as H. M. fall at the extreme end on a continuum of forgetfulness, but even those of us with normal memories know from

GET INVOLVED! Your Sensory Register at Work

In a dark room or closet, swing a flashlight rapidly in a circle. You will see an unbroken circle of light instead of a series of separate points. The reason: The successive images remain briefly in the sensory register.

Travis Gering

personal experience how frustratingly brief short-term retention can be. We look up a telephone number, are distracted for a moment, and have to look it up again. We meet someone and two minutes later find ourselves groping for the person's name. Is it any wonder that short-term memory has been called a "leaky bucket"?

According to most memory models, if the bucket did not leak it would quickly overflow, because at any given moment, short-term memory can hold only so many items. Years ago, George Miller (1956) estimated its capacity to be "the magical number seven plus or minus two." Conveniently, postal codes and phone numbers fall in this range; 16-digit credit card numbers do not. Since then, estimates of STM's capacity have ranged from two items to 20, with one estimate putting the "magical number" at four (Cowan, 2001; Cowan et al., 2008). Everyone agrees, however, that the number of items that short-term memory can handle at any one time is small. ◉▸

Given the limits on short-term memory, how do we remember the beginning of a spoken sentence until the speaker reaches the end? After all, most sentences are longer than just a few words. Most information-processing models of memory propose that we bind small bits of information into larger units, or **chunks**. The real capacity of STM, it turns out, is not a few bits of information but a few chunks (Gilchrist & Cowan, 2012). A chunk can be a word, a phrase, a sentence, or even an image, and it depends on previous experience. For most Canadians, the acronym CBC and the number 1867 are each one chunk, but CCB and 8617 are not (unless they are your initials or your pin). A chunk can be visual: If you know football, when you see a play unfolding, you might see a single chunk of information—say, a wishbone formation—and be able to remember it. If you do not know football, you will see only a field full of players, and you probably won't be able to remember their positions when you look away.

But even chunking cannot keep short-term memory from eventually filling up. Information that will be needed for longer periods must be transferred to long-term memory or it will be displaced by new information and spill out of the bucket. Particularly meaningful items may transfer quickly, but other information will usually require more processing—unless we do something to keep it in STM for a while, as we will discuss shortly.

Working Memory. In the original three-box model, short-term memory functioned basically as a buffer for holding and rehearsing information until it could be transferred to or from long-term memory. But this view did not account for the sense of effort we feel when trying to solve a problem. Does $2 \times (3 + 5) / 4 = 4$? Solving that

◉▸ **Simulate** the **Experiment** *Digit Span* in **MyPsychLab**

chunk A meaningful unit of information; it may be composed of smaller units.

These card players are having a great time using their working memories.

Jupiter Images

problem feels as though we are not simply holding on to information but also *working* with it, which is why psychologists today think that STM is really part of a **working memory** system. STM keeps its job as a temporary holding bin, but another more active part—an "executive"—controls attention, focusing it on the information we need for the task at hand and warding off distracting information (Baddeley, 1992, 2007; Engle, 2002). In the previous problem, your working memory must contain the numbers and instructions for operating on them, and also carry out those operations and retain the intermediate results from each step.

People who do well on tests of working memory tend to do well on intelligence tests and on tasks requiring complex cognition and the control of attention, such as understanding what you read, following directions, taking notes, playing bridge, learning new words, estimating how much time has elapsed, and many other real-life tasks (Broadway & Engle, 2011). When they are engrossed in challenging activities that require their concentration and effort, they stay on task longer, and their minds are less likely than other people's to wander (Kane et al., 2007). (See also Chapter 9.)

The ability to bring information from long-term memory into short-term memory or to use working memory is not disrupted in patients like H. M. They can do arithmetic, relate events that predate their injury, and do anything else that requires retrieval of information from long-term into short-term memory. Their problem is with the flow of information in the other direction, from short-term to long-term memory.

Long-Term Memory: Memory's Storage System

The third box in the three-box model of memory is **long-term memory (LTM)**. The capacity of long-term memory seems to have no practical limits. The vast amount of information stored there enables us to learn, get around in the environment, and build a sense of identity and a personal history.

Organization in Long-Term Memory. Because long-term memory contains so much information, it must be organized in some way, so that we can find the particular items we are looking for. One way to organize words (or the concepts they represent) is by the *semantic categories* to which they belong. *Chair*, for example, belongs to the category *furniture*. In a study done many years ago, people had to memorize 60 words that came from four semantic categories: animals, vegetables, names, and professions. The words were presented in random order, but when people were allowed to recall the items in any order they wished, they tended to recall them in clusters corresponding to the four categories (Bousfield, 1953). This finding has been replicated many times.

Evidence on the storage of information by semantic category also comes from cases of people with brain damage. In one such case, a patient called M. D. appeared to have made a complete recovery after suffering several strokes, with one odd exception: He had trouble remembering the names of fruits and vegetables. M. D. could easily name a picture of an abacus or a sphinx, but he drew a blank when he saw a picture of an orange or a carrot. He could sort pictures of animals, vehicles, and other objects into their appropriate categories, but did poorly with pictures of fruits and vegetables. On the other hand, when M. D. was *given* the names of fruits and vegetables, he immediately pointed to the corresponding pictures

working memory In many models of memory, a cognitively complex form of short-term memory; it involves active mental processes that control retrieval of information from long-term memory and interpret that information appropriately for a given task.

long-term memory (LTM) In the three-box model of memory, the memory system involved in the long-term storage of information.

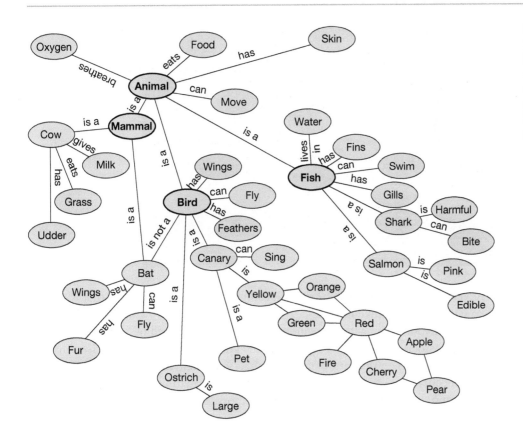

FIGURE 10.4 Part of a Conceptual Grid in Long-Term Memory
Many models of memory represent the contents of long-term semantic memory as an immense network or grid of concepts and the relations among them. This illustration shows part of a hypothetical grid for *animals*.

(Hart, Berndt, & Caramazza, 1985). Apparently, M. D. still had information about fruits and vegetables, but his brain lesion prevented him from using their names to get to the information when he needed it, unless someone else provided the names. This evidence suggests that information in memory about a particular concept (such as *orange*) is linked in some way to information about the concept's semantic category (such as *fruit*).

Indeed, many models of long-term memory represent its contents as a vast network of interrelated concepts and propositions (Anderson, 1990; Collins & Loftus, 1975). In these models, a small part of a conceptual network for *animals* might look something like the one in Figure 10.4. The way people use these networks, however, depends on experience and education. In rural Liberia, the more schooling children have, the more likely they are to use semantic categories in recalling lists of objects (Cole & Scribner, 1974). This makes sense, because in school, children must memorize a lot of information in a short time, and semantic grouping can help. Unschooled children, having less need to memorize lists, do not cluster items and do not remember them as well. But this does not mean that unschooled children have poor memories. When the task is one that is meaningful to them, such as recalling objects that were in a story or a village scene, they remember extremely well (Mistry & Rogoff, 1994).

We organize information in long-term memory not only by semantic groupings but also in terms of the way words sound or look. Have you ever tried to recall some name, that was on *tip of your tongue?* These *tip-of-the-tongue (TOT) states* occur across many languages and cultures; users of sign language call them "tip of the finger" states (Thompson, Emmorey, & Gollan, 2005). Scientists value them as a sort of slow-motion video of memory processes (A. Brown, 2012). People in a TOT state tend to come up with words that resemble the right one in sound, meaning, or form (e.g., number of syllables) before finally recalling the one they're searching for, which indicates that information in long-term memory is organized in those terms (R. Brown &

Culture affects the encoding, storage, and retrieval of information in long-term memory. Navajo healers, who use stylized, symbolic sand paintings in their rituals, must commit to memory dozens of intricate visual designs, because no exact copies are made and the painting is destroyed after each ceremony.

Emil Muench/Getty Images

McNeill, 1966). For the name *Kevin* they might say, "Wait, it starts with a K and has two syllables . . . Kenny? Kerran? . . ."

Information in long-term memory may also be organized by its familiarity, relevance, or association with other information. The method used in any given instance probably depends on the nature of the memory; you would no doubt store information about the major cities of Europe differently from information about your first date. To understand the organization of long-term memory, then, we must know what kinds of information can be stored there.

The Contents of Long-Term Memory. Most theories of memory distinguish skills or habits ("knowing how") from abstract or representational knowledge ("knowing that"). **Procedural memories** are memories of knowing how to do something—comb your hair, use a pencil, solve a jigsaw puzzle, knit a sweater, or swim. Many researchers consider procedural memories to be implicit, because once skills and habits are learned well, they do not require much conscious processing. **Declarative memories** involve knowing that something is true, as in knowing that Ottawa is the capital of Canada; they are usually assumed to be explicit.

Declarative memories come in two varieties: semantic memories and episodic memories (Tulving, 1985). **Semantic memories** are internal representations of the world, independent of any particular context. They include facts, rules, and concepts—items of general knowledge. On the basis of your semantic memory of the concept *cat*, you can describe a cat as a small, furry mammal that typically spends its time eating, sleeping, prowling, and staring into space, even though a cat may not be present when you give this description, and you probably won't know how or when you first learned it.

Episodic memories are internal representations of personally experienced events. When you remember how your cat once surprised you in the middle of the night by pouncing on you as you slept, you are retrieving an episodic memory. Figure 10.5 summarizes these kinds of memories.

Episodic memory allows us to travel not only backward in time, but also forward, to imagine possible future experiences (Schacter, 2012). We mine our episodic memories to construct scenarios of what might happen and then rehearse how we might behave. In fact, regions of the brain known to be involved when we retrieve personal memories, notably the hippocampus and parts of the prefrontal cortex and temporal lobe, are also activated when we imagine future events (Addis, Wong, & Schachter, 2007). Patients who cannot retrieve any episodic memories because of damage to the hippocampus often cannot envision future episodes either, even in response to such simple

procedural memories Memories for the performance of actions or skills ("knowing how").

declarative memories Memories of facts, rules, concepts, and events ("knowing that"); they include semantic and episodic memories.

semantic memories Memories of general knowledge, including facts, rules, concepts, and propositions.

episodic memories Memories of personally experienced events and the contexts in which they occurred.

FIGURE 10.5 Types of Long-Term Memories
This diagram summarizes the distinctions among long-term memories. A procedural memory might be of learning how to ride a bike; a declarative memory might be knowing that Ottawa is the capital of Canada. Can you come up with your own examples of each memory type?

questions as "What will you do tomorrow?" (Hassabis & Maguire, 2007). The "time-travel" function of episodic memories is often beneficial and motivating, because people tend to forget negative episodic memories faster than positive ones, leaving us with a forgiving past and rosy future (Szpunar, Addis, & Schacter, 2012).

From Short-Term to Long-Term Memory: A Puzzle.

The three-box model of memory is often invoked to explain an interesting phenomenon called the **serial-position effect**. If you are shown a list of items and are then asked immediately to recall them, your recall will be best for items at the beginning of the list (the *primacy effect*) and at the end of the list (the *recency effect*); the items in the middle of the list will tend to drop away (Bhatarah, Ward, & Tan, 2008; Johnson & Miles, 2009). If we plot the results, we see a U-shaped curve as shown in Figure 10.6. A serial-position effect occurs when you meet a lot of people at a party and find you can recall the names of the first few and the last few, but almost no one in between.

Primacy and recency effects apparently occur for different reasons. Primacy effects happen because the first few items in a list are rehearsed many times and so are likely to make it to long-term memory and remain memorable. Recency effects occur because at the time of recall, they are plucked out of short-term memory, where they are still sitting. The items in the middle of a list are not so well retained because by the time they get into short-term memory, it is already crowded with the first few items. As a result, middle items often drop out of short-term memory before they can be stored in long-term memory. Indeed, a functional MRI study found that recognition memory for words early in a list activated areas in the hippocampus associated with retrieval from long-term memory, but recognition for words that came near the end of the list did not (Talmi et al., 2005).

The problem with this explanation is that the recency effect sometimes occurs even after a considerable delay, when the items at the end of a list should no longer be in short-term memory (Davelaar et al., 2004). Moreover, the serial position effect can occur not just with semantic memories but also episodic ones—memories of past personal experiences, such as the soccer games you played in over the last season. The serial-position curve, therefore, remains something of a puzzle.

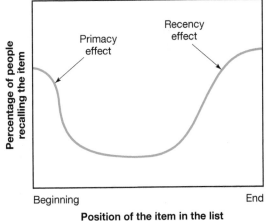

Position of the item in the list

FIGURE 10.6 The Serial-Position Effect
When people try to recall a list of similar items immediately after learning it, they tend to remember the first and last items best and the ones in the middle worst.

Simulate the **Experiment**
Serial Position Effect in **MyPsychLab**

serial-position effect The tendency for recall of the first and last items on a list to surpass recall of items in the middle of the list.

Learning Objectives

12 Define consolidation and explain how it occurs.

13 List three areas of the brain involved in memory. For each area, give everyday examples of the types of memory each part is involved in.

14 Ilustrate the effects of stress hormones on memory.

The Biology of Memory

We have been discussing memory solely in terms of information processing, but what is happening in the brain while all of that processing is going on?

Changes in Neurons and Synapses

Explore the Concept
Virtual Brain: Learning and Memory in **MyPsychLab**

Forming a memory involves chemical and structural changes at the level of synapses, and these changes differ for short-term memory and long-term memory.

In short-term memory, changes within neurons temporarily alter their ability to release neurotransmitters, the chemicals that carry messages from one cell to another (see Chapter 4). Evidence comes from studies with sea snails, sea slugs, and other organisms that have small numbers of easily identifiable neurons (Kandel, 2001; Kandel & Schwartz, 1982). These primitive animals can be taught simple conditioned responses, such as withdrawing or not withdrawing parts of their bodies in response to a light touch. When the animal retains the skill for only the short term, the neuron or neurons involved temporarily show an increase or decrease in readiness to release neurotransmitter molecules into a synapse.

In contrast, long-term memory involves lasting structural changes in the brain. To mimic what they think may happen during the formation of a long-term memory, researchers apply brief, high-frequency electrical stimulation to groups of neurons in the brains of animals or to brain cells in a laboratory culture. In various areas, especially the hippocampus, this stimulation increases the strength of synaptic responsiveness, a phenomenon known as **long-term potentiation** (Bliss & Collingridge, 1993; Whitlock et al., 2006). Certain receiving neurons become more responsive to transmitting neurons, making synaptic pathways more excitable. This idea is far from new, as a Canadian researcher at McGill University, D. O. Hebb, suggested such a thing in 1949 in his book *The Organization of Behaviour*. Hebb suggested that changes in neural activity occur due to a process similar to classical conditioning. It was this theory that prompted the original discoverers of long-term potentiation, Bliss and Lomo (1973), to look for the phenomenon.

Most (though not all) researchers believe that long-term potentiation underlies many and perhaps all forms of learning and memory. Both calcium and the neurotransmitter glutamate seem to play a key role in this process, causing receiving neurons in the hippocampus to become more receptive to the next signal that comes along (Lisman, Yasuda, & Raghavachari, 2012). It is a little like increasing the diameter of a funnel's neck to permit more flow through the funnel. In addition, during long-term potentiation, dendrites grow and branch out, and certain types of synapses increase in number (Greenough, 1984). At the same time, in another process, some neurons become *less* responsive than they were previously (Bolshakov & Siegelbaum, 1994).

Most of these changes take time, which probably explains why long-term memories remain vulnerable to disruption for a while after they are stored (Sutherland, Sparks, & Lehmann, 2010). The neural and synaptic changes that occur when memories are formed are distributed through the brain and involve areas of the brain that appear to learn best when experiences are repeated again and again. Memories become more permanent, a process known as **consolidation**, by the brain repeating the experience by replaying the neural activity for hours after its occurrence (Marrone et al., 2008; Euston, Tatsuno, & McNaughton, 2007). In Chapter 5, we discuss the probable role of sleep in ensuring consolidation of new information.

Where Memories are Made

Scientists have used microelectrodes, brain-scan technology, and other techniques to identify the brain structures responsible for the formation and storage of specific types of memories. The amygdala is involved in the formation, consolidation, and retrieval of memories of fearful and other emotional events (Buchanan, 2007; see Chapter 11). Indeed, enhanced activation of the amygdala is associated with the vividness of flashbulb memories and may be a key mechanism in the production of flashbulb memories (Sharot et al., 2007). Areas in the frontal lobes of the brain are especially active during short-term and working-memory tasks (Goldman-Rakic, 1996; Mitchell & Johnson, 2009). The prefrontal cortex and areas adjacent to the hippocampus in the temporal lobe are also important for the efficient encoding of pictures and words.

But it is the hippocampus that has the starring role in many aspects of memory. It is critical to the formation of long-term declarative memories ("knowing that"); as we have seen in the case of H. M., damage to this structure can cause amnesia for new facts and events. The hippocampus is also critical in recalling past experiences (Pastalkova et al., 2008; Corkin, 2002). In a surprise to many researchers, Suzanne Corkin (2002) reported that H. M. also had severe difficulties recalling past experiences, with impairments in recalling detailed memories of his mother or father or in the events that made up any part of his life before the surgery. This observation flies in the face of the very popular theory of memory consolidation, which suggests that memories take a long time to form, but once formed they become independent of the hippocampus (Squire, 2007). It is because of research that suggests that the hippocampus plays a key role in the formation of new memories and in the recall of episodic memories, no

long-term potentiation A long-lasting increase in the strength of synaptic responsiveness, thought to be a biological mechanism of long-term memory.

consolidation The process by which a long-term memory becomes durable and relatively stable.

Watch the **Video**
Neurological Basis of Memory: Howard Eichenbaum in **MyPsychLab**

FIGURE 10.7 Brain Activity in Explicit and Implicit Memory
As these composite functional MRI scans show, patterns of brain activity differ depending on the type of memory task involved. When people had an explicit memory for dot patterns they had seen earlier, areas in the visual cortex, temporal lobes, and frontal lobes (indicated by orange in the lower photos) were more active. When people's implicit memories were activated, areas in the visual cortex (blue in the upper photos) were relatively inactive (Reber, Stark, & Squire, 1998).

Cold Spring Harbor Laboratory Press

matter how old they are (Steinvorth, Levine, & Corkin, 2005; Sutherland, Sparks, & Lehmann, 2010) that we are now developing a new theory of how memories are formed, stored, and maintained. As we noted above, it appears that the hippocampus replays the neural events that occurred during learning, and that this repetition (often during sleep) is how memories are formed (Euston, Tatsuno, & McNaughton, 2007).

A team of researchers has identified how neurons in the hippocampus may become involved in specific memories. They implanted electrodes into the brains of 13 people about to undergo surgery for severe epilepsy. (This is standard procedure because it enables doctors to pinpoint the location of the brain activity causing the seizures.) As the patients were being prepped, they watched a series of 5- to 10-second film clips of TV shows such as *Seinfeld* or *The Simpsons*, or of animals and landmarks. The researchers recorded which neurons in the hippocampus were firing as the patients watched; for each patient, particular neurons might become highly active during particular videos and respond only weakly to others. After a few minutes, the patients were asked to recall what they had seen. They remembered almost all of the clips, and as they recalled each one, the very neurons that had been active when they first saw it were reignited (Gelbard-Sagiv et al., 2008).

The formation and retention of procedural memories (memory for skills and habits) seem to involve other brain structures and pathways. In work with rabbits, Richard Thompson (1983, 1986) showed that one kind of procedural memory—a simple, classically conditioned response to a stimulus, such as an eye blink in response to a tone—depends on activity in the cerebellum. Human patients with damage in the cerebellum are incapable of this type of conditioning (Daum & Schugens, 1996).

The formation of declarative and procedural memories in different brain areas could explain a curious finding about patients like H. M. Despite their inability to form new declarative memories, with sufficient practise such patients can acquire new procedural memories that enable them to solve a puzzle, read mirror-reversed words, or play tennis—even though they do not recall the training sessions in which they learned these skills. Apparently, the parts of the brain involved in acquiring new procedural memories have remained intact. Patients such as H.M. retain some implicit memory for verbal material, as measured by priming tasks, suggesting that the brain has separate systems for implicit and explicit tasks. As Figure 10.7 shows, this view has been bolstered by brain scans, which reveal differences in the location of brain activity when ordinary people perform explicit or implicit memory tasks (Reber, Stark, & Squire, 1998; Squire et al., 1992).

The brain circuits that take part in the *formation* and *retrieval* of long-term memories, however, are not the same as those involved in long-term *storage* of those memories. Although the hippocampus is vital for the formation and retrieval of memories, the storage of memories appears to be the responsibility of the cerebral cortex (Battaglia et al., 2011). In fact, memories may be stored in the same cortical areas that were involved in the original perception of the information. When people remember pictures, visual parts of the brain become active; when people remember sounds, auditory areas become active, just as they did when the information was first perceived (Nyberg et al., 2000; Thompson & Kosslyn, 2000).

The typical "memory" is a complex cluster of information. When you recall meeting a man yesterday, you remember his greeting, his tone of voice, how he looked, and where he was. Even a single concept, such as *shovel*, includes a lot of information about its length, what it's made of, and what it's used for. These different pieces of information are probably processed separately and stored at different locations that are distributed across wide areas of the brain, with all the sites participating in the representation of the event or concept as a whole. The

REVIEW 10.1 Some Brain Areas Involved in Memory

No simple summary of brain areas associated with memory can do this complex topic justice. Here are just a few of the areas and functions that have been studied.

Brain Area	Associated Memory Function
Amygdala	Formation, consolidation, and retrieval of emotional memories
Frontal lobes	Short-term memory and working-memory tasks
Prefrontal cortex, parts of temporal lobes	Efficient encoding of words and pictures, working memory, source monitoring
Hippocampus	Formation of long-term declarative memories; aids in the retrieval of specific memories; may bind together diverse elements of a memory so that it can be retrieved later as a coherent entity
Cerebellum	Formation and retention of simple classically conditioned responses
Cerebral cortex	Storage of long-term memories, possibly in areas involved in the original perception of the information

hippocampus may somehow bind together the diverse aspects of a memory at the time it is formed, so that even though these aspects are stored in different cortical sites, the memory can later be retrieved as one coherent entity (Squire & Zola-Morgan, 1991).

Review 10.1 shows the structures that we have discussed and summarizes some of the memory-related functions associated with them. But we have given you just a few small nibbles from the smorgasbord of findings now available. Neuroscientists hope that someday they will be able to describe the entire stream of events in the brain that occur from the moment you say to yourself "I must remember this" to the moment you actually do remember . . . or find that you can't.

Hormones, Emotion, and Memory

Have you ever smelled fresh cookies and recalled a tender scene from your childhood? Do you have a vivid memory of seeing a particularly horrifying horror movie? Emotional memories such as these are often especially intense, and the explanation resides partly in our hormones.

Hormones released by the adrenal glands during stress and emotional arousal, including epinephrine (adrenaline) and norepinephrine, can enhance memory. If you give people a drug that prevents their adrenal glands from producing these hormones, they will remember less about emotional stories they heard than a control group will (Cahill et al., 1994). Conversely, if you give animals norepinephrine right after learning, their memories will improve. The link between emotional arousal and memory makes evolutionary sense: Arousal tells the brain that an event or piece of information is important enough to encode and store for future use.

However, extreme arousal is not necessarily a good thing. When animals or people are given very high doses of stress hormones, their memories for learned tasks sometimes suffer instead of improving; a moderate dose may be optimal (Andreano & Cahill, 2006). Two psychologists demonstrated the perils of high stress and anxiety in a real-life setting: the Horror Labyrinth of the London Dungeon (Valentine & Mesout, 2009). The labyrinth is a maze of disorienting mirrored walls set in Gothic vaults. As visitors walk through it, they hear strange noises and screams, and various alarming things suddenly appear, including a "scary person"—an actor dressed in a dark robe, wearing makeup to appear scarred and bleeding. Volunteers wore a wireless heart-rate monitor as they walked through the labyrinth, so that their stress and anxiety levels could be recorded.

The higher their stress and anxiety, the less able they were to accurately describe the "scary person" later, and the fewer correct identifications they made of him in a lineup.

Such effects on memory do not matter much at an amusement attraction, but they can have serious consequences when crime victims, police officers, and combat soldiers must recall details of a highly stressful experience, such as a shootout or the identity of an enemy interrogator (Morgan et al., 2007). The unintended effects of misleading suggestions, combined with the effects of extreme stress on memory, mean that we should be especially cautious about intelligence obtained from imprisoned people who may have been tortured, such as Omar Khadr (Loftus, 2011).

Assuming that adrenal hormones do not become *too* high, how might these hormones enhance storage of information in the brain? One possibility is that norepinephrine affects glutamate receptors on the surfaces of nerve cells, increasing the strength of incoming signals (Hu et al., 2007; McGaugh, 1990). Another is that adrenal hormones cause the level of glucose (a sugar) to rise in the bloodstream, and from there the glucose can readily enter the brain. Once in the brain, glucose may enhance memory either directly or by altering the effects of neurotransmitters. If so, increasing the amount of glucose available to the brain should enhance memory. Indeed, this "sweet memories" effect does occur both in aged rats and mice and in human beings. In one encouraging study, healthy older people fasted overnight, drank a glass of lemonade sweetened with either glucose or saccharin, and then took two memory tests. The saccharin-laced drink had no effect on their performance, but lemonade with glucose greatly boosted their ability to recall a taped passage 5 or 40 minutes after hearing it (Manning, Hall, & Gold, 1990).

Before you reach for a candy bar, you should know that the effective dose of glucose is narrow; too much can impair cognitive functioning instead of helping it. The "sweet memories" effect also depends on your metabolism, what you have eaten that day, and the level of glucose in your brain before you ingest it. In this area, as in others in the biology of memory, we have much to learn. No one knows yet exactly how the brain stores information, how different memory circuits link up with one another, or how a student is able to locate and retrieve information at the drop of a multiple-choice item.

Recite & Review

Recite: Let's see what your memory has consolidated. Say out loud everything you can about brain changes during short-term memory, *long-term potentiation, consolidation*, the importance of the hippocampus, the long-term storage of memories, and hormonal influences on memory.

Review: Next, go back and read this section again.

Now take this *Quick Quiz:*

1. Is long-term potentiation associated with (a) increased responsiveness of certain receiving neurons to transmitting neurons or (b) a decrease in receptors on certain receiving neurons?

2. The cerebellum has been associated with _____ memories; the hippocampus has been associated with _____ memories.

3. *True or false:* Hormone research suggests that if you want to remember well, you should be as relaxed as possible while learning.

4. After reading about glucose and memory, should you immediately start gulping down lemonade? Why or why not?

Answers:

1. a **2.** procedural, declarative **3.** false **4.** You should not pig out on sugar yet. You do not know what amount might be effective for you, given your metabolism, brain levels of glucose, and dietary habits. And you need to consider the health risks of consuming sugary foods with lots of calories and little nutritional value.

Learning Objectives

15 Explain why mnemonics and maintenance rehearsal are not as effective as elaborative rehearsal.

16 Based on what you know about how the brain remembers, deduce why retrieval practice and deep encoding are the best ways to study.

How We Remember

In everyday life, people who want to give their powers of memory a boost sometimes use **mnemonics** [neh-MON-iks], formal strategies and tricks for encoding, storing, and retaining information. (Mnemosyne, pronounced neh-MOZ-eh-nee, was the ancient Greek goddess of memory.) Some mnemonics take the form of easily memorized rhymes (e.g., "Thirty days hath September/April, June, and November . . ."). Others use formulas (e.g., "Every good boy does fine" for remembering which notes are on the lines of the treble clef in musical notation). Still others use visual images or word associations. They may also reduce the amount of information by chunking it, which is why many companies use words for their phone numbers instead of unmemorable numbers.

Some stage performers with amazing recall rely on far more complicated mnemonics. We are not going to spend time on them here, though, because for ordinary memory tasks, such tricks are often no more effective than rote repetition, and sometimes they are actually worse (Wang, Thomas, & Ouellette, 1992). Most memory researchers do not use such mnemonics themselves (Hébert, 2001). After all, why bother to memorize a grocery list using a fancy mnemonic when you can write down what you need to buy?

Well, then, what does work? Let's look at some techniques that are based on well-established principles of memory that help us encode and store information to help it stick in our minds and be there when we need it.

Effective Encoding

Our memories, as we have seen, are not exact replicas of experience. Sensory information is summarized and encoded as words or images almost as soon as it is detected. When you hear a lecture, you may hang on every word (we hope you do), but you do not memorize those words verbatim. You extract the main points and encode them. ✳

To remember information well, you have to encode it accurately in the first place. With some kinds of information, accurate encoding takes place automatically, without effort. Think about where you usually sit in your psychology class. When were you last there? You can probably provide this information easily, even though you never made a deliberate effort to encode it. But many kinds of information require *effortful encoding*: the plot of a novel, the procedures for assembling a cabinet, the arguments for and against a proposed law. To retain such information, you might have to select the main points, label concepts, or associate the information with personal experiences or with material you already know. Experienced students know that most of the information in any course requires effortful encoding, otherwise known as studying. The mind does not gobble up information automatically; you must make the material digestible.

✳ Explore the Concept *What Do You Remember?* in MyPsychLab

Rehearsal

An important technique for keeping information in short-term memory and increasing the chances of long-term retention is *rehearsal*, the review or practice of material while you are learning it. When people are prevented from rehearsing, the contents of

GET INVOLVED! Pay Attention!

It seems obvious, but often we fail to remember because we never encoded the information in the first place. Which of these loonies is the real one? (The answer is at the end of this chapter.) If you are a Canadian, you have seen lots of loonies, yet you will probably have trouble recognizing the real one because you have never paid close attention to and encoded the details of its design (Nickerson & Adams, 1979).

Pearson Education

---

maintenance rehearsal Rote repetition of material in order to maintain its availability in memory.

elaborative rehearsal Association of new information with already stored knowledge and analysis of the new information to make it memorable.

When actors learn a script, they do not rely on maintenance rehearsal alone. They also use elaborative rehearsal and deep processing, analyzing the meaning of their lines and associating their lines with imagined information about the character they are playing.

Keith morris/Alamy

their short-term memories quickly fade (Peterson & Peterson, 1959). You are taking advantage of rehearsal when you look up a phone number and then repeat it over and over to keep it in short-term memory until you no longer need it. And when you can't remember a phone number because your phone always remembers it for you, you are learning what happens when you *don't* rehearse!

A poignant demonstration of the power of rehearsal once occurred during a session with H. M. (Ogden & Corkin, 1991). The experimenter gave H. M. five digits to repeat and remember, but then she was unexpectedly called away. When she returned after more than an hour, H. M. was able to repeat the five digits correctly. He had been rehearsing them the entire time.

Short-term memory holds many kinds of information, including visual information and abstract meanings. But most people, or at least most hearing people, seem to favour speech for encoding and rehearsing the contents of short-term memory. The speech may be spoken aloud or to oneself. When people make errors on short-term memory tests that use letters or words, they often confuse items that sound the same or similar, such as *d* and *t*, or *bear* and *bare*. These errors suggest that they have been rehearsing verbally.

Some strategies for rehearsing are more effective than others. **Maintenance rehearsal** involves merely the rote repetition of the material. This kind of rehearsal is fine for keeping information in STM, but it will not always lead to long-term retention. A better strategy if you want to remember for the long haul is **elaborative rehearsal**, also called *elaboration of encoding* (Cermak & Craik, 1979; Craik & Tulving, 1975). Elaboration involves associating new items of information with material that has already been stored or with other new facts. It can also involve analyzing the physical, sensory, or semantic features of an item.

Suppose that you are studying the concept of working memory. Simply memorizing the definition is unlikely to help much. But if you can elaborate the concept, you are more likely to remember it. The word *working* should remind you that working memory is involved in tasks that require effort and attention. And what benefits do effort and attention bring? Yes, that is why working memory is related to the ability to concentrate, resist distraction, and solve problems. Many students try to pare down what they are learning to the bare essentials, but knowing more details about something makes it more memorable; that is what elaboration means.

A related strategy for prolonging retention is **deep processing**, or the processing of meaning (Craik & Lockhart, 1972). If you process only the physical or sensory features of a stimulus, such as how the word *hypothalamus* is spelled and how it sounds, your processing will be shallow even if it is elaborated. If you recognize patterns and assign labels to objects or events ("*Hypo* means 'below,' so the *hypothalamus* must be *below* the thalamus"), your processing will be somewhat deeper. If you fully analyze the meaning of what you are trying to remember (perhaps by encoding the functions and importance of the hypothalamus), your processing will be deeper yet. *Shallow processing* is sometimes useful; when you memorize a poem, for instance, you will want to pay attention to (and elaborately encode) the sounds of the words and the patterns of rhythm in the poem and not just the poem's meaning. Usually, though, deep processing is more effective. That is why, if you try to memorize information that has little or no meaning for you, the information may not stick. ⊙►

deep processing In the encoding of information, the processing of meaning rather than simply the physical or sensory features of a stimulus.

⊙► **Simulate** the **Experiment**
Depth of Processing in **MyPsychLab**

Retrieval Practice

Many students think that the way to remember course material is simply to study it once thoroughly, or maybe twice, so they can retrieve the correct answers on an exam. Unfortunately, within just a few weeks or months after the exam, some of those answers will have vanished like steam on a bathroom mirror. *Retrieval practice*, the repeated retrieval of an item of information from memory, is necessary if a memory is to undergo consolidation and remain available for a long time. After all, that's the goal of learning.

In a university course, a good way to ensure retrieval practice is to take short quizzes after you have learned some material but before the big exam. In a series of experiments in which students learned words in foreign languages, once a student had learned a word it was (1) repeatedly studied but dropped from further testing, (2) repeatedly tested but dropped from further studying, or (3) dropped from studying and testing. To the surprise of the students themselves, studying after learning had no effect on their subsequent ability to recall the foreign words. But repeated *testing*, which caused them to repeatedly retrieve the words from memory, had a large benefit (Karpicke, 2012; Karpicke & Roediger, 2008). So when your professors want to keep quizzing you, it's only for your own good!

Remembering the Secrets of Learning

The very first "secret of learning" is to use the 3R method—read, recite, review—and we've helped you do that by building it into every one of our quizzes. Remember, though, successful learning techniques encourage you to process deeply, to use your imagination, to use elaborative rehearsal, to test yourself, and to think about what you are hearing or reading. And they all have something important in common: They teach you to be an active rather than a passive learner. Your memory isn't a sponge that simply soaks up whatever is poured on it. Memory requires you to transform new information into something you can understand, use, . . . and remember.

HOW TO REMEMBER BETTER

Effortful Encoding → Processing → Deep Processing / Elaborative Rehearsal / Active Studying (Read-Recite-Review) → Retrieval Practice

Learning Objectives

17 Discuss why forgetting may be adaptive.

18 Define three mechanisms that underlie forgetting.

19 Explain the controversy around repressed and recovered memories.

Why We Forget

Have you ever, in the heat of some deliriously happy moment, said to yourself, "I'll never forget this, never, *never*, NEVER"? Do you find that you can more clearly remember saying those words than the deliriously happy moment itself? Sometimes you encode an event, you rehearse it, you analyze its meaning, you tuck it away in long-term storage, and still you forget it. Is it any wonder that most of us have wished, at one time or another, for a "photographic memory"?

Actually, having a perfect memory is not the blessing that you might suppose. The Russian psychologist Alexander Luria (1968) once told of a journalist, S., who could reproduce giant grids of numbers both forward and backward, even after the passage of 15 years. To accomplish his astonishing feats, he used mnemonics, especially the formation of visual images. But you should not envy him, for he had a serious problem: He could not forget even when he wanted to. Along with the diamonds of experience, he kept dredging up the pebbles. Images he had formed to aid his memory kept creeping into consciousness, distracting him and interfering with his ability to concentrate. At times he even had trouble holding a conversation because the other person's words would set off a jumble of associations. Eventually, S. took to supporting himself by travelling from place to place, demonstrating his mnemonic abilities for audiences. ◉

Or consider two modern cases: Brad Williams and Jill Price both have extraordinary memories and have offered scientists the opportunity to study their abilities. When given any date going back for decades, they are able to say instantly what they were doing, what day of the week it was, and whether anything of great importance happened on that date. Mention November 7, 1991, to Williams, and he says (correctly), "Let's see; that would be around when [basketball star] Magic Johnson

Watch the **Video** *The Big Picture: The Woman Who Cannot Forget* in **MyPsychLab**

announced he had HIV. Yes, a Thursday. There was a big snowstorm here the week before." Neither Williams nor Price uses mnemonics or can say where their accurate memories come from. Although Williams and his family regard his abilities as a source of amusement, Price describes her nonstop recollections as a mixed blessing (Parker, Cahill, & McGaugh, 2006). The phenomenon of constant, uncontrollable recall, she wrote, is "totally exhausting. Some have called it a gift, but I call it a burden. I run my entire life through my head every day and it drives me crazy!!!"

Paradoxically, then, forgetting is adaptive: We need to forget some things if we wish to remember efficiently. Piling up facts without distinguishing the important from the trivial is just confusing. Nonetheless, most of us forget more than we want to and would like to know why.

In the early days of psychology, in an effort to measure pure memory loss independent of personal experience, Hermann Ebbinghaus (1885/1913) memorized long lists of nonsense syllables, such as *bok*, *waf*, or *ged*, and then tested his retention over a period of several weeks. Most of his forgetting occurred soon after the initial learning and then levelled off (see Figure 10.8a). Generations of psychologists adopted Ebbinghaus's method of studying memory, but his method did not tell them much about the kinds of memories that people care about most.

A century later, Marigold Linton decided to find out how people forget real events rather than nonsense syllables. Like Ebbinghaus, she used herself as a subject, but she charted the curve of forgetting over years rather than days. Every day for 12 years she recorded on a four- by six-inch card two or more things that had happened to her that day. Eventually, she accumulated a catalogue of thousands of discrete events, both trivial ("I have dinner at the Canton Kitchen: delicious lobster dish") and significant ("I land at Orly Airport in Paris"). Once a month, she took a random sampling of all the cards accumulated to that point, noted whether she could remember the events on them, and tried to date the events. Linton (1978) expected the kind of rapid forgetting reported by Ebbinghaus. Instead, as you can see in Figure 10.8b, she found that long-term forgetting was slower and proceeded at a much more constant pace, as details gradually dropped out of her memories.

Of course, some memories, especially those that mark important transitions, are more memorable than others. But why did Marigold Linton, like the rest of us, forget so many details? Psychologists have proposed five mechanisms to account for forgetting: decay, replacement of old memories by new ones, interference, cue-dependent forgetting, and psychological amnesia brought on by repression.

FIGURE 10.8 Two Kinds of Forgetting Curves
Hermann Ebbinghaus, who tested his own memory for nonsense syllables, found that his forgetting was rapid at first and then tapered off (a). In contrast, when Marigold Linton tested her own memory for personal events over a period of several years, her retention was excellent at first, but then it fell off at a gradual but steady rate (b).

Motor skills, which are stored as procedural memories, can last a lifetime; they rarely decay.

Karen Preuss/The Image Works

FIGURE 10.9 The Stop-Sign Study When people who saw a car with a yield sign (left) were later asked if they had seen "the stop sign" (a misleading question), many said they had. Similarly, when those shown a stop sign were asked if they had seen "the yield sign," many said yes. These false memories persisted even after the participants were told about the misleading questions, suggesting that misleading information had erased their original mental representations of the signs (Loftus, Miller, & Burns, 1978).

Dr. Elizabeth Loftus

Decay

One commonsense view, the **decay theory**, holds that memories simply fade with time if they are not accessed now and then. We have already seen that decay occurs in sensory memory and that it occurs in short-term memory as well unless we keep rehearsing the material. However, the mere passage of time does not account so well for forgetting in long-term memory. People commonly forget things that happened only yesterday while remembering events from many years ago. Indeed, some memories, both procedural and declarative, can last a lifetime. If you learned to swim as a child, you will still know how to swim at age 30, even if you have not been in a pool or lake for 22 years. We are also happy to report that some school lessons have great staying power. In one study, people did well on a Spanish test some 50 years after taking Spanish in high school, even though most had hardly used Spanish at all in the intervening years (Bahrick, 1984). Decay alone cannot entirely explain lapses in long-term memory.

Replacement

Another theory holds that new information entering memory can wipe out old information, just as recording over a USB key obliterates the original material. In a study supporting this view, researchers showed people slides of a traffic accident and used leading questions to get them to think that they had seen a stop sign when they had really seen a yield sign, or vice versa (see Figure 10.9). People in a control group who were not misled in this way were able to identify the sign they had actually seen. Later, all the participants were told the purpose of the study and were asked to guess whether they had been misled. Almost all of those who had been misled continued to insist that they had *really, truly* seen the sign whose existence had been planted in their minds (Loftus, Miller, & Burns, 1978). The researchers interpreted this finding to mean that the subjects had not just been trying to please them and that people's original perceptions had in fact been erased by the misleading information.

Interference

A third theory holds that forgetting occurs because similar items of information interfere with one another in either storage or retrieval; the information may get into memory and stay there, but it becomes confused with other information. Such interference, which occurs in both short- and long-term memory, is especially common when you have to recall isolated facts such as names, addresses, passwords, and area codes.

Suppose you are at a party and you meet someone named Julie. A little later you meet someone named Judy. You go on to talk to other people, and after an hour, you

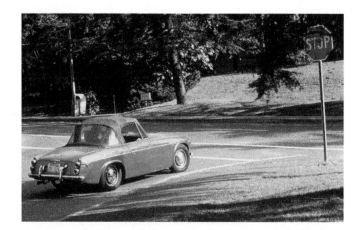

again bump into Julie, but by mistake you call her Judy. The second name has interfered with the first. This type of interference, in which new information interferes with the ability to remember old information, is called **retroactive interference**:

retroactive interference Forgetting that occurs when recently learned material interferes with the ability to remember similar material stored previously.

proactive interference Forgetting that occurs when previously stored material interferes with the ability to remember similar, more recently learned material.

cue-dependent forgetting The inability to retrieve information stored in memory because of insufficient cues for recall.

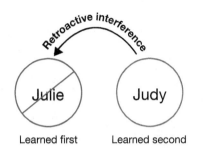

Retroactive interference is illustrated by the story of an absentminded professor of ichthyology (the study of fish) who complained that whenever he learned the name of a new student, he forgot the name of a fish. But whereas with replacement, the new memory erases the old and makes it irretrievable, in retroactive interference the loss of the old memory is sometimes just temporary. With a little concentration, that professor could probably recall his new students and his old fish.

Interference also works in the opposite direction. Old information (such as the foreign language you learned in high school) may interfere with the ability to remember current information (such as the new language you are trying to learn now). This type of interference is called **proactive interference**:

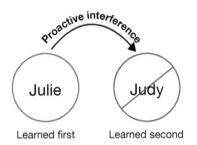

Over a period of weeks, months, and years, proactive interference may cause more forgetting than retroactive interference does, because we have stored up so much information that can potentially interfere with anything new.

Cue-Dependent Forgetting

Often, when we need to remember, we rely on *retrieval cues*, items of information that can help us find the specific information we're looking for. If you are trying to remember the last name of an actor you saw in an old film, it might help to know the actor's first name or another movie the actor starred in.

When we lack retrieval cues, we may feel as if we are lost in the mind's library. In long-term memory, this type of memory failure, called **cue-dependent forgetting**, may be the most common type of all. Willem Wagenaar (1986), who, like Marigold Linton, recorded critical details about events in his life, found that within a year he had forgotten 20% of those details; after five years, he had forgotten 60%. Yet when he gathered cues from witnesses about 10 events that he thought he had forgotten, he was able to recall something about all 10, which suggests that some of his forgetting was cue dependent.

Cues that were present when you learned a new fact or had an experience are apt to be especially useful later as retrieval aids. That may explain why remembering is often easier when you are in the same physical environment as you were when an event

Charlie Chaplin's film *City Lights* provides a classic illustration of state-dependent memory. After Charlie saves a drunken millionaire's life, the two spend the rest of the evening carousing. But the next day, after sobering up, the millionaire fails to recognize Charlie and gives him the cold shoulder. Then, once again, the millionaire gets drunk, and once again greets Charlie as a pal. (Note: Your memory will be best if you are sober during both encoding and recall!)

Mary Evans; Ronald Grant/Everett Collection

occurred: Cues in the present context match those from the past. Ordinarily, this overlap helps us remember the past more accurately. But it may also help account for the eerie phenomenon of *déjà vu*, the fleeting sense of having been in *exactly* the same situation that you are in now (*déjà vu* means "already seen" in French). Some element in the present situation, familiar from some other context that you cannot identify—even a dream, a novel, or a movie—may make the entire situation seem so familiar that it feels like it happened before (Brown, 2004). In other words, *déjà vu* may be a kind of mistaken recognition memory. Similar feelings of familiarity can actually be produced in the laboratory. When something about newly presented words, shapes, or photographs resembles elements of stimuli seen previously, people report that the new words, shapes, or photographs are familiar even though they can't recall the original ones (Cleary, 2008).

In everyday forgetting, your mental or physical state may act as a retrieval cue, evoking a **state-dependent memory**. If you were afraid or angry at the time of an event, you may remember that event best when you are once again in the same emotional state (Lang et al., 2001). Your memories can also be biased by whether or not your current mood is consistent with the emotional nature of the material you are trying to remember, a phenomenon known as **mood-congruent memory** (Bower & Forgas, 2000; Buchanan, 2007; Fiedler et al., 2011). You are more likely to remember happy events, and forget or ignore unhappy ones, when you are feeling happy than when you are feeling sad. Likewise, you are apt to remember unhappy events better and remember more of them when you are feeling unhappy, which in turn creates a vicious cycle. The more unhappy memories you recall, the more depressed you feel, and the more depressed you feel, the more unhappy memories you recall . . . so you stay stuck in your depression and make it even worse (Joormann & Gotlib, 2007; Wenzel, 2005).

The Repression Controversy

state-dependent memory The tendency to remember something when the rememberer is in the same physical or mental state as during the original learning or experience.

mood-congruent memory The tendency to remember experiences that are consistent with one's current mood and overlook or forget experiences that are not.

amnesia The partial or complete loss of memory for important personal information.

A final theory of forgetting is concerned with **amnesia**, the loss of memory for important personal information. Amnesia most commonly results from organic conditions such as brain disease or head injury, and is often temporary. However, for some individuals brain injury or disease results in profound and long-lasting memory deficits. Researchers at Baycrest Medical Centre in Toronto have relied on implicit memory to teach these individuals to use smartphones to compensate for their impaired explicit memory. Recent studies have demonstrated that, for both the affected individuals and their families, smartphones are effective prostheses that help them remember important events in their lives (Svoboda et al., 2010; Svoboda & Richards, 2009).

In *psychogenic amnesia*, however, the causes of forgetting are psychological, such as a need to escape feelings of embarrassment, guilt, shame, disappointment, or emotional shock. Psychogenic amnesia begins immediately after the precipitating event, involves massive memory loss including loss of personal identity, and usually ends suddenly, after just a few weeks. Despite its frequent portrayal in films and novels, in real life it is quite rare (McNally, 2003).

Psychologists generally accept the notion of psychogenic amnesia. *Traumatic amnesia*, however, is far more controversial. Traumatic amnesia allegedly involves the burying of specific traumatic events for a long period of time, often for many years. When the memory returns, it is supposedly immune to the usual processes of distortion and confabulation, and is recalled with perfect accuracy. The notion of traumatic amnesia originated with the psychoanalytic theory of Sigmund Freud, who argued that the mind defends itself from unwelcome and upsetting memories through the mechanism of **repression**, the involuntary pushing of threatening or upsetting information into the unconscious (see Chapter 14).

Most memory researchers reject the argument that a special unconscious mechanism called "repression" is necessary to explain either psychogenic or traumatic amnesia (Rofé, 2008). Richard McNally (2003) reviewed the experimental and clinical evidence and concluded, "The notion that the mind protects itself by repressing or dissociating memories of trauma, rendering them inaccessible to awareness, is a piece of psychiatric folklore devoid of convincing empirical support." The problem for most people who have suffered disturbing experiences is not that they cannot remember, but rather that they cannot forget: The memories keep intruding. There is no case on record of anyone who has repressed the memory of being in a concentration camp, being in combat, or being the victim of an earthquake or a terrorist attack, although details of even these horrible experiences are subject to distortion and fading over time, as are all memories.

Further, repression is hard to distinguish from normal forgetting. People who seem to forget disturbing experiences could be intentionally keeping themselves from retrieving their painful memories by distracting themselves whenever a memory is reactivated. Or they may be focusing consciously on positive memories instead. Perhaps, understandably, they are not rehearsing unhappy memories, so those memories fade with time. Perhaps they are simply avoiding the retrieval cues that would evoke the memories. But a reluctance to think about an upsetting experience is not the same as an *inability* to remember it (McNally, 2003).

The debate over traumatic amnesia and repression erupted into the public arena in the 1990s, when claims of recovered memories of sexual abuse began to appear. Many women and some men came to believe, during psychotherapy, that they could recall long-buried memories of having been sexually victimized for many years, and in bizarre ways. For therapists who accepted the notion of repression, such claims were entirely believable (Brown, Scheflin, & Whitfield, 1999; J. Herman, 1992). But most researchers today believe that almost all of these memories were false, having been evoked by therapists who were unaware of the research we described earlier on the power of suggestion and the dangers of confabulation (Lindsay & Read, 1994; McNally, 2003; Schacter, 2001). By asking leading questions, and by encouraging clients to construct vivid images of abuse, revisit those images frequently, and focus on emotional aspects of the images, such therapists unwittingly set up the very conditions that encourage confabulation and false memories.

Since the 1990s, accusations have steadily declined and many accusers have reconciled with their families (McHugh et al., 2004). Yet the concept of repression lingers on.

repression In psychoanalytic theory, the selective, involuntary pushing of threatening or upsetting information into the unconscious.

💡 **THINKING CRITICALLY**

Consider other interpretations.

How should critical thinkers evaluate someone's claim that they repressed memories of bizarre, traumatic experiences that went on for years, and only remembered what happened decades later, in therapy? What other explanations can account for these apparent memories?

Many of its original proponents have turned to the term "dissociation" to account for memory failures in traumatized individuals, the idea being that upsetting memories are split off (dissociated) from everyday consciousness (see Chapter 15). But a review of the research has found no good evidence that early trauma causes such dissociation (Giesbrecht et al., 2008; Huntjens, Verschuere, & McNally, 2012).

Of course, it is obviously possible for someone to forget a single unhappy or deeply unpleasant experience and not recall it for years, just as going back to your elementary school might trigger a memory of the time that you did something embarrassing in front of your whole class. How then should we respond to an individual's claim to have recovered memories of years of traumatic experiences that were previously "repressed"? How can we distinguish true memories from false ones?

Clearly, a person's recollections are likely to be trustworthy if there is corroborating evidence available, such as medical records, police or school reports, or the accounts of other people who had been present at the time. But in the absence of supporting evidence, we may have to tolerate uncertainty, because a person might have a detailed, emotionally rich "memory" that feels completely real but that has been unintentionally confabulated (Bernstein & Loftus, 2009). In such cases, it is important to consider the content of the recovered memory and how it was recovered.

Thus, given what we know about memory, we should be skeptical if the person says that he or she has memories from the first year or two of life; as we will see in the next section, this is not possible, physiologically or cognitively. We should be skeptical if, over time, the person's memories become more and more implausible; for instance, the person says that sexual abuse continued day and night for 15 years without ever being remembered and without anyone else in the household ever noticing anything amiss. We should also be skeptical if a person suddenly recovers a traumatic memory as a result of therapy or after hearing about supposed cases of recovered memory in the news or reading about one in a best-selling autobiography. And we should hear alarm bells go off if a therapist used suggestive techniques, such as hypnosis, dream analysis, "age regression," guided imagery, and leading questions, to "recover" the memories. These techniques are all known to increase confabulation (see Chapter 16).

Recite & Review

Recite: Make sure you don't have amnesia for the preceding material by reciting out loud everything you can about the *decay theory*, replacement of old information, *retroactive interference*, *proactive interference*, *cue-dependent forgetting*, *state-dependent memory*, *mood-congruent memory*, *amnesia*, and *repression*.

Review: Next, go back and reread this section.

Now take this *Quick Quiz:*

1. Wilma has been a long-time fan of the actor Ryan Gosling. Later, she meets an interesting guy named Bryan Gosling, but she keeps calling him Ryan. Why?

2. When a man at his twentieth high school reunion sees his old friends, he recalls incidents he thought were long forgotten. Why?

3. What mechanisms other than repression could account for a person's psychogenic amnesia?

Answers:

1. proactive interference **2.** The sight of his friends provides retrieval cues for the incidents. **3.** The person could be intentionally avoiding the memory by using distraction or focusing on positive experiences; failure to rehearse the memory may be causing it to fade; or the person may be avoiding retrieval cues that would evoke the memory.

Autobiographical Memories

For most of us, our memories about our own experiences are by far the most fascinating. We use them to entertain ("Did I ever tell you about the time . . . ?") and to connect with others ("Remember that time we . . . ?"). We analyze them to learn more about who we are. We modify and embellish them to impress others, and some people even publish them.

Childhood Amnesia: The Missing Years

A curious aspect of autobiographical memory is that most adults cannot recall any events from earlier than age two; and even after that, memories are sketchy at best until about age six (Jack & Hayne, 2010). A few people can vaguely recall significant events that occurred when they were as young as two years old, such as the birth of a sibling, but not earlier ones (Fivush & Nelson, 2004; Usher & Neisser, 1993). As adults, we cannot remember taking our first steps, or uttering our first halting sentences. We are victims of **childhood amnesia** (sometimes called *infantile amnesia*).

Childhood amnesia is disturbing to many people, so disturbing that some adamantly deny it, claiming to remember events from the second or even the first year of life. But like other false memories, these are merely reconstructions based on photographs, family stories, and imagination. The "remembered" event may not have even taken place. Swiss psychologist Jean Piaget (1952) once reported a memory of nearly being kidnapped at the age of two. Piaget remembered sitting in his pram, watching his nurse as she bravely defended him from the kidnapper. He remembered the scratches she received on her face. He remembered a police officer with a short cloak and white baton who finally chased the kidnapper away. But when Piaget was 15, his nurse wrote to his parents confessing that she had made up the entire story. Piaget noted, "I therefore must have heard, as a child, the account of this story . . . and projected it into the past in the form of a visual memory, which was a memory of a memory, but false."

Of course, we all retain procedural memories from the toddler stage, when we first learned to use a fork, drink from a cup, and pull a wagon. We also retain semantic memories acquired early in life: the rules of counting, the names of people and things, knowledge about objects in the world, words and meanings. Moreover, toddlers who are only one to two years old often reveal nonverbally that they remember past experiences (for example, by imitating something they saw earlier); and some four-year-olds can remember experiences that occurred before age 2½ (Bauer, 2002; McDonough & Mandler, 1994; Tustin & Hayne, 2010). What young children do not do well is encode and retain their early episodic memories—memories of particular events—and carry them into later childhood or adulthood. They cannot start doing this consistently until about age 4½ (Fivush & Nelson, 2004).

> **THINKING CRITICALLY**
>
> Avoid emotional reasoning.
>
> Many people get upset at the idea that their earliest experiences are lost to memory and angrily insist that memories from the first two years must be accurate. How can research help us think clearly about this issue?

childhood (infantile) amnesia The inability to remember events and experiences that occurred during the first two or three years of life.

This infant, whose leg is attached by a string to a colourful mobile, will learn within minutes to make the mobile move by kicking it. She may still remember the trick a week later, an example of procedural memory (Rovee-Collier, 1993). However, when she is older, she will not remember the experience itself; she will fall victim to childhood amnesia.

Carolyn Rovee-Collier

Freud thought that childhood amnesia was a special case of repression, but memory researchers today think that repression has nothing to do with it, and they point to better explanations:

1 **Brain development.** The prefrontal cortex, and other brain regions involved in the formation or storage of events, are not well developed until a few years after birth (McKee & Squire, 1993; Newcombe, Lloyd, & Balcomb, 2012). The research of Paul Frankland, at the University of Toronto, suggests that childhood amnesia results from the rapid addition of new neurons in the brain in key areas (Frankland, Kohler, & Jossellyn, 2013; Josselyn & Frankland, 2012). In addition, the brains of infants and toddlers are busily attending to all the new experiences of life, but this very fact makes it difficult for them to focus on just one event and shut out everything else that's going on—the kind of focus necessary for encoding and remembering (Gopnik, 2009).

2 **Cognitive development.** Before you can carry memories about yourself with you into adulthood, you have to have a self to remember. The emergence of a self-concept usually does not take place before age 2 (Howe, Courage, & Peterson, 1994). In addition, the cognitive schemas used by preschoolers are very different from those used by older children and adults. Only after acquiring language and starting school do children form schemas that contain the information and cues necessary for recalling earlier experiences (Howe, 2000). Young children's limited vocabularies and language skills also prevent them from narrating some aspects of an experience to themselves or others. Later, after their linguistic abilities have matured, they still cannot use those abilities to recall earlier, preverbal memories, because those memories were not encoded linguistically (Simcock & Hayne, 2002).

3 **Social development.** Preschoolers have not yet mastered the social conventions for reporting events, nor have they learned what is important to others. As a result, they focus on the routine aspects of an experience rather than the distinctive ones that will provide retrieval cues later, and they encode their experiences far less elaborately than adults do. Instead, they tend to rely on adults' questions to provide retrieval cues ("Where did we go for breakfast?" or "Who did you go trick-or-treating with?"). This dependency on adults may prevent them from building up a stable core of remembered material that will be available later on (Fivush & Nelson, 2005). But as children get older, their conversations with parents help them develop their own autobiographical memories, and thus play an important role in ending childhood amnesia (Reese, Jack, & White, 2010).

Nonetheless, our first memories, even when they are not accurate, may provide useful insights into our personalities, current concerns, ambitions, and attitudes toward life. What are *your* first memories—or, at least, what do you think they are? What might they tell you about yourself?

Memory and Narrative: The Stories of Our Lives

The communications researcher George Gerbner once observed that human beings are unique because we are the only animal that tells stories—and lives by the stories we tell. This view of human beings as the "storytelling animal" has had a huge impact in cognitive psychology. The *narratives* we compose to simplify and make sense of our lives have a profound influence on our plans, memories, love affairs, hatreds, ambitions, and dreams.

Thus we say, "I have no academic motivation because I flunked the third grade." We say, "Let me tell you the story of how we fell in love." We say, "When you hear what happened, you'll understand why I felt entitled to take such cold-hearted revenge." These stories are not necessarily fictions; rather, they are attempts to orga-nize and give meaning to the events of our lives. But because these narratives rely heavily on memory, and because memories are reconstructed and are constantly shift-ing in response to current needs, beliefs, and experiences, our autobiographies are also, to some degree, works of interpretation and imagination. Adult memories thus reveal as much about the present as they do about the past.

When you construct a narrative about an incident in your life, you have many choices about how to do it. The spin you put on a story depends on who the audience is; you are apt to put in, leave out, understate, and embellish different things depending on whether you are telling about an event in your life to a therapist, your boss, or friends on Facebook. Your story is also influenced by your purpose in relating it: to convey facts, entertain, or elicit sympathy. As a result of these influences, distortions are apt to creep in, even when you think you are being accurate. And once those distor-tions are part of the story, they are likely to become part of your memory of the events themselves (Marsh & Tversky, 2004).

Your culture also affects how you encode and tell your story. Canadians live in a culture that emphasizes individuality, personal feelings, and self-expression. Their earli-est childhood memories reflect that fact: They tend to report lengthy, emotionally elaborate memories of events, memories that focus on—who else?—themselves. In contrast, Chinese students, who live in a culture that emphasizes group harmony, social roles, and personal humility, tend to report early memories of family or neighbourhood activities, conflicts with friends or relatives that were resolved, and emotionally neutral events (Wang, 2008).

Once you have formulated a story's central theme ("My father never liked us"; "My partner was always competitive with me"), that theme may then serve as a cog-nitive schema that guides what you remember and what you forget (Mather, Shafir, & Johnson, 2000). Teenagers who have strong and secure attachments to their mothers remember previous quarrels with their moms as being less intense and conflicted than they reported at the time, whereas teenagers who have more ambiv-alent and insecure attachments remember such quarrels as being worse than they were (Feeney & Cassidy, 2003). A story's theme may also influence our judgments of events and people in the present. If you have a fight with your lover, the central theme in your story about the fight might be negative ("He was a jerk") or neutral

Recite & Review

Recite: It's time to say out loud everything you can about *childhood amnesia* and the influ-ence of narratives in autobiographical memory.

Review: Next, go back and read this section again.

Now take this *Quick Quiz:*

1. A friend of yours claims to remember her birth, her first tooth, and her first birthday party. She is most likely to be (a) lying, (b) confabulating, (c) repressing, (d) revealing wishful thinking, (e) accurately remembering.

2. Give three explanations for childhood amnesia (be specific).

3. Why are the themes in our life stories so important?

Answers:

1. b, d. 2. the immaturity of certain brain structures, making it difficult for very young children to focus attention, encode, and remember; cognitive factors such as immature cognitive schemas, lack of linguistic skills, and lack of a self-concept; lack of knowledge of social conventions for encoding and reporting events 3. They guide what we remember and forget about our personal pasts, and affect our judgments of events and people.

("It was a mutual misunderstanding"). This theme may bias you to blame or forgive your partner long after you have forgotten what the conflict was about (McGregor & Holmes, 1999). You can see that the spin you give a story is critical, so be careful about the stories you tell!

If you have been reading this chapter actively, you should be able to recall the many factors that can trip you up when you call upon your memory to add a plot twist to your life story, to remember a fact, or to idly daydream about a past event: confabulation, source misattribution, poor encoding and rehearsal strategies, interference, inadequate retrieval cues, suggestibility, and biases. By now, therefore, you should not be surprised that memory can be as fickle as it can be accurate. As cognitive psychologists have shown repeatedly, we are not merely actors in our personal life dramas; we also write the scripts.

Taking Psychology with You

THINKING CRITICALLY IN EVERYDAY LIFE

Memory and Myth

Psychological research is having a significant impact on people's ability to think critically about memory. Most notably, awareness of the fallibility of memory is growing among police, interrogators, prosecutors, and judges. At the start of this chapter, we promised to tell you what happened in the case of Thomas Sophonow, who was convicted of the murder of Barbara Stoppel on the strength of eyewitness testimony.

In 2000, the Winnipeg police announced that DNA evidence obtained from the crime scene did not match that of Thomas Sophonow and that they had a new suspect in the murder. In 2001, the Province of Manitoba struck an inquiry into the Sophonow case and found that the investigators had made many critical errors, including in how they questioned eyewitnesses. Thomas Sophonow was awarded $2.6 million in compensation for his wrongful imprisonment.

The case of Thomas Sophonow, though, is far from unique. In Canada alone, there have been similar high-profile cases: Guy Paul Morin, David Milgaard, Steven Truscott, and Donald Marshall Jr., to name a few. When psychological scientists examined 40 cases in which wrongful conviction had been established beyond a doubt, they found that 90% of those cases had involved a false identification by one or more eyewitnesses (Wells et al., 1998). Of course, not all eyewitness testimony is erroneous. But the potential for errors in identification shows how important it is to gather evidence carefully, ensure adequate legal representation for defendants, conduct police interviews using proper procedures, reduce pressure on witnesses, and obtain a DNA analysis whenever possible.

Inspired by the Innocence Project at the Cardozo School of Law in New York City, grassroots organizations of lawyers and students have been successfully challenging questionable convictions in the United States and Canada. Since the early 1990s, these efforts have led to the exoneration of nearly 300 innocent people, some of whom had been condemned to death (see individual cases at http://www.innocenceproject.org/). In 2006, a documentary film, *After Innocence*, chronicled seven cases of wrongful imprisonment; the men involved are still struggling to get their convictions expunged from their records. Other investigative projects around the world have produced similar accomplishments.

How would you feel if your testimony resulted in the conviction of an innocent person? Would you be able to admit your mistake, or would you, as most people do, cling more stubbornly than ever to the accuracy of your memory? Clearly eyewitnesses can and do make mistakes; ethnic differences can increase these mistakes; even memories of shocking or traumatic experiences are vulnerable to distortion and influence by others; and our confidence in our memories is not a reliable guide to their accuracy. Remember, many eyewitnesses are very confident, and the relation between confidence in memories and the accuracy of these memories is very poor.

Human memory has both tremendous strengths and tremendous weaknesses. Because our deepest sense of ourselves relies on our memories, this is a difficult truth to accept. It is so much easier to give in to emotional reasoning ("I just feel that my memory is absolutely, 100% true!") and not consider other explanations ("Could my brother's account of that family quarrel be more accurate than mine?"). But if we can do so, we will be able to respect the great power of memory and at the same time retain humility about our capacity for error, confabulation, and self-deception.

Summary

Reconstructing the Past

- Unlike a smartphone, human memory is highly selective and is *reconstructive*: People add, delete, and change elements in ways that help them make sense of information and events. They often experience *source misattribution*, the inability to distinguish information stored during an event from information added later. Even vivid *flashbulb memories* tend to become less accurate or complete over time.

- Because memory is so often reconstructive, it is subject to *confabulation*, the confusion of imagined events with actual ones. Confabulation is especially likely when people have thought, heard, or told others about the imagined event many times and thus experience *imagination inflation*, the image of the event contains many details, or the event is easy to imagine. Confabulated memories can feel vividly real yet be false.

Memory and the Power of Suggestion

- The reconstructive nature of memory also makes memory vulnerable to suggestion. Eyewitness testimony is especially vulnerable to error when the suspect's ethnicity differs from that of the witness, when leading questions are put to witnesses, or when witnesses are given misleading information.

- Like adults, children often remember the essential aspects of an event accurately but can also be suggestible, especially when responding to biased interviewing by adults— when they are asked questions that blur the line between fantasy and reality, are asked leading questions, are told what "other kids" had supposedly said, and are praised for making false allegations.

In Pursuit of Memory

- The ability to remember depends in part on the type of performance called for. In tests of *explicit memory* (conscious recollection), *recognition* is usually better than *recall*. In tests of *implicit memory*, which is measured by indirect methods such as *priming* and the *relearning method*, past experiences may affect current thoughts or actions even when these experiences are not consciously remembered.

- In *information-processing models*, memory involves the *encoding*, *storage*, and *retrieval* of information. The *three-box model* proposes three interacting systems: the sensory register, short-term memory, and long-term memory. Some cognitive scientists prefer a *parallel distributed processing (PDP)* or *connectionist* model, which represents knowledge as connections among numerous interacting processing units, distributed in a vast network and all operating in parallel. But the three-box model continues to offer a convenient way to organize the major findings on memory.

The Three-Box Model of Memory

- In the three-box model, incoming sensory information makes a brief stop in the *sensory register*, which momentarily retains it in the form of sensory images.

- *Short-term memory (STM)* retains new information for up to 30 seconds by most estimates (unless rehearsal takes place). The capacity of STM is extremely limited but can be extended if information is organized into larger units by *chunking*. Early models of STM portrayed it mainly as a bin for the temporary storage of information, but many models now envision it as a part of a more general *working-memory* system, which includes an "executive" that controls the retrieval of information from long-term memory and focuses on information needed for the task being performed. Working memory permits us to control attention, resist distraction, and therefore maintain information in an active, accessible state.

- *Long-term memory (LTM)* contains an enormous amount of information that must be organized to make it manageable. Words (or the concepts they represent) are often organized by semantic categories. Many models of LTM represent its contents as a network of interrelated concepts. The way people use these networks depends on experience and education. Research on *tip-of-the-tongue (TOT) states* shows that words are also indexed in terms of sound and form.

- *Procedural memories* ("knowing how") are memories for how to perform specific actions; *declarative memories* ("knowing that") are memories for abstract or representational knowledge. Declarative memories include *semantic memories* (general knowledge) and *episodic memories* (memories for personally experienced events). Episodic memories allow us to retrieve past events in order to imagine the future.

- The three-box model is often invoked to explain the *serial-position effect* in memory, but although it can explain the *primacy effect*, it cannot explain why a *recency effect* sometimes occurs after a considerable delay.

The Biology of Memory

- Short-term memory involves temporary changes within neurons that alter their ability to release neurotransmitters, whereas long-term memory involves lasting structural changes in neurons and synapses. *Long-term potentiation*, an increase in the strength of synaptic responsiveness, seems to be an important mechanism of long-term memory. Neural changes associated with long-term potentiation take time to develop, which helps explain why long-term memories require a period of *consolidation*.

- The amygdala is involved in the formation, consolidation, and retrieval of emotional memories. Areas of the frontal lobes are especially active during short-term and working-memory tasks. The prefrontal cortex and parts of the temporal lobes are involved in the efficient encoding of words and pictures. The hippocampus plays a critical role in the formation and retrieval of long-term declarative memories. Other areas, such as the cerebellum, are crucial for the formation of procedural memories. Studies of patients with amnesia suggest that different brain systems are active during explicit and implicit memory tasks. The long-term storage of declarative memories possibly takes place in cortical areas that were active during the original perception of the information or event. The various components of a memory are probably stored at different sites, with all of these sites participating in the representation of the event as a whole.

- Hormones released by the adrenal glands during stress or emotional arousal, including epinephrine and norepinephrine, enhance memory. These adrenal hormones cause the level of glucose to rise in the bloodstream, and glucose may enhance memory directly or by altering the effects of neurotransmitters. But very high hormone levels can interfere with the retention of information; a moderate level is optimal for learning new tasks.

How We Remember

- *Mnemonics* can enhance retention, but for ordinary memory tasks, complex memory tricks are often ineffective or even counterproductive.

- To remember material well, we must encode it accurately in the first place. Some kinds of information, such as material in this course, require *effortful*, as opposed to automatic, encoding. Rehearsal of information keeps it in short-term memory and increases the chances of long-term retention. *Elaborative rehearsal* is more likely to result in transfer to long-term memory than is *maintenance rehearsal*, and *deep processing* is usually a more effective retention strategy than *shallow processing*. *Retrieval practice* is necessary if a memory is going to be consolidated, and therefore last and be available for a long time. The *read-recite-review strategy* encourages active learning and produces better results than simply reading and rereading material.

Why We Forget

- Forgetting can occur for several reasons. Information in sensory and short-term memory appears to *decay* if it does not receive further processing. New information may erase and replace old information in long-term memory. *Proactive* and *retroactive interference* may take place. *Cue-dependent forgetting* may occur when *retrieval cues* are inadequate. The most effective retrieval cues are those that were present at the time of the initial experience. A person's mental or physical state may also act as a retrieval cue, evoking a *state-dependent memory*. We tend to remember best those events that are congruent with our current mood (*mood-congruent memory*).

- *Amnesia*, the forgetting of important personal information, usually occurs because of disease or injury to the brain. *Psychogenic amnesia*, which involves a loss of personal identity and has psychological causes, is rare. *Traumatic amnesia*, which allegedly involves the forgetting of specific traumatic events for long periods of time, is highly controversial, as is *repression*, the psychodynamic explanation of traumatic amnesia. Because these concepts lack good empirical support, psychological scientists are skeptical about their validity and about the accuracy of "recovered memories." Critics argue that many therapists, unaware of the power of suggestion and the dangers of confabulation, have encouraged false memories of victimization.

Autobiographical Memories

- Most people cannot recall any events from earlier than the age of two. The reasons for such *childhood amnesia* include the immaturity of certain brain structures, making it difficult for very young children to focus attention, encode, and remember; cognitive factors such as immature cognitive schemas, lack of linguistic skills, and lack of a self-concept; and lack of knowledge of social conventions for encoding and reporting events.

- A person's *narrative* "life story" organizes the events of his or her life and gives them meaning.

Taking Psychology with You

- DNA evidence has exonerated many men who were falsely convicted of rape and murder, making the public and members of the criminal-justice system more aware of the limitations of eyewitness testimony and the fallibility of memory.

Facial expressions do not always convey the emotion being felt. A posed, social smile like Nobel laureate Alice Munro (left) may be expressed in a variety of situations. And look at the face of Jennifer Jones, who has just won the gold medal in curling—we assume that she is actually joyful rather than sad, which is suggested by her face.

Left: ZUMA Press Inc/Alamy. Right: Adrian Dennis/Staff/Getty Images.

designed to test for depth perception, which emerges early in infancy. But in one experiment, 1-year-old babies were put on a more ambiguous cliff that did not drop off sharply and thus did not automatically evoke fear, as the original cliff did. In this case, the babies' behaviour depended on their mothers' expressions: 74% crossed the cliff when their mothers put on a happy, reassuring expression, but not a single infant crossed when the mother showed an expression of fear (Sorce et al., 1985). If you have ever watched a toddler take a tumble and then look at his or her parent before deciding whether to cry or to forget it, you will understand the influence of parental facial expressions. And you can see why they have had such survival value for babies: An infant needs to be able to read the parent's facial signals of alarm or safety because young children do not yet have the experience necessary for judging danger.

Facial Expressions in Context. There are important cultural and social limits to the supposedly universal readability of facial expressions. When you perceive another person's facial expression, you are being influenced by what else is happening in the situation, by your own emotional state, and by the cultural context (Barrett, Mesquita, & Gendron, 2011). People are better at identifying emotions expressed by others in their own ethnic, national, or regional group than they are at recognizing the emotions of foreigners (Elfenbein & Ambady, 2003). Within a culture, facial expressions can have different meanings depending on the situation; a smile can mean "I'm happy!" or "I don't want to make you angry while I tell you this." Likewise, people often interpret identical facial expressions—even of universal emotions such as disgust, sadness, and anger—in very different ways, depending on what else they are observing in the social context; thus, almost everyone recognizes the expression of disgust if all they see is a face. But when they see a picture of the same disgusted expression on a man with his arm raised as if to strike, they will say the expression is anger (Aviezer et al., 2008). Moreover, although infants and young children can obviously *display* facial expressions of various emotions, they have to learn how to identify those expressions in adults. At first, they seem to have only two general categories: positive (happy) and negative (notably fear, as in the example of the visual cliff, and anger). They do not recognize adults' expressions of sadness until they are about 3, and disgust at about age 5; until then, they will usually misinterpret these expressions as anger (Widen & Russell, 2010).

Finally, of course, facial expressions are only part of the emotional picture. Emotions exist without facial expressions, and facial expressions need not convey emotions. People can feel sad, anxious, or angry without letting it show—and, conversely, they can use facial expressions to lie about their feelings. In Shakespeare's play *Henry VI*, the villain who will become the evil King Richard III says:

> Why, I can smile, and murder while I smile;
> And cry content to that which grieves my heart;
> And wet my cheeks with artificial tears,
> And frame my face to all occasions.

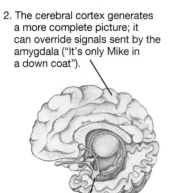

2. The cerebral cortex generates a more complete picture; it can override signals sent by the amygdala ("It's only Mike in a down coat").

1. The amygdala scrutinizes information for its emotional importance ("It's a bear! Be afraid! Run!").

Emotion and the Brain. Various parts of the brain are involved in the different components of emotional experience: recognizing another person's emotion, feeling a specific emotion, expressing an emotion, and acting on an emotion. People who have a stroke that affects brain areas involved in the experience of disgust are often unable to feel disgusted. One young man with stroke damage in these regions had little or no emotional response to images and ideas that would be disgusting to most people, such as faeces-shaped chocolate (Calder et al., 2000). Are you making a disgusted expression as you read that? He couldn't.

Most emotions motivate a response (an *action tendency*) of some sort: to embrace or approach the person who instills joy in you, attack a person who makes you angry, withdraw from a food that disgusts you, or flee from a person or situation that frightens you (Frijda, Kuipers, & ter Schure, 1989). The prefrontal regions of the brain are involved in these impulses to approach or withdraw. Regions of the *right* prefrontal region are specialized for the impulse to withdraw or escape (as in disgust and fear). Regions of the *left* prefrontal cortex are specialized for the motivation to approach others (as in happiness, a positive emotion, and anger, a negative one) (Carver & Harmon-Jones, 2009; Harmon-Jones, Peterson, & Harris, 2009). People who have greater-than-average activation of the left areas, compared with the right, have more positive feelings, a quicker ability to recover from negative emotions, and a greater ability to suppress negative emotions (Urry et al., 2004). People with damage to this area often lose the capacity for joy and people who are highly anxious may benefit from stimulation of this area (Balconi & Ferrari, 2013).

Parts of the prefrontal cortex are also involved in the *regulation* of emotion, helping us modify and control our feelings, keeping us on an even keel and responding appropriately to others (Jackson et al., 2003). A degenerative disease that destroys cells in parts of the frontal lobes causes not only a loss of cells, say researchers, but a "loss of self." It blunts the sufferer's ability to respond to the emotions of others, understand why they and others feel as they do, and adjust their own emotional responses appropriately: A loving mother becomes indifferent to her child's injury; a businessman does embarrassing things and doesn't notice the reaction of others (Levenson & Miller, 2007).

The amygdala plays a key role in emotion, especially anger and fear (see Chapter 4). The amygdala is responsible for evaluating sensory information, determining its emotional importance, and making the initial decision to approach or withdraw from a person or situation (Adolphs, 2001; LeDoux, 1996). The amygdala instantly assesses danger or threat, which is a good thing, because otherwise you could be standing in the street asking, "Is it wise to cross now, while that very large truck is coming toward me?" The amygdala's initial response may then be overridden by a more accurate appraisal from the cortex. This is why you jump with fear when you suddenly feel a hand on your back in a dark alley, and why your fear evaporates when the cortex registers that the hand belongs to a friend whose lousy idea of humour is to scare you in a dark alley.

If either the amygdala or critical areas of the cortex are damaged, abnormalities result in the ability to experience fear or recognize it in others. A patient known as S. M. has a rare disease that destroyed her amygdala, and as a result she cannot feel fear—not toward snakes, not when watching scary movies, not even when she was attacked in a park by a man with a knife (Feinstein et al., 2011). People with damage in

GET INVOLVED!   Turn on Your Right Hemisphere

These faces have expressions of happiness on one side and sadness on the other. Look at the nose of each face; which face looks happier? Which face looks sadder?

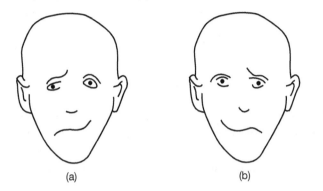

(a)   (b)

You are likely to see face *b* as the happier one and face *a* as the sadder one. The reason is that in most people the left side of a picture is processed by the right side of the brain, where recognition of emotional expression primarily occurs (Oatley, Keltner, & Jenkins, 2006).

the cortex may have difficulty turning off their own fear responses, causing anxiety and obsessive-compulsive disorders (see Chapter 15).

Mirror, Mirror, in the Brain: Neurons for Imitation and Empathy. In 1992, a team of Italian neuroscientists accidentally made an astonishing discovery. They had implanted wires in the brains of macaque monkeys, in regions involved in planning and carrying out movement. Every time a monkey moved and grasped an object, the cells fired and the monitor registered a sound. One day, a graduate student heard the monitor go off when the monkey was simply observing him eating an ice-cream cone. The neuroscientists looked more closely, and found that certain neurons in the monkeys' brains were firing not only when the monkeys were picking up peanuts and eating them but also when the monkeys were merely observing their human caretakers doing exactly the same thing (Ferrari, Rozzi, & Fogassi, 2005). These neurons responded only to very specific actions: A neuron that fired when a monkey grasped a peanut would also fire when the scientist grasped a peanut but not when the scientist grasped something else (Rizzolatti & Sinigaglia, 2010). The scientists called these cells **mirror neurons**. Incredibly, human mirror neurons do not simply recognize another person's action; they respond only when the action is *intentional* rather than accidental (Iacoboni, 2008; Iacoboni et al., 2005).

In humans, mirror neurons enable us to identify what others are feeling, to understand other people's intentions, and to imitate their actions and gestures, even in infancy (Iacoboni, 2008; Fogassi & Ferrari, 2007; Green, Kochukhova, & Gredebäck, 2014; Nyström, 2008). When you see another person in pain, one reason you feel a jolt of empathy is that mirror neurons involved in pain are firing. When you watch a spider crawl up someone's leg, one reason you have a creepy sensation is that your mirror neurons are firing—the same ones that would fire if the spider were crawling up your own

mirror neurons Brain cells that fire when a person or animal observes others carrying out an action; they are involved in empathy, language comprehension, imitation, and reading emotions.

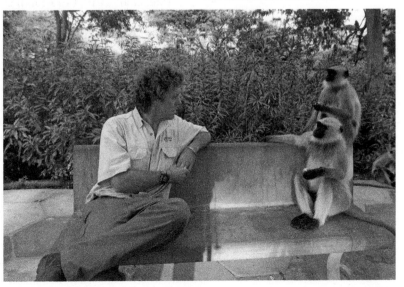

Mirror neurons are surely at work in this conversation.

Pete Oxford/Nature Picture Library

These volunteers, videotaped in a study of conversational synchrony, are obviously in sync with one another, even though they have just met. The degree to which two people's gestures and expressions are synchronized reflects the rapport they feel with one another. Such synchrony can also create a contagion of moods (Grahe & Bernieri, 1999).

Frank J. Bernieri

leg. And when you see another person's facial expression, your own facial muscles will often subtly mimic it, activating a similar emotional state (Dimberg, Thunberg, & Elmehed, 2000).

When you have an emotional response to music, mirror neurons are involved (Chapin et al., 2010). Mirror neurons thus appear to be the underlying mechanism for human empathy, nonverbal rapport, and *mood contagion*, the spreading of an emotion from one person to another. Mood contagion occurs when two people feel rapport with one another's *positive* emotions, nonverbal signals, and posture: Their gestures become more synchronized, they behave more cooperatively, and they feel more cheerful (Wiltermuth & Heath, 2009). This phenomenon may be the reason that synchronized human activities—marches, bands, dancing—are socially and emotionally beneficial. Mood contagion also occurs to negative emotions—which means that our friends and neighbours may have more power over our moods than we realize.

The discovery of mirror neurons is exciting, but their functions are still hotly debated (Gallese et al., 2011). For example, these neurons seem strongly involved in empathy, but empathy has social limits: Mirror neurons go to sleep when people look at individuals they dislike or are prejudiced against. If you like a person, mimicking their facial movements and gestures will increase that liking, but if you dislike the person, trying to perk up your mirror neurons by mimicking won't improve matters at all (Stel et al., 2010; van Baaren et al., 2009).

The Energy of Emotion. Once the brain areas associated with emotion are activated, the next stage of the emotional relay is the release of hormones to enable you to respond quickly. When you are under stress or feeling an intense emotion, the sympathetic division of the autonomic nervous system spurs the adrenal glands to send out *epinephrine* and *norepinephrine* (see Chapter 4). These chemical messengers produce arousal and alertness. The pupils dilate, widening to allow in more light; the heart beats faster; blood pressure increases; breathing speeds up; and blood sugar rises. These changes provide the body with the energy needed to take action, whether you are happy and want to get close to someone you love, or are scared and want to escape a person who is frightening you (Löw et al., 2008).

Epinephrine in particular provides the energy of an emotion, that familiar tingle of excitement. At high levels, it can create the sensation of being "seized" or "flooded" by an emotion that is out of your control. In a sense, you are out of control, because you cannot consciously alter your heart rate and blood pressure. However, you can learn to control your actions when you are under the sway of an emotion (even intense

REVIEW 11.1 **Emotion and the Body**

Facial Expressions	Reflect internal feelings, influence internal feelings (facial feedback), communicate feelings, signal intentions, affect behaviour and feelings of others (mood contagion), conceal or pretend an emotion (lie).
The Brain	Specific areas are involved in specific emotions (e.g., disgust) and in different aspects of emotion (e.g., recognizing facial expressions in others, expressing an emotion oneself).
Amygdala	Determines emotional importance of incoming sensory information; is responsible for the initial decision to approach or withdraw; is involved in learning, recognizing, and expressing fear.
Cortex	Appraises the significance of emotional information from the amygdala. The left prefrontal cortex is associated with "approach" emotions (e.g., happiness, anger); the right prefrontal cortex with "withdrawal" emotions (e.g., fear, sadness).
Mirror Neurons	Found in various parts of the brain, these cells fire in response to the actions or emotions of another person, possibly creating synchrony, promoting empathy, and generating mood contagion.
Autonomic Nervous System	Activates the hormones epinephrine and norepinephrine, which produce energy and alertness. Certain emotions are associated with distinctive patterns of autonomic nervous system activity.

anger, as we discuss in "Taking Psychology with You"). As arousal subsides, anger may pale into annoyance, ecstasy into contentment, fear into suspicion, past emotional whirlwinds into calm breezes.

Although epinephrine and norepinephrine are released during many emotional states, emotions also differ from one another physiologically: Fear, disgust, anger, sadness, surprise, and happiness are associated with different patterns of brain activity and autonomic nervous system activity, as measured by heart rate, electrical conductivity of the skin, and finger temperature (Damasio et al., 2000; Levenson, 1992). These distinctive patterns may explain why people all over the world use similar terms to describe the primary emotions, saying they feel "hot and bothered" when they are angry or "cold and clammy" when they are afraid. These metaphors capture what is going on in their bodies.

In sum, the physiology of emotion involves characteristic facial expressions; activity in specific parts of the brain, notably the amygdala, specialized parts of the prefrontal cortex, and mirror neurons; and sympathetic nervous system activity that prepares the body for action (see Review 11.1).

BIOLOGY and
Lie Detection

On the TV crime drama *Lie to Me*, a psychologist ("the world's leading detection expert") stated he could tell immediately whether a bad guy was lying. What a great skill! Lots of people want to know if someone is lying: teachers, employers, the government. The problem is that justice depends not only on finding out "whodunnit" but also on protecting those who didn't do anything. The challenge for social scientists and for law enforcement is to better identify liars without falsely accusing truth tellers.

Unfortunately, the idea that some people have a "natural" ability to detect the lies of others is not supported by evidence. Even highly

THINKING CRITICALLY

Analyze assumptions and biases.

Many people assume that because physiological changes, such as an elevated heart rate, are involved in emotional states, physiological measurements can tell us whether someone is afraid, guilty, or lying. Is this assumption valid? What evidence does it overlook?

educated and trained individuals have only about a 54% chance of detecting a lie (Bond & DePaulo, 2008). (For the rest of us, the success rate is 50%, the same as flipping a coin.) People may speak hesitantly in telling a story, seem stressed in their speech, or avoid looking the interrogator in the eye for many reasons (DePaulo et al., 2003; Leo, 2008; Vrij, Granhag, & Porter, 2010). They may be frightened, not know what answers are expected, have nervous mannerisms, or come from a culture that regards direct eye contact as confrontational or rude. However, recent research has shown that some factors that many Canadians might think would affect our ability to detect lies, do not. In a clever experiment, students viewed women who were either veiled (either wearing a niqab or hijab) or not. Perhaps surprisingly, the students were more accurate at when veiled women were lying than when the same women were not veiled (Leach et al., 2014). ◉

👁━Watch the Video
Special Topics: Detecting Lies
in **MyPsychLab**

For centuries, people have tried to determine when a person is lying by detecting physiological responses that cannot be controlled consciously. This is the idea behind the *polygraph machine* (lie detector), which was invented in 1915 by a Harvard professor named William Marston. The polygraph is based on the assumption that a lie generates emotional arousal. A person who is guilty and fearful of being found out will therefore have increased activity in the autonomic nervous system while responding to incriminating questions: a faster heart rate, increased respiration rate, and increased electrical conductance of the skin.

Law enforcement officers are still enthusiastic about the polygraph, but most psychological scientists regard polygraph tests as invalid because no physiological patterns of autonomic arousal are specific to lying (Leo, 2008; Lykken, 1998). Machines cannot tell whether you are feeling guilty, angry, nervous, amused, or revved up from an exciting day. Innocent people may be tense and nervous about the whole procedure. They may react to the word *bank*, not because they robbed a bank but because they recently bounced a cheque; in either case, the machine will record a lie. The reverse mistake is also common: People who are motivated to escape detection can often beat the machine by tensing muscles or thinking about an exciting experience during neutral questions.

FIGURE 11.2 Misjudging the Innocent

This graph shows the average percentages across three studies of classifications by lie detectors. Nearly half of the innocent people were classified as guilty, and a significant number of guilty people were classified as innocent. The suspect's guilt or innocence had been independently confirmed by other means, such as by admissions by the actual perpetrators (Iacono & Lykken, 1997).

The polygraph will correctly catch many liars and guilty people. The main problem is that it also falsely identifies many innocent people as having lied (see Figure 11.2). For this reason, in 1987 the Supreme Court of Canada decided that the results of polygraph tests would no longer be admissible as evidence in Canadian courts.

Because of the unreliability of the polygraph, researchers are trying to find other ways of measuring physiological signs of lying. The Computer Voice Stress Analyzer and Layered Voice Analysis are based on the assumption that the human voice contains telltale signals that betray a speaker's emotional state and intent to deceive. Its promoters claim high degrees of accuracy, but research has mostly yielded negative findings (Harnsberger et al., 2009; Leo, 2008). Like the polygraph, voice analyzers detect physiological changes that may indicate fear, anger, or other signs of stress rather than lying, and they often falsely label true statements as lies.

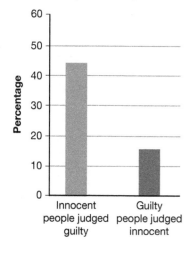

The hottest new effort at lie detection is brain imaging. Some researchers are trying to find "brain fingerprints" by using fMRIs of brain activity to see whether they can infer that a person is lying from characteristic patterns of brain activity. Some companies are already advertising that they can predict with better than 90% certainty whether or not someone is telling the truth. Don't buy it. Areas of the brain that light up on a fMRI when people are allegedly lying are also those involved with many other cognitive functions, including memory, self-awareness, and self-monitoring (Greely & Illes, 2007). And because of the normal variability among people in their autonomic and brain reactivity, innocent but highly reactive people are still likely to be mislabelled guilty by these tests (Stix, 2008). A 2011 report from the British Royal Society's committee on neuroscience and law concluded that using brain scanners to determine whether a witness is lying is premature, because of their unreliability, and to date the courts have agreed.

More promising methods of lie detection are cognitive rather than biological. One approach increases the "cognitive load" on the suspect, because liars have more things to keep straight in their minds—the truth, the lie they told, and the story they concocted to cover it up. When the interviewer increases that mental load, as by asking the suspect to tell the story backward, liars make more mistakes (Vrij et al., 2011).

To date no technique is foolproof at catching the guilty, and the main reason is the flawed assumption that universal and identifiable biological or cognitive signs reveal when a person is lying accurately (Gamer & Ambach, 2014). We're telling the truth!

Recite & Review

Recite: A little surge of hormonal energy should help you say aloud what you can about *emotion*, *primary and secondary emotions*, *facial feedback*, *mirror neurons* and the mirror system, mood contagion, the parts of the brain involved in emotion, epinephrine and norepinephrine, and the polygraph and other methods of "lie detection."

Review: Next, read this section once more.

Now take this *Quick Quiz:*

1. Three-year-old Olivia sees her dad dressed as a gorilla and runs away in fear. What brain structure is probably involved in her emotional reaction?

2. Mia is watching an old Laurel and Hardy film, which makes her chuckle and makes her want to see more funny movies. Which side of her prefrontal cortex is likely to be most active?

3. Rajiv is watching *Horrible Hatchet Homicides in Halifax*. What cells in his brain are making him wince when the hero is being attacked?

4. Rajiv is watching *Horrible Hatchet Homicides in Halifax, II*. What hormones are causing his heart to pound and his palms to sweat when the murderer is stalking an unsuspecting victim?

Answers:

1. the amygdala 2. the left 3. mirror neurons 4. epinephrine and norepinephrine

Emotion and the Mind

Two friends of ours returned from a mountain-climbing trip to Nepal. One said, "I was ecstatic! The crystal-clear skies, the millions of stars, the friendly people, the majestic mountains, the harmony of the universe!" The other said, "I was miserable! The bedbugs and fleas, the lack of toilets, the yak-butter tea, the awful food, the unforgiving mountains!" Same trip, two different emotional reactions to it. Why?

In the first century CE, the Stoic philosophers suggested an answer: People do not become angry or sad or ecstatic because of actual events, but because of their explanations of those events. Modern psychologists have verified the Stoics' ideas experimentally. Many years ago, Stanley Schachter and Jerome Singer (1962) argued that the experience of emotion depends both on physiological arousal and on how you interpret and explain that arousal. In their classic experiment, participants were told that they were being given a vitamin but were actually given either epinephrine or saline. Participants who were told that the vitamin could have side effects consistent with epinephrine (for example, increased heart rate) interpreted their change in physical

appraisals A person's perceptions, beliefs, attributions, and goals, that determine which emotion he or she will feel in a given circumstance; they are a central component of emotion and the emotional experience.

state as being due to the injection and not due to an emotional state. However, some participants were not told of the possible side effects of epinephrine. When these participants were paired with confederates who acted emotionally, they tended to interpret the changes in their heart rate as reflecting emotional states. Thus, Schachter and Singer suggest that although your body may be churning away in high gear, unless you can explain and label those changes, you will not feel a true emotion. This idea spurred other investigators to study how emotions are created and influenced by **appraisals**: beliefs, perceptions of the situation, expectations, goals, and attributions that people make to explain their own and other people's behaviour (see Chapter 8) (Moors et al., in press; Fairholme et al., 2009; Lindquist & Barrett, 2008). Human beings, after all, are the only species that can say, "The more I thought about it, the madder I got." We think ourselves into an emotional state, and sometimes we think ourselves out of it.

The importance of appraisals in emotion explains why two people often have different emotional reactions to the same situation. In a classic test of Schachter and Singer's theory, Dutton and Aron (1974) employed a rather unorthodox methodology to manipulate arousal in their male participants—they employed a very high suspension bridge over the Capilano Gorge in North Vancouver. The male hikers participating in the experiment met an attractive female research assistant in one of two conditions. Some met her while crossing the (scary) suspension bridge, whereas others met her while standing on the lower and more stable bridge. Following this meeting, the male hikers were asked to rate the attractiveness of the female research assistant. Those males who met her on the scary bridge rated her as more attractive. In a clever twist, the researchers also had the female research assistant leave her phone number with all the participants. Just as the attractiveness ratings would suggest, the males who met her on the scary bridge were more likely to actually call her for a date later on. Therefore, the feelings of arousal that the male hikers experienced on the scary bridge were interpreted as *attraction*. If she had not been present, these feelings of arousal probably would have been interpreted as *fear*.

Psychologists have studied how thoughts affect all kinds of emotions. For example, imagine that you get an A on your psychology midterm; how will you feel? Or perhaps you get a D on that midterm; how will you feel then? Most people assume that success brings happiness and failure brings unhappiness, but the emotions you feel will depend more on how you explain your grade than on what you actually get. Do you

When male hikers met a female research assistant on a scary suspension bridge, they found her more attractive than did males who met the same female on a lower, more stable bridge, just as the Schachter-Singer theory would predict.

Francesca Russell/Getty Images

GET INVOLVED! Examining Your Emotions after an Exam

After your next midterm, write down your feelings at the end of the exam, how well you think you are going to do, and the reasons for the predicted grade. Do you attribute the grade to your own efforts or perhaps a lack of effort? How do your feelings influence your predicted grade? When you get the results, do those explanations change? That is, do you continue to attribute your performance to your effort (especially if you did well) or do you blame your instructor for being too hard or "unfair" (especially if you didn't do as well as you thought)? How are these explanations related to your feelings about your grade?

attribute your grade to your own efforts (or lack of them) or to the teacher, fate, or luck? Students who believe they perform well because of their own efforts tend to feel proud, competent, and satisfied. Those who believe they perform well because of a lucky fluke tend to feel gratitude, surprise, or guilt ("I don't deserve this"). Those who blame others tend to feel angry (Weiner, 1986). ◉

Appraisal patterns also differ across cultures. Japanese and Canadians tend to differ in their appraisals of the causes and responsibility for errors and for success. As a result, Japanese are more likely to blame themselves when something goes wrong and to experience shame, whereas Canadians are more likely to blame others and experience anger. In the case of success, Canadians are more likely to take credit and feel proud, whereas Japanese are more likely to regard their success as reflecting the situation and opportunity—and feel lucky (Imada & Ellsworth, 2011).

Here is a more surprising example of how thoughts affect emotions. Of two Olympic finalists, one who wins a second-place silver medal and one who wins a third-place bronze medal, who will feel happier? Won't it be the silver medalist? Nope. In a study of athletes' reactions to placing second and third at national and international competitions, bronze medallists were happier than the silver medallists (Medvec, Madey, & Gilovich, 1995). Apparently, the athletes were comparing their performance to what might have been. The second-place winners, comparing themselves to the gold medalists, were unhappy that they didn't get the gold. But the third-place winners, comparing themselves to those who did more poorly, were happy that they earned a medal at all!

Cognitions and physiology are inextricably linked in the experience of emotion. Thoughts affect emotions, and emotional states influence thoughts (Fairholme et al., 2009; Keltner, Ellsworth, & Edwards, 1993). Blaming others for your woes can make you feel angry, but once you are angry you may be more inclined to think the worst of other people's motives; when you are sad, you are more likely to feel that the rotten situation made them do what they did. The complicated mix of emotions that people feel when they have "disappointing wins" (outcomes that were not as good as they had expected) or "relieving losses" (bad outcomes that could have been worse) shows how powerfully thought affects emotional responses.

An infant's primitive emotions do not have much mental sophistication: "Hey, I'm mad because no one is feeding me!" As a child's cerebral cortex matures, however, appraisals become more complex, and so do emotions: "Hey, I'm mad

◉—⌐Watch the **Video**
Emotion Regulation: James Coan
in **MyPsychLab**

THINKING CRITICALLY

Analyze assumptions and biases.

Reuters

Most people assume that second-place winners feel happier about their performance than third-place winners do. Yet when psychologists questioned this assumption, they found that usually the opposite is true, as the text explains. In this European swimming competition, silver medalist Vitaly Romanovich of Russia (left) is clearly feeling a lot grumpier than both the gold medallist Federico Colbertaldo of Italy (centre) and bronze medalist Samuel Pizzetti of Italy—he can't even bring himself to display his medal!

Children need to be old enough to have a sense of self before they can feel the moral emotions of shame, guilt, or remorse.

Darama/Corbis

because this situation is entirely unfair!" Some emotions, such as shame and guilt, depend completely on the maturation of higher cognitive capacities and do not occur until a child is two or three years old (and never in some people). These *self*-conscious emotions require the emergence of a sense of self and the ability to perceive that you have behaved badly or let another person down (Baumeister, Stillwell, & Heatherton, 1994; Tangney et al., 1996).

Appraisals, therefore, are essential to the creation of most emotions. But when people decide that it is shameful for a man to dance on a table with a lampshade on his head, or for a woman to walk down a street with her arms and legs uncovered, from where do their ideas about shame originate? If you are a person who loudly curses others when you are angry, where did you learn that cursing is acceptable? To answer these questions, we turn to the role of culture.

Recite & Review

Recite: How are your thoughts affecting your feelings about reciting what you can about the role of *appraisals* in generating emotions? How do thoughts affect emotions and emotions affect thoughts?

Review: Next, reread this section, so that you can appraise your own understanding accurately.

Now take this *Quick Quiz:*

1. Dara and Dinah get Bs on their psychology midterm, but Dara is ecstatic and proud, and Dinah is furious. What expectations and attributions are probably affecting their emotional reactions?

2. At a party, you see a stranger flirting with your date. You are flooded with jealousy. What cognitions might be causing this emotion? *Be specific.* What alternative thoughts might reduce your jealous feelings?

Answers:

1. Dara was probably expecting a lower grade and is attributing her B to her own efforts; Dinah was probably expecting a higher grade and is attributing her B to the instructor's unfairness, bad luck, or other external reasons. 2. Possible thoughts causing jealousy are "My date finds other people more attractive," "That person is trying to steal my date," or "My date's behaviour is humiliating me." But you could be thinking, "It's a compliment to me that other people find my date attractive," or "It pleases me that my date is getting such deserved attention."

Learning Objectives

5. Discuss how language and culture shape emotional experience(s).

6. Provide two examples of prototypical emotions.

7. Define display rules. Assess how cultural differences in display rules can lead to misunderstandings.

8. Summarize the differences between the genders in emotional expression.

Emotion and Culture

A young wife leaves her house one morning to draw water from the local well as her husband watches from the porch. On her way back from the well, a male stranger stops her and asks for some water. She gives him a cupful and then invites him home to dinner. He accepts. The husband, wife, and guest have a pleasant meal together. In a gesture of hospitality, the husband invites the guest to spend the night with his wife. The guest accepts. In the morning, the husband leaves early to bring home breakfast. When he returns, he finds his wife again in bed with the visitor.

At what point in this story will the husband feel angry? The answer depends on his culture (Hupka, 1981, 1991). A North American husband would feel rather angry at a wife who had an extramarital affair, and a wife would feel rather angry at being offered to a guest as if she were a lamb chop. A Pawnee husband of the nineteenth century would be enraged at any man who dared ask his wife for water. An Ammassalik Inuit husband finds it perfectly honourable to offer his wife to a stranger, but only once; he would be angry to find his wife and the guest having a second encounter. And a century ago, a Toda husband in India would not have been angry at all because the Todas allowed both husband and wife to take lovers. Both spouses might feel angry, though, if one of them had a *covert* affair, without announcing it publicly.

In most cultures, people feel angry in response to insult and the violation of social rules, but as this story shows, they often disagree about what comprises an insult or what the correct rule is. In this section, we will explore how culture influences the emotions we feel and the ways in which we express them.

How Culture Shapes Emotions

Are some emotions specific to particular cultures and not found elsewhere? What does it mean that some languages have words for subtle emotional states that other languages lack? The Germans have *schadenfreude*, a feeling of joy at another's misfortune. The Japanese speak of *hagaii*, helpless anguish tinged with frustration. Tahitians have *mehameha*, a trembling sensation felt when ordinary categories of perception are suspended—at twilight, in the brush, watching fires glow without heat. In the West, an event that cannot be identified is usually greeted with fear, yet *mehameha* does not describe what Westerners call fear or terror (Levy, 1984).

> ### 💡 THINKING CRITICALLY
>
> Ask questions.
>
> What does it mean if one language has a term for an emotion that another language lacks, like *schadenfreude* or *hagaii*? Are people whose languages include these words actually more likely to feel the emotion, or just to have a term that describes it?

Do these interesting linguistic differences mean that Germans are more likely than others actually to feel *schadenfreude* or the Japanese to feel *hagaii*? Or are they just more willing to give these subtle emotions a single name? Most people in all cultures are capable of feeling certain innate emotions, the ones that have physiological hallmarks in the brain and nervous system. But people in different cultures might indeed differ in their abilities to experience emotional blends and variations such as *schadenfreude*.

The difference between innate emotions and more complex cultural variations is reflected in languages all over the world. In Chapter 9, we noted that a *prototype* is a typical representative of a class of things. People everywhere consider some emotions to be prototypical examples of the concept of *emotion*: Thus, most people will say that *anger* and *sadness* are more representative of an emotion than are *irritability* and *nostalgia*. Prototypical emotions are reflected in the emotion words that young children learn first: *happy*, *sad*, *mad*, and *scared*. As children develop, they begin to draw emotional distinctions that are less prototypical and more specific to their language and culture, such as *ecstatic*, *depressed*, *hostile*, or *anxious* (Hupka, Lenton, & Hutchison, 1999; Russell & Fehr, 1994; Shaver, Wu, & Schwartz, 1992). And their appraisals of a given situation or provocation will also vary—as we saw earlier in describing the difference between Canadians and Japanese—depending on their culture's values, norms, and traditions. In this way, children and adults come to experience the nuances of emotional feeling that their cultures emphasize. The result is many varieties of emotion, some shading into one another, which have labels in some languages but not in others.

display rules Social and cultural rules that regulate when, how, and where a person may express (or suppress) emotions.

All emotions depend on the culture and context that produce them and shape their expression. Anger may be universal, but the way it is experienced will vary from culture to culture—whether it feels good or bad, useful or destructive. And cultures determine much of what people feel emotional *about*. For example, disgust is universal, but the content of what produces disgust changes as an infant matures, and it varies across cultures (Rozin, Lowery, & Ebert, 1994). People in some cultures learn to become disgusted by bugs (which other people find beautiful or tasty), unfamiliar sexual practices, dirt, death, contamination by a handshake with a stranger, or particular foods (e.g., meat if they are vegetarian, or all animal products such as honey or leather if they are vegan).

Communicating Emotions

Anger is considered a primary emotion in western societies. But in some cultures, such as the Inuit, anger is not tolerated because it threatens the community's need for closeness. Inuit mothers often calmly ignore an angry baby, conveying the message that complaining is not welcome. No one suggests that members of Inuit society do not feel anger—but regardless of culture, it is clear that the the expression of emotions is rarely a matter of "I say what I feel." You may be obliged to disguise what you feel. **Display rules** are cultural norms for how, when and where you express the emotions that you feel (Ekman et al., 1987; Gross, 1998).

Even the smile, which seems a straightforward signal of friendliness, has many meanings and uses that are not universal (LaFrance, 2011). North Americans smile more frequently than Germans, not because North Americans are inherently friendlier but because they differ in their notions of when a smile is appropriate. After a business meeting, North Americans often complain that the Germans were cold and aloof, and the Germans often complain that the North Americans were excessively cheerful, hiding their real feelings under the mask of a smile (Hall & Hall, 1990). The Japanese smile even more than North Americans do, to disguise embarrassment, anger, or other negative emotions whose public display is considered rude and improper. ◉

◉—⌐**Watch** the **Video**
Mixed Emotions: Jeffrey Larsen
in **MyPsychLab**

Display rules also govern *body language*, nonverbal signals of body movement, posture, gesture, and gaze (Birdwhistell, 1970). Many aspects of body language are specific to particular languages and cultures, which makes even the simplest gesture subject to misunderstanding and offence. The sign associated with the University of Texas

Around the world, the cultural rules for expressing emotions differ. The display rule for a formal Japanese wedding portrait is "no direct expressions of emotion," but not every member of this family has learned that rule yet.

Philip Jones Griffiths/Magnum Photos

Arms and hands communicate interest, emphasis, and emotion, just as words do.

Zoreslava/Shutterstock

football team, the Longhorns, is to extend the index finger and the pinkie. In Italy and other parts of Europe, it means you're saying a man's wife has been unfaithful to him—a serious insult.

Display rules tell us not only what to do when we are feeling an emotion, but also how and when to show an emotion we do not feel. Most people are expected to demonstrate sadness at funerals, happiness at weddings, and affection toward relatives. What if we don't actually feel sad, happy, or affectionate? Acting out an emotion we do not really feel because we believe it is socially appropriate is called **emotion work**. It is part of our efforts to regulate our emotions when we are with others (Gross, 1998). Sometimes emotion work is a job requirement. Flight attendants, waiters, and customer-service representatives must put on a happy face to convey cheerfulness, even if they are privately angry about a rude or drunken customer. Bill collectors must put on a stern face to convey threat, even if they feel sorry for the person they are collecting money from (Hochschild, 2003).

emotion work Expression of an emotion, often because of a role requirement, that a person does not really feel.

Gender and Emotion

"Women are too emotional," men often complain. "Men are too uptight," women often reply. This is a familiar gender stereotype. But what does "too emotional" mean? We need to define our terms and examine our assumptions. And we need to consider the larger culture in which men and women live, which shapes the rules and norms that govern how the sexes are supposed to behave.

Although women are more likely than men to suffer from clinical depression (see Chapter 15), neither sex feels any of the everyday emotions more often than the other, whether the emotion is anger, worry, embarrassment, anxiety, love, or grief (Archer, 2004; Deffenbacher et al., 2003; Fischer et al., 1993; C. Harris, 2003; Kring & Gordon, 1998; Shields, 2005). The major difference between the sexes has less to do with whether they feel emotions than with how and when their emotions are expressed, and how others perceive those expressions. For instance, when men cry in a work context, they are perceived as emotional whereas women are perceived as less competent (Fischer, Eagly, & Oosterwijk, 2013).

> **THINKING CRITICALLY**
>
> Define your terms.
>
> People say that women are the emotional sex, but they often fail to define their terms. What does *emotional* mean? Does it refer to how quickly or intensely people react, the kinds of thoughts that provoke them, or how emotions are expressed?

In western cultures, both sexes unconsciously associate "angry" with male and "happy" with female. When researchers showed students a series of computer-generated, fairly androgynous faces with a range expressions, angry to happy, the students consistently rated the angry faces as being masculine and the happy faces as feminine (Becker et al., 2007). This stereotyped link between gender and emotion may explain why a man who expresses anger in a professional context is considered high status, but a professional woman who does exactly the same thing loses status. She's considered to be an angry person, someone "out of control" (Brescoll & Uhlmann, 2008). Powerful women thus often face a dilemma: express anger when a subordinate or adversary has done something illegal or incompetent (and risk being thought "over-emotional") or behave calmly (and risk being seen as "cold and unemotional").

Conversely, women who don't smile when others expect them to are often disliked, even if they are actually smiling as often as men would. This may be why North American women, on average, smile more than men do, gaze at their listeners more, have more emotionally expressive faces, use more expressive hand and body movements, and touch others more (DePaulo, 1992; Kring & Gordon, 1998). Women smile more than men to pacify others, convey deference to someone of higher status, or smooth over conflicts (Hess, Adams, & Kleck, 2005; LaFrance, 2011; Shields, 2005).

Women also talk about their emotions more than men do. They are far more likely to cry and to acknowledge emotions that reveal vulnerability and weakness, such as "hurt feelings," fear, sadness, loneliness, shame, and guilt (Grossman & Wood, 1993; Timmers, Fischer, & Manstead, 1998). In contrast, most North American men express only one emotion more freely than women do: anger toward strangers, especially other men. Otherwise, men are expected to control and mask negative feelings. When they are worried or afraid, they are more likely than women to use vague terms, saying that they feel moody, frustrated, or on edge (Fehr et al., 1999).

However, the influence of a particular situation often overrides gender rules. You won't find many gender differences in emotional expressiveness at a football game or the Stanley Cup final! An important situational constraint on emotional expression is the status of the participants (Kenny et al., 2010; Snodgrass, 1992). A man is as likely as a woman to control his temper when the target of anger is someone with higher status or power; few people will readily sound off at a professor, police officer, or employer. And both women *and* men have a greater interest in being able to read the nonverbal cues of those who have higher status and more power than they do (Kraus, Côté, & Keltner, 2010).

Even where gender differences exist, they are not universal. Italian, French, Spanish, and Middle Eastern men and women can have entire conversations using highly expressive hand gestures and facial expressions. In contrast, in Asian cultures, both sexes are

Both sexes feel emotionally attached to friends, but often they express their affections differently. From childhood on, girls tend to prefer "face-to-face" friendships based on shared feelings; boys tend to prefer "side-by-side" friendships based on shared activities.

Left: Myrleen Pearson/Alamy. Right: Robb Kendrick/ Aurora Photos.

taught to control emotional expression (Matsumoto, 1996; Mesquita & Frijda, 1992). Israeli and Italian men are more likely than women to mask feelings of sadness, but British, Spanish, Swiss, and German men are *less* likely than their female counterparts to inhibit this emotion (Wallbott, Ricci-Bitti, & Bänninger-Huber, 1986).

In sum, the answer to "Which sex is more emotional?" is this: sometimes men, sometimes women, and sometimes neither, depending on the circumstances and the cultural context.

Recite & Review

Recite: Say aloud what you know about the influence of culture on emotion, *display rules*, *emotion work*, body language, and the factors related to gender differences and similarities in emotionality.

Review: Please do not display anger at our request to reread this section.

Now take this *Quick Quiz:*

1. Maureen is working in a fast-food restaurant and is becoming irritated with a customer who isn't ordering fast enough. She is supposed to be pleasant to all customers, but instead she snaps, "Hey, whaddaya want to order, slowpoke?" To keep her job and her temper, Maureen needs practice in _____.

2. In a class discussion, a student says something that embarrasses a student from another culture. The second student smiles to disguise his discomfort; the first student, thinking he is not being taken seriously, gets angry. This misunderstanding reflects the students' different _____ for the expression of embarrassment and anger.

3. *True or false:* Throughout the world, women are more emotionally expressive than men.

Answers:

1. emotion work 2. display rules 3. false

Learning Objectives

9 Describe the three phases of stress as defined by Selye. Provide a real-life example of each phase.

10 Summarize how stress affects the body and immune system.

11 Discuss how optimism and a sense of control can alleviate stress.

12 Define primary and secondary control. Explain how culture interacts with these forms of control.

The Nature of Stress

As we have seen, emotions take many forms, varying in complexity and intensity, and depend on physiology, cognitive processes, and cultural rules. These same three factors can help us understand those situations in which negative emotions become chronically stressful, and those in which chronic stress creates negative emotions.

When people say they are "under stress," they mean all sorts of things: They are having recurring conflicts with a parent, are feeling frustrated and angry about their lives, are fighting with a partner, are overwhelmed with caring for a sick child, can't keep up with work obligations, or have just lost a job. Are these stressors linked to illness—to migraines, stomachaches, flu, or more life-threatening diseases such as cancer? And do they affect everyone in the same way?

Stress and the Body

The modern era of stress research began in 1956, when Canadian endocrinologist Hans Selye published *The Stress of Life.* Environmental stressors such as heat, cold, toxins, and danger, Selye wrote, disrupt the body's equilibrium. The body then mobilizes its resources to fight off these stressors and restore normal functioning. Selye described the body's response to stressors of all kinds as a **general adaptation syndrome**, a set of physiological reactions that occur in three phases: ✳

✳ Explore the Concept *Do You Fly or Fight?* in MyPsychLab

1 **The alarm phase,** in which the body mobilizes the sympathetic nervous system to meet the immediate threat. The threat could be anything from taking a test you haven't studied for to running from a rabid dog. As we saw earlier, the release of adrenal hormones, epinephrine and norepinephrine, occurs with any intense emotion. It boosts energy, tenses muscles, reduces sensitivity to pain, shuts down digestion (so that blood will flow more efficiently to the brain, muscles, and skin), and increases blood pressure. Decades before Selye, psychologist Walter Cannon (1929) described these changes as the "fight-or-flight" response, a phrase still in use.

Stress hormones elevated — Blood flow increases — Heart rate speeds up — Digestion slows — Muscles tense

2 **The resistance phase,** in which your body attempts to resist or cope with a stressor that cannot be avoided. During this phase, the physiological responses of the alarm phase continue, but these very responses make the body more vulnerable to other stressors. When your body has mobilized to deal with a heat wave or pain from a broken leg, you may find you are more easily annoyed by minor frustrations. In most cases, the body will eventually adapt to the stressor and return to normal.

3 **The exhaustion phase,** in which persistent stress depletes the body of energy, thereby increasing vulnerability to physical problems and illness. The same reactions that allow the body to respond effectively in the alarm and resistance phases are unhealthy as long-range responses. Tense muscles can cause headache and neck pain. Increased blood pressure can become chronic hypertension. If normal digestive processes are interrupted or shut down for too long, digestive disorders may result.

Selye did not believe that people should aim for a stress-free life. Some stress, he said, is positive and productive, even if it also requires the body to produce short-term energy: competing in an athletic event, falling in love, working hard on a project you enjoy. And some negative stress is simply unavoidable; it's called life.

Current Approaches. One of Selye's most important observations was that the very biological changes that are adaptive in the short run, because they permit the body to respond quickly to danger, can become hazardous in the long run (McEwen, 2007). Modern researchers are learning how this happens.

When you are under stress, your brain's hypothalamus sends messages to the endocrine glands along two major pathways. One, as Selye observed, activates the sympathetic division of the autonomic nervous system for "fight or flight," producing the release of epinephrine and norepinephrine from the inner part (medulla) of the adrenal glands. In addition, the hypothalamus initiates activity along the **HPA axis**

general adaptation syndrome According to Hans Selye, a series of physiological reactions to stress occurring in three phases: alarm, resistance, and exhaustion.

HPA (hypothalamus–pituitary–adrenal cortex) axis A system activated to energize the body to respond to stressors. The hypothalamus sends chemical messengers to the pituitary gland, which in turn prompts the adrenal cortex to produce cortisol and other hormones.

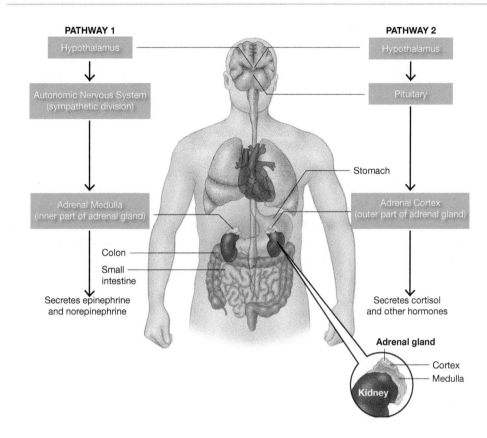

PATHWAY 1
Hypothalamus → Autonomic Nervous System (sympathetic division) → Adrenal Medulla (inner part of adrenal gland) → Secretes epinephrine and norepinephrine

PATHWAY 2
Hypothalamus → Pituitary → Adrenal Cortex (outer part of adrenal gland) → Secretes cortisol and other hormones

Stomach
Colon
Small intestine

Adrenal gland
Cortex
Medulla
Kidney

FIGURE 11.3 The Brain and Body Under Stress
When a person is in danger or under stress, the hypothalamus sends messages to the endocrine glands along two major pathways. In one, the hypothalamus activates the sympathetic division of the autonomic nervous system, which stimulates the adrenal medulla to produce epinephrine and norepinephrine. The result is the many bodily changes associated with "fight or flight." In the other pathway, messages travel along the HPA axis to the adrenal cortex, which produces cortisol and other hormones. The result is increased energy and protection from tissue inflammation in case of injury.

(HPA stands for hypothalamus–pituitary–adrenal cortex). The hypothalamus releases chemical messengers that communicate with the pituitary gland, which in turn sends messages to the outer part (cortex) of the adrenal glands. The adrenal cortex secretes **cortisol** and other hormones that elevate blood sugar and protect the body's tissues from inflammation in case of injury (see Figure 11.3). ✳

One result of HPA axis activation is increased energy, which is crucial for short-term responses to stress (Kemeny, 2003). But if cortisol and other stress hormones stay high too long, they can lead to hypertension, immune disorders, other physical ailments, and emotional problems such as depression. Elevated levels of cortisol also motivate animals (and presumably humans, too) to seek out rich comfort foods and store the extra calories as abdominal fat.

The cumulative effects of external sources of stress may partially explain why people at the lower rungs of the socioeconomic ladder have worse health and higher mortality rates for almost every disease and medical condition than do those at the top regardless of ethnicity, gender, or where they live in Canada (Adler & Snibbe, 2003; Health Canada, 2008). Poverty disproportionately affects single-parent families (especially those headed by women), families on social assistance, and urban families of Canada's indigenous peoples (Anand et al., 2001; McIntyre, Connor, & Warren, 2000).

✳▫ **Explore** the **Concept**
Virtual Brain: Stress and Health
in **MyPsychLab**

cortisol A hormone secreted by the adrenal cortex that elevates blood sugar and protects the body's tissues in case of injury; if chronically elevated due to stress, it can lead to hypertension, immune disorders, other illnesses, and possibly depression.

Alas, the same stress hormones that help in the short run can have unwanted long-term consequences.

Cathy Guisewite/UNIVERSAL PRESS SYNDICATE

Although the health risks associated with poverty in Canada cannot be easily attributed to health care access, in practice, poor Canadians may be less likely to go to the doctor when they are ill or to fill prescriptions to treat their illnesses (Williamson & Fast, 1998). Obviously this may be because many poor Canadians may not have money to buy medications or to pay for transportation to the doctor (Williamson & Fast, 1998). However, research conducted at McGill University has found that poor Canadians are also more likely to have high-fat diets, to consume inadequate quantities of vitamins and minerals, and to be obese—factors that are associated with numerous health risks (e.g., Johnson-Down et al., 1997). As well, impoverished Canadians may experience higher levels of discrimination and the environmental stress of living in areas with higher crime rates, fewer community services, run-down housing, and greater exposure to hazards such as chemical contamination (Health Canada, 2008; Taylor, Repetti, & Seeman, 1997; Wandersman & Nation, 1998). In fact, some researchers suggest that poverty can be thought of as a series of accumulated stressors and that living within an impoverished community only intensifies these stressors (Kupersmidt et al., 1995; McLoyd, 1998). These effects snowball for children, with accumulated negative effects on their physical health, mental health, and cognitive abilities (such as memory) extending to adolescence and adulthood (Evans & Kim, 2007; Evans & Schamberg, 2009). In 2007, one in 10 children (defined as individuals under the age of 18) in Canada lived in poverty (The Vanier Institute of the Family, 2010). Persistent childhood stress takes its toll on health both through biological mechanisms, such as chronically elevated cortisol, and behavioural ones. Children living with chronic stress often become hyper-vigilant to danger, mistrust others, have poor relationships, are unable to regulate their emotions, abuse drugs, and don't eat healthy food. No wonder that by the time they are adults, they have an elevated risk of cardiovascular disease, autoimmune disorders, diabetes, and early mortality (Evans & Schamberg, 2009; Miller, Chen, & Parker, 2011). ◉

⊙—⌐Watch the Video
Special Topics: Health Disparities in **MyPsychLab**

Because work is central in most people's lives, the effects of persistent unemployment can threaten health for people at all income levels, even increasing their vulnerability to the common cold. In one study, heroic volunteers were given either ordinary nose drops or nose drops containing a cold virus, and then were quarantined for five days. The people most likely to get a cold's miserable symptoms were those who had been underemployed or unemployed for at least a month. As Figure 11.4 shows, the longer the work problems lasted, the greater the likelihood of illness (Cohen et al., 1998).

Nonetheless, the physiological changes caused by stress do not occur to the same extent in everyone. People's responses to stress vary according to their learning history,

FIGURE 11.4 Stress and the Common Cold
Chronic stress lasting a month or more boosts the risk of catching a cold. The risk is increased among people undergoing problems with their friends or loved ones; it is highest among people who are out of work (Cohen et al., 1998).

gender, preexisting medical conditions, and genetic predisposition for high blood pressure, heart disease, obesity, diabetes, or other health problems (Belsky & Pluess, 2009a; McEwen, 2000, 2007). This is why some people respond to the same stressor with much greater increases in blood pressure, heart rate, and hormone levels than other individuals do, and their physical changes take longer to return to normal. These hyper-responsive individuals may be the ones most at risk for eventual illness.

The Immune System: PNI. Researchers in the field of *health psychology* (and its medical relative, behavioural medicine) investigate all aspects of how mind and body affect each other to preserve wellness or cause illness. Some health psychologists have teamed up with other researchers to create an interdisciplinary specialty with the cumbersome name, **psychoneuroimmunology or PNI** for short. The "psycho" part stands for psychological processes such as emotions and perceptions; "neuro" for the nervous and endocrine systems; and "immunology" for the immune system, which enables the body to fight disease and infection.

The immune system consists of fighter cells that look more fantastical than any alien creature Hollywood could design. This one is about to engulf and destroy a cigarette-shaped parasite that causes a tropical disease.

Juergen Berger/Science Source

PNI researchers are especially interested in the white blood cells of the immune system, which are designed to recognize foreign or harmful substances (*antigens*), such as flu viruses, bacteria, and tumour cells, and then destroy or deactivate them. The immune system deploys different kinds of white blood cells as weapons, depending on the nature of the enemy. Natural killer cells are important in tumour detection and rejection, and are involved in protection against the spread of cancer cells and viruses. Helper T cells enhance and regulate the immune response; they are the primary target of the HIV virus that causes AIDS. Chemicals produced by the immune cells are sent to the brain, and the brain in turn sends chemical signals to stimulate or restrain the immune system. Anything that disrupts this communication loop, whether drugs, surgery, or chronic stress, can weaken or suppress the immune system (Segerstrom & Miller, 2004). ◉

Some PNI researchers have gotten right down to the level of cell damage to see how stress can lead to illness, aging, and even premature death. At the end of every chromosome is a protein complex called a *telomere* that, in essence, tells the cell how long it has to live. Every time a cell divides, enzymes whittle away a tiny piece of the telomere; when it is reduced to almost nothing, the cell stops dividing and dies. Chronic stress, especially if it begins in childhood, appears to shorten the telomeres (Epel, 2009; Monaghan, 2014). One team of researchers compared two groups of healthy 20- to 50-year-old women: 19 who had healthy children and 39 who were primary caregivers of a child who was seriously and chronically ill (e.g., a child with cerebral palsy). Of course, the mothers of the sick children felt that they were under stress, but they also had significantly greater cell damage than did the mothers of healthy children. In fact, the cells of the highly stressed women looked like those of women at least ten years older, and their telomeres were much shorter (Epel et al., 2004). But don't despair—meditation practice not only reduced stress and stress-induced immune responses, but also increased enzymes that repaired telomeres (Epel et al., 2009; Jacobs et al., 2011; Lin, Epel, & Blackburn, 2009).

◉─ **Watch** the **Video**
The Basics: Stress and Your Health
in **MyPsychLab**

Stress and the Mind

Before you try to persuade your instructors that the stress of constant studying is bad for your health, consider this mystery: The large majority of individuals who are living with stressors, even serious ones such as loss of a job or the death of a loved one, do not get sick (Bonanno, 2004; Taylor, Repetti, & Seeman, 1997). What protects them? What attitudes and qualities are most strongly related to health, well-being, and long life?

psychoneuroimmunology (PNI) The study of the relationships among psychology, the nervous and endocrine systems, and the immune system.

Optimism. When something bad happens to you, what is your first reaction? Do you tell yourself that you will somehow come through it okay, or do you gloomily mutter, "More proof that if something can go wrong for me, it will"? In a fundamental way, optimism—the general expectation that things will go well in spite of occasional setbacks—makes life possible. If people are in a jam but believe things will get better eventually, they will keep striving to make that prediction come true. Even despondent fans of the Toronto Maple Leafs, who have not won the Stanley Cup since 1967, maintain optimism that "there's always next year."

At first, studies of optimism reported (optimistically!) that optimism is better for health, well-being, and even longevity than is pessimism (Carver & Scheier, 2002; Maruta et al., 2000). You can see why popularizers in the media ran far with this ball, some claiming that having an optimistic outlook would prolong the life of people suffering from serious illnesses. Unfortunately, that hope proved false: A team of Australian researchers who followed 179 patients with lung cancer over a period of eight years found that optimism made no difference in who lived or in how long they lived (Schofield et al., 2004). Indeed, for every study showing the benefits of optimism, another shows that it can actually be harmful: Among other things, optimists are more likely to keep gambling, even when they lose money, and they can be more vulnerable to depression when the hoped-for outcome does not occur (McNulty & Fincham, 2012). Optimism also backfires when it keeps people from preparing themselves for complications of surgery ("Oh, everything will be fine") or causes them to underestimate risks to their health (Friedman & Martin, 2011).

Pessimists naturally accuse optimists of being unrealistic, and often that is true! For optimism to reap its benefits, it must be grounded in reality, spurring people to take better care of themselves and to regard problems and bad news as difficulties they can overcome. Realistic optimists are more likely than pessimists to be active problem solvers, get support from friends, and seek information that can help them (Brissette, Scheier, & Carver, 2002; Geers, Wellman, & Lassiter, 2009). They keep their sense of humour, plan for the future, and reinterpret the situation in a positive light. Pessimists, in contrast, often do self-destructive things: They drink too much, smoke, fail to wear seat belts, drive too fast, and refuse to take medication for illness. However, so do unrealistic optimists.

Watch the **Video** *What's In It For Me?: Psychological Resilience* in **MyPsychLab**

THINKING CRITICALLY
Consider other interpretations.

Most people think stress is something "out there" that just happens to them. However, there is another way of looking at stress—as something in you, something that depends on your thoughts and emotion. Do you see your work as an endless set of assignments you will never complete or as challenging tasks to master? The answer will affect how stressed you are.

Conscientiousness and Control. Thus, it is not optimism by itself that predicts health and well-being. You can recite "Everything is good! Everything will work out!" 20 times a day, but it won't get you much (except odd glances from your classmates). Optimism needs a behavioural partner.

In one of the longest longitudinal studies ever conducted in psychology—90 years!—researchers were able to follow the lives of more than 1500 children originally studied by Lewis Terman, beginning in 1921 (see Chapter 9). Terman followed these children, affectionately called the "Termites," long into their adulthood, and when he died in 1956 other researchers took up the project. Health psychologists Howard Friedman and Leslie Martin (2011) found that the secret to longevity for the Termites was *conscientiousness*, the ability to persist in pursuit of goals, get a good education, work hard but enjoy the work and its challenges, and be responsible. Conscientious people are optimists, in the sense that they believe their efforts will pay off, and they act in ways to make that expectation come true. The findings on the Termites, who were largely a homogeneous cohort that was white and middle class, have been replicated across more than 20 independent samples that differed in terms of ethnicity and social class (Deary, Weiss, & Batty, 2010).

Conscientiousness is related to another important cognitive ingredient in health: having an internal locus of control. **Locus of control** refers to your general expectation about whether you can control the things that happen to you (Rotter, 1990). People who have an *internal locus of control* ("internals") tend to believe that they are responsible for what happens to them. Those who have an *external locus of control* ("externals") tend to believe that their lives are controlled by luck, fate, or other people. Having an internal locus of control, especially concerning things you can do *right now* rather than vague future events, is associated with good health, academic achievement, political activism, and emotional well-being (Frazier et al., 2011; Roepke & Grant, 2011; Strickland, 1989).

Most people can tolerate all kinds of stressors if they feel able to control them or predict the outcome. Consider crowding: Mice get really nasty when they're crowded, but many people love crowds, voluntarily getting squashed in Maple Leaf Square to watch the Raptors during the playoffs. Human beings show signs of stress not when they are actually crowded but when they *feel* crowded (Evans, Lepore, & Allen, 2000). Cortisol *is* elevated when people feel that they are being judged negatively by others or have no control over the task at hand (Dickerson & Kemeny, 2004; Miller, Chen, & Zhou, 2007). But people who have the greatest control over their work pace and activities, such as executives and managers, have fewer illnesses and stress symptoms than do employees who have little control, who feel trapped doing repetitive tasks, and who have a low chance of promotion (Karasek & Theorell, 1990). The greatest threat to health and well-being occurs when people feel caught in a situation they cannot escape, one that goes on without a foreseeable end.

Feeling in control affects the immune system, which may be why it helps to speed up recovery from surgery and some diseases (E. Skinner, 1996). People who have an

locus of control A general expectation about whether the results of your actions are under your own control (internal locus) or beyond your control (external locus).

THINKING CRITICALLY

Examine the evidence.

Who has more stress: corporate managers in highly competitive jobs or assembly-line workers in routine and predictable jobs? People who are bossed suffer more from job stress than their bosses do, especially if the employees cannot control many aspects of their work (Karasek & Theorell, 1990).

internal locus of control are better able than externals to resist infection by cold viruses and even the health-impacting effects of poverty and discrimination (Cohen, Tyrrell, & Smith, 1993; Krieger & Sidney, 1996; Lachman & Weaver, 1998). As with optimism, feeling in control also makes people more likely to take action to improve their health when necessary. In studies of patients recovering from heart attacks, those who believed the heart attack occurred because they smoked, didn't exercise, or had a stressful job were more likely to change their bad habits and recover quickly. In contrast, those who thought their illness was due to bad luck or fate—factors outside their control—were less likely to generate plans for recovery and more likely to resume their old unhealthy habits (Affleck et al., 1987; Ewart, 1995).

Overall, then, a sense of control is a good thing, but critical thinkers might want to ask: Control over what? It is surely not beneficial for people to believe they can control absolutely every aspect of their lives; some things, such as death, taxes, or being a random victim of a crime, are out of anyone's control. Health and well-being are not enhanced by self-blame ("Whatever goes wrong with my health is my fault") or the belief that all disease can be prevented by doing the right thing ("If I take vitamins and hold the right positive attitude, I'll never get sick"). ◉

◉─[Watch the Video *What's In It For Me?: The Challenge Of Quitting Bad Health Habits* in **MyPsychLab**

CULTURE and *Control*

Eastern and western cultures tend to hold different attitudes toward the ability and desirability of controlling one's own life. In general, western cultures celebrate **primary control**, in which people try to influence events by trying to exert direct control over them: If you are in a bad situation, you change it, fix it, or fight it. The eastern approach emphasizes **secondary control**, in which people try to accommodate to a bad situation by changing their own aspirations or desires: If you have a problem, you live with it or act in spite of it (Rothbaum, Weisz, & Snyder, 1982).

A Japanese psychologist once offered some examples of Japanese proverbs that teach the benefits of yielding to the inevitable (Azuma, 1984): *To lose is to win* (giving in, to protect the harmony of a relationship, demonstrates the superior trait of generosity); *willow trees do not get broken by piled-up snow* (no matter how many problems pile up in your life, flexibility will help you survive them); and *the true tolerance is to tolerate the intolerable* (some "intolerable" situations are facts of life that no amount of protest will change). You can imagine how long "To lose is to win" would survive on the football field, or how long most Canadians would be prepared to tolerate the intolerable! Yet an important part of coping, for any of us, is learning to accept limited resources, irrevocable losses, and circumstances over which we have little or no direct influence—all aspects of secondary control (E. Skinner, 2007).

People who are ill or under stress can reap the benefits of both western and eastern forms of control by avoiding either–or thinking: by taking responsibility for future actions while not blaming themselves unduly for past ones. Among first-year students who are doing poorly in their classes, future success depends on maintaining enough primary control to keep working hard and learning to study better, *and* on the ability to come to terms with the fact that success is not going to drop into their laps without effort (Hall et al., 2006). Among women who are recovering from sexual assault or coping with cancer, adjustment is related to a woman's belief that she is not to blame for being raped or for getting sick but that she *is* in charge of taking care of herself from then on (Frazier, 2003; Taylor, Lichtman, & Wood, 1984). "I felt that I had lost control of my body somehow," said one cancer survivor, "and the way for me to get back some control was to find out as much as I could." This

primary control An effort to modify reality by changing other people, the situation, or events; a "fighting back" philosophy.

secondary control An effort to accept reality by changing your own attitudes, goals, or emotions; a "learn to live with it" philosophy.

way of thinking allows people to avoid guilt and self-blame while retaining a belief that they can take steps to get better.

Many problems require us to decide what we can change and to accept what we cannot; perhaps the secret of healthy control lies in knowing the difference.

. . . .

Recite & Review

Recite: Reduce your stress before the next exam by saying out loud what you know about the *general adaptation syndrome, the HPA axis* and its role in stress, *cortisol, psychoneuroimmunology* and the immune system, the effects of optimism, conscientiousness, *locus of control*, and *primary* and *secondary control*.

Review: Next, be conscientious and read this section again.

Now take this *Quick Quiz:*

1. Steve is unexpectedly called on in class to discuss a question. He hasn't the faintest idea of the answer, and he feels his heart pound and his palms sweat. According to Selye, Steve is in the _____ phase of his stress response.

2. Maria has worked as a file clerk for 17 years in a job that is closely supervised and boring. Her boss must make many rapid-fire decisions every day and is always complaining of the pressures of responsibility. Which of them probably has the more stressful job? (a) Maria, (b) the boss, (c) both equally, (d) neither job is stressful (*Bonus:* Why?)

3. Anika usually takes credit for doing well on her work assignments and blames her failures on lack of effort. Benecia attributes her successes to luck and blames her failures on the fact that she is an indecisive Gemini. Anika has an _____ locus of control whereas Benecia has an _____ locus.

4. Adapting to the reality that you have a chronic medical condition is an example of (primary/secondary) control; joining a protest to make a local company clean up its hazardous wastes is an example of (primary/secondary) control.

5. On television, a self-described health expert explains that "No one gets sick if they don't want to be sick," because we can all control our bodies. As a critical thinker, how should you assess this claim?

Answers:

1. alarm 2. a, because Maria has less control than her boss does over every aspect of her work. 3. internal; external 4. secondary; primary 5. First, you would want to define your terms: What does "control" mean, and what kind of control is the supposed expert referring to? People can control some things, such as how much they exercise and whether they smoke, and they can control some aspects of treatment once they become ill, but they cannot control everything that happens to them. Second, you would examine the assumption that control is always a good thing; the belief that we have total control over our lives could lead to depression and unwarranted self-blame when illness strikes.

Learning Objectives

13 Evaluate the statement "Negative emotions are bad for your health."

14 Characterize the impact that hostility and depression have on heart disease.

15 Describe positive psychology and how positive emotions can affect health.

16 Interpret the ways in which confession and forgiveness can improve health.

Stress and Emotion

Perhaps you have heard people say things like "She was so depressed, it's no wonder she got sick" or "He's always so angry, he's going to give himself a heart attack one day." Are negative emotions, especially anger and depression, hazardous to your health?

First, we can eliminate the popular belief in a "cancer-prone" personality. (This notion was initially promoted by the tobacco industry to draw attention away from smoking as a leading cause of cancer.) Research has thoroughly discredited this belief; studies of thousands of people around the world, from Japan to Finland, have found no link between personality traits and risk of cancer (Nakaya et al., 2003).

Second, we need to separate the effects of negative emotions on healthy people from the effects of such emotions on people who are ill. Once a person already has a virus or medical condition or is living in a chronically stressful situation, negative emotions such as anxiety and helplessness can indeed increase the risk of illness and affect the speed of recovery (Kiecolt-Glaser et al., 1998). People who become depressed after a heart attack are significantly more likely to die from cardiac causes in the following year, even controlling for severity of the disease and other risk factors (Frasure-Smith et al., 1999). But can anger and depression be causes of illness on their own?

Hostility and Depression: Do They Hurt?

One of the first modern efforts to link emotions and illness occurred in the 1970s, with research on the "Type A" personality, a set of qualities thought to be associated with heart disease: ambition, impatience, anger, working hard, and having high standards for oneself. Later research ruled out all of these factors except one: The toxic ingredient in the Type A personality turned out to be hostility (Myrtek, 2007). Indeed, working hard and having high standards proved to be important factors in good health and longevity, as the Termite study showed (Friedman & Martin, 2011).

By "hostility," we do not mean the irritability or anger that everyone feels on occasion, but *cynical* or *antagonistic hostility*, which characterizes people who are mistrustful of others and always ready to provoke mean, furious arguments. In a classic study of male physicians who had been interviewed as medical students 25 years earlier, those who were chronically angry and resentful were five times as likely as non-hostile men to get heart disease, even when other risk factors such as smoking and a poor diet were taken into account (Ewart & Kolodner, 1994; Williams, Barefoot, & Shekelle, 1985) (see Figure 11.5). These findings have been replicated in other large-scale studies, with men and women of many different ethnicities (Krantz et al., 2006; Williams et al., 2000). Proneness to anger is a significant risk factor all on its own for impairments of the immune system, elevated blood pressure, heart disease, and even slower healing of wounds (Chida & Hamer, 2008; Gouin et al., 2008; Suinn, 2001).

Clinical depression, too, is linked to at least a doubled risk of later heart attack and cardiovascular disease (Frasure-Smith & Lespérance, 2005; Schulz et al., 2000). But what accounts for that link? A large prospective study found that depressed people were more likely to accumulate fat in the belly and midriff (perhaps because of the elevated cortisol that often occurs with depression), where it is more likely to increase the risk of diabetes and heart disease (Vogelzangs et al., 2008). Thus, one reason that depression might lead to heart disease over time would not be depression itself, but more likely the behaviours that depression can produce in some of its sufferers.

For some time, researchers thought that depression might also lead to cancer, but now it looks as though the reverse is true—that cancer can cause depression, and not just because the diagnosis is "depressing." Cancerous tumours, as well as the immune system that is fighting them, produce high levels of a chemical that can cause the emotional and behavioural symptoms of depression. Rats that have cancer, of which they are unaware,

Watch the Video
Heart Disease in **MyPsychLab**

FIGURE 11.5 Hostility and Heart Disease
Anger is more hazardous to health than a heavy workload. Men who had the highest hostility scores as young medical students were the most likely to have coronary heart disease 25 years later (Williams, Barefoot, & Shekelle, 1985).

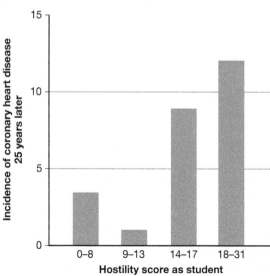

float passively in water instead of swimming for safety, and show other signs of anxiety and apathy (Pyter et al., 2009). It appears that the tumour *itself* acts as a stressor that can result in changes in the brain that are associated with depression (Xiu, Lin, & Wei, 2010). ◉

◉—Watch the Video
The Big Picture: Health Psychology in **MyPsychLab**

Positive Emotions: Do They Help?

Just as negative emotions can be unhealthful, positive emotions may be healthful, Consider the findings from a study of 180 Catholic nuns. Researchers examined autobiographies composed by the nuns when they were about 22 years old to see whether the quality of their writing predicted the onset of Alzheimer's disease later in life. (It did.) When other researchers scored the writings for their emotional content, they found a strong association between the frequency of positive emotions described—such as happiness, love, hope, gratitude, contentment, amusement—and longevity six decades later (Danner, Snowdon, & Friesen, 2001). The nuns whose life stories contained the most words describing positive emotions lived, on average, nine years longer than nuns who reported the fewest positive feelings. These differences in longevity could not have been due to the stress of poverty, raising children, or particular experiences. The women all had the same experiences and standard of living, at least after they entered the convent. Of course, finding a group of very old people who are happy does not mean that happiness contributed to their longevity; as people age, they often become less angry and more content (see Chapter 13). For instance, a longitudinal study of Harvard men found that some life paths led the men to be happy *and* well and others to be sad *and* ill. Happiness did not cause wellness, and sadness did not cause illness (Vaillant, 2002).

Nonetheless, positive emotions could be physically beneficial because they soften or counteract the high arousal caused by negative emotions or chronic stressors. They may dispose people to think more creatively about their opportunities and choices and, as with optimism and internal locus of control, motivate people to take action to achieve their goals (Kok, Catalino, & Fredrickson, 2008). People who express positive feelings are also more likely to attract friends and supporters than are people who are always bitter and brooding, and, as we will see, social support is one of the most powerful contributors to good health (Friedman & Martin, 2011; Ong, 2010; Pressman & Cohen, 2005).

An emerging area of psychology, *positive psychology*, seeks to examine the ways in which positive emotions such as happiness and positive personality traits enhance well-being, health, and resilience (Seligman & Csikszentmihalyi, 2000; Hart & Sasso, 2011). Research demonstrates that when experiencing severe stressors, people who adopt a proactive coping style experience less depression and report more positive experiences than those who do not (Greenglass, 2002; Greenglass & Fiksenbaum, 2009). This proactive coping is not naive, "Polyanna"-ish optimism, but rather a realistic assessment of all possible outcomes, both good and bad. Such an evaluation allows people to develop possible responses and to assess how well they are progressing (Churchill & Davis, 2010; Davis & Asliturk, 2011).

Emotional Inhibition and Expression

If negative emotions are risky, you might assume that the safest thing to do when you feel angry, depressed, or worried is to try to suppress those feelings. For small problems and annoyances, suppression is usually just fine! But anyone who has tried to banish an unwelcome thought or bitter memory knows how hard it can be to do this. When you are trying to avoid a thought, you are in fact processing the thought more frequently; you are rehearsing it. That is why, when you are obsessed with someone you were once romantically involved with, trying not to think of the person actually prolongs your emotional responsiveness to him or her (Wegner & Gold, 1995).

The continued inhibition of thoughts and emotions actually requires physical effort that can be stressful to the body. People who are able to express matters of great emotional importance to them show elevated levels of disease-fighting white blood cells, whereas people who suppress such feelings tend to have decreased levels (Petrie, Booth, & Pennebaker, 1998). There is also a social cost to suppressing important feelings. In a longitudinal study that followed first-year university students as they adjusted to being in a new environment, those who expressed their worries and fears openly with other students ended up with better relationships and greater satisfaction, compared to those who said they preferred to keep their emotions to themselves (Srivastava et al., 2009).

Another familiar, and negative, feeling when someone is in a new environment is loneliness. Ken Cramer and colleagues (Cramer & Neyedley, 1998) from the University of Windsor found that male students, who may feel the need to conceal their feelings to conform to traditional sex roles, are in fact lonelier than female students. It has also been found that lonely students, regardless of sex, are less likely to stay in school, tend to trust others less, and change their eating patterns more than students who are not lonely (Rotenberg, 1994, 1998; Rotenberg & Flood, 1999; Rotenberg & Kmill, 1992; Rotenberg & Morrison, 1993; Rotenberg et al., 2010). As well, lonely people have been found to be the harshest judges, of themselves and others (Rotenberg & MacKie, 1999). Thus, lonely people may, because of their judgmental attitudes, discourage others from getting close to them—thus keeping the cycle of loneliness going.

Everyone has secrets and private moments of sad reflection. But when you feel sad or fearful for too long, keeping your feelings to yourself may increase your stress.

Jeff Greenberg/PhotoEdit Inc.

The Benefits of Confession.

Given the findings on the harmful effects of feeling negative emotions and also the difficulty and costs of suppressing them, what is a person supposed to do with them? One way to reduce the wear and tear of negative emotions comes from research on the benefits of confession: divulging (even if only to yourself) private thoughts and feelings that make you ashamed, worried, frightened, or sad (Pennebaker, 2002, 2011). A randomized controlled trial following 156 patients after their first heart attack found that those who wrote about their feelings about the heart attack fared better and improved more quickly than a control group who wrote about neutral daily activities (Willmott et al., 2011). And first-year university students who privately wrote down their "deepest thoughts and feelings" about coming to college reported greater short-term homesickness and anxiety, compared to students who wrote about trivial topics. But by the end of the school year, they had had fewer bouts of flu and fewer visits to the infirmary than did the control group (Pennebaker, Colder, & Sharp, 1990).

This method is especially powerful when people write about traumatic experiences. When a group of university students was asked to write about a personal, traumatic experience for 20 minutes a day for four days, many told stories of sexual coercion, physical beatings, humiliation, or parental abandonment. Yet most had never discussed these experiences with anyone. The researchers collected data on the students' physical symptoms, white blood cell counts,

GET INVOLVED! True Confessions

To see whether the research on the benefits of confession will be helpful to you, take a moment to write down your deepest thoughts and feelings about being in university, your past, a secret, your future—anything you have never told anyone. Do this again tomorrow and then again for a few days in a row. Note your feelings after writing too. Are you upset, troubled, sad, or relieved? Does your account change over time? Research suggests that if you do this exercise now, you may have fewer colds, headaches, and trips to the doctor over the next few months (Pennebaker, Colder, & Sharp, 1990).

emotions, and visits to the health centre. On every measure, the students who wrote about traumatic experiences were better off than those who wrote only about neutral topics (Pennebaker, Kiecolt-Glaser, & Glaser, 1988). Subsequent research has confirmed the benefits of expressing and working through memories of traumatic events head-on, rather than trying to suppress intrusive, troubling thoughts (Dalgleish, Hauer, & Kuyken, 2008; see Chapter 16).

The benefits of writing occur primarily when the revelation produces insight and understanding, thereby fostering the ability to distance oneself from the bad experience and end the stressful repetition of obsessive thoughts and unresolved feelings (Kross & Ayduk, 2011; Lepore, Ragan, & Jones, 2000). One young woman, who had been molested at the age of 9 by a boy a year older, at first wrote about her feelings of embarrassment and guilt. By the third day, she was writing about how angry she felt at the boy. By the last day, she had begun to see the whole event differently; he was a child too, after all. When the study was over, she said, "Before, when I thought about it, I'd lie to myself. . . . Now, I don't feel like I even have to think about it because I got it off my chest. I finally admitted that it happened."

The Benefits of Letting Grievances Go. Another way of letting go of negative emotions is to give up the thoughts that produce them and adopt a perspective that might lead to forgiveness. When people rehearse their grievances and hold on to their grudges, their blood pressure, heart rate, and skin conductance rise. Forgiving thoughts (as in the preceding example—"He was a child too") reduce these signs of physiological arousal and restore feelings of control (Whited, Wheat, & Larkin, 2010; Witvliet, Ludwig, & Vander Laan, 2001). (See Figure 11.6.) Forgiveness, like confession when it works, helps people see events in a new light. It promotes empathy, the ability to see the situation from another person's perspective. It strengthens and repairs ongoing relationships (Fehr, Gelfand, & Nag, 2010). But it is important not to oversimplify: Forgiveness is not a cure-all and not always a good thing; it depends on the context in which the conflict occurs (McNulty & Fincham, 2012). In a study of women at a domestic violence shelter, the women who forgave their abusive partners were more likely to return to them, and within marriage, forgiveness predicted continued psychological and physical violence (McNulty, 2011).

Forgiveness does *not* mean that the offended person denies, ignores, or excuses the offence, which might be serious. It does mean that the victim is able, finally, to come to terms with the injustice and let go of obsessive feelings of hurt, rage, and vengefulness. As the Chinese proverb says, "He who pursues revenge should dig two graves."

FIGURE 11.6 Heartfelt Forgiveness Participants in a study were asked to think of someone who they felt had offended or hurt them. Then they were asked to imagine unforgiving reactions (rehearsing the hurt and harbouring a grudge) and forgiving reactions (feeling empathy, forgiving). People's heart rates increased much more sharply and took longer to return to normal when their thoughts were unforgiving.

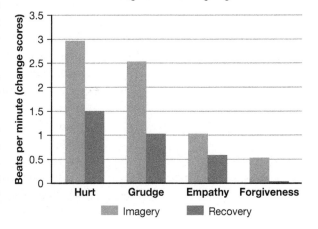

Recite & Review

Recite: You will never forgive yourself if you don't recite aloud what you know about hostility, depression and health, the benefits of writing down secret feelings that have never been expressed, and the benefits of forgiveness.

Review: Next, read this section again.

Now take this *Quick Quiz:*

1. Which aspect of Type A behaviour is most hazardous to the heart? (a) working hard, (b) being in a hurry, (c) cynical hostility, (d) irritability in traffic, (e) general grumpiness

2. Amber has many worries about being in her highly competitive nursing program, but she is afraid to tell anyone. What might be the healthiest solution for her? (a) trying not to think about her feelings, (b) writing down her feelings and then rereading and rethinking what she wrote, (c) talking frequently to anyone who will listen, (d) tweeting her friends about her moods

3. We are giving away an answer to #2, but why might answer *d* not be helpful to Amber?

Answers:

1. c 2. b 3. Sending tweets (or posting her feelings on her Facebook page) might make Amber momentarily feel good, but she probably won't retrieve those messages later to reread and rethink about what she wrote; and rethinking her story is the important element.

Learning Objectives

17 List four methods for reducing or managing stress.

18 Compare emotion-focused coping with problem-focused coping. Give examples of when each coping style occurs and assess its utility.

19 Explore three ways of coping with unsolvable problems. Give examples of each.

20 Discuss the importance and limitations of social support.

Coping with Stress

We have noted that most people who are under stress, even those living in difficult situations, do not become ill. In addition to feeling optimistic and in control, and not wallowing around in negative emotions, how do they manage to cope?

The most immediate way to deal with the physiological tension of stress and negative emotions is to take time out and reduce the body's physical arousal. Many people, from infants to the old, respond beneficially to the soothing touch of massage (Moyer, Rounds, & Hannum, 2004). Others employ the Buddhist practice of *mindfulness meditation*, which fosters emotional tranquility (see Chapter 16). The goal is to learn to accept feelings of anger, sadness, or anxiety without judging them or trying to get rid of them (a form of secondary control) (Davidson et al., 2003). Many meditation practices exist; a common one is to focus on your breathing, and as thoughts intrude acknowledge them but then send them away and return to your breaths. Doing this even in brief sessions over several weeks produces changes in brain activity associated with positive emotions and increases feelings of control. Over an extended time, meditation seems to stimulate greater activity of the enzymes involved in the length of telomeres and increases the longevity of key immune cells (Jacobs et al., 2011; Moyer et al., 2011). ◉

Another central way of reducing negative emotions and lowering the risk of illness is exercise. Exercise is as beneficial for improving mood (especially depression and

◉——Watch **the Video** *In the Real World: Reducing Stress, Improving Health* in **MyPsychLab** anxiety) as taking aspirin is for getting rid of a headache (Otto & Smits, 2012). People who are physically fit have improved cardiovascular health and cognitive function, and lower risk of diabetes, than people who are less fit, even when all are under the same pressures. People who exercise regularly and moderately also show lower physiological arousal to stressors (Vita et al., 1998). Exercise even seems able to slow the progression of degenerative diseases, such as Parkinson's (Gitler, 2011) and may be important in slowing dementia (Ben Ayed, 2014).

These activities, along with any others that calm your body and focus your mind—dance, prayer, music, cooking—are all good for health. But if your house has burned down or you need a serious operation, other coping strategies will be necessary. ✳

✳⎡**Explore** the **Concept**
How Do You Deal with Your Emotions?
in **MyPsychLab**

Solving the Problem

Years ago, at the age of 23, a friend of ours named Simi Linton was struck by tragedy. Linton, her new husband, and her best friend were in a horrific car accident. When she awoke in a hospital room, with only a vague memory of the crash, she learned that her husband and friend had been killed and that she herself had suffered permanent spinal injury and would never walk again.

How in the world does anyone recover from such a devastating event? Some people advise survivors of disaster or tragedy to "get it out of your system" or to "get in touch with your feelings." But survivors know they feel miserable. What should they *do*? This question gets to the heart of the difference between *emotion-focused* and *problem-focused coping* (Lazarus, 2000a; Lazarus & Folkman, 1984). Emotion-focused coping concentrates on the emotions the problem has caused, whether anger, anxiety, or grief. For a period of time after any tragedy or disaster, it is normal to give in to these emotions and feel overwhelmed by them. In this stage, people often need to talk obsessively about the event in order to come to terms with it, make sense of it, and decide what to do about it (Lepore, Ragan, & Jones, 2000).

These two friends know all about surviving and thriving.

Jeff Greenberg/Alamy

Eventually, most people become ready to concentrate on solving the problem itself. The specific steps in problem-focused coping depend on the nature of the problem: whether it is a pressing but one-time decision; a continuing difficulty, such as living with a disability; or an anticipated event, such as having an operation. Once the problem is identified, the coper can learn as much as possible about it from professionals, friends and books or others in the same predicament (Clarke & Evans, 1998). Becoming informed increases the feeling of control and may speed recovery (Doering et al., 2000).

As for Simi Linton, she learned how to do just about everything in her wheelchair (including dancing!), and she went back to school. She got a PhD in psychology, remarried, and became a highly respected teacher, counsellor, writer, and activist committed to improving conditions and opportunities for people with disabilities (Linton, 2006).

Rethinking the Problem

Some problems cannot be solved; these are the unavoidable facts of life, such as an inability to have children, losing your job, or developing a chronic illness. Now what? Health psychologists have identified three effective cognitive coping methods: 👁

👁⎡**Watch** the **Video**
Fighting Stress in **MyPsychLab**

1 **Reappraising the situation.** Although you may not be able to get rid of a stressor, you can choose to think about it differently, a process called *reappraisal*.

Reappraisal can turn anger into sympathy, worry into determination, and feelings of loss into feelings of opportunity. Maybe that job you lost was dismal but you were too afraid to quit and look for another; now you can. Reappraisal improves well-being and reduces negative emotions (Gross & John, 2003; Haga, Kraft, & Corby, 2009; Moskowitz et al., 2009).

2 **Learning from the experience.** Most victims of traumatic events and life-threatening illnesses report that the experience made them stronger, more resilient, and even better human beings because they grew and learned from the event (McFarland & Alvaro, 2000). Those who draw lessons from the inescapable tragedies of life, and find meaning in them, thrive as a result of adversity instead of simply surviving it (Davis, Nolen-Hoeksema, & Larson, 1998; Folkman & Moskowitz, 2000). The ability to find meaning in adversity may even slow the course of serious diseases. In a longitudinal study of men with HIV who had been recently bereaved, those who "tried not to think about it" showed sharper declines in immune function than men who found meaning and purpose in the loss. The latter said they had acquired greater appreciation of the loved one, a perception of life as being fragile and precious, or other benefits. "I would say that his death lit up my faith," said one man (Taylor, Kemeny, et al., 2000).

3 **Making social comparisons.** In a difficult situation, successful copers often compare themselves to others whom they feel are less fortunate. Even if they have fatal diseases, they find someone who is worse off (Taylor & Lobel, 1989; Wood, Michela, & Giordano, 2000). One person with AIDS said in an interview, "I made a list of all the other diseases I would rather not have than AIDS. Lou Gehrig's disease; being in a wheelchair; rheumatoid arthritis, when you are in knots and in terrible pain." Sometimes successful copers also compare themselves to those who are doing better than they are (Collins, 1996). They might say, "Look at her—she's had such family troubles and survived that awful bout with cancer, and she's happier than ever with her life. How did she do it?" or "He and I have the same kinds of problems. How come he's doing so much better in school than I am? What does he know that I don't?" Such social comparisons are beneficial when they provide a person with information about ways of coping, managing an illness, or improving a stressful situation (Suls, Martin, & Wheeler, 2002).

Drawing on Social Support

A final way to deal with negative emotions and stress is to reach out to others. Your health depends not only on what is going on in your body and mind but also on what is going on in your relationships: what you take from them, and what you give to them. When social groups provide individuals with a sense of meaning, purpose, and belonging, they produce positive psychological benefits for their members' health and well-being (Haslam et al., 2009; Uchino, 2009). Being involved in social networks and a close community is one of the most powerful predictors of having a long and healthy life (Friedman & Martin, 2011). Why?

When Friends Help You Cope . . . Think of all the ways in which family members, friends, neighbours, and co-workers can help you. They can offer concern and affection. They can help you evaluate problems and plan a course of action. They can offer resources and services such as lending you money or a car, or taking notes in class for you when you are sick. Most of all, they are sources of attachment and connection, which everyone needs throughout life.

Friends can even improve your health. In general, work-related stress and unemployment increase a person's vulnerability to the common cold, but having a lot of

THINKING CRITICALLY

Avoid emotional reasoning, examine the evidence—and then tolerate uncertainty!

It is difficult for animal lovers to avoid emotional reasoning about the benefits of pets. No wonder they welcome the news that having a pet lowers your blood pressure and is good for your health in other ways too. When one psychologist examined the evidence, he indeed found plenty of studies showing that pets have these benefits; unfortunately, he found just as much evidence that pets have either no long-term benefits or even harmful and negative effects (Herzog, 2011). Before jumping to conclusions, therefore, we have to tolerate some uncertainty until we better understand the conditions under which pets do benefit human health and well-being, and when they can be sources of stress themselves.

friends and social contacts helps to reduce that risk (Cohen et al., 2003). Social support is especially important for people who have stressful jobs that require high cardiovascular responsiveness day after day, such as firefighters. Having social support helps the heart rate and stress hormones return to normal more quickly after a stressful episode (Roy, Steptoe, & Kirschbaum, 1998).

When social support comes from a loving partner, its benefits on the immune system are especially powerful. In one study of 16 couples, the wives had to lie in an MRI machine, periodically receiving a mild but stressful electric shock on their ankle (Coan, Schaefer, & Davidson, 2006). During the procedure, some women received a touch on the hand from a stranger; others held hands with their husbands. The women's brain images showed activation in the hypothalamus and other regions involved with pain, physical arousal, and negative emotions. Yet, as you can see in Figure 11.7, the moment the women felt a husband's reassuring hand, their brain activation subsided in all the regions that had been revved up to cope with threat and fear. Holding hands with a stranger, although comforting, did not produce as great a decrease in brain activation as did a husband's touch.

When a touch is affectionate and welcome, it elevates some "therapeutic" hormones, especially *oxytocin*, the hormone that induces relaxation and is associated with mothering and attachment. In fact, human bodies may be designed not only for a "fight-or-flight" response to stress and challenge, but also a "tend-and-befriend" response—being friendly and conciliatory, seeking out a friend or loved one, taking care of others (Taylor & Master, 2011). Animal studies find that early nurturing by parents or other adults who "tend and befriend" the young can affect the sensitivity of the HPA axis, making the infants more resilient to later chronic stressors (Young & Francis, 2008). Such findings may help explain why, without such nurturing, stressed children become more vulnerable to illness, and why a significant minority of children who grow up under adverse conditions do not develop health problems: They have been protected by having warm, nurturing mothers (Miller et al., 2011).

However, once again it is important not to oversimplify, by concluding that people can defeat any illness if they just have the right amount and kind of social support. Some years ago, a psychiatrist claimed, on the basis of a preliminary study, that women with advanced breast cancer lived longer if they joined support groups, but the study has been discredited and was never replicated (Coyne et al., 2009).

FIGURE 11.7 Hugs and Health
Women had to lie in an MRI machine while receiving mild but stressful shocks on their ankle. Those who showed the highest activation of the hypothalamus and other regions of the brain involved in stress and anxiety went through the test alone. A stranger's calming touch reduced activation somewhat, and a husband's touch reduced it even more. The women in "super couples," those who felt the closest to their husbands (right bar), showed the lowest signs of stress (Coan, Schaefer, & Davidson, 2006).

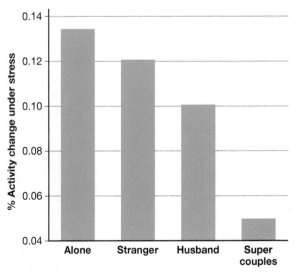

Therapy does not prolong survival, although it often is emotionally and socially beneficial to individual members.

Moreover, not all cultural groups define "social support" the same way or benefit from the same kind. People from Asians backgrounds may be more reluctant than westerners to ask for help explicitly from friends, colleagues, and family and to disclose feelings of distress to others. Being culturally attuned to the harmony of their relationships (see Chapter 14), many Asians are concerned about the potentially negative and embarrassing effects of self-disclosure or of seeking help. As a result, they often feel more stressed and have elevated stress hormones when they are required to ask for help or reveal their private feelings (Kim, Sherman, & Taylor, 2008). But Asians do not differ from westerners in their reliance on, and need for, *implicit* social support—the knowledge that someone will be there to help if they need it. ◉

◉—⌐**Watch** the **Video**

Thinking Like a Psychologist: Personality and Health in **MyPsychLab**

. . . And Coping with Friends.   Needless to say, sometimes other people aren't helpful. Sometimes they themselves are the source of unhappiness, stress, and anger. Even Facebook, which brings so much pleasure and feelings of connection to millions of people, has a dark side. "Everyone" seems so happy and successful, listing all their accomplishments, babies, promotions, etc., that many people feel worse about themselves after spending time scrolling through their friends' updates. A series of studies of first-year college students found that most of them consistently underestimated their friends' and peers' moods and negative experiences, and overestimated how much fun their peers were having. As a result of comparisons to allegedly happier Facebook friends, many came away feeling more lonely and dejected themselves; women were especially vulnerable to feelings of inadequacy (Jordan et al., 2011).

In close relationships, the same person who is a source of support can also become a source of stress, especially if the two parties are arguing all the time. Being in an unhappy, bitter, uncommunicative relationship can significantly impair health (Friedman & Martin, 2011). It makes the partners depressed and angry, affects their health habits, elevates stress hormones, and also directly influences

Friends can be our greatest source of warmth, support, and fun . . . and also sources of exasperation, anger, and misery.

Everett Collection

their cardiovascular, endocrine, and immune systems (Kiecolt-Glaser & Newton, 2001). Couples who argue in a hostile fashion—criticizing, interrupting, or insulting each other, and becoming angry and defensive—show significant elevations of cortisol and poorer immune function afterward (Kiecolt-Glaser et al., 2005). Couples who argue in a positive fashion—trying to find common ground, compromising, listening to each other's concerns, and using humour to defuse tension—do not show these impairments. As one student of ours observed, "This study gives new meaning to the accusation 'You make me sick!'"

In addition to being sources of conflict, friends and relatives may be unsupportive simply out of ignorance or awkwardness. Sometimes they actively block your efforts to change bad health habits, such as by binge drinking or smoking, or by making fun of you or pressuring you to conform to what "everyone" does. They may try to cheer you up, saying, "Everything will be fine," rather than let you talk about your fears or find solutions.

Finally, we should not forget the benefits of giving support, rather than always being on the receiving end. Julius Segal (1986), a psychologist who worked with Holocaust survivors, hostages, refugees, and other survivors of catastrophe, wrote that a key element in their recovery was compassion for others: "healing through helping." Why? The ability to look outside yourself is related to all of the successful coping mechanisms we have discussed. It encourages you to solve problems instead of blaming others or just venting your emotions, helps you reappraise the situation by seeing it from another person's perspective, fosters forgiveness, and allows you to gain perspective on your own problems (Brown et al., 2003). Healing through helping thus helps everyone to accept difficult situations that are facts of life.

Recite & Review

Recite: Take advantage of social support, and find a friend to whom you can describe the benefits of meditation and exercise, cognitive strategies for coping with stressful problems, and the benefits and potential harms of close relationships.

Review: Next, reappraise your feelings about reviewing this material, and reread it.

Now take this *Quick Quiz:*

1. You accidentally broke your glasses. Which response is an example of reappraisal? (a) "I am such a stupid, clumsy idiot!" (b) "I never do anything right." (c) "What a shame, but I've been wanting new frames anyway." (d) "I'll forget about it in aerobics class."

2. Finding out what your legal and financial resources are when you have been victimized by a crime is an example of (a) problem-focused coping, (b) emotion-focused coping, (c) distraction, (d) reappraisal.

3. "This class drives me crazy, but I'm better off than my friends who aren't in university" is an example of (a) distraction, (b) social comparison, (c) denial, (d) empathy.

4. What hormone is elevated when happy couples hug one another?

5. Your roommate has turned your room into a garbage dump, filled with rotten leftover food and unwashed clothes. Assuming that you don't like living with rotting food and dirty clothes, what coping strategies described in this section might help you?

Answers:

social support, perhaps by offering your friends a pizza if they help you clean up.
compare your roommate to others who are worse ("At least mine is generous and friendly"). And you might mobilize some
You could reappraise the seriousness of the problem ("I only have to live with this person until the end of the term") or
1. c 2. a 3. b 4. oxytocin 5. You might solve the problem by finding a compromise (e.g., cleaning the room together).

REVIEW 11.2   Factors That Increase the Risk of Illness

Factors	Examples
Environmental	Poverty, lack of access to health care, exposure to toxins, crime, discrimination
Experiential	Childhood neglect, traumatic events, chronic job stress, unemployment
Biological	Viral or bacterial infections, disease, genetic vulnerability, toxins
Psychological	Hostility, chronic major depression, emotional inhibition, low levels of conscientiousness, external locus of control (fatalism), feeling powerless
Behavioural	Smoking, poor diet, lack of exercise, abuse of alcohol and other drugs, lack of sleep
Social	Lack of supportive friends, low involvement in meaningful groups, being in a hostile, bitter relationship

As you can see in Review 11.2, the factors that affect health and illness range from those we can't do anything about to those that we can. Successful coping does not mean eliminating all sources of stress or all difficult emotions. It does not mean constant happiness or a life without anger, grief, and frustration. The healthy person faces problems, deals with them, learns from them, and gets beyond them. To wish for a life without stress, or a life without emotion, would be like wishing for a life without friends. The result might be calm, but it would be joyless. Chronic problems, difficult decisions, and occasional tragedies are inescapable. How we handle them is the test of our humanity.

Taking Psychology with You

THINKING CRITICALLY IN EVERYDAY LIFE

How Much Control Do We Have over Our Emotions and Our Health?

Clara Harris killed her husband in "the heat of anger." Could she have controlled herself? When we are feeling extreme emotions or when major stressors require the body to cope with threat, fear, or danger, the body whirls into action to give us the energy to respond. Just about everyone has had the unpleasant experience of a racing heart, sweaty palms, and other emotional symptoms upon seeing a former lover with a new partner. But does that mean we have no control over our emotions—that if we yell, scream, or become violent when we're angry, it's not our fault?

How about our health? People do have some control over the psychological and social factors involved in the onset and course of many illnesses, such as negative emotions, pessimism, and lack of supportive friends. And we can choose to do the three things that are the strongest behavioural predictors of longevity and health, which are not psychological at all: not

smoking (or quitting), eating a healthful diet, and exercising regularly. But does that mean that if we become sick, it's our own fault?

Life is full of stressful experiences, emotional problems, and disastrous bolts out of the blue that we cannot predict or avoid. At such times, critical thinking becomes especially important, because the temptation is great to slide into over-simplified, either–or thinking: For example, if you are angry about some injustice, *either* you try to squelch your feelings *or* you take them out on the nearest innocent target. If you become ill, *either* you accept traditional medical procedures *or* you use alternative psychological ones, such as visual imagery, meditation, and support groups. It seems easier to jump to one explanation or solution and stick with it, without examining the evidence (pro and con) for its effectiveness. In stressful times, everyone is inclined to let emotional reasoning cloud their good judgment.

Usually, though, solutions and ways of coping do not require either–or answers. People can follow traditional medical treatments while *engaging* the power of optimism, meditation, and social support in their recovery and well-being. In the case of managing anger, Clara Harris could surely have found a course of action between suppressing her feelings completely and driving her SUV over her husband in a parking lot!

Hostile anger, as we have seen in this chapter, is particularly hazardous to health, but what should people do when they are enraged? When we examine the evidence, we find that the pop-psych advice to "ventilate your anger and get it out of your system" often backfires: Many people feel worse both physically and mentally after an angry confrontation. When people brood and ruminate about their anger, talk to others incessantly about how angry they are, or ventilate their feelings in hostile acts, their blood pressure shoots up, they often feel angrier, and they behave even *more* aggressively later than if they had just let their feelings of anger subside (Bushman et al., 2005; Tavris, 1989). Conversely, when people learn to control their tempers and express anger constructively, they usually feel better, not worse; calmer, not angrier.

When people are feeling angry, they may not be able to control that racing heart or the emotion itself, but they can control what they do next: They can take five, calm down, and

> ❝The pop-psych advice to 'ventilate your anger and get it out of your system' often backfires: Many people feel worse both physically and mentally after an angry confrontation. ❞

cool off rather than acting impulsively and maing matters worse. They can use their critical-thinking skills to avoid emotional reasoning and check their perceptions of the situation for accuracy. People who are quick to feel anger tend to interpret other people's actions as intentional offences. People who are slow to anger tend to give others the benefit of the doubt, and they are not as focused on their own injured pride.

Critical thinkers might also learn to think carefully about how to express anger, and make a calm decisions about how to proceed, so that they will get the results they want. Many people say harsh and hurtful things in anger simply to make the other person feel bad. But shouting "You moron! How could you be so stupid!" is not likely to get the person to apologize, let alone to change his or her behaviour. If the goal is to improve a bad situation or achieve justice, learning how to express anger so that the other person will listen is essential.

In short, we may not be able to control the stressors in our lives or the intensity of some emotions we feel after great loss, injustice, or tragedy, but we human beings have something almost better: The ability to think about our actions and to control what we do next.

Summary

MyPsychLab can help you get a better grade. Test your knowledge and grasp difficult concepts through
- Custom study plans: See where you are strong and where you are wrong
- Multimedia, including videos and interactive simulations
- Dynamic Study Modules: flashcards for self-study that ensure you achieve mastery of course concepts

The Nature of Emotion

- Emotions evolved to bind people together, motivate them to achieve their goals, and help them make decisions and plans. The experience of *emotion* involves physiological changes in the face, brain, and autonomic nervous system; cognitive processes such as appraisal and interpretation; *action tendencies*; and subjective feelings. In turn, emotions and their expression are influenced and shaped by cultural norms and regulations.

- Some facial expressions—anger, fear, sadness, happiness, disgust, surprise, contempt, and possibly pride—are widely recognized across cultures. They foster communication with others, signal our intentions to others, enhance infant

survival, and, as studies of *facial feedback* show, help us to identify our own emotional states. But an accurate reading of others' facial expressions increases among members of the same ethnicity, and depends on the social context. Also, because people can and do disguise their emotions, their expressions do not always communicate accurately.

- Many aspects of emotion are associated with specific parts of the brain. The amygdala is responsible for initially evaluating the emotional importance of incoming sensory information and is especially involved in fear. The cerebral cortex provides the cognitive ability to override this initial appraisal. Emotions generally involve the motivation to approach or withdraw; regions of the *left* prefrontal cortex appear to be specialized for the motivation to approach others (as with happiness and anger), whereas regions of the *right* prefrontal region are specialized for withdrawal or escape (as with disgust and fear).

- *Mirror neurons* throughout the brain are activated when people observe others, especially other people of the same group or others they like. These neurons seem to be involved in empathy, imitation, synchrony, and *mood contagion.*

- During the experience of any emotion, *epinephrine* and *norepinephrine* produce a state of physiological arousal to prepare the body for an output of energy.

- As discussed in "Biology and Lie Detection," the most popular method of lie detection is the *polygraph machine*, but it has low reliability and validity because no patterns of autonomic nervous system activity are specific to lying; it has a high rate of labelling innocent people as guilty. Other methods, such as voice stress analyses, have similar drawbacks.

- Cognitive approaches to emotion emphasize the perceptions and *appraisals* that are involved in different emotions. Thoughts and emotions operate reciprocally, each influencing the other. Some emotions, such as shame and guilt, require complex cognitive capacities.

Emotion and Culture

- Many psychologists believe that all human beings share the ability to experience certain basic emotions, a view supported by research on emotion *prototypes*. However, cultural differences in values, norms, and appraisals generate emotion blends and culture-specific emotional feelings. Culture affects almost every aspect of emotional experience, including which emotions are considered appropriate or wrong, and what people feel emotional about.

- Culture strongly influences *display rules*, including those governing nonverbal *body language*, that regulate how and whether people express their emotions. *Emotion work* is the effort a person makes to display an emotion he or she does not feel but feels obliged to convey.

- Women and men are equally likely to feel all emotions, although gender rules shape differences in emotional expression. North American women on average are more expressive than men, except for expressing anger at strangers. But both sexes are less expressive toward a person of higher status, both sexes will do the emotion work their job requires, and some situations foster expressiveness in everybody. Gender differences also vary across cultures.

The Nature of Stress

- The relation between emotions and stress is both physiological and psychological. Chronic negative emotions can become chronically stressful, and chronic stress can create negative emotions.

- Hans Selye argued that environmental stressors such as heat, pain, and danger produce a *general adaptation syndrome*, in which the body responds in three stages: *alarm, resistance,* and *exhaustion.* If a stressor persists, it may overwhelm the body's ability to cope, and illness may result. Modern research has added to Selye's work. When a person is under stress or in danger, the hypothalamus sends messages to the endocrine glands along two major pathways. One activates the sympathetic division of the autonomic nervous system, releasing adrenal hormones from the inner part of the adrenal glands. In the other, the hypothalamus initiates activity along the *HPA axis.* Chemical messengers travel from the hypothalamus to the pituitary, and in turn to the outer part (cortex) of the adrenal glands. The adrenal cortex secretes *cortisol* and other hormones that increase energy. Excess levels of cortisol can become harmful in the long run.

- When the stressors of poverty and unemployment become chronic, they can increase people's stress levels and increase their chances of illness. But responses to stress differ across individuals, depending on the type of stressor and the individual's own genetic predispositions.

- Health psychologists and researchers in the interdisciplinary field of *psychoneuroimmunology* (PNI) are studying the interaction among psychological factors, the nervous and endocrine systems, and the immune system (particularly the white blood cells that destroy harmful foreign bodies, called *antigens*). Chronic stress can even shorten *telomeres*, a protein on the end of the chromosome that determines cell life.

- Psychological factors affect people's responses to stress. Realistic optimism, conscientiousness, and having an *internal locus of control* improve immune function and also increase a person's ability to tolerate pain, live with ongoing problems, and recover from illness, possibly because they motivate people to take better care of themselves. As discussed in "Culture and Control," cultures differ in the kind of control they emphasize and value: *primary control*, trying to change the stressful situation, or *secondary control*, learning to accept and accommodate to the stressful situation.

Stress and Emotion

- Researchers have sought links between emotions, stress, and illness. There is no "cancer-prone personality," but chronic anger, especially in the form of *cynical* or *antagonistic* hostility, is a strong risk factor in heart disease. Major depression also increases the risk of later heart disease.

- People who consciously suppress their emotions (caused by serious matters) are at greater risk of illness than people who acknowledge and cope with negative emotions. The effort to suppress worries, secrets, and memories of upsetting experiences can become stressful to the body. Two ways of letting go of negative emotions include confession and forgiveness. The goal is to achieve insight and understanding, and to let go of grudges.

Coping with Stress

- The first step in coping with stress and negative emotions is to reduce their physical effects, such as through *mindfulness meditation* and exercise, both of which have significant physical and mental benefits. The second is to focus on solving the problem (*problem-focused coping*) rather than on venting the emotions caused by the problem (*emotion-focused coping*). A third approach is to rethink the problem, which involves *reappraisal*, learning from the experience, and comparing oneself to others.

- Social support is essential in maintaining physical health and emotional well-being; it even prolongs life and speeds recovery from illness. A touch or a hug from a supportive partner calms the alarm circuits of the brain and raises levels of *oxytocin*, which may result in reduced heart rate and blood pressure. However, friends and family can also be sources of stress. In close relationships, couples who fight in a hostile and negative way show impaired immune function. Giving support to others is also associated with health and hastens recovery from traumatic experiences.

Taking Psychology with You

- We may not always be able to control the physiological arousal produced by stress or intense emotions such as anger, but we generally are able to decide how to behave. Coping with stress does not mean trying to live without pain or problems. It means learning how to live with them.

Key Terms

emotion **378**
primary emotions **378**
secondary emotions **379**
facial feedback **380**
mirror neurons **383**

appraisals **388**
display rules **392**
emotion work **393**
general adaptation syndrome (Selye) **396**

HPA axis **396**
cortisol **397**
psychoneuroimmunology (PNI) **399**
locus of control **401**

primary control **402**
secondary control **402**

12 Motivation

418

Ask questions. . . be willing to wonder

What accounts for the worldwide epidemic of obesity?

Why do we fall in love, and why with that person?

Why are some people straight and others gay?

After a setback, why do some people persist in their goals and others give up?

In 1992, Silken Laumann won a bronze medal at the Barcelona Olympics. Most stories of outstanding Olympic achievement are about gold medals. Indeed, just three months before the event, she was favoured to scull her way to the gold. However, in a horrible training accident, Silken severely injured one of her legs. By some accounts, the leg was "half-amputated." Following five hasty reconstructive surgeries and a skin graft, her physicians told her that her Olympic dreams would not become reality. In fact, they even told her that she might never be able to row again, even recreationally. In an incredible demonstration of motivation, Silken chose to endure the pain of catch-up training shortly before the big event. This determination paid off. She earned a place in the final and pushed her ailing body to the limit, earning Canada's most famous Olympic bronze medal.

In 1875, a teenager named Annie Oakley defeated Frank Butler, the star of the Buffalo Bill Wild West Show, in an arranged sharp-shooting competition. "It was her first big match—my first defeat," wrote Butler. "The next day I came back to see the little girl who had beaten me, and it was not long until we married." He became her manager, and for the next 50 years they travelled together across Europe and North America, where her skills with a gun made her the toast of both continents. Throughout his life, Frank published love poems until their deaths, within 18 days of one another, in 1926 (Kreps, 1990).

What motivated Silken Laumann to risk permanent disability and successfully compete for an Olympic medal? What kept Annie Oakley and Frank Butler in love for 50 years, when so many other romantic passions die in five years—or five weeks?

The word *motivation*, like the word *emotion*, comes from the Latin root meaning "to move," and the psychology of motivation is indeed the study of what moves us, why we do what we do. To psychologists, **motivation** refers to a process within a person or animal that causes that organism to move toward a goal or away from an unpleasant situation. The motive may be to satisfy a psychological goal, say, by getting married or avoiding marriage; it may be to satisfy a biological need, say, by eating a sandwich to reduce hunger; or it may be to fulfill a psychological ambition, say, by being the first to row across the Atlantic in a dinghy (it's been done).

For many decades, the study of motivation was dominated by a focus on biological *drives*, such as those to acquire food and water, to have sex, to seek novelty, and to avoid cold and pain. Some psychologists still think that people are motivated by certain drives, especially sex and hunger. But drive theories cannot

motivation An inferred process within a person or animal that causes movement either toward a goal or away from an unpleasant situation.

intrinsic motivation The pursuit of an activity for its own sake.

extrinsic motivation The pursuit of an activity for external rewards, such as money or fame.

set point The genetically influenced weight range for an individual; it is maintained by biological mechanisms that regulate food intake, fat reserves, and metabolism.

⊙—⌐Watch the Video
The Big Picture: Motivation and Emotion in **MyPsychLab**

account for the full complexity of human motivation, because people are conscious creatures who think and plan ahead, set goals for themselves, and plot strategies to reach those goals. People are motivated to eat, for instance, but that information doesn't tell us why some individuals with strong political commitments will go on hunger strikes to protest injustice. ⊙

In this chapter, we will examine four central areas of human motivation: food, love, sex, and achievement. We will see how happiness and well-being are affected by the kinds of goals we set for ourselves, and by whether we are spurred to reach them because of **intrinsic motivation,** the desire to do something for its own sake and the pleasure it brings, or **extrinsic motivation,** the desire to pursue a goal for external rewards.

Learning Objectives

1 Articulate the biological mechanisms that make it difficult for obese people to lose weight and keep it off.

2 Describe how notions of the ideal male and female body change over time and across cultures.

3 Explain why people all over the world are getting fatter.

4 Tabulate the major forms of eating disorders, and why they are increasing among young men as well as women.

The Hungry Animal: Motives to Eat

Some people are skinny; others are plump. Some are shaped like string beans; others look more like pears. Some can eat anything they want without gaining an ounce; others struggle unsuccessfully their whole lives to shed pounds. Some hate being fat, and others think that fat is just fine. How much do genes, psychology, and environment affect our motivation to eat or not to eat? ✳

✳—⌐Explore the Concept
Virtual Brain: Hunger and Eating in **MyPsychLab**

The Biology of Weight

At one time, most psychologists thought that being overweight was a sign of emotional disturbance. If you were fat, it was because you hated your mother, feared intimacy, or were trying to fill an emotional hole in your psyche by loading up on rich desserts. The evidence for psychological theories of overweight, however, came mainly from self-reports and from flawed studies that lacked control groups or objective measures of how much people were actually eating. When researchers did controlled experiments, they learned that fat people, on average, are no more and no less emotionally disturbed than average-weight people. Even more surprising, they found that heaviness is not always caused by overeating (Stunkard, 1980). Many heavy people do eat large quantities of food, but so do some thin people. In one study, in which volunteers gorged themselves for months, it was as hard for slender people to gain weight as it is for most heavy people to lose weight. The minute the study was over, the slender people lost weight as fast as dieters gained it back (Sims, 1974).

Genetic Influences on Weight and Body Shape. The explanation that emerged from such findings was that a biological mechanism keeps your body weight at a genetically influenced **set point,** the weight you stay at when you are not trying to gain or lose (Lissner et al., 1991). The set point can vary about 10% in either direction. For example,

THINKING CRITICALLY

Analyze assumptions and biases.

Obesity is caused mainly by psychological problems and lack of willpower, isn't it? When researchers questioned this common assumption, they were in for a surprise.

Body weight and shape are strongly affected by genetic factors. Set-point theory helps explain why the Pimas of the American Southwest gain weight easily but lose it slowly, whereas the Bororo nomads of Nigeria can eat a lot of food yet remain slender.

Left: Magnum photos. Right: Hemis/Alamy.

a woman with a set point of 150 pounds might weigh anywhere from 135 to 165. But if her weight dips below 135 or goes above 165, her body will produce either an insatiable urge to eat or a loss of appetite to bring its fat levels back into line. Set-point research has focused on how the body regulates appetite, eating, and weight gain and loss. Everyone has a genetically programmed *basal metabolism rate*, the rate at which the body burns calories for energy, and a fixed number of fat cells, which store fat for energy and can change in size. Obese people have about twice the number of fat cells as normal-weight adults do, and their fat cells are bigger (Spalding et al., 2008). When people lose weight, they don't lose the fat cells; the cells just get thinner, and easily plump up again.

A complex interaction of metabolism, fat cells, and hormones keeps people at the weight their bodies are designed to be, much as a thermostat keeps a house at a constant temperature. When a heavy person diets, the body's metabolism slows down to conserve energy and fat reserves (Ravussin et al., 1988). When a thin person overeats, metabolism speeds up, burning energy. In one study, in which 16 slender volunteers ate 1000 extra calories every day for eight weeks, their metabolisms sped up to burn the excess calories. They were like hummingbirds, in constant movement: fidgeting, pacing, changing their positions frequently while seated, and so on (Levine, Eberhardt, & Jensen, 1999).

Set-point theory predicts that the heritability of weight and body fat should be high, and indeed it is: In twin and adoption studies, heritability estimates fall between 0.40 and 0.70 (Comuzzie & Allison, 1998). Pairs of adult identical twins who grew up in different families are just as similar in body weight and shape as twins raised together. And when identical twins gain weight, they gain it in the same place: Some pairs store extra pounds around their waists, others on their hips and thighs (Bouchard et al., 1990). Genes also determine how much "brown fat" a person has in addition to the usual white fat. Brown fat is an energy-burning type of fat that seems important in regulating body weight and blood sugar. It is lacking in obese people, which may be one reason that fat people can't burn all the calories they consume (Cypess et al., 2009). However, production of brown fat is also triggered by cold and exercise, which, in mice at least, turns ordinary white fat brown (Ouellet et al., 2012). Brown fat cells are fascinating; when they run out of their own sources of energy, they suck fat out of the rest of the body to keep their proprietor warm.

Genes are also involved in some types of obesity. In a study of 171 Pima Indians in Arizona, two-thirds of the women and half of the men became obese over time, and the slower their metabolisms, the greater the weight gain. After adding anywhere from 20 to 45 pounds, however, the Pimas stopped gaining weight. Their metabolism rates rose, and their weights stabilized at the new, higher level (Ravussin et al., 1988). Many Pimas apparently have a set point for plumpness. Similarly, the Inuit of the Canadian Arctic (Young, 1996) and other indigenous peoples of Canada have much higher rates of obesity than other Canadians (Harris et al., 1997; Katzmarzyk & Malina, 1998, 1999; Orr et al., 1998). Furthermore, obesity in these groups has serious consequences—including Type II diabetes. Among the indigenous peoples of Canada,

Among the Inuit of the Canadian Arctic, obesity and Type II diabetes are largely the result of ingesting too many calories (high-fat foods, sugars, and carbohydrates). Although Inuit cultures ate fatty food traditionally (whale blubber, for instance), it was in limited supply—especially the sugar and carbohydrates. In modern Inuit society, the supply of fats, sugars, and carbohydrates is virtually unlimited.

Mike Bedell Photography

Both of these mice have a mutation in the *ob* gene, which usually makes mice chubby, like the one on the left. But when leptin is injected daily, the mice eat less and burn more calories, causing the chubby one to become slim, like his friendly pal. Unfortunately, leptin injections have not had the same results in most human beings. It only helps humans who lack leptin for genetic reasons.

Remi Banali/ZUMA Press Gamma

the rate of Type II diabetes is higher than among any other group in the world (Harris et al., 1997).

A few years ago, a team of researchers isolated a genetic variation that causes mice to become obese (Zhang et al., 1994). The usual form of the gene, called *obese*, or *ob* for short, causes fat cells to secrete a protein, which researchers have named *leptin* (from the Greek *leptos*, "slender"). Leptin travels through the blood to the brain's hypothalamus, which is involved in the regulation of appetite. When leptin levels are normal, people eat just enough to maintain their weight. When a mutation of the *ob* gene causes leptin levels to be too low, however, the hypothalamus thinks the body lacks fat reserves and signals the individual to overeat (Zhang et al., 1994). Injecting leptin into leptin-deficient mice reduces the animals' appetites, speeds up their metabolisms, and makes them more active; as a result, the animals shed weight (Friedman, 2003). Some extremely obese individuals who lack leptin for genetic reasons likewise benefit from injections of the hormone. A 90-kilogram (200-pound) nine-year-old girl, whose legs were so large she could hardly walk, dramatically reduced her food intake and weight to normal levels after treatment with leptin (Farooqi et al., 2002, 2007).

Studies of mice suggest that leptin plays its most crucial role early in life, by altering the brain chemistry that influences how much an animal or person later eats. More specifically, leptin helps regulate body weight by strengthening neural circuits in the hypothalamus that reduce appetite and by weakening circuits that stimulate it (Elmquist & Flier, 2004). During a critical period in infancy, leptin influences the formation of those neural connections, and the set point is, well, set (Bouret, Draper, & Simerly, 2004). Some researchers speculate that because of this early neural plasticity, overfeeding infants while the hypothalamus is developing may later produce childhood obesity.

Researchers have identified a number of other genes that are linked to being overweight (Farooqi & O'Rahilly, 2004; Frayling et al., 2007; Friedman, 2003; Herbert et al., 2006; Stice et al., 2008). For example, they have discovered a gene that modulates production of a protein that apparently converts excess calories into heat rather than fat. Possession of this gene may be one reason why slim people stay slim even when they temporarily overeat (Arsenijevic et al., 2000).

Findings such as these often raise the public's hopes for a breakthrough drug that will help people lose weight easily and quickly. One pharmaceutical company thought leptin would be the answer: Take leptin, lose weight! Alas, for most obese people, and for people who are merely overweight, taking leptin does not produce much weight loss (Comuzzie & Allison, 1998). Just to make life more complicated, leptin is only one influence on body weight. Dozens of genes and body chemicals are involved in appetite, metabolism rates, and weight regulation. You have receptors in your nose and mouth that keep urging you to eat more ("The food is right there! It's good! Eat!"), receptors in your gut telling you to quit ("You've had enough already!"), and leptin and other chemicals telling you that you have stored enough fat or not enough. One hormone makes you hungry and eager to eat more, and another turns off your appetite after a meal, making you eat less. The hormone ghrelin makes you hungry and eager to eat more, and leptin turns off your appetite after a meal, making you eat less. This complex set-point system seems to explain why dieters who lose weight so rarely keep it off. Even a year after their weight loss, the bodies of dieters are still leptin deficient, sending out hormonal signals to eat more and restore the lost pounds (Kissileff et al., 2012).

As if all this weren't enough, your brain will get high on sugary foods even if your tongue can't taste them or enjoy their texture. Sweets increase pleasure-inducing dopamine levels in the brain, making you crave more rich food (de Araujo et al., 2008). (Forget about trying to fool your brain with artificial sweeteners; they just make you want the real thing.) Some obese individuals may have underactive reward circuitry, which leads them to overeat to boost their dopamine levels (Stice et al., 2008). When heavy people joke (or lament) that they are "addicted" to rich food, they may literally be right.

The complexity of the mechanisms governing appetite and weight explains why appetite-suppressing drugs inevitably fail in the long run: They target only one of the many factors that conspire to keep you the weight you are.

The Overweight Debate. If genes are so strongly implicated in weight and body shape, and if most people have normal set points, why are so many people, all over the world, getting fatter? Increases in obesity rates have occurred in both sexes, all social classes, and all age groups, and in many other countries (Popkin, 2009). More than half of all North American adults, and at least 25% of all children and teenagers, are now overweight or obese. The increase has been greatest among the very fat: The number of North Americans who are at least 100 pounds overweight has quadrupled since the 1980s. Increases in obesity rates have occurred in both sexes, all social classes, all age groups, and in many countries (Taubes, 1998). The United Nations, so used to dealing with problems of starvation and malnutrition, has announced that "obesity is the dominant unmet global health issue," especially in the United States, Canada, Great Britain, Mexico, Egypt, North Africa, Japan, and Australia, and even in coastal China and Southeast Asia.

The prevalence of obesity in Canada has increased in the past few years (Millar & Stephens, 1993); in 1994, it was estimated that 26% of women and 35% of men in Canada were obese, and that by government standards, half of the adult population was overweight (MacDonald et al., 1997; Trakas, Lawrence, & Shear, 1999). So people are a little plump; what does it matter? For the year 1994, obesity was estimated to directly cost Canadian taxpayers more than $1.8 billion in health care; approximately 2.4% of the health-care budget was spent treating obesity or diseases directly resulting from obesity (Birmingham et al., 1999). This increase in obesity is not restricted to Canadians, as it has also been observed in the United Kingdom, the United States, and other western cultures (Flegal, 1999).

The reasons have little to do with the prevalence of obesity genes, which cannot have changed much in just a couple of decades. In fact, among recent immigrants to Canada, the longer they have lived in this country, the greater the chance that they will become overweight or obese (Cairney & Ostbye, 1999). These people have not changed their genes—just their addresses and thus their diets.

Many health researchers are worried about this trend because obesity is considered a leading risk factor in diabetes, high blood pressure, heart disease, stroke, cancer, infertility, sleep apnea, and many other disorders. But are there comparable health risks to being overweight by, say, 20 to 30 pounds? What if a person is genetically predisposed to be fat, though not obese? Lately some scientists have been cautioning against the emotional reasoning that so often accompanies discussions of this subject in North America, where "thin is in." They believe that for most people, the real health culprit is not overweight but lack of fitness. Fat people who are physically fit are healthier and have lower risk of illness, on average, than thin people who are sedentary (Campos, 2004). Because many overweight people have sedentary habits, few scientists have thought to separate these two factors. In a representative sample of more than 5000 American adults over the age of 20, about 24% of the normal-weight adults were metabolically unhealthy—that is, they had high blood pressure, "bad" cholesterol, elevated triglycerides, and other risk factors for heart disease—whereas 51% of the overweight adults and nearly 32% of the obese adults were metabolically healthy (Wildman et al., 2008). ◉

Watch the **Video**
Nutrition in **MyPsychLab**

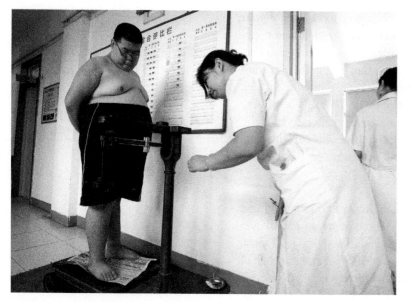

Obesity is a global problem. Children around the world are eating more like North Americans—too much food, and too much fast food.

DIEGO AZUBEL/EPA/Newscom

Scientists are currently debating the extent of the problem and what can be done about it. One scientist, Jeffrey Friedman, the primary discoverer of the gene for leptin, said in an interview that the obesity epidemic is mainly a result of the fact that fat people are getting fatter; thin people have remained pretty much the same (Kolata, 2004). Thin people do not balloon into obesity, he observes—remember those hummingbird metabolisms that so many of them have—nor can fat people lose weight permanently through willpower, because body weight is genetically determined. Other scientists agree that genes play a powerful role, but they observe that changes in the environment and culture are the reason why so many people are putting on the pounds. After all, in between the extremes of thin and fat are the millions of people whose weights have risen 10 to 30 to 50 pounds, and that's not trivial. What has caused that increase?

Whatever the health implications of being overweight, a puzzle remains: If genes and all the chemical factors and fat cells they regulate are so strongly implicated in weight and body shape, why are so many people, all over the world, getting fatter? In Mexico in 1989, for example, fewer than 10% of its citizens were overweight; the country's greatest concern was poverty and hunger. Yet by 2006, 71% of Mexican women and 66% of the men were overweight or obese, with corresponding increases in diabetes and other diseases (Popkin, 2009). What has caused that increase in Mexico and so many other nations in so short a time?

Another major influence on weight is exercise, which boosts the body's metabolic rate, even in people who are genetically susceptible to obesity (Esparza et al., 2000). When obese women are put on severely restricted diets, their metabolic rates drop sharply, as set-point theory would predict. But when they combine the diet with moderate physical activity—daily walking—they lose weight and their metabolic rates rise almost to previous levels (Wadden et al., 1990).

Environmental Influences on Weight

The leading culprits causing the worldwide rise in weight have to do with five sweeping changes in the environment (Critser, 2002; Popkin, 2009; Taubes, 2008): 👁

👁⎯Watch the Video
The Problem of Childhood Obesity
in **MyPsychLab**

1 **The increased abundance of fast food and processed foods** that are inexpensive, readily available, and high in sugar, starch, fat, and carbohydrates (Taubes, 2008). Human beings are genetically predisposed to gain weight when rich food is abundant because, in our species' evolutionary past, starvation was all too often a real possibility. Therefore, a tendency to store calories in the form of fat provided a definite survival advantage. Unfortunately, evolution did not produce a comparable mechanism to prevent people who do not have hummingbird metabolisms from gaining weight when food is easily available, tasty, rich, varied, and cheap. That, of course, is precisely the situation today, surrounded as we are by three-quarter–pound burgers, fries, chips, tacos, candy bars, pizzas, and pop.

One research team observed the direct effects of the proximity of fast-food outlets on obesity. They followed thousands of grade 9 schoolchildren before and after a new fast-food restaurant opened near their schools. Those whose schools were within a block of a burger or pizza outlet were more likely to become obese in the next year than students whose schools were a 400 metres or more away (Currie et al., 2009). Proximity to fast food seems to be a major cause of the "freshman 15" as well. In a study at two very different universities, one in the American Midwest and the other in the East, more than 70% of all freshmen gained significant amounts of weight in their first year (Lloyd-Richardson et al., 2009).

2 **The widespread consumption of high-sugar, high-calorie soft drinks.** Throughout most of human history, the proportion of calories consumed in beverages (milk, wine, fruit juice, and the like) was very low, and thus the human body did not evolve a mechanism that would compensate for fluid intake by lowering food intake. Then, fifty years ago, soft drinks, which are loaded with sugar and calories, began spreading across the globe. Putting sweeteners into drinks has led to a weight gain of up to 14 pounds per person in those who drink two to three pops a day (Popkin, 2009).

3 **The sharp decline in exercise and other expenditures of energy** because of remote controls, a preference for sedentary activities such as watching videos and television, and the speed and convenience of driving rather than walking or biking.

4 **The increased portion sizes of food and drink.** Servings of food and drink have become supersized, double or triple what they were only one generation ago. Even babies and toddlers up to two years of age are being fed as much as 30% more calories than they need (Fox et al., 2004). In France, people eat rich food but much less of it than North Americans do (Rozin et al., 2003). Their notion of what a proper portion is—for yogurt, pop, a salad, a sandwich, anything—is much lower than in Canada.

5 **The abundance of highly varied foods.** When diets are predictable and routine, people habituate to what they are eating and eat less of it. That is why all diets that restrict people to eating only a few kinds of foods (only watermelon, only protein, only whatever) are successful at first. As soon as food becomes more varied, however, people eat more and gain more weight (Remick, Polivy, & Pliner, 2009). In fact, people will even eat more M&Ms when they are available in a bowl containing 10 colours than when the same number of candies are in a bowl containing only seven colours (Wansink, 2006).

GET INVOLVED! What's Controlling How Much You Eat?

Many people believe that what they eat and how much they eat is regulated by how hungry they feel. But the motivation to eat is complicated. Here are some invisible external influences on your eating habits (Wansink, 2006):

- **Package size:** People eat more from a large container (say, of popcorn) than a small one.

- **Plate size:** People eat more when they serve themselves on large plates rather than small ones.

- **Cues for how much has been eaten:** People eat more from a buffet when waiters quickly replace their dirty dishes, thereby eliminating tell-tale signs of how much food has already been consumed.

- **Kitchen and table layouts:** People eat more when food and snacks are displayed prominently, are varied, and are easily accessible.

- **Distraction:** People eat more when they are being distracted by friends and the environment.

The next time you are out with friends, take notes on how much everyone is eating (including yourself), and notice whether any of the above influences are at work. If you are trying to lose weight, how can you alter your own "food environment" to correct for these influences?

CULTURE and *the Ideal Body*

Norms, Gender, and Weight

Eating habits and activity levels are shaped by a culture's customs and standards of what the ideal body should look like: fat or thin, muscular or soft? In many places around the world, especially where famine and crop failures are common, fat is taken as a sign of health, of affluence in men, and of sexual desirability in women (Stearns, 1997). Among the Calabari of Nigeria, brides are put in special fattening huts where they do nothing but eat, so as to become fat enough to please their husbands.

Studies of English Canadians suggest that we hold negative attitudes toward obese people (LeBow, 1988; LeBow et al., 1989; Morrison & O'Connor, 1999). Interestingly, when asked what type of body they prefer, most anglophone Canadians indicate that they prefer smaller body shapes than their own, while people of the Ojibway–Cree First Nations indicate that they also prefer smaller body shapes than their own, but not as small as those preferred by the Anglos. This was despite the fact that only 16% of *both* groups indicated they were happy with their current physique (Gittelsohn et al., 1996). Obviously, researchers must conduct more studies of indigenous peoples of Canada before concluding whether all indigenous peoples hold similar body-image values.

Ironically, while people of all ethnicities and social classes have been getting fatter, the cultural ideal for women in the United States, Canada, and Europe has been getting thinner. Why have these changes in cultural norms occurred? One explanation is that white men and women are more likely than blacks or Latinos to associate overweight with softness, laziness, and weakness (Crandall & Martinez, 1996). In particular, the curvy, big-breasted female body is associated in people's minds with femininity, nurturance, and motherhood. Hence, big breasts have been fashionable in eras that celebrate women's role as mothers, such as after the Second World War, when women were encouraged to give up their wartime jobs and have many children (Stearns, 1997). However, among many whites, femininity has also often been associated, alas, with incompetence. Thus, whenever women have entered traditionally male spheres of

Should a woman be voluptuous and curvy or slim as a reed? Should a man be thin and smooth or strong and buff? What explains cultural changes in attitudes toward the ideal body? During the 1950s, actresses like Jayne Mansfield embodied the postwar ideal: curvy, buxom, and "womanly." In the 1980s and 1990s, many women struggled to be skinny and boyish; today, they want to be thin but also have prominent breasts. Men, too, have been caught up in body-image changes. The 1960s' ideal was the soft and scrawny hippie; today's ideal man is tough and muscular.

education and work, as they did in the 1920s and again beginning in the 1970s, bright, ambitious women have tried to look boyishly thin and muscular in order to avoid being perceived as soft, feminine, and dumb (Silverstein & Perlick, 1995). Today's big-breasted but otherwise skinny female ideal may reflect today's norm: Women are supposed to be both professionally competent *and* maternal.

The cultural ideal for North American men has changed, too. Until relatively recently, most heavily muscled men were labourers and farmers, so being physically strong and muscular was considered unattractive, a sign of being working class. In the past decade, pressures have increased for middle-class men to be buff and strong (Bordo, 2000). Today, having a strong, muscular body is a sign of affluence rather than poverty. It means a man has the money and the time to join a gym and work out. (Some fashion designers, though, are using male models that are as skinny and gaunt as their female counterparts.)

Another factor that must be considered is the difference in weight satisfaction levels between men and women. Although more Canadian men than women are overweight or obese, more Canadian women are currently dieting, even when their weight is in the healthy range (Green et al., 1997). Research studying Canadian teenagers has found that most girls (69%) wanted to lose weight, while most boys (54%) wanted to gain weight (Barr, 1995), regardless of their actual weight. It seems that these cultural norms of what women and men should look like appear by the teen years and persist into adulthood. Programs designed to promote acceptance of healthy weights in men and women must consider these gender differences in attitudes and, potentially, culture; otherwise, they may not succeed.

The Body As Battleground: Eating Disorders

Because the motivation to eat, or not eat, is so complicated, you can see why many people, especially women, find themselves caught in a battle between their biology and their culture. Evolution has designed women to store fat, which is necessary for the onset of menstruation, healthy childbearing, nursing, and, after menopause, the production and storage of estrogen. In cultures that think women should be very thin, therefore, many women become obsessed with weight and are continually dieting, forever fighting their bodies' need for a little healthy roundness.

Some people lose that battle, developing serious eating disorders that reflect an irrational terror of being fat. In **bulimia**, the person binges (eats vast quantities of rich food) and then purges by inducing vomiting or using laxatives. In **anorexia**, the person eats hardly anything and therefore becomes dangerously thin; anorexics have severely distorted body images, thinking they are fat even when they are emaciated. Although many people with these disorders recover, others damage their health permanently, or, in the case of anorexia, die of heart or kidney failure or complications of osteoporosis. Their weakened bones simply collapse. ◉

Bulimia and anorexia are the most well-known eating disorders, and occur most often among young white women. But more than 40% of all cases of eating disorders occur among men, the elderly, ethnic minority groups, young children, and athletes, and do not fit the diagnostic criteria for bulimia or anorexia (Thomas, Vartanian, & Brownell, 2009). For example, people with binge-eating disorder binge without purging; others chew whatever food they want but spit it out without swallowing; others are normal weight but take no joy in eating because they worry obsessively about gaining a pound; some develop phobias about eating certain kinds of food. All of these disorders involve an unhealthy attitude toward food, weight, and the body.

Genes may play a role in the development of eating disorders, particularly anorexia nervosa, which has been found across cultures and throughout history (Striegel-Moore & Bulik, 2007), but so do psychological factors, including depression and anxiety, low

◉——|Watch the Video
Speaking Out: Natasha: Living with Anorexia Nervosa in **MyPsychLab**

bulimia An eating disorder characterized by episodes of excessive eating (bingeing) followed by forced vomiting or use of laxatives (purging).

anorexia (anorexia nervosa) An eating disorder characterized by fear of being fat, a distorted body image, radically reduced consumption of food, and emaciation.

THINKING CRITICALLY

Ask questions: Define your terms.

Remy de la Mauvinie/AP Images

Jennifer Graylock/AP Images

What is the difference between being slender and being too thin? Does the fashion model on the left look good to you or does she look emaciated? Likewise, what is the difference between being "pleasantly plump" and being too fat? Nikki Blonsky, the exuberant star of the movie *Hairspray*, is overweight but physically fit. Does she look good to you or does she look too fat?

self-esteem, perfectionism, a distorted body image, drug use, and perceived pressure from peers to lose weight (Presnell, Bearman, & Stice, 2004; Ricciardelli & McCabe, 2004; Sherry & Hall, 2009). Cultural factors are also important. For example, bulimia is rare to nonexistent in non-western cultures and has only become a significant problem in Western cultures with the rise of the thin ideal for women (Keel & Klump, 2003). A meta-analysis of experimental and correlational studies found that women's exposure to the media ideal of impossibly thin women fosters the belief that "thin is beautiful" and increases the risk of disordered eating (Grabe, Ward, & Hyde, 2008; Slevec & Tiggemann, 2011). American culture is also rife with "bodysnarking"—the relentlessly critical and snide appraisals of other people's bodies that get posted on blogs, YouTube, Facebook, and Twitter, and are constant topics for entertainment magazines and talk shows.

Female ballet dancers and actors, jockeys of both sexes, some other athletes, and of course models are under enormous professional pressure to be thin. (In 2006, many fashion models had become so gaunt and emaciated that the Fashion Week organizers in Madrid, Spain, announced they would ban ultrathin models, women with a body mass index lower than 18.) In the United States, a recent meta-analysis found that women's levels of dissatisfaction with their bodies, once highest for Anglo women, now cross all ethnic lines; Asian-American, black, Hispanic, and Anglo women are virtually alike (Grabe & Hyde, 2006). Unhappiness with one's body, in turn, increases the likelihood of disordered eating. In a study of women students from Hong Kong, Taiwan, and Japan who were studying in the United States, those who had internalized Western notions of the ultrathin ideal were more likely to develop eating disorders (Stark-Wroblewski, Yanico, & Lupe, 2005).

Eating disorders and body-image distortions among boys and men are increasing too, though they take different forms. Just as anorexic women see their gaunt bodies as being too fat, some men have the delusion that their muscular bodies are too puny. So they abuse steroids and exercise or pump iron compulsively (Pope, Phillips, & Olivardia, 2000; Thompson & Cafri, 2007). Many North American men mistakenly think that most women prefer extremely muscular guys, partly because media images of muscular men in North America often show them with bared pecs or abs. As a result, some men develop a distorted body image in which they think they are not muscular and strong enough. In contrast, Chinese men in Taiwan and pastoral nomads of northern Kenya do not think the heavily muscled male body is especially desirable or attractive, and these cultures do not promote media images of muscular males. Men in these cultures have fewer body-image disorders than North American men do and virtually no interest in muscle-building drugs (Campbell, Pope, & Filiault, 2005; Yang, Gray, & Pope, 2005). 👁

In sum, within a given environment, genetic predispositions for a certain body weight and metabolism interact with psychological needs, cultural norms, and individual habits to shape, in this case quite literally, who we are.

👁⊣**Watch** the **Video**
In the Real World: Eating Disorders
in **MyPsychLab**

Recite & Review

Recite: Is all this information about eating making you hungry for knowledge? If so, say aloud what you know about *motivation*, *intrinsic and extrinsic motivation*, set point, brown fat, leptin, ghrelin, five major environmental reasons for the rising rates of obesity and overweight, other environmental suspects, cultural influences on weight, *bulimia*, *anorexia*, and other forms of eating problems.

Review: Enjoy a nice apple and reread this section.

Now take this *Quick Quiz:*

Is all this information about eating making you hungry for knowledge?

1. *True or false:* Most fat people are heavy because their emotional problems cause them to overeat.

2. What theory seems to explain why thin people rarely become fat and fat people have so much trouble losing weight?

3. Which hormone stimulates appetite, and which helps regulate appetite by telling the hypothalamus that the body has stored enough fat?

4. Rising rates of overweight and obesity can best be explained by (a) genetic changes over the past few decades, (b) a lack of willpower, (c) an abundance of high-calorie food and sedentary lifestyles, (d) the increase in eating disorders.

5. Bill, who is thin, reads in the newspaper that genes set the range of body weight and shape. "Oh, good," he exclaims, "now I can eat all the junk food I want; I was born to be skinny." What's wrong with Bill's conclusion?

✔⊣**Study** and **Review**
in **MyPsychLab**

Answers:

1. false **2.** set-point theory **3.** ghrelin, leptin **4.** c **5.** Bill is right to recognize that there may be limits to how heavy he can become. But he is oversimplifying and jumping to conclusions. Many people who have a set point for leanness will gain considerable weight if they don't exercise. Also, junk food is unhealthy for reasons that have nothing to do with becoming overweight.

In the musical comedy *Annie Get Your Gun,* Annie Oakley lets Frank Butler beat her in a sharp-shooting competition as she sings, "You can't get a man with a gun." But she did. In real life, she beat him in the contest, they fell in love, married, and worked together.

The Darke County Historical Society & Garst Museum

The Social Animal: Motives to Love

Do you have a favourite love story? Is it one where the couple falls madly in love at first sight and, after a couple of silly misunderstandings, lives happily ever after, without a single quarrel or miserable moment? Or is it more like the story of Annie Oakley and Frank Butler, one of lifelong mutual respect and companionship? What *is* love, anyway—the crazy, passionate, heart-palpitating feeling of falling for another person, or the steady, stable feeling of deep and abiding attachment and trust?

The Biology of Love

Psychologists who study love (a tough job, but someone has to do it) distinguish *passionate* ("*romantic*") *love,* characterized by a whirlwind of intense emotions and sexual passion, from *companionate love,* characterized by affection and trust. Passionate love is the stuff of crushes, infatuations, "love at first sight," and the early stage of love affairs. It may burn out completely or evolve into companionate love. Passionate love is known in all cultures and has a long history. Wars and duels have been fought because of it, people have committed suicide because of it, great love affairs have begun, and been torn apart, because of it. Yet, although the experience of romantic love is universal, many cultures have not regarded it as the proper basis for anything serious—such as marriage (Hatfield & Rapson, 2008).

In this era of PET scans, fMRIs, and biotechnical advances, it was inevitable that researchers would seek to explain passionate love by rummaging around in the brain. There are olfactory cues in a potential partner's scent that can turn you on (or off). There are physical cues in the potential partner's voice and body shape, and even in how similar his or her face is to yours. There is the dopamine jolt of reward, from the same dopamine that makes anticipation of a fabulous meal or an addictive drug so pleasurable, and there are the arousal and excitement provided by adrenaline (Aron et al., 2005; Cozolino, 2006). And then there are key hormones that turn that first phase of exhilaration into the longer-lasting phase of attachment and bonding. Neuroscientists hope to find answers to the great mysteries of attraction: why people are often hopelessly smitten with someone who is "unsuitable," why the heart seems to overrule the head in matters of love ("He/she is perfectly nice, but I just didn't feel any *chemistry*"), and why many people feel obsessed with a new beloved and can barely sleep or eat when they are apart.

Many biologically oriented researchers believe that the neurological origins of passionate love begin in infancy, in the baby's attachment to the mother. In this view, maternal and romantic love, the deepest of human attachments, share a common evolutionary purpose—preserving the species—and so they share common neural mechanisms, the ones that make attachment and pair-bonding feel good. And, in fact, certain key neurotransmitters and hormones that are involved in pleasure and reward are activated in the mother–baby pair-bond and again later in the pair-bond of adult lovers and even of passionate friends (Bartels & Zeki, 2004; Diamond, 2004).

Two important hormones for social bonding are vasopressin and oxytocin, which play a crucial role in the attachment-caregiving system, influencing feelings and expressions of love, caring, and trust not only between mothers and babies but also between friends and between lovers (Poulin, Holman, & Buffone, 2012; Walum et al., 2008; Taylor, Klein, et al., 2000). In one extraordinary study, researchers administered oxytocin in a nasal spray to volunteers, who were later more likely than control subjects to trust one another in various risky interactions (Kosfeld et al., 2005). In another study, couples given oxytocin increased their nonverbal expressions of love for one another—gazing, smiling, and fondling—in contrast to couples given a placebo (Gonzaga et al., 2006). Conversely, when prairie voles, a monogamous species, are given a drug that blocks oxytocin, they continue to mate, but they don't get attached to their partners (Ross et al., 2009). We can just imagine what the pharmaceutical industry will try to do with this information!

Studies of animals also find that the characteristic feelings and actions that occur during attachment are mediated by reward circuits in the brain and involve the release of **endorphins**, the brain's natural opiates (see Chapter 4). When baby mice and other animals are separated from their mothers, they cry out in distress, and the mother's touch (or lick) releases endorphins that soothe the infant. But when puppies, guinea pigs, and chicks are injected with low doses of either morphine or endorphins, the animals show much less distress than usual when separated from their mothers; the chemicals seem to be a biological replacement for Mom (Panksepp et al., 1980). And when mice are genetically engineered to lack certain opioid receptors, they become less attached to their mothers and do not show signs of distress when separated from them. This is the same kind of social aloofness that autistic children display (Moles, Kieffer, & D'Amato, 2004). These findings suggest that endorphin-stimulated euphoria may be a child's initial motive for seeking affection and cuddling—that, in effect, a child attached to a parent is a child addicted to love. The addictive quality of adult passionate love, including the physical and emotional distress that lovers feel when they are apart, may involve the same biochemistry (Diamond, 2004).

Using functional magnetic resonance imaging (fMRI), neuroscientists have found other neurological similarities between infant–mother love and adult romantic love. Two researchers, for example, have found that certain parts of the brain light up when people look at images of their sweethearts, in contrast to other parts that are activated when they see pictures of friends or furniture. And these are the same areas that are activated when mothers see images of their own children as opposed to pictures of other children (Bartels & Zeki, 2004).

Clearly, then, the bonds of attachment are biologically based. Yet, as always, it is important to avoid biological reductionism and the conclusion that "love is all in our hormones" or "love occurs in this corner of the brain but not that one." Human love affairs involve many other factors that affect whom we choose, how we get along, and whether we stay with a partner over the years.

The Psychology of Love

Many romantics believe there is only one true love awaiting them. Considering that there are seven billion people on the planet, the odds of finding said person are a bit daunting! What if you're in Omaha or Winnipeg and your true love is in Dubrovnik or Kankakee? You could wander for years and never cross paths. ◉

Fortunately, evolution has made it possible to form deep and lasting attachments without travelling the world. In fact, the first major predictor of whom we love is plain proximity. In what is known as the **proximity effect**, the people who are nearest to you

The biology of the baby–mother bond may be the origin of adult romantic love, with its exchange of loving gazes and depth of attachment.

Michaeljung/Fotolia

◉—⌐Watch the Video
What's in It for Me? Attraction
in **MyPsychLab**

endorphins [en-DOR-fins] Chemical substances in the nervous system that are similar in structure and action to opiates; they are involved in pain reduction, pleasure, and memory and are known technically as *endogenous opioid peptides*.

proximity effect The people who are nearest to you geographically are most likely to be dearest to you, too.

Internet dating services capitalize on the fact that like attracts like. "What type turns you on?," asks this ad. Usually, the type that is similar to you.

Alamy

are most likely to be dearest to you, too. We choose our friends and lovers from the set of people who live close by, or who study or work near us. Of course, today's love-seekers can use the internet to find remote kindred spirits, but proximity remains a highly desirable attribute; dating sites can filter out anyone who is geographically undesirable. The **similarity effect** holds that likeness—in looks, attitudes, beliefs, values, personality, and interests—is the second key predictor of whom we love (Berscheid & Reis, 1998). Although it is commonly believed that opposites attract, the fact is that we tend to choose friends and loved ones who are most like us. Many students use Facebook to find romantic prospects who share their love of poker, the TV show *Game of Thrones*, the hip-hop artist K'naan, or any other passion.

The internet has made similarity-matching possible on all kinds of dimensions. There are thousands of dating websites, matching couples by age, political attitudes, religion or secularism, sexual orientation, and many other criteria. There are sites for people with disabilities, preferences for particular sexual activities, and even beloved pets. Some prominent matchmaking sites administer questionnaires and personality inventories, claiming to use scientific principles to pair up potential soulmates (Sprecher et al., 2008). These efforts vary in effectiveness. Can you think why? One reason is that many people think they know exactly what they "must have" in a partner, and then they meet someone who has few of those qualities but a whole bunch of others that suddenly become essential. (A woman we know thought she must have a man who was taller than she, until she met the love of her life, who is three inches shorter.) Another reason, though, is that the premises of some of these scientific-sounding matchmaking sites may be faulty, especially those based on unvalidated personality types and anecdotal testimonials (King, Austin-Oden, & Lohr, 2009). But one underlying premise of most internet-matching sites is basically right—like attracts like.

The Attachment Theory of Love.

Once you find someone to love, *how* do you love? According to Phillip Shaver and Cindy Hazan (1993), adults, just like babies, can be secure, anxious, or avoidant in their attachments (see Chapter 13). Securely attached lovers are rarely jealous or worried about being abandoned. They are more compassionate and helpful than insecurely attached people and are quicker to understand and forgive their partners if the partner does something thoughtless or annoying (Mikulincer et al., 2005; Mikulincer & Shaver, 2007). Anxious lovers are always agitated about their relationships; they want to be close but worry that their partners will leave them. Other people often describe them as clingy, which may be why they are more likely than secure lovers to suffer from unrequited love (Aron, Aron, & Allen, 1998). Avoidant people distrust and avoid intimate attachments.

Where do these differences come from? According to the **attachment theory of love**, people's attachment styles as adults derive in large part from how their parents cared for them (Dinero et al., 2008; Mikulincer & Shaver, 2007; Fraley & Shaver, 2000; Mikulincer & Goodman, 2006). Children form internal "working models" of relationships: Can I trust others? Am I worthy of being loved? Will my parents leave me? If a child's parents were cold and rejecting and provided little or no emotional and physical comfort, the child learns to expect other relationships to be the same. If children form secure attachments to trusted parents, they become more trusting of others, expecting to form other secure attachments with friends and lovers in adulthood (Feeney & Cassidy, 2003).

The distribution of the three basic styles of attachment among adults is in fact very similar to that found for infants: about 64% are secure, 25% are avoidant, and 11% are

similarity effect Similarity—in looks, attitudes, beliefs, values, personality, and interests—is attractive to human beings; we tend to choose friends and loved ones who are most like us.

attachment theory of love People's attachment styles as adults derive in large part from how their parents cared for them.

anxious. Further, the kinds of relationships people have as adults are strongly related to their reports of how their parents treated them (Mickelson, Kessler, & Shaver, 1997). In one observational study of young adults in family interactions, their ratings of their families' warmth and sensitivity were positively related to how they behaved with their own romantic partners and to their own degree of attachment security (Dinero et al., 2008). Securely attached adults report having had warm, close relationships with their parents. Although they recognize their parents' flaws, they describe their parents as having been more loving and kind than insecurely attached people do. Anxious people feel more ambivalence toward their parents, especially their mothers, and also describe their parents ambivalently, as having been both harsh and kind. And people with an avoidant attachment style describe their parents in almost entirely negative terms. These individuals are most likely to report having had cold, rejecting parents, extended periods of separation from their mothers, or childhood environments that prevented them from forging close ties with others (Hazan & Shaver, 1994; Klohnen & Bera, 1998).

The avoidant style is particularly resistant to change, because people who are busy avoiding one another never learn to trust someone long enough to become securely attached (Klohnen & Bera, 1998). However, even avoidant or anxiously attached people can have successful, stable relationships if they find securely attached partners who will put up with their insecurities (Kirkpatrick & Davis, 1994; Koski & Shaver, 1997). Although those who display an avoidant style are not necessarily pathological, this style is commonly reported by people who also display pathological behaviours. For example, at Queen's University, Jamieson and Marshall (2000) found that nonfamilial child molesters were five times more likely to report an avoidant relationship than those in the community sample.

Keep in mind, though, that a person's own temperament could also account for the consistency of attachment styles from childhood to adulthood, as well as for the working models of relationships that are formed during childhood (Gillath et al., 2008). Certainly some parents are cold, punitive, and rejecting. But a child who is temperamentally fearful or whose reward circuits do not function normally may reject even a kind parent's efforts to console and cuddle. That child may therefore come to believe that all relationships are untrustworthy.

Gender, Culture, and Love

Which sex is more romantic? Which sex truly understands true love? Which sex falls in love but won't commit?

Pop-psych books are full of answers, along with advice for dealing with all those love-challenged heartbreakers who love you and leave you (fools that they are). But all stereotypes oversimplify. Neither sex loves more than the other in terms of love at first sight, passionate love, or companionate love over the long haul (Dion & Dion, 1993; Fehr, 1993; Hatfield & Rapson, 1996/2005). Men and women are equally likely to suffer the heart-crushing torments of unrequited love. They are equally likely to be securely or insecurely attached (Feeney & Cassidy, 2003). Both sexes suffer mightily when a love relationship ends, assuming they did not want it to.

However, women and men do differ, on average, in how they *express* love. Males in many cultures learn early that revelations of emotion can be construed as evidence of vulnerability and weakness, which are considered unmasculine (see Chapter 11). Thus, men in such cultures often develop ways of revealing love that differ from the ways women do. In contemporary Western society, many women express feelings of love in words, whereas many men express these feelings in actions—doing things for the partner, supporting the family financially, or just sharing the same activity, such as watching TV or a football game together (Shields, 2002;

THINKING CRITICALLY

Define your terms.

Many people define love as an overwhelming romantic passion. What are the consequences of defining love that way? What other definitions might lead to greater satisfaction in a relationship over time?

Economic and social changes are transforming gender roles in all developed nations. But marriage for financial security is still the only option for many women from impoverished nations—like this bride, whose husband chose her from a mail-order catalogue.

Susan Meiselas/Magnum photos

Baumeister & Bratslavsky, 1999; Cancian, 1987; Swain, 1989). Similarly, many women tend to define intimacy as shared revelations of feelings, but many men define intimacy as just hanging out together.

These gender differences in ways of expressing the universal motives of love and intimacy do not just pop up out of nowhere; they reflect social, economic, and cultural forces. For example, for many years, Western men were more romantic than women in their choice of partner, and women in turn were far more pragmatic than men. One reason was that a woman did not just marry a man; she married a standard of living. Therefore, she could not afford to marry someone unsuitable or waste her time in a relationship that was not going anywhere, even if she loved the guy. She married, in short, for extrinsic reasons rather than intrinsic ones. In contrast, a man could afford to be sentimental in his choice of partner. In the 1960s, two-thirds of a sample of university men said they would not marry someone they did not love, but only one-fourth of the women ruled out the possibility (Kephart, 1967).

As women entered the workforce and as two incomes became necessary in most families, however, the gender difference in romantic love faded, and so did economic motivations to marry, all over the world. Nowadays, in every developed nation, only tiny numbers of women and men would consider marrying someone they did not love, even if the person had all the right qualities. Pragmatic reasons for marriage, with romantic love being a remote luxury, persist only in countries where the extended family still controls female sexuality and the financial terms of marriage (Hatfield & Rapson, 1996/2005). Yet even in these countries, such as India and Pakistan, the tight rules governing marriage choices are loosening. So are the rules forbidding divorce, even in extremely traditional nations such as Japan and South Korea (Rosin, 2012).

As you can see, our motivations to love may start with biology and the workings of the brain, but they are shaped and directed by our early experiences with parents, the culture we live in, the historical era that shapes us, and something as utterly unromantic as economic dependency or self-sufficiency.

✓•⎯Study and Review

in **MyPsychLab**

Recite & Review

Recite: Assuming you are passionate about learning, recite aloud what you know about biological factors in love and attachment, *endorphins*, *proximity effect*, *similarity effect*, oxytocin, vasopressin, the two major predictors of whom we love, the benefits and problems of online dating, the *attachment theory of love*, the ingredients and definitions of love, and why motives for marriage have changed in recent history.

Review: Next, reread this section; that shouldn't be a tough assignment.

Now take this *Quick Quiz:*

Are you passionately committed to quizzes yet?

1. How are adult passionate love and infant–mother love biologically similar?

2. The two major predictors of whom we love are _____ and _____.

3. Tiffany is wildly in love with Timothy, and he with her, but she can't stop worrying about his fidelity and doubting his love. She wants to be with him constantly, but when she feels jealous, she pushes him away and finds it hard to forgive him. According to the attachment theory of love, which style of attachment does Tiffany have?

4. *True or false:* Until recently, men in Western societies were more likely than women to marry for love.

Answers:

1. Both involve the release of neurotransmitters, vasopressin and oxytocin, and endorphins that make attachment literally feel good, by activating the pleasure–reward circuits in the brain. 2. proximity and similarity 3. anxious 4. True

Learning Objectives

9 Identify which part of the anatomy is the "sexiest sex organ."

10 Explain why pleasure is only one of many motives for having sex.

11 Describe how culture affects sexual practices.

The Erotic Animal: Motives for Sex

Most people believe that sex is a biological drive, merely a matter of doing what comes naturally. "What's there to discuss about sexual motivation?" they say. "Isn't it all intrinsic, inborn, inevitable, and inherently pleasurable?"

It is certainly true that in most other species, sexual behaviour is genetically programmed. Without instruction, a male stickleback fish knows exactly what to do with a female stickleback, and a whooping crane knows when to whoop. But as sex researcher Leonore Tiefer (2004) has observed, for human beings "sex is not a natural act." For one thing, the activities that one culture considers natural—such as mouth-to-mouth kissing or oral sex—are often considered unnatural in another culture or historical time. Second, people have to learn from experience and culture what they are supposed to do with their sexual desires and how they are expected to behave. And third, people's motivations for sexual activity are by no means always and only for intrinsic pleasure. Human sexuality is influenced by a blend of biological, psychological, and cultural factors. As Canadians, we live in a relatively sexually active culture. The average Canadian adult has sex around 150 times a year, which is the fourth-highest frequency among 22 countries surveyed (Durex, 2002). This rate of activity has a downside, though. Canadians tend to start having sex at earlier ages than is evident in other countries, which leads to relatively higher rates of teenage pregnancy.

Desire and sensuality are lifelong pleasures.

Tyler Olson/Fotolia

Watch the Video
The Big Picture: The Power of Sex in **MyPsychLab**

The Biology of Desire

Biological researchers have contributed to our understanding of sexual motivation by sweeping away the cobwebs of superstition and ignorance about how the body works.

Hormones and Sexual Response. One biological factor that seems to promote sexual desire in both sexes is the hormone testosterone, an androgen (masculinizing hormone) that both sexes produce (see Chapter 4). Its role has been documented in studies of men who have been given synthetic hormones that suppress the production of testosterone; of men and women who have abnormally low testosterone levels; and of women who have kept diaries of their sexual activity while also having their hormone levels periodically measured (Bradford & Pawlak, 1993; Dabbs, 2000). This fact has created a market for the legal and illegal use of androgens. The assumption is that if the goal is to reduce sexual desire, for example in sex offenders, testosterone should be lowered, say, through chemical castration; if the goal is to increase sexual desire in women and men who complain of low libido, testosterone should be increased—like adding fuel to your gas tank. Yet these efforts often fail to produce the expected results (Berlin, 2003; M. Anderson, 2005). Why?

One reason is that the symptoms of androgen deficiency (low libido, fatigue, lack of well-being) are also those of depression and marital problems. There is also no consensus on how much sexual activity is "not enough" or on the difference between normally low and abnormally deficient levels of testosterone. Measures of testosterone taken at different intervals do not correlate strongly because the hormone fluctuates. Moreover, hormones and behaviour travel a two-way street: Testosterone does contribute to sexual arousal, but sexual activity also produces higher levels of testosterone (Sapolsky, 1997). And, in a significant number of cases, the side effects of androgen range from unpleasant to harmful (International Consensus Conference, 2002), and side effects are unlikely to increase desire.

Another reason is that in primates, unlike other mammals, sexual motivation requires more than hormones; it is also affected by social experience and context (Wallen, 2001). That is why desire can persist in sex offenders who have lost testosterone, and why desire might remain low in people who have been given testosterone. Indeed, artificially administered testosterone does not do much more than a placebo to increase sexual satisfaction in healthy people, nor does a drop in testosterone invariably cause a loss of sexual motivation or enjoyment. For example, in studies of women who had had their uteruses or ovaries surgically removed or who were going through menopause, use of a testosterone patch increased their sexual activity to only one more time a month over the placebo group (Buster et al., 2005).

Arousal and Orgasm.   Physiological research has dispelled a lot of nonsense written about female sexuality, such as the once-common notions that "good" women don't have orgasms or that mature women should have the "right kind" of orgasm (Ehrenreich, 1978). The first modern attack on these beliefs came from Alfred Kinsey and his associates (1948, 1953) in their pioneering books on male and female sexuality. Kinsey's team surveyed thousands of people about their sexual attitudes and behaviour, and they also reviewed the existing research on sexual physiology. In *Sexual Behaviour in the Human Female*, they observed that "males would be better prepared to understand females, and females to understand males, if they realized that they are alike in their basic anatomy and physiology." For example, the penis and the clitoris develop from the same embryonic tissues; they differ in size, of course, but not in sensitivity. Kinsey did believe, however, that women overall have a "lesser sexual capacity" than men, reflected in women's lower frequency of masturbation and orgasm. Although he acknowledged that many women are taught to avoid, dislike, or feel ambivalent about sex, he tended to attribute this gender difference to biology.

The idea that men and women are sexually similar in any way was extremely shocking in 1953. At that time many people believed that women were not as sexually motivated as men and that women cared more about affection than sexual satisfaction—notions soundly refuted by Kinsey's interviews. The national hysteria that accompanied the Kinsey Reports seems hard to believe today. Yet it is still difficult for social scientists to conduct serious, methodologically sound research on the development of human sexuality. As John Bancroft, the current head of the Kinsey Institute, has observed, because many American adults need to believe that young children have no sexual feelings, they interpret any evidence of normal sexual expression in childhood (such as masturbation or "playing doctor") as a symptom of sexual abuse. And because many adults are uncomfortable about sexual activity among

THINKING CRITICALLY

Avoid emotional reasoning.

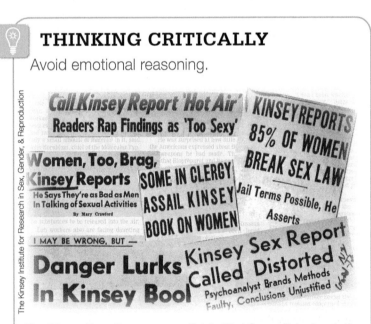

The Kinsey Institute for Research in Sex, Gender, & Reproduction

The "Kinsey Report" on women, officially titled *Sexual Behaviour in the Human Female*, was not exactly greeted with praise and acceptance— or with clear thinking. Many people were so emotionally upset by the findings that many women enjoy sex and have had premarital sex that they chose to attack Kinsey instead of coolly appraising his research.

teenagers, they try to restrict or eliminate it by prohibiting sex education and promoting abstinence; then they reject research showing that such prohibitions actually increase the behaviour they consider taboo (Bancroft, 2006; Levine, 2002).

The next wave of sex research began in the 1960s with the laboratory research of physician William Masters and his associate Virginia Johnson (1966). In studies of physiological changes during sexual arousal and orgasm, Masters and Johnson confirmed that male and female orgasms are indeed remarkably similar and that all orgasms are physiologically the same, regardless of the source of stimulation. But Masters and Johnson disagreed with Kinsey's assertion that women have a lesser sexual capacity than men. On the contrary, they argued, women's capacity for sexual response "infinitely surpasses that of men" because women, unlike most men, are able to have repeated orgasms until exhaustion or a ringing telephone makes them stop.

However, just as Kinsey might have underestimated women's sexual capacity, Masters and Johnson might have overestimated it. Their research was limited by the selection of a sample consisting only of men and women who were easily orgasmic, and they did not investigate how people's physiological responses might vary according to their age, experience, and culture (Tiefer, 2004). Thus, in their eagerness to show that the physiology of arousal and orgasm was the same in both sexes, Masters and Johnson tended to overlook individual differences. Since Masters and Johnson's studies, sex researchers have learned much more about individual variation in sexual physiology and responsiveness (Ellison, 2000; Laumann et al., 1994). For example, people vary not only in their propensity for sexual excitation and responsiveness, but also in their ability to inhibit and control that excitement (Bancroft et al., 2009). That is, some people are all accelerator and no brakes, and others are slow to accelerate but quick to brake.

If you have ever taken a sex-ed class, you may have had to memorize Masters and Johnson's description of the "four stages of the sexual response cycle": desire, arousal (excitement), orgasm, resolution. Unfortunately, the impulse to oversimplify—treating these four stages as if they were akin to the invariable cycles of a washing machine—led to a mistaken inference of universality. It later turned out that not everyone has an orgasm even following great excitement, and that in many women, desire follows arousal (Laan & Both, 2008).

> ### 💡 THINKING CRITICALLY
>
> Don't oversimplify.
>
> Given that a minimum level of testosterone is important in sexual desire, many people assume that adding testosterone will increase desire and removing it will lower desire. Why does this assumption oversimplify the issue?

Sex and the "Sex Drive." The question of whether men and women are alike or different in some underlying, biologically based sex drive continues to provoke lively debate. Although women on average are certainly as capable as men of sexual pleasure, men have higher rates of almost every kind of sexual behaviour, including masturbation, erotic fantasies, and orgasm (Oliver & Hyde, 1993; Peplau, 2003; Schmitt et al., 2012). These sex differences occur even when men are forbidden by cultural or religious rules to engage in sex at all; for example, Catholic priests have more of these sexual experiences than Catholic nuns do (Baumeister, Catanese, & Vohs, 2001). Men are also more likely than women to admit to having sex because "I was slumming" or "The opportunity presented itself" (Meston & Buss, 2007).

Biological psychologists argue that these differences occur universally because the hormones and brain circuits involved in sexual behaviour differ for men and women. They maintain that for men, the wiring for sex overlaps with that for dominance and aggression, which is why sex and aggression are more likely to be linked in men than women. For women, the circuits and hormones governing sexuality and nurturance seem to overlap, which is why sex and love are more likely to be linked in women than in men (Diamond, 2008).

Other psychologists, however, maintain that most gender differences in sexual behaviour reflect women's and men's different roles and experiences in life and have little or nothing to do with biologically based drives or brain circuits (Eagly & Wood, 1999; Tiefer, 2008). Sex surveys generally find that men and women are, overall, more alike than different, for example in preferring sex with love (Laumann et al., 1994). In the sociocultural view, as long as large numbers of women learn to fear, dislike, or avoid sex, whether through cultural and familial messages or through coercive or otherwise unpleasant sexual experiences, it is impossible to know what women's sexual drive might really be like (Kaschak & Tiefer, 2002). ◉

A middle view is that men's sexual behaviour is more biologically influenced than is women's, whereas women's sexual desires and responsiveness are more affected by circumstances, the specific relationship, and cultural norms (Baumeister, 2000; Peplau et al., 2000; Schmitt et al., 2012).

The Psychology of Desire

Psychologists are fond of observing that the sexiest sex organ is the brain, where perceptions begin. People's values, fantasies, and beliefs profoundly affect their sexual desire and behaviour. That is why a touch on the knee by an exciting new date feels terrifically sexy, but the same touch by a creepy stranger on a bus feels disgusting. It is why a worried thought can kill sexual arousal in a second, and why a fantasy can be more erotic than reality.

The Many Motives for Sex. To most people, the primary motives for sex are pretty obvious: to enjoy the pleasure of it, to express love and intimacy, or to make babies. But there are other motives too, not all of them so positive: for money or perks, duty or feelings of obligation, rebellion, power over the partner, submission to the partner in order to avoid his or her anger or rejection, and so on.

One survey of nearly 2000 people yielded 237 motives for having sex, and nearly every one of them had been rated as the most important motive for someone. Most men and women listed the same top 10, including attraction to the partner, love, fun, and physical pleasure. But some said, "I wanted to feel closer to God," "I was drunk," "to get rid of a headache" (that was #173), "to help me fall asleep," "to make my partner feel powerful," "to return a favour," "because someone dared me," or to hurt an enemy or a rival ("I wanted to make him pay so I slept with his girlfriend"; "I wanted someone else to suffer from herpes as I do"). In this survey, men were more likely than women to say they use sex to gain status, enhance their reputation (e.g., because the partner was normally "out of my league"), or get things (such as a promotion) (Meston & Buss, 2007).

Across the many studies of motives for sex, there appear to be several major categories (Cooper, Shapiro, & Powers, 1998; Meston & Buss, 2007):

- *Pleasure:* the satisfaction and physical pleasure of sex.
- *Intimacy:* emotional closeness with the partner; spiritual transcendence.
- *Insecurity:* reassurance that you are attractive or desirable.
- *Partner approval:* the desire to please or appease the partner; the desire to avoid the partner's anger or rejection.
- *Peer approval:* the wish to impress friends, be part of the group, and conform to what everyone else seems to be doing.
- *Attaining a goal:* to get status, money, revenge, or to "even the score."

In this research, men and women did not differ in their motives for intimacy, but men more strongly endorsed all the other motives, especially peer approval. The older people were, the more likely they were to have sex for intimacy and for self-enhancement (pleasure), and the less likely they were to have sex for peer or partner approval. White

▶—|**Watch** the **Video**
The Basics: Sex and Gender Differences
in **MyPsychLab**

The many motivations for sex range from sex for profit to sex for fun.

Top: John Ferguson/Newscom. Bottom: Carol Ford/Getty Images.

adolescents were more often motivated by a desire for intimacy than black adolescents were, and black teenagers were more often motivated by coping and peer pressure.

People's motives for having sex affect many aspects of their sexual behaviour, including whether they engage in sex in the first place, whether they enjoy it, whether they have unprotected or otherwise risky sex, and whether they have few or many partners (Browning et al., 2000). Extrinsic motives, such as having sex for purposes of coping and gaining approval, are most strongly associated with risky sexual behaviour, including having many partners, not using birth control, and pressuring a partner into sex (Cooper, Shapiro, & Powers, 1998; Hamby & Koss, 2003; Impett, Gable, & Peplau, 2005).

Unfortunately, significant numbers of women and men are having sex for extrinsic rather than intrinsic motives. In one study, university students in dating relationships kept a daily diary of their sexual experiences; 50% of the women and 26% of the men reported consenting to unwanted sexual activity during that time (O'Sullivan & Allgeier, 1998). Men typically do so because of peer pressure, inexperience, a desire for popularity, or a fear of seeming homosexual or unmasculine. Women typically do so because they do not want to lose the relationship; because they feel obligated, once the partner has spent time and money on them; because the partner makes them feel guilty; or because they want to satisfy the partner and avoid conflict (Impett, Gable, & Peplau, 2005).

People's motives for consenting to unwanted sex depend in part on their own feelings of security in the relationship. In a study of 125 university women, one-half to two-thirds of Asian-American, white, and Latina women had consented to having sex when they didn't really want to, and all of the black women said they had. Do you remember the attachment theory of love discussed earlier? Anxiously attached women were the most willing to consent to unwanted sex, especially if they feared their partners were less committed than they were. They reported that they often had sex out of feelings of obligation and to prevent the partner from leaving. Securely attached women also occasionally had unwanted sex, but their reasons were different: to gain sexual experience, to satisfy their curiosity, or to actively please their partners and further the intimacy between them (Impett, Gable, & Peplau, 2005).

Sexual Coercion and Rape. One of the most persistent differences in the sexual experiences of women and men has to do with their perceptions of, and experiences with, sexual coercion. At Carleton University, DeKeseredy and Kelly (1993) tested a large sample of female undergraduate students and found that 29% reported having experienced at least one incident of sexual assault. In a nationally representative survey of more than 3000 Americans aged 18 to 59, nearly 25% of the women said that a man had forced them to do something sexually that they did not want to do, but only about 3% of the men said they had ever forced a woman into a sexual act. While this percentage is low, studies conducted among Canadian and American university students reveal that men are far more likely than women to admit to coercing a partner into sex—using alcohol or other drugs, or threats or actual physical force (O'Sullivan, Byers, & Finkelman, 1998).

The most extreme form of sexual coercion, of course, is rape. College and university women tend to define rape as being forced into intercourse by an acquaintance or stranger, or as having been molested as a child. They are least likely to call their experience rape if they were sexually assaulted by a boyfriend, were drunk or otherwise drugged, or were forced to have oral or digital sex (Kahn, 2004). About half of all women who report a sexual assault that meets the legal definition of rape—being forced to engage in sexual acts against their will—do not label it as rape (McMullin & White, 2006; Peterson & Muehlenhard, 2011). Furthermore, the vast majority of these crimes go unpunished. Only 6% of all sexual assaults in Canada are reported to the police (Statistics Canada, 1993). This underreporting might be due to the fact that most women know their attackers; 80% of assaulted women know their male attackers in some capacity (Kinnon, 1981). In fact, 31% of the assaults occur within a dating or acquaintance relationship (Kinnon, 1981). Other women are motivated to avoid labelling the experience with such a charged word because they are embarrassed, or simply because they don't want to think of someone they know personally as being a "rapist" (Koss, 2011; Peterson & Muehlenhard, 2011).

What causes some men to rape? Sociobiologists often answer by analogy with other animals: For example, because male scorpion flies (and males of other species) force themselves on females, human rape must have the same evolutionary origins and reproductive purposes—for the male to fertilize as many females as possible (Thornhill & Palmer, 2000). But among human beings, rape is often committed by high-status men, including sports heroes and other celebrities, who could easily find consenting sexual partners. All too frequently its victims are children or the elderly, who do not reproduce. And sadistic rapists often injure or kill their victims, hardly a way to perpetuate one's genes. The human motives for rape thus appear to be primarily psychological:

- *Narcissism and hostility toward women.* Sexually aggressive males are often narcissistic, are unable to empathize with women, and feel entitled to have sexual relations with whatever woman they choose. They misperceive women's behaviour in social situations, equate feelings of power with sexuality, and accuse women of provoking them (Bushman et al., 2003; Malamuth et al., 1995; Zurbriggen, 2000). One interesting study compared men who had forcibly raped a woman with men who used manipulative techniques to have sex and with men who had had consensual sex only. The rapists were more likely to have grown up in violent households, were more accepting of male violence, and were less likely to endorse love as a motive for sex than were men in the manipulation and consent groups (Lyndon, White, & Kadlec, 2007).

- *A desire to dominate, humiliate, or punish the victim.* This motive is apparent among soldiers who rape captive women during war and then often kill them (Olujic, 1998). Similarly, reports of the systematic rapes of female cadets at the U.S. Air Force Academy suggest that the rapists' motives were to humiliate the women and get women to leave the Academy. Aggressive motives also occur in the rape of men by other men, usually by anal penetration (King & Woollett, 1997). This form of rape typically occurs in youth gangs, where the intention is to humiliate rival gang members, and in prison, where again the motive is to conquer and degrade the victim.

- *Sadism.* A minority of rapists are violent criminals who get pleasure out of inflicting pain on their victims and who often murder them in planned, grotesque ways (Turvey, 2008).

You can see that the answer to the question "Why do people have sex?" is not at all obvious. It is not a simple matter of "doing what's natural." In addition to the intrinsic motives of intimacy, pleasure, procreation, and love, extrinsic motives include intimidation, dominance, insecurity, appeasing the partner, approval from peers, and the wish to prove oneself a real man or a desirable woman.

Think about kissing. Westerners like to think about kissing, and to do it, too. But if you think kissing is natural, try to remember your first serious kiss and all you had to learn about noses, breathing, and the position of teeth and tongue. The sexual kiss is so complicated that some cultures have never gotten around to it. They think that kissing another person's mouth—the very place that food enters!—is disgusting (Tiefer, 2004). Others have elevated the sexual kiss to high art; why do you suppose one version is called French kissing?

As the kiss illustrates, having the physical equipment to perform a sexual act is not all there is to sexual motivation. People have to learn what is supposed to turn them on (or off), which parts of the body and what activities are erotic (or repulsive), and even how to have pleasurable sexual relations (Laumann & Gagnon, 1995).

Thus, to men in cultures where women are required to cover up completely in public, the sight of a woman's ankle can be arousing; to Western men today, an ankle doesn't do it. In some cultures, oral sex is regarded as a bizarre sexual deviation; in others, it is considered not only normal but also supremely desirable. In many cultures, men believe that women who have experienced the sexual pleasure of kissing or being caressed, or who enjoy orgasms, will become unfaithful, so sexual relations are limited to quick intercourse; in others, men's satisfaction and pride depend on knowing the woman is sexually satisfied too. In some cultures, sex itself is seen as something joyful and beautiful, an art to be cultivated as one might cultivate the skill of gourmet cooking. In others, it is considered ugly and dirty, something to be gotten through as quickly as possible.

How do cultures transmit their rules and requirements about sex to their members? During childhood and adolescence, people learn their culture's *gender roles*, collections of rules that determine the proper attitudes and behaviour for men and women. Just as an actor in the role of Hamlet needs a script to learn his part, a person following a gender role needs a **sexual script** that instructs men and women on how to behave in sexual situations (Gagnon & Simon, 1973; Laumann & Gagnon, 1995). If you are a teenaged girl, are you supposed to be sexually adventurous and assertive or sexually modest and passive? What if you are a teenaged boy? What if you are an older woman or man? The answers differ from culture to culture, as members act in accordance with the sexual scripts for their gender, age, religion, social status, and peer group.

In many parts of the world, boys acquire their attitudes about sex in a competitive atmosphere where the goal is to impress other males, and they talk and joke about masturbation and other sexual experiences with their friends. While their traditional sexual scripts are encouraging them to value physical sex, traditional scripts are teaching girls to value relationships and make themselves attractive (Matlin, 2012). At an early age, girls learn that the closer they match the cultural ideal of beauty, the greater their power, sexually and in other ways. They learn that they will be scrutinized and evaluated according to their looks, which of course is the meaning of being a "sex object" (Impett et al., 2011). What many girls and women may not realize is that the more sexualized their clothing, the more likely they are to be seen as incompetent and unintelligent (Graff, Murnen, & Smolak, 2012). Many girls learn that their role is to be sexually desirable (which is good), but not to indulge in their own sexual pleasures (which would be bad). Modern scripts for women in many places are changing, however, as illustrated by the sexual scripts followed by the characters in *Grey's Anatomy* or *Sex and the City*. But an analysis of 25 prime-time television shows that are most popular with teenagers found that the familiar male and female scripts are alive and well: Male characters frequently act out the traditional male script by actively and aggressively pursuing sex; many female characters still play the part of "sex object" and are judged by their sexual conduct (Kim et al., 2007). ◉

Gay men and lesbians follow sexual scripts, too. But theirs tend to be more flexible than heterosexual scripts in establishing rules for the relationship because most partners are not following a traditional gender role (Kurdek, 2005; Peplau & Spalding, 2000).

Jaroslav Kocian/Getty Images

THINKING CRITICALLY
Consider other interpretations.

Many people think that all sexual behaviour, including kissing, is universal and caused by a simple physiological drive. What other explanations are possible?

◉⎯Watch the Video
Special Topics: Cultural Norms and Sexual Behaviour in **MyPsychLab**

sexual script Set of implicit rules that specify proper sexual behaviour for a person in a given situation, varying with the person's gender, age, religion, social status, and peer group.

These teenagers are following the sexual scripts for their gender and culture—the boys, by ogling and making sexual remarks about girls in order to impress their peers, and the girls, by preening and wearing makeup to look good for boys.

Left: Jupiter Images. Right: Cassy Muronaka/ PhotoEdit Inc.

Scripts can be powerful determinants of behaviour. Because black women now account for 58% of reported AIDS cases among women in the United States, researchers have sought to understand how sexual scripts might be reducing their likelihood of practising safe sex. In interviews with 14 black women aged 22 to 39, researchers found that the women's behaviour was governed by scripts fostering these beliefs: *Men control relationships*; *women sustain relationships*; *male infidelity is normal*; *men control sexual activity*; *women want to use condoms, but men control condom use* (Bowleg, Lucas, & Tschann, 2004). As one woman summarized, "The ball was always in his court." These scripts, the researchers noted, are rooted in black North American history and the recurring scarcity of men available for long-term commitments. The scripts originated to preserve the stability of the family, but today they encourage some women to establish and maintain sexual relationships at the expense of their own needs and safety.

Gender, Culture, and Sex

As we discussed in Chapter 3, evolutionary psychologists believe that gender roles and sexual scripts simply reflect hardwired biological sex differences that resulted from natural selection. In contrast, social and cultural psychologists believe that gender roles and sexual scripts reflect a culture's economic, demographic, and social arrangements. As evidence for their point of view, they have found that when those arrangements change, so do women's and men's attitudes and behaviour. A meta-analysis of 530 studies, involving nearly 270 000 individuals, showed that in North America, young people's sexual attitudes and behaviour changed dramatically between 1943 and 1999, with the largest changes occurring among girls and young women (Wells & Twenge, 2005). Approval of premarital sex leapt from 12% to 73% among young women, and from 40% to 79% among young men; feelings of sexual guilt decreased sharply for both sexes; and, for women, average age at first intercourse dropped from 19 to 15 over the five decades, with small fluctuations.

Most people choose sexual partners by using the same criteria they apply in the search for love partners: similarity and proximity (availability). What happens, then, when large-scale demographic changes result in a lopsided ratio of heterosexual men and women? In China and India, countries in which most parents value boys and disparage girls, the ratio of young men to women is now about 120 to 100, a result of decades of abortions of female fetuses. In contrast, among black North Americans there are more women than available men, because so many young black men are unemployed, are in prison, or die young.

More than 20 years ago, an important book assessed the social and sexual consequences of these uneven ratios in different cultures, and at different points in human history (Guttentag & Secord, 1983). When men are scarce, the ball is always in their court: Men are more likely to have multiple sexual partners, divorce rates and numbers of single-parent families increase, and women become more independent. Regardless of the point in history or the place on the globe, when women are scarce, men vie for wives, divorce rates drop, both sexes have fewer sexual partners, and women become less independent. A more recent study found that societies (like Afghanistan's) that have large numbers of young, unemployed, and unattached men are also more vulnerable to internal disruption, violence, and extremist groups (like the Taliban) (Hudson & den Boer, 2004).

Sexual attitudes and motives likewise change along with women's economic status. The ball is no longer always in the man's court, and as a result, girls and young women increasingly feel free to control their own sexual lives (Rosin, 2012). Whenever women have needed marriage to ensure their social and financial security, they have regarded sex as a bargaining chip, an asset to be rationed rather than an activity to be enjoyed for its own sake (Hatfield & Rapson, 1996/2005). A woman with no economic resources of her own cannot afford to casually seek sexual pleasure if that means risking an unwanted pregnancy, the security of marriage, her reputation in society, her physical safety, or, in some cultures, her very life. When women become self-supporting and able to control their own fertility, however, they are more likely to want sex for pleasure rather than as a means to another goal. When women are not financially dependent on men and have goals of economic self-sufficiency, it is easier for them to refuse sex as well as to leave an abusive relationship or situation. By 2010, the percentage of girls ages 15 to 17 who had had sexual intercourse dropped from 37.2 to 27; teen pregnancies and reports of acquaintance rape also reached a record low (Rosin, 2012).

Lopsided sex ratios and other social factors also help account for the different sexual practices, values, and norms that occur within a nation. One research team, surveying a random sample of more than 2000 people in Chicago, has used the term *sex market* to describe a geographical and cultural boundary within which people seek partners (Laumann et al., 2004). Big cities will have many different sex markets, formed by the ethnicity, age, status, and sexual orientation of their "shoppers." A bisexual black man, an immigrant Latina woman, a single young white woman, and an older gay man will seek out different sex markets that determine where and how they will find sexual partners: through work, religious institutions, bars, friends, social institutions, the internet, and so on. Sex markets vary tremendously in the sexual behaviour they consider appropriate, the sexual scripts they endorse for their members, and the meanings they attribute to sex—which is why so many groups in North America are quarrelling about what is right or normal sexual behaviour. Although big cities consist of many different sex markets, people rarely travel across them. They prefer the familiarity and proximity of the market they know best.

In the TV series *Sex and the City*, the women shopped for men the way they shopped for shoes. This rewriting of the traditional sexual script for women drew both fans and critics.

Photo ITAR-TASS Itar-Tass Photos/Newscom

GET INVOLVED! Is the Double Standard Still Alive?

Think of all the words you know to describe a sexually active woman and then think of words for a sexually active man. Is one list longer than the other? Are the two lists equally negative or positive in their connotations? What does this exercise tell you about the survival of the double standard and your culture's sexual scripts?

BIOLOGY and *Sexual Orientation*

Elusive Causes, Recent Clues

Why is it that most people become heterosexual, some homosexual, and others bisexual? Many psychological explanations for homosexuality have been proposed over the years, but none of them has been supported. Homosexuality is not a result of having a smothering mother, an absent father, or emotional problems. It is not caused by same-sex sexual play in childhood or adolescence, which is actually quite common (Lamb, 2002). It is not caused by seduction by an older adult (Rind, Tromovich, & Bauserman, 1998). It is not caused by parental practices or role models. Most gay men recall that they rejected the typical boy role and boys' toys and games from an early age, in spite of enormous pressures from their parents and peers to conform to the traditional male role (Bailey & Zucker, 1995). Conversely, the overwhelming majority of children of gay parents do not become gay, as a learning model would predict, although they are more likely than the children of straight parents to be open-minded about homosexuality and gender roles (Bailey et al., 1995; Patterson, 1992, 2006).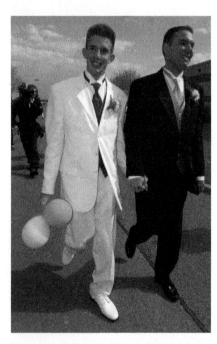

Many researchers, therefore, have been turning to biological explanations of sexual orientation. One line of supporting evidence is that homosexual behaviour—including courtship displays, sexual activity, and the rearing of young by two males or two females—has been documented in some 450 species, including bottlenose dolphins, penguins, and primates (Bagemihl, 1999). Sexual orientation also seems to be moderately heritable, particularly in men (Bailey, Dunne, & Martin, 2000; Rahman & Wilson, 2003). But the large majority of gay men and lesbians do not have a close gay relative, and their siblings, including twins, are overwhelmingly likely to be heterosexual (Peplau et al., 2000).

In the early 1990s, a few studies of gay men reported associations between sexual orientation and specific areas of the brain (Allen & Gorski, 1992; LeVay, 1991). These studies got lots of press, but they were not replicated (Byne, 1995). Researchers have also examined the role of prenatal exposure to androgens and how this might affect brain organization and partner preference (McFadden, 2008; Rahman & Wilson, 2003). Female babies accidentally exposed in the womb to masculinizing hormones are more likely than other girls to become bisexual or lesbian and to prefer typical boys' toys and activities (Collaer & Hines, 1995; Meyer-Bahlburg et al., 1995). However, most androgenized girls do not become lesbians, and most lesbians were not exposed in the womb to atypical prenatal hormones (Peplau et al., 2000).

One new line of research is investigating the possibility that other prenatal events might predispose a child toward a same-sex orientation. For example, more than a dozen studies have found that the probability of a man's becoming gay rises significantly according to the number of older brothers he has—gay or not—when these brothers are born of the same mother. (Remember, though, that the percentage of males who become homosexual is very small.) A recent study of 944 homosexual and heterosexual men suggests that this "brother effect" has nothing to do with family environment, but rather with conditions within the womb before birth (Bogaert, 2006). In this study, the only factor that predicted sexual orientation was having older biological brothers; growing up with older stepbrothers or adoptive brothers (or

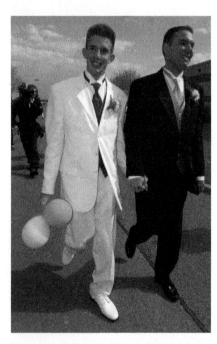

Watch the Video
Thinking Like a Psychologist: Sexual Orientation in **MyPsychLab**

Marc Hall (left), with his boyfriend Jean-Paul Doumond. An Ontario court ruled that Hall should be allowed to bring his boyfriend to his Catholic high school prom in Oshawa on May 10, 2002. Why are some people homosexual in spite of enormous social pressures to be heterosexual, including laws and customs that typically deny them the benefits accorded to straights?

Tony Bock/Toronto Star

sisters) had no influence at all. The increased chance of homosexuality occurred even when men had older brothers born to the same mother but raised in a different home. No one yet has any idea, however, what prenatal influence might account for these results.

Several other intriguing biological findings are also associated with sexual orientation. In two studies, a team of Swedish scientists exposed people to two odours: a testosterone derivative found in men's sweat and an estrogen-like compound found in women's urine. It appears that when a hormone is from the sex you are *not* turned on by, your olfactory system registers it but your hypothalamus and through that, your sexual arousal and response system, do not register it. Thus, the brain activity of homosexual women in response to the odours was similar to that of heterosexual men, and the brain activity of gay men was similar to that of heterosexual women (Berglund, Lindström, & Savic, 2006; Savic, Berglund, & Lindström, 2005). But the researchers wisely noted that their study could not answer questions of cause and effect. "We can't say whether the differences are because of pre-existing differences in their brains, or if past sexual experiences have conditioned their brains to respond differently," said the lead researcher.

The basic problem with trying to find a single origin of sexual orientation is that sexual identity and behaviour take different forms, and they don't correlate strongly (Savin-Williams, 2006). Some people are heterosexual in behaviour but have homosexual fantasies and even define themselves as gay or lesbian. Some men, such as prisoners, are homosexual in behaviour because they lack opportunities for heterosexual sex, but they do not define themselves as gay and prefer women as sexual partners. In some cultures, teenage boys go through a homosexual phase that they do not define as homosexual and that does not affect their future relations with women (Herdt, 1984). Some gay men are feminine in interests and manner, but many are not; some lesbians are "butch" (i.e., masculine in interests and manner) but many other lesbians are not (Singh et al., 1999).

Moreover, although some lesbians have an exclusively same-sex orientation their whole lives, many have more fluid sexual orientations: They have sex with the person they fall in love with, male or female (Peplau et al., 2000). Some women are lesbian for a particular time in their lives, as reflected in the joking term LUG—lesbian until graduation (Diamond, 2003). A researcher interviewed 100 lesbian and bisexual women over a 10-year span, and found that only one-third reported consistent attraction only to other women; two-thirds also felt attracted to men. For most of these women, love was truly blind as far as gender was concerned; their sexual behaviour depended on whether they loved the partner, not what sex he or she was (Diamond, 2008). Similarly, when men and women watch erotic films, men are more influenced than women are by the sex of the people having sex, whereas women are more influenced than men are by the context in which the sex occurs. Thus, most straight men are turned off by watching gay male couples coupling, most gay men are turned off by watching heterosexual couples, and most straight and lesbian women are turned on by watching anyone of either sex, as long as the context is erotic (Rupp & Wallen, 2008). In Lesotho,

THINKING CRITICALLY

Examine the evidence.

Nicole Bengiveno/Redux Pictures

Many people think that homosexuality is abnormal, unnatural, or a matter of preference, but there is ample evidence of same-sex sexual activity in more than 450 nonhuman species. These young male penguins, Squawk and Milou, entwine their necks, kiss, call to each other, and have sex—and they firmly reject females. Another male pair in the same zoo, Silo and Roy, seemed so desperate to incubate an egg together that they put a rock in their nest and sat on it. Their human keeper was so touched that he gave them a fertile egg to hatch. Silo and Roy sat on it for the necessary 34 days until their chick, Tango, was born, and then they raised Tango beautifully. "They did a great job," said the zookeeper.

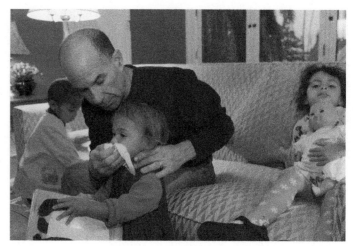

Gay and lesbian couples have all the joys and problems of straight couples. Phyllis Lyon and Del Martin (left) lived together for 56 years. In 2008, two months after they were finally legally allowed to marry, Del Martin died. On the right, Tom Howard is shown with the three children he is raising with his partner. Howard left his job as a professor in order to be a stay-at-home dad. Why does the issue of legalizing gay and lesbian marriage evoke so much emotion and controversy?

Left: Liz Mangelsdorf/Corbis. Right: Stephanie Diani/The New York Times, Redux Pictures.

in South Africa, women have intimate relations with other women, including passionate kissing and oral sex, but they do not define these acts as sexual, as they do when a man is the partner (Kendall, 1999).

Biological factors cannot account for the diversity of such customs or for the diversity of experience among gay men and lesbians. At present, therefore, we must tolerate uncertainty about the origins of sexual orientation. Perhaps the origins will turn out to differ, on average, for males and females, and also differ among individuals, whatever their primary orientation.

Now, how are you reacting to these findings? Your responses are probably affected by your feelings about the subject. Many gay men and lesbians welcome biological research on the grounds that it supports what they have been saying all along: Sexual orientation is not a matter of choice but a fact of nature. Others fear that people who are prejudiced against homosexuals will use this research to argue that gay people have a biological defect that should be eradicated. But people who are hostile to homosexuals can use any theory, biological or psychological, to justify their wish to eliminate homosexuality. They have often used learning theories to argue, mistakenly, that "if it's learned, it can be unlearned," and thus to subject gay men, and even "unboyish" boys as young as three years old, to harsh and punitive forms of behaviour modification (Burke, 1996).

Political storms about sex research are no less heated today than they were in Kinsey's time. Some conservative and evangelical Christians, including the Traditional Values Coalition, are trying to block research on sexual behaviour they say the Bible disapproves of, such as masturbation, homosexuality, and any form of sexual behaviour outside of marriage. Other conservative Christians, however, call on modern research to make the case that homosexuality is not a preference but a natural disposition. In their book *What God Has Joined Together: A Christian Case for Gay Marriage*, David Myers and Letha Scanzoni (2005) argue that the Bible's seven brief comments opposing same-sex behaviour are really condemnations of the exploitation of children, promiscuity, idolatry, and acting against one's nature, and that these verses pale in importance beside the Bible's thousands of verses about love, compassion, and empathy.

As you see, research on sexuality can be used for many purposes and political goals, depending on the values and attitudes of the culture in which such findings emerge and people's own religious passions or personal beliefs. But as long as people are morally opposed to homosexuality, preconceptions and prejudice are likely to cloud their reactions to anything that psychologists learn about it.

Recite & Review

Recite: Were you motivated to learn about sexual motivation? Say aloud what you know about biological factors in sexuality; psychological motives for sex, rape, and coercion; *sexual scripts* and their influence on sexual behaviour; and the possible factors involved in sexual orientation.

Review: Next, reread this section.

Now take this *Quick Quiz:*

Were you motivated to learn about sexual motivation?

1. Biological research finds that (a) homosexual behaviour is found in hundreds of animal species, (b) male and female sexual responses are physiologically very different, (c) all women can have multiple orgasms, (d) women have a stronger sex drive than men do, contrary to the stereotype.

2. Research on the motives of rapists finds that rape is usually a result of (a) thwarted sexual desire, (b) hostility or a need for peer approval, (c) crossed signals, (d) female provocation.

3. When men are scarce, what are some consequences for the sexual behaviour of both sexes?

4. Under what conditions are women most likely to use sex as a "bargaining chip"? (a) when they are employed and thus have their own money to bargain with, (b) when they don't know how to play poker, (c) when they are using birth control, (d) when they are financially dependent.

5. *True or false:* Exclusively psychological theories of the origins of homosexuality have never been supported.

Answers:

1. a 2. b 3. Men are more likely to have multiple sexual partners, divorce rates and single-parent families increase, and women become more independent. 4. d 5. True

✓•⎯**Study** and **Review**

in **MyPsychLab**

Learning Objectives

12 List the three kinds of goals most likely to boost the motivation to succeed.

13 Define the important difference between mastery goals and performance goals.

14 Explain how the desire to achieve is affected by the opportunity to achieve.

15 Identify which aspects of a job are more important than money in increasing satisfaction with work.

The Competent Animal: Motives to Achieve

Almost every adult works. But work does not only mean paid employment. Students work at studying. Homemakers work, often more hours than salaried employees, at running a household. Artists, poets, and actors work, even if they are paid erratically (or not at all). Most people are motivated to work in order to meet the basic needs for food and shelter. Yet survival does not explain why some people want to do their work well and others just want to get it done. And it does not explain why some people work to make a basic living and then put their passions for achievement into unpaid activities—learning to become an accomplished trail rider or travelling to Madagascar to catch sight of a rare bird for their bird-watching list. What keeps everybody doing what they do?

Thematic Apperception Test (TAT)
A projective test that asks respondents to interpret a series of drawings showing scenes of people; usually scored for unconscious motives, such as the need for achievement, power, or affiliation.

approach goals Goals framed in terms of desired outcomes or experiences, such as learning to scuba dive.

avoidance goals Goals framed in terms of avoiding unpleasant experiences, such as trying not to look foolish in public.

Psychologists, particularly those in the field of industrial/organizational psychology, have measured the psychological qualities that spur achievement and success and also the environmental conditions that influence productivity and satisfaction. Their findings apply not only to understanding why people thrive or wilt at their jobs, but also to understanding people's aspirations and achievements in general.

The Effects of Motivation on Work

In the early 1950s, David McClelland and his associates (1953) speculated that some people have a *need for achievement* that motivates them as much as hunger motivates people to eat. To measure the strength of this motive, McClelland used a variation of the **Thematic Apperception Test (TAT)**, which requires the test-taker to make up a story about a set of ambiguous pictures, such as a young man sitting at a desk. (The TAT is one of many *projective tests*, which are based on the assumption that a person will project unconscious motives and feelings onto an ambiguous stimulus; see Chapter 16.) The strength of the achievement motive, said McClelland (1961), is captured in the fantasies the test-taker reveals. High achievers tell stories of challenge and success; lower achievers tell stories of idyllic vacations at the beach.

The TAT is one of the few projective tests that has modest empirical support for the measurement of achievement motivation. But it does not have strong *test–retest reliability*, meaning that people's responses are easily influenced by what is going on at that moment in their lives rather than by some inner drive to succeed (Lilienfeld, Wood, & Garb, 2000). Some people might tell stories of achieving against all odds, not because they are determined to do so, but because they are idly daydreaming about dazzling the world on *Canadian Idol*. But the method launched many investigations into the question of why some people seem to have a drive to make it no matter what, and others drift along.

The Importance of Goals. Today the predominant approach to understanding achievement motivation emphasizes goals rather than inner drives: What you accomplish depends on the goals you set for yourself and the reasons you pursue them (Dweck & Grant, 2008). Not just any old goals will promote achievement, though. A goal is most likely to improve your motivation and performance when three conditions are met (Higgins, 1998; Locke & Latham, 2002, 2006):

- *The goal is specific.* Defining a goal vaguely, such as "doing your best," is as ineffective as having no goal at all. You need to be specific about what you are going to do and when you are going to do it: "I will write four pages of this paper today."

- *The goal is challenging but achievable.* You are apt to work hardest for tough but realistic goals. The highest, most difficult goals produce the highest levels of motivation and performance, unless, of course, you choose impossible goals that you can never attain.

- *The goal is framed in terms of getting what you want rather than avoiding what you do not want.* **Approach goals** are positive experiences that you seek directly, such as getting a better grade or learning to scuba dive. **Avoidance goals** involve the effort to avoid unpleasant experiences, such as trying not to make a fool of yourself at parties or trying to avoid being dependent. ◉

All the motives discussed in this chapter are affected by approach versus avoidance goals. People who frame their goals in specific, achievable approach terms (e.g., "I'm going to lose weight by jogging three times a week") feel better about themselves, are happier, feel more competent, are more optimistic, and are less depressed than people who frame the same goals in avoidance terms (e.g., "I'm going to lose weight by

◉—⌐**Watch** the **Video**
Attitudes and Job Satisfaction
in **MyPsychLab**

GET INVOLVED! (Re)Framing Your Goals

As the text discusses, people sometimes frame their goals in vague, unrealistic, or negative ways. Think of two goals you would like to accomplish. For example, you might consider goals related to studying more efficiently, improving communication with a family member, solving problems in a particular relationship, or becoming more physically fit. Now phrase each of your two goals in a way that makes it (1) specific, (2) challenging but achievable, and (3) something to be approached rather than avoided. How can framing your goals in this way improve your motivation to reach them?

cutting out rich foods") (Coats, Janoff-Bulman, & Alpert, 1996; Updegraff, Gable, & Taylor, 2004). Framing goals in terms of approach or avoidance can even affect the quality of close relationships. For example, people who have sex for *approach* motives—to enjoy their own physical pleasure, to promote a partner's happiness, or to seek enhanced intimacy—tend to have happier and less conflicted relationships than those who have sex to *avoid* a partner's loss of interest or quarrels with the partner (Impett & Tolman, 2006; Impett, Peplau, & Gable, 2005).

Can you guess why approach goals produce better results than avoidance goals? Approach goals allow you to focus on what you can actively do to accomplish them and on the intrinsic pleasure of the activity. Avoidance goals make you focus on what you have to give up (Elliot & Sheldon, 1998).

In the case of work, defining your goals will move you along the road to success, but what happens when you hit a pothole? Some people give up when a goal becomes difficult or they are faced with a setback, whereas others become even more determined to succeed. The crucial difference between them is why they are working for that goal: to show off in front of others or to learn the task for the satisfaction of it.

People who are motivated by *performance goals* are concerned primarily with being judged favourably and avoiding criticism. Those who are motivated by *mastery (learning) goals* are concerned with increasing their competence and skills and finding intrinsic pleasure in what they are learning (Grant & Dweck, 2003; Senko, Durik, & Harackiewicz, 2008). When people who are motivated by performance goals do poorly, they will often decide the fault is theirs and stop trying to improve. Because their goal is to demonstrate their abilities, they set themselves up for grief when they temporarily fail, as all of us must if we are to learn anything new. In contrast, people who are motivated to master new skills will generally regard failure and criticism as sources of useful information that will help them improve. They know that learning takes time.

Why do some children choose performance goals and others choose mastery goals? In a study of 128 grade 5 students, the children worked independently on sets of puzzle problems (Mueller & Dweck, 1998). The experimenter scored their results, told them all they had done well, and gave them one of two additional types of feedback: She praised some of them for their ability ("You must be smart to do these problems!") and others for their effort ("You must have worked hard at these problems!"). The children then worked on a more difficult set of problems, but this time the experimenter told them they had done a lot worse. Finally, the children described which goals they preferred to work for: performance (e.g., doing "problems that aren't too hard, so I don't get many wrong") or mastery (e.g., doing "problems that I'll learn a lot from, even if I won't look so smart").

The children praised for being smart rather than for working hard tended to lose the pleasure of learning and focused instead on how well they were doing. After these children failed the second set of problems, they tended to give up on

Why will some children become engrossed in a project and work on it for hours, whereas others give up in frustration if they can't get it just right?

Daniel Bosler/Getty Images

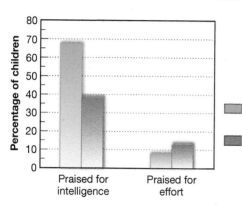

FIGURE 12.1 Mastery and Motivation

Children praised for "being smart" rather than for "working hard" tend to lose the pleasure of learning and focus on how well they are doing. Nearly 70% of grade 5 students who were praised for intelligence later chose performance goals (green bars) rather than learning goals, compared to fewer than 10% of those who were praised for their efforts (Mueller & Dweck, 1998). Notice also that the children praised for intelligence were much more likely to lie to others about how well they had done (purple bars)—since their goal was showing off, not learning.

subsequent ones, enjoyed them less, and actually performed less well than children who had been praised for their efforts. As you can see in Figure 12.1, nearly 70% of the grade 5 students who were praised for their intelligence later chose performance goals rather than learning goals, compared to fewer than 10% of those who were praised for their efforts. When children realize that all effort is subject to improvement, however, they realize that they can always try again. That is the key to mastery. As one learning-oriented child said to the experimenters, "Mistakes are our friends" (Dweck & Sorich, 1999).

Mastery goals are powerful intrinsic motivators at all levels of education and throughout life. Students who are in university primarily to master new areas of knowledge choose more challenging projects, persist in the face of difficulty, use deeper and more elaborate study strategies, are less likely than other students to cheat, and enjoy learning more than do students who are there only to get a degree and a meal ticket (Elliot & McGregor, 2001; Grant & Dweck, 2003). As usual, though, we should avoid oversimplifying: Olympic athletes, world-class musicians, and others who are determined to become the best in their field blend performance and mastery goals.

Expectations and Self-Efficacy. How hard you work for something also depends on your expectations. If you are fairly certain of success, you will work harder to reach your goal than if you are fairly certain of failure.

A classic experiment showed how quickly experience affects these expectations. Young women were asked to solve 15 anagram puzzles. Before working on each one, they had to estimate their chances of solving it. Half of the women started off with very easy anagrams, but half began with insoluble ones. Sure enough, those who started with the easy ones increased their estimates of success on later ones. Those who began with the impossible ones decided they would all be impossible. These expectations, in turn, affected the young women's ability to actually solve the last 10 anagrams, which were the same for everyone. The higher the expectation of success, the more anagrams the women solved (Feather, 1966). Once acquired, therefore, expectations can create a *self-fulfilling prophecy* (Merton, 1948): Your expectations make you behave in ways that make the expectation come true. You expect to succeed, so you work hard—and succeed. Or you expect to fail, so you don't do much work—and do poorly.

Your expectations are further influenced by your level of confidence in yourself and your abilities (Dweck & Grant, 2008; Judge, 2009). No one is born with a feeling of confidence, or *self-efficacy*. You acquire it through experience in mastering new skills, overcoming obstacles, and learning from occasional failures. Self-efficacy also

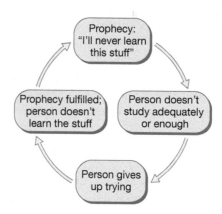

comes from having successful role models who teach you that your ambitions are possible and from having people around to give you constructive feedback and encouragement (Bandura, 2006).

People who have a strong sense of self-efficacy are quick to cope with problems rather than stewing and brooding about them. Studies in North America, Europe, and Russia find that self-efficacy has a positive effect on just about every aspect of people's lives: how well they do on a task, the grades they earn, how persistently they pursue their goals, the kinds of career choices they make, their ability to solve complex problems, their motivation to work for political and social goals, their health habits, and even their chances of recovery from heart attack (Bandura et al., 2001; Maddux, 1995; Stajkovic & Luthans, 1998). Meta-analyses of decades of research find that self-efficacy and the setting of ambitious but achievable goals are indeed the strongest predictors of learning and accomplishment (Lanaj, Chang, & Johnson, 2012; Sitzmann & Ely, 2011).

The Effects of Work on Motivation

Imagine that you live in a town that has one famous company, Boopsie's Biscuits & Buns. Everyone in the town is grateful for the 3B company and goes to work there with high hopes. Soon, however, an odd thing starts happening to many employees. They complain of fatigue and irritability. They are taking lots of sick leave. Productivity declines. What's going on at Boopsie's Biscuits & Buns? Is everybody suffering from sheer laziness?

Most observers would answer that something is wrong with those employees. But what if something is wrong with Boopsie's? Some people undoubtedly do lack motivation, but accomplishment does not depend on internal motives alone. Psychologists also want to know how the work we do, as well as the conditions under which we do it, nurtures or crushes our motivation to succeed.

For example, one simple but powerful external factor that affects many people's motivation to work in a particular field is the proportion of men and women in that occupation (Kanter, 2006). When occupations are segregated by gender, many people form gender stereotypes about the requirements of such careers: Female jobs require kindness and nurturance; male jobs require strength and smarts. These stereotypes, in turn, stifle many people's aspirations to enter a nontraditional career and also create prejudices in employers (Agars, 2004; Cejka & Eagly, 1999; Eccles, 2011).

> **THINKING CRITICALLY**
>
> Ask questions.
>
> If a person isn't doing well at work, North Americans tend to ask, "What's the matter with that person's motivation? How come that person is a lazy slug?" What other questions would lead to different answers about why the employee seems so lazy?

Thus, when law, veterinary medicine, and bartending were almost entirely male professions, and nursing, teaching, and child care were almost entirely female, few women aspired to enter the "male" professions and few men to enter the "female" ones. As job segregation began breaking down, however, people's career motivations changed. Today, it isn't at all unusual to see a female lawyer, vet, or bartender, or a male nurse or even nanny.

And although women are still a minority in engineering, math, and science, their numbers are rising: In 1970–1971, women earned 0.6% of the doctorates in engineering, 7.6% of those in mathematics, and 16.3% of those in biological sciences. By 2001–2002, the percentages had jumped to 17.3%, 29%, and 44.3%, respectively (Cox & Alm, 2005). As these numbers have increased, the view that women are not suited to engineering, math, and science has been fading, though slowly.

Working Conditions. Once they are in a job, what motivates people to do well? Why do others lose their motivation altogether? To begin with, achievement depends on having the *opportunity* to achieve. When someone does not do well at work, others are apt to say it is the individual's own fault because he or she lacks the internal drive to make it. But what the person may really lack is a fair chance to make it, and this is especially true for those who have been subjected to systematic discrimination (Sabattini & Crosby, 2009). Once they have entered a career, people may become more motivated to advance up the ladder or less so, depending on how many rungs they are permitted to climb. Women used to be rare in politics, but today it's not news that they are counsellors, mayors, MPs, or prime ministers.

Several aspects of the work environment are likely to increase work motivation and satisfaction and reduce the chances of emotional burnout (Bakker, 2011; Bond et al., 2004; Maslach, Schaufeli, & Leiter, 2001; Rhoades & Eisenberger, 2002):

- The work feels meaningful and important to employees.
- Employees have control over many aspects of their work, such as setting their own hours and making decisions.
- Tasks are varied rather than repetitive.
- The company maintains clear and consistent rules.
- Employees have supportive relationships with their superiors and co-workers.
- Employees receive useful feedback about their work, so they know what they have accomplished and what they need to do to improve.
- The company offers opportunities for its employees to learn and advance.

Did you notice anything missing from that list of beneficial working conditions? Where is money, supposedly the great motivator? Actually, work motivation is related not to the amount of money you get, but to how and when you get it. The strongest motivator is *incentive pay*, bonuses that are given upon completion of a goal rather than as an automatic raise (Locke et al., 1981). Incentive pay increases people's feelings of competence and accomplishment ("I got this raise because I deserved it"). This doesn't mean that people should accept low pay so that they will like their jobs better or that they should never demand cost-of-living raises!

Companies that foster these conditions tend to have more productive and satisfied employees. Workers tend to become more creative in their thinking and feel better about themselves and their work than they do if they feel stuck in routine jobs that give them no control or flexibility over their daily tasks.

Conversely, when people are put in situations that frustrate their desire and ability to succeed, they become dissatisfied and stressed out, and their desire to succeed declines (Jenkins, 1994). For example, while the rising number of women entering the sciences is heartening news, many are not staying. A study of nearly 2500 women and

Like employees, students can have poor working conditions that affect their motivation. They may have to study in crowded quarters or may have young siblings who interrupt and distract them.

Buccina Studios/Getty Images

men in science, engineering, and technology found that although women made up 41% of the entry-level jobs, more than half of them had left their jobs by age 35, and a fourth had abandoned science altogether. The women who lost their motivation to work in these fields reported feeling isolated (many said they were the only woman in their work group), and two-thirds said they had been sexually harassed (Hewlitt, Luce, & Servon, 2008). Other reasons included being paid less than men for the same work and having working conditions that did not allow them to handle their family obligations. Mothers are still more likely than fathers to reduce their work hours, modify their work schedules, and report feeling distracted on the job because of child-care concerns (Sabattini & Crosby, 2009).

In sum, work motivation and satisfaction depend on the right fit between qualities of the individual and conditions of the work.

Recite & Review

Recite: To work on your understanding of work motivation, say aloud what you recall about the *Thematic Apperception Test (TAT)*, the three conditions under which goals are most effective, *approach* and *avoidance goals*, performance and mastery goals, self-fulfilling prophecies, self-efficacy, and the work conditions that increase motivation.

Review: Next, give your motivation a jolt and reread this material.

Now take this *Quick Quiz:*

Work on your understanding of work motivation.

1. Horatio wants to earn a black belt in karate. Which way(s) of thinking about this goal are most likely to help him reach it? (a) "I should do the best I can," (b) "I should make sure not to lose many matches," (c) "I will set specific goals that are tough but attainable," (d) "I will set specific goals that I know I can reach easily," (e) "I will strive to achieve key milestones on the way to my goal."

2. Ramón and Ramona are learning to ski. Every time she falls, Ramona says, "This is the most humiliating experience I've ever had! Everyone is watching me behave like a clumsy dolt!" When Ramón falls, he says, "&*!!@$@! I'll show these dratted skis who's boss!" Why is Ramona more likely than Ramón to give up? (a) She *is* a clumsy dolt, (b) She is less competent at skiing, (c) She is focused on learning, (d) She is focused on performance.

3. Which of these factors significantly increases work motivation? (a) specific goals, (b) regular pay, (c) feedback, (d) general goals, (e) being told what to do, (f) being able to make decisions, (g) the chance of promotion, (h) having routine, predictable work.

Answers:

1. c, e 2. d 3. a, c, f, g

✓●—[**Study** and **Review**
in **MyPsychLab**

Learning Objectives

16 Explain why people are poor at predicting what will make them happy or miserable.

17 Articulate why money can't buy happiness.

18 Describe three basic kinds of motivational conflicts.

Motives, Values, and Well-Being

When you think about setting goals for yourself, here is a crucial psychological finding to keep in mind: People are really bad at predicting what will make them happy and what will make them miserable, and at estimating how long those feelings will last (Wilson & Gilbert, 2005). In one study, college students were asked how happy or unhappy they imagined they would feel after being randomly assigned to live in a dorm they thought was "desirable" or "undesirable" (Dunn, Wilson, & Gilbert, 2003). The students predicted that their dorm assignments would have a huge impact on their overall level of happiness and that being assigned to an undesirable dorm would essentially wreck their

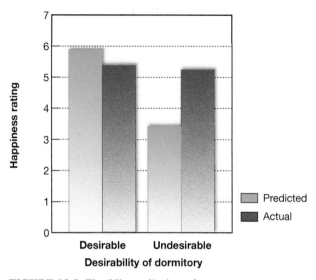

FIGURE 12.2 The Misprediction of Emotion
In a real-life longitudinal study, college students about to be randomly assigned to a dorm had to predict how happy or unhappy they would feel about being assigned to a house they had ranked as "desirable" or "undesirable." Most students thought they would be much less happy in an "undesirable" dorm, but in fact, one year later, there was no difference between the two groups (Dunn, Wilson, & Gilbert, 2003).

satisfaction for the whole year. In fact, as you can see from Figure 12.2, one year later everyone had nearly identical levels of happiness no matter where they were living.

Perhaps the undesirable dorms turned out to be unexpectedly pleasant, with cool people living in them? No. The students had focused on the wrong factors when imagining their future feelings of happiness in the houses; they had placed far more importance on what the house looked like and on its location than on its inhabitants. But in fact it's people who make a place fun or unpleasant to live in, and all the houses had likable people in them. Because the students could not foresee this, or how much they would like their new roommates, they mispredicted their future happiness.

This result has been replicated in many contexts: The good is rarely as good as we imagine it will be, and the bad is rarely as terrible. The reason is that people adjust quickly to happy changes—new relationships, a promotion, even winning the lottery—and fail to anticipate that they will cope with bad experiences just as quickly. They will make sense of unexpected events, cope with tragedies, and make excuses for loved ones who hurt them. Yet people make many decisions based on false assumptions about how they will feel in the future. For example, they might spend more money than they can afford on a car or sound system because they think that this is what will make them truly happy.

What, then, does make people happy? In all the domains of human motivation we have examined, a key conclusion emerges: People who are motivated by the intrinsic satisfaction of an activity are happier and more satisfied than those motivated solely by extrinsic rewards (Deci & Ryan, 1985; Kasser & Ryan, 2001). We also saw how intrinsic motivation in any domain will rise or fall depending on the goals we choose and the way we think of them. Goals, in turn, are determined by our values about what is important in life: freedom, religion, equality, wealth, fame, wisdom, serenity, salvation, sexual passion, the desire to improve the world, or anything else. Psychological research cannot tell us which values to choose, but it does help illuminate the consequences of our choices.

For example, many North Americans are more motivated to make money than to find activities they enjoy. Psychotherapist Allen Kanner noticed this difference in attitude among the children he saw in his practice: Ten years earlier, the children he treated had told him they wanted to be astronauts, baseball players, ballerinas, and doctors when they grew up, while the children he was currently treating told him they just wanted to be rich. They didn't want to play with conventional toys, but only with better, newer toys (Kanner & Kasser, 2003). Yet research finds repeatedly that having positive, intrinsically enjoyable *experiences* makes most people happier than having *things*: Doing is more satisfying than buying (Van Boven & Gilovich, 2003). Although people imagine that greater wealth will bring greater happiness, once they are at a level that provides basic comfort and security, more isn't necessarily better. They adjust quickly to the greater wealth and then think they need even more of it to be happier (Gilbert, 2006a).

Whichever values and goals you choose, if they are in conflict, the discrepancy can produce emotional stress and unhappiness. Two motives conflict when the satisfaction of one leads to the inability to act on the other—when, that is, you want to have your cake and eat it, too. Researchers have identified three kinds of motivational conflicts (Lewin, 1948):

✳ Explore the Concept
What Motivates You? in MyPsychLab

1 **Approach–approach conflicts** occur when you are equally attracted to two or more possible activities or goals. For example, you would like to be a veterinarian *and* a rock singer; you would like to go out Tuesday night with friends *and* study like mad for an exam Wednesday.

2 **Avoidance–avoidance conflicts** require you to choose the lesser of two evils because you dislike both alternatives. Novice parachute jumpers, for example, must choose between the fear of jumping and the fear of losing face if they don't jump.

3 **Approach–avoidance conflicts** occur when a single activity or goal has both a positive and a negative aspect. For example, you want to be a powerful executive but you worry about losing your friends if you succeed. In culturally diverse nations, differing cultural values produce many approach–avoidance conflicts, as our students have revealed. A Chicano student said he wants to become a lawyer, but his parents, valuing family closeness, worry that if he goes to graduate school, he will become independent and feel superior to his working-class family. A black student from a poor neighbourhood, in university on scholarship, is torn between wanting to leave his background behind him forever and returning to help his home community. And a white student wants to be a marine biologist, but her friends tell her that only nerdy guys and dweebs go into science.

Conflicts like these are inevitable, part of the price and pleasure of living. But if conflicts remain unresolved, they can take an emotional toll. In students, high levels of conflict and ambivalence about goals and values are associated with anxiety, depression, headaches and other symptoms, and more visits to the health centre (Emmons & King, 1988). In contrast, students who strive for goals that are consistent with the qualities they value are healthier and have a greater sense of meaning and purpose in life than do those who are pursuing goals discrepant with their core values (Sheldon & Houser-Marko, 2001).

Are some psychological goals more important to our well-being than others? The humanist psychologist Abraham Maslow (1970) thought so. Maslow envisioned people's motives as forming a pyramid, a *hierarchy of needs*. At the bottom level of the pyramid were basic survival needs for food, sleep, and water; at the next level were security needs, for shelter and safety; at the third level were social needs, for belonging and affection; at the fourth level were esteem needs, for self-respect and the respect of others; and at the top were needs for self-actualization and self-transcendence. Maslow argued that your needs must be met at each level before you can even think of the matters posed by the level above it. You can't worry about achievement if you are hungry, cold, and poor. You can't become self-actualized if you haven't satisfied your needs for self-esteem and love. Human beings behave badly, he argued, only when their lower needs are frustrated.

This theory, which seemed so logical and optimistic about human progress, became immensely popular. Motivational speakers still often refer to it, using colourful pictures of Maslow's pyramid. But the theory, which was based mostly on Maslow's observations and intuitions, has had little empirical support (Sheldon et al., 2001; Smither, 1998). On the contrary, people may have *simultaneous* needs for comfort and safety and also for attachments, self-esteem, and competence. And individuals who have met their lower needs do not inevitably seek higher ones, nor is it the case that people behave badly only when their lower needs are frustrated. Higher needs may even supersede lower ones. History is full of examples of people who would rather die of torture or starvation than sacrifice their convictions, or who would rather explore, risk, or create new art than be safe and secure at home. 👁

A different way of thinking about universal psychological needs has been developed by researchers who studied large samples of students in the United States and South Korea (Sheldon et al., 2001). Although students are not actually typical of all human beings, and two cultures do not represent all cultures on the planet, the findings are provocative and support many of the points in this chapter. The top four psychological needs turned out to be *autonomy* (feeling that you are making choices based on your "true interests and values"), *competence* (feeling able to master challenges), *relatedness* (feeling close to others who are important to you), and *self-esteem* (having self-respect). Other needs were of lesser importance, including pleasure, self-actualization (which was at the top of Maslow's list), popularity, and, at the bottom, once again . . . money and luxury.

👁—⌐Watch the Video
What's in It for Me? Meeting Our Needs
in **MyPsychLab**

As we have seen in this chapter, there are many motives that spur us to action, but psychological well-being depends on finding activities and choosing goals that are intrinsically satisfying and on developing the self-efficacy to achieve them. The motives and goals that inspire us, and the choices we make in their pursuit, are what give our lives passion, colour, and meaning. Choose them wisely.

✓•—Study and Review
in **MyPsychLab**

Recite & Review

Recite: We hope you don't feel any conflict over the goal of learning this material. Recite what you know about the misprediction of emotion, findings about money and happiness, the three kinds of conflict, and Abraham Maslow's pyramid of needs.

Review: Next, read this section again.

Now take this *Quick Quiz:*

Do you wish to approach or avoid this quiz?

1. Max has applied for a study-abroad program, but couldn't get into his first choice, a drama school in London. He is feeling so miserable about the rejection that he is thinking of staying home. "Why should I go to a second-rate school somewhere else?," he reasons. What is the matter with his reasoning?

2. A Pakistani student says she desperately wants an education and a career as a pharmacist, but she also does not want to disobey her parents who have arranged a marriage for her back home. Which kind of conflict does she have?

3. Maslow's popular hierarchy of needs has several flaws. What are they?

Answers:

1. Max assumes that how he feels now is how he will feel in the future. He can't imagine the more likely scenario, that he will find things to like about any program he enters. 2. approach–avoidance 3. It was not based on extensive empirical research; it has not been well supported by research; the needs he proposed can be simultaneous rather than hierarchi- cal; higher needs often supersede lower ones.

Taking Psychology with You

THINKING CRITICALLY IN EVERYDAY LIFE

How to Attain Your Goals

What are your values? What would you most like to achieve and accomplish in your life? Love, wealth, security, passion, freedom, fame, the desire to improve the world, being the best in a sport or other skill? Something else? What are your short-term goals: Would you like to improve your love life? Get better grades? Enjoy school more? Lose weight? Become a better tennis player?

There is a whole world of "motivational speakers," books, and tapes that offer inspiration, enthusiasm, and a few magic steps to change your life, but we hope that by now you will apply critical thinking to their promises. Enthusiastic inspiration is fine as far as it goes, but it doesn't usually transfer into helping you make real-life changes. In contrast, think about some of the lessons of motivational research that you have learned in this chapter:

Seek activities that are intrinsically pleasurable, even if they don't pay off. If you really, really want to study Swahili or Swedish even though these languages are not in your pre-law requirements, try to find a way to do it. If you are not enjoying your major or your job, consider finding a career that would be more intrinsically pleasurable, or at least make sure you have other projects and activities that you do enjoy for their own sake.

Focus on learning goals, not only on performance goals. In general, you will be better able to cope with setbacks if your goal is to learn rather than to show how good you are. Regard failure as a chance to learn rather than as a sign of incompetence.

Assess your working conditions. Everyone has working conditions. Whether you are a student, a self-employed writer, or a homemaker, if your motivation and well-being are starting to wilt, check out your environment. Are you getting support from others? Do you have opportunities to develop ideas and vary your routine, or are you expected to do the same thing day after day? Are there barriers that might limit your advancement in your chosen field?

Take steps to resolve motivational conflicts. Are you torn between competing goals? For instance, are you unhappily stuck between the goal of achieving independence and a desire to be cared for by your parents? The reconciliation of conflicts like these is important for your well-being (Emmons & King, 1988).

Most important, think critically about the goals you have chosen for yourself: Are they what you want to do or what someone else wants you to do? Do they reflect your values? If you are not happy with your body, your relationships, or your work, why not? Think about it.

Summary

MyPsychLab can help you get a better grade. Test your knowledge and grasp difficult concepts through
- Custom study plans: See where you are strong and where you are wrong
- Multimedia, including videos and interactive simulations
- Dynamic Study Modules: flashcards for self-study that ensure you achieve mastery of course concepts

- *Motivation* refers to an inferred process within a person or animal that causes that organism to move toward a goal—to satisfy a biological need or achieve a psychological ambition—or away from an unpleasant situation. A few primary *drives* are based on physiological needs, but all human motives are affected by psychological, social, and cultural factors. Motivation may be *intrinsic*, for the inherent pleasure of an activity, or *extrinsic*, for external rewards.

The Hungry Animal: Motives to Eat

- Overweight and obesity are not simply a result of failed willpower, emotional disturbance, or overeating. Hunger, weight, and eating are regulated by a set of bodily mechanisms, such as *basal metabolism rate* and number of fat cells, that keep people close to their genetically influenced *set point*. Genes influence body shape, distribution of fat, and whether the body will convert excess calories into fat. Genes may also account for certain types of obesity; for example, the *ob* gene regulates *leptin*, which enables the hypothalamus to regulate appetite and metabolism. The hormone ghrelin spurs appetite and leptin reduces it.

- Genetics alone cannot explain why rates of overweight and obesity are rising all over the world among all social classes, ethnicities, and ages. The reasons reflect the interaction of an evolved genetic disposition to gain weight when rich food is plentiful and an environment that provides cheap, varied, high-calorie food and rewards sedentary lifestyles.

Eating habits and activity levels are also affected by cultural standards of what the ideal body should look like—heavy or thin, soft or muscular.

- When genetic predispositions clash with culture, physical and mental problems can result. In cultures that foster overeating and regard overweight as a sign of attractiveness and health, obesity is acceptable, but obesity increases the risk of various physical problems. In cultures that foster unrealistically thin bodies, eating disorders increase, especially *bulimia* and *anorexia*. These disorders are far more common in women than in men, but as pressures on men to have muscular bodies have increased, rates of body-image problems and eating disorders among men are increasing too.

The Social Animal: Motives to Love

- All human beings have a need for connection, attachment, and love. Psychologists who study love distinguish *passionate* (*"romantic"*) *love* from *companionate love*. Biologically oriented researchers believe that the neurological origins of passionate love begin in the baby's attachment to the mother. Attachment stimulates the release of various brain chemicals, including the hormone vasopressin and oxytocin, associated with bonding and trust, and *endorphins*, which create rushes of pleasure and reward.

- Two strong predictors of whom people will love are *proximity* and *similarity*. Once in love, people form different kinds of attachments. *Attachment theory* views adult love relationships, like those of infants, as being secure, avoidant, or anxious. People's attachment styles tend to be stable from childhood to adulthood and affect their close relationships.

- For most people, love consists of passion, intimacy, and commitment. Men and women are equally likely to feel love and need attachment, but they differ, on average, in how they express feelings of love and how they define intimacy. In Western societies, women often express love in words, whereas men express it in actions. But as women have entered the workforce in large numbers and pragmatic (extrinsic) reasons for marriage have faded, the two sexes have become more alike in endorsing romantic love as a requirement for marriage.

The Erotic Animal: Motives for Sex

- Biological research finds that testosterone influences sexual desire in both sexes, although hormones do not cause sexual behaviour in a simple, direct way. The Kinsey surveys of male and female sexuality and the laboratory research of William Masters and Virginia Johnson showed that physiologically, there is no right kind of orgasm for women to have, and that both sexes are capable of sexual arousal and response.

- Some researchers believe that men have a higher frequency of many sexual behaviours, on average, because they have a stronger sex drive than women do. Others believe that gender differences in sexual motivation and behaviour are a result of differences in roles, cultural norms, and opportunity. A compromise view is that men's sexuality is more biologically influenced than is women's, whereas female sexuality is more governed by circumstances, relationships, and cultural norms.

- Men and women have sex to satisfy many different psychological motives, including pleasure, intimacy, coping, self-affirmation, the partner's approval, or peer approval. Extrinsic motives for sex, such as the need for approval, are associated with riskier sexual behaviour than intrinsic motives are. Both sexes may agree to intercourse for nonsexual motives: Men sometimes feel obligated to make a move to prove their masculinity, and women sometimes feel obliged to give in to preserve the relationship. People's motives for consenting to unwanted sex vary depending on their feelings of security and commitment in the relationship.

- A major gender difference in sexual experience has to do with rape and perceptions of sexual coercion: What many women regard as coercion is not always seen as such by men. Men who rape do so for diverse reasons, including peer pressure; anger, revenge, or a desire to humiliate the victim; narcissism and hostility toward women; and sometimes sadism.

- Cultures differ widely in determining what parts of the body people learn are erotic, which sexual acts are considered erotic or repulsive, and whether sex itself is good or bad. Cultures transmit these ideas through *gender roles* and *sexual scripts*, which specify appropriate behaviour during courtship and sex, depending on a person's gender, age, and sexual orientation.

- As in the case of love, gender differences (and growing similarities) in sexuality are strongly affected by cultural and economic factors, such as the ratio of women to men and the resulting availability of partners. As gender roles have become more alike, so has the sexual behaviour of men and women, with women wanting sex for pleasure rather than as a bargaining chip. Big cities have many different "sex markets," geographical and cultural areas in which people seek partners, and people tend not to cross them.

- As discussed in "Biology and Sexual Orientation," traditional psychological explanations for homosexuality have not been supported. Genetic and hormonal factors seem to be involved, although the evidence is stronger for gay men than for lesbians. The larger the number of older biological brothers a man has, the greater his likelihood of becoming homosexual, suggesting that prenatal events might be involved. In spite of the evidence of a biological contribution to sexual orientation, there is great variation in the expression of homosexuality around the world, and women's sexual orientation seems more fluid than men's. Research on this issue is sensitive because people's reactions to scientific findings on the origins of homosexuality are affected by their emotional and religious feelings about the topic.

The Competent Animal: Motives to Achieve

- The study of achievement motivation began with research using the *Thematic Apperception Test (TAT)*. People who are motivated by a high *need for achievement* set high but realistic standards for success and excellence. The TAT has empirical problems, but it launched the study of the factors that motivate achievement.

- People achieve more when they have specific, focused goals; when they set high but achievable goals for themselves; and when they have *approach goals* (seeking a positive outcome) rather than *avoidance goals* (avoiding an unpleasant outcome). People who focus on approach goals have greater well-being, better health, and even better intimate and sexual relationships than those who focus on avoidance goals.

- Work motivation also depends on circumstances of the job itself. Working conditions that promote motivation and satisfaction are those that provide workers with a sense of meaningfulness, control, variation in tasks, clear rules, feedback, and social support. *Incentive pay* is more effective than predictable raises in elevating work motivation. Other conditions that affect people's work motivation are the gender ratio of members in an occupation and whether the job provides opportunities for promotion and success.

Motives, Values, And Well-Being

• Satisfaction and well-being increase when people enjoy the intrinsic satisfaction of an activity and when their goals and values are in harmony. Having positive, intrinsically enjoyable experiences makes most people happier than having things. In an *approach–approach conflict*, a person is equally attracted to two goals. In an *avoidance–avoidance conflict*, a person is equally repelled by two goals. An *approach–avoidance conflict* is the most difficult to resolve because the person is both attracted to and repelled by the same goal. Prolonged conflict can lead to physical symptoms and reduced well-being.

• Abraham Maslow believed that human motives could be ranked in a *hierarchy of needs*, from basic biological needs for survival to higher psychological needs for self-actualization. This popular theory has not been well supported empirically. A more recent approach suggests that people have four major psychological needs, for autonomy, relatedness, competence, and self-esteem.

Taking Psychology with You

• Motivational research suggests that people are happiest and most fulfilled when they seek intrinsically pleasurable activities, focus on learning, improve their working conditions, resolve competing goals, and choose the goals that reflect their most important values.

Key Terms

motivation **419**
intrinsic motivation **420**
extrinsic motivation **420**
set point **420**

bulimia **427**
anorexia **427**
endorphins **431**
proximity effect **431**

similarity effect **432**
attachment theory of love **432**
sexual script **441**

Thematic Apperception Test (TAT) **448**
approach goals **448**
avoidance goals **448**

13 Development over the Lifespan

Ask questions. . . be willing to wonder

How does a baby's thinking differ from an adult's?

———

What makes the years from 18 to 25 unlike adolescence or adulthood?

———

Is mental decline inevitable in old age?

———

Do childhood experiences affect us for our entire lives?

In 1996, Arceli Keh, then age 63, gave birth to a healthy baby girl. The child was conceived through in vitro fertilization, with sperm from Keh's 60-year-old husband and an egg donated by a younger woman. Keh and her family were delighted, but some fertility experts and ethicists had misgivings. Many said that 50 or 55 should be the maximum age for inseminating a woman with donor eggs, not because older women can't be good mothers, but because having a teenager when you are in your 70s would be difficult for mother and child. How, they worried, would Arceli Keh, at age 78, manage a teenage girl? In 2011, Arceli Keh *was* 78, her husband 75, their daughter Cynthia 14, and all were doing well. "Having my baby gave me a new lease on life," Keh told a reporter. "I'm more energetic than most women my age because I have to be."

Arceli Keh soon lost her title of "world's oldest mother" to Carmela Bousada, who, after being inseminated with an embryo from donor egg and sperm, delivered twin boys a week before her 67th birthday. (When her own mother died at the age of 101, Bousada decided it was "the right time" to have children.) In contrast to Keh's experience, Bousada, who had no husband or other children, died of stomach cancer when her twins were only three years old.

When, if ever, is a human being "too old" to have a baby, whether by in vitro fertilization or adoption? Would it make any difference if the mother were "only" 55 years old? 50? Do you feel the same about older fathers as you do about older mothers? Consider that former Prime Minister Pierre Trudeau became a father at 71 or that Guinness World Records reports that the oldest father in the world was almost 93 years old (92 years, 10 months)! Is there a "right time" to become a parent? For that matter, is there a right time to do anything in life—go to school, get married, retire, . . . die?

The universal human journey from birth to death was once far more predictable than it is today. Getting an education, choosing a job, starting a family, and advancing up the ladder to retirement were all events that tended to happen in sequence. But because of demographic changes, an unpredictable economy, advances in reproductive technology, and many other forces, millions of people are now doing things out of order, if they do them at all. Today, getting an education, having children, changing careers, or starting a family may occur in almost any decade of adulthood.

Developmental psychologists study physiological and cognitive changes across the lifespan and how these are affected by a person's genetic predispositions, culture, circumstances, and experiences. Some focus on children's mental and social development, including **socialization**, the process by which children

socialization The process by which children learn the behaviours, attitudes, and expectations required of them by their society or culture.

461

Development depends on the genetic hand you are dealt at birth, the resources and opportunities your parents provide for you, experiences that happen to you, and the unexpected events of history. What futures might you imagine for these three children? At the end of this chapter, you'll see who they are.

Left: Corbis. Centre: AP Images. Right: Getty Images.

learn the rules and behaviour expected of them by society. Others specialize in the study of adolescents, adults, or the very old. In this chapter, we will explore some of their major findings, starting at the very beginning of human development, with the period before birth, and continuing through adulthood into old age.

Learning Objectives

1. List the stages of development from fertilization to birth.

2. Compile a list of factors (with examples) that can affect prenatal development.

3. Discuss how culture can affect the development of infants.

4. Analyze the differences among the varieties of infant attachment.

From Conception through the First Year

A baby's development, before and after birth, is a marvel of *maturation*, the sequential unfolding of genetically influenced behaviour and physical characteristics. In only 9 months of a mother's pregnancy, a fetus grows from a dot this big (.) to a squalling bundle of energy who looks just like Aunt Sarah. In another 15 months, that bundle of energy grows into a babbling toddler who is curious about everything. No other time in human development brings so many changes so fast.

Prenatal Development

Prenatal development begins at fertilization, when the male sperm unites with the female ovum (egg); the fertilized single-celled egg is called a *zygote*. The zygote soon begins to divide, and in 10 to 14 days, it has become a cluster of cells that attaches itself to the wall of the uterus. The outer portion of this cluster will form part of the placenta and umbilical cord, and when implantation is completed about two weeks after fertilization, the inner portion becomes the *embryo*. The placenta, connected to the embryo by the umbilical cord, serves as the growing embryo's link for food from the mother. It allows nutrients to enter and wastes to exit, and it screens out some, but not all, harmful substances. At eight weeks after conception, the embryo is only 4 cm long. During the fourth to eighth weeks, the hormone testosterone is secreted by the rudimentary testes in embryos that are genetically male; without this hormone, the embryo will develop to be anatomically female. After eight weeks, the organism, now called a *fetus*, further develops the organs and systems that existed in rudimentary form in the embryonic stage. ✳

Although the womb is a fairly sturdy protector of the growing embryo or fetus, the prenatal environment—which is influenced by the mother's own health, allergies, and diet—can affect the course of development; for example, by predisposing an infant to later obesity or immune problems (Coe & Lubach, 2008). Most people don't realize it, but fathers play a role in prenatal development, too. Because of genetic mutations in sperm, fathers over 50 have three times the risk of conceiving a child who develops schizophrenia as fathers under age 25 do (Malaspina, 2001); teenage fathers have an increased risk that their babies will be born prematurely or have low birth weight; babies of men exposed to solvents and other chemicals in the workplace are more likely to be miscarried or stillborn, or to develop cancer later in life; and having an older father increases the probability that a child will have autism or bipolar disorder (Frans et al., 2008; Kong et al., 2012; Reichenberg et al., 2006).

During a woman's pregnancy, some harmful influences can cross the placental barrier and affect the fetus (O'Rahilly & Müller, 2001). These influences include the following:

1 **German measles** (rubella), especially early in the pregnancy, can affect the fetus's eyes, ears, and heart. The most common consequence is deafness. Rubella is preventable if the mother is vaccinated at least three months before pregnancy.

2 **X-rays or other radiation, pollutants, and toxic substances** can cause fetal deformities and cognitive abnormalities that can last throughout life. Exposure to lead is associated with attention problems and lower IQ scores, as is exposure to mercury (found most commonly in contaminated fish), pesticides, and high air pollution (Newland & Rasmussen, 2003; Perera et al., 2006; Raloff, 2011; see Chapter 3).

3 **Sexually transmitted diseases** can cause mental retardation, blindness, and other physical disorders. Genital herpes affects the fetus only if the mother has an outbreak at the time of delivery, which exposes the newborn to the virus as the baby passes through the birth canal. (This risk can be avoided by having a caesarean section.) HIV, the virus that causes AIDS, can also be transmitted to the fetus, especially if the mother has developed AIDS and has not been treated during pregnancy.

4 **Cigarette smoking** during pregnancy increases the likelihood of miscarriage, premature birth, an abnormal fetal heartbeat, and an underweight baby. The negative effects may last long after birth, showing up in increased rates of infant sickness, sudden infant death syndrome (SIDS), and, in later childhood, hyperactivity, learning difficulties, asthma, and even antisocial behaviour (Button, Thapar, & McGuffin, 2005). Despite these dangers, more than half of all smokers continue to smoke while pregnant (Schneider et al., 2010), with approximately 5% of women smoking more than 10 cigarettes per day (Public Health Agency of Canada, 2009). These numbers are alarming, when you consider that between 23–28% of pregnant women who smoke do not report that they smoke when asked (Dietz et al., 2010; Webb et al., 2003).

5 **Maternal stress** can affect the fetus, increasing the risk of later cognitive and emotional problems and vulnerability to adult diseases such as hypertension (Talge, Neal, & Glover, 2007; Weinstock, 2005; see Chapter 11). Babies of mothers who developed post-traumatic stress disorder in the aftermath of the World Trade Center attacks on 9/11 were more likely to have abnormal cortisol levels themselves at one year of age, and also to weigh less at birth, both indicators of future health problems (Yehuda et al., 2005).

✳ **Explore** the **Concept**
Virtual Brain: Development of the Brain in **MyPsychLab**

6 **Drugs** can be harmful to the fetus, whether they are illicit ones such as cocaine and heroin, or legal substances such as alcohol, antibiotics, antidepressants, antihistamines, tranquilizers, acne medication, prescription opiate painkillers, and diet pills (Healy, 2012; Lester, LaGasse, & Seifer, 1998; Stanwood & Levitt, 2001). Regular consumption of alcohol can kill neurons throughout the fetus's developing brain and impair the child's later mental abilities, attention span, and academic achievement (Ikonomidou et al., 2000; Streissguth, 2001). Having more than two drinks a day significantly increases the risk of *fetal alcohol syndrome (FAS)* or *fetal alcohol spectrum disorder (FASD)*, which is associated with low birth weight, a smaller brain, facial deformities, lack of coordination, and developmental disabilities.

Before you think that FASD is not a problem in Canada—think again. More than 75% of Canadian women report having consumed alcohol during the last year and over 50% of all pregnancies are unplanned (Canadian Addictions Survey, 2004). Further, FASD is the leading known cause of developmental disability in Canada (Public Health Agency of Canada, 2009; Poole, 2008). However, FAS and FASD are two of the most preventable of birth defects. The Public Health Agency of Canada has put forth a comprehensive four-part plan to reduce FASD and its impact in the community, not only through pre-conception education but with support during pregnancy and afterwards (Poole, 2008). Although the rate of FAS and FASD has not appreciably decreased in 20 years (Habbick et al., 1996), it is clear that early intervention, education, and ongoing support are key ways to reduce frequency and improve outcomes for all involved.

In addition to avoiding these teratogens, a pregnant woman can do much to have a healthy baby. She can maintain a healthy weight, take prenatal vitamins (especially folic acid, which prevents neural defects in the brain and spinal cord), and get regular prenatal care (Abu-Saad & Fraser, 2010).

The Infant's World

Newborn babies could never survive on their own, but they are far from being passive and inert. Many abilities, tendencies, and characteristics are universal in human beings and are present at birth or develop very early, given certain experiences. Newborns begin life with several *motor reflexes*, automatic behaviours that are necessary for survival. They will suck on anything suckable, such as a nipple or finger. They will tightly grasp a finger pressed on their tiny palms. They will turn their heads toward a touch on the cheek or corner of the mouth and search for something to suck on, a handy rooting reflex that allows them to find the breast or bottle. Many of these reflexes eventually disappear, but others—such as the knee-jerk, eye-blink, and sneeze reflexes—remain.

Infants are born with a grasping reflex; they will cling to any offered finger. And they need the comfort of touch, which their adult caregivers love to provide.

Tony Wear/Shutterstock

Babies are also equipped with a set of inborn perceptual abilities (see Chapter 6). They can see, hear, touch, smell, and taste (bananas and sugar water are in, rotten eggs are out). A newborn's visual focus range is only about 20 centimetres, the average distance between the baby and the face of the person holding the baby, but visual ability develops rapidly. Newborns can distinguish contrasts, shadows, and edges. And they can discriminate their mother or other primary caregiver on the basis of smell, sight, or sound almost immediately. Even more impressive, as mentioned in Chapter 3, babies are born with an interest in novelty and some basic cognitive skills, including a fundamental sense of numbers (they know that three things are more than two things) (Izard et al., 2009).

Experience, however, plays a crucial role in shaping an infant's mind, brain, and gene expression right from the get-go. Infants who get little touching will grow more slowly and release less growth hormone than their amply cuddled peers, and throughout their lives, they have stronger reactions to stress and are more prone to depression and its cognitive deficits (Diamond & Amso, 2008; Field, 2009). Although infants everywhere develop according to the same maturational sequence, many aspects of their development depend on cultural customs that govern how their parents hold, touch, feed, and talk to them (Rogoff, 2003). For example, in Canada and other western countries, babies are expected to sleep for eight uninterrupted hours by the age of four or five months. This milestone is considered a sign of neurological maturity, although many babies wail when the parent puts them in the crib at night and leaves the room. But among Mayan peoples, rural Italians, African villagers, Indian Rajput villagers, and urban Japanese, this nightly clash of wills rarely occurs because the infant sleeps with the mother for the first few years of life, waking and nursing about every four hours. These differences in babies' sleep arrangements reflect cultural and parental values. Mothers in these cultures believe that sleeping with the baby forges a close bond; in contrast, many urban North American and German parents believe it is important to foster the child's independence as soon as possible (Keller et al., 2005; Morelli et al., 1992). However, family sleeping arrangements may be more fluid that we thought—in a study of over 900 North American families, almost half reported that their children slept with them at least some of the time (Barajas et al., 2011).

Most Navajo babies calmly accept being strapped to a cradle board (left), whereas other North American babies will often protest vigorously (right). Yet, despite cultural differences in such practices, babies everywhere eventually sit up and walk.

Doris Pinney Brenner

Attachment

Emotional attachment is a universal capacity of all primates and is crucial for health and survival all through life. The mother is usually the first and primary object of attachment for an infant, but in many cultures (and other species), babies become just as attached to their fathers, siblings, and grandparents (Hrdy, 1999).

Interest in the importance of early attachment began with the work of British psychiatrist John Bowlby (1969, 1973), who observed the devastating effects on babies raised in orphanages without touches or snuggling, and on other children raised in conditions of severe deprivation or neglect. The babies were physically healthy but emotionally despairing, remote, and listless. By becoming attached to their caregivers, Bowlby said, children gain a secure base from which they can explore the environment and a haven of safety to return to when they are afraid. Ideally, infants will find a balance between feeling securely attached to the caregiver and feeling free to explore and learn in new environments. Recent research suggests that Bowlby's observations remain valid (Gunnar et al., 2007). Reactive Attachment Disorder, a failure to form normal attachment with primary caregivers, has been documented by following the outcomes of children raised in orphanages under conditions of severe deprivation (O'Connor et al., 2000). Long-term study of these children suggests that there are profound, long-lasting emotional and cognitive consequences of early deprivation (Colvert, Rutter, Beckett, et al., 2008; Colvert, Rutter, Kreppner, et al., 2008).

Contact Comfort. Attachment begins with physical touching and cuddling between infant and parent. **Contact comfort**, the pleasure of being touched and held, is not only crucial for newborns; it continues to be important throughout life, releasing a flood of pleasure-producing and stress-reducing endorphins (see Chapter 12). In hospital settings, even the mildest touch by a nurse or physician on a patient's arm or forehead is reassuring psychologically and lowers blood pressure.

Margaret and Harry Harlow first demonstrated the importance of contact comfort by raising infant rhesus monkeys with two kinds of artificial mothers (Harlow, 1958; Harlow & Harlow, 1966). One, which they called the "wire mother," was a forbidding construction of wires and warming lights, with a milk bottle connected to it. The other, the "cloth mother," was constructed of wire but covered in foam rubber and cuddly

contact comfort In primates, the innate pleasure derived from close physical contact; it is the basis of the infant's first attachment.

FIGURE 13.1 The Comfort of Contact

Infants need cuddling as much as they need food. In Margaret and Harry Harlow's studies, infant rhesus monkeys were reared with a cuddly terry-cloth "mother" and with a bare wire "mother" that provided milk (left). The infants would cling to the terry-cloth mother when they were not being fed. But when an unfamiliar and scary toy (a mechanical spider or a large teddy bear) was placed in the enclosure, the infant monkey would run to the terry-cloth mother for comfort.

Science Source

◉ ⌐ **Watch** the **Video**
Classic Footage of Harlow's Monkeys: Contact Comfort in **MyPsychLab**

◉ ⌐ **Watch** the **Video**
Separation Anxiety in **MyPsychLab**

STYLES OF ATTACHMENT

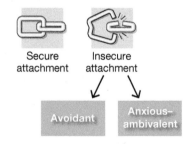

Secure attachment   Insecure attachment

Avoidant   Anxious–ambivalent

separation anxiety The distress that most children develop, at about six to eight months of age, when their primary caregivers temporarily leave them with strangers.

terry-cloth (see Figure 13.1). At the time, many psychologists thought that babies become attached to their mothers simply because mothers provide food (Blum, 2002). But the Harlows' baby monkeys ran to the terry-cloth mother when they were frightened or startled, and snuggling up to it calmed them down. Human children also seek contact comfort when they are in an unfamiliar situation, are scared by a nightmare, or fall and hurt themselves. ◉

Separation and Security. Once babies are emotionally attached to the mother or other caregiver, separation can be a wrenching experience. Between six and eight months of age, babies become wary or fearful of strangers. They wail if they are put in an unfamiliar setting or are left with an unfamiliar person. And they show **separation anxiety** if the primary caregiver temporarily leaves them. This reaction usually continues until the middle of the second year, but many children show signs of distress until they are about three years old (Hrdy, 1999). All children go through this phase, though cultural child-rearing practices influence how strongly the anxiety is felt and how long it lasts (see Figure 13.2). In cultures where babies are raised with lots of adults and other children, separation anxiety is not as intense or as long-lasting as it can be in cultures where babies form attachments primarily or exclusively with the mother (Rothbaum et al., 2000). ◉

To study the nature of the attachment between mothers and babies, Mary Ainsworth (1973, 1979) devised an experimental method called the *Strange Situation*. A mother brings her baby into an unfamiliar room containing lots of toys. After a while, a stranger comes in and attempts to play with the child. The mother leaves the baby with the stranger. She then returns and plays with the child, and the stranger leaves. Finally, the mother leaves the baby alone for three minutes and returns. In each case, observers note how the baby behaves with the mother, with the stranger, and when the baby is alone.

Ainsworth divided the children into three categories on the basis of their reactions to the Strange Situation. Some babies were *securely attached*: They cry or protest if the parent left the room; they welcome her back and then play happily again; they are clearly more attached to the mother than to the stranger. Other babies were *insecurely attached*, and this insecurity can take two forms. Some children may be *avoidant*, not caring if the mother leaves the room, making little effort to seek contact with her on her return, and treating the stranger about the same as the mother. Or the child may be *anxious* or *ambivalent*, resisting contact with the mother at reunion but protesting loudly if she leaves. Some anxious-ambivalent babies cry to be picked up and then demand to be put down or they may behave as if they are angry with the mother and resist her efforts to comfort them.

FIGURE 13.2 The Rise and Fall of Separation Anxiety
At around six months of age, many babies begin to show separation anxiety when the person who is their main source of attachment tries handing them over to someone else or leaves the room. This anxiety typically peaks at about a year of age and then steadily declines. But the proportion of children responding this way varies across cultures. It is high among rural African children and low among children raised in a communal Israeli kibbutz, where children become attached to many adults. (Data from Kagan, Kearsley, & Zelazo, 1978.)

What Causes Insecure Attachment? Ainsworth believed that the difference between secure, avoidant, and anxious-ambivalent attachment lies primarily in the way mothers treat their babies during the first year. Mothers who are sensitive to their babies' needs, she said, create securely attached infants; mothers who are insensitive to their babies create insecurely attached infants. To many, this implied that babies needed exactly the right kind of mothering from day one to become securely attached, and that putting a child in daycare would retard this development—notions that have caused considerable insecurity among mothers!

Ainsworth's measure of attachment, however, did not take the baby's experience into account. Babies who become attached to many adults, because they live in large extended families or have spent a lot of time with adults in daycare, may seem to be avoidant in the Strange Situation because they don't panic when their mothers leave. But perhaps they have simply learned to be comfortable with strangers. Moreover, although there is a modest correlation between a mother's sensitivity to her child and the security of her child's attachment, this doesn't tell us which causes what, or whether something else causes both sensitivity and secure attachment. Programs designed to help new mothers become less anxious and more attuned to their babies do help some moms become more sensitive, but these programs only modestly affect the child's degree of secure attachment (Bakermans-Kranenburg et al., 2008).

The emphasis on maternal sensitivity also overlooks the fact that most children, all over the world, form a secure attachment to their mothers in spite of wide variations in child-rearing practices (LeVine & Norman, 2008; Mercer, 2006). For instance, German babies are frequently left on their own for a few hours at a stretch by mothers who believe that even babies should become self-reliant. And among the Efe of Africa, babies spend about half their time away from their mothers in the care of older children and other adults (Tronick, Morelli, & Ivey, 1992). Yet German and Efe children are not insecure, and they develop as normally as children who spend more time with their mother.

Likewise, time spent in daycare—from less than 10 hours a week to more than 30—has no effect on the security of a child's attachment (McKim et al., 1999; NICHD Early Child Care Research Network, 2006). In fact, children in daycare did better on some measures of cognition and language skills. Recently, Canadian researchers examined the question again and compared babies whose mothers went back to work before they were a year old with those who stayed home for longer (Baker & Milligan, 2010). They found very few differences between the two groups of children in terms of motor skill, temperament, or acquisition of developmental milestones. ◉

What factors, then, do promote insecure attachment?

- *Abandonment and deprivation in the first year or two of life*. Institutionalized babies are more likely than adopted children to have later problems with

◉ **Watch** the **Video**
Parent-Child Attachments: Ross Thompson in **MyPsychLab**

Longitudinal studies find that good daycare does not affect the security of children's attachments and often produces many social and intellectual benefits.

Getty Images, Inc.

attachment, whereas babies adopted before age 1 or 2 eventually become as securely attached as their non-adopted peers (Rutter et al., 2004; van den Dries et al., 2009).

- *Parenting that is abusive, neglectful, or erratic because the parent is chronically irresponsible or clinically depressed.* A South African research team observed 147 mothers with their two-month-old infants and followed up when the babies were 18 months old. Many of the mothers who had suffered from postpartum depression became either too intrusive with their infants or too remote and insensitive. In turn, their babies were more likely to be insecurely attached at 18 months (Tomlinson, Cooper, & Murray, 2005).

- *The child's own genetically influenced temperament.* Babies who are fearful and prone to crying from birth are more likely to show insecure behaviour in the Strange Situation, suggesting that their later insecure attachment may reflect a temperamental predisposition (Gillath et al., 2008; Seifer et al., 1996; see Chapter 14).

- *Stressful circumstances in the child's family.* Infants and young children may temporarily shift from secure to insecure attachment, becoming clingy and fearful of being left alone, if their families are undergoing a period of stress, as during parental divorce or a parent's chronic illness (Belsky et al., 1996; Mercer, 2006).

The bottom line, however, is that infants are biologically disposed to become attached to their caregivers. Normal, healthy attachment will occur within a wide range of cultural, family, and individual variations in child-rearing customs. Although, sadly, things can go wrong in prenatal development and in the first year after birth, the plasticity of the brain and human resilience can often overcome early deprivation or even harm. We will revisit the issue of resilience at the end of this chapter, and in "Taking Psychology with You" we will consider other information that might alleviate the anxieties many parents feel about whether they are doing the right thing. ◉

◉—|Watch the Video
Challenges of Becoming a New Parent in **MyPsychLab**

Recite & Review

Recite: We hope you are feeling secure enough to state out loud what you know about *socialization,* prenatal development, the major kinds of harmful influences on a fetus, infant abilities, *contact comfort, separation anxiety,* secure and insecure attachment, and factors that promote insecure attachment.

Review: Next, reread this section.

Now take this *Quick Quiz:*

1. Name as many potentially harmful influences on fetal development as you can.

2. Rachel is playing happily on a jungle gym at her daycare centre when she falls off and badly scrapes her knee. She runs to her caregiver for a consoling hug. Rachel seeks _____.

3. *True or false*: To develop normally, infants must sleep in their own cribs, apart from their mothers.

4. A baby left in the Strange Situation does not protest when his mother leaves the room, and he seems to ignore her when she returns. According to Ainsworth, what style of attachment does this behaviour reflect?

5. In Question 4, what else besides the child's style of attachment could account for the child's reaction?

Answers:

1. German measles early in pregnancy; exposure to radiation or toxic substances such as lead or mercury; sexually transmitted diseases; the mother's use of cigarettes, alcohol, or other drugs 2. contact comfort 3. false 4. insecure (avoidant) 5. the child's own temperament and familiarity with being temporarily left alone

from that experience to distinguish the intentional versus accidental reaches of others (Sommerville, Woodward, & Needham, 2005).

4 **Cognitive development is influenced by a child's culture.** One of Piaget's contemporaries, the Russian psychologist Lev Vygotsky (1896–1934), disagreed with Piaget and emphasized the sociocultural influences on children's cognitive development. Vygotsky (1962) believed that children develop mental representations of the world through culture, language, and the environment, and that adults play a major role in this process by constantly guiding and teaching their children. As a result, he said, instead of going through invariant stages, a child's cognitive development may proceed in any number of directions. Vygotsky was correct. Culture—the world of tools, language, rituals, beliefs, games, and social institutions—shapes and structures children's cognitive development, fostering some abilities and not others (Tomasello, 2000). For instance, nomadic hunters excel in spatial abilities, because spatial orientation is crucial for finding water and successful hunting routes. In contrast, children who live in settled agricultural communities, such as the Baoulé of the Ivory Coast, develop rapidly in the ability to quantify but are much slower in developing spatial reasoning.

Despite these modifications, Piaget left an enduring legacy: the insight that children are not passive vessels into which education and experience are poured. Children actively interpret their worlds, using their developing abilities to assimilate new information and figure things out.

Experience and culture influence cognitive development. Children who work with clay, wood, and other materials, such as this young potter in India, tend to understand the concept of conservation sooner than children who have not had this kind of experience.

Science Source

Recite & Review

Recite: Use your human capacity for language (and thought) to speak aloud what you have learned about the meaning of *language*; the debate between Chomsky and his critics over whether there is a universal grammar; *telegraphic speech*, Piaget's stages, *object permanence*, the principle of *conservation*, the *theory of mind*, and the major modifications of Piaget's theory.

Review: Next, reread this section.

Now take this *Quick Quiz:*

1. The central distinction between human language and other communication systems is that language (a) allows for the generation of an infinite number of new utterances, (b) is spoken, (c) is learned only after explicit training, (d) expresses meaning directly.
2. Some of Chomsky's critics believe that instead of figuring out grammatical rules when acquiring language, children learn _____.
3. Understanding that two rows of six dimes are equal in number, even if one row is flat and the other is stacked up, is an example of _____.
4. Understanding that a toy exists even after mom puts it in her purse is an example of

   _____.
5. A five-year-old boy who tells his dad that "Sally said she saw a bunny but she was lying" has developed a _____.

Answers:

1. a 2. the probability that any given word or syllable will follow another one 3. conservation 4. object permanence 5. theory of mind

Moral Development

How do children learn to tell right from wrong, resist the temptation to behave selfishly, and obey the rules of social conduct? In the 1960s, Lawrence Kohlberg (1964), inspired by Piaget's work, argued that children's ability to understand right from wrong, and other forms of moral reasoning, evolved along with the rest of their cognitive abilities, progressing through three levels. In studies of how children reason about moral dilemmas, he found that very young children obey rules because they fear being punished if they disobey, and later because they think it is in their best interest to obey. At about age 10, their moral judgments shift to ones based on conformity and loyalty to others, and then to an understanding of the rule of law. In adulthood, a few individuals go on to develop a moral standard based on universal human rights. Martin Luther King, Jr. fought against laws supporting segregation, Mohandas Gandhi advocated nonviolent solutions to injustice in India, and Nellie McClung fought for women's rights.

Kohlberg was right that moral reasoning ability increases during the school years. Unfortunately so do cheating, lying, cruelty, and the cognitive ability to rationalize these actions. Accordingly, developmental psychologists today place greater emphasis on how children learn to regulate their own emotions and behaviour (Mischel & Ayduk, 2004). Most children learn to inhibit their wishes to hit their younger siblings, steal a classmate's toy, or scream at the top of their lungs if they don't get their way. The child's emerging ability to understand right from wrong, and to behave accordingly, depends on the emergence of conscience and moral emotions such as shame, guilt, and empathy (Kochanska et al., 2005).

As we saw in discussing criticisms of Piaget's theory, even very young children are capable of feeling empathy for others and taking another person's point of view. Children do not obey rules only because they are afraid of what will happen to them if they disobey, but also because they understand right and wrong. By five, they know it is wrong to hurt someone even if a teacher tells them to (Turiel, 2002). Therefore, many psychologists conclude that the capacity for differentiating right from wrong may be inborn. Evolutionary psychologists argue that this "moral sense" underlies the basic beliefs, judgments, and behaviour that are considered moral almost everywhere, and that it originated in cooperative, altruistic strategies that permitted our forebears to resolve conflicts and get along (Delton et al., 2011; Krebs, 2008).

Can the moral sense and a desire to behave well with others be nurtured or extinguished by specific methods of child rearing? For decades, most developmental psychologists assumed that the answer was "Of course!" and they set about trying to pinpoint which parental techniques create well-behaved, kind, unselfish children. Then came a flood of behavioural-genetic studies that led to a very different assumption: The effects of the parents' methods depend (of course!) on the kind of child they have—one who heeds discipline or one who is resistant and hostile.

How do children internalize moral rules? How do they learn that cheating, stealing, and grabbing a younger sibling's toy are wrong?

Getty Images, Inc.

Today, many researchers are seeking a middle ground by studying gene-environment interactions (Schmidt et al., 2009). As we discuss in Chapter 15, aggressive, antisocial adolescents often have a history of maltreatment and abuse in childhood *and* a gene variant linked to aggressive behaviour. Good parenting, however, can help to override a genetic vulnerability. One controversial hypothesis suggests that infants and toddlers who show high levels of distress and irritability are actually more responsive to, and influenced by, styles of parenting than easygoing babies are. Easygoing babies are "dandelions"; they survive in almost any circumstances they encounter, because they are, well, easygoing. "Orchid children," in contrast, are highly sensitive to their environments; under adversity, they wither (Ellis & Boyce, 2008). When temperamentally difficult babies have impatient, rejecting, or coercive parents, they later tend to become aggressive and even more difficult and defiant. When they have patient, supportive, firm parents, they become better natured and happier (Belsky, Bakermans-Kranenburg, & van IJzendoorn, 2007; Belsky & Pluess, 2009b). ◉

Keeping the complexity of this issue in mind, let's look at how parental discipline methods interact with a child's temperament in the development of conscience and moral behaviour.

Getting Children to Be Good. When you did something wrong as a child, did the adults in your family spank you, shout at you, threaten you, or explain the error of your ways? Many parents try to enforce moral standards and good behaviour by relying on **power assertion**, which includes threats, physical punishment, depriving the child of privileges, and generally taking advantage of being bigger, stronger, and more powerful. Of course, a parent may have no alternative other than "Do it because I say so!" if the child is too young to understand a rule or impishly keeps trying to break it. Moreover, the culture and context in which the discipline occurs makes an enormous difference. Is the parent–child relationship fundamentally loving and trusting or is it one full of hostility and fighting? Does the child interpret the parents' actions as being fair and caring, or unfair and cruel?

When power assertion consists of sheer parental bullying, cruel insults ("You are so stupid, I wish you'd never been born"), and frequent physical punishment, it is

◉—Watch the Video
The Real World: Parenting Styles and Socialization in **MyPsychLab**

power assertion A method of child rearing in which the parent uses punishment and authority to correct the child's misbehaviour.

Power assertion is the use of physical force, threats, insults, or other kinds of power to get the child to obey ("Do it because I say so!" "Stop that right now!"). The child may obey, but only when the parent is present—and the child often feels resentful.

Tony Freeman/PhotoEdit Inc.

The parent who uses induction appeals to the child's good nature, empathy, love for the parent, and sense of responsibility toward others and offers explanations of rules ("You're too grown up to behave like that"; "Fighting hurts your little brother"). The child tends to internalize reasons for good behaviour.

Stephanie Rausser/Getty Images

induction A method of child rearing in which the parent appeals to the child's own abilities, sense of responsibility, and feelings for others in correcting the child's misbehaviour.

associated with greater aggressiveness in children and reduced empathy (Alink et al., 2009; Gershoff, 2002; Moore & Pepler, 2006). As we discuss in Chapter 7, physical punishment often backfires, especially when it is used inappropriately or harshly; it spirals out of control, causing the child to become angry and resentful. Moreover, harsh but ineffective discipline methods are often transmitted to the next generation: Aggressive parents teach their children that the way to discipline children is by behaving aggressively (Capaldi et al., 2003).

What is the alternative? In contrast to power assertion, a parent can use **induction**, appealing to the child's own abilities, empathy, helpful nature, affection for others, and sense of responsibility ("You made Doug cry; it's not nice to bite"; "Poking Clementine in her eyes could really hurt her, you don't want to hurt your friend"). Or the parent might appeal to the child's own helpful inclinations ("I know you're a person who likes to be nice to others") rather than citing external reasons to be good ("You'd better be nice or you won't get dessert").

Self-Control and Conscience. One of the most important social-emotional skills that children need to acquire is *self regulation*, the ability to suppress their immediate impulses and wishes. Self regulation predicts a child's ability to *delay gratification* to gain later benefits. The original classic study of delayed gratification used a "marshmallow test": Preschoolers were offered a choice between eating one marshmallow right away or having two marshmallows if they could wait a few minutes while the experimenter stepped out of the room (Mischel, Shoda, & Rodriguez, 1989). Dozens of studies have been done since, including follow-ups on what became of the children in the first experiments, and the results are clear: Children who are able to resist the single marshmallow (or other prize) in favour of getting a larger reward later are better able to control negative emotions, pay attention to the task at hand, and do well in school. Indeed, the early ability to postpone gratification has effects on health, success, and well-being that last for *decades* (Casey et al., 2011; Eigsti et al., 2006; Ponitz et al., 2009).

Children's ability to regulate their impulses and delay gratification is a major milestone in the development of conscience and moral behaviour.

Nancy Richmond/The Image Works

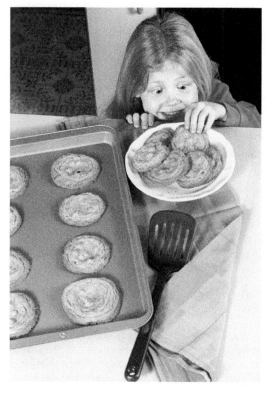

Where does this skill come from? Partly from temperament and personality, because children who can control their emotions and impulses usually do so across situations (de Ridder et al., 2012; Raffaelli, Crockett, & Shen, 2005). Partly from learning: Children and young people can learn to improve their ability to delay gratification by focusing on the later benefits, by distracting themselves from focusing on the appealing prize, and by mentally "cooling" the hot, appealing features of the prize (e.g., by imagining the marshmallow as a cloud or a little cotton ball, rather than as a sweet treat). And partly from the way their parents treat them.

A longitudinal study of 106 preschool children explored the links between parental discipline, the child's self-control, and the emergence of conscience (Kochanska & Knaack, 2003). The children who were most able to regulate their impulses early in life were the least likely to get in trouble later by fighting or destroying things, and the most likely to have a high conscience score. Self regulation was negatively correlated with the mother's use of power assertion, meaning that mothers who ordered their children to "behave" tended to have children who were impulsive and aggressive (see also Alink et al., 2009). However, cause and effect worked in both directions. Some mothers relied on power assertion *because* their children were impulsive, defiant, and aggressive and would not listen to them. This pattern of findings teaches us to avoid oversimplification by concluding that "It's all in what the mother does" or that "It's all in the child's personality." Mothers and children, it seems, raise each other.

Recite & Review

Recite: Exercise self-control by reciting out loud what you know about the development of moral reasoning and its relation to moral emotions and behaviour, "orchid" and "dandelion" children, *power assertion* versus *induction*, and delay of gratification and its benefits.

Review: Next, reread this material.

Now take this *Quick Quiz:*

1. Which method of disciplining a child who is hitting his younger brother is most likely to teach empathy? (a) induction, (b) indulgence, (c) power assertion, (d) spanking

2. What early ability predicts the development of conscience later on?

Answers:

1. a 2. delay of gratification, the ability to control one's immediate impulses and wishes

Learning Objectives

9 Compare and contrast gender identity with gender typing.

10 Describe what an intersex condition is.

11 Provide the biological explanation of why most little boys and girls are "sexist" in their choice of toys, at least for a while. Contrast this with the cognitive explanation for gender segregation.

Gender Development

No parent ever excitedly calls a relative to exclaim, "It's a baby! It's a black-haired baby!" The baby's sex is the first thing everyone notices and announces. How soon do children notice that boys and girls are different sexes and understand which sex they themselves are? How do children learn the rules of masculinity and femininity, the things that boys do that are different from what girls do? Why, as one friend of ours observed, do most preschool children act like the "gender police," insisting, say, on what boys and girls "have to" wear or play with? And why do some children come to feel they don't belong to the sex everyone else thinks they do? ✳

✳ **Explore** the **Concept**
How Does Gender Affect You?
in **MyPsychLab**

Gender Identity

Let's start by clarifying some terms. **Gender identity** refers to a child's sense of being male or female, of belonging to one sex and not the other. **Gender typing** is the process of socializing children into their gender roles, and thus reflects society's ideas about which abilities, interests, traits, and behaviours are appropriately masculine or feminine. A person can have a strong gender identity and not be gender typed: A man may be confident in his maleness and not feel threatened by doing "unmasculine" things such as needlepoint; a woman may be confident in her femaleness and not feel threatened by doing "unfeminine" things such as serving in combat.

In the past, psychologists tried to distinguish the terms *sex* and *gender*, reserving "sex" for the physiological or anatomical attributes of males and females and "gender" for differences that are learned. Thus, they might speak of a sex difference in the frequency of baldness but a gender difference in fondness for romantic comedies. Today, these two terms are often used interchangeably because, as we have noted repeatedly in this book, nature and nurture are inextricably linked (Roughgarden, 2004).

gender identity The fundamental sense of being male or female; it is independent of whether the person conforms to the social and cultural rules of gender.

gender typing The process by which children learn the abilities, interests, and behaviours associated with being masculine or feminine in their culture.

Throughout history and across cultures, some people have broken out of conventional gender categories. Some women have lived as men, as did the eighteenth-century pirates Ann Bonny and Mary Read. Some men have lived as women: The Muxes (pronounced moo-shays) of southern Mexico are males who consider themselves female, live as females, and are a socially accepted category (centre). Increasingly in today's culture, some individuals do not wish to identify as traditionally male or female. Thomas Beatie (right) was born a genetic female and later had a sex-change operation. Because he had a womb, he was able to become the first "pregnant man" in the world.

Left: The Granger Collection. Center: Reuters. Right: AP Images.

intersex conditions (intersexuality) Conditions in which chromosomal or hormonal anomalies cause a child to be born with ambiguous genitals, or genitals that conflict with the infant's chromosomes.

The complexity of sex and gender development is especially apparent in people who do not fit the familiar categories of male and female. Every year, thousands of babies are born with **intersex conditions**, formerly known as *hermaphroditism*. In these conditions, chromosomal or hormonal anomalies cause the child to be born with ambiguous genitals, or genitals that conflict with the infant's chromosomes. A child who is genetically female might be born with an enlarged clitoris that looks like a penis. A child who is genetically male might be born with androgen insensitivity, a condition that causes the external genitals to appear female.

As adults, many intersexed individuals call themselves *transgender*, a term describing a broad category of people who do not fit comfortably into the usual categories of male and female, masculine and feminine. Some transgender people are comfortable living with the physical attributes of both sexes, considering themselves to be "gender queer" and even opting not to be referred to as either *he* or *she*. Some feel uncomfortable in their sex of rearing and wish to be considered a member of the other sex. You have probably also heard the term *transsexual*, describing people who are not intersexed yet who feel that they are male in a female body or vice versa; their gender identity is at odds with their anatomical sex or appearance. Many transsexuals try to make a full transition to the other sex through surgery or hormones. Intersexed people and transsexuals have lived in virtually all cultures throughout history (Denny, 1998; Roughgarden, 2004).

Influences on Gender Development

To understand the typical course of gender development, as well as the variations, developmental psychologists study the interacting influences of biology, cognition, and learning on gender identity and gender typing.

Biological Influences. Starting in the preschool years, boys and girls congregate primarily with other children of their sex, and most prefer the toys and games of their own sex. They will play together if required to, but given their druthers, they usually choose to play with same-sex friends. The kind of play that young boys and girls enjoy also differs, on average. Little boys, like young males in all primate species, are more likely than females to go in for physical roughhousing, risk taking, and aggressive displays. These sex differences occur all over the world, almost regardless of whether adults encourage boys and girls to play together or separate them (Lytton & Romney, 1991; Maccoby, 1998, 2002). Many parents lament that although they try to give their children the same toys, it makes no difference; their sons want trucks and guns and their daughters want dolls.

Biological scientists believe that these play and toy preferences have a basis in prenatal hormones, particularly the presence or absence of prenatal androgens (masculinizing hormones). Girls who were exposed to higher-than-normal prenatal androgens in the womb are later more likely than nonexposed girls to prefer "boys' toys" such as cars and fire engines, and they are also more physically aggressive than other girls (Berenbaum & Bailey, 2003). A study of more than 200 healthy children in the general population also found a relation between fetal testosterone and play styles. (Testosterone is produced in fetuses of both sexes, although it is higher on average in males.) The higher the levels of fetal testosterone, as measured in the amniotic fluid of the children's mothers during pregnancy, the higher the children's later scores on a measure of male-typical play (Auyeung et al., 2009). In studies of rhesus monkeys, who of course are not influenced by their parents' possible gender biases, male monkeys, like human boys, consistently and strongly prefer to play with wheeled toys rather than cuddly plush toys, while female monkeys, like human girls, are more varied in their toy preferences (Hassett, Siebert, & Wallen, 2008). ◉

Do these findings have anything to do with gender identity, the core sense of being male or female? A psychologist reviewed hundreds of cases of children whose sex of rearing was discrepant with their anatomical or genetic sex. He learned that the answer is enormously complex, because a person's gender identity depends on the interactions of genes, prenatal hormones, anatomical structures, and experiences in life (Zucker, 1999). Consider a longitudinal study of 16 genetic males who had a rare condition that caused them to be born without a penis. The babies were otherwise normal males, with testicles and appropriate androgen levels. Two of the boys were raised as male and developed a male gender identity. Fourteen had been socially and surgically assigned to the female sex, according to the custom when they were born. Of those 14, eight have declared themselves male, five are living as females, and one has an unclear gender identity (Reiner & Gearhart, 2004).

Look familiar? In a scene typical of many homes and daycares, the boy likes to play with trucks and the girl with dolls. Whether or not such behaviour is biologically based, the gender rigidity of the early years does not inevitably continue into adulthood unless cultural rules reinforce it.

Michelle D Bridwell/PhotoEdit Inc.

◉—⌐**Watch** the **Video**
Play Styles in **MyPsychLab**

THINKING CRITICALLY

Tolerate uncertainty.

Most people fall into the categories "male" or "female." This makes it difficult for parents and doctors to be certain about how best to treat infants who are born with intersex conditions. Should such infants be assigned surgically to one sex or the other, or should they be left alone until they are grown? In the absence of clear answers, how would you make this decision?

Cognitive Influences. Cognitive psychologists explain the mystery of children's gender segregation and toy and play preferences by studying children's changing cognitive abilities. Even before babies can speak, they can discriminate between the two sexes. By the age of nine months, most babies can discriminate male from female faces (Fagot & Leinbach, 1993), and they can match female faces with female voices (Poulin-Dubois et al., 1994). By the age of 18 to 20 months, most toddlers have a concept of gender labels. They can accurately identify their own gender and that of people in picture books and begin correctly using the words *boy*, *girl*, and *man* (interestingly, *lady* and *woman* come later) (Zosuls et al., 2009).

Once children can label themselves and others consistently as being a boy or a girl, shortly before age two, they change their behaviour to conform to the category they belong to. Many begin to prefer same-sex playmates and sex-traditional toys without being explicitly taught to do so (Martin, Ruble, & Szkrybalo, 2002; Zosuls et al., 2009).

gender schema A cognitive schema (mental network) of knowledge, beliefs, metaphors, and expectations about what it means to be male or female.

They become more gender-typed in their toy play, games, aggressiveness, and verbal skills than children who still cannot consistently label males and females. Most notably, girls stop behaving aggressively (Fagot, 1993). It is as if they go along behaving like boys until they know they are girls. At that moment, they seem to decide: "Girls don't do this. I'm a girl; I'd better not either."

It's great fun to watch three- to five-year-old children struggle to figure out what makes boys and girls different: "The ones with eyelashes are girls; boys don't have eyelashes," said one four-year-old girl to her aunt in explaining her drawing. After dinner at an Italian restaurant, a four-year-old boy told his parents that he'd got the answer: "Men eat pizza and women don't" (Bjorkland, 2000).

By about age five, most children develop a stable gender identity, a sense of themselves as being male or female regardless of what they wear or how they behave. Only then do they understand that what boys and girls do does not necessarily indicate what sex they are: A girl remains a girl even if she can climb a tree (or eats pizza!), and a boy remains a boy even if he has long hair. At this age, children consolidate their knowledge, with all of its mistakes and misconceptions, into a **gender schema**, a mental network of beliefs and expectations about what it means to be male or female and about what each sex is supposed to wear, do, feel, and think (Bem, 1993; Martin & Ruble, 2004). Gender schemas even include metaphors. For example, after age four, children of both sexes will usually say that rough, spiky, black, or mechanical things are male and that soft, pink, fuzzy, or flowery things are female; that black bears are male and pink poodles are female (Leinbach, Hort, & Fagot, 1997). Gender schemas are most rigid between ages five and seven; at this age, it's really hard to dislodge a child's notion of what boys and girls can do (Martin, Ruble, & Szkrybalo, 2002). But the content of these schemas is not innate. A hundred years ago, an article in *The Ladies Home Journal* advised: "The generally accepted rule is pink for the boys, and blue for the girls. The reason is that pink, being a more decided and stronger color, is more suitable for the boy, while blue, which is more delicate and dainty, is prettier for the girl" (Paoletti, 2012). The invention of gender-specific "rules" of clothing for babies and young children was a creation of late twentieth-century marketing.

Many people retain inflexible gender schemas throughout their lives, feeling uncomfortable or angry with those who break out of traditional roles—let alone with transgendered individuals who don't fit either category or want to change the one they grew up with. However, with experience and cognitive sophistication, older children often become more flexible in their gender schemas, especially if they have friends of the other sex and if their families and cultures encourage such flexibility (Martin & Ruble, 2004).

Cultures and religions, too, differ in their schemas for the roles of women and men. In all western industrialized nations, it is taken for granted that women and men alike should be educated; indeed, laws mandate a minimum education for both sexes. But in cultures where female education is prohibited in the name of religious law, as in parts of Pakistan, girls such as Malala Yousafzai who wish to attend school receive death threats and Malala herself was shot in the head and neck to try and halt her advocacy for the rights of women and girls. Gender schemas can be very powerful, and events that challenge their legitimacy can be enormously threatening.

Crystal Smith transcribed a number of commercials directed to "boys" or "girls," and made these "word clouds" out of the result. You can see at once how advertisers cater to exaggerated gender schemas.

Crystal Smith, The Achilles Effect

Learning Influences. A third influence on gender development is the environment, which is full of subtle and not-so-subtle messages about what girls and boys are supposed to do. Behavioural and social-cognitive learning theorists study how the process of gender socialization instills these messages in children (Bussey & Bandura, 1999). They find that gender socialization begins at the moment of birth. Many parents are careful to dress

GET INVOLVED! Gender and Generations

Gender norms have been changing rapidly, and one way to see this for yourself is to interview older members of your family. Ask at least one man and one woman these questions: (1) When you were growing up, was there anything your parents did not permit you to do because of your sex? (2) Is there any job you think is unsuitable for a man or a woman to do? (3) Did you ever experience discrimination because of your sex? Now consider how you would answer those questions. Do your answers agree with theirs? Why or why not?

their baby in outfits they consider to be the correct colour and pattern for his or her sex. Clothes don't matter to the infant, of course, but they are signals to adults about how to treat the child. Adults often respond to the same baby differently, depending on whether the child is dressed as a boy or a girl. Remember the media frenzy when Kathy Witterick and David Stocker announced that they were going to raise a genderless baby, named 'Storm'? Their refusal to publically announce the gender of their child made national headlines.

Parents, teachers, and other adults convey their beliefs and expectations about gender even when they are entirely unaware that they are doing so. When parents believe that boys are naturally better at math or sports and that girls are naturally better at English, they unwittingly communicate those beliefs by how they respond to a child's success or failure. They may tell a son who did well in math, "You're a natural math whiz, Lee!" But if a daughter gets good grades, they may say, "Wow, you really worked hard in math, Leigh, and it shows!" The implication is that girls have to try hard but boys have a natural gift. Messages like these are not lost on children. Both sexes tend to lose interest in activities that are supposedly not natural for them, even when they all start out with equal abilities (Dweck, 2006; Frome & Eccles, 1998)

In today's fast-moving world, however, society's messages to men and women keep shifting. As a result, gender development has become a lifelong process, in which

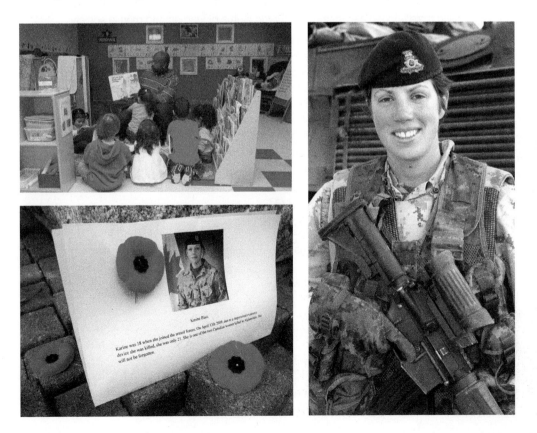

Shocking images or nothing new? The idea of women serving in the military and men teaching preschoolers would once have startled most people and offended others. As women soldiers became common, they lost the power to shock, at least if they remained in service jobs. But the wars in Iraq and Afghanistan again changed the gender rules, creating a generation of female soldiers who fight on the front lines with their male peers. Both Karine Blais (left) and Nichola Kathleen Sarah Goddard (right) were among the 158 Canadians who were killed while on active duty fighting the Taliban in Afghanistan.

Left top: Cathy Guisewite/Universal Uclick. Left bottom: Gary Nylander/The Canadian Press Images. Right: Department of National Defence/Handout/Reuters.

gender schemas, attitudes, and behaviour evolve as people have new experiences and as society itself changes (Rosin, 2012). Five-year-old children may behave like sexist piglets while they are trying to figure out what it means to be male or female. Their behaviour is shaped by a combination of hormones, genetics, cognitive schemas, parental and social lessons, religious and cultural customs, and experiences. But their gender-typed behaviour as five-year-olds usually has little to do with how they will behave at 25 or 45. In fact, by early adulthood, men and women show virtually no average differences in cognitive abilities, personality traits, self-esteem, or psychological well-being (Hyde, 2007).

That is why children can grow up in an extremely gender-typed family and yet, as adults, find themselves in careers or relationships or identities they would never have imagined for themselves. If five-year-olds are the gender police, many adults end up breaking the law.

Recite & Review

Recite: Say aloud what you remember about *gender identity*, *gender typing*, *intersex conditions*, and transgender and transsexual people; biological, cognitive, and learning influences on gender; and *gender schemas*.

Review: Rereading this section is appropriate for all sexes and genders.

Now take this *Quick Quiz:*

1. True or false: All intersexed people are transsexual.

2. A biological psychologist would say that a three-year-old boy's love of going "vroom, vroom" with his truck collection is probably largely a result of _____.

3. Which statement about gender schemas is false? (a) They are present in early form by one year of age; (b) they are permanent conceptualizations of what it means to be masculine or feminine; (c) they eventually expand to include many meanings and associations to being male and female; (d) they reflect the status of women and men in society.

4. Herb hopes his four-year-old daughter will become a scientist like him, but she refuses to play with the toy microscope he bought her and insists that she will be a princess when she grows up. What conclusions can Herb draw about his daughter's future career?

Answers:

1. false 2. prenatal hormones, specifically androgens 3. b 4. Not many. His daughter's rigid gender-typed behaviour is typical when children are acquiring gender schemas, but it does not necessarily predict much of anything about her adult interests or occupation.

Learning Objectives

12 Define adrenarche.

13 Chart the physiological changes of adolescence.

14 List two key aspects of brain development that occur in adolescence.

15 Evaluate the statement that adolescents today can be characterized as "Generation Me."

adrenarche [a-DREN-ar-kee] A time in middle childhood when the adrenal glands begin producing the adrenal hormone DHEA and other hormones that affect cognitive and social development.

Adolescence

In middle childhood (ages six to 12), children go through a period called **adrenarche** (a-DREN-ar-kee), when the adrenal glands begin pumping out hormones that affect brain development, most notably an androgen called DHEA (Campbell, 2011).

These hormones divert glucose in the brain to foster the maturation of brain regions vital to interpreting social and emotional cues. Indeed, children's brains during these years are at their most flexible and responsive to learning. Children become able to control their impulses, reason better, focus and plan for the future, and understand mortality and death. Their friendships flourish. All over the world, cultures acknowledge that middle childhood is an important station on the road to adulthood: Adults begin giving children responsibilities—hunting, gardening, care of younger children, chores—though these tasks vary in seriousness (Lancy & Grove, 2011). Ariaal girls in northern Kenya work the hardest, putting in 9.6 hours of farm work daily; but among the Pumé, a foraging group in Venezuela, preadolescent girls do almost nothing. "Pumé girls spend their time socializing, talking and laughing with their friends, beading and resting," observed the researchers who lived among them (Kramer & Greaves, 2011).

And then . . . adolescence strikes. *Adolescence* refers to the period of development between **puberty**, the age at which a person becomes capable of sexual reproduction, and adulthood. in some cultures and eras, the time span between puberty and adulthood is only a few months; a sexually mature boy or girl is expected to marry and assume adult tasks. In modern western societies, however, teenagers are not considered emotionally mature enough to assume the full rights, responsibilities, and roles of adulthood.

The Physiology of Adolescence

Until puberty, boys and girls produce roughly the same levels of androgens (masculinizing hormones) and estrogens (feminizing hormones). At puberty, however, the brain's pituitary gland begins to stimulate hormone production in the gonads and adrenal glands. From then on, boys have a higher level of androgens than girls do, and girls have a higher level of estrogens than boys do.

In boys, the gonads are the testes (testicles), which produce sperm; in girls, the gonads are the ovaries, which release eggs. During puberty, these organs mature and the individual becomes capable of reproduction. In girls, signs of sexual maturity are the development of breasts and **menarche**, the onset of menstruation. In boys, the signs are the onset of nocturnal emissions and the growth of the testes, scrotum, and penis. Hormones are also responsible for the emergence of *secondary sex characteristics*, such as a deepened voice and facial and chest hair in boys and pubic hair in both sexes.

The onset of puberty depends on both biological and environmental factors. Menarche depends on a female's having a critical level of body fat, which is necessary to sustain a pregnancy and which triggers the hormonal changes associated with puberty. An increase in body fat among children in developed countries may help explain why the average age of puberty declined in Europe and North America until the mid-twentieth century. In North America, the average age of menarche now occurs at about 12.5 years; in Europe it is 13; in many parts of Africa, menarche is typical of young women between the ages of 14 and 17 (Anderson, Dallal, & Must, 2003; Tanner, 1990; Wheeler, 1991). However, other signs of puberty in girls, such as pubic hair and breast buds, have been appearing at younger and younger ages; boys, too, are entering puberty six months to two years sooner than previously estimated.

Individuals vary enormously in the onset and length of puberty. Some girls go through menarche at 9 or 10, or even earlier, and some boys are still growing in height after age 19. Early-maturing boys generally have a more positive view of their bodies than late-maturing boys do, and their relatively greater size and

puberty The age at which a person becomes capable of sexual reproduction.

menarche [men-AR-kee] The onset of menstruation during puberty.

To their embarrassment, children typically reach puberty at different times. These girls are all the same age, but they differ considerably in physical maturity.

Richard Hutchings/Science Source

strength give them a boost in sports and the prestige that being a good athlete brings young men. But they are also more likely to smoke, drink alcohol, use other drugs, and break the law than later-maturing boys (Cota-Robles, Neiss, & Rowe, 2002). Some early-maturing girls have the prestige of being socially popular, but they are also more likely to fight with their parents, drop out of school, have a negative body image, abuse drugs, have poorer relationships, and be angry or depressed (Westling, Andrews, & Peterson, 2012; Westling et al., 2008). Early menarche itself does not cause these problems; rather, it tends to accentuate existing behavioural problems and family conflicts. Girls who go through puberty relatively late, in contrast, have a more difficult time at first, but by the end of adolescence, many are happier with their appearance and are more popular than their early-maturing classmates (Caspi & Moffitt, 1991; Stattin & Magnusson, 1990).

BIOLOGY and *the Adolescent Brain*

When does a teenager become capable of thinking like an adult? This is not just an academic question; it can be a matter of life or death. In many American states, teenaged criminals are tried and sentenced as adults. In 2005, the American Supreme Court banned the death penalty for juveniles as cruel and unusual punishment, and in 2012, it ruled that mandatory sentences of life without parole are likewise excessive. The ruling on the death penalty decision was based in part on evidence showing that adolescents often get into trouble because their brains are neurologically immature (Albert & Steinberg, 2011; Steinberg, 2007). Indeed, full neurological and cognitive maturity often does not occur until about age 25, much later than commonly believed. For that reason, Laurence Steinberg and Elizabeth Scott (2003) argued that many teenagers who commit crimes should be considered "less guilty by reason of adolescence." In Canada, there is no death penalty, although the *Youth Criminal Justice Act* suggests that for major offences (e.g., murder), youths who are 14 or older can be transferred to adult court for trial. Since its introduction in 2001, there has been a significant reduction in the incarceration of young offenders in Canada (Statistics Canada, 2007).

When people think of physical changes in adolescence, they usually think of hormones and maturing bodies. But the adolescent brain undergoes significant developmental changes, notably a major pruning of synapses. This pruning occurs primarily in the prefrontal cortex, which is responsible for impulse control and planning, and the limbic system, which is involved in emotional processing (Spear, 2000a, 2000b). In Chapter 15 we will see that errors in the pruning process during adolescence may be involved in the onset of schizophrenia in vulnerable individuals.

Another change involves myelinization, which provides insulation for neurons and improves the efficiency of

THINKING CRITICALLY

Examine the evidence.

Sharon Graham Sargent/The Canadian Press Images

In April 2006, the bodies of Marc, Debra, and Jacob Richardson were found in their house in Medicine Hat. A 12-year-old* from Medicine Hat and her 23-year-old boyfriend, Jeremy Steinke, were convicted of murdering her parents and brother. Was she responsible for these heartless crimes? Many people assume that by late adolescence, individuals are legally, socially, and physically adult, but some researchers in neuroscience and developmental psychology disagree.

Given her age, her name cannot be revealed.

neural transmission (see Chapter 4), strengthening the connections between the emotional areas of the brain and the reasoning prefrontal cortex. This process may continue through the late teens or early twenties, which would help explain why the strong emotions of the adolescent years often overwhelm rational decision making and cause some teenagers to behave more impulsively than adults. It would explain why adolescents are more vulnerable to peer pressure that encourages them to try risky, dumb, or dangerous things—why taunts of "I dare you!" and "You're chicken!" have more power over a 15-year-old than a 25-year-old. Even when teenagers know they are doing the wrong thing, many lack the reasoning ability to foresee the consequences of their actions down the line (Reyna & Farley, 2006).

If adolescence is literally a state of diminished responsibility, how should the courts treat underage offenders? Should 12-years olds be less accountable than 14-year-olds or 18-year-olds? What do you think?

The Psychology of Adolescence

The media love sensational stories about teenagers who are angry or violent, live in emotional turmoil, feel lonely, have low self-esteem, and are running wild sexually.

Yet in reality, overall feelings of self-esteem do not suddenly plummet after the age of 13 for boys or girls (Gentile et al., 2009), and the rate of violent crimes committed by adolescents has been dropping steadily since 1993. What about sex? According to Statistics Canada, today's teenagers may actually be more conservative than their parents were at their age. In 1996, 47% of teens aged 15 to 19 had had sex; in 2005, that number dropped to 43% (Rotermann, 2008). The age at which people first had sex had also increased, with less than 8% of teens reporting that they had had sex before the age of 15 (Rotermann, 2008). Only the rate of births to teenage girls has risen in the last few years, a result of declining contraceptive use. As for sexting (the practice of emailing nude pictures to friends), although parents and prosecutors are alarmed, *Maclean's* (Kingston, 2009) reports that fewer than 25% of Canadian teens reporting that they had ever sent nude or semi-nude pictures of themselves electronically. That being said, the tragic suicides of Amanda Todd (who committed suicide after an internet predator bullied her and spread revealing pictures of her) and Rehtaeh Parsons (who was also bullied on the internet by the posting of sexual, and non-consensual, content) suggest that although sexting may be infrequent in Canada, the inappropriate use of these images to bully may have dire consequences. Indeed, in the United States, similar distribution of such images by 14- and 15-year-olds has resulted in arrests for creating and distributing child pornography (no such cases have yet been tried in Canada).

Similarly, studies of representative samples of adolescents find that only a small minority are seriously troubled, angry, or unhappy. Most teenagers have supportive families, a sense of purpose and self-confidence, good friends, and the skill to cope with their problems. Nevertheless, three kinds of problems are more common during adolescence than during childhood or adulthood: conflict with parents, mood swings and depression, and higher rates of reckless, rule-breaking, and risky behaviour (Steinberg, 2007). Rule breaking often occurs because teenagers are developing their own standards and values by trying on the styles, actions, and attitudes of their peers, in contrast to those of their parents.

Peers become especially important to adolescents because they represent the values and style of the generation that teenagers identify with, the generation that they will share experiences with as adults (Bukowski, 2001; Harris, 2009). Many people report that feeling rejected by their peers when they were teenagers was more devastating than punitive treatment by parents. According to a government-sponsored review of whether and how online technologies affect child safety, the most frequent dangers that teenagers face on the internet are not pornography or even predatory adults, and definitely not sexting. "Bullying and harassment, most often by peers, are the most frequent threats that minors face, both online and offline," the report found (Berkman Center for Internet & Society, 2008).

Adolescents who are lonely, depressed, anxious, or angry tend to express these concerns in ways characteristic of their sex. Boys are more likely than girls to externalize their problems in acts of aggression and other antisocial behaviour. Girls are more likely than boys to internalize their feelings and problems by becoming withdrawn, blaming themselves for whatever goes wrong, or developing eating disorders (Wicks-Nelson & Israel, 2003). Although, as we said, there are no gender differences in overall self-esteem, a gender gap in two specific *areas* of self-esteem emerges in adolescence, reflecting the externalizing/internalizing difference in habits of coping. Girls are more dissatisfied than boys with their bodies and general appearance; boys are more dissatisfied than girls with their social behaviour at school and with friends (Gentile et al., 2009).

Keep in mind that the "psychology of adolescence" depends profoundly on the larger culture in which teenagers live. During the 1960s and early 1970s, a period of great social upheaval during which many teenagers rebelled against their parents' lives and values, some observers wrote as if teenage rebellion were a universal, biologically driven phase; today, most teenagers remain close to their parents and see no reason to rebel against them. In this light, consider the role of culture's influence on a particular personality trait, narcissism. Narcissism is not the same thing as self-esteem; it is a combination of excessive self-regard and a lack of empathy or interest in others (Twenge & Campbell, 2009). And it is not the kind of understandable self-focus that is common among adolescents and young adults who are worried about their future relationships and work lives (Roberts, Edmonds, & Grijalva, 2010).

You may not welcome this information, but Jean Twenge and her colleagues (2008; 2012) have amassed considerable evidence that narcissism has been rising among today's cohort of college students and younger teenagers, to such a degree that they refer to this cohort as "Generation Me." University students' scores on the Narcissistic Personality Inventory, which measures a grandiose sense of importance, entitlement, and cynicism (narcissists agree that "I wish somebody would someday write my

Recite & Review

Recite: State out loud all you remember about *adrenarche, puberty, adolescence, menarche,* the biology of the adolescent brain, and the kinds of problems more common in adolescence than in childhood or adulthood.

Review: Next, reread this section.

Now take this *Quick Quiz:*

1. What is the difference between *puberty* and *adolescence*?

2. Extreme turmoil and rebellion in adolescence are (a) nearly universal, (b) the exception rather than the rule, or (c) rare.

3. What changes occur in the brain during adolescence?

Answers:

1. Puberty refers to the physiological process of sexual maturation; adolescence is a social category marking the years between puberty and adulthood. 2. b 3. pruning of synapses, myelinization, and strengthening of connections between the emotional parts of the brain and the prefrontal cortex

biography" and "I find it easy to manipulate people"), have steadily increased between the years 1966 and 2009, (Twenge et al., 2012; Twenge et al., 2008; Twenge & Foster, 2010). Why? One answer, they suggest, is that we live in a time in which western culture has become more self-focused and less other-directed. In one revealing measure of this change, researchers coded the lyrics of the ten most popular songs of the year from 1980 to 2007, counting the number of first-person singular pronouns (*I, me, mine*). These self-references, such as Jennifer Hudson's "I Remember Me" or Ashlee Simpson's "I Am Me" ("I am me and I won't change for anyone"—really? not for anyone?) have been steadily rising (DeWall et al., 2011). How are you reacting to this information? Does it sound totally wrong or does it strike a chord?

Learning Objectives

16 Describe the eight crises that are the hallmark of the lifespan approach proposed by Erik Erikson.

17 Compare and contrast "emerging adulthood" with adolescence.

18 Give examples of some common midlife changes for women and men.

19 Evaluate the statement that cognitive decline is a normal part of aging. Recommend three strategies for avoiding cognitive decline in your older years.

Adulthood

According to ancient Greek legend, the Sphinx was a monster—half lion, half woman—who terrorized passersby on the road to Thebes. The Sphinx would ask each traveller a question and then murder those who failed to answer correctly. (The Sphinx was a pretty tough grader.) The question was this: What animal walks on four feet in the morning, two feet at noon, and three feet in the evening? Only one traveller, Oedipus, knew the solution to the riddle. The animal, he said, is Man, who crawls on all fours as a baby, walks upright as an adult, and limps in old age with the aid of a staff.

The Sphinx was the first lifespan theorist. Since then, many philosophers, writers, and scientists have speculated on the course of adult development. Are the changes of adulthood predictable, like those of childhood? What are the major psychological issues of adult life? Is mental and physical deterioration in old age inevitable?

Stages and Ages

One of the first modern theorists to propose a lifespan approach to psychological development was psychoanalyst Erik H. Erikson (1902–1994). Erikson (1950/1963, 1982) wrote that all individuals go through eight stages in their lives. Each stage is characterized by what he called a "crisis," a particular psychological challenge that ideally should be resolved before the individual moves on:

Explore the **Concept**
Erikson's Psychosocial Stages of Development in **MyPsychLab**

- *Trust versus mistrust* is the challenge that occurs during the baby's first year, when the baby depends on others to provide food, comfort, cuddling, and warmth. If these needs are not met, the child may never develop the essential trust of others necessary to get along in the world.

- *Autonomy (independence) versus shame and doubt* is the challenge that occurs when the child is a toddler. The young child is learning to be independent and must do so without feeling too ashamed or uncertain about his or her actions.

- *Initiative versus guilt* is the challenge that occurs as a preschooler develops. The child is acquiring new physical and mental skills, setting goals, and enjoying newfound talents, but must also learn to control impulses. The danger lies in developing too strong a sense of guilt over his or her wishes and fantasies.

- *Competence versus inferiority* is the challenge for school-age children, who are learning to make things, use tools, and acquire the skills for adult life. Children who fail these lessons of mastery and competence may come out of this stage feeling inadequate and inferior.

- *Identity versus role confusion* is the great challenge of adolescence, when teenagers must decide who they are, what they are going to do, and what they hope to make of their lives. Erikson used the term *identity crisis* to describe what he considered to be the primary conflict of this stage. Those who resolve it will emerge with a strong identity, ready to plan for the future. Those who do not will sink into confusion, unable to make decisions.

- *Intimacy versus isolation* is the challenge of young adulthood. Once you have decided who you are, said Erikson, you must share yourself with another and learn to make commitments. No matter how successful you are at work, you are not complete until you are capable of intimacy.

- *Generativity versus stagnation* is the challenge of the middle years. Now that you know who you are and have an intimate relationship, will you sink into complacency and selfishness, or will you experience generativity—creativity and renewal? Parenthood is the most common route to generativity, but people can be productive, creative, and nurturing in other ways, in their work or their relationships with the younger generation.

- *Ego integrity versus despair* is the final challenge of late adulthood and old age. As they age, people strive to reach the ultimate goals of wisdom, spiritual tranquility, and acceptance of their lives. Just as the healthy child will not fear life, said Erikson, the healthy adult will not fear death.

Erikson recognized that cultural and economic factors affect people's progression through these stages. Some societies make the passages relatively easy. If you know you are going to be a farmer like your parents and you have no alternative, you are unlikely to have an adolescent identity crisis (unless you hate farming). However, if you have many choices or if, on the contrary, the economy has made it difficult to find any good job, the transition can become prolonged (Schwartz, 2004). Similarly, cultures that place a high premium on independence and individualism will make it difficult for many of their members to resolve Erikson's sixth crisis, that of intimacy versus isolation. ◉

◉—|Watch the **Video**
Classic Footage of Erik Erikson in **MyPsychLab**

Now that people's lives have become less traditional and predictable, these psychological issues may also occur in different orders or return even after having been resolved. For example, although in western societies adolescence is often a time of confusion about identity and aspirations, an identity crisis is not limited to the teen years. A man who has worked in one job for 20 years, and then is laid off at 45 and must find an entirely new career, may have an identity crisis too. Likewise, competence is not mastered once and for all in childhood. People learn new skills and lose old ones throughout their lives, and their sense of competence rises and falls accordingly. And people who are highly generative, in terms of being committed to helping their communities or the next generation, tend to do volunteer work or choose

According to Erik Erikson, children must master the crisis of competence and older adults must resolve the challenge of generativity. This child and her grandmother are certainly helping each other with their life tasks. But are the needs for competence and generativity significant at only one stage of life?

Buena Vista Images/Lifesize/Getty Images

occupations that allow them to contribute to society throughout their lives (McAdams, 2006). As one psychologist observed many years ago, "There is not one process of aging, but many; there is not one life course followed, but multiple courses. . . . The variety is as rich as the historic conditions people have faced and the current circumstances they experience" (Pearlin, 1982).

Stage theories, therefore, do not adequately describe how adults grow and change, or remain the same, across the lifespan. Yet Erikson was right to show that development does not stop at adolescence or young adulthood; it is an ongoing process. His ideas were influential because he placed adult development in the context of family, work, and society, and he specified many of the essential concerns of adulthood: trust, competence, identity, generativity, and the ability to enjoy life and accept death. Modern psychologists who study lifespan development recognize that social and cultural factors affect the way each of these adult concerns is expressed and mastered. Collectively, they reflect the timeless and universal human concerns of adulthood (Dunkel & Sefcek, 2009).

THINKING CRITICALLY

Avoid emotional reasoning.

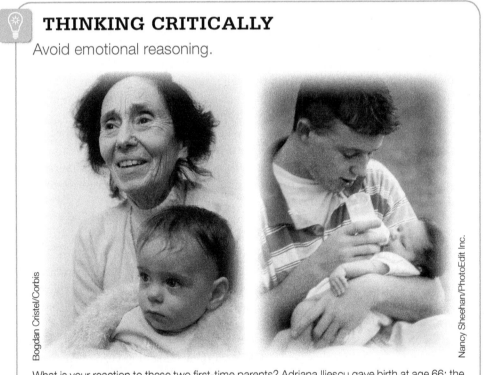

Bogdan Cristel/Corbis

Nancy Sheehan/PhotoEdit Inc.

What is your reaction to these two first-time parents? Adriana Iliescu gave birth at age 66; the young man became a father at 15. Many people react negatively to individuals who they feel are "off time" for the transition to parenthood. How young is too young and how old is too old to become a parent?

The Transitions of Life

When nearly everyone your age goes through the same experience or enters a new role at the same time—going to school, having a baby, retiring—adjusting to these transitions is relatively easy. Conversely, if you aren't doing these things and hardly anyone you know is doing them either, you will not feel out of step. Today, however, most people will face unanticipated transitions—events that happen without warning, such as being fired from a job. And many people have to deal with changes that they expect to happen that do not: not getting a job after university, not getting married at the age they expected, not getting promoted, not being able to afford to retire, or realizing that they cannot have children (Schlossberg & Robinson, 1996). With this in mind, let's consider some of the major transitions of life.

Emerging Adulthood.

In industrialized nations, major demographic changes have postponed the timing of career decisions, marriage or cohabitation, and parenthood until a person's late twenties or even thirties, on the average. Many young people between the ages of 18 and 25 are in some form of post-secondary education and at least partly dependent financially on their parents. This phenomenon has created a phase of life that some call *emerging adulthood* (Arnett, 2004). When emerging adults are asked whether they feel they have reached adulthood, the majority answer: in some ways yes, in some ways no. ◉

In certain respects, emerging adults have moved beyond adolescence into maturity, becoming more emotionally controlled, more confident, less dependent, and less angry and alienated (Azmitia, Syed, & Radmacher, 2008; Roberts, Caspi, & Moffitt, 2001). But they are also the group most likely to live unstable lives and feel unrooted. Emerging adults move more often than people in other demographic groups do—back to their parents' homes and then out again, from one city to another, from living with roommates to living on their own. And their rates of risky behaviour (such as binge drinking, having unprotected sex, and driving at high speeds or while drunk) are higher than those of any other age group, including adolescents (Arnett, 2004).

Of course, not all young people in this age group are alike. Some groups within the larger society, such as Latter Day Saints, promote early marriage and parenthood. And young people who are poor, who have dropped out of school, who had a child at 16, or who have few opportunities to get a good job will not have the income or leisure to explore many options. But the overall shift in all industrialized nations toward a global economy, increased education, and delayed career and family decisions means that emerging adulthood is likely to grow in importance as a distinct phase of prolonged exploration and freedom.

The Middle Years.

For most women and men, the mid-life years between 35 and 65 are the prime of life (MacArthur Foundation, 1999; Mroczek & Spiro, 2005). Contrary to the many jokes about "midlife crises," in which a formerly conventional adult changes partner, job, and car and runs off to Tahiti, these years are typically a time of the greatest psychological well-being, good health, productivity, and community involvement. They are also often a time of reflection and reassessment. People look back on what they have accomplished, take stock of what they regret not having done, and think about what they want to do with their remaining years. When crises occur, it is for reasons not related to aging but to specific life-changing events, such as illness or the loss of a job or partner (Wethington, 2000).

But doesn't menopause make most mid-life women depressed, irritable, and irrational? **Menopause**, which usually occurs between ages 45 and 55, is the cessation of menstruation after the ovaries stop producing estrogen and progesterone. Menopause does produce physical symptoms in many women, notably hot flashes, as the vascular system adjusts to the decrease in estrogen. But only about 10% of all women have unusually severe physical symptoms.

The negative view of menopause as a syndrome that causes depression and other negative emotional reactions is based on women who have undergone early menopause following a hysterectomy (removal of the uterus) or who have had a lifetime history of depression. But these women are not typical. According to many surveys of thousands of healthy, randomly chosen women in the general population, most women view menopause with relief that they no longer have to worry about pregnancy or menstrual periods. The vast majority have only a few physical symptoms (which can be

◉─[Watch the Video
What's in It for Me?: Identity
in **MyPsychLab**

menopause The cessation of menstruation and of the production of ova; it is usually a gradual process lasting up to several years.

annoying and bothersome but are temporary) and most do not become depressed; only 3% even report regret at having reached menopause (McKinlay, McKinlay, & Brambilla, 1987). In one study of 1000 postmenopausal women, fewer than half reported physical symptoms and only 5% of those complained of mood symptoms (Ness, Aronow, & Beck, 2006).

Although women lose their fertility after menopause and men theoretically remain fertile throughout their lives, men have a biological clock too. Testosterone diminishes, although it never drops as sharply in men as estrogen does in women. The sperm count may also gradually drop, and the sperm that remain are more susceptible to genetic mutations that can increase the risk of certain diseases in children conceived by older fathers, as we saw earlier (Wyrobek et al., 2006).

The physical changes of mid-life do not by themselves predict how people will feel about aging or how they will respond to it (Schaie & Willis, 2002). People's views of aging are profoundly influenced by the culture they live in and by the promises of technology to prolong life and health—some realistic, some still science fiction. Is aging something natural and inevitable, to be accepted gracefully? Or is it a process to be fought tooth and nail, with every chemical, surgical, and genetic weapon we can lay our hands on? If we can live to 100, why not have a baby at 70? To what extent should society pay for life-extending interventions? These issues will be hotly debated in the years to come.

Old Age

When does old age start? In Canada, the average life expectancy for men is 79 years of age, whereas the average life expectancy for women is 83 years (Statistics Canada, 2012). As our life expectancies increase, many gerontologists are beginning to divide the elderly into the following categories: the young old (ages 60–75); the old old (ages 75–85); and the oldest old (ages 85+). Today, the fastest-growing segment of the population in Canada is the oldest old. For instance, in 1971, 8% of Canadians were over age 65, whereas in 2000, 13% of Canadians were over age 65. From 1952 to 2006, the number of Canadians who were over 100 increased from 175 to 4635 people (most of whom were women) and in the most recent census in 2011 there were 5825 centarians, a stunning increase (Statistics Canada, 2012)! Some estimates suggest that by 2061, there will be more than 78 000 Canadians who will be more than 100 years old (Statistics Canada, 2012). How will these people fare? *Gerontologists*, researchers who study aging and the old, have been investigating the likely consequences of this massive demographic change.

One consequence of the demographic changes facing Canadians is that the phase of retirement will change significantly. When people expected to live only until their early seventies, retirement at 65 was associated with loss—a withdrawal from work and fulfilling activities, with not much to look forward to but illness and old age. Today, thanks to the enormous cohort of healthy baby boomers and a changed economy, retirement might last 20 or 30 years. Thus it is no longer simply a life transition from working to not working. People in the phase of what some psychologists are calling "positive retirement" often find a new career, volunteer work, or new, engrossing activities (Halpern, 2008). Indeed, the Government of Canada is introducing new changes to pensions that reflect longer lifespans and longer times working (Service Canada, 2013).

Still, various aspects of intelligence, memory, decision making, and other forms of mental functioning do decline significantly with age. Older adults start score lower on tests of reasoning, spatial ability, and complex problem solving than do younger adults. The ability to produce and spell familiar words declines, a change that often causes great frustration and annoyance (Burke & Shafto, 2004). It takes older people longer to retrieve words and names, dates, and other information; in fact, the speed of

◉─┤**Watch** the **Video**
DSM in Context: Speaking Out: Alvin: Living with Dementia in **MyPsychLab**

fluid intelligence The capacity to reason and use information to solve problems; it is relatively independent of education.

crystallized intelligence Cognitive skills and specific knowledge acquired over a lifetime; it is heavily dependent on education and tends to remain stable over time.

THINKING CRITICALLY

Consider other explanations.

People assume that aging inevitably produces senility, depression, weakness, and a decline in mental abilities. What else could be causing these problems?

cognitive processing in general slows down. However, older people vary in this respect, with some declining significantly and others remaining sharp (Lövdén et al., 2010; Salthouse, 2012). ◉

Fortunately, not all cognitive abilities worsen with age. **Fluid intelligence** is the capacity for deductive reasoning and the ability to use new information to solve problems. It reflects in part an inherited predisposition, and it parallels other biological capacities in its growth and later decline (Bosworth & Schaie, 1999; Li et al., 2004). **Crystallized intelligence** consists of knowledge and skills built up over a lifetime, the kind of intelligence that gives us the ability to do arithmetic, define words, or take political positions. It depends heavily on education and experience, and it tends to remain stable or even improve over the lifespan (see Chapter 9). This is why physicians, lawyers, teachers, farmers, musicians, insurance agents, politicians, psychologists, and people in many other occupations can continue working well into old age (Halpern, 2008). Also, older adults are often able to compensate for age-related declines by recruiting parts of the brain that are not commonly activated when young people do the same tasks—an example of the brain's impressive plasticity (flexibility) (Huang et al., 2012).

Many of the physical and mental losses that do occur in old age are physiologically and genetically based and are seen in all societies, but others have to do with cultural, behavioural, and psychological factors (Park & Gutchess, 2006). Psychologists have made great strides in separating conditions once thought to be an inevitable part of old age from those that are preventable or treatable:

- Apparent senility in the elderly is often caused by malnutrition, prescription medications, harmful combinations of medications, and even over-the-counter drugs (such as sleeping pills and antihistamines), all of which can be hazardous to older people.

- Weakness, frailty, and even many of the diseases associated with old age are often caused by being inactive and sedentary (Booth & Neufer, 2005).

- Depression, passivity, and memory problems may result from the loss of meaningful activity, intellectual stimulation, goals to pursue, and control over events (Hess, 2005; Schaie & Zuo, 2001).

The two images of old age: More and more old people are living healthy, active, mentally stimulating lives. But with increasing longevity, many people are also falling victim to degenerative diseases such as Alzheimer's.

Left: Gupton Charles. Right: Angela Hampton/ Alamy.

Older people can profit from aerobic exercise and strength training, which maintain physical strength and flexibility, boost the brain's blood supply, and promote the development of new cells in the hippocampus and other areas of the brain. The result is improved functioning in memory, planning, concentration, and making schedules (Colcombe & Kramer, 2003; Erickson et al., 2011; Hertzog et al., 2008). Mental stimulation also fosters the growth of neural connections in the brain, even well into old age. Older adults can sometimes do as well on memory tests as people in their twenties, when given instruction and training. In one project, older people who had shown a decline in inductive reasoning and spatial ability over a 14-year span were given five hours of training in these skills. This brief intervention produced significant improvements in two-thirds of the sample, and many people performed at or above the level of skill they had had 14 years earlier. More impressive, the effects were still apparent up to seven years later (Kramer & Willis, 2002). Cognitive enrichment cannot prevent most cases of serious cognitive decline and dementia, but the declines may be delayed (Gatz, 2007; Hertzog et al., 2008).

Perhaps the best news is that as people get older, most become better able to regulate negative feelings and emphasize the positive. The frequency of intense negative emotions is highest among people aged 18 to 34, then drops sharply to age 65. After 65, it levels off, rising only slightly among old people facing crises of illness and bereavement (Charles & Carstensen, 2004; Urry & Gross, 2010). Apparently, many people do grow wiser, or at least more tranquil, with age.

Some researchers who study aging are therefore optimistic. In their view, people who have challenging occupations and interests, who remain active mentally, who exercise regularly, and who adapt flexibly to change and loss are more likely than others to maintain their cognitive abilities and well-being. "Use it or lose it," they say, and they are hopeful that research into the brain's remarkable plasticity will one day produce successful interventions to prevent or delay cognitive decline (Lövdén et al., 2010). In a study of people who were 100 years old at the *start* of the investigation, fully 73% of them were free of dementia at the time of their deaths

Remember the cute children pictured at the beginning of this chapter? They are Adolph Hitler, Queen Elizabeth II, and Albert Einstein. Now that you have read this chapter, what kinds of genetic, familial, and historical influences can you think of that might explain what made these three famous people so remarkably different?

(in one case, at age 111) (Hagberg & Samuelsson, 2008). Why? Genome-wide association studies are beginning to identify the specific molecular circuits that are associated with good memory in some very old individuals such as these (Barnes, 2011). Other gerontologists are less upbeat. "When you've lost it, you can't use it," they reply. They are worried about the growing numbers of people living into their 90s and beyond, when rates of cognitive impairment and dementia rise dramatically (Salthouse, 2006). The challenge for society is to prepare for the many people who will be living into advanced old age by helping as many as possible to keep using their brains instead of losing them.

✓•—[**Study** and **Review**
in **MyPsychLab**

Recite & Review

Recite: Assuming that you aren't old enough for cognitive decline, state aloud what you know about Erikson's eight stages (including the identity crisis), emerging adulthood, *menopause*, cognitive functioning in old age, *fluid* versus *crystallized intelligence*, and emotional regulation in later years.

Review: Next, reread this section.

Now take this *Quick Quiz:*

1. What new phase of life development has emerged because of demographic changes, and what years does it include?

2. Most women react to menopause by (a) feeling depressed, (b) regretting the loss of femininity, (c) going a little crazy, (d) feeling relieved or neutral.

3. Which of these statements about the decline of mental abilities in old age is *false*? (a) It can often be lessened with training programs; (b) it inevitably declines sharply; (c) it is sometimes a result of malnutrition, medication, or disease rather than aging; (d) it is slowed when people live in stimulating environments.

4. Suddenly, your 80-year-old grandmother has become confused and delusional. Before concluding that old age has made her senile, what other explanations should you rule out?

Answers:

1. emerging adulthood, ages 18 to 25 2. d 3. b 4. You should be sure she is not malnourished and you should rule out the possibility that she is taking too many medications, including nonprescription drugs.

Learning Objectives

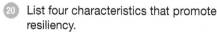

20 List four characteristics that promote resiliency.

The Wellsprings of Resilience

Most people take it for granted that the path from childhood to adolescence to adulthood is a fairly straight one. We think of the lasting attitudes, habits, and values our parents taught us. We continue to have deep attachments to our families, even when we are fighting with them. And many people carry with them the scars of emotional wounds they suffered as children. Children who have been beaten, neglected, or constantly subjected to verbal or physical abuse by their parents are more likely than other children to have emotional problems, become delinquent and violent, commit crimes, have low IQs, drop out of school, and develop mental disorders and chronic stress-related illnesses (Emery & Laumann-Billings, 1998; Margolin & Gordis, 2004; Repetti, Taylor, & Seeman, 2002).

And yet when researchers began to question the entrenched assumption that early trauma always has long-lasting negative effects and considered the evidence for alternative views, they got quite a different picture. Most children are resilient, eventually overcoming even the effects of war, childhood illness, having abusive or alcoholic parents, early deprivation, or being sexually molested (Kaufman & Zigler, 1987; Nelson et al., 2007; Rathbun, DiVirgilio, & Waldfogel, 1958; Rind, Tromovitch, & Bauserman, 1998; Rutter et al., 2004; Werner, 1989; West & Prinz, 1987). Most adults eventually recover after a disaster, too. For example, a study of thousands of Jewish immigrants to Canada and the States who had survived the Holocaust found, in most, resiliency and successful integration into their new lives rather than persisting traumatic distress (Helmreich, 1992).

It is widely assumed that people who recover from adversity must be rare and have special qualities. But the surprising evidence shows that resilience is actually quite ordinary (Masten, 2001). Many of the children who outgrow early deprivation and trauma have easygoing temperaments or personality traits, such as self-efficacy and self-control, which help them roll with even severe punches. They have a secure attachment style, which helps them work through traumatic events in a way that heals their wounds and restores hope and emotional balance (Mikulincer, Shaver, & Horesh, 2006). If children lack secure attachments with their own parents, they may be rescued by love and attention from their siblings, peers, extended family members, or other caring adults. And some have experiences outside the family—in schools, places of worship, or other organizations—that give them a sense of competence, moral support, solace, religious faith, and self-esteem (Cowen et al., 1990; Garmezy, 1991).

Perhaps the most powerful reason for the resilience of so many children, and for the changes that all of us make throughout our lives, is that we are constantly interpreting our experiences. We can decide to repeat the mistakes our parents made or break free of them. We can decide to remain prisoners of childhood or to strike out in new directions at age 20, 50, or 70. As the world continues to change in unpredictable ways, the territory of adulthood will continue to expand, providing new frontiers as well as fewer signposts and road maps to guide us. Increasingly, age will be what we make of it.

> ## THINKING CRITICALLY
> Analyze assumptions and biases.
>
> Many people are convinced that childhood traumas always cause emotional problems in adulthood. What is wrong with this assumption, and what evidence does it overlook?

Recite & Review

Recite: State aloud what you know about the four characteristics of resiliency.

Review: Next, reread this section.

Now take this *Quick Quiz:*

What are the four characteristics of resiliency?

Answers:

1. easygoing temperament, secure attachment style, supportive experiences outside the family, and how one interprets one's experiences.

Taking Psychology with You

Bringing Up Baby

Every year or so, another best-selling book arrives to tell parents they've been doing it all wrong. Countless books have advised parents to treat their children in very specific, if contradictory, ways: Pick them up, don't pick them up; respond when they cry, don't respond when they cry; let them sleep with you, never let them sleep with you; be affectionate, be stern; be highly sensitive to their every need so they will securely attach to you, don't overreact to their every mood or complaint or you will spoil them. Be a Chinese "tiger mother"; no, wait, be a laid-back French mother. A billion-dollar industry has emerged to calm (and inflame) parental worries, offering expensive strollers, toys, "fetal education," and baby sign-language programs—all to create the perfect child (Paul, 2008).

No need to panic. Critical thinkers can call upon two lines of evidence, described in this chapter, to protect themselves from the guilt-mongers and marketers. One is that babies and young children thrive under a wide variety of child-rearing methods. The second is that babies bring their own temperaments and other genetic predispositions to the matter of how best to raise them.

Well, then, how should you treat your children? Should you be strict or lenient, powerful or permissive? Should you require your child to stop having tantrums, to clean up his or her room, to be polite? Should you say, "Oh, nothing I do will matter, anyway" or "If I don't get 100% compliance on every order, this kid is going to boot camp"? Child development research does suggest certain general principles that can help parents find that middle way and foster their children's confidence and helpfulness:

Set high expectations that are appropriate to the child's age and temperament, *and teach the child how to meet them.* Some parents make few demands on their children, either unintentionally or because they believe a parent should not impose standards. Others make many demands, such as requiring children to be polite, help with chores, control their anger, be thoughtful of others, and do well in school. The children of parents who make few demands tend to be aggressive, impulsive, and immature. The children of parents who have high but realistic expectations tend to be helpful and above average in competence and self-confidence (Damon, 1995).

Explain, explain, explain.

Induction, telling a child why you have applied a rule, teaches a child to be responsible. Punitive methods ("Do it or I'll spank you") may result in compliance, but the child will tend to disobey as soon as you are out of sight. Explanations also teach children how to reason and understand. While setting standards for your children, you can also allow them to express disagreements and feelings. This does not mean you have to argue with a four-year-old about the merits of table manners or permit antisocial and destructive behaviour. Once you have explained a rule, you need to enforce it consistently.

Encourage empathy.

Call the child's attention to the effects of his or her actions on others and appeal to the child's sense of fair play and desire to be good. As we saw, even very young children are capable of empathy. Vague orders, such as "Don't fight," are less effective than showing the child how fighting disrupts and hurts others.

Notice, approve of, and reward good behaviour.

Many parents punish the behaviour they dislike, but that very punishment brings the child attention, which is often rewarding to the child. It is much more effective to praise the behaviour you do want, which teaches the child what is expected.

Remember the critical-thinking guideline "don't oversimplify."

The challenge is to avoid the twin fallacies of "It's all genetic" and "If I just do all the right things, whatever they are, my child will be intelligent, kind, and successful." Even with the best skills and intentions, you cannot control everything that happens to your child or remodel your child's temperamental dispositions. Besides, as children grow up, they are influenced by their peers and generation and by particular experiences that shape their interests and motivation. But you do have the power to make your children's lives miserable or secure. You also have the profound power to affect the *quality* of the relationship you will have with your child throughout life: one filled with conflict and resentment, or one that is close and loving.

Summary

- *Developmental psychologists* study how people grow and change over the lifespan. Many study *socialization*, the process by which children learn the rules and behaviour society expects of them.

From Conception through the First Year

- *Maturation* is the unfolding of genetically influenced behaviour and characteristics. Prenatal development begins at fertilization, when the male sperm unites with the female ovum (egg) to form a single-celled egg called a *zygote*. During the first eight weeks of prenatal development, the organism is called an *embryo*; after that, it is known as a *fetus*. Harmful influences that can adversely affect the fetus's development include German measles, toxic substances, some sexually transmitted diseases, cigarettes, alcohol (which can cause *fetal alcohol syndrome* and cognitive deficits), illegal drugs, over-the-counter medications, and chronic maternal stress. Fathers affect prenatal development too; the sperm of teenage boys and men over 50 may have mutations that increase the risk of miscarriage, birth defects, and certain diseases in their offspring.

- Babies are born with *motor reflexes*, a number of perceptual abilities, and rudimentary cognitive skills. Cultural practices affect the timing of physical milestones.

- Babies' innate need for *contact comfort* gives rise to emotional attachment to their caregivers, and by the age of six to eight months, infants begin to feel *separation anxiety*. Studies of the *Strange Situation* have distinguished *secure* from *insecure* attachment; insecurity can take one of two forms, *avoidant* or *anxious-ambivalent* attachment.

- Styles of attachment are relatively unaffected by the normal range of child-rearing practices, and also by whether or not babies spend time in daycare. Insecure attachment is promoted by parents' rejection, mistreatment, or abandonment of their infants; by a mother's postpartum depression, which may affect her ability to care for the baby; by the child's own fearful, insecure temperament; or by stressful family situations.

Cognitive Development

- Human beings are the only species that uses *language* to express and comprehend an infinite number of novel utterances, think about the past and future, and describe things or people who are not present. An innate capacity for language may have evolved in humans because it enhanced the chances of survival and the establishment of social bonds.

- Noam Chomsky argued that the human brain contains a mental module that is sensitive to a *universal grammar* (features common to all languages). In support of this view, children from different cultures go through similar stages of language development; adults do not consistently correct their children's syntax; and groups of children who have never been exposed to adult language often invent their own. However, many psycholinguists no longer believe there is a universal grammar, because languages also vary around the world. Instead, they say, language is a cultural tool, shaped by the world in which children grow up.

- Some models of language acquisition, *computer neural networks*, do not assume an innate capacity at all; instead, they assume that children learn the statistical probability that any given word or syllable will follow another. Parental practices, such as recasting a child's incorrect sentence, also aid in language acquisition. It is likely, therefore, that biological readiness and experience interact in the development of language.

- Language acquisition begins in the womb, as even newborns can distinguish the language their mothers spoke during pregnancy from an unfamiliar language. Infants are responsive to the pitch, intensity, and sound of language, which may be why adults in many cultures speak to babies in *parentese*, using higher-pitched words and exaggerated intonation of vowels. At four to six months of age, babies begin to recognize the sounds of their own language. They go through a babbling phase from age six months to one year, and at about one year, they start saying single words and using symbolic gestures, which continue to be important for language, thinking, and problem solving. At age two, children speak in two- or three-word *telegraphic* sentences that convey a variety of messages.

- Jean Piaget argued that cognitive development depends on an interaction between maturation and a child's experiences in the world. Children's thinking changes and adapts through *assimilation* and *accommodation*. Piaget proposed four stages of cognitive development: *sensorimotor* (birth to age two), during which the child learns *object permanence*; *preoperational* (ages two to seven), during which language and symbolic thought develop, although the child remains *egocentric* in reasoning; *concrete operations* (ages seven to 12), during which the child comes to understand *conservation*; and *formal operations* (age 12 to adulthood), during which abstract reasoning develops.

- Today we know that the changes from one stage to another are not as clear-cut as Piaget implied; development is more continuous and overlapping. Babies and young children have greater cognitive abilities, at earlier ages, than Piaget thought, perhaps because of the "core knowledge" they are born with. Young children are not always egocentric in their thinking. By the age of four or five, they have developed a *theory of mind* to account for their own and other people's behaviour. And, as Piaget's contemporary Lev Vygotsky had pointed out, cultural and parental practices affect the pace and content of cognitive development.

Moral Development

- Lawrence Kohlberg proposed that as children mature cognitively, they go through three levels of moral reasoning. But people can reason morally without behaving morally. Developmental psychologists study how children learn to internalize standards of right and wrong and to behave accordingly. This ability depends on the emergence of conscience and the moral emotions of guilt, shame, and empathy, and on the ability of children to learn to regulate their impulses, wishes, and feelings.

- As a strategy for teaching children to behave, a parent's use of *power assertion* is associated with a child's aggressiveness and lack of empathy. *Induction* is associated with children who develop empathy, internalize moral standards, and can resist temptation. But all methods of discipline interact with the child's own temperament.

- The capacity of very young children to *delay gratification* and control their feelings is associated with the development of internalized moral standards and conscience. This ability is enhanced by mothers who use induction as a primary form of discipline. It may also reflect a personality trait, because it tends to emerge very early in life and to be consistent over time and across situations.

Gender Development

- Gender development includes the emerging awareness of *gender identity*, the understanding that a person is biologically male or female regardless of what he or she does or wears, and *gender typing*, the process by which boys and girls learn what it means to be masculine or feminine in their culture. Some individuals are born with *intersex* physical conditions, living with the physical attributes of both sexes, and consider themselves to be *transgender*. *Transsexuals* feel that they are male in a female body or vice versa; their gender identity is at odds with their anatomical sex.

- Universally, young children tend to prefer same-sex toys and playing with other children of their own sex. Biological psychologists account for this phenomenon in terms of genes and prenatal androgens, which appear to be involved in gender-typed play. Cognitive psychologists study how children develop *gender schemas* for the categories "male" and "female," which in turn shape their gender-typed behaviour. Gender schemas tend to be inflexible at first. Later they become more flexible as the child cognitively matures and assimilates new information, if the child's culture promotes flexible gender schemas. Learning theorists study the direct and subtle reinforcers and social messages that foster gender typing.

- Gender development changes over the lifespan, depending on people's experiences with work and family life and larger events in society and their culture.

Adolescence

- Middle childhood (ages six to 12) is an important phase in which children around the world begin to be assigned various adult responsibilities. During *adrenarche*, the adrenal glands begin pumping out hormones that affect brain development. *Adolescence* begins with the physical changes of *puberty*. In girls, puberty is signalled by *menarche* and the development of breasts; in boys, it begins with the onset of nocturnal emissions and the development of the testes, scrotum, and penis. Hormones produce *secondary sex characteristics*, such as pubic hair in both sexes and a deeper voice in males.

- As discussed in "Biology and the Adolescent Brain," the adolescent brain undergoes a major pruning of synapses, and myelinization, which improves the efficiency of neural transmission and connections among developing areas. These neurological changes may not be complete until the early twenties, which would help explain why the strong emotions of the adolescent years sometimes overwhelm rational decision making and why teenagers often behave more impulsively than adults and may have implications for how teenagers who break the law should be treated.

- Most North American adolescents do not go through extreme emotional turmoil, anger, or rebellion and they do like their parents. They do not suffer from unusually low self-esteem or its opposite, extreme narcissism. However, conflict with parents, mood swings and depression, and reckless or rule-breaking behaviour increase. The peer group becomes especially influential, which is why peer bullying is often the source of teenagers' greatest unhappiness. Boys tend to externalize their problems in acts of aggression and other antisocial behaviour; girls tend to internalize their problems by becoming depressed or developing eating disorders.

Adulthood

- Erik Erikson proposed that life consists of eight stages, each with a unique psychological challenge, or crisis, that must be resolved, such as an *identity crisis* in adolescence. Erikson identified many of the essential concerns of adulthood and showed that development is a lifelong process. However, psychological issues or crises are not confined to particular chronological periods or stages.

- When most people in an age group go through the same event at about the same time, transitions are easier than when people feel out of step. In western nations, major demographic changes have caused young adults to postpone the timing of career decisions, marriage or commitment to a partner, and parenthood. Many people between the ages of 18 and 25, especially if they are not financially independent, find themselves in a life phase often called *emerging adulthood.*

- The middle years are generally not a time of turmoil or crisis but the prime of most people's lives. In women, *menopause* begins in the late forties or early fifties. Many women have temporary physical symptoms, but most do not regret the end of fertility or become depressed and irritable. In middle-aged men, hormone production slows down and sperm counts decline; fertility continues, but with increased risk of fetal abnormalities.

- *Gerontologists* have revised our ideas about old age, now that people are living longer and healthier lives and entering an extended phase of "positive retirement." The speed of cognitive processing slows down, and *fluid intelligence* parallels other biological capacities in its eventual decline. *Crystallized intelligence*, in contrast, depends heavily on culture, education, and experience, and it tends to remain stable over the lifespan.

- Many supposedly inevitable results of aging, such as senility, depression, and physical frailty, are often avoidable. They may result from disease, medication, or poor nutrition, and also from lack of stimulation, control of one's environment, and physical strength and fitness. Exercise and mental stimulation promote the growth of synapses in the human brain, even well into old age, although some mental losses are inevitable.

The Wellsprings of Resilience

- Children who experience violence or neglect are at risk of many problems later in life, but most children are resilient and are able to overcome early adversity. Psychologists now study not only the sad consequences of neglect, poverty, and violence but also the reasons for resilience under adversity.

Taking Psychology with You

- Many child-rearing experts claim to have "the" way to make children smarter, nicer, and more successful. Research in child development can help people think critically about such claims and also offers some general guidelines: Set high but realistic expectations, explain the reasons for your rules, encourage empathy, and reward good behaviour.

Key Terms

socialization **461**
contact comfort **465**
separation anxiety **466**
language **469**
telegraphic speech **473**
object permanence **474**

conservation **474**
theory of mind **476**
power assertion **479**
induction **480**
gender identity **481**
gender typing **481**

intersex conditions
  (intersexuality) **482**
gender schema **484**
adrenarche **486**
puberty **487**
menarche **487**

menopause **494**
fluid intelligence **496**
crystallized intelligence **496**

14 Theories of Personality

Ask questions. . . be willing to wonder

How accurate are those tests that tell you what "personality type" you are?

——

When people talk about "repressing" a memory or being "in denial," where does that language come from?

——

If you hear that shyness or another personality trait is "inherited," does that mean it can't be changed?

——

Why is the same person often so different with family, with friends, and in the classroom?

personality A distinctive and relatively stable pattern of behaviour, thoughts, motives, and emotions that characterizes an individual.

trait A characteristic of an individual, describing a habitual way of behaving, thinking, or feeling.

She was the eldest daughter of eight children in an Italian immigrant family. Only six years old when her mother died, she became the dutiful caretaker of her siblings. She faithfully attended Catholic school, and throughout childhood she was deeply religious. But her earliest passion was to dance, and when her reluctant father finally allowed her to take lessons, her instructors immediately recognized and encouraged her talent. As a young woman, driven to succeed, she dropped out of college and made her way to New York with a one-way ticket and $35 in her purse. She found part-time work, met some musicians, connected with some influential DJs . . . and became the superstar the world knows as Madonna.

Today, Madonna works tirelessly and demands total control over her shows. Her friends and associates have observed that she also obsessively controls her films, public appearances, and even her private life in the service of her public image. And that image is a continual work in progress: good-girl virgin in white, androgynous robot, provocative sex symbol, glamour queen, devoted Catholic, practitioner of the Kabbalah (a mystical wing of Judaism), doting mother. At the 2009 Oscars, the newly divorced Madonna, age 50, turned up with a new facelift and a new, 22-year-old boyfriend. Who is Madonna? The flamboyant performer who loves to shock or a regular mom, sex symbol, or spiritual seeker? Was she born to be an exhibitionist, or did she create a persona to make herself famous? Which personality traits best describe her: extroverted, ambitious, outrageous, motherly, obsessive, funny, selfish, rebellious? Who is the "real" Madonna amid the changing public images? *Is* there a real one?

In this chapter, we will see how psychologists answer such questions—how they define and study personality. **Personality** refers to a distinctive pattern of behaviour, mannerisms, thoughts, motives, and emotions that characterizes an individual over time and across different situations. This pattern consists of many distinctive **traits**, habitual ways of behaving, thinking, and feeling: shy, outgoing, friendly, hostile, gloomy, confident, and so on.

We will begin with the oldest theory of personality, the psychodynamic view, so that you will have a sense of how influential it was, why it still appeals to some, and why many of its ideas have become outdated. Next we will consider evidence for the newest theory, the genetic view. Few scientists think anymore that babies are tiny lumps of clay, shaped entirely by their experiences, or that parents alone determine whether their infant becomes an adventurer, a sourpuss, a worrywart . . . or an extrovert like Madonna. On the other hand, even if half of the human variation in personality traits is due to genetics, what is responsible for the other half?

To answer that question, we will then examine leading approaches to personality that are neither psychodynamic nor biological: the environmental approach, which emphasizes the role of social learning, situations, parents, and peers; the cultural approach, which emphasizes cultural influences on traits and behaviour; and the humanist and narrative approaches, which emphasize self-determination and people's own view of themselves. 👁

👁—▯**Watch** the **Video**
The Big Picture: What Is Personality? in **MyPsychLab**

Learning Objectives

① Explain Freud's theory of the structure and development of personality.

② Describe Carl Jung's theory of the collective unconscious and how it applies to Harry Potter's arch-enemy, Lord Voldemort.

③ Articulate the nature of the "objects" in the object-relations approach to personality.

④ Discuss why many psychologists reject most psychodynamic ideas.

Sigmund Freud (1856–1939).

Alamy

psychoanalysis A theory of personality and a method of psychotherapy developed by Sigmund Freud; it emphasizes unconscious motives and conflicts.

psychodynamic theories Theories that explain behaviour and personality in terms of unconscious energy dynamics within the individual.

Psychodynamic Theories of Personality

A man apologizes for "displacing" his frustrations at work onto his family. A woman suspects that she is "repressing" a childhood trauma. An alcoholic reveals that he is no longer "in denial" about his drinking. A teacher informs a divorcing couple that their eight-year-old child is "regressing" to immature behaviour. All of this language about displacing, repressing, denying, and regressing can be traced to the first psychodynamic theory of personality, Sigmund Freud's theory of **psychoanalysis**.

Freud's theory is called **psychodynamic** because it emphasizes the movement of psychological energy within the person, in the form of attachments, conflicts, and motivations. (Freud did not use "dynamic" in today's sense, to mean "powerful" or "energetic." *Dynamics* is a term from physics that refers to the motion and balance of systems under the action of external or internal forces.) Today's psychodynamic theories differ from Freudian theory and from one another, but they all share an emphasis on unconscious processes going on within the mind. They also share an assumption that adult personality and ongoing problems are formed primarily by experiences in early childhood. These experiences produce unconscious thoughts and feelings, which later form characteristic habits, conflicts, and often self—defeating behaviour.

Freud and Psychoanalysis

To enter the world of Sigmund Freud is to enter a realm of unconscious motives, passions, guilty secrets, unspeakable yearnings, and conflicts between desire and duty. These unseen forces, Freud believed, have far more power over our personalities than our conscious intentions do. The unconscious reveals itself, said Freud, in art, dreams, jokes, apparent accidents, and slips of the tongue (which have come to be called

"Freudian slips"). According to Freud (1920/1960), the British member of Parliament who referred to the "honourable member from Hell" when he meant to say "from Hull" was revealing his actual unconscious appraisal of his colleague. ✴

✴ ⌐Explore the Concept
Freud: Id, Ego, and Superego
in **MyPsychLab**

The Structure of Personality. In Freud's theory, personality consists of three major systems: the id, the ego, and the superego. Any action we take or problem we have results from the interaction and degree of balance among these systems (Freud, 1905b, 1920/1960, 1923/1962).

The **id**, which is present at birth, is the reservoir of unconscious psychological energies and the motives to avoid pain and obtain pleasure. The id contains two competing instincts: the life, or sexual, instinct (fuelled by psychic energy called the **libido**) and the death, or aggressive, instinct. As energy builds up in the id, tension results. The id may discharge this tension in the form of reflex actions, physical symptoms, or uncensored mental images and unbidden thoughts.

The **ego**, the second system to emerge, is a referee between the needs of instinct and the demands of society. It bows to the realities of life, putting a rein on the id's desire for sex and aggression until a suitable, socially appropriate outlet for them can be found. The ego, said Freud, is both conscious and unconscious, and it represents "reason and good sense."

The **superego**, the last system of personality to develop, is the voice of conscience, representing morality and parental authority. The superego judges the activities of the id, handing out good feelings of pride and satisfaction when you do something well and handing out miserable feelings of guilt and shame when you break the rules. The superego is partly conscious but largely unconscious.

According to Freud, the healthy personality must keep all three systems in balance. Someone who is too controlled by the id is governed by impulse and selfish desires. Someone who is too controlled by the superego is rigid, moralistic, and bossy. Someone who has a weak ego is unable to balance personal needs and wishes with social duties and realistic limitations.

If a person feels anxious or threatened when the wishes of the id conflict with social rules, the ego has weapons at its command to relieve the tension. These unconscious strategies, called **defence mechanisms**, deny or distort reality, but they also protect us from conflict and anxiety. They become unhealthy only when they cause self-defeating behaviour and emotional problems. Here are five of the primary defences identified by Freud and later analysts (A. Freud, 1967; Vaillant, 1992):

1 **Repression** occurs when a threatening idea, memory, or emotion is blocked from consciousness. A woman who had a frightening childhood experience that she cannot remember, for example, is said to be repressing her memory of it. Freud used the term *repression* to mean both unconscious expulsion of disturbing material from awareness and conscious suppression of such material. But modern analysts tend to think of it only as an unconscious defence mechanism.

2 **Projection** occurs when a person's own unacceptable or threatening feelings are repressed and then attributed to someone else. A person who is embarrassed about having sexual feelings toward members of a different ethnic group, for example, may project this discomfort onto them, saying, "Those people are dirty-minded and oversexed."

3 **Displacement** occurs when people direct their emotions (especially anger) toward things, animals, or other people that are not the real object of their feelings. A boy who is forbidden to express anger toward his father, for example, may "take it out" on his toys or his younger sister. When displacement serves a higher cultural or socially useful purpose, as in the creation of art or inventions, it is called *sublimation*. Freud argued that society has a duty to help people sublimate their unacceptable

id In psychoanalysis, the part of personality containing inherited psychic energy, particularly sexual and aggressive instincts.

libido (li-BEE-do) In psychoanalysis, the psychic energy that fuels the life or sexual instincts of the id.

ego In psychoanalysis, the part of personality that represents reason, good sense, and rational self-control.

superego In psychoanalysis, the part of personality that represents conscience, morality, and social standards.

defence mechanisms Methods used by the ego to prevent unconscious anxiety or threatening thoughts from entering consciousness.

A Freudian would say that woman's this is nail-biting a sign of an oral fixation.

Diego cervo/Fotolia

impulses for the sake of civilization. Sexual passion, for example, may be sublimated into the creation of art or literature.

4 **Regression** occurs when a person reverts to a previous phase of psychological development. An eight-year-old boy who is anxious about his parents' divorce may regress to earlier habits of thumb sucking or clinging. Adults may regress to immature behaviour when they are under pressure—for example, by having temper tantrums when they don't get their way.

5 **Denial** occurs when people refuse to admit that something unpleasant is happening, such as mistreatment by a partner; that they have a problem, such as drinking too much; or that they are feeling a forbidden emotion, such as anger. Denial protects a person's self-image and preserves the illusion of invulnerability: "It can't happen to me."

The Development of Personality. Freud argued that personality develops in a series of **psychosexual stages**, in which sexual energy takes different forms as the child matures. Each new stage produces a certain amount of frustration, conflict, and anxiety. If these are not resolved properly, normal development may be interrupted, and the child may remain *fixated*, or stuck, at the current stage.

For example, said Freud, some people remain fixated at the *oral* stage, which occurs during the first year of life, when babies experience the world through their mouths. As adults, they will seek oral gratification in smoking, overeating, nail biting, or chewing on pencils; some may become clinging and dependent, like a nursing child. Others remain fixated at the *anal* stage, at ages two to three, when toilet training and control of bodily wastes are the key issues. They may become "anal retentive," holding everything in, obsessive about neatness and cleanliness. Or they may become just the opposite, "anal expulsive"—messy and disorganized.

For Freud, however, the most crucial stage for the formation of personality was the *phallic* (Oedipal) stage, which lasts roughly from age three to age five or six. During this stage, said Freud, the child unconsciously wishes to possess the parent of the other sex and to get rid of the parent of the same sex. Children often proudly announce, "I'm going to marry Daddy (or Mommy) when I grow up," and they reject the same-sex "rival." Freud labelled this phenomenon the **Oedipus complex**, after the Greek legend of King Oedipus, who unwittingly killed his father and married his mother.

Boys and girls, Freud believed, go through the Oedipal stage differently. Boys are discovering the pleasure and pride of having a penis, so when they see a naked girl for the first time, they are horrified. Their unconscious exclaims (in effect), "Her penis has been cut off! Who could have done such a thing to her? Why, it must have been her powerful father. And if he could do it to her, my father could do it to me!" This realization, said Freud, causes the boy to repress his desire for his mother and identify with his father. He accepts his father's authority and the father's standards of conscience and morality; the superego has emerged.

Freud admitted that he did not quite know what to make of girls, who, lacking the penis, could not go through the same steps. He speculated that a girl, upon discovering male anatomy, would panic that she had only a puny clitoris instead of a stately penis. She would conclude that she had already lost her penis. As a result, Freud said, girls do not have the powerful motivating fear that boys do to give up their Oedipal feelings and develop a strong superego; they have only a lingering sense of "penis envy."

Freud believed that when the Oedipus complex is resolved, at about age five or six, the child's personality is fundamentally formed. Unconscious conflicts with parents,

psychosexual stages In Freud's theory, the idea that sexual energy takes different forms as the child matures; the stages are oral, anal, phallic (Oedipal), latency, and genital.

Oedipus complex In psychoanalysis, a conflict occurring in the phallic (Oedipal) stage, in which a child desires the parent of the other sex and views the same-sex parent as a rival.

unresolved fixations and guilts, and attitudes toward the same and the other sex will continue to replay themselves throughout life. The child settles into a supposedly non-sexual *latency* stage, in preparation for the *genital* stage, which begins at puberty and leads to adult sexuality.

In Freud's view, then, your adult personality is shaped by how you progressed through the early psychosexual stages, which defence mechanisms you developed to reduce anxiety, and whether your ego is strong enough to balance the conflict between the id (what you would like to do) and the superego (your conscience).

As you might imagine, Freud's ideas were not exactly received with yawns. Sexual feelings in five-year-olds! Repressed longings in respectable adults! Unconscious meanings in dreams! Penis envy! This was strong stuff in the early years of the twentieth century, and before long psychoanalysis had captured the public imagination in Europe and North America. But it also produced a sharp rift with the emerging schools of empirical psychology.

This rift continues to divide scholars today. Many believe that the overall framework of Freud's theory is timeless and brilliant, even if some specific ideas have proven faulty (Westen, 1998). Others think that psychoanalytic theory is nonsense, with little empirical support, and that Freud was not the theoretical genius, impartial scientist, or even successful clinician that he claimed to be. On the contrary, Freud often bullied his patients into accepting his explanations of their symptoms and ignored all evidence disconfirming his ideas (Borch-Jacobsen & Shamdasani, 2012; McNally, 2003; Powell & Boer, 1995; Webster, 1995).

On the positive side, Freud welcomed women into the profession of psychoanalysis, wrote eloquently about the devastating results for women of society's suppression of their sexuality, and argued, ahead of his time, that homosexuality was neither a sin nor a perversion but a "variation of the sexual function" and "nothing to be ashamed of" (Freud, 1961). Freud was thus a mixture of intellectual vision and blindness, sensitivity and arrogance. His provocative ideas left a powerful legacy to psychology, one that others began to tinker with immediately.

Recite & Review

Recite: Tell your imaginary analyst as much as you can about *personality* and *traits*, *psychodynamic theories*, *psychoanalysis*, especially Freud's notions about the *id*, *libido*, *ego*, and *superego*; *defence mechanisms*; and the five *psychosexual stages* of personality development, including the *Oedipus complex* and the major scientific criticisms of psychodynamic theories.

Review: Next, go back and read this section again.

Now take this *Quick Quiz:*

Have Freudian concepts registered your in unconscious?

Which Freudian concepts do the following events suggest?

1. A four-year-old girl wants to snuggle on Daddy's lap but refuses to kiss her mother.

2. A celibate priest writes poetry about sexual passion.

3. A man who is angry with his boss shouts at his kids for making noise.

4. A racist justifies segregation by saying that black men are only interested in sex with white women.

5. A nine-year-old boy who moves to a new city starts having tantrums.

Answers:

1. Oedipus complex 2. sublimation 3. displacement 4. projection 5. regression

collective unconscious In Jungian theory, the universal memories and experiences of humankind, represented in the symbols, stories, and images (archetypes) that occur across all cultures.

archetypes [AR-ki-tipes] Universal, symbolic images that appear in art, myths, stories, and dreams; to Jungians, they reflect the collective unconscious.

Other Psychodynamic Approaches

Some of Freud's followers stayed in the psychoanalytic tradition and modified Freud's theories from within. Women, as you might imagine, were not too pleased about "penis envy." Clara Thompson (1943/1973) and Karen Horney [HORN-eye] (1926/1973) argued that it was insulting and unscientific to claim that half the human race is dissatisfied with its anatomy. When women feel inferior to men, they said, we should look for explanations in the disadvantages that women live with and their second-class status. Other psychoanalysts broke away from Freud, or were actively rejected by him, and went off to start their own schools.

Jungian Theory. Carl Jung (1875–1961) was originally one of Freud's closest friends and a member of his inner circle, but the friendship ended with a furious quarrel about the nature of the unconscious. In addition to the individual's own unconscious, said Jung (1967), all human beings share a vast **collective unconscious**, containing universal memories, symbols, images, and themes, which he called **archetypes**.

An archetype can be an image, such as the "magic circle," called a mandala in Eastern religions, which Jung thought symbolizes the unity of life and "the totality of the self." Or it can be a figure found in fairy tales, legends, and popular stories, such as the Hero, the nurturing Earth Mother, the Powerful Father, or the Wicked Witch. It can even be an aspect of the self. For example, the *shadow* archetype reflects the prehistoric fear of wild animals and represents the bestial, evil side of human nature. Scholars have found that some basic archetypes, such as the Hero and the Earth Mother, do appear in the stories and images of virtually every society (Campbell, 1949/1968; Neher, 1996). Jungians would recognize dragons, Darth Vader, the Dark Lord Sauron, Dracula, and Harry Potter's tormentor Lord Voldemort as expressions of the shadow archetype. In Canada, we regard Karla Homolka, who aided her husband, Paul Bernardo, in the sexual assault and murder of several teenage girls in Ontario, as an example of the wicked witch or shadow archetype. Few figures in Canadian history elicit as repulsed a reaction among so many people as do these two. ◉

Although Jung shared with Freud a fascination with the darker aspects of the personality, he had more confidence in the positive, forward-moving strengths of the ego. He believed that people are motivated not only by past conflicts but also by their future goals and their desire to fulfill themselves. Jung was also among the first to identify extroversion/introversion as a basic dimension of personality. Nonetheless, many of Jung's ideas were more suited to mysticism and philosophy than to empirical

◉ | **Watch** the **Video**
Classic Footage of Carl Jung on Unconcious in **MyPsychLab**

In the Jungian view, the Joker is a modern of archetype evil, along with Darth Vader, Lord Voldemort, Dracula, and the Wicked Witch of the West. Historically, the Hero archetype has always been male, but that's clearly changing, as fans of *Battlestar Galactica* know. Captain Kara Thrace bravely fights the odds to save the world, just as those guys with Bat-, Spider-, and Super- in their names do.

Left: DC Comics/ZUMA Press/Newscom. Right: SCI-FI CHANNEL/Album/Newscom.

psychology, which may be why so many Jungian ideas became popular with New Age movements.

Jung had a psychotic breakdown after his split with Freud. And he revealed his own "dark side" when he supported the Nazis, writing vicious attacks on Jews and claiming that their collective unconscious differed from that of Gentiles (so much for its universality). But he continued to treat patients and attract many worshipful followers by virtue of his charisma (Hayman, 2001). Like Freud, therefore, Jung left a troubling personal legacy along with theories that appealed to legions of believers.

The Object-Relations School. Freud essentially regarded the baby as if it were an independent, greedy little organism ruled by its own instinctive desires; other people were relevant only insofar as they gratified the infant's drives or blocked them. But by the 1950s, increased awareness of the importance of human attachments led to a different view of infancy, put forward by the **object-relations school**, which was developed in Great Britain by Melanie Klein, D. W. Winnicott, and others. To object-relations theorists, the central problem in life is to find a balance between the need for independence and the need for others. This balance requires constant adjustment to separations and losses: small ones such as disagreements during quarrels, moderate ones such as leaving home for the first time, and major ones such as divorce or death. The way we react to these separations, according to object-relations analysts, is largely determined by our experiences in the first year or two of life. In order to get the mother's recognition, the baby will find parts of himself or herself that the mother appreciates and values. If the baby's need for recognition goes unheeded, the baby's personality will be warped. The infant may develop what Winnicott called a "false self," because certain parts of the baby's "true self" remain undeveloped (Orbach, 2009).

The reason for the clunky word "object" in object-relations, instead of the warmer word "human" or "parent," is that the infant's attachment is not only to a real person (usually the mother) but also to the infant's evolving perception of her. The child creates a *mental* representation of the mother—someone who is kind or fierce, protective or rejecting. The child's representations of important adults, whether realistic or distorted, unconsciously affect personality throughout life, influencing whether the person relates to others with trust or suspicion, acceptance or criticism.

Object-relations theorists have applied this approach in many ways: for example, to predict whether a client will benefit from psychotherapy (Mallinckrodt, Porter, & Kivlighan, 2005), to help people deal with disability and other losses in life (Goldstein, 2002), and even to try to explain why some distrustful, cynical people harass others on the internet (Whitty & Carr, 2006).

The object-relations school also departs from Freudian theory regarding the nature of male and female development (Sagan, 1988; Winnicott, 1957/1990). In the object-relations view, children of both sexes identify first with the mother. Girls, who are the same sex as the mother, do not need to separate from her; the mother treats a daughter as an extension of herself. But boys must break away from the mother in order to develop a masculine identity; the mother encourages a son to be independent and separate. Thus men, in this view, develop more rigid boundaries between themselves and other people than women do.

According to object-relations theory, a baby constructs unconscious representations of his or her parents that will influence the child's relations with others throughout life.

Getty Image

object-relations school A psychodynamic approach that emphasizes the importance of the infant's first two years of life and the baby's formative relationships, especially with the mother.

Evaluating Psychodynamic Theories

Although modern psychodynamic theorists differ in many ways, they share a general belief that to understand personality we must explore its unconscious dynamics and origins. Many psychologists in other fields, however, regard most psychodynamic ideas as literary metaphors rather than as scientific explanations (Cioffi, 1998; Crews, 1998). They point out that most of the cornerstone assumptions in psychoanalytic theory, such as the notion that the mind "represses" traumatic experiences, have not been supported scientifically (McNally, 2003; Rofé, 2008; see Chapter 10). Object-relations analysts make all kinds of assumptions about what an infant feels and wants, but how do they know that a "true self" is being suppressed? Moreover, psychological scientists have shown that psychodynamic theories are guilty of three scientific failings:

Arekmalang/Fotolia

Freud claimed, without much empirical evidence, that all little girls suffer from "penis envy." But studies of preschool girls and boys find that young children of *both* sexes are curious about, and often imagine having, the reproductive abilities of the other sex (Linday, 1994).

THINKING CRITICALLY

Examine the evidence.

1 **Violating the principle of falsifiability.** As we saw in Chapter 2, a theory that is impossible to disconfirm in principle is not scientific. Many psychodynamic concepts about unconscious motivations are, in fact, impossible to confirm or disconfirm. Followers often accept an idea because it seems intuitively right or their experience seems to support it. Anyone who doubts the idea or offers disconfirming evidence is then accused of being "defensive" or "in denial."

2 **Drawing universal principles from the experiences of a few atypical patients.** Freud and most of his followers generalized from a few individuals, often patients in therapy, to all human beings. Of course, sometimes case studies can generate valid insights about human behaviour. The problem occurs when the observer fails to confirm his or her observations by studying larger, more representative samples and including appropriate control groups. For example, some psychodynamically oriented therapists, believing in Freud's notion of a childhood "latency" stage, have assumed that if a child masturbates or enjoys sex play, the child has probably been sexually molested. But research finds that masturbation and sexual curiosity are not found just in abused children; these are normal and common childhood behaviours (Bancroft, 2006; Friedrich et al., 1998).

3 **Basing theories of personality development on the retrospective accounts of adults.** Most psychodynamic theorists did not observe random samples of children at different ages, as modern child psychologists do, to construct their theories of development. Instead they worked backward, creating theories based on themes in adults' recollections of childhood. The analysis of memories can be an illuminating way to achieve insights about our lives; in fact, it is the only way we can think about our own lives! But memory is often inaccurate, influenced as much by what is going on in our

lives now as by what happened in the past. If you are currently not getting along with your mother, you may remember all the times when she was hard on you and forget the counterexamples of her kindness.

Retrospective analysis has another problem: It creates an *illusion* of causality between events. People often assume that if A came before B, then A must have caused B. For example, if your mother spent three months in the hospital when you were five years old and today you feel shy and insecure in university, an object-relations analyst might draw a connection between the two facts. But a lot of other things could be causing your shyness and insecurity, such as being away from home for the first time at a large and impersonal institution. When psychologists conduct longitudinal studies, following people from childhood to adulthood, they often get a very different picture of causality from the one that emerges by looking backward (see Chapter 13).

Despite these serious problems, some psychodynamic concepts have been empirically tested and validated. Researchers have identified unconscious processes in thought, memory, and behaviour (Bargh & Morsella, 2008). They have found evidence for the major defence mechanisms, such as projection, denial, and displacement (Baumeister, Dale, & Sommer, 1998; Cramer, 2000; Marcus-Newhall et al., 2000). They have demonstrated the interaction of mind and body in the generation of stress-related physical problems. And they have confirmed the important psychodynamic idea that we are often unaware of the motives behind our own puzzling or self-defeating actions.

> ## THINKING CRITICALLY
> Analyze assumptions.
>
> Freud and his followers assumed they could derive general principles of personality by studying patients in therapy, that childhood traumas inevitably have lifelong emotional consequences, and that memories are reliable guides to the past. What is wrong with these assumptions?

Recite & Review

Recite: State aloud what you know about Jung's theory of the *collective unconscious* and its *archetypes*; and the *object-relations school*.

Review: Next, if you are not feeling defensive, reread this section.

Now take this *Quick Quiz:*

Are you feeling defensive about answering this quiz?

1. An eight-year-old boy is hitting classmates and disobeying his teacher. Which of the following explanations of his behaviour might come from a Freudian, Jungian, or object-relations analyst? (a) The boy is expressing his shadow archetype. b) The boy is expressing the aggressive energy of the id and has not developed enough ego control. (c) The boy has had unusual difficulty separating from his mother and is compensating by behaving aggressively.

2. What criticism of all three of the preceding explanations might a psychological scientist make?

3. In the 1950s and 1960s, many psychoanalysts, working with unhappy gay men who had sought therapy, concluded that homosexuality was a mental illness. What violation of the scientific method were they committing?

Answers:

1. a. Jungian b. Freudian c. object-relations analyst **2.** All three explanations are nonfalsifiable; that is, there is no way to disconfirm them or confirm them. They are just subjective interpretations. **3.** The analysts were drawing conclusions from patients in therapy and failing to test these conclusions with gay men who were not in therapy or with heterosexuals. When such research was done using appropriate control groups, it turned out that gay men were not more mentally disturbed or depressed than heterosexuals (Hooker, 1957).

●━│**Watch** the **Video** *Thinking Like a Psychologist: Measuring Personality* in **MyPsychLab**

Learning Objectives

⑤ Decide whether you can trust tests that tell you what "personality type" you are.

⑥ Explain how psychologists can tell which personality traits are more central or important than others.

⑦ List the five dimensions of personality that describe people the world over.

The Modern Study of Personality

People love to fit themselves and their friends into "types"; they have been doing it forever. Early Greek philosophers thought our personalities fell into four fundamental categories depending on mixtures of body fluids. For example, if you were an angry, irritable sort of person, you supposedly had an excess of choler, and even now the word *choleric* describes a hothead. And if you were sluggish and unemotional, you supposedly had an excess of phlegm, making you a "phlegmatic" type. ●

Popular Personality Tests

That particular theory is long gone, but other unscientific tests of personality types still exist, aimed at predicting how people will do at work, whether they will get along with others, or whether they will succeed as leaders. One such test, the Myers-Briggs Type Indicator, is hugely popular in business, at motivational seminars, and with matchmaking services; at least 2.5 million Americans a year take it (Gladwell, 2004). The test assigns people to one of 16 different types, depending on how the individual scores on the dimensions of introverted or extroverted, logical or intuitive. Unfortunately, the Myers-Briggs test is not much more reliable than measuring body fluids; one study found that fewer than half of the respondents scored as the same type a mere five weeks later. And there is little evidence that knowledge of a person's type reliably predicts behaviour on the job or in relationships (Barbuto, 1997; Paul, 2004; Pittenger, 1993). Equally useless from a scientific point of view are many of the tests used by business and government to predict which "types" are apt to steal, take drugs, or be disloyal on the job (Ehrenreich, 2001).

In contrast, there are many measures of personality traits that are scientifically valid and useful in research. These **objective tests (inventories)** are standardized questionnaires requiring written responses, typically to multiple-choice or true–false items. They provide information about literally hundreds of different aspects of personality, including needs, values, interests, self-esteem, emotional problems, and typical ways of responding to situations. Using well-constructed inventories, psychologists have identified hundreds of traits, ranging from sensation seeking (the enjoyment of risk) to "erotophobia" (the fear of sex). ●

Core Personality Traits

Are some personality traits more important or central than others? Do some of them overlap or cluster together? For Gordon Allport, one of the most influential psychologists in the empirical study of personality, the answer to both questions was yes. Allport (1961) recognized that not all traits have equal weight and significance in people's lives. Most of us, he said, have five to ten *central* traits that reflect a characteristic way of behaving, dealing with others, and reacting to new situations. For instance, some people see the world as a hostile, dangerous place, whereas others see it as a place for fun and frolic. *Secondary* traits, in contrast, are more changeable aspects of personality, such as music preferences, habits, casual opinions, and the like.

●━│**Watch** the **Video** *In the Real World: Putting Popular Personality Assessments to the Test* in **MyPsychLab**

objective tests (inventories) Standardized questionnaires requiring written responses; they typically include scales on which people are asked to rate themselves.

Raymond B. Cattell (1973) advanced the study of this issue by applying a statistical method called **factor analysis**. Performing a factor analysis is like adding water to flour: It causes the material to clump up into little balls. When applied to traits, this procedure identifies clusters of correlated items that seem to be measuring some common, underlying factor. Today, hundreds of factor-analytic studies support the existence of a cluster of five central "robust factors," known informally as the *Big Five* (Chang, Connelly, & Geeza, 2012; McCrae & Costa, 2008; McCrae et al., 2005; Paunonen, 2003; Roberts & Mroczek, 2008): ◉

factor analysis A statistical method for analyzing the intercorrelations among various measures or test scores; clusters of measures or scores that are highly correlated are assumed to measure the same underlying trait or ability (factor).

◉—⌐**Watch** the **Video**
Classic Footage of Gordon Allport on Personality Traits in **MyPsychLab**

1 **Extroversion versus introversion** describes the extent to which people are outgoing or shy. It includes such traits as being sociable or reclusive, adventurous or cautious, socially dominant or more passive, eager to be in the limelight or inclined to stay in the shadows.

2 **Neuroticism (negative emotionality) versus emotional stability** describes the extent to which a person suffers from such traits as anxiety, an inability to control impulses, and a tendency to feel negative emotions such as anger, guilt, contempt, and resentment. Neurotic individuals are worriers, complainers, and defeatists, even when they have no major problems. They are always ready to see the sour side of life and none of its sweetness.

3 **Agreeableness versus antagonism** describes the extent to which people are good-natured or irritable, cooperative or abrasive, secure or suspicious and jealous. It reflects the tendency to have friendly relationships or hostile ones.

Where do you think this man would score on extroversion?

Benedicte Desrus/Alamy

4 **Conscientiousness versus impulsiveness** describes the degree to which people are responsible or undependable, persevering or quick to give up, steadfast or fickle, tidy or careless, self-disciplined or impulsive.

5 **Openness to experience versus resistance to new experience** describes the extent to which people are curious, imaginative, questioning, and creative or conforming, unimaginative, predictable, and uncomfortable with novelty.

Culture can affect the prominence of these personality factors and how they are reflected in language (Toomela, 2003). Nonetheless, in spite of some semantic and cultural variations, the Big Five have emerged as distinct, central personality dimensions throughout the world, in countries as diverse as Britain, Canada, the Czech Republic, China, Ethiopia, Turkey, the Netherlands, Japan, Spain, the Philippines, Germany, Portugal, Israel, Korea, Russia, and Australia (Digman & Shmelyov, 1996; Katigbak et al., 2002; McCrae et al., 2005; Somer & Goldberg, 1999). One monumental research venture gathered data from thousands of people across 50 cultures. In this massive project, as in many smaller ones, the five personality factors emerged whether people were asked for self-reports or were assessed by others (McCrae et al., 2005; Terracciano & McCrae, 2006).

Although the Big Five are quite stable over a lifetime, especially once a person hits 30, there are some

People's personalities are often reflected in how they arrange their work spaces!

Paul Thomas/Getty Images

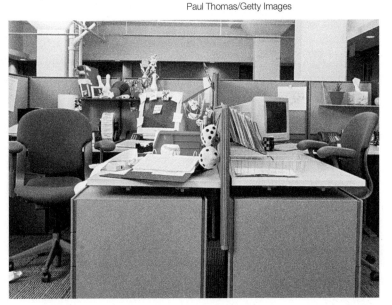

exceptions. In later adulthood people tend to become less extroverted and less open to new experiences, and, with the right experiences, many young people eventually become more self-confident and emotionally stable (Roberts & Mroczek, 2008). There is also some good news for crabby neurotics, especially young ones. Data from an enormous cross-sectional sample involving more than 1 200 000 children, adolescents, and adults, ages 10 to 65, revealed that whereas adult trends are overwhelmingly in the direction of greater maturity and adjustment, maturity plummets between late childhood and adolescence (Soto et al., 2011). Another survey of thousands of people in 10 countries, and a meta-analysis of 92 longitudinal studies, found that young people aged 16 to 21 are the most neurotic (emotionally negative) and the least

GET INVOLVED! Rate Your Traits

For each of the 10 items that follow, write a number from 1 to 7 indicating the extent to which you see that trait as being characteristic of you, where 1 = "I *disagree* strongly that this trait describes me" to 7 = "I *agree* strongly that this trait describes me." Use the midpoint, 4, if you neither agree nor disagree that the trait describes you. (This self-test was designed by Samuel D. Gosling.)

1. _____ Extroverted, enthusiastic
2. _____ Critical, quarrelsome
3. _____ Dependable, self-disciplined
4. _____ Anxious, easily upset
5. _____ Open to new experiences
6. _____ Reserved, quiet
7. _____ Sympathetic, warm
8. _____ Disorganized, careless
9. _____ Calm, emotionally stable
10. _____ Conventional, uncreative

To score yourself on the Big Five traits, use this key:

Extroversion:	High on question 1, low on question 6
Neuroticism:	High on question 4, low on question 9
Agreeableness:	High on question 7, low on question 2
Conscientiousness:	High on question 3, low on question 8
Openness:	High on question 5, low on question 10

Now ask a friend or relative to rate you on each of the 10 items. How closely does that rating match your own? If there is a discrepancy, what might be the reason for it?

FIGURE 14.1 Consistency and Change in the Personality over Lifespan
Although the Big Five traits are fairly stable, changes do occur over the lifespan. As you can see, neuroticism (negative emotionality) is highest among young adults and then declines, whereas conscientiousness is lowest among young adults and then steadily increases (Costa et al., 1999).

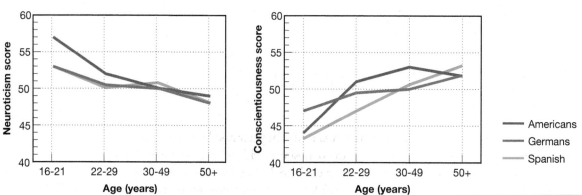

agreeable and conscientious. But fortunately, people tend to become more agreeable and conscientious and less negative between ages 30 and 40 (see Figure 14.1) (Costa et al., 1999; Roberts, Walton, & Viechtbauer, 2006). Because these changes have been found in many countries, they may reflect the universality of adult experiences—such as work and family responsibilities—or common maturational changes over the lifespan.

The Big Five do not provide a complete picture of personality, of course. Clinical psychologists note that important traits involved in mental disorders are missing, such as psychopathy (lack of remorse and empathy), self-absorption, and obsessionality (Westen & Shedler, 1999). Personality researchers note that other important traits are missing, such as religiosity, dishonesty, humorousness, independence, and conventionality (Abrahamson, Baker, & Caspi, 2002; Paunonen & Ashton, 2001). But most researchers today agree that the Big Five do lie at the core of key personality variations among individuals, and not only human individuals, either.

Recite & Review

Recite: Out loud, say as much as you can about *objective tests (inventories)*, *factor analysis*, and the "Big Five" personality traits.

Review: Next, show that you have the trait of conscientiousness by rereading this section.

Now take this *Quick Quiz:*

Show that you have the trait of conscientiousness by taking this quiz.

1. What is the advantage of inventories over projective tests in measuring personality?

2. Raymond Cattell advanced the study of personality by (a) developing case-study analysis, (b) using factor analysis, (c) devising the Myers-Briggs Type Indicator.

3. Which of the following are *not* among the Big Five personality factors? (a) introversion, (b) agreeableness, (c) psychoticism, (d) openness to experience, (e) intelligence, (f) neuroticism, (g) conscientiousness

4. Which one of the Big Five typically decreases by age 40? (a) agreeableness, (b) extroversion, (c) openness to experience, (d) neuroticism

Answers:

1. In general, they have better reliability and validity. 2. b 3. c, e 4. d

Learning Objectives

8 Explain whether animals have "personalities" just as people do.

9 Articulate the extent to which temperamental and personality differences among people are influenced by genes.

10 Describe why people who have highly heritable personality traits are not necessarily stuck with them forever.

Genetic Influences on Personality

A mother we know was describing her two children: "My daughter has always been difficult, intense, and testy," she said, "but my son is the opposite, placid and good-natured. They came out of the womb that way." Was this mother right? Is it possible to be born touchy or good-natured? What aspects of personality might have an inherited component?

Researchers measure genetic contributions to personality in three ways: by studying personality traits in other species, by studying the temperaments of human infants and children, and by doing heritability studies of twins and adopted individuals. These methods, to date, permit us only to *infer* the existence of relevant genes—just as, if you find your toddler covered in chocolate, it's pretty safe to infer that candy is somewhere close by. Scientists hope that the actual genes underlying key traits will one day be discovered, and dozens of possible associations between specific genes and personality traits have already been reported (Fox, Nichols, et al., 2005; Plomin et al., 2001). You will be hearing lots more about genetic discoveries in the coming years, so it is important to understand what they mean and don't mean.

BIOLOGY and *Animal Traits*

Do Puppies Have Personalities?

When we think of an individual who has a personality, we usually think of a human being. But members of many other species, including bears, dogs, hyenas, goats, cats, and of course our fellow primates, also vary in their characteristic ways of responding to the environment and to one another (Weinstein, Capitanio, & Gosling, 2008). Some chimpanzees are warm, friendly, and cooperative; others are conniving and mean. Some are "extroverts," bold and impulsive; others are "introverts," shy and cautious (Fairbanks, 2001). Apparently, then, you don't have to be a person to have a personality.

Recently, researchers have been crossing the border between traditional personality research and physiology, genetics, ecology, and ethology (the study of animals in their natural habitats) to investigate the nature of "personality" in our fellow animals (Fairbanks, 2001). These investigators argue that just as it has been evolutionarily adaptive for human beings to vary in their temperaments and ways of responding to the world and those around them (see Chapter 3), so it has been for animals. It would be beneficial for a species if some, but not all, of its members were bold or impulsive enough to risk life and limb to confront a stranger or experiment with a new food, and if some of its members were appropriately cautious.

In an imaginative set of studies, Samuel D. Gosling and his colleagues (2003) recruited dog owners and their dogs in a local park. All the owners provided personality assessments of their dogs and filled out the same personality inventory for themselves. The owners then designated another person who knew them and their dogs and who could judge the personalities of both. In a second study, the owners brought their dogs to an enclosed section of the park where three independent observers rated the dogs so that the researchers could compare the owners' judgments of their dogs' personalities with the observers' ratings. And in a third study, the investigators took photos of the dogs at play in order to examine the effects of breed and appearance on the animals' personalities.

Future studies that blur the "border" between humans and other species will help researchers to better understand the complex interaction of genetic, biological, and environmental effects on personality.

Maxx images

In their previous work with dogs and 11 other species, the psychologists had found evidence of all the Big Five traits except conscientiousness, which requires considerable cognitive ability and to date has turned up only in humans and chimpanzees (Gosling & John, 1999). In this research too, they found four doggie dimensions of extroversion, agreeableness, emotional reactivity (neuroticism), and openness to experience. The dog owners, their friends, and the neutral observers all agreed quite strongly in their ratings of the dogs' personalities along these four dimensions. So when you hear your dog-crazy friend say, "Barkley is such a shy and nervous little pup, whereas Barker is outgoing and sociable," she is probably right.

temperaments Physiological dispositions to respond to the environment in certain ways; they are present in infancy and in many nonhuman species and are assumed to be innate.

Heredity and Temperament

Let's turn now to human personalities. Even in the first weeks after birth, human babies differ in activity level, mood, responsiveness, heart rate, and attention span (Fox, Henderson, et al., 2005). Some are irritable and cranky; others are placid and calm. Some will cuddle up in an adult's arms and snuggle; others squirm and fidget, as if they cannot stand being held. Some smile easily; others fuss and cry. These differences appear even when you control for possible prenatal influences, such as the mother's nutrition, drug use, or problems with the pregnancy. The reason is that babies are born with genetically determined **temperaments**, dispositions to respond to the environment in certain ways (Clark & Watson, 2008). Temperaments include *reactivity* (how excitable, arousable, or responsive a baby is), *soothability* (how easily the baby is calmed when upset), and positive and negative emotionality. Temperaments are quite stable over time and are the clay out of which later personality traits are moulded (Clark & Watson, 2008; Else-Quest et al., 2006; Rothbart, Ahadi, & Evans, 2000).

Jerome Kagan (1997) has spent years studying the temperament of reactivity, following children from infancy to adolescence. About 20% of all children are either highly reactive or nonreactive; the other 80% fall somewhere in between. Highly reactive infants, even at four months of age, are excitable, nervous, and fearful; they overreact to any little thing, even a colourful picture placed in front of them. As toddlers, they tend to be wary and fearful of new things—toys that make noise, odd-looking robots—even when their moms are right there with them. At five years, many of these

Extreme shyness and fear of new situations tend to be biologically based, stable aspects of temperament, both in human beings and in monkeys. On the left, a timid infant rhesus monkey cowers behind a friend in the presence of an outgoing stranger.

Left: Dr. Stephen J. Suomi. Right: JGI/Jamie Grill/Getty Images children are still timid and uncomfortable in new situations. At seven years, many still have symptoms of anxiety. They are afraid of being kidnapped, they need to sleep with the light on, and they are afraid of sleeping in an unfamiliar house—even if they have never experienced any sort of trauma.

In contrast, nonreactive infants, Kagan (1998) says, are "California, laid-back babies." They lie there without fussing; they rarely cry; they babble happily. As toddlers, they are outgoing and curious about new toys and events. They continue to be easygoing and extroverted throughout childhood.

Children at these two extremes differ physiologically, too (Rothbart, Ahadi, & Evans, 2000). During mildly stressful tasks, reactive children are more likely than nonreactive children to have increased heart rates, heightened brain activity, and high levels of stress hormones. The same physiological attributes appear in shy, anxious infant rhesus monkeys (Suomi, 1991). Starting early in life, these "uptight" monkeys respond with anxiety to novelty and challenge, just as highly reactive children do. They too have high heart rates and elevated stress hormones.

You can see how biologically based temperaments might form the basis of the later personality traits we call extroversion, agreeableness, or neuroticism.

Heredity and Traits

A third way to study genetic contributions to personality is to estimate the **heritability** of specific traits within groups of children or adults. As we discuss in Chapter 3, heritability refers to the proportion of the total variation in a trait that is attributable to genetic variation within a group. Estimates of heritability come from behavioural–genetic studies of adopted children and of identical and fraternal twins reared apart and together. (If you need to review these methods and how they are used to estimate the role of genetics, see pages 85–89.) 👁

Findings from adoption and twin studies have provided compelling support for a genetic contribution to personality. Identical twins reared apart will often have unnerving similarities in gestures, mannerisms, and moods; indeed, their personalities often seem as similar as their physical features. If one twin tends to be optimistic, glum, or excitable, the other will probably be that way too (Braungert et al., 1992; Plomin, DeFries, & Knopik, 2013). Researchers have begun to identify some of the different patterns of brain activity that underlie such traits. For example, just about everyone feels some discomfort when facing the unknown. But people who score high on neuroticism find uncertainty almost intolerable at a neurological level; their brains show high reactivity in certain key areas (Hirsch & Inzlicht, 2008).

Behavioural–genetic findings have produced remarkably consistent results on the heritability of traits. For the Big Five and for many other traits, from aggressiveness to overall happiness, heritability is about 0.50 (Bouchard, 1997a; Jang et al., 1998; Lykken & Tellegen, 1996; Waller et al., 1990; Weiss, Bates, & Luciano, 2008). This means that within a group of people, about 50% of the variation in such traits is attributable to genetic differences among the individuals in the group. These findings have been replicated in many countries.

Evaluating Genetic Theories

We think you will agree that these behavioural–genetic findings are pretty amazing. "It will doubtless seem incredible to many readers that variables such as social class, educational opportunities, religious training, and parental love and discipline have no substantial influence on adult personality," wrote Robert McCrae and Paul Costa in 1988, "but imagine for a moment that it is correct. Psychologists hope that one intelligent use of such findings will be to help people become more accepting of

👁—⎤Watch the Video
Special Topics: Twins and Personality
in **MyPsychLab**

heritability A statistical estimate of the proportion of the total variance in some trait that is attributable to genetic differences among individuals within a group.

THINKING CRITICALLY

Tolerate uncertainty.

Identical twins Gerald Levey (left) and Mark Newman were separated at birth and raised in different cities. When they were reunited at 31, they discovered some astounding similarities. Both were volunteer firefighters, wore moustaches, and were unmarried. Both liked to hunt, watch old John Wayne movies, and eat Chinese food. They drank the same brand of beer, held the can with the little finger curled, and crushed the can when it was empty. It's tempting to conclude that all of these similarities are due to heredity, but we should also consider other explanations: Some could result from shared environmental factors such as social class and upbringing and some could be due merely to chance. For any given set of twins, we can never know for sure.

themselves and their children. Although we can all learn to make improvements and modifications to our personalities, most of us probably will never be able to *transform* our personalities completely because of our genetic dispositions and temperaments—a realization that might make people more realistic about what psychotherapy can do for them, and about what they can do for their children" (as cited in Efran, Greene, & Gordon, 1998).

On the other hand, it is important not to oversimplify by assuming that "It's all in our genes!" A genetic *predisposition* does not necessarily imply genetic *inevitability*. A person might have a gene that, for example, predisposes him or her to depression, but without certain environmental stresses or circumstances, the person will probably never become depressed (see Chapter 15). When people oversimplify, they mistakenly assume that personality problems that have a genetic component are permanent—say, that someone is "born to be bad" or to be a miserable grump forever (Dweck, 2008). Oversimplification can also lead people to incorrectly assume that if a problem, such as depression or shyness, has a genetic contribution, it will respond only to medication, so there is no point trying other interventions; we discuss this fallacy further in Chapter 16.

As Robert Plomin (1989), a leading behavioural geneticist, observed, "The wave of acceptance of genetic influence on behaviour is growing into a tidal wave that threatens to engulf the second message of this research: These same data provide the best available evidence for the importance of environmental influences." Let us now see what some of those influences might be.

THINKING CRITICALLY

Don't oversimplify.

Some personality traits, such as shyness, are highly heritable. Some people think that means "genes are everything"; a shy person can never learn to be comfortable in new situations, so there's no point trying to change. What is a more accurate way to think about the impact of heredity on personality?

Recite & Review

Recite: Tell the nearest dog or baby (real or imagined) as much as you can about personality in animals, *temperaments*, and the *heritability* of personality traits.

Review: Although there is no quiz-taking gene, you do have the ability to reread this section as a check on your memory.

Now take this *Quick Quiz:*

We hope you a few have quiz-taking genes.

1. What three broad lines of research support the hypothesis that personality differences are due in part to genetic differences?

2. In behavioural–genetic studies, the heritability of personality traits, including the Big Five, is typically about (a) 0.50, (b) 0.90, (c) 0.10 to 0.20, (d) zero.

3. Researchers announce that their study of identical twins has revealed a high heritability for divorce (McGue & Lykken, 1992). Given that our prehistoric ancestors hadn't yet invented marriage, let alone divorce, what on earth could this finding mean?

Answers:

1. Research on animal personalities, human temperaments, and the heritability of traits. **2.** a **3.** There obviously cannot be a "divorce gene," but perhaps personality factors with a heritable component, such as neuroticism and hostility, make it harder for a person to get along with a partner and thereby increase the likelihood of getting divorced (Rogge et al., 2006).

Learning Objectives

11 Describe how social-cognitive theory accounts for Madonna's "personality" changes (and everyone else's).

12 List the extent to which parents can—and can't—influence their children's personalities.

13 Describe how your peers shape certain of your personality traits, and suppress others.

Environmental Influences on Personality

The environment may be half of the influence on variations in personality, but what *is* the environment, exactly? In this section, we will consider the relative influence of three aspects of the environment: the particular situations you find yourself in, how your parents treat you, and who your peers are.

Situations and Social Learning

The very definition of a trait is that it is consistent across situations. But people often behave one way with their parents and a different way with their friends, one way at home and a different way in other situations. In learning terms, the reason for people's inconsistency is that different behaviours are rewarded, punished, or ignored in different contexts. For example, you are likely to be more extroverted in an audience of screaming, cheering *American Idol* fans than at home with relatives who would regard such noisy displays with alarm and condemnation. This is why some behaviourists think it does not even make much sense to talk about "personality."

Social-cognitive learning theorists, however, argue that people do acquire central personality traits from their learning history and their resulting expectations and beliefs. (To refresh your memory of learning principles and of how strict behaviourists differ from social-cognitive learning theorists, see Chapter 7.) A child who studies hard and gets good grades, attention from teachers, admiration from friends, and praise from parents will come to expect that hard work in other situations will also pay off. That child will become, in terms of personality traits, "ambitious" and "industrious." A child who studies hard and gets poor grades, is ignored by teachers and parents, and is rejected by friends for being a grind will come to expect that working hard isn't worth it. That child will become, in terms of personality traits, "unambitious" or "unmotivated."

Today, most personality researchers recognize that people can have a core set of stable traits *and* that their behaviour can vary across situations (Fleeson, 2004). There is a continual interaction between your particular qualities and the situation you are in. Your temperaments, habits, and beliefs influence how you respond to others, whom you hang out with, and the situations you seek (Bandura, 2001; Cervone & Shoda, 1999; Mischel & Shoda, 1995). In turn, the situation influences your behaviour and beliefs, rewarding some behaviours and extinguishing others. In social-cognitive learning theory, this process is called **reciprocal determinism**.

The two-way process of reciprocal determinism (as opposed to the one-way determinism of "genes determine everything" or "everything is learned") helps

THINKING CRITICALLY
Don't oversimplify.

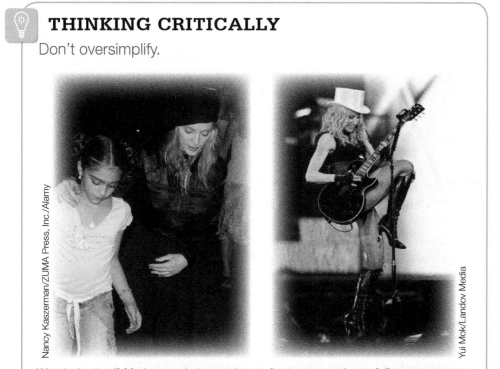

Who is the "real" Madonna—doting mother or flamboyant performer? By understanding reciprocal determinism, we can avoid oversimplifying. Our genetic dispositions and personality traits cause us to choose some situations over others, but situations then influence which aspects of our personalities we express.

reciprocal determinism In social-cognitive theories, the two-way interaction between aspects of the environment and aspects of the individual in the shaping of personality traits.

nonshared environment Unique aspects of a person's environment and experience that are not shared with family members.

answer a question asked by everyone who has a sibling: What makes children who grow up in the same family so different, apart from their genes? The answer seems to be: an assortment of experiences that affect each child differently, chance events that cannot be predicted, situations that children find themselves in, and peer groups that the children belong to (Harris, 2006; Plomin, 2011; Rutter et al., 2001). Behavioural geneticists refer to these unique and chance experiences that are not shared with other family members as the **nonshared environment**: for example, being in Mrs. Miller's class in grade 4 (which might inspire you to become a scientist), winning the lead in the school play (which might push you toward an acting career), or being bullied at school (which might have caused you to see yourself as weak and powerless). All these experiences work reciprocally with your own interpretation of them, your temperament, and your perceptions (did Mrs. Miller's class excite you or bore you?).

Keeping the concept of reciprocal determinism in mind, let us take a look at two of the most powerful environmental influences in people's lives: their parents and their friends.

Parental Influence—and Its Limits

If you check out parenting books online or in a bookstore, you will find that in spite of the zillion different kinds of advice they offer, they share one entrenched belief: Parental child-rearing practices are the strongest influence, maybe even the *sole* influence, on children's personality development. For many decades, few psychologists thought to question this assumption, and many still accept it. Yet the belief that personality is primarily determined by how parents treat their children has begun to crumble under the weight of three kinds of evidence (Harris, 2006, 2009; Plomin, 2011):

THINKING CRITICALLY

Examine the evidence.

Most people assume that parents are almost entirely responsible for their children's personality and behaviour. What evidence challenges this popular belief?

1 **The shared environment of the home has little if any influence on most personality traits.** In behavioural–genetic research, the "shared environment" includes the family you grew up with and the experiences and background you shared with your siblings and parents. If these had as powerful an influence as commonly assumed, studies should find a strong correlation between the personality traits of adopted children and those of their adoptive parents. In fact, the correlation is weak to nonexistent, indicating that the influence of childrearing practices and family life is very small compared to the influence of genetics (Cohen, 1999; Plomin, 2011). It is only the nonshared environment that has a strong impact.

2 **Few parents have a single child-rearing style that is consistent over time and that they use with all their children.** Developmental psychologists have tried for many years to identify the effects of specific child-rearing practices on children's personality traits. The problem is that parents are inconsistent from day to day and over the years. Their child-rearing practices vary, depending on their own stresses, moods, and marital satisfaction (Holden & Miller, 1999). As one child we know said to her exasperated mother, "Why are you so mean to me today, Mommy? I'm this naughty every day." Moreover, parents tend to adjust their methods of child rearing according to the temperament of the child; they are often more lenient with easygoing children and more punitive with difficult ones.

3 **Even when parents try to be consistent in the way they treat their children, there may be little relation between what they do and how the children turn out.** Some children of troubled and abusive parents are resilient and do not suffer lasting emotional damage, and some children of the kindest and most nurturing parents succumb to drugs, mental illness, or gangs.

Of course, parents do influence their children in lots of ways that are unrelated to the child's personality. They contribute to their children's religious beliefs, intellectual and occupational interests, motivation to succeed, skills, values, and adherence to traditional or modern notions of masculinity and femininity (Beer, Arnold, & Loehlin, 1998; Krueger, Hicks, & McGue, 2001). Above all, what parents do profoundly affects the quality of their relationship with their children—whether their children feel loved, secure, and valued or humiliated, frightened, and worthless (Harris, 2009).

Parents also have some influence even on traits in their children that are highly heritable. In one longitudinal study that followed children from age three to age 21, those who were impulsive, uncontrollable, and aggressive at age three were far more likely than calmer children to grow up to be impulsive, unreliable, and antisocial and more likely to commit crimes (Caspi, 2000). Early temperament was a strong and consistent predictor of these later personality traits. But not *every* child came out the same way. What protected some of those at risk, and helped them move in a healthier direction, was having parents who made sure they stayed in school, supervised them closely, and gave them consistent discipline.

Nevertheless, it is clear that, in general, parents have less influence on a child's personality than many people think. Because of reciprocal determinism, the relationship runs in both directions, with parents and children continually influencing one another. Moreover, as soon as children leave home, starting in preschool, parental influence on children's behaviour *outside* the home begins to wane. The nonshared environment—peers, chance events, and circumstances—takes over.

The Power of Peers

When two psychologists surveyed 275 freshmen at Cornell University, they found that most of them had secret lives and private selves that they never revealed to their parents (Garbarino & Bedard, 2001). On Facebook, too, many teenagers report having committed crimes, drinking, doing drugs, cheating in school, sexting, and having sex, all without their parents having a clue. (They assume, incorrectly, that what they reveal is "private" and read only by their several hundred closest friends.) This phenomenon of showing only one facet of your personality to your parents and an entirely different one to your peers becomes especially apparent in adolescence.

Children, like adults, live in two environments: their homes and their world outside the home. At home, children learn how their parents want them to behave and what they can get away with; as soon as they go to school, however, they conform to the dress, habits, language, and rules of their peers. Most adults can remember how terrible they felt when their classmates laughed at them for pronouncing a word "the wrong way" or doing something "stupid" (i.e., not what the rest of the kids were doing), and many recall the pain of being excluded. To avoid the controlling forces of being laughed at or rejected, most children will do what they can to conform to the norms and rules of their immediate peer group (Harris, 2009). Children who were law-abiding in grade 5 may start breaking the law in high school, if that is what it takes—or what they think it takes—to win the respect of their peers.

GET INVOLVED! Situation and Self

Are you a different person when you are alone, with your parents, hanging out with friends, in class, or at a party? If so, in what ways? Do you have a secret self that you do not show to your family? Consider the Big Five factors, or any other personality traits that are important to you, as you answer these questions.

It has been difficult to tease apart the effects of parents and peers because parents usually try to arrange things so that their children's environments duplicate their own values and customs. To see which has the stronger influence on personality and behaviour, therefore, we must look at situations in which the peer group's values clash with the parents' values. For example, when parents value academic achievement and their child's peers think that success in school is only for sellouts or geeks, whose view wins? The answer, typically, is peers (Arroyo & Zigler, 1995; Harris, 2009). Conversely, children whose parents gave them no encouragement or motivation to succeed may find themselves with peers who are working like mad to get into college or university, and start studying hard themselves.

Thus, peers play a tremendous role in shaping our personality traits and behaviour, causing us to emphasize some attributes or abilities and downplay others. Of course, as the theory of reciprocal determinism would predict, our temperaments and dispositions also cause us to select particular peer groups (if they are available) instead of others, and our temperaments influence how we behave within the group. But once we are among peers, most of us go along with them, moulding facets of our personalities to the pressures of the group.

In sum, core personality traits may stem from genetic dispositions, but they are profoundly shaped by learning, peers, situations, experience, and, as we will see next, the largest environment of all: the culture.

Recite & Review

Now take this *Quick Quiz:*

Do your peers take these quizzes? Does the answer determine whether you will?

1. What three lines of evidence have challenged the belief that parents are the major influence on their children's personalities?

2. Which contributes most to the variation among siblings in their personality traits? (a) the unique experiences they have that are not shared with their families, (b) the family environment that all of them share, or (c) the way their parents treat them

3. Eight-year-old Dwayne is pretty shy at home, where he is the middle of 12 children, but extroverted at school, where he is the leader of his friends. What might be the reason for his personality change?

Answers:

1. The shared family environment has little if any influence on personality; few parents have a consistent child-rearing style; and even when parents try to be consistent in the way they treat their children, there may be little relation between what they do and how the children turn out. 2. a 3. Peer groups have a powerful influence on which personality traits are encouraged and expressed, and peers can even override the child's situation at home.

Learning Objectives

14. Describe how culture influences your personality, and even whether you think have you a stable one.

15. Explain why men in the South and West are more likely to get angry when insulted than other American men.

16. Appreciate cultural influences on personality without stereotyping.

Cultural Influences on Personality

culture A program of shared rules that governs the behaviour of members of a community or society and a set of values, beliefs, and attitudes shared by most members of that community.

If you get an invitation to come to a party at seven, at what time do you arrive? Conscientiousness about time is an individual personality trait. However, **culture** has a profound effect on people's behaviour, attitudes, and the traits they value or disdain. Culture provides rules that govern our behaviour and values that shape our beliefs (see Chapter 8). And it is just as powerful an influence on personality and behaviour as any biological process.

Culture, Values, and Traits

Quick! Answer this question: "Who are you?"

Your answer will be influenced by your cultural background, and particularly by whether your culture emphasizes individualism or community (Hofstede & Bond, 1988; Kanagawa, Cross, & Markus, 2001; Markus & Kitayama, 1991; Triandis, 1996, 2007). In **individualist cultures**, the independence of the individual often takes precedence over the needs of the group, and the self is often defined as a collection of personality traits ("I am outgoing, agreeable, and ambitious") or in occupational terms ("I am a psychologist"). In **collectivist cultures**, group harmony often takes precedence over the wishes of the individual, and the self is defined in the context of relationships and the community ("I am the son of a farmer, descended from three generations of storytellers on my mother's side and five generations of farmers on my father's side . . ."). In one fascinating study that showed how embedded this dimension is in language and how it shapes our thinking, bicultural individuals born in China tended to answer "Who am I?" in terms of their own individual attributes when they were writing in English—but they described themselves in terms of their relations to others when they were writing in Chinese (Ross, Xun, & Wilson, 2002).

As Table 14.1 shows, individualist and collectivist ways of defining the self influence many aspects of life, including which personality traits we value, how and whether we express emotions, how much we value having relationships or maintaining freedom, and how freely we express angry or aggressive feelings (Forbes et al., 2009; Oyserman & Lee, 2008). With its multicultural population, Canada is a unique environment within which to see both perspectives. Romin Tafarodi and colleagues at the University of Toronto examined the interaction between both individualist and collectivist cultural affiliations on self-esteem. Overall, their findings indicate that whether or not we feel good about ourselves stems largely from how our culture defines our specific role in society—as either individuals struggling to compete with others to reach personal goals, or as one of many in the larger community helping each other to reach common goals (Tafarodi, 1998; Tafarodi & Milne, 2002; Tafarodi, Lang, & Smith, 1999; Tafarodi, Tam, & Milne, 2001).

Individualist and collectivist orientations affect us in countless subtle but powerful ways. For example, in one study, Chinese and American pairs had to play a communication game that required each partner to be able to take the other's

individualist cultures Cultures in which the self is regarded as autonomous, and individual goals and wishes are prized above duty and relations with others.

collectivist cultures Cultures in which the self is regarded as embedded in relationships, and harmony with one's group is prized above individual goals and wishes.

Individualistic Americans exercise by running, walking, bicycling, and skating, all in different directions and wearing different clothes. Collectivist Japanese employees at their hiring ceremony exercise in identical fashion.

Left: Geraint Lewis/Alamy. Right: Patti McConville/Alamy.

TABLE 14.1 Some Average Differences between Individualist and Collectivist Cultures

Members of Individualist Cultures	Members of Collectivist Cultures
Define the self as autonomous, independent of groups.	Define the self as an interdependent part of groups.
Give priority to individual, personal goals.	Give priority to the needs and goals of the group.
Value independence, leadership, achievement, self-fulfillment.	Value group harmony, duty, obligation, security.
Give more weight to an individual's attitudes and preferences than to group norms as explanations of behaviour.	Give more weight to group norms than to individual attitudes as explanations of behaviour.
Attend to the benefits and costs of relationships; if costs exceed advantages, a person is likely to drop a relationship.	Attend to the needs of group members; if a relationship is beneficial to the group but costly to the individual, the individual is likely to stay in the relationship.

Source: Triandis, 1996.

perspective. Eye-gaze measures showed that the Chinese players were almost always able to look at the target from their partner's perspective, whereas the American players often completely failed at this task (Wu & Keysar, 2007). Of course, members of both cultures understand the difference between their own view of things and another person's, but the collectivist-oriented Chinese pay closer attention to other people's nonverbal expressions, the better to monitor and modify their own responses.

Because people from collectivist cultures are concerned with adjusting their own behaviour depending on the social context, they tend to regard personality and the sense of self as being more flexible than people from individualist cultures do. In a study comparing Japanese and Americans, the Americans reported that their sense of self changes only 5 to 10% in different situations, whereas the Japanese said that 90 to 99% of their sense of self changes (de Rivera, 1989). For the group-oriented Japanese, it is important to enact *tachiba*, to perform your social roles correctly so that there will

In many cultures, children are expected to contribute to the family income and to take care of their younger siblings. These experiences encourage helpfulness over independence.

Alamy

be harmony with others. Americans, in contrast, tend to value "being true to yourself" and having a "core identity."

Culture and Traits. When people fail to understand the influence of culture on behaviour, they often attribute another person's mysterious or annoying actions to individual personality traits when they are really due to cultural norms. Take cleanliness. How often do you bathe? Once a day, once a week? Do you regard baths as healthy and invigorating or as a disgusting wallow in dirty water? How often, and where, do you wash your hands—or feet? A person who would seem obsessively clean in one culture might seem an appalling slob in another (Fernea & Fernea, 1994).

Or consider helpfulness. Many years ago, in a classic cross-cultural study of children in Kenya, India, Mexico, the Philippines, Japan, the United States, and five other countries, researchers measured how often children behaved altruistically (offering help, support, or unselfish suggestions) or egoistically (seeking help and attention or wanting to dominate others) (Whiting & Edwards, 1988; Whiting & Whiting, 1975). American children were the least altruistic on all measures and the most egoistic. The most altruistic children came from societies in which children are assigned many tasks, such as caring for younger children and gathering and preparing food. These children knew that their work made a genuine contribution to the well-being or economic survival of the family. In cultures that value individual achievement and self-advancement, taking care of others has less importance, and altruism as a personality trait is not cultivated to the same extent.

Or consider tardiness. Individuals differ in whether they try to be places "on time" or are always late, but cultural norms affect how individuals regard time in the first place. In northern Europe, Canada, the United States, and most other individualistic cultures, time is organized into linear segments in which people do one thing "at a time" (Hall, 1983; Hall & Hall, 1990; Leonard, 2008). The day is divided into appointments, schedules, and routines, and because time is a precious commodity, people don't like to "waste" time or "spend" too much time on any one activity (hence the popularity of multitasking). In such cultures, being on time is taken as a sign of conscientiousness or thoughtfulness and being late as a sign of indifference or intentional disrespect. Therefore, it is considered the height of rudeness (or high status) to keep someone waiting. But in Mexico, southern Europe, the Middle East, South America, and Africa, time is organized along parallel lines. People do many things at once, and the needs of friends and family supersede mere appointments; they think nothing of waiting for hours or days to see someone. The idea of having to be somewhere "on time," as if time were more important than a person, is unthinkable.

CULTURE and *Violence*
The Cultivation of Male Aggression

Many people think that men are more violent than women because men have higher levels of testosterone. But if that is so, then why, given that men everywhere have testosterone, do rates of male aggressiveness vary enormously across cultures and throughout history? Why are rates of violence higher in some regions of the United States than others?

To answer these questions, Richard Nisbett (1993) began by examining the historical record. He found that the American South, along with some western regions of the country originally settled by Southerners, have much higher rates of white homicide and other violence than the rest of the country has—but only particular kinds of violence: the use of fists or guns to protect a man's sense of honour, protect his property, or respond to perceived insults. Nisbett considered various explanations, such as poverty or racial tensions. But when he controlled for regional differences in poverty and the percentage of blacks in the population, by county, "Southernness" remained an independent predictor of homicide. Nisbett also ruled out a history of slavery as an explanation: Regions of the South that had the highest concentrations of slaves in the past have the lowest white homicide rates today.

Nisbett hypothesized that the higher rates of violence in the South derive from economic causes: The higher rates occur in cultures that were originally based on herding, in contrast to cultures based on agriculture. Why would this be so? People who depend economically on agriculture tend to develop and promote cooperative strategies for survival. But people who depend on their herds are extremely vulnerable; their livelihoods can be lost in an instant by the theft of their animals. To reduce the likelihood of theft, Nisbett theorized, herders learn to be hyperalert to any threatening act (real or perceived) and respond to it immediately with force. This would explain why cattle rustling and horse thievery were capital crimes in the Old West, and why Mediterranean and Middle Eastern herding cultures even today place a high value on male aggressiveness. And indeed, when Nisbett looked at agricultural practices *within* the South, he found that homicide rates were more than twice as high in the hills and dry plains areas (where herding occurs) as in farming regions.

The emphasis on aggressiveness and vigilance in herding communities, in turn, fosters a *culture of honour*, in which even small disputes and trivial insults (trivial to people from other cultures, that is) put a man's reputation for toughness on the line,

⚡ THINKING CRITICALLY

Analyze assumptions and biases.

Many people assume that men can't help being violent because of their biology. Yet, on average, men in agricultural economies are far more cooperative and nonviolent than men in herding economies. Amish farmers have always had very low rates of violence, whereas in the Old West, the cattle-herding cowboy culture was a violent one. (Fortunately, the shootout here is a reenactment.)

requiring him to respond with violence to restore his status (Cohen, 1998). Although the herding economy has become much less important in the South and West, the legacy of its culture of honour remains. These regions have rates of honour-related homicides (such as murder to avenge a perceived insult to one's family) that are *five times higher* than in other regions of the country. Cultures of honour also have higher rates of domestic violence. Both sexes in such cultures believe it is appropriate for a man to physically assault a woman if he believes she is threatening his honour and reputation by being unfaithful or by leaving him (Vandello & Cohen, 2008). Why do these practices continue long after they are functional, considering that most young Southern college men aren't herding cattle on their campuses? In a series of experiments, Southern men were more likely than Northern men to assume that their male peers believe that aggressive action is *required* to restore honour. Thus the cultural practice is perpetuated because "everyone else" seems to demand it (Vandello, Cohen, & Ransom, 2008).

Nisbett and his colleagues also wanted to demonstrate how these external cultural norms literally "get under the skin" to affect physiology and personality. They brought 173 Northern and Southern male students into their lab and conducted three experiments to measure how these students would respond psychologically and physiologically to being insulted (Cohen et al., 1996). They explained that the experiment would assess the students' performance on various tasks and that the experimenter would be taking saliva samples to measure everyone's blood sugar levels throughout the procedure. Actually, the saliva samples were used to measure levels of cortisol, a hormone associated with high levels of stress, and testosterone, which is associated with dominance and aggression. At one point in the experiment, a confederate of the experimenter, who seemed to be another student participant, bumped into each man and called him an insulting name (a seven-letter word beginning with "a," if you want to know).

As you can see in Figure 14.2, Northerners responded calmly to the insult; if anything, they thought it was funny. But many Southerners were immediately inflamed and their levels of cortisol and testosterone shot up. They were more likely to feel that their masculinity had been threatened, and they were more likely to retaliate aggressively than Northerners were. Southerners and Northerners who were not insulted were alike on most measures, with the exception that the Southerners were actually more polite and deferential. It appears that they have more obliging manners than Northerners—until they are insulted. Then, look out.

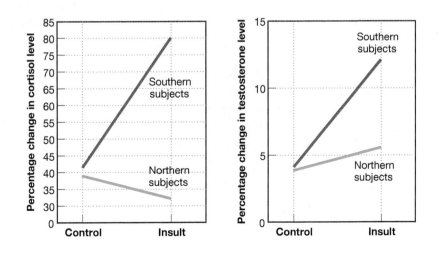

FIGURE 14.2 Aggression Cultures and of Honour

As these two graphs show, when young men from Northern states were insulted in an experiment, they shrugged it off, thinking it was funny or unimportant. But for young Southern men, levels of the stress hormone cortisol and of testosterone shot up—and they were more likely to retaliate aggressively (Cohen et al., 1996).

In cultures of honour, in sum, when "being a man" is defined by competitiveness and strength, some men will constantly try to prove their masculinity and status in displays of aggression (Bosson & Vandello, 2011).

Being raised in a culture of honour, however, is only one cause of male aggression. Another cause has to do with the dangers that a culture faces. In cultures in which competition for resources is fierce and survival is difficult, men are "toughened up" and pushed to take risks, even with their lives (Gilmore, 1990). In contrast, among the Ifaluk, the Tahitians, and the people of Sudest Island near New Guinea, where resources are abundant and there are no serious hazards or enemies to worry about, men do not feel they have to prove themselves and they are not raised to be tough and aggressive (Lepowsky, 1994; Levy, 1984). When a society becomes more peaceful, so do its men.

. . . .

Evaluating Cultural Approaches

A woman we know, originally from England, married a Lebanese man. They were happy together but had the usual number of marital misunderstandings and squabbles. After a few years, they visited his family home in Lebanon, where she had never been before. "I was stunned," she told us. "All the things I thought he did because of his *personality* turned out to be because he's *Lebanese*! Everyone there was just like him!"

Our friend's reaction illustrates both the contributions and the limitations of cultural studies of personality. She was right in recognizing that some of her husband's behaviour was attributable to his culture; for example, his Lebanese notions of time were very different from her English notions. But she was wrong to infer that the Lebanese are all "like him": Individuals are affected by their culture, but they vary within it.

Cultural psychologists face the problem of how to describe cultural influences on personality without oversimplifying or stereotyping (Church & Lonner, 1998). As one student of ours put it, "How come when we students speak of 'the' Japanese or 'the' blacks or 'the' whites or 'the' Latinos, it's called stereotyping, and when you do it, it's called 'cross-cultural psychology'?" This question shows excellent critical thinking! The study of culture does not rest on the assumption that all members of a culture behave the same way or have the same personality traits. As we have seen, people vary according to their temperaments, beliefs, and learning histories, and this variation occurs within every culture.

Moreover, regional variations occur in every society. Canada may be an "individualist" culture overall, but Quebec and the Maritime provinces, with their history of strong regional identity, are more collectivist than the rugged, independent Western province of Alberta.

Cultural psychologists also face the risk of exaggerating the contrasts between cultures. In spite of their differences, all cultures reflect adaptations to universal human needs, such as those for love, attachment, family, work, identity, and self-esteem. As one cultural psychologist put it, "Human beings are not blank slates on which any cultural form can be written" (Cohen, 2001). Yet the existence of cross-cultural universals and of individual variations within cultures does not negate the importance of cultural rules that, on average, make Swedes different from Bedouins, or Cambodians different from Italians. The traits that we value, our sense of self versus community, and our notions of the right way to behave—all key aspects of personality—begin with the culture in which we are raised.

THINKING CRITICALLY

Don't oversimplify.

Many people will collectively characterize the personality of people from Alberta, or from Toronto. How can we think about the cultural factors that influence personality traits without stereotyping?

Recite & Review

Recite: Find a culturally comfortable way to say out loud what you remember about *reciprocal determinism*, *nonshared environment*, *culture*, *individualist* versus *collectivist* cultures, cultures of honour, and cultural influences on personality traits.

Review: Because you live in an educational culture that values doing well in academic courses, ensure your own best performance by rereading this section.

Now take this *Quick Quiz:*

At the moment, you live in a culture that values the importance of quizzes.

1. Are cultures whose members regard the "self" as a collection of stable personality traits individualist or collectivist?

2. Which cultural practice tends to foster the traits of helpfulness and altruism? (a) every family member "does his or her own thing," (b) parents insist that children obey, (c) children contribute to the family welfare, (d) parents remind children often about the importance of being helpful

3. Why, according to one theory, do men in the American South and West respond more aggressively to perceived insults than other American men do?

Answers:

1. individualist 2. c 3. These men come from regions in which economies based on herding gave rise to "cultures of honour," requiring males to be vigilant and aggressive toward potential threats.

Learning Objectives

17 Contrast how humanist approaches to personality differ from psychodynamic and genetic ones.

18 List the contributions of Abraham Maslow, Carl Rogers, and Rollo May to understanding our "inner lives."

19 Explain how your life story affects your personality—and vice versa.

20 Contrast how psychological scientists evaluate humanist and narrative views of personality.

The Inner Experience

A final way to look at personality starts from each person's own point of view, from the inside out. Biology may hand us temperamental dispositions that benefit or limit us, the environment may deal us some tough or fortunate experiences, our parents may treat us as we would or would not have wished, but the sum total of our personality is how we, individually, weave all of these elements together.

Humanist Approaches

One such approach to personality comes from **humanist psychology**, which was launched as a movement in the early 1960s. The movement's chief leaders—Abraham Maslow (1908–1970), Carl Rogers (1902–1987), and Rollo May (1909–1994)—argued that it was time to replace psychoanalysis and behaviourism with a "third force" in psychology, one that would draw a fuller picture of human potential and personality. Psychologists who take a humanist approach to personality emphasize our uniquely human capacity to determine our own actions and futures.

Abraham Maslow. The trouble with psychology, said Maslow (1970, 1971), was that it had ignored many of the positive aspects of life, such as joy, laughter, love, happiness,

humanist psychology A psychological approach that emphasizes personal growth, resilience, and the achievement of human potential.

You are never too old for self-actualization. Hulda Crooks, shown here at age 91 climbing Mt. Fuji, took up mountain climbing at 54. "It's been a great inspiration for me," she said. "When I come down from the mountain I feel like I can battle in the valley again." She died at the age of 101.

Itsuo Inouye/AP Images

and *peak* experiences, rare moments of rapture caused by the attainment of excellence or the experience of beauty. The traits that Maslow thought most important to personality were not the Big Five, but rather the qualities of the *self-actualized person*—the person who strives for a life that is meaningful, challenging, and satisfying (see Chapter 12).

For Maslow, personality development could be viewed as a gradual progression toward self-actualization. Most psychologists, he argued, had a lopsided view of human nature, a result of their emphasis on studying emotional problems and negative traits such as neuroticism or insecurity. As Maslow (1971) wrote, "When you select out for careful study very fine and healthy people, strong people, creative people . . . then you get a very different view of mankind. You are asking how tall can people grow, what can a human being become?"

Carl Rogers. As a clinician, Carl Rogers (1951, 1961) was interested not only in why some people cannot function well but also in what he called the "fully functioning individual." How you behave, he said, depends on your subjective reality, not on the external reality around you. Fully functioning people experience *congruence*, or harmony, between the image they project to others and their true feelings and wishes. They are trusting, warm, and open, rather than defensive or intolerant. Their beliefs about themselves are realistic.

To become fully functioning people, Rogers maintained, we all need **unconditional positive regard**, love and support for the people we are, without strings (conditions) attached. This doesn't mean that Winifred should be allowed to kick her brother when she is angry with him or that Wilbur may throw his dinner out the window because he doesn't like pot roast. In these cases, a parent can correct the child's behaviour without withdrawing love from the child. The child can learn that the behaviour, not the child, is what is bad. "House rules are 'no violence,' children," is a very different message from "You are horrible children for behaving so badly."

Unfortunately, Rogers observed, many children are raised with *conditional* positive regard: "I will love you if you behave well, and I won't love you if you behave badly." Adults often treat each other this way, too. People treated with conditional regard begin to suppress or deny feelings or actions that they believe are unacceptable to those they love. The result, said Rogers, is incongruence, a sense of being out of touch with your feelings, of not being true to your real self, which in turn produces low self-regard, defensiveness, and unhappiness. A person experiencing incongruence scores high on neuroticism, becoming bitter and negative.

Rollo May. May shared with the humanists a belief in free will. But he also emphasized some of the inherently difficult and tragic aspects of the human condition, including loneliness, anxiety, and alienation. May brought to American psychology elements of the European philosophy of **existentialism**, which emphasizes such inevitable challenges of human existence as the search for the meaning of life, the need to confront death, and the necessity of taking responsibility for our actions.

Free will, wrote May, carries a price in anxiety and despair, which is why so many people try to escape from freedom into narrow certainties and blame others for their misfortunes. For May, our personalities reflect the ways we cope with the struggles to find meaning in existence, to use our freedom wisely, and to face suffering and death bravely. May popularized the humanist idea that we can choose to make the best of ourselves by drawing on inner resources such as love and courage, but he added that we can never escape the harsh realities of life and loss.

Narrative Approaches

In the past two decades, another approach to personality has focused on the importance of the *life* narrative, the story that each of us develops over time to explain ourselves and make meaning of everything that has happened to us (Bruner, 1990; McAdams, 2008;

unconditional positive regard To Carl Rogers, love or support given to another person with no conditions attached.

existentialism A philosophical approach that emphasizes the inevitable dilemmas and challenges of human existence.

Existential psychologists remind us of the inevitable struggles of human existence, as such the fight against loneliness and alienation.

Shelly Perry/iStockphoto

McAdams & Pals, 2006; Sarbin, 1997a, 1997b). In the narrative view, your distinctive personality rests on the story you tell to answer the question "Who am I?"

Because the narrative approach emphasizes how the stories we tell give us an identity, shape our behaviour, and motivate us to pursue or abandon our goals, it integrates the many diverse influences on personality that we have discussed in this chapter. Do you believe you are a victim of bad childhood experiences or a survivor of them? Do you believe that your mood swings are caused by a biochemical imbalance or an imbalanced love affair? When you talk about your life to others, do you play the hero or the passive bystander?

The life narrative you create for yourself reflects your needs and justifies the actions you take, or fail to take, to solve your problems. It affects whether you even feel that you can solve your problems and transform your life (McAdams, 2008). For example, therapist David Epston worked with an immigrant woman named Marisa, who had been abused and rejected all her life. "To tell a story about your life turns it into a history," he told her, "one that can be left behind, and makes it easier for you to create a future of your own design" (as cited in O'Hanlon, 1994). Marisa came to see that she could tell a new story about her experiences, one that did not emphasize the tragedies that had befallen her but rather her triumphs in overcoming them. "My life has a future now," she told Epston. "It will never be the same again."

In the narrative view, your stories about how you see and explain yourself are the essence of your personality, capturing everything that has happened to you and all the factors that affect your biology, psychology, and relationships. They are what make you unique in all the world.

Evaluating Humanist and Narrative Approaches

As with psychodynamic theories, the major scientific criticism of humanist psychology is that many of its assumptions are untestable. Freud looked at humanity and saw destructive drives, selfishness, and lust. Maslow and Rogers looked at humanity and saw cooperation, selflessness, and love. May looked at humanity and saw fear of freedom, loneliness, and the struggle for meaning. These differences, say critics, may tell us more about the observers than about the observed.

Many humanist concepts, although intuitively appealing, are hard to define operationally (see Chapter 2). How can we know whether a person is self-fulfilled or self-actualized?

How can we tell whether a woman's decision to quit her job and become a professional rodeo rider represents an "escape from freedom" or a freely made choice? And what exactly is unconditional positive regard? If it is defined as unquestioned support of a child's efforts at mastering a new skill, or as assurance that the child is loved in spite of his or her mistakes, then it is clearly a good idea. But in the popular culture, it has often been interpreted as an unwillingness ever to say no to a child or to offer constructive criticism and set limits, which children need.

Despite such concerns, humanist psychologists have added balance to the study of personality. A contemporary specialty known as "positive psychology" (see Chapter 1) follows in the footsteps of humanism by focusing on the qualities that enable people to be optimistic and resilient in times of stress (Gable & Haidt, 2005; Seligman & Csikszentmihaly, 2000). Influenced in part by the humanists, psychologists are studying many positive human traits, such as courage, altruism, the motivation to excel, and self-confidence. Developmental psychologists are studying ways to foster children's empathy and creativity. And some researchers are studying the emotional and existential effects of the fear of death.

As for narrative approaches, research is flourishing, showing how the stories we tell about ourselves play a crucial role in shaping our distinctive personalities (McAdams & Pals, 2006). Cognitive psychologists emphasize how our stories shape and distort our memories. Psychotherapists are exploring the ways in which clients who tell self-defeating life stories might turn them around, creating more hopeful and positive ones. Social and cultural psychologists examine how a culture or society's dominant myths and shared stories influence people's ambitions and expectations, political views, and beliefs that the world can be improved or will never change.

The humanist, existential, and narrative views of personality share one central message: We have the power to choose our own destinies, even when fate delivers us into tragedy. Across psychology, this message has fostered an appreciation of resilience in the face of adversity.

Recite & Review

Recite: Choose to exercise free will and autonomy by reciting out loud what you know about *humanist psychology*, Abraham Maslow and his notions of peak experiences and self-actualization, Carl Rogers and *unconditional positive regard*, Rollo May and *existentialism*, and narrative approaches to personality.

Review: Next, reread this section.

Now take this *Quick Quiz:*

Exercise free will, as a humanist would advise you to, by choosing to take this quiz.

1. According to Carl Rogers, a man who loves his wife only when she is looking her best is giving her _____ positive regard.

2. The humanist who described the importance of having peak experiences was (a) Abraham Maslow, (b) Rollo May, (c) Carl Rogers.

3. A humanist and a Freudian psychoanalyst are arguing about human nature. What underlying assumptions about psychology and human potential are they likely to bring to their discussion? How can they resolve their differences without either–or thinking?

Answers:

1. conditional **2.** a **3.** The Freudian assumes that human nature is basically selfish and destructive; the humanist assumes that it is basically loving and cooperative. They can resolve this either–or debate by recognizing that human beings have both capacities, and that the situation and culture often determine which capacity is expressed at a given time.

Now that you have read about the major influences on personality (see Review 14.1), how would you explain why Madonna is who she is? Some aspects of her character and temperament, such as extroversion and conscientiousness, seem likely to have a genetic component. Her personality was perhaps also shaped, however, by unique experiences in her childhood and young adulthood that were not shared with her siblings: having the opportunity to take dance classes, later seizing the chance and running away to New York. Madonna's chameleon-like persona, which changes every couple of years, is further shaped and rewarded by today's culture, which often values image over reality, transience over permanence, style over substance, celebrity over obscurity. Psychodynamic theorists might wonder whether Madonna's unconscious motivations for success and her constant changing of public personalities stem from the shock of losing her mother when she was only six; Madonna was her mother's first name, too. Humanists might remind us that we do not know anything about the real Madonna, because the faces she presents to the public might reveal nothing at all about her inner, private self. And psychologists who study life narratives would have a full-time job keeping up with the stories that Madonna spins about herself!

REVIEW 14.1 The Major Influences on Personality

Psychodynamic		Unconscious dynamics shape human motives, guilts, conflicts, and defences.
Genetic		Children are born with particular temperaments, and most traits are highly influenced by genes.
Environmental Experience		Learning, situations, and unique experiences affect which traits are encouraged and which genes are expressed.
	Parents	Modify and shape a child's temperament and genetic predispositions; affect gender roles, attitudes, and self-concept; affect the quality of the relationship with the child.
	Peer group	Influences an individual's values, behaviour, ambitions, goals, and so on.
	Situation	Determines which behaviours are rewarded and which are punished or ignored, thereby shaping the expression or suppression of particular traits.
	Chance events	May influence a person's experiences and choices in unexpected ways, thus encouraging the development of some traits over others.
Cultural		Cultural norms specify which traits are valued, affect basic notions of the self and personality, and shape behaviours from aggressiveness to altruism.
Humanist		Despite genetic, environmental, cultural, and psychodynamic influences, people can exercise free will to become the kind of person they want to be.
Narrative		Personality rests on the stories people create to explain their lives (e.g., whether they see themselves as victims or survivors); these stories can change.

✱⌐Explore the Concept
What Has Shaped Your Personality?
in MyPsychLab

For Madonna and for all the rest of us, genetic influences, learned habits, cultural norms, unconscious fears and conflicts, and visions of possibility, filtered through our interior sense of self and our life story, give each of us the stamp of our personality, the qualities that make us feel uniquely . . . us.   ✱

Taking Psychology with You

THINKING CRITICALLY IN EVERYDAY LIFE

How to Avoid the "Barnum Effect"

How well does the following paragraph describe you? *Some of your aspirations tend to be pretty unrealistic. At times you are extroverted, affable, and sociable, while at other times you are introverted, wary, and reserved. You pride yourself on being an independent thinker and do not accept others' opinions without satisfactory proof. You prefer a certain amount of change and variety, and you become dissatisfied when hemmed in by restrictions and limitations. At times you have serious doubts as to whether you have made the right decision or done the right thing.*

When people believe that this description was written just for them, as the result of a personalized horoscope or handwriting analysis, they all say the same thing: "It describes me *exactly*!" Everyone thinks this description is accurate because it is vague enough to apply to almost everyone and it is flattering. Don't we all consider ourselves to be "independent thinkers"?

This is why many psychologists worry about the "Barnum effect" (Snyder & Shenkel, 1975). P. T. Barnum was the great circus showman who said, "There's a sucker born every minute." He knew that the formula for success was to "have a little something for everybody," which is just what unscientific personality profiles, horoscopes, and handwriting analyse (graphology) have in common. They have "a little something for everyone" and are therefore nonfalsifiable.

For example, graphologists claim that they can identify your personality traits from the form and distribution of your handwritten letters. Wide spacing between words means you feel isolated and lonely. If your lines drift upward, you are an "uplifting" optimist, and if your lines droop downward, you are a pessimist who feels you are being "dragged down." If you make large capital *I*'s, you have a large ego.

Graphologists are not the same as handwriting experts, who are trained to determine, say, whether a document is a forgery. Graphologists, like astrologers, usually know little or nothing about the scientific method, how to correct for their biases, or how to empirically test their claims. That is why the

many different graphological approaches usually conflict. For example, according to one system, a certain way of crossing *t*'s reveals someone who is vicious and sadistic; according to another, it reveals a practical joker (Beyerstein, 1996).

Whenever graphology *has* been tested empirically, it has failed. A meta-analysis of 200 published studies found no validity or reliability to graphology in predicting work performance, aptitudes, or personality. No school of graphology fared better than any other, and no graphologist was able to perform better than untrained amateurs making guesses from the same writing samples (Dean, 1992; Klimoski, 1992).

If graphology were just an amusing game, no one would worry about it, but unfortunately it can have harmful consequences. Graphologists have been hired by companies to predict a person's leadership ability, attention to detail, willingness to be a good team player, and more. They pass judgment on people's honesty, generosity, and even supposed criminal tendencies. How would you feel if you were turned down for a job because some graphologist branded you a potential thief on the basis of your alleged "desire-for-possession hooks" on your *S*'s?

If you do not want to be a victim of the Barnum effect, research offers this advice to help you think critically about graphology and its many cousins:

Beware of all-purpose descriptions that could apply to anyone. Sometimes you doubt your decisions; who among us has not? Sometimes you feel outgoing and sometimes shy; who does not? Do you "have sexual secrets that you are afraid of confessing"? Just about everybody does.

Beware of your own selective perceptions. Most of us are so impressed when an astrologer, psychic, or graphologist gets something right that we overlook all the descriptions that are plain wrong. Be aware of the confirmation bias—the tendency to explain away all the descriptions that don't fit.

Resist flattery and emotional reasoning. This is a hard one! It is easy to reject a profile that describes you as selfish or stupid. Watch out for the ones that make you feel good by telling you how wonderful and smart you are, what a great leader you will be, or how modest you are about your exceptional abilities.

If you keep your ability to think critically with you, you won't end up paying hard cash for soft answers or taking a job you dislike because it fits your "personality type." In other words, you'll have proven Barnum wrong.

Summary

MyPsychLab can help you get a better grade. Test your knowledge and grasp difficult concepts through

- Custom study plans: See where you are strong and where you are wrong
- Multimedia, including videos and interactive simulations
- Dynamic Study Modules: flashcards for self-study that ensure you achieve mastery of course concepts

- *Personality* refers to an individual's distinctive and relatively stable pattern of behaviour, motives, thoughts, and emotions. Personality is made up of many different *traits*, characteristics that describe a person across situations.

Psychodynamic Theories of Personality

- Sigmund Freud was the founder of *psychoanalysis*, which was the first *psychodynamic* theory. Modern psychodynamic theories share an emphasis on unconscious processes and a belief in the formative role of childhood experiences and early unconscious conflicts.

- To Freud, the personality consists of the *id* (the source of sexual energy, which he called the *libido*, and the aggressive instinct), the *ego* (the source of reason), and the *superego* (the source of conscience). *Defence* mechanisms protect the ego from unconscious anxiety. They include, among others, repression, projection, displacement (one form of which is sublimation), regression, and denial.

- Freud believed that personality develops in a series of *psychosexual* stages, with the *phallic* (Oedipal) stage most crucial. During this stage, Freud believed, the *Oedipus* complex occurs, in which the child desires the parent of the other sex and feels rivalry with the same-sex parent. When the Oedipus complex is resolved, the child identifies with the same-sex parent, but females retain a lingering sense of inferiority and "penis envy"—a notion later contested by female psychoanalysts such as Clara Thompson and Karen Horney.

- Carl Jung believed that people share a *collective* unconscious that contains universal memories and images, or *archetypes*, such as the *shadow* (evil) and the Earth Mother.

- The *object-relations school* emphasizes the importance of the first two years of life rather than the Oedipal phase; the infant's representations of important figures, especially the mother,

rather than sexual needs and drives; and the problem in male development of breaking away from the mother.

- Psychodynamic approaches have been criticized for violating the principle of falsifiability; for overgeneralizing from atypical patients to everyone; and for basing theories on the unreliable memories and retrospective accounts of adults, which can create an *illusion of causality*. However, some psychodynamic ideas have received empirical support, including the existence of nonconscious processes and defences.

The Modern Study of Personality

- Most popular tests that divide personality into "types" are not valid or reliable. In research, psychologists typically rely on *objective tests (inventories)* to identify and study personality traits and disorders.

- Gordon Allport argued that people have a few *central traits* that are key to their personalities and a greater number of *secondary traits* that are less fundamental. Raymond Cattell used *factor analysis* to identify clusters of traits that he considered the basic components of personality. There is strong evidence, from studies around the world, for the *Big Five* dimensions of personality: extroversion versus introversion, neuroticism (negative emotionality) versus emotional stability, agreeableness versus antagonism, conscientiousness versus impulsiveness, and openness to experience versus resistance to new experience. Although these dimensions are quite stable over time and across circumstances, some of them do change over the lifespan, reflecting maturational development or common adult responsibilities.

Genetic Influences on Personality

- As discussed in "Biology and Animal Traits," members of many other species, including octopuses, pigs, hyenas, bears, horses, dogs, and all primates, vary in the same characteristic traits as humans do—such as shyness, aggressiveness, extroversion, agreeableness, and neuroticism. This evidence suggests that certain key personality traits (and the Big Five factors) have an evolutionary, biological basis.

- In human beings, individual differences in *temperaments*, such as reactivity, soothability, and positive or negative emotionality, appear to be inborn, emerging early in life and influencing subsequent personality development. Temperamental differences in extremely reactive and nonreactive children may be due to variations in the responsiveness of the sympathetic nervous system to change and novelty.

- Behavioural–genetic data from twin and adoption studies suggest that the *heritability* of many adult personality traits is about 0.50. Genetic influences create dispositions and set limits on the expression of specific traits. But even traits that are highly heritable are often modified throughout life by circumstances, chance, and learning.

Environmental Influences on Personality

- People often behave inconsistently in different circumstances when behaviours that are rewarded in one situation are punished or ignored in another. According to *social-cognitive learning theory*, personality results from the interaction of the environment and aspects of the individual, in a pattern of *reciprocal determinism*.

- Behavioural geneticists have found that an important influence on personality is the *nonshared environment*, the unique experiences that each child in a family has.

- Three lines of evidence challenge the popular assumption that parents have the greatest impact on their children's personalities and behaviour: (1) Behavioural–genetic studies find that shared family environment has little if any influence on variations in most personality traits; (2) few parents have a consistent child-rearing style over time and with all their children; and (3) even when parents try to be consistent, there may be little relation between what they do and how the children turn out. However, parents can modify their children's temperaments, prevent children at risk of delinquency and crime from choosing a path of antisocial behaviour, influence many of their children's values and attitudes, and teach them to be kind and helpful. And, of course, parents profoundly affect the quality of their relationship with their children.

- One major environmental influence on personality comes from a person's peer groups, which can be more powerful than parents. Most children and teenagers behave differently with their parents than with their peers.

Cultural Influences on Personality

- Many qualities that western psychologists treat as individual personality traits are heavily influenced by *culture*. People from *individualist cultures* define themselves in different terms than those from *collectivist cultures*, and they perceive their "selves" as more stable across situations. Cultures vary in their norms for many behaviours, such as cleanliness and notions of time. Altruistic children tend to come from cultures in which their families assign them many tasks that contribute to the family's well-being or economic survival.

- As discussed in "Culture and Violence," male aggression is not simply a result of male hormones; it is also influenced by the economic requirements of the culture a man grows up in, which in turn shape men's beliefs about when violence is necessary. Herding economies foster male aggressiveness more than agricultural economies do. Men in *cultures of honour*, including certain regions of the American South and West, are more likely to become angry when they feel insulted and to behave aggressively to restore their sense of honour than are men from other cultures; when they are insulted, their levels of cortisol and testosterone rise quickly, whereas men from other cultures generally do not show this reaction.

- Cultural theories of personality face the problem of describing broad cultural differences and their influences on personality without promoting stereotypes or overlooking universal human needs.

The Inner Experience

- *Humanist psychologists* focus on a person's subjective sense of self and the free will to change. They emphasize human potential and the strengths of human nature, as in Abraham Maslow's concepts of *peak experiences* and *self-actualization*. Carl Rogers stressed the importance of *unconditional positive regard* in creating a fully functioning person. Rollo May brought *existentialism* into psychology, emphasizing some of the inherent challenges of human existence that result from having free will, such as the search for meaning in life.

- As another way of understanding personality from the "inside," some personality psychologists study *life narratives*, the stories people create to explain themselves and make sense of their lives. These stories may serve to suppress changes in our lives or encourage them.

- Some ideas from humanist psychology are subjective and difficult to measure, but others have fostered research on positive aspects of personality, such as optimism, hope, and resilience under adversity. Research on the importance of life narratives has influenced the study of personality, memory, health, and psychotherapy.

- Genetic influences, life experiences and learned habits, cultural norms, unconscious fears and conflicts, and our private, inner sense of self all combine in complex ways to create our distinctive personalities.

Taking Psychology with You

- Critical thinkers can learn to avoid the "Barnum effect"—being a sucker for fake inventories, horoscopes, handwriting analysis, and other pseudoscientific "tests" of personality.

Key Terms

personality **505**
trait **505**
psychoanalysis **506**
psychodynamic theories **506**
id **507**
libido **507**
ego **507**

superego **507**
defence mechanisms **507**
psychosexual stages (oral, anal, phallic, latency, genital) **508**
Oedipus complex **508**
collective unconscious **510**
archetypes **510**

object-relations school **511**
objective tests (inventories) **514**
factor analysis **515**
temperaments **519**
heritability **520**
reciprocal determinism **523**

nonshared environment **524**
culture **526**
individualist cultures **527**
collectivist cultures **527**
humanist psychology **533**
unconditional positive regard **534**
existentialism **534**

15 Psychological Disorders

Ask questions. . . be willing to wonder

Are mental disorders the same in every culture?

———

Why do some people get over a traumatic experience fairly quickly, yet others develop PTSD?

———

Why do some people get depressed for no reason, while others have reason, but don't get depressed?

———

What's the matter with psychopaths that makes them capable of such heartless deception and cruelty?

———

Can problem drinkers ever learn to drink moderately?

Margaret Mary Ray believed with all her heart that late-night talk-show host David Letterman was in love with her. Caught up in this delusion, she stalked Letterman day and night for a decade, writing him letters and repeatedly breaking into his house. She camped out on his tennis court and once stole his car. The tabloids treated her delusions as a running joke. Finally, she gave up. She wrote to her mother, "I'm all travelled out," and put herself in front of a coal train. She was killed instantly.

You don't have to be a psychologist to know that something was terribly wrong with Margaret Mary Ray. When people think of "mental illness," they usually think of individuals like her—people with delusions or people who behave in bizarre ways, such as walking the streets wearing layers of clothing on a hot summer day.

Most psychological problems are far less dramatic than the public's impression of them and far more common. Some people go through episodes of complete inability to function, yet get along fine between those episodes. Many people function adequately every day, yet suffer constant melancholy, always feeling below par. And some people cannot control their worries or tempers. In this chapter, you will learn about the many psychological problems that cause people unhappiness and anguish. You will learn about the severe disorders that really do make people unable to control their behaviour. But you will also learn why psychologists and psychiatrists often find it difficult to agree on a diagnosis, and why diagnosing mental problems is not the same as diagnosing medical problems such as diabetes or appendicitis.

One of the most common worries that people have is "Am I normal?" It is normal to fear being abnormal—especially when you are reading about psychological problems! But it is also normal to have problems. All of us on occasion have difficulties that seem too much to handle, and it is often unclear precisely when "normal" problems shade into "abnormal" ones.

Learning Objectives

1 Explain why insanity is not the same thing as having a mental disorder.

2 Describe how mental disorders differ from normal problems.

3 Discuss why the standard professional guide to the diagnosis of mental disorders is controversial.

4 Explain why popular "projective" tests like the Rorschach Inkblot Test are not reliable.

Defining and Diagnosing Disorder

Many people confuse unusual behaviour—behaviour that deviates from the norm—with mental disorder, but the two are not the same. A person may behave in ways that are statistically rare (collecting ceramic pigs, being a genius at math, committing murder) without having a mental illness. Conversely, some mental disorders, such as depression and anxiety, are extremely common. ⊙➤

People also confuse mental disorder and insanity. In the law, the definition of *insanity* rests primarily on whether a person is aware of the consequences of his or her actions and can control his or her behaviour. But *insanity* is a legal term only; a person may have a mental illness and yet be considered sane by the court.

If frequency of the problem is not a guide, and insanity reflects only one extreme kind of mental illness, how then should we define a "mental disorder"?

Dilemmas of Definition

One problem is that the definition of a disorder depends on whether we are taking society's point of view, the view of people who are affected by the troubled individual, or the perspective of troubled individuals themselves.

1 **Mental disorder as a violation of cultural standards.** One definition emphasizes the roles and rules of the culture. Every society sets up standards for its members to follow, and those who break the most important rules governing appropriate behaviour are usually considered deviant or disturbed. However, many of these rules are specific to a particular time or group. For example, it is not uncommon for bereaved people to have momentary visions of a deceased relative or to "hear" the loved one's voice. But in most of North America, these hallucinations are considered abnormal, and people who have them often fear they might be "crazy." In contrast, the Chinese, the Hopi, and members of many other cultures, regard such visions as perfectly normal.

2 **Mental disorder as emotional distress.** A second approach identifies mental disorder in terms of a person's suffering—as from depression, anxiety, incapacitating fears, or problems with drugs. In this definition, a behaviour that is unendurable or upsetting for one person, such as lack of interest in sex, may be acceptable and normal for another. But this definition does not cover the behaviour of people who are clearly disturbed and dangerous to others, yet who are not troubled about their actions. ⊙➤

3 **Mental disorder as behaviour that is self-destructive or harmful to others.** A third approach emphasizes the negative consequences of a person's behaviour. Some behaviour is harmful to the individual sufferer, such as the behaviour of a woman who is so afraid of crowds that she cannot leave her house, a man who

⊙➤ **Simulate** the **Experiment**
Psychology Experiments Survey: Are You Normal? in **MyPsychLab**

⊙➤ **Simulate** the **Experiment**
Psychological Disorders in **MyPsychLab**

drinks so much that he cannot keep a job, or a student who is so anxious that she cannot take exams. In other cases, the individual may report feeling fine and deny that anything is wrong, yet will behave in ways that are disruptive, dangerous, or out of touch with reality—as when a child sets fires, a compulsive gambler loses the family savings, or a woman hears voices telling her to stalk a celebrity. ⊙➤

In this chapter, we define **mental disorder** broadly, as any behaviour or emotional state that causes a person to suffer, is self-destructive, seriously impairs the person's ability to work or get along with others, or endangers others or the community. By this definition, many people will have some mental-health problem in the course of their lives, or their loved ones will. A nationwide survey of more than 9000 randomly selected adults in the United States found that only about 7% of the population suffer from mental illnesses that are "seriously debilitating." But nearly half, at some time in their lives, temporarily fall prey to severe anxiety, depression, drug abuse, and other problems that can make their lives miserable (Kessler et al., 2005). In Canada, mental disorders are the leading cause of disability in people aged 15 to 44 (WHO, 2004).

Dilemmas of Diagnosis

Even armed with a general definition of mental disorder, psychologists have found that classifying mental disorders into distinct categories is not an easy job. In this section we will see why this is so.

Classifying Disorders: The DSM. The standard reference manual used to diagnose mental disorders is the *Diagnostic and Statistical Manual of Mental Disorders (DSM)*, published by the American Psychiatric Association (1994, 2000, 2013). The latest edition of the manual is the DSM-5, which was released in 2013. The importance of this manual in the field of psychology and psychiatry is substantial. In fact, it

⊙➤ **Simulate** the **Experiment**
Psychology Experiments Survey: How Do You Take Care of Your Mental Health? in **MyPsychLab**

mental disorder Any behaviour or emotional state that causes an individual great suffering, is self-destructive, seriously impairs the person's ability to work or get along with others, or endangers others or the community.

THINKING CRITICALLY

Define your terms.

Bojan Brecelj/Corbis   Al Campanie/The Image Works   Elena Dorfman/Redux Pictures

What's normal? In many places around the world, it is normal for women and men to create scars on their bodies for decoration or symbolic meaning. In Papua New Guinea, all young men go through an initiation rite in which small, deep cuts are made on their backs to create permanent scars that signify a crocodile's scales (left). In contrast, in most places it is abnormal to mutilate oneself for the sole purpose of inflicting injury and pain, as the patient on the right has done. But what about the decorative scars on the arm of the 23-year-old woman from upstate New York (middle), who had them made by a "body artist"? She also has scars on her leg and her stomach, along with 29 piercings. Is her behaviour "normal" or "abnormal"?

is often referred to as "the Bible of psychiatry." The DSM's primary aim is *descriptive:* to provide clear diagnostic categories so that clinicians and researchers can agree on which disorders they are talking about and then can study and treat these disorders.

Disorders documented in the DSM-5 are "clustered" together using the following chapters:

1. Neurodevelopmental Disorders
2. Emotional (Internalizing) Disorders
3. Somatic Disorders
4. Externalizing Disorders
5. Neurocognitive Disorders
6. Personality Disorders

The DSM has had an extraordinary impact worldwide. Virtually all textbooks in psychiatry and psychology base their discussions of mental disorders on the DSM. Lawyers and judges often refer to the manual's list of mental disorders, even though the DSM warns that its categories "may not be wholly relevant to legal judgments." With most new editions of the manual, the number of mental disorders has grown. The first edition, in 1952, was only 86 pages long and contained about 100 diagnoses. The DSM-IV, published in 1994 and slightly revised in 2000 (DSM-IV-TR), is 900 pages long and contains nearly 400 diagnoses of mental disorder. The DSM-5 is 947 pages and describes slightly fewer disorders than the DSM-IV-TR. The previous edition of the DSM had been widely criticized for the growing list of disorders, and it appears as though this criticism had some effect on the DSM-5!

What is the reason for this increase in mental disorders since 1952? Supporters of the new categories answer that it is important to distinguish disorders precisely in order to treat them properly. However, the DSM is an American publication, and health care in the United States is privatized to a much greater extent than is the case in Canada. Critics point to an economic reason: Insurance companies require clinicians to assign their clients an appropriate DSM code number for the diagnosed disorder, which puts pressure on compilers of the manual to add more diagnoses so that physicians and psychologists can be compensated.

THINKING CRITICALLY

Analyze assumptions and biases.

Many people assume that diagnosing mental disorders is as straightforward and objective as diagnosing appendicitis. Is this assumption correct?

Problems with the DSM. Because of the DSM's powerful influence, critics maintain that it is important to be aware of its limitations and some inherent problems in the very effort to classify and label mental disorders:

1 **The danger of overdiagnosis.** "If you give a small boy a hammer," wrote Abraham Kaplan (1967), "it will turn out that everything he runs into needs pounding." Likewise, say critics, if you give mental-health professionals a diagnostic label, it will turn out that everyone they run into has the symptoms of the new disorder.

Consider "attention deficit/hyperactivity disorder" (ADHD), a diagnostic label given to children and adults who are impulsive, messy, restless, and easily frustrated and who have trouble concentrating. Since ADHD was added to the DSM, it has become the fastest-growing disorder in both Canada and the United States, where it is diagnosed at least 10 times as often as it is in Europe. Critics therefore fear that parents, teachers, and mental-health professionals are overusing this diagnosis, especially on boys, who make up 80 to 90% of all ADHD cases. The critics argue that normal boyish behaviour—being rambunctious, refusing to nap, being playful, not listening to teachers in school—is being turned into a psychological problem (Cummings & O'Donohue, 2008; Panksepp, 1998). A longitudinal study of more than a hundred four- to six-year-olds found that the number of children who met the criteria for

ADHD declined over time (Lahey et al., 2005). Some remained highly impulsive and unable to concentrate, but others, it seems, simply matured!

Likewise, the fastest-growing diagnosis given to young children is bipolar disorder, once thought to occur only in adolescents and adults; the number of diagnoses rose from 20 000 to 800 000 in just one year (Moreno et al., 2007). Many experts think that only about 20% of the children currently diagnosed as bipolar meet the strict criteria for the disorder (Leibenluft & Rich, 2008).

2 **The power of diagnostic labels.** Being given a diagnosis reassures people who are seeking an explanation for their emotional symptoms or problems ("Whew! So *that's* what I've got!"). But once a person has been given a diagnosis, other people begin to see that person primarily in terms of the label; it sticks like lint. For example, when a rebellious, disobedient teenager is diagnosed as having "oppositional defiant disorder," people tend to see him as a person with a permanent, official condition; something is wrong with his personality. They then overlook other possible explanations of his actions: Maybe he is "defiant" because he has been mistreated or his parents don't listen to him. And once he is labelled, observers tend to ignore changes in his behaviour and the times when he is not being defiant.

3 **The confusion of serious mental disorders with normal problems.** The DSM is not called "The Diagnostic and Statistical Manual of Mental Disorders and a Whole Bunch of Everyday Problems." However, the DSM includes everyday problems, including "disorder of written expression" (having trouble writing clearly), or "religious or spiritual problem," or even "post-traumatic embitterment disorder." Some critics fear that by lumping together such normal difficulties with true mental illnesses, such as schizophrenia, the DSM implies that everyday problems are comparable to disorders—and equally likely to require treatment (Houts, 2002).

4 **The illusion of objectivity and universality.** Finally, some psychologists argue that the whole enterprise of the DSM is a vain attempt to impose a veneer of science on an inherently subjective process (Houts, 2002; Kutchins & Kirk, 1997; Tiefer, 2004). Many decisions about what to include as a disorder, say these critics, are based not on empirical evidence but on group consensus. The problem is that group consensus often reflects prevailing attitudes and prejudices rather than objective evidence.

It is easy to identify prejudices in *past* notions of mental problems. In the early years of the nineteenth century, a physician named Samuel Cartwright argued that many slaves were suffering from *drapetomania*, an urge to escape from slavery (Kutchins & Kirk, 1997; Landrine, 1988). (He made up the word from *drapetes*, the Latin word for "runaway slave," and *mania*, meaning "mad" or "crazy.") Thus, doctors could assure slave owners that a mental illness, not the intolerable condition of slavery, made slaves seek freedom. Today, of course, "drapetomania" seems foolish and cruel.

Over the years, psychiatrists have quite properly rejected many other "disorders" that reflected cultural prejudices and lacked empirical validation, such as lack of vaginal orgasm, childhood masturbation disorder, and homosexuality (Wakefield, 2011). But critics argue that many disorders still in the DSM are just as affected by contemporary prejudices and values. Today you don't have a disorder if you want to have sex "too often" (once called, in women, "nymphomania"), but you do if you do not want to have sex "often enough" (hypoactive sexual desire disorder) (Groneman, 2000). Emotional problems allegedly associated with menstruation remain in the DSM, but behavioural problems associated with testosterone have never even been considered for inclusion. In short, critics maintain, many diagnoses still depend on a cultural consensus—not

Harriet Tubman (on the left) helped others escape from slavery on the "underground railroad." Slaveholders welcomed the idea that Tubman and others who insisted on their freedom had a mental disorder called "drapetomania."

Getty Images, Inc.

on empirical evidence—about what constitutes normal behaviour, as well as what constitutes a mental disorder.

Advantages of the DSM. Defenders of the DSM agree that the boundaries between "normal problems" and "mental disorders" are fuzzy and often difficult to determine (Kessler et al., 2005). They also recognize that many psychological symptoms fall along a continuum, ranging from mild to severe (Helzer et al., 2008; McNally, 2011). This is one reason that the DSM-5 will classify many disorders along a spectrum of symptoms rather than as discrete categories. But they believe that when the manual is used correctly and diagnoses are made with valid objective tests, the DSM improves the reliability of diagnosis (Beutler & Malik, 2002; Widiger & Clark, 2000). This is important, they maintain, because the DSM's categories help clinicians distinguish among disorders that share certain symptoms (such as anxiety, irritability, or delusions) in order to select the most appropriate treatment.

....

CULTURE and *Mental Illness*
Are Mental Problems the Same Everywhere?

Researchers are making great progress in separating mental disorders that are universal—usually involving genetic vulnerabilities, brain disease, or brain damage—from those that are specific to particular cultural contexts, norms, and traditions. In response to critics who argue that almost all diagnoses of mental disorder are matters of consensus, clinicians point out that certain disorders occur everywhere. From the Inuit to the Pacific Islanders to the Yoruba of Nigeria, some individuals have schizophrenic delusions, are severely depressed, cannot control their aggressive behaviour, or have panic attacks (Butcher, Lim, & Nezami, 1998; Kleinman, 1988).

However, culture does influence and shape the particular symptoms a sufferer of these disorders will have, and how the disorder expresses itself (Barlow, Chorpita, & Turovsky, 1996). In Latin America and Southern Europe, a person having a panic attack may report feelings of choking, being smothered, and fear of dying. In America, the fear of "going crazy" is a more common symptom than elsewhere. In Greenland, some fishermen suffer from "kayak-angst": a sudden attack of dizziness and fear that occurs while they are fishing in small, one-person kayaks (Amering & Katschnig, 1990). Likewise, depression occurs all over the world, but members of various ethnic groups differ in what symptoms they reveal (drinking, crying, withdrawing . . .), in their willingness to talk about their feelings and seek help, and in the likelihood of committing suicide. In the United States, the group at highest risk of suicide is Native American men, and the group at lowest risk is black women (Goldston et al., 2008).

One difficulty in diagnosing mental disorders is raised by culture-specific presentation of *syndromes*. The latest edition of the DSM includes some variations of symptom presentation, depending on the cultural perspective. By all accounts, this represents a vast improvement over previous editions of the DSM.

Consider this example. In Japanese culture, people are extremely sensitive to matters of social harmony and concerned about not offending other people; *taijin kyo-fusho* is a disorder in which a person feels intensely frightened and irrationally medical exams, and children who have participated in lab experiments have failed to find consistent evidence that props improve young children's ability to make accurate reports. On the contrary, these props actually elevate the risk of false reports of touching (Poole, Bruck, & Pipe, 2011). You can see how someone who did not understand the problems with projective tests might end up making inferences about a child's behaviour that were dangerously wrong.

Another situation in which projective tests are used widely yet often inappropriately is in child-custody assessments. Understandably, when faced with divorcing partners who are bitterly quarrelling, calling each other names, and accusing each other of being a terrible parent, the courts long for an objective way to determine which one is better suited to have custody. But when a panel of psychological scientists impartially examined the leading psychological assessment measures, most of which are projective tests, they found that "these measures assess ill-defined constructs, and they do so poorly, leaving no scientific justification for their use in child custody evaluations" (Emery, Otto, & O'Donohue, 2005).

Objective Tests. Many clinicians also use **objective tests (inventories)**, standardized questionnaires that ask about the test taker's behaviour and feelings. Some inventories, such as the Beck Depression Inventory, the Spielberger State–Trait Anger Inventory, and the Taylor Manifest Anxiety Scale, assess specific emotional problems. The most widely used test for assessing personality and emotional disorders, the *Minnesota Multiphasic Personality Inventory (MMPI)*, is organized into 10 categories, or *scales*, covering such problems as depression, paranoia, schizophrenia, and introversion. Four additional *validity scales* indicate whether a test taker is likely to be lying, defensive, or evasive while answering the items.

Inventories are generally more reliable and more valid than either projective methods or subjective clinical judgments (Dawes, 1994; Meyer et al., 2001). But inventories also have some limitations; one continuing problem is that they often fail to take into account differences among cultural, regional, and socioeconomic groups. In response to this criticism, the developers of the MMPI released a major revision, the MMPI-2, with norms based on a sample that was more representative in terms of ethnicity, region, age, and gender (Butcher et al., 1989; Lucio et al., 1999). Explicit tests of whether this new structure actually represents personality in current clinical and nonclinical groups of people have been quite encouraging. At the University of Toronto, Michael Bagby and his colleagues gave the MMPI-2 test to more than 600 people (clinical and nonclinical participants) and found that its structure provided an accurate framework for describing personality in both groups of people (Bagby et al., 2002). However, despite these recent revisions of the MMPI the problem persists; for example, Mexican, Puerto Rican, and Argentine respondents score differently from non-Hispanic Americans, on average, on the Masculinity–Femininity Scale. This difference does not reflect emotional problems but rather traditional Latino attitudes toward sex roles (Cabiya et al., 2000). Also, the MMPI and other objective tests have a significant rate of false positives; that is, they sometimes label a person's responses as evidence of mental disorder when no serious problem actually exists (Guthrie & Mobley, 1994; Leib, 2008). And, finally, objective tests such as the MMPI are often inappropriately used in business, industry, legal settings, and schools by persons who are not well trained in testing.

We turn now to a closer examination of some of the disorders described in the DSM. Of course, we cannot cover all of them in one chapter, so we have singled out several that illustrate the range of psychological problems that afflict humanity, from the common to the very rare.

objective tests (inventories)
Standardized objective questionnaires requiring written responses; they typically include scales on which people are asked to rate themselves.

✓•⊏ **Study** and **Review**
in **MyPsychLab**

Recite & Review

Recite: Your mental health will be enhanced if you will say, out loud, what you know about insanity, *mental disorder*, the DSM (including its uses and limitations), culture-bound syndromes, *projective tests*, *objective tests*, and the MMPI.

Review: Next, reread this section.

Now take this *Quick Quiz:*

1. Ruthie is afraid to leave her apartment unless she is with a close friend or relative, yet she says she feels fine and she angrily resists her friends' advice that she get help. What definition of mental disorder does Ruthie's behaviour meet?

2. The primary purpose of the DSM is to (a) provide descriptive criteria for diagnosing mental disorders, (b) help psychologists assess normal as well as abnormal behaviour, (c) describe the causes of common disorders, (d) keep the number of diagnostic categories of mental disorders to a minimum.

3. List four criticisms of the DSM.

4. What is the advantage of inventories, compared with clinical judgments and projective tests, in diagnosing mental disorders?

Answers:

1. Mental disorder as behaviour that is self-destructive. 2. a 3. It can foster overdiagnosis; it overlooks the influence of diagnostic labels on the perceptions of clinicians and the behaviour of clients; it confuses serious mental disorders with everyday problems in living, and it falsely implies that its diagnoses apply universally and are always based on objective evidence. 4. Inventories have better reliability and validity.

Learning Objectives

5 Explain the difference between ordinary anxiety and an anxiety disorder.

6 Describe why the most disabling of all phobias is known as the "fear of fear."

7 Compare why some people recover quickly after a trauma whereas others develop posttraumatic stress disorder.

Anxiety Disorders

Anyone who is waiting for important news or living in an unpredictable situation quite sensibly feels *anxiety*, a general state of apprehension or psychological tension. And anyone who is in a dangerous and unfamiliar situation, such as making a first parachute jump or facing a peevish python, quite sensibly feels flat-out fear. In the short run, these emotions are adaptive because they energize us to cope with danger. They ensure that we don't make that first jump without knowing how to operate the parachute, and that we get away from that snake as fast as we can.

But sometimes fear and anxiety become detached from any actual danger, or these feelings continue even when danger and uncertainty are past. The result may be *chronic anxiety*, marked by long-lasting feelings of apprehension and doom; *panic attacks*, short-lived but intense feelings of anxiety; *phobias*, excessive fears of specific things or situations; or *obsessive-compulsive disorder*, in which repeated thoughts and rituals are used to ward off anxiety. ((•●

Anxiety and Panic

The chief characteristic of **generalized anxiety disorder** is continuous, uncontrollable anxiety or worry—a feeling of foreboding and dread—that occurs on a majority of days during a six-month period and that is not brought on by physical causes such as

((•●⊏ **Listen** to the **Chapter Audio**
Anxiety Disorders in **MyPsychLab**

generalized anxiety disorder A continuous state of anxiety marked by feelings of worry and dread, apprehension, difficulties in concentration, and signs of motor tension.

disease, drugs, or drinking too much coffee. Symptoms include restlessness or feeling keyed up, difficulty concentrating, irritability, jitteriness, sleep disturbance, and unwanted, intrusive worries.

Some people suffer from generalized anxiety disorder without having lived through any specific anxiety-producing event. They may have a physiological tendency to experience anxiety symptoms—sweaty palms, a racing heart, shortness of breath—when they are in challenging or uncontrollable situations. Genes may also be involved in causing abnormalities in the amygdala, the core structure for the acquisition of fear (see Chapter 11), and in the prefrontal cortex, which is associated with the ability to realize when danger has passed (Lonsdorf et al., 2009). As we saw in Chapter 13, temperamentally shy children are already predisposed to react with anxiety in novel situations. Other chronically anxious people may have a history, starting in childhood, of being unable to control or predict their environments (Barlow, 2000; Mineka & Zinbarg, 2006). Whatever the origin of generalized anxiety disorder, its sufferers have mental biases in the way they attend to and process threatening information. They perceive everything as an opportunity for disaster, a cognitive habit that fuels their worries and keeps their anxiety bubbling along (Mitte, 2008). ◉

posttraumatic stress disorder (PTSD) An anxiety disorder in which a person who has experienced a traumatic or life-threatening event has symptoms such as psychic numbing, reliving of the trauma, and increased physiological arousal.

◉—⎤Watch the **Video**
Clinical Anxiety in **MyPsychLab**

Posttraumatic Stress Disorder. Stress symptoms, including insomnia, agitation, and jumpiness, are entirely normal in the immediate aftermath of any crisis or trauma, such as war, rape, torture, natural disasters, sudden bereavement, or terrorist attacks. But if the symptoms persist for one month or longer and begin to impair a person's functioning, the sufferer may have **posttraumatic stress disorder (PTSD)**. Typical symptoms of PTSD include reliving the trauma in recurrent, intrusive thoughts; a sense of detachment from others and a loss of interest in familiar activities; and increased physiological arousal, reflected in insomnia, irritability, and impaired concentration.

At the University of Western Ontario, Ruth Lanius and her colleagues (2002) used fMRI technology to study the neural circuitry of seven people who suffered from PTSD as the result of sexual abuse. The trouble is, PTSD symptoms can be intermittent rather than continuous, making them very difficult to study. To make sure that the participants were experiencing symptoms of PTSD, researchers read them a story about sexual abuse during the brain scan. Participants who reported a sense of detachment, or a "dissociative response," after they heard the story were exhibiting symptoms of PTSD. The scans showed that this detachment was accompanied by increased activity across all four lobes of the participants' brains, with most activity concentrated in the prefrontal cortex and the cortex in and around the limbic brain structures (such as the cingulated cortex, amygdala, and hippocampus). This result supports the finding that PTSD is associated with changes in activity levels of particular brain structures. ◉

Interestingly, in PTSD sufferers, the hippocampus is apt to be smaller than average (McNally, 2003). The hippocampus is crucially involved in autobiographical memory. An abnormally small one may figure in the difficulty of some trauma survivors to react to their memories as events from their past, which may be why they keep reliving them in the present. Originally, researchers thought that severe trauma caused neuron

◉—⎤Watch the **Video**
PTSD 9/11 in **MyPsychLab**

💡 **THINKING CRITICALLY**

Ask questions.

David Turnle/Corbis

This grief-stricken soldier has just learned that the body bag on the flight with him contains the remains of a close friend who was killed in action. Understandably, many soldiers suffer posttraumatic stress symptoms. But why do most eventually recover, whereas others have PTSD for many years?

panic disorder An anxiety disorder in which a person experiences recurring panic attacks, periods of intense fear, and feelings of impending doom or death, accompanied by physiological symptoms such as rapid heart rate and dizziness.

damage or loss of cells in the hippocampus, producing PTSD symptoms—impaired memory, recurrent fears, and so forth. But this hypothesis has been refuted. One team used MRIs to measure hippocampal size in identical twins, only one of whom in each pair had been in combat in Vietnam. If trauma shrinks the hippocampus, then the size of the hippocampus should have been different in the veterans who developed PTSD and their identical twins. But this was not what the researchers found. Two things were necessary for a vet to develop chronic PTSD: serving in combat *and* having a smaller hippocampus than normal (Gilbertson et al., 2002). Twins who had smaller hippocampi but no military service did not develop PTSD, and neither did the twins who *did* experience combat but who had normal-sized hippocampi.

Most people who live through a traumatic experience eventually recover without developing PTSD. For example, one major national survey of Americans found that about 60% had experienced a traumatic event, but only 8% of the men and 20% of the women developed PTSD (Kessler et al., 1995). Some experts predicted an epidemic of PTSD after 9/11, but it never materialized (Bonanno et al., 2010). Why, then, if most people recover from a traumatic experience, do some continue to have PTSD symptoms for years, sometimes for decades?

One answer may involve a genetic predisposition. Behavioural–genetic studies of twins in the general population as well as among combat veterans have found that PTSD symptoms have a heritable component (Stein et al., 2002; Yehuda et al., 2009).

Another answer may be that people who develop long-lasting PTSD often have a prior history of psychological problems and other traumatic experiences with poor emotional adjustment to them (Ozer et al., 2003). One reason for their poor adjustment is that they are more likely to have self-defeating, anxiety-producing ways of thinking in general—for example, they tend to "catastrophize" about every little thing that goes wrong, to believe they are inadequate, and to feel that no one can be trusted (Bovin & Marx, 2011; Bryant & Guthrie, 2005). Many PTSD sufferers also lack the social, psychological, and neurological resources to deal with their difficult experiences. They are more likely than resilient people to have the personality trait of neuroticism and to have lower-than-average intelligence, which may impair their ability to cope cognitively with trauma (McNally, 2003).

In sum, many cases of PTSD seem to be a result of impaired cognitive and neurological functioning that existed *before* the trauma took place, triggered by the eventual traumatic experience.

Panic Disorder.   Another kind of anxiety disorder is **panic disorder**, in which a person has recurring attacks of intense fear or panic, often with feelings of impending doom or death. These panic attacks may last from a few minutes to (more rarely) several hours. Symptoms include trembling and shaking, dizziness, chest pain or discomfort, rapid heart rate, feelings of unreality, hot and cold flashes, sweating, and—as a result of all these scary physical reactions—a fear of dying, going crazy, or losing control. Many sufferers fear they are having a heart attack.

Although panic attacks seem to come out of nowhere, they in fact usually occur in the aftermath of stress, prolonged emotion, specific worries, or frightening experiences (McNally, 1998). For example, a friend of the authors was on a plane that was a target of a bomb threat while airborne at 33 000 feet. He coped beautifully at the time, but two weeks later, seemingly out of nowhere, he had a panic attack.

Such delayed attacks after life-threatening scares are common. The essential difference between people who develop panic disorder and those who do not lies in *how they interpret their bodily reactions* (Barlow, 2000). Healthy

Panic attack: Anxiety symptoms that seem "out of the blue"

Interpretation → "Oh my God, I'm dying!" → Panic disorder

Interpretation → "Oh, it's just stress; it will pass." → No disorder people who have occasional panic attacks see them correctly as a result of a passing crisis or period of stress, comparable to another person's migraines. But people who develop panic disorder regard the attack as a sign of illness or impending death, and they begin to live their lives in restrictive ways, trying to avoid future attacks. ●

Watch the Video
Panic Disorder in **MyPsychLab**

Fears and Phobias

Are you afraid of bugs, snakes, or dogs? Are you vaguely uncomfortable with them or so afraid that you can't stand to be around one? A **phobia** is an exaggerated fear of a specific situation, activity, or thing. Some common phobias—such as fear of snakes, insects, heights (acrophobia), thunder (brontophobia), or being trapped in enclosed spaces (claustrophobia)—may have evolved to be easily acquired in human beings because these fears reflected real dangers for the species (Öhman & Mineka, 2003). Other phobias, such as a fear of cats (ailurophobia) or the colour purple (porphyrophobia), may be acquired through classical conditioning or even through observation of a frightening event that is happening to someone else (Mineka & Zinbarg, 2006). Still other phobias, such as fear of dirt and germs (mysophobia) or of the number 13 (triskaidekaphobia), may reflect personality differences or cultural traditions. Whatever its source, a phobia is truly frightening and often incapacitating for its sufferer. It is not just a tendency to say "ugh" at tarantulas or skip the snake display at the zoo. ●

Watch the Video
Phobias in **MyPsychLab**

People who have a *social phobia* become extremely anxious in situations in which they will be observed by others—eating in a restaurant, speaking in front of a group or crowd, having to perform for others. They worry that they will do or say something that will be excruciatingly humiliating or embarrassing. These phobias are more severe forms of the occasional shyness and social anxiety that everyone experiences. For people with a social phobia, the mere thought of being in a new situation with unfamiliar people is scary enough to cause sweating, trembling, nausea, and an overwhelming feeling of inadequacy. So they don't go, increasing their isolation and imagined fears.

By far the most disabling fear disorder is **agoraphobia**. In ancient Greece, the *agora* was the social, political, business, and religious centre of town, the public meeting place away from home. The fundamental fear in agoraphobia is of being trapped in a crowded public place, where escape might be difficult or where help might be unavailable if the person has a panic attack. Individuals with agoraphobia report many specific fears—of being in a crowded movie theatre, driving in traffic or tunnels, or going to parties—but the underlying fear is of being away from a safe place, usually home, or a safe person, usually a parent or partner.

Agoraphobia typically begins with a panic attack that seems to have no cause. The attack is so unexpected and scary that the agoraphobic-to-be begins to avoid situations that he or she thinks may provoke another one. For example, a woman the authors know had a panic attack while driving on a highway. This was a perfectly normal post-traumatic response to the suicide of her husband a few weeks earlier. But thereafter she avoided highways—as if the highway, and not the suicide, had caused the attack. Because so many of the actions associated with agoraphobia arise as a mistaken effort

GET INVOLVED! What Scares You?

Everyone fears something. Stop for a moment to think about what you fear most. Is it heights? Snakes? Speaking in public? Ask yourself these questions: (1) How long have you feared this thing or situation? (2) How would you respond if you could not avoid this thing or situation? (3) How much would you be willing to rearrange your life to avoid this feared thing or situation? After considering these questions, would you regard your fear as a full-blown phobia or merely a normal source of apprehension?

phobia An exaggerated, unrealistic fear of a specific situation, activity, or object.

agoraphobia A set of phobias, often set off by a panic attack, involving the basic fear of being away from a safe place or person.

obsessive-compulsive disorder (OCD) An anxiety disorder in which a person feels trapped in repetitive, persistent thoughts (*obsessions*) and repetitive, ritualized behaviours (*compulsions*) designed to reduce anxiety.

◉─|Watch the **Video**
John: OCD in **MyPsychLab**

to avoid a panic attack, psychologists regard agoraphobia as a "fear of fear" rather than simply a fear of places.

Obsessions and Compulsions

Obsessive-compulsive disorder (OCD) is characterized by recurrent, persistent, unwished-for thoughts or images (*obsessions*) or by repetitive, ritualized, stereotyped behaviours that the person feels must be carried out to avoid disaster (*compulsions*). Of course, many people have trivial compulsions and practise superstitious rituals; baseball players are famous for them—one won't change his socks and another will eat chicken every day while he is on a hitting streak. Obsessions and compulsions become a disorder when they become uncontrollable and interfere with a person's life. ◉

People who have obsessive thoughts often find them frightening or repugnant: thoughts of killing a child, of becoming contaminated by a handshake, or of having unknowingly hurt someone in a traffic accident. Obsessive thoughts take many forms, but they are alike in reflecting impaired ways of reasoning and processing information.

People who suffer from compulsions likewise feel they have no control over them. The most common compulsions are hand washing, counting, touching, and checking. A woman *must* check the furnace, lights, locks, oven, and fireplace three times before she can sleep; or a man *must* wash his hands and face precisely eight times before he leaves the house. OCD sufferers usually realize that their behaviour is senseless, and they are often tormented by their rituals. But if they try to forgo the ritual, they feel mounting anxiety that is relieved only by giving in to it. For one young man with OCD, stairs became a treadmill he could not get off: "At first I'd walk up and down the stairs only three or four times," he recalled. "Later I had to run up and down 63 times in 45 minutes. If I failed, I had to start all over again from the beginning" (as cited in King, 1989).

In many people with OCD, the prefrontal cortex is depleted of serotonin, which creates a kind of cognitive rigidity—an inability to let go of certain thoughts, and behavioural rigidity, an inability to alter compulsive behaviour after getting negative feedback (Chamberlain et al., 2008; Clarke et al., 2004). In addition, several parts of the brain are hyperactive in people with OCD. One area of the frontal lobes sends messages of impending danger to other areas involved in controlling the movement of the limbs and preparing the body to feel fear and respond to external threats. Normally, once danger is past or a person realizes that there is no cause for fear, the brain's alarm signal turns off. In people with OCD, however, false alarms keep clanging and the emotional networks keep sending out mistaken "fear!" messages (Schwartz et al., 1996). The sufferer feels in a constant state of danger and tries repeatedly to reduce the resulting anxiety.

Pathological hoarders fill their homes with newspapers, bags of old clothing, used tissue boxes—all kinds of junk. They are tormented by fears of throwing out something they will need later. A PET-scan study that compared obsessive hoarders with people with obsessive symptoms found that hoarders had less activity in parts of the brain involved in decision making, problem solving, spatial orientation, and memory (Saxena et al., 2004). Perhaps these deficits explain why hoarders keep things (their inability to decide what to throw away creates a constant struggle) and why they often keep their papers and junk in the living room, in the kitchen, or even on the bed. They have trouble remembering where things are and thus feel the need to have them in sight.

This is an example of Hoarding Disorder, which the DSM-5 lists as a new diagnostic category. The person who lived here was unable to throw away any papers or magazines without feeling tremendous anxiety.

Chet Gordon/The Image Works

Recite & Review

Recite: There is no "speaking out loud to yourself disorder," so go ahead and recite what you know about *generalized anxiety disorder*, *posttraumatic stress disorder*, *panic disorder*, *phobias*, *agoraphobia*, and *obsessive-compulsive disorder*.

Review: Next, read this section again.

Now take this *Quick Quiz,* by matching each term on the left with its description on the right.

1. social phobia
2. generalized anxiety disorder
3. posttraumatic stress disorder
4. agoraphobia
5. compulsion
6. obsession

  a. need to perform a ritual
  b. fear of fear; of being trapped with no way of escape
  c. continuing sense of doom
  d. repeated, unwanted thoughts
  e. fear of meeting new people
  f. anxiety following severe shock

Answers:

1.e 2.c 3.f 4.b 5.a 6.d

✓●─ **Study** and **Review**
in **MyPsychLab**

Learning Objectives

8 Document the difference between major depression and the blues.

9 List four contributing factors in depression.

10 Describe how some people can think themselves into depression.

Mood Disorders

Mood disorders include disturbances in mood ranging from extreme depression to extreme mania. Of course, most people feel sad from time to time, and also joyful. And most people, at some time in their lives, will know the wild grief that accompanies tragedy and bereavement.

Depression

Anxiety, painful though it is, is at least a sign that a person is engaged in the future: It reflects the belief that something bad will happen. But depressed people feel burned out about the future: They are sure that nothing good will ever happen. Some people go through life with constant but low-grade unhappiness; they can do what they need to but nearly always report their mood as sad or "down in the dumps." Others suffer from **major depression**, a serious mood disorder that involves emotional, behavioural, cognitive, and physical changes severe enough to disrupt a person's ordinary functioning. The writer William Styron, who fought and recovered from major depression, used the beginning of Dante's classic poem *The Divine Comedy* to convey his suffering:

> *In the middle of the journey of our life*
> *I found myself in a dark wood,*
> *For I had lost the right path.*

"For those who have dwelt in depression's dark wood," wrote Styron (1990) in *Darkness Visible*, "and known its inexplicable agony, the return from the abyss is not

major depression A mood disorder involving disturbances in emotion (excessive sadness), behaviour (loss of interest in one's usual activities), cognition (thoughts of hopelessness), and body function (fatigue and loss of appetite).

Even people who are rich, successful, and adored by millions can suffer from major depression. The suicide of Nirvana's lead singer, Kurt Cobain, shocked and saddened his many fans.

Joe Giron/Corbis

◉ **Watch** the **Video**
William: Double Depression
Listening to Blues Test
in **MyPsychLab**

✳ **Explore** the **Concept**
Bipolar Disorder in **MyPsychLab**

◉ **Watch** the **Video**
Bipolar Disorder in **MyPsychLab**

bipolar disorder A mood disorder in which episodes of both depression and mania (excessive euphoria) occur.

vulnerability-stress models Approaches that emphasize how individual vulnerabilities interact with external stresses or circumstances to produce mental disorders.

unlike the ascent of the poet, trudging upward and upward out of hell's black depths and at last emerging into what he saw as 'the shining world.'"

People with major depression feel despairing and hopeless. They may think often of death or suicide. They feel unable to get up and do things; it takes an enormous effort even to get dressed. Their thinking patterns feed their bleak moods. They exaggerate minor failings, ignore or discount positive events, and interpret any little thing that goes wrong as evidence that nothing will ever go right. Emotionally healthy people who are sad or grieving do not see themselves as completely worthless and unlovable. Depressed people interpret losses as signs of failure and conclude that they will never be happy again.

Depression is accompanied by physical changes as well. The depressed person may overeat or stop eating, have difficulty falling asleep or sleeping through the night, have trouble concentrating, and feel tired all the time. Some sufferers have other physical reactions, such as headaches or inexplicable pain.

Major depression occurs at least twice as often among women as among men, all over the world. However, because women are more likely than men to talk about their feelings and more likely to seek help, depression in males is probably underdiagnosed. Men who are depressed often try to mask their feelings by withdrawing, abusing drugs, or behaving violently (Canetto, 1992; Kessler et al., 1995). As Susan Nolen-Hoeksema, a leading depression researcher, put it, "Women think and men drink." ◉

Bipolar Disorder

At the opposite pole from depression is *mania*, an abnormally high state of exhilaration. You might think it's impossible to feel too good, but mania is not the normal joy of being in love or winning the Pulitzer Prize. Instead of feeling fatigued and listless, the manic person is excessively wired and often irritable when thwarted. Instead of feeling hopeless and powerless, the person feels powerful and is full of plans; but these plans are usually based on delusional ideas, such as thinking that he or she has solved the world's problems. People in a state of mania often get into terrible trouble, going on extravagant spending sprees, making impulsive and bad decisions, or having risky sexual adventures. ✳

When people experience at least one episode of mania alternating with episodes of depression, they are said to have **bipolar disorder** (formerly called *manic-depressive disorder*). This is a rarer problem than depression and distinctly different. Although more women than men suffer from depression, bipolar disorder occurs equally in both sexes. The great humorist Mark Twain had bipolar disorder, which he described as "periodical and sudden changes of mood . . . from deep melancholy to half-insane tempests and cyclones." Other writers, artists, musicians, and scientists have suffered from this disorder (Jamison, 1992). During the highs, many of these artists create their best work, but the price of the lows is disastrous relationships, bankruptcy, and sometimes suicide. As noted earlier, bipolar disorder, once thought to emerge only in adulthood, is now being widely diagnosed among young children and adolescents, although the symptoms and mood swings often look different from those in adults and the diagnosis in children remains controversial (Holden, 2008). ◉

Origins of Depression

Psychologists have investigated many contributing factors to major depression: genetic factors, life experiences, problems with close attachments, and cognitive habits. Few researchers think that any one of these factors alone produces chronic depression. Most researchers now emphasize **vulnerability-stress models** of mental disorders, in which a person's vulnerabilities (in genetic predispositions, personality traits, or habits of thinking) interact with stressful events (such as sexual victimization, violence, or loss of a close relationship) to produce any given case (Hankin & Abramson, 2001). Let's consider the evidence for each contributing factor in depression:

1 **Genetic factors.** Studies of adopted children and twins support the notion that major depression is a moderately heritable disorder (Bierut et al., 1999). Psychologists are hunting for the genes that might be involved, although it is unlikely that a single gene directly or inevitably "causes" severe depression. As in the case of posttraumatic stress disorder, a genetic predisposition must interact with stressful events to create the disorder.

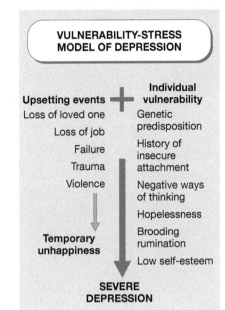

VULNERABILITY-STRESS
MODEL OF DEPRESSION

Upsetting events ➕ Individual vulnerability
Loss of loved one — Genetic predisposition
Loss of job — History of insecure attachment
Failure —
Trauma — Negative ways of thinking
Violence — Hopelessness

Temporary unhappiness — Brooding rumination

Low self-esteem

SEVERE DEPRESSION

Psychologists have identified one gene (called 5-HTT) that comes in two forms: a long form that apparently helps protect people from depression, and a short form that makes them more vulnerable to it (Caspi et al., 2003). In a study of 847 New Zealanders who were followed from birth to age 26, the researchers found that 43% of those who possessed two copies of the short form of this gene (one from each parent) became severely depressed in the aftermath of major stress (such as the loss of a job, disabling injuries, a death in the family, or abuse suffered in childhood). Yet only 17% of those with two copies of the long form of this gene became depressed, even when they suffered the same stresses. And people who inherited one long form of the gene from one parent and a short form from the other fell in between in their susceptibility to depression (33%). Genes may exert their effects on depression by affecting levels of serotonin and other neurotransmitters in the brain. Genes may also affect production of the stress hormone cortisol, which, at high levels, can damage cells in the hippocampus and amygdala (Sapolsky, 2000; Sheline, 2000). In depressed patients, the system that regulates reactions to stress is in overdrive; it doesn't shut down when it should, and it keeps overproducing cortisol (Plotsky, Owens, & Nemeroff, 1998). Nonetheless, genes cannot account for all cases of depression; even among the New Zealanders with the greatest genetic vulnerability, more than half did not become depressed. Nor do genes seem to account for the sex difference in depression rates. In the New Zealand study, women were no more likely than men to have the short form of the 5-HTT gene.

Nonetheless, research into gene-environment interactions continues. Children who are at high genetic risk for developing depression (or aggressive disorders or alcohol abuse) may grow up just fine if they have good parents who monitor and control their children's vulnerabilities to these disorders (Dick et al., 2011; Dougherty et al., 2011). Moreover, the relative influence of genetic and environmental factors varies over the lifespan. A review of eight studies of identical twins found that although genetic predispositions predicted the twins' levels of depression and anxiety in childhood and young adulthood, by middle adulthood environmental factors and life experiences had become more powerful influences (Kendler et al., 2011).

Depleting animals of serotonin does not induce depression, nor does increasing brain serotonin necessarily alleviate it. The fact that some antidepressants raise serotonin levels (see Chapter 16) does not mean that low serotonin levels caused the depression—a common but mistaken inference (Kirsch, 2010; Lacasse & Leo, 2005).

2 **Life experiences and circumstances.** One powerful experience that often generates depression is violence. Adolescents of both sexes who are exposed to high rates of violence report higher levels of depression and more attempts to commit suicide than those who are not subjected to constant violence in their lives or communities (Mazza & Reynolds, 1999). Domestic violence also contributes to the higher rates of depression among women. One major longitudinal study followed men and women from ages 18 to 26, and compared those in physically abusive relationships with those in nonabusive ones. Although depressed women are more likely to enter abusive relationships to begin with, involvement in a violent relationship independently increased their rates of depression and anxiety—but, interestingly, not men's

(Ehrensaft, Moffitt, & Caspi, 2006). Women are also more likely than men to be sexually abused as children and young adults, which creates a higher risk of depression in adulthood (Weiss, Longhurst, & Mazure, 1999).

However, the common belief that the higher rates of depression among adult women is due to their having been sexually molested in childhood has not been supported. This belief originated with retrospective studies, where researchers asked already-depressed adult women about events in their pasts. But prospective studies, which follow children into adulthood, lead to a different conclusion. In one, nearly 700 children with substantiated cases of physical and sexual abuse and neglect before age 11 were matched with a control group of non-abused and non-neglected children. All were followed into their late twenties. Physical beatings and neglect were strongly related to depression and other problems in young adults, but, surprisingly, childhood sexual abuse was not (Widom, DuMont, & Czaja, 2007).

In addition, the conditions of people's lives—the roles they occupy, their status, their satisfaction with work and family—can affect their likelihood of becoming depressed. Men are more likely than women to be both married and working full time, a combination of roles that is strongly associated with mental health and lower rates of depression (Brown, 1993). Women are more likely than men to live in poverty and suffer from discrimination, two additional sources of depression (Belle & Doucet, 2003).

Childhood maltreatment, independent of all other childhood and adult risk factors, is associated with a particularly high risk of adult depressive episodes lasting a year or more (Brown & Harris, 2008). A mechanism that might explain this increased risk is that prolonged stress in childhood puts the body's responses to stress in overdrive, so that it overproduces the stress hormone cortisol (Gotlib et al., 2008; see Chapter 11). Depressed people have high levels of cortisol, which can affect the hippocampus and amygdala, causing mood and memory abnormalities.

3 **Losses of important relationships.** A third line of investigation emphasizes the loss of important relationships in setting off depression in vulnerable individuals. Many depressed people have a history of separations and losses, both past and present; insecure attachments; and rejection by parents or peers (Hammen, 2009; Nolan, Flynn, & Garber, 2003; Weissman, Markowitz, & Klerman, 2000). As we noted earlier, however, people with a history of happy and secure attachments may also fall into prolonged depression because of the loss of a beloved partner (Wakefield et al., 2007).

4 **Cognitive habits.** Finally, depression involves specific, negative ways of thinking about one's situation (Beck, 2005). Typically, depressed people believe that their situation is *permanent* ("Nothing good will ever happen to me") and *uncontrollable* ("I'm depressed because I'm ugly and horrible and I can't do anything about it"). Expecting nothing to get better, they do nothing to improve their lives and therefore remain unhappy. They feel hopeless and pessimistic, believing that nothing good will ever happen to them and that they are powerless to change the future (Abramson, Metalsky, & Alloy, 1989; Seligman, 1991). When depressed and nondepressed people are put into a sad mood and given a choice between looking at sad faces or happy faces, depressed people choose the sad faces—a metaphor for how they process the world in general, attending to everything that confirms the gloominess of life rather than any of its joys (Joormann & Gotlib, 2007). And when asked to recall happier times, nondepressed people cheer up. But depressed people feel even worse, as if the happy memory makes them feel that they will never be happy again (Joormann, Siemer, & Gotlib, 2007).

The cognitive biases associated with depression are not just correlates of the disorder. Longitudinal studies show that they play a causal role, interacting with severe life stresses to generate further depressive episodes (Hallion & Ruscio, 2011; Monroe et al., 2007). One of the strongest bad cognitive habits associated with depression is *rumination*—brooding about everything that is wrong in your life, sitting alone thinking about how unmotivated you feel, and persuading yourself that no one loves you or ever will. People with ruminating cognitive styles that foster hopelessness are at greater risk of developing full-blown major depression than are people who are able to distract themselves, look outward, and seek solutions (Chorpita & Barlow, 1998). They have trouble preventing these thoughts from entering and remaining in their memory, which keeps them stewing in negative perceptions and unhappy past events (Joormann, Levens, & Gotlib, 2011; Kuster, Orth, & Meier, 2012). Beginning in adolescence, women are much more likely than men to develop a ruminating, intro-spective style, rehearsing the reasons for their unhappiness. This tendency contrib-utes both to longer-lasting depressions in women and to the sex difference in reported rates, as you can see in Figure 15.1 (Nolen-Hoeksema, 2004).

The factors we have described, ranging from genetics to jobs, from what happens in people's lives to how they think about it, combine in different ways to produce any given case of depression. That is why the same precipitating event can affect two people entirely differently: why one is able to roll with the punches of life and another is knocked flat.

FIGURE 15.1 Gender and Depression

Women are far more likely than men to ruminate and brood when they are sad. This mental habit, however, can easily turn into depression. As the correlations show, the relationship between gender and depression is itself almost insignificant. But women are more likely to ruminate, and rumi-nation, especially when combined with stressful experiences, is very highly correlated with depression (Nolen-Hoeksema, 2004).

✓●—⌐**Study** and **Review**

in **MyPsychLab**

Recite & Review

Recite: Stop ruminating about your study habits, and state what you remember about *major depression*, *bipolar disorder*, and the *vulnerability-stress model* of mental disorders.

Review: Next, reread this section.

Now take this *Quick Quiz:*

Don't let another quiz make you vulnerable to depression!

1. Biological researchers find that depressed people have unusually high levels of the stress hormone _____.

2. Depressed people tend to believe that the reasons for their unhappiness are (a) controlla-ble, (b) temporary, (c) out of their hands, (d) caused by the situation.

3. A news headline announces that a gene has been identified as the cause of depression. Does this mean that everyone with the gene will become depressed? How should critical thinkers interpret this research?

Answers:

1. cortisol 2. c 3. No, it means that people with the gene are *more likely* to become depressed if they also undergo severely stressful experiences. Critical thinkers would also want to make sure the research is replicated, and they would realize that not all kinds of depression might be influenced by genetics.

Learning Objectives

11 Describe what a charming but heartless tycoon and a remorseless killer have in common.

12 Explain why some people are incapable of feeling guilt or pangs of conscience.

Personality Disorders

Personality disorders involve unchanging, maladaptive traits that cause great distress or an inability to get along with others. The DSM-5- describes such a disorder as "impairments in personality (self and interpersonal) functioning and the presence of pathological person-ality traits" Personality disorders are not caused by medical conditions, stress, drug abuse, or situations that temporarily induce a person to behave in ways that are out of character.

Narcissus fell in love with his own image, and now he has a personality disorder named after him—just what a narcissist would expect!

Universal Images Group Limited/Alamy

⊙▶ Simulate the **Experiment**
Psychological Disorders in **MyPsychLab**

paranoid personality disorder
A disorder characterized by unreasonable, excessive suspiciousness and mistrust, and irrational feelings of being persecuted by others.

narcissistic personality disorder
A disorder characterized by an exaggerated sense of self-importance and self-absorption.

borderline personality disorder
A disorder characterized by intense but unstable relationships, a fear of abandonment by others, an unrealistic self-image, and emotional volatility.

psychopathy A personality disorder characterized by a lack of remorse, empathy, anxiety, and other social emotions; the use of deceit and manipulation; and impulsive thrill seeking.

Problem Personalities

Personality disorders come in many varieties. **Paranoid personality disorder** involves pervasive, unfounded suspiciousness and mistrust of other people, irrational jealousy, secretiveness, and doubt about the loyalty of others. People with paranoid personalities have delusions of being persecuted by everyone from their closest relatives to government agencies, and their beliefs are immune to disconfirming evidence.

Narcissistic personality disorder involves an exaggerated sense of self-importance and self-absorption. The word *narcissism* gets its name from the Greek myth of Narcissus, a beautiful young man who fell in love with his own image. Narcissistic individuals are preoccupied with fantasies of their own importance, power, and brilliance. They demand constant attention and admiration and feel entitled to special favours, without, however, being willing to reciprocate.

Borderline personality disorder characterizes people who have a history of intense but unstable relationships in which they alternate between idealizing the partner and then devaluing the partner. They frantically try to avoid real or imagined abandonment by others, even if the "abandonment" is only a friend's brief vacation. They have profoundly unrealistic self-images. They are self-destructive and impulsive, often spending too much, abusing drugs, cutting themselves, and threatening to commit suicide. And they are emotionally volatile, careening from anger to euphoria to anxiety.

Notice that although these descriptions evoke flashes of recognition ("I know that type!"), it is hard to know where value judgments end (say, that someone is self-absorbed or suspicious) and a clear disorder begins (Maddux & Mundell, 1997). Cultures differ, too, in how they draw the line. For example, Western society often encourages people to pursue dreams of unlimited success, physical beauty, and ideal love, but such dreams might be considered signs of serious disturbance in a more group-oriented society. How would you distinguish between having a narcissistic personality disorder and being a normal member of a group or culture that encourages putting your own needs ahead of those of your family and friends and puts a premium on youth and beauty?

Criminals and Psychopaths

Throughout history, people have been fascinated and horrified by the "bad seeds" among them—people who, even as children, are ready to break the rules and seem unable to be socialized. Societies have also recognized and feared the few members in their midst who lack all human connection to anyone else, people who can cheat, con, and kill without flinching. (In the 1800s these individuals were said to be afflicted with "moral insanity.") ⊙▶

In 1976, in his influential book *The Mask of Sanity*, Hervey Cleckley popularized and standardized the term *psychopath* to describe a person who lacks all conscience. A key characteristic of **psychopathy**, said Cleckley, is an inability to feel normal emotions. Psychopaths are incapable not only of remorse but also of fear of punishment and of shame, guilt, and empathy for the misery they cause others. Because they lack emotional connections to others, they often behave cruelly and irresponsibly—usually more for the thrill than for personal gain.

If caught in a lie or a crime, psychopaths may seem sincerely sorry and promise to make amends, but it is all an act. They can be utterly charming, but they use their charm to manipulate and deceive others (Cleckley, 1976; Hare, Hart, & Harpur, 1991). Some psychopaths are violent and sadistic, able to kill a pet, a child, or a random adult without a twinge of regret, but others direct their energies into con games or career advancement, abusing other people emotionally or economically rather than physically (Robins, Tipp, & Przybeck, 1991). A leading researcher in this field, Robert Hare, calls corporate psychopaths "snakes in suits."

Psychopaths are believed to exist in all cultures and throughout history, although they are more prevalent in individualistic western societies. Even a close-knit culture such as the Yupik in Canada has a word for them—*kunlangeta* (Seabrook, 2008). An anthropologist once asked a member of the tribe what the group would do with a *kunlangeta*, and he said, "Somebody would have pushed him off the ice when nobody else was looking." Psychopaths are feared and detested everywhere.

In the 1990s, the clinicians who were revising the DSM decided to replace the term *psychopathy* with **antisocial personality disorder (APD)**, which applies to people who show "a pervasive pattern of disregard for, and violation of, the rights of others." People with APD repeatedly break the law; they are impulsive and seek quick thrills; they show reckless disregard for their own safety or that of others; they often get into physical fights or assault others; and they are irresponsible, failing to hold jobs or meet obligations (Widiger et al., 1996). Crucially for the diagnosis, they have had a history of these behavioural problems since childhood; they aren't just teenage delinquents who have been hanging out with a bad peer group. In people with APD, as one researcher found, rule breaking and irresponsibility start in early childhood and then take different forms at different ages: "biting and hitting at age 4, shoplifting and truancy at age 10, selling drugs and stealing cars at age 16, robbery and rape at age 22, and fraud and child abuse at age 30" (Moffitt, 1993).

The DSM made the change in labelling to emphasize the *behavioural* signs of antisocial personality disorder. But to many clinicians, the defining essence of psychopaths is their heartlessness and conniving charm. People who commit violent crimes may be antisocial, reckless, and irresponsible, these clinicians point out, yet differ greatly in their motivations for behaving this way. People with APD also vary widely in their capacity for empathy, remorse, guilt, anxiety, or loyalty (Hare, Hart, & Harpur, 1991). Thus, not all people with APD are psychopaths. Conversely, as we just noted, not all psychopaths are "antisocial" and aggressive in the typical ways that people with APD are. However, sometimes the two disorders converge, as in the case of sadistic, "cold-blooded" killers.

While at the University of British Columbia, Robert Hare developed a widely used, 20-item checklist for assessing psychopathy: the Psychopathy Checklist, Revised (PCL-R) (Hare, 1990). It is clear that APD and psychopathy are similar conditions with similar diagnostic criteria. In fact, some have questioned whether the two can be dissociated (Zagon, 1995). However, Hare argues that the two conditions are readily

antisocial personality disorder (APD) A personality disorder characterized by a lifelong pattern of irresponsible, antisocial behaviour such as lawbreaking, violence, and other impulsive, reckless acts.

Some psychopaths are sadistic and violent. Gary L. Ridgway (left), the deadliest convicted serial killer in U.S. history, strangled 48 women, placing their bodies in "clusters" around the country. He did this because, he said coolly, he wanted to keep track of them. "I killed so many women, I have a hard time keeping them straight," he told the court. But others are confident men who use charm and elaborate scams to deceive and defraud. Christopher Rocancourt (right, with model Naomi Campbell) conned celebrities and others out of millions of dollars by adopting false identities, including movie producer, Brazilian race driver, Russian prince, son of Sophia Loren, and financier. He was caught in Canada and spent a year in a correctional centre—hosting media interviews and writing his autobiography.

Left: Elaine Thompson/AP Images. Right: Evan Agostini/AP Images.

dissociable, and the accurate diagnosis of APD is useful in psychiatric settings when one wants to predict a variety of antisocial behaviours, such as substance abuse. Further, he points out that most psychopaths meet the criteria for APD, but most people with APD are not psychopaths (Hare, 1996). Accurately differentiating between the conditions is perhaps most important in legal settings. A convicted killer who meets the diagnostic criteria for APD but not psychopathy is not nearly as likely to reoffend as a psychopath (Hare & Neumann, 2008).

Researchers have identified a number of factors involved in these disorders:

1 **Abnormalities in the central nervous system.** Something certainly seems to be amiss in the emotional wiring of psychopaths, the wiring that allows all primates, not just human beings, to feel connected to others of their kind. When that wiring goes awry, even some chimpanzees will behave in ways that are comparable to the actions of human psychopaths. They, too, deceive and manipulate others to get their way and they are unmoved by the suffering of others of their kind (Lilienfeld, Gershon, et al., 1999).

The psychopath's inability to feel emotional arousal—empathy, guilt, fear of punishment, and anxiety under stress—suggests some aberration in the central nervous system (Hare, 1965, 1996; Lykken, 1995; Raine et al., 2000). Indeed, psychopaths do not respond physiologically to the threat of punishment the way other people do; this may be why they can behave fearlessly in situations that would scare others to death. Normally, when a person is anticipating danger, pain, or punishment, the electrical conductance of the skin changes, a classically conditioned response that indicates anxiety or fear. But psychopaths are slow to develop such responses, which suggests that they are unable to feel the anxiety necessary for learning that their actions will have unpleasant consequences (see Figure 15.2). Their lack of empathy for others who are suffering also seems to have a physiological basis. When psychopaths are shown pictures of people crying and in distress, their skin conductance barely shifts, in contrast to nonpsychopaths, whose skin conductance shoots up (Blair et al., 1997).

This emotional flatness may help distinguish psychopaths from other aggressive people with antisocial personality disorder (Lorber, 2004). For example, antisocial, violent adolescents who have normal levels of physiological arousal in response to danger and threat, and whose responses can be classically conditioned, do not usually get involved in a life of crime as adults, suggesting that they "outgrow" the disorder with maturity (Raine & Liu, 1998). But those who are likely to become career criminals have the same unusually low levels of physiological arousal that psychopaths do.

2 **Impaired frontal-lobe functioning.** One trait shared by psychopaths and people with APD is impulsivity, an inability to control responses to frustration and provocation (Luengo et al., 1994; van Goozen et al., 2007; Raine, 1996). Such an inability, which often leads to breaking rules and laws, may have a biological basis. Many psychopaths have abnormalities in the prefrontal cortex, which, as we saw in Chapter 4, is responsible for planning and impulse control. They don't do as well as other individuals on neuropsychological tests of frontal-lobe functioning, and they have less grey matter in the frontal lobes than other people do (Dinn & Harris, 2000; Raine, 2008). One PET-scan study found that cold-blooded "predatory" murderers had less brain activity in the frontal lobe than did men who murdered in the heat of passion or controls who had not murdered anybody (Raine et al., 1998).

One reason for these frontal-lobe abnormalities may be brain damage resulting from physical neglect, accidents, battering, or injury. Men convicted of violent crimes are more likely than nonviolent criminals and noncriminals to have been severely battered as children (Lewis, 1992; Milner & McCanne, 1991;

FIGURE 15.2 Emotions and Antisocial Personality Disorder
In several experiments, people with antisocial personality disorder (APD) were slow to develop classically conditioned responses to anticipated danger, pain, or shock—responses that indicate normal anxiety. This deficit may be related to the ability of psychopaths to behave in destructive ways without remorse or regard for the consequences (Hare, 1965, 1993).

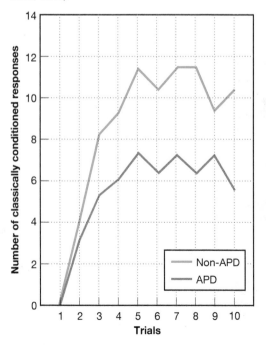

abuse (Gleaves, 1996). In this view, the trauma produces a mental "splitting" (dissociation): One personality emerges to handle everyday experiences, another personality (called an "alter") emerges to cope with the bad ones. MPD patients are frequently described as having lived for years with several alters of which they were unaware until therapy.

On the other side are those who believe that most cases of MPD are unwittingly generated by clinicians themselves, during their interactions with vulnerable clients who have other psychological problems (Lilienfeld & Lohr, 2003). Researchers have shown that "dissociative amnesia," the mechanism that supposedly causes traumatized children to repress their ordeal and develop several identities as a result, lacks historical and empirical support (see Chapter 10). Truly traumatic experiences are remembered all too long and all too well (McNally, 2003; Pope et al., 2007). These researchers point out that before 1980, only a handful of MPD cases had ever been diagnosed anywhere in the world; yet by the mid-1990s, tens of thousands of cases had been reported. (See Table 15.1.) MPD became a lucrative business, benefitting hospitals that opened MPD clinics, therapists who had a new disorder to treat, and psychiatrists and patients who wrote best-selling books. Skeptics think the sudden increase in cases was a sign that the disorder was being wildly overdiagnosed by its proponents. Clinicians who deeply believed in the prevalence of MPD may have even been creating the disorder in their clients through the power of suggestion, sometimes bordering on coercion, and through techniques like hypnosis (McHugh, 2008; Merskey, 1995; Rieber, 2006; Spanos, 1996).

You can see this pressure at work in the comments of psychiatrist Richard Kluft (1987), who wrote that efforts to determine the presence of MPD—that is, to get the person to reveal a "dissociated" personality—may require "between two-and-a-half and four hours of continuous interviewing. Interviewees must be prevented from taking breaks to regain composure. . . . In one recent case of singular difficulty, the first

Why did the number of "alters" reported by people with MPD increase over the years? In the earliest cases, multiple personalities came only in pairs. In the 1886 story of Dr. Jekyll and Mr. Hyde, the kindly Dr. Jekyll turned into the murderous Mr. Hyde. At the height of the MPD epidemic in North America in the 1990s, people were claiming to have several dozen, even hundreds, of alters, including demons, children, extraterrestrials, and animals.

Everett Collection

TABLE 15.1 The Rise of Multiple Personality Disorder

1789	An early case is reported of a young German woman with several "personalities," including a French woman and a little boy.
1816	The first recorded case of "multiple personality" appears in the United States (Mary Reynolds).
1875	The condition is renamed "multiple personality" in France.
1886	Robert Louis Stevenson's *Strange Case of Dr. Jekyll and Mr. Hyde* popularizes the notion of two personalities in one body.
1957	*The Three Faces of Eve* is published and the film is released.
1960	Eight cases have been reported.
1976	The movie *Sybil* is released.
1980	The DSM includes the MPD diagnosis for the first time.
1980	The book *Michelle Remembers* claims that "Satanic ritual abuse" is a leading cause of MPD.
1980–1991	Media coverage escalates in popular books and on talk shows that feature MPD "victims."
1985	Psychiatrist Richard Kluft claims to have treated 250 MPD patients.
1986	6000 cases have been reported in North America.
1987	The first MPD inpatient treatment unit is established at Rush Presbyterian Hospital in Chicago; others follow across the country.
1995	More than 40 000 cases have been reported in North America.
1995	Diane Humenansky becomes the first psychiatrist found guilty of malpractice for inducing multiple personalities in a vulnerable patient.
1996– present	Other successful lawsuits are filed against major proponents of the MPD diagnosis and against treatment units in hospitals. Hospitals begin closing these units. Epidemic of cases subsides.

Sources: Acocella, 1999; Kenny, 1986; Loftus, 1996; Nathan, 1994; Pendergrast, 1995.

💡 **THINKING CRITICALLY**

Consider other interpretations.

A man appeared on *60 Minutes* to talk about his new book, in which he described his 11 personalities—male and female, old and young. These emerged, he said, because he was sexually abused as a child. What else might explain how and why he developed "MPD"?

✳️ Explore the Concept
Dissociative Identity Disorder
in MyPsychLab

sign of dissociation was noted in the sixth hour, and a definitive spontaneous switching of personalities occurred in the eighth hour." Mercy! After eight hours of "continuous interviewing" without a single break, how many of us wouldn't do what the interviewer wanted?

Clinicians who conducted such interrogations argued that they were merely *permitting* other personalities to reveal themselves. However, in numerous malpractice cases across the country, courts have ruled, on the basis of the testimony of scientific experts in psychiatry and psychology, that it was more likely that these clinicians were actively *creating* personalities through suggestion and sometimes outright intimidation (Loftus, 1996). The MPD clinics in hospitals closed, psychiatrists became more wary, and the number of cases dropped sharply almost overnight. ✳️

The Sociocognitive Explanation. No one disputes that some troubled, highly imaginative individuals can produce many different "personalities" when asked. But the *sociocognitive explanation* of MPD holds that this phenomenon is simply an extreme form of the ability we all have to present different aspects of our personalities to others (Lilienfeld et al., 1999). In this view, the diagnosis of MPD provides a culturally acceptable way for some troubled people to make sense of their problems (Hacking, 1995; Showalter, 1997). It allows them to account for sexual or criminal behaviour that they now regret or find intolerably embarrassing; they can claim their "other personality did it." In turn, therapists who are looking for MPD reward such patients with attention and praise for revealing more and more personalities (Piper & Merskey, 2004).

The story of the rise and fall of MPD offers an important lesson in critical thinking, because unskeptical media coverage of sensational MPD cases played a major role in fostering the rise of MPD diagnoses. When Canadian psychiatrist Harold Merskey (1992) reviewed the published cases of MPD, he was unable to find a single one in which a patient developed MPD without being influenced by the therapist's suggestions or reports about the disorder in books and the media. Even the famous case of "Sybil," a huge hit as a book, film, and television special, was a hoax. Sybil never had a traumatic childhood of sexual abuse, she did not have multiple personality disorder,

✔️ Study and Review
in MyPsychLab

Recite & Review

Recite: Tell what you know about *dissociative identity disorder* (*multiple personality disorder*).

Review: Next, reread this section.

Any one of your personalities may now take this *Quick Quiz:*

In August 2003, Donna Walker was arrested for trying to convince an Indiana couple that she was their long-missing daughter. She claimed that her "bad girl" personality (Allison) was responsible for this deception and also for her long history of perpetrating hoaxes on police, friends, and the media. Her "good girl" personality (Donna), she said, was a victim of childhood sexual abuse who spent years working as an FBI informant. The FBI verified that Walker had worked for them, although some of her reports were fabricated. One agent said that Walker has as many as seven personalities who come and go. As a critical thinker, what questions would you want to ask about Walker and her multiple-personality defence?

Answers:

Some possible questions to ask: Is there corroborating evidence for Walker's claims? (She said she was sexually abused from ages four to 13 by a family member and then by the minister of her church, and that she was sent to a psychiatric hospital at age 13.) How much of the rest of her life story can be independently corroborated? Did Walker claim to have "other personalities" only when she was in a jam with the law or was there evidence of MPD throughout her life? Could she have another mental disorder, such as schizophrenia or antisocial personality disorder?

and her "symptoms" were largely generated by her psychiatrist (Borch-Jacobson, 1997, 2009; Rieber, 2006; Nathan, 2011).

The story of MPD teaches us to think critically about disorders that become trendy: to consider other explanations, to examine assumptions and biases, and to demand good evidence.

Learning Objectives

19 Describe the difference between schizophrenia and a "split personality."

20 List the five key signs of schizophrenia.

21 Explain whether schizophrenia is partly heritable.

22 Describe why schizophrenia might begin in the womb yet not emerge until adolescence.

Schizophrenia

> To be schizophrenic is best summed up in a repeating dream that I have had since childhood. In this dream I am lying on a beautiful sunlit beach but my body is in pieces. . . . I realize that the tide is coming in and that I am unable to gather the parts of my dismembered body together to run away. . . . This to me is what schizophrenia feels like; being fragmented in one's personality and constantly afraid that the tide of illness will completely cover me. (As cited in Rollin, 1980.)

In 1911, Swiss psychiatrist Eugen Bleuler coined the term **schizophrenia** to describe cases in which the personality loses its unity. Contrary to popular belief, people with schizophrenia do not have a "split" or "multiple" personality. As this haunting quotation illustrates, schizophrenia is a fragmented condition in which words are split from meaning, actions from motives, perceptions from reality. It is an example of a **psychosis**, a mental condition that involves distorted perceptions of reality and an inability to function in most aspects of life.

Symptoms of Schizophrenia

Schizophrenia is the cancer of mental illness: elusive, complex, and varying in form. The disorder involves the following symptoms: ✳

1 **Bizarre delusions.** A schizophrenic may believe, for example, that dogs are extraterrestrials disguised as pets. Some people with schizophrenia have delusions of identity, believing that they are Moses, Jesus, or another famous person. Some have paranoid delusions, taking innocent events—a stranger's cough, a helicopter overhead—as evidence that everyone is plotting against them. They often report that their thoughts have been inserted into their heads by someone controlling them or are being broadcast on television. Some, like Margaret Mary Ray, whose story opened this chapter, have delusions that a celebrity loves them.

2 **Hallucinations, false sensory experiences that feel intensely real.** By far the most common hallucination among people with schizophrenia is hearing voices; it is virtually a hallmark of the disease. Some sufferers of schizophrenia are so tormented by these voices that they commit suicide to escape them. One man described how he heard as many as 50 voices cursing him, urging him to steal other people's brain cells, or ordering him to kill himself. Once he picked up a ringing telephone and heard them screaming, "You're guilty!" over and over. They yelled "as loud as humans with megaphones," he told a reporter. "It was utter despair. I felt scared. They were always around" (Goode, 2003).

schizophrenia A psychotic disorder marked by delusions, hallucinations, disorganized and incoherent speech, inappropriate behaviour, and cognitive impairments.

psychosis An extreme mental disturbance involving distorted perceptions and irrational behaviour; it may have psychological or organic causes. (Plural: *psychoses*.)

✳ Explore the **Concept**
Types and Symptoms of Schizophrenia in **MyPsychLab**

Bryan Charnley painted 17 self-portraits, with comments, reflecting his battle with schizophrenia. He painted the one above in March 1991, when his mind was clear. In June, he committed suicide.

Terence Charnley

👁—Watch the Video *The Three Faces of Eve* in **MyPsychLab**

3 **Disorganized, incoherent speech.** Schizophrenics may give voice to an illogical jumble of ideas and symbols, linked by meaningless rhyming words or by remote associations, called *word salads*. A patient of Bleuler's wrote, "Olive oil is an Arabian liquor-sauce which the Afghans, Moors and Moslems use in ostrich farming. The Indian plantain tree is the whiskey of the Parsees and Arabs. Barley, rice and sugar cane called artichoke, grow remarkably well in India. The Brahmins live as castes in Baluchistan. The Circassians occupy Manchuria and China. China is the Eldorado of the Pawnees" (Bleuler, 1911/1950).

4 **Grossly disorganized and inappropriate behaviour.** A schizophrenic's behaviour may range from childlike silliness to unpredictable and violent agitation. The person may wear three overcoats and gloves on a hot day, start collecting garbage, or hoard scraps of food.

5 **Impaired cognitive abilities.** People with schizophrenia do much worse than healthy people in almost every cognitive domain, especially verbal learning and recall of words and stories, language, perception, working memory, selective attention, and problem solving (Barch, 2003; Dominguez et al., 2009; Uhlhaas & Silverstein, 2005). Their speech is often impoverished; they make only brief, empty replies in conversation because of diminished thought rather than an unwillingness to speak. Many of these cognitive impairments emerge in vulnerable children long before an actual schizophrenic breakdown occurs, and they last after the patient's psychotic symptoms subside as a result of medication (Heinrichs, 2005). 👁

Other symptoms may appear months before hallucinations or delusions do, and they often persist even when more dramatic symptoms are in remission. For example, many people with schizophrenia lose the motivation to take care of themselves and interact with others; they may stop working or bathing, and become isolated and withdrawn. They seem emotionally "flat"; their facial expressions are unresponsive and they make poor eye contact. Some completely withdraw into a private world, sitting for hours without moving, a condition called *catatonic stupor*. (Catatonic states can also produce frenzied, purposeless behaviour that goes on for hours.)

The cognitive and social deficits in schizophrenia may emerge early, in late childhood or early adolescence (Tarbox & Pogue-Geile, 2008), but the first full-blown psychotic episode typically occurs in late adolescence or early adulthood. In some

April 20: "[I am feeling] paranoid. The person upstairs was reading my mind and speaking back to me to keep me in a sort of ego crucifixion. . . . I felt this was because I was discharging very strong vibrations."

Terence Charnley

May 6: "I had no tongue, no real tongue, and could only flatter. . . . The nail in the mouth expresses this. The people around me cannot understand how I was so stupid and cannot forgive me . . . thus I am a target. The nails in my eyes express that I cannot see whereas other people seem to have extrasensory perception and I am blind in this respect."

Terence Charnley

May 18: "My mind seemed to be thought broadcasting [and] it was beyond my will to do anything about it. I summed this up by painting my brain as an enormous mouth. . . . The trouble seemed to stem from a broken heart so I painted a great mass of gore there. . . . I feel I am giving off strong personality vibrations, hence the wavy lines emanating from my head."

Terence Charnley

individuals, the breakdown occurs suddenly; in others, it is more gradual, a slow change in personality. The more breakdowns and relapses the individual has had, the poorer the chances for complete recovery. Yet, contrary to stereotype, many people with schizophrenia do recover from this illness and go on to hold good jobs and have successful relationships, especially if they have strong family support and access to community programs (Harding, 2005; Hopper et al., 2007; Jobe & Harrow, 2010).

The mystery of this disease is that some people with schizophrenia are almost completely impaired in all spheres; others do well in certain areas. Still others have normal moments of lucidity in otherwise withdrawn lives. One adolescent crouched in a rigid catatonic posture in front of a television for the month of October; later, he was able to report on all the highlights of the World Series he had seen. A middle-aged man, hospitalized for 20 years, believing he was a prophet of God and that monsters were coming out of the walls, was able to interrupt his ranting to play a good game of chess (Wender & Klein, 1981).

Simulate the **Experiment**
Schizophrenia Overview in **MyPsychLab**

Origins of Schizophrenia

Any disorder that has so many variations and symptoms will pose many problems for those trying to find its origins. Early psychodynamic and learning theories, which held that schizophrenia results from being raised by an erratic, cold, rejecting mother or from living in an unpredictable environment, have not been supported. Most researchers now believe that schizophrenia is caused by genetic problems that produce subtle abnormalities in the brain. As usual, however, genes must interact with certain stressors in the environment during prenatal development, birth, or adolescence. Here is some evidence on the contributing factors:

Watch the **Video** *Genetic Schizophrenia* in **MyPsychLab**

1 Genetic predispositions. A person has a much greater risk of developing schizophrenia if an identical twin develops the disorder, even if the twins are reared apart (Gottesman, 1991; Gottesman et al., 2010; Heinrichs, 2005). Children with one schizophrenic parent have a lifetime risk of 12%, and children with two schizophrenic parents have a life-time risk of 27 to 46%, compared to a risk in the general population of only 1 to 2% (see Figure 15.4). In a Finnish study of identical twins, fully 83% of the variation in the risk of becoming schizophrenic was due to combined genetic factors and only 17% to unique environmental factors (Cannon et al., 1998). Researchers all over the world are trying to track down the genes that might be involved in specific symptoms, such as hallucinations, sensitivity to sounds, and cognitive impairments (Desbonnet, Waddington, & O'Tuathaigh, 2009; Tomppo et al., 2009). One team has identified one such gene, called DISC1 or "disrupted-in-schizophrenia." Chromosomal aberrations on this gene are involved in schizophrenia and bipolar disorder, which share severe disturbances of emotion and cognition (Millar et al., 2005; Walker & Tessner, 2008).

2 Structural brain abnormalities. Most individuals with schizophrenia have abnormalities in the brain, including a decrease in the volume of the temporal lobe or hippocampus, reduced neuronal connections in the prefrontal cortex, or enlargement of the *ventricles*, spaces in the brain that are filled with cerebrospinal fluid (see Figure 15.5) (Black et al., 2004; Heinrichs, 2005; Zorrilla et al., 1997). Schizophrenics are also more likely than healthy individuals to have abnormalities in the thalamus, the traffic-control centre that filters sensations and focuses attention (Andreasen et al., 1994; Gur et al., 1998). Schizophrenics also may have abnormalities in the auditory cortex and Broca's and Wernicke's areas, all involved in speech perception and processing. Such abnormalities might explain the nightmare of voice hallucinations.

FIGURE 15.4 Genetic Vulnerability to Schizophrenia
This graph, based on combined data from 40 European twin and adoption studies conducted over seven decades, shows that the closer the genetic relationship to a person with schizophrenia, the higher the risk of developing the disorder. (Based on Gottesman, 1991.)

Lifetime risk of developing schizophrenia

FIGURE 15.5 Schizophrenia and the Brain
People with schizophrenia are more likely to have enlarged ventricles (spaces) in the brain than healthy people are. These MRI scans of 28-year-old male identical twins show the difference in the size of ventricles between the healthy twin (left) and the one with schizophrenia (right).

National Institute of Mental Health

Healthy   Schizophrenic

👁‑🎞 Watch the **Video** *Rodney: Schizophrenia* in **MyPsychLab**

((•‑🔊 Listen to the **Chapter Audio** *Schizophrenia and Smoking* in **MyPsychLab**

FIGURE 15.6 The Adolescent Brain and Schizophrenia
These dramatic images highlight areas of brain-tissue loss in adolescents with schizophrenia. Using a new method that detects fine changes, neuroscientists tracked the loss of grey matter over five years. The areas of greatest tissue loss (regions that control memory, hearing, motor functions, and attention) are shown in red and magenta; a healthy brain (top) looks almost entirely blue (Thompson et al., 2001).

University of California, Los Angeles, School of Medicine

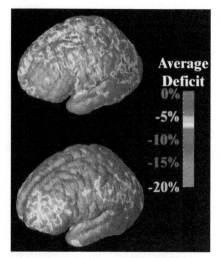

3 **Neurotransmitter abnormalities.** Schizophrenia has been associated with abnormalities in several neurotransmitters, including serotonin, glutamate, and dopamine (Sawa & Snyder, 2002). However, similar neurotransmitter abnormalities are also found in many other mental disorders, such as depression, OCD, and alcoholism, making it difficult to know whether these abnormalities play a specific role in schizophrenia. 👁

4 **Prenatal problems or birth complications.** Damage to the fetal brain significantly increases the likelihood of schizophrenia later in life. Such damage may occur if the mother suffers from malnutrition; schizophrenia rates rise during times of famine, as happened in China and elsewhere (St. Clair et al., 2005). Damage may also occur if the mother gets the flu virus during the first four months of prenatal development, which triples the risk of schizophrenia (Brown et al., 2004; Mednick, Huttunen, & Machón, 1994). And it may occur if there are complications during birth that injure the baby's brain or deprive it of oxygen (Cannon et al., 2000). However, prenatal stress—on the mother or the fetus—is a risk factor for the development of other psychological disorders later in life, too, not only schizophrenia (Huizink, Mulder, & Buitelaar, 2004). ((•

5 **Adolescent abnormalities in brain development.** The last factor contributing to schizophrenia occurs in adolescence, when the brain undergoes a natural pruning away of synapses. Normally, this pruning helps make the brain more efficient in handling the new challenges of adulthood. But it appears that schizophrenic brains aggressively prune away too many synapses, which may explain why the first full-blown schizophrenic episode typically occurs in adolescence or early adulthood. Healthy teenagers lose about 1% of the brain's grey matter between ages 13 and 18. But as you can see in Figure 15.6, adolescents with schizophrenia show much more extensive and rapid tissue loss, primarily in the sensory and motor regions (Thompson et al., 2001). "We were stunned to see a spreading wave of tissue loss that began in a small region of the brain," said Paul Thompson, who headed the study that tracked the loss of grey matter in the brain over five years. "It moved across the brain like a forest fire, destroying more tissue as the disease progressed." The reason for the excessive pruning is not yet known, but it may involve genetic dispositions, fetal brain damage, or stressful life experiences (McGlashan & Hoffman, 2000).

Thus, the developmental pathway of schizophrenia is something of a relay. It starts with a genetic predisposition, which must combine with prenatal risk factors or birth complications that affect brain development. The resulting vulnerability then awaits events in adolescence—synaptic pruning within the brain (Walker & Tessner, 2008) or external stressors—that serve as a trigger for the disease (Conklin & Iacono, 2002). This model explains why one identical twin may develop schizophrenia but not the other: Both may have the genetic susceptibility, but only one may have been exposed to other risk factors in the womb, birth complications, or stressful life events. These factors may combine in different ways as well, explaining why some schizophrenics recover and others do not. The riddle of schizophrenia is likely to be several riddles, waiting to be solved.

Recite & Review

Recite: Say aloud what you remember about *schizophrenia*, *psychosis*, and catatonic stupor.

Review: Next, read the section on schizophrenia again.

Now take this *Quick Quiz:*

1. What are the five major kinds of symptoms in schizophrenia?
2. What are the three likely stages in the "relay" that produces schizophrenia?

✔●—**Study** and **Review**
in **MyPsychLab**

Answers:

1. delusions, hallucinations, disorganized speech, inappropriate behaviour, and impaired cognitive abilities 2. genetic predispositions; prenatal risk factors or birth complications; events during adolescence, such as excessive pruning of synapses in the brain or external stressors

Mental Disorder and Personal Responsibility

We have come to the end of a long walk along the spectrum of psychological problems—from those that are normal conditions of life, such as occasional anxiety or "caffeine-induced sleep disorder," to mental disorders that can be severely disabling, such as major depression or schizophrenia.

One of the great debates generated by all diagnoses of mental disorder concerns the question of personal responsibility. In law and in everyday life, many people reach for a psychological reason to exonerate themselves of responsibility for their actions.

Romance writer Janet Dailey, who, when caught, admitted she had plagiarized whole passages from another writer's work, said she was suffering from "a psychological problem that I never even suspected I had." Many people—as an excuse for some habit that is immoral, illegal, or fattening—claim they are "addicted" to the behaviour, whether it is sex, shopping, eating chocolate, jogging, or spending hours on the internet. These activities may be highly pleasurable, to be sure, but are they "addictions" in the customary meaning of the word?

Some psychologists think these activities are indeed comparable to drug addiction or to any other compulsive behaviour: They can be maladaptive, disrupting the lives of those who spend thousands of hours shopping or having adventures in cyberspace instead of the real world; they can cause emotional distress to the individual or to his or her friends and family. Other psychologists, however, think that students who spend too much time online are no different from previous generations who also found plenty of ways to distract themselves and avoid the common problems facing students everywhere—insecurity, worry about grades, a disappointing social life. This is not a "mental disorder," they say, it's a normal problem, called "Learning to Pass Courses and Figure Out Life." Certainly,

THINKING CRITICALLY

Ask questions.

The legal system is based on the assumption of personal responsibility, but it also recognizes that some people cannot control their behaviour. When does a mental disorder become an excuse to "get away with murder," and when does it truly diminish a person's legal and moral responsibility?

Andrea Yates was convicted of the murder of her children and sent to a mental institution. Do you agree that this was the appropriate punishment? Why or why not?

Steve Ueckert/Pool/AP Images

some students who use internet addiction as an excuse for not studying are making an obvious effort to avoid responsibility for a bad grade. Others may be spending too much time on the internet as a way of coping with depression, anxiety, or another emotional problem.

The difficulty of knowing where to draw the line of responsibility is apparent in the tragic story of Andrea Yates, a Texas woman who killed her five young children in a state of extreme despair. She had suffered from clinical depression and psychotic episodes for years and in her blackest depressions became mute and catatonic. She tried to kill herself twice. Her father, two brothers, and a sister had suffered varying degrees of mental illness, including depression. Yates was overwhelmed by raising and home schooling all her children by herself, with no help from her reportedly domineering husband, who permitted her two hours a week of personal time. Although she suffered a postpartum psychotic episode after the birth of their fourth child and a clinical psychologist warned against her having another baby, her husband refused to consider birth control, although not for religious reasons. "We want as many as nature will allow," he said (Yardley, 2001). In 2002, Yates was convicted of murder and sentenced to life in prison after a jury rejected her claim that she was so psychotic that she thought she was saving the souls of her children by killing them. That conviction was overturned on appeal. In 2006, another jury found her not guilty by reason of insanity and she was sent to a mental institution. The defence saw this verdict as a triumph for the understanding of mental illness; the prosecution saw it as a failure of justice.

Does Andrea Yates deserve our condemnation for her horrible acts of murder or our pity? Was her punishment appropriate? We noted at the beginning of this chapter that "insanity" refers only to the defendant's ability to know right from wrong at the time the crime was committed. It is used in only a tiny percentage of all criminal cases. But in some jurisdictions, a defendant may claim to have "diminished responsibility" for a crime. This claim does not exonerate the defendant, but it may result in reduced charges, for example from premeditated first-degree murder to manslaughter. A diminished-capacity defence holds that the defendant lacked the mental capacity to form a calculated and malicious plan but instead was impaired by mental illness or the great provocation of the situation. In some jurisdictions, diminished capacity and other mitigating factors are considered only at the sentencing phase, once the defendant has been found guilty.

When thinking about the relationship of mental disorder to personal responsibility, we face a dilemma. The law recognizes, rightly, that people who are mentally incompetent, delusional, or disturbed should not be judged by the same standards as mentally healthy individuals. At the same time, society has an obligation to protect its citizens from harm and to reject easy excuses for violations of the law. To balance these two positions, we need to find ways to ensure that people who commit crimes or behave reprehensibly face the consequences of their behaviour. We must also ensure that people who are suffering from psychological problems have the compassionate support of society in their search for help. After all, psychological problems of one kind or another are challenges that all of us will face at some time in our lives.

Taking Psychology with You

When a Friend Is Suicidal

Suicide can be frightening to those who find themselves fantasizing about it, and it is devastating to the family and friends of those who go through with it. In Canada, it is the

ninth leading cause of death, far surpassing homicide (Statistics Canada, 1997). The suicide rate is highest among white men over the age of 65, but suicide rates have nearly tripled in the past 40 years among adolescents and young adults, especially among college and university students and black teenagers. In the United States, about 1300 college or university students commit suicide every year, and nearly 32 000 more make an unsuccessful attempt (Farrell, 2005).

Women are more likely than men to attempt suicide, primarily as a cry for help, whereas men are four times more likely than women to succeed. But this gender difference depends on culture and circumstances. In Finland, for example, more males than females attempt suicide; and in Canada and the United States, men in prison have high rates of attempted suicide (Canetto & Sakinofsky, 1998). Moreover, men's efforts to commit suicide are not always obvious: Some men provoke confrontations with the police, hoping to be shot; some intentionally kill themselves in car accidents; and men are more likely than women to destroy themselves with drugs.

Because of the many widespread myths about suicide, it is important to become informed and know what to do in a crisis:

- *Take all suicide threats seriously.* Some people assume they can't do anything when a friend talks about committing suicide. "He'll just do it at another place, another time," they think. In fact, most suicides occur during an acute crisis. Once the person gets through the crisis, the desire to die fades.

  Others believe that if a friend is *talking* about committing suicide, he or she won't really *do* it. This belief is also false. Few people commit suicide without signalling their intentions. Most are ambivalent: "I want to kill myself, but I don't want to be dead—at least not forever." Most suicidal people want relief from the terrible pain of feeling that nobody cares and that life is not worth living. Getting these thoughts and fears out in the open is an important first step.

- *Know the danger signs.* A person is at risk of trying to commit suicide if he or she has tried to do it before; has become withdrawn and listless; has a history of depression; reveals specific plans for carrying out the suicide or gives away cherished possessions; expresses no concern about religious prohibitions or the impact on family members; and has access to a lethal method, such as a gun.

- *Get involved: Ask questions and get help.* If you believe a friend is suicidal, do not be afraid to ask, "Are you thinking of suicide?" This question does not "put the idea" in anyone's mind. If your friend is contemplating the action, he or she will probably be relieved to talk about it, which in turn will reduce feelings of isolation and despair. Don't try to talk your friend out of it by debating whether suicide is right or wrong, and don't put on phony cheerfulness. If your friend's words scare you, say so. By allowing your friend to unburden his or her grief, you help the person get through the immediate crisis.

- *Do not leave your friend alone.* If necessary, get the person to a clinic or a hospital emergency room, or contact a crisis centre. Links to local suicide prevention centres (complete with phone numbers) can be found here: **http://suicideprevention.ca/thinking-about-suicide/find-a-crisis-centre/**. Don't worry about doing the wrong thing. In an emergency, the worst thing you can do is nothing at all.

- If you are the one who is contemplating suicide, remember that you are not alone and that help is a phone call or an email away. You can call the national hotline number (mentioned above) or your school's counselling services. For more information, the U.S. Centers for Disease Control and Prevention has a website that provides facts about suicide (**www.cdc.gov/safeusa/suicide.htm**). Many students fear getting help because they think no one will understand, they fear they will be made fun of by their friends, or they believe they cannot be helped. Wrong, wrong, wrong.

In her book *Night Falls Fast: Understanding Suicide*, Kay Jamison (1999), a psychologist who suffers from bipolar disorder, explored this difficult subject from the standpoint of both a mental-health professional and a person who has "been there." In describing the aftermath of her own suicide attempt, she wrote: "I do know . . . that I should have been dead but was not—and that I was fortunate enough to be given another chance at life, which many others were not."

Summary

MyPsychLab can help you get a better grade. Test your knowledge and grasp difficult concepts through
- Custom study plans: See where you are strong and where you are wrong
- Multimedia, including videos and interactive simulations
- Dynamic Study Modules: flashcards for self-study that ensure you achieve mastery of course concepts

Defining and Diagnosing Disorder

- When defining *mental disorder*, mental-health professionals emphasize the violation of cultural standards, the emotional suffering caused by the behaviour, and whether the behaviour is harmful to others or society.

- The *Diagnostic and Statistical Manual of Mental Disorders (DSM)*, which is used throughout the world, is designed to provide objective criteria and categories for diagnosing mental disorder. Critics argue that the diagnosis of mental disorders, unlike those of medical diseases, is inherently a subjective process that can never be entirely objective. They believe the DSM fosters overdiagnosis, overlooks the influence of diagnostic labels on clients and therapists, confuses serious mental disorders with everyday problems in living, and creates an illusion of objectivity and universality.

• Supporters of the DSM believe that when the DSM criteria are used correctly and when empirically validated objective tests are used, reliability in diagnosis improves. The DSM now lists many *culture-bound syndromes* in addition to disorders (such as depression and schizophrenia) that are found all over the world.

• In diagnosing psychological disorders, clinicians often use *projective tests* such as the *Rorschach Inkblot Test* or, with children, anatomically detailed dolls. These methods have low reliability and validity, creating problems when they are used in the legal arena, as in custody disputes, or in diagnosing disorders. In general, *objective tests (inventories)*, such as the *MMPI*, are more reliable and valid than projective ones.

Anxiety Disorders

• *Generalized anxiety disorder* involves continuous, chronic *anxiety*, with signs of nervousness, worry, and irritability. When anxiety results from exposure to uncontrollable or unpredictable danger, it can lead to *posttraumatic stress disorder (PTSD)*, which involves mentally reliving the trauma, emotional detachment, and increased physiological arousal.

• Most people who live through a traumatic experience eventually recover without developing PTSD. But a minority do. The reasons for their increased vulnerability to posttraumatic symptoms include having a history of psychological problems and other traumatic experiences, lacking social support and psychological resources, having lower-than-average intelligence, having a relatively smaller hippocampus than normal, and having a genetic vulnerability.

• *Panic disorder* involves sudden, intense attacks of profound fear. Panic attacks are common in the aftermath of stress or frightening experiences; those who go on to develop a disorder tend to interpret the attacks as a sign of impending disaster.

• *Phobias* are unrealistic fears of specific situations, activities, or things. Common *social phobias* include fears of speaking in public, going on a date, or being observed by others. *Agoraphobia*, the fear of being away from a safe place or person, is the most disabling phobia—a "fear of fear." It often begins with a panic attack, which the person tries to avoid in the future by staying close to "safe" places or people.

• *Obsessive-compulsive disorder (OCD)* involves recurrent, unwished-for thoughts or images (obsessions) and repetitive, ritualized behaviours (compulsions) that a person feels unable to control. Some people with OCD have depleted levels of serotonin in their prefrontal cortex, which may contribute to their cognitive rigidity. Parts of the brain involved in fear and responses to threat are also more active than normal in people with OCD; the "alarm mechanism," once activated, does not turn off when danger is past. A separate compulsive disorder is pathological hoarding, which may involve deficiencies in other parts of the brain.

Mood Disorders

• Symptoms of *major depression* include distorted thinking patterns, low self-esteem, physical ailments such as fatigue and loss of appetite, and prolonged grief and despair. Women are twice as likely as men to suffer from major depression, but depression in men may be underdiagnosed. In *bipolar disorder*, a person experiences episodes of both depression and *mania* (excessive euphoria). It is equally common in both sexes.

• *Vulnerability-stress models* of depression (or any other disorder) look at interactions between individual vulnerabilities and stressful experiences. Some people have a genetic predisposition to become depressed when they undergo severe stress, and others may be genetically protected. Genes may affect levels of serotonin and the stress hormone cortisol. For some vulnerable individuals, repeated losses of important people can set off episodes of major depression. Life experiences that increase the risk of depression include violence, problems with work and family, poverty, discrimination, and sexual abuse. Cognitive habits also play an important role: believing that the origin of one's unhappiness is permanent and uncontrollable, feeling hopeless and pessimistic, and brooding or ruminating about one's problems.

Personality Disorders

• *Personality disorders* are characterized by rigid, self-destructive traits that cause distress or an inability to get along with others. They include, among others, *paranoid, narcissistic, borderline*, and *antisocial personality disorders*.

• The term *psychopath* describes people who lack conscience and emotional connection to others; they don't feel remorse, shame, guilt, or anxiety over wrongdoing; and they can charm and con others with ease. *Antisocial personality disorder (APD)* applies to people with a lifelong pattern of aggressive, reckless, impulsive, and criminal behaviour. Not all psychopaths have APD, and not all people with APD are psychopaths, but in some individuals the two disorders converge. Researchers have identified abnormalities in the central nervous system and prefrontal cortex that are associated with lack of emotional responsiveness and with impulsivity. APD has a genetic component, but biological vulnerabilities must interact with stressful or violent environments to produce the disorder.

people to function and respond to psychotherapy. Yet many psychiatrists and drug companies are trumpeting the benefits of medication without informing the public of its limitations, so some words of caution are in order.

Most people are unaware of how a publication bias—the tendency for journals to publish positive findings but not negative or ambiguous ones—affects what we know. Independent researchers reviewed unpublished data submitted to the U.S. Food and Drug Administration (FDA) on 12 popular antidepressants. Of the 74 studies they examined, 38 reported positive results, and all but one of those was later published. Of the remaining studies with negative or mixed results, only 14 were published—and most of them were given a positive spin (Turner et al., 2008). In 2003, British drug authorities reported that nine unpublished studies of Paxil found that it tripled the risk of suicidal thoughts and suicide attempts in young people who were taking the drug compared to those given a placebo (G. Harris, 2003). Paxil and other SSRIs can cause a severe form of restlessness and agitation in the first few weeks they are taken, and this reaction might push vulnerable young people to a precipice. Today, the U.S. Food and Drug Administration (FDA) has cautioned against prescribing SSRIs to anyone under 18.

Most worrisome for the future of impartial research is that most researchers who are studying the effectiveness of medication have strong financial ties to the pharmaceutical industry in the forms of lucrative consulting fees, funding for studies, stock investments, and patents. Indeed, funding for some research is available only from pharmaceutical companies, which may require investigators to sign contracts allowing the companies to determine whether, where, and when the research findings will be published. (For example, Pfizer delayed publication of research it had sponsored in the United States showing that Viagra was ineffective for women; eventually, an independent Canadian study reported the same results [Basson et al., 2002].) Studies that are independently funded often do not get the strong positive results that industry-funded drug trials do (Angell, 2004; Healy, 2002; Krimsky, 2003). In this section, therefore, we want to give you an idea of what you are not hearing from the drug companies.

1 **The placebo effect.** New drugs, like new psychotherapies, often promise quick and effective cures. But the **placebo effect** ensures that many people will respond positively to a new drug just because of the enthusiasm surrounding it and because of their own expectations that the drug will make them feel better. After a while, when placebo effects decline, many drugs turn out to be neither as effective as promised nor as widely applicable. This has happened repeatedly with each new generation of tranquilizer and each new "miracle" antipsychotic drug and antidepressant, including Clozaril and Prozac (Healy, 2012; Moncrieff, 2001). In fact, some investigators maintain that much of the effectiveness of antidepressants is due to a placebo effect (Khan et al., 2003; Kirsch, 2009). Even researchers who quarrel with that strong conclusion acknowledge that the drugs are less effective than commonly believed. Overall, only about half of all depressed patients respond positively to any given antidepressant medication, and of those, only about 40% are actually responding to the specific biological effects of the drugs (Hollon, Thase, & Markowitz, 2002). In a meta-analysis of more than 5000 patients in 47 clinical trials, investigators found that the placebo effect was "exceptionally large," accounting for more than 80% of the alleviation of symptoms. The drugs were most effective for patients with severe depression (Kirsch et al., 2008). New research in neuroscience is illuminating the reason why placebos work for some people: The psychological expectation of improvement actually produces some of the same brain changes that medication does (Benedetti et al., 2005; see Chapter 6).

placebo effect The apparent success of a medication or treatment due to the patient's expectations or hopes than rather to the drug or treatment itself.

> ### THINKING CRITICALLY
> Avoid emotional reasoning.
>
> You hear a researcher claiming that a new drug is "a breakthrough drug for depression" or for anxiety or for some other problem. Such announcements always generate a lot of excitement. Why should people be cautious before concluding that a new drug is the miracle they are longing for it to be? What information is the public often not getting from the company making the drug?

therapeutic window The amount of a drug that is enough but not too much, taking into account the fact that the same dose of a drug may be metabolized differently in men and women, old people and young people, and different ethnic groups.

2 **High relapse and dropout rates.** A person may have short-term success with antipsychotic or antidepressant drugs. However, in part because of these drugs' unpleasant side effects, one-half to two-thirds of people stop taking them. When they do, they are quite likely to relapse, especially if they have not learned how to cope with their problems (Hollon, Thase, & Markowitz, 2002).

3 **Dosage problems.** The challenge with drugs is to find the **therapeutic window**, the amount that is enough but not too much. This problem is compounded by the fact that the same dose of a drug may be metabolized differently in men and women, old people and young people, and different ethnic groups. When psychiatrist Keh-Ming Lin moved from Taiwan to the United States, he was amazed to learn that the dosage of antipsychotic drugs given to American patients with schizophrenia was often 10 times higher than the dose for Chinese patients. In subsequent studies, Lin and his colleagues confirmed that Asian patients require significantly lower doses of the medication for optimal treatment (Lin, Poland, & Chien, 1990). Similarly, black people suffering from depression or bipolar disorder seem to need lower dosages of tricyclic antidepressants and lithium than other ethnic groups do (Strickland et al., 1991, 1995). Groups may differ in the dosages they can tolerate because of variations in metabolic rates, amount of body fat, the number or type of drug receptors in the brain, or cultural practices such as smoking and eating certain foods.

4 **Disregard for effective, possibly better, nonmedical treatments.** Because ads promise such wonderful results, medication often seems the best way to deal with an emotional or behavioural problem. Yet nonmedical treatments may work just as well or better. For example, two psychologists examined data on more than 168 000 children with attention deficit disorder who had been referred to a behavioural-care facility for treatment. More than 60% of the boys and 23% of the girls were on Ritalin or another drug. But after six sessions of behaviour therapy for the children and 10 sessions for the parent, only 11% of the boys and 2% of the girls remained on medication (Cummings & Wiggins, 2001).

The popularity of drugs has also been fuelled in the United States by pressure from managed-care organizations, which prefer to pay for one patient visit for a prescription rather than 10 visits for psychotherapy, and by drug company advertising. In 1997 the FDA permitted pharmaceutical companies to advertise directly to consumers, a practice still forbidden in Canada and Europe; sales of new drugs skyrocketed because of consumer demand.

5 **Unknown long-term risks.** We saw that antipsychotic drugs can have dangerous and even fatal consequences if taken for many years. Antidepressants have been assumed to be quite safe, but the effects of taking them indefinitely are still unknown. The general public and even many physicians do not realize that new drugs are often tested on only a few hundred people for only a few weeks or months, even when the drug is one that patients might take for years (Angell, 2004). (The cost of bringing most new drugs to market is very high, and manufacturers feel they cannot afford to wait years to determine whether there might be long-term hazards.) Many physicians and laypeople, feeling reassured if a drug is effective in the short run, overlook the possibility of long-term dangers, as well as the potential risks of drug interactions. Yet psychiatrists, understandably frustrated by the failure of existing antipsychotics and antidepressants to help all of their clients, are increasingly prescribing "cocktails" of medications—this one for anxiety, plus this one for depression, plus another to manage the side effects. They report anecdotal success in some cases, but as yet there has been virtually no research on the benefits and risks of these combination approaches.

6 **Untested off-label uses.** Most consumers do not realize that once a drug is approved by Health Canada, doctors are then permitted to prescribe it for other conditions and to populations other than those on which it was originally tested. That

is why antidepressants are now being marketed for "social phobias"; why Prozac, when its patent expired, was renamed Sarafem and marketed to women for "premenstrual dysphoric disorder"; why Ritalin, widely given to school-aged children, is now being prescribed for two- and three-year-olds; why the number of antidepressants given to preschoolers has doubled; and why antipsychotics such as Risperdal are being used for nonpsychotic disorders such as impulsive aggression.

Medications have saved lives and improved the lives of thousands of people suffering from severe mental illness as well as those suffering from milder forms of depression, anxiety, and other emotional problems. Yet the cautions we have listed are the reason why it is important to think critically about this issue. In coming years, you will be hearing about many "promising medications" for such common psychological problems as memory loss, eating disorders, smoking, and alcoholism (Miller, 2008). Every major pharmaceutical company is working on one or more of these, and you are likely to hear enthusiastic researchers promising "We'll have it within five years!" But we hope you will resist the impulse to jump on any new-drug bandwagon. Drugs for mental disorders are neither totally miraculous, as some of their promoters say, nor totally worthless, as some of their critics maintain. Critical thinkers must weigh the benefits and limitations of medication for psychological problems, wait for the data on safety and effectiveness, and resist the temptation to oversimplify.

Direct Brain Intervention

For most of human history, a person suffering from mental illness often got a rather extreme form of "help." A well-meaning tribal healer or, in later centuries, a doctor would try to release the "psychic pressures" believed to be causing the symptoms by drilling holes in the victim's skull. It didn't work! However, the basic impulse—to try to cure mental illness by intervening directly in the brain—has continued.

One approach, **psychosurgery**, is designed to surgically destroy selected areas of the brain thought to be responsible for emotional disorders or disturbed behaviour. The most famous form of modern psychosurgery was invented in 1935, when a Portuguese neurologist, Antonio Egas Moniz, drilled two holes into the skull of a mental patient and used a specially designed instrument to cut or crush nerve fibres running from the prefrontal lobes to other areas. Moniz called this operation a "leukotomy," which means "white matter cutting." Moniz developed this procedure before the invention of psychoactive medications for the treatment of mental illness, and argued that his surgical procedure should be used extremely conservatively. His wishes were not granted. In 1945, American physician Walter Freeman adapted the "leukotomy" procedure (now called a prefrontal lobotomy), aggressively promoted it, and eventually performed more than 3500 operations himself, including one on John F. Kennedy's sister Rosemary. Similarly, thousands of lobotomies were performed in Canada during the same time period (Simmons, 1987). The procedure, which had been intended to reduce a patient's emotional symptoms without impairing intellectual ability, tragically left many patients apathetic, withdrawn, and unable to care for themselves (Valenstein, 1986). Despite Freeman's reckless adaptation and administration of the original leukotomy procedure, Moniz won a Nobel Prize for his work.

Today, psychosurgery is rare, but some neurosurgeons have not given up on the effort to cure mental illness by operating on the brain. Some are burning holes in the frontal lobes of the brain (cingulotomies) as a last resort on people with intractable cases of obsessive-compulsive disorder and severe depression, people who have not responded to drugs or psychotherapy (Cosgrove & Rauch, 2003). Unfortunately, reports of success are largely anecdotal and no controlled studies have been conducted on any of the new forms of psychosurgery (Lopes et al., 2004).

Instead of operating on the brain, therefore, other psychiatrists and neurologists prefer to stimulate it electrically. The oldest method is **electroconvulsive therapy (ECT)**,

psychosurgery Any surgical procedure that destroys selected areas of the brain believed to be involved in emotional disorders or violent, impulsive behaviour.

electroconvulsive therapy (ECT) A procedure used in cases of prolonged and severe major depression, in which a brief brain seizure is induced.

or "shock therapy," which is used for the treatment of severe depression, although no one knows how or why it works. An electrode is placed on one side of the head (rarely on both), and a brief current is turned on. The current triggers a seizure that typically lasts one minute, causing the body to convulse. Today, unlike in the past, patients are given muscle relaxants and anesthesia, so they sleep through the procedure and their convulsions are minimized. ECT has helped some people who are suicidal and who have not responded to medication or any other treatments. The World Psychiatric Association has endorsed ECT as safe and effective, especially for people with crippling depression and suicidal impulses and for those who have not responded to other treatments (Shorter & Healy, 2008). However, the mood-improving effect of ECT is usually short-lived, and the depression almost always returns within a few weeks or months (U.S. Food and Drug Administration, 2011; Hollon, Thase, & Markowitz, 2002). And ECT is ineffective with other disorders, such as schizophrenia or alcoholism, though it is occasionally misused for these conditions. Critics of ECT have long argued that the method is often used improperly and that it can in fact damage the brain and impair memory. However, it is largely accepted that ECT works, even if its mechanism of action is poorly understood, and the practice is still accepted by the Canadian Psychiatric Association (Flint & Gagnon, 2002).

While this debate continues, researchers are looking for milder ways to electrically stimulate the brains of severely depressed individuals. One method, transcranial magnetic stimulation (TMS), involves the use of a pulsing magnetic coil held to a person's skull over the left prefrontal cortex. This area of the brain is less active in people with depression, and repeated TMS seems to give it a boost. The patient stays awake, and the procedure does not cause memory loss or other side effects (Wasserman & Lisanby, 2001). In one well-controlled study of depressed patients who had not improved on medication, those who were given TMS treatments every day for four weeks were more likely to improve than those given a "sham" treatment with no

THINKING CRITICALLY

Tolerate uncertainty.

George Ruhe/Redux Pictures

A researcher demonstrates transcranial magnetic stimulation (TMS). One neurosurgeon who uses this technology with depressed patients told a reporter why he thinks the results have been unpredictable so far. "The effect is very dependent on who is delivering the TMS," he said. "The way you hold the coil, where you put it, the rotation, the angle" affect what happens in the brain. As a critical thinker, what warning lights should go off in your own brain when you read a statement like that? One answer: If a method depends more on who is doing it than on what is being done, the placebo effect is likely to be the reason for any benefits, rather than the technology itself. Until controlled studies are done, we need to tolerate some uncertainty about whether TMS will prove to be effective.

stimulation (Fitzgerald et al., 2003). Nonetheless, as yet, no one knows why magnetic stimulation might ease a patient's emotional suffering. It is still experimental, and since claims of its success are based only on patients' self-reports, the powerful placebo effect of treatment cannot be ruled out (Lozano et al., 2008). The company that developed this $25 000-per-patient device has hired psychiatrists to lobby for it, mounted a vigorous marketing campaign to get it approved, and funded virtually all of the so-far unsuccessful efforts to show that it works (Barglow, 2008).

Recite & Review

Recite: You have just read about many kinds of biological treatments. Take a breath, and say everything you can recall about *antipsychotic drugs*, *antidepressant drugs (MAOIs, tricyclics, SSRIs)*, *tranquilizers*, and *lithium carbonate*; the cautions about drug treatments; the *placebo effect*, *therapeutic window*, and *psychosurgery*, and *electroconvulsive therapy*.

Review: Next, given all the information you need to digest, reread the section.

Now take this *Quick Quiz:*

No amount of electric shock will stimulate test-taking ability.

1. Match these treatments with the problems for which they are typically used.

   i. antipsychotic drugs   **a.** suicidal depression

   ii. antidepressant drugs   **b.** bipolar disorder

   iii. lithium carbonate   **c.** schizophrenia

   iv. electroconvulsive therapy   **d.** depression and anxiety

                                        e. obsessive-compulsive disorder

2. Give four reasons to be cautious about claims that drugs for psychological disorders are miracle cures.

3. Tanya has had occasional episodes of depression that seem to be getting worse. Her physician prescribes an antidepressant. Before taking it, what questions should Tanya ask herself and the doctor?

Answers:

1. i. c; ii. d, e; iii. b; iv. a **2.** Placebo effects are common; dropout and relapse rates are high; appropriate dosages can be difficult to determine and can vary by sex, age, and ethnicity; and some drugs have unknown or long-term risks **3.** Has the physician prescribed the drug without taking her full medical and psychological history? Has the physician considered other possible reasons for her depression? Would psychotherapy be appropriate, either with or without medication? Does the medication have any unpleasant side effects or long-term risks? Will the doctor continue to monitor her reactions to the drug on a regular basis?

Learning Objectives

④ Describe the major approaches to psychotherapy.

⑤ Detail how behaviour therapists can help you change bad habits and cognitive therapists can help you get rid of self-defeating thoughts.

⑥ Explain why humanist and existential therapists focus on the "here and now" instead of the "why and how."

⑦ List the benefits of treating a whole family instead of only one of its members.

Major Schools of Psychotherapy

All good psychotherapists want to help clients think about their lives in new ways and find solutions to the problems that plague them. In this section we will consider the major schools of psychotherapy. To illustrate the philosophy and methods of each one, we will focus on a fictional fellow named Murray. Murray is a smart guy whose problem is all too familiar to many students: He procrastinates. He just can't seem to settle down and write his term papers. He keeps getting incompletes, and before long the incompletes turn to Fs. Why does Murray procrastinate, manufacturing his own misery? What kind of therapy might help him? ●

Psychodynamic Therapy

Sigmund Freud was the father of the "talking cure," as one of his patients called it. In his method of **psychoanalysis**, patients talk not about their immediate problems but about their dreams and their memories of childhood. Freud believed that intensive analysis of these dreams and memories would give patients insight into the unconscious reasons for their symptoms. With insight and emotional release, the person's symptoms would disappear.

In orthodox psychoanalysis, which is rarely practised today, the client meets with the therapist as often as several times a week for a period of years. The client lies on a sofa, with the analyst sitting out of view, and says whatever comes to mind without censoring, a technique called *free association*. The analyst listens to the client's free associations and dreams, but rarely comments. There is no rush to solve the problem that brought the client into therapy. In fact, a person may come in complaining of a symptom, such as anxiety or headaches, and the therapist may not get around to that symptom for months or even years. The analyst views the symptom as only the tip of the mental iceberg.

psychoanalysis A theory of personality and a method of psychotherapy, originally formulated by Sigmund Freud, that emphasizes unconscious motives and conflicts.

Freud's psychoanalytic method has evolved into many different *psychodynamic therapies*, which share the goal of exploring the unconscious dynamics of personality, such as defences and conflicts (see Chapter 13). Proponents of these therapies often refer to them as *"depth" therapies* because the goal is to delve into the deep, unconscious processes believed to be the source of the patient's problems, rather than to concentrate on "superficial" symptoms and conscious beliefs. As we saw in Chapter 13, one modern psychodynamic approach is based on object-relations theory, which emphasizes the unconscious influence of people's earliest mental representations of their parents and how these affect reactions to separations and losses throughout life.

transference In psychodynamic therapies, a critical process in which the client transfers unconscious emotions or reactions, such as emotional feelings about his or her parents, onto the therapist.

A major element of most psychodynamic therapies, from Freudian to present forms, is **transference**, the client's transfer (displacement) of emotional elements of

Psychodynamic therapists emphasize the clinical importance of transference, the process by which the client transfers emotional feelings toward other important people in his or her life (usually the parents) onto the therapist. Therapists know that "love's arrow" isn't really intended for them!

his or her inner life—usually feelings about the client's parents—outward onto the analyst. Have you ever found yourself responding to a new acquaintance with unusually quick affection or dislike, and later realized it was because the person reminded you of a relative whom you loved or loathed? That experience is similar to transference. In therapy, a woman who has failed to resolve her Oedipal love for her father might believe she has fallen in love with the analyst. A man who is unconsciously angry at his mother for rejecting him might become furious with his analyst for going on vacation. Through analysis of transference in the therapy setting, psychodynamic therapists believe, clients can see their emotional conflicts in action and work through them (Schafer, 1992; Westen, 1998). Experimental studies have found that transference is not limited to psychotherapy; mental representations of significant others are stored in memory and are often activated in new encounters (Andersen & Berk, 1998; Andersen & Chen, 2002).

Today, most psychodynamic therapists reject the orthodox psychoanalytic approach of having the silent analyst listen to a client free associating. They face the client, they are more goal directed, and they limit therapy to a specific number of sessions, say, 10 or 20. Perhaps they might help our friend Murray gain the insight that he procrastinates as a way of expressing anger toward his parents. He might realize that he is angry because they insist that he study for a career he dislikes. Ideally, Murray will come to this insight by himself. If the analyst suggests it, Murray might feel too defensive to accept it.

Behaviour and Cognitive Therapy

Unlike psychodynamic therapists, psychologists who practise behaviour therapy or cognitive therapy would not worry much about Murray's past, his parents, or his unconscious anxieties. Psychologists who practise behaviour therapy would get right to the problem: What are the reinforcers in Murray's environment that are maintaining his behaviour? "Mur," they would say, "forget about insight. You have lousy study habits." Psychologists who practise cognitive therapy would focus on helping Murray understand how his beliefs about studying, writing papers, and success are woefully unrealistic. Often these two approaches are combined.

Behavioural Techniques. **Behaviour therapy** is based on applied behavioural analysis, the application of techniques derived from the behavioural principles of classical and operant conditioning that we discussed in Chapter 7. (You may want to review those principles before going on.) Here are some of these methods (Kazdin, 2001; Martin & Pear, 2011):

1. **Exposure.** The most widely used behavioural approach for treating fears and panic is **graduated exposure**. When people are afraid of some situation, object, or upsetting memory, they usually do everything they can to avoid confronting or thinking of it. Naturally, this only makes the fear worse. Exposure treatments, either in the client's imagination or in actual situations, are aimed at reversing this tendency. In graduated exposure, the client controls the degree of confrontation with the source of the fear. For example, someone who is trying to avoid thinking of a traumatic event might be asked to imagine the event over and over, until it no longer evokes the same degree of panic. A more dramatic form of exposure is **flooding**, in which the therapist takes the client directly into the feared situation and remains there until the client's panic and anxiety decline. Thus a person suffering from agoraphobia might be taken into a department store or a subway, an action that would normally be terrifying to contemplate. Notice how different this approach is from the psychodynamic one, in which the goal is to uncover the presumably unconscious reason that the person with agoraphobia feels afraid of going out. 👁

behaviour therapy A form of therapy that applies principles of classical and operant conditioning to help people change self-defeating or problematic behaviours.

graduated exposure In behaviour therapy, a method in which a person suffering from a phobia or panic attacks is gradually taken into the feared situation or gradually exposed to a traumatic memory until the anxiety subsides.

flooding In behaviour therapy, a form of exposure treatment in which the client is taken directly into the feared situation and remains there until his or her panic subsides.

👁—⌐**Watch** the **Video**
Anxiety Treatment: Edna Foa
in **MyPsychLab**

In this virtual reality version of systematic desensitization, people with spider phobias are gradually exposed to computerized but extremely lifelike images of spiders in a realistic, three-dimensional environment (Wiederhold & Wiederhold, 2000).

Mary Levin/University of Washington

2 **Systematic desensitization. Systematic desensitization** is an older behavioural method, a step-by-step process of breaking down a client's conditioned associations with a feared object or experience (Wolpe, 1958). It is based on the classical-conditioning procedure of *counterconditioning*, in which a stimulus (such as a dog) for an unwanted response (such as fear) is paired with some other stimulus or situation that elicits a response incompatible with the undesirable one (see Chapter 7). In this case, the incompatible response is usually relaxation. The client learns to relax deeply while imagining or looking at a sequence of feared stimuli, arranged in a hierarchy from the least frightening to the most frightening. The hierarchy itself is provided by the client. The sequence for a person who is terrified of spiders might be to read the classic children's story *Charlotte's Web*, then look at pictures of small, cute spiders, then look at pictures of tarantulas, then move on to observing a real spider, and so on. At each step the person must become relaxed before going on. Eventually, the fear responses are extinguished.

Some behaviour therapists have developed virtual-reality (VR) programs to desensitize clients to various phobias, notably of flying, heights, spiders, and public speaking, and to help clients reduce anxiety (Gregg & Tarrier, 2007). Others are experimenting with VR to treat combat veterans who are suffering from intractable posttraumatic stress symptoms. In a U.S. program called Virtual Iraq, vets get a combination of exposure and desensitization. They wear a helmet with video goggles and earphones to hear the sounds of war, and then play a modified version of the VR game Full Spectrum Warrior adapted to the Iraq experience (S. Halpern, 2008).

3 **Behavioural self-monitoring.** Before people can change their behaviour, they have to identify the reinforcers that are supporting their unwanted habits: attention from others, temporary relief from tension or unhappiness, or tangible rewards such as money or a good meal. One way to do this is through **behavioural self-monitoring**, in which the client keeps a record of the behaviour that he or she wishes to change. A man who wants to curb his overeating may not be aware of how much he eats throughout the day to relieve tension; a behavioural record might show that he eats more junk food in the late afternoon than he realized. A mother might complain that her child "always" has temper tantrums; a behavioural record will show when, where, and with whom they occur. Once the unwanted behaviour is identified, along with the reinforcers that have been maintaining it, a treatment program can be designed to change it. For instance, the man might find other ways to reduce stress and make sure that he is nowhere near junk food in the late afternoon. The mother can learn to respond to her child's tantrum not with her attention (or a cookie to buy silence) but with a time-out: banishing the child to a corner where no positive reinforcers are available.

4 **Skills training.** It is not enough to tell someone "Don't be shy" if the person does not know how to make small talk with others, or "Don't yell!" if the person does not know how to express feelings calmly. Therefore, some behaviour therapists use operant-conditioning techniques, modelling, and role-playing to teach the skills a client might lack. For example, a shy person might learn how to converse in social settings by focusing on other people rather than on his or her own insecurity. **Skills-training** programs have been designed for all kinds of behavioural problems, such as teaching parents how to discipline their children, impulsive adults how to manage anger, and people with schizophrenia how to get along in the world. These skills are also being taught in virtual worlds, such as Second Life. After face-to-face sessions with a therapist, the client creates an avatar to explore a virtual environment and

systematic desensitization In behaviour therapy, a step-by-step process of desensitizing a client to a feared object or experience; it is based on the classical-conditioning procedure of *counterconditioning*.

behavioural self-monitoring In behaviour therapy, a method of keeping careful data on the frequency and consequences of the behaviour to be changed.

skills training In behaviour therapy, an effort to teach the client skills that he or she may lack, as well as new constructive behaviours to replace self-defeating ones.

GET INVOLVED! Cure Your Fears

In Chapter 15, a Get Involved exercise asked you to identify your greatest fear. Now see whether systematic desensitization procedures will help you conquer it. Write down a list of situations that evoke your fear, starting with one that produces little anxiety (e.g., seeing a photo of a tiny spider) and ending with the most frightening one possible (e.g., looking at live tarantulas at the pet store). Then find a quiet room where you will have no distractions or interruptions, sit in a comfortable reclining chair, and relax all the muscles of your body. Breathe slowly and deeply. Imagine the first, easiest scene, remaining as relaxed as possible. Do this until you can confront the image without becoming the least bit anxious. When that happens, go on to the next scene in your hierarchy. Do not try this all at once; space out your sessions over time. Does it work?

experiment with new behaviours; the therapist can be monitoring the client's psychological and even physiological reactions at the same time. One widely used therapy for autistic children applies principles of operant conditioning to reduce the child's inappropriate or self-destructive behaviour and help the child acquire specific social and linguistic skills (Green, 1996a, 1996b).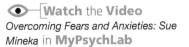

A behaviourist would treat Murray's procrastination in several ways. Murray might not know how he actually spends his time when he is avoiding his studies. Afraid that he hasn't time to do everything, he does nothing. Monitoring his own behaviour with a diary would let Murray know exactly how he spends his time, and how much time he should realistically allot to a project. Instead of having a vague, impossibly huge goal, such as "I'm going to reorganize my life," Murray would establish specific small goals, such as reading the two books necessary for an English paper and writing one page of an assignment. If Murray does not know how to write clearly, however, even writing one page might feel overwhelming; he might also need some skills training, such as a basic composition class. Most important, the therapist would change the reinforcers that are maintaining Murray's "procrastination behaviour"—perhaps the immediate gratification of partying with friends—and replace them with reinforcers for getting the work done.

Cognitive Techniques. As we saw in Chapter 11, gloomy thoughts can generate an array of negative emotions and self-defeating behaviours. The underlying premise of **cognitive therapy** is that constructive thinking can do the opposite, reducing or dispelling anger, fear, and depression. This is not a new idea. It originated 2000 years ago, with the Stoic philosophers, and was popularized in North America in the "mind cure" movement of the nineteenth century (Caplan, 1998). Cognitive therapists help clients identify the beliefs and expectations that might be unnecessarily prolonging their unhappiness, conflicts, and other problems (Persons, Davidson, & Tompkins, 2001). Clients examine the evidence for their beliefs—say, that everyone is mean and selfish, that ambition is hopeless, or that love is doomed. They learn to consider other explanations for the behaviour of people who annoy them: for example, perhaps their father's strict discipline was intended not to control but to protect them. By requiring people to identify their assumptions and biases, examine the evidence, and consider other interpretations, cognitive therapy, as you can see, teaches critical thinking.

One of the best-known contemporary schools of cognitive therapy is Albert Ellis's **rational emotive behaviour therapy (REBT)** (Ellis, 1993; Ellis & Blau, 1998). In this approach, which reflects Ellis's own no-nonsense, get-on-with-it attitude, the therapist uses rational arguments to directly challenge a client's unrealistic beliefs or expectations. Ellis has pointed out that people who are

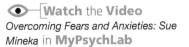
Watch the **Video**
Overcoming Fears and Anxieties: Sue Mineka in **MyPsychLab**

Cognitive therapists encourage clients to emphasize the positive (the early sunny signs of spring) rather than always focusing on the negative (the lingering icy clutch of winter). Poet Michael Casey described the first daffodil that bravely rises through the snow as "a gleam of laughter in a sullen face."

Yanchenko/Fotolia

cognitive therapy A form of therapy designed to identify and change irrational, unproductive ways of thinking and, hence, to reduce negative emotions.

rational emotive behaviour therapy (REBT) A form of cognitive therapy devised by Albert Ellis, designed to challenge the client's unrealistic thoughts.

emotionally upset often *overgeneralize*: They decide that one annoying act by someone means that person is totally bad in every way, or that a normal mistake they made is evidence that they are rotten to the core. Many people also *catastrophize*, transforming a small problem into disaster: "I failed this test, and now I'll flunk out of school, and no one will ever like me, and even my cat will hate me, and I'll never get a job." Ellis also observed that many people drive themselves crazy with notions of what they "must" do. The therapist challenges these thoughts directly, showing the client why they are irrational and misguided.

Another leading form of cognitive therapy, devised by Aaron Beck (1976, 2005), avoids direct challenges to the client's beliefs. Beck pioneered the application of cognitive therapy for depression. As we saw in Chapter 15, depression often arises from specific pessimistic thoughts—for example, that the sources of your misery are permanent and that nothing good will ever happen to you again. For Beck, these beliefs are not "irrational"; rather, they are unproductive or based on misinformation. A therapist using Beck's approach would ask you to test your beliefs against the evidence. If you say, "But I *know* no one likes me," the therapist might say, "Oh, yes? How do you know? Do you really not have a single friend? Has anyone in the past year been nice to you?"

Similarly, the University of Waterloo's Donald Meichenbaum developed a form of cognitive-behaviour therapy called "stress inoculation" to treat anxiety (Meichenbaum & Deffenbacher, 1988). Some degree of anxiety is normal—and sometimes even helpful. When imagining ourselves dealing with a difficult task, most of us will feel some anxiety. This anxiety can help motivate us, and perhaps even help us perform better than we would have had we been more relaxed. However, excessive anxiety can be crippling, keeping us from working efficiently and finishing our projects. Stress inoculation training was designed to reduce anxiety in both academic settings, especially in taking tests, and nonacademic settings. It consists of three stages. During the *education phase*, the individual is taught about the nature of anxiety, and the client and therapist work together to identify the situations that generate anxiety for the client. In the *rehearsal phase*, the person is taught how to better manage anxiety, and he or she practises being exposed to threatening situations in safe surroundings. During the *implementation phase*, the client deals with anxiety-provoking stimuli in real-world situations. Stress inoculation has become a widely accepted technique for controlling anxiety.

A cognitive therapist might treat Murray's procrastination by having Murray write down his thoughts about work, read the thoughts as if someone else had said them, and then write a rational response to each one. This technique would encourage Murray to examine the validity of his assumptions and beliefs. Many procrastinators are

GET INVOLVED! Mind over Mood

See whether cognitive-therapy techniques can help you control your moods. Think of a time recently when you felt a particularly strong emotion, such as depression, anger, or anxiety. On a piece of paper, record (1) the situation—who was there, what happened, and when; (2) the intensity of your feeling at the time, from weak to strong; and (3) the thoughts that were going through your mind (e.g., "She never cares about what I want to do"; "He's going to leave me").

Now examine your thoughts. What is the worst thing that could happen if those thoughts are true? Are your thoughts accurate or are you "mind-reading" another person's intentions and motives? Is there another way to think about this situation or the other person's behaviour? If you practise this exercise repeatedly, you may learn how your thoughts affect your moods—and find out that you have more control over your feelings than you realized (Greenberger & Padesky, 1995).

perfectionists; if they cannot do something perfectly, they will not do it at all. Unable to accept their limitations, they set impossible standards and catastrophize:

Negative Thought	**Rational Response**
If I don't get an A+ on this paper, my life will be ruined.	My life will be a lot worse if I keep getting incompletes. It's better to get a B or even a C than to do nothing.
My professor is going to think I'm an idiot when he reads this. I'll feel humiliated by his criticism.	He hasn't accused me of being an idiot yet. If he makes some criticisms, I can learn from them and do better next time.

Strict behaviourists consider thoughts to be "behaviours" that are modifiable by learning principles; they do not regard thoughts themselves as causes of behaviour. But most psychologists believe that thoughts and behaviour influence each other, which is why cognitive-behaviour therapy (CBT) is more common than either cognitive or behaviour therapy alone. In recent years, some CBT practitioners, inspired by Eastern philosophies such as Buddhism, have begun to question the goal of changing a client's self-defeating thoughts. They argue that it is difficult if not impossible to get rid of unwanted thoughts and feelings, especially when people have been rehearsing them for years. They therefore propose a form of CBT based on "mindfulness" and "acceptance": Clients learn to explicitly identify and accept whatever negative thoughts and feelings arise, without trying to eradicate them or letting them derail healthy behaviour (Hayes, Follette, & Linehan, 2004). For example, instead of trying to persuade a client who is afraid of making public speeches that her fear is irrational, therapists who adopt this approach would encourage her to accept the anxious thoughts and feelings without judging them—or herself—harshly. Then she can focus on coping techniques and ways of giving speeches despite her anxiety.

Humanist and Existential Therapy

Humanist therapy, like its parent philosophy humanism, starts from the assumption that human nature is basically good and that people behave badly or develop problems when they are warped by self-imposed limits. Humanist therapists, therefore, want to know how clients subjectively see their own situations and how they construe the world around them. These therapists generally do not dig into the client's past but instead focus on helping the person develop the will and confidence to change and achieve his or her goals. That is why these therapists explore what is going on "here and now," not past issues of "why and how."

In **client-centred (nondirective) therapy**, developed by Carl Rogers, the therapist's role is to listen to the client's needs in an accepting, nonjudgmental way and offer what Rogers called *unconditional* positive regard (see Chapter 13). Whatever the client's specific complaint is, the goal is to build the client's self-esteem and self-acceptance and help the client find a more productive way of seeing his or her problems. Thus a Rogerian might assume that Murray's procrastination masks his low self-regard and that Murray is out of touch with his real feelings and wishes. Perhaps he is not passing his courses because he is trying to please his parents by majoring in pre-law, when secretly he would rather become an artist.

Rogers (1951, 1961) believed that effective therapists must be warm and genuine. For Rogerians, *empathy*, the therapist's ability to understand and accept what the client says, is the crucial ingredient of successful therapy. The therapist shows a basic level of empathy by listening carefully and being able to restate the client's remarks accurately: "You tell me

humanist therapy A form of psychotherapy based on the philosophy of humanism, which emphasizes the client's free will to change rather than past conflicts.

client-centred (nondirective) therapy A humanist approach, devised by Carl Rogers, which emphasizes the therapist's empathy with the client and the use of unconditional positive regard.

Watch the **Video**
In the Real World: Cognitive Behavioural Therapy in **MyPsychLab**

Watch the **Video**
Classic Footage of Carl Rogers on the Role of a Therapist in **MyPsychLab**

Jim Varney/Science Source

existential therapy A form of therapy designed to help clients explore the meaning of existence and face the great questions of life, such as death, freedom, alienation, and loneliness.

that you feel frustrated, Murray, because no matter how hard you try, you don't succeed." And the therapist shows advanced empathy by understanding the *meaning* of the client's remarks: "Working that hard without results must really make you unhappy and maybe make you feel a bit sorry for yourself." The client, according to humanist therapists, will eventually internalize the therapist's support and become more self-accepting.

Existential therapy helps clients explore the meaning of existence and face with courage the great questions of life, such as death, freedom, alienation from oneself and others, loneliness, and meaninglessness. Existential therapists, like humanist therapists, believe that our lives are not inevitably determined by our pasts or our circumstances; we have the power and free will to choose our own destinies. As Irvin Yalom (1989) explained, "The crucial first step in therapy is the patient's assumption of responsibility for his or her life predicament. As long as one believes that one's problems are caused by some force or agency outside oneself, there is no leverage in therapy."

Yalom argues that the goal of therapy is to help clients cope with the inescapable realities of life and death and the struggle for meaning. However grim our experiences may be, he believes, "they contain the seeds of wisdom and redemption." Perhaps the most remarkable example of a man able to find seeds of wisdom in a barren landscape was Victor Frankl (1905–1997), who developed a form of existential therapy after surviving a Nazi concentration camp. In that pit of horror, Frankl (1955) observed, some people maintained their sanity because they were able to find meaning in the experience, shattering though it was.

Some observers believe that, ultimately, all therapies are existential. In different ways, therapy helps people determine what is important to them, what values guide them, and what changes they will have the courage to make. An existential therapist might help Murray think about the significance of his procrastination, what his ultimate goals in life are, and how he might find the strength to carry out his ambitions.

Family and Couples Therapy

Murray's situation is getting worse. His father has begun to call him Tomorrow Man, which upsets his mother, and his younger brother, the math major, has been calculating how much tuition money Murray's incompletes are costing. His older sister, Isabel, the biochemist who's never had an incomplete in her life, now proposes that they all go to a family therapist. "Murray's not the only one in this family with complaints," she says.

A practitioner of *family therapy* would maintain that Murray's problem developed in the context of his family, that it is sustained by the dynamics of his family, and that any change he makes will affect all members of his family (McDaniel, Lusterman, & Philpot, 2001; Nichols & Schwartz, 2008). One of the most famous early family therapists, Salvador Minuchin (1984), compared the family to a kaleidoscope, a changing pattern of mosaics in which the pattern is larger than any one piece. In this view, efforts to isolate and treat one member of the family without the others are doomed. Only if all family members reveal their differing perceptions of each other can mistakes and misperceptions be identified. A teenager, for instance, may see his mother as crabby and nagging when actually she is tired and worried. A parent may see a child as rebellious when in fact the child is lonely and desperate for attention.

Family members are usually unaware of how they influence one another. By observing the entire family, the family therapist hopes to discover tensions and imbalances in power and communication. For example, in some families a child may have a chronic illness or a psychological problem, such as anorexia, that affects the workings of the whole family.

Some family therapists use photographs to help people identify themes and problems in their family histories. Does this picture convey a happy and cohesive family to you or a divided one? Shortly after it was taken, the couple divorced; the father took custody of the children . . . and the mother kept the dog (Entin, 1992).

Alan Entin, Ph.D.

One parent may become overinvolved with the sick child while the other parent retreats, and each may start blaming the other. The child, in turn, may cling to the illness or disorder as a way of expressing anger, keeping the parents together, getting the parents' attention, or asserting control (Cummings & Davies, 2011).

Some family therapists look for patterns of behaviour across generations. The therapist and client may create a family tree showing psychologically significant events across as many generations as possible (McGoldrick, Gerson, & Shellenberger, 1999). This method may reveal historical patterns, as you can see in Figure 16.1.

Even when it is not possible to treat the whole family, some therapists will treat individuals in a **family-systems perspective**, which recognizes that people's behaviour in a family is as interconnected as that of two dancers (Bowen, 1978; Cox & Paley, 2003). Clients learn that if they change in any way, even for the better, their families may protest noisily or may send subtle messages that read, "Change back!" Why? Because when one family member changes, each of the others must change too. As the saying goes, it takes two to tango, and if one dancer stops, so must the other. But most people do not like change. They are comfortable with old patterns and habits, even those that cause them trouble. They want to keep dancing the same old dance, even if their feet hurt.

When members of a couple argue frequently about issues that never seem to get resolved, they may be best helped by going together to *couples* therapy, which is designed to help couples manage the inevitable conflicts that occur in all relationships (Christensen & Jacobson, 2000). One of the most common problems that couples complain about is the "demand-withdraw" pattern, in which one partner badgers the other about some perceived failing, demanding that he or she change. The more the badgering partner demands, the more the target withdraws, sulks, or avoids the subject (Baucom et al., 2011; Christensen & Jacobson, 2000). Couples therapists generally insist on seeing both partners so that they will hear both sides of the story. They cut through the blaming and attacking ("She never listens to me!" "He never does anything!") and instead focus on helping the couple resolve their differences, get over hurt and blame, and make specific behavioural changes to reduce anger and conflict. Recently, however, many couples therapists have been moving away from the "fix all

family-systems perspective An approach to doing therapy with individuals or families by identifying how each family member forms part of a larger interacting system.

FIGURE 16.1 One Family's History of Mental Illness
Family trees of mental disorders can reveal patterns across generations. Alice Faye Redd was convicted of defrauding elderly investors of $10 million, money she then lost in lavish spending and extravagant investment schemes. Prosecution and defence psychiatrists agreed that she suffered from bipolar disorder. Alice Redd's daughter constructed this multigenerational family record of depression and suicide in an effort to have her mother committed for treatment, but the court sentenced Redd to 15 years in prison.

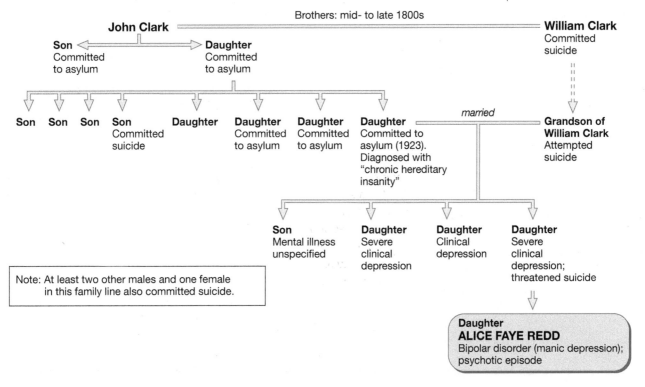

the differences" approach and are instead helping couples learn to accept and live with qualities in both partners that aren't going to change much (Baucom et al., 2011; Hayes, 2004). For example, a wife can stop trying to turn her calm, steady husband into a spontaneous adventurer ("After all, that's what I originally loved about him—he's as steady as a rock") and a husband can stop trying to make his shy wife more assertive ("I have always loved her remarkable serenity").

Family and couples therapists may use psychodynamic, behavioural, cognitive, or humanist approaches in their work; they share only a focus on the family or the couple. In Murray's case, a family therapist would observe how Murray's procrastination fits his family dynamics. Perhaps it allows Murray to get his father's attention and his mother's sympathy. Perhaps it keeps Murray from facing his greatest fear: that if he does finish his work, it will not measure up to his father's impossibly high standards. The therapist will not only help Murray change his work habits, but also help his family deal with a changed Murray.

The kinds of psychotherapy we have discussed are all quite different in theory, and so are their techniques (see Review 16.2). Yet in practice, many psychotherapists take an *integrative approach to psychotherapy*, drawing on methods and ideas from various schools and avoiding strong allegiances to any one theory. This flexibility enables them to treat clients with whatever methods are most appropriate and effective. For example, some therapists may use behavioural methods to quickly help a client suffering from a phobia, but they may also apply principles from "depth" psychology to help the client explore the role the phobia has come to play in his or her life. One internet-based survey of more than 2400 psychotherapists found that two-thirds said they practise cognitive-behaviour therapy—and that the single most influential therapist they

REVIEW 16.2   The Major Schools of Therapy Compared

	Primary Goal	Methods
Psychodynamic	Insight into unconscious motives and feelings that prolong symptoms	Probing unconscious motives, examining the process of transference, exploring childhood experiences
Cognitive-Behavioural		
Behavioural	Modification of self-defeating behaviours	Graduated exposure (flooding), systematic desensitization, behavioural records, skills training
Cognitive	Modification of irrational or unvalidated beliefs	Prompting the client to test beliefs against evidence; exposing the faulty reasoning in catastrophizing and mind-reading; sometimes helping the client accept unpleasant thoughts and feelings and live with them
Humanist and Existential		
Humanist	Insight; self-acceptance and self-fulfillment; new, optimistic perceptions of oneself and the world	Providing a nonjudgmental setting in which to discuss issues; use of empathy and unconditional positive regard by the therapist
Existential	Finding meaning in life and accepting inevitable losses	Varies with the therapist; philosophic discussions about the meaning of life, the client's goals, finding the courage to survive loss and suffering
Family and Couples		
Family	Modification of family patterns	May use any of the preceding methods to change family patterns that perpetuate problems and conflicts
Couples	Resolution of conflicts, breaking out of destructive habits	May use any of the preceding methods to help the couple communicate better, resolve conflicts, or accept what cannot be changed

followed was Carl Rogers and that they often incorporate ideas of mindfulness and acceptance (Cook, Biyanova, & Coyne, 2009).

In discussing theories of personality in Chapter 14, we described the importance of the life narrative—the story that each of us develops to explain who we are and how we got that way (McAdams & Pals, 2006). In a fundamental way, all successful therapies, regardless of their approach, share a key element: They are able to motivate the client into wanting to change, and they replace a client's pessimistic or unrealistic life narrative with one that is more hopeful or attainable (Howard, 1991; Schafer, 1992).

Recite & Review

Recite: Don't procrastinate, the way Murray would; recite what you recall about the major schools of psychotherapy and their primary methods: *psychoanalysis, transference, behaviour therapy* and its techniques, *graduated exposure, flooding, systematic desensitization, behavioural self-monitoring, skills training, cognitive therapy, rational emotive behaviour therapy (REBT), client-centred (nondirective) therapy, humanist and existential therapies,* and *family-systems perspective.*

Review: Read this section again, to make sure you are clear about the differences among the different approaches.

Now take this *Quick Quiz:*

Don't be a procrastinator like our friend Murray; take this quiz now.

Match each method or concept with the therapy associated with it.

1. transference	**a.** cognitive therapy
2. systematic desensitization	**b.** psychodynamic therapy
3. facing the fear of death	**c.** humanist therapy
4. reappraisal of thoughts	**d.** behaviour therapy
5. unconditional positive regard	**e.** family therapy
6. exposure to feared situation	**f.** existential therapy
7. avoidance of "catastrophizing"	
8. analysis of generational patterns	

Answers:

1.b 2.d 3.f 4.a 5.c 6.d 7.a 8.e

Learning Objectives

8 Describe the meaning of "scientist–practitioner gap" and why it has been widening.

9 Identify which form of psychotherapy is most likely to help if you are anxious or depressed.

10 Articulate why psychotherapy can sometimes be harmful.

Evaluating Psychotherapy

Poor Murray! He is getting a little baffled by all these therapies. He wants to make a choice soon; there's no sense in procrastinating about that, too! Is there any scientific evidence, he wonders, that might help him decide which therapy—or therapist—will be best for him?

Psychotherapy is, first and foremost, a relationship. Its success depends on the bond the therapist and client establish between them, called the **therapeutic alliance**.

therapeutic alliance The bond of confidence and mutual understanding established between therapist and client, which allows them to work together to solve the client's problems.

When both parties respect and understand each other and agree on the goals of treatment, the client is more likely to improve, regardless of the specific techniques the therapist uses (Klein et al., 2003).

CULTURE and *Psychotherapy*

Does a Therapist–Client "Match" Matter?

Many therapists and clients establish successful therapeutic alliances in spite of coming from different backgrounds. But sometimes cultural differences cause misunderstandings that result from ignorance or prejudice (Comas-Dìaz, 2006; Sue et al., 2007). A lifetime of experience with racism and a general "cultural distrust" may keep some indigenous peoples of Canada from revealing feelings that they believe a white therapist would not understand or accept (Whaley & Davis, 2007). Similarly, indigenous Canadian therapists frequently have to deal with clients who are uncomfortable with them. Misunderstandings and prejudice may be one reason why clients are more likely to stay in therapy when their therapists' ethnicity matches their own. If such clients stay in therapy and do not drop out early, however, most are as likely to do as well with an "unmatched" therapist as with a matched one. But a cultural "match" is also important because it often makes it more likely that clients and therapists share perceptions of what the client's problem is, agree on the best way of coping, and have the same expectations about what therapy can accomplish (Zone et al., 2005).

In establishing a bond with clients, therapists must distinguish normal cultural patterns from individual psychological problems. An Irish-American family therapist, Monica McGoldrick (2005), described some problems that are typical of Irish-American families. These problems arise from Irish history and religious beliefs, and they are deeply ingrained. She observed:

> In general, the therapist cannot expect the family to turn into a physically affectionate, emotionally intimate group, or to enjoy being in therapy very much,

> The notion of Original Sin—that you are guilty before you are born—leaves them with a heavy sense of burden. Someone not sensitized to these issues may see this as pathological. It is not. But it is also not likely to change and the therapist should help the family tolerate this inner guilt rather than try to get rid of it.

However, therapy is not always a one-on-one interaction. Group therapies are often employed, particularly with some cultural groups. In Canada, group therapy has been a particularly popular approach with indigenous Canadian clients, in part because the practice bears more similarity to traditional healing practices. However, the composition of a group structured in a manner that mirrors the social, racial, cultural, and class structure of Euro-Canadian society is problematic for treating relatively traditional indigenous Canadians (Waldram & Wong, 1995).

More and more psychotherapists are becoming "sensitized to the issues" caused by cultural differences (Arredondo et al., 2005; Sue et al., 2007). For example, many Latino and Asian clients are likely to react to a formal interview with a therapist with relative passivity and deference, leading some therapists to misdiagnose this cultural norm as a problem with shyness. In Latin American cultures, *susto*, or "loss of the soul," is a common response to extreme grief or fright; the person believes that his or her soul has departed along with that of the deceased relative. A psychotherapist unfamiliar with this

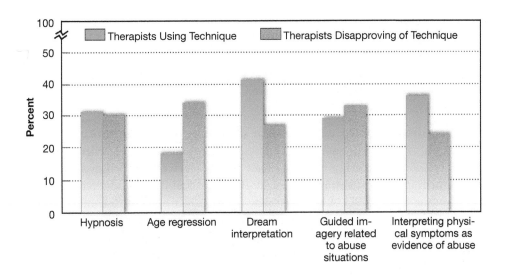

FIGURE 16.3 Psychologists' Attitudes toward the Use of Suggestive Techniques for Recovering Memories of Sexual Abuse
Between one-fourth and one-third of licensed clinical psychologists have used suggestive methods regularly "to help clients recall memories of sexual abuse," although these techniques can produce confabulation and false memories. The percentages are from two combined samples of American clinical psychologists with PhDs, randomly drawn from names listed in the National Register of Health Service Providers in Psychology (Poole et al., 1995). The numbers have not changed appreciably in recent years.

and one-third of them—have used one or more of these inappropriate techniques specifically to help clients "retrieve" memories of sexual abuse, as you can see in Figure 16.3 (Poole et al., 1995). Research in Canada and the United States finds that the percentages have not declined appreciably in recent years (Katz, 2001; Nunez, Poole, & Memon, 2002; Polusny & Follette, 1996).

Table 16.1 lists a number of therapies that have been shown, through randomized controlled trials or meta-analysis, to have a significant risk of harming their clients.

2 **Inappropriate or coercive influence, which can create new problems for the client.** In a healthy therapeutic alliance, therapist and client come to agree on an explanation for the client's problems. Of course, the therapist will influence this explanation, according to his or her training and philosophy. Some therapists, however, cross the line. They so zealously believe in the prevalence of certain problems or

TABLE 16.1 Potentially Harmful Therapies

Intervention	Potential Harm
Critical Incident Stress Debriefing (CISD)	Heightened risk of PTSD
Scared Straight interventions	Worsening of conduct problems
Facilitated communication	False allegations of sexual and child abuse
Attachment therapies	Death and serious injury to children
Recovered-memory techniques (e.g., dream analysis)	Induction of false memories of trauma, family breakups
"Multiple personality disorder"-oriented therapy	Induction of "multiple" personalities
Grief counselling for people with normal bereavement reactions	Increased depressive symptoms
Expressive-experiential therapies	Worsening and prolonging painful emotions
Boot-camp interventions for conduct disorder	Worsening of aggression and conduct problems
DARE (Drug Abuse and Resistance Education)	Increased use of alcohol and other drugs

Source: Lilienfeld (2007)

disorders that they actually induce the client to produce the symptoms they are looking for (Mazzoni, Loftus, & Kirsch, 2001; McHugh, 2008; McNally, 2003; Nathan, 2011; Watters & Ofshe, 1999). Therapist influence, and sometimes downright coercion, is a likely reason for the huge numbers of people who were diagnosed with multiple personality disorder in the 1980s and 1990s (see Chapter 15) and for an epidemic of recovered memories of sexual abuse during this period (see Chapter 10).

3 **Prejudice or cultural ignorance on the part of the therapist.** Some therapists may be prejudiced against some clients because of the client's gender, culture, religion, or sexual orientation. They may be unaware of their prejudices, yet express them in nonverbal ways that make the client feel ignored, disrespected, and devalued (Sue et al., 2007). A therapist may try to induce a client to conform to the therapist's standards and values, even if they are not appropriate for the client or in the client's best interests. For example, for many years gay men and lesbians who entered therapy were told that homosexuality was a mental illness that could be cured. Some of the so-called treatments were harsh, such as electric shock for "inappropriate" arousal. Although these methods were discredited many years ago (Davison, 1976), other "reparative" therapies that supposedly turn gay men and lesbians into heterosexuals still surface from time to time. They are often promoted in campaigns by conservative Christians who believe that homosexuality is a sin, with testimonials

Recite & Review

Recite: Say aloud whatever you remember about the *therapeutic alliance*, cultural issues in psychotherapy, *the scientist–practitioner gap*, *randomized controlled trials*, problems for which cognitive or behaviour therapy is the treatment of choice, and factors that increase the risk of harm in psychotherapy.

Review: Next, read this section as often as you need to, until you have a deep understanding of what makes psychotherapy successful or can make it harmful.

Now take this *Quick Quiz:*

Find out whether you are an educated consumer of quizzes.

1. Which of the following is the most important predictor of successful therapy? (a) how long it lasts, (b) the insight it provides the client, (c) the bond between therapist and client, (d) whether the therapist and client are matched according to gender

2. In general, which type of psychotherapy is most effective for anxiety and depression?

3. What kind of psychologist is trained to help people cope with chronic illness or disability or recover from injury?

4. What are four possible sources of harm in psychotherapy?

5. Ferdie is spending too much time playing softball and not enough time studying, so he signs up for "sportaholic therapy (ST)." The therapist tells him the cure for his "addiction" is to quit softball cold turkey and tap his temples three times whenever he feels the urge to play. After a few months, Ferdie announces that ST isn't helping and he's going to stop coming. The therapist gives him testimonials of other clients who swear by ST, explaining that Ferdie's doubts are actually a sign that the therapy is working. What are some problems with this argument? (*Bonus:* What kind of therapy might help Ferdie manage his time better?)

Answers:

1. c 2. cognitive-behaviour therapy 3. rehabilitation psychologist 4. the use of empirically unsupported techniques, prejudice or biased treatment, inappropriate or coercive influence, and unethical behaviour 5. The therapist has violated the principle of falsifiability (see Chapter 2). If Ferdie is helped by the treatment, that shows it works; if he is not helped, that still shows it works but Ferdie is "denying" its benefits. Also, Ferdie is not hearing testimonials from people who have dropped out of ST and were not helped by it. (*Bonus:* A good behavioural time-management program might help, so Ferdie can play softball *and* get other things done, too.)

from alleged converts. But there is no reliable empirical evidence from scientifically designed studies supporting these claims, and both the American Psychological Association and the American Psychiatric Association have gone on record opposing reparative therapies on ethical and scientific grounds. The former organization has issued "Guidelines for Psychological Practice with Lesbian, Gay, and Bisexual Clients" (American Psychological Association, 2012).

4 **Sexual intimacies or other unethical behaviour on the part of the therapist.** The Canadian Psychological Association's ethical guidelines prohibit therapists from having any sexual intimacies with their clients or violating other professional boundaries. Occasionally, some therapists behave like cult leaders, persuading their clients that their mental health depends on staying in therapy and severing their connections to their "toxic" families (Singer, 2003; Watters & Ofshe, 1999). Such "psychotherapy cults" are created by the therapist's use of techniques that foster the client's isolation, prevent the client from terminating therapy, and reduce the client's ability to think critically (see Chapter 8).

To avoid these risks and benefit from what good, effective psychotherapy has to offer, people looking for the right therapy must become educated consumers—able and willing to use the critical-thinking skills we have emphasized throughout this book.

The Value and Values of Psychotherapy

Modern psychotherapy has been of enormous value to many people. But psychotherapists themselves have raised some important questions about the values inherent in what they do (Cushman, 1995; Hillman & Ventura, 1992). How much personal change is possible, and do some therapists promise their clients too much? Does psychotherapy, by encouraging people to look inward to their feelings and woes, foster a preoccupation with the self over relationships and the importance of contributing to the larger world? Does it promise unrealistic notions of endless happiness and complete self-fulfillment? ◉

Many people in North America have an optimistic, can-do, let's-fix-this-fast attitude toward all problems, whether mental, physical, or social. In contrast, as discussed in Chapter 15, Eastern cultures have a less optimistic view of change, and they tend to be more tolerant of events they regard as being outside of human control. In the Japanese practice of Morita therapy, therefore, clients are taught to accept and live with their most troubling emotions, instead of trying to eradicate these psychological weeds from the lawn of life (Reynolds, 1987). Some western psychotherapists also now teach techniques of mindful meditation and greater self-acceptance instead of constant self-improvement, and they have been successful with problems ranging from depression to borderline personality disorder (Hayes, 2004; Kabat-Zinn, 1994; Linehan, 1993; Segal, Williams, & Teasdale, 2001). Most people get all the help they need from talking things over with good friends or with others who are in the same situation they are. But if you have a persistent problem that you do not know how to solve, one that causes you considerable unhappiness and that has lasted six months or more, it may be time to look for help. As the research in this chapter suggests, consumers who are thinking about psychotherapy should consider these important matters:

◉ **Watch** the **Video** *Recent Trends in Treatment: Sue Mineka* in **MyPsychLab**

> 💡 **THINKING CRITICALLY**
>
> Ask questions.
>
> The benefits of psychotherapy are well documented, but we can ask questions about its implicit message. Does psychotherapy foster unrealistic expectations of personal change? When should clients think about living with problems or situations they cannot change?

- *Choosing a therapist.* Make sure you are dealing with a reputable individual with appropriate credentials and training. Your school counselling centre is a good place to start. You might also seek out a university psychology clinic, where you can get therapy with a graduate student in training; these students are closely supervised and the fees will be lower. If you know the kind of therapy you want, check your local listings; many therapists are listed according to the kind of therapy they do.

- *Choosing a therapy.* As we have seen, not all therapies are equally effective for all problems. You should not spend four years in psychodynamic therapy for panic attacks, which can generally be helped in a few sessions of cognitive-behaviour therapy. Likewise, if you have a specific emotional problem, such as depression, anger, or anxiety, or if you are coping with chronic health problems, look for a cognitive or behaviour therapist. However, if you just want to discuss your life with a wise and empathic counsellor, the kind of therapy may not matter so much. If a physician or psychiatrist prescribes drugs, it is best to talk to a competent psychotherapist or counsellor about your problems and what intervention might help you before you begin medication.

- *Deciding when to leave.* For the common emotional problems of life, short-term treatment is usually sufficient. Some people are helped in only one or two sessions; about half improve within eight to 11 sessions, and three-fourths improve within six months to a year. After a year, further change is usually minimal (Kopta et al., 1994). However, people with more severe mental disorders do often require and benefit from continued therapeutic care (Shadish et al., 2000).

If you begin a time-limited treatment, such as a seven-session airplane-phobia program, you ought to stick with it to the end. In unlimited therapy, however, you have the right to determine when enough is enough, especially if the therapist has been unable to help you with your problem after a considerable length of time.

If you have made a real effort to work with a therapist and there has been no result after ample time and effort, the reason could have as much to do with the treatment or the therapist as with you.

In the hands of an empathic and knowledgeable practitioner, psychotherapy can help you make decisions and clarify your values and goals. It can teach you new skills and new ways of thinking. It can help you get along better with your family and break out of destructive family patterns. It can get you through bad times when no one seems to care or to understand what you are feeling. It can teach you how to manage depression, anxiety, and anger.

However, despite its many benefits, psychotherapy cannot transform you into someone you're not. It cannot turn an introvert into an extrovert. It cannot cure an emotional disorder overnight. It cannot provide a life without problems. And it is not intended to substitute for experience—for work that is satisfying, relationships that are sustaining, activities that are enjoyable. As Socrates knew, the unexamined life is not worth living. Yet, as we would add, the unlived life is not worth examining.

Taking Psychology with You

THINKING CRITICALLY IN EVERYDAY LIFE

How to Evaluate Self-Help Groups and Books

Not all psychological problems require the aid of a professional. Nowadays, thousands of programs and books are designed to help people help themselves. More than 2000

self-help books are published every year, and an estimated seven to 15 million adults belong to self-help groups. Do these books and groups help?

Self-help groups are available (online and in person) for alcoholics and relatives of alcoholics; people suffering from depression, anorexia, or schizophrenia; women with breast cancer; parents of murdered children; diabetics; rape victims; step-parents; relatives of people with Alzheimer's; and people with just about any other concern you can think of (Davison, Pennebaker, & Dickerson, 2000). Members say that the primary benefits are the awareness that they are not alone, encouragement when they are feeling down, and help in feeling better about themselves.

Self-help groups offer understanding, empathy, and solutions to shared problems. Such groups can be reassuring and supportive in ways that family, friends, and psychotherapists sometimes may not be. For example, people with disabilities face unique challenges that involve coping not only with physical problems but also with the condescension, hostility, and prejudice of many nondisabled people (Linton, 1998). Other disabled people, who share these challenges, can offer the right kind of empathy and useful advice.

Self-help groups do not provide psychotherapy, and they are not designed to help people with serious psychological difficulties. They are not regulated by law or by professional standards, and they vary widely in their philosophies and methods. Some are accepting and tolerant, offering support and spiritual guidance. Others are confrontational and coercive, and members who disagree with the premises of the group may be made to feel deviant, crazy, or "in denial." If you choose to become part of a support group, make sure it falls into the first category.

As for self-help books, there is one for every problem, from how to toilet train your children to how to find happiness. When self-help books propose a specific, well-supported program for the reader to follow, they can actually be as effective as treatment administered by a therapist—*if* the reader follows through with the program (Rosen, Glasgow, & Moore, 2003). Unfortunately, most books do not do this. After serving as chair of the APA's Task Force on Self-Help Therapies, Gerald Rosen (1981) concluded, "Psychologists have published untested materials, advanced exaggerated claims, and accepted the use of misleading titles that encourage unrealistic expectations regarding outcome." That was many years ago, and the situation is worse today. The information in this chapter suggests some guidelines for evaluating a self-help book:

- The book's advice should be based on sound scientific theory and should propose a program that has been empirically supported. It should not be based on the author's pseudoscientific theories, armchair observations, or political views. These criteria rules out, among other kinds of books, most of the love manuals in which the author's own tales of woe become the basis of an entire philosophy of love, marriage, and happiness. Personal accounts by people who have survived difficulties can be helpful and inspirational, of course, but an author's own experience is not grounds for generalizing to everyone.

- The book should not promise the impossible. This rules out books that promise perfect sex, total love, or high self-esteem in 30 days. It also rules out books or tapes that promote techniques whose effectiveness has been disconfirmed by research, such as dream analysis or "subliminal" messages.

- The advice should be organized in a systematic program. It should be given step by step, not as a vague pep talk to "take charge of your life" or "find love in your heart," and the reader should be told how to evaluate his or her progress.

Some books do meet these criteria. One is *Changing for Good* (Prochaska, Norcross, & DiClemente, 1994), which describes the ingredients of effective change that apply to people in and out of therapy. But as long as people yearn for a magic bullet to cure their problems, quick-fix solutions will find a ready audience.

Summary

Biological Treatments for Mental Disorders

- Over the centuries, people trying to understand and treat psychological disorders have alternated between biological and psychological explanations. Today, biological treatments are in the ascendance because of research findings on the genetic and biological causes of some disorders and because of economic and social factors.

- The medications most commonly prescribed for mental disorders include *antipsychotic drugs*, used in treating schizophrenia and other psychotic disorders; *antidepressant drugs*, used in treating depression, anxiety disorders, and obsessive-compulsive disorder; *tranquilizers*, often prescribed for emotional problems; and *lithium carbonate*, a salt used to treat bipolar disorder.

- Drawbacks of drug treatment include the *placebo effect*; high dropout and relapse rates among people who take medications without also learning how to cope with their problems; the difficulty of finding the correct dose (the *therapeutic window*) for each individual, compounded by the fact that a person's ethnicity, sex, and age can influence a drug's effectiveness; the long-term risks of medication, known and unknown; and the risk of possible drug interactions when several are being taken. Medication can be helpful and can even save lives, but in an age in which commercial interests are heavily invested in promoting drugs for psychological problems, the public is largely unaware of drugs' limitations and potential risks. Medication should not be prescribed uncritically and routinely, especially when nondrug therapies can work as well as drugs for many mood and behavioural problems.

- When drugs and psychotherapy have failed to help seriously disturbed people, some psychiatrists have intervened directly in the brain. *Psychosurgery*, which destroys selected areas of the brain thought to be responsible for a psychological problem, is rarely done today. *Electroconvulsive therapy (ECT)*, in which a brief current is sent through the brain, has been used successfully to treat suicidal depression. However, controversy exists about its effects on the brain and the appropriateness of its use. A newer method, transcranial magnetic stimulation (TMS), in which a magnetic coil is applied over the left prefrontal cortex, is being studied as a way of treating severe depression.

Major Schools of Psychotherapy

- *Psychodynamic ("depth") therapies* include Freudian *psychoanalysis* and its modern variations, such as approaches based on object-relations theory. These therapies explore unconscious dynamics by using *free association* and by focusing on the process of *transference* to break through the patient's defences.

- Practitioners of *behaviour therapy* draw on classical and operant principles of learning, called applied behavioural analysis. Behaviour therapists use such methods as *graduated exposure*, and sometimes immediate exposure, called *flooding*; systematic desensitization, based on *counterconditioning*; *behavioural self-monitoring*; and *skills training*.

- Practitioners of *cognitive therapy* aim to change the irrational thoughts involved in negative emotions and self-defeating actions. Albert Ellis's *rational emotive behaviour therapy (REBT)*

and Aaron Beck's form of cognitive therapy are two leading cognitive approaches.

- *Humanist therapy* holds that human nature is essentially good and attempts to help people feel better about themselves by focusing on here-and-now issues and on their capacity for change. Carl Rogers's *client-centred (nondirective) therapy* emphasizes the importance of the therapist's empathy and ability to provide *unconditional positive regard*. *Existential therapy* helps people cope with the dilemmas of existence, such as the meaning of life and the fear of death.

- *Family therapy* holds the view that individual problems develop in the context of the whole family network. It has a *family-systems perspective*, understanding that any one person's behaviour in the family affects everyone else, sometimes across generations. In *couples therapy*, the therapist usually sees both partners in a relationship to help them resolve ongoing quarrels and disputes or to help them accept and live with qualities of both partners that are unlikely to change.

- In practice, most therapists take an *integrative approach to psychotherapy*, drawing on many methods and ideas. Whatever their approach, successful therapies help people form more adaptive "life stories."

Evaluating Psychotherapy

- Successful therapy requires a *therapeutic alliance* between the therapist and the client, so that they understand each other and can work together. The clients who benefit most from psychotherapy are motivated to solve their problems; hostile, negative individuals are more resistant to treatment. For their part, good therapists are empathic and constructive. When therapist and client are of different ethnicities, the therapist must be able to distinguish normal cultural patterns from signs of mental illness, and both parties must be aware of potential prejudice and misunderstandings.

- A *scientist–practitioner gap* has developed because of the different assumptions held by researchers and many clinicians regarding the value of empirical research for doing psychotherapy and for assessing its effectiveness. The gap has led to a proliferation of scientifically unsupported psychotherapies.

- In assessing the effectiveness of psychotherapy, researchers need to control for the placebo effect and the *justification of effort* effect. They rely on *randomized controlled trials* to determine which therapies are empirically supported. For example, randomized controlled trials have shown that postcrisis debriefing programs are usually ineffective at best and can even slow recovery for some survivors.

• Some psychotherapies are better than others for specific problems. Behaviour therapy and cognitive-behaviour therapy are the most effective for depression, anxiety disorders, anger problems, certain health problems (such as pain, insomnia, and eating disorders), and childhood and adolescent behaviour problems. Family-systems therapies, especially when combined with behavioural techniques as in *multisystemic therapy*, are helpful for children and young adults with schizophrenia and for aggressive adolescents. Some problems and target populations, such as sex offenders, respond best to combined therapeutic approaches. Some methods, such as *motivational interviewing*, have been able to change a client's willingness to begin a program of change in only a session or two.

Taking Psychology with You

• Because of the growing number of therapy providers and therapies that lack empirical validation, people seeking mental health services need to choose a therapist very carefully. Further, some therapeutic approaches are better suited to specific problems, and one should be quite selective when choosing self-help groups or books.

Key Terms

antipsychotic drugs (neuroleptics) **586**
antidepressant drugs **587**
tranquilizers **588**
lithium carbonate **588**
placebo effect **589**
therapeutic window **590**

psychosurgery **591**
electroconvulsive therapy (ECT) **591**
psychoanalysis **594**
transference **594**
behaviour therapy **595**
graduated exposure **595**
flooding **595**

systematic desensitization **596**
behavioural self-monitoring **596**
skills training **596**
cognitive therapy **597**
rational emotive behaviour therapy (REBT) **597**
humanist therapy **599**

client-centred (nondirective) therapy **599**
existential therapy **600**
family-systems perspective **601**
therapeutic alliance **603**
randomized controlled trials **607**

Appendix

STATISTICAL METHODS

Nineteenth-century English statesman Benjamin Disraeli reportedly once named three forms of dishonesty: "lies, damned lies, and statistics." It is certainly true that people can lie with the help of statistics. It happens all the time: Advertisers, politicians, and others with some claim to make either use numbers inappropriately or ignore certain critical ones. People also use numbers to convey a false impression of certainty and objectivity when the true state of affairs is uncertainty or ignorance. But it is people, not statistics, that lie. When statistics are used correctly, they neither confuse nor mislead. On the contrary, they expose unwarranted conclusions, promote clarity and precision, and protect us from our own biases and blind spots.

If statistics are useful anywhere, it is in the study of human behaviour. If human beings were all alike, and psychologists could specify all the influences on behaviour, there would be no need for statistics. But any time we measure human behaviour, we are going to wind up with different observations or scores for different individuals. Statistics can help us spot trends amid the diversity.

This appendix will introduce you to some basic statistical calculations used in psychology. Reading the appendix will not make you a statistician, but it will acquaint you with some ways of organizing and assessing research data. If you suffer from a "number phobia," relax: You do not need to know much math to understand this material. However, you should have read Chapter 2, which discussed the rationale for using statistics and described various research methods. You may want to review the basic terms and concepts covered in that chapter. Be sure that you can define *hypothesis, sample, independent variable, dependent variable, random assignment, experimental group, control group, descriptive statistics, inferential statistics, test of statistical significance,* and *effect size.* (Correlation coefficients, which are described in some detail in Chapter 2, will not be covered here.)

To read the tables in this appendix, you will also need to know the following symbols:

N = total number of observations or scores in a set

X = observation or score

Σ = Greek capital letter sigma, read as "the sum of"

√ = square root of

(*Note:* Boldfaced terms in this appendix are defined in the glossary at the end of the book.)

Organizing Data

Before we can discuss statistics, we need some numbers. Imagine that you are a psychologist and that you are interested in that most pleasing of human qualities, a sense of humour. You suspect that a well-developed funny bone can protect people from the negative emotional effects of stress. You already know that in the months following a stressful event, people who score high on sense-of-humour tests tend to feel less tense and moody than more sobersided individuals do. You realize, though, that this correlational evidence does not prove cause and effect. Perhaps people with a healthy sense of humour have other traits, such as flexibility or creativity, that act as the true stress buffers. To find out whether humour itself really softens the impact of stress, you do an experiment.

First, you randomly assign subjects to two groups, an experimental group and a control group. To keep our calculations simple, let's assume there are only 15 people per group. Each person individually views a silent film that most North Americans find fairly stressful, one showing Australian aboriginal boys undergoing a puberty rite involving genital mutilation. Subjects in the experimental group are instructed to make up a humorous monologue while watching the film. Those in the control group are told to make up a straightforward narrative. After the film, each person answers a mood questionnaire that measures current feelings of tension, depression, aggressiveness, and anxiety. A person's overall score on the questionnaire can range from 1 (no mood disturbance) to 7 (strong mood disturbance). This procedure provides you with 15 "mood disturbance" scores for each group. Have people who tried to be humorous reported less disturbance than those who did not?

Constructing a Frequency Distribution

Your first step might be to organize and condense the "raw data" (the obtained scores) by constructing a **frequency distribution** for each group. A frequency distribution shows how often each possible score actually occurred. To construct one, you first order all the possible scores from highest to lowest. (Our mood disturbance scores will be ordered from 7 to 1.) Then you tally how often each score was actually obtained. Table A.1 gives some hypothetical raw data for the two groups, and Table A.2 shows the two frequency distributions based on these data. From these distributions, you can

TABLE A.1 Some Hypothetical Raw Data

These scores are for the hypothetical humour-and-stress study described in the text.

Experimental group	4, 5, 4, 4, 3, 6, 5, 2, 4, 3, 5, 4, 4, 3, 4
Control group	6, 4, 7, 6, 6, 4, 6, 7, 7, 5, 5, 5, 7, 6, 6

TABLE A.2 Two Frequency Distributions

The scores are from Table A.1.

Experimental Group			Control Group		
Mood Distur-bance Score	Tally	Frequency	Mood Distur-bance Score	Tally	Frequency
7		0	7	////	4
6	/	1	6	ʍ /	6
5	///	3	5	///	3
4	ʍ //	7	4	//	2
3	///	3	3		0
2	/	1	2		0
1		0	1		0
		N = 15			N = 15

that depicts numerical relationships. Graphs appear at several points in this book, and are routinely used by psychologists to convey their findings to others. From graphs, we can get a general impression of what the data are like, note the relative frequencies of different scores, and see which score was most frequent.

In a graph constructed from a frequency distribution, the possible score values are shown along a horizontal line (the *x-axis* of the graph) and frequencies along a vertical line (the *y-axis*), or vice versa. To construct a **histogram**, or **bar graph**, from our mood scores, we draw rectangles (bars) above each score, indicating the number of times it occurred by the rectangle's height (Figure A.1).

A slightly different kind of "picture" is provided by a **frequency polygon**, or **line graph**. In a frequency polygon, the frequency of each score is indicated by a dot placed directly over the score on the horizontal axis, at the appropriate height on the vertical axis. The dots for the various scores are then joined together by straight lines, as in Figure A.2 on the next page. When necessary an "extra" score, with a frequency of zero, can be added at each end of the horizontal axis, so that the polygon will rest on this axis instead of floating above it.

A word of caution about graphs: They may either exaggerate or mask differences in the data, depending on which units are used on the vertical axis. The two graphs in Figure A.3, although they look quite different, actually depict the same data. Always read the units on the axes of a graph; otherwise, the shape of a histogram or frequency polygon may be misleading.

see that the two groups differed. In the experimental group, the extreme scores of 7 and 1 did not occur at all, and the most common score was the middle one, 4. In the control group, a score of 7 occurred four times, the most common score was 6, and no one obtained a score lower than 4.

Because our mood scores have only seven possible values, our frequency distributions are quite manageable. Suppose, though, that your questionnaire had yielded scores that could range from 1 to 50. A frequency distribution with 50 entries would be cumbersome and might not reveal trends in the data clearly. A solution would be to construct a *grouped frequency distribution* by grouping adjacent scores into equal-sized *classes* or *intervals*. Each interval could cover, say, five scores (1–5, 6–10, 11–15, and so forth). Then you could tally the frequencies within each *interval*. This procedure would reduce the number of entries in each distribution from 50 to only 10, making the overall results much easier to grasp. However, information would be lost. For example, there would be no way of knowing how many people had a score of 43 versus 44.

Graphing the Data

As everyone knows, a picture is worth a thousand words. The most common statistical picture is a **graph**, a drawing

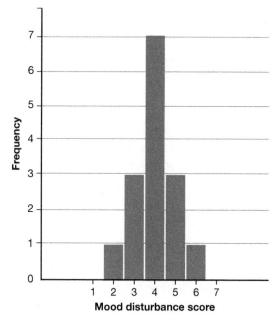

FIGURE A.1 A Histogram
This graph depicts the distribution of mood disturbance scores shown on the left side of Table A.2.

scattered about the mean; a small one means that most scores are clustered near the mean.

4. Raw scores can be transformed into other kinds of scores. *Percentile scores* indicate the percentage of people who scored at or below a given raw score. *Z-scores* (*standard scores*) indicate how far a given raw score is above or below the mean of the distribution.

5. Many variables have a distribution approximating a *normal distribution*, depicted as a *normal curve*. The normal curve has a convenient property: When standard deviations are used as the units on the horizontal axis, the percentage of scores falling between any two points on the horizontal axis is always the same. Not all types of observations are distributed normally, however. Some distributions are *skewed* to the left or right.

6. Inferential statistics can be used to test the *null hypothesis* and to tell a researcher whether a result differed significantly from what might have been expected purely by chance. Basically, hypothesis testing involves estimating where the obtained result would have fallen in a theoretical *sampling distribution* based on studies of the entire population in question. If the result would have been far out in one of the tails of the distribution, it is considered statistically significant. A statistically significant result may or may not be psychologically interesting or important, so many researchers are using methods to determine how strongly the independent variable is influencing the dependent variable.

Key Terms

frequency distribution *A-1*
graph *A-2*
histogram/bar graph *A-2*
frequency polygon/line graph *A-2*
descriptive statistics *A-3*
measure of central tendency *A-3*
mean *A-3*
median *A-3*
mode *A-4*
measure of variability *A-4*
range *A-4*
standard deviation *A-4*
deviation score *A-4*
percentile score (centile rank) *A-5*
z-score (standard score) *A-5*
normal distribution *A-6*
normal curve *A-6*
right- and left-skewed distributions *A-6*
inferential statistics *A-7*
null hypothesis *A-7*
alternative hypothesis *A-7*
sampling distribution *A-7*
statistically significant *A-8*

Glossary

absolute threshold   The smallest quantity of physical energy that can be reliably detected by an observer.

acculturation   The process by which members of minority groups come to identify with and feel part of the mainstream culture.

action potential   A brief change in electrical voltage that occurs between the inside and the outside of an axon when a neuron is stimulated; it produces an electrical impulse.

activation–synthesis theory   The theory that dreaming results from the cortical synthesis and interpretation of neural signals triggered by activity in the lower part of the brain.

adrenal hormones   Hormones that are produced by the adrenal glands and that are involved in emotion and stress.

adrenarche [a-DREN-ar-kee]   A time in middle childhood when the adrenal glands begin producing the adrenal hormone DHEA and other hormones that affect cognitive and social development.

affect heuristic   The tendency to consult one's emotions instead of estimating probabilities objectively.

agoraphobia   A set of phobias, often set off by a panic attack, involving the basic fear of being away from a safe place or person.

algorithm   A problem-solving strategy guaranteed to produce a solution even if the user does not know how it works.

Gordon Allport   One of the most influential psychologists in the empirical study of personality.

alternative hypothesis   The rival hypothesis to the null hypothesis, and the hypothesis that is accepted if the null is rejected. Expresses the possibility that, on average, the experimental group will have different scores than the control group.

amnesia   The partial or complete loss of memory for important personal information.

amygdala [uh-MIG-dul-uh]   A brain structure involved in the arousal and regulation of emotion and the initial emotional response to sensory information.

anabolic steroids   Synthetic derivatives of testosterone that are taken in pill form or by injection to increase muscle mass and strength.

anorexia (anorexia nervosa)   An eating disorder characterized by fear of being fat, a distorted body image, radically reduced consumption of food, and emaciation.

antidepressant drugs   Drugs used primarily in the treatment of mood disorders, especially depression and anxiety.

antipsychotic drugs (neuroleptics)   Drugs used primarily in the treatment of schizophrenia and other psychotic disorders; they are often used off label and inappropriately for other disorders such as dementia and impulsive aggressiveness.

antisocial personality disorder (APD)   A personality disorder characterized by a lifelong pattern of irresponsible, antisocial behaviour such as lawbreaking, violence, and other impulsive, reckless acts.

applied psychology   The study of psychological issues that have direct practical significance; also, the application of psychological findings.

appraisals   A person's perceptions, beliefs, attributions, and goals, that determine which emotion he or she will feel in a given circumstance; they are a central component of emotion and the emotional experience.

approach–approach conflicts   Conflicts that occur when you are equally attracted to two or more possible activities or goals.

approach–avoidance conflicts   Conflicts that occur when a single activity or goal has both a positive and a negative aspect.

approach goals   Goals framed in terms of desired outcomes or experiences, such as learning to scuba dive.

arithmetic mean   An average that is calculated by adding up a set of quantities and dividing the sum by the total number of quantities in the set.

attachment theory of love   People's attachment styles as adults derive in large part from how their parents cared for them.

attribution theory   The theory that people are motivated to explain their own and other people's behaviour by attributing causes of that behaviour to a situation or a disposition.

autonomic nervous system   The subdivision of the peripheral nervous system that regulates the internal organs and glands.

availability heuristic   The tendency to judge the probability of a type of event by how easy it is to think of examples or instances.

avoidance goals   Goals framed in terms of avoiding unpleasant experiences, such as trying not to look foolish in public.

axon   A neuron's extending fibre that conducts impulses away from the cell body and transmits them to other neurons.

basic concepts   Concepts that have a moderate number of instances and that are easier to acquire than those having few or many instances.

basic psychology   The study of psychological issues in order to seek knowledge for its own sake rather than for its practical application.

Bayesian statistics   Statistics that involve a formula for calculating the likelihood of a hypothesis being true and meaningful, taking into account relevant prior knowledge.

behaviour modification   The application of operant conditioning techniques to teach new responses or to reduce or eliminate maladaptive or problematic behaviour; also called *applied behaviour analysis*.

behaviour therapy   A form of therapy that applies principles of classical and operant conditioning to help people change self-defeating or problematic behaviours.

behavioural genetics   An interdisciplinary field of study concerned with the genetic bases of individual differences in behaviour and personality.

behavioural self-monitoring   In behaviour therapy, a method of keeping careful data on the frequency and consequences of the behaviour to be changed.

behaviourism   An approach to psychology that emphasizes the study of observable behaviour and the role of the environment and prior experience as determinants of behaviour.

binocular cues   Visual cues to depth or distance requiring two eyes.

biological perspective   A psychological approach that emphasizes bodily events and changes associated with actions, feelings, and thoughts.

biological rhythm A periodic, more or less regular fluctuation in a biological system; it may or may not have psychological implications.

bipolar disorder A mood disorder in which episodes of both depression and mania (excessive euphoria) occur.

borderline personality disorder A disorder characterized by intense but unstable relationships, a fear of abandonment by others, an unrealistic self-image, and emotional volatility.

brain stem The part of the brain at the top of the spinal cord, consisting of the medulla and the pons.

brightness Lightness or luminance; the dimension of visual experience related to the amount of light emitted from or reflected by an object.

bulimia An eating disorder characterized by episodes of excessive eating (bingeing) followed by forced vomiting or use of laxatives (purging).

case study A detailed description of a particular individual being studied or treated.

Raymond Cattell Devised the factor analysis statistical method for analyzing personality traits.

cell body The part of the neuron that keeps it alive and determines whether or not it will fire.

central nervous system (CNS) The portion of the nervous system consisting of the brain and spinal cord.

cerebellum A brain structure that regulates movement and balance, is involved in remembering simple skills and acquired reflexes, and plays a role in cognitive and emotional learning.

cerebral cortex A collection of several thin layers of cells covering the cerebrum; it is largely responsible for higher mental functions. *Cortex* is Latin for "bark" or "rind."

cerebral hemispheres The two halves of the cerebrum.

cerebrum [suh-REE-brum] The largest brain structure, consisting of the upper part of the brain; divided into two hemispheres, it is in charge of most sensory, motor, and cognitive processes. From the Latin for "brain."

childhood (infantile) amnesia The inability to remember events and experiences that occurred during the first two or three years of life.

chromosomes Within every cell, rod-shaped structures that carry the genes.

chronotype A person's pattern of sleep and wakefulness throughout a typical day.

chunk A meaningful unit of information; it may be composed of smaller units.

circadian [sur-CAY-dee-un] rhythm A biological rhythm with a period (from peak to peak or trough to trough) of about 24 hours; from the Latin *circa*, "about," and *dies*, "a day."

classical conditioning The process by which a previously neutral stimulus becomes associated with a stimulus that already elicits a response and, in turn, acquires the capacity to elicit a similar or related response. Also called Pavlovian or respondent conditioning.

client-centred (nondirective) therapy A humanist approach, devised by Carl Rogers, which emphasizes the therapist's empathy with the client and the use of unconditional positive regard.

cochlea [KOCK-lee-uh] A snail-shaped, fluid-filled organ in the inner ear, containing the structure where the receptors for hearing are located.

coefficient of correlation A measure of correlation that ranges in value from −1.00 to +1.00.

cognitive dissonance A state of tension that occurs when a person simultaneously holds two cognitions that are psychologically inconsistent or when a person's belief is incongruent with his or her behaviour.

cognitive ethology The study of cognitive processes in nonhuman animals.

cognitive perspective A psychological approach that emphasizes mental processes in perception, memory, language, problem solving, and other areas of behaviour.

cognitive schema An integrated mental network of knowledge, beliefs, and expectations concerning a particular topic or aspect of the world.

cognitive therapy A form of therapy designed to identify and change irrational, unproductive ways of thinking and, hence, to reduce negative emotions.

concept A mental category that groups objects, relations, activities, abstractions, or qualities having common properties.

conditioned response (CR) The classical-conditioning term for a response that is elicited by a conditioned stimulus; it occurs after the conditioned stimulus is associated with an unconditioned stimulus.

conditioned stimulus (CS) The classical-conditioning term for an initially neutral stimulus that comes to elicit a conditioned response after being associated with an unconditioned stimulus.

conditioning A basic kind of learning that involves associations among environmental stimuli and an organism's responses.

cones Visual receptors involved in colour vision.

confabulation Confusion of an event that happened to someone else with one that happened to you, or a belief that you remember something when it never actually happened.

confidence interval A statistical measure that provides, with a specified probability, a range of values within which a population mean is likely to lie.

confirmation bias The tendency to look for or pay attention only to information that confirms one's own belief.

conservation The understanding that the physical properties of objects—such as the number of items in a cluster or the amount of liquid in a glass—can remain the same even when their form or appearance changes.

consolidation A process by which the synaptic changes associated with recently stored memories become durable and stable, causing memory to become more reliable.

contact comfort In primates, the innate pleasure derived from close physical contact; it is the basis of the infant's first attachment.

continuous reinforcement A reinforcement schedule in which a particular response is always reinforced.

control condition In an experiment, a comparison condition in which participants are not exposed to the same treatment as in the experimental condition.

convergence The turning inward of the eyes, which occurs when they focus on a nearby object.

corpus callosum [CORE-puhs cah-LOW-suhm] The bundle of nerve fibres connecting the two cerebral hemispheres.

correlation A measure of how strongly two variables are related to one another.

correlational study A descriptive study that looks for a consistent relationship between two phenomena.

cortisol A hormone secreted by the adrenal cortex that elevates blood sugar and protects the body's tissues in case of injury; if chronically elevated due to stress, it can lead to hypertension, immune disorders, other illnesses, and possibly depression.

counterconditioning In classical conditioning, the process of pairing a conditioned stimulus with a stimulus that elicits a response that is incompatible with an unwanted conditioned response.

critical thinking The ability and willingness to assess claims and make objective judgments on the basis of well-supported reasons and evidence rather than emotion or anecdote.

cross-sectional study A study in which people (or animals) of different ages are compared at a given time.

crystallized intelligence Cognitive skills and specific knowledge acquired over a lifetime; it is heavily dependent on education and tends to remain stable over time.

cue-dependent forgetting The inability to retrieve information stored in memory because of insufficient cues for recall.

culture A program of shared rules that govern the behaviour of people in a community or society, and a set of values, beliefs, and customs shared by most members of that community.

dark adaptation A process by which visual receptors become maximally sensitive to dim light.

Charles Darwin (1809–1882) British naturalist who pioneered the theory of evolution of species.

decay theory The theory that information in memory eventually disappears if it is not accessed; this theory applies better to short-term than to long-term memory.

declarative memories Memories of facts, rules, concepts, and events ("knowing that"); they include semantic and episodic memories.

deep processing In the encoding of information, the processing of meaning rather than simply the physical or sensory features of a stimulus.

defence mechanisms Methods used by the ego to prevent unconscious anxiety or threatening thoughts from entering consciousness.

deindividuation In groups or crowds, the loss of awareness of one's own individuality.

dendrites A neuron's branches that receive information from other neurons and transmit it toward the cell body.

dependent variable A variable that an experimenter predicts will be affected by manipulations of the independent variable.

depressants Drugs that slow activity in the central nervous system.

descriptive methods Methods that yield descriptions of behaviour but not necessarily causal explanations.

descriptive statistics Statistical procedures that organize and summarize research data.

deviation score Scores found by subtracting the mean from each individual score.

***Diagnostic and Statistical Manual of Mental Disorders* (DSM)** The standard reference manual used to diagnose mental disorders, published by the American Psychiatric Association.

dialectical reasoning A process in which opposing facts or ideas are weighed and compared, with a view to determining the best solution or resolving differences.

difference threshold The smallest difference in stimulation that can be reliably detected by an observer when two stimuli are compared; also called *just noticeable difference (jnd)*.

diffusion of responsibility In groups, the tendency of members to avoid taking action because they assume that others will.

discriminative stimulus A stimulus that signals when a particular response is likely to be followed by a certain type of consequence.

display rules Social and cultural rules that regulate when, how, and where a person may express (or suppress) emotions.

dissociation A split in consciousness in which one part of the mind operates independently of other parts.

dissociative identity disorder A controversial disorder marked by the apparent appearance within one person of two or more distinct personalities, each with its own name and traits; formerly known as *multiple personality disorder (MPD)*.

DNA (deoxyribonucleic acid) The chromosomal molecule that transfers genetic characteristics by way of coded instructions for the structure of proteins.

doctrine of specific nerve energies The principle that different sensory modalities exist because signals received by the sense organs stimulate different nerve pathways leading to different areas of the brain.

double-blind study An experiment in which neither the people being studied nor the individuals running the study know who is in the control group and who is in the experimental group until after the results are tallied.

effect size An objective, standardized way of describing the strength of the independent variable's influence on the dependent variable.

ego In psychoanalysis, the part of personality that represents reason, good sense, and rational self-control.

elaborative rehearsal Association of new information with already stored knowledge and analysis of the new information to make it memorable.

electroconvulsive therapy (ECT) A procedure used in cases of prolonged and severe major depression, in which a brief brain seizure is induced.

electroencephalogram (EEG) A recording of neural activity detected by electrodes.

embryonic stage Stage of prenatal development that begins once implantation is completed, about two weeks after fertilization, and lasts until the eighth week after conception.

emotion A state of arousal involving facial and bodily changes, brain activation, cognitive appraisals, subjective feelings, and tendencies toward action.

emotional intelligence The ability to identify your own and other people's emotions accurately, express your emotions clearly, and regulate emotions in yourself and others.

emotion regulation Modifying and controlling what we feel.

emotion work Expression of an emotion, often because of a role requirement, that a person does not really feel.

empirical Relying on or derived from observation, experimentation, or measurement.

endocrine glands Internal organs that produce hormones and release them into the bloodstream.

endogenous Generated from within rather than by external cues.

endorphins [en-DOR-fins] Chemical substances in the nervous system that are similar in structure and action to opiates; they are involved in pain reduction, pleasure, and memory and are known technically as *endogenous opioid peptides*.

entrainment The synchronization of biological rhythms with external cues, such as fluctuations in daylight.

entrapment A gradual process in which individuals escalate their commitment to a course of action to justify their investment of time, money, or effort.

episodic memories Memories of personally experienced events and the contexts in which they occurred.

equilibrium The sense of balance.

Erik Erikson (1902–1994) One of the first modern theorists to propose a lifespan approach to psychological development. Erikson proposed that all individuals go through eight stages in their lives, each characterized by a particular "crisis" that ideally should be resolved before the individual moves on.

ethnic identity A person's identification with a racial or ethnic group.

ethnocentrism The belief that one's own ethnic group, nation, or religion is superior to all others.

event-related potentials (ERP) A technique that isolates the neural activity associated with a specific stimulus ("event").

evolution A change in gene frequencies within a population over many generations; a mechanism by which genetically influenced characteristics of a population may change.

evolutionary psychology A field of psychology emphasizing evolutionary mechanisms that may help explain human commonalities in cognition, development, emotion, social practices, and other areas of behaviour.

existential therapy A form of therapy designed to help clients explore the meaning of existence and face the great questions of life, such as death, freedom, alienation, and loneliness.

experiment A controlled test of a hypothesis in which the researcher manipulates one variable to discover its effect on another.

experimenter effects Unintended changes in study participants' behaviour due to cues that the experimenter inadvertently conveys.

explicit memory Conscious, intentional recollection of an event or of an item of information.

extinction The weakening and eventual disappearance of a learned response. In classical conditioning, it occurs when the conditioned stimulus is no longer paired with the unconditioned stimulus; in operant conditioning, it occurs when a response is no longer followed by a reinforcer.

extrinsic motivation The pursuit of an activity for external rewards, such as money or fame.

extrinsic reinforcers Reinforcers that are not inherently related to the activity being reinforced.

facial feedback The process by which the facial muscles send messages to the brain about the basic emotion being expressed.

factor analysis A statistical method for analyzing the intercorrelations among various measures or test scores; clusters of measures or scores that are highly correlated are assumed to measure the same underlying trait, ability, or aptitude (factor).

familiarity effect The tendency of people to feel more positively toward a person, item, product, or other stimulus the more familiar they are with it.

family-systems perspective An approach to doing therapy with individuals or families by identifying how each family member forms part of a larger interacting system.

feature detector cells Cells in the visual cortex that are sensitive to specific features of the environment.

feminist psychology A psychological approach that analyzes the influence of social inequities on gender relations and on the behaviour of the two sexes.

fetal stage Stage of prenatal development from eight weeks after conception until birth, during which the fetus further develops the organs and systems that existed in rudimentary form in the embryonic stage.

field research Descriptive or experimental research conducted in a natural setting outside the laboratory.

flooding In behaviour therapy, a form of exposure treatment in which the client is taken directly into the feared situation and remains there until his or her panic subsides.

fluid intelligence The capacity to reason and use information to solve problems; it is relatively independent of education.

fMRI (functional magnetic resonance imaging) A type of magnetic resonance imaging used to study brain activity associated with specific thoughts and behaviours.

framing effect The tendency for people's choices to be affected by how a choice is presented, or framed, such as whether it is worded in terms of potential losses or gains.

fraternal (dizygotic) twins Twins that develop from two separate eggs fertilized by different sperm; they are no more alike genetically than are any other pair of siblings.

frequency distribution Shows how often a possible score or observation actually occurred.

frequency polygon/line graph A graph composed of dots placed directly over the score on the horizontal axis at the appropriate height on the vertical axis. When these dots are joined by a line, the frequency polygon becomes a line graph.

Sigmund Freud (1856–1939) Austrian neurologist who pioneered the field of psychoanalysis.

frontal lobes Lobes at the front of the brain's cerebral cortex; they contain areas involved in short-term memory, higher-order thinking, initiative, social judgment, and (in the left lobe, typically) speech production.

functionalism An early psychological approach that emphasized the function or purpose of behaviour and consciousness.

fundamental attribution error The tendency, in explaining other people's behaviour, to overestimate personality factors and underestimate the influence of the situation.

***g* factor** A general intellectual ability assumed by many theorists to underlie specific mental abilities and talents.

ganglion cells Neurons in the retina of the eye that gather information from receptor cells (by way of intermediate bipolar cells); their axons make up the optic nerve.

gate-control theory of pain The theory that the experience of pain depends in part on whether pain impulses get past a neurological "gate" in the spinal cord and thus reach the brain.

gender identity The fundamental sense of being male or female; it is independent of whether the person conforms to the social and cultural rules of gender.

gender schema A cognitive schema (mental network) of knowledge, beliefs, metaphors, and expectations about what it means to be male or female.

gender typing The process by which children learn the abilities, interests, and behaviours associated with being masculine or feminine in their culture.

general adaptation syndrome According to Hans Selye, a series of physiological responses to stressors that occur in three phases: alarm, resistance, and exhaustion.

generalized anxiety disorder A continuous state of anxiety marked by feelings of worry and dread, apprehension, difficulties in concentration, and signs of motor tension.

genes The functional units of heredity; they are composed of DNA and specify the structure of proteins.

genetic marker A segment of DNA that varies among individuals, has a known location on a chromosome, and can function as a genetic landmark for a gene involved in a physical or mental condition.

genome The full set of genes in each cell of an organism (with the exception of sperm and egg cells).

Gestalt principles Principles that describe the brain's organization of sensory information into meaningful units and patterns.

glia [GLY-uh or GLEE-uh] Cells that support, nurture, and insulate neurons, remove debris when neurons die, enhance the formation and maintenance of neural connections, and modify neuronal functioning.

graduated exposure In behaviour therapy, a method in which a person suffering from a phobia or panic attacks is gradually taken into the feared situation or gradually exposed to a traumatic memory until the anxiety subsides.

graph A statistical drawing that depicts the numerical relationships between among variables.

groupthink The tendency for all members of a group to think alike for the sake of harmony and to suppress disagreement.

heuristic A rule of thumb that suggests a course of action or guides problem solving but does not guarantee an optimal solution.

higher-order conditioning In classical conditioning, a procedure in which a neutral stimulus becomes a conditioned stimulus through association with an already established conditioned stimulus.

hindsight bias The tendency to overestimate one's ability to have predicted an event once the outcome is known; the "I knew it all along" phenomenon.

hippocampus A brain structure involved in the storage of new information in memory.

histogram/bar graph A graph of bars drawn above each score; the height of the bars indicate the frequency of a score occurring.

hormones Chemical substances, secreted by organs called *glands*, that affect the functioning of other organs.

HPA (hypothalamus–pituitary–adrenal cortex) axis A system activated to energize the body to respond to stressors. The hypothalamus sends chemical messengers to the pituitary, which in turn prompts the adrenal cortex to produce cortisol and other hormones.

hue The dimension of visual experience specified by colour names and related to the wavelength of light.

humanist psychology A psychological approach that emphasizes personal growth and the achievement of human potential rather than the scientific understanding and assessment of behaviour.

humanist therapy A form of psychotherapy based on the philosophy of humanism, which emphasizes the client's free will to change rather than past conflicts.

hypnosis A procedure in which the practitioner suggests changes in the sensations, perceptions, thoughts, feelings, or behaviour of the participant.

hypothalamus A brain structure involved in emotions and drives vital to survival; it regulates the autonomic nervous system.

hypothesis A statement that attempts to predict or to account for a set of phenomena; scientific hypotheses specify relationships among events or variables and are empirically tested.

id In psychoanalysis, the part of personality containing inherited psychic energy, particularly sexual and aggressive instincts.

identical (monozygotic) twins Twins that develop when a fertilized egg divides into two parts that develop into separate embryos.

implicit learning Learning that occurs when you acquire knowledge about something without being aware of how you did so and without being able to state exactly what it is you have learned.

implicit memory Unconscious retention in memory, as evidenced by the effect of a previous experience or previously encountered information on current thoughts or actions.

inattentional blindness Failure to consciously perceive something you are looking at because you are not attending to it.

independent variable A variable that an experimenter manipulates.

individualist cultures Cultures in which the self is regarded as autonomous, and individual goals and wishes are prized above duty and relations with others.

induction A method of child rearing in which the parent appeals to the child's own abilities, sense of responsibility, and feelings for others in correcting the child's misbehaviour.

inferential statistics Statistical procedures that allow researchers to draw inferences about how statistically meaningful a study's results are.

informed consent The doctrine that anyone who participates in human research must do so voluntarily and must know enough about the study to make an intelligent decision about whether to participate.

instinctive drift During operant learning, the tendency for an organism to revert to instinctive behaviour.

intelligence An inferred characteristic of an individual, usually defined as the ability to profit from experience, acquire knowledge, think abstractly, act purposefully, or adapt to changes in the environment.

intelligence quotient (IQ) A measure of intelligence originally computed by dividing a person's mental age by his or her chronological age and multiplying by 100; it is now derived from norms provided for standardized intelligence tests.

intermittent (partial) schedule of reinforcement A reinforcement schedule in which a particular response is sometimes but not always reinforced.

internal desynchronization A state in which biological rhythms are not in phase (synchronized) with one another.

intersex conditions (intersexuality) Conditions in which chromosomal or hormonal anomalies cause a child to be born with ambiguous genitals, or genitals that conflict with the infant's chromosomes.

intrinsic motivation The pursuit of an activity for its own sake.

intrinsic reinforcers Reinforcers that are inherently related to the activity being reinforced.

William James (1842–1910) American philosopher, physician, and psychologist and a leader of functionalism.

Carl Jung (1875–1961) Originally one of Freud's collaborators; Jung proposed the idea of the collective unconscious and pioneered the school of Jungian analysis.

justification of effort The tendency of individuals to increase their liking for something that they have worked hard or suffered to attain; a common form of dissonance reduction.

just-world hypothesis The notion that many people need to believe that the world is fair and that justice is served, that bad people are punished and good people rewarded.

kinesthesis [KIN-es-THEE-sís] The sense of body position and movement of body parts; also called *kinesthesia*.

language A system that combines meaningless elements such as sounds or gestures to form structured utterances that convey meaning.

latent learning A form of learning that is not immediately expressed in an overt response; it occurs without obvious reinforcement.

lateralization Specialization of the two cerebral hemispheres for particular operations.

learning A relatively permanent change in behaviour (or behavioural potential) due to experience.

learning perspective A psychological approach that emphasizes how the environment and experience affect a person's or animal's actions; it includes behaviourism and social-cognitive learning theories.

lesion method   The removal or disabling of a brain structure to gain better understanding of its function; this method is used only in animals.

libido [li-BEE-do]   In psychoanalysis, the psychic energy that fuels the life or sexual instincts of the id.

lithium carbonate   A drug frequently given to people suffering from bipolar disorder.

localization of function   Specialization of particular brain areas for particular functions.

locus of control   A general expectation about whether the results of your actions are under your own control (internal locus) or beyond your control (external locus).

longitudinal study   A study in which people (or animals) are followed and periodically reassessed over a period of time.

long-term memory (LTM)   In the three-box model of memory, the memory system involved in the long-term storage of information.

long-term potentiation   A long-lasting increase in the strength of synaptic responsiveness, thought to be a biological mechanism of long-term memory.

loudness   The dimension of auditory experience related to the intensity of a pressure wave.

lucid dream   A dream in which the dreamer is aware of dreaming.

maintenance rehearsal   Rote repetition of material in order to maintain its availability in memory.

major depression   A mood disorder involving disturbances in emotion (excessive sadness), behaviour (loss of interest in one's usual activities), cognition (thoughts of hopelessness), and body function (fatigue and loss of appetite).

Abraham Maslow (1908–1970)   One of three chief leaders of the humanist psychology movement; Maslow believed in the importance of peak experiences and self-actualization.

Maslow's hierarchy of needs   A pyramid expressing the relative importance of different motives for people: at the bottom level of the pyramid are basic survival needs, for food, sleep, and water; at the next level are security needs, for shelter and safety; at the third level are social needs, for belonging and affection; at the fourth level are esteem needs, for self-respect and the respect of others; and at the top are needs for self-actualization and self-transcendence.

Rollo May (1909–1994)   One of three chief leaders of the humanist psychology movement; an existentialist who believed in free will but also emphasized some of the inherently difficult and tragic aspects of the human condition, including loneliness, anxiety, and alienation.

mean   *See* arithmetic mean.

measure of central tendency   Measures of central tendency characterize an entire set of data in terms of a single representative number that approximates the midpoint.

measure of variability   Identifies whether scores are clustered closely around the mean or widely scattered.

median   The midpoint in a set of scores or observations ordered from highest to lowest.

medulla [muh-DUL-uh]   A structure in the brain stem responsible for certain automatic functions, such as breathing and heart rate.

melatonin   A hormone, secreted by the pineal gland, that is involved in the regulation of daily biological (circadian) rhythms.

menarche [men-ARR-kee]   The onset of menstruation during puberty.

menopause   The cessation of menstruation and of the production of ova; it is usually a gradual process lasting up to several years.

mental age (MA)   A measure of mental development expressed in terms of the average mental ability at a given age.

mental disorder   Any behaviour or emotional state that causes an individual great suffering, is self-destructive, seriously impairs the person's ability to work or get along with others, or endangers others or the community.

mental image   A mental representation that mirrors or resembles the thing it represents; mental images occur in many and perhaps all sensory modalities.

mental modules   A collection of specialized and independent sections of the brain, developed to handle specific survival problems, such as the need to locate food or find a mate.

mental set   A tendency to solve problems using procedures that worked before on similar problems.

meta-analysis   A set of techniques for combining data from a number of related studies to determine the explanatory strength of a particular independent variable.

metacognition   The knowledge or awareness of one's own cognitive processes, and the ability to monitor and control those processes.

mirror neurons   Brain cells that fire when a person or animal observes others carrying out an action; they are involved in empathy, language comprehension, imitation, and reading emotions.

mnemonics [neh-MON-iks]   Strategies and tricks for improving memory, such as the use of a verse or a formula.

mode   In a set of scores, the score that occurs most often.

monocular cues   Visual cues to depth or distance that can be used by one eye alone.

mood-congruent memory   The tendency to remember experiences that are consistent with one's current mood and overlook or forget experiences that are not.

motivation   An inferred process within a person or animal that causes movement either toward a goal or away from an unpleasant situation.

MRI (magnetic resonance imaging)   A method for studying body and brain tissue, using magnetic fields and special radio receivers.

mutation   Changes in genes, sometimes due to an error in the copying of the original DNA sequence during the division of the cells that produce sperm and eggs.

myelin sheath   A fatty insulation that may surround the axon of a neuron.

narcissistic personality disorder   A disorder characterized by an exaggerated sense of self-importance and self-absorption.

narcolepsy   A sleep disorder involving sudden and unpredictable daytime attacks of sleepiness or lapses into REM sleep.

natural selection   The evolutionary process in which individuals with genetically influenced traits that are adaptive in a particular environment tend to survive and to reproduce in greater numbers than do other individuals; as a result, their traits become more common in the population.

negative correlation   An association between increases in one variable and decreases in another.

negative reinforcement   A reinforcement procedure in which a response is followed by the removal, delay, or decrease in intensity of an unpleasant stimulus; as a result, the response becomes stronger or more likely to occur.

nerve   A bundle of nerve fibres (axons and sometimes dendrites) in the peripheral nervous system.

neurogenesis The production of new neurons from immature stem cells.

neuromodulators Neurochemicals that modulate the functioning of neurons and neurotransmitters.

neuron A cell that conducts electrochemical signals; the basic unit of the nervous system; also called a *nerve cell*.

neurotransmitter A chemical substance that is released by a transmitting neuron at the synapse and that alters the activity of a receiving neuron.

nonconscious processes Mental processes occurring outside of and not available to conscious awareness.

normal curve The symmetrical bell-shaped form that appears when normal distribution is plotted in a frequency polygon.

normal distribution A probability distribution that takes a symmetrical shape around the mean after a large number of observations, sometimes called a "bell curve." A theoretical construct of a pattern that appears from a very large number of observations.

norms In test construction, established standards of performance.

norms (social) Rules that regulate social life, including explicit laws and implicit cultural conventions.

null hypothesis Expresses the possibility that the experimental manipulations will have no effect on the subjects' behaviour.

objective tests (inventories) Standardized objective questionnaires requiring written responses; they typically include scales on which people are asked to rate themselves.

object permanence The understanding, which develops throughout the first year, that an object continues to exist even when you cannot see it or touch it.

observational learning A process in which an individual learns new responses by observing the behaviour of another (a model) rather than through direct experience; sometimes called *vicarious conditioning*.

observational study A study in which the researcher carefully and systematically observes and records behaviour without interfering with the behaviour; it may involve either naturalistic or laboratory observation.

obsessive-compulsive disorder (OCD) An anxiety disorder in which a person feels trapped in repetitive, persistent thoughts (*obsessions*) and repetitive, ritualized behaviours (*compulsions*) designed to reduce anxiety.

Occam's Razor The principle of choosing the solution that accounts for the most evidence while making the fewest unverified assumptions.

occipital [ahk-SIP-uh-tuhl] lobes Lobes at the lower back part of the brain's cerebral cortex; they contain areas that receive visual information.

Oedipus complex In psychoanalysis, a conflict occurring in the phallic (Oedipal) stage, in which a child desires the parent of the other sex and views the same-sex parent as a rival.

operant conditioning The process by which a response becomes more likely to occur or less so, depending on its consequences.

operational definition A precise definition of a term in a hypothesis, which specifies the operations for observing and measuring the process or phenomenon being defined.

opiates Drugs, derived from the opium poppy, that relieve pain and commonly produce euphoria.

opponent-process theory A theory of colour perception that assumes that the visual system treats pairs of colours as opposing or antagonistic.

organ of Corti [core-tee] A structure in the cochlea containing hair cells that serve as the receptors for hearing.

overregularizations Non-random errors in grammar that show a child has grasped a grammatical rule.

oxytocin A hormone, secreted by the pituitary gland, that stimulates uterine contractions during childbirth, facilitates the ejection of milk during nursing, and seems to promote, in both sexes, attachment and trust in relationships.

panic disorder An anxiety disorder in which a person experiences recurring panic attacks, periods of intense fear, and feelings of impending doom or death, accompanied by physiological symptoms such as rapid heart rate and dizziness.

papillae [pa-PILL-ee] Knoblike elevations on the tongue, containing the taste buds (singular: papilla).

parallel distributed processing (PDP) model A model of memory in which knowledge is represented as connections among thousands of interacting processing units, distributed in a vast network, and all operating in parallel. Also called a *connectionist model*.

paranoid personality disorder A disorder characterized by unreasonable, excessive suspiciousness and mistrust, and irrational feelings of being persecuted by others.

parasympathetic nervous system The subdivision of the autonomic nervous system that operates during relaxed states and that conserves energy.

parietal [puh-RYE-uh-tuhl] lobes Lobes at the top of the brain's cerebral cortex; they contain areas that receive information on pressure, pain, touch, and temperature, and handle attention and awareness of spatial relations.

percentile score (centile rank) A percentile score gives the percentage of people who scored at or below a given raw score.

perception The process by which the brain organizes and interprets sensory information.

perceptual constancy The accurate perception of objects as stable or unchanged despite changes in the sensory patterns they produce.

perceptual set A habitual way of perceiving, based on expectations.

peripheral nervous system (PNS) All portions of the nervous system outside the brain and spinal cord; it includes sensory and motor nerves.

personality A distinctive and relatively stable pattern of behaviour, thoughts, motives, and emotions that characterizes an individual.

PET scan (positron-emission tomography) A method for analyzing biochemical activity in the brain, for example by using injections of a glucose-like substance containing a radioactive element.

phantom pain The experience of pain in a missing limb or other body part.

phobia An exaggerated, unrealistic fear of a specific situation, activity, or object.

phrenology The now discredited theory that different brain areas account for specific character and personality traits, which can be "read" from bumps on the skull.

Jean Piaget (1896–1980) Swiss psychologist who studied child development, created the "flower-blooming" school of cognitive development, and proposed the theory of cognitive stages.

pitch The dimension of auditory experience related to the frequency of a pressure wave; the height or depth of a tone.

pituitary gland A small endocrine gland at the base of the brain that releases many hormones and regulates other endocrine glands.

placebo An inactive substance or fake treatment used as a control in an experiment or given by a medical practitioner to a patient.

placebo effect The apparent success of a medication or treatment due to the patient's expectations or hopes rather than to the drug or treatment itself.

plasticity The brain's ability to change and adapt in response to experience—for example, by reorganizing or growing new neural connections.

pons A structure in the brain stem involved in, among other things, sleeping, waking, and dreaming.

positive correlation An association between increases in one variable and increases in another—or between decreases in one and in another.

positive reinforcement A reinforcement procedure in which a response is followed by the presentation of, or increase in intensity of, a reinforcing stimulus; as a result, the response becomes stronger or more likely to occur.

postdecision dissonance In the theory of cognitive dissonance, tension that occurs when you believe you may have made a bad decision.

posttraumatic stress disorder (PTSD) An anxiety disorder in which a person who has experienced a traumatic or life-threatening event has symptoms such as psychic numbing, reliving of the trauma, and increased physiological arousal.

power assertion A method of child rearing in which the parent uses punishment and authority to correct the child's misbehaviour.

prejudice A strong, unreasonable dislike or hatred of a group, based on a negative stereotype.

primary control An effort to modify reality by changing other people, the situation, or events; a "fighting back" philosophy.

primary emotions Emotions that are considered to be universal and biologically based.

primary punisher A stimulus that is inherently punishing; an example is electric shock.

primary reinforcer A stimulus that is inherently reinforcing, typically satisfying a physiological need; an example is food.

priming A method used to measure unconscious cognitive processes, in which a person is exposed to information and is later tested to see whether the information affects behaviour or performance on another task or in another situation.

principle of falsifiability The principle that a scientific theory must make predictions that are specific enough to expose the theory to the possibility of disconfirmation; that is, the theory must predict not only what will happen but also what will not happen.

proactive interference Forgetting that occurs when previously stored material interferes with the ability to remember similar, more recently learned material.

procedural memories Memories for the performance of actions or skills ("knowing how").

projective tests Psychological tests used to infer a person's motives, conflicts, and unconscious dynamics on the basis of the person's interpretations of ambiguous stimuli.

proposition A unit of meaning that is made up of concepts and expresses a single idea.

prototype An especially representative example of a concept.

proximity effect The people who are nearest to you geographically are most likely to be dearest to you, too.

psychedelic drugs Consciousness-altering drugs that produce hallucinations, change thought processes, or disrupt the normal perception of time and space.

psychiatrist A medical doctor (MD) who has completed a three-year residency in psychiatry to learn how to diagnose and treat mental disorders under the supervision of more experienced physicians.

psychoactive drug A drug capable of influencing perception, mood, cognition, or behaviour.

psychoanalysis A theory of personality and a method of psychotherapy developed by Sigmund Freud; it emphasizes unconscious motives and conflicts.

psychoanalyst A person who practises psychoanalysis, has obtained specialized training at a psychoanalytic institute, and has undergone extensive psychoanalysis personally.

psychobabble Pseudoscience and quackery covered by a veneer of psychological and scientific-sounding language.

psychodynamic perspective A psychological approach that emphasizes unconscious dynamics within the individual, such as inner forces, conflicts, or the movement of instinctual energy.

psychodynamic theories Theories that explain behaviour and personality in terms of unconscious energy dynamics within the individual.

psycholinguists Researchers who study the psychology of language.

psychological practice Providing health or mental-health services.

psychological tests Procedures used to measure and evaluate personality traits, emotional states, aptitudes, interests, abilities, and values.

psychology The discipline concerned with behaviour and mental processes and how they are affected by an organism's physical state, mental state, and external environment; the term is often represented by Ψ, the Greek letter *psi* (usually pronounced "sigh").

psychometrics The measurement of mental abilities, traits, and processes.

psychometric psychologist Practitioner who designs and evaluates tests of mental abilities, aptitudes, interests, and personality.

psychoneuroimmunology (PNI) The study of the relationships among psychology, the nervous and endocrine systems, and the immune system.

psychopathy A personality disorder characterized by a lack of remorse, empathy, anxiety, and other social emotions; the use of deceit and manipulation; and impulsive thrill seeking.

psychosexual stages In Freud's theory, the idea that energy sexual different forms takes as the child the matures; the stages are oral, anal, phallic (Oedipal), latency, and genital.

psychosis An extreme mental disturbance involving distorted perceptions and irrational behaviour; it may have psychological or organic causes. (Plural: psychoses.)

psychosurgery Any surgical procedure that destroys selected areas of the brain believed to be involved in emotional disorders or violent, impulsive behaviour.

psychotherapist Unregulated person who does any kind of psychotherapy.

puberty The age at which a person becomes capable of sexual reproduction.

punishment The process by which a stimulus or event weakens or reduces the probability of the response that it follows.

random assignment A procedure for assigning people to experimental and control groups in which each individual has the same probability as any other of being assigned to a given group.

randomized controlled trials Research designed to determine the effectiveness of a new medication or form of therapy, in which people with a given problem or disorder are randomly assigned to one or more treatment groups or to a control group.

range A measure of variability found by subtracting the lowest score from the highest one.

rapid eye movement (REM) sleep Sleep periods characterized by eye movement, loss of muscle tone, and dreaming.

rational emotive behaviour therapy (REBT) A form of cognitive therapy devised by Albert Ellis, designed to challenge the client's unrealistic thoughts.

reasoning The drawing of conclusions or inferences from observations, facts, or assumptions.

recall The ability to retrieve and reproduce from memory previously encountered material.

recognition The ability to identify previously encountered material.

reinforcement The process by which a stimulus or event strengthens or increases the probability of the response that it follows.

relearning method A method for measuring retention that compares the time required to relearn material with the time used in the initial learning of the material.

reliability In test construction, the consistency of scores derived from a test, from one time and place to another.

REM behaviour disorder A disorder in which the muscle paralysis that normally occurs during REM sleep is absent or incomplete, and the sleeper is able to act out his or her dreams.

representative sample A group of individuals, selected from a population for study, that matches the population on important characteristics such as age and sex.

repression In psychoanalytic theory, the selective, involuntary pushing of threatening or upsetting information into the unconscious.

reticular activating system (RAS) A dense network of neurons found in the core of the brain stem; it arouses the cortex and screens incoming information.

retina Neural tissue lining the back of the eyeball's interior, which contains the receptors for vision.

retinal disparity The slight difference in lateral separation between two objects as seen by the left eye and the right eye.

retroactive interference Forgetting that occurs when recently learned material interferes with the ability to remember similar material stored previously.

right- and left-skewed distributions A skewed distribution has a large number of scores clustering at one end or the other of the horizontal axis.

rods Visual receptors that respond to dim light.

Carl Rogers (1902–1987) One of three chief leaders of the humanist psychology movement; he posited the importance of the fully functioning individual and unconditional positive regard.

role A given social position that is governed by a set of norms for proper behaviour.

sampling distribution Expresses the possibility that, if only chance were operating, the various experimental results would form a normal distribution.

saturation Vividness or purity of colour; the dimension of visual experience related to the complexity of light waves.

schizophrenia A psychotic disorder marked by delusions, hallucinations, disorganized and incoherent speech, inappropriate behaviour, and cognitive impairments.

seasonal affective disorder (SAD) A controversial disorder in which a person experiences depression during the winter and an improvement of mood in the spring.

secondary control An effort to accept reality by changing your own attitudes, goals, or emotions; a "learn to live with it" philosophy.

secondary emotions Emotions that are specific to certain cultures or that depend on cognitive complexity.

secondary punisher A stimulus that has acquired punishing properties through association with other punishers.

secondary reinforcer A stimulus that has acquired reinforcing properties through association with other reinforcers.

secondary traits Changeable aspects of personality.

selective attention The focusing of attention on selected aspects of the environment and the blocking out of others.

semantic memories Memories of general knowledge, including facts, rules, concepts, and propositions.

semicircular canals Sense organs in the inner ear that contribute to equilibrium by responding to rotation of the head.

sensation The detection of physical energy emitted or reflected by physical objects; it occurs when energy in the external environment or the body stimulates receptors in the sense organs.

sense receptors Specialized cells that convert physical energy in the environment or the body to electrical energy that can be transmitted as nerve impulses to the brain.

sensory adaptation The reduction or disappearance of sensory responsiveness when stimulation is unchanging or repetitious.

sensory deprivation The absence of normal levels of sensory stimulation.

sensory register A memory system that momentarily preserves extremely accurate images of sensory information.

separation anxiety The distress that most children develop, at about six to eight months of age, when their primary caregivers temporarily leave them with strangers.

serial-position effect The tendency for recall of the first and last items on a list to surpass recall of items in the middle of the list.

set point The genetically influenced weight range for an individual; it is maintained by biological mechanisms that regulate food intake, fat reserves, and metabolism.

sex hormones Hormones that regulate the development and functioning of reproductive organs and that stimulate the development of male and female sexual characteristics; they include androgens, estrogens, and progesterone.

sexual script Set of implicit rules that specify proper sexual behaviour for a person in a given situation, varying with the person's gender, age, religion, social status, and peer group.

shaping An operant-conditioning procedure in which successive approximations of a desired response are reinforced.

short-term memory (STM) In the three-box model of memory, a limited-capacity memory system involved in the retention of information for brief periods; it is also used to hold information retrieved from long-term memory for temporary use.

signal-detection theory A psychophysical theory that divides the detection of a sensory signal into a sensory process and a decision process.

significance tests Statistical tests that show how likely it is that a study's results occurred merely by chance.

similarity effect Similarity—in looks, attitudes, beliefs, values, personality, and interests—is attractive to human beings; we tend to choose friends and loved ones who are most like us.

single-blind study An experiment in which participants do not know whether they are in an experimental or a control group, but the researchers do.

skills training In behaviour therapy, an effort to teach the client skills that he or she may lack, as well as new constructive behaviours to replace self-defeating ones.

sleep apnea A disorder in which breathing briefly stops during sleep, causing the person to choke and gasp and momentarily awaken.

social cognition An area in social psychology concerned with social influences on thought, memory, perception, and beliefs.

social-cognitive theories Theories that emphasize how behaviour is learned and maintained through observation and imitation of others, positive consequences, and cognitive processes such as plans, expectations, and beliefs.

social Darwinism The notion that the wealthy and successful are more reproductively fit than other people.

social identity The part of a person's self-concept that is based on his or her identification with a nation, religious or political group, occupation, or other social affiliation.

socialization The process by which children learn the behaviours, attitudes, and expectations required of them by their society or culture.

sociobiology An interdisciplinary field that emphasizes evolutionary explanations of social behaviour in animals, including human beings.

sociocultural perspective A psychological approach that emphasizes social and cultural influences on behaviour.

somatic nervous system The subdivision of the peripheral nervous system that connects to sensory receptors and to skeletal muscles; sometimes called the *skeletal nervous system*.

source misattribution The inability to distinguish an actual memory of an event from information you learned about the event elsewhere.

spinal cord A collection of neurons and supportive tissue running from the base of the brain down the centre of the back, protected by a column of bones (the spinal column).

spontaneous recovery The reappearance of a learned response after its apparent extinction.

standard deviation A commonly used measure of variability that indicates the average difference between scores in a distribution and their mean.

standardize In test construction, to develop uniform procedures for giving and scoring a test.

state-dependent memory The tendency to remember something when the rememberer is in the same physical or mental state as during the original learning or experience.

statistically significant A result that has a less than 5% likelihood of occurring by chance.

stem cells Immature cells that renew themselves and have the potential to develop into mature cells; given encouraging environments, stem cells from early embryos can develop into any cell type.

stereotype A summary impression of a group, in which a person believes that all members of the group share a common trait or traits (positive, negative, or neutral).

stereotype threat A burden of doubt a person feels about his or her performance, due to negative stereotypes about his or her group's abilities.

stimulants Drugs that speed up activity in the central nervous system.

stimulus discrimination The tendency to respond differently to two or more similar stimuli. In classical conditioning, it occurs when a stimulus similar to the conditioned stimulus fails to evoke the conditioned response; in operant conditioning, the tendency of a response to occur in the presence of one stimulus but not in the presence of other similar stimuli that differ from it on some dimension.

stimulus generalization After conditioning, the tendency to respond to a stimulus that resembles one involved in the original conditioning. In classical conditioning, it occurs when a stimulus that resembles the conditioned stimulus elicits the conditioned response; in operant conditioning, the tendency for a response that has been reinforced (or punished) in the presence of one stimulus to occur (or be suppressed) in the presence of other similar stimuli.

structuralism An early psychological approach that emphasized the analysis of immediate experience into basic elements.

subconscious processes Mental processes occurring outside of conscious awareness but accessible to consciousness when necessary.

successive approximations In the operant-conditioning procedure of shaping, behaviours that are ordered in terms of increasing similarity or closeness to the desired response.

superego In psychoanalysis, the part of personality that represents conscience, morality, and social standards.

suprachiasmatic [soo-pruh-kye-az-MAT-ick] **nucleus (SCN)** An area of the brain containing a biological clock that governs circadian rhythms.

surveys Questionnaires and interviews that ask people directly about their experiences, attitudes, or opinions.

sympathetic nervous system The subdivision of the autonomic nervous system that mobilizes bodily resources and increases the output of energy during emotion and stress.

synapse The site where transmission of a nerve impulse from one nerve cell to another occurs; it includes the axon terminal, the synaptic cleft, and receptor sites in the membrane of the receiving cell.

synesthesia A condition in which stimulation of one sense also evokes another.

tacit knowledge Strategies for success that are not explicitly taught but that instead must be inferred.

taste buds Nests of taste-receptor cells.

telegraphic speech A child's first word combinations, which omit (as a telegram did) unnecessary words.

thalamus A brain structure that relays sensory messages to the cerebral cortex.

theory An organized system of assumptions and principles that purports to explain a specified set of phenomena and their interrelationships.

theory of mind A system of beliefs about the way one's own mind and the minds of others work, and of how individuals are affected by their beliefs and feelings.

therapeutic alliance The bond of confidence and mutual understanding established between therapist and client, which allows them to work together to solve the client's problems.

therapeutic window The amount of a drug that is enough but not too much, taking into account the fact that the same dose of a drug may be metabolized differently in men and women, old people and young people, and different ethnic groups.

timbre The distinguishing quality of a sound; the dimension of auditory experience related to the complexity of the pressure wave.

tolerance Increased resistance to a drug's effects accompanying continued use.

trait A characteristic of an individual, describing a habitual way of behaving, thinking, or feeling.

tranquilizers Drugs commonly but often inappropriately prescribed for patients who complain of unhappiness, anxiety, or worry.

transcranial direct current stimulation (tDCS) A technique that applies a very small electric current to stimulate or suppress activity in parts of the cortex; it enables researchers to identify the functions of a particular area.

transcranial magnetic stimulation (TMS) A method of stimulating brain cells using a powerful magnetic field produced by a wire coil placed on a person's head; it can be used by researchers to temporarily inactivate neural circuits.

transference In psychodynamic therapies, a critical process in which the client transfers unconscious emotions or reactions, such as emotional feelings about his or her parents, onto the therapist.

triarchic [try-ARE-kick] theory of intelligence A theory of intelligence that emphasizes analytic, creative, and practical abilities.

trichromatic theory A theory of colour perception that proposes three mechanisms in the visual system, each sensitive to a certain range of wavelengths; their interaction is assumed to produce all the different experiences of hue.

unconditioned response (UR) The classical-conditioning term for a response elicited by an unconditioned stimulus.

unconditioned stimulus (US) The classical-conditioning term for a stimulus that already elicits a certain response without additional learning.

validity The ability of a test to measure what it was designed to measure.

validity effect The tendency of people to believe that a statement is true or valid simply because it has been repeated many times.

variables Characteristics of behaviour or experience that can be measured or described by a numeric scale.

volunteer bias A shortcoming of findings derived from a sample of volunteers instead of a representative sample; the volunteers may differ from those who did not volunteer.

vulnerability-stress models Approaches that emphasize how individual vulnerabilities interact with external stresses or circumstances to produce mental disorders.

Lev Vygotsky (1896–1934) Psychologist who emphasized the sociocultural influences of language and culture on children's cognitive development.

Wechsler Adult Intelligence Scale (WAIS) Intelligence test for adults devised by David Wechsler that produces a general IQ score and also provides specific scores for different kinds of ability.

Wechsler Intelligence Scale for Children (WISC) Intelligence test for children devised by David Wechsler that produces a general IQ score and also provides specific scores for different kinds of ability.

Benjamin Lee Whorf A linguist and anthropologist who proposed that language moulds cognition and perception.

withdrawal Physical and psychological symptoms that occur when someone addicted to a drug stops taking it.

working memory In many models of memory, a cognitively complex form of short-term memory; it involves active mental processes that control retrieval of information from long-term memory and interpret that information appropriately for a given task.

Wilhelm Wundt (1832–1920) German trained in medicine and philosophy, who wrote many volumes on psychology, physiology, natural history, ethics, and logic, and was the first person to announce (in 1873) that he intended to make psychology a science; his laboratory was the first to have its results published in a scholarly journal.

z-score (standard score) A z-score tells you how far a given raw score is above or below the mean, using the standard deviation as the unit of measurement.

References

Note: Coloured type indicates a Canadian researcher or a researcher associated with a Canadian university.

Abel, G. G., Mittelman, M., Becker, J. V., et al. (1988). Predicting child molesters' response to treatment. *Annals of the New York Academy of Sciences, 528,* 223–234.

Abrahamson, A. C., Baker, L. A., & Caspi, A. (2002). Rebellious teens? Genetic and environmental influences on the social attitudes of adolescents. *Journal of Personality and Social Psychology, 83,* 1392–1408.

Abrams, D. B., & Wilson, G. T. (1983). Alcohol, sexual arousal, and self-control. *Journal of Personality and Social Psychology, 45,* 188–198.

Abu-Saad, K., & Fraser, D. (2010). Maternal nutrition and birth outcomes. *Journal of Epidemiologic Reviews, 32*(1), 5–25.

Adachi, P. J. C., & Willoughby, T. (2011). The effect of violent video games on aggression: Is it more than just the violence? *Aggression and Violent Behavior, 16,* 55–62.

Adair, J. G., & Vohra, N. (2003). The explosion of knowledge, references, and citations: Psychology's unique response to a crisis. *American Psychologist, 58,* 15–23.

Adams, J. L. (2001). *Conceptual blockbusting: A guide to better ideas* (4th ed.). New York: Perseus Books.

Addis, D. R., Wong, A. T., & Schacter, D. L. (2007). Remembering the past and imagining the future: Common and distinct neural substrates during event construction and elaboration. *europsychologia, 45,* 1363–1377.

Ader, R. (2000). True or false: The placebo effect as seen in drug studies is definitive proof that the mind can bring about clinically relevant changes in the body: The placebo effect: If it's all in your head, does that mean you only think you feel better? *Advances in Mind-Body Medicine, 16,* 7–11.

Adler, N. E., & Snibbe, A. C. (2003). The role of psychosocial processes in explaining the gradient between socioeconomic status and health. *Current Directions in Psychological Science, 12,* 119–123.

Adolphs, R. (2001). Emotion, social cognition, and the human brain. Invited address presented at the annual meeting of the American Psychological Society, Toronto, Canada.

Affleck, G., Tennen, H., Croog, S., & Levine, S. (1987). Causal attribution, perceived control, and recovery from a heart attack. *Journal of Social and Clinical Psychology, 5,* 339–355.

Agars, M. D. (2004). Reconsidering the impact of gender stereotypes on the advancement of women in organizations. *Psychology of Women Quarterly, 28,* 103–111.

Agrawal, Y., Platz, E. A., & Niparko, J. K. (2008). Prevalence of hearing loss and differences by demographic characteristics among US adults. *Archives of Internal Medicine, 168,* 1522–1530.

Aguiar, P., Vala, J., Correia, I., & Pereira, C. (2008). Justice in our world and in that of others: Belief in a just world and reactions to victims. *Social Justice Research, 21,* 50–68.

Ainsworth, M. D. S. (1973). The development of infant–mother attachment. In B. M. Caldwell & H. N. Ricciuti (Eds.), *Review of child development research* (Vol. 3). Chicago, IL: University of Chicago Press.

Ainsworth, M. D. S. (1979). Infant–mother attachment. *American Psychologist, 34,* 932–937.

Albert, D., & Steinberg, L. (2011). Judgment and decision making in adolescence. *Journal of Research on Adolescence, 21,* 211–224.

Alcock, J. E. (2011, March/April). Back from the future: Parapsychology and the Bem affair. *Skeptical Inquirer,* 31–39.

Alford, C. Fred. (2001). *Whistleblowers: Broken lives and organizations.* Ithaca, NY: Cornell University Press.

Alford, J. R., Funk, C. L., & Hibbing, J. R. (2005). Are political orientations genetically transmitted? *American Political Science Review, 99,* 153–167.

Alink, L. R. A., Mesman, J., van Zeijl, J., et al. (2009). Maternal sensitivity moderates the relation between negative discipline and aggression in early childhood. *Social Development, 18,* 99–120.

Allen, L. S., & Gorski, R. A. (1992). Sexual orientation and the size of the anterior commissure in the human brain. *Proceedings of the National Academy of Sciences, 89,* 7199–7202.

Allport, G. W. (1954/1979). *The nature of prejudice.* Reading, MA: Addison-Wesley.

Allport, G. W. (1961). *Pattern and growth in personality.* New York, NY: Holt, Rinehart and Winston.

Almad, A. A., & Maragakis, N. J. (2012). Glia: an emerging target for neurological disease therapy. *Stem Cell Research & Therapy, 3,* 37.

Amabile, T. M. (1983). *The social psychology of creativity.* New York, NY: Springer-Verlag.

Amabile, T. M., & Khaire, M. (2008). Creativity and the role of the leader. *Harvard Business Review, 86.* Retrieved from http://hbr.harvardbusiness.org/2008/10/creativity-and-the-role-of-the-leader/ar/1

Ambady, N. (2011, May/June). The mind in the world: Culture and the brain. *APS Observer, 24.*

Amedi, A., Merabet, L., Bermpohl, F., & Pascual-Leone, A. (2005). The occipital cortex in the blind: Lessons about plasticity and vision. *Current Directions in Psychological Science, 14,* 306–311.

American Psychiatric Association. (1994). *The diagnostic and statistical manual of mental disorders* (4th ed.). Washington, DC: American Psychiatric Association.

American Psychiatric Association. (2000). *The diagnostic and statistical manual of mental disorders, IV-TR.* Washington, DC: American Psychiatric Association.

American Psychiatric Association. (2013). *Diagnostic and statistical manual of mental disorders* (5th ed). Arlington, VA: American Psychiatric Publishing.

American Psychological Association. (2012). Guidelines for psychological practice with lesbian, gay, and bisexual clients. *American Psychologist, 67,* 10–42.

Amering, M., & Katschnig, H. (1990). Panic attacks and panic disorder in cross-cultural perspective. *Psychiatric Annals, 20,* 511–516.

Anand, S. S., Yusuf, S., Jacobs, R., et al. (2001). Risk factors, atherosclerosis, and cardiovascular disease among Aboriginal people in Canada: The study of health assessment and risk evaluation in Aboriginal peoples (SHARE-AP). *Lancet, 358*(9288), 1147–1153.

Anastasi, A., & Urbina, S. (1997). *Psychological testing* (7th ed.). Upper Saddle River, NJ: Prentice-Hall.

Andersen, S. M., & Berk, M. S. (1998). Transference in everyday experience: Implications of experimental research for relevant clinical phenomena. *Review of General Psychology, 2,* 81–120.

Andersen, S. M., & Chen, S. (2002). The relational self: An interpersonal social-cognitive theory. *Psychological Review, 109,* 619–645.

Anderson, A. (2005). *The way we argue now: A study in the cultures of theory.* Princeton, NJ: Princeton University Press.

Anderson, C. A., Berkowitz, L., Donnerstein, E., et al. (2003). The influence of media violence on youth. *Psychological Science in the Public Interest, 4*(3), [whole issue].

Anderson, C. A., Shibuya, A., Ihori, N., et al. (2010). Violent video game effects on aggression, empathy, and prosocial behavior in eastern and western countries: A meta-analytic review. *Psychological Bulletin, 136,* 151–173.

Anderson, J. R. (1990). *The adaptive nature of thought.* Hillsdale, NJ: Erlbaum.

Anderson, M. (2005). Is lack of sexual desire a disease? Is testosterone the cure? *Medscape Ob/Gyn & Women's Health.* Retrieved from http://www.medscape.com/viewarticle/512218

Anderson, S. E., Dallal, G. E., & Must, A. (2003). Relative weight and race influence average age at menarche: Results from two nationally representative surveys of US girls studied 25 years apart. *Pediatrics, 111,* 844–850.

Anderson-Barnes, V. C., McAuliffe, C., Swanberg, K. M., & Tsao, J. W. (2009, October). Phantom limb pain: A phenomenon of proprioceptive memory? *Medical Hypotheses, 73,* 555–558.

Andics, A., Gácsi, M., Faragó, T., Kis, A., & Miklósi, Á. (2014). Voice-sensitive regions in the dog and human brain are revealed by comparative fMRI, *Current Biology, 24,* 574–578.

Andreano, J. M., & Cahill, L. (2006). Glucocorticoid release and memory consolidation in men and women. *Psychological Science, 17,* 466–470.

Angell, M. (2004). *The truth about the drug companies: How they deceive us and what to do about it.* New York, NY: Random House.

Anglin, P., & Meng, R. (2000). Evidence on grades and grade inflation at Ontario's universities. *Canadian Public Policy, 26*(3), 361–368.

Antonuccio, D. O., Danton, W. G., DeNelsky, G. Y., et al. (1999). Raising questions about antidepressants. *Psychotherapy and Psychosomatics, 68,* 3–14.

Antrobus, J. (1991). Dreaming: Cognitive processes during cortical activation and high afferent thresholds. *Psychological Review, 98,* 96–121.

Antrobus, J. (2000). How does the dreaming brain explain the dreaming mind? *Behavioral and Brain Sciences, 23,* 904–907.

Archer, J. (2004). Sex differences in aggression in real-world settings: A meta-analytic review. *Review of General Psychology, 8,* 291–322.

Archer, S. N., Robilliard, D. L., Skene, D. J., et al. (2003). A length polymorphism in the circadian clock gene Per3 is linked to delayed sleep phase syndrome and extreme diurnal preference. *Sleep, 26,* 413–415.

Arendt, H. (1963). *Eichmann in Jerusalem: A report on the banality of evil.* New York, NY: Viking.

Arkes, H. R. (1993). Some practical judgment and decision-making research. In N. J. Castellan, Jr., et al. (Eds.), *Individual and group decision making: Current issues.* Hillsdale, NJ: Erlbaum.

Arkes, H. R., Boehm, L. E., & Xu, G. (1991). The determinants of judged validity. *Journal of Experimental Social Psychology, 27,* 576–605.

Arnett, J. J. (2004). Emerging adulthood: The winding road from the late teens through the twenties. New York, NY: Oxford University Press.

Arnon, I., & Clark, E. V. (2011). Why *"on your feet"* is better than *"feet"*: Children's word production is facilitated in familiar sentence-frames. *Language Learning & Development, 7,* 107–129.

Aron, A., Aron, E. N., & Allen, J. (1998). Motivations for unreciprocated love. *Personality and Social Psychology Bulletin, 24,* 787–796.

Aron, A., Fisher, H., Mashek, D. J., et al. (2005). Reward, motivation, and emotion systems associated with early-stage intense romantic love. *Journal of Neurophysiology, 94,* 327–337.

Aronson, E. (2000). *Nobody left to hate.* New York, NY: Freeman.

Aronson, E. (2008). *The social animal* (10th ed.). New York, NY: Worth.

Aronson, E. (2012). *The social animal* (11th ed.). New York: Worth.

Aronson, E., & Mills, J. (1959). The effect of severity of initiation on liking for a group. *Journal of Abnormal and Social Psychology, 59,* 177–181.

Aronson, J. (2010). Jigsaw and the nurture of human intelligence. In M. H. Gonzales, C. Tavris, & J. Aronson (Eds.), *The scientist and the humanist: A festschrift in honor of Elliot Aronson.* New York, NY: Psychology Press.

Arredondo, P., & Perez, P. (2003). Counseling paradigms and Latina/o Americans. In F. Harper & J. McFadden (Eds.), *Culture and counseling: New approaches.* Boston, MA: Allyn & Bacon.

Arredondo, P., Rosen, D. C., Rice, T., et al. (2005). Multicultural counseling: A 10-year content analysis of the *Journal of Counseling & Development. Journal of Counseling and Development, 83,* 155–161.

Arroyo, C. G., & Zigler, E. (1995). Racial identity, academic achievement, and the psychological well-being of economically disadvantaged adolescents. *Journal of Personality and Social Psychology, 69,* 903–914.

Arsenijevic, D., Onuma, H., Pecqueur, C., et al. (2000, December 26). Disruption of the uncoupling protein-2 gene in mice reveals a role in immunity and reactive oxygen species production. *Nature Genetics, 4,* 387–388.

Arum, R., & Roksa, J. (2011). *Academically adrift: Limited learning on college campuses.* Chicago: University of Chicago Press.

Asch, S. E. (1952). *Social psychology.* Englewood Cliffs, NJ: Prentice-Hall.

Asch, S. E. (1965). Effects of group pressure upon the modification and distortion of judgments. In H. Proshansky & B. Seidenberg (Eds.), *Basic studies in social psychology.* New York, NY: Holt, Rinehart and Winston.

Aserinsky, E., & Kleitman, N. (1955). Two types of ocular motility occurring in sleep. *Journal of Applied Physiology, 8,* 1–10.

Atkinson, R. C., & Shiffrin, R. M. (1968). Human memory: A proposed system and its control processes. In K. W. Spence & J. T. Spence (Eds.), *The psychology of learning and motivation: Vol. 2. Advances in research and theory.* New York, NY: Academic Press.

Atran, S. (2010). *Talking to the enemy.* New York: HarperCollins.

Auyeung, B., Baron-Cohen, S., Ashwin, E., et al. (2009). Fetal testosterone predicts sexually differentiated childhood behavior in girls and in boys. *Psychological Science, 20,* 144–148.

Aviezer, H., Hassin, R. R., Ryan, J., et al. (2008). Angry, disgusted, or afraid? Studies on the malleability of emotion perception. *Psychological Science, 19,* 724–732.

Axel, R. (1995). The molecular logic of smell. *Scientific American, 273,* 154–159.

Azmitia, M., Syed, M., & Radmacher, K. (2008). On the intersection of personal and social identities: Introduction and evidence from a longitudinal study of emerging adults. In M. Azmitia, M. Syed, & K. Radmacher (Eds.), *The intersections of personal and social identities. New Directions for Child and Adolescent Development, 120,* 1–16. San Francisco: Jossey-Bass.

Azuma, H. (1984). Secondary control as a heterogeneous category. *American Psychologist, 39,* 970–971.

Baas, M., De Dreu, C. K. W., & Nijstad, B. A. (2008). A meta-analysis of 25 years of mood-creativity research: Hedonic tone, activation, or regulatory focus? *Psychological Bulletin, 134,* 779–806.

Baddeley, A. D. (1992). Working memory. *Science, 255,* 556–559.

Baddeley, A. D. (2007). *Working memory, thought, and action.* New York, NY: Oxford.

Bagemihl, B. (1999). *Biological exuberance: Animal homosexuality and natural diversity.* New York, NY: St. Martin's Press.

Bahill, A. T., & Karnavas, W. J. (1993). The perceptual illusion of baseball's rising fastball and breaking curveball. *Journal of Experimental Psychology: Human Perception & Performance, 19,* 3–14.

Bahrick, H. P. (1984). Semantic memory content in permastore: Fifty years of memory for Spanish learned in school. *Journal of Experimental Psychology: General, 113,* 1–29.

Bahrick, H. P., Bahrick, P. O., & Wittlinger, R. P. (1975). Fifty years of memory for names and faces: A cross-sectional approach. *Journal of Experimental Psychology: General, 104,* 54–75.

Bailey, J. M., Bobrow, D., Wolfe, M., & Mikach, S. (1995). Sexual orientation of adult sons of gay fathers. *Developmental Psychology, 31,* 124–129.

Bailey, J. M., Dunne, M. P., & Martin, N. G. (2000). Genetic and environmental influences on sexual orientation and its correlates in an Australian twin sample. *Journal of Personality and Social Psychology, 78,* 524–536.

Bailey, J. M., Gaulin, S., Agyei, Y., & Gladue, B. A. (1994). Effects of gender and sexual orientation on evolutionarily relevant aspects of human mating psychology. *Journal of Personality and Social Psychology, 66,* 1081–1093.

Bailey, J. M., & Zucker, K. J. (1995). Childhood sex-typed behavior and sexual orientation: A conceptual analysis and quantitative review. *Developmental Psychology, 31,* 43–55.

Baillargeon, R. (1994). How do infants learn about the physical world? *Current Directions in Psychological Science, 5,* 133–140.

Baillargeon, R. (2004). Infants' physical world. *Current Directions in Psychological Science, 13,* 89–94.

Bains, J. S., & Oliet, S. H. R. (2007). Glia: they make your memories stick. *Trends in Neurosciences, 30*(8), 417–424.

Baker, M., & Milligan, K. (2010). Evidence from maternity leave expansions of the impact of maternal care on early child development. *The Journal of Human Resources, 45,* 1–32.

Baker, T. B., McFall, R. M., & Shoham, V. (2008). Current status and future prospects of clinical psychology: Toward a scientifically principled approach to mental and behavioral health care. *Psychological Science in the Public Interest, 9,* entire issue.

Bakermans-Kranenburg, M. J., Breddels-van Baardewijk, P., Juffer, F., et al. (2008). Insecure mothers with temperamentally reactive infants: A chance for intervention. In F. Juffer, M. J. Bakermans-Kranenburg, & M. H. van IJzendoorn (Eds.), *Promoting positive parenting: An attachment-based intervention.* New York, NY: Taylor & Francis.

Bakker, A. B. (2011). An evidence-based model of work engagement.

Balcetis, E., Dunning, D., & Miller, R. L. (2008). Do collectivists know themselves better than individualists? Cross-cultural studies of the holier than thou phenomenon. *Journal of Personality and Social Psychology, 95,* 1252–1267.

Balconi, M., & Ferrari, C. (2013). Left DLPFC rTMS stimulation reduced the anxiety bias effect or how to restore the positive memory processing in high-anxiety subjects. *Psychiatry Research, 209,* 554–559.

Balter, M. (2012). "Killjoys" challenge claims of clever animals. *Science, 335,* 1036–1037.

Bancroft, J. (2006). Normal sexual development. In H. E. Barbaree & W. L. Marshall (Eds.), *The juvenile sex offender* (2nd ed.). New York, NY: Guilford.

Bancroft, J., Graham, C. A., Janssen, E., Sanders, S. A. (2009). The dual control model: Current status and future directions. *Journal of Sex Research, 46,* 121–142.

Bandura, A. (1977). *Social learning theory.* Englewood Cliffs, NJ: Prentice-Hall.

Bandura, A. (1986). *Social foundations of thought and action: A social cognitive theory.* Englewood Cliffs, NJ: Prentice-Hall.

Bandura, A. (1999). Moral disengagement in the perpetration of inhumanities. *Personality and Social Psychology Review, 3,* 193–209.

Bandura, A. (2001). Social cognitive theory: An agentic perspective. *Annual Review of Psychology, 52,* 1–26. Palo Alto, CA: Annual Reviews.

Bandura, A. (2006). Toward a psychology of human agency. *Perspectives on Psychological Science, 1,* 164–180.

Bandura, A., Caprara, G. V., Barbaranelli, C., Pastorelli, C., & Regalia, C. (2001). Sociocognitive self-regulatory mechanisms governing transgressive behavior. *Journal of Personality and Social Psychology, 80,* 125–135.

Bandura, A., Ross, D., & Ross, S. A. (1963). Vicarious reinforcement and imitative learning. *Journal of Abnormal and Social Psychology, 67,* 601–607.

Banks, M. S. (with P. Salapatek). (1984). Infant visual perception. In P. Mussen. (Series Ed.), M. M. Haith & J. J. Campos. (Vol. Eds.), *Handbook of child psychology: Vol. II. Infancy and developmental psychobiology* (4th ed.). New York, NY: Wiley.

Barajas, R. G., Martin, A., Brooks-Gunn, J., & Hale, L. (2011). Mother-child bed-sharing in toddlerhood and cognitive and behavioral outcomes. *Pediatrics, 128,* e339–e347.

Barash, D. P. (2001, April 20). Deflating the myth of monogamy. *The Chronicle of Higher Education,* B16–B17.

Barash, D. P., & Lipton, J. E. (2001). *The myth of monogamy: Fidelity and infidelity in animals and people.* New York, NY: W. H. Freeman.

Barbuto, J. E. (1997). A critique of the Myers-Briggs Type Indicator and its operationalization of Carl Jung's psychological types. *Psychological Reports, 80,* 611–625.

Bargary, G., & Mitchell, K. J. (2008). Synaesthesia and cortical connectivity. *Trends in Neurosciences, 31,* 335–342.

Bargh, J. A. (1999, January 29). The most powerful manipulative messages are hiding in plain sight. *The Chronicle of Higher Education,* B6.

Bargh, J. A., & Morsella, E. (2008). The unconscious mind. *Perspectives on Psychological Science, 3,* 73–79.

Barglow, P. (2008). Corporate self interest and vagus nerve stimulation for depression. *Skeptical Inquirer, 32.5,* 35–40.

Barlow, D. H. (2004). Psychological treatments. *American Psychologist, 59,* 869–878.

Barlow, D. H., Chorpita, B. F., & Turovsky, J. (1996). Fear, panic, anxiety, and disorders of emotion. In D. A. Hope et al. (Eds.), *Nebraska Symposium on Motivation, 1995: Perspectives on anxiety, panic, and fear.* Lincoln: University of Nebraska Press.

Barnes, C. (2011, September 1). Secrets of aging. *The Scientist,* online at http://the-scientist.com/2011/09/01/secrets-of-aging/

Baron-Cohen, S., & Harrison, J. E. (Eds.). (1997). *Synaesthesia: Classic and contemporary readings.* Cambridge, MA: Blackwell.

Barr, S. I. (1995). Dieting attitudes and behavior in urban high school students: Implications for calcium intake. *Journal of Adolescent Health, 16,* 458–464.

Barrett, D. (2001). *The committee of sleep.* New York, NY: Crown/Random House.

Barrett, L. F., Mesquita, B., & Gendron, M. (2011). Context in emotion perception. *Current Directions in Psychological Science, 20,* 286–290.

Barry, P. (2007). Genome 2.0: Mountains of new data are challenging old views. *Science News, 172,* 154–156.

Barsky, S. H., Roth, M. D., Kleerup, E. C., et al. (1998). Histopathologic and molecular alterations in bronchial epithelium in habitual smokers of marijuana, cocaine, and/or tobacco. *Journal of the National Cancer Institute, 90,* 1198–1205.

Bartels, A., & Zeki, S. (2004). The neural correlates of material and romantic love. *NeuroImage, 21,* 1155–1166.

Bartlett, F. C. (1932). *Remembering.* Cambridge, England: Cambridge University Press.

Bartoshuk, L. M. (1998). *Born to burn: Genetic variation in taste.* Paper presented at the annual meeting of the American Psychological Association, San Francisco, CA.

Bassetti, C., Vella, S., Donati, F., et al. (2000). SPECT during sleepwalking. *Lancet, 356,* 484–485.

Basson, R., McInnis, R., Smith, M. D., Hodgson, G., & Koppiker, N. (2002). Efficacy and safety of sidenafil citrate in women with sexual dysfunction associated with female sexual arousal disorder. *Journal of Women's Health and Gender-Based Medicine, 11,* 367–377.

Battaglia, F. P., Benchenane, K., Sirota, A., et al. (2011). The hippocampus: hub of brain network communication for memory. *Trends in Cognitive Sciences, 15,* 310–318.

Baucom, K. J. W., Sevier, M., Eldridge, K. A., et al. (2011). Observed communication in couples two years after integrative and traditional behavioral couple therapy: Outcome and link with five-year follow-up. *Journal of Consulting and Clinical Psychology 79,* 565–576.

Bauer, P. (2002). Long-term recall memory: Behavioral and neuro-developmental changes in the first 2 years of life. *Current Directions in Psychological Science, 11,* 137–141.

Baumeister, R. F. (2000). Gender differences in erotic plasticity: The female sex drive as socially flexible and responsive. *Psychological Bulletin, 126,* 347–374.

Baumeister, R. F., & Bratslavsky, E. (1999). Passion, intimacy, and time: Passionate love as a function of change in intimacy. *Personality and Social Psychology Review, 3,* 49–67.

Baumeister, R. F., Brewer, L. E., Tice, D. M., & Twenge, J. M. (2007). The need to belong: Understanding the interpersonal and inner effects of social exclusion. *Social and Personality Psychology Compass, 1,* 506–520.

Baumeister, R. F., Campbell, J. D., Krueger, J. I., & Vohs, K. D. (2003). Does high self-esteem cause better performance, interpersonal success, happiness, or healthier lifestyles? *Psychological Science in the Public Interest, 4*(1), [whole issue].

Baumeister, R. F., Catanese, K. R., & Vohs, K. D. (2001). Is there a gender difference in strength of sex drive? Theoretical views, conceptual distinctions, and a review of relevant evidence. *Personality and Social Psychology Review, 5,* 242–273.

Baumeister, R. F., Dale, K., & Sommer, K. L. (1998). Freudian defense mechanisms and empirical findings in modern social psychology: Reaction formation, projection, displacement, undoing, isolation, sublimation, and denial. *Journal of Personality, 66,* 1081–1124.

Baumeister, R. F., Stillwell, A. M., & Heatherton, T. F. (1994). Guilt: An interpersonal approach. *Psychological Bulletin, 115,* 243–267.

Baumrind, D., Larzelere, R. E., & Cowan, P. (2002). Ordinary physical punishment—Is it harmful? Commentary on Gershoff's Review. *Psychological Bulletin, 128,* 580–589.

Beauchamp, G. K., & Mennella, J. A. (2011). Flavor perception in human infants: Development and functional significance. *Digestion, 83,* 1–6.

Bechara, A., Dermas, H., Tranel, D., & Damasio, A. R. (1997). Deciding advantageously before knowing the advantageous strategy. *Science, 275,* 1293–1294.

Beck, A. T. (1976). *Cognitive therapy and the emotional disorders.* New York, NY: International Universities Press.

Beck, A. T. (2005). The current state of cognitive therapy: A 40-year retrospective. *Archives of General Psychiatry, 62,* 953–959.

Beck, D. M. (2010). The appeal of the brain in the popular press. *Perspectives on Psychological Science, 5,* 762–766.

Becker, D. V., Kenrick, D. T., Neuberg, S. L., et al. (2007). The confounded nature of angry men and happy women. *Journal of Personality and Social Psychology, 92,* 179–190.

Beer, J. M., Arnold, R. D., & Loehlin, J. C. (1998). Genetic and environmental influences on MMPI factor scales: Joint model fitting to twin and adoption data. *Journal of Personality and Social Psychology, 74,* 818–827.

Belsky, J., Bakermans-Kranenburg, M. J., & van IJzendoorn, M. H. (2007). For better *and* for worse: Differential susceptibility to environmental influences. *Current Directions in Psychological Science, 16,* 300–304.

Belsky, J., Hsieh, K. H., & Crnic, K. (1996). Infant positive and negative emotionality: One dimension or two? *Developmental Psychology, 32,* 289–298.

Belsky, J., & Pluess, M. (2009). The nature (and nurture?) of plasticity in early human development. *Perspectives on Psychological Science, 4,* 345–351.

Bem, D. (2011). Feeling the future: Experimental evidence for anomalous retroactive influences on cognition and affect. *Journal of Personality and Social Psychology, 100,* 407–425.

Bem, D. J., & Honorton, C. (1994). Does psi exist? Replicable evidence for an anomalous process of information transfer. *Psychological Bulletin, 115,* 4–18.

Bem, S. L. (1993). *The lenses of gender.* New Haven, CT: Yale University Press.

Ben Ayed, I. (2014). Influence d'un exercice aérobie sur la performance cognitive chez des patients MCI: étude de cas. *Science & Sports, 29,* 42–45.

Benedetti, F., & Levi-Montalcini, R. (2001). *Opioid and non-opioid mechanisms of placebo analgesia.* Paper presented at the annual meeting of the American Psychological Society, Toronto, Canada.

Benedetti, F., Mayberg, H. S., Wager, T. D., et al. (2005). Neurobiological mechanisms of the placebo effect. *The Journal of Neuroscience, 45,* 10390–10402.

Benjamin, L. T., Jr. (1998). Why Gorgeous George, and not Wilhelm Wundt, was the founder of psychology: A history of popular psychology in America. Invited address presented at the National Institute on the Teaching of Psychology, St. Petersburg Beach, FL.

Benjamin, L. T., Jr. (2003). Why can't psychology get a stamp? *Journal of Applied Psychoanalytic Studies, 5,* 443–454.

Bennett, C. M., Baird, A. A., Miller, M. B., & Wolford, G. L. (2010). Neural correlates of interspecies perspective taking in the post-mortem Atlantic Salmon: An argument for multiple comparisons correction. *Journal of Serendipitous and Unexpected Results. 1*, 1–5.

Beran, M. J., & Beran, M. M. (2004). Chimpanzees remember the results of one-by-one addition of food items to sets over extended time periods. *Psychological Science, 15*, 94–99.

Berenbaum, S. A., & Bailey, J. M. (2003). Effects on gender identity of prenatal androgens and genital appearance: Evidence from girls with congenital adrenal hyperplasia. *Journal of Clinical Endocrinology and Metabolism, 88*, 1102–1106.

Berger, F., Gage, F. H., & Vijayaraghavan, S. (1998). Nicotinic receptor-induced apoptotic cell death of hippocampal progenitor cells. *Journal of Neuroscience, 18*, 6871–6881.

Berglund, H., Lindström, P., & Savic, I. (2006). Brain response to putative pheromones in lesbian women. *Proceedings of the National Academy of Sciences, 103*, 8269–8274.

Berkman Center for Internet & Society. (2008, December 31). Enhancing child safety and online technologies: Final report of the Internet Safety Task Force. Retrieved from http://cyber.law.harvard.edu/sites/cyber.law.harvard.edu/files/ISTTF_Final_Report.pdf

Berlin, F. S. (2003). Sex offender treatment and legislation. *Journal of the American Academy of Psychiatry and the Law, 31*, 510–513.

Bermudo-Soriano, Carlos Riaza, Perez-Rodriguez, M. Mercedes, Vaquero-Lorenzo, Concepcion, & Baca-Garcia, Enrique. (2012). Pharmacology, new perspectives in glutamate and anxiety. *Biochemistry and Behavior, 100*, 752–774.

Bernstein, D. M., & Loftus, E. F. (2009). How to tell if a particular memory is true or false. *Perspectives on Psychological Science, 4*, 370–374.

Berntsen, D., & Thomsen, D. K. (2005). Personal memories for remote historical events: Accuracy and clarity of flashbulb memories related to World War II. *Journal of Experimental Psychology: General, 134*, 242–257.

Berscheid, E., & Reis, H. T. (1998). Attraction and close relationships. In D. T. Gilbert, S. T. Fiske, & G. Lindzey (Eds.), *The handbook of social psychology, Vol. 2* (4th ed.). New York, NY: McGraw-Hill.

Best, J. (2001). *Damned lies and statistics.* Berkeley: University of California Press.

Beutler, L. E. (2000). David and Goliath: When empirical and clinical standards of practice meet. *American Psychologist, 55*, 997–1007.

Beutler, L. E., & Malik, M. L. (Eds.). (2002). *Rethinking the DSM: A psychological perspective.* Washington, DC: American Psychological Association.

Beyerstein, B. L. (1996). Graphology. In G. Stein (Ed.), *The encyclopedia of the paranormal.* Amherst, NY: Prometheus Books.

Beyerstein, B. L. (1999). Fringe psychotherapies: The public at risk. In W. Sampson (Ed.), *A guide to alternative medicine.* London, England: Gordon and Breach.

Bhatarah, P., Ward, G., & Tan, L. (2008). Examining the relationship between free and immediate serial recall: The serial nature of recall and the effect of test expectancy. *Memory & Cognition, 36*, 20–34.

Bianchi, S. M., Robinson, J. P., & Milkie, M. A. (2006). *Changing rhythms of American family life.* New York, NY: Russell Sage Foundation.

Binder, J., Zagefka, H., Brown, R., et al. (2009). Does contact reduce prejudice or does prejudice reduce contact? A longitudinal test of the contact hypothesis among majority and minority groups in three European countries. *Journal of Personality and Social Psychology, 96*, 843–856.

Birdwhistell, R. L. (1970). *Kinesics and context: Essays on body motion communication.* Philadelphia: University of Pennsylvania Press.

Birkhead, T. (2001). *Promiscuity: An evolutionary history of sperm competition.* Cambridge, MA: Harvard University Press.

Birmingham, C. L., Muller, J. L., Palepu, A., et al. (1999). The cost of obesity in Canada. *Canadian Medical Association Journal, 160*, 483–488.

Bischof, M., & Bassetti, C. L. (2004). Total dream loss: A distinct neuropsychological dysfunction after bilateral PCA stroke. *Annals of Neurology.* doi:10.1002/ana.20246

Biss, R. K., & Hasher, L. (2012). Happy as a lark: Morning-type younger and older adults are higher in positive affect. *Emotion, 12*, 437–441.

Biswal, B. B., Mennes, M., Zuo, X., et al. (2010). Toward discovery science of human brain function. *Proceedings of the National Academy of Sciences of the United States of America, 107*, 4734–4739.

Bittman, M., Rutherford, L., Brown, J., & Unsworth, L. (2011). Digital natives? New and old media and children's outcomes. *Australian Journal of Education, November, 55*, 161–175.

Bjork, R. A. (2000). Human factors 101: How about just trying things out? *APS Observer, 13*(3), 30.

Bjorkland, D. F. (2000). *Children's thinking: Developmental function and individual differences.* Belmont, CA: Wadsworth.

Blackmore, S. (2001). Giving up the ghosts: End of a personal quest. *Skeptical Inquirer, 25*(2), 25.

Blagrove, M. (1996). Problems with the cognitive psychological modeling of dreaming. *Journal of Mind and Behavior, 17*, 99–134.

Blakemore, C., & Cooper, G. F. (1970). Development of the brain depends on the visual environment. *Nature, 228*, 477–478.

Blass, T. (Ed.). (2000). *Obedience to authority: Current perspectives on the Milgram paradigm.* Mahwah, NJ: Erlbaum.

Bliss, T. V., & Collingridge, G. L. (1993). A synaptic model of memory: Long-term potentiation in the hippocampus. *Nature, 361*(6407), 31–39.

Bliss, T. V., & Lomo, T. (1973). Long-lasting potentiation of synaptic transmission in the dentate area of the anaesthetized rabbit following stimulation of the perforant path. *Journal of Physiology (London), 232*(2), 331–356.

Bloom, M. (2005). *Dying to kill: The allure of suicide terror.* New York, NY: Columbia University Press.

Blum, D. (2002). *Love at Goon Park: Harry Harlow and the science of affection.* Cambridge, MA: Perseus Books.

Bluming, A., & Tavris, C. (2009). Hormone replacement therapy: Real concerns and false alarms. *The Cancer Journal, 15*, 93–104.

Boesch, C. (1991). Teaching among wild chimpanzees. *Animal Behavior, 41*, 530–532.

Bogaert, A. F. (2006, June 28). Biological versus nonbiological older brothers and men's sexual orientation. *Proceedings of the National Academy of Sciences.* doi:10.1073/pnas.0511152103

Bohannon, J. N., & Stanowicz, L. (1988). The issue of negative evidence: Adult responses to children's language errors. *Developmental Psychology, 24*, 684–689.

Bolshakov, V. Y., & Siegelbaum, S. A. (1994). Postsynaptic induction and presynaptic expression of hippocampal long-term depression. *Science, 264*, 1148–1152.

Bonanno, G. A. (2004). Loss, trauma, and human resilience. *American Psychologist, 59*, 20–28.

Bond, C. F., & DePaulo, B. M. (2008). Individual differences in judging deception: Accuracy and bias. *Psychological Bulletin, 134*, 477–492.

Bond, M. A., Punnett, L., Pyle, J. L., et al. (2004). Gendered work conditions, health, and work outcomes. *Journal of Occupational Health Psychology, 91*, 28–45.

Bond, R., & Smith, P. B. (1996). Culture and conformity: A meta-analysis of studies using Asch's (1952, 1956) line judgment task. *Psychological Bulletin, 119*, 111–137.

Boot, W. R., Blakely, D. P., & Simons, D. J. (2011, September 13). Do action video games improve perception and cognition? *Frontiers in Psychology, 2*, 226.

Booth, F. W., & Neufer, P. D. (2005). Exercise controls gene expression. *American Scientist, 93*, 28–35.

Bootzin, R. R. (2009, March). Update on the psychological science accreditation system. Association for Psychological Science, *Observer;* 20–21.

Borch-Jacobsen, M., & Shamdasani, S. (2012). *The Freud files: An inquiry into the history of psychoanalysis.* New York: Cambridge University Press.

Bordo, S. (2000). *The male body.* New York, NY: Farrar, Straus and Giroux.

Boring, E. G. (1953). A history of introspection. *Psychological Bulletin, 50*, 169–187.

Born, J., & Wilhelm, I. (2012). System consolidation of memory during sleep. *Psychological Research, 76*, 192–203.

Bornstein, R. F., Leone, D. R., & Galley, D. J. (1987). The generalizability of subliminal mere exposure effects: Influence of stimuli perceived without awareness on social behavior. *Journal of Personality and Social Psychology, 53*, 1070–1079.

Boroditsky, L. (2003). Linguistic relativity. In L. Nadel (Ed.), *Encyclopedia of cognitive science.* London, England: Nature Publishing Group.

Boroditsky, L., Schmidt, L., & Phillips, W. (2003). Sex, syntax, and semantics. In D. Gentner & S. Goldin-Meadow (Eds.), *Language in mind: Advances in the study of language and thought.* Cambridge, MA: MIT Press.

Bosson, J. K., & Vandello, J. A. (2011). Precarious manhood and its links to action and aggression. *Current Directions in Psychological Science, 20*, 82.

Bosworth, H. B., & Schaie, K. W. (1999). Survival effects in cognitive function, cognitive style, and sociodemographic variables in the Seattle Longitudinal Study. *Experimental Aging Research, 25*, 121–139.

Bouchard, C., Tremblay, A., Despres, J. P., et al. (1990). The response to long-term overfeeding in identical twins. *New England Journal of Medicine, 322,* 1477–1482.

Bouchard, T. J., Jr. (1995). *Nature's twice-told tale: Identical twins reared apart—what they tell us about human individuality.* Paper presented at the annual meeting of the Western Psychological Association, Los Angeles, CA.

Bouchard, T. J., Jr. (1997a). The genetics of personality. In K. Blum & E. P. Noble (Eds.), *Handbook of psychiatric genetics.* Boca Raton, FL: CRC Press.

Bouchard, T. J., Jr. (1997b). IQ similarity in twins reared apart: Findings and responses to critics. In R. J. Sternberg & E. Grigorenko (Eds.), *Intelligence: Heredity and environment.* New York, NY: Cambridge University Press.

Bouchard, T. J., Jr. (2004). Genetic influence on human psychological traits: A survey. *Current Directions in Psychological Science, 13,* 148–151.

Bouchard, T. J., Jr., & McGue, M. (1981). Familial studies of intelligence: A review. *Science, 212,* 1055–1058.

Bouret, S. G., Draper, S. J., & Simerly, R. B. (2004). Trophic action of leptin on hypothalamic neurons that regulate feeding. *Science, 304,* 108–110.

Bousfield, W. A. (1953). The occurrence of clustering in the recall of randomly arranged associates. *Journal of General Psychology, 49,* 229–240.

Bower, B. (1998). All fired up: Perception may dance to the beat of collective neuronal rhythms. *Science News, 153,* 120–121.

Bower, G. H., & Forgas, J. P. (2000). Affect, memory, and social cognition. In E. Eich et al. (Eds.), *Cognition and emotion.* New York, NY: Oxford University Press.

Bowers, K. S., Regehr, G., Balthazard, C., & Parker, K. (1990). Intuition in the context of discovery. *Cognitive Psychology, 22,* 72–110.

Bowlby, J. (1969). *Attachment and loss. Vol. 1. Attachment.* New York, NY: Basic Books.

Bowlby, J. (1973). *Attachment and loss: Vol. 2. Separation.* New York, NY: Basic Books.

Bowleg, L., Lucas, K. J., & Tschann, J. M. (2004). "The ball was always in his court": An exploratory analysis of relationship scripts, sexual scripts, and condom use among African American women. *Psychology of Women Quarterly, 28,* 70–82.

Bowles, S. (2008). Policies designed for self-interested citizens may undermine "the moral sentiments": Evidence from economic experiments. *Science, 320,* 1605–1609.

Bradford, J. M., & Pawlak, A. (1993). Effects of cyproterone acetate on sexual arousal patterns of pedophiles. *Archives of Sexual Behavior, 22,* 629–641.

Brandt, M. J. (2011). Sexism and gender inequality across 57 societies. *Psychological Science, 22,* 1413–1418.

Braun, K. A., Ellis, R., & Loftus, E. F. (2002). Make my memory: How advertising can change our memories of the past. *Psychology & Marketing, 19,* 1–23.

Braungert, J. M., Plomin, R., DeFries, J. C., & Fulker, D. W. (1992). Genetic influence on tester-rated infant temperament as assessed by Bayley's Infant Behavior Record: Nonadoptive and adoptive siblings and twins. *Developmental Psychology, 28,* 40–47.

Bregman, A. S. (1990). *Auditory scene analysis: The perceptual organization of sound.* Cambridge, MA: MIT Press.

Breland, K., & Breland, M. (1961). The misbehavior of organisms. *American Psychologist, 16,* 681–684.

Brennan, P. A., & Mednick, S. A. (1994). Learning theory approach to the deterrence of criminal recidivism. *Journal of Abnormal Psychology, 103,* 430–440.

Brescoll, V. L., & Uhlmann, E. L. (2008). Can an angry woman get ahead? Status conferral, gender, and expression of emotion in the workplace. *Psychological Science, 19,* 268–275.

Brewer, M. B., & Gardner, W. (1996). Who is this "we"? Levels of collective identity and self representations. *Journal of Personality and Social Psychology, 71,* 83–93.

Brezina, V. (2010). Beyond the wiring diagram: signalling through complex neuromodulatory networks. *Philosophical transactions of the Royal Society of London. Series B, Biological sciences, 365,* 2363–2374.

Brissette, I., Scheier, M. F., & Carver, C. S. (2002). The role of optimism in social network development, coping, and psychological adjustment during a life transition. *Journal of Personality and Social Psychology, 82,* 102–111.

Broadway, J. M., & Engle, R. W. (2011). Lapsed attention to elapsed time? Individual differences in working memory capacity and temporal reproduction. *Acta Psychologica, 137,* 115–126.

Brockner, J., & Rubin, J. Z. (1985). *Entrapment in escalating conflicts: A social psychological analysis.* New York, NY: Springer-Verlag.

Bröder, A. (1998). Deception can be acceptable. *American Psychologist, 53,* 805–806.

Brooks-Gunn, J. (1986). Differentiating premenstrual symptoms and syndromes. *Psychosomatic Medicine, 48,* 385–387.

Brosnan, S. F., & de Waal, F. B. M. (2003). Monkeys reject unequal pay. *Nature, 425,* 297–299.

Brown, A. S. (2004). *The déjà vu experience: Essays in cognitive psychology.* New York, NY: Psychology Press.

Brown, A. S. (2012). *The tip of the tongue state.* New York: Psychology Press.

Brown, D., Scheflin, A. W., & Whitfield, C. L. (1999). Recovered memories: The current weight of the evidence in science and in the courts. *Journal of Psychiatry and Law, 27,* 5–156.

Brown, G. K., Ten Have, T., Henriques, G. R., et al. (2005, August 3). Cognitive therapy for the prevention of suicide attempts. *Journal of the American Medical Association, 294,* 563–570.

Brown, G. R., Laland, K. N., & Mulder, M. B. (2009). Bateman's principles and human sex roles. *Trends in Ecology & Evolution, 24,* 297–304.

Brown, R. (1986). *Social psychology* (2nd ed.). New York, NY: Free Press.

Brown, R., & Kulik, J. (1977). Flashbulb memories. *Cognition, 5,* 73–99.

Brown, R., & McNeill, D. (1966). The "tip of the tongue" phenomenon. *Journal of Verbal Learning and Verbal Behavior, 5,* 325–337.

Brown, R., & Middlefell, R. (1989). Fifty-five years of cocaine dependence [letter]. *British Journal of Addiction, 84,* 946.

Brown, R. P., & Josephs, R. A. (1999). A burden of proof: Stereotype relevance and gender differences in math performance. *Journal of Personality and Social Psychology, 76,* 246–257.

Brown, S. L., Nesse, R. M., Vinokur, A. D., & Smith, D. M. (2003). Providing social support may be more beneficial than receiving it: Results from a prospective study of mortality. *Psychological Science, 14,* 320–327.

Browning, J. R., Hatfield, E., Kessler, D., & Levine, T. (2000). Sexual motives, gender, and sexual behavior. *Archives of Sexual Behavior, 29,* 135–153.

Bruck, M. (2003). *Effects of suggestion on the reliability and credibility of children's reports.* Invited address at the annual meeting of the American Psychological Society, Atlanta, GA.

Bruder, C. E. G., Piotrowski, A., Gijsbers, A. A., et al. (2008). Phenotypically concordant and discordant monozygotic twins display different DNA copy-number-variation profiles. *American Journal of Human Genetics, 82,* 763–771.

Bruinius, H. (2006). *Better for all the world: The secret history of forced sterilization and America's quest for racial purity.* New York, NY: Alfred A. Knopf.

Bruner, J. S. (1990). *Acts of meaning.* Cambridge, MA: Harvard University Press.

Bryant, G. A., & Barrett, H. C. (2007). Recognizing intentions in infant-directed speech. *Psychological Science, 18,* 746–751.

Bryden, M. P. (1982). *Laterality: Functional asymmetry in the intact brain.* San Diego: Academic Press.

Buchanan, T. W. (2007). Retrieval of emotional memories. *Psychological Bulletin, 133,* 761–779.

Buchert, R., Thomasius, R., Nebeling, B., et al. (2003). Long-term effects of "ecstasy" use on serotonin transporters of the brain investigated by PET. *Journal of Nuclear Medicine, 44,* 375–384.

Buck, L., & Axel, R. (1991). A novel multigene family may encode odorant receptors: A molecular basis for odor recognition. *Cell, 65,* 175–187.

Buhrmester, M., Kwang, T., & Gosling, S. D. (2011). Amazon's Mechanical Turk: A new source of inexpensive, yet high-quality, data? *Perspectives on Psychological Science.* doi:10.1177/1745691610393980.

Bukowski, W. M. (2001). Friendship and the worlds of childhood. In D. W. Nangle & C. A. Erdley (Eds.), *The role of friendship in psychological adjustment. New directions for child and adolescent development, No. 91.* San Francisco, CA: Jossey-Bass.

Buller, D. J. (2005). *Adapting minds: Evolutionary psychology and the persistent quest for human nature.* Cambridge MA: MIT Press.

Burgaleta, M., Head, K., Álvarez-Linera, J., Martínez, K., et al. (2012). Sex differences in brain volume are related to specific skills, not to general intelligence. *Intelligence, 40,* 60–68.

Burger, J. M. (2009). Replicating Milgram: Would people still obey today? *American Psychologist, 64,* 1–11.

Burke, B. L., Arkowitz, H., & Menchola, M. (2003). The efficacy of motivational interviewing: A meta-analysis of controlled clinical trials. *Journal of Consulting and Clinical Psycholology, 71,* 843–861.

Burke, D. M., & Shafto, M. A. (2004). Aging and language production. *Current Directions in Psychological Science, 13,* 21–24.

Burke, P. (1996). *Gender shock.* New York, NY: Basic Books.

Burnham, D., Kitamura, C., & Vollmer-Conna, U. (2002, May 24). What's new, pussycat? On talking to babies and animals. *Science, 296,* 1435.

Bushman, B. J., & Anderson, C. A. (2001). Media violence and the American public: Scientific facts versus media misinformation. *American Psychologist, 56,* 477–489.

Bushman, B. J., Bonacci, A. M., Pedersen W. C., et al. (2005). Chewing on it can chew you up: Effects of rumination on triggered displaced aggression. *Journal of Personality and Social Psychology, 88,* 969–983.

Bushman, B., Bonacci, A. M., van Dijk, M., & Baumeister, R. F. (2003). Narcissism, sexual refusal, and aggression: Testing a narcissistic reactance model of sexual coercion. *Journal of Personality and Social Psychology, 84,* 1027–1040.

Bushman, B. J., Ridge, R. D.,. Das, E., et al. (2007). When God sanctions killing. *Psychological Science, 18,* 204–207.

Buss, D. M. (1994). *The evolution of desire: Strategies of human mating.* New York, NY: Basic Books.

Buss, D. M. (1995). Evolutionary psychology: A new paradigm for psychological science. *Psychological Inquiry, 6,* 1–30.

Buss, D. M. (1996). Sexual conflict: Can evolutionary and feminist perspectives converge? In D. M. Buss & N. Malamuth (Eds.), *Sex, power, conflict: Evolutionary and feminist perspectives.* New York, NY: Oxford University Press.

Buss, D. M. (1999). *Evolutionary psychology: The new science of the mind.* Boston, MA: Allyn & Bacon.

Buss, D. M., & Barnes, M. L. (1986). Preferences in human mate selection. *Journal of Personality and Social Psychology, 50,* 559–570.

Buss, D. M., & Schmitt, D. P. (2011). Evolutionary psychology and feminism. *Sex Roles, 64,* 768–787.

Bussey, K., & Bandura, A. (1999). Social-cognitive theory of gender development and differentiation. *Psychological Review, 106,* 676–713.

Buster, J. E., Kingsberg, S. A., Aguirre, O., et al. (2005). Testosterone patch for low sexual desire in surgically menopausal women: A randomized trial. *Obstetrics and Gynecology, 105*(Pt 1), 944–952.

Butcher, J. N., Lim, J., & Nezami, E. (1998). Objective study of abnormal personality in cross-cultural settings: The MMPI-2. *Journal of Cross-Cultural Psychology, 29,* 189–211.

Butler, S., Chalder, T., Ron, M., et al. (1991). Cognitive behaviour therapy in chronic fatigue syndrome. *Journal of Neurology, Neurosurgery & Psychiatry, 54,* 153–158.

Button, T. M. M., Thapar, A., & McGuffin, P. (2005). Relationship between antisocial behaviour, attention-deficit hyperactivity disorder and maternal prenatal smoking. *British Journal of Psychiatry, 187,* 155–160.

Buunk, B., Angleitner, A., Oubaid, V., & Buss, D. M. (1996). Sex differences in jealousy in evolutionary and cultural perspective: Tests from the Netherlands, Germany, and the United States. *Psychological Science, 7,* 359–363.

Byers-Heinlein, K., Burns, T. C., & Werker, J. F. (2010). The roots of bilingualism in newborns. *Psychological Science, 21,* 343–348.

Byne, W. (1995). Science and belief: Psychobiological research on sexual orientation. *Journal of Homosexuality, 28,* 303–344.

Cacioppo, J. T., Berntson, G. G., Lorig, T. S., et al. (2003). Just because you're imaging the brain doesn't mean you can stop using your head: A primer and set of first principles. *Journal of Personality and Social Psychology, 85,* 650–661.

Cadinu, M., Maass, A., Rosabianca, A., & Kiesner, J. (2005). Why do women underperform under stereotype threat? Evidence for the role of negative thinking. *Psychological Science, 16,* 472–578.

Cahill, L. (2005, May). His brain, her brain. *Scientific American, 292,* 40–47.

Cahill, L., Prins, B., Weber, M., & McGaugh, J. L. (1994). ß-adrenergic activation and memory for emotional events. *Nature, 371,* 702–704.

Cahill, L., Uncapher, M., Kilpatrick, L., et al. (2004). Sex-Related hemispheric lateralization of amygdala function in emotionally influenced memory: An FMRI investigation. *Learning & Memory, 11,* 261–266.

Cairney, J., & Ostbye, T. (1999). Time since immigration and excess body weight. *Canadian Journal of Public Health–Revue Canadienne de Santé Publique, 90,* 120–124.

Calder, A. J., Keane, J., Manes, F., Antoun, N., & Young, A. W. (2000). Impaired recognition and experience of disgust following brain injury. *Nature Neuroscience, 3,* 1077–1078.

Camerer, Colin F. (2003). Strategizing in the brain. *Science, 300,* 1673–1675.

Cameron, J., Banko, K. M., & Pierce, W. D. (2001). Pervasive negative effects of rewards on intrinsic motivation: The myth continues. *Behavior Analyst, 24,* 1–44.

Campbell, B. C. (2011). Adrenarche and middle childhood. Human Nature, 22, 327–349.

Campbell, B. C., Pope, H. G., & Filiault, S. (2005). Body image among Ariaal men from Northern Kenya. *Journal of Cross-Cultural Psychology, 36,* 371–379.

Campbell, F. A., & Ramey, C. T. (1995). Cognitive and school outcomes for high risk students at middle adolescence: Positive effects of early intervention. *American Educational Research Journal, 32,* 743–772.

Campbell, J. (1949/1968). *The hero with 1,000 faces* (2nd ed.). Princeton, NJ: Princeton University Press.

Campos, P. (2004). *The obesity myth: Why America's obsession with weight is hazardous to your health.* New York, NY: Gotham Books.

Canadian Institutes of Health Research, Natural Sciences and Engineering Research Council of Canada, and Social Sciences and Humanities Research Council of Canada. *Tri-Council Policy Statement: Ethical Conduct for Research Involving Humans.*

Cancian, F. M. (1987). *Love in America: Gender and self-development.* Cambridge, England: Cambridge University Press.

Cannon, W. B. (1929). *Bodily changes in pain, hunger, fear and rage* (2nd ed.). New York, NY: Appleton.

Capaldi, D. M., Pears, K. C., Patterson, G. R., & Owen, L. D. (2003). Continuity of parenting practices across generations in an at-risk sample: A prospective comparison of direct and mediated associations. *Journal of Abnormal Child Psychology, 31,* 127–142.

Caplan, E. (1998). *Mind games: American culture and the birth of psychotherapy.* (See Chapter 4: Inventing psychotherapy: The American Mind Cure movement, 1830–1900.) Berkeley: University of California Press.

Carey, B. (2011). You might already know this . . . *The New York Times,* D1, 3.

Carnagey, N. L., & Anderson, C. A. (2005). The effects of reward and punishment in violent video games on aggressive affect, cognition, and behavior. *Psychological Science, 16,* 882–889.

Cartwright, R. (1977). *Night life: Explorations in dreaming.* Englewood Cliffs, NJ: Prentice-Hall.

Cartwright, R. D. (1996). Dreams and adaptations to divorce. In D. Barrett (Ed.), *Trauma and dreams.* Cambridge, MA: Harvard University Press.

Cartwright, R. D., Young, M. A., Mercer, P., & Bears, M. (1998). Role of REM sleep and dream variables in the prediction of remission from depression. *Psychiatry Research, 80,* 249–255.

Carver, C. S., & Harmon-Jones, E. (2009). Anger is an approach-related affect: Evidence and implications. *Psychological Bulletin, 135,* 183–204.

Carver, C. S., & Scheier, M. F. (2002). Optimism. In C. R. Snyder & S. J. Lopes (Eds.), *The handbook of positive psychology.* New York, NY: Oxford University Press.

Casey, B. J., Somerville, L. H., Gotlib, I. H., et al. (2011). Behavioral and neural correlates of delay of gratification 40 years later. *Proceedings of the National Academy of Science, 108,* 14998–15003.

Caspi, A. (2000). The child is father of the man: Personality continuities from childhood to adulthood. *Journal of Personality and Social Psychology, 78,* 158–172.

Caspi, A., & Moffitt, T. E. (1991). Individual differences are accentuated during periods of social change: The sample case of girls at puberty. *Journal of Personality and Social Psychology, 61,* 157–168.

Cassin, S. E., von Ranson, K. M., Heng, K., et al. (2008). Adapted motivational interviewing for women with binge eating disorder: A randomized controlled trial. *Psychology of Addictive Behaviors, 22,* 417–425.

Cattell, R. B. (1973). *Personality and mood by questionnaire.* San Francisco, CA: Jossey-Bass.

Ceci, S. J., & Bruck, M. (1995). *Jeopardy in the courtroom: A scientific analysis of children's testimony.* Washington, DC: American Psychological Association.

Cejka, M. A., & Eagly, A. H. (1999). Gender-stereotypic images of occupations correspond to the sex segregation of employment. *Personality and Social Psychology Bulletin, 25,* 413–423.

Cermak, L. S., & Craik, F. I. M. (Eds.). (1979). *Levels of processing in human memory.* Hillsdale, NJ: Erlbaum.

Cervone, D., & Shoda, Y. (1999). Beyond traits in the study of personality coherence. *Current Directions in Psychological Science, 8,* 27–32.

Chabat, D. R., Rainville, C., Kupers, R., & Ptito, M. (2007). Tactile-'visual' acuity of the tongue in early blind individuals. *Neuroreport, 18,* 1901–1904.

Chambless, D. L., & Ollendick, T. H. (2001). Empirically supported psychological interventions: Controversies and evidence. *Annual Review of Psychology, 52,* 685–716.

Chambless, D. L., & the Task Force on Psychological Interventions. (1998). Update on empirically validated therapies II. *The Clinical Psychologist, 51,* 3–16.

Champagne, F. A. (2009). *Nurturing nature: Epigenetics and the transmission of behavior across generations.* Invited address at the annual meeting of the Association for Psychological Science, San Francisco, CA.

Chan, B. L., Witt, R., Charrow, A. P., et al. (2007). Mirror therapy for phantom limb pain [correspondence]. *New England Journal of Medicine, 357,* 2206–2207.

Chandrashekar, J., Hoon, M. A., Ryba, N. J. P., & Zuker, C. S. (2006). The receptors and cells for mammalian taste. *Nature, 444,* 288–294.

Chang, A. M., Buch, A. M., Bradstreet, D. S., et al. (2011). Human diurnal preference and circadian rhythmicity are not associated with the CLOCK 3111C/T gene polymorphism. *Biological Rhythms, 26,* 276–279.

Chang, L., Connelly, B. S., & Geeza, A. A. (2012). Separating method factors and higher order traits of the big five: A meta-analytic multitrait–multimethod approach. *Journal of Personality and Social Psychology, 102,* 408–426.

Chapin, H., Jantzen, K., Kelso, J. A. S., et al. (2010). Dynamic emotional and neural responses to music depend on performance expression and listener experience. *PLoS ONE, 5:* e13812. doi:10.1371/journal.pone.0013812

Charles, S. T., & Carstensen, L. L. (2004). A life-span view of emotional functioning in adulthood and old age. In P. Costa (Ed.), *Recent advances in psychology and aging* (Vol. 15). Amsterdam, the Netherlands: Elsevier.

Chaudhari, N., Landin, A. M., & Roper, S. D. (2000). A metabotropic glutamate receptor variant functions as a taste receptor. *Nature Neuroscience, 3,* 113–119.

Chaves, J. F. (1989). Hypnotic control of clinical pain. In N. P. Spanos & J. F. Chaves (Eds.), *Hypnosis: The cognitive-behavioral perspective.* Buffalo, NY: Prometheus Books.

Cheesman, J., & Merikle, P. M. (1986). Distinguishing conscious from unconscious perceptual processes. *Canadian Journal of Psychology, 40*(4), 343–367.

Chen, Z., Williams, K. D., Fitness, J., & Newton, N. C. (2008). When hurt will not heal. *Psychological Science, 19,* 789–795.

Cheney, D. L., & Seyfarth, R. M. (1985). Vervet monkey alarm calls: Manipulation through shared information? *Behavior, 94,* 150–166.

Cheung, B. Y., Chudek, M., & Heine, S. J. (2011). Evidence for a sensitive period for acculturation: Younger immigrants report acculturating at a faster rate. *Psychological Science, 22,* 147–152.

Chida, Y., & Hamer, M. (2008). Chronic psychosocial factors and acute physiological responses to laboratory-induced stress in healthy populations: A quantitative review of 30 years of investigations. *Psychological Bulletin, 134,* 829–885.

Chipuer, H. M., Rovine, M. J., & Plomin, R. (1990). LISREL modeling: Genetic and environmental influences on IQ revisited. *Intelligence, 14,* 11–29.

Choi, I., Dalal, R., Kim-Prieto, C., & Park, H. (2003). Culture and judgment of causal relevance. *Journal of Personality and Social Psychology, 84,* 46–59.

Chomsky, N. (1957). *Syntactic structures.* The Hague, the Netherlands: Mouton.

Chomsky, N. (1980). Initial states and steady states. In M. Piatelli-Palmerini (Ed.), *Language and learning: The debate between Jean Piaget and Noam Chomsky.* Cambridge, MA: Harvard University Press.

Christensen, A., & Jacobson, N. S. (2000). *Reconcilable differences.* New York, NY: Guilford.

Christie, G. J., Cook, C. M., Ward, B. J., Tata, M. S., Sutherland J., Sutherland R. J., Saucier, D. M. (2013). Mental rotational ability is correlated with spatial but not verbal working memory performance and P300 amplitude in males. *PLoS One, 8*(2):e57390. doi:10.1371/journal.pone.0057390.

Christopher, A. N., & Wojda, M. R. (2008). Social dominance orientation, right-wing authoritarianism, sexism, and prejudice toward women in the workforce. *Psychology of Women Quarterly, 32,* 65–73.

Church, A. T., & Lonner, W. J. (1998). The cross-cultural perspective in the study of personality: Rationale and current research. *Journal of Cross-Cultural Psychology, 29,* 32–62.

Churchill, A. C., & Davis, C. G. (2010). Realistic orientation and the transition to motherhood. *Journal of Social and Clinical Psychology, 22,* 97–114.

Cialdini, R. B. (2009). We have to break up. *Perspectives on Psychological Science, 4,* 5–6.

Cioffi, F. (1998). *Freud and the question of pseudoscience.* Chicago, IL: Open Court.

Claidière, N., & Whiten, A. (2012). Integrating the study of conformity and culture in humans and nonhuman animals. *Psychological Bulletin 138,* 126–145.

Clancy, S. A. (2005). *Abducted: How people come to believe they were kidnapped by aliens.* Cambridge, MA: Harvard University Press.

Clark, E. V., & Estigarribia, B. (2011). Using speech and gesture to inform young children about unfamiliar word meanings. *Gesture, 11,* 1–23.

Clark, L. A., & Watson, D. (2008). Temperament: An organizing paradigm for trait psychology. In O. P. John, R. W. Robbins, & L. A. Pervin (Eds.), *Handbook of personality: Theory and research* (3rd ed.). New York, NY: Guilford.

Clarke, P., & Evans, S. H. (1998). *Surviving modern medicine.* Rutgers, NJ: Rutgers University Press.

Cleary, A. M. (2008). Recognition memory, familiarity, and déjà vu experiences. *Current Directions in Psychological Science, 17,* 353–357.

Cloninger, C. R. (1990). *The genetics and biology of alcoholism.* Cold Springs Harbor, ME: Cold Springs Harbor Press.

Coan, J. A., Schaefer, H., & Davidson, R. J. (2006). Lending a hand: Social regulation of the neural response to threat. *Psychological Science, 17*(12), 1032–1039.

Coats, E. J., Janoff-Bulman, R., & Alpert, N. (1996). Approach versus avoidance goals: Differences in self-evaluation and well-being. *Personality and Social Psychology Bulletin, 22,* 1057–1067.

Coe, C. L., & Lubach, G. R. (2008). Fetal programming: Prenatal origins of health and illness. *Current Directions in Psychological Science, 17,* 36–41.

Cohen, D. (1998). Culture, social organization, and patterns of violence. *Journal of Personality and Social Psychology, 75,* 408–419.

Cohen, D. (2001). Cultural variation: Considerations and implications. *Psychological Bulletin, 127*(4), 451–471.

Cohen, D. B. (1999). Stranger in the nest: Do parents really shape their child's personality, intelligence, or character? New York, NY: Wiley.

Cohen, D., Nisbett, R. E., Bowdle, B. F., & Schwarz, N. (1996). Insult, aggression, and the Southern culture of honor: An "experimental ethnography." *Journal of Personality and Social Psychology, 70,* 945–960.

Cohen Kadosh, R., Henik, A., Catena, A., et al. (2009). Induced cross-modal synaesthetic experience without abnormal neuronal connections. *Psychological Science, 20,* 258–265.

Cohen, S., Doyle, W. J., Turner, R., et al. (2003). Sociability and susceptibility to the common cold. *Psychological Science, 14,* 389–395.

Cohen, S., Frank, E., Doyle, W. J., et al. (1998). Types of stressors that increase susceptibility to the common cold in healthy adults. *Health Psychology, 17,* 214–223.

Cohen, S., Tyrrell, D. A., & Smith, A. P. (1993). Negative life events, perceived stress, negative affect, and susceptibility to the common cold. *Journal of Personality and Social Psychology, 64,* 131–140.

Colcombe, S., & Kramer, A. F. (2003). Fitness effects on the cognitive function of older adults: A meta-analytic study. *Psychological Science, 14,* 125–130.

Cole, M., & Scribner, S. (1974). *Culture and thought.* New York, NY: Wiley.

Collaer, M. L., & Hines, M. (1995). Human behavioral sex differences: A role for gonadal hormones during early development? *Psychological Bulletin, 118,* 55–107.

Collignon, O., Dormal, G., Albouy, G., Vandewalle, G., Voss, P., Phillips, C., & Lepore, F. (2013). Impact of blindness onset on the functional organization and the connectivity of the occipital cortex. *Brain.* doi:10.1093/brain/awt176

Collins, A. M., & Loftus, E. F. (1975). A spreading-activation theory of semantic processing. *Psychological Review, 82,* 407–428.

Collins, B. E., & Brief, D. E. (1995). Using person-perception vignette methodologies to uncover the symbolic meanings of teacher behaviors in the Milgram paradigm. *Journal of Social Issues, 51,* 89–106.

Collins, R. L. (1996). For better or worse: The impact of upward social comparison on self-evaluations. *Psychological Bulletin, 119,* 51–69.

Colvert, E., Rutter, M., Beckett, C., et al. (2008). Emotional difficulties in early adolescence following severe early deprivation: Findings from the English and Romanian adoptees study. *Development and Psychopathology, 20,* 547–567.

Colvert, E., Rutter, M., Kreppner, J., et al. (2008). Do theory of mind and executive function deficits underlie the adverse outcomes associated with profound early deprivation? Findings from the English and Romanian adoptees study. *Journal of Abnormal Child Psychology, 36,* 1057–1068.

Comas-Díaz, L. (2006). Latino healing: The integration of ethnic psychology into psychotherapy. *Psychotherapy: Theory, Research, Practice, Training, 43,* 436–453.

Comuzzie, A. G., & Allison, D. B. (1998). The search for human obesity genes. *Science, 280,* 1374–1377.

Conroy, J. (2000). *Unspeakable acts, ordinary people: The dynamics of torture.* New York, NY: Knopf.

Corriveau, K. H., Fusaro, M., & Harris, P. L. (2009). Going with the flow: Preschoolers prefer nondissenters as informants. *Psychological Science, 20,* 372–377.

Cook, J. M., Biyanova, T., & Coyne, J. C. (2009). Influential psychotherapy figures, authors, and books: An Internet survey of over 2,000 psychotherapists. *Psychotherapy: Theory, Research, Practice, Training, 46,* 42–51.

Cooper, M. L., Shapiro, C. M., & Powers, A. M. (1998). Motivations for sex and risky sexual behavior among adolescents and young adults: A functional perspective. *Journal of Personality and Social Psychology, 75,* 1528–1558.

Corcoran, M. E., Saucier, D. M., Zhang, X., et al. (2005). Cannabinoids and kindling. In M. E. Corcoran & S. L. Moshe (Eds.), *Kindling 6.* New York, NY: Springer-Kluwer.

Corkin, S. (1984). Lasting consequences of bilateral medial temporal lobectomy: Clinical course and experimental findings in H. M. *Seminars in Neurology, 4,* 249–259.

Corkin, S. (2002). What's new with the amnesic patient HM? *Nature Reviews Neuroscience, 3,* 153–160.

Corkin, S., Amaral, D. G., Gonzalez, R. G., et al. (1997). H. M.'s medial temporal lobe lesion: Findings from magnetic resonance imaging. *Journal of Neuroscience, 17,* 3964–3979.

Cosgrove, G. R., & Rauch, S. L. (2003). Stereotactic cingulotomy. *Neurosurgery Clinics of North America, 14,* 225–235.

Cosmides, L., Tooby, J., & Barkow, J. H. (1992). Introduction: Evolutionary psychology and conceptual integration. In J. H. Barkow, L. Cosmides, & J. Tooby (Eds.), *The adapted mind: Evolutionary psychology and the generation of culture.* New York, NY: Oxford University Press.

Costa, P. T., Jr., McCrae, R. R., Martin, T. A., et al. (1999). Personality development from adolescence through adulthood: Further cross-cultural comparisons of age differences. In V. J. Molfese & D. Molfese (Eds.), *Temperament and personality development across the life span.* Hillsdale, NJ: Erlbaum.

Costantino, G., & Malgady, R. G. (1996). Culturally sensitive treatment: Cuento and hero/heroine modeling therapies for Hispanic children and adolescents. In E. D. Hibbs & P. S. Jensen (Eds.), *Psychosocial treatments for child and adolescent disorders: Empirically based strategies for clinical practice.* Washington, DC: American Psychological Association.

Cota-Robles, S., Neiss, M., & Rowe, D. C. (2002). The role of puberty in violent and nonviolent delinquency among Anglo American, Mexican American, and African American boys. *Journal of Adolescent Research, 17,* 364–376.

Council, J. R., Kirsch, I., & Grant, D. L. (1996). Imagination, expectancy and hypnotic responding. In R. G. Kunzendorf, N. K. Spanos, & B. J. Wallace (Eds.), *Hypnosis and imagination.* Amityville, NY: Baywood.

Courage, M. L., & Howe, M. L. (2002). From infant to child: The dynamics of cognitive change in the second year of life. *Psychological Bulletin, 128,* 250–277.

Cowan, N. (2001). The magical number 4 in short-term memory: A reconsideration of mental storage capacity. *Behavioral and Brain Sciences, 24,* 87–185.

Cowan, N., Morey, C. C., Chen, Z., et al. (2008). Theory and measurement of working memory capacity limits. In B. H. Ross (Ed.), *The psychology of learning and motivation.* San Diego, CA: Elsevier.

Cowan, R. S. (2008). *Heredity and hope: The case for genetic screening.* Cambridge, MA: Harvard University Press.

Cowen, E. L., Wyman, P. A., Work, W. C., & Parker, G. R. (1990). The Rochester Child Resilience Project (RCRP): Overview and summary of first year findings. *Development and Psychopathology, 2,* 193–212.

Cox, W. M., & Alm, R. (2005, February 28). Scientists are made, not born. *The New York Times* op-ed page. Retrieved from http://www.nytimes.com/2005/02/28/opinion/28cox.html

Coyne, J. A. (2009). *Why evolution is true.* New York, NY: Viking.

Coyne, J. C., Thombs, B. D., Stefanek, M., & Palmer, S. C. (2009). Time to let go of the illusion that psychotherapy extends the survival of cancer patients. *Psychological Bulletin, 135,* 179–182.

Cozolino, L. (2006). *The neuroscience of human relationships: Attachment and the developing social brain.* New York, NY: Norton.

Craik, F. I. M., & Lockhart, R. (1972). Levels of processing: A framework for memory research. *Journal of Verbal Learning and Verbal Behavior, 11,* 671–684.

Craik, F. I. M., & Tulving, E. (1975). Depth of processing and the retention of words in episodic memory. *Journal of Experimental Psychology: General, 104,* 268–294.

Crair, M. C., Gillespie, D. C., & Stryker, M. P. (1998). The role of visual experience in the development of columns in cat visual cortex. *Science, 279,* 566–570.

Cramer, K. M., & Neyedley, K. A. (1998). Mediating the sex difference in loneliness: The role of masculinity and femininity. *Sex Roles, 38,* 645–653.

Cramer, P. (2000). Defense mechanisms in psychology today: Further processes for adaptation. *American Psychologist, 55,* 637–646.

Crandall, C. S., & Martinez, R. (1996). Culture, ideology, and antifat attitudes. *Personality and Social Psychology Bulletin, 22,* 1165–1176.

Crawford, M., & Marecek, J. (1989). Psychology constructs the female: 1968–1988. *Psychology of Women Quarterly, 13,* 147–165.

Crews, F. (Ed.). (1998). *Unauthorized Freud: Doubters confront a legend.* New York, NY: Viking.

Crits-Christoph, P., Wilson, G. T., & Hollon, S. D. (2005). Empirically supported psychotherapies: Comment on Westen, Novotny, and Thompson-Brenner (2004). *Psychological Bulletin, 131,* 412–417.

Critser, G. (2002). *Supersize.* New York, NY: Houghton-Mifflin.

Cronbach, L. (1990). *Essentials of psychological testing* (5th ed.). New York, NY: Harper & Row.

Cruz, V. T., Nunes, B., Reis, A. M., & Pereira, J. R. (2005). Cortical remapping in amputees and dysmelic patients: A functional MRI study. *NeuroRehabilitation, 18,* 299–305.

Cumming, G. (2012). *Understanding the new statistics: Effect sizes, confidence intervals, and meta-Analysis.* New York, NY: Routledge.

Cumming, G., Fidler, F., Leonard, M., et al. (2007). Statistical reform in psychology: Is anything changing? *Psychological Science, 18,* 230–232.

Cummings, E. M., & Davies, P. T. (2011). *Marital conflict and children: An emotional security perspective.* New York: Guilford.

Cummings, N. A., & Wiggins, J. G. (2001). A collaborative primary care/behavioral health model for the use of psychotropic medication with children and adolescents. *Issues in Interdisciplinary Care, 3,* 121–128.

Cunningham, W. A., & Brosch, T. (2012). Motivational salience: Amygdala tuning from traits, needs, values, and goals. *Current Directions in Psychological Science, 21,* 54–59.

Currie, J., DellaVigna, S., Moretti, E., & Pathania, V. (2009, April). The effect of fast food restaurants on obesity. Unpublished paper. Retrieved from http://www.econ.berkeley.edu/moretti/obesity.pdf

Curtiss, S. (1977). *Genie: A psycholinguistic study of a modern-day "wild child."* New York, NY: Academic Press.

Curtiss, S. (1982). Developmental dissociations of language and cognition. In L. Obler & D. Fein (Eds.), *Exceptional language and linguistics.* New York, NY: Academic Press.

Cushman, P. (1995). *Constructing the self, constructing America: A cultural history of psychotherapy.* New York, NY: Addison-Wesley.

Cypess, A. M., Lehman, S., Williams, G., et al. (2009, April 9). Identification and importance of brown adipose tissue in adult humans. *New England Journal of Medicine, 360,* 1509–1517.

Czeisler, C. A., Duffy, J. F., Shanahan, T. L., et al. (1999). Stability, precision, and near-24-hour period of the human circadian pacemaker. *Science, 284,* 2177–2181.

Dabbs, J. M., Jr. (2000). *Heroes, rogues, and lovers: Testosterone and behavior.* New York, NY: McGraw-Hill.

Dadds, M. R., Bovbjerg, D. H., Redd, W. H., & Cutmore, T. R. H. (1997). Imagery in human classical conditioning. *Psychological Bulletin, 122,* 89–103.

Daley, T. C., Whaley, S. E., Sigman, M. D., et al. (2003). IQ on the rise: The Flynn Effect in rural Kenyan children. *Psychological Science, 14,* 215–219.

Dalgleish, T. (2004). Cognitive approaches to posttraumatic stress disorder: The evolution of multirepresentational theorizing. *Psychological Bulletin, 130,* 228–260.

Dalgleish, T., Hauer, B., & Kuyken, W. (2008). The mental regulation of autobiographical recollection in the aftermath of trauma. *Current Directions in Psychological Science, 17,* 259–263.

Dalton, K. S., Morris, D. L., Delanoy, D. I., et al. (1996). Security measures in an automated ganzfeld system. *Journal of Parapsychology, 60,* 129–147.

Daly, M., & Wilson, M. (1983). *Sex, evolution, and behavior* (2nd ed.). Belmont, CA: Wadsworth.

Damak, S., Rong, M., Yasumatsu, K., et al. (2003). Detection of sweet and umami taste in the absence of taste receptor T1r3. *Science, 301,* 850–853.

Damasio, A. R. (1994). *Descartes' error: Emotion, reason, and the human brain.* New York, NY: Grosset/Putnam.

Damasio, A. R. (2003). *Looking for Spinoza: Joy, sorrow, and the feeling brain.* San Diego, CA: Harcourt.

Damasio, A. R., Grabowski, T. J., Bechara, A., et al. (2000). Subcortical and cortical brain activity during the feeling of self-generated emotions. *Nature Neuroscience, 3,* 1049–1056.

Ellis, A. (1993). Changing rational-emotive therapy (RET) to rational emotive behavior therapy (REBT). *Behavior Therapist, 16,* 257–258.

Ellis, A., & Blau, S. (1998). Rational emotive behavior therapy. *Directions in Clinical and Counseling Psychology, 8,* 41–56.

Ellis, B. J., & Boyce, W. T. (2008). Biological sensitivity to context. *Current Directions in Psychological Science, 17,* 183–187.

Ellison, C. R. (2000). *Women's sexualities.* Oakland, CA: New Harbinger.

Elmquist, J. K., & Flier, J. S. (2004, April 2). The fat–brain axis enters a new dimension. *Science, 304,* 63–64.

Else-Quest, N. M., Hyde, J. S., Goldsmith, H. H., & Can Hulle, C. A. (2006). Gender differences in temperament: A meta-analysis. *Psychological Bulletin, 132,* 33–72.

Emberson, L. L., Lupyan, G., Goldstein, M. H., & Spivey, M. J. (2010). Overheard cell-phone conversations: When less speech is more distracting. *Psychological Science, 21,* 1383–1388.

Emery, R. E., & Laumann-Billings, L. (1998). An overview of the nature, causes, and consequences of abusive family relationships. *American Psychologist, 53,* 121–135.

Emmons, R. A., & King, L. A. (1988). Conflict among personal strivings: Immediate and long-term implications for psychological and physical well-being. *Journal of Personality and Social Psychology, 54,* 1040–1048.

Engle, R. W. (2002). Working memory capacity as executive attention. *Current Directions in Psychological Science, 11,* 19–23.

Entin, A. D. (1992). *Family photographs: Visual icons and emotional history.* Paper presented at the annual meeting of the American Psychological Association, Washington, DC.

Epel, E. S. (2009). Telomeres in a life-span perspective: A new "psychobiomarker"? *Current Directions in Psychological Science, 18,* 6–10.

Epel, E. S., Blackburn, E. H., Lin, J., et al. (2004, December 7). Accelerated telomere shortening in response to life stress. *Proceedings of the National Academy of Science, 101,* 17312–17315.

Epel, E. S., Daubenmier, J., Moskowitz, J. T., et al. (2009). Can meditation slow rate of cellular aging? Cognitive stress, mindfulness, and telomeres. *Annals of the New York Academy of Sciences, 1172,* 34–53.

Erceg-Hurn, D. M., & Mirosevich, V. M. (2008). Modern robust statistical methods. *American Psychologist, 63,* 591–601.

Erickson, K. I., Voss, M. W., Prakash, R. S., et al. (2011). Exercise training increases size of hippocampus and improves memory. *Proceedings of the National Academy of Sciences, 108,* 3017–3022.

Erikson, E. H. (1950/1963). *Childhood and society* (2nd ed.). New York, NY: Norton.

Erikson, E. H. (1982). *The life cycle completed.* New York, NY: Norton.

Ervin-Tripp, S. (1964). Imitation and structural change in children's language. In E. H. Lenneberg (Ed.), *New directions in the study of language.* Cambridge, MA: MIT Press.

Escera, C., Cilveti, R., & Grau, C. (1992). Ultradian rhythms in cognitive operations: Evidence from the P300 component of the event-related potentials. *Medical Science Research, 20,* 137–138.

Esparza, J., Fox, C., Harper, I. T., et al. (2000, January 24). Daily energy expenditure in Mexican and USA Pima Indians: Low physical activity as a possible cause of obesity. *International Journal of Obesity and Related Metabolic Disorders, 1,* 55–59.

Euston, D. R., Tatsuno, M., & McNaughton, B. L. (2007). Fast-forward playback of recent memory sequences in prefrontal cortex during sleep. *Science, 318,* 1147–1150.

Evans, G. W., & Kim, P. (2007). Childhood poverty and health. *Psychological Science, 18,* 953–957.

Evans, G. W., Lepore, S. J., & Allen, K. M. (2000). Cross-cultural differences in tolerance for crowding: Fact or fiction? *Journal of Personality and Social Psychology, 79,* 204–210.

Evans, G. W., & Schamberg, M. A. (2009, March 30). Childhood poverty, chronic stress, and adult working memory. *Proceedings of the National Academy of Sciences, 106.*

Evans, N., & Levinson, S. C. (2009). The myth of language universals: Language diversity and its importance for cognitive science. *Behavioral and Brain Sciences, 32,* 429–492.

Everett, D. L. (2012). *Language: The cultural tool.* New York: Pantheon.

Ewart, C. K. (1995). Self-efficacy and recovery from heart attack. In J. E. Maddux (Ed.), *Self-efficacy, adaptation, and adjustment: Theory, research, and application.* New York, NY: Plenum.

Ewart, C. K., & Kolodner, K. B. (1994). Negative affect, gender, and expressive style predict elevated ambulatory blood pressure in adolescents. *Journal of Personality and Social Psychology, 66,* 596–605.

Eyferth, K. (1961). [The performance of different groups of the children of occupation forces on the Hamburg-Wechsler Intelligence Test for Children.] *Archiv für die Gesamte Psychologie, 113,* 222–241.

Fagan, J. F., III. (1992). Intelligence: A theoretical viewpoint. *Current Directions in Psychological Science, 1,* 82–86.

Fagot, B. I. (1993, June). *Gender role development in early childhood: Environmental input, internal construction.* Invited address presented at the annual meeting of the International Academy of Sex Research, Monterey, CA.

Fagot, B. I., & Leinbach, M. D. (1993). Gender-role development in young children: From discrimination to labeling. *Developmental Review, 13,* 205–224.

Fairbanks, L. A. (2001). Individual differences in response to a stranger: Social impulsivity as a dimension of temperament in vervet monkeys (*Cercopithecus aethiops sabaeus*). *Journal of Comparative Psychology, 115,* 22–28.

Fairholme, C. P., Boisseau, C. L., Ellard, K. K., et al. (2009). Emotions, emotion regulation, and psychological treatment: A unified perspective. In A. M. Kring & D. M. Sloan (Eds.), *Emotion regulation and psychopathology.* New York, NY: Guilford.

Fallon, J. H., Keator, D. B., Mbogori, J., et al. (2004). Hostility differentiates the brain metabolic effects of nicotine. *Cognitive Brain Research, 18,* 142–148.

Fallone, G., Acebo, C., Seifer, R., & Carskadon, M. A. (2005). Experimental restriction of sleep opportunity in children: Effects on teacher ratings. *Sleep, 28,* 1280–1286.

Falk, C. F., Heine, S. J., & Takemura, K. (2014). Cultural Variation in the Minimal Group Effect. *Journal of Cross-Cultural Psychology, 45,* 265.

Farah, M. J. (2012). Neuroethics: The ethical, legal, and societal impact of neuroscience. *Annual Review of Psychology, 63,* 571–591.

Farooqi, I. S., Matarese, G., Lord, G. M., et al. (2002). Beneficial effects of leptin on obesity, T cell hyporesponsiveness, and neuroendocrine/metabolic dysfunction of human congenital leptin deficiency. *Journal of Clinical Investigation, 110,* 1093–1103.

Farooqi, I. S., & O'Rahilly, S. (2004). Monogenic human obesity syndromes. *Recent Progress in Hormone Research, 59,* 409–424.

Farooqi, S., Bullmore, E., Keogh, J., et al. (2007, Sept. 7). Leptin regulates striatal regions and human eating behavior. *Science, 317,* 1355–1355.

Fausto-Sterling, A. (1997). Beyond difference: A biologist's perspective. *Journal of Social Issues, 53,* 233–258.

Feather, N. T. (1966). Effects of prior success and failure on expectations of success and subsequent performance. *Journal of Personality and Social Psychology, 3,* 287–298.

Feeney, B. C., & Cassidy, J. (2003). Reconstructive memory related to adolescent–parent conflict interactions. *Journal of Personality and Social Psychology, 85,* 945–955.

Fehr, B. (1993). How do I love thee… Let me consult my prototype. In S. Duck (Ed.), *Individuals in relationships* (Vol. 1). Newbury Park, CA: Sage.

Fehr, B., Baldwin, M., Collins, L., et al. (1999). Anger in close relationships: An interpersonal script analysis. *Personality and Social Psychology Bulletin, 25,* 299–312.

Fehr, E., & Fischbacher, U. (2003). The nature of human altruism. *Nature, 425,* 785–791.

Fehr, R., Gelfand, M. J., & Nag, M. (2010). The road to forgiveness: A meta-analytic synthesis of its situational and dispositional correlates. *Psychological Bulletin, 136,* 894–914.

Fein, S., & Spencer, S. J. (1997). Prejudice as self-image maintenance: Affirming the self through derogating others. *Journal of Personality and Social Psychology, 73,* 31–44.

Feinberg, A. P. (2008). Epigenetics at the epicenter of modern medicine. *Journal of the American Medical Association, 299,* 1345–1350.

Feinberg, O., Willer, R, M., & Keltner, D. (2012). Flustered and faithful: Embarrassment as a signal of prosociality. *Journal of Personality and Social Psychology, 102,* 81–97.

Feinstein, J. S., Adolphs, R., Damasio, A., & Tranel, D. (2011). The human amygdala and the induction and experience of fear. *Current Biology, 21,* 34–38.

Ferguson, C. (2009). Media violence effects: Confirmed truth or just another X-file? *Journal of Forensic Psychology Practice, 9,* 103–126.

Ferguson, C. J. (2007). The good, the bad and the ugly: A meta-analytic review of positive and negative effects of violent video games. *Psychiatric Quarterly, 78,* 309–316.

Ferguson, C. J., & Kilburn, J. (2010). Much ado about nothing: The misestimation and overinterpretation of violent video game effects in eastern and western nations: Comment on Anderson et al. *Psychological Bulletin, 136*, 174–178.

Fernald, A., & Mazzie, C. (1991). Prosody and focus in speech to infants and adults. *Developmental Psychology, 27*, 209–221.

Fernandez, E., & Turk, D. C. (1992). Sensory and affective components of pain: Separation and synthesis. *Psychological Bulletin, 112*, 205–217.

Fernea, E., & Fernea, R. (1994). Cleanliness and culture. In W. J. Lonner & Malpass (Eds.), *Psychology and culture*. Boston, MA: Allyn & Bacon.

Ferrari, P. F., Rozzi, S., & Fogassi, L. (2005). Mirror neurons responding to observation of actions made with tools in monkey ventral premotor cortex. *Journal of Cognitive Neuroscience, 17*, 212–226.

Festinger, L. (1957). *A theory of cognitive dissonance*. Evanston, IL: Row, Peterson.

Festinger, L., & Carlsmith, J. M. (1959). Cognitive consequences of forced compliance. *Journal of Abnormal and Social Psychology, 58*, 203–210.

Festinger, L., Pepitone, A., & Newcomb, T. (1952). Some consequences of deindividuation in a group. *Journal of Abnormal and Social Psychology, 47*, 382–389.

Festinger, L., Riecken, H. W., & Schachter, S. (1956). *When prophecy fails*. Minneapolis: University of Minnesota Press.

Fidler, F., & Loftus, G. R. (2009). Why figures with error bars should replace *p* values: Some conceptual arguments and empirical demonstrations. *Journal of Psychology, 217*, 27–37.

Fiedler, K., Nickel, S., Muehlfriedel, T., & Unkelbach, C. (2001). Is mood congruency an effect of genuine memory or response bias? *Journal of Experimental Social Psychology, 37*, 201–214.

Field, T. (2009). The effects of newborn massage: United States. In T. Field et al. (Eds.), *The newborn as a person: Enabling healthy infant development worldwide*. Hoboken, NJ: John Wiley & Sons.

Fields, H. (1991). Depression and pain: A neurobiological model. *Neuropsychiatry, Neuropsychology, and Behavioral Neurology, 4*, 83–92.

Fields, R. D. (2004, April). The other half of the brain. *Scientific American*, 54–61.

Fiez, J. A. (1996). Cerebellar contributions to cognition. *Neuron, 16*, 13–15.

Fine, C. (2010). From scanner to sound bite: Issues in interpreting and reporting sex differences in the brain. *Current Directions in Psychological Science, 19*, 280–283.

Fine, I., Wade, A. R., Brewer, A. A., et al. (2003). Long-term deprivation affects visual perception and cortex. *Nature Neuroscience, 6*, 915–916.

Fischer, A. H., Eagly, A. H., & Oosterwijk, S. (2013). The meaning of tears: Which sex seems emotional depends on the social context. *European Journal of Social Psychology, 43*, 505–515.

Fischer, P., Krueger, J. I., Greitemeyer, T., et al. (2011). The bystander-effect: A meta-analytic review on bystander intervention in dangerous and non-dangerous emergencies. *Psychological Bulletin, 137*, 517–537.

Fischer, P. C., Smith, R. J., Leonard, E., et al. (1993). Sex differences on affective dimensions: Continuing examination. *Journal of Counseling and Development, 71*, 440–443.

Fischhoff, B. (1975). Hindsight is not equal to foresight: The effect of outcome knowledge on judgment under uncertainty. *Journal of Experimental Psychology: Human Perception and Performance, 1*, 288–299.

Fitzgerald, P. B., Brown, T. L., Marston, N. A., et al. (2003). Transcranial magnetic stimulation in the treatment of depression: A double-blind, placebo-controlled trial. *Archives of General Psychiatry, 60*, 1002–1008.

Fivush, R., & Nelson, K. (2004). Culture and language in the emergence of autobiographical memory. *Psychological Science, 15*, 573–582.

Fivush, R., & Nelson, K. (2005). Parent-child reminiscing locates the self in the past. *British Journal of Developmental Psychology, 24*, 235–251.

Flavell, J. H. (1999). Cognitive development: Children's knowledge about the mind. *Annual Review of Psychology, 50*, 21–45.

Flegal, K. M. (1999). The obesity epidemic in children and adults: Current evidence and research issues. *Medicine and Science in Sports and Exercise, 31* (Supplement 11), S509–S514.

Fleeson, W. (2004). Moving personality beyond the person-situation debate. *Current Directions in Psychological Science, 13*, 83–87.

Flint, A. J., & Gagnon, N. (2002). Effective use of electroconvulsive therapy in late-life depression. *Canadian Journal of Psychiatry, 47*, 734–741.

Flynn, J. R. (1987). Massive IQ gains in 14 nations: What IQ tests really measure. *Psychological Bulletin, 95*, 29–51.

Flynn, J. R. (1999). Searching for justice: the discovery of IQ gains over time. *American Psychologist, 54*, 5–20.

Fogassi, L., & Ferrari, P. F. (2007). Mirror neurons and the evolution of embodied language. *Current Directions in Psychological Science, 16*, 136–141.

Folkman, S., & Moskowitz, J. T. (2000). Positive affect and the other side of coping. *American Psychologist, 55*, 647–654.

Forbes, G., Zhang, X., Doroszewicz, K., & Haas, K. (2009). Relationships between individualism-collectivism, gender, and direct or indirect aggression: A study in China, Poland, and the US. *Aggressive Behavior, 35*, 24–30.

Forgas, J. P. (1998). On being happy and mistaken: Mood effects on the fundamental attribution error. *Journal of Personality and Social Psychology, 75*, 318–331.

Forgas, J. P., & Bond, M. H. (1985). Cultural influences on the perception of interaction episodes. *Personality and Social Psychology Bulletin, 11*, 75–88.

Foster, J. L., Huthwaite, T., Yesberg, J. A., et al. (2012). Repetition, not number of sources, increases both susceptibility to misinformation and confidence in the accuracy of eyewitnesses. *Acta Psychologica, 139*, 320–326.

Foulkes, D. (1999). *Children's dreaming and the development of consciousness*. Cambridge, MA: Harvard University Press.

Fouts, R. S. (with Stephen T. Mills). (1997). *Next of kin: What chimpanzees have taught me about who we are*. New York, NY: Morrow.

Fouts, R. S., & Rigby, R. L. (1977). Man–chimpanzee communication. In T. A. Seboek (Ed.), *How animals communicate*. Bloomington: University of Indiana Press.

Fox, M. K., Pac, S., Devaney, B., & Jankowski, L. (2004). Feeding Infants and Toddlers Study: What foods are infants and toddlers eating? *Journal of the American Dietetic Association, 104*, 22–30.

Fox, N. A., Henderson, H. A., Marshall, P. J., et al. (2005). Behavioral inhibition: Linking biology and behavior within a developmental framework. *Annual Review of Psychology, 56*, 235–262.

Fox, N. A., Nichols, K. E., Henderson, H. A., et al. (2005). Evidence for a gene-environment interaction in predicting behavioral inhibition in middle childhood. *Psychological Science, 16*, 921–926.

Fraga, M. F., Ballestar, E., Paz, M. F., et al. (2005). Epigenetic differences arise during the lifetime of monozygotic twins. *Proceedings of the National Academy of Sciences, 102*, 10604–10609.

Fraley, R. C., & Shaver, P. R. (2000). Adult romantic attachment: Theoretical developments, emerging controversies, and unanswered questions. *Review of General Psychology, 4*, 132–154.

Frankl, V. E. (1955). *The doctor and the soul: An introduction to logotherapy*. New York, NY: Knopf.

Frankland, P. W., Kohler, S., & Josselyn, S. A. (2013). Hippocampal neurogenesis and forgetting. *Trends in Neurosciences, 36*, 497–503.

Frans, E. M., Sandin, S., Reichenberg, A., et al. (2008). Advancing paternal age and bipolar disorder. *Archives of General Psychiatry, 65*, 1034–1040.

Frasure-Smith, N., & Lespérance, F. (2005). Depression and coronary heart disease: Complex synergism of mind, body, and environment. *Current Directions in Psychological Science, 14*, 39–43.

Frasure-Smith, N., Lespérance, F., Juneau, M., et al. (1999). Gender, depression, and one-year prognosis after myocardial infarction. *Psychosomatic Medicine, 61*, 26–37.

Frayling, T. M., Timpson, N. J., Weedon, M. N., et al. (2007, May 11). A common variant in the *FTO* gene is associated with body mass index and predisposes to childhood and adult obesity. *Science, 316*, 889–894.

Frazier, P., Keenan, N., Anders, S., et al. (2011). Perceived past, present, and future control and adjustment to stressful life events. *Journal of Personality and Social Psychology, 100*, 749–765.

Frazier, P. A. (2003). Perceived control and distress following sexual assault: A longitudinal test of a new model. *Journal of Personality and Social Psychology, 84*, 1257–1269.

Fredrickson, B. L., & Losada, M. F. (2005). Positive affect and the complex dynamics of human flourishing. *American Psychologist, 60*, 678–686.

Frensch, P. A., & Rünger, D. (2003). Implicit learning. *Current Directions in Psychological Science, 12*, 13–18.

Freud, A. (1967). *Ego and the mechanisms of defense (The writings of Anna Freud, Vol. 2)* (Rev. ed.). New York, NY: International Universities Press.

Freud, S. (1900/1953). The interpretation of dreams. In J. Strachey (Ed.), *The standard edition of the complete psychological works of Sigmund Freud* (Vols. 4 and 5). London, England: Hogarth Press.

Freud, S. (1905a). Fragment of an analysis of a case of hysteria. In J. Strachey (Ed. and Trans.), *The standard edition of the complete psychological works of Sigmund Freud* (Vol. 7). London, England: Hogarth Press.

Freud, S. (1905b). Three essays on the theory of sexuality. In J. Strachey (Ed.), *Standard edition* (Vol. 7).

Freud, S. (1920/1960). *A general introduction to psychoanalysis* (J. Riviere, Trans.). New York, NY: Washington Square Press.

Freud, S. (1923/1962). *The ego and the id* (J. Riviere, Trans.). New York, NY: Norton.

Freud, S. (1961). *Letters of Sigmund Freud, 1873–1939.* (E. L. Freud, Ed.). London, England: Hogarth Press.

Fridlund, A. J. (1994). *Human facial expression: An evolutionary view.* San Diego, CA: Academic Press.

Friedman, H. S., & Martin, L. R. (2011). *The longevity project.* New York: Hudson Street Press.

Friedman, J. M. (2003). A war on obesity, not the obese. *Science, 299,* 856–858.

Friedrich, W., Fisher, J., Broughton, D., et al. (1998). Normative sexual behavior in children: A contemporary sample. *Pediatrics, 101,* 1–8. Retrieved from http://www.pediatrics.org/cgi/content/full/101/4/e9

Frijda, N. H., Kuipers, P., & ter Schure, E. (1989). Relations among emotion, appraisal, and emotional action readiness. *Journal of Personality and Social Psychology, 57,* 212–228.

Frome, P. M., & Eccles, J. S. (1998). Parents' influence on children's achievement-related perceptions. *Journal of Personality and Social Psychology, 74,* 435–452.

Frye, R. E., Schwartz, B. S., & Doty, R. L. (1990). Dose-related effects of cigarette smoking on olfactory function. *Journal of the American Medical Association, 263,* 1233–1236.

Fryer, R. G. (2011). Financial incentives and student achievement: Evidence from randomized trials. *The Quarterly Journal of Economics, 126,* 1755–1798.

Fuchs, C. S., Stampfer, M. J., Colditz, G. A., et al. (1995, May 11). Alcohol consumption and mortality among women. *New England Journal of Medicine, 332,* 1245–1250.

Gable, S. L., & Haidt, J. (2005). What (and why) is positive psychology? *Review of General Psychology, 9,* 103–110.

Gaertner, S. L., Mann, J. A., Dovidio, J. F., et al. (1990). How does cooperation reduce intergroup bias? *Journal of Personality and Social Psychology, 59,* 692–704.

Gagnon, J., & Simon, W. (1973). *Sexual conduct: The social sources of human sexuality.* Chicago, IL: Aldine.

Gal, D., & Rucker, D. D. (2010). When in doubt, shout! Paradoxical influences of doubt on proselytizing. *Psychological Science, 21,* 1701–1707.

Galanter, E. (1962). Contemporary psychophysics. In R. Brown, E. Galanter, H. Hess, & G. Mandler (Eds.), *New directions in psychology.* New York, NY: Holt, Rinehart and Winston.

Gallese, V., Gernsbacher, M. A., Heyes, C., et al. (2011). Mirror neuron forum. *Perspectives on Psychological Science, 6,* 369–407.

Galotti, K. (1989). Approaches to studying formal and everyday reasoning. *Psychological Bulletin, 105,* 331–351.

Galotti, K. M. (2007). Decision structuring in important real-life choices. *Psychological Science, 18,* 320–325.

Gamer, M., & Ambach, W. (2014). Deception research today. *Frontiers in Psychology,* 25 March 2014. doi:10.3389/fpsyg.2014.00256d

Gao, J.-H., Parsons, L. M., Bower, J. M., et al. (1996). Cerebellum implicated in sensory acquisition and discrimination rather than motor control. *Science, 272,* 545–547.

Garbarino, J., & Bedard, C. (2001). *Parents under siege.* New York, NY: The Free Press.

Garcia, J., & Gustavson, C. R. (1997, January). Carl R. Gustavson (1946–1996): Pioneering wildlife psychologist. *APS Observer,* 34–35.

Garcia, J., & Koelling, R. A. (1966). Relation of cue to consequence in avoidance learning. *Psychonomic Science, 4,* 23–124.

Garcia-Sierra, A., Rivera-Gaxiola, M., Percaccio, C. R., et al. (2011). Bilingual language learning: An ERP study relating early brain responses to speech, language input, and later word production. *Journal of Phonetics, 39,* 546–557.

Gardner, R. A., & Gardner, B. T. (1969). Teaching sign language to a chimpanzee. *Science, 165,* 664–672.

Garmezy, N. (1991). Resilience and vulnerability to adverse developmental outcomes associated with poverty. *American Behavioral Scientist, 34,* 416–430.

Garry, M., Manning, C. G., Loftus, E. F., & Sherman, S. J. (1996). Imagination inflation: Imagining a childhood event inflates confidence that it occurred. *Psychonomic Bulletin & Review, 3,* 208–214.

Garry, M., & Polaschek, D. L. L. (2000). Imagination and memory. *Current Directions in Psychological Science, 9,* 6–10.

Garven, S., Wood, J. M., Malpass, R. S., & Shaw, J. S., III. (1998). More than suggestion: The effect of interviewing techniques from the McMartin Preschool case. *Journal of Applied Psychology, 83,* 347–359.

Gatz, M. (2007). Genetics, dementia, and the elderly. *Current Directions in Psychological Science, 16,* 123–127.

Gauthier, I., Skudlarksi, P., Gore, J. C., & Anderson, A. W. (2000). Expertise for cars and birds recruits brain areas involved in face recognition. *Nature Neuroscience, 3,* 191–197.

Gauthier, I., Tarr, M. J., Anderson, A. W., et al. (1999). Activation of the middle fusiform "face area" increases with expertise in recognizing novel objects. *Nature Neuroscience, 2,* 568–573.

Gawande, A. (2009, March 30). Hellhole. *The New Yorker,* 36–45.

Gazzaniga, M. S. (1967). The split brain in man. *Scientific American, 217*(2), 24–29.

Gazzaniga, M. S. (1988a). *Mind matters.* Boston, MA: Houghton-Mifflin.

Gazzaniga, M. S. (1998b). *The mind's past.* Berkeley: University of California Press.

Gazzaniga, M. S. (2005). *The ethical brain.* Washington, DC: Dana Press.

Gazzaniga, M. S. (2008). *Human: The science behind what makes us unique.* New York, NY: Ecco/Harper Collins.

Geary, D. C., & Huffman, K. J. (2002). Brain and cognitive evolution: Forms of modularity and the functions of mind. *Psychological Bulletin, 128,* 667–698.

Geers, A. L., Wellman, J. A., & Lassiter, G. D. (2009). Dispositional optimism and engagement: The moderating influence of goal prioritization. *Journal of Personality and Social Psychology, 96,* 913–932.

Gelbard-Sagiv, H., Mukamel, R., Harel, M., et al. (2008, October 3). Internally generated reactivation of single neurons in human hippocampus during free recall. *Science, 322,* 96–101.

Gentile, B., Grabe, S., Dolan-Pascoe, B., et al. (2009). Gender differences in domain-specific self-esteem: A meta-analysis. *Review of General Psychology, 13,* 34–45.

Gentner, D., & Goldin-Meadow, S. (Eds.). (2003). *Language in mind: Advances in the study of language and thought.* Cambridge, MA: MIT Press.

Gerken, L. A., Wilson, R., & Lewis, W. (2005). Infants can use distributional cues to form syntactic categories. *Journal of Child Language, 32,* 249–268.

Gershoff, E. T. (2002). Parental corporal punishment and associated child behaviors and experiences: A meta-analytic and theoretical review. *Psychological Bulletin, 128,* 539–579.

Gibbs, R. B. (2010). Estrogen therapy and cognition: A review of the cholinergic hypothesis. *Endocrine Review, 31,* 224–253.

Gibson, E., & Walk, R. (1960). The "visual cliff." *Scientific American, 202,* 80–92.

Giesbrecht, T., Lynn, S. J., Lilienfeld, S. O., & Merckelbach, H. (2008). Cognitive processes in dissociation: An analysis of core theoretical assumptions. *Psychological Bulletin, 134,* 617–647.

Gigerenzer, G., Gaissmaier, W., Kurz-Milcke, E., et al. (2008). Helping doctors and patients make sense of health statistics. *Psychological Science in the Public Interest, 8,* 53–96.

Gilbert, D. (2006a). *Stumbling on happiness.* New York, NY: Knopf.

Gilbert, D. (2006b, July 2). If only gay sex caused global warming. *Los Angeles Times,* Comment section, M1, M6.

Gilchrist, A. L., & Cowan, N. (2012). Chunking. In V. Ramachandran (Ed.), *Encyclopedia of human behavior* (Vol. 1). San Diego: Academic Press.

Gilestro, G. F., Tononi, G., & Cirelli, C. (2009). Widespread changes in synaptic markers as a function of sleep and wakefulness in *Drosophila. Science, 324,* 109–112.

Gillath, O., Shaver, P. R., Baek, J. M., & Chun, D. S. (2008). Genetic correlates of adult attachment style. *Personality and Social Psychology Bulletin, 34,* 1396–1405.

Gilmore, D. D. (1990). *Manhood in the making: Cultural concepts of masculinity.* New Haven, CT: Yale University Press.

Ginsberg, J., Mohebbi, M. H., Patel, R. S., et al. (2008). Detecting influenza epidemics using search engine query data. *Nature, 457,* 1012–1014.

Ginty, A. T., & Conklin, S. M. (2012). Preliminary evidence that acute long-chain omega-3 supplementation reduces cardiovascular reactivity to mental stress: A randomized and placebo controlled trial. *Biological Psychology, 89,* 269–272.

Gist, R., Lubin, B., & Redburn, B. G. (1998). Psychosocial, ecological, and community perspectives on disaster response. *Journal of Personal and Interpersonal Loss, 3,* 25–51.

Gitler, A. D. (2011, November 4). Another reason to exercise. *Science, 334,* 606–607.

Gittelsohn, J., Harris, S. B., Thorne-Lyman, A. L., et al. (1996). Body image concepts differ by age and sex in an Ojibway–Cree community in Canada. *Journal of Nutrition, 126,* 2990–3000.

Gladwell, M. (2004, September 20). Personality plus. *The New Yorker,* 42–48.

Glick, P. (2006). Ambivalent sexism, power distance, and gender inequality across cultures. In S. Guimond (Ed.), *Social comparison and social psychology: Understanding cognition, intergroup relations, and culture.* New York, NY: Cambridge University Press.

Glick, P., Fiske, S. T., Mladinic, A., et al. (2000). Beyond prejudice as simple antipathy: Hostile and benevolent sexism across cultures. *Journal of Personality and Social Psychology, 79,* 763–775.

Glick, P., Lameiras, M., Fiske, S. T., et al. (2004). Bad but bold: Ambivalent attitudes toward men predict gender inequality in 16 nations. *Journal of Personality and Social Psychology, 86,* 713–728.

Golden, R. M., Gaynes, B. N., Ekstrom, R. D., et al. (2005). The efficacy of light therapy in the treatment of mood disorders: A review and meta-analysis of the evidence. *American Journal of Psychiatry, 162,* 656–662.

Golder, S. A., & Macy, M. W. (2011). Diurnal and seasonal mood vary with work, sleep, and daylength across diverse cultures. *Science, 333,* 1878–1881.

Goldin-Meadow, S. (2003). *The resilience of language.* New York, NY: Psychology Press.

Goldin-Meadow, S., Cook, S. W., & Mitchell, Z. A. (2009). Gesturing gives children new ideas about math. *Psychological Science, 20,* 267–272.

Goldman-Rakic, P. S. (1996). *Opening the mind through neurobiology.* Invited address at the annual meeting of the American Psychological Association, Toronto, Canada.

Goldstein, A. J., de Beurs, E., Chambless, D. L., & Wilson, K. A. (2000). EMDR for panic disorder with agoraphobia: Comparison with waiting list and credible attention-placebo control conditions. *Journal of Consulting and Clinical Psychology, 68,* 947–956.

Goldstein, E. G. (2002). *Object relations theory and self psychology in social work practice.* New York, NY: Free Press.

Goldstein, J. M., Seidman, L. J., Horton, N. J., et al. (2001). Normal sexual dimorphism of the adult human brain assessed by in vivo magnetic resonance imaging. *Cerebral Cortex, 11,* 490–497.

Goldstein, M., & Miklowitz, D. (1995). The effectiveness of psychoeducational family therapy in the treatment of schizophrenic disorders. *Journal of Marital and Family Therapy, 21,* 361–376.

Goldstein, N. J., Cialdini, R. B., & Griskevicius, V. (2008). A room with a viewpoint: Using social norms to motivate environmental conservation in hotels. *Journal of Consumer Research, 35,* 472–482.

Goldston, D. B., Molock, S. D., Whitbeck, L. B., et al. (2008). Cultural considerations in adolescent suicide prevention and psychosocial treatment. *American Psychologist, 63,* 14–31.

Goldstone, R. L., Roberts, M. E., & Gureckis, T. M. (2008). Emergent processes in group behavior. *Current Directions in Psychological Science, 17,* 10–15.

Golinkoff, R. M., & Hirsh-Pasek, K. (2006). Baby wordsmith: From associationist to social sophisticate. *Current Directions in Psychological Science, 15,* 30–33.

Gonsalves, B. D., & Cohen, N. J. (2010). Brain imaging, cognitive processes, and brain networks. *Perspectives on Psychological Science, 5,* 744–752.

Gonzaga, G. C., Turner, R. A., Keltner, D., et al. (2006). Romantic love and sexual desire in close relationships. *Emotion, 6,* 163–179.

Good, C., Aronson, J., & Harder, J. A. (2008). Problems in the pipeline: Stereotype threat and women's achievement in high-level math courses. *Journal of Applied Developmental Psychology, 29,* 17–28.

Goodwyn, S., & Acredolo, L. (1998). Encouraging symbolic gestures: A new perspective on the relationship between gesture and speech. In J. Iverson & S. Goldin-Meadow (Eds.), *The nature and functions of gesture in children's communication.* San Francisco, CA: Jossey-Bass.

Gopnik, A. (2009). *The philosophical baby.* New York, NY: Farrar, Straus and Giroux.

Gopnik, M., Choi, S., & Baumberger, T. (1996). Cross-linguistic differences in early semantic and cognitive development. *Cognitive Development, 11,* 197–227.

Gorn, G. J. (1982). The effects of music in advertising on choice behavior: A classical conditioning approach. *Journal of Marketing, 46,* 94–101.

Gosling, S. D., & John, O. P. (1999). Personality dimensions in nonhuman animals: A cross-species review. *Current Directions in Psychological Science, 8,* 69–75.

Gosling, S. D., Kwan, V. S. Y., & John, O. P. (2003). A dog's got personality: A cross-species comparative approach to personality judgments in dogs and humans. *Journal of Personality and Social Psychology, 85,* 1161–1169.

Gospic, K., Mohlin, E., Fransson, P., Petrovic, P., Johannesson, M., & Ingvar, M. (2011). Limbic justice—Amygdala involvement in immediate rejection in the ultimatum game. *PLoS Biology, 9*(5): e1001054. doi:10.1371/journal. pbio.1001054.

Gottfredson, L. S. (2002). g: Highly general and highly practical. In R. J. Sternberg & E. L. Grigorenko (Eds.), *The general intelligence factor: How general is it?* Mahwah, NJ: Erlbaum.

Gougoux, F., Zatorre, R. J., Lassonde, M., et al. (2005). A functional neuroimaging study of sound localization: Visual cortex activity predicts performance in early-blind individuals. *PLoS Biology, 3,* 324–333.

Gouin, J. P., Kiecolt-Glaser, J. K., Malarkey, W. B., & Glaser, R. (2008). The influence of anger expression on wound healing. *Brain, Behavior, and Immunity, 22,* 699–708.

Gould, S. J. (1985, June). The median isn't the message. *Discover, 6,* 40–42.

Gould, S. J. (1994, November 28). Curveball. [Review of *The Bell Curve,* by Richard J. Herrnstein and Charles Murray.] *The New Yorker,* 139–149.

Gould, S. J. (1996). *The mismeasure of man* (Rev. ed.). New York, NY: Norton.

Gourevitch, P. (2009, May 4). The life after. *The New Yorker,* 36–49.

Grabe, S., & Hyde, J. S. (2006). Ethnicity and body dissatisfaction among women in the United States: A meta-analysis. *Psychological Bulletin, 132,* 622–640.

Grabe, S., Ward, L. M., & Hyde, J. S. (2008). The role of the media in body image concerns among women: A meta-analysis of experimental and correlational studies. *Psychological Bulletin, 134,* 460–476.

Graeber, M. B., & Streit, W. J. (2010). Microglia: Biology and pathology. *Acta Neuropathologica, 119,* 89–105.

Graff, K., Murnen, S. K., & Smolak, L. (2012, March 12). Too sexualized to be taken seriously? Perceptions of a girl in childlike vs. sexualizing clothing. *Sex Roles, OnLine First.* doi:10.1007/s11199-012-0145-3.

Graham, J., Haidt, J., & Nosek, B. A. (2009). Liberals and conservatives rely on different sets of moral foundations. *Journal of Personality and Social Psychology, 96,* 1029–1046.

Graham, J. W. (1986). Principled organizational dissent: A theoretical essay. *Research in Organizational Behavior, 8,* 1–52.

Grahe, J. E., & Bernieri, F. J. (1999). The importance of nonverbal cues in judging rapport. *Journal of Nonverbal Behavior, 23,* 253–269.

Grant, H., & Dweck, C. S. (2003). Clarifying achievement goals and their impact. *Journal of Personality and Social Psychology, 85,* 541–553.

Gray, K., & Wegner, D. M. (2008). The sting of intentional pain. *Psychological Science, 19,* 1260–1261.

Greely, H., Sahakian, B., Harris, J., et al. (2008). Towards responsible use of cognitive-enhancing drugs by the healthy. *Nature, 455,* 702–705. doi:10.1038/456702a

Greely, H. T., & Illes, J. (2007). Neuroscience-based lie detection: The urgent need for regulation. *American Journal of Law & Medicine, 35.*

Green, D., Kochukhova, O., & Gredebäck, G. (2014). Extrapolation and direct matching mediate anticipation in infancy. *Infant Behavior & Development, 37,* 111–118.

Green, G. (1996a). Behavioral treatment of autistic persons: A review of research from 1980 to the present. *Research in Developmental Disabilities, 17,* 433–465.

Green, G. (1996b). Early behavioral intervention for autism: What does research tell us? In C. Maurice, G. Green, & S. C. Luce (Eds.), *Behavioral intervention for young children with autism.* Austin, TX: PRO-ED.

Green, J. P., & Lynn, S. J. (2010). Hypnotic responsiveness: Expectancy, attitudes, fantasy proneness, absorption, and gender. *Clinical and Experimental Hypnosis, 59,* 103–121.

Green, K. L., Cameron, R., Polivy, J., et al. (1997). Weight dissatisfaction and weight loss attempts among Canadian adults. Canadian Heart Health Survey Research Group. *Canadian Medical Association Journal, 157*(Suppl. 1), S17–S25.

Greenberg, J., Solomon, S., & Arndt, J. (2008). A basic but uniquely human motivation: Terror management. In J. Shah & W. Gardner (Eds.), *Handbook of motivation science.* New York, NY: Guilford Press.

Greenberger, D., & Padesky, C. A. (1995). *Mind over mood: A cognitive therapy treatment manual for clients.* New York, NY: Guilford.

Greenberger, E., Lessard, J., Chen, C., & Farruggia, S. P. (2008). Self-entitled college students: Contributions of personality, parenting, and motivational factors. *Journal of Youth & Adolescence, 37,* 1193–1204.

Greenglass, E. R. (2002). Proactive coping and quality of life management. In E. Frydenberg (Ed.), *Beyond coping: Meeting goals, visions, and challenges.* London: Oxford University Press.

Greenglass, E. R., & Fiksenbaum, L. (2009). Proactive coping, positive affect, and well-being: Testing for mediation using path analysis. *European Psychologist, 14,* 29–39.

Greenough, W. T. (1984). Structural correlates of information storage in the mammalian brain: A review and hypothesis. *Trends in Neurosciences, 7,* 229–233.

Greenough, W. T., & Anderson, B. J. (1991). Cerebellar synaptic plasticity: Relation to learning vs. neural activity. *Annals of the New York Academy of Sciences, 627,* 231–247.

Greenough, W. T., & Black, J. E. (1992). Induction of brain structure by experience: Substrates for cognitive development. In M. Gunnar & C. A. Nelson (Eds.), *Behavioral developmental neuroscience: Vol. 24. Minnesota Symposia on Child Psychology.* Hillsdale, NJ: Erlbaum.

Greenwald, A. G., McGhee, D. E., & Schwartz, J. L. K. (1998). Measuring individual differences in implicit cognition: The Implicit Association Test. *Journal of Personality and Social Psychology, 74,* 1464–1480.

Greenwald, A. G., Poehlman, T. A., Uhlmann, E. L., & Banaji, M. R. (2009). Understanding and using the Implicit Association Test: III. Meta-analysis of predictive validity. *Journal of Personality and Social Psychology, 97,* 17–41.

Greenwald, A. G., Spangenberg, E. R., Pratkanis, A. R., & Eskenazi, J. (1991). Double-blind tests of subliminal self-help audiotapes. *Psychological Science, 2,* 119–122.

Gregg, L., & Tarrier, N. (2007). Virtual reality in mental health: A review of the literature. *Social Psychiatry and Psychiatric Epidemiology, 42,* 343–54.

Gregory, R. L. (1963). Distortion of visual space as inappropriate constancy scaling. *Nature, 199,* 678–679.

Griffin, D. R. (2001). *Animal minds: Beyond cognition to consciousness.* Chicago, IL: University of Chicago Press.

Grimshaw, G. M., Kwasny, K. M., Covell, E., & Johnson, R. A. (2003). The dynamic nature of language lateralization: Effects of lexical and prosodic factors. *Neuropsychologia, 41,* 1008–1019.

Grinspoon, L., & Bakalar, J. B. (1993). *Marihuana, the forbidden medicine.* New Haven, CT: Yale University Press.

Groneman, C. (2000). *Nymphomania: A history.* New York, NY: Norton.

Gross, J. J. (1998). The emerging field of emotion regulation: An integrative review. *Review of General Psychology, 2,* 271–299.

Gross, J. J., & John, O. P. (2003). Individual differences in two emotion regulation processes: Implications for affect, relationships, and well-being. *Journal of Personality and Social Psychology, 85,* 348–362.

Grossman, M., & Wood, W. (1993). Sex differences in intensity of emotional experience: A social role interpretation. *Journal of Personality and Social Psychology, 65,* 1010–1022.

Guilford, J. P. (1988). Some changes in the structure-of-intellect model. *Educational and Psychological Measurement, 48,* 1–4.

Gunnar, M. R., van Dulmen, M. H., & International Adoption Project Team. (2007). Behaviour problems in postinstitutionalized internationally adopted children. *Developmental Psychopathology, 19,* 129–148.

Gur, R. C., Gunning-Dixon, F., Bilker, W. B., & Gur, R. E. (2002). Sex differences in temporo-limbic and frontal brain volumes of healthy adults. *Cerebral Cortex, 12,* 998–1003.

Guralnick, M. J (Ed.). (1997). *The effectiveness of early intervention.* Baltimore, MD: Brookes.

Gustavson, C. R., Garcia, J., Hankins, W. G., & Rusiniak, K. W. (1974). Coyote predation control by aversive conditioning. *Science, 184,* 581–583.

Guttentag, M., & Secord, P. (1983). *Too many women?* Beverly Hills, CA: Sage.

Guzman-Marin, R., Suntsova, N., Methippara, M., et al. (2005). Sleep deprivation suppresses neurogenesis in the adult hippocampus of rats. *European Journal of Neuroscience, 22,* 2111–2116.

Habbick, B. F., Nanson, J. L., Snyder, R. E., et al. (1996). Foetal alcohol syndrome in Saskatchewan: Unchanged incidence in a 20-year period. *Canadian Journal of Public Health, 87*(3), 204–207.

Haber, R. N. (1970, May). How we remember what we see. *Scientific American, 222,* 104–112.

Hafer, C. L. (2000a). Do innocent victims threaten the belief in a just world? Evidence from a modified Stroop task. *Journal of Personality and Social Psychology, 79*(2), 165–173.

Hafer, C. L. (2000b). Investment in long-term goals and commitment to just means drive the need to believe in a just world. *Personality and Social Psychology Bulletin, 26,* 1059–1073.

Hafer, C. L., & Bègue, L. (2005). Experimental research on just-world theory: Problems, developments and future challenges. *Psychological Bulletin, 131*(1), 128–167.

Haga, S. M., Kraft, P., & Corby, E. K. (2009). Emotion regulation: Antecedents and well-being outcomes of cognitive reappraisal and expressive suppression in cross-cultural samples. *Journal of Happiness Studies, 10,* 271–291.

Hagberg, B., & Samuelsson, G. (2008). Survival after 100 years of age: A multivariate model of exceptional survival in Swedish centenarians. *Journals of Gerontology: Series A (Biological Sciences and Medical Sciences), 63,* 1219–1226.

Hahn, R., Fuqua-Whitley, D., Wethington, H., et al. (2008). Effectiveness of universal school-based programs to prevent violent and aggressive behaviour: A systematic review. *Child: Care, Health, & Development, 34,* 139.

Haidt, J. (2012). *The righteous mind: Why good people are divided by politics and religion.* New York: Pantheon Books.

Haimov, I., & Lavie, P. (1996). Melatonin—A soporific hormone. *Current Directions in Psychological Science, 5,* 106–111.

Hall, C. (1953). A cognitive theory of dreams. *Journal of General Psychology, 49,* 273–282.

Hall, E. T. (1959). *The silent language.* Garden City, NY: Doubleday.

Hall, E. T. (1976). *Beyond culture.* New York, NY: Anchor.

Hall, E. T. (1983). *The dance of life: The other dimension of time.* Garden City, NY: Anchor Press/Doubleday.

Hall, E. T., & Hall, M. R. (1987). *Hidden differences: Doing business with the Japanese.* Garden City, NY: Anchor Press/Doubleday.

Hall, E. T., & Hall, M. R. (1990). *Understanding cultural differences.* Yarmouth, ME: Intercultural Press.

Hall, G. S. (1899). A study of anger. *American Journal of Psychology, 10,* 516–591.

Hall, N. C., Perry, R. P., Ruthig, J. C., et al. (2006). Primary and secondary control in achievement settings: A longitudinal field study of academic motivation, emotions, and performance. *Journal of Applied Social Psychology, 36,* 1430–1470.

Halliday, G. (1993). Examination dreams. *Perceptual and Motor Skills, 77,* 489–490.

Halpern, D. (2002). *Thought and knowledge: An introduction to critical thinking* (4th ed.). Hillsdale, NJ: Erlbaum.

Halpern, D. F. (2008). Psychologists are redefining retirement as a new phase of life. *The General Psychologist, 43,* 22–29.

Halpern, S. (2008, May 19). Virtual Iraq. *The New Yorker,* 32–37.

Hamby, S. L., & Koss, M. P. (2003). Shades of gray: A qualitative study of terms used in the measurement of sexual victimization. *Psychology of Women Quarterly, 27,* 243–255.

Hampshire, A., Highfield, R. R., Parkin, B. L., & Owen, A. M. (2012). Fractionating human intelligence. *Neuron, 76,* 1225–1237.

Haney, C., Banks, C., & Zimbardo, P. (1973). Interpersonal dynamics in a simulated prison. *International Journal of Criminology and Penology, 1,* 69–97.

Haney, C., & Zimbardo, P. (1998). The past and future of U.S. prison policy: Twenty-five years after the Stanford Prison Experiment. *American Psychologist, 53,* 709–727.

Hare, B., Brown, M., Williamson, C., & Tomasello, M. (2002). The domestication of social cognition in dogs. *Science, 298,* 1634–1636.

Hare, W. (2009, March/April). What open-mindedness requires. *Skeptical Inquirer, 33,* 36–39.

Hare-Mustin, R. T. (1991). Sex, lies, and headaches: The problem is power. In T. J. Goodrich (Ed.), *Women and power: Perspectives for therapy.* New York, NY: Norton.

Hare-Mustin, R. T., & Marecek, J. (1990). Gender and the meaning of difference: Postmodernism and psychology. In R. Hare-Mustin & J. Maracek (Eds.), *Psychology and the construction of gender.* New Haven, CT: Yale University Press.

Haritos-Fatouros, M. (1988). The official torturer: A learning model for obedience to the authority of violence. *Journal of Applied Social Psychology, 18,* 1107–1120.

Harlow, H. F. (1958). The nature of love. *American Psychologist, 13,* 673–685.

Harlow, H. F., & Harlow, M. K. (1966). Learning to love. *American Scientist, 54,* 244–272.

Harlow, H. F., Harlow, M. K., & Meyer, D. R. (1950). Learning motivated by a manipulation drive. *Journal of Experimental Psychology, 40,* 228–234.

Harmon-Jones, E., Peterson, C. K., & Harris, C. R. (2009). Jealousy: Novel methods and neural correlates. *Emotion, 9,* 113–117.

Harnsberger, J. D., Hollien, H., Martin Camilo, A., & Hollien, K. A. (2009). Stress and deception in speech: Evaluating Layered Voice Analysis. *Journal of Forensic Sciences, 54,* 642–650.

Harris, C. (2003). Factors associated with jealousy over real and imagined infidelity: An examination of the social-cognitive and evolutionary psychology perspectives. *Psychology of Women Quarterly, 27,* 319–329.

Harris, G. (2003, August 7). Debate resumes on the safety of depression's wonder drugs. *The New York Times,* A1, C4.

Harris, J. R. (2006). *No two alike: Human nature and human individuality.* New York, NY: Norton.

Harris, J. R. (2009). *The nurture assumption* (2nd ed.). New York, NY: Free Press.

Harris, L. T., & Fiske, S. T. (2006). Dehumanizing the lowest of the low: Neuroimaging responses to extreme outgroups. *Psychological Science, 17*(10), 847–853.

Harris, S. B., Gittelson, J., Hanley, A., et al. (1997). The prevalence of NDDM and associated risk factors in native Canadians. *Diabetes Care, 20,* 185–187.

Hart, A. J., Whalen, P. J., Shin, L. M., et al. (2000). Differential response in the human amygdala to racial outgroup vs. ingroup face stimuli. *NeuroReport, 11,* 2351–2355.

Hart, J., Jr., Berndt, R. S., & Caramazza, A. (1985, August 1). Category-specific naming deficit following cerebral infarction. *Nature, 316,* 339–340.

Hart, K. E., & Sasso, T. (2011). Mapping the contours of contemporary positive psychology. *Canadian Psychology, 52,* 82–92.

Haslam, S. A., Jetten, J., Postmes, T., & Haslam, C. (2009). Social identity, health and well-being: An emerging agenda for applied psychology. *Applied Psychology: An International Review, 58,* 1–23.

Haslam, S. A., & Reicher, S. (2003, Spring). Beyond Stanford: Questioning a role-based explanation of tyranny. *Society for Experimental Social Psychology Dialogue, 18,* 22–25.

Hassabis, D., & Maguire, E. A. (2007). Deconstructing episodic memory with construction. *Trends in Cognitive Sciences, 11,* 299–306.

Hassett, J. M., Siebert, E. R., Wallen, K. (2008). Sex differences in rhesus monkey toy preferences parallel those of children. *Hormones and Behavior, 54,* 359–364.

Hatfield, E., & Rapson, R. L. (1996/2005). *Love and sex: Cross-cultural perspectives.* Boston, MA: University Press of America.

Hatfield, E., & Rapson, R. L. (2008). Passionate love and sexual desire: Multidisciplinary perspectives. In J. P. Forgas & J. Fitness (Eds.), *Social relationships: Cognitive, affective, and motivational processes.* New York, NY: Psychology Press.

Haut, J. S., Beckwith, B. E., Petros, T. V., & Russell, S. (1989). Gender differences in retrieval from long-term memory following acute intoxication with ethanol. *Physiology and Behavior, 45,* 1161–1165.

Havas, D. A., Glenberg, A. M., Gutowski, K. A., et al. (2010). Cosmetic use of botulinum toxin-A affects processing of emotional language. *Psychological Science, 21,* 895–900.

Havas, D. A., & Matheson, J. (2013). The functional role of the periphery in emotional language comprehension. *Frontiers in Psychology,* 27 May 2013, doi:10.3389/fpsyg.2013.00294

Hawkins, E. H., Cummins, L. H., & Marlatt, G. A. (2004). Preventing substance abuse in American Indian and Alaska Native Youth: Promising strategies for healthier communities. *Psychological Bulletin, 130,* 304–323.

Hawkins, S. A., & Hastie, R. (1990). Hindsight: Biased judgments of past events after the outcomes are known. *Psychological Bulletin, 107,* 311–327.

Hayes, S. C. (2004). Acceptance and commitment therapy and the new behavior therapies: Mindfulness, acceptance, and relationship. In S. C. Hayes, V. M. Follette, & M. M. Linehan (Eds.), *Mindfulness and acceptance: Expanding the cognitive-behavioral tradition.* New York, NY: Guilford.

Hayes, S. C., Follette, V. M., & Linehan, M. M. (Eds.). (2004). *Mindfulness and acceptance: Expanding the cognitive-behavioral tradition.* New York, NY: The Guilford Press.

Hayman, R. (2001). *A life of Jung.* New York, NY: W. W. Norton.

Hazan, C., & Diamond, L. M. (2000). The place of attachment in human mating. *Review of General Psychology, 4,* 186–204.

Hazan, C., & Shaver, P. R. (1994). Attachment as an organizational framework for research on close relationships. *Psychological Inquiry, 5,* 1–22.

He, F., & Sun, Y. E. (2007). Glial cells more than support cells? *The International Journal of Biochemistry and Cell Biology, 39,* 661–665.

Head, J., Neumann, E., Helton, W. S., & Shears, C. (2013). Novel Word Processing. *The American Journal of Psychology, 126,* 323–333.

Health Canada. (2004). *Canadian Addictions Survey (CAS): A national survey of Canadians' use of alcohol and other drugs: prevalence of use and related harms: highlights.* Ottawa.

Health Canada. (2008). *Reach for the top: A report by the advisor on healthy children & youth.* Retrieved April 1, 2008, from http://www.hc-sc.gc.ca/hl-vs/pubs/child-enfant/advisor-conseillere/appendices_e.html

Health Canada. (2009). *Childhood immunization.* Retrieved July 10, 2010, from http://www.hc-sc.gc.ca/hl-vs/iyh-vsv/med/immuniz-eng.php

Healy, D. (2002). *The creation of psychopharmacology.* Cambridge, MA: Harvard University Press.

Healy, D. (2012). *Pharmageddon.* Berkeley, CA: University of California Press.

Hebb, D. O. (1949). *The organization of behavior.* New York, NY: Wiley-Interscience.

Hébert, R. (September, 2001). Code overload: Doing a number on memory. *APS Observer, 14,* 1, 7–11.

Hedden, T., Ketay, S., Aron, A., et al. (2008). Cultural influences on neural substrates of attentional control. *Psychological Science, 19,* 12–17.

Hein, G., Silani, G., Preuschoff, K., et al. (2010). Neural responses to ingroup and outgroup members' suffering predict individual differences in costly helping. *Neuron, 68,* 149–160.

Heine, S. J., & Lehman, D. R. (1997). The cultural construction of self-enhancement: An examination of group-serving biases. *Journal of Personality and Social Psychology, 72*(6), 1268–1283.

Helmreich, W. (1992). *Against all odds: Holocaust survivors and the successful lives they led.* New York, NY: Simon & Schuster.

Helson, R., Roberts, B., & Agronick, G. (1995). Enduringness and change in creative personality and the prediction of occupational creativity. *Journal of Personality and Social Psychology, 6,* 1173–1183.

Helzer, J. E., Wittchen, H. U., Krueger, R. F., & Kraemer, H. C. (2008). Dimensional options for *DSM-V*: The way forward. In J. E. Helzer, H. C. Kramer, & R. F. Krueger (Eds.), *Dimensional approaches in diagnostic classification: Refining the research agenda for* DSM-V. Washington, DC: American Psychiatric Association.

Henderlong, J., & Lepper, M. (2002). The effects of praise on children's intrinsic motivation: A review and synthesis. *Psychological Bulletin, 128,* 774–795.

Henggeler, S. W., Schoenwald, S. K., Borduin, C. M., et al. (1998). *Multisystemic treatment of antisocial behavior in children and adolescents.* New York, NY: Guilford Press.

Henrich, J., Boyd, R., Bowles, S., Camerer, C., Fehr, E., Gintis, H., & McElreath, R. (2001). In Search of Homo Economicus: Behavioral Experiments in 15 Small-Scale Societies. *The American Economic Review, 91,* 73–78.

Henrich, J., Heine, Steven, J., & Norenzayan, A. (2010, June 15). The weirdest people in the world? *Behavioral and Brain Sciences, 33,* 61–83.

Herbert, A., Gerry, N. P., McQueen, M. B., et al. (2006, April 14). A common genetic variant is associated with adult and childhood obesity. *Science, 312,* 279–283.

Herculano-Houzel, S. (2009). The human brain in numbers: A linearly scaled-up primate brain. *Frontiers of Human Neuroscience, 3,* 31.

Herdt, G. (1984). *Ritualized homosexuality in Melanesia.* Berkeley: University of California Press.

Herek, G. M., & Capitanio, J. P. (1996). "Some of my best friends": Intergroup contact, concealable stigma, and heterosexuals' attitudes toward gay men and lesbians. *Personality and Social Psychology Bulletin, 22,* 412–424.

Herman, J. (1992). *Trauma and recovery.* New York, NY: Basic Books.

Herman, J. H. (1992). Transmutative and reproductive properties of dreams: Evidence for cortical modulation of brainstem generators. In J. Antrobus & M. Bertini (Eds.), *The neuropsychology of dreaming.* Hillsdale, NJ: Erlbaum.

Herman, L. M., Kuczaj, S. A., & Holder, M. D. (1993). Responses to anomalous gestural sequences by a language-trained dolphin: Evidence for processing of semantic relations and syntactic information. *Journal of Experimental Psychology: General, 122,* 184–194.

Herman, L. M., & Morrel-Samuels, P. (1996). Knowledge acquisition and asymmetry between language comprehension and production: Dolphins and apes as general models for animals. In M. Bekoff & D. Jamieson et al. (Eds.), *Readings in animal cognition.* Cambridge, MA: MIT Press.

Heron, W. (1957). The pathology of boredom. *Scientific American, 196*(1), 52–56.

Herrnstein, R. J., & Murray, C. (1994). *The bell curve: Intelligence and class structure in American life.* New York, NY: Free Press.

Hertzog, C., Kramer, A. F., Wilson, R. S., & Lindenberger, U. (2008). Enrichment effects on adult cognitive development: Can the functional capacity of older adults be preserved and enhanced? *Psychological Science in the Public Interest, 9,* 1–65.

Herz, R. S., & Cupchik, G. C. (1995). The emotional distinctiveness of odor-evoked memories. *Chemical Senses, 20,* 517–528.

Herzog, H. (2011). The impact of pets on human health and psychological well-being: Fact, fiction, or hypothesis?" *Current Directions in Psychological Science, 20,* 236–239.

Hess, T. M. (2005). Memory and aging in context. *Psychological Bulletin, 131,* 383–406.

Hess, U., Adams, R. B., Jr., & Kleck, R. (2005). Who may frown and who should smile? Dominance, affiliation, and the display of happiness and anger. *Cognition and Emotion, 19,* 515–536.

Hess, U., & Thibault, P. (2009). Darwin and emotional expression. *American Psychologist, 64,* 120–128.

Hewlitt, S. A., Luce, C. B., & Servon, L. J. (2008, June). Stopping the exodus of women in science. *Harvard Business Review, 86*(6), 22–24, 139. Retrieved from http://hbr.org/2008/06/stopping-the-exodus-of-women-in-science/ar/1

Higgins, E. T. (1998). Promotion and prevention: Regulatory focus as a motivational principle. *Advances in Experimental Social Psychology, 30,* 1–46.

Hilgard, E. R. (1977). *Divided consciousness: Multiple controls in human thought and action.* New York, NY: Wiley-Interscience.

Hilgard, E. R. (1986). *Divided consciousness: Multiple controls in human thought and action* (2nd ed.). New York, NY: Wiley.

Hillman, J., & Ventura, M. (1992). *We've had a hundred years of psychotherapy—and the world's getting worse.* San Francisco, CA: HarperCollins.

Hilts, P. J. (1995). *Memory's ghost: The strange tale of Mr. M. and the nature of memory.* New York, NY: Simon & Schuster.

Hines, T. M. (1998). Comprehensive review of biorhythm theory. *Psychological Reports, 83,* 19–64.

Hirsch, H. V. B., & Spinelli, D. N. (1970). Visual experience modifies distribution of horizontally and vertically oriented receptive fields in cats. *Science, 168,* 869–871.

Hirsh, J. B., Galinsky, A. D., & Zhong, C.B. (2011). Drunk, powerful, and in the dark: How general processes of disinhibition produce both prosocial and antisocial behavior. *Perspectives on Psychological Science, 6,* 415–427.

Hirsch, J. B., & Inzlicht, M. (2008). The devil you know: Neuroticism predicts neural response to uncertainty. *Psychological Science, 19,* 962–967.

Hobson, J. A. (1988). *The dreaming brain.* New York, NY: Basic Books.

Hobson, J. A. (1990). Activation, input source, and modulation: A neurocognitive model of the state of the brain mind. In R. R. Bootzin, J. F. Kihlstrom, & D. L. Schacter (Eds.), *Sleep and cognition.* Washington, DC: American Psychological Association.

Hobson, J. A., Pace-Schott, E. F., & Stickgold, R. (2000). Dreaming and the brain: Toward a cognitive neuroscience of conscious states. *Behavioral and Brain Sciences, 23,* 793–842, 904–1018, 1083–1121.

Hobson, J. A., Sangsanguan, S., Arantes, H., & Kahn, D. (2011). Dream logic: The inferential reasoning paradigm. *Dreaming, 21,* 1–15.

Hochschild, A. R. (2003). *The managed heart: Commercialization of human feeling* (2nd ed.). Berkeley, CA: University of California Press.

Hodson, G. (2011). Do ideologically intolerant people benefit from intergroup contact? *Current Directions in Psychological Science, 20,* 154–159.

Hoekstra, H. E., Hirschmann, R. J., & Bundey, R. A., et al. (2006). A single amino acid mutation contributes to adaptive color pattern in beach mice. *Science 313,* 101–104.

Hoffmann, D. E., & Rothenberg, K. H. (2005). When should judges admit or compel genetic tests? *Science, 310,* 241–242.

Hoffrage, U., Hertwig, R., & Gigerenzer, G. (2000). Hindsight bias: A by-product of knowledge updating? *Journal of Experimental Psychology: Learning, Memory, & Cognition, 26,* 566–581.

Hofstede, G., & Bond, M. H. (1988). The Confucius connection: From cultural roots to economic growth. *Organizational Dynamics,* 5–21.

Holden, G. W., & Miller, P. C. (1999). Enduring and different: A meta-analysis of the similarity in parents' child rearing. *Psychological Bulletin, 125,* 223–254.

Holland, R. W., Hendriks, M., & Aarts, H. (2005). Smells like clean spirit: Nonconscious effects of scent on cognition and behavior. *Psychological Science, 16,* 689–693.

Hollon, S. D., Thase, M. E., & Markowitz, J. C. (2002). Treatment and prevention of depression. *Psychological Science in the Public Interest, 3,* 39–77.

Hood, B. (2009). *SuperSense: Why we believe in the unbelievable.* San Francisco, CA: HarperOne.

Hooker, E. (1957). The adjustment of the male overt homosexual. *Journal of Projective Techniques, 21,* 18–31.

Horgan, J. (1995, November). Get smart, take a test: A long-term rise in IQ scores baffles intelligence experts. *Scientific American, 273,* 12, 14.

Horn, J. L., & Cattell, R. B. (1966). Refinement and test of the theory of fluid and crystallized general intelligences. *Journal of Educational Psychology, 57,* 253–270.

Horney, K. (1973). The flight from womanhood. *The International Journal of Psycho-Analysis, 7,* 324–339. Reprinted in J. B. Miller (Ed.), *Psychoanalysis and women.* New York, NY: Brunner/Mazel.

Hornung, R. W., Lanphear, B. P., & Dietrich, K. N. (2009). Age of greatest susceptibility to childhood lead exposure: A new statistical approach. *Environmental Health Perspectives, 117,* 1309–1312.

Horrey, W. J., & Wickens, C. D. (2006). Examining the Impact of Cell Phone Conversations on Driving Using Meta-Analytic Techniques. *Human Factors: The Journal of Human Factors and Ergonomics Society, 48,* 196–205.

Houston, D. M., & Jusczyk, P. W. (2003). Infants' long-term memory for the sound patterns of words and voices. *Journal of Experimental Psychology: Human Perception & Performance, 29,* 1143–1154.

Houts, A. C. (2002). Discovery, invention, and the expansion of the modern Diagnostic and Statistical Manuals of Mental Disorders. In L. E. Beutler & M. L. Malik (Eds.), *Rethinking the DSM: A psychological perspective.* Washington, DC: American Psychological Association.

Howard, G. S. (1991). Culture tales: A narrative approach to thinking, cross-cultural psychology, and psychotherapy. *American Psychologist, 46,* 187–197.

Howe, M. L. (2000). *The fate of early memories: Developmental science and the retention of childhood experiences.* Washington, DC: American Psychological Association.

Howe, M. L., Courage, M. L., & Peterson, C. (1994). How can I remember when "I" wasn't there? Long-term retention of traumatic experiences and emergence of the cognitive self. *Consciousness and Cognition, 3,* 327–355.

Hrdy, S. B. (1988). Empathy, polyandry, and the myth of the coy female. In R. Bleier (Ed.), *Feminist approaches to science.* New York, NY: Pergamon.

Hrdy, S. B. (1994). What do women want? In T. A. Bass (Ed.), *Reinventing the future: Conversations with the world's leading scientists.* Reading, MA: Addison-Wesley.

Hrdy, S. B. (1999). *Mother nature.* New York, NY: Pantheon.

Hu, H., Real, E., Takamiya, K., et al. (2007). Emotion enhances learning via norepinephrine regulation of AMPA-receptor trafficking. *Cell, 131,* 160–173.

Hu, P., Stylos-Allan, M., & Walker, M. (2006). Sleep facilitates consolidation of emotional declarative memory. *Psychological Science, 17,* 891–898.

Huang, C. M., Polk, T. A., Goh, J. O., & Park, D. C. (2012). Both left and right posterior parietal activations contribute to compensatory processes in normal aging. *Neuropsychologia, 50,* 55–66.

Huang, L., Shanker, Y. G., Dubauskaite, J., et al. (1999). Ggamma13 colocalizes with gustducin in taste receptor cells and mediates IP3 responses to bitter denatonium. *Nature Neuroscience, 2,* 1055–1062.

Hubel, D. H., & Wiesel, T. N. (1962). Receptive fields, binocular interaction and functional architecture in the cat's visual cortex. *Journal of Physiology (London), 160,* 106–154.

Hubel, D. H., & Wiesel, T. N. (1968). Receptive fields and functional architecture of monkey striate cortex. *Journal of Physiology (London), 195,* 215–243.

Hudson, V. M., & den Boer, A. M. (2004). *Bare branches: The security implications of Asia's surplus male population.* Cambridge, MA: MIT Press.

Hugdahl, K., & Westerhausen, R. (2010). *The two halves of the brain: Information processing in the cerebral hemispheres.* New York: MIT Press.

Huggins, M. K., Haritos-Fatouros, M., & Zimbardo, P. G. (2003). *Violence workers: Police torturers and murderers reconstruct Brazilian atrocities.* Berkeley, CA: University of California Press.

Huntington's Disease Collaborative Research Group. (1993). A novel gene containing a trinucleotide repeat that is expanded and unstable on Huntington's disease chromosomes. *Cell, 72,* 971–983.

Huntjens, R. J. C., Verschuere, B., & McNally, R. J. (2012). Inter-identity autobiographical amnesia in patients with dissociative identity disorder. *PloS One, 7*(7): e40580.

Hupka, R. B. (1981). Cultural determinants of jealousy. *Alternative Lifestyles, 4,* 310–356.

Hupka, R. B. (1991). The motive for the arousal of romantic jealousy. In P. Salovey (Ed.), *The psychology of jealousy and envy*. New York, NY: Guilford Press.

Hupka, R. B., Lenton, A. P., & Hutchison, K. A. (1999). Universal development of emotion categories in natural language. *Journal of Personality and Social Psychology, 77*, 247–278.

Hur, Y. M., Bouchard, T. J., Jr., & Lykken, D. T. (1998). Genetic and environmental influence on morningness-eveningness. *Personality and Individual Differences, 25*, 917–925.

Huron, D. (1991). Review of *Auditory scene analysis: The perceptual organization of sound* by Albert S. Bregman. *Psychology of Music, 19*(1), 77–82.

Hyde, J. S. (2005). The gender similarities hypothesis. *American Psychologist, 60*, 581–592.

Hyde, J. S. (2007). New directions in the study of gender similarities and differences. *Current Directions in Psychological Science, 16*, 259–263.

Hyman, I. E., Jr., & Pentland, J. (1996). The role of mental imagery in the creation of false childhood memories. *Journal of Memory and Language, 35*, 101–117.

Iacoboni, M. (2008). *Mirroring people: The new science of how we connect with others.* New York, NY: Farrar, Straus and Giroux.

Iacoboni, M., Molnar-Szakacs, I., Gallese, V., et al. (2005). Grasping the intentions of others with one's own mirror neuron system. *Public Library of Science: Biology 3*(3): e79. doi:10.1371/journal.pbio.003079

Iacono, W. G., & Lykken, D. T. (1997). The scientific status of research on polygraph techniques: The case against polygraph tests. In D. L. Faigman, D. Kaye, M. J. Saks, & J. Sanders (eds.), *Modern scientific evidence: The law and science of expert testimony*. St. Paul, MN: West.

Ikonomidou, C., Bittigau, P., Ishimaru, M. J., et al. (2000, February 11). Ethanol-induced apoptotic neurodegeneration and fetal alcohol syndrome. *Science, 287*, 1056–1060.

Imada, T., & Ellsworth, P. C. (2011). Proud Americans and lucky Japanese: Cultural differences in appraisal and corresponding emotion. *Emotion, 11*, 329–345.

Impett, E. A., Gable, S., & Peplau, L. A. (2005). Giving up and giving in: The costs and benefits of daily sacrifice in intimate relationships. *Journal of Personality and Social Psychology, 89*, 327–344.

Impett, E. A., Henson, J. M., Breines, J. G., et al. (2011). Embodiment feels better: Girls' body objectification and well-being across adolescence. *Psychology of Women Quarterly, 35*, 46–58.

Impett, E. A., Peplau, L. A., & Gable, S. (2005). Approach and avoidance sexual motives: Implications for personal and interpersonal well-being. *Personal Relationships, 12*, 465–482.

Impett, E. A., & Tolman, D. L. (2006). Late adolescent girls' sexual experiences and sexual satisfaction. *Journal of Adolescent Research, 21*, 628–646.

Innocenti, G. M., & Price, D. J. (2005). Exuberance in the development of cortical networks. *Nature Reviews Neuroscience, 6*, 955–965.

International Consensus Conference. (2002, June). *Female androgen deficiency syndrome: Definition, diagnosis, and classification*. International Consensus Conference, Princeton, NY. Retrieved from http://www.medscape.com/viewprogram/302

Inzlicht, M., & Ben-Zeev, T. (2000). A threatening intellectual environment: Why females are susceptible to experiencing problem-solving deficits in the presence of males. *Psychological Science, 11*, 365–371.

Ishigami, Y., & Klein, R. M. (2009). Is a hands-free phone safer than a handheld phone? *Journal of Safety Research, 40*, 157–164.

Islam, M. R., & Hewstone, M. (1993). Intergroup attributions and affective consequences in majority and minority groups. *Journal of Personality and Social Psychology, 64*, 936–950.

Ito, T. A., & Urland, G. R. (2003). Race and gender on the brain: Electrocortical measures of attention to the race and gender of multiply categorizable individuals. *Journal of Personality and Social Psychology, 85*, 616–626.

Izard, C. E. (1990). Facial expressions and the regulation of emotions. *Journal of Personality and Social Psychology, 58*, 487–498.

Izard, C. E. (1994). Innate and universal facial expressions: Evidence from developmental and cross-cultural research. *Psychological Bulletin, 115*, 288–299.

Izard, C. E. (2007). Basic emotions, natural kinds, emotion schemas, and a new paradigm. *Perspectives on Psychological Science, 2*, 260–280.

Izard, V., Sann, C., Spelke, E. S., & Streri, A. (2009). Newborn infants perceive abstract numbers. *Proceedings of the National Academy of Sciences, 106*, 10382–10385.

Izumikawa, M., Minoda, R., Kawamoto, K. A., et al. (2005). Auditory hair cell replacement and hearing improvement by *Atoh1* gene therapy in deaf mammals. *Nature Medicine, 11*, 271–276.

Jackson, D. C., Mueller, C. J., Dolski, I., et al. (2003). Now you feel it, now you don't: Frontal brain electrical asymmetry and individual differences in emotion regulation. *Psychological Science, 14*, 612–617.

Jacobs, T. L., Epel, E. S., Lin, J., et al. (2011). Intensive meditation training, immune cell telomerase activity, and psychological mediators. *Psychoneuroendocrinology, 36*, 664–681.

Jacobsen, P. B., Bovbjerg, D. H., Schwartz, M. D., et al. (1995). Conditioned emotional distress in women receiving chemotherapy for breast cancer. *Journal of Consulting & Clinical Psychology, 63*, 108–114.

James, W. (1890/1950). *Principles of psychology* (Vol. 1). New York, NY: Dover.

James, W. (1902/1936). *The varieties of religious experience*. New York, NY: Modern Library.

Jamieson, S., & Marshall, W. L. (2000). Attachment styles and violence in child molesters. *Journal of Sexual Aggression, 5*(2): 88–98.

Jang, K. L., McCrae, R. R., Angleitner, A., et al. (1998). Heritability of facet-level traits in a cross-cultural twin sample: Support for a hierarchical model of personality. *Journal of Personality and Social Psychology, 74*, 1556–1565.

Janis, I. L. (1982). *Groupthink: Psychological studies of policy decisions and fiascos* (2nd ed.). Boston, MA: Houghton-Mifflin.

Janis, I. L. (1989). *Crucial decisions: Leadership in policymaking and crisis management*. New York, NY: Free Press.

Jenkins, J. G., & Dallenbach, K. M. (1924). Obliviscence during sleep and waking. *American Journal of Psychology, 35*, 605–612.

Jenkins, S. R. (1994). Need for power and women's careers over 14 years: Structural power, job satisfaction, and motive change. *Journal of Personality and Social Psychology, 66*, 155–165.

Jensen, A. R. (1969). How much can we boost IQ and scholastic achievement? *Harvard Educational Review, 39*, 1–123.

Jensen, A. R. (1981). *Straight talk about mental tests*. New York, NY: Free Press.

Jensen, A. R. (1998). *The g factor: The science of mental ability*. Westport, CT: Praeger/Greenwood.

Jewell, R. T., McPherson, M. A., & Tieslau, M. A. (2013). Whose fault is it? Assigning blame for grade inflation in higher education. *Applied Economics, 45*, 1185–1200.

Johanek, L. M., Meyer, R. A., Friedman, R. M., et al. (2008). A role for polymodal C-fiber afferents in nonhistaminergic itch. *The Journal of Neuroscience, 28*, 7659–7669.

Johns, M., Schmader, T., & Martens, A. (2005). Knowing is half the battle: Teaching stereotype threat as a means of improving women's math performance. *Psychological Science, 16*, 175–179.

Johnson, A. J., & Miles, C. (2009). Serial position effects in 2-alternative forced choice recognition: functional equivalence across visual and auditory modalities. *Memory, 17*, 84–91.

Johnson, M. K., Hashtroudi, S., & Lindsay, D. S. (1993). Source monitoring. *Psychological Bulletin, 114*, 3–28.

Johnson, M. K., Raye, C. L., Mitchell, K. J., & Ankudowich, E. (2011). The cognitive neuroscience of true and false memories. In R. F. Belli (Ed.), *True and false recovered memories: Toward a reconciliation of the debate* (Vol. 58). New York: Springer.

Johnson-Down, L., O'Loughlin, J., Koski, K. G., & Gray-Donald, K. (1997). High prevalence of obesity in low income and multiethnic schoolchildren: A diet and physical activity assessment. *Journal of Nutrition, 127*(12), 2310–2315.

Jones, E. E. (1990). *Interpersonal perception*. New York, NY: Macmillan.

Jones, M. C. (1924). A laboratory study of fear: The case of Peter. *Pedagogical Seminary, 31*, 308–315.

Jones, S. (1994). *The language of genes*. New York, NY: Anchor/Doubleday.

Joormann, J., & Gotlib, I. H. (2007). Selective attention to emotional faces following recovery from depression. *Journal of Abnormal Psychology, 116*, 80–85.

Jordan, A. H., Monin, B., Dweck, C. S., et al. (2011). Misery has more company than people think: Underestimating the prevalence of others' negative emotions. *Personality and Social Psychology Bulletin, 37*, 120–135.

Jordan, K. E., & Brannon, E. M. (2006). The multisensory representation of number in infancy. *Proceedings of the National Academy of Sciences, 103*, 3486–3489.

Josselyn, S. A., & Frankland, P. W. (2012). Infantile amnesia: A neurogenic hypothesis. *Learning and Memory, 19*, 423–433.

Jost, J. T. (2006). The end of the end of ideology. *American Psychologist, 61*, 651–670.

Jost, J. T., & Amodio, D. M. (2012). Political ideology as motivated social cognition: Behavioral and neuroscientific evidence. *Motivation and Emotion, 36*, 55–64.

Jost, J. T., Glaser, J., Kruglanski, A. W., & Sulloway, F. J. (2003). Political conservatism as motivated social cognition. *Psychological Bulletin, 129,* 339–375.

Jost, J. T., Nosek, B. A., & Gosling, S. D. (2008). Ideology: Its resurgence in social, personality, and political psychology. *Perspectives on Psychological Science, 3,* 126–136.

Judd, C. M., Park, B., Ryan, C. S., et al. (1995). Stereotypes and ethnocentrism: Diverging interethnic perceptions of African American and white American youth. *Journal of Personality and Social Psychology, 69,* 460–481.

Judge, T. A. (2009). Core self-evaluations and work success. *Current Directions, 18,* 18–22.

Junco, R., & Cotten, S. R. (2012). No A 4 U: The Relationship Between Multitasking and Academic Performance. *Computers and Education, 59,* 505-514.

Jung, C. (1967). *Collected works.* Princeton, NJ: Princeton University Press.

Jusczyk, P. W. (2002). How infants adapt speech-processing capacities to native-language structure. *Current Directions in Psychological Science, 11,* 15–18.

Jussim, L., Cain, T. R., Crawford, J. T., et al. (2009). The unbearable accuracy of stereotypes. In T. Nelson (Ed.), *The handbook of prejudice, stereotyping, and discrimination.* New York, NY: Psychology Press.

Kabat-Zinn, J. (1994). *Wherever you go, there you are: Mindfulness meditation in everyday life.* New York, NY: Hyperion.

Kagan, J. (1989). *Unstable ideas: Temperament, cognition, and self.* Cambridge, MA: Harvard University Press.

Kagan, J. (1997). Temperament and the reactions to unfamiliarity. *Child Development, 68,* 139–143.

Kagan, J. (1998). *Three seductive ideas.* Cambridge, MA: Harvard University Press.

Kagan, J., Kearsley, R. B., & Zelazo, P. R. (1978). *Infancy: Its place in human development.* Cambridge, MA: Harvard University Press.

Kahn, A. S. (2004). 2003 Carolyn Sherif Award Address: What college women do and do not experience as rape. *Psychology of Women Quarterly, 28,* 9–15.

Kahneman, D. (2002). Maps of bounded rationality: A perspective on intuitive judgment and choice. *Nobel Prize lecture.* Retrieved February 11, 2008, from http://nobelprize.org/nobel_prizes/economics/laureates/2002/kahnemann-lecture.pdf

Kahneman, D. (2003). A perspective on judgment and choice: Mapping bounded rationality. *American Psychologist, 58,* 697–720.

Kahneman, D. (2011). *Thinking, fast and slow.* New York: Farrar, Straus and Giroux.

Kaminski, J., Call, J., & Fisher, J. (2004). Word learning in a domestic dog: Evidence for "fast mapping." *Science, 304,* 1682–1683.

Kanagawa, C., Cross, S. E., & Markus, H. R. (2001). "Who am I?" The cultural psychology of the conceptual self. *Personality and Social Psychology Bulletin, 27,* 90–103.

Kandel, E. R. (2001). The molecular biology of memory storage: A dialogue between genes and synapses. *Science, 294,* 1030–1038.

Kandel, E. R., & Schwartz, J. H. (1982). Molecular biology of learning: Modulation of transmitter release. *Science, 218,* 433–443.

Kane, M. J., Brown, L. H., McVay, J. C., et al. (2007). For whom the mind wanders, and when: An experience-sampling study of working memory and executive control in daily life. *Psychological Science, 18,* 614–621.

Kanner, A., & Kasser, T. (2003). *Psychology and consumer culture: The struggle for a good life in a materialistic society.* Washington, DC: American Psychological Association.

Kanter, R. M. (2006). Some effects of proportions on group life: Skewed sex ratios and responses to token women. In J. N. Levine & R. L. Moreland (Eds.), *Small groups. Key Readings in Social Psychology.* New York, NY: Psychology Press.

Kanwisher, N. (2000). Domain specificity in face perception. *Nature Neuroscience, 3,* 759.

Kaplan, A. (1967). A philosophical discussion of normality. *Archives of General Psychiatry, 17,* 325–330.

Kaplan, M. S., Morales, M., & Becker, J. V. (1993). The impact of verbal satiation of adolescent sex offenders: A preliminary report. *Journal of Child Sexual Abuse, 2,* 81–88.

Karasek, R., & Theorell, T. (1990). *Healthy work: Stress, productivity, and the reconstruction of working life.* New York, NY: Basic Books.

Karney, B., & Bradbury, T. N. (2000). Attributions in marriage: State or trait? A growth curve analysis. *Journal of Personality and Social Psychology, 78,* 295–309.

Karni, A., Tanne, D., Rubenstein, B. S., et al. (1994). Dependence on REM sleep of overnight improvement of a perceptual skill. *Science, 265,* 679–682.

Karpicke, J. D. (2012). Retrieval-based learning: Active retrieval promotes meaningful learning. *Current Directions in Psychological Science, 21,* 157–163.

Karpicke, J. D., & Roediger, H. L., III. (2008, February 15). The critical importance of retrieval for learning. *Science, 319,* 966–968.

Kaschak, E., & Tiefer, L. (Eds.). (2002). *A new view of women's sexual problems.* Binghamton, NY: Haworth Press.

Kaschak, M. P., Kutta, T. J., & Jones, J. L. (2011). Structural priming as implicit learning: Cumulative priming effects and individual differences. *Psychonomic Bulletin & Review, 18,* 1133–1139.

Kasser, T., & Ryan, R. M. (2001). Be careful what you wish for: Optimal functioning and the relative attainment of intrinsic and extrinsic goals. In P. Schmuck & K. M. Sheldon (Eds.), *Life goals and well-being.* Lengerich, Germany: Pabst Science Publishers.

Kassinove, H. (Ed.). (1995). *Anger disorders: Definition, diagnosis, treatment.* Washington, DC: Taylor & Francis.

Katigbak, M. S., Church, A. T., Guanzon-Lapeña, Ma. A., et al. (2002). Are indigenous personality dimensions culture specific? Philippine inventories and the Five-Factor model. *Journal of Personality and Social Psychology, 82,* 89–101.

Katz, Z. (2001). Canadian psychologists' education, trauma history, and the recovery of memories of childhood sexual abuse [doctoral dissertation]. Simon Fraser University. *Dissertations Abstracts International, 61,* 3848.

Katzmarzyk, P. T., & Malina, R. M. (1998). Obesity and relative subcutaneous fat distribution among Canadians of First Nation and European ancestry. *International Journal of Obesity and Related Metabolic Disorders, 22,* 1127–1131.

Kaufman, J., & Zigler, E. (1987). Do abused children become abusive parents? *American Journal of Orthopsychiatry, 57,* 186–192.

Kazdin, A. E. (2001). *Behavior modification in applied settings* (6th ed.). Belmont, CA: Wadsworth.

Kazdin, A. E. (2008). Evidence-based treatment and practice: New opportunities to bridge clinical research and practice, enhance the knowledge base, and improve patient care. *American Psychologist, 63,* 146–150.

Keating, C. F. (1994). World without words: Messages from face and body. In W. J. Lonner & R. Malpass (Eds.), *Psychology and culture.* Needham Heights, MA: Allyn & Bacon.

Keel, P. K., & Klump, K. L. (2003). Are eating disorders culture-bound syndromes? Implications for conceptualizing their etiology. *Psychological Bulletin, 129,* 747–769.

Keen, S. (1986). *Faces of the enemy: Reflections of the hostile imagination.* San Francisco, CA: Harper & Row.

Keizer, K., Lindenberg, S., & Steg, L. (2008, December 12). The spreading of disorder. *Science, 322,* 1681–1685.

Keller, H., Abels, M., Lamm, B., et al. (2005). Ecocultural effects on early infant care: A study in Cameroon, India, and Germany. *Ethos, 33,* 512–541.

Kely, D. D. (1981). Chapter 40. In E. R. Kandel & J. H. Schwartz, (Eds.), *Principles of Neural Science,* New York: Elsevier North Holland.

Kelman, H. C., & Hamilton, V. L. (1989). *Crimes of obedience: Toward a social psychology of authority and responsibility.* New Haven, CT: Yale University Press.

Keltner, D., & Buswell, B. N. (1997). Embarrassment: Its distinct form and appeasement functions. *Psychological Bulletin, 122,* 250–270.

Keltner, D., Ellsworth, P. C., & Edwards, K. (1993). Beyond simple pessimism: Effects of sadness and anger on social perception. *Journal of Personality and Social Psychology, 64,* 740–752.

Kemeny, M. E. (2003). The psychobiology of stress. *Current Directions in Psychological Science, 12,* 124–129.

Kempermann, G. (2006). *Adult neurogenesis: Stem cells and neuronal development in the adult brain.* New York, NY: Oxford University Press.

Kendall (1999). Women in Lesotho and the (Western) construction of homophobia. In E. Blackwood & S. E. Wieringa (Eds.), *Female desires: Same-sex relations and transgender practices across cultures.* New York, NY: Columbia University Press.

Kennedy, D., & Norman, C. (2005). Introduction to special issue: What don't we know? *Science, 309,* 75.

Kenny, D, A., Snook, A., Boucher, E., & Hancock, J. T. (2010). Interpersonal sensitivity, status, and stereotype accuracy. *Psychological Science, 21,* 1735–1739.

Kenrick, D. T., Sundie, J. M., Nicastle, L. D., & Stone, G. O. (2001). Can one ever be too wealthy or too chaste? Searching for nonlinearities in mate judgment. *Journal of Personality and Social Psychology, 80,* 462–471.

Kephart, W. M. (1967). Some correlates of romantic love. *Journal of Marriage and the Family, 29,* 470–474.

Kessler, R. C., Chiu, W. T., Demler, O., Merikangas, K. R., & Walters, E. E. (2005). Prevalence, severity, and comorbidity of 12-month *DSM-IV* disorders in the National Comorbidity Survey Replication. *Archives of General Psychiatry, 62,* 590–592.

Khan, A., Detke, M., Khan, S. R., & Mallinckrodt, C. (2003). Placebo response and antidepressant clinical trial outcome. *Journal of Nervous and Mental Diseases, 191,* 211–218.

Kibbe, M. M., & Leslie, A. M. (2011). What do infants remember when they forget? Location and identity in 6-month-olds' memory for objects. *Psychological Science, 22,* 1500–1505.

Kida, T. (2006). *Don't believe everything you think: The 6 basic mistakes we make in thinking.* Amherst, NY: Prometheus Books.

Kiecolt-Glaser, J. K., Loving, T. J., Stowell, J. R., et al. (2005). Hostile marital interactions, proinflammatory cytokine production, and wound healing. *Archives of General Psychiatry, 62,* 1377–1384.

Kiecolt-Glaser, J. K., & Newton, T. L. (2001). Marriage and health: His and hers. *Psychological Bulletin, 127,* 472–503.

Kihlstrom, J. F. (1994). Hypnosis, delayed recall, and the principles of memory. *International Journal of Clinical and Experimental Hypnosis, 40,* 337–345.

Kihlstrom, J. F. (1995). *From a subject's point of view: The experiment as conversation and collaboration between investigator and subject.* Invited address presented at the annual meeting of the American Psychological Society, New York, NY.

Kim, H. L., Streltzer, J., & Goebert, D. (1999). St. John's wort for depression: A meta-analysis of well-defined clinical trials. *Journal of Nervous and Mental Diseases, 187,* 532–538.

Kim, H. S., Sherman, D. K., & Taylor, S. E. (2008). Culture and social support. *American Psychologist, 63,* 518–526.

Kim, J. L., Sorsoli, C. L., Collins, K., et al. (2007). From sex to sexuality: Exposing the heterosexual script on primetime network television. *Journal of Sex Research, 44,* 145–157.

King, A. E., Austin-Oden, D., & Lohr, J. M. (2009, January). Browsing for love in all the wrong places. *Skeptic, 15,* 48–55.

King, M., & Woollett, E. (1997). Sexually assaulted males: 115 men consulting a counseling service. *Archives of Sexual Behavior, 26,* 579–588.

King, P. M., & Kitchener, K. S. (1994). *Developing reflective judgment: Understanding and promoting intellectual growth and critical thinking in adolescents and adults.* San Francisco, CA: Jossey Bass.

King, P. M., & Kitchener, K. S. (2002). The reflective judgment model: Twenty years of research on epistemic cognition. In B. K. Hofer & P. R. Pintrich (Eds.), *Personal epistemology: The psychology of beliefs about knowledge and knowing.* Mahway, NJ: Erlbaum.

Kingston, A. (2009, March 12). The sexting scare. Though no 'epidemic,' it raises big issues for parents and the law. *Macleans.* Retrieved from http://www2.macleans.ca/2009/03/12/the-sexting-scare

Kinnon, D. (1981). *Report on sexual assault in Canada.* Ottawa: Canadian Advisory Council on the Status of Women.

Kinoshita, S., & Peek-O'Leary, M. (2005). Does the compatibility effect in the race Implicit Association Test reflect familiarity or affect? *Psychonomic Bulletin & Review, 12,* 442–452.

Kinsey, A. C., Pomeroy, W. B., & Martin, C. E. (1948). *Sexual behavior in the human male.* Philadelphia, PA: Saunders.

Kinsey, A. C., Pomeroy, W. B., Martin, C. E., & Gebhard, P. H. (1953). *Sexual behavior in the human female.* Philadelphia, PA: Saunders.

Kirkpatrick, L. A., & Davis, K. A. (1994). Attachment style, gender, and relationship stability: A longitudinal analysis. *Journal of Personality and Social Psychology, 66,* 502–512.

Kirsch, I. (1997). Response expectancy theory and application: A decennial review. *Applied and Preventive Psychology, 6,* 69–70.

Kirsch, I. (2004). Conditioning, expectancy, and the placebo effect: Comment on Stewart-Williams and Podd (2004). *Psychological Bulletin, 130,* 341–343.

Kirsch, I. (2009). *The emperor's new drugs: Exploding the antidepressant myth.* London: The Bodley Head.

Kirsch, I., Deacon, B. J., Huedo-Medina, T. B., et al. (2008). Initial severity and antidepressant benefits: A meta-analysis of data submitted to the Food and Drug Administration. *PLoS Medicine, 5,* e45.

Kirsch, I., & Lynn, S. J. (1995). The altered state of hypnosis: Changes in the theoretical landscape. *American Psychologist, 50,* 846–858.

Kish, S. J. (2003). What is the evidence that Ecstasy (MDMA) can cause Parkinson's disease? *Movement Disorders, 18,* 1219–1223.

Kissileff, H. R., Thornton, J. C., Torres M. I., et al. (2012). Leptin reverses declines in satiation in weight-reduced obese humans. *American Journal of Clinical Nutrition, 95,* 309–317.

Kitchener, K. S., Lynch, C. L., Fischer, K. W., & Wood, P. K. (1993). Developmental range of reflective judgment: The effect of contextual support and practice on developmental stage. *Developmental Psychology, 29,* 893–906.

Klauer, S. G., Dingus, T. A., Neale, V. L., et al. (2006). *The impact of driver inattention on near-crash/crash risk: An analysis using the 100-car naturalistic driving study data.* Performed by Virginia Tech Transportation Institute, Blacksburg, VA, sponsored by National Highway Traffic Safety Administration, Washington, DC. DOT HS 810 594. Retrieved from http://www.nhtsa.gov/DOT/NHTSA/NRD/Multimedia/PDFs/Crash%20Avoidance/2006/DriverInattention.pdf

Klein, D. N., Schwartz, J. E., Santiago, N. J., et al. (2003). Therapeutic alliance in depression treatment: Controlling for prior change and patient characteristics. *Journal of Consulting & Clinical Psychology, 71,* 997–1006.

Klein, R., & Armitage, R. (1979). Rhythms in human performance: 1 1/2-hour oscillations in cognitive style. *Science, 204,* 1326–1328.

Kleinke, C. L., Peterson, T. R., & Rutledge, T. R. (1998). Effects of self-generated facial expressions on mood. *Journal of Personality and Social Psychology, 74,* 272–279.

Kleinman, A. (1988). *Rethinking psychiatry: From cultural category to personal experience.* New York, NY: Free Press.

Klimoski, R. (1992). Graphology and personnel selection. In B. Beyerstein & D. Beyerstein (Eds.), *The write stuff: Evaluations of graphology—The study of handwriting analysis.* Buffalo, NY: Prometheus Books.

Klingberg, T. (2010). Training and plasticity of working memory. *Trends in Cognitive Sciences, 14,* 317–324.

Klohnen, E. C., & Bera, S. (1998). Behavioral and experiential patterns of avoidantly and securely attached women across adulthood: A 31-year longitudinal perspective. *Journal of Personality and Social Psychology, 74,* 211–223.

Knowles, L. P. (Spring 2010). Stem Cell Patents. *Stem Cell Network, For the Public, Ethics and Policy,* Spring 2010. Retrieved August 13, 2013, from http://www.stemcellnetwork.ca/uploads/File/whitepapers/Stem-Cell-Patents.pdf

Kochanska, G., Forman, D. R., Aksan, N., & Dunbar, S. B. (2005). Pathways to conscience: Early mother–child mutually responsive orientation and children's moral emotion, conduct, and cognition. *Journal of Child Psychology and Psychiatry, 46,* 19–34.

Kochanska, G., & Knaack, A. (2003). Effortful control as a personality characteristic of young children: Antecedents, correlates, and consequences. *Journal of Personality, 71,* 1087–1112.

Kohlberg, L. (1964). Development of moral character and moral ideology. In M. Hoffman & L. W. Hoffman (Eds.), *Review of child development research.* New York, NY: Russell Sage Foundation.

Köhler, W. (1925). *The mentality of apes.* New York, NY: Harcourt, Brace.

Köhler, W. (1929). *Gestalt psychology.* New York, NY: Horace Liveright.

Köhler, W. (1959). *Gestalt psychology today.* Presidential address to the American Psychological Association, Cincinnati, OH. Reprinted in E. R. Hilgard (Ed.), *American psychology in historical perspective: Addresses of the presidents of the American Psychological Association, 1892–1977.* Washington, DC: American Psychological Association, 1978.

Kohsaka, A., Laposky, A. D., Ramsey, K. M., et al. (2007). High-fat diet disrupts behavioral and molecular circadian rhythms in mice. *Cell Metabolism, 6,* 414–421.

Kok, B. E., Catalino, L. I., & Fredrickson, B. L. (2008). The broadening, building, buffering effects of positive emotions. In S. J. Lopez (Ed.), *Positive psychology: Exploring the best in people* (Vol 2). Westport, CT: Praeger Publishers/Greenwood.

Kolata, G. (2004, June 8). The fat epidemic: He says it's an illusion. *The New York Times,* Science section, D5.

Kolb, B., Gibb, R., & Robinson, T. E. (2003). Brain plasticity and behavior. *Current Directions in Psychological Science, 12,* 1–5.

Kolb, B., & Teskey, G. C. (2012). Age, experience, injury, and the changing brain. *Developmental Psychobiology, 54,* 311–325.

Kopta, S. M., Howard, K. I., Lowry, J. L., & Beutler, L. E. (1994). Patterns of symptomatic recovery in psychotherapy. *Journal of Consulting and Clinical Psychology, 62,* 1009–1016.

Kornell, N. (2009). Metacognition in humans and animals. *Current Directions in Psychological Science, 18,* 11–15.

Kosfeld, M., Heinrichs, M., Zak, P. J., et al. (2005). Oxytocin increases trust in humans. *Nature, 435,* 673–676.

Koski, L. R., & Shaver, P. R. (1997). Attachment and relationship satisfaction across the lifespan. In R. J. Sternberg & M. Hojjatt (Eds.), *Satisfaction in close relationships.* New York, NY: Guilford.

Koss, M. (2011). Hidden, unacknowledged, acquaintance, and date rape: Looking back, looking forward. *Psychology of Women Quarterly, 35,* 348–354.

Kosslyn, S. M. (1980). *Image and mind.* Cambridge, MA: Harvard University Press.

Kosslyn, S. M., Thompson, W. L., Costantini-Ferrando, M. F., et al. (2000). Hypnotic visual illusion alters color processing in the brain. *American Journal of Psychiatry, 157,* 1279–1284.

Kounios, J., & Beeman, M. (2009). The *aha!* moment: The cognitive neuroscience of insight. *Current Directions in Psychological Science, 18,* 210–216.

Kraha, A., & Boals, A. (2014). Why so negative? Positive flashbulb memories for a personal event. *Memory, 22,* 442–449.

Kramer, A. F., & Willis, S. L. (2002). Enhancing the cognitive vitality of older adults. *Current Directions in Psychological Science, 11,* 173–177.

Kramer, K. L., & Greaves, R. D. (2011). Juvenile subsistence effort, activity levels, and growth patterns: Middle childhood among Pumé foragers. *Human Nature, 22,* 303–326.

Krantz, D. S., Olson, M. B., Francis, J. L., et al. (2006). Anger, hostility, and cardiac symptoms in women with suspected coronary artery disease: The women's ischemia syndrome evaluation (WISE) study. *Journal of Women's Health, 15,* 1214–1223.

Kraus, M. W., Côté, S., & Keltner, D. (2010). Social class, contextualism, and empathic accuracy. *Psychological Science, 21,* 1716–1723.

Krebs, D. L. (2008). Morality: An evolutionary account. *Perspectives on Psychological Science, 3,* 149–172.

Kreps, B. (1990). *Subversive thoughts, authentic passions.* San Francisco, CA: Harper & Row.

Krieger, N., & Sidney, S. (1996). Racial discrimination and blood pressure: The CARDIA study of young black and white adults. *American Journal of Public Health, 86,* 1370–1378.

Krimsky, S. (2003). *Science in the private interest.* Lanham, MD: Rowman & Littlefield.

Kring, A. M., & Gordon, A. H. (1998). Sex differences in emotion: Expression, experience, and physiology. *Journal of Personality and Social Psychology, 74,* 686–703.

Kripke, D. F. (1974). Ultradian rhythms in sleep and wakefulness. In E. D. Weitzman (Ed.), *Advances in sleep research* (Vol. 1). Flushing, NY: Spectrum.

Kroll, B. M. (1992). *Teaching hearts and minds: College students reflect on the Vietnam War in literature.* Carbondale: Southern Illinois University Press.

Kross, E., & Ayduk, O. (2011). Making meaning out of negative experiences by self-distancing. *Current Directions in Psychological Science, 20*(3), 187–191.

Kross, E., Berman, M. G., Mischel, W., et al. (2011). Social rejection shares somatosensory representations with physical pain. *Proceedings of the National Academy of Sciences, 108,* 6270–6275.

Krueger, R. F., Hicks, B. M., & McGue, M. (2001). Altruism and antisocial behavior: Independent tendencies, unique personality correlates, distinct etiologies. *Psychological Science, 12,* 397–402.

Krupa, D. J., Thompson, J. K., & Thompson, R. F. (1993). Localization of a memory trace in the mammalian brain. *Science, 260,* 989–991.

Krützen, M., Mann, J., Heithaus, M. R., et al. (2005). Cultural transmission of tool use in bottlenose dolphins. *Proceedings of the National Academy of Sciences, 102:* 8939–8943. doi:10.1073/pnas.0500232102

Krystal, J. H., Rosenheck, R. A., Kramer, J. A., et al. (2011, August 3). Adjunctive risperidone treatment for antidepressant-resistant symptoms of chronic military service–related PTSD: A randomized trial. *Journal of the American Medical Association, 306,* 493.

Kuhl, P. K., Williams, K. A., Lacerda, F., et al. (1992, January 31). Linguistic experience alters phonetic perception in infants by 6 months of age. *Science, 255,* 606–608.

Kuhn, D., Weinstock, M., & Flaton, R. (1994). How well do jurors reason? Competence dimensions of individual variation in a juror reasoning task. *Psychological Science, 5,* 289–296.

Kuncel, N. R., Hezlett, S. A., & Ones, D. S. (2004). Academic performance, career potential, creativity, and job performance: Can one construct predict them all? *Journal of Personality and Social Psychology, 86,* 148–161.

Kunda, Z. (1990). The case for motivated reasoning. *Psychological Bulletin, 108,* 480–498.

Kupersmidt, J. B., Griesler, P. C., DeRosier, M. E., et al. (1995). Childhood aggression and peer relations in the context of family and neighborhood factors. *Child Development, 66*(2), 360–375.

Kurdek, L. A. (2005). What do we know about gay and lesbian couples? *Current Directions in Psychological Science, 14,* 251–254.

Kutchins, H., & Kirk, S. A. (1997). *Making us crazy: DSM. The psychiatric bible and the creation of mental disorders.* New York, NY: Free Press.

Laan, E., & Both, S. (2008). What makes women experience desire? In L. Tiefer (Ed.), The New View campaign against the medicalization of sex (Special Issue). *Feminism and Psychology, 18,* 505–514.

LaBerge, S., & Levitan, L. (1995). Validity established of DreamLight cues for eliciting lucid dreaming. *Dreaming: Journal of the Association for the Study of Dreams, 5,* 159–168.

Lacasse, J. R., & Leo, J. (2005, December). Serotonin and depression: A disconnect between the advertisements and the scientific literature. *PLoS Medicine, 2*(12): e392. doi:10.1371/journal.pmed.0020392

Lachman, M. E., & Weaver, S. L. (1998). The sense of control as a moderator of social class differences in health and well-being. *Journal of Personality and Social Psychology, 74,* 763–773.

Lachman, S. J. (1996). Processes in perception: Psychological transformations of highly structured stimulus material. *Perceptual and Motor Skills, 83,* 411–418.

LaFrance, M. (2011). *Lip service.* New York: W. W. Norton.

Lahey, B. B., Pelham, W. E., Loney, J., et al. (2005). Instability of the DSM-IV subtypes of ADHD from preschool through elementary school. *Archives of General Psychiatry, 62,* 896–902.

Lamb, S. (2002). *The secret lives of girls.* New York, NY: The Free Press.

Lanaj, K., Chang, C.-H., & Johnson, R. E. (2012). Regulatory focus and work-related outcomes: A review and meta-analysis. *Psychological Bulletin, 138,* 998–1034.

Lancy, D. F., & Grove, M. A. (2011). Getting noticed: Middle childhood in cross-cultural perspective. *Human Nature, 22,* 281–302.

Landrigan, C. P., Fahrenkopf, A. M., Lewin, D., et al. (2008). Effects of the Accreditation Council for Graduate Medical Education duty hour limits on sleep, work hours, and safety. *Pediatrics, 122,* 250–258.

Landrine, H. (1988). Revising the framework of abnormal psychology. In P. Bronstein & K. Quina (Eds.), *Teaching a psychology of people.* Washington, DC: American Psychological Association.

Lang, A. J., Craske, M. G., Brown, M., & Ghaneian, A. (2001). Fear-related state dependent memory. *Cognition & Emotion, 15,* 695–703.

Langer, E. J., Blank, A., & Chanowitz, B. (1978). The mindlessness of ostensibly thoughtful action: The role of placebic information in interpersonal interaction. *Journal of Personality and Social Psychology, 36,* 635–642.

Lanphear, B. P., Hornung, R., Ho, M., et al. (2002). Environmental lead exposure during early childhood. *Journal of Pediatrics, 140,* 49–47.

Lanphear, B. P., Hornung, R., Khoury, J., et al. (2005). Low-level environmental lead exposure and children's intellectual function: An international pooled analysis. *Environmental Health Perspectives, 113,* 894–899.

Lansdown, T. C., & Stephens, A. N. (2013). Couples, contentious conversations, mobile telephone use and driving. *Accident Analysis & Prevention, 50,* 416–422.

Lany, J., & Gómez, R. L. (2008). Twelve-month-old infants benefit from prior experience in statistical learning. *Psychological Science, 19,* 1247–1252.

Lau, H., Alger, S., & Fishbein, W. (2008, November). *Naps and relational memory—a daytime nap facilitates extraction of general concepts.* Paper presented at the annual meeting of the Society for Neuroscience, Washington, DC.

Laumann, E. O., Ellingson, S., Mahay, J., Paik, A., & Youm, Y. (Eds.). (2004). *The sexual organization of the city.* Chicago, IL: University of Chicago Press.

Laumann, E. O., & Gagnon, J. H. (1995). A sociological perspective on sexual action. In R. G. Parker & J. H. Gagnon (Eds.), *Conceiving sexuality: Approaches to sex research in a postmodern world.* New York, NY: Routledge.

Laumann, E. O., Gagnon, J. H., Michael, R. T., & Michaels, S. (1994). *The social organization of sexuality.* Chicago, IL: University of Chicago Press.

Laurence, J. R., & Perry, C. (1988). *Hypnosis, will, and memory: A psycho-legal history.* New York, NY: Guilford Press.

Lavie, P. (1976). Ultradian rhythms in the perception of two apparent motions. *Chronobiologia, 3,* 21–218.

Lavie, P. (2001). Sleep-wake as a biological rhythm. *Annual Review of Psychology, 52,* 277–303.

Lazarus, R. S. (2000a, Spring). Reason and our emotions: A hard sell. *The General Psychologist, 35,* 16–20.

Lazarus, R. S., & Folkman, S. (1984). *Stress, appraisal, and coping.* New York, NY: Springer.

Leach, A. M., Ammar, N., England, D. N., Remigio, L. M. (2014, April). *Detecting lies in veiled witnesses.* Paper presented at the Mediterranean Interdisciplinary Forum on Social Sciences and Humanities, Beirut, Lebanon.

Leach, A.-M., Cutler, B. L., & Van Wallendael, L. (2009). Lineups and Eyewitness Identification. *Annual Review of Law and Social Science, 5,* 157–178.

LeBow, M. D. (1988). Attitudes, perceptions, and practices of Canadian school children towards obesity. *Journal of Obesity and Weight Regulation,* 7(1), 43–55.

LeBow, M. D., Ness, D., Makarenko, P., & Lam, T. (1989). Attitudes, perceptions, and practices of Canadian teenagers towards obesity. *Journal of Obesity and Weight Regulation, 8,* 53–65.

LeDoux, J. E. (1996). *The emotional brain.* New York, NY: Simon & Schuster.

Lee, S. J., & McEwen, B. S. (2001). Neurotrophic and neuroprotective actions of estrogens and their therapeutic implications. *Annual Review of Pharmacology & Pharmacological Toxicology, 41,* 569–591.

Lefton, L. A., Boyes, M., & Ogden, N. (2000). *Psychology* (Canadian ed.). Needham Heights, MA: Allyn & Bacon, Inc.

d (2011). *Neuromania: On the limits of brain science.* New York: Oxford University Press.

Leibenluft, E., & Rich, B. A. (2008). Pediatric bipolar disorder. *Annual Review of Clinical Psychology, 4,* 163–187.

Leichsenring, F., & Rabung, S. (2008, October 1). Effectiveness of long-term psychodynamic therapy: A meta-analysis. *Journal of the American Medical Association, 300,* 1551–1565.

Leinbach, M. D., Hort, B. E., & Fagot, B. I. (1997). Bears are for boys: Metaphorical associations in young children's gender stereotypes. *Cognitive Development, 12,* 107–130.

Lent, R., Azevedo, F. A. C., Andrade-Moraes, C. H., & Pinto, A. V. O. (2012). How many neurons do you have? Some dogmas of quantitative neuroscience under revision. *The European Journal of Neuroscience, 35,* 1–9.

Leo, R. A. (2008). *Police interrogation and American justice.* Cambridge, MA: Harvard University Press.

Leonard, K. M. (2008). A cross-cultural investigation of temporal orientation in work organizations: A differentiation matching approach. *International Journal of Intercultural Relations, 32,* 479–492.

Lepore, S. J., Ragan, J. D., & Jones, S. (2000). Talking facilitates cognitive-emotional processes of adaptation to an acute stressor. *Journal of Personality and Social Psychology, 78,* 499–508.

Lepowsky, M. (1994). *Fruit of the motherland: Gender in an egalitarian society.* New York, NY: Columbia University Press.

Leppänen, J., & Nelson, C. A. (2012). Early development of fear processing. *Current Directions in Psychological Science, 21,* 200–204.

Lepper, M. R., Greene, D., & Nisbett, R. E. (1973). Undermining children's intrinsic interest with extrinsic rewards. *Journal of Personality and Social Psychology, 28,* 129–137.

Leproult, R., Copinschi, G., Buxton, O., & Van Cauter, E. (1997). Sleep loss results in an elevation of cortisol levels the next evening. *Sleep, 20,* 865–870.

Leproult, R., Van Reeth, O., Byrne, M. M., et al. (1997). Sleepiness, performance, and neuroendocrine function during sleep deprivation: Effects of exposure to bright light or exercise. *Journal of Biological Rhythms, 12,* 245–258.

Lerner, M. J. (1980). *The belief in a just world: A fundamental delusion.* New York, NY: Plenum.

Lester, B. M., LaGasse, L. L., & Seifer, R. (1998, October 23). Cocaine exposure and children: The meaning of subtle effects. *Science, 282,* 633–634.

LeVay, S. (1991). A difference in hypothalamic structure between heterosexual and homosexual men. *Science, 253,* 1034–1037.

Levenson, R. W. (1992). Autonomic nervous system differences among emotions. *Psychological Science, 3,* 23–27.

Levenson, R. W., Ekman, P., & Friesen, W. V. (1990). Voluntary facial action generates emotion-specific autonomic nervous system activity. *Psychophysiology, 27,* 363–384.

Levenson, R. W., & Miller, B. L. (2007). Loss of cells—loss of self. *Current Directions in Psychological Science, 16,* 289–294.

Levin, D. T. (2000). Race as a visual feature: Using visual search and perceptual discrimination tasks to understand face categories and the cross-race recognition deficit. *Journal of Experimental Psychology: General, 129,* 559–574.

Levine, J., & Suzuki, D. (1993). *The secret of life: Redesigning the living world.* Boston, MA: WGBH Educational Foundation.

Levine, J. (2002). *Harmful to minors.* Minneapolis: University of Minnesota Press.

Levine, J. A., Eberhardt, N. L., & Jensen, M. D. (1999, January 8). Role of non-exercise activity thermogenesis in resistance to fat gain in humans. *Science, 283,* 212–214.

LeVine, R. A., & Norman, K. (2008). Attachment in anthropological perspective. In R. A. LeVine & R. S. New (Eds.), *Anthropology and child development: A cross-cultural reader.* Malden, MA: Blackwell.

Levine, R. V. (2003, May–June). The kindness of strangers. *American Scientist, 91,* 227–233.

Levine, R. V., Norenzayan, A., & Philbrick, K. (2001). Cross-cultural differences in helping strangers. *Journal of Cross-Cultural Psychology, 32,* 543–560.

Levy, B. (1996). Improving memory in old age through implicit self-stereotyping. *Journal of Personality and Social Psychology, 71,* 1092–1107.

Levy, D. A. (2010). *Tools of critical thinking: Metathoughts for psychology* (2nd ed.). Long Grove, IL: Waveland.

Levy, J., Trevarthen, C., & Sperry, R. W. (1972). Perception of bilateral chimeric figures following hemispheric deconnection. *Brain, 95,* 61–78.

Levy, R. I. (1984). The emotions in comparative perspective. In K. R. Scherer & P. Ekman (Eds.), *Approaches to emotion.* Hillsdale, NJ: Erlbaum.

Lewin, K. (1948). *Resolving social conflicts.* New York, NY: Harper.

Lewontin, R. C. (1970). Race and intelligence. *Bulletin of the Atomic Scientists, 26*(3), 2–8.

Lewontin, R. C. (2001, March 5). *Genomania: A disorder of modern biology and medicine.* Invited address at the University of California, Los Angeles, CA.

Lewontin, R. C., Rose, S., & Kamin, L. J. (1984). *Not in our genes: Biology, ideology, and human nature.* New York, NY: Pantheon.

Lewy, A. J., Ahmed, S., Jackson, J. L., & Sack, R. L. (1992). Melatonin shifts human circadian rhythms according to a phase response curve. *Chronobiology International, 9,* 380–392.

Lewy, A. J., Lefler, B. J., Emens, J. S., & Bauer, V. K. (2006). The circadian basis of winter depression. *Proceedings of the National Academy of Sciences, 103,* 7414–7419.

Li, S.-C., Lindenberger, U., Hommel, B., et al. (2004). Transformations in the couplings among intellectual abilities and constituent cognitive processes across the life span. *Psychological Science, 15,* 155–163.

Lieberman, J. A., Stroup, T. S., McEvoy, J. P., et al. (2005, September 22). Effectiveness of antipsychotic drugs in patients with chronic schizophrenia. *New England Journal of Medicine, 353,* 1209–1223.

Lieberman, M. (2000). Intuition: A social cognitive neuroscience approach. *Psychological Bulletin, 126,* 109–137.

Lien, M.-C., Ruthruff, E., & Johnston, J. C. (2006). Attentional limitations in doing two tasks at once: The search for exceptions. *Current Directions in Psychological Science, 16,* 89–93.

Lilienfeld, S. O. (1996, January/February). EMDR treatment: Less than meets the eye? *Skeptical Inquirer,* 25–31.

Lilienfeld, S. O. (2007). Psychological treatments that cause harm. *Perspectives on Psychological Science, 2,* 53–70.

Lilienfeld, S. O., Gershon, J., Duke, M., Marino, L., & De Waal, F. B. M. (1999). A preliminary investigation of the construct of psychopathic personality (psychopathy) in chimpanzees (*Pan troglodytes*). *Journal of Comparative Psychology, 113,* 365–375.

Lilienfeld, S. O., Lynn, S. J., Kirsch, I., et al. (1999). Dissociative identity disorder and the sociocognitive model: Recalling the lessons of the past. *Psychological Bulletin, 125,* 507–523.

Lilienfeld, S. O., Lynn, S. J., & Lohr, J. M. (Eds.). (2003). *Science and pseudoscience in clinical psychology.* New York, NY: Guilford.

Lilienfeld, S. O., Wood, J. M., & Garb, H. N. (2000). The scientific status of projective techniques. *Psychological Science in the Public Interest, 1,* 27–66.

Lin, J., Epel, E. S., & Blackburn, E. H. (2009). Telomeres, telomerase stress and aging. In G. G. Bernston & J. T. Cacioppo (Eds.), *Handbook of Neuroscience for the Behavioral Sciences.* New York, NY: Wiley.

Lin, K.-M., Poland, R. E., & Chien, C. P. (1990). Ethnicity and psychopharmacology: Recent findings and future research directions. In E. Sorel (Ed.), *Family, culture, and psychobiology.* New York, NY: Legas.

Lin, L., Hungs, M., & Mignot, E. (2001). Narcolepsy and the HLA region. *Journal of Neuroimmunology, 117,* 9–20.

Linday, L. A. (1994). Maternal reports of pregnancy, genital, and related fantasies in preschool and kindergarten children. *Journal of the American Academy of Child and Adolescent Psychiatry, 33,* 416–423.

Lindquist, K. A., & Barrett, L. F. (2008). Constructing emotion. *Psychological Science, 19,* 898–903.

Lindsay, D. S., Hagen, L., Read, J. D., et al. (2004). True photographs and false memories. *Psychological Science, 15,* 149–154.

Lindsay, D. S., & Read, J. D. (1994). Psychotherapy and memories of childhood sexual abuse: A cognitive perspective. *Applied Cognitive Psychology, 8,* 281–338.

Linehan, M., M. (1993). *Cognitive-behavioral treatment of borderline personality disorder.* New York, NY: Guilford Press.

Linton, M. (1978). Real-world memory after six years: An in vivo study of very long-term memory. In M. M. Gruneberg, P. E. Morris, & R. N. Sykes (Eds.), *Practical aspects of memory*. London, England: Academic Press.

Linton, S. (1998). *Claiming disability: Knowledge and identity*. New York, NY: New York University Press.

Linton, S. (2006). *My body politic*. Ann Arbor: University of Michigan Press.

Lipps, J. H. (2004, January/February). Judging authority. *Skeptical Inquirer*, 35–37.

Lisman, J., Yasuda, R., & Raghavachari, S. (2012). Mechanisms of CaMKII action in long-term potentiation. *Nature Reviews Neuroscience, 13*, 169–182.

Lissner, L., Odell, P. M., D'Agostino, R. B., et al. (1991, June 27). Variability of body weight and health outcomes in the Framingham population. *New England Journal of Medicine, 324*, 1839–1844.

Lloyd-Richardson, E. E., Bailey, S., Fava, J. L., Wing, R., Tobacco Etiology Research Network. (TERN). (2009). A prospective study of weight gain during the college freshman and sophomore years. *Preventive Medicine, 48*, 256–261.

LoBue, V., & DeLoache, J. S. (2008). Detecting the snake in the grass. *Psychological Science, 19*, 284–289.

Locke, E. A., & Latham, G. P. (2002). Building a practically useful theory of goal setting and task motivation. *American Psychologist, 57*, 705–717.

Locke, E. A., & Latham, G. P. (2006). New directions in goal-setting theory. *Current Directions in Psychological Science, 15*, 265–268.

Locke, E. A., Shaw, K., Saari, L., & Latham, G. (1981). Goal-setting and task performance: 1969–1980. *Psychological Bulletin, 90*, 125–152.

Loehlin, J. C., Horn, J. M., & Willerman, L. (1996). Heredity, environment, and IQ in the Texas adoption study. In R. J. Sternberg & E. Grigorenko (Eds.), *Intelligence: Heredity and environment*. New York, NY: Cambridge University Press.

Loftus, E. F. (2011). Intelligence gathering post-9/11. *American Psychologist, 66*, 532–541.

Loftus, E. F., & Greene, E. (1980). Warning: Even memory for faces may be contagious. *Law and Human Behavior, 4*, 323–334.

Loftus, E. F., & Guyer, M. J. (2002). Who abused Jane Doe? *Skeptical Inquirer*. Part 1: May/June, 24–32. Part 2: July/August, 37–40.

Loftus, E. F., Miller, D. G., & Burns, H. J. (1978). Semantic integration of verbal information into a visual memory. *Journal of Experimental Psychology: Human Learning and Memory, 4*, 19–31.

Loftus, E. F., & Palmer, J. C. (1974). Reconstruction of automobile destruction: An example of the interaction between language and memory. *Journal of Verbal Learning and Verbal Behavior, 13*, 585–589.

Loftus, E. F., & Pickrell, J. E. (1995). The formation of false memories. *Psychiatric Annals, 25*, 720–725.

Lohr, J. M., Montgomery, R. W., Lilienfeld, S. O., & Tolin, D. F. (1999). Pseudoscience and the commercial promotion of trauma treatments. In R. Gist & B. Lubin (Eds.), *Response to disaster: Psychosocial, community, and ecological approaches*. Philadelphia, PA: Brunner/Mazel (Taylor & Francis).

Lohr, J. M., Tolin, D. F., & Lilienfeld, S. O. (1998). Efficacy of eye movement desensitization and reprocessing: Implications for behavior therapy. *Behavior Therapy, 29*, 123–156.

Lonner, W. J. (1995). Culture and human diversity. In E. Trickett, R. Watts, & D. Birman (Eds.), *Human diversity: Perspectives on people in context*. San Francisco, CA: Jossey-Bass.

Lonner, W. J., & Malpass, R. S. (Eds.). (1994). *Psychology and culture*. Needham Heights, MA: Allyn & Bacon.

Lonsdorf, T. B., Weike, A. I., Nikamo, P., et al. (2009). Genetic gating of human fear learning and extinction: Possible implications for gene-environment interaction in anxiety disorder. *Psychological Science, 20*, 198–206.

Lopes, A. C., de Mathis, M. E., Canteras, M. M., et al. (2004). Update on neurosurgical treatment for obsessive compulsive disorder [original article in Portuguese]. *Rev bras Psiquiatr, 26*, 62–66.

López, S. R. (1995). Testing ethnic minority children. In B. B. Wolman (Ed.), *The encyclopedia of psychology, psychiatry, and psychoanalysis*. New York, NY: Holt.

Lövdén, M., Bächman, L., Lindenberger, U., et al. (2010). A theoretical framework for the study of adult cognitive plasticity. *Psychological Bulletin, 136*, 659–676.

Löw, A., Lang, P. J., Smith, J. C., & Bradley, M. M. (2008). Both predator and prey: Emotional arousal in threat and reward. *Psychological Science, 19*, 865–873.

Lozano, A. M., Mayberg, H. S., Giacobbe, P., et al. (2008). Subcallosal cingulate gyrus deep brain stimulation for treatment-resistant depression. *Biological Psychiatry, 64*, 461–467.

Lubinski, D. (2004). Introduction to the special section on cognitive abilities: 100 years after Spearman's (1904) "'General intelligence,' objectively determined and measured." *Journal of Personality and Social Psychology, 86*, 96–111.

Lucchina, L. A., Curtis, O. F., Putnam, P., et al. (1998). Psychophysical measurement of 6-n-propylthiouracil (PROP) taste perception. *Annals of the New York Academy of Sciences, 855*, 816–819.

Luders, E., Narr, K. L., Thompson, P. M., et al. (2004). Gender differences in cortical complexity. *Nature Neuroscience, 7*, 799–800.

Lugaresi, E., Medori, R., Montagna, P., et al. (1986, October 16). Fatal familial insomnia and dysautonomia with selective degeneration of thalamic nuclei. *New England Journal of Medicine, 315*, 997–1003.

Luhrmann, T. M. (2000). *Of two minds: The growing disorder in American psychiatry*. New York, NY: Knopf.

Luo, Y., & Baillargeon, R. (2010). Toward a mentalistic account of early psychological reasoning. *Current Directions in Psychological Science, 19*, 301–307.

Luria, A. R. (1968). *The mind of a mnemonist* (L. Soltaroff, Trans.). New York, NY: Basic Books.

Luria, A. R. (1980). *Higher cortical functions in man* (2nd Rev. ed.). New York, NY: Basic Books.

Lykken, D. T. (1998). *A tremor in the blood: Uses and abuses of the lie detector*. New York, NY: Plenum Press.

Lykken, D. T., & Tellegen, A. (1996). Happiness is a stochastic phenomenon. *Psychological Science, 7*, 186–189.

Lyndon, A. E., White, J. W., & Kadlec, K. M. (2007). Manipulation and force as sexual coercion tactics: Conceptual and empirical differences. *Aggressive Behavior, 33*, 291–303.

Lynn, S. J., & Green, J. P. (2011). The sociocognitive and dissociation theories of hypnosis: Toward a rapprochement. *Clinical and Experimental Hypnosis, 59*, 277–293.

Lynn, S. J., Rhue, J. W., & Weekes, J. R. (1990). Hypnotic involuntariness: A social cognitive analysis. *Psychological Review, 97*, 69–184.

Lytton, H., & Romney, D. M. (1991). Parents' differential socialization of boys and girls: A meta-analysis. *Psychological Bulletin, 109*, 267–296.

Maas, J. B. (1998). *Power sleep*. New York, NY: Villard.

Maass, A., Cadinu, M., Guarnieri, G., & Grasselli, A. (2003). Sexual harassment under social identity threat: The computer harassment paradigm. *Journal of Personality and Social Psychology, 85*, 853–870.

MacArthur Foundation Research Network on Successful Midlife Development. (1999). Report of latest findings. (Orville G. Brim, director, 2145 14th Avenue, Vero Beach, FL 32960.)

Maccoby, E. E. (1998). *The two sexes: Growing up apart, coming together*. Cambridge, MA: Belknap Press/Harvard University Press.

Maccoby, E. E. (2002). Gender and group process: A developmental perspective. *Current Directions in Psychological Science, 11*, 54–58.

MacDonald, S. M., Reeder, B. A., Chen, Y., Despres, J. P., & the Canadian Heart Health Surveys Research Group. (1997). Obesity in Canada: A descriptive analysis. *Canadian Medical Association Journal, 157*(Supplement 1), S3–S9.

Mack, A. (2003). Inattentional blindness: Looking without seeing. *Current Directions in Psychological Science, 12*, 180–184.

Macleod, J., Oakes, R., Copello, A., et al. (2004). Psychological and social sequelae of cannabis and other illicit drug use by young people: A systematic review of longitudinal, general population studies. *The Lancet, 363*, 1568–1569.

Macrae, C. N., & Bodenhausen, G. V. (2000). Social cognition: Thinking categorically about others. *Annual Review of Psychology, 51*, 93–120.

Maddux, J. E. (Ed.). (1995). *Self-efficacy, adaptation, and adjustment: Theory, research, and application*. New York, NY: Plenum.

Madsen, K. M., Hviid, A., Vestergaard, M., et al. (2002). A population-based study of measles, mumps, and rubella vaccination and autism. *New England Journal of Medicine, 347*, 1477–1482.

Malamuth, N. M., Linz, D., Heavey, C. L., et al. (1995). Using the confluence model of sexual aggression to predict men's conflict with women: A 10-year follow-up study. *Journal of Personality and Social Psychology, 69*, 353–369.

Malaspina, D. (2001). Paternal factors and schizophrenia risk: De novo mutations and imprinting. *Schizophrenia Bulletin, 27*, 379–393.

Mallinckrodt, B., Porter, M. J., & Kivlighan, D. M. (2005). Client attachment to therapist, depth of in-session exploration, and object relations in brief psychotherapy. *Psychotherapy: Theory, Research, Practice, Training, 42*, 85–100.

Manning, C. A., Hall, J. L., & Gold, P. E. (1990). Glucose effects on memory and other neuropsychological tests in elderly humans. *Psychological Science, 1*, 307–311.

Marchman, V. A., & Fernald, A. (2008). Speed of word recognition and vocabulary knowledge in infancy predict cognitive and language outcomes in later childhood. *Developmental Science, 11,* F9–F16.

Marcus, G. (2004). *The birth of the mind: How a tiny number of genes creates the complexities of human thought.* New York, NY: Basic Books.

Marcus, G. F., Pinker, S., Ullman, M., et al. (1992). Overregularization in language acquisition. *Monographs of the Society for Research in Child Development,* 57(Serial No. 228), 1–182.

Marcus-Newhall, A., Pedersen, W. C., Carlson, M., & Miller, N. (2000). Displaced aggression is alive and well: A meta-analytic review. *Journal of Personality and Social Psychology, 78,* 670–689.

Margolin, G., & Gordis, E. B. (2004). Children's exposure to violence in the family and community. *Current Directions in Psychological Science, 13,* 152–155.

Markowitz, J. S., Donovan, J. L., DeVane, C. L., et al. (2003, September 17). Effect of St John's wort on drug metabolism by induction of cytochrome P450 3A4 enzyme. *Journal of the American Medical Association, 290,* 1519–1520.

Markus, H. R., & Kitayama, S. (1991). Culture and the self: Implications for cognition, emotion, and motivation. *Psychological Review, 98,* 224–253.

Marlatt, G. A., & Rohsenow, D. J. (1980). Cognitive processes in alcohol use: Expectancy and the balanced placebo design. In N. K. Mello (Ed.), *Advances in substance abuse* (Vol. 1). Greenwich, CT: JAI Press.

Marrone, D. F., Ramirez-Amaya, V., & Barnes, C. A. (2012). Neurons generated in senescence maintain capacity for functional integration. *Hippocampus, 22,* 1134–1142.

Marrone, D. F., Schaner, M. J., McNaughton, B. L., Worley, P. F., & Barnes, C. A. (2008). Immediate-Early Gene Expression at Rest Recapitulates Recent Experience. *The Journal of Neuroscience, 28,* 1030–1033.

Marsh, E. J., & Tversky, B. (2004). Spinning the stories of our lives. *Applied Cognitive Psychology, 18,* 491–503.

Martin, C. L., & Ruble, D. (2004). Children's search for gender cues. *Current Directions in Psychological Science, 13,* 67–70.

Martin, C. L., Ruble, D. N., & Szkrybalo, J. (2002). Cognitive theories of early gender development. *Psychological Bulletin, 128,* 903–933.

Martin, G., & Pear, J. (2007). *Behavior modification: What it is and how to do it* (8th ed.). New York, NY: Prentice Hall.

Martin, L. J., & Carron, A. V. (2012). Team Attributions in Sport: A Meta-Analysis. *Journal of Applied Sport Psychology, 24,* 157–174.

Martinez, G. M., Chandra, A., Abma, J. C., et al. (2006). *Fertility, contraception, and fatherhood: Data on men and women from Cycle 6 of the 2002 National Survey of Family Growth.* DHHS Publication No. (PHS) 2006-1978. Washington, DC: Centers for Disease Control.

Martino, G., & Marks, L. E. (2001). Synesthesia: Strong and weak. *Current Directions in Psychological Science, 10,* 61–69.

Maruta, T., Colligan R. C., Malinchoc, M., & Offord, K. P. (2000). Optimists vs. pessimists: Survival rate among medical patients over a 30-year period. *Mayo Clinic Proceedings, 75,* 140–143.

Masand, P. S. (2000). Side effects of antipsychotics in the elderly. *Journal of Clinical Psychiatry, 61*(Suppl. 8), 43–49.

Maslach, C., Schaufeli, W. B., & Leiter, M. P. (2001). Job burnout. *Annual Review of Psychology, 52,* 397–422.

Maslow, A. H. (1970). *Motivation and personality* (2nd ed.). New York, NY: Harper & Row.

Maslow, A. H. (1971). *The farther reaches of human nature.* New York, NY: Viking.

Mason, M. P. (2008). *Head cases: Stories of brain injury and its aftermath.* New York, NY: Farrar, Straus & Giroux.

Masson, M. E. J., & Loftus, G. R. (2003). Using confidence intervals for graphically based data interpretation. *Canadian Journal of Experimental Psychology/Revue canadienne de psychologie expérimentale, 57,* 203–220.

Masten, A. S. (2001). Ordinary magic: Resilience processes in development. *American Psychologist, 56,* 227–238.

Masters, W. H., & Johnson, V. E. (1966). *Human sexual response.* Boston, MA: Little, Brown.

Masuda, T., & Nisbett, R. E. (2001). Attending holistically versus analytically: Comparing the context sensitivity of Japanese and Americans. *Journal of Personality and Social Psychology, 81,* 922–934.

Mather, M., Shafir, E., & Johnson, M. K. (2000). Misremembrance of options past: Source monitoring and choice. *Psychological Science, 11,* 132–138.

Matlin, M, (2012). *The psychology of women* (7th ed.). Belmont, CA: Cengage.

Matsumoto, D. (1996). *Culture and psychology.* Pacific Grove, CA: Brooks-Cole.

Matsumoto, D., & Yoo, S. H. (2006). Toward a new generation of cross-cultural research. *Perspectives on Psychological Science, 1,* 234–250.

Matthews, G., Zeidner, M., & Roberts, R. D. (2003). *Emotional intelligence: Science and myth.* Cambridge, MA: MIT Press/Bradford Books.

Maurer, D., Lewis, T. L., Brent, H. P., & Levin, A. V. (1999). Rapid improvement in the acuity of infants after visual input. *Science, 286,* 108–110.

Mauser, G. (1995). Do Canadians use firearms in self-protection? *Canadian Journal of Criminology, 37*(4), 556–561.

Mauser, G. A., & Buckner, H. T. (1997). Canadian attitudes toward gun control: The real story. A Mackenzie Institute Occasional Paper, The Mackenzie Institute.

Max, M., Shanker, Y. G., Huang, L., et al. (2001). Tas1r3, encoding a new candidate taste receptor, is allelic to the sweet responsiveness locus Sac. *Nature Genetics, 28,* 58–63.

Mayer, J. (2009). *The dark side: The inside story of how the war on terror turned into a war on American ideals* (reprint edition). New York, NY: Anchor.

Mayer, J. D., & Salovey, P. (1997). What is emotional intelligence? In P. Salovey & D. Sluyter (Eds.), *Emotional development and emotional intelligence: Implications for educators.* New York, NY: Basic Books.

Mayou, R. A., Ehlers, A., & Hobbs, M. (2000). Psychological debriefing for road traffic accident victims. *British Journal of Psychiatry, 176,* 589–593.

Mazzoni, G. A., Loftus, E. F., & Kirsch, I. (2001). Changing beliefs about implausible autobiographical events: A little plausibility goes a long way. *Journal of Experimental Psychology: Applied, 7,* 51–59.

Mazzoni, G. A., Loftus, E. F., Seitz, A., & Lynn, S. J. (1999). Changing beliefs and memories through dream interpretation. *Applied Cognitive Psychology, 13,* 125–144.

McAdams, D. P. (2006). *The redemptive self: Stories Americans live by.* New York, NY: Oxford University Press.

McAdams, D. P. (2008). Personal narratives and the life story. In O. P. John, R. W. Robbins, & L. A. Pervin (Eds.), *Handbook of personality: Theory and research* (3rd ed.). New York, NY: Guilford.

McAdams, D. P., & Pals, J. L. (2006). A new Big Five: Fundamental principles for an integrative science of personality. *American Psychologist, 61,* 204–217.

McCabe, D. P., & Castel, A. D. (2008). Seeing is believing: The effect of brain images on judgments of scientific reasoning. *Cognition, 107,* 343–352.

McClearn, G. E., Johanson, B., Berg, S., et al. (1997). Substantial genetic influence on cognitive abilities in twins 80 or more years old. *Science, 176,* 1560–1563.

McClelland, D. C., Atkinson, J. W., Clark, R. A., & Lowell, E. L. (1953). *The achievement motive.* New York, NY: Appleton-Century-Crofts.

McClelland, J. L. (1994). The organization of memory: A parallel distributed processing perspective. *Revue Neurologique, 150,* 570–579.

McClelland, J. L. (2011). Memory as a constructive process: The parallel-distributed processing approach. In S. Nalbantian, P. Matthews, & J. L. McClelland (Eds.), *The memory process: Neuroscientific and humanistic perspectives.* Cambridge, MA: MIT Press.

McCrae, R. R. (1987). Creativity, divergent thinking, and openness to experience. *Journal of Personality and Social Psychology, 52,* 1258–1265.

McCrae, R. R., & Costa, P. T. (2008). The five-factor theory of personality. In O. P. John, R. W. Robbins, & L. A. Pervin (Eds.), *Handbook of personality: Theory and research* (3rd ed.). New York, NY: Guilford.

McCrae, R. R., Terracciano, A., & members of the Personality Profiles of Cultures Project. (2005). Universal features of personality traits from the observer's perspective: Data from 50 cultures. *Journal of Personality and Social Psychology, 88,* 547–561.

McDaniel, M. A., Howard, D. C., & Einstein, G. O. (2009). The Read-Recite-Review study strategy: Effective and portable. *Psychological Science, 20,* 516–522.

McDaniel, S. H., Lusterman, D.-D., & Philpot, C. L. (Eds.). (2001). *Casebook for integrating family therapy: An ecosystemic approach.* Washington, DC: American Psychological Association.

McDonough, L., & Mandler, J. M. (1994). Very long-term recall in infancy. *Memory, 2,* 339–352.

McElroy, S. L., & Keck, P. E., Jr. (2000). Pharmacologic agents for the treatment of acute bipolar mania. *Biological Psychiatry, 48,* 539–557.

McEwen, B. S. (2000). Allostasis and allostatic load: Implications for neuropsychopharmacology. *Neuropsychopharmacology, 22,* 108–124.

McEwen, B. S. (2007). Physiology and neurobiology of stress and adaptation: Central role of the brain. *Physiological Review, 87,* 873–904.

McFadden, D. (2008). What do sex, twins, spotted hyenas, ADHD, and sexual orientation have in common? *Perspectives on Psychological Science, 3,* 309–322.

McFarland, C., & Alvaro, C. (2000). The impact of motivation on temporal comparisons: Coping with traumatic events by perceiving personal growth. *Journal of Personality and Social Psychology, 79,* 327–343.

McGaugh, J. L. (1990). Significance and remembrance: The role of neuromodulatory systems. *Psychological Science, 1,* 15–25.

McGoldrick, M. (2005). Irish families. In M. McGoldrick, J. Giordano, & N. Garcia-Preto (Eds.), *Ethnicity and family therapy* (3rd ed.). New York, NY: Guilford.

McGoldrick, M., Gerson, R., & Shellenberger, S. (1999). *Genograms: Assessment and intervention* (2nd ed.). New York, NY: W. W. Norton.

McGrayne, S. B. (2011). *The theory that would not die: How Bayes' rule cracked the Enigma code, hunted down Russian submarines and emerged triumphant from two centuries of controversy.* New Haven, CT: Yale University Press.

McGregor, I., & Holmes, J. G. (1999). How storytelling shapes memory and impressions of relationship events over time. *Journal of Personality and Social Psychology, 76,* 403–419.

McGue, M., Bouchard, T. J., Jr., Iacono, W. G., & Lykken, D. T. (1993). Behavioral genetics of cognitive ability: A life-span perspective. In R. Plomin & G. E. McClearn (Eds.), *Nature, nurture, and psychology.* Washington, DC: American Psychological Association.

McGue, M., & Lykken, D. T. (1992). Genetic influence on risk of divorce. *Psychological Science, 3,* 368–373.

McHugh, P. R. (2008). *Try to remember: Psychiatry's clash over meaning, memory, and mind.* New York, NY: Dana Press.

McHugh, P. R., Lief, H. I., Freyd, P. P., & Fetkewicz, J. M. (2004). From refusal to reconciliation: Family relationships after an accusation based on recovered memories. *Journal of Nervous and Mental Disease, 192,* 525–531.

McIntyre, L., Connor, S. K., & Warren, J. (2000). Child hunger in Canada: Results of the 1994 National Longitudinal Survey of Children and Youth. *Canadian Medical Association Journal, 163*(8), 961–965.

McKee, R. D., & Squire, L. R. (1992). Equivalent forgetting rates in long-term memory for diencephalic and medial temporal lobe amnesia. *Journal of Neuroscience, 12,* 3765–3772.

McKee, R. D., & Squire, L. R. (1993). On the development of declarative memory. *Journal of Experimental Psychology: Learning, Memory, and Cognition, 19,* 397–404.

McKemy, D. D., Neuhausser, W. M., & Julius, D. (2002). Identification of a cold receptor reveals a general role for TRP channels in thermosensation. *Nature, 416,* 52–58.

McKim, M. K., Cramer, K. M., Stuart, B., & O'Connor, D. L. (1999). Infant care decisions and attachment security: The Canadian Transition to Child Care Study. *Canadian Journal of Behavioural Science, 31,* 92–106.

McKinlay, J. B., McKinlay, S. M., & Brambilla, D. (1987). The relative contributions of endocrine changes and social circumstances to depression in mid-aged women. *Journal of Health and Social Behavior, 28,* 345–363.

McLoyd, V. C. (1998). Socioeconomic disadvantage and child development. *American Psychologist, 53*(2), 185–204.

McMullin, D., & White, J. W. (2006). Long-term effects of labeling a rape experience. *Psychology of Women Quarterly, 30,* 96–105.

McNally, R. J. (1994). *Panic disorder: A critical analysis.* New York, NY: Guilford.

McNally, R. J. (2003). *Remembering trauma.* Cambridge, MA: Harvard University Press.

McNally, R. J. (2011). *What is mental illness?* Cambridge, MA: Harvard University Press.

McNally, R. J., Bryant, R. A., & Ehlers, A. (2003). Does early psychological intervention promote recovery from posttraumatic stress? *Psychological Science in the Public Interest, 4,* 45–79.

McNulty, J. K. (2011). The dark side of forgiveness: The tendency to forgive predicts continued psychological and physical aggression in marriage. *Journal of Family Psychology, 24,* 787–790.

McNulty, J. K., & Fincham, F. D. (2012). Beyond positive psychology? Toward a contextual view of psychological processes and well-being. *American Psychologist, 67,* 101–110.

Mealey, L. (1996). Evolutionary psychology: The search for evolved mental mechanisms underlying complex human behavior. In J. P. Hurd (Ed.), *Investigating the biological foundations of human morality* (Vol. 37). Lewiston, NY: Edwin Mellen Press.

Mealey, L. (2000). *Sex differences: Developmental and evolutionary strategies.* San Diego, CA: Academic Press.

Mednick, S. A. (1962). The associative basis of the creative process. *Psychological Review, 69,* 220–232.

Mednick, S. C., Nakayama, K., Cantero, J. L., et al. (2002). The restorative effect of naps on perceptual deterioration. *Nature Neuroscience, 5,* 677–681.

Medvec, V. H., Madey, S. F., & Gilovich, T. (1995). When less is more: Counterfactual thinking and satisfaction among Olympic medalists. *Journal of Personality and Social Psychology, 69,* 603–610.

Meeus, W. H. J., & Raaijmakers, Q. A. W. (1995). Obedience in modern society: The Utrecht studies. In A. G. Miller, B. E. Collins, & D. E. Brief (Eds.), Perspectives on obedience to authority: The legacy of the Milgram experiments. *Journal of Social Issues, 51*(3), 155–175.

Mehl, M. R., Vazire, S., Ramírez-Esparza, N., & Pennebacker, J. W. (2007). Are women really more talkative than men? *Science, 317,* 82.

Meichenbaum, D. H., & Deffenbacher, J. L. (1988). Stress inoculation training. *Counselling Psychologist, 16*(1), 69–90.

Meindl, J. R., & Lerner, M. J. (1985). Exacerbation of extreme responses to an out-group. *Journal of Personality and Social Psychology, 47,* 71–84.

Meissner, C. A., & Brigham, J. C. (2001). Thirty years of investigating the own-race bias in memory for faces: A meta-analytic review. *Psychology, Public Policy, & Law, 7,* 3–35.

Meltzoff, A. N., & Gopnik, A. (1993). The role of imitation in understanding persons and developing a theory of mind. In S. Baron-Cohen, H. Tager-Flusberg, & D. Cohen (Eds.), *Understanding other minds.* New York, NY: Oxford University Press.

Melzack, R. (1992, April). Phantom limbs. *Scientific American, 266,* 120–126. [Reprinted in the special issue Mysteries of the Mind, 1997.]

Melzack, R. (1993). Pain: Past, present and future. *Canadian Journal of Experimental Psychology, 47,* 615–629.

Melzack, R., & Wall, P. D. (1965). Pain mechanisms: A new theory. *Science, 13,* 971–979.

Mendoza-Denton, R., & Page-Gould, E. (2008). Can cross-group friendships influence minority students' well-being at historically white universities? *Psychological Science, 19,* 933–939.

Mennella, J. A., Jagnow, C. P., & Beauchamp, G. K. (2001). Prenatal and postnatal flavor learning by human infants. *Pediatrics, 107,* E88.

Mercer, J. (2006). *Understanding attachment.* Westport, CT: Praeger.

Merikle, P. M., & Skanes, H. E. (1992). Subliminal self-help audiotapes: A search for placebo effects. *Journal of Applied Psychology, 77,* 772–776.

Merton, R. K. (1948). The self-fulfilling prophecy. *Antioch Review, 8,* 193–210.

Mesquita, Batja, & Frijda, Nico H. (1992). Cultural variations in emotions: A review. *Psychological Bulletin, 112,* 179–204.

Meston, C. M., & Buss, D. M. (2007). Why humans have sex. *Archives of Sexual Behavior, 36,* 477–507.

Metcalfe, J. (2009). Metacognitive judgments and control of study. *Current Directions in Psychological Science, 18,* 159–163.

Meyer-Bahlburg, H. F. L., Ehrhardt, A. A., Rosen, L. R., et al. (1995). Prenatal estrogens and the development of homosexual orientation. *Developmental Psychology, 31,* 12–21.

Mezulis, A. H., Abramson, L. Y., Hyde, J. S., & Hankin, B. L. (2004). Is there a positivity bias in attributions? *Psychological Bulletin, 130,* 711–747.

Michael, R. B., Garry, M., & Kirsch, I. (2012). Suggestion, cognition, and behavior. *Current Directions in Psychological Science, 21,* 151–156.

Mickelson, K. D., Kessler, R. C., & Shaver, P. R. (1997). Adult attachment in a nationally representative sample. *Journal of Personality and Social Psychology, 73,* 1092–1106.

Mieda, M., Willie, J. T., Hara, J., et al. (2004). Orexin peptides prevent cataplexy and improve wakefulness in an orexin neuron-ablated model of narcolepsy in mice. *Proceedings of the National Academy of Science, 101,* 4649–4654.

Miklowitz, D. J. (2007). The role of the family in the course and treatment of bipolar disorder. *Current Directions in Psychological Science, 16,* 192–196.

Mikulincer, M., & Goodman, G. (Eds.). (2006). *Dynamics of romantic love: Attachment, caregiving, and sex.* New York, NY: Guilford.

Mikulincer, M., & Shaver, P. R. (2007). *Attachment in adulthood: Structure, dynamics, and change.* New York, NY: Guilford Press.

Mikulincer, M., Shaver, P. R., Gillath, O., & Nitzberg, R. E. (2005). Attachment, caregiving, and altruism: Boosting attachment security increases compassion and helping. *Journal of Personality and Social Psychology, 89,* 817–839.

Mikulincer, M., Shaver, P. R., & Horesh, N. (2006). Attachment bases of emotion regulation and posttraumatic adjustment. In D. K. Snyder, J. A. Simpson, &

J. N. Hughes (Eds.), *Emotion regulation in couples and families: Pathways to dysfunction and health*. Washington, DC: American Psychological Association.

Milgram, S. (1963). Behavioral study of obedience. *Journal of Abnormal and Social Psychology, 67*, 371–378.

Milgram, S. (1974). *Obedience to authority: An experimental view*. New York, NY: Harper & Row.

Millar, W. J., & Stephens, T. (1993). Social status and health risks in Canadian adults: 1985 and 1991. *Health Report, 5*, 143–156.

Miller, G. (2000). *The mating mind: How sexual choice shaped the evolution of human nature*. New York, NY: Doubleday.

Miller, G. (2008, April 11). Tackling alcoholism with drugs. *Science, 320*, 168–170.

Miller, G. (2011, January 21). ESP paper rekindles discussion about statistics. *Science, 331*, 272–273.

Miller, G. A. (1956). The magical number seven, plus or minus two: Some limits on our capacity for processing information. *Psychological Review, 63*, 81–97.

Miller, G. E., Chen, E., & Parker, K. J. (2011). Psychological stress in childhood and susceptibility to the chronic diseases of aging: Moving toward a model of behavioral and biological mechanisms. *Psychological Bulletin, 137*, 959–997.

Miller, G. E., Chen, E., & Zhou, E. S. (2007). If it goes up, must it come down? Chronic stress and the hypothalamic-pituitary-adrenocortical axis in humans. *Psychological Bulletin, 133*, 25–45.

Miller, G. E., Lachman, M. E., Chen, E., et al. (2011). Pathways to resilience: Maternal nurturance as a buffer against the effects of childhood poverty on metabolic syndrome. *Psychological Science, 22*, 1591–1599.

Miller, W. R., & Rollnick, S. (2002). *Motivational interviewing: Preparing people for change* (2nd ed.). New York, NY: Guilford Press.

Miller-Jones, D. (1989). Culture and testing. *American Psychologist, 44*, 360–366.

Milner, B. (1970). Memory and the temporal regions of the brain. In K. H. Pribram & D. E. Broadbent (Eds.), *Biology of memory*. New York, NY: Academic Press.

Milton, J., & Wiseman, R. (1999). Does psi exist? Lack of replication of an anomalous process of information transfer. *Psychological Bulletin, 125*, 387–391.

Milton, J., & Wiseman, R. (2001). Does psi exist? Reply to Storm and Ertel (2001). *Psychological Bulletin, 127*, 434–438.

Mineka, S., & Zinbarg, R. (2006). A contemporary learning theory perspective on the etiology of anxiety disorders: It's not what you thought it was. *American Psychologist, 61*, 10–26.

Minuchin, S. (1984). *Family kaleidoscope*. Cambridge, MA: Harvard University Press.

Mischel, W. (1973). Toward a cognitive social learning reconceptualization of personality. *Psychological Review, 80*, 252–253.

Mischel, W. (2009, May 24). *The new genetics and what it means for psychological science*. Introduction to the presidential symposium at the annual meeting of the Association for Psychological Science, San Francisco, CA.

Mischel, W., & Ayduk, O. (2004). Willpower in a cognitive-affective processing system: The dynamics of delay of gratification. In R. F. Baumeister & K. D. Vohs (Eds.), *Handbook of self-regulation: Research, theory, and applications*. New York, NY: Guilford Press.

Mischel, W., & Shoda, Y. (1995). A cognitive affective system theory of personality: Reconceptualizing situations, dispositions, dynamics, and invariance in personality structures. *Psychological Review, 102*, 246–268.

Mischel, W., Shoda, Y., & Rodriguez, M. L. (1989). Delay of gratification in children. *Science, 244*, 933–938.

Mistry, J., & Rogoff, B. (1994). Remembering in cultural context. In W. J. Lonner & R. Malpass (Eds.), *Psychology and culture*. Needham Heights, MA: Allyn & Bacon.

Mitchell, D. B. (2006). Nonconscious priming after 17 years: Invulnerable implicit memory? *Psychological Science, 17*, 925–929.

Mitchell, K. J., & Johnson, M. K. (2009). Source monitoring 15 years later: What have we learned from fMRI about the neural mechanisms of source memory? *Psychological Bulletin, 135*, 638–677.

Mitte, K. (2005). Meta-analysis of cognitive-behavioral treatments for generalized anxiety disorder: A comparison with pharmacotherapy. *Psychological Bulletin, 131*, 785–795.

Mitterer, H., & de Ruiter, J. P. (2008). Recalibrating color categories using world knowledge. *Psychological Science, 19*, 629–634.

Miyamoto, Y., Nisbett, R. E., & Masuda, T. (2006). Culture and the physical environment: Holistic versus analytic perceptual affordances. *Psychological Science, 17*, 113–119.

Mnookin, S. (2011). *The panic virus: A true story of medicine, science, and fear*. New York, NY: Simon & Schuster.

Modigliani, A., & Rochat, F. (1995). The role of interaction sequences and the timing of resistance in shaping obedience and defiance to authority. In A. G. Miller, B. E. Collins, & D. E. Brief (Eds.), Perspectives on obedience to authority: The legacy of the Milgram experiments. *Journal of Social Issues, 51*(3), 107–125.

Moghaddam, F. M. (2005). The staircase to terrorism: A psychological exploration. *American Psychologist, 60*, 161–169.

Moles, A., Kieffer, B., & D'Amato, F. (2004). Deficit in attachment behavior in mice lacking the μ-opioid receptor gene. *Science, 304*, 1983–1986.

Monaghan, P. (2014). Organismal stress, telomeres and life histories. *Journal of Experimental Biology, 217*, 57–66.

Monahan, J. L., Murphy, S. T., & Zajonc, R. B. (2000). Subliminal mere exposure: Specific, general, and diffuse effects. *Psychological Science, 11*, 462–466.

Moncrieff, J. (2001). Are antidepressants overrated? A review of methodological problems in antidepressant trials. *Journal of Nervous and Mental Disease, 189*, 288–295.

Montmayeur, J. P., Liberies, S. D., Matsunami, H., & Buck, L. B. (2001). A candidate taste receptor gene near a sweet taste locus. *Nature Neuroscience, 4*, 492–498.

Moore, R. Y. (1997). Circadian rhythms: Basic neurobiology and clinical applications. *Annual Review of Medicine, 48*, 253–266.

Moore, T. E. (1992, Spring). Subliminal perception: Facts and fallacies. *Skeptical Inquirer, 16*, 273–281.

Moore, T. E. (1995). Subliminal self-help auditory tapes: An empirical test of perceptual consequences. *Canadian Journal of Behavioural Science, 27*, 9–20.

Moore, T. E., & Pepler, D. J. (2006). Wounding words: Maternal verbal aggression and children's adjustment. *Journal of Family Violence, 21*, 89–93.

Moors, A., Ellsworth, P. C., Scherer, K., & Frijda, N. (in press). Appraisal theories of emotion: State of the art and future development. *Emotion Review*.

Morell, V. (2008, March). Minds of their own. *National Geographic, 213*, 36–61.

Morelli, G. A., Rogoff, B., Oppenheim, D., & Goldsmith, D. (1992). Cultural variation in infants' sleeping arrangements: Questions of independence. *Developmental Psychology, 28*, 604–613.

Moreno, C., Laje, G., Blanco, C., et al. (2007). National trends in the outpatient diagnosis and treatment of bipolar disorder in youth. *Archives of General Psychiatry, 64*, 1032–1039.

Morgan, C. A., Hazlett, G., Baranoski, M., et al. (2007). Accuracy of eyewitness identification is significantly associated with performance on a standardized test of face recognition. *International Journal of Law and Psychiatry, 30*, 213–223.

Morin, C. M., Vallières, A., Guay, B., et al. (2009). Cognitive behavioral therapy, singly and combined with medication, for persistent insomnia. *Journal of the American Medical Association, 301*, 2005–2015.

Morrison, T. G., & O'Connor, W. E. (1999). Psychometric properties of a scale measuring negative attitudes toward overweight individuals. *Journal of Social Psychology, 139*, 436–445.

Morton, L. L., Allen, J. D., & Williams, N. (1994). Hemisphericity and information processing North American native (Objiwa) and non-native adolescents. *International Journal of Neuroscience, 75*(3–4), 189–202.

Morton, T. A., Postmes, T., Haslam, S. A., & Hornsey, M. J. (2009). Theorizing gender in the face of social change: Is there anything essential about essentialism? *Journal of Personality and Social Psychology, 96*, 653–664.

Moscovitch, M., Winocur, G., & Behrmann, M. (1997). What is special about face recognition? Nineteen experiments on a person with visual object agnosia and dyslexia but normal face recognition. *Journal of Cognitive Neuroscience, 9*, 555–604.

Moskowitz, J. T., Hult, J. R., Bussolari, C., & Acree, M. (2009). What works in coping with HIV? A meta-analysis with implications for coping with serious illness. *Psychological Bulletin, 135*, 121–141.

Moyer, C. A., Donnelly, M. P. W., Anderson, J. C., et al. (2011). Frontal electroencephalographic asymmetry associated with positive emotion is produced by brief meditation training. *Psychological Science, 22*, 1277–1279.

Moyer, C. A., Rounds, J., & Hannum, J. W. (2004). A meta-analysis of massage therapy research. *Psychological Bulletin, 130*, 3–18.

Mozell, M. M., Smith, B. P., Smith, P. E., et al. (1969). Nasal chemoreception in flavor identification. *Archives of Otolaryngology, 90*, 367–373.

Mroczek, D. K., & Spiro, A., III. (2005). Changes in life satisfaction during adulthood: Findings from the veterans affairs normative aging study. *Journal of Personality and Social Psychology, 88*, 189–202.

Mueller, C. M., & Dweck, C. S. (1998). Praise for intelligence can undermine children's motivation and performance. *Journal of Personality and Social Psychology, 75*, 33–52.

Mueller, U., Rowe, J. B., Rittman, T., Lewis, C., Robbins, T. W., & Sahakian, B. J. (2013). Effects of modafinil on non-verbal cognition, task enjoyment and creative thinking in healthy volunteers. *Neuropharmacology, 64,* 490–495.

Mukamal, K. J., Conigrove, K. M., Mittleman, M. A., et al. (2003). Roles of drinking pattern and type of alcohol consumed in coronary heart disease in men. *New England Journal of Medicine, 348,* 109–118.

Müller, C. P., & Schumann, G. (2011). Drugs as instruments: A new framework for non-addictive psychoactive drug use. Behavioral and Brain *Sciences, 34,* 293–310.

Müller, R.-A., Courchesne, E., & Allen, G. (1998). The cerebellum: So much more [letter] *Science, 282,* 879–880.

Murray, C. (2008). Real education: Four simple truths for bringing America's schools back to reality. New York, NY: Crown Forum.

Myers, D. G., & Scanzoni, L. D. (2005). *What God has joined together: The Christian case for gay marriage.* San Francisco, CA: HarperSanFrancisco.

Myrtek, M. (2007). Type A behavior and hostility as independent risk factors for coronary heart disease. In J. Jordan et al. (Eds.), *Contributions toward evidence-based psychocardiology: A systematic review of the literature.* Washington, DC: American Psychological Association.

Na, J., & Kitayama, S. (2011). Spontaneous trait inference is culture-specific: Behavioral and neural evidence. *Psychological Science, 22,* 1025–1032.

Nachman, M. W., Hoekstra, H. E., & D'Agostino, S. L. (2003). The genetic basis of adaptive melanism in pocket mice. *Proceedings of the National Academy of Science, 100,* 5268–5273.

Nakaya, N., Tsubono, Y., Hosokawa, T., et al. (2003). Personality and the risk of cancer. *Journal of the National Cancer Institute, 95,* 799–805.

Nash, M. R. (1987). What, if anything, is regressed about hypnotic age regression? A review of the empirical literature. *Psychological Bulletin, 102,* 42–52.

Nash, M. R. (2001, July). The truth and the hype of hypnosis. *Scientific American, 285,* 46–49, 52–55.

Nash, M. R., & Barnier, A. J. (2007). *The Oxford handbook of hypnosis.* Oxford, England: Oxford University Press.

Nash, M. R., & Nadon, R. (1997). Hypnosis. In D. L. Faigman, D. Kaye, M. J. Saks, & J. Sanders (Eds.), *Modern scientific evidence: The law and science of expert testimony.* St. Paul, MN: West.

Nathan, D. (2011). *Sybil exposed: The extraordinary story behind the famous multiple personality case.* New York: Free Press.

National Science Board. (2000). *Science & engineering indicators 2000.* Arlington, VA: National Science Foundation. [A reprint of the relevant section of this chapter can be found in the January/February 2001 issue of *Skeptical Inquirer,* pp. 12–15.]

Navarrete, C. D., Olsson, A., Ho, A. K., et al. (2009). Fear extinction to an outgroup face: The role of target gender. *Psychological Science, 20,* 155–158.

Neal, D. T., & Chartrand, T. L. (2011). Embodied emotion perception: Amplifying and dampening facial feedback modulates emotion perception accuracy. *Social Psychological and Personality Science, 2,* 673–678.

Needleman, H. L., Riess, J. A., Tobin, M. J., et al. (1996). Bone lead levels and delinquent behavior. *Journal of the American Medical Association, 275,* 363–369.

Neher, A. (1996). Jung's theory of archetypes: A critique. *Journal of Humanistic Psychology, 36,* 61–91.

Neisser, U. (Ed.). (1998). *The rising curve: Long-term gains in IQ and related measures.* Washington, DC: American Psychological Association.

Neisser, U., & Harsch, N. (1992). Phantom flashbulbs: False recollections of hearing the news about *Challenger.* In E. Winograd & U. Neisser (Eds.), *Affect and accuracy in recall: Studies of "flashbulb memories."* New York, NY: Cambridge University Press.

Nelson, C. A., III, Zeanah, C. H., Fox, N. A., et al. (2007). Cognitive recovery in socially deprived young children: The Bucharest early intervention project. *Science, 318,* 1937–1940.

Nelson, G., Westhues, A., & MacLeod, J. (2003). A meta-analysis of longitudinal research on preschool prevention programs for children. *Prevention & Treatment, 6*(1), article 31. Retrieved from http://webarchive.nationalarchives.gov.uk/+/http://www.hm-treasury.gov.uk/d/cypreview2006_cphva7.pdf

Ness, J., Aronow, W. S., & Beck, G. (2006). Menopausal symptoms after cessation of hormone replacement therapy. *Maturitas, 53,* 356–361.

Nesse, R. M., & Ellsworth, P. C. (2009). Evolution, emotion, and emotional disorders. *American Psychologist, 64,* 129–139.

Newcombe, N. S., Lloyd, M. E., & Balcomb, F. (2012). Contextualizing the development of recollection: Episodic memory and binding in young children. In

S. Ghetti & P. J. Bauer (Eds.), *Origins and development of recollection: Perspectives from psychology and Neuroscience.* New York: Oxford University Press.

Newland, M. C., & Rasmussen, E. B. (2003). Behavior in adulthood and during aging is affected by contaminant exposure in utero. *Current Directions in Psychological Science, 12,* 212–217.

NICHD Early Child Care Research Network. (2006). Infant-mother attachment classification: Risk and protection in relation to changing maternal caregiving quality. *Developmental Psychology, 42,* 38–58.

Nichols, M. P., & Schwartz, R. C. (2008). *Family therapy: Concepts and methods* (8th ed.). Boston, MA: Allyn & Bacon.

Nickerson, R. A., & Adams, M. J. (1979). Long-term memory for a common object. *Cognitive Psychology, 11,* 287–307.

Nickerson, R. S. (1998). Confirmation bias: A ubiquitous phenomenon in many guises. *Review of General Psychology, 2,* 175–220.

Nisbett, R. E. (1993). Violence and U.S. regional culture. *American Psychologist, 48,* 441–449.

Nisbett, R. E. (2009). *Intelligence and how to get it: Why schools and culture count.* New York, NY: W. W. Norton.

Nisbett, R. E., Aronson, J., Blair, C., et al. (2012). Intelligence: New findings and theoretical developments. *The American Psychologist, 67,* 130–159.

Nisbett, R. E., & Ross, L. (1980). *Human inference: Strategies and shortcomings of social judgment.* Englewood Cliffs, NJ: Prentice-Hall.

Nishimoto, S., Vu, A. T., Naselaris, T., et al. (2011). Reconstructing visual experiences from brain activity evoked by natural movies. *Current Biology, 21,* 1641–1646.

Nitsche, M. A., Cohen, L. G., Wassermann, E. M., et al. (2008). Transcranial direct current stimulation: State of the art 2008. *Brain Stimulation, 1,* 206–223.

Nivet, E., Vignes, M., Girard, S. D., et al. (2011). Engraftment of human nasal olfactory stem cells restores neuroplasticity in mice with hippocampal lesions. *The Journal of Clinical Investigation, 121,* 2808–2820.

Noble, M., Mayer-Pröschel, M., Davies, J. E., et al. (2011). Cell therapies for the central nervous system: How do we identify the best candidates? *Current Opinion in Neurology, 24,* 570–576.

Nolan, S. A., Flynn, C., & Garber, J. (2003). Prospective relations between rejection and depression in young adolescents. *Journal of Personality and Social Psychology, 85,* 745–755.

Nonaka, S., Hough, C. J., & Chuang, D.-M. (1998, March 3). Chronic lithium treatment robustly protects neurons in the central nervous system against excitotoxicity by inhibiting N-methyl-D-aspartate receptor-mediated calcium influx. *Proceedings of the National Academy of Sciences, 95,* 2642–2647.

Norcross, J. C., Kohout, J. L., & Wicherski, M. (2005). Graduate study in psychology: 1971 to 2004. *American Psychologist, 60,* 959–975.

Norman, D. A. (1988). *The psychology of everyday things.* New York, NY: Basic Books.

Nosek, B. A., Greenwald, A. G., & Banaji, M. R. (2007). The Implicit Association Test at 7: A methodological and conceptual review. In J. A. Bargh (Ed.), *Social psychology and the unconscious.* New York, NY: Psychology Press.

Nunez, N., Poole, D. A., & Memon, A. (2002). Psychology's two cultures revisited: Implications for the integration of science with practice. *Scientific Review of Mental Health Practice, 1.*

Nunn, J. A., Gregory, L. J., Brammer, M., et al. (2002). Functional magnetic resonance imaging of synesthesia: Activation of V4/V8 by spoken words. *Nature neuroscience, 5,* 371–375.

Nyberg, L., Habib, R., McIntosh, A. R., & Tulving, E. (2000). Reactivation of encoding-related brain activity during memory retrieval. *Proceedings of the National Academy of Sciences, 97,* 11120–11124.

Nyström, P. (2008). The infant mirror neuron system studied with high density EEG. *Social Neuroscience, 3,* 334–347.

Oaten, M., Stevenson, R. J., & Case, T. I. (2009). Disgust as a disease-avoidance mechanism. *Psychological Bulletin, 125,* 303–321.

Oatley, K., Keltner, D., & Jenkins, J. M. (2006). *Understanding emotions* (2nd ed.). Malden, MA: Blackwell.

O'Connor, T. G., Rutter, M., Beckett, C., et al. (2000). English and Romanian Adoptees Study Team. The effects of global severe privation on cognitive competence: Extension and longitudinal follow-up. *Child Development, 71*(2), 376–390.

Offit, P. A. (2008). *Autism's false prophets: Bad science, risky medicine, and the search for a cure.* New York, NY: Columbia University Press.

Ofshe, R. J., & Watters, E. (1994). *Making monsters: False memory, psychotherapy, and sexual hysteria.* New York, NY: Scribners.

Ogden, J. (2012). *Trouble in mind: Stories from a neuropsychologist's casebook.* New York: Oxford University Press.

Ogden, J. A., & Corkin, S. (1991). Memories of H. M. In W. C. Abraham, M. C. Corballis, & K. G. White (Eds.), *Memory mechanisms: A tribute to G. V. Goddard.* Hillsdale, NJ: Erlbaum.

O'Hanlon, B. (1994, November/December). The third wave. *Family Therapy Networker,* 18–29.

Öhman, A., & Mineka, S. (2001). Fears, phobias, and preparedness: Toward an evolved module of fear and fear learning. *Psychological Review, 108,* 483–522.

Oliver, M. B., & Hyde, J. S. (1993). Gender differences in sexuality: A meta-analysis. *Psychological Bulletin, 114,* 29–51.

Olson, J. M., Vernon, P. A., Harris, J. A., & Jang, K. L. (2001). The heritability of attitudes: A study of twins. *Journal of Personality and Social Psychology, 80,* 845–850.

Olson, M. A. (2009). Measures of prejudice. In T. Nelson (Ed.), *The handbook of prejudice, sterotyping, and discrimination.* New York, NY: Psychology Press.

Olsson, A., Ebert, J., Banaji, M., & Phelps, E. A. (2005). The role of social groups in the persistence of learned fear. *Science, 309,* 785–787.

Olsson, A., & Phelps, E. (2004). Learned fear of "unseen" faces after Pavlovian, observational, and instructed fear. *Psychological Science, 15,* 822–828.

Olujic, M. B. (1998). Embodiment of terror: Gendered violence in peacetime and wartime in Croatia and Bosnia-Herzegovina. *Medical Anthropology Quarterly, 12,* 31–50.

O'Neill, S., & Zajac, R. (2012). The role of repeated interviewing in children's responses to cross-examination-style questioning. *British Journal of Psychology.* doi:10.1111/j.2044-295.2011.02096.x.

Ong, A. D. (2010). Pathways linking positive emotion and health in later life. *Current Directions in Psychological Science, 19,* 358–362.

Ophir, E., Nass, C., & Wagner, A. D. (2009). Cognitive control in media multitaskers. *Proceedings of the National Academy of Sciences.* doi:10.1073/pnas.0903620106

O'Rahilly, R., & Müller, F. (2001). *Human embryology and teratology.* New York, NY: Wiley.

Orbach, S. (2009). *Bodies.* London, England: Profile Books.

Orians, G. H., & Heerwagen, J. H. (1992). Evolved responses to landscapes. In J. Barkow, L. Cosmides, & J. Tooby (Eds.), *The adapted mind* (pp. 555–579). New York, NY: Oxford University Press.

Orr, P. H., Martin, B. D., Patterson, K., & Moffat, M. E. (1998). Prevalence of diabetes mellitus and obesity in the Keewatin District of the Canadian Arctic. *International Journal of Circumpolar Health, 57* (Supplement 1), 340–347.

Ó Scalaidhe, S. P., Wilson, F. A. W., & Goldman-Rakic, P. S. (1997). A real segregation of face-processing neurons in prefrontal cortex. *Science, 278,* 1135–1138.

O'Sullivan, L. F., & Allgeier, Elizabeth, R. (1998). Feigning sexual desire: Consenting to unwanted sexual activity in heterosexual dating relationships. *Journal of Sex Research, 35,* 234–243.

O'Sullivan, L. F., Byers, E. S., & Finkelman, L. (1998). A comparison of male and female college students' experiences of sexual coercion. *Psychology of Women Quarterly, 22,* 177–195.

Osland, T. M., Bjorvatn, B., Steen, V. M., & Pallesen, S. (2011). Association study of a variable-number tandem repeat polymorphism in the clock gene PERIOD3 and chronotype in Norwegian university students. *Chronobiology International, 28,* 764–770.

Otto, M. W., Behar, E., Smits, J. A. J., & Hoffmann, S. G. (2009). Combining pharmacological and cognitive behavioral therapy in the treatment of anxiety disorders. In M. M. Antony & M.B. Stein (Eds.), *Oxford handbook of anxiety and related disorders.* New York: Oxford University Press.

Otto, M., & Smits, J. A. J. (2012). *Exercise for mood and anxiety.* New York: Oxford University Press.

Ouellet, V., Labbé, S. M., Blondin, D. P., et al. (2012). Brown adipose tissue oxidative metabolism contributes to energy expenditure during acute cold exposure in humans. *The Journal of Clinical Investigation, 122,* 545–552.

Oxnam, R. B. (2005). *A Fractured Mind.* New York: Hyperion.

Oyserman, D., & Lee, S. W. S. (2008). Does culture influence what and how we think? Effects of priming individualism and collectivism. *Psychological Bulletin, 134,* 311–342.

Özgen, E. (2004). Language, learning, and color perception. *Current Directions in Psychological Science, 13,* 95–98.

Packer, D. J. (2008). Identifying systematic disobedience in Milgram's obedience experiments: A meta-analytic review. *Perspectives on Psychological Science, 3,* 301–304.

Packer, D. J. (2009). Avoiding groupthink: Whereas weakly identified members remain silent, strongly identified members dissent about collective problems. *Psychological Science, 20,* 619–626.

Pagel, J. F. (2003). Non-dreamers. *Sleep Medicine, 4,* 235–241.

Pail, G., Huf, W., Pjrek, E., et al. (2011). Bright-light therapy in the treatment of mood disorders. *Neuropsychobiology, 64,* 152–162.

Panksepp, J., Herman, B. H., Vilberg, T., et al. (1980). Endogenous opioids and social behavior. *Neuroscience and Biobehavioral Reviews, 4,* 473–487.

Paoletti, J. (2012). *Pink and blue: Telling the girls from the boys in America.* Bloomington, IN: University of Indiana Press.

Parada, M., Corral, M., Mota, N., et al. (2012). Executive functioning and alcohol binge drinking in university students. *Addictive Behaviors, 37,* 167–172.

Park, D., & Gutchess, A. (2006). The cognitive neuroscience of aging and culture. *Current Directions in Psychological Science, 15,* 105–108.

Park, R. L. (2000). *Voodoo science: The road from foolishness to fraud.* New York, NY: Oxford University Press.

Parker, E. S., Birnbaum, I. M., & Noble, E. P. (1976). Alcohol and memory: Storage and state dependency. *Journal of Verbal Learning and Verbal Behavior, 15,* 691–702.

Parker, E. S., Cahill, L., & McGaugh, J. L. (2006). A case of unusual autobiographical remembering. *Neurocase, 12,* 35–49.

Parlee, M. B. (1994). The social construction of premenstrual syndrome: A case study of scientific discourse as cultural contestation. In M. G. Winkler & L. B. Cole (Eds.), *The good body: Asceticism in contemporary culture.* New Haven, CT: Yale University Press.

Pascual-Leone, A., Amedi, A., Fregni, F., & Merabet, L. B. (2005). The plastic human brain cortex. *Annual Review of Neuroscience, 28,* 377–401.

Pastalkova, E., Itskov, V., Amarasingham, A., & Buzsáki, G. (2008, September 5). Internally generated cell assembly sequences in the rat hippocampus. *Science, 321,* 1322–1327.

Patterson, C. J. (1992). Children of lesbian and gay parents. *Child Development, 63,* 1025–1042.

Patterson, D. R., & Jensen, M. P. (2003). Hypnosis and clinical pain. *Psychological Bulletin, 129,* 495–521.

Patterson, F., & Linden, E. (1981). *The education of Koko.* New York, NY: Holt, Rinehart and Winston.

Patterson-Kane, E. G., Harper, D., & Hunt, M. (2001). Cage preferences of laboratory rats. *Laboratory Animals, 35,* 74–79.

Paul, A. M. (2004). *The cult of personality.* New York, NY: The Free Press.

Paul, P. (2008). *Parenting, Inc.: How the billion-dollar baby business has changed the way we raise our children.* New York, NY: Henry Holt.

Paul, R. W. (1984, September). Critical thinking: Fundamental to education for a free society. *Educational Leadership,* 4–14.

Paunonen, S. V. (2003). Big Five factors or personality and replicated predictions of behavior. *Journal of Personality & Social Psychology, 84,* 411–422.

Paunonen, S. V., & Ashton, M. C. (2001). Big Five factors and facets and the prediction of behavior. *Journal of Personality and Social Psychology, 81,* 524–539.

Pavlov, I. P. (1927). *Conditioned reflexes* (G. V. Anrep, Trans.). London, England: Oxford University Press.

Payne, J. D., Stickgold, R., Swanberg, K., & Kensinger, E. A. (2008). Sleep preferentially enhances memory for emotional components of scenes. *Psychological Science, 19,* 781–788.

Pearlin, L. (1982). Discontinuities in the study of aging. In T. K. Hareven & K. J. Adams (Eds.), *Aging and life course transitions: An interdisciplinary perspective.* New York, NY: Guilford.

Peier, A. M., Moqrich, A., Hergarden, A. C., et al. (2002). A TRP channel that senses cold stimuli and menthol. *Cell, 108,* 705–715.

Pellegrini, A. D., & Galda, L. (1993). Ten years after: A reexamination of symbolic play and literacy research. *Reading Research Quarterly, 28,* 163–175.

Peng, Y., McCann-Hiltz, D., & Goddard, E. (2004). Consumer demand for meat in Alberta, Canada: Impact of BSE. Retrieved February 11, 2008, from http://ageconsearch.umn.edu/bitstream/123456789/15505/1/sp04pe07.pdf

Pennebaker, J. W. (2002). Writing, social processes, and psychotherapy: From past to future. In S. J. Lepore & J. M. Smyth (Eds.), *The writing cure: How expressive writing promotes health and emotional well-being.* Washington, DC: American Psychological Association.

Pennebaker, J. W. (2011). *The secret life of pronouns: What our words say about us.* New York: Bloomsbury.

Pennebaker, J. W., Colder, M., & Sharp, L. K. (1990). Accelerating the coping process. *Journal of Personality and Social Psychology, 58*, 527–528.

Pennebaker, J. W., Kiecolt-Glaser, J., & Glaser, R. (1988). Disclosure of traumas and immune function: Health implications for psychotherapy. *Journal of Consulting and Clinical Psychology, 56*, 239–245.

Pennisi, E. (2005). Why do humans have so few genes? *Science, 309*, 80.

Peplau, L. A. (2003). Human sexuality: How do men and women differ? *Current Directions in Psychological Science, 12*, 37–40.

Peplau, L. A., & Spalding, L. R. (2000). The close relationships of lesbians, gay men and bisexuals. In C. Hendrick & S. Hendrick (Eds.), *Close relationships: A sourcebook*. Thousand Oaks, CA: Sage.

Peplau, L. A., Spalding, L. R., Conley, T. D., & Veniegas, R. C. (2000). The development of sexual orientation in women. *Annual Review of Sex Research, 10*, 70–99.

Pepperberg, I. (2000). *The Alex studies: Cognitive and communicative abilities of grey parrots*. Cambridge, MA: Harvard University Press.

Pepperberg, I. M. (2002). Cognitive and communicative abilities of grey parrots. *Current Directions in Psychological Science, 11*, 83–87.

Pepperberg, I. M. (2006). Grey parrot (*Psittacus erithacus*) numerical abilities: Addition and further experiments on a zero-like concept. *Journal of Comparative Psychology, 120*, 1–11.

Pepperberg, I. M. (2008). *Alex and me*. New York: HarperCollins.

Perera, F. P., Rauh, V., Whyatt, R. M., et al. (2006). Effect of prenatal exposure to airborne polycyclic aromatic hydrocarbons on neurodevelopment in the first three years of life among inner-city children. *Environmental Health Perspectives*. doi:10.1289/ehp.9084

Persinger, M. A., & Makarec, K. (1987). Temporal lobe epileptic signs and correlative behaviors displayed by normal populations. *Journal of General Psychology, 114*(2), 179–195.

Persons, J., Davidson, J., & Tompkins, M. A. (2001). *Essential components of cognitive-behavior therapy for depression*. Washington, DC: American Psychological Association.

Peterson, C., Seligman, M. E. P., Yurko, K. H., et al. (1998). Catastrophizing and untimely death. *Psychological Science, 9*, 127–130.

Peterson, D. R. (2003). Unintended consequences: Ventures and misadventures in the education of professional psychologists. *American Psychologist, 58*, 791–800.

Peterson, L. R., & Peterson, M. J. (1959). Short-term retention of individual verbal items. *Journal of Experimental Psychology, 58*, 193–198.

Peterson, Z. D., & Muehlenhard, C. L. (2011). A match-andmotivation model of how women label their nonconsensual sexual experiences. *Psychology of Women Quarterly, 35*, 558–570.

Petersson, K. M., Silva, C., Castro-Caldas, A., et al. (2007). Literacy: a cultural influence on functional left-right differences in the inferior parietal cortex. *European Journal of Neuroscience, 26*, 791–799.

Petkova, V. I., & Ehrsson, H. H. (2008). If I were you: Perceptual illusion of body swapping. *PLoS ONE, 3*: e3832. doi:10.1371/journal.pone.0003832

Petrie, K. J., Booth, R. J., & Pennebaker, J. W. (1998). The immunological effects of thought suppression. *Journal of Personality and Social Psychology, 75*, 1264–1272.

Pettigrew, T. T., & Tropp, L. R. (2006). A meta-analytic test of intergroup contact theory. *Journal of Personality and Social Psychology, 90*, 751–783.

Pfungst, O. (1911/1965). *Clever Hans (The horse of Mr. von Osten): A contribution to experimental animal and human psychology*. New York, NY: Holt, Rinehart and Winston.

Phinney, J. S. (1996). When we talk about American ethnic groups, what do we mean? *American Psychologist, 51*, 918–927.

Piaget, J. (1929/1960). *The child's conception of the world*. Paterson, NJ: Littlefield, Adams.

Piaget, J. (1952). *Play, dreams, and imitation in childhood*. New York, NY: W. W. Norton.

Piaget, J. (1984). Piaget's theory. In P. Mussen (Series Ed.) & W. Kessen (Vol. Ed.), *Handbook of child psychology: Vol. 1. History, theory, and methods* (4th ed.). New York: Wiley.

Pierce, W. D., Cameron, J., Banko, K. M., & So, S. (2003). Positive effects of rewards and performance standards on intrinsic motivation. *Psychological Record, 53*, 561–579.

Pika, S., & Mitani, J. (2006). Referential gesture communication in wild chimpanzees (*Pan troglodytes*). *Current Biology, 16*, 191–192.

Pinker, S. (1994). *The language instinct: How the mind creates language*. New York, NY: Morrow.

Pinker, S. (1997). *How the mind works*. New York, NY: Norton.

Pinker, S. (2002). *The blank slate: The modern denial of human nature*. New York, NY: Viking.

Pittenger, D. J. (1993). The utility of the Myers-Briggs Type Indicator. *Review of Educational Research, 63*, 467–488.

Plant, E. A., & Devine, P. G. (1998). Internal and external motivation to respond without prejudice. *Journal of Personality and Social Psychology, 75*, 811–832.

Plomin, R. (1989). Environment and genes: Determinants of behavior. *American Psychologist, 44*, 105–111.

Plomin, R. (2011). Commentary: Why are children in the same family so different? Non-shared environment three decades later. *International Journal of Epidemiology, 40*, 582–592.

Plomin, R., & Crabbe, J. (2000). DNA. *Psychological Bulletin, 126*, 806–828.

Plomin, R., & DeFries, J. C. (1985). *Origins of individual differences in infancy: The Colorado Adoption Project*. New York, NY: Academic Press.

Plomin, R., DeFries, J. C., & Knopik, V. S. (2013). *Behavioral Genetics* (6th ed.). New York: Worth.

Plomin, R., DeFries, J. C., McClearn, G. E., & McGuffin, P. (2001). *Behavioral genetics* (4th ed.). New York, NY: Worth.

Plotnik, J. M., de Waal, F. B. M., & Reiss, D. (2006). Self-recognition in an Asian elephant. *Proceedings of the National Academy of Sciences, 103*(45), 17053–17057.

Pobric, G., Mashal, N., Faust, M., & Lavidor, M. (2008). The role of the right cerebral hemisphere in processing novel metaphoric expressions: A transcranial magnetic stimulation study. *Journal of Cognitive Neuroscience, 20*, 170–181.

Polusny, M. A., & Follette, V. M. (1996). Remembering childhood sexual abuse: A national survey of psychologists' clinical practices, beliefs, and personal experiences. *Professional Psychology: Research and Practice, 27*, 41–52.

Ponitz, C. C., McClelland, M. M., Matthews, J. S., & Morrison, F. J. (2009). A structured observation of behavioral self-regulation and its contribution to kindergarten outcomes. *Developmental Psychology, 45*, 605–619.

Poole, D. A., & Lamb, M. E. (1998). *Investigative interviews of children*. Washington, DC: American Psychological Association.

Poole, D. A., Lindsay, D. S., Memon, A., & Bull, R. (1995). Psychotherapy and the recovery of memories of childhood sexual abuse: U.S. and British practitioners' opinions, practices, and experiences. *Journal of Consulting and Clinical Psychology, 63*, 426–437.

Poole, Nancy A., (2008). Fetal Alcohol Spectrum Disorder (FASD) Prevention: Canadian perspectives. Public Health Agency of Canada, Cat # HP5-73/2008. Retrieved from: http://www.phac-aspc.gc.ca/hp-ps/dca-dea/prog-ini/fasd-etcaf/publications/cp-pc/pdf/cp-pc-eng.pdf.

Pope, H. G., & Katz, D. L. (1992). Psychiatric effects of anabolic steroids. *Psychiatric Annals, 22*, 24–29.

Pope, H. G., Jr., Phillips, K. A., & Olivardia, R. (2000). *The Adonis complex: The secret crisis of male body obsession*. New York, NY: Free Press.

Popkin, B. M. (2009). *The world is fat: The fads, trends, policies, and products that are fattening the human race*. New York, NY: Avery.

Portenoy, R. K. (1994). Opioid therapy for chronic nonmalignant pain: Current status. In H. L. Fields & J. C. Liebeskind (Eds.), *Progress in pain research and management. Pharmacological approaches to the treatment of chronic pain: Vol. 1.* Seattle, WA: International Association for the Study of Pain.

Postmes, T., & Spears, R. (1998). Deindividuation and antinormative behavior: A meta-analysis. *Psychological Bulletin, 123*, 238–259.

Postuma, R. B., Gagnon, J. F., Vendette, M., et al. (2008). Quantifying the risk of neurodegenerative disease in idiopathic REM sleep behavior disorder. *Neurology*, published online December 24, doi:10.1212/01.wnl.0000340980.19702.6e

Potter, W. J. (1987). Does television viewing hinder academic achievement among adolescents? *Human Communication Research, 14*, 27–46.

Poulin, M. J., Holman, E. A., & Buffone, A. (2012). The neurogenetics of nice: Receptor genes for oxytocin and vasopressin interact with threat to produce prosocial behavior. *Psychological Science, 23*, 446–452.

Poulin-Dubois, D., Serbin, L. A., Kenyon, B., & Derbyshire, A. (1994). Infants' intermodal knowledge about gender. *Developmental Psychology, 30*, 436–442.

Powell, R. A., & Boer, D. P. (1995). Did Freud misinterpret reported memories of sexual abuse as fantasies? *Psychological Reports, 77*, 563–570.

Premack, D., & Premack, A. J. (1983). *The mind of an ape*. New York, NY: Norton.

Presnell, K., Bearman, S. K., & Stice, E. (2004). Risk factors for body dissatisfaction in adolescent boys and girls: A prospective study. *International Journal of Eating Disorders, 36*, 389–401.

Pressman, S. D., & Cohen, S. (2005). Does positive affect influence health? *Psychological Bulletin, 131,* 925–971.

Preston, J., & Epley, N. (2005). Explanations versus applications: The explanatory power of valuable beliefs. *Psychological Science, 16,* 826–832.

Price, D. D., Finniss, D. G., & Benedetti, F. (2008). A comprehensive review of the placebo effect: Recent advances and current thought. *Annual Review of Psychology, 59,* 565–590.

Primack, B. A., Silk, J. S., DeLozier, C. R., et al. (2011). Using ecological momentary assessment to determine media use by individuals with and without major depressive disorder. *Archives of Pediatrics & Adolescent Medicine, 165,* 360–365.

Principe, G., Kanaya, T., Ceci, S. J., & Singh, M. (2006). Believing is seeing: How rumors can engender false memories in preschoolers. *American Psychologist, 17,* 243–248.

Prochaska, J. O., Norcross, J. C., & DiClemente, C. C. (1994). *Changing for good.* New York, NY: Morrow.

Proffitt, D. R. (2006). Distance perception. *Current Directions in Psychological Science, 3,* 131–135.

Pronin, E. (2008, May 30). How we see ourselves and how we see others. *Science, 320,* 1177–1180.

Pronin, E., Gilovich, T., & Ross, L. (2004). Objectivity in the eye of the beholder: Divergent perceptions of bias in self versus others. *Psychological Review, 111,* 781–799.

Ptito, M., Moesgaard, S. M., Gjedde, A., & Kupers, R. (2005). Cross-modal plasticity revealed by electrotactile stimulation of the tongue in the congenitally blind. *Brain, 128,* 606–614.

Public Health Agency of Canada (2006). Canadian National Report on Immunization, 2006. Retrieved July 10, 2010, from http://www.phac-aspc.gc.ca/publicat/ccdr-rmtc/06vol32/32s3/2vaccine-eng.php

Public Health Agency of Canada. (2009). What mothers say: The Canadian maternity experiences survey. Retrieved from: http://www.phac-aspc.gc.ca/rhs-ssg/pdf/survey-eng.pdf

Public Health Agency of Canada (2012). Thimerosal in Vaccines and Autism. http://www.phac-aspc.gc.ca/im/q_a_thimerosal-eng.php.

Punamaeki, R.-L., & Joustie, M. (1998). The role of culture, violence, and personal factors affecting dream content. *Journal of Cross-Cultural Psychology, 29,* 320–342.

Pynoos, R. S., & Nader, K. (1989). Children's memory and proximity to violence. *Journal of the American Academy of Child and Adolescent Psychiatry, 28,* 236–241.

Pyszczynski, T., Rothschild, Z., & Abdollahi, A. (2008). Terrorism, violence, and hope for peace: A terror management perspective. *Current Directions in Psychological Science, 17,* 318–322.

Pyter, L. M., Pineros, V., Galang, J. A., et al. (2009, June 2). Peripheral tumors induce depressive-like behaviors and cytokine production and alter hypothalamic-pituitary-adrenal axis regulation. *Proceedings of the National Academy of Sciences, 106,* 9069–9074.

Quinlivan, D. S., Neuschatz, J. S., Cutler, B. L., Wells, G. L., McClung, J., & Harker, D. L. (2012). Do pre-admonition suggestions moderate the effect of unbiased lineup instructions? *Legal and Criminological Psychology, 17,* 165–176.

Quinn, D. M., & Spencer, S. J. (2001). The interference of stereotype threat with women's generation of mathematical problem-solving strategies. *Journal of Social Issues, 57,* 55–71.

Quinn, P., & Bhatt, R. (2005). Learning perceptual organization in infancy. *Psychological Science, 16,* 511–515.

Radel, R., & Clément-Guillotin, C. (2012). Evidence of motivational influences in early visual perception: Hunger modulates conscious access. *Psychological Science, 23,* 232–234.

Radford, B. (2005, June). Psychic predictions (and rationalizations) fail again. *Skeptical Briefs, 15,* 529.

Raffaelli, M., Crockett, L. J., & Shen, Y.-L. (2005). Developmental stability and change in self-regulation from childhood to adolescence. *The Journal of Genetic Psychology, 166,* 54–75.

Rahman, Q., & Wilson, G. D. (2003). Born gay? The psychobiology of human sexual orientation. *Personality and Individual Differences, 34,* 1337–1382.

Raloff, J. (2011). Environment: Chemicals linked to kids' lower IQs: Studies identify effects from pesticides still used on farms. *Science News, 179,* 15.

Ramachandran, V. S., & Altschuler, E. L. (2009). The use of visual feedback, in particular mirror visual feedback, in restoring brain function. *Brain, 132,* 1693–1710.

Ramachandran, V. S., & Blakeslee, S. (1998). *Phantoms in the brain.* New York, NY: William Morrow.

Ramey, C. T., & Ramey, S. L. (1998). Early intervention and early experience. *American Psychologist, 53,* 109–120.

Randall, D. K. (2012). *Dreamland: Adventures in the strange world of sleep.* New York: Norton.

Range, F., Aust, U., Steurer, M., & Huber, L. (2008). Visual categorization of natural stimuli by domestic dogs. *Animal Cognition, 11,* 339–347.

Rasch, B., & Born, J. (2008). Reactivation and consolidation of memory during sleep. *Current Directions in Psychological Science, 17,* 188–192.

Rasch, B., Büchel, C., Gais, S., & Born, J. (2007). Odor cues during slow-wave sleep prompt declarative memory consolidation. *Science, 315,* 1426–1429.

Rasch, B., Pommer, J., Diekelmann, S., & Born, J. (2009). Pharmacological REM sleep suppression paradoxically improves rather than impairs skill memory. *Nature Neuroscience, 12,* 396–397. doi:10.1038/nn.2206

Raser, J. M., & O'Shea, E. K. (2005). Noise in gene expression: Origins, consequences, and control. *Science, 309,* 2010–2013.

Rathbun, C., DiVirgilio, L., & Waldfogel, S. (1958). A restitutive process in children following radical separation from family and culture. *American Journal of Orthopsychiatry, 28,* 408–415.

Rauschecker, J. P. (1999). Making brain circuits listen. *Science, 285,* 1686–1687.

Ravussin, E., Lillioja, S., Knowler, W., et al. (1988). Reduced rate of energy expenditure as a risk factor for body-weight gain. *New England Journal of Medicine, 318,* 467–472.

Ray, W. A., Chung, C. P., Murray, K. T., et al. (2009). Atypical antipsychotic drugs and the risk of sudden cardiac death. *New England Journal of Medicine, 360,* 225–235.

Raz, A., Fan, J., & Posner, M. I. (2005). Hypnotic suggestion reduces conflict in the human brain. *Proceedings of the National Academy of Science, 102,* 9978–9983.

Raz, A., Kirsch, I., Pollard, J., & Nitkin-Kamer, Y. (2006). Suggestion reduces the Stroop effect. *Psychological Science, 17,* 91–95.

Reber, P. J., Stark, C. E. L., & Squire, L. R. (1998). Contrasting cortical activity associated with category memory and recognition memory. *Learning & Memory, 5,* 420–428.

Redd, W. H., Dadds, M. R., Futterman, A. D., et al. (1993). Nausea induced by mental images of chemotherapy. *Cancer, 72,* 629–636.

Redelmeier, D. A., & Tversky, A. (1996). On the belief that arthritis pain is related to the weather. *Proceedings of the National Academy of Sciences, 93,* 2895–2896.

Redick, T. S., Shipstead, Z., Harrison, T. L., et al. (2012, June 18). No evidence of intelligence improvement after working memory training: A randomized, placebo-controlled study. *Journal of Experimental Psychology: General.* doi:10.1037/a0029082.

Reedy, F. E., Bartoshuk, L. M., Miller, I. J., et al. (1993). Relationships among papillae, taste pores, and 6-n-propylthiouracil (PROP) suprathreshold taste sensitivity. *Chemical Senses, 18,* 618–619.

Reese, E., Jack, F., & White, N. (2010). Origins of adolescents' autobiographical memories. *Cognitive Development, 25,* 352–367.

Regard, M., & Landis, T. (1997). "Gourmand syndrome": Eating passion associated with right anterior lesions. *Neurology, 48,* 1185–1190.

Reichenberg, A., Gross, R., Weiser, M., Bresnahan, M., et al. (2006). Advancing paternal age and autism. *Archives of General Psychiatry, 63,* 1026–1032.

Reid, R. L. (1991). Premenstrual syndrome. *New England Journal of Medicine, 324,* 1208–1210.

Reiner, W. G., & Gearhart, J. P. (2004, January 22). Discordant sexual identity in some genetic males with cloacal exstrophy assigned to female sex at birth. *New England Journal of Medicine, 350,* 333–341.

Remick, A. K., Polivy, J., & Pliner, P. (2009). Internal and external moderators of the effect of variety on food intake. *Psychological Bulletin, 135,* 434–451.

Rensink, R. (2004). Visual sensing without seeing. *Psychological Science, 15,* 27–32.

Repantis, D., Schlattmann, P., Laisney, O., & Heuser, I. (2010). Modafinil and methylphenidate for neuroenhancement in healthy individuals. A systematic review. *Pharmacological Research, 62,* 187–206.

Repetti, R. L., Taylor, S. E., & Seeman, T. E. (2002). Risky families: Family social environments and the mental and physical health of offspring. *Psychological Bulletin, 128,* 330–366.

Rescorla, R. A. (1988). Pavlovian conditioning: It's not what you think it is. *American Psychologist, 43,* 151–160.

Reyna, V., & Farley, F. (2006). Risk and rationality in adolescent decision making. *Psychological Science in the Public Interest, 7,* 1–44.

Reynolds, B. A., & Weiss, S. (1992). Generation of neurons and astrocytes from isolated cells of the adult mammalian central nervous system. *Science, 255,* 1707–1710.

Reynolds, D. K. (1987). *Water bears no scars: Japanese lifeways for personal growth.* New York, NY: Morrow.

Reynolds, K., Lewis, L. B., Nolen, J. D. L., et al. (2003). Alcohol consumption and risk of stroke: A meta-analysis. *Journal of the American Medical Association, 289,* 579–588.

Rhoades, L., & Eisenberger, R. (2002). Perceived organizational support: A review of the literature. *Journal of Applied Psychology, 87,* 698–714.

Ricciardelli, L. A., & McCabe, M. P. (2004). A biopsychosocial model of disordered eating and the pursuit of muscularity in adolescent boys. *Psychological Bulletin, 130,* 179–205.

Rice, M. L. (1990). Preschoolers' QUIL: Quick incidental learning of words. In G. Conti-Ramsden & C. E. Snow (Eds.), *Children's language* (Vol. 7). Hillsdale, NJ: Erlbaum.

Richardson-Klavehn, A., & Bjork, R. A. (1988). Measures of memory. *Annual Review of Psychology, 39,* 475–543.

Ridley, M. (2000). *Genome. The autobiography of a species in 23 chapters.* New York, NY: HarperCollins.

Ridley-Johnson, R., Cooper, H., & Chance, J. (1983). The relation of children's television viewing to school achievement and I.Q. *Journal of Educational Research, 76,* 294–297.

Rind, B., Tromovitch, P., & Bauserman, R. (1998). A meta-analytic examination of assumed properties of child sexual abuse using college samples. *Psychological Bulletin, 124,* 22–53.

Rizzolatti, G., & Sinigaglia, C. (2010). The functional role of the parietofrontal mirror circuit: Interpretations and misinterpretations. *Nature Reviews Neuroscience, 11,* 264–274.

Ro, T., Farnè, A., Johnson, R., et al. (2007). Feeling sounds after a thalamic lesion. *Annals of Neurology, 62,* 433–441.

Roberson, D., Davies, I., & Davidoff, J. (2000). Color categories are not universal: Replications and new evidence in favor of linguistic relativity. *Journal of Experimental Psychology: General, 129,* 369–398.

Roberts, B. W., Caspi, A., & Moffitt, T. E. (2001). The kids are alright: Growth and stability in personality development from adolescence to adulthood. *Journal of Personality and Social Psychology, 81,* 670–683.

Roberts, B. W., Edmonds, G., & Grijalva, E. (2010). It is developmental me, not generation me: Developmental changes are more important than generational changes in narcissism. *Perspectives on Psychological Science, 5,* 97–102.

Roberts, B. W., & Mroczek, D. (2008). Personality trait change in adulthood. *Current Directions in Psychological Science, 17,* 31–35.

Roberts, B. W., Walton, K. E., & Viechtbauer, W. (2006). Patterns of mean-level change in personality traits across the life course: A meta-analysis of longitudinal studies. *Psychological Bulletin, 132,* 1–25.

Roberts, J. V. (2000). Changing public attitudes towards corporal punishment: The effects of statutory reform in Sweden. *Child Abuse & Neglect, 24,* 1027–1035.

Robins, R. W., Gosling, S. D., & Craik, K. H. (1999). An empirical analysis of trends in psychology. *American Psychologist, 54,* 117–128.

Robinson, B. (1988). Final report to the Canadian Psychological Association Board of Directors. Psy.D. Task Force.

Robinson, T., Wilde, M. L., Navracruz, L. C., et al. (2001). Effects of reducing children's television and video game use on aggressive behavior: A randomized controlled trial. *Archives of Pediatric and Adolescent Medicine, 155,* 13–14.

Rodriguez, P., Wiles, J., & Elman, J. L. (1999). A recurrent neural network that learns to count. *Connection Science, 11,* 5–40.

Roediger, H. L. (1990). Implicit memory: Retention without remembering. *American Psychologist, 45,* 1043–1056.

Roediger, H. L., & McDermott, K. B. (1995). Creating false memories: Remembering words not presented in lists. *Journal of Experimental Psychology, Learning, Memory, & Cognition, 21,* 803–814.

Roepke, S. K., & Grant, I. (2011). Toward a more complete understanding of the effects of personal mastery on cardiometabolic health. *Health sychology, 30,* 615–632.

Rofé, Y. (2008). Does repression exist? Memory, pathogenic, unconscious and clinical evidence. *Review of General Psychology, 12,* 63–85.

Rogers, C. (1951). *Client-centered therapy: Its current practice, implications, and theory.* Boston, MA: Houghton-Mifflin.

Rogers, C. (1961). *On becoming a person.* Boston, MA: Houghton-Mifflin.

Rogers, R. W., & Prentice-Dunn, S. (1981). Deindividuation and anger-mediated interracial aggression: Unmasking regressive racism. *Journal of Personality and Social Psychology, 41,* 63–73.

Rogge, R. D., Bradbury, T. N., Hahlweg, K., et al. (2006). Predicting marital distress and dissolution: Refining the two-factor hypothesis. *Journal of Family Psychology, 20,* 156–159.

Rogoff, B. (2003). *The cultural nature of human development.* New York, NY: Oxford University Press.

Rojstaczer, S., & Healy, C. (2012). Where A is ordinary: The evolution of American college and university grading, 1940–2009. *Teachers College Record, 114,* 7. www.tcrecord.org/library, ID Number: 16473.

Romanczyk, R. G., Arnstein, L., Soorya, L. V., & Gillis, J. (2003). The myriad of controversial treatments for autism: A critical evaluation of efficacy. In S. O. Lilienfeld, S. J. Lynn, & J. M. Lohr (Eds.), *Science and pseudoscience in clinical psychology.* New York, NY: Guilford.

Rosch, E. H. (1973). Natural categories. *Cognitive Psychology, 4,* 328–350.

Rosen, G. M. (1981). Guidelines for the review of do-it-yourself treatment books. *Contemporary Psychology, 26,* 189–191.

Rosen, G. M., Glasgow, R. E., & Moore, T. E. (2003). Self-help therapy: The science and business of giving psychology away. In S. O. Lilienfeld, S. J. Lynn, & J. M. Lohr (Eds.), *Science and pseudoscience in clinical psychology.* New York, NY: Guilford.

Rosenblum, E. B. (2005). *The genetics of reptile color evolution at the community level.* Invited symposium address, meeting of Evolution 2005, Fairbanks, Alaska.

Rosenthal, N. E. (2009). Issues for DSM-V: Seasonal affective disorder and seasonality. *The American Journal of Psychiatry, 166,* 852–853.

Rosenthal, R. (1994). Interpersonal expectancy effects: A 30-year perspective. *Current Directions in Psychological Science, 3,* 176–179.

Rosenzweig, M. R. (1984). Experience, memory, and the brain. *American Psychologist, 39,* 365–376.

Rosin, H. (2012). *The end of men: And the rise of women.* New York: Riverhead Books.

Ross, H. E., Freeman, S. M., Spiegel, L. L., et al. (2009). Variation in oxytocin receptor density in the nucleus accumbens has differential effects on affiliative behaviors in monogamous and polygamous voles. *Journal of Neuroscience, 29,* 1312–1318.

Ross, L. (2010). Dealing with conflict: Experiences and experiments. In M. H. Gonzales, C. Tavris, & J. Aronson (Eds.), *The scientist and the humanist: A festschrift in honor of Elliot Aronson.* New York, NY: Psychology Press.

Ross, M., Xun, W. Q. E., & Wilson, A. E. (2002). Language and the bicultural self. *Personality and Social Psychology Bulletin, 28,* 1040–1050.

Rotenberg, K. J. (1994). Loneliness and interpersonal trust. *Journal of Social and Clinical Psychology, 13,* 152–173.

Rotenberg, K. J. (1998). Stigmatization of transitions in loneliness. *Journal of Social and Personal Relationships, 15,* 565–576.

Rotenberg, K. J., Addis, N., Betts, L. R., et al. (2010). The relation between trust beliefs and loneliness during early childhood, middle childhood, and adulthood. *Personality and Social Psychology Bulletin, 36,* 1086–1100.

Rotenberg, K. J., & Flood, D. (1999). Loneliness, dysphoria, dietary restraint, and eating behaviour. *International Journal of Eating Disorders, 25,* 55–64.

Rotenberg, K. J., & Kmill, J. (1992). Perception of lonely and nonlonely persons as a function of individual differences in loneliness. *Journal of Social and Personal Relationships, 9,* 325–330.

Rotenberg, K. J., & MacKie, J. (1999). Stigmatization of social and intimacy loneliness. *Psychological Reports, 84,* 147–148.

Rotermann, M. (2008). Trends in teen sexual behaviour and condom use. Component of Statistics Canada Catalogue no. 82-003-X. Retrieved from http://www.statcan.gc.ca/pub/82-003-x/2008003/article/10664-eng.pdf

Rothbart, M. K., Ahadi, S. A., & Evans, D. E. (2000). Temperament and personality: Origins and outcomes. *Journal of Personality and Social Psychology, 78,* 122–135.

Rothbaum, F., Weisz, J., Pott, M., et al. (2000). Attachment and culture: Security in the United States and Japan. *American Psychologist, 55,* 1093–1104.

Rothbaum, F. M., Weisz, J. R., & Snyder, S. S. (1982). Changing the world and changing the self: A two-process model of perceived control. *Journal of Personality and Social Psychology, 42,* 5–37.

Rothermund, K., & Wentura, D. (2004). Underlying processes in the Implicit Association Test: Dissociating salience from associations. *Journal of Experimental Psychology: General, 133,* 139–165.

Rotter, J. B. (1990). Internal versus external control of reinforcement: A case history of a variable. *American Psychologist, 45,* 489–493.

Roughgarden, J. (2004). *Evolution's rainbow: Diversity, gender, and sexuality in nature and people.* Berkeley: University of California Press.

Rouw, R., & Scholte, S. S. (2007). Increased structural connectivity in grapheme-color synesthesia. *Nature Neuroscience, 10,* 792–797.

Rovee-Collier, C. (1993). The capacity for long-term memory in infancy. *Current Directions in Psychological Science, 2,* 130–135.

Rowe, M. L., & Goldin-Meadow, S. (2009, February 13). Differences in early gesture explain SES disparities in child vocabulary size at school entry. *Science, 323,* 951–953.

Roy, M. P., Steptoe, A., & Kirschbaum, C. (1998). Life events and social support as moderators of individual differences in cardiovascular and cortisol reactivity. *Journal of Personality and Social Psychology, 75,* 1273–1281.

Rozin, P., & Haidt, J. (2014). The domains of disgust and their origins: Contrasting biological and cultural evolutionary accounts. *Trends in Cognitive Sciences, 17,* 367–368.

Rozin, P., Kabnick, K., Pete, E., et al. (2003). The ecology of eating: Smaller portion sizes in France than in the United States help explain the French paradox. *Psychological Science, 14,* 450–454.

Rozin, P., Lowery, L., & Ebert, R. (1994). Varieties of disgust faces and the structure of disgust. *Journal of Personality and Social Psychology, 66,* 870–881.

Ruggiero, V. R. (1988). *Teaching thinking across the curriculum.* New York, NY: Harper & Row.

Ruggiero, V. R. (2004). *The art of thinking: A guide to critical and creative thought* (7th ed.). Pearson/Longman.

Rumbaugh, D. M. (1977). *Language learning by a chimpanzee: The Lana project.* New York, NY: Academic Press.

Rumbaugh, D. M., Savage-Rumbaugh, E. S., & Pate, J. L. (1988). Addendum to "Summation in the chimpanzee (*Pan troglodytes*)." *Journal of Experimental Psychology: Animal Behavior Processes, 14,* 118–120.

Rumelhart, D. E., McClelland, J. L., & the PDP Research Group. (1986). *Parallel distributed processing: Explorations in the microstructure of cognition* (Vols. 1 and 2). Cambridge, MA: MIT Press.

Rupp, H. A., & Wallen, K. (2008). Sex differences in response to visual sexual stimuli: A review. *Archives of Sexual Behavior, 37,* 206–218.

Rushton, J. P. (1988). Race differences in behavior: A review and evolutionary analysis. *Personality and Individual Differences, 9,* 1009–1024.

Rushton, J. P., & Jensen, A. R. (2005). Thirty years of research on race differences in cognitive ability. *Psychology, Public Policy, and Law, 11,* 235–294.

Russell, J. A., & Fehr, B. (1994). Fuzzy concepts in a fuzzy hierarchy: Varieties of anger. *Journal of Personality and Social Psychology, 67,* 186–205.

Rutter, M., O'Connor, T. G., & the English and Romanian Adoptees (ERA) Study Team. (2004). Are there biological programming effects for psychological development? Findings from a study of Romanian adoptees. *Developmental Psychology, 40,* 81–94.

Rutter, M., Pickles, A., Murray, R., & Eaves, L. (2001). Testing hypotheses on specific environmental causal effects on behavior. *Psychological Bulletin, 127,* 291–324.

Rymer, R. (1993). *Genie: An abused child's flight from silence.* New York, NY: HarperCollins.

Sabattini, L., & Crosby, F. (2009). Work ceilings and walls: Work-life and "family-friendly" policies. In M. Barreto, M. Ryan, & M. Schmitt (Eds.), *The glass ceiling in the 21st century: Understanding barriers to gender equality.* Washington, DC: American Psychological Association.

Sack, R. L., & Lewy, A. J. (1997). Melatonin as a chronobiotic: Treatment of circadian desynchrony in night workers and the blind. *Journal of Biological Rhythms, 12,* 595–603.

Sackett, P. R., Hardison, C. M., & Cullen, M. J. (2004). On interpreting stereotype threat as accounting for African American–white differences on cognitive tests. *American Psychologist, 59,* 7–13.

Sacks, O. (1985). *The man who mistook his wife for a hat and other clinical tales.* New York, NY: Simon & Schuster.

Saffran, J. R., Aslin, R. N., & Newport, E. L. (1996). Statistical learning by 8-month-old infants. *Science, 274,* 1926–1928.

Sagan, E. (1988). *Freud, women, and morality: The psychology of good and evil.* New York, NY: Basic Books.

Sage, C., Huang, M., Karimi, K., et al. (2005). Proliferation of functional hair cells in vivo in the absence of the retinoblastoma protein. *Science, 307,* 114–118.

Sahley, C. L., Rudy, J. W., & Gelperin, A. (1981). An analysis of associative learning in a terrestrial mollusc: 1. Higher-order conditioning, blocking, and a transient US preexposure effect. *Journal of Comparative Physiology, 144,* 1–8.

Salovey, P., & Grewal, D. (2005). The science of emotional intelligence. *Current Directions in Psychological Science, 14,* 281–285.

Salthouse, T. A. (2006). Mental exercise and mental aging: Evaluating the validity of the "use it or lose it" hypothesis. *Perspectives on Psychological Science, 1,* 68–87.

Salthouse, T. A. (2012). Does the level at which cognitive change occurs change with age? *Psychological Science, 23,* 18–23.

Saltz, B. L., Woerner, M. G., Kane, J. M., et al. (1991). Prospective study of tardive dyskinesia incidence in the elderly. *Journal of the American Medical Association, 266*(17), 2402–2406.

Sameroff, A. J., Seifer, R., Barocas, R., et al. (1987). Intelligence quotient scores of 4-year-old children: Social-environmental risk factors. *Pediatrics, 79,* 343–350.

Sampson, R. J, Sharkey, P., & Raudenbush, S. W. (2008). Durable effects of concentrated disadvantage among verbal ability of African-American children. *Proceedings of the National Academy of Sciences, 105,* 845–853.

Sandel, M. (2007). *The case against perfection: Ethics in the age of genetic engineering.* Cambridge, MA: Belknap/Harvard University Press.

Sanfey, A. G., Rilling, J. K., & Aronson, J. K. (2003). The neural basis of economic decision-making in the Ultimatum Game. *Science, 300,* 1755–1758.

Sapolsky, R. M. (1997). *The trouble with testosterone.* New York, NY: Touchstone.

Sarbin, T. R. (1991). Hypnosis: A fifty year perspective. *Contemporary Hypnosis, 8,* 1–15.

Sarbin, T. R. (1997a). The poetics of identity. *Theory & Psychology, 7,* 67–82.

Sarbin, T. R. (1997b). The power of believed-in imaginings. *Psychological Inquiry, 8,* 322–325.

Sarris, J. (2013). St. John's Wort for the Treatment of Psychiatric Disorders. *Complementary and Integrative Therapies for Psychiatric Disorders, 36,* 65–72.

Saucier, D. M., & Cain, D. P. (1995). NMDA-dependent long-term potentiation is not required for spatial learning in the water maze. *Nature, 378,* 186–189.

Saucier, G. (2000). Isms and the structure of social attitudes. *Journal of Personality and Social Psychology, 78,* 366–385.

Savage-Rumbaugh, S., & Lewin, R. (1994). *Kanzi: The ape at the brink of the human mind.* New York, NY: Wiley.

Savage-Rumbaugh, S., Shanker, S., & Taylor, T. (1998). *Apes, language and the human mind.* New York, NY: Oxford University Press.

Savic, I., Berglund, H., & Lindström, P. (2005, May 17). Brain response to putative pheromones in homosexual men. *Proceedings of the National Academy of Sciences, 102,* 7356–7361.

Savin-Williams, R. C. (2006). Who's gay? Does it matter? *Current Directions in Psychological Science, 15,* 40–44.

Scarr, S. (1993). Biological and cultural diversity: The legacy of Darwin for development. *Child Development, 64,* 1333–1353.

Scarr, S., Pakstis, A. J., Katz, S. H., & Barker, W. B. (1977). Absence of a relationship between degree of white ancestry and intellectual skill in a black population. *Human Genetics, 39,* 69–86.

Scarr, S., & Weinberg, R. A. (1994). Educational and occupational achievement of brothers and sisters in adoptive and biologically related families. *Behavioral Genetics, 24,* 301–325.

Schachter, S., & Singer, J. E. (1962). Cognitive, social, and physiological determinants of emotional state. *Psychological Review, 69,* 379–399.

Schacter, D. L. (2001). *The seven sins of memory: How the mind forgets and remembers.* Boston, MA: Houghton-Mifflin.

Schacter, D. L. (2012). Constructive memory: Past and future. *Dialogues in Clinical Neuroscience, 14,* 7–18.

Schacter, D. L., Chiu, C. Y., & Ochsner, K. N. (1993). Implicit memory: A selective review. *Annual Review of Neuroscience, 16,* 159–182.

Schaeffer, C. M., & Borduin, C. M. (2005). Long-term follow-up to a randomized clinical trial of multisystemic therapy with serious and violent juvenile offenders. *Journal of Consulting and Clinical Psychology, 73,* 445–453.

Schafer, R. (1992). *Retelling a life: Narration and dialogue in psychoanalysis.* New York, NY: Basic Books.

Schaie, K. W., & Willis, S. L. (2002). *Adult development and aging* (5th ed.). Upper Saddle River, NJ: Prentice Hall.

Schaie, K. W., & Zuo, Y. L. (2001). Family environments and cognitive functioning. In R. J. Sternberg & E. Grigorenko (Eds.), *Cognitive development in context.* Hillsdale, NJ: Erlbaum.

Schank, R. (with Peter Childers). (1988). *The creative attitude*. New York, NY: Macmillan.

Scharfman, H. E., & Hen, R. (2007). Is more neurogenesis always better? *Science, 315*, 336–338.

Schellenberg, E. G. (2004). Music lessons enhance IQ. *Psychological Science, 15*, 511–514.

Scherer, K. R. (1997). The role of culture in emotion-antecedent appraisal. *Journal of Personality and Social Psychology, 73*, 902–922.

Schlossberg, N. K., & Robinson, S. P. (1996). *Going to plan B*. New York, NY: Simon & Schuster/Fireside.

Schmelz, M., Schmidt, R., Bickel, A., et al. (1997). Specific C-receptors for itch in human skin. *Journal of Neuroscience, 17*, 8003–8008.

Schmidt, F. L., & Hunter, J. (2004). General mental ability in the world of work: Occupational attainment and job performance. *Journal of Personality and Social Psychology, 86*, 162–173.

Schmidt, L. A., Fox, N. A., Perez-Edgar, K., & Hamer, D. H. (2009). Linking gene, brain, and behavior: DRD4, frontal asymmetry, and temperament. *Psychological Science, 20*, 831–837.

Schmitt, D. P. (2003). Universal sex differences in the desire for sexual variety: Tests from 52 nations, 6 continents, and 13 islands. *Journal of Personality and Social Psychology, 85*, 85–104.

Schmitt, D. P., Jonason, P. K., Byerley, G. J., et al. (2012). A reexamination of sex differences in sexuality: New studies reveal old truths. *Current Directions in Psychological Science, 21*, 135–139.

Schneider, S., Huy, C., Schutz, J., & Diehl, K. (2010). Smoking cessation during pregnancy: A systematic literature review. *Drug and Alcohol Review, 29*, 81–90.

Schnell, L., & Schwab, M. E. (1990, January 18). Axonal regeneration in the rat spinal cord produced by an antibody against myelin-associated neurite growth inhibitors. *Nature, 343*, 269–272.

Schoenfeld, T. J., & Gould, E. (2013). Differential Effects of Stress and Glucocorticoids on Adult Neurogenesis. *Current Topics in Behavioral Neurosciences, 15*, 139–164.

Schofield, P., Ball, D., Smith, J. G., et al. (2004). Optimism and survival in lung carcinoma patients. *Cancer, 100*, 1276–1282.

Schulz, R., Beach, S. R., Ives, D. G., et al. (2000). Association between depression and mortality in older adults: The Cardiovascular Health Study. *Archives of Internal Medicine, 160*, 1761–1768.

Schwartz, B. (2004). *The paradox of choice: Why more is less*. New York, NY: Ecco Press.

Schwartz, S. J., Unger, J. B., Zamboanga, B. L., & Szapocznik, J. (2010). Rethinking the concept of acculturation. *American Psychologist, 65*, 237–251.

Sears, P., & Barbee, A. H. (1977). Career and life satisfactions among Terman's gifted women. In J. C. Stanley, W. C. George, & C. H. Solano (Eds.), *The gifted and the creative: A fifty-year perspective*. Baltimore, MD: Johns Hopkins University Press.

Sebastián-Gallés, N., Albareda-Castellot, B., Weikum, W. M., et al. (2012). A bilingual advantage in visual language discrimination in infancy. *Psychological Science, 23*, 994–999.

Segal, J. (1986). *Winning life's toughest battles*. New York, NY: McGraw-Hill.

Segal, Z. V., Williams, J., Mark G., & Teasdale, J. D. (2001). *Mindfulness-based cognitive therapy for depression: A new approach to preventing relapse*. New York, NY: Guilford Press.

Segall, M. H., Dasen, P. P., Berry, J. W., & Poortinga, Y. H. (1999). *Human behavior in global perspective* (2nd ed.). Boston, MA: Allyn & Bacon.

Segall, M. H., Campbell, D. T., & Herskovits, M. J. (1966). *The influence of culture on visual perception*. Indianapolis, IN: Bobbs-Merrill.

Segerstrom, S. C., & Miller, G. E. (2004). Psychological stress and the human immune system: A meta-analytic study of 30 years of inquiry. *Psychological Bulletin, 130*, 601–630.

Seidenberg, M. S., MacDonald, M. C., & Saffran, J. R. (2002). Does grammar start where statistics stop? *Science, 298*, 553–554.

Seifer, R., Schiller, M., Sameroff, A., et al. (1996). Attachment, maternal sensitivity, and infant temperament during the first year of life. *Developmental Psychology, 32*, 12–25.

Sekuler, R., & Blake, R. (1994). *Perception* (3rd ed.). New York, NY: Knopf.

Seligman, M. E. P., & Csikszentmihaly, M. (2000). Positive psychology: An introduction. *American Psychologist, 55*, 5–14.

Seligman, M. E. P., & Hager, J. L. (1972, August). Biological boundaries of learning: The sauce-béarnaise syndrome. *Psychology Today*, 59–61, 84–87.

Seligman, M. E. P., Schulman, P., DeRubeis, R. J., & Hollon, S. D. (1999). The prevention of depression and anxiety. *Prevention & Treatment, 2*, Retrieved from http://www.ppc.sas.upenn.edu/depprevseligman1999.pdf

Senghas, A., Kita, S., & Özyürek, A. (2004). Children creating core properties of language: Evidence from an emerging sign language in Nicaragua. *Science, 305*, 1779–1782.

Senko, C., Durik, A. M., & Harackiewicz, J. M. (2008). Historical perspectives and new directions in achievement goal theory: Understanding the effects of mastery and performance-approach goals. In J. Y. Shah & W. L. Gardner (Eds.), *Handbook of motivation science*. New York, NY: Guilford.

Serpell, R. (1994). The cultural construction of intelligence. In W. J. Lonner & R. S. Malpass (Eds.), *Psychology and culture*. Needham Heights, MA: Allyn & Bacon.

Service Canada (2013). *Ages of eligibility for the Old Age Security pension and benefits*. Retrieved from: http://www.servicecanada.gc.ca/eng/services/pensions/oas/changes/index.shtml

Shadish, W. R., Matt, G. E., Navarro, A. M., & Phillips, G. (2000). The effects of psychological therapies under clinically representative conditions: A meta-analysis. *Psychological Bulletin, 126*, 512–529.

Shapiro, F. (1994). EMDR: In the eye of a paradigm shift. *Behavior Therapist, 17*, 153–156.

Shapiro, F. (1995). *Eye movement desensitization and reprocessing: Basic principles, protocols, and procedures.* New York, NY: Guilford.

Shariff, A. F., & Tracy, J. L. (2009). Knowing who's boss: Implicit perceptions of status from the nonverbal expression of pride source. *Emotion, 9*, 631–639.

Shariff, A. F., & Tracy, J. L. (2011). What are emotion expressions for? *Current Directions in Psychological Science, 20*, 395–399.

Sharman, S. J., Manning, C. G., & Garry, M. (2005). Explain this: Explaining childhood events inflates confidence for those events. *Applied Cognitive Psychology, 19*, 16–74.

Sharot, T., Martorella, E. A., Delgado, M. R., & Phelps, E. A. (2007). How personal experience modulates the neural circuitry of memories of September 11. *Proceedings of the National Academy of Science, 104*, 389–394.

Shatz, M., & Gelman, R. (1973). The development of communication skills: Modifications in the speech of young children as a function of the listener. *Monographs of the Society for Research in Child Development, 38*.

Shaver, P. R., & Hazan, C. (1993). Adult romantic attachment: Theory and evidence. In D. Perlman & W. H. Jones (Eds.), *Advances in personal relationships* (Vol. 4). London, England: Kingsley.

Shaver, P. R., Wu, S., & Schwartz, J. C. (1992). Cross-cultural similarities and differences in emotion and its representation: A prototype approach. In M. S. Clark (Ed.), *Review of Personality and Social Psychology* (Vol. 13). Newbury Park, CA: Sage.

Shea, C. (2001, September). White man can't contextualize. *Lingua Franca*, 44–47, 49–51.

Sheldon, K. M., Elliot, A. J., Kim, Y., & Kasser, T. (2001). What is satisfying about satisfying events? Testing 10 candidate psychological needs. *Journal of Personality and Social Psychology, 80*, 325–339.

Sheldon, K. M., & Houser-Marko, L. (2001). Self-concordance, goal attainment, and the pursuit of happiness: Can there be an upward spiral? *Journal of Personality and Social Psychology, 80*, 152–165.

Shepard, R. N., & Metzler, J. (1971). Mental rotation of three-dimensional objects. *Science, 171*, 701–703.

Sherif, M. (1958). Superordinate goals in the reduction of intergroup conflicts. *American Journal of Sociology, 63*, 349–356.

Sherif, M., Harvey, O. J., White, B. J., Hood, W., & Sherif, C. (1961). *Intergroup conflict and cooperation: The Robbers Cave experiment*. Norman: University of Oklahoma Institute of Intergroup Relations.

Sherman, D. K., & Kim, H. S. (2005). Is There an "I" in "Team"? The Role of the Self in Group-Serving Judgments. *Journal of Personality and Social Psychology, 88*, 108–120.

Shermer, M. (1997). *Why people believe weird things: Pseudoscience, superstition, and other confusions of our time*. New York, NY: Freeman.

Sherry, J. L. (2001). The effects of violent video games on aggression: A meta-analysis. *Human Communication Research, 27*, 409–431.

Sherry, S. B., & Hall, P. A. (2009). The perfectionism model of binge eating: Tests of an integrative model. *Journal of Personality and Social Psychology, 96*, 690–709.

Shields, S. A. (2002). *Speaking from the heart: Gender and the social meaning of emotion*. New York, NY: Cambridge University Press.

Shields, S. A. (2005). The politics of emotion in everyday life: "Appropriate" emotion and claims on identity. *Review of General Psychology, 9*, 3–15.

Shields, Stephanie A., & Dicicco, Elaine C. (2011). The social psychology of sex and gender: From gender differences to doing gender. *Psychology of Women Quarterly, 35*, 491–499.

Shih, M., Pittinsky, T. L., & Ambady, N. (1999). Stereotype susceptibility: Identity salience and shifts in quantitative performance. *Psychological Science, 10*, 80–83.

Shors, T. J. (2009, March). Saving new brain cells. *Scientific American*, 46–54.

Shorter, E., & Healy, D. (2008). *Shock therapy: A history of electroconvulsive treatment in mental illness*. New Brunswick, NJ: Rutgers University Press.

Sidanius, J., Pratto, F., & Bobo, L. (1996). Racism, conservatism, affirmative action, and intellectual sophistication: A matter of principled conservatism or group dominance? *Journal of Personality and Social Psychology, 70*, 476–490.

Sidanius, J., Van Laar, C., Levin, S., & Sinclair, S. (2004). Ethnic enclaves and the dynamics of social identity on the college campus: The good, the bad, and the ugly. *Journal of Personality and Social Psychology, 87*, 96–110.

Siegel, R. K. (1989). *Intoxication: Life in pursuit of artificial paradise*. New York, NY: Dutton.

Siegler, R. S. (2006). Microgenetic analyses of learning. In D. Kuhn & R. S. Siegler (Eds.), *Handbook of child psychology: Vol. 2. Cognition, perception, and language* (6th ed.). New York, NY: Wiley.

Silverstein, B., & Perlick, D. (1995). *The cost of competence: Why inequality causes depression, eating disorders, and illness in women*. New York, NY: Oxford University Press.

Simcock, G., & Hayne, H. (2002). Breaking the barrier: Children fail to translate their preverbal memories into language. *Psychological Science, 13*, 225–231.

Simmons, H. G. (1987). Psychosurgery and the abuse of psychiatric authority in Ontario. *Journal of Health Politics, Policy, and Law, 12*, 537–550.

Simner, M. L. (1998). Use of the TOEFL as a standard for university admission: A position statement by the Canadian Psychological Association. *European Journal of Psychological Assessment, 14*, 261–265.

Simon, H. A. (1955). A behavioral model of rational choice. *Quarterly Journal of Economics, 69*, 99–118.

Simons, D. J., & Chabris, C. F. (1999). Gorillas in our midst: Sustained inattentional blindness for dynamic events. *Perception, 28*, 1059–1974.

Simons, D. J., & Chabris, C. F. (2011). What people believe about how memory works: A representative survey of the U.S. population. *PLoS One, 6*: e22757.

Simonton, D. K., & Song, A. (2009). Eminence, IQ, physical and mental health, and achievement domain. *Psychological Science, 20*, 429–434.

Sims, E. A. (1974). Studies in human hyperphagia. In G. Bray & J. Bethune (Eds.), *Treatment and management of obesity*. New York, NY: Harper & Row.

Sinaceur, M., Heath, C., & Cole, S. (2005). Emotional and deliberative reactions to a public crisis: Mad cow disease in France. *Psychological Science, 16*, 247–254.

Singer, M. T. (2003). *Cults in our midst* (Rev. ed.). New York, NY: Wiley.

Singh, D., Vidaurri, M., Zambarano, R. J., & Dabbs, J. M., Jr. (1999). Lesbian erotic role identification: Behavioral, morphological, and hormonal correlates. *Journal of Personality and Social Psychology, 76*, 1035–1049.

Sitzmann, T., & Ely, K. (2011). A meta-analysis of self-regulated learning in work-related training and educational attainment: What we know and where we need to go. *Psychological Bulletin, 137*, 421–442.

Skinner, B. F. (1938). *The behavior of organisms: An experimental analysis*. New York, NY: Appleton-Century-Crofts.

Skinner, B. F. (1948/1976). *Walden two*. New York, NY: Macmillan.

Skinner, B. F. (1956). A case history in the scientific method. *American Psychologist, 11*, 221–233.

Skinner, B. F. (1972). The operational analysis of psychological terms. In *B. F. Skinner, cumulative record* (3rd ed.). New York, NY: Appleton-Century-Crofts.

Skinner, B. F. (1990). Can psychology be a science of mind? *American Psychologist, 45*, 1206–1210.

Skinner, E. A. (1996). A guide to constructs of control. *Journal of Personality and Social Psychology, 71*, 549–570.

Skinner, E. A. (2007). Secondary control critiqued: Is it secondary? Is it control? *Psychological Bulletin, 133*, 911–916.

Skinner, J. B., Erskine, A., Pearce, S. A., et al. (1990). The evaluation of a cognitive behavioural treatment programme in outpatients with chronic pain. *Journal of Psychosomatic Research, 34*, 13–19.

Slater, M., Antley, A., Davison, A., et al. (2006). A virtual reprise of the Stanley Milgram obedience experiments. *PLoS One 1*(1): e39.

Slavin, R. E., & Cooper, R. (1999). Improving intergroup relations: Lessons learned from cooperative learning programs. *Journal of Social Issues, 55*, 647–663.

Slevec, J., & Tiggemann, M. (2011). Media exposure, body dissatisfaction, and disordered eating in middle-aged women: A test of the sociocultural model of disordered eating. *Psychology of Women Quarterly, 35*, 617–627.

Sloane, S., Baillargeon, R., & Premack, D. (2012). Do infants have a sense of fairness? *Psychological Science, 23*, 196–204.

Slovic, P., Finucane, M. L., Peters, E., & MacGregor, D. G. (2002). The affect heuristic. In T. Gilovich, D. Griffin, & D. Kahneman (Eds.), *Heuristics and biases: The psychology of intuitive judgment*. New York, NY: Cambridge University Press.

Slovic, P., & Peters, E. (2006). Risk perception and affect. *Current Directions in Psychological Science, 15*, 322–325.

Small, G. (2008). *iBrain: Surviving the technological alteration of the modern mind*. New York, NY: Collins Living.

Smilek, D., Dixon, M. J., Cudahy, C., & Merikle, P. (2002). Synesthetic color experiences influence memory. *Psychological Science, 13*, 548–552.

Smith, D. N. (1998). The psychocultural roots of genocide: Legitimacy and crisis in Rwanda. *American Psychologist, 53*, 743–753.

Smith, J. F., & Kida, T. (1991). Heuristics and biases: Expertise and task realism in auditing. *Psychological Bulletin, 109*, 472–489.

Smith, M. E., & Farah, M. J. (2011). Are prescription stimulants "smart pills"? The epidemiology and cognitive neuroscience of prescription stimulant use by normal healthy individuals. *Psychological Bulletin, 137*, 717–741.

Smith, P. B., & Bond, M. H. (1994). *Social psychology across cultures: Analysis and perspectives*. Boston, MA: Allyn & Bacon.

Smither, R. D. (1998). *The psychology of work and human performance* (3rd ed.). New York, NY: Longman.

Snodgrass, S. E. (1992). Further effects of role versus gender on interpersonal sensitivity. *Journal of Personality and Social Psychology, 62*, 154–158.

Snowdon, C. T. (1997). The "nature" of sex differences: Myths of male and female. In P. A. Gowaty (Ed.), *Feminism and evolutionary biology*. New York, NY: Chapman and Hall.

Snyder, C. R., & Shenkel, R. J. (1975, March). The P. T. Barnum effect. *Psychology Today*, 52–54.

Sommer, R. (1969). *Personal space: The behavioral basis of design*. Englewood Cliffs, NJ: Prentice-Hall.

Sommer, R. (1977, January). Toward a psychology of natural behavior. *APA Monitor*. (Reprinted in *Readings in psychology 78/79*. Guilford, CT: Dushkin, 1978.)

Sommerville, J. A., Woodward, A. L., & Needham, A. (2005). Action experience alters 3-month-old infants' perception of others' actions. *Cognition, 96*, B1–B11.

Sorce, J. F., Emde, R. N., Campos, J., & Klinnert, M. D. (1985). Maternal emotional signaling: Its effect on the visual cliff behavior of 1-year-olds. *Developmental Psychology, 21*, 195–200.

Soto, C. J., John, O. P., Gosling, S. D., & Potter, J. (2011). Age differences in personality traits from 10 to 65: Big Five domains and facets in a large cross-sectional sample. *Journal of Personality and Social Psychology 100*, 330–348.

Spalding, K. L., Arner, E., Westermark, P. O., et al. (2008, June 5). Dynamics of fat cell turnover in humans. *Nature, 453*, 783–787.

Spanos, N. P. (1991). A sociocognitive approach to hypnosis. In S. J. Lynn & J. W. Rhue (Eds.), *Theories of hypnosis: Current models and perspectives*. New York, NY: Guilford Press.

Spanos, N. P. (1996). *Multiple identities and false memories: A sociocognitive perspective*. Washington, DC: American Psychological Association.

Spanos, N. P., Burgess, C. A., Roncon, V., et al. (1993). Surreptitiously observed hypnotic responding in simulators and in skill-trained and untrained high hypnotizables. *Journal of Personality and Social Psychology, 65*, 391–398.

Spanos, N. P., Menary, E., Gabora, N. J., et al. (1991). Secondary identity enactments during hypnotic past-life regression: A sociocognitive perspective. *Journal of Personality and Social Psychology, 61*, 308–320.

Spanos, N. P., Stenstrom, R. J., & Johnson, J. C. (1988). Hypnosis, placebo, and suggestion in the treatment of warts. *Psychosomatic Medicine, 50*, 245–260.

Spanswick, S., Lehmann, H., & Sutherland, R. J. (2011). A novel model of hippocampal cognitive deficits, slow neurodegeneration, and neuroregeneration. *Journal of Biomedicine and Biotechnology*, Article ID 527201. doi:10.1155/2011/527201

Spear, L. P. (2000a). Neurobiological changes in adolescence. *Current Directions in Psychological Science, 9*, 111–114.

Spear, L. P. (2000b). The adolescent brain and age-related behavioral manifestations. *Neuroscience and Biobehavioral Review, 24*, 417–463.

Spearman, C. (1927). *The abilities of man*. London, England: Macmillan.

Spelke, E. S., & Kinzler, K. D. (2007). Core knowledge. *Developmental Science, 10*, 89–96.

Sperling, G. (1960). The information available in brief visual presentations. *Psychological Monographs, 74*(498).

Sperry, R. W. (1964). The great cerebral commissure. *Scientific American, 210*(1), 42–52.

Sperry, R. W. (1982). Some effects of disconnecting the cerebral hemispheres. *Science, 217*, 1223–1226.

Spitz, H. H. (1997). *Nonconscious movements: From mystical messages to facilitated communication*. Mahwah, NJ: Erlbaum.

Sprecher, S., Schwartz, P., Harvey, J., & Hatfield, E. (2008). The businessoflove.com: Relationship initiation at Internet matchmaking services. In S. Sprecher, A. Wenzel, & J. Harvey (Eds.), *The handbook of relationship initiation.* New York, NY: Psychology Press.

Sprecher, S., Sullivan, Q., & Hatfield, E. (1994). Mate selection preferences: Gender differences examined in a national sample. *Journal of Personality and Social Psychology, 66*, 1074–1080.

Spring, B., Chiodo, J., & Bowen, D. J. (1987). Carbohydrates, tryptophan, and behavior: A methodological review. *Psychological Bulletin, 102*, 234–256.

Squier, L. H., & Domhoff, G. W. (1998). The presentation of dreaming and dreams in introductory psychology textbooks: A critical examination with suggestions for textbook authors and course instructors. *Dreaming, 8*, 149–168.

Squire, L. R. (2007, April 6). Rapid consolidation. *Science, 316*, 57–58.

Squire, L. R., Ojemann, J. G., Miezin, F. M., et al. (1992). Activation of the hippocampus in normal humans: A functional anatomical study of memory. *Proceedings of the National Academy of Science, 89*, 1837–1841.

Squire, L. R., & Zola-Morgan, S. (1991). The medial temporal lobe memory system. *Science, 253*, 1380–1386.

Srivastava, S., Tamir, M., McGonigal, K. M., et al. (2009). The social costs of emotional suppression: A prospective study of the transition to college. *Journal of Personality and Social Psychology, 96*, 883–897.

Staats, C. K., & Staats, A. W. (1957). Meaning established by classical conditioning. *Journal of Experimental Psychology, 54*, 74–80.

Stajkovic, A. D., & Luthans, F. (1998). Self-efficacy and work-related performance: A meta-analysis. *Psychological Bulletin, 124*, 240–261.

Stanley, D., Phelps, E., & Banaji, M. (2008). The neural basis of implicit attitudes. *Current Directions in Psychological Science, 17*, 164–170.

Stanovich, K. (2010). *How to think straight about psychology* (9th ed.). Boston, MA: Allyn & Bacon.

Stanwood, G. D., & Levitt, P. (2001). *The effects of cocaine on the developing nervous system*. In C. A. Nelson & M. Luciana (Eds.), *Handbook of developmental cognitive neuroscience*. Cambridge, MA: The MIT Press.

Stark-Wroblewski, K., Yanico, B. J., & Lupe, S. (2005). Acculturation, internalization of Western appearance norms, and eating pathology among Japanese and Chinese international student women. *Psychology of Women Quarterly, 29*, 38–46.

Statistics Canada. (1993). The Violence against Women Survey. *The Daily*, November 18, 1993.

Statistics Canada. (2005). *Insomnia*. Health Report 17(1), Catalogue 82-003-XPE2005001. Ottawa.

Statistics Canada. (2007, March 14). Youth custody and community services. *The Daily*. Retrieved June 20, 2007, from http://www.statcan.ca/Daily/English/070314/d070314d.htm

Statistics Canada. (2008, April 2). 2006 Census: Ethnic origin, visible minorities, place of work and mode of transportation. *The Daily*. Retrieved from http://www.statcan.ca/Daily/English/080402/d080402a.htm

Statistics Canada (2012). CANSIM, table 102-0512 and Catalogue no. 84-537-XIE. Last modified: 2012-05-31. Retrieved from: http://www.statcan.gc.ca/tables-tableaux/sum-som/l01/cst01/health26-eng.htm

Statistics Canada (2012). Centarians in Canada. Catalogue no. 98-311-X2011003.

Statistics Canada (2013). Immigration and Ethnocultural Diversity in Canada. National Household Survey, 2011. Catalogue no. 99-010-X2011001.

Stattin, H., & Magnusson, D. (1990). *Pubertal maturation in female development*. Hillsdale, NJ: Erlbaum.

Staub, E. (1999). The roots of evil: Social conditions, culture, personality, and basic human needs. *Personality and Social Psychology Review, 3*, 179–192.

Stearns, P. N. (1997). *Fat history: Bodies and beauty in the modern West*. New York, NY: New York University Press.

Steele, C. M. (1992, April). Race and the schooling of black Americans. *Atlantic Monthly*, 68–78.

Steele, C. M. (1997). A threat in the air: How stereotypes shape intellectual identity and performance. *American Psychologist, 52*, 613–629.

Steele, C. M., & Aronson, J. (1995). Stereotype threat and the intellectual test performance of African-Americans. *Journal of Personality and Social Psychology, 69*, 797–811.

Stein, L. J., Cowart, B. J., & Beauchamp, G. K. (2012). The development of salty taste acceptance is related to dietary experience in human infants: A perspective study. *American Journal of Clinical Nutrition, 95*, 123–129.

Steinberg, L. (2007). Risk taking in adolescence. *Current Directions in Psychological Science, 16*, 55–59.

Steinberg, L., & Scott, E. S. (2003). Less guilty by reason of adolescence. *American Psychologist, 58*, 1009–1018.

Steiner, R. A. (1989). *Don't get taken!* El Cerrito, CA: Wide-Awake Books.

Steinvorth, S., Levine, B., & Corkin, S. (2005). Medial temporal lobe structures are needed to re-experience remote autobiographical memories: Evidence from H. M. and W. R. *Neuropsychologia, 43*, 479–496.

Stel, M., Blascovich, J., McCall, C., et al. (2010). Mimicking disliked others: Effects of a priori liking on the mimicry-liking link. *European Journal of Social Psychology, 40*, 867–880.

Stenberg, C. R., & Campos, J. (1990). The development of anger expressions in infancy. In N. Stein, B. Leventhal, & T. Trabasso (Eds.), *Psychological and biological approaches to emotion*. Hillsdale, NJ: Erlbaum.

Stepanski, E., & Perlis, M. (2000). Behavioral sleep medicine: An emerging subspecialty in health psychology. *Journal of Psychosomatic Research, 49*, 343–347.

Stephan, W. G., Ageyev, V., Coates-Shrider, L., et al. (1994). On the relationship between stereotypes and prejudice: An international study. *Personality and Social Psychology Bulletin, 20*, 277–284.

Sternberg, R. J. (1988). *The triarchic mind: A new theory of human intelligence*. New York, NY: Viking.

Sternberg, R. J. (2004). Culture and intelligence. *American Psychologist, 59*, 325–338.

Sternberg, R. J. (2012). The triarchic theory of successful intelligence. In D. P. Flanagan & P. L. Harrison (Eds.), *Contemporary intellectual assessment: Theories, tests, and issues* (3rd ed.). New York: Guilford Press.

Sternberg, R. J. (2014). Teaching about the nature of intelligence. *Intelligence, 42*, 176–179.

Sternberg, R. J., Forsythe, G. B., Hedlund, J., et al. (2000). *Practical intelligence in everyday life*. New York, NY: Cambridge University Press.

Sternberg, R. J., Wagner, R. K., Williams, W. M., & Horvath, Joseph A. (1995). Testing common sense. *American Psychologist, 50*, 912–927.

Stevenson, H. W., Chen, C., & Lee, S. Y. (1993, January 1). Mathematics achievement of Chinese, Japanese, and American children: Ten years later. *Science, 259*, 53–58.

Stevenson, H. W., & Stigler, J. W. (1992). *The learning gap*. New York, NY: Summit.

Stewart-Williams, S., & Podd, J. (2004). The placebo effect: Dissolving the expectancy versus conditioning debate. *Psychological Bulletin, 130*, 324–340.

Stice, E., Spoor, S., Bohon, C., & Small, D. M. (2008, October 17). Relation between obesity and blunted striatal response to food is moderated by *Taq*lA A1 allele. *Science, 322*, 449–452.

Stickgold, R. (2005). Sleep-dependent memory consolidation. *Nature, 437*, 1272–1278.

Stiles, C., Murray, S., & Kentish-Barnes, C. (2011, October 28). *Udderly Robotic* [Radio Broadcast]. Country Life. Wellington: Radio New Zealand National.

Stix, G. (2008, August). Lighting up the lies. *Scientific American*, 18–19.

Stoch, M. B., & Smythe, P. M. (1963). Does undernutrition during infancy inhibit brain growth and subsequent intellectual development? *Archives of Diseases in Childhood, 38*, 546–552.

Strahan, E. J., Spencer, S. J., & Zanna, M. P. (2002). Subliminal priming and persuasion: Striking while the iron is hot. *Journal of Experimental Social Psychology, 38*(6), 556–568.

Straus, M. A. (2005). Children should never, ever, be spanked no matter what the circumstances. In D. R. Loseke, R. J. Gelles, & M. M. Cavanaugh (Eds.), *Current Controversies about Family Violence* (2nd ed.). Thousand Oaks, CA: Sage.

Strauss, E., Wada, J., & Hunter, M. (1994). Callosal morphology and performance on intelligence tests. *Journal of Clinical and Experimental Neuropsychology, 16*(1), 79–83.

Strayer, D. L., & Drews, F. A. (2007). Cell-phone-induced driver distraction. *Current Directions in Psychology, 16,* 128–131.

Strayer, D. L., Drews, F. A., & Crouch, D. J. (2006). A comparisonc of the cell phone driver and the drunk driver. *Human Factors, 48,* 381–391.

Streissguth, A. P. (2001). Recent advances in fetal alcohol syndrome and alcohol use in pregnancy. In D. P. Agarwal & H. K. Seitz (Eds.), *Alcohol in health and disease.* New York, NY: Marcel Dekker.

Streyffeler, L. L., & McNally, R. J. (1998). Fundamentalists and liberals: Personality characteristics of Protestant Christians. *Personality and Individual Differences, 24,* 579–580.

Strickland, B. R. (1989). Internal–external control expectancies: From contingency to creativity. *American Psychologist, 44,* 1–12.

Strickland, T. L., Lin, K. M., Fu, P., et al. (1995). Comparison of lithium ratio between African-American and Caucasian bipolar patients. *Biological Psychiatry, 37,* 325–330.

Strickland, T. L., Ranganath, V., Lin, K. M., et al. (1991). Psychopharmacological considerations in the treatment of black American populations. *Psychopharmacology Bulletin, 27,* 441–448.

Striegel-Moore, R. H., & Bulik, C. M. (2007). Risk factors for eating disorders. *American Psychologist, 62,* 181–198.

Stunkard, A. J. (Ed.). (1980). *Obesity.* Philadelphia, PA: Saunders.

Suddendorf, T., & Whiten, A. (2001). Mental evolution and development: Evidence for secondary representation in children, great apes, and other animals. *Psychological Bulletin, 127,* 629–650.

Sue, D. W., Capodilupo, C. M., Torino, G. C., et al. (2007). Racial microaggressions in everyday life: Implications for clinical practice. *American Psychologist, 62,* 271–286.

Suedfeld, P. (1975). The benefits of boredom: Sensory deprivation reconsidered. *American Scientist, 63*(1), 60–69.

Sugiyama, M., Hattori, H., Inoue, T., Wakaita, H., Hibi, H., & Ueda, M. (2013). Stem cells from human exfoliated deciduous teeth enhance recovery from focal cerebral ischemia in rats. *Journal of Oral and Maxillofacial Surgery, Medicine, and Pathology,* (online May, 2013). http://dx.doi.org/10.1016/j.ajoms.2013.04.014

Suinn, R. M. (2001). The terrible twos—Anger and anxiety. *American Psychologist, 56,* 27–36.

Sullivan, M. J. L., Tripp, D. A., & Santor, D. (1998). *Gender differences in pain and pain behaviour: The role of catastrophizing.* Paper presented at the annual meeting of the American Psychological Association, San Francisco, CA.

Suls, J., Martin, R., & Wheeler, L. (2002). Social comparison: Why, with whom, and with what effect? *Current Directions in Psychological Science, 11,* 159–163.

Suomi, S. J. (1991). Uptight and laid-back monkeys: Individual differences in the response to social challenges. In S. Branch, W. Hall, & J. E. Dooling (Eds.), *Plasticity of development.* Cambridge, MA: MIT Press.

Surowiecki, J. (2004). *The wisdom of crowds.* New York, NY: Doubleday.

Sutherland, R. J., Sparks, F. T., & Lehmann, H. (2010). Hippocampus and retrograde amnesia in the rat model: A modest proposal for the situation of systems consolidation. *Neuropsychologia, 48,* 2357–2369.

Svoboda, E., & Richards, B. (2009). Compensating for anterograde amnesia: A new training method that capitalizes on emerging smartphone technologies. *Journal of the International Neuropsychological Society, 15,* 629–638.

Svoboda, E., Richards, B., Polsinelli, A., & Guger, S. (2010). A theory-driven training programme in the use of emerging commercial technology: Application to an adolescent with severe memory impairment. *Neuropsychological Rehabilitation, 20*(4), 562–586. doi:10.1080/09602011003669918

Swain, S. (1989). Covert intimacy: Closeness in men's friendships. In B. J. Risman & P. Schwartz (Eds.), *Gender in intimate relationships.* Belmont, CA: Wadsworth.

Swenson, C. C., Henggeler, S. W., Taylor, I. S., & Addison, O. W. (2005). *Multisystemic therapy and neighborhood partnerships: Reducing adolescent violence and substance abuse.* New York, NY: Guilford Press.

Symons, D. (1979). *The evolution of human sexuality.* New York, NY: Oxford University Press.

Szpunar, K. K., Addis, D. R., & Schacter, D. L. (2012). Memory for emotional simulations: Remembering a rosy future. *Psychological Science, 23,* 24–29.

Tafarodi, R. W. (1998). Paradoxical self-esteem and selectivity in the processing of social information. *Journal of Personality and Social Psychology, 74,* 1118–1196.

Tafarodi, R. W., Lang, J. M., & Smith, A. J. (1999). Self-esteem and the cultural trade-off: Evidence for the role of individualism-collectivism. *Journal of Cross-Cultural Psychology, 30,* 620–640.

Tafarodi, R. W., & Milne, A. B. (2002). Decomposing global self-esteem. *Journal of Personality, 70,* 443–483.

Tafarodi, R. W., Tam, J., & Milne, A. B. (2001). Selective memory and the persistence of paradoxical self-esteem. *Personality and Social Psychology Bulletin, 27,* 1179–1189.

Tajfel, H., Billig, M. G., Bundy, R. P., & Flament, C. (1971). Social categorization and intergroup behavior. *European Journal of Social Psychology, 1,* 149–178.

Tajfel, H., & Turner, J. C. (1986). The social identity theory of intergroup behavior. In S. Worchel & W. G. Austin (Eds.), *Psychology of intergroup relations.* Chicago, IL: Nelson-Hall.

Takahashi, K., Tanabe, K., Ohnuki, M., et al. (2007). Induction of pluripotent stem cells from adult human fibroblasts by defined factors. *Cell, 131,* 861–872.

Talarico, J. M. (2009). Freshman flashbulbs: Memories of unique and first-time events in starting college. *Memory, 17,* 256–265.

Talarico, J. M., & Rubin, D. C. (2003). Confidence, not consistency, characterizes flashbulb memories. *Psychological Science, 14,* 455–461.

Talarico, J. M., & Rubin, D. C. (2007). Flashbulb memories are special after all; in phenomenology, not accuracy. *Applied Cognitive Psychology, 21,* 557–578.

Talbot, M. (2008, May 12). Birdbrain: The woman behind the world's chattiest parrots. *The New Yorker.* Retrieved from http://www.newyorker.com/reporting/2008/05/12/080512fa_fact_talbot

Talbot, M. (2009, April 27). Brain gain: The underground world of neuroenhancing drugs. *The New Yorker,* 32–43.

Talge, N. M., Neal, C., & Glover, V. (2007). Antenatal maternal stress and long-term effects on child neurodevelopment: how and why? *Journal of Child Psychology and Psychiatry, 48,* 245–261.

Tallis, R. (2011). *Aping mankind: Neuromania, Darwinitis, and the misrepresentation of humanity.* Durham, England: Acumen.

Talmi, D., Grady, C. L., Goshen-Gottstein, Y., & Moscovitch, M. (2005). Neuroimaging the serial position curve: A test of single-store versus dual-store models. *Psychological Science, 16,* 716–723.

Tang, Y., Zhang, W., Chen, K., et al. (2006). Arithmetic processing in the brain shaped by cultures. *Proceedings of the National Academy of Sciences, 103,* 10775–10780.

Tangney, J. P., Wagner, P. E., Hill-Barlow, D., et al. (1996). Relation of shame and guilt to constructive versus destructive responses to anger across the lifespan. *Journal of Personality and Social Psychology, 70,* 797–809.

Tanner, J. (1990). *Fetus into man: Physical growth from conception to maturity.* Cambridge, MA: Harvard University Press.

Taubes, G. (1998). As obesity rates rise, experts struggle to explain why. *Science, 280,* 1367–1368.

Taubes, G. (2008). *Good calories, bad calories: Fats, carbs, and the controversial science of diet and health.* New York, NY: Anchor.

Tavris, C. (1989). *Anger: The misunderstood emotion* (Rev. ed.). New York, NY: Simon & Schuster/Touchstone.

Tavris, C, & Aronson, E. (2007). *Mistakes were made (but not by me).* Orlando, FL: Houghton Mifflin Harcourt.

Tay, R. (2009). The Effectiveness of Automated and Manned Traffic Enforcement. *International Journal of Sustainable Transportation, 3,* 178–186.

Taylor, A. K., & Kowalski, P. (2004). Naïve psychological science: The prevalence, strength, and sources of misconceptions. *Psychological Record, 54,* 15–25.

Taylor, S., Thordarson, D. S., Maxfield, L., et al. (2003). Comparative efficacy, speed, and adverse effects of three PTSD treatments: Exposure therapy, EMDR, and relaxation training. *Journal of Consulting and Clinical Psychology, 71,* 330–338.

Taylor, S. E., Kemeny, M. E., Reed, G. M., et al. (2000). Psychological resources, positive illusions, and health. *American Psychologist, 55,* 99–109.

Taylor, S. E., Klein, L. C., Lewis, B. P., et al. (2000). Biobehavioral responses to stress in females: Tend-and-befriend, not fight-or-flight. *Psychological Review, 107,* 411–429.

Taylor, S. E., Lichtman, R. R., & Wood, J. V. (1984). Attributions, beliefs about control, and adjustment to breast cancer. *Journal of Personality and Social Psychology, 46,* 489–502.

Taylor, S. E., & Lobel, M. (1989). Social comparison activity under threat: Downward evaluation and upward contacts. *Psychological Review, 96,* 569–575.

Taylor, S. E., & Master, S. L. (2011). Social responses to stress: The tend-and-befriend model. In Contrada, R. J., & Baum, A. (Eds.). *The handbook of stress science: Biology, psychology, and health* (pp. 101–109). New York: Springer.

Taylor, S. E., Repetti, R., & Seeman, T. (1997). Health psychology: What is an unhealthy environment and how does it get under the skin? *Annual Review of Psychology, 48,* 411–447.

Terhune, D. B., Tai, S., Cowey, A., et al. (2011). Enhanced cortical excitability in grapheme-color synesthesia and its modulation. *Current Biology, 21,* 2006–2009.

Terman, L. M., & Oden, M. H. (1959). *Genetic studies of genius: Vol. 5. The gifted group at mid-life.* Stanford, CA: Stanford University Press.

Terracciano, A., & McCrae, R. R. (2006, February). National character does not reflect mean personality traits levels in 49 cultures: Reply. *Science, 311,* 777–779.

The Vanier Institute (2010). *Families count. Profiling Canada's families.* Ottawa: Vanier Institute of the Family.

Thomas, A. K., & Dubois, S. J. (2011). Reducing the burden of stereotype threat eliminates age differences in memory distortion. *Psychological Science, 12,* 1515–1517.

Thomas, J. J., Vartanian, L. R., & Brownell, K. D. (2009). The relationship between eating disorder not otherwise specified (EDNOS) and officially recognized eating disorders: Meta-analysis and implications for DSM. *Psychological Bulletin, 135,* 407–433.

Thomas, Michael S. C., & Johnson, Mark H. (2008). New advances in understanding sensitive periods in brain development. *Current Directions in Psychological Science, 17,* 1–5.

Thompson, C. (1943/1973). Penis envy in women. *Psychiatry, 6,* 123–125. (Reprinted in J. B. Miller (Ed.), *Psychoanalysis and women.* New York, NY: Brunner/Mazel, 1973.)

Thompson, J. K., & Cafri, G. (Eds.). (2007). *The muscular ideal: Psychological, social, and medical perspectives.* Washington, DC: American Psychological Association.

Thompson, R., Emmorey, K., & Gollan, T. H. (2005). "Tip of the fingers" experiences by deaf signers. *Psychological Science, 16,* 856–860.

Thompson, R. F. (1983). Neuronal substrates of simple associative learning: Classical conditioning. *Trends in Neurosciences, 6,* 270–275.

Thompson, R. F. (1986). The neurobiology of learning and memory. *Science, 233,* 941–947.

Thompson, R. F., & Kosslyn, S. M. (2000). Neural systems activated during visual mental imagery: A review and meta-analyses. In A. W. Toga & J. C. Mazziotta (Eds.), *Brain mapping: The systems.* San Diego, CA: Academic Press.

Thorndike, E. L. (1898). Animal intelligence: An experimental study of the associative processes in animals. *Psychological Review Monograph Supplement, 2* (Whole No. 8).

Thorndike, E. L. (1903). *Educational psychology.* New York, NY: Columbia University Teachers College.

Thornhill, R., & Palmer, C. T. (2000). *A natural history of rape: Biological bases of sexual coercion.* Cambridge, MA: MIT Press.

Tiefer, L. (2004). *Sex is not a natural act, and other essays* (Rev. ed.). Boulder, CO: Westview.

Tiefer, L. (2008). Sexual problems. In Clouse, A. (Ed.), *Women's health in clinical practice: A handbook for primary care.* Totowa, NJ: Humana Press.

Tierney, Kevin J., & Connolly, Maeve K. (2013). A review of the evidence for a biological basis for snake fears in humans. *The Psychological Record, 63,* 919–928.

Timmann, D., Drepper, J., Frings, M., et al. (2010). The human cerebellum contributes to motor, emotional and cognitive associative learning. A review. *Cortex, 46*(7), 845–857.

Timmers, M., Fischer, A. H., & Manstead, A. S. R. (1998). Gender differences in motives for regulating emotions. *Personality and Social Psychology Bulletin, 24,* 974–985.

Tinti, C., Schmidt, S., Sotgiu, I., et al. (2009). The role of importance/consequentiality appraisal in flashbulb memory formation: The case of the death of Pope John Paul III. *Applied Cognitive Psychology, 23,* 236–253.

Tolman, E. C. (1938). The determiners of behavior at a choice point. *Psychological Review, 45,* 1–35.

Tolman, E. C., & Honzik, C. H. (1930). Introduction and removal of reward and maze performance in rats. *University of California Publications in Psychology, 4,* 257–275.

Tomasello, M. (2000). Culture and cognitive development. *Current Directions in Psychological Science, 9,* 37–40.

Tomasello, M. (2003). Constructing a language: *A usage-based theory of language acquisition.* Cambridge, MA: Harvard University Press.

Tomasello, M. (2008). *Origins of human communication.* Cambridge, MA: MIT Press.

Tomlinson, M., Cooper, P., & Murray, L. (2005). The mother–infant relationship and infant attachment in a South African peri-urban settlement. *Child Development, 76,* 1044–1054.

Toomela, A. (2003). Relationships between personality structure, structure of word meaning, and cognitive ability: A study of cultural mechanisms of personality. *Journal of Personality and Social Psychology, 85,* 723–735.

Tormala, Z. L., & Petty, R. E. (2002). What doesn't kill me makes me stronger: The effects of resisting persuasion on attitude certainty. *Journal of Personality and Social Psychology, 83,* 1298–1313.

Tourangeau, R., & Yan, T. (2007). Sensitive questions in surveys. *Psychological Bulletin, 133,* 859–883.

Tracy, J. L., & Robins, R. W. (2007). Emerging insights into the nature and function of pride. *Current Directions in Psychological Science, 16,* 147–151.

Tracy, J. L., & Robins, R. W. (2008). The nonverbal expression of pride: Evidence for cross-cultural recognition. *Journal of Personality and Social Psychology, 94,* 516–530.

Trakas, K., Lawrence, K., & Shear, N. H. (1999). Utilization of health care resources by obese Canadians. *Canadian Medical Association Journal, 160,* 1457–1462.

Transport Canada. (1998). *Seat belt use in Canada: 1998 survey results.* Retrieved from http://www.tc.gc.ca/roadsafety/stats/sbuse98/English/sb98sume.htm

Triandis, H. C. (1996). The psychological measurement of cultural syndromes. *American Psychologist, 51,* 407–415.

Triandis, H. C. (2007). Culture and psychology: A history of the study of their relationship. In S. Kitayama & D. Cohen (Eds.), *Handbook of cultural psychology.* New York, NY: Guilford Press.

Trivers, R. (1972). Parental investment and sexual selection. In B. Campbell (Ed.), *Sexual selection and the descent of man.* New York, NY: Aldine de Gruyter.

Trivers, R. (2004). Mutual benefits at all levels of life [book review.] *Science, 304,* 965.

Tronick, E. Z., Morelli, G. A., & Ivey, P. K. (1992). The Efe forager infant and toddler's pattern of social relationships: Multiple and simultaneous. *Developmental Psychology, 28,* 568–577.

Tucker-Drob, E. M. (2012). Preschools reduce early academic-achievement gaps: A longitudinal twin approach. *Psychological Science, 23,* 310–319.

Tulving, E. (1985). How many memory systems are there? *American Psychologist, 40,* 385–398.

Turati, C. (2004). Why faces are not special to newborns: An alternative account of the face preference. *Current Directions in Psychological Science, 13,* 5–8.

Turiel, E. (2002). *The culture of morality.* Cambridge, England: Cambridge University Press.

Turkheimer, E., Haley, A., Waldron, M., D'Onofrio, B., & Gottesman, I. I. (2003). Socioeconomic status modifies heritability of IQ in young children. *Psychological Science, 14,* 623–628.

Turner, C. F., Ku, L., Rogers, S. M., et al. (1998). Adolescent sexual behavior, drug use, and violence: Increased reporting with computer survey technology. *Science, 280,* 867–873.

Turner, E. H., Matthews, A. M., Linardatos, E., et al. (2008). Selective publication of antidepressant trials and its influence on apparent efficacy. *New England Journal of Medicine, 358,* 252–60.

Turvey, B. E. (2008). Serial crime. In B. E. Turvey (Ed.), *Criminal profiling: An introduction to behavioral evidence analysis* (3rd ed.). San Diego, CA: Elsevier Academic Press.

Tustin, K., & Hayne, H. (2010). Defining the boundary: Age-related changes in childhood amnesia. *Developmental Psychology, 46,* 1049–1061.

Tversky, A., & Kahneman, D. (1973). Availability: A heuristic for judging frequency and probability. *Cognitive Psychology, 5,* 207–232.

Tversky, A., & Kahneman, D. (1981). The framing of decisions and the psychology of choice. *Science, 211,* 453–458.

Twenge, J. (2009). Change over time in obedience: The jury's still out, but it might be decreasing. *American Psychologist, 64,* 28–31.

Twenge, J. M., & Campbell, W. K. (2009). *The narcissism epidemic.* New York: Free Press.

Twenge, J. M., Campbell, W. K., & Freeman, E. C. (2012). Generational differences in young adults' life goals, concern for others, and civic orientation, 1966–2009. *Journal of Personality and Social Psychology, 102,* 1045–1062.

Twenge, J. M., & Foster, J. D. (2010). Birth cohort increases in narcissistic personality traits among American college students, 1982–2009. *Social Psychological and Personality Science, 1,* 99–106.

Twenge, J. M., Konrath, S., Foster, J. D., et al. (2008). Egos inflating over time: A cross-temporal meta-analysis of the Narcissistic Personality Inventory. *Journal of Personality, 76,* 875–901.

Tyrer, P., Oliver-Africano, P. C., Ahmed, Z., et al. (2008, January 5). Risperidone, haloperidol, and placebo in the treatment of aggressive challenging behaviour in patients with intellectual disability: A randomised controlled trial. *Lancet, 371,* 57–63.

Uchino, B. N. (2009). Understanding the links between social support and physical health: A life-span perspective with emphasis on the separability of perceived and received support. *Perspectives on Psychological Science, 4*(3), 236–255.

Ullian, E. M., Chrisopherson, K. S., & Barres, B. A. (2004). Role for glia in synaptogenesis. *Glia, 47,* 209–216.

Updegraff, J. A., Gable, S. L., & Taylor, S. E. (2004). What makes experiences satisfying? The interaction of approach-avoidance motivations and emotions in well-being. *Journal of Personality and Social Psychology, 86,* 496–504.

Urry, H. L., & Gross, J. J. (2010). Emotion regulation in older age. *Current Directions in Psychological Science, 19,* 352–357.

Urry, H. L., Nitschke, J. B., Dolski, I., et al. (2004). Making a life worth living: Neural correlates of well-being. *Psychological Science, 15,* 367–372.

U. S. Food and Drug Administration (2011). Executive Summary Prepared for the January 27–28, 2011 meeting of the neurological devices panel to discuss the classification of electroconvulsive therapy devices (ECT). Available online at www.fda.gov/downloads/AdvisoryCommittees/CommitteesMeetingMaterials/MedicalDevicesAdvisoryCommittee/neurologicalDevicesPanel/UCM240933.pdf

Usher, J. A., & Neisser, U. (1993). Childhood amnesia and the beginnings of memory for four early life events. *Journal of Experimental Psychology: General, 122,* 155–165.

Uttal, W. R. (2001). *The new phrenology: The limits of localizing cognitive processes in the brain.* Cambridge, MA: MIT Press/Bradford Books.

Vaillant, G. E. (Ed.). (1992). *Ego mechanisms of defense.* Washington, DC: American Psychiatric Press.

Vaillant, G. E. (2002). *Aging well.* Boston: Little, Brown.

Valenstein, E. (1986). *Great and desperate cures: The rise and decline of psychosurgery and other radical treatments for mental illness.* New York, NY: Basic Books.

Valentine, T., & Mesout, J. (2009). Eyewitness identification under stress in the London dungeon. *Applied Cognitive Psychology, 23,* 151–161.

Van Baaren, R., Janssen, L., Chartrand, T. L., & Dijksterhuis, A. (2009). Where is the love? The social aspects of mimicry. *Philosophical Transactions of the Royal Society of London, B: Biological Sciences, 364,* 2381–2389.

Van Boven, L., & Gilovich, T. (2003). To do or to have? That is the question. *Journal of Personality and Social Psychology, 85,* 1193–1202.

Van Cantfort, T. E., & Rimpau, J. B. (1982). Sign language studies with children and chimpanzees. *Sign Language Studies, 34,* 15–72.

Van de Castle, R. (1994). *Our dreaming mind.* New York, NY: Ballantine Books.

Vandello, J. A., & Cohen, D. (2008). U.S. Southern and Northern differences in perceptions of norms about aggression: Mechanisms for the perpetuation of a culture of honor. *Social and Personality Psychology Compass, 2,* 652–667.

Vandello, J. A., Cohen, D., Ransom, S. (2008). U.S. Southern and Northern differences in perceptions of norms about aggression: Mechanisms for the perpetuation of a culture of honor. *Journal of Cross-Cultural Psychology, 39,* 162–177.

Vandenberg, B. (1985). Beyond the ethology of play. In A. Gottfried & C. C. Brown (Eds.), *Play interactions.* Lexington, MA: Lexington Books.

van den Dries, L., Juffer, F., van IJzendoorn, M. H., & Bakermans-Kranenburg, M. J. (2009). Fostering security? A meta-analysis of attachment in adopted children. *Children and Youth Services Review, 31,* 410–421.

van der Toorn, J., Tyler, T. R., & Jost, J. T. (2011). More than fair: Outcome dependence, system justification, and the perceived legitimacy of authority figures. *Journal of Experimental Social Psychology, 47,* 127–138.

Van Emmerik, A. A., Kamphuis, J. H., Hulsbosch, A. M., & Emmelkamp, P. M. G. (2002, September 7). Single session debriefing after psychological trauma: A meta-analysis. *The Lancet, 360,* 766–771.

Van Horn, J. D., Irimia, A., Torgerson, C. M., et al. (2012) Mapping connectivity damage in the case of Phineas Gage. *PLoS One 7, 5:* e37454.

van IJzendoorn, M. H., Juffer, F., & Klein Poelhuis, C. W. (2005). Adoption and cognitive development: A meta-analytic comparison of adopted and nonadopted children's IQ and school performance. *Psychological Bulletin, 131,* 301–316.

van Laar, C., Levin, S., & Sidanius, J. (2008). Ingroup and outgroup contact: A longitudinal study of the effects of cross-ethnic friendships, dates, roommate relationships and participation in segregated organizations. In U. Wagner, L. R. Tropp, G. Finchilescu, & C. Tredoux (Eds.), *Improving intergroup relations: Building on the legacy of Thomas F. Pettigrew.* Malden, MA: Blackwell.

Van Ommeren, M., Saxena, S., & Saraceno, B. (2005, January). Mental and social health during and after acute emergencies: Emerging consensus? *Bulletin of the World Health Organization, 83,* 71–76.

van Schaik, C. (2006, April). Why are some animals so smart? *Scientific American,* 64–71.

Vecera, S. P., Vogel, E., K., & Woodman, G. F. (2002). Lower region: A new cue for figure-ground assignment. *Journal of Experimental Psychology: General, 131,* 194–205.

Velliste, M., Perel, S., Spalding, M. C., et al. (2008). Cortical control of a prosthetic arm for self-feeding. *Nature, 453,* 994–995.

Vertes, R. P., & Siegel, J. M. (2005). Time for the sleep community to take a critical look at the purported role of sleep in memory processing. *Sleep, 28,* 1228–1229.

Vita, A. J., Terry, R. B., Hubert, H. B., & Fries, J. F. (1998). Aging, health risks, and cumulative disability. *New England Journal of Medicine, 338,* 1035–1041.

Vogelzangs, N., Kritchevsky, S. B., Beekman, A. T., et al. (2008). Depressive symptoms and change in abdominal obesity in older persons. *Archives of General Psychiatry, 65,* 1386–1393.

Voigt, B. F., Kudaravalli, S., Wen, X., & Pritchard, J. K. (2006). A map of recent positive selection in the human genome. *PLoS Biology, 4,* e72.

Volkow, N. D., Chang, L, Wang, G. J., et al. (2001). Association of dopamine transporter reduction with psychomotor impairment in methamphetamine abusers. *American Journal of Psychiatry, 158,* 377–382.

Voyer, D., Voyer, S., & Bryden, M. P. (1995). Magnitude of sex differences in spatial abilities: A meta-analysis and consideration of critical variables. *Psychological Bulletin, 117,* 250–270.

Vrij, A., Granhag, P. A., Mann, S., & Leal, S. (2011). Outsmarting the liars: Toward a cognitive lie detection approach. *Current Directions in Psychological Science, 20,* 28–32.

Vrij, A., Granhag, P. A., & Porter, S. (2010). Pitfalls and opportunities in nonverbal and verbal lie detection. *Psychological Science in the Public Interest, 11,* 89–121.

Vroon, P. (1997). *Smell: The secret seducer* [P. Vincent, Trans.] New York, NY: Farrar, Straus & Giroux.

Vul, E., Harris, C., Winkielman, P., & Pashler, Harold. (2009). Puzzlingly high correlations in fMRI studies of emotion, personality, and social cognition. *Perspectives on Psychological Science, 4,* 274–290.

Vul, E., & Pashler, H. (2008). Measuring the crowd within. *Psychological Science, 19,* 645–647.

Vygotsky, L. (1962). *Thought and language.* Cambridge, MA: MIT Press.

Wadden, T. A., Foster, G. D., Letizia, K. A., & Mullen, J. L. (1990, August 8). Long-term effects of dieting on resting metabolic rate in obese outpatients. *Journal of the American Medical Association, 264,* 707–711.

Wade, C. (2006). Some cautions about jumping on the brain-scan bandwagon. *APS Observer, 19,* 23–24.

Wagenaar, W. A. (1986). My memory: A study of autobiographical memory over six years. *Cognitive Psychology, 18,* 225–252.

Wagenmakers, E. J., Wetzels, R., Borsboom, D., et al. (2011). Why psychologists must change the way they analyze their data: The case of psi. *Journal of Personality and Social Psychology, 100,* 426–432.

Wagner, C. C., & Ingersoll, K. S. (2008). Beyond cognition: Broadening the emotional base of motivational interviewing. *Journal of Psychotherapy Integration, 18,* 191–206.

Wagner, U., Gais, S., Haider, H., et al. (2004). Sleep inspires insight. *Nature, 427,* 352–355.

Wakefield, J. (2011). The DSM-5's proposed new categories of sexual disorder: The problem of false positives in sexual diagnosis. *Journal of Clinical Social Work.* doi:10.1007/s10615-011-0353-2.

Wakefield, J. C. (1992). Disorder as harmful dysfunction: A conceptual critique of DSM-III-R's definition of mental disorder. *Psychological Review, 99,* 232–247.

Waldram, J. B., & Wong, S. (1995). Group therapy of Aboriginal offenders in a Canadian forensic psychiatric facility. *American Indian and Alaska Native Mental Health Research, 6*(2), 34–56.

Walker, A. (1994). Mood and well-being in consecutive menstrual cycles: Methodological and theoretical implications. *Psychology of Women Quarterly, 18,* 271–290.

Walker, D. L., Ressler, K. J., Lu, K. T., & Davis, M. (2002). Facilitation of conditioned fear extinction by systemic administration or intra-amygdala infusions of D-cycloserine as assessed with fear-potentiated startle in rats. *The Journal of Neuroscience, 22,* 2343–2351.

Walker-Andrews, A. S. (1997). Infants' perception of expressive behaviors: Differentiation of multimodal information. *Psychological Bulletin, 121,* 437–456.

Wallace-Wells, B. (2009, February 5). Bitter pill. *Rolling Stone,* 56–63, 74–76.

Wallbott, H. G., Ricci-Bitti, P., & Bänninger-Huber, E. (1986). Non-verbal reactions to emotional experiences. In K. R. Scherer, H. G. Wallbott, & A. B. Summerfield (Eds.), *Experiencing emotion: A cross-cultural study*. Cambridge, England: Cambridge University Press.

Wallen, K. (2001). Sex and context: Hormones and primate sexual motivation. *Hormones and Behavior, 40*, 339–357.

Waller, N. G., Kojetin, B. A., Bouchard, T. J., Jr., et al. (1990). Genetic and environmental influences on religious interests, attitudes, and values: A study of twins reared apart and together. *Psychological Science, 1*, 138–142.

Walton, G. M., & Cohen, G. L. (2011, March 18). A brief social belonging intervention improves academic and health outcomes of minority students. *Science, 331*, 1447–1451.

Walum, H., Westberg, L., Henningsson, S., et al. (2008). Genetic variation in the vasopressin receptor 1a gene (AVPR1A) associates with pair-bonding behavior in humans. *Proceedings of the National Academy of Sciences, 105*, 14153–14156.

Wampold, B. (2001). *The great psychotherapy debate: Models, methods, and findings*. Mahwah, NJ: Erlbaum.

Wandersman, A., & Nation, M. (1998). Urban neighborhoods and mental health: Psychological contributions to understanding toxicity, resilience, and interventions. *American Psychologist, 53*, 647–656.

Wang, A. Y., Thomas, M. H., & Ouellette, J. A. (1992). The keyword mnemonic and retention of second-language vocabulary words. *Journal of Educational Psychology, 84*, 520–528.

Wang, Q. (2008). Being American, being Asian: The bicultural self and autobiographical memory in Asian Americans. *Cognition, 107*, 743–751.

Wang, R., & Bianchi, S. (2009). ATUS fathers' involvement in childcare. *Social Indicator Research, 93*, 141–145.

Wansink, B. (2006). *Mindless eating*. New York, NY: Bantam.

Warren, G. H., & Raynes, A. E. (1972). Mood changes during three conditions of alcohol intake. *Quarterly Journal of Studies on Alcohol, 33*, 979–989.

Wasserman, E. W., & Lisanby, S. H. (2001). Therapeutic application of repetitive transcranial magnetic stimulation: A review. *Clinical Neurophysiology, 112*, 1367–1377.

Watanabe, S. (2001). Van Gogh, Chagall and pigeons: Picture discrimination in pigeons and humans. *Animal Cognition, 4*, 1435–9448.

Watanabe, S. (2010). Pigeons can discriminate "good" and "bad" paintings by children. *Animal Cognition, 13*, 75–85.

Watkins, L. R., & Maier, S. F. (2003). When good pain turns bad. *Current Directions in Psychological Science, 12*, 232–236.

Watson, J. B. (1925). *Behaviorism*. New York, NY: Norton.

Watson, J. B., & Rayner, R. (1920). Conditioned emotional reactions. *Journal of Experimental Psychology, 3*, 1–14. (Reprinted May 2000 in *American Psychologist, 55*, 313–317.)

Watters, E., & Ofshe, R. (1999). *Therapy's delusions*. New York, NY: Scribner.

Weaver, C. N. (2008). Social distance as a measure of prejudice among ethnic groups in the United States. *Journal of Applied Social Psychology, 38*, 778–795.

Webb, D. A., Boyd, N. R., Messina, D., & Windsor, R. A. (2003). The discrepancy between self-reported smoking status and urine continine levels among women enrolled in prenatal care at four publicly funded clinical sites. *Journal of Public Health Management and Practice, 9*(4), 322–325.

Webster, R. (1995). *Why Freud was wrong*. New York, NY: Basic Books.

Wechsler, D. (1955). *Manual for the Wechsler Adult Intelligence Scale*. New York, NY: Psychological Corporation.

Wegner, D. M., Fuller, V. A., & Sparrow, B. (2003). Clever hands: Uncontrolled intelligence in facilitated communication. *Journal of Personality and Social Psychology, 85*, 5–19.

Wegner, D. M., & Gold, D. B. (1995). Fanning old flames: Emotional and cognitive effects of suppressing thoughts of a past relationship. *Journal of Personality and Social Psychology, 68*, 782–792.

Wehr, T. A., Duncan, W. C., Sher, L., et al. (2001). A circadian signal of change of season in patients with seasonal affective disorder. *Archives of General Psychiatry, 58*, 1108–1114.

Weil, A. T. (1972/1986). *The natural mind: A new way of looking at drugs and the higher consciousness*. Boston, MA: Houghton-Mifflin.

Weil, A. T. (1974a, June). Parapsychology: Andrew Weil's search for the true Geller. *Psychology Today*, 45–50.

Weil, A. T. (1974b, July). Parapsychology: Andrew Weil's search for the true Geller: Part II. The letdown. *Psychology Today*, 74–78, 82.

Weiner, B. (1986). *An attributional theory of motivation and emotion*. New York, NY: Springer-Verlag.

Weinstein, T. A., Capitanio, J. P., & Gosling, S. D. (2008). Personality in animals. In O. P. John, R. W. Robbins, & L. A. Pervin (Eds.), *Handbook of personality: Theory and research*. New York, NY: Guilford.

Weinstock, Marta (2005). The potential influence of maternal stress hormones on development and mental health of the offspring. *Brain, Behavior, and Immunity, 19*, 296–308.

Weiss, A., Bates, T. C., & Luciano, M. (2008). Happiness is a personal(ity) thing. *Psychological Science, 19*, 205–210.

Weisz, J. R., Weiss, B., Han, S. S., et al. (1995). Effects of psychotherapy with children and adolescents revisited: A meta-analysis of treatment outcome studies. *Psychological Bulletin, 117*, 450–468.

Wellman, H. M., Cross, D., & Watson, J. (2001). Meta-analysis of theory-of-mind development: The truth about false belief. *Child Development, 72*, 655–684.

Wells, B. E., & Twenge, J. (2005). Changes in young people's sexual behavior and attitudes, 1943–1999: A cross-temporal meta-analysis. *Review of General Psychology, 9*, 249–261.

Wells, G. L., & Olson, E. A. (2003). Eyewitness testimony. *Annual Review of Psychology, 54*, 277–295.

Wells, G. L., Small, M., Penrod, S., et al. (1998). Eyewitness identification procedures: Recommendations for lineups and photospreads. *Law and Human Behavior, 22*, 602–647.

Wenzel, A. (2005). Autobiographical memory tasks in clinical research. In A. Wenzel & D. C. Rubin (Eds.), *Cognitive methods and their application to clinical research*. Washington, DC: American Psychological Association.

Werner, E. E. (1989). High-risk children in young adulthood: A longitudinal study from birth to 32 years. *American Journal of Orthopsychiatry, 59*, 72–81.

Wertheimer, M. (1958). Principles of perceptual organization. In D. C. Beardslee & M. Wertheimer (Eds.), *Readings in perception*. Princeton, NJ: Van Nostrand. [Original work published 1923.]

West, M. O., & Prinz, R. J. (1987). Parental alcoholism and childhood psychopathology. *Psychological Bulletin, 102*, 204–218.

West, R. E., & Young, R. J. (2002). Do domestic dogs show any evidence of being able to count? *Animal Cognition, 5*, 183–186.

Westen, D. (1998). The scientific legacy of Sigmund Freud: Toward a psychodynamically informed psychological science. *Psychological Bulletin, 124*, 333–371.

Westen, D., Novotny, C. M., & Thompson-Brenner, H. (2004). The empirical status of empirically supported psychotherapies: Assumptions, findings, and reporting in controlled clinical trials. *Psychological Bulletin, 130*, 631–663.

Westen, D., & Shedler, J. (1999). Revising and assessing axis II, Part II: Toward an empirically based and clinically useful classification of personality disorders. *American Journal of Psychiatry, 156*, 273–285.

Westling, E., Andrews, J. A., Hampson, S. E., & Peterson, M. (2008). Pubertal timing and substance use: The effects of gender, parental monitoring and deviant peers. *Journal of Adolescent Health, 42*, 555–563.

Westling, E., Andrews, J. A., & Peterson, M. (2012). Gender differences in puberty timing, social competence, and cigarette use: A test of the early maturation hypothesis. *Journal of Adolescent Health, 51*, 150–155.

Wethington, E. (2000). Expecting stress: Americans and the "midlife crisis." *Motivation & Emotion, 24*, 85–103.

Wetzels, R., Matzke, D., Lee, M. D., et al. (2011). Statistical evidence in experimental psychology: An empirical comparison using 855 t tests. *Perspectives on Psychological Science, 6*, 291–298.

Whaley, A. L., & Davis, K. E. (2007). Cultural competence and evidence-based practice in mental health services. *American Psychologist, 62*, 563–574.

Wheeler, M. D. (1991). Physical changes of puberty. *Endocrinology and Metabolism Clinics of North America, 20*(1), 1–14.

Wheeler, M. E., & Fiske, S. T. (2005). Controlling racial prejudice: Social-cognitive goals affect amygdala and stereotype activation. *Psychological Science, 16*, 56–63.

Whited, M. C., Wheat, A. L., & Larkin, K. T. (2010). The influence of forgiveness and apology on cardiovascular reactivity and recovery in response to mental stress. *The Journal of Behavioral Medicine, 33*, 293–304.

Whiting, B. B., & Edwards, C. P. (1988). *Children of different worlds: The formation of social behavior*. Cambridge, MA: Harvard University Press.

Whiting, B., & Whiting, J. (1975). *Children of six cultures*. Cambridge, MA: Harvard University Press.

Whitlock, J. R., Heynen, A. J., Shuler, M. G., & Bear, M. F. (2006, August 25). Learning induces long-term potentiation in the hippocampus. *Science, 313*, 1093–1098.

Whitty, M. T., & Carr, A. N. (2006). New rules in the workplace: Applying object-relations theory to explain problem Internet and email behaviour in the workplace. *Computers in Human Behavior, 22,* 235–250.

Whorf, B. L. (1956). *Language, thought and reality.* Cambridge, MA: MIT Press. [Original work published 1940.]

Wicks-Nelson, R., & Israel, A. C. (2003). *Behavior disorders of childhood* (5th ed.). Upper Saddle River, NJ: Prentice Hall.

Widen, S. C., & Russell, J. A. (2010). Differentiation in preschooler's categories of emotion. *Emotion, 10,* 651–661.

Widiger, T., & Clark, L. A. (2000). Toward DSM-V and the classification of psychopathology. *Psychological Bulletin, 126,* 946–963.

Widom, C. S., DuMont, K., & Czaja, S. J. (2007). A prospective investigation of major depressive disorder and comorbidity in abused and neglected children grown up. *Archives of General Psychiatry, 64,* 49–56.

Wiederhold, B. K., & Wiederhold, M. D. (2000). Lessons learned from 600 virtual reality sessions. *CyberPsychology & Behavior, 3,* 393–400.

Wildman, R. P., Muntner, P., Reynolds, K., et al. (2008, August 11). The obese without cardiometabolic risk factor clustering and the normal weight with cardiometabolic risk factor clustering: Prevalence and correlates of 2 phenotypes among the US population. *Archives of Internal Medicine, 168,* 1617–1624.

Williams, K. D. (2009). Ostracism: Effects of being excluded and ignored. *Advances in Experimental Social Psychology, 41,* 279–314.

Williams, K. D., & Nida, S. (2011). Ostracism: Consequences and coping. *Current Directions in Psychological Science, 20,* 71–75.

Williams, L. A., & DeSteno, D. (2009). Pride: Adaptive social emotion or seventh sin? *Psychological Science, 20,* 284–288.

Williams, R. B., Jr., Barefoot, J. C., & Shekelle, R. B. (1985). The health consequences of hostility. In M. A. Chesney & R. H. Rosenman (Eds.), *Anger and hostility in cardiovascular and behavioral disorders.* New York, NY: Hemisphere.

Williamson, D. L., & Fast, J. E. (1998). Poverty and medical treatment: When public policy compromises accessibility. *Canadian Journal of Public Health, 89*(2), 120–124.

Willmott, L., Harris, P., Gellaitry, G., et al. (2011). The effects of expressive writing following first myocardial infarction: A randomized controlled trial. *Health Psychology, 30*(5), 642–650.

Wilner, D., Walkley, R., & Cook, S. (1955). *Human relations in interracial housing.* Minneapolis: University of Minnesota Press.

Wiltermuth, S. S., & Heath, C. (2009). Synchrony and cooperation. *Psychological Science, 20,* 1–5.

Wilson, E. O. (1975). *Sociobiology: The new synthesis.* Cambridge, MA: Belknap/Harvard University Press.

Wilson, G. T., & Fairburn, C. G. (1993). Cognitive treatments for eating disorders. *Journal of Consulting and Clinical Psychology, 61,* 261–269.

Wilson, S. J., & Lipsey, M. W. (2007). School-based interventions for aggressive and disruptive behavior: Update of a meta-analysis. *American Journal of Preventive Medicine, 33,* S130–S143.

Wilson, T. (2011). *Redirect: The surprising new science of psychological change.* New York: Little, Brown.

Wilson, T. D., & Gilbert, D. T. (2005). Affective forecasting: Knowing what to want. *Current Directions in Psychological Science, 14,* 131–134.

Winick, M., Meyer, K. K., & Harris, R. C. (1975). Malnutrition and environmental enrichment by early adoption. *Science, 190,* 1173–1175.

Winnicott, D. W. (1957/1990). *Home is where we start from.* New York, NY: Norton.

Wirz-Justice, A., Benedetti, F., Berger, M., et al. (2005). Chronotherapeutics (light and wake therapy) in affective disorders. *Psychological Medicine, 35,* 939–944.

Wispé, L. G., & Drambarean, N. C. (1953). Physiological need, word frequency, and visual duration thresholds. *Journal of Experimental Psychology, 46,* 25–31.

Witkiewitz, K., & Marlatt, G. A. (2004). Relapse prevention for alcohol and drug problems: That was Zen, this is Tao. *American Psychologist, 59,* 224–235.

Witvliet, C. vanOyen, Ludwig, T. E., & Vander Laan, K. L. (2001). Granting forgiveness or harboring grudges: Implications for emotion, physiology, and health. *Psychological Science, 12,* 117–123.

Wolfson, A. R., and Carskadon, M. A. (1998). Sleep schedules and daytime functioning in adolescents. *Child Development, 69,* 875–887.

Wolpe, J. (1958). *Psychotherapy by reciprocal inhibition.* Palo Alto, CA: Stanford University Press.

Wood, E., Tyndall, M. W., Kerr, T., et al. (2002). Safer injection facilites for injection drug users: The debate continues. *Canadian Medical Association Journal, 166*(4), 422.

Wood, J. V., Michela, J. L., & Giordano, C. (2000). Downward comparison in everyday life: Reconciling self-enhancement models with the mood-cognition priming model. *Journal of Personality and Social Psychology, 79,* 563–579.

Wood, W., Lundgren, S., Ouellette, J. A., et al. (1994). Minority influence: A meta-analytic review of social influence processes. *Psychological Bulletin, 115,* 323–345.

Woodward, A. L. (2009). Infants' grasp of others' intentions. *Current Directions in Psychological Science, 18,* 53–57.

Woody, E. Z., & Bowers, K. S. (1994). A frontal assault on dissociated control. In S. J. Lynn & J. W. Rhue (Eds.), *Dissociation: Clinical, theoretical and research perspectives.* New York, NY: Guilford.

Woody, E. Z., & Sadler, P. (2012). Dissociation theories of hypnosis. In M. R. Nash, M. Nash, & A. Barnier (Eds.), *The Oxford handbook of hypnosis: Theory, research, and Practice.* New York: Oxford University Press.

World Health Organization (WHO) (2004). Annex Table 3: Burden of disease in DALYs by cause, sex, and mortality stratum in WHO regions, estimates for 2002. *The World Health Report 2004: Changing History.* Geneva, Switzerland: WHO.

Wright, S. C., Taylor, D. M., & Ruggiero, K. M. (1996). Examining the potential for academic achievement among Inuit children: Comparisons on the Raven Coloured Progressive Matrices. *Journal of Cross Cultural Psychology, 27*(6), 733–753.

Wu, S., & Keysar, B. (2007). The effect of culture on perspective taking. *Psychological Science, 18,* 600–606.

Wynne, C. D. L. (2004). *Do animals think?* Princeton, NJ: Princeton University Press.

Wyrobek, A. J., Eskenazi, B., Young, S., et al. (2006, June 9). Advancing age has differential effects on DNA damage, chromatin integrity, gene mutations, and aneuploidies in sperm. *Proceedings of the National Academy of Sciences, 103,* 9601–9606.

Xiu, L. J., Lin, H. M., & Wei, P. K. (2010). The effect of chronic mild stress on tumor-bearing rats' behavior and its mechanism. *Neuroscience Letters, 473,* 1–4.

Xu, N., Burnham, D., Kitamura, C., Vollmer-Conna, U. (2013). Vowel hyper-articulation in parrot-, dog- and infant-directed speech. *Anthrozoos: A Multidisciplinary Journal of the Interactions of People & Animals, 26,* 373–380.

Yalom, I. D. (1989). *Love's executioner and other tales of psychotherapy.* New York, NY: Basic Books.

Yang, C. F. J., Gray, P., & Pope, H. G., Jr. (2005). Male body image in Taiwan versus the West: Yanggang Zhiqi meets the Adonis Complex. *American Journal of Psychiatry, 162,* 263–269.

Yapko, M. (1994). *Suggestions of abuse: True and false memories of childhood sexual trauma.* New York, NY: Simon & Schuster.

Yehuda, R., Engel, S. M., Brand, S. R., et al. (2005). Transgenerational effects of posttraumatic stress disorder in babies of mothers exposed to the World Trade Center attacks during pregnancy. *The Journal of Clinical Endocrinology & Metabolism, 90,* 4115–4118.

Young, L. J., & Francis, D. D. (2008). The biochemistry of family commitment and youth competence: Lessons from animal models. In K. Kline (Ed.), *Authoritative communities: The scientific case for nurturing the whole child.* New York, NY: Springer Science + Business Media.

Young, M. P., & Yamane, S. (1992). Sparse population coding of faces in the inferotemporal cortex. *Science, 256,* 1327–1331.

Young, T. K. (1996). Obesity, central fat patterning, and their metabolic correlated among Inuit of the central Canadian Arctic. *Human Biology, 68,* 245–263.

Young, T., Finne, L., Peppard, P. E., et al. (2008). Sleep-disordered breathing and mortality: Eighteen-year follow-up of the Wisconsin Sleep Cohort. *Sleep, 31,* 1071–1078.

Yu, M., & Stiffman, A. R. (2007). Culture and environment as predictors of alcohol abuse/dependence symptoms in American Indian youths. *Addictive Behaviors, 32,* 2253–2259.

Yuan, S., & Fisher, C. (2009). "Really? She blicked the baby?" Two-year-olds learn combinatorial facts about verbs by listening. *Psychological Science, 20,* 619–626.

Zaehle, T., Sandmann, P., Thorne, J. D., et al. (2011). Transcranial direct current stimulation of the prefrontal cortex modulates working memory performance: Combined behavioural and electrophysiological evidence. *BMC Neuroscience, 12,* 1–11.

Zajac, R., & Henderson, N. (2009). Don't it make my brown eyes blue: Co-witness misinformation about a target's appearance can impair target-absent line-up performance. *Memory, 17*, 266–278.

Zajonc, R. B. (1968). Attitudinal effects of mere exposure. *Journal of Personality and Social Psychology, 9*, Monograph Supplement 2, 1–27.

Zeki, S., Romaya, J. P., Benincasa, D. M.T., & Atiyah, M. F. (2014). The experience of mathematical beauty and its neural correlates. *Frontiers in Human Neuroscience, 8*, 68.

Zhang, Y., Hoon, M. A., Chandrashekar, J., et al. (2003). Coding of sweet, bitter, and umami tastes: Different receptor cells sharing similar signaling pathways. *Cell, 112*, 293–301.

Zhang, Y., Proenca, R., Maffei, M., et al. (1994). Positional cloning of the mouse obese gene and its human homologue. *Nature, 372*(6505), 425–432.

Zhu, L. X., Sharma, S., Stolina, M., et al. (2000). Delta-9-tetrahydrocannabinol inhibits antitumor immunity by a CB2 receptor-mediated, cytokine-dependent pathway. *Journal of Immunology, 165*, 373–380.

Zimbardo, P. G., & Leippe, M. R. (1991). *The psychology of attitude change and social influence*. New York, NY: McGraw-Hill.

Zimmer, L., & Morgan, J. P. (1997). *Marijuana myths, marijuana fact: A review of the scientific evidence*. New York, NY: Lindesmith Center.

Zimmerman, F. J., Christakis, D. A., & Meltzoff, A. N. (2007). Associations between media viewing and language development in children under age 2 years. *Journal of Pediatrics, 151*, 364–368.

Zone, N., Sue, S., Chang, J., et al. (2005). Beyond ethnic match: Effects of client–therapist cognitive match in problem perception, coping orientation, and therapy goals on treatment outcomes. *Journal of Community Psychology, 33*, 569–585.

Zosuls, K. M., Ruble, D. N., Tamis-LeMonda, C. S., et al. (2009). The acquisition of gender labels in infancy: Implications for gender-typed play. *Developmental Psychology, 45*, 688–701.

Zou, Z., & Buck, L. (2006). Combinatorial effects of odorant mixes in olfactory cortex. *Science, 311*, 1477–1481.

Zucker, K. J. (1999). Intersexuality and gender identity differentiation. *Annual Review of Sex Research, 10*, 1–69.

Zurbriggen, E. L. (2000). Social motives and cognitive power-sex associations: Predictors of aggressive sexual behavior. *Journal of Personality and Social Psychology, 78*, 559–581.

Credits

Table, Text, and Figure Credits

Chapter 1 *Page 16:* Excerpt from Gestalt Psychology Today. First published in American Psychologist, 14, 727–734. 1959; *Page 24:* Excerpt from "Why can't psychology get a stamp?" by Ludy T. Benjamin in Journal of Applied Psychoanalytic Studies October 2003, Volume 5, Issue 4, pp 443–454.

Chapter 2 *Page 35:* Excerpt from "Feeling the Future: Experimental Evidence for Anomalous Retroactive Influences on Cognition and Affect" by Darryl J. Bem in JOURNAL OF PERSONALITY AND SOCIAL PSYCHOLOGY 2011, Vol. 100, No. 3, 407–425. Copyright © 2011 American Psychological Association; *Page 36:* Excerpt from "HOW TO THINK STRAIGHT ABOUT PSYCHOLOGY, 10E" by Keith E. Stanovich. Published by Pearson, © 2011; *Page 37:* Excerpt from "SCIENCE AND PSEUDOSCIENCE IN CLINICAL PSYCHOLOGY". Published by Guilford Press, © 2005. Excerpt from "Clever Hands: Uncontrolled Intelligence Facilitated Communication" by Daniel M. Wegner, Betsy Sparrow, Valerie A. Fuller. Published by American Psychological Association, © 2003; *Page 39:* Excerpt from "MISTAKES WERE MADE (BUT NOT BY ME)" by Carol Tavris. Published by Mariner Books, © 2008; *Page 40:* Excerpt from "The Weirdest People in the World?" by Joseph Henrich, Steven J. Heine, Ara Norenzayan. Published by Cambridge University Press, © 2010; *Page 45:* Excerpt from "Sensitive Questions in Surveys" by Roger Tourangeau, Ting Yan. Published by American Psychological Association, © 2007; *Page 46:* Excerpt from "Adolescent Sexual Behavior, Drug Use, and Violence: Increased Reporting with Computer Survey Technology" by C. F. Turner, L. Ku, S. M. Rogers, L. D. Lindberg, J. H. Pleck, F. L. Sonenstein. Published by American Association For The Advancement of Science, © 1998; *Page 46–47:* From "Should We Trust Web-Based Studies? A Comparative Analysis of Six Preconceptions About Internet Questionnaires" by Samuel D. Gosling, Simine Vazire, Sanjay Srivastava and Oliver P. John., American Psychologist 93, February/March 2004, Vol. 59, No. 2, 93–104. Copyright © 2004 by the American Psychological Association, Inc.; *Page 47:* Excerpt from "Fifty-Five Years of Cocaine Dependence" by R. Brown, R. Middlefell. Published by BRITISH JOURNAL OF ADDICTION © 1989; *Page 48:* Excerpt from "The Relation of Children's Television Viewing to School Achievement and I.Q" by Robyn Ridley-Johnson, Harris Cooper, June Chance. Published by JOURNAL OF EDUCATIONAL RESEARCH © 1983; *Page 55:* Excerpt from "PSYCHOLOGY AND CULTURE" by Walter J. Lonner, Roy S. Malpass. Published by Allyn and Bacon, © 1994; Excerpt from "Toward a New Generation of Cross-Cultural Research" by David Matsumoto and Seung Hee Yoo. Published by Sage Publication, © 2006; *Page 58:* Excerpt from "Why Figures with Error Bars Should Replace P Values: Some Conceptual Arguments and Empirical Demonstrations" by Fiona Fidler and Geoffrey R. Loftus. Published by American Psychological Association (APA), © 2009. Excerpt from "UNDERSTANDING THE NEW STATISTICS: EFFECT SIZES, CONFIDENCE INTERVALS, AND META-ANALYSIS" by Geoff Cumming. Published by Routledge Publishing, © 2011; *Page 60:* Excerpt from "UNDERSTANDING THE NEW STATISTICS: EFFECT SIZES, CONFIDENCE INTERVALS, AND META-ANALYSIS" by Geoff Cumming. Published by Routledge Publishing, Inc, © 2011; *Page 61:* Excerpt from "Bayesian Versus Orthodox Statistics: Which Side Are You On?" by Zoltan Dienes. Published by Sage Publication © 2011; Excerpt from "You Might Already Know This" by Benedict Carey, The New York Times, January 10, 2011. © 2011. Excerpt from "Statistical Evidence in Experimental Psychology: An Empirical Comparison Using

855 t Tests" by Ruud Wetzels, Dora Matzk, Michael D. Lee, Jeffrey N. Rouder, Geoffrey J. Iverson and Eric-Jan Wagenmakers, Perspectives on Psychological Science, May 2011, 6(3) 291–298. Copyright © The Author(s) 2011. Published by Sage Publication; *Page 65:* Excerpt from "Cage Size Preference in Rats in the Laboratory" by E. G. Patterson-Kane, D. N. Harper & M. Hunt. Published by Sage Publication © 2002.

Chapter 3 *Page 71:* Excerpt from "BEHAVIORISM" by John B. Watson. Published by WEST Press © 2008; *Page 78:* Excerpt from "THE LANGUAGE INSTINCT: HOW THE MIND CREATES LANGUAGE" by Steven Pinker. Published by HarperCollins Publishers © 2010; *Page 84:* Excerpt from "ADAPTING MINDS: EVOLUTIONARY PSYCHOLOGY AND THE PERSISTENT QUEST FOR HUMAN NATURE" by David J. Buller. Published by MIT Press © 2006.

Chapter 4 *Page 101:* Excerpt from "Gourmand Syndrome: Eating Passion Associated with Right Anterior Lesions" by Regard M, Landis T. Published by American Academy of Neurology © 1997. Excerpt from "HEAD CASES: STORIES OF BRAIN INJURY AND ITS AFTERMATH" by Michael Paul Mason. Published by Farrar, Straus and Giroux © 2008. Excerpt from "Cortical Control of a Prosthetic Arm for Self Feeding" by Meel Velliste, Sagi Perel, M. Chance Spalding, Andrew S. Whitford, Andrew B. Schwartz. Published by Macmillan Publishers © 2008. Excerpt from "Reconstructing Visual Experiences from Brain Activity Evoked by Natural Movies" by Shinji Nishimoto, An T. Vu, Thomas Naselaris, Yuval Benjamini, Bin Yu, Jack L. Gallant. Published by Elsevier © 2011; *Page 106:* Excerpt from "Role of Glia In Synaptogenesis" by Ullian, E. M; Chrisopherson, K. S; Barres, B. A. Published by John Wiley © 2004. Excerpt from "RMicroglia: Biology and Pathology" by Manuel B. Graeber, Wolfgang J. Streit. Published by Springer Publishing © 2010. Excerpt from "The Other Half of the Brain" by R. Douglas Fields, Scientific American, April 2004, 290: 54–61. Copyright © 2004; *Page 108:* Excerpt from "Axonal Regeneration in the Rat Spinal Cord Produced by an Antibody Against Myelin-Associated Neurite Growth Inhibitors" by Schnell L, Schwab ME. Nature,1990 Jan 18; 343(6255): 269–72. Copyright © 1990. Excerpt from "Generation of Neurons and Astrocytes from Isolated Cells of the Adult Mammalian Central Nervous System" by Brent A. Reynolds & Samuel Weiss. Published by American Association For The Advancement of Science © 1992. Excerpt from "Introduction of Pluripotent Stem Cells from Adult Human Fibroblasts by Defined Factor" by K. Takahashi, K. Tanabe, M. Ohnuki, M. Narita, T. Ichisaka, K. Tomoda, S. Yamanaka. Cell, Volume 131, Issue 5, 30 November 2007, Pages 861–872 Copyright © 2006. Excerpt from "Engraftment of Human Nasal Olfactory Stem Cells Restores Neuroplasticity in Mice with Hippocampal Lesions". Published by American Society Of Clinical Investigation © 2011; *Page 109:* Excerpt from "Cell Therapies for the Central Nervous System: How Do We Identify the Best Candidates?" by Noble, Marka; Mayer-Pröschel, Margota; Davies, Jeannette E.b; Davies, Stephen J.A.b; Pröschel, Christop. Published by Lippincott Williams & Wilkins © 2011; *Page 113:* Excerpt from "Emerging Perspectives on Distinctions Between Romantic Love and Sexual Desire" by Lisa M. Diamond. Published by Sage Publication; *Page 114:* Excerpt from "The Role of the Right Cerebral Hemisphere in Processing Novel Metaphoric Expressions: A Transcranial Magnetic Stimulation Study" by G. Pobric, N. Mashal, M. Faust, and M. Lavidor. Journal of Cognitive Neuroscience, January 2008, Vol. 20, No. 1, Pages 170–181. Copyright © 2008 Massachusetts Institute of Technology. Excerpt from "Transcranial Direct Current Stimulation: State of the Art 2008" by Michael A. Nitsche, Leonardo G. Cohen, Eric M. Wassermann, Alberto Priori,

Nicolas Lang, Andrea Antal, Walter Paulus, Friedhelm Hummel, Paulo S. Boggio, Felipe Fregni, Alvaro Pascual-Leone. Published by Elsevier © 2008; *Page 115:* Excerpt from "Transcranial Direct Current Stimulation of the Prefrontal Cortex Modulates Working Memory Performance: Combined Behavioural and Electrophysiological Evidence" by T. Zaehle, P. Sandmann, J. D. Thorne, L. Jäncke, and C.S. Herrmann. BMC Neuroscience 2011, 12:2. Copyright © 2011. Excerpt from "Bilingual Language Learning: An ERP Study Relating Early Brain Responses to Speech, Language Input, and Later Word Production" by Adrian Garcia-Sierraa, Maritza Rivera-Gaxiolaa, Cherie R. Percaccioa, Barbara T. Conboyb, Harriett Romoc, Lindsay Klarmana, Sophia Ortizc, Patricia K. Kuhl. Published by Elsevier © 2011; *Page 117:* Excerpt from "BRAIN SCANS AND BIOMEDICAL IDENTITY" by Joseph Dumit. Published by Princeton University Press, © 2004. Excerpt from "Seeing is Believing: The Effect of Brain Images on Judgments of Scientific Reasoning" by David P. McCabe, Alan D. Castel. Published by Elsevier © 2008. Excerpt from "Puzzlingly High Correlations in fMRI Studies of Emotion, Personality, and Social Cognition" by Edward Vul, Christine Harris, Piotr Winkielman and Harold Pashler, PERSPECTIVES ON PSYCHOLOGICAL SCIENCE, May 2009 vol. 4 no. 3 274–290. Excerpt from "Neural Correlates of Interspecies Perspective Taking in the Post-Mortem Atlantic Salmon: An Argument for Multiple Comparisons Correction" by Craig M. Bennett, Abigail A. Baird, Michael B. Miller, and George L. Wolford. Published by JOURNAL OF SERENDIPITOUS and UNEXPECTED RESULTS. Excerpt from "The Appeal of the Brain in the Popular Press" by Diane M. Beck. Published by Sage Publication © 2010; *Page 119:* Excerpt from "Cerebellar Contributions to Cognition" by Timmann D., Drepper J., Frings M., Maschke M., Richter S., Gerwig M., Kolb F. P. Published by Cell Press © 2007; *Page 120:* Excerpt from "Motivational Salience: Amygdala Tuning From Traits, Needs, Values, and Goals" by William A. Cunningham and Tobias Brosch. Published by Sage Publication © 2012; *Page 122:* Excerpt from "The Return Of Phineas Gage: Clues About The Brain From The Skull Of A Famous Patient" by Hanna Damasio, Thomas Grabowski, Randall Frank, Albert M.Galaburda, Antonio R. Damasio. Published by American Association For The Advancement of Science © 1994; *Page 125:* Excerpt from "The Great Cerebral Commissure" by R. W. Sperry. Published by Scientific America © 1964; *Page 127:* Excerpt from "THE TWO HALVES OF THE BRAIN: INFORMATION PROCESSING IN THE CEREBRAL HEMISPHERES" by Kenneth Hugdahl, René Westerhausen. Published by MIT Press © 2010. Excerpt from "LATERALITY: FUNCTIONAL ASYMMETRY IN THE INTACT BRAIN" by M. P. Bryden. Published by Elsevier © 1983. Excerpt from "The Dynamic Nature of Language Lateralization: Effects of Lexical and Prosodic Factors" by G. M. Grimshaw, K. M. Kwasny, E. Covell and R. A. Johnson, NEUROPSYCHOLOGIA, Volume 41, Issue 8, 2003, Pages 1008–1019; *Page 129:* Excerpt from "Treatment-Induced Cortical Reorganization After Stroke in Humans" by Joachim Liepert, Heike Bauder, Wolfgang H. R. Miltner, Edward Taub and Cornelius Weiller, STROKE 2000; 31: 1210–1216. Copyright © 2000. Published by American Heart Association. Excerpt from "Exuberance In the Development of Cortical Networks" by Giorgio M. Innocenti and David J. Price. Published by Macmillan Publishers © 2005; *Page 130:* "Adapting to Blindness" by Frederic Gougoux, Robert J. Zatorre, Maryse Lassonde, Patrice Voss and Franco Lepore from A Functional Neuroimaging Study of Sound Localization: Visual Cortex Activity Predicts Performance in Early-Blind Individuals, PLoS Biol 3(2): e27. Copyright © 2005 by PLoS (Public Library of Science). Used by permission of PLoS (Public Library of Science). Excerpt from "The Mind In The World: Culture and The Brain" by Ambady Nalini. Published by Association For Psychological Science; *Page 134:* Excerpt from "Brain Gain: The Underground World of Neuroenhancing Drugs" by MARGARET TALBOT. Published by Conde Nast © 2009. Excerpt from "Towards Responsible Use of Cognitive-Enhancing Drugs by The Healthy" by Henry Greely, Barbara Sahakian, John Harris, Ronald C. Kessler,

Michael Gazzaniga, Philip Campbell & Martha J. Farah. Published by Macmillan Publishers © 2008.

Chapter 5 *Page 141:* Excerpt from "Sleep-Wake as a Biological Rhythm" by P. Lavie, Annual Review of Psychology, Vol. 52: 277–303 (Volume publication date February 2001) Copyright © 2001; *Page 142:* Excerpt from "Melatonin as a Chronobiotic: Treatment of Circadian Desynchrony in Night Workers and the Blind" by Robert L. Sack and Alfred A. Lewy from Journal of Biological Rhythms, December 1997 vol. 12, no. 6 595–603. Copyright © 1997; *Page 153:* Excerpt from "Role of Rem Sleep and Dream Variables in the Prediction of Remission from Depression" by R. Cartwright, M. A. Young, P. Mercer, M. Bears from Psychiatry Research, Volume 80, Issue 3, 21 September 1998, Pages 249–255. Copyright © 1998; *Page 155:* Excerpt from "DREAMING: AN INTRODUCTION TO THE SCIENCE OF SLEEP" by J. Allan Hobson. Copyright © 2002 by J. Allan Hobson. Published by Oxford University Press. Excerpt from "THE DREAMING BRAIN" by J. Allan Hobson. Copyright © 1988 by J. Allen Hobson. Published by Basic Books.

Chapter 6 *Page 206:* Excerpt from "White Men Can't Contextualize" by Christopher Shea from LINGUA FRANCA, September 2001 - Volume 11, No. 6, 44–47, 49–51. Copyright © 2001; *Page 215:* Excerpt from "Giving Up Ghosts: End of Personal Quest" by Susan Blackmore from SKEPTICAL INQUIRER 25, no. 2 (2001): 25. Copyright © 2001.

Chapter 7 *Page 250:* Excerpt from "Violent Video Game Effects On Aggression, Empathy, and Prosocial Behavior in Eastern and Western Countries: A Meta-Analytic Review" by Anderson, C. A., Shibuya, A., Ihori, N., Swing, E. L., Bushman, B. J., Sakamoto, A., Rothstein, H. R., Saleem, M. from PSYCHOLOGICAL BULLETIN, 136, 151–173. Copyright © 2010.

Chapter 8 *Page 255:* Quote by Adolf Eichmann from SOCIAL PSYCHOLOGY 2E by Roger Brown. Copyright © 1986 by The Free Press; *Page 259:* Excerpts from "OBEDIENCE TO AUTHORITY; AN EXPERIMENTAL VIEW" by Stanley Milgram. Published by HarperCollins Publishing, © 2009; *Page 260:* Excerpt by Haslam, S. A. and Reicher, S. D. from The Stanford Prison Study video and "Nature" Of Conformity: What Milgram And Zimbardo's Studies Really Show. Used by permission of S. Alexander Haslam & Stephen D. Reicher. Excerpt from "Words from Beyond Stanford: Questioning A Role Based Explanation of Tyranny" by Alexander Haslam and Stephen Reicher from Beyond Stanford: Questioning A Role Based Explanation of Tyranny, SOCIETY FOR EXPERIMENTAL SOCIAL PSYCHOLOGY DIALOGUE, 18, 22–25. Published by S. Alexander Haslam & Stephen D. Reicher, © 2003; *Page 272:* Excerpt from "Culture And Conformity: A Meta-Analysis Of Studying Using Asch's (1952b, 1956) line judgement task" by Rod Bond and Peter B. Smith. Published by PSYCHOLOGICAL BULLETIN, © 1996; *Page 292:* Excerpt from "HIDDEN DIFFERENCES: DOING BUSINESS WITH THE JAPANESE" by Edward Twitchell Hall, Mildred Reed Hall. Published by Anchor Books © 1990; *Page 293:* Excerpt from "The Fine Art of Hiding What You Mean to Say" by MICHAEL SLACKMAN. Published in New York Times © 2006.

Chapter 9 *Page 304:* Excerpt from "DEVELOPING REFLECTIVE JUDGMENT: UNDERSTANDING AND PROMOTING INTELLECTUAL GROWTH AND CRITICAL THINKING IN ADOLESCENTS AND ADULTS" by Karen Strohm Kitchener & Patricia M. King. Published by Jossey Bass Publishing, © 1994. Excerpt from "THE RIGHTEOUS MIND: WHY GOOD PEOPLE ARE DIVIDED BY POLITICS AND RELIGION" by Jonathan Haidt. Published by Pantheon Books Publishing, © 2013; *Page 329:* Excerpt from "Birdbrain: The Woman Behind The World's Chattiest Parrots" by Margaret Talbot. Published by Conde Nast. © 2008; *Page 333:* Excerpt from Conceptual Blockbusting by James L. Adams, copyright © 1986. Reprinted by permission of Basic Books, a member of The Perseus Books Group.

Chapter 10 *Page 338:* Excerpt from "MEMORY MECHANISMS: A TRIBUTE TO G. V. GODDARD" by K. Geoffrey White, Michael Corballis. Published by Psychology Press, © 1990; *Page 342:* Excerpt from "More than Suggestion: The Effect of Interviewing Techniques From The McMartin Preschool Case" by Garven, Sena; Wood, James M.; Malpass, Roy S.; & Shaw, John S. Published by JOURNAL OF APPLIED PSYCHOLOGY, © 1998; *Page 343:* Excerpt from "Effects of suggestion on the reliability and credibility of children's reports. Invited address at the annual meeting of the American Psychological Society, Atlanta" by Maggie Bruck. Published by American Psychological Society; *Page 367:* Excerpt from Remembering Trauma by Richard McNally. Copyright © 2003, 2005 by the President and Fellows of Harvard College.

Chapter 11 *Page 377:* Excerpt from "Wife Testifies She Was 'in a Fog' Just Before Her Car Struck Husband" by Nick Madigan from New York Times, February 08, 2003. Copyright © 2003; *Page 383:* "Get Involved! Turn on Your Right Hemisphere" from Understanding Emotions, 2e by Keith Oatley, Dacher Keltner and Jennifer M. Jenkins. Copyright © 2006 by John Wiley & Sons, Inc. Used by permission of John Wiley & Sons, Inc.

Chapter 12 *Page 437:* Excerpt from HUMAN SEXUAL RESPONSE by William H. Masters & Virginia E. Johnson. Published by Ishi Press © 2010.

Chapter 13 *Page 484:* Data from "CHILDREN'S THINKING: DEVELOPMENTAL FUNCTION AND INDIVIDUAL DIFFERENCES" by David F. Bjorklund. Published by Wadsworth Publishing Company, © 2000. Data from "PINK AND BLUE: TELLING THE BOYS FROM THE GIRLS IN AMERICA" by Jo B. Paoletti. Published by Indiana University Presss, © 2012; *Page 487:* Excerpt from "Juvenile Subsistence Effort, Activity Levels, and Growth Patterns" by Karen L. Kramer and Russell D. Greaves, Human Nature 22(3):303–326 (2011); *Page 493:* Data from "AGING AND LIFE COURSE TRANSITIONS: AN INTERDISCIPLINARY PERSPECTIVE" by Tamara K. Hareven, Kathleen J. Adams. Published by Guilford Publications, © 1982.

Chapter 14 *Page 516:* "GET INVOLVED! Rate Your Traits" from A Very Brief Measure of the Big Five Personality Domains. JOURNAL OF RESEARCH IN PERSONALITY by Gosling, Samuel D., Rentfrow, P. J., and Swann, William B. Copyright © 2003 by Elsevier. Used by permission of Elsevier; *Page 521:* Excerpt from "Environment and Genes: Determinants of Behavior" by Robert Plomin from AMERICAN PSYCHOLOGIST. Published by American Psychological Association (APA), © 1989; *Page 528:* Table 14.01 "Some Average Differences Individualist between Collectivist and Cultures" by Harry C. Triandis from The Psychological Measurement of Cultural Syndromes, AMERICAN PSYCHOLOGIST, 51. Published by Association for Psychological Science, © 1996; *Page 534:* Excerpt from "THE FARTHER REACHES OF HUMAN NATURE" by Abraham H. Maslow, © 1993; *Page 535:* Excerpt from "The Third Wave. Family Therapy" by Bill O'Hanlon. Published by NETWORKER, © 1994.

Chapter 15 *Page 546:* Excerpt on The Danger of Overdiagnosis by Abraham Kaplan from Psychological Disorders; *Page 549:* Excerpt from "Culture: A Significant Advance" on DIAGNOSTIC AND STATISTICAL MANUAL OF MENTAL DISORDERS, Fifth Edition (DSM 5) published by American Psychiatric Association. American Psychiatric Association, Copyright © 2013; *Page 551:* Excerpt from "A Critical Assessment of Child Custody Evaluations: Limited Science and a Flawed System" by Robert E. Emery, Randy K. Otto, William T. O'Donohue, published in PSYCHOLOGICAL, SCIENCE IN THE PUBLIC INTEREST, Vol. 06, 01–29, July 2005. Published by Association for Psychological Science, © 2005; *Page 556:* Excerpt from "The Chemistry of Doubt (obsessive-compulsive disorder)" by Pamela King in PSYCHOLOGY TODAY, October 1, 1989. Copyright © 2002; *Page 557:* "Translated Lines of the Poem The Divine Comedy" from DARKNESS VISIBLE: A MEMOIR OF MADNESS by William Styron. Copyright © 2010 by Open Road Media. Used by permission of Open Road Media. Excerpt from "DARKNESS VISIBLE: A MEMOIR OF MADNESS" by William Styron. Published by Open Road Media, Copyright © 1990; *Page 563:* Excerpt from "Adolescence-Limited and Life-Course-Persistent Antisocial Behavior: A Developmental Taxonomy" by Terrie E. Moffitt. Published by Psychological Review, Copyright © 1993; *Pages 573–574:* Excerpt from "The Simulation and Dissimulation of Multiple Personality Disorder, AMERICAN JOURNAL OF CLINICAL HYPNOSIS", by Richard P. Kluft. Published by American Society of Clinical Hypnosis, Copyright © 1987; *Page 575:* Excerpt from "COPING WITH SCHIZOPHRENIA" edited by Henry Rollins. Published by Lawrence Verry Incorporated, Copyright © 1980; *Page 576:* Excerpt from "Dementia Praecox or the Group of Schizophrenia" by Eugen Bleuler. Copyright © 1911/1950, published by International Universities Press. Excerpts from "Bryan Charnley website (www.bryancharnley.info)". Copyright © 1991 by SANE. Used by permission of SANE; *Page 577:* Figure from "SCHIZOPHRENIA GENESIS: THE ORIGINS OF MADNESS. NEW YORK: FREEMAN", by Irving I. Gottesman. Published by W. H. Freeman, Copyright © 1991; *Page 581:* Excerpt from "NIGHT FALLS FAST: UNDERSTANDING SUICIDE", by Kay R. Jamison. Published by Knopf, Copyright © 1999.

Chapter 16 *Page 600:* Excerpt from "LOVE'S EXECUTIONER AND OTHER TALES OF PSYCHOTHERAPY" by Irvin D. Yalom. Published by Basic Books; *Page 604:* Excerpt from "ETHNICITY AND FAMILY THERAPY" by Monica McGoldrick, Joe Giordano, Nydia Garcia-Preto. Published by Basic Books, © 2005; *Page 607:* Excerpt from "Current Status and Future Prospects of Clinical Psychology: Toward a Scientifically Principled Approach To Mental and Behavioral Health Care" by Baker T.B., McFall, R.M., Shoham, V. from PSYCHOLOGICAL SCIENCE IN THE PUBLIC INTEREST, 9 (2) 67–103. Copyright © 2009; *Page 608:* From "Psychological Debriefing for Road Traffic Accident Victims" by Mayou, R. A., Ehlers, A., and Hobbs, M. The British Journal of Psychiatry (2000) 176: 589–593. Copyright © 2000. Used by permission of British Journal of Psychiatry.